The Oxford Handbook of Acceptance and Commitment Therapy

OXFORD LIBRARY OF PSYCHOLOGY
AREA EDITORS

Clinical Psychology
David H. Barlow

Cognitive Neuroscience
Kevin N. Ochsner and Stephen M. Kosslyn

Cognitive Psychology
Daniel Reisberg

Counseling Psychology
Elizabeth M. Altmaier and Jo-Ida C. Hansen

Developmental Psychology
Philip David Zelazo

Health Psychology
Howard S. Friedman

History of Psychology
David B. Baker

Methods and Measurement
Todd D. Little

Neuropsychology
Kenneth M. Adams

Organizational Psychology
Steve W. J. Kozlowski

Personality and Social Psychology
Kay Deaux and Mark Snyder

OXFORD LIBRARY OF PSYCHOLOGY

The Oxford Handbook of Acceptance and Commitment Therapy

Edited by

Michael P. Twohig, Michael E. Levin, and Julie M. Petersen

OXFORD
UNIVERSITY PRESS

OXFORD
UNIVERSITY PRESS

Oxford University Press is a department of the University of Oxford. It furthers the University's objective of excellence in research, scholarship, and education by publishing worldwide. Oxford is a registered trade mark of Oxford University Press in the UK and certain other countries.

Published in the United States of America by Oxford University Press
198 Madison Avenue, New York, NY 10016, United States of America.

CIP data is on file at the Library of Congress
ISBN 978–0–19–755007–6

DOI: 10.1093/oxfordhb/9780197550076.001.0001

The manufacturer's authorised representative in the EU for product safety is Oxford University Press España S.A. of El Parque Empresarial San Fernando de Henares, Avenida de Castilla, 2 – 28830 Madrid (www.oup.es/en or product.safety@oup.com). OUP España S.A. also acts as importer into Spain of products made by the manufacturer.

CONTENTS

Conclusion

CONTRIBUTORS

Niloofar Afari, PhD
Professor, Department of Psychiatry, University of California, San Diego

Joanna J. Arch, PhD
Associate Professor, Psychology and Neuroscience, University of Colorado, Boulder

Myles Arendtson, BA
Graduate Student, School of Psychological and Behavioral Sciences, Southern Illinois University, Carbondale

Jacqueline A-Tjak, PhD
Clinical Psychologist, A-Tjak Cursussen, Emmer-Compascuum

Anthony Biglan, PhD
Senior Scientist, Oregon Research Institute, Eugene

Ellen J. Bluett, PhD
Clinical Associate Professor of Behavioral Science, Family Medicine Residency of Western Montana, University of Montana, Missoula

Jonathan B. Bricker, PhD
Professor, Division of Public Health Sciences, Fred Hutchinson Cancer Center and University of Washington, Seattle

Amanda N. Chastain, MA, BCBA
Senior Research Associate, University of Southern California, Los Angeles

Joseph Ciarrochi, PhD
Professor, Institute of Positive Psychology and Education, Australian Catholic University, Austinmer

Lisa W. Coyne, PhD
Assistant Professor, Psychiatry Department, Harvard Medical School, Boston

Katrina M. Daigle, MA, MS, PhD Candidate
Psychology Department, Suffolk University, Boston

Lilian Dindo, PhD
Associate Professor, Medicine, Baylor College of Medicine, Houston

Claudia Drossel, PhD
Associate Professor, Psychology, Eastern Michigan University, Ypsilanti

Karlyn A. Edwards, PhD
Postdoctoral Fellow, Department of Anesthesiology, Perioperative, and Pain Medicine, Stanford University, Palo Alto

Stacy Ellenberg, PhD
Clinical Psychology, Postdoctoral Fellow, MindWell Center, Ithaca

Elizabeth H. Eustis, PhD
Research Assistant Professor, Department of Psychological and Brain Sciences Boston University, Boston

Neal Falletta-Cowden, MA
Psychology, Behavior Analysis, University of Nevada, Reno

Christina R. Felonis, BA
Doctoral Student in Clinical Psychology, Department of Psychology, Drexel University, Philadelphia

Lauren B. Finkelstein, MA
Doctoral Student in Clinical Psychology, Department of Psychology and Neuroscience, University of Colorado, Boulder

Paul E. Flaxman, PhD
Reader in Organizational Psychology, Department of Psychology, City University of London, London

Caleb Fogle, MS
Student in Clinical Psychology, Southern Illinois University, Carbondale

Michelle Forman, MS
University of Nevada, Reno

Sara Freeman, MS
LCMHC Therapist, Mood Treatment Center, Greensboro

Brandon A. Gaudiano, PhD
Professor Psychiatry and Human Behavior, Brown University, Providence

Duncan Gillard, DEdPsy
Senior Psychologist and Creative Director, Connect Wellbeing in Education LLP, Bristol

Bárbara Gil-Luciano, PhD
Associate Professor, Cofounder of Universidad de Nebrija, Madrid Institute of Contextual Psychology (MICPSY), Madrid

Mikala A. Grimaldi, BS
OCD and Anxiety Behavior Specialist, Clinical Research Coordinator, New England Center for OCD and Anxiety, Boston

Colin Harte, PhD
Postdoctoral Researcher, Federal University of São Carlos, Brazil and Paradigma – Centro de Ciências e Technologia do Comportamento, Brazil

Louise Hayes, PhD
Licensed Clinical Psychologist, Director, DNA-V International, University of Almería, Melbourne

Steven C. Hayes, PhD
Foundation Professor of Psychology, Psychology, University of Nevada, Reno

Matthew S. Herbert, PhD
Research Psychologist and Assistant Professor, Research Development Service and Department of Psychiatry, Veterans Affairs San Diego Healthcare System and University of California, San Diego

Dermot Barnes-Holmes, PhD
Professor, Department of Psychology, Ghent University, Belgium

Duckhyun Jo, MA
Doctoral Student, Department of Psychology, University of Hawaii, Honolulu

Adrienne Juarascio, PhD
Assistant Professor, Department of Psychological and Brain Sciences, Drexel University, Philadelphia

Maria Karekla, PhD
Assistant Professor, Department of Psychology, University of Cyprus, Cyprus

Katariina Keinonen, PhD
Senior Lecturer, Department of Psychology, University of Jyväskylä, Jyväskylä

Megan Kelly, PhD
Professor, Department of Psychiatry, University of Massachusetts Chan Medical School, Worcester

Päivi Lappalainen, PhD
Postdoctoral Researcher, Department of Psychology, University of Jyväskylä, Jyväskylä

Raimo Lappalainen, PhD
Professor, Department of Psychology, University of Jyväskylä, Jyväskylä

Eric B. Lee, PhD
Assistant Professor, School of Psychological and Behavioral Sciences, Southern Illinois University, Carbondale

Dayna Lee-Baggley, PhD
Registered Psychologist, Assistant Professor, Family Medicine, Dalhousie University, Halifax

Jenna LeJeune, PhD
Licensed Psychologist, President Portland Psychotherapy Clinic, Training, and Research Center, Portland

Michael E. Levin, PhD
Professor, Department of Psychology, Utah State University, Logan

Jason Lillis, PhD
Associate Professor (Research), Alpert Brown Medical School, The Miriam Hospital and College of Psychology, Providence

Carmen Luciano, PhD
Professor, Department of Psychology, University of Almería, Almería

Jason Luoma, PhD
CEO, Portland Psychotherapy Clinic, Research and Training Center, Portland

Akihiko Masuda, PhD
Professor, Department of Psychology, University of Hawaii at Manoa, Honolulu

Lance M. McCracken
Professor, Clinical Psychology, Department of Psychology, Uppsala University, Uppsala

Louise McHugh, PhD
Professor, School of Psychology, University College Dublin, Dublin

Rhonda M. Merwin, PhD
Associate Professor, Department of Psychiatry and Behavioral Sciences, Duke University Medical Center, Durham

Lucas Morgan, PhD
Clinical Supervisor, Ola Lāhui Behavioral Health, Honolulu

Ashley A. Moskovich, PhD
Assistant Professor, Department of Psychiatry and Behavioral Sciences, Duke University Medical Center, Durham

Amy R. Murrell, PhD
Licensed Psychologist and Affiliate Faculty, Private Practice and Department of Psychology, Murrell Psychological Services, LLC and University of Memphis, Memphis

Clarissa W. Ong, PhD
Research Scientist, Department of Psychological and Brain Sciences, Boston University, Boston

Carly Onnink, BS
Research Assistant, Department of Psychiatry and Behavioral Sciences, Duke University Medical Center, Durham

Julie M. Petersen, MS
Doctoral Student, Department of Psychology, Utah State University, Logan

Angela Pisoni, MA, PhD Candidate
Department of Psychiatry and Behavioral Sciences, Duke University Medical Center, Durham

Arianna Prudenzi, PhD
MSc, BSc Research Fellow, School of Psychology, Institute for Mental Health, University of Birmingham, Birmingham

Joanne Qina'au, MA
Doctoral Student, Department of Psychology, University of Hawaii at Manoa, Honolulu

Tyler L. Renshaw, PhD
Associate Professor, Psychology Department, Utah State University, Logan

Anthony J. Roberson, PhD
Assistant Professor, Department of Clinical, Health, and Applied Sciences, University of Houston-Clear Lake, Houston

Francisco J. Ruiz, PhD
Associate Professor, Faculty of Psychology, Fundación Universitaria Konrad Lorenz, Bogotá

Emily K. Sandoz, PhD
BCBA, Emma Louise LeBlanc Burguieres/BORSF Endowed Professor of Social Sciences, Psychology Department, University of Louisiana at Lafayette, Lafayette

Rebecca Schneider, PhD
Assistant Professor, Department of Psychiatry and Behavioral Sciences, Emory University School of Medicine, Atlanta

Miguel A. Segura-Vargas
Graduate Student, Master's in Psychology, Theory and Research, Faculty of Psychology and Educational Sciences KU Leuven, Leuven

Brooke M. Smith, PhD
Assistant Professor, Department of Psychology, Western Michigan University, Kalamazoo

Gregory S. Smith, PhD, BCBA-D
Assistant Clinical Professor, Department of Applied Behavior Analysis, University of Dayton, Dayton, OH

Samuel D. Spencer, MA
Doctoral Candidate, Department of Psychology, University of Hawaii at Manoa, Honolulu

Paakhi Srivastava, PhD
Assistant Research Professor and Clinic Director, Center for Weight, Eating and Lifestyle, Drexel University, Philadelphia

Alison Stapleton, BA, PhD Candidate
School of Psychology, University College Dublin, Dublin

Maria Stavrinaki, PhD
Clinical Psychologist, Department of Psychology, University of Cyprus, Nicosia

Thomas G. Szabo, PhD, BCBA-D, LBA
Assistant Professor, Department of Psychology, Capella University, Minneapolis

Jonathan Tarbox, PhD, BCBA
Associate Professor of Teaching and Program Director, Department of Psychology, University of Southern California, Los Angeles

Niklas Törneke, MD
Psychiatrist, NT Psykiatri AB, Köpingsvik

Michael P. Twohig, PhD
Professor, Department of Psychology, Utah State University, Logan

Julia R. Van Liew, PhD
Assistant Professor, Behavioral Medicine, Medical Humanities, and Bioethics, Des Moines University, Des Moines

Stephanie Vinal, MS
Doctoral Student, Department of Psychology, Utah State University, Logan

Kevin E. Vowles, PhD
Professor, School of Psychology, Queen's University of Belfast, Belfast

Andy Wall, BS
Graduate Student, School of Psychological and Behavioral Sciences, Southern Illinois University, Carbondale

Robyn D. Walser, PhD
Assistant Professor, Staff Psychologist, Director, Department of Psychology University of California, Berkeley, National Center for PTSD, TL Consultation Services, Berkeley

Thomas J. Waltz, PhD, LP
Associate Professor, Department of Psychology, Eastern Michigan University, Ypsilanti

Sean N. Weeks, MS
Doctoral Candidate, Department of Psychology, Utah State University, Logan

Emily Rachel Wharton, PsyD
Psychologist, Palo Alto Veterans Affairs, Redwood City

Rikard K. Wicksell, PhD
Associate Professor, Department of Clinical Neuroscience, Division of Psychology, Karolinska Institutet, Stockholm

Kelly G. Wilson, PhD
Professor Emeritus of Psychology, Department of Psychology, University of Mississippi, Oxford, Mississippi

Olivia B. Wons, MS, PhD Student
Department of Psychological and Brain Sciences, Drexel University, Philadelphia

Lucie Zernerova, PhD
Research Associate, Department of Psychology, City, University of London, London

Robert D. Zettle, PhD
Professor and Director of Clinical Training, Department of Psychology, Wichita State University, Wichita

INTRODUCTION

Michael P. Twohig, Michael E. Levin, and Julie M. Petersen

The founding of acceptance and commitment therapy (ACT) and contextual behavioral sciences (CBS) involved many players. Obviously, Dr. Steven Hayes, first at the University of North Carolina, Greensboro, and later at the University of Nevada, Reno, was the strongest voice in its creation, but the conceptualization of human behavior, including emphasizing the importance of internal experiences, and the use of behavior analysis for clinical issues existed prior to ACT (Chapter 1). Dr. Hayes and colleagues were among the many scholars who developed the theoretical groundings that would become the basis of ACT and CBS. The first empirical publication on ACT arguably occurred in 1986 (Zettle & Hayes, 1986), with a follow-up study in 1989 (Zettle & Rains, 1989). The clinical trial research nearly stopped, and Dr. Hayes and many other researchers, most notably, Dr. Dermot Barnes-Holmes, led the way in building the basic science of human language and cognition that guides and supports ACT (Chapter 4). The work on ACT was still occurring at the University of Nevada at Reno, which led to the first published manual on the therapy in 1999. This manual allowed people all over the world to learn ACT.

Around the year 2000, outcome studies on ACT began to appear again, but the work only trickled in until 2004 when the journal *Behavior Therapy* published Dr. Hayes's presidential address before the Association for Behavioral and Cognitive Therapies as well as a full special issue of ACT outcome studies. It was around this time that ACT began to spread across the globe, with many researchers focusing on it and clinicians learning to put it into practice. In 2005, the Association for Contextual Behavioral Science (ACBS) was created as a home for those interested in ACT, relational frame therapy (RFT), and contextual behavioral approaches more broadly. Many aspects of this organization highlight the fact that the goal of ACBS was to create a home for individuals to work together and support each other in moving contextual science and services forward.

This strong theoretical, basic scientific, and applied base, as well as an organization to facilitate dissemination and collaboration, has led to ACT's exceptional growth. As of the writing of this introductory chapter, we have become aware of more than 1000 randomized trials. ACT is being very actively studied and disseminated in many countries throughout the world and within large systems of care such as the World Health Organization as well as Department of Veterans Affairs hospitals throughout the United States. ACBS has grown to over 9000 members across the world. There was a time when it was easy to keep track of developments associated with ACT and the state of the science, but that is no longer the case as ACT research and clinical innovations continue to grow. ACT has become global. Many laboratories have been set up that are working on various aspects of ACT and contextual behavioral science more broadly. Among these advances are in-depth lines of research iteratively refining and testing ACT for particular problems and settings; translational research on the underlying basic principles and theoretical processes of change; large-scale implementation work deploying ACT through systems of care; and various other features of this dynamic, widely applied treatment. When massive levels of growth occur, it is wise to organize the material. With the support of Oxford University Press, we have been able to produce this handbook on ACT, which we have chosen to break into five sections.

In the first section, we cover the theoretical and conceptual work that informs ACT, including theory and basic science (Chapters 1–5). In the second, we cover the main methods and constructs that are key to ACT, including psychological flexibility and the six ACT processes of change (Chapters 6–13). Third, we cover ACT as it applies to major disorders and problem areas (Chapters 14–24). Fourth, we look at ACT as it has been implemented across unique settings and populations (Chapters 25–31). And in the fifth section, authors offer thoughts on future directions for CBT and ACT (Chapters 32–33). This edited book includes the contributions of many of the leading scholars in these areas. This 33-chapter book will bring the reader up to date on ACT and its CBS foundations.

Conceptual Formation

While this book is titled *The Oxford Handbook of Acceptance and Commitment Therapy* and largely focuses on ACT, it is to be noted that this therapy exists within a specific philosophical and theoretical foundation that is central to an understanding of it. This is why the *Conceptual Formation* section contains five chapters. Many people are aware that ACT places a strong focus on concepts such as acceptance and mindfulness, but those who are newer to this therapy likely do not understand where and why we focus on those processes of change. This is similar to how behavior analysis taught parents the procedure of time-in/time-out to help them teach their children to be safe and to self-regulate. We did not need to teach parents about schedules of reinforcement, extinction, or habituation, but without those principles, our treatment of how to implement such procedures would have lacked a lot of precision, depth, and understanding. The theory and basic science guided the practical application.

ACT is heavily tied to and influenced by behavioral analysis and functional contextual thinking. The core tenets of functional contextual thinking are that all events must be considered in their historical, current, and future contexts and should be analyzed as whole events. Simply stated, no action can be looked at in isolation or outside of the responder's learning history, current pressures, or future expectations. It is much more important to look at the function of a response (i.e., its intended and actual effects) in terms of its topography (i.e., how the form of the behavior could be described). Speaking of function, the other main tenet of functional contextual thinking is that the goals of work are defined by the person doing it. Thus, there is no "right" goal for one's work; setting the objective is up to the person doing it. It has been stated that the goals of functional contextualism as a science are prediction and influence with precision, scope, and depth. That is, we want to know why something is occurring, but only enough to give us the ability to influence it. We also want to do that work in a way that our understandings will be clear and consistent with the best science in our own field and that of others. This combination of factors helps ensure a pragmatic, progressive science that directly informs efforts to improve well-being and reduce human suffering, which we call contextual behavioral science (see Chapter 2).

Behavior analysis has offered psychological science wonderful methods to predict and influence behavior through translational research that scales basic principles such as reinforcement into applied procedures (see Chapter 3). It has led to amazing successes in many areas of human behavior. While it emphasized more simplistic actions such as learning to write, read, or speak, behavior analysis even handled more complicated patterns of behavior that contribute to problems, including psychosis, sexual dysfunction, and substance use. But the cognitive revolution certainly surpassed behavior analysis in many areas of applied psychology, largely because behavior analysts did not have good ways to address the cognitive and emotional aspects of human beings.

A movement within behavior analysis was initiated to address these more complicated human issues, while integrating with traditional clinical work without giving up the principles we hold dear. This movement was loosely called clinical behavior analysis (Chapter 5). Stimulus equivalence, rule-governed behavior, and RFT were all developments within behavior analysis showing language had an amazing ability to affect basic behavioral principles. Stimulus equivalence showed that reinforcing functions could pass between stimuli that were trained to be the same, without having to learn each stimulus association directly. RFT added to this insight by showing that stimuli could be related to each other in many other ways besides equivalence and that certain features of the environment indicated what type of relational response and what functions should also be transferred between stimuli (see Chapter 4 for an overview of RFT). Finally, rule-governed behavior showed us that due to our cognitive abilities, we do not always respond to the contingencies in our environment, leading us to instead respond to verbally created versions of contingencies that are formed through our abilities to have a relational response.

From a clinical level, this movement showed us that we needed to help our clients contextualize the influence of cognition on our behavior. We needed to allow cognitions to influence us when they are helpful and not influence us when they are against our goals. Concepts such as acceptance defusion and being present (or mindfulness) were helpful tools in treating our minds like warning signals rather than firm rules. But because all of these considerations were very context and function dependent, we needed some guidance on when to listen and when not to—this is where values are helpful in ACT. We could not choose actions based on their topography; rather, we had to choose based on function. Using values as our guide, we could instruct clients to listen to the thought if it moved them toward their values and to ignore them when it did not. We are still guided by all the principles and procedures we have learned from behavior analysis to help the client either increase or decrease behaviors linked to our values (i.e., things we care about). ACT is behavior analysis that addresses and incorporates the role of language and cognition. Thus, it can arguably be considered a version of clinical behavior analysis.

The chapters in this first section of the book will provide readers with a strong conceptual understanding of the philosophy of science, basic research, and translational theory that underlies and guides ACT. This section includes a historical overview of how ACT developed (Chapter 1); of CBS and how it provides a foundation for ACT (Chapter 2); of basic behavioral principles (Chapter 3); and of RFT as a modern behavior-analytic theory of cognition (Chapter 4). All these strands are finally brought together into a discussion of ACT as clinical behavior analysis and how these principles can be applied to address the complex human behaviors seen clinically (Chapter 5). Although this section will provide critical orientation to readers newer to ACT on the underlying conceptual foundations, it also includes cutting-edge research and innovations in theory refinement that can help guide established ACT researchers and clinicians in their ongoing work.

General ACT Methods

ACT is part of the behavioral and cognitive-behavioral tradition, but it is unique in that it is heavily influenced by functional contextual thinking. Several key aspects align with behavior analysis and behavior therapy, but RFT heavily influences how cognitive and emotional activity is addressed. Specifically, an individual's ability to relationally respond to stimuli (public or private) is both a blessing and a curse. On the one hand, relational responding allows us to make sense of novel situations and to respond in effective ways by applying what is known from previous situations to novel ones. On the other hand, this ability is often overblown and misapplied. For example, the fear one experiences when asking someone on a date is likely out of proportion to the worst-case consequence of asking (the person saying "no"). A core tenet of ACT is that this exaggerated relational responding frequently occurs with internal experiences, thus, fostering a need to avoid such experiences. For example, the emotion we call anxiety is objectively not harmful, but people run from it as though it poses a great danger. For example, in one known case, a person who struggled with panic attacks jumped out of a moving car so as not to be "trapped" in an oncoming traffic jam.

RFT too literally conceptualizes such behavior as responding to a stimulus (such as anxiety), or stated another way, as being too heavily influenced by the stimulus properties brought on by relational responding. Rigid responding to inner experiences can lead to experiential avoidance, which is generally defined as behaviors that regulate or avoid inner experiences when doing so decreases quality of life. Many psychological disorders have experiential avoidance at their core. Experiential avoidance is fostered by other psychological processes such as cognitive fusion, not being present, and not following one's values, which themselves also contribute to psychological suffering and disorders. Therefore, we more commonly conceptualize psychological issues from an ACT stance as being largely about psychological inflexibility. Psychological inflexibility occurs when a person buys into thoughts, is not present, avoids internal experiences, and is unclear and does not approach the things they care about (i.e., their actions are excessively guided by regulating internal experiences, at the expense of what is effective or meaningful in the big picture).

ACT, in turn, largely addresses issues of psychological inflexibility. In the behavioral commitment process, ACT has a large part in skill building, but if a great deal of skill building is needed, the therapy should center more on skills and less on building psychological flexibility. We build psychological flexibility through six processes of change: acceptance, defusion, being present, self as context, values, and behavioral commitments. These processes can be categorized in many ways, but a simple one that is tied to RFT is that some processes act upon relational responding and others act on functional responding. Specifically, processes such as acceptance and defusion largely help bring the individual into more objective elements of the stimulus (the aspects that are less language based). In contrast, processes such as values and behavioral commitments are more about increasing the reinforcing value for certain actions and decreasing it for others.

The chapters in this second section of the handbook are organized on the basis of each of the six key processes of the ACT model for addressing psychological inflexibility (Chapters 8–13) as well as on the basis of psychological flexibility broadly (Chapter 7), along with how to assess and plan treatment using these processes (Chapter 6). These chapters provide an up-to-date overview of the theoretical model, measurement of these processes of change, research targeting specific processes, examination of how each process is targeted clinically, and challenges and future directions for research and clinical practice.

Specific Applications of ACT

While ACT is intended to be a broader, transdiagnostic intervention, specific adaptations have been made that depend on the clinical presentation. In problem-specific applications of ACT, we tend to target those aspects of psychological inflexibility that are most impacted by the presenting problem (e.g., values-based choices, fusion with internal experiences). For example, in depression, psychological inflexibility is most likely strongest in the face of low mood (e.g., values, self-as-content; see Chapter 14), whereas in obsessive-compulsive and related disorders (OCRDs), it is more present in a person's inability to break the cycle of compulsive behavior in response to an obsession (e.g., acceptance and defusion; see Chapter 16). As another example, ACT for health management in obesity may focus on the meaning behind health behavior change (e.g., committed action and values; see Chapter 18). Thus, ACT for depression, OCRDs, and health management use the same theoretical foundation but lean on different processes and adjunctive treatment tools, which we will detail further in this Introduction.

An ACT conceptualization of depression suggests high psychological inflexibility similar to that of other psychopathology models. However, ACT's focus for depression is less on mood or cognitions. Instead, in ACT for depression, values and self-compassion are used to establish hope (i.e., depression does not have to go away for one to have a meaningful life), alongside defusion and self-as-context, in order to separate oneself from negative self-images and cognitions in the service of a meaningful life (e.g., a person can feel depressed *and* go to the grocery store). Thus, ACT for depression hones in on the concept of a person being more than their thoughts and feelings (i.e., self-as-context).

Similar to depressive symptoms such as low mood or negative cognitions, the presence of obsessions or urges (i.e., the urge to pick skin or pull hair) in OCRDs is not inherently problematic. ACT for OCRDs focuses on promoting psychological flexibility so that the emphasis shifts to values rather than compulsive behavior. For example, ACT for OCRDs encourages an individual to choose meaningful action over what their obsession may urge them to do (e.g., play with their child on the playground in the service of being a good parent *while* having obsessions about contamination and harm). In the treatment of OCRDs, ACT is commonly used to support engagement in techniques such as habit reversal training (HRT) and/or exposure therapy. Thus, more emphasis is placed on the client's willingness to experience OCRD symptoms (i.e., obsessions, the urge to pull hair) in the service of a meaningful life.

As a final example, ACT processes are used in the health and weight management of individuals with obesity in order to promote health behavior change in clients—much as ACT for OCRDs may focus on using ACT to help break cycles of compulsive behavior using HRT or exposures. ACT processes are utilized to help improve healthy living (e.g., defusion from thoughts like "you can exercise tomorrow"). With this goal in mind, ACT focuses on promoting healthy eating and portion sizes through processes such as present moment awareness (e.g., mindful eating) and acceptance/defusion around challenging internal and external experiences related to physical activity and self-monitoring of health behaviors. Therefore, ACT is used adjunctively to motivate and help individuals stick to their health goals.

Although ACT contains common underpinnings (e.g., the six processes, emphasis on increasing psychological flexibility), it is uniquely utilized across depression, OCRDs, and health management in obesity. While the same processes are used, they are flexibly applied alongside other therapeutic techniques and target the specific elements of psychological inflexibility that are most relevant to each problem.

As ACT research and practice has continued to develop over the past few decades, these applications to specific problem areas have become more refined and specialized. Researchers and clinicians have found key adaptations that overcome the unique challenges that arise when treating given problem areas and that make ACT more acceptable and effective for the clients being served. In addition to the aforementioned areas, this book covers other specific areas such as anxiety and trauma (Chapter 15), eating disorders (Chapter 17), chronic pain (Chapter 20), medical conditions (Chapter 21), alcohol and drug use disorders (Chapter 22), smoking cessation (Chapter 23), psychosis (Chapter 24), and nonclinical applications in the workplace (Chapter 19). We have specifically focused on problem areas that have a particularly well-established evidence base for the efficacy of ACT and where this work has led to refinements in how ACT is adapted and delivered to address the unique needs of these clients. These chapters include a discussion of how the ACT model applies to the given problem area; research on how psychological inflexibility contributes to the problem; research on the efficacy of ACT for treating a particular problem; an overview of how ACT is applied (with a focus on more unique adaptations and treatment strategies for this area); and challenges and future directions for research and clinical practice. Overall, we hope this book provides readers with a clear understanding of how ACT has been applied in specific areas that may be of interest, both in research and clinically, and in areas for future growth.

Implementation of ACT

ACT is designed to be a functional and contextual intervention, flexible for adaptations across different settings and populations. Through its focus on processes of change applied to idiographic case conceptualization rather than manualized protocols for specific disorders, ACT provides a great deal of flexibility in how it is implemented to meet the needs of specific settings and populations (Levin et al., 2019). This book covers a wide range of settings and populations to illustrate how ACT is flexibly disseminated and implemented, including for youth (Chapter 27), through technology (Chapter 28) and cultural adaptations (Chapter 30). These three areas present very different adaptation needs; however, through some flexible adaptations, ACT can still be presented in a theoretically consistent and appealing manner.

For example, when implementing ACT with youth, it is crucial to consider the child/adolescent's developmental level and social context (e.g., families, friends) (Halliburton & Cooper, 2015). While the goal of ACT with youth is still to promote psychological flexibility, this construct looks different in youth as compared to adults. For example, youths are still developing and do not have the same sense of valuing as adults do. Thus, the goal of ACT with youth is to lay the groundwork for psychological flexibility and connect them to vitality and their sense of self in the moment. Several different models of ACT can be used with youth; the chapter in the present moment volume focuses on DNA-V (see Chapter 27). DNA-V turns the processes of ACT into "characters" (i.e., the Discoverer, Noticer, and Advisor) that are more easily digestible for youth (L. Hayes & Ciarrochi, 2015). However, this adaptation ultimately does not change ACT's underlying principles and philosophy. Rather, it repackages them so that they are more developmentally sensitive and digestible for youth.

As another example, ACT is often adapted for automated mobile and/or online interventions, allowing larger numbers of people to access care without common barriers (e.g., finances, distance, stigma; Andersson et al., 2018). ACT in traditional treatment settings is typically process-based and experiential, making heavy use of the therapeutic relationship in the moment. However, ACT implemented via automated technology requires adaptations to similarly target psychological flexibility without the presence (or with minimal presence) from a treatment provider. Online ACT can often be more didactic and is typically broken up into individual modules to teach the different processes of ACT. However, structured lessons do not necessarily mean less flexibility or experiential exercises; technological adaptations for ACT can often involve experiential self-guided exercises as well as individual guidance from coaches, chat features, and so forth. Similar to working with youth, adaptations of ACT for technology do not change the intervention at a theoretical level. Rather, the focus is on how to similarly move psychological flexibility in this unique format.

The last example we will highlight here is the use of ACT across cultures. ACT has been successfully studied and implemented internationally (Gloster et al., 2020). Part of the success comes from ACT's functional and contextual emphasis—doing what is workable and appropriate for each setting (e.g., DNA-V for youth, structured lessons in self-help interventions). Thus, cultural adaptations of ACT have a similar function. For example, ACT metaphors can and should be easily changed to make them more culturally understandable and appropriate (e.g., Hawaiian adaptations of the Passengers on the Bus metaphor as described in Chapter 30). In implementing ACT across cultures, clinicians rely on the theory of ACT (e.g., targeting psychological flexibility) to guide their behaviors, noting how both they and their client are situated in the past and present of cultural influence (e.g., the potential power dynamic of an older therapist and younger client). Thus, psychological flexibility remains the ultimate treatment goal, but the methods used are adjusted according to the cultural setting. Again, this is similar to how a clinician may adapt ACT to make it appropriate for youth or for a technological intervention.

On the whole, implementation of ACT across settings and groups has the same primary goal: reduce suffering by improving psychological flexibility. The road to arriving at this destination varies depending on the setting or group. This book covers a variety of implementation topics, including ACT training (Chapter 25), schools (Chapter 26), youth (Chapter 27), technology (Chapter 28), groups (Chapter 29), cultural adaptation (Chapter 30), and applications in behavior analysis (Chapter 31). These chapters are included given the breadth and depth of research and clinical development that has occurred in these areas and their unique challenges and features in implementing ACT. These topics exemplify how ACT can be adapted in a variety of ways to meet the needs of particular settings and populations, while remaining faithful to the treatment as defined functionally in targeting psychological flexibility. They also highlight areas for further innovation and development in these domains and provide models for how ACT can similarly be adapted for other contexts.

Conclusion

This book includes two chapters on the future of ACT and CBS. The first, by Wicksell et al. (Chapter 32), offers guidance in key areas where ACT research needs to grow. The second chapter, by Hayes et al. (Chapter 33), is based on the recommendations of the ACBS taskforce on Strategies and Tactics of Contextual Behavioral Science Research. This guiding document outlines areas of growth for research on ACT and other areas of CBS based on the underlying scientific strategy (Hayes et al., 2021). These papers point out that even though ACT has seen huge growth over the last 20-some years, many issues remain to be addressed. Some of these issues are as simple as a particular disorder, age group, cultural group, or setting. Others are much larger and long-term, including full inclusion and representation of all groups in the applied and research world.

The greatest strength of ACT and ACBS lies in their diverse numbers. Because ACBS has been an egalitarian organization since the beginning, it has been able to grow throughout the world. Sometimes the work grows simultaneously in different countries, and so it is only after much time that work is translated and findings are compared. At other times, the work is easily broadcast and is influencing all researchers. The pure amount of work that is occurring and the varying world views and mind-sets keep the work moving in novel directions. This work now also spans several decades, with many ongoing lines of research contributing a wealth of knowledge in key areas of basic science, theory, and applications to particular problem areas and settings. Hopefully, a comprehensive book like the present one, with its diverse array of contributing authors, will offer some guidance and clarity to help clinicians and researchers orient themselves to the current status of ACT and contribute to its ongoing movement in a systematic and meaningful direction.

References

Andersson, G. (2018). Internet interventions: Past, present and future. *Internet Interventions, 12*, 181–188.

Gloster, A. T., Walder, N., Levin, M., Twohig, M., & Karekla, M. (2020). The empirical status of acceptance and commitment therapy: A review of meta-analyses. *Journal of Contextual Behavioral Science, 18*, 181–192.

Halliburton, A. E., & Cooper, L. D. (2015). Applications and adaptations of acceptance and commitment therapy (ACT) for adolescents. *Journal of Contextual Behavioral Science, 4*, 1–11.

Hayes, L. L., & Ciarrochi, J. V. (2015). *The thriving adolescent: Using acceptance and commitment therapy and positive psychology to help teens manage emotions, achieve goals, and build connection*. New Harbinger Publications.

Hayes, S. C., Merwin, R. M., McHugh, L., Sandoz, E., A-tjak, J., Ruiz, F. J., .Barnes-Holmes, D., Bricker, J. B., Ciarrochi, J., Dixon, M. R., Po-Lun Fung, K., Gloster, A. T., Gobin, R. L., Gould, E. R., Hofmann, S. G., Kasujja, R., Karekla, M., Luciano, C., & McCracken, L. M. (2021). Report of the ACBS Task Force on the strategies and tactics of contextual behavioral science research. *Journal of Contextual Behavioral Science, 20*, 172–183.

Levin, M. E., Smith, B. M., & Smith, G. S. (2019). The potential benefits of flexibility for dissemination and implementation: Acceptance and commitment therapy as an example. *Perspectives on Behavior Science, 42*, 223–232.

Zettle, R. D., & Hayes, S. C. (1986). Dysfunctional control by client verbal behavior: The context of reason-giving. *The Analysis of Verbal Behavior, 4*, 30–38.

Zettle, R. D., & Rains, J. C. (1989). Group cognitive and contextual therapies in treatment of depression. *Journal of Clinical Psychology, 45*, 436–445.

SECTION 1

Conceptual Foundation

CHAPTER

1 Progression of ACT

Robert D. Zettle *and* Kelly G. Wilson

Abstract

Acceptance and commitment therapy (ACT) in the context of its historical and progressive development unfolded within three phases over the past 40 years. Events and influences in an initial phase that culminated in the development of comprehensive distancing as a precursor to ACT in the early 1980s preceded philosophical, theoretical, and conceptual refinements that took place during the next phase of ACT's progression. These advancements, including the further explication of functional contextualism, rule governance, and relational responding, contributed to the emergence of ACT as a coherent transdiagnostic intervention by the turn of this century. Ever increasing outcome and process research within the last two decades during ACT's third and most recent stage of progression have been instrumental in solidifying its current empirical status and expanding globalization.

Key Words: history, comprehensive distancing, ACT, functional contextualism, rule governance, relational frame theory

Progression of ACT

As reflected by its title, this article provides an overview of the current status of acceptance and commitment therapy (ACT; S. C. Hayes, Strosahl, & Wilson, 2012) situated within an historical account of the events that have led up to it. In short, we seek to show where ACT is at the moment and the paths that it took to arrive there. We particularly offer an update of the progression of ACT that has occurred since the initial publications concerning its development 10–15 years ago (Cullen, 2008; Zettle, 2005) and a more recent historical overview (Hooper & Larsson, 2015, Ch. 3).

ACT is often presented most simply as the application of a psychological flexibility model of human functioning comprising six interrelated processes: (1) acceptance, (2) defusion, (3) flexible present moment awareness, (4) self-as-context, (5) chosen values, and (6) committed action (S. C. Hayes et al., 2012). For our purposes here, we prefer to define ACT as (1) a psychological approach to the alleviation of human suffering and the promotion of human well-being, (2) based on functional contextualism, and (3) informed by relational frame theory (RFT; S. C. Hayes, Barnes-Holmes, & Roche, 2001) as an associated account of human language and cognition. We will accordingly refer to the progression over time in what might be regarded as technical/methodological, philosophical, and theoretical dimensions or strands within ACT, and how all three became integrated and interwoven with each other in forging its identity and determining its current status. As will be seen, ACT as we know it today, developed from a psychological approach known as comprehensive distancing (Zettle, 2005) that was philosophically based on radical behaviorism (Skinner, 1974) and informed theoretically by Skinner's (1969) conceptualization of rule-governed behavior.

Disclaimers

Before embarking on our journey, we would like to offer two disclaimers that are applicable to any historical account such as ours. First, key events within such narratives are in hindsight often presented in a more linear and coherent fashion (see Table 1.1) than how they actually

Table 1.1 Timeline of Key Events in the Progression of ACT

Date	Event
1982	Rule-governed behavior is extended as a behavior-analytic conceptual model for cognitive-behavioral interventions (Zettle & Hayes, 1982).
	First laboratory analogue study of comprehensive distancing's impact on pain tolerance is conducted and presented (S. C. Hayes, Korn, Zettle, Rosenfarb, & Cooper, 1982).
1984	Results of first randomized clinical trial of comprehensive distancing compared to cognitive therapy for depression are presented (Zettle & Hayes, 1984).
	"Making Sense of Spirituality" paper is published describing deictic framing and process of establishing transcendent perspective taking (S. C. Hayes, 1984).
1985	Introductory presentation of RFT (S. C. Hayes & Brownstein, 1985).
	Observer exercise added to the comprehensive distancing protocol.
1986	Parameters of contextualism as a broader world view within which radical behaviorism may be subsumed are presented (S. C. Hayes & Brownstein, 1986).
1987	First chapter-length presentation of comprehensive distancing (S. C. Hayes, 1987).
1989	Rule governance is fully reconceptualized within RFT (S. C. Hayes, 1989: S. C. Hayes & Hayes, 1989).
1991	First uses of "acceptance and commitment therapy" (Wilson, Khorakiwala, & Hayes, 1991) and ACT (Wilson & Taylor, 1991) in paper presentation titles.
1993	Functional contextualism is proposed as the philosophical foundation for ACT (S. C. Hayes, 1993).
	First use of acceptance and commitment therapy in a publication title (S. C. Hayes & Wilson, 1993).
1999	First book-length presentation of ACT published (S. C. Hayes, Strosahl, & Wilson, 1999).
2001	First-book length presentation of RFT published (S. C. Hayes et al., 2001).
2003	ACT and RFT list serves are started.
	First World Conference on ACT, RFT, & The New Behavioral Psychology is held in Linkoping, Sweden.
2005	Association for Contextual Behavioral Science is established.
	Get Out of Your Mind and into Your Life published (S. C. Hayes, 2005).
2008	First meta-analysis of ACT published (Öst, 2008).
2011	Development of the Acceptance and Action Questionnaire-II (AAQ-II; Bond et al., 2011).
2012	*The Journal of Contextual Behavioral Science* is established.
	Second edition of *Acceptance and Commitment Therapy* published (S. C. Hayes et al., 2012).

unfolded in real time. Accordingly, the development of ACT might be more appropriately viewed as the culmination of a reticulated process that more closely resembles solving a challenging crossword puzzle (S. C. Hayes, Zettle, Barnes-Holmes, & Biglan, 2016) than proving a geometric theorem. In particular, the delineation of functional contextualism did not precede the formulation of RFT, which in turn, then resulted in the creation of ACT (S. C. Hayes et al., 2016). Separate as well as coordinated progress in each of the three dimensions or strands that define ACT contributed to its overall development. Some of these advancements were more obvious and had rather immediate impacts, while others were more subtle with delayed influences.

Second, the history we offer is uniquely our own; indeed, it is difficult to see how it could be otherwise. The contributions and vision of single individuals are often critical in the development of many therapeutic approaches that end up being "branded" [e.g., Freud (1916) in the case of psychoanalysis and Beck (1976) for cognitive therapy], and ACT is no exception. Accordingly, suffice it to say that we would not be writing this article had it not been for our particular relationships with Steve Hayes that began at different junctures during the progression of ACT. Recently, he has reflected on some of his more personal experiences that were instrumental in its origination (S. C. Hayes, 2019).

Our Histories

The relationship between Robert D. Zettle (RDZ) and Steve goes back to the fall of 1976 when both arrived at the University of North Carolina at Greensboro (UNC-G). RDZ was beginning his first year in the clinical psychology program there, and Steve, who at the time had not yet defended his dissertation, had just been hired as a new assistant professor and assigned as RDZ's faculty advisor. It quickly became obvious that the two shared an interest from a behavior analytic perspective in better understanding the impact of human language and verbal behavior on clinical phenomena. It was an influence that Steve acknowledges had been ignited in him at least three years earlier by Willard Day (S. C. Hayes, 2001). RDZ became Steve's first doctoral student and for his dissertation completed what is retrospectively commonly regarded as the first randomized clinical trial of what later came to be recognized as ACT (Zettle, 1984). Both left UNC-G not long after its completion to accept academic appointments, RDZ at Wichita State University and Steve at the University of Nevada, Reno (UNR), where his relationship with Kelly G. Wilson (KGW) began.

KGW entered the graduate program in clinical psychology at UNR in the fall of 1989, at which point the Reno lab was well established. Steve had brought several graduate students with him from UNC-G and had attracted several others since his arrival at UNR in 1986. It was a highly productive time on multiple fronts. KGW's interests mapped well onto the breadth of lab interests at the time. He participated in qualitative clinical research on proto-ACT inspired by Willard Day's (1969) "behavioral phenomenology," engaged in basic human operant research on RFT (Wilson & Hayes, 1996), participated in seminars and conferences aimed at fleshing out functional contextualism, published theoretical work on ACT and RFT (S. C. Hayes & Wilson, 1993, 1994), and co-wrote and administered two National Institutes of Drug Abuse (NIDA) funded grants, ultimately co-authoring the first book-length ACT manual just prior to departing for an academic post at the University of Mississippi (S. C. Hayes et al., 1999).

We hope that the account that follows will be sufficiently consistent and coherent to be seen as plausible, while acknowledging that others who have been witnesses to and/or possible contributors to the development of ACT have their own and possibly somewhat different stories to tell. We thus make no claims that our narrative is "true" in the sense of elemental realism, although we have endeavored to appropriately document events and elements within it whenever possible. Rather, we will defer to readers to determine where between fiction and "history," as that term is most commonly used, our account falls. Regardless of where it might be placed, it may in our view be deemed as "true" to the extent that it is useful, as suggested by Skinner (1980, p. 308) in his comparison of historical and fictional narratives: "In most of the uses we make of history, fiction will serve as well. We demand consistency and plausibility in lieu of truth and thus preserve what really matters, a bit of vicarious experience." Like the King advised in *Alice's Adventures in Wonderland*, we will "begin at the beginning and go on till [we] come to the end: then stop" (Carroll, 1865).

The Beginning: 1976–1986

In order to present the historical context in which ACT emerged, our story begins just as the first wave of behavior therapy, which had been dominated by interventions based on operant and respondent conditioning principles, was about to be replaced by a second wave featuring cognitive-behavioral approaches (S. C. Hayes, 2004).

Rush et al. (1977) Paper

A key event in this transition, particularly given developments that had preceded it, was the Rush, Beck, Kovacs, and Hollon (1977) randomized clinical trial, which favorably compared cognitive therapy (Beck, Rush, Shaw, & Emery, 1979) to imipramine. This study was particularly noteworthy as it was the first one to report that a psychological approach was superior to medication in treating a psychiatric disorder. By the time of its publication, the need to more effectively address the role of human language and cognition in the initiation, maintenance, and treatment of abnormal behavior had become increasingly apparent to many first-wave behavior therapists, especially those serving adult outpatients. At a theoretical/conceptual level, however, more visible accounts of verbal-cognitive processes that had been offered by disgruntled behavior therapists (e.g., Mahoney, 1974) were much more mechanistic and mentalistic than behavior analytic in their orientation. At a technical level, related ways of weakening the dysfunctional impact of language and cognition within what by now had come to be regarded as "cognitive-behavior modification" (Meichenbaum, 1977) were largely limited to thought-stopping (e.g., Rimm, 1973) and coping self-statements as part of self-instructional training (Meichenbaum, 1972).

In our view, the Rush et al. (1977) paper transformed how behavior therapy was conceptualized and practiced at the time for at least three reasons. One, any psychotherapeutic approach shown to be more efficacious than pharmacotherapy, especially in treating depression as the most common presenting adult outpatient complaint, understandably received the attention of behavior therapists given their commitment to evidence-based practice. Second, apart from distinctions drawn by Beck (1970) between cognitive and behavior therapy, his treatment package included enough behavioral techniques, such as activity scheduling (Beck et al., 1979, Chapter 7), with which behavior therapists were already familiar, for it to be received as not too different or foreign. However, third and perhaps most importantly, what cognitive therapy offered that was new, namely cognitive restructuring, was a more sophisticated and apparently more efficacious means, relative to thought stopping and self-instructional training, of altering the cognitive control of negative thinking. Not surprisingly, cognitive restructuring as a treatment technique was soon added to existing behavior therapy protocols, thereby giving rise to cognitive-behavior therapy (CBT), even though its relative impact and ostensible mechanisms of action were later called into question based on component and process analyses of cognitive therapy (Jacobson et al., 1996; Zettle & Hayes, 1986, 1987).

Behavior Analysis and CBT

With the advent of this second wave of cognitive-behavioral approaches, any presence and influence that behavior analysis had in the development and practice of operant-based interventions within the first wave were diluted even further. It should be noted that Ferster (1967, 1972) had offered a behavior-analytic perspective on verbal psychotherapy that has since been cited as contributing to the development of functional analytic psychotherapy (R. J. Kohlenberg & Tsai, 1991). However, this work, did not readily point to any innovative changes to behavioral therapeutic practice at the time and by the mid- to late 1970s had clearly been overshadowed by a number of the developments already discussed. As a result, turning to the writings of Skinner (1957, 1969) appeared to be the most fruitful approach to take by those wishing to mount a radical behavioral counter-response to the conceptual challenges and practical changes presented by the "cognitive revolution" taking place within behavior therapy.

Even though Skinner considered *Verbal Behavior* (1957) his most important work (Salzinger, 1990), it became apparent that this work was of limited utility due to its focus on the behavior of speakers while relatively neglecting that of listeners. In short, Skinner's conceptual analyses of speaking, for example, might help explain why a depressed client's thinking exemplifies Beck's (1967, 1987) negative cognitive triad, but not why or how such thinking then influences the emotional reactions and overt behavior of that same client as a listener. Even more importantly, such a limited account had no substantive clinical value in guiding effective ways to weaken such pernicious cognitive control.

By comparison, Skinner's (1969) formulation of rule-governed behavior, especially when modified and expanded, initially proved to be more useful in several respects in suggesting a radical behavioral framework in which to conceptualize cognitive therapy and related approaches (Zettle & Hayes, 1982). For one, it shifted more focus to the behavior of listeners, including instances in which rule-followers and rule-givers share the same skin. A problematic issue, however, quickly became apparent and was not completely resolved until later when it was extensively addressed by RFT (see Barnes-Holmes et al., 2001, as well as Article 4 this volume). This problem concerned Skinner's (1966, 1969) topographical definition of rules as "contingency-specifying stimuli." When this issue was at least temporarily addressed by recasting rules as verbal discriminative stimuli, rule-governed behavior more broadly could be meaningfully reconceptualized as comprising three different functional units (pliance, tracking, and augmenting) under the control of two distinct sets of contingencies, one naturalistic and the other arbitrary and socially mediated.

An expansive conceptual framework that pointed to multiple controlling variables for rule-following, and to a lesser degree for rule formulation, had some rather important practical and theoretical implications. For one, it suggested that coping self-statements may function as plys, or rules whose following is mediated by a verbal-social community, and thus have limited efficacy unless delivered and followed in a public context. This finding had already been reported (Zettle & Hayes, 1979) and subsequently replicated by other related studies (e.g., S. C. Hayes & Wolf, 1984; Rosenfarb & Hayes, 1984).

Comprehensive Distancing

More importantly for the development of ACT, examining cognitive therapy through the lens of rule governance also suggested a new therapeutic approach. This approach, referred to as comprehensive distancing (CD), was further influenced by the personal struggles of S. C. Hayes (2019) with panic attacks at the time. This forerunner of ACT sought to expand the process of distancing from cognitions as the "first critical step" within cognitive therapy (Hollon & Beck, 1979, p. 189) in which clients are encouraged to respond to their depressing thoughts as mere psychological events rather than as immutable facts prior to restructuring them. Many readers will recognize the similarities to emphases on acceptance, defusion, and even mindfulness within ACT, and to what is more often referred to as "decentering" (Bernstein et al., 2015; Safran & Segal, 1996) within mindfulness-based cognitive therapy (Segal, Williams, & Teasdale, 2002).

Formulating rules, thinking, reason-giving (Zettle & Hayes, 1986), and similar verbal activities from a behavior-analytic perspective cannot function as causes for other actions insofar as they cannot be directly manipulated (S. C. Hayes & Brownstein, 1986). Nonetheless, they may participate in controlling relationships with other behavior when sufficiently supported by verbal-social contingencies. For example, a range of destructive and dysfunctional actions may be socially acceptable when justified by a narrative of plausible reasons (S. C. Hayes, 1987). This analysis further suggested the viability of creating a special verbal-social community within the context of therapy in which deleterious cognitive control could be systematically weakened, for example, through acceptance and defusion, without resorting necessarily to change in cognitive content.

Initial empirical support for CD was provided by a laboratory experiment increasing cold pressor-induced pain tolerance (S. C. Hayes et al., 1982) that was published 17 years later (S. C. Hayes, Bissett, et al., 1999), a randomized clinical trial comparing it favorably to cognitive therapy for depression (Zettle & Hayes, 1984), and a series of unsystematic case studies (S. C. Hayes, 1987). While CD included many of the treatment components and techniques that are commonly part of the contemporary practice of ACT, there were also at least two noteworthy omissions. Behavioral homework was included in CD, but because it was not linked to values, it ostensibly functioned more like mood-enhancing behavioral activation (e.g., Martell, Addis, & Jacobson, 2001) than valued action. In short, relatively speaking, CD was more of an acceptance and willingness therapy than an acceptance *and commitment to valued action* therapy.

Also missing from CD was the *Observer* exercise (S. C. Hayes et al., 2012, pp. 233–237) that is often used to complement the *Chessboard* metaphor (which was included) in fostering self-as-context within ACT. This exercise was not added until at least two years later at the suggestion of a graduate student in the Hayes lab (S. C. Hayes, personal communication, March 28, 2005), not coincidentally around the same time of the "Making Sense of Spirituality" paper (S. C. Hayes, 1984). This publication is understandably included in a collection of Hayes's (2015) canonical papers and merits special mention as beginning the link that would later be solidified between RFT and ACT. It makes no explicit mention of deictic framing, but it elucidates the processes from which the "behavior of seeing seeing from a perspective" (S. C. Hayes, 1984, p. 103) results in a transcending sense of self.

An even bigger boost in retrospect to the relationship being fostered between CD and RFT occurred near the end of what might be regarded as ACT's decade-long, initial developmental stage with the unveiling of RFT by S. C. Hayes and Brownstein (1985). Sidman's (1971) report of untrained equivalence classes that emerged between printed words and pictures, as well as between spoken and printed words, in teaching reading to a teen with a severe intellectual disability, was recognized as a prototype for how a more expansive repertoire of arbitrary applicable relational responding could be acquired as operant behavior. The S. C. Hayes and Brownstein paper also positioned RFT to ultimately subsume rule governance by reconceptualizing rules as verbal stimuli that serve a discriminative function because of their "participation in relational frames established by the verbal community for the purpose of producing such effects" (1985, p. 19).

The End of the Beginning

In summary, by 1986, CD as a precursor to ACT had been developed as (1) a psychological approach to the alleviation of human suffering, (2) based on radical behaviorism and (3) informed by a theoretical model of rule governance. At this juncture, Hayes would relocate to UNR to focus more during the next decade and a half on delineating functional contextualism as a broader philosophical foundation for ACT and RFT as a related conceptual framework in further informing its development. Unfortunately, on a sad and more personal note, especially for RDZ, these advancements would occur without any further contributions from Aaron Brownstein who suddenly passed away far too early in the spring of 1986 (Shull, 1986). Aaron was an astute experimental behavior analyst, but one just as, if not even more interested, in understanding complex human behavior, including clinical phenomena (e.g., Greenspoon & Brownstein, 1967a, 1967b), as he was with the actions of rats and pigeons in Skinner boxes. Although the present article cites only two references in which Aaron was Steve's co-author, with one of them (Hayes & Brownstein, 1986) published posthumously, both were foundational to the development of functional contextualism (Hayes & Brownstein, 1986) and RFT (Hayes & Brownstein, 1985), and thus, albeit less directly, major influences in the progression of ACT as well. If there is an "unsung hero" in our story, he's Aaron Brownstein.

Laying the Groundwork: 1986–2000

Grasping the progression of ACT during this period would be difficult without some understanding of the extraordinary social network in which the development occurred. Hayes came to Reno in 1986 in a leadership position as the Director of Training of the Clinical PhD program, later transitioning to Department Chair. Under his leadership, the behavioral presence in the department grew with the addition of Bill and Victoria Follette to the faculty in 1989, the founding of the Behavior Analysis Program by Linda Hayes in 1990, and the subsequent hiring of behavior analysis faculty (L. J. Hayes et al., 2016). The department embodied an extraordinary unity of purpose in the development of behavior analysis theoretically, philosophically, and in various applications. Although there was considerable interest in ACT and CD proto-ACT, which certainly drew the attention of incoming clinical students, that work was very much a product of the behavioral thinking aimed at broadening and deepening the behavioral tradition.

Steve and Linda Hayes were running a lab in tandem when KGW arrived, and the lab meetings became as much a debate society as they were a place to organize the business of a research lab. Assorted elements of the behavioral tradition were poured together there. Willard Day, who had been a faculty member at UNR—had died in the spring of 1989, but his entirely unique view of a behavior theory and philosophy was very much alive (Day, 1969). As referenced earlier, Day had inspired Hayes to examine the behavior analysis of language deeply, but he was also a serious student of the philosophy of science. Indeed, he had taken a sabbatical year to travel to Oxford and read philosophy during the period in which Gilbert Ryle was Waynflete Professor of Metaphysics.

Hayes's move to Reno was not random. He joined the faculty there while Willard was still alive and active, recognizing it as an historically appropriate place for developing a broad and rich behavioral tradition. The examination of contextualism and a deeper look at pragmatism were natural activities in that environment. That seriousness in the study of behavior theory and philosophy was ever present in a series of seminars, one of which, co-taught by Steve and Linda Hayes, focused solely on Steven Pepper's (1942) work. The seminar contained five students, Steve and Linda, as well as Jim Owen, a radical behaviorist faculty member from the UNR Speech and Language Department. It was not so much a university course as it was an ongoing debate as we examined psychology through the lens of Pepper's work. There was no unanimity of view. Table pounding, shouted arguments, and sometimes preposterous thought experiments were common. Linda Hayes launched a series of small seminars throughout the 1990s with a distinctive Kantorian flavor on behavioral philosophy and verbal behavior. These conversations were not confined to the lab and classroom. Rather, they spilled over into the hallways, at lunch, evenings at the Hayes's residence, as well as through social gatherings at various homes of students and faculty organized under a series of names, including "Food and Philosophy" and "Beer and Behaviorism," that involved readings and discussions of wildly varying topics relevant to psychology and philosophy.

It was in this context that the groundwork for ACT clinical innovation developed. The broader fleshing out of clinical behavior analysis occurred in a context centered in basic behavior analysis as well as in other perspectives on the use of behavioral thinking to applied problems. Notably, both Bill and Victoria Follette brought with them considerable exposure to the work of Bob Kohlenberg and a functional-analytic psychotherapy perspective (R. J. Kohlenberg & Tsai, 1991). And of course, Barbara Kohlenberg was among the graduate students who had come to Reno from UNC-G with Steve.

The Debut of ACT

By the early 1990s, the philosophical and theoretical systems in which CD had been situated had been supplanted; radical behaviorism had been superseded by functional contextualism; and a Skinnerian model of rule governance had been replaced with RFT. The stage was accordingly set to transform CD into ACT. Comprehensive distancing was always something of a troubling name. Insiders knew that the "distancing" in CD was not initiated to "get away from" troubling thoughts or to get enough separation to see them more objectively and rationally. Instead, its purpose was to create sufficient psychological space within which clients could make contact more broadly with difficult emotional content. Such expanded contact might include recognition of content patterning, contexts that provoked such content, connection of difficult content within personal history, and critically, the functional role such content played in organizing behavior.

A name that requires an explanation is by its nature troublesome. The acronym ACT emerged in the Hayes lab at Reno when a several week-long brainstorming session produced a variety of acronyms, including CAT (contextual analytic therapy) and RAP (radical acceptance psychotherapy). Our best recollection is that the acronym came first, perhaps as a scramble of CAT. ACT had the right flavor as a therapy that was all about getting into action. The acronym lent itself to the spirit of the work, but also as short-hand for the treatment: Accept, Choose, and Take action. ACT also had the advantage that it could be spoken as a word consistent with the treatment—act, not A-C-T. And ultimately as a therapy name, acceptance and commitment therapy was intuitively understandable and consistent with the developing work.

Who actually came up with the ACT acronym and name is lost to KGW, who was there, as well as to Steve Hayes, who was consulted. As best as we can document in official conference programs, the first reference to acceptance and commitment therapy appeared in the title of a paper presented at the Association for Behavior Analysis (ABA) conference in May 1991 (Wilson et al., 1991). This would place the date of the name change to the fall of 1990, as this was the deadline for the ABA conference paper proposals. A few papers appeared in the vitas at the November 1990 Association for the Advancement of Behavior Therapy Conference; however, those were certainly title changes that happened at or right before their presentations. It took another three years for the name "acceptance and commitment therapy" to first appear in the title of a publication (S. C. Hayes & Wilson, 1994) rather than conference presentations.

Apart from a mere alteration in name, some strategic and technical changes were made to CD that resulted in ACT as we know it today. Probably the most prominent of these changes was the addition of values to the protocols and the explicit linking of committed action to values. Hayes's personal struggle with panic was his entry point to ACT. KGW came to the work while he was recovering from severe substance dependence; acceptance was important, but purpose and meaning as described by Victor Frankl (1965) were central. Behavior therapists are always interested in selecting the most potent available reinforcers. Understanding them for verbally competent individuals necessarily required a behavioral examination of verbally constructed values and interventions suited to that analysis. At the end of the 1990 academic year, KGW proposed a comprehensive examination on a behavioral analysis of Frankl's noogenic neuroses and constructed the first values protocols for a NIDA treatment development grant in 1993. Values first appeared in published form in two articles appearing in *The Behavior Analyst* (S. C. Hayes & Wilson, 1993; 1994).

Theoretical Developments

Following the publication of an entire book dedicated to Aaron Brownstein and rule-governed behavior (S. C. Hayes, 1989), the reconceptualization that had begun with the Hayes and Brownstein (1985) paper and expanded by Hayes (1987) moved even further away from a traditional Skinnerian perspective to one that was more clearly based within RFT. Especially noteworthy in this volume was a chapter written by Hayes and Hayes (1989) whose stated purpose was "to apply a relational perspective to the issue of rule-governance. Behavior controlled by verbal stimuli is a different kind of behavior because it involves different psychological processes" (p. 177). In this endeavor, several basic elements of RFT were referenced that predated the expanded coverage they would later receive within the S. C. Hayes et al. (2001) text; aka "the purple book." In particular, mutual entailment, combinatorial entailment, transfer of stimulus functions, and contextual control over relational responding (i.e., C_{rel} and C_{func}) were all explicated in accounting for "the verbal action of the listener as a basis for rule-governance" (p. 153).

This emergent thinking in rule governance and RFT was a hot topic within the lab at Reno and spawned a variety of basic experimental laboratory research, including an experimental analysis of the development of relational responding in infants (Lipkens, 1992). There were also studies examining relational responding in complex human behavior, including network structure (e.g., B. S. Kohlenberg, 1994; Wilson & Hayes, 1996), transformation of motivational functions (Ju, 2000), and propagation and durability of networks among pathology-relevant stimuli (Wilson, 1998). These studies represented a quite organic follow-up from the dissertations that had been completed in Hayes's lab at UNC-G on language development, stimulus equivalence, and rule-governed behavior, including those by Devaney (1985), Rosenfarb (1986), Wulfert (1987), and, importantly, the publication of David Steele's dissertation, which was arguably the first clearly relational frame theory-oriented experimental analysis, (though it was not called RFT at the time; Steele & Hayes, 1991).

Philosophical Developments

Expanding beyond a strict Skinnerian conceptualization of rule-governed behavior quite understandably led to a closer critical examination of radical behaviorism itself as the philosophical framework within which it was embedded. The building out of a behavioral community at Reno provided a fertile environment for launching a theoretical and philosophical discussion with similarly interested individuals from around the world, resulting in a series of books and conferences, including *Dialogues on Verbal Behavior* (L. J. Hayes & Chase, 1991), *Understanding Verbal Relations* (S. C. Hayes & Hayes, 1992), *Varieties of Scientific Contextualism* (S. C. Hayes, Hayes, Reese, & Sarbin, 1993), *Behavior Analysis of Language and Cognition* (L. J. Hayes, Hayes, Ono, & Sato, 1994), and *Investigations in Behavioral Epistemology* (L. J. Hayes & Ghezzi, 1997). In an edited volume focused on elucidating scientific contextualism (S. C. Hayes et al., 1993), Hayes argued that contextualism as one of Pepper's (1942) four world views could be meaningfully divided into descriptive and functional variants. While Skinner's (1974) radical behaviorism clearly can be regarded as contextualistic, Hayes regarded it as dogmatic in that it reflected the purposes of science to predict and control behavior rather than Skinner's own selection of that particular goal. Functional contextualism in which goals are explicitly linked to the clearly articulated preanalytic values of predicting and influencing behavior was instead recommended as a philosophical foundation for psychological interventions, thus allowing for a functional contextualism with goals other than prediction and influence.

Clinical Developments

During the 1990s, mainstream CBT was highly focused on treatment outcome studies. CBT treatment protocols were devised for psychiatric diagnoses, with outcomes studied in randomized clinical trials (RCTs) funded by the National Institutes of Health (NIH). The workgroup at Reno had taken a very different turn, as reflected in the intensive work on theory, philosophy, and basic empirical work discussed previously. Although grant-funded RCTs were not the focus, three NIH studies were funded during this time period that were all developmental and exploratory in nature. The first study was a protocol development grant from NIDA funded in 1993 examining the application of ACT to poly-substance abuse, in which the first values protocols were formalized. That grant was followed by a subsequent RCT extending that protocol development, funded in 1997. Both of these grants were directed by KGW. Finally, a study involving the treatment of nicotine dependent participants was funded in 2000, spearheaded by Elizabeth Gifford, that explored an integration of ACT and functional-analytic psychotherapy principles. Finally, Steve Hayes served as a consultant to a training project at a large Seattle-based health maintenance organization. The result was an innovative field effectiveness study in which the treatment was not studied per se, but rather the focus was the exposure of a cohort of therapists to ACT training over an intensive year of training and supervision. The study importantly involved a diverse mental health population being seen in primary care and a community mental health clinic with neither fixed diagnoses nor protocol length (Strosahl, Hayes, Bergan, & Romano, 1998).

In addition to these grant-funded efforts, small, unfunded dissertation studies examined a broad array of presenting concerns in a variety of clinical settings. Bach (2000) tested a brief protocol with patients presenting with psychotic symptoms at a regional psychiatric hospital. Geiser (1992) treated chronic pain patients at a Reno pain clinic. This period also produced a series of analogue studies examining components thought to be central to ACT, such as acceptance, thought suppression, and metaphor (Afari, 1996; McCurry, 1991; Pistorello, 1998; Walser, 1998). Khorakiwala's (1991) dissertation used a variant of Willard Day's behavioral phenomenology in a qualitative analysis of processes of change in proto-ACT.

From the start, the development of ACT was an iterative and reticulated process. ACT development was never merely a therapy development project. Rather ACT began and continues to be a component of a much broader effort. The focus was on careful theory and philosophy, enriched by experimental analyses, and qualitative research on therapy processes, stretching from the lab to the clinic and back again. All this was with an eye toward laying a foundation for a broadly applicable theory of human suffering, struggle, and its remediation. This work did not go unnoticed. During the 1990s, Dermot Barnes-Holmes, soon joined by Yvonne Barnes-Holmes, launched what would become the most productive human operant lab in the world, beginning in Cork, Ireland. Frank Bond applied ACT principles to workplace environments and published the first organizational behavior management application of ACT, giving rise to a stream of related research (Bond & Bunce, 2000). Carmen Luciano produced an active lab in Almeria, Spain, with research stretching from basic research to clinical applications. All of these interactions, stretching from basic theory and philosophy, from the lab to the clinic, culminated in the publication of the first book-length description of ACT (S. C. Hayes et al., 1999) and set the foundation for a global treatment development effort.

Making a Mark on the World: 2000–Present

By this juncture in our story, the first book-length presentation of ACT had been published (S. C. Hayes et al., 1999) and a comparable one covering RFT (S. C. Hayes et al., 2001) was about to appear, leading to the international dissemination of ACT and a rather rapid proliferation in several types of research related to it. In retrospect, such sudden growth and visibility, as will be seen, perhaps quite understandably eventually led to considerable pushback by ACT's critics and skeptics.

The Globalization of ACT

The Association for Contextual Behavioral Science (ACBS) was established in 2005 as the primary organizational home for researchers as well as practitioners of ACT and RFT. Very quickly, however, it also attracted an increasingly broader array of contextually minded clinicians and scientists. ACBS currently has over 9000 members (n.d.-h) representing a diverse range of interests within contextual behavioral science; including evolution science, comparative psychology, climate change, the use of psychedelics, and psychodynamic psychotherapy.

ACBS provides access to a wide array of materials and resources about ACT, including notices of training opportunities, as well as postings of publications and assessment instruments, in addition to treatment manuals and protocols. Even prior to the formal founding of ACBS, a concerted effort had already been underway to disseminate ACT beyond its origination in the United States. Although ACBS was not incorporated until 2005, it was born in tragedy. Steve Hayes was preparing to fly to Sweden to do a workshop for Psykolog Partners, a Swedish company that provided a variety of mental health services. The day Dr. Hayes was to fly, he got a call canceling his flight. In fact, every flight in the United States was canceled that day—Tuesday, September 11, 2001. Undaunted, Psykolog Partners went beyond rescheduling the workshop and organized the first proto-ACBS conference, held in Linköping, Sweden, in August 2003. Since 2006, when ACBS assumed responsibility for organizing world conferences, over half of them by design have been held outside the United States—in the United Kingdom, the Netherlands, Italy, Australia, Germany, Spain, Canada, and Ireland—in an effort to make ACT research and practice more accessible to the rest of the world (n.d.-g). While U.S. residents still constitute the largest membership subgroup within ACBS (17%), as of this writing, another 92 nations, or roughly 47% of the world's countries, from every continent save Antarctica, are now represented.

ACBS has worked hard at inclusion. Membership dues are values-based. The member gets to choose their dues, with individuals from wealthier countries being encouraged to pay higher dues. The ACBS website is wiki, allowing all members to access and share treatment and educational materials. ACBS has resisted certification of therapists. It does recognize ACT trainers through a peer review process, but this is not a profit-making effort.

Evidence of the strategy's success in establishing an international community is provided by the current composition of 40 affiliated ACBS chapters worldwide (n.d.-f). The majority of them (i.e., 26, or 65%) are outside the United States and have been variously organized nationally (e.g., Argentina and Finland), regionally (e.g., Australia and New Zealand), and, in some instances, by linguistic communities (e.g., Dutch speakers in Belgium and the Netherlands and French speakers in Belgium and France). ACT has grown by resisting exclusivity, instead promoting an organization of contextual therapies. Many of these chapters have already hosted successful conferences of their own or have plans to do so, thus further increasing ACT's local and regional presence and influence. ACT's international visibility has also been increased, albeit to perhaps not the same degree, by the creation of organizational affiliates of ACBS (n.d.-e), as, for example, in Africa, India, the United Arab Emirates, and Western Balkans; where chapters have not yet been firmly established. ACT's increased globalization and worldwide reach is reflected not only by the diversity of the ACBS membership list, but over the past 5 years by 11 related intervention projects that have been conducted in countries that appear on lists of low- to middle-income countries (ACBS, n.d.-c). One of the most recent examples of this outreach was the implementation and evaluation of an ACT-based, self-help intervention for South Sudanese refugees (Tol et al., 2020).

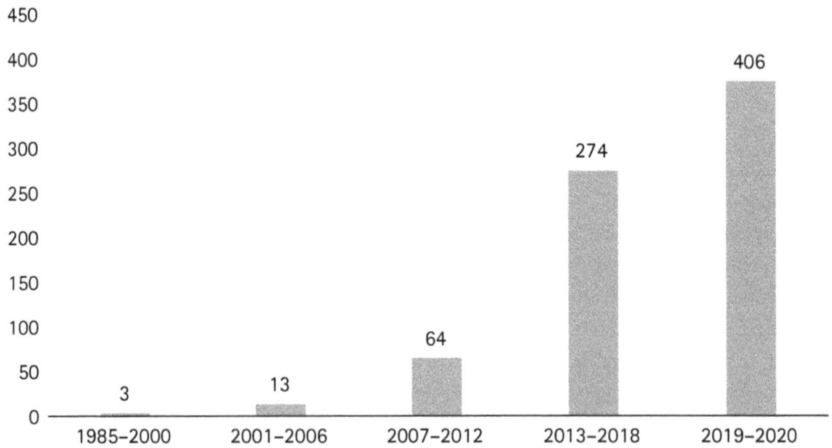

Figure 1.1 *Cumulative Number of ACT Outcome Publications*

Note. The figure includes "in press" publications listed as of May 2022 at https://contextualscience.org/ACT_Randomized_Controlled_Trials.

Research Progression of ACT

The increasing number of projects conducted in impoverished regions of the world has been part of a broader exponential growth of ACT-related research within several domains occurring over the last two decades. (see Figure 1.1)

OUTCOME RESEARCH

For ease of discussion, we will provide separate overviews of research that has evaluated the efficacy and effectiveness of ACT during this most recent stage of its progression.

EFFICACY RESEARCH

As seen in the accompanying figure, the number of publications from 1985 to 2000 (i.e., four) that compared the efficacy of ACT to other interventions and/or various control conditions increased by nearly 300% during the next 5 years. The growth has increased exponentially over the last two decades to where there are as of this writing over 900 efficacy studies that have either been published or are "in press." Although measures of symptomatic relief have been the primary outcome variables in such investigations, researchers increasingly have also examined improvements in quality of life (S. C. Hayes, Luoma, Bond, Mausda, & Lillis, 2006) and, even more recently, increases in flourishing as additional dependent measures in evaluating ACT's impact (Bohlmeijer, Lamers, & Fledderus, 2015).

By 2010, enough randomized trials of ACT had been accumulated that systematic reviews and meta-analyses of its efficacy began appearing. Most of these initial evaluations, unlike later and more recent ones (ACBS, n.d.-k), focused on ACT more broadly rather than on its treatment of specific presenting problems (e.g., Veehof, Oskam, Schreurs, & Bohlmeijer, [2011] for chronic pain, Bluett, Homan, Morrison, Levin, & Twohig, [2014] for anxiety disorders and OCD, and Howell and Passmore [2019] for depression). Two meta-analyses that received more attention and reaction within the ACT community than most were critical ones by Öst (2008, 2014). In his first publication, Öst (2008) concluded that ACT trials did not merit recognition as an empirically supported treatment, despite significant and moderate effect sizes, because of a relative lack of methodological rigor compared to traditional CBT studies. In response to a subsequent rejoinder to his criticisms (Gaudiano, 2009), Öst (2009) conceded that ACT research was not funded at levels comparable to CBT trials, but maintained that the American Psychological Association's recognition of ACT as having "moderately strong" empirical support for treatment of depression was unjustified.

A second and updated meta-analysis by Öst (2014) 6 years later was even more critical of ACT. In this work, Öst concluded that there had been no methodological improvements in outcome research over that period of time. Moreover, he noted a deterioration in overall effect size, resulting in no basis for regarding ACT as a "well-established" treatment for any disorder. A robust response from a team of ACT researchers (Atkins et al., 2017) that catalogued a plethora of factual and interpretational errors that likely biased Öst's conclusions was followed by an equally spirited rebuttal (Öst, 2017) that to date has effectively ended the back-and-forth sparring.

Perhaps both motivated by and despite Öst's criticisms, ACT researchers have become increasingly successful in obtaining external funding (ACBS, n.d.-i). Moreover, efficacy research on ACT has progressed to the point that the Society of Clinical Psychology (SCP) has recognized the therapy as an evidence-based treatment approach for multiple psychiatric disorders. More specifically, SCP (Division 12 of the American Psychological Association) has affirmed ACT's transdiagnostic status by concluding that it enjoys strong empirical support in the treatment of chronic pain (n.d.-a), and modest support in addressing depression (n.d.-b), mixed anxiety (n.d.-c), obsessive-compulsive disorder (n.d.-d), and psychotic symptoms (n.d.-e).

EFFECTIVENESS RESEARCH

One of the more noteworthy evaluations of ACT's effectiveness within the last decade resulted from its inclusion in a national dissemination and training initiative for treatment of depression implemented by the U.S. Department of Veterans Affairs (VA; Walser, Karlin, Trockel, Mazina, & Taylor, 2013). What has been referred to as the "roll-out" has now trained hundreds of VA therapists in ACT, who in turn, have implemented it with thousands of their veteran clients. Indirect comparisons to controlled trials of ACT for depression (Zettle, 2015) as well as to traditional CBT within the same VA program (Karlin et al., 2012) in both reducing depressive symptoms and in enhancing quality of life have been favorable.

More recent research suggests that the effectiveness of ACT may be reasonably robust when offered outside the United States in a group format for both inpatients and outpatients with varying clinical presentations. Similar to the results of the VA roll-out, a German clinical trial found that ACT and CBT were equally effective in treating inpatient depression (Samaan et al., 2020), while an Australian study documented the effectiveness of ACT with a transdiagnostic outpatient sample (Pinto et al., 2017).

PROCESS OF CHANGE RESEARCH

Beginning with the earliest outcome studies (Zettle & Hayes, 1986; Zettle & Rains, 1989), ACT researchers have been committed to not only investigating its therapeutic impact, but variables that may mediate such change (ACBS, n.d.-d). The most recent systematic review of ACT mediational studies specifically focused on those published from 2006 to 2015 in updating an earlier review by S. C. Hayes et al. (2006). Stockton et al. (2019) found general support for ACT's purported mechanisms of change but also noted some methodological limitations. They reported that not all six processes posited to contribute to psychological flexibility (S. C. Hayes et al., 2006) were examined to the same degree. Since the introduction (S. C. Hayes et al., 2004) and subsequent revision of the Acceptance Action Questionnaire (Bond et al., 2011) and translation into several different languages (ACBS, n.d.-a), acceptance has been the specific process that has received the most attention as a possible mediator of therapeutic change. However, with the recent development of psychometrically sound measures for self-as-context (Yu, McCracken, & Norton, 2016; Zettle et al., 2018), future mediational research now has the means available to evaluate the full range of processes within the model on which ACT is based.

LABORATORY-BASED COMPONENT RESEARCH

Investigations of ACT's possible mechanisms of action have also progressed through laboratory-based component studies. This strategy is a long-standing one within ACT-related research, going back almost 40 years (S. C. Hayes et al., 1982), in which analogues of treatment components linked to specific processes within the psychological flexibility model are experimentally manipulated as independent variables. For example, participants have been instructed to "just notice" and "make room" for distressing thoughts related to shock-induced pain while continuing a valued task in investigating processes of acceptance and committed action (Gutiérrez, Luciano, Rodríguez, & Fink, 2004). As with the other ACT research domains reviewed, a sufficient number of such analogue studies have been completed over time to conduct meta-analyses of them. The most recent one of which we are aware found broad-based support for the psychological flexibility model, with larger effect sizes noted for component conditions that were more experientially based (e.g., use of metaphors and exercises) than those presented by a rationale alone (Levin, Hildebrandt, Lillis, & Hayes, 2012).

Breadth of ACT Applications

The common depiction of ACT as a transdiagnostic approach (e.g., Dindo, Van Liew, & Arch, 2017; Muto & Mitamura, 2011) both reflects and obscures the wide array of presenting problems and concerns to which it has increasingly been applied over the last two decades. Such a description appropriately underscores that ACT practitioners and proponents over the course of its development typically have often opted for breadth over depth of coverage in applying it to mental health conditions. This progression, for example, can be contrasted with that of cognitive therapy that focused almost exclusively on establishing itself as a treatment of depression before being extended to other disorders (e.g., Clark & Beck, 2010). While ACT for anxiety and related concerns have received the most attention (ACBS; n.d.-k), it has, as noted earlier, also demonstrated its efficacy in treatment of chronic pain, depression, obsessive-compulsive disorder, and psychotic symptoms to be recognized by SCP as an evidence-based intervention for these clinical presentations as well. Other behavioral health concerns addressed by ACT, though less intensively, have included substance abuse, eating disorders, marital discord, borderline personality disorder, and trichotillomania (ACBS, n.d.-k).

While ACT can thus be reasonably regarded as an efficacious transdiagnostic approach for mental health concerns, doing so fails to recognize its expanded applications to medical conditions and other areas of human suffering and functioning. ACT, for example, has shown benefits in assisting those dealing with an array of medical and neurological concerns including stroke, asthma, HIV, tinnitus, fibromyalgia, diabetes, smoking, cancer, and multiple sclerosis (ACBS, n.d.-k). Going all the way back to the third published comparative outcome study of ACT (Bond & Bunce, 2000), it has also addressed human concerns, such as worksite stress management, which have presented themselves in more everyday contexts apart from mental health centers and medical clinics. What has increasingly been referred to as acceptance and commitment *training* (Moran, 2015), for instance, has been extended to job-site performance and safety, parenting, and skill coaching, among other areas (ACBS, n.d.-k).

Insofar as ACT rests on a broad-based model of human functioning that highlights the role of psychological flexibility, its breadth of application is not arbitrarily constrained. A further reflection of this diversity is that the majority of the current 39 special interest groups (SIGs) within ACBS (n.d.-j) are concerned with some aspect or dimension of ACT. Some of the SIGs focus on particular presenting problems (e.g., ACT and Autism, Applying ACT to Addictions, and Pain SIG), several are organized around specific populations (e.g., ACT for Military, ACT for the Christian Client, and Aging in Context) or practice settings (e.g., ACT in Education, College/University Student Mental Health, ACT in Primary Care), while still others are composed of those with shared professional or personal identities (e.g., ACT and Judaism, Occupational Therapy and ACT, and Social Work SIG).

Variety of Implementation Formats

Beginning with the publication of the first ACT-based, transdiagnostic self-help book (S. C. Hayes & Smith, 2005), over the past decade and a half there has been a progressive increase in developing creative ways to make the treatment approach more accessible and one that goes beyond the traditional face-to-face, client-therapist format. These alternative delivery systems have included the use of computer-based protocols, smartphones, apps, and other forms of telehealth in addition to bibliotherapy (ACBS, n.d.-b). This trend is likely to accelerate further, given the current global pandemic and its aftermath. A recent meta-analysis of self-help as a format for delivering ACT documented small effect sizes for depression and anxiety that were enhanced when supplemented with clinician guidance (French, Golijani-Moghaddam, & Schröder, 2017). This overall evaluation parallels the conclusions of an even more recent systematic review and meta-analysis of internet-based ACT (Thompson, Destree, Albertella, & Fontenelle, 2021).

Forging a Mature Identity

A final sequence of events that occurred within the relatively recent history of ACT warrants inclusion in our narrative because of its impact in forming ACT's mature self-identity. If there was a single trigger for this process, it was the argument that ACT exemplified an increasingly emergent third wave of CBT embracing the use of mindfulness and acceptance strategies that also differed from the previous generation of more traditional CBT approaches on both philosophical and technical grounds (S. C. Hayes, 2004). As noted, the philosophical foundation of ACT, in particular, is functional contextualism rather than some variant of mechanism (Pepper, 1942) that appears to at least implicitly underlie most traditional forms of CBT, such as Beckian cognitive therapy (S. C. Hayes, 2004). Additionally, ACT and other third-wave approaches favor secondary change techniques to alter the function or relationship that clients have with their problematic private events (e.g., defusion and mindfulness practices) over seeking to modify their form or content (e.g., disputation and cognitive restructuring).

The assertion that a new wave of CBT was occurring was greeted with rather passionate and sometimes heated pushback from threatened proponents representing the second generation of more traditional CBT (Hoffmann & Asmundson, 2008). From our perspective, this was a concerted effort to keep the young ACT whippersnapper in its place. What followed was a rather predictable sequence in which ACT was summarily dismissed as nothing new or different, and most certainly, nothing that was possibly better (cf. S. C. Hayes, 2008). One argument that ACT was little more than old wine in new bottles asserted that it was not that substantially different from both traditional CBT (Arch & Craske, 2008; Hofmann & Asmundson, 2008) and Morita therapy (1998; Hofmann, 2008; Leahy, 2008).

The larger acrimonious debate about the identity of ACT and its status within the CBT family, however, did serve as an impetus for more comparative research. This research ultimately helped empirically resolve the debate in ACT's favor and thereby help establish its "street cred." While outcome research typically found the efficacy of ACT to be comparable to traditional CBT (e.g., Arch et al., 2012; Craske et al., 2014; Forman, Herbert, Moitra, Yeomans, & Geller, 2007), thus supporting the criticism that ACT was not better, related mediational research also was generally consistent in suggesting that at least some of its mechanisms of action were uniquely different (Forman et al., 2012; Niles et al., 2014). Perhaps the most telling reflection of the rapprochement that eventually emerged from this maturational stage in ACT's development is that two of the primary "combatants" during this process are now collaborating in advocating a process-based approach to CBT writ large that incorporates both shared and unique clinical competencies integral to both ACT and more traditional CBT (S. C. Hayes & Hofmann, 2018).

Summary and Concluding Remarks

While we have concluded our narrative, it is hardly the termination of ACT's ongoing story, which will continue to be told by others into the future (see Article 32 this volume, for example). As reflected by Skinner's (1980) comparison of historical and fictional accounts, we hope we have preserved "what really matters" about the progression of ACT. As we see it, that would be an understanding of the historical and current contextual variables instrumental in development of the therapy. A reticulated process interweaving the threads of technical/methodological, philosophical, and theoretical/conceptual advancements informed by basic and applied research findings began with humble efforts to view verbal psychotherapy through a behavior-analytic lens. Over 40 years later, it has culminated in a therapeutic approach and a related model of human functioning that has currently demonstrated an international impact in alleviating human suffering and promoting well-being. This is an ongoing endeavor, however, with much more work to be undertaken and further progress to be made. In our view, ACT has already shown considerable promise in meeting the challenge of the human condition (S. C. Hayes, Barnes-Holmes, & Wilson, 2014). We trust it will continue to do so as long, as it does not forget where it came from while keeping an eye on the prize.

References

Afari, N. (1996). *A study of paradoxical cognitive responding in thought suppression.* University of Nevada, Reno, ProQuest Dissertations Publishing, 9716666.

Arch, J. J., & Craske, M. G. (2008). Acceptance and commitment therapy and cognitive behavioral therapy for anxiety disorders: Different treatments, similar mechanisms? *Clinical Psychology: Science and Practice, 15,* 263–279.

Arch, J. J., Eifert, G. H., Davies, C., Vilardaga, J. C. P., Rose, R. D., & Craske, M. G. (2012). Randomized clinical trial of cognitive behavioral therapy (CBT) versus acceptance and commitment therapy (ACT) for mixed anxiety disorders. *Journal of Consulting and Clinical Psychology, 80,* 750–765.

Association for Contextual Behavioral Science. (n.d.-a). *ACT measures in languages other than English.* Retrieved from https://contextualscience.org/act_measures_in_languages_other_than_english

Association for Contextual Behavioral Science. (n.d.-b). *ACT self-help studies including those based on computers, phones, smartphones, and books.* Retrieved from https://contextualscience.org/act_selfhelp_studies_including_those_based_on_computers_phones_smartphones

Association for Contextual Behavioral Science. (n.d.-c). *ACT studies in low and middle income countries.* Retrieved from https://contextualscience.org/act_studies_in_low_and_middle_income_countries

Association for Contextual Behavioral Science. (n.d.-d). *ACT studies with mediational data.* Retrieved from https://contextualscience.org/act_studies_with_mediational_data

Association for Contextual Behavioral Science. (n.d.-e). *Affiliates.* Retrieved from https://contextualscience.org/affiliates

Association for Contextual Behavioral Science (n.d.-f). *Chapters.* Retrieved from https://contextualscience.org/chapters

Association for Contextual Behavioral Science. (n.d.-g). *Conferences.* Retrieved from https://contextualscience.org/conferences

Association for Contextual Behavioral Science. (n.d.-h). *Member directory.* Retrieved from https://contextualscience.org/civicrm/profile?gid=21&reset=1&force=1

Association for Contextual Behavioral Science. (n.d.-i). *Ongoing ACT grants.* Retrieved from https://contextualscience.org/ongoing_act_grants

Association for Contextual Behavioral Science. (n.d.-j). *Special interest groups.* Retrieved from https://contextualscience.org/special_interest_groups

Association for Contextual Behavioral Science. (n.d.-k). *State of the ACT evidence.* Retrieved from https://contextualscience.org/state_of_the_act_evidence

Atkins, P. W. B., Ciarocchi, J., Gaudiano, B. A., Bricker, J. B., Donald, J., Rovner, G., . . . Hayes, S. C. (2017). Departing from the essential features of a high quality systematic review of psychotherapy: A response to Öst (2014) and recommendations for improvement. *Behavior Research and Therapy, 97,* 259–272.

Bach, P. A. (2000). *Acceptance and commitment therapy in the treatment of symptoms of psychosis.* University of Nevada, Reno, ProQuest Dissertations Publishing, 9995329.

Barnes-Holmes, D., O'Hora, D., Roche, B., Hayes, S. C., Bissett, R. T., & Lyddy, F. (2001). Understanding and verbal regulation. In S. C. Hayes, D. Barnes-Holmes, & B. Roche (Eds.), *Relational frame theory: A post-Skinnerian account of human language and cognition* (pp. 103–117). Kluwer/Plenum.

Beck, A. T. (1967). *Depression: Clinical, experimental, and theoretical aspects.* New York: Harper and Row.

Beck, A. T. (1970). Cognitive therapy: Nature and relation to behavior therapy. *Behavior Therapy, 1,* 184–200.

Beck, A. T. (1976). *Cognitive therapy and the emotional disorders.* Madison, CT: International Universities Press.

Beck, A. T. (1987). Cognitive models of depression. *Journal of Cognitive Psychotherapy, 1,* 5–7.
Beck, A. T., Rush, A. J., Shaw B. F., & Emery, G. (1979). *Cognitive therapy of depression.* New York: Guilford Press.
Bernstein, A., Hadash, Y., Lichtash, Y., Tanay, G., Shepherd, K., & Fresco, D. M. (2015). Decentering and related constructs: A critical review and metacognitive processes model. *Perspectives on Psychological Science, 10,* 599–617.
Bluett, E. J., Homan, K. J., Morrison, K. L., Levin, M. E., & Twohig, M. P. (2014). Acceptance and commitment therapy for anxiety and OCD spectrum disorders: An empirical review. *Journal of Anxiety Disorders, 6,* 612–624.
Bohlmeijer, E. T., Lamers, S. M. A., & Fledderus, M. (2015). Flourishing in people with depressive symptomatology increases with acceptance and commitment therapy: Post- hoc analyses of a randomized controlled trial. *Behavior Research and Therapy, 65,* 101–106.
Bond, F. W., & Bunce, D. (2000). Mediators of change in emotion-focused and problem-focused worksite stress management interventions. *Journal of Occupational Health Psychology, 5,* 156–163.
Bond, F. W., Hayes, S. C., Baer, R. A., Carpenter, K. M., Guenole, N., Orcutt, H. K., . . . Zettle, R. D. (2011). Preliminary psychometric properties of the Acceptance and Action Questionnaire-II: A revised measure of psychological inflexibility and experiential avoidance. *Behavior Therapy, 42,* 676–688.
Carroll, L. (1865). *Alice's adventures in wonderland.* New York: Macmillan.
Clark, D. A., & Beck, A. T. (2010). *Cognitive therapy of anxiety disorders: Science and practice.* New York: Guilford Press.
Craske, M. G., Niles, A. N., Burklund, L. J., Wolitzky-Taylor, K. B., Plumb-Vilardaga, J. C., Arch, J. J. . . . Lieberman, M. D. (2014). Randomized controlled trial of cognitive behavioral therapy and acceptance and commitment therapy for social phobia: Outcomes and moderators. *Journal of Consulting and Clinical Psychology, 82,* 1034–1048.
Cullen, C. (2008). Acceptance and commitment therapy (ACT): A third wave behavior therapy. *Behavioural and Cognitive Psychotherapy, 36,* 667–673.
Day, W. F. (1969). Radical behaviorism in reconciliation with phenomenology. *Journal of the Experimental Analysis of Behavior, 12,* 315–328.
Devaney, J. M. (1985). *Stimulus equivalence and language development in children.* The University of North Carolina at Greensboro, ProQuest Dissertations Publishing, 8701324.
Dindo, L., Van Liew, J. R., & Arch, J. J. (2017). Acceptance and commitment therapy: A transdiagnostic behavioral intervention for mental health and medical conditions. *Neurotherapeutics, 14,* 546–553.
Ferster, C. B. (1967). Arbitrary and natural reinforcement. *Psychological Record, 17,* 341–347.
Ferster, C. B. (1972). An experimental analysis of clinical phenomena. *Psychological Record, 22,* 1–16.
Forman, E. M., Chapman, J. F., Herbert, J. D., Goetter, E. M., Yuen, E. K., & Moitra, E. (2012). Using session-by-session measurement to compare mechanisms of action for acceptance and commitment therapy and cognitive therapy. *Behavior Therapy, 43,* 341–354.
Forman, E. M., Herbert, J. D., Moitra, E., Yeomans, P. D., & Geller, P. A. (2007). A randomized controlled effectiveness trial of acceptance and commitment therapy and cognitive therapy for anxiety and depression. *Behavior Modification, 31,* 772–799.
Frankl, V. E. (1965). *Man's search for meaning: An introduction to logotherapy.* Boston: Beacon Press.
French, K., Golijani-Moghaddam, N., & Schröder, T. (2017). What is the evidence for the efficacy of self-help acceptance and commitment therapy? A systematic review and meta-analysis. *Journal of Contextual Behavioral Science, 6,* 360–374.
Freud, S. (1916). *Vorlesungen zur einführung in die psychoanalyse* [Introductory lectures on psychoanalysis]. Budapest: Internationaler Psychoanalytischer Verlag.
Gaudiano, B. A. (2009). Öst's (2008) methodological comparison of clinical trials of acceptance and commitment therapy versus cognitive behavioral therapy: Matching apples with oranges? *Behavior Research and Therapy, 47,* 1066–1070.
Geiser, D. S. (1992). *A comparison of acceptance-focused and control-focused psychological treatments in a chronic pain treatment center.* University of Nevada, Reno, ProQuest Dissertations Publishing, 9315546.
Greenspoon, J., & Brownstein, A. J. (1967a). Awareness in verbal conditioning. *Journal of Experimental Research in Personality, 2,* 295–308.
Greenspoon, J., & Brownstein, A. J. (1967b). Psychotherapy from the standpoint of a behaviorist. *Psychological Record, 17,* 401–416.
Gutiérrez, O., Luciano, C., Rodríguez, M., & Fink, B. C. (2004). Comparison between an acceptance-based and a cognitive-control-based protocol for coping with pain. *Behavior Therapy, 35,* 767–783.
Hayes, L. J., & Chase, P. N. (Eds.). (1991). *Dialogues on verbal behavior.* Oakland, CA: Context Press.
Hayes, L. J., & Ghezzi, P. M. (Eds.). (1997). *Investigations in behavioral epistemology.* Oakland, CA: Context Press.
Hayes, L. J., Hayes, S. C., Ono, K., & Sato, M. (1994). *Behavior analysis of language and cognition.* Oakland, CA: Context Press

Hayes, L. J., Houmanfar, R. A., Ghezzi, P. M., Williams, W. L., Locey, M., & Hayes, S. C. (2016). The origin and evolution of the behavior analysis program at the University of Nevada, Reno. *The Behavior Analyst, 39*, 167–173. https://doi.org/10.1007/s40614-016-0061-x

Hayes, S. C. (1984). Making sense of spirituality. *Behaviorism, 12*, 99–110.

Hayes, S. C. (1987). A contextual approach to therapeutic change. In N. S. Jacobson (Ed.), *Psychotherapists in clinical practice: Cognitive and behavioral perspectives* (pp. 327–387). New York: Guilford Press.

Hayes, S. C. (Ed.). (1989). *Rule-governed behavior: Cognition, contingencies, and instructional control.* New York: Plenum.

Hayes, S. C. (1993). Analytic goals and the varieties of scientific contextualism. In S. C. Hayes, L. J. Hayes, H. W. Reese, & T. R. Sarbin (Eds.), *Varieties of scientific contextualism* (pp. 11–27). Oakland, CA: Context Press.

Hayes, S. C. (2001). A personal prologue. In S. C. Hayes, D. Barnes-Holmes, & B. Roche (Eds.), *Relational frame theory: A post-Skinnerian account of human language and cognition* (pp. vii–ix). New York: Kluwer/Plenum.

Hayes, S. C. (2004). Acceptance and commitment therapy, relational frame theory, and the third wave of behavioral and cognitive therapies. *Behavior Therapy, 35*, 639–665.

Hayes, S. C. (2005). *Get out of your mind and into your life.* Oakland, CA: New Harbinger.

Hayes, S. C. (2008). Climbing our hills: A beginning conversation on the comparison of acceptance and commitment therapy and traditional cognitive behavioral therapy. *Clinical Psychology: Science and Practice, 15*, 286–295.

Hayes, S, C. (2015). *The act in context: The canonical papers of Steven C. Hayes.* Oxfordshire, UK: Routledge.

Hayes, S. C. (2019). *A liberated mind: How to pivot toward what matters.* New York: Avery.

Hayes, S. C., Barnes-Holmes, D., & Roche, B. (Eds.). (2001). *Relational frame theory: A post- Skinnerian account of human language and cognition.* New York: Kluwer/Plenum.

Hayes, S. C., Barnes-Holmes, D., & Wilson, K. G. (2014). Contextual behavioral science: Creating a science more adequate to the challenge of the human condition. *Journal of Contextual Behavioral Science, 1*, 1–16.

Hayes, S. C., Bissett, R. T., Korn, Z., Zettle, R. D., Rosenfarb, I. S., Cooper, L. D., & Grundt, A. M. (1999). The impact of acceptance versus control rationales on pain tolerance. *Psychological Record, 49*, 33–47.

Hayes, S. C., & Brownstein, A. J. (1985, May). *Verbal behavior, equivalence classes, and rules: New definitions, data, and directions* [Paper presentation]. Association for Behavior Analysis 11th Annual Convention, Columbus, OH.

Hayes, S. C., & Brownstein, A. J. (1986). Mentalism, behavior-behavior relations, and a behavior analytic view of the purposes of science. *The Behavior Analyst, 9*, 175–190.

Hayes, S. C., & Hayes, L. J. (1989). The verbal action of the listener as a basis for rule- governance. In S. C. Hayes (Ed.), *Rule-governed behavior: Cognition, contingencies, and instructional control* (pp. 153–190). New York: Plenum.

Hayes, S. C., & Hayes, L. J. (Eds.). (1992). *Understanding verbal relations.* Oakland, CA: Context Press/New Harbinger.

Hayes, S. C., Hayes, L. J., Reese, H. W., & Sarbin, T. R. (Eds.). (1993). *Varieties of scientific contextualism.* Oakland, CA: Context Press.

Hayes, S. C., & Hofmann, S. G. (2018). *Process-based CBT: The science and core clinical competencies of cognitive behavioral therapy.* Oakland, CA: Context Press.

Hayes, S. C., Korn, Z., Zettle, R. D., Rosenfarb, I., & Cooper, L. (1982, November). *Cognitive therapy and rule-governed behavior: The effects of comprehensive distancing on pain tolerance* [Poster presentation]. Association for Advancement of Behavior Therapy 16th Annual Convention, Los Angeles, CA, United States.

Hayes, S. C., Luoma, J. B., Bond, F. W., Mausda, A., & Lillis, J. (2006). Acceptance and commitment therapy: Model, processes and outcomes. *Behavior Research and Therapy, 44*, 1–25.

Hayes, S. C., & Smith, S. (2005). *Get out of your mind and into your life: The new acceptance and commitment therapy.* Oakland, CA: New Harbinger.

Hayes, S. C., Strosahl, K. D., & Wilson, K. G. (1999). *Acceptance and commitment therapy: An experiential approach to behavior change.* New York: Guilford Press.

Hayes, S. C., Strosahl, K. D., & Wilson, K. G. (2012). *Acceptance and commitment therapy: The process and practice of mindful change* (2nd ed.). New York: Guilford Press.

Hayes, S. C., Strosahl, K. D., Wilson, K. G., Bissett, R. T., Pistorello, J., Toarmino, D., . . . McCurry, S. M. (2004). Measuring experiential avoidance: A preliminary test of a working model. *The Psychological Record, 54*, 553–578.

Hayes, S. C., & Wilson, K. G. (1993). Some applied implications of a contemporary behavior-analytic account of verbal events. *The Behavior Analyst, 16*, 283–301.

Hayes, S. C., & Wilson, K. G. (1994). Acceptance and commitment therapy: Altering the verbal support for experiential avoidance. *The Behavior Analyst, 17*, 289–303.

Hayes, S. C., & Wolf, M. R. (1984). Cues, consequences, and therapeutic talk: Effect of social context and coping statements on pain. *Behavior Research and Therapy, 22*, 385–392.

Hayes, S. C., Zettle, R. D., Barnes-Holmes, D., & Biglan, A. (2016). Examining the partially completed crossword puzzle: The nature and status of contextual behavioral science. In R. D. Zettle, S. C. Hayes, D. Barnes-Holmes, & A. Biglan (Eds.), *The Wiley handbook of contextual behavioral science* (pp. 1–6). New York: Wiley Blackwell.

Hofmann, S. G. (2008). Acceptance and commitment therapy: New wave or Morita therapy? *Clinical Psychology: Science and Practice, 15,* 280–285.

Hofmann, S. G., & Asmundson, G. J. G. (2008). Acceptance and mindfulness-based therapy: New wave or old hat? *Clinical Psychology Review, 28,* 1–16.

Hollon, S. D., & Beck, A. T. (1979). Cognitive therapy of depression. In P. C. Kendall & S. D. Hollon (Eds.), *Cognitive-behavioral interventions: Theory, research, and procedures* (pp. 153–203). New York: Academic Press.

Hooper, N., & Larsson, A. (2015). *The research journey of acceptance and commitment therapy (ACT).* London: Palgrave Macmillan.

Howell, A. J., & Passmore, H. (2019). Acceptance and commitment therapy (ACT) to reduce depression: A systematic review and meta-analysis. *Journal of Affective Disorders, 260,* 728–737.

Jacobson, N. S., Dobson, K. S., Truax, P. A., Addis, M. E., Koerner, K., Gollan, J. K., . . . Prince, S. E. (1996). A component analysis of cognitive-behavioral treatment of depression. *Journal of Consulting and Clinical Psychology, 64,* 295–304.

Ju, W. C. (2000). *Toward an empirical analysis of verbal motivation: A possible preparation for distinguishing discriminative and motivational functions of verbal stimuli.* University of Nevada, Reno, ProQuest Dissertations Publishing, 9985720.

Karlin, B. E., Brown, G. B., Trockel, M., Cunning, D., Zeiss, A. M., & Taylor, C. B. (2012). National dissemination of cognitive behavioral therapy for depression in the Department of Veterans Affairs Health Care System: Therapist and patient-level outcomes. *Journal of Consulting and Clinical Psychology, 80,* 707–718.

Khorakiwala, D. (1991). *An analysis of the process of client change in a contextual approach to therapy.* University of Nevada, Reno, ProQuest Dissertations Publishing. 9131276.

Kohlenberg, B. S. (1994). *Transfer of function through equivalence: Modification effects based upon modality and contextual control.* University of Nevada, Reno, ProQuest Dissertations Publishing, 9511783.

Kohlenberg, R. J., & Tsai, M. (1991). *Functional analytic psychotherapy: Creating intense and curative therapeutic relationships.* New York: Plenum.

Leahy, R. L. (2008). A closer look at ACT. *The Behavior Therapist, 31,* 148–150.

Levin, M. E., Hildebrandt, M. J., Lillis, J., & Hayes, S. C. (2012). The impact of treatment components suggested by the psychological flexibility model: A meta-analysis of laboratory-based component studies. *Behavior Therapy, 43,* 741–756.

Lipkens, R. (1992). *A behavior analysis of complex human functioning: Analogical reasoning.* University of Nevada, Reno, ProQuest Dissertations Publishing, 9230123.

Mahoney, M. J. (1974). *Cognition and behavior modification.* Pensacola, FL: Ballinger.

Martell, C. R., Addis, M. E., & Jacobson, N. S. (2001). *Depression in context: Strategies for guided action.* New York: W. W. Norton.

McCurry, S. M. (1991). *Client use of metaphor in a contextual form of therapy.* University of Nevada, Reno, ProQuest Dissertations Publishing, 9126403.

Meichenbaum, D. H. (1972). Cognitive modification of test anxious college students. *Journal of consulting and Clinical Psychology, 39,* 370–380.

Meichenbaum, D. H. (1977). *Cognitive-behavior modification: An integrative approach.* New York: Plenum.

Moran, D. J. (2015). Acceptance and commitment training in the workplace. *Current Opinion in Psychology, 2,* 26–31.

Morita, S. (1998). *Morita therapy and the true nature of anxiety-based disorders (shinkeishitsu).* (A. Kondo, Trans., P. LeVine, Ed.). New Paltz: State University of New York Press.

Muto, T., & Mitamura, T. (2011). Acceptance and commitment therapy as a transdiagnostic approach: Toward shifting to a "concurrent-habits" paradigm. *Japanese Journal of Psychosomatic Medicine, 51,* 1105–1110.

Niles, A. N., Burklund, L. J., Arch, J. J., Lieberman, M. D., Saxbe, D., & Craske, M. G. (2014). Cognitive mediators of treatment for social anxiety disorder: Comparing acceptance and commitment therapy and cognitive-behavioral therapy. *Behavior Therapy, 45,* 664–677.

Öst, L.-G. (2008). Efficacy of the third wave of behavioral therapies: A systematic review and meta-analysis. *Behavior Research and Therapy, 46,* 296–321.

Öst, L.-G. (2009). Inventing the wheel once more or learning from the history of psychotherapy research methodology: Reply to Gaudiano's comments on Öst's (2008) review. *Behavior Research and Therapy, 47,* 1071–1073.

Öst, L.-G. (2014). The efficacy of acceptance and commitment therapy: An updated systematic review and meta-analysis. *Behavior Research and Therapy, 61,* 105–121.

Öst, L.-G. (2017). Rebuttal of Atkins et al. (2017) critique of the Öst (2014) meta-analysis of ACT. *Behavior Research and Therapy, 97,* 273–281.

Pepper, S. C. (1942). *World hypotheses: A study in evidence.* Berkeley: University of California Press.

Pinto, R. A., Kienhuis, M., Slevison, M., Chester, A., Sloss, A., & Yap, K. (2017). The effectiveness of an outpatient acceptance and commitment therapy group program for a transdiagnostic population. *Clinical Psychologist, 21,* 33–43.

Pistorello, J. (1998). *Acceptance, suppression, and monitoring of personally-relevant unwanted thoughts in women diagnosed with borderline personality disorder.* University of Nevada, Reno, ProQuest Dissertations Publishing, 9833383.

Rimm, D. C. (1973). Thought stopping and covert assertion in the treatment of phobias. *Journal of Consulting and Clinical Psychology, 41,* 466–467.

Rosenfarb, I. S. (1986). *The use of therapist rules, self-rules, and contingency shaped feedback in the treatment of social skills deficits in adults.* The University of North Carolina at Greensboro, ProQuest Dissertations Publishing, 871229.

Rosenfarb, I., & Hayes, S. C. (1984). Social standard setting: The Achilles' heel of informational accounts of therapeutic change. *Behavior Therapy, 15,* 515–528.

Rush, A. J., Beck, A. T., Kovacs, M., & Hollon, S. (1977). Comparative efficacy of cognitive therapy and imipramine in the treatment of depressed outpatients. *Cognitive Therapy and Research, 1,* 17–37.

Safran, J., & Segak, Z. V. (1996). *Interpersonal process in cognitive therapy.* New York: Rowman and Littlefield.

Salzinger, K. (1990). B. F. Skinner (1904–1990). *American Psychological Society Observer, 5,* 1–4.

Samaan, M., Diefenbacher, A., Schade, C., Dambacher, C., Pontow, I-M., Pakenham, K., & Fydrich, T. (2020). A clinical effectiveness trial comparing ACT and CBT for inpatients with depressive and mixed mental disorders. *Psychotherapy Research, 31,* 355–368. https://doi.org/10.1080/10503307.2020.1802080

Segal, Z. V., Williams, J. M. G., & Teasdale, J. D. (2002). *Mindfulness-based cognitive therapy for depression: A new approach for preventing relapse.* New York: Guilford Press.

Shull, R. L. (1986). In memoriam: Aaron Joseph Brownstein (1932–1986). *The Behavior Analyst, 9,* 239–240.

Sidman, M. (1971). Reading and auditory-visual equivalences. *Journal of Speech and Hearing Research, 14,* 5–13.

Skinner, B. F. (1957). *Verbal behavior.* New York: Appleton.

Skinner, B. F. (1966). An operant analysis of problem solving. In B. Kleinmuntz (Ed.), *Problem-solving: Research, method, and theory* (pp. 225–257). New York: Wiley.

Skinner, B. F. (1969). *Contingencies of reinforcement: A theoretical analysis.* New York: Appleton.

Skinner, B. F. (1974). *About behaviorism.* New York: Knopf.

Skinner, B. F. (1980). *Notebooks.* (R. Epstein, Ed.). New York: Prentice-Hall.

Society of Clinical Psychology. (n.d.-a). *Treatment: Acceptance and commitment therapy for chronic pain.* Retrieved from https://www.div12.org/treatment/acceptance-and-commitment-therapy-for-chronic-pain/

Society of Clinical Psychology. (n.d.-b). *Treatment: Acceptance and commitment therapy for depression.* Retrieved from https://www.div12.org/treatment/acceptance-and-commitment-therapy-for-depression/

Society of Clinical Psychology. (n.d.-c). *Treatment: Acceptance and commitment therapy for mixed anxiety disorders.* Retrieved from https://www.div12.org/treatment/acceptance-and-commitment-therapy-for-mixed-anxiety-disorders/

Society of Clinical Psychology. (n.d.-d). *Acceptance and commitment therapy for obsessive-compulsive disorder status: Modest research support.* Retrieved from https://www.div12.org/treatment/acceptance-and-commitment-therapy-for-obsessive-compulsive-disorder/

Society of Clinical Psychology. (n.d.-e). *Acceptance and commitment therapy for psychosis status: Modest research support.* Retrieved from https://www.div12.org/treatment/acceptance-and-commitment-therapy-for-psychosis/

Steele, D. L. & Hayes, S. C. (1991). Stimulus equivalence and arbitrarily applicable relational responding. *Journal of the Experimental Analysis of Behavior, 56,* 519–555. doi: 10.1901/jeab.1991.56-519

Stockton, D., Kellett, S., Berrios, R., Sirios, F., Wilkinson, N., & Miles, G. (2019). Identifying the underlying mechanisms of change during acceptance and commitment therapy (ACT): A systematic review of contemporary mediation studies. *Behavioral and Cognitive Psychotherapy, 47,* 332–362.

Strosahl, K. D., Hayes, S. C., Bergan, J., & Romano, P. (1998). Assessing the field effectiveness of acceptance and commitment therapy: An example of the manipulated training research method. *Behavior Therapy, 29,* 35–63.

Thompson, E. M., Destree, L., Albertella, L., & Fontenelle, L. F. (2021). Internet-based acceptance and commitment therapy: A transdiagnostic systematic review and meta- analysis for mental health outcomes. *Behavior Therapy, 52,* 492–507.

Tol, W. A., Leku, M. R., Lakin, D. P., Carswell, K., Augustinavicius, J., Adaku, A., . . . van Ommeren, M. (2020). Guided self-help to reduce psychological distress in South Sudanese female refugees in Uganda: A cluster randomized trial. *Lancet Global Health, 8,* 254–263.

Veehof, M. M., Oskam, M., Schreurs, K. M. G., & Bohlmeijer, E. T. (2011). Acceptance-based interventions for the treatment of chronic pain: A systematic review and meta-analysis. *Pain, 152*, 533–542.
Walser, R. D. (1998). *The effects of suppression and acceptance on thought and emotion.* University of Nevada, Reno, ProQuest Dissertations Publishing, 9916965.
Walser, R. D., Karlin, B. E., Trockel, M., Mazina, B., & Taylor, C. B. (2013). Training and implementation of acceptance and commitment therapy for depression in the Veterans Health Administration: Therapist and patient outcomes. *Behavior Research and Therapy, 51*, 555–563.
Wilson, K. G. (1998). *Relational acquisition of stimulus function in substance dependence: A preliminary examination of drug versus nondrug related equivalence classes.* University of Nevada, Reno, ProQuest Dissertations Publishing, 9916966.
Wilson, K. G., & Hayes, S. C. (1996). Resurgence of derived stimulus relations. *Journal of the Experimental Analysis of Behavior, 66*, 267–281.
Wilson, K. G., Khorakiwala, D., & Hayes, S. C. (1991, May). Change in acceptance and commitment therapy. In K. G. Wilson (Chair), *Radical behavioral psychotherapy process research* [Symposium]. Association for Behavior Analysis 17th Annual Convention, Atlanta, GA, United States.
Wilson, K. G., & Taylor, N. (1991, November). Why the "acceptance" in acceptance and commitment therapy (ACT)? In S. C. Hayes (Chair), *Acceptance as change: Acceptance as a strategy of clinical intervention* [Symposium]. Association for Advancement of Behavior Therapy 25th Annual Convention, New York City.
Wulfert, E. (1987). *Higher-order control over equivalence classes and response sequences: An experimental analogue of simple syntactic relations.* The University of North Carolina at Greensboro, ProQuest Dissertations Publishing, 8719189.
Yu, L., McCracken, L. M., & Norton, S. (2016). The Self-Experiences Scale (SEQ): Preliminary analyses for a measure of self in people with chronic pain. *Journal of Contextual Behavioral Science, 5*, 127–133.
Zettle, R. D. (1984). *Cognitive therapy of depression: A conceptual and empirical analysis of component and process issues.* [Unpublished doctoral dissertation]. University of North Carolina at Greensboro.
Zettle, R. D. (2005). The evolution of a contextual approach to therapy: From comprehensive distancing to ACT. *International Journal of Behavioral Consultation and Therapy, 1*, 77–89.
Zettle, R. D. (2015). Acceptance and commitment therapy for depression. *Current Opinion in Psychology, 2*, 65–69.
Zettle, R. D., Gird, S. E., Webster, B. K., Carrasquillo-Richardson, N., Swails, J. A., & Burdsal, C. A. (2018). The Self-as-Context Scale: Development and preliminary psychometric properties. *Journal of Contextual Behavioral Science, 10*, 64–74.
Zettle, R. D., & Hayes, S. C. (1979, December). Coping self-statements as a self-control procedure. In R. O. Nelson (Chair), *Environmental determinants of self-control and cognitive behavior therapy techniques* [Symposium]. Association for Advancement of Behavior Therapy 13th Annual Convention, San Francisco, CA, United States.
Zettle, R. D., & Hayes, S. C. (1982). Rule-governed behavior: A potential theoretical framework for cognitive-behavioral therapy. In P. C. Kendall (Ed.), *Advances in cognitive- behavioral research and therapy* (pp. 73–118). New York: Academic Press.
Zettle, R. D., & Hayes, S. C. (1984, August). Cognitive therapy of depression: Behavioral analysis of component and process issues. In S. C. Hayes (Chair), *Behavior analytic perspectives on current issues in clinical psychology*[Symposium]. American Psychological Association 92nd Annual Convention, Toronto, ON, Canada.
Zettle, R. D., & Hayes, S. C. (1986). Dysfunctional control by client verbal behavior: The context of reason-giving. *The Analysis of Verbal Behavior, 4*, 30–38.
Zettle, R. D., & Hayes, S. C. (1987). Component and process analysis of cognitive therapy. *Psychological Reports, 64*, 939–953.
Zettle, R. D., & Rains, J. C. (1989). Group cognitive and contextual therapies in treatment of depression. *Journal of Clinical Psychology, 45*, 438–445.

CHAPTER 2

Implementing ACT as Contextual Behavioral Science

Emily K. Sandoz *and* Caleb Fogle

Abstract

Acceptance and commitment therapy (ACT) has been explicitly grounded in particular philosophical and theoretical perspectives since its development. At a macro level, these foundations not only contextualize current iterations of ACT (i.e., explaining why ACT is the way that it is), but also guide adaptations and continued refinement of ACT (i.e., to shape how ACT is continually evolving). However, there are also important implications for moment-to-moment implementation of ACT. This article provides a brief review of early foundations with explicit implications for ACT implementation, including both contextualism and its relationship with other world views, and behavior analysis as grounded in both radical behaviorism and interbehavioral psychology. Modern contextual behavioral science (CBS) is described in detail as behavior analysis with functional contextual underpinnings. Also described are the philosophical assumptions that characterize this perspective, along with the implications of these assumptions for ACT therapists. This article seeks to support ACT therapists in implementing ACT with intention and effectiveness.

Key Words: contextualism, radical behaviorism, interbehaviorism, contextual behavioral science, philosophy, behavior analysis, monism, epistemology, analytic goal, truth criterion

Since its earliest iteration, acceptance and commitment therapy (ACT; Hayes, Strosahl, & Wilson, 1999; 2012) has clearly set out its philosophical and theoretical roots. Notably, this has distinguished ACT in two ways—both in how these roots themselves diverge from dominant positions in psychological treatment and in the fact that they are so frequently and explicitly delineated. ACT's roots have been described in terms of the philosophical world view referred to as contextualism (specifically, functional contextualism) and the theoretical orientation of behavior analysis. Together, these distinguish the scientific paradigm that guides the research, practice, and professional activity related to ACT—contextual behavioral science. Most simply defined, contextual behavioral science (CBS; Hayes, Barnes-Holmes, & Wilson, 2012) is behavior analysis with explicit functional contextual philosophical underpinnings.

In this way, using ACT as a treatment package involves, in part, viewing both extant empirical findings and direct observations in the therapy room through the lenses of functional contextualism and behavior analysis. This approach not only clarifies observations and findings that are explicitly consistent with ACT and its underlying model of psychopathology (i.e., that support the psychological flexibility model), but also allows the ACT practitioner to make sense of and integrate observations and findings that are not obviously consistent from an ACT perspective. Together, the philosophical and theoretical foundations inherent in a

CBS perspective provide an explicit approach for organizing both general information gleaned from the ever-growing and changing scientific record and specific data gathered in the context of clinical assessment. This article reviews the philosophical and theoretical foundations of ACT, discusses how they integrate to comprise CBS, and offers implications for the ACT therapist along the way.

Philosophical Foundations of CBS and ACT

Like many scientific disciplines, the behavioral sciences continually undergo transitions and divisions relating to philosophies of science (Mason, Sripada, & Stich, 2010). Disciplines and subdisciplines are differentiated by their answers to philosophical questions. For example, in psychology, subdisciplines are differentiated by how they respond to questions such as "Are mental capacities innate?" (e.g., *nativism*), "How do humans make decisions?" (e.g., *rationality*), and "How is psychological functioning organized within individuals?" (e.g., *modularity*). These philosophical underpinnings affect the culture of psychology, and indeed behavioral science as a whole, by influencing the conduct of research at every level, the interpretation and dissemination of findings, and the refinement of theories. They also, as in applied psychology, impact the broader dissemination and implementation of said findings and theories.

One way of organizing and conceptualizing philosophical perspectives that has been influential in the emergence of CBS is Stephen Pepper's (1942) work categorizing *world hypotheses,* which are world views or conceptual systems. From Pepper's perspective, world views are observed, preanalytic commonalities that are obvious in human beings' necessarily biased attempts, both scientific and otherwise, to understand, explain, and investigate the world. By clarifying and simplifying these proposed epistemological systems according to their root metaphors and units of analysis, Pepper suggests we can understand and avoid the failures of communication that come from having unexpressed but conflicting philosophical assumptions. For Pepper, each of the four relatively adequate world views adopt one of four *root metaphors,* used to exemplify the workings of the world through a commonsense concept. In addition, each root metaphor extends into one of three *truth criteria,* which are standards for determining what theories about the world are understood as true. The four world hypotheses Pepper identifies are mechanism, formism, organicism, and contextualism. Each of these world views has implications for research and practice within behavioral science, and, in particular, for behavior therapy.

Mechanism

The first world hypothesis that Pepper (1942) outlines is *mechanism.* The root metaphor adopted by mechanism is the machine. From this perspective, the world is viewed as containing parts parallel to gears, pullies, and screws, which relate to one another in specific ways with particular force. A behavior scientist who embraces the mechanistic world hypothesis may attempt to explain a phenomenon (e.g., emotions) by explaining mechanisms (i.e., components acting in relation to other components) that seem to underlie its existence. Terms are applied to these components, and theories describe how they relate. For example, a researcher who embraces this world hypothesis may explain the lack of emotional awareness exhibited by a child diagnosed with autism as a result of inactive mirror neurons (see Dapretto et al., 2006). These theories and terms are evaluated in terms of how they match observations of particular components and relations between them (e.g., neurons firing in certain patterns, skin conductance change, subjective reporting of cognitive contents, or parenting style). In this way, the truth criterion within mechanisms is *correspondence.* From this perspective, a statement about the world is true to the extent that it accurately describes, or corresponds with, the actual world and its components. This view of truth is dominant within science, and indeed, psychology research and practice typically assume a mechanistic view.

In the context of behavior therapy, applying a mechanistic perspective might involve identifying thoughts, feelings, and overt behaviors, interacting in a particular way, that correspond with components of a psychological disorder. It might involve identifying patterns in which these components or relationships among them change to facilitate remission in a way that corresponds with a theory of psychological wellness. In the therapy process, the therapist emphasizing mechanism might aim to implement actions that correspond to the technologies purported by the theory to influence those patterns.

Formism

The second world hypothesis that Pepper (1942) outlines is *formism*. The root metaphor adopted by formism is similarity. From this perspective, the world is viewed as a collection of distinct items—parts that vary in fundamental characteristics so that they are essentially distinct from other parts, and such that they can be assigned to categories based on the degree of similarity and difference. A behavior scientist who embraces the formist world hypothesis may attempt to group phenomena by identifying an observed feature or collection of features that vary, grouping variations according to how alike they are, then naming those features that covary with a particular term (e.g., syndromal classification of psychological disorders). In this way, similar to mechanism, the truth criterion within formism is correspondence. That is, from a formist perspective, a classification or categorization is true to the extent that it accurately corresponds to how actual distinct parts in the world are alike and different.

In the context of behavior therapy, applying a formist perspective might involve grouping the observed patterns of thoughts, feelings, and overt behaviors according to how they correspond with diagnostic categories, personality variables, and other labeled categories. In this way, the therapist would attempt to ultimately account for as many aspects of the client's behavior and reported experience as possible by describing them in scientific terms. It might also involve considerations of variability between the client's behavior and established sociocultural or developmental norms as a way of determining what is pathological. In the process, the therapist emphasizing formism might aim to implement actions that allow for the discovery and categorization of new aspects of the client's behavior or experience.

Organicism

The third world hypothesis that Pepper (1942) outlines is *organicism*. The root metaphor adopted by organicism is the growing, developing organism. From this perspective, the world is viewed as a dynamic, integrated whole that changes in a constant and orderly way over time. A behavior scientist who embraces the organicist world hypothesis may attempt to understand a phenomenon by observing the system in which it participates, including how it evolves over time and in tandem with other, related phenomena (e.g., stage theories of human development). The truth criterion within organicism is *coherence*. That is, from an organicist perspective, a fact about a phenomenon is true to the extent that it coheres with the description of the system of which it is purportedly a member, and a description of a system is true to the extent that it coheres with descriptions of the facts.

In the context of behavior therapy, applying an organicist perspective might involve viewing observed thoughts, feelings, and overt behaviors as interrelated aspects of a constantly evolving repertoire. That whole repertoire might be viewed as inseparable from the dynamic system in which it is evolving, ranging from the immediately observable therapeutic relationship to more abstract sociocultural systems. In addition, both the client's behavior and experiences and the numerous systems in which they participate are viewed as immediate iterations of events with inseparable histories and futures. In process, the therapist emphasizing organicism might aim to implement actions that allow for an increasingly complex understanding of the client, in terms of the systems in which they participate.

Contextualism

The fourth and final view that Pepper (1942) outlines is *contextualism*. The root metaphor within contextualism is the act-in-context. From this perspective, the world is viewed as an integrated whole where any naming of particular events involves abstracting from the whole. In this way, no act or event can be understood except in relation to the context in which it occurs. A behavior scientist who embraces the contextualist world hypothesis may attempt to understand a phenomenon by observing it in the many specific contexts in which it occurs (and perhaps, the contexts in which it does not). Instead of an event being described in terms of its absolute unique features, it is described in terms of its relationships to the rest of the whole from which it is abstracted. Of course, this effort could never be completed, as this perspective views the whole as primary, meaning the context for an event would include all events outside of that which is being described. Thus, the truth criterion within contextualism is *effective action*. That is, from a contextualist perspective, the contextual account is sufficient when the description of the act-in-context allows the analyst to further work toward previously defined goals for the analysis. In some cases, the contextualist may even adopt other world hypotheses temporarily if they foster an account that more readily meets their goals. In other words, the pragmatism of the contextual worldview extends even to its foundations, allowing for incorporation of other root metaphors and truth criteria where they allow for a more actionable technical account.

In the context of behavior therapy, applying a contextualist perspective might involve observing thoughts, feelings, and overt behaviors in terms of their relationships with the contexts in which they occur. The most direct approach to this would involve assessing and intervening on the client's behavior primarily in terms of the observed therapeutic context. In the process, the therapist emphasizing contextualism might aim to create the context in therapy for evoking difficult thoughts, feelings, and overt behaviors and adding to that context to teach new, more effective behavioral patterns consistent with therapeutic goals.

Practical Integration of World Hypotheses

Part of Pepper's (1942) explicit intention with this description of world hypotheses was to account for the difficulty some scientific traditions have with communicating and integrating findings across different epistemological systems. Truth, however, is rarely determined by a single criterion, especially in the applied sector. For contextual behavior therapists, for example, the effective application of a particular theoretical orientation likely requires that the theory is coherent. Further, the assessment of whether or not action is effective likely involves some evaluation of the extent to which the observed outcomes correspond to an idea of what effective means. Even though effective action might be the primary truth criterion that contextual behavior therapists adopt, both coherence and correspondence are involved to some extent. This is particularly workable for the contextual behavior therapist, who is easily able to integrate other perspectives if the efforts they foster are better suited to therapeutic goals (i.e., if they foster effective action), and allow for the ultimate aim of integrating new observations into the contextual account. This consideration may be important, as many therapists describe an eclectic theoretical orientation (e.g., Cook, Biyanova, Elhai, Schnurr, & Coyne 2010), which involves incorporating into their practice interventions based on scientific findings from a variety of world views. Contextualism offers a way to do so that promotes the pragmatic use of philosophy and theory without requiring theoretical eclecticism—and in a way that necessarily involves sensitivity to what is working (cf. Safran & Messer, 1997).

Implications of Contextualist Philosophical Foundations in ACT

Contextualism is foundational to the practice of ACT. The ACT therapist working from strong functional contextual philosophical underpinnings is empowered to:

1. directly observe behavior as it unfolds in the therapeutic context,
2. analyze observed behavior in terms of its relationship with contexts introduced in assessment,
3. select as therapeutic goals behaviors that are likely to be more effective in such contexts,
4. select interventions based on this analysis of behavior in context,
5. analyze the functional impact of these interventions on behavior in a moment-to-moment way, and
6. alter interventions iteratively as necessary to improve their impact on behavior.

In other words, the ACT therapist aims to build sensitivity, creativity, and generativity into every aspect of the therapeutic interaction by *playing the function game*—that is, listening and watching the relationships among the contexts they create with each behavior they engage in and the responses of the client. For example, the therapist may observe that when they ask the client about intimacy with other people, the client disengages from conversation (e.g., breaks eye contact, lowers their vocal tone). The ACT therapist may ask the client to notice their discomfort, or even ask them to describe the different thoughts and feelings they are experiencing in the moment. And to the extent that the client struggles to do so, the therapist might identify these behaviors (i.e., noticing and expressing thoughts and feelings) in the context of this topic (i.e., intimacy) as treatment targets, building interventions that support the client engaging in these behaviors in this context.

Of course, the contextual therapist may also find themselves comparing what they observe to clinically relevant terms or theories (i.e., *playing the correspondence game*, e.g., by considering a particular DSM-5 diagnosis) or checking the soundness of the clinical conceptualization (i.e., *playing the coherence game*, e.g., by recalling previous reports of experiences of inconsistency in caregiving in the home). Indeed, they may shift their emphasis to correspondence or coherence with intention, judging this to be temporarily more workable to support the therapeutic goals. In short, the ACT therapist working from strong functional contextual philosophical underpinnings notices when they shift away from the *function game* and shifts back. Effectiveness with this process is further supported by fluency with ACT's theoretical foundations in behavior analysis, including both radical behaviorism and interbehavioral psychology.

Theoretical Foundations of CBS and ACT

Pepper's (1942) description of world hypotheses has likely been most impactful to the practice of behavior therapy in the extent to which it was used in attempts to characterize the philosophical foundations of behavior analysis when precursors to ACT were just being developed. This extended conversation began with a review of Pepper's primary text on the topic published in a behavior-analytic journal (Hayes, Hayes, & Reese, 1988), which purported contextualism to be the epistemological core of behavior analysis and served to clarify both philosophical and theoretical underpinnings of ACT.

In some ways, this characterization seems obvious. Behavior analysis distinguishes itself from dominant perspectives in psychology by committing to a natural science of behavior (see Morris, 1984). That is, behavior analysis seeks to understand individual behavior in terms of natural, physical processes rather than in terms of other behaviors. For example, a behavior analyst might note a number of different behaviors that emerge together across the varying levels of analysis. Physiological arousal, intrusive thoughts of past threats, and aggressive behavior, for instance, all tend to co-occur. However, the behavior analyst would not propose that physiological arousal or thoughts of past threats *cause* aggressive behavior. Instead, they would pursue causes for behavior that are outside of the behavioral stream (see Wilson, 2001 on theoretical constructs). In this way, behavior analysis necessarily relies in large part on contextual events to explain, and intervene to change, behavior. Contextual analysis is central to both radical behaviorism and interbehavioral psychology; these two theoretical approaches within behavior analysis have made considerable contributions to the development of CBS and ACT.

Radical Behaviorism

Modern behavior analysis relies heavily on Skinnerian radical behaviorism (see Skinner, 1974), which holds that behavior is understood in terms of its relationships with antecedent (i.e., the occasion in which the behavior occurs) and consequential contexts (i.e., the consequences that reinforce the behavior). From the radical behavioral perspective, behaviors vary in their sensitivity to consequential contexts. *Respondent behaviors* are those that are insensitive to consequential contexts, that is, behaviors that are primarily under antecedent control (e.g., a dog appears tense with ears pulled back when fireworks are set off in the neighborhood or a client experiences an increase in heart rate upon hearing their name announced in the waiting room). *Operant behaviors*, on the other hand, are sensitive to both aspects of contextual control, antecedent and consequential. For example, a dog might sit by the door when their owner gets the leash as this has resulted in quick access to their walk outside, or a client might disclose an increase in heart rate when the therapist asks how they are, as acknowledging arousal has resulted in expressions of support. The functional relationships among contexts and behaviors are referred to as contingencies. In this way, the basic unit of analysis in radical behaviorism is the *three-term contingency*—the antecedent context, the behavior, and the reinforcing context. Further, both respondent and operant contingencies can be sensitive to additional layers of contextual control, or fourth terms (e.g., establishing or motivating operations; Michael, 1982; setting events; Wahler & Fox, 1981), in that they function differently under different conditions. In this way, any event in behavior analysis is understood functionally rather than in terms of its form. Behaviors are understood and defined functionally—that is, they are understood in terms of the context in which they occur. Likewise, contexts are understood functionally—that is, they are understood in terms of the behaviors they evoke. Even relations among behaviors or between contexts and behaviors are understood in terms of the contexts in which they occur.

For example, the behavior analyst observing physiological arousal, intrusive thoughts of past threats, and aggressive behavior might determine that these behaviors most likely take place in situations in which they are being evaluated (antecedent). They also might note that the aggressive behaviors tend to result in escape from the conversation (consequence), particularly when the conversation is personal rather than professional (antecedent operation). In this way, the behavior analyst has determined the functional relationship between the context and this class of behaviors. Intervention might involve changing the context to reduce the likelihood of any one of these behaviors (e.g., using more constructive feedback that is not explicitly evaluative or intentionally persisting in the conversation even when aggressive behavior begins). It also might involve changing the context to alter the relationships among the behaviors. Specifically, the behavior analyst might create the antecedent context that evokes the response class then add to that context to train new skills (e.g., intentionally creating an evaluative context, watching for elicitation of physiological arousal and intrusive thoughts, and prompting asking clarifying questions or repeating their understanding of the feedback received). To the extent that the situation still evokes arousal and intrusive thoughts, but does not occasion aggressive behavior, the learning has involved the changing of *relations among behaviors*, not merely the likelihood of the whole class.

Finally, radical behaviorism is also explicitly pragmatic in terms of the evaluation of analyses via their function. For example, Skinner (1984) suggested that psychological definitions be analyzed, from a behavioral perspective, as behavior in context, such that an operational definition for a psychological term can be understood as simply the conditions under which that term is used. In this way, psychological terms from any nonbehavioral scientific tradition can be operationalized and conceptualized behaviorally by examining the context in which those terms are used. For example, a behavioral conceptualization of mindfulness would involve consideration of the conditions under which the term *mindfulness* is used.

Interbehavioral Psychology

Another well-developed behavior-analytic theoretical approach that contributed to the development of CBS and ACT was Kantorian *interbehavioral psychology* (see Kantor, 1958). Grounded in a robust philosophical system called *interbehaviorism*, the basic unit of analysis in interbehavioral psychology is interbehavior, also known as the interbehavioral field or the *psychological event*. Any one *psychological event* is defined as an integrated field, which is composed of bidirectional, functional, dynamic interactions among (1) response functions (i.e., behavior) and (2) stimulus functions (i.e., context), along with (3) the settings in which those interactions occur, (4) the sensory medium of contact allowing for those interactions, and (5) the historical context present in the current iteration of the evolving interaction. Just as with field theories in other scientific traditions, all aspects of the interbehavioral field are not only functionally defined in terms of their relationships with one another, but are also said to comprise an ever-evolving, unitary whole. Reconsidering the examples above, we find that the client's heart rate is participating in a psychological event that includes bidirectional interactions among their heart rate, their name being called, their perception of such in this particular therapist's office from this particular assistant on this particular day, and all previous iterations of functionally similar interactions. The client disclosing the increase in their heart rate is participating in a psychological event that includes bidirectional interactions among their heart rate and disclosure thereof, the therapist's asking how they are, listening, and expressing their support, their perceiving these particular behaviors from this particular therapist on this particular day, and all previous iterations of functionally similar interactions. In this way, interbehavioral psychology encourages an analysis of complex instances of behavior (or interbehavior) as they occur in everyday settings and as can be described with a common language.

Sandoz (2020) has presented three examples of where an interbehavioral perspective, in particular, might have clinical implications in CBS interventions. First, the functional relationship obtaining[1] between the therapist's behavior (setting context for the client's behavior) and the client's behavior (setting context for the therapist's behavior) can be approached as the primary unit of analysis of the therapy process. In this approach, instead of each aspect of the contingency being analyzed separately, the therapeutic relationship, conceptualized as the co-creative and evolving interaction between therapist and client, is what is observed and intervened upon in therapy. Second, thoughts and feelings can be included as part of a class of coordinated responses unfolding in a dynamic stream, and their subtlety (i.e., the difficulty involved in their observation) is a function of the therapeutic relationship. In this approach, the therapist is freed from the burden of accounting for "private" contexts or behaviors "within" the client and instead focuses on strategically developing the relationship to support increasing familiarity and facility with their understanding of both the client's behavior and their impact on such. Third, the learning history can be approached as an aspect of the present, evident in the functional relations obtaining between the client's coordinated responses and the therapy context. In this approach, the therapist creates the conditions in therapy that are functionally similar to those in the client's life, observing the client's history in the emerging patterns,, and then adds to those conditions to expand upon those functions.

Implications of Behavior-Analytic Theoretical Foundations in ACT

Behavior analysis is foundational to the practice of ACT, much as contextual analysis is central to the ideals governing *applications* of behavior analysis. For example, applied behavior analysis (ABA) is often described in terms of seven dimensions that differentiate it from other intervention efforts in psychology (Baer, Wolf, & Risley, 1968): applied, behavioral, analytic, technological, conceptually systematic, effective, and generalizable. In this way, applied behavior analysis is itself functionally defined and evaluated. Interventions are not behavior analytic because of the specific terms used, theories employed by the therapist, or the format or setting of the intervention. Exactly what a behavior-analytic intervention involves and exactly how the specific impact is evaluated depend on a number of features of the context including the client's repertoire, the sociocultural context, and the intervention format.

For example, applications of behavior analysis that are language-based (e.g., "talk therapy") in their characterization of and intervention on problem behavior are referred to as *clinical behavior analysis* (CBA; Kohlenberg, Tsai, & Dougher, 1993; see Dougher, 2000). CBA tends to employ techniques that appear quite different from applications of behavior analysis interventions in other settings. CBA-oriented therapists, however, would equally aspire to the same seven dimensions.

In this way, the ACT therapist working from strong CBA underpinnings is empowered to evaluate and develop their work functionally according to the extent to which it is:

1. *applied* in that they target phenomena of social significance for the client;
2. *behavioral* in that they aim to measure, as precisely as possible, the client's behaviors of interest;
3. *analytic* in that they aim to demonstrate that any favorable behavior change is attributable to the intervention;
4. *technological* in that they describe intervention methods in precise functional terms (i.e., specifying contingent relationships among the client's behavior, the therapist's behavior, and other aspects of the intervention);
5. *conceptually systematic* in that they derive their interventions from basic principles;
6. *effective* in that they objectively demonstrate a practically and/or clinically significant effect for the client; and
7. *generalizable* in that they directly target broad behavior change over time and across contexts.

In other words, the ACT therapist aims to choose target behaviors (or interbehaviors) in terms of the extent to which they matter to the client and will be specifically effective in their lives. The ACT therapist aims to include regular measurement of those behaviors (or interbehaviors) with as much precision as possible without losing nuance. The ACT therapist aims to investigate the acute and specific impact of their intervention. They approach empirically supported treatment as involving not only the implementation of treatments demonstrated to work in the scientific literature, but also the tracking of processes and outcomes for particular clients, at certain times, in terms of specific targeted behaviors. The ACT therapist aims to describe observed behaviors (or interbehaviors) as completely as possible in terms of the direct relationships with the therapeutic context. The ACT therapist aims to develop and alter their interventions based on direct observations and consistent with basic principles. And finally, the ACT therapist aims to demonstrate a general impact of their interventions across a range of important domains of functioning.

Functional Contextualism: Defining Contextual Behavioral Science

Despite the seemingly obvious contextualistic orientation of both theoretical approaches like radical behaviorism and interbehavioral psychology (e.g., see Morris, 1984), as well as of applications of behavior analysis, responses to the characterization of contextualism as the "philosophical core" of behavior analysis (Hayes et al., 1988) have varied widely. Some behavior analysts have exhibited enthusiasm for the contextual foundations of behavior analysis being made explicit (e.g., Morris, 1988; 1993). Others rejected this characterization, describing more sophisticated forms of mechanism they believed characterized those adopted by behavior analysis (e.g., Delprato, 1993; Shull & Lawrence, 1993). Still others suggested behavior analysis adopts a contextualistic epistemology (i.e., contextualist assumptions about how we know what is), but a mechanistic *ontology* (i.e., mechanistic assumptions about what is; Reese, 1993). Finally, some analysts responded by proposing a brand of behavior analysis in which the contextualistic epistemology might be extended to a contextualistic ontology, where the untestable, fundamental assumption about reality is that it is indistinguishable from the behavioral event itself, including both contextual and behavioral factors (e.g., Barnes & Roche, 1994). With this, it became apparent to some that behavior analysis was not monolithic in its world view and that explication of a behavior analysis with explicit contextual philosophical underpinnings might be needed (e.g., see Hayes, Hayes, Reese, & Sarbin, 1993).

As behavior analysis contended with its philosophical roots, functional contextualism was named as a distinct philosophical position within the contextualist world view in behavior analysis and *contextual behavioral science* established as behavior analysis with functional contextual underpinnings. Functional contextualism was first described primarily in terms of its distinction from descriptive contextualism (Hayes, 1993). In short, it was proposed that contextualism varies along the extent to which the pragmatic truth criterion of effective action is emphasized over and above the root metaphor of the act-in-context and the emphasis of the unitary whole as primary. Interbehavioral psychology was offered as exemplary of descriptive contextualism, emphasizing the root metaphor of the act-in-context and the emphasis of the unitary whole as primary to such an extent that analyses did not have practical utility. However, this characterization has been revealed as problematic in two ways (see Hayes & Fryling, 2019). First, descriptive contextualism does not adequately represent the philosophical underpinnings of interbehavioral psychology. Interbehavioral psychology is based in interbehaviorism, a fully developed philosophy of science that is consistent with Pepper's (1942) contextual world view but is considerably more precise in its positions and expansive in its implications. Second, Pepper (1942) offered his world views not as complete philosophies of science, but as categorizations of the patterns he saw among various approaches to observation and sense-making (both scientific and otherwise).

In time, however, functional contextualism was further specified in terms of its philosophical assumptions, including its units of analysis, epistemology, ontology, and truth criterion (e.g., see Hayes, Barnes-Holmes, et al., 2012). This created the necessary foundation for not just the initial development of ACT, but also its ongoing refinement. For example, the specification of functional contextualism also provided the foundation for the development of *relational frame theory* (Hayes, Barnes-Holmes, & Roche, 2001), a behavior-analytic theory of language and cognition that has been employed both to explain ACT and to support its evolution (e.g., see Harte & Barnes-Holmes, this volume). In addition, the specification of functional contextualism and contextual behavioral science offered further implications for the practice of ACT.

Implications of the Act-in-Context as the Unit of Analysis in ACT

Functional contextualism focuses on analysis of the behavior of organisms, interacting with the immediate situation, as an iteration of the history of all their relevant context–behavior interactions. In this way, functional contextualism adopts the root metaphor of contextualism, the act-in-context, as its primary unit of analysis. In this way, as with the psychological event in Interbehavioral Psychology, behavior and context are approached as unitary aspects of the same phenomena, defined in terms of their evolving relationship to one another and thus, unable to be fully separated without losing definition. Instead, behavior, context, and the acute functional relationship among them are distinguished from one another (and from other aspects of the environment or the behavioral stream) only for the practical purposes of examination consistent with analytic goals. For example, the client's disclosure of their heart pounding (behavior) is not wholly differentiable from the therapist's asking how they are (antecedent context) or expressing support (consequential context). Further, none of these are wholly differentiable from aspects of the physical environment in which the conversation takes place or from the many other behaviors that make up the client's stream of behavior. The contextual therapist will make these distinctions, however artificial, because of the way it positions them, as a manipulable part of the immediate context, to intervene to influence the client's behavior.

This perspective empowers the ACT therapist working from strong functional contextual underpinnings to recognize their role as a primary part of the situational context for each behavior they observe in session and thus to:

1. act in ways that sample contexts that are functionally similar to those in the client's life so that they can sample and directly observe functionally defined behaviors of importance determined by the client's learning history;
2. act in ways that add to the context, contributing to their functionally relevant learning history to expand the client's repertoire in said contexts;
3. analyze their own behavior in the specific therapeutic context co-created with the client in terms of the context set by the client's behavior and their learning history with such contexts, setting goals for therapist development specific to the client;
4. center the therapeutic relationship in the intervention and evaluate their impact on its effectiveness (cf. Sandoz, 2020).

Functional contextualism extends its understanding of the act-in-context beyond the individual behavior of the whole organism, allowing units of analysis to vary with the level of the analysis. For example, some phenomena of interest (e.g., familial conflict, academic retention, systemic oppression) may be best described and measured behaviorally at the group level. From a functional contextual perspective, group-level behavior can be analyzed with the dyad, family, organization, or community serving as the behaving organism, and in terms of the relevant immediate and historical contexts in which this group-level activity unfolds. On the other hand, some phenomena of interest (e.g., dopaminergic activity) may be best described and measured behaviorally in terms of suborganismic processes. From a functional contextual perspective, specific physiological, genetic, and epigenetic processes can be analyzed as behaviors of the suborganismic system, in terms of the immediate and historical contexts in which they unfold. By retaining the act-in-context as a flexible unit of analysis applicable at multiple levels, functional contextualism avoids both reductionism and expansionism, allowing for any level of analysis as necessary to achieve analytic goals.

This perspective empowers the ACT therapist working from strong functional contextual underpinnings to:

5. scale their interventions to individual therapy, couples therapy, family therapy, group therapy, and milieu therapy formats;
6. scale their observations of individual behavior to particular aspects of the activity being observed in the dynamic and complex behavioral stream (e.g., watching micro-expressions or listening for vocal tremor);
7. create interventions that are sensitive to information about behavior at levels of analysis outside of their expertise and/or immediate observational field (e.g., incorporating data on neurological functioning or cultural contingencies in the design of intervention and selection of targets for observation);

Implications of a Monist Account of Behavior in ACT

Functional contextualism's flexibility with level of analysis also implies (and to some extent, requires) a monistic account of behavior where the behavioral stream is assumed to be unitary and inclusive of any and all activities of the organism. This behavior is contrasted with a dualist account, where analyses of behavior include events that are not only not observed but are in-kind unobservable (e.g., the Unconscious; see Wilson, 2001). Instead, from a functional contextual perspective, the behavioral stream includes behaviors whose observation is limited by privacy or subtlety (e.g., thoughts, feelings, physical sensations). These are not treated as different kinds of events than those behaviors that are easily publicly observed. The monism of functional contextualism can also be thought to include the unitary conceptualization of the act-in-context, where behavior, context, and their respective functions are approached as inseparable and distinguished only for purposes of analysis. In this way, an analysis that includes only relationships among behavior (e.g., this thought accompanies this feeling, both of which accompany this behavior) is incomplete until context is incorporated. Finally, functional contextualism's monism considers the specification of behavior, context, and function a complete analysis in its own right.

If the analysis specifies behavior (or behaviors and the relations among them), context, and function, the analysis is actionable without the appeal to hypothetical constructs that collapse patterns of context and behavior into personal characteristics (e.g., self-esteem, morality, intelligence). For example, the functional contextualist analyzing a student's academic performance might note patterns in certain social contexts that suggest intelligence, but these would be approached as behaviors to be analyzed rather than explanations of the performance observed. In this way, the complete analysis would include the aspects of context that account for the academic performance, the "intelligent" social behavior, and the relationship among them. Such analyses would then be evaluable in terms of the actions derived from the analysis and their effects. In this way, the adequately complete functional contextual analysis has immediate and direct implications for both contextual change and the outcome expected.

This perspective empowers the ACT therapist working from strong functional contextual underpinnings to:

8. develop a working understanding of whole, complex functional classes of co-occurring responses that are probable in the client's repertoire and are characterized by particular behaviors that make for adequate observation;
9. shift attention among co-occurring behaviors that comprise the functional response class to those that are observable in the moment, that vary with functional shifts in context, and that serve the goals of the assessment or intervention;
10. contextualize co-occurring behaviors and the relationships among them by analyzing them in terms of their immediately observable and manipulable contexts;
11. translate relevant theories that rely on unobservable and/or hypothetical constructs into descriptions of context–behavior relationships that are either actionable or dismissable.

In other words, in session, ACT therapists watch for patterns in what kinds of behaviors tend to co-occur in session with respect to particular contextual shifts that comprise the intervention (e.g., questions or instructions). For example, the therapist might observe rapid eye blinking, looking up and away, tension in the voice, and descriptions of obstacles, all of which tend to come together in session when the therapist asks about future plans or intentions. ACT therapists selectively attend to those behaviors that are observable, that vary with functional shifts in context, and that are relevant to the goals of the intervention. The therapist might find the vocal tension and description of obstacles as the formal aspects of the response class that they most easily discriminate in session. ACT therapists also discern what contextual changes accompany shifts in the behavioral stream among response classes, thus increasingly understanding them functionally with every interaction. The therapist might note that they can reliably evoke vocal tension and descriptions of obstacles by asking about the future—a necessary aspect of the relationship that will allow for the therapist to build out the client's repertoire in such contexts. Lastly, ACT therapists notice hypothetical constructs that emerge as part of their experience of the client (e.g., insecure attachment, ego strength, confirmation bias), and translate them into actionable accounts. The therapist might note that the label "imposter syndrome" seems to fit their observations of the client's behavior (rapid eye blinking, looking up and away, tension in the voice, and descriptions of obstacles) in the contexts that evoke thoughts of the future. They might then translate this to mean that self-deprecation, a sense of not belonging, and fear of failure may be part of this response class, and probe such the next time any members of the response class are exhibited (e.g., "How do you react to yourself in this vision of everything falling apart in the future?").

Implications of a Strong Epistemology and Disinterest in Ontology in ACT

Robust philosophies of science typically go beyond identifying the focus of their analyses to include explication of *epistemological* assumptions about what is known and *ontological* assumptions about what is. Functional contextualism, however, approaches knowing in the same way as it approaches any behavior—as an act-in-context. Expanding upon Skinner's (1984) radical behaviorist approach on the operational definition of psychological terms, functional contextualism proposes that all scientific behavior is understood in terms of its context. Even as the scientist or therapist notes a behavioral phenomenon they intend to observe, they are abstracting this phenomenon from the unitary whole; this abstraction occurs in a specific immediate context and with respect to their history with such contexts. Further, this specific abstraction has consequences that may be more or less consistent with preestablished analytic goals. The same goes for developing an assessment method, a clinical conceptualization or research hypothesis, analytic or interpretive strategy, or interpretive conclusions. What is known is inseparable from the activity of knowing, which is understood in terms of its relationships with context and evaluated in terms of its effectiveness.

Whether in functional contextualism or in behavior analysis before it, this epistemological stance has resulted in what has been termed a "disinterest" in ontology (Hayes, Barnes-Holmes, et al., 2012, p. 4). In short, the pursuit of terms and theories that correspond with categories in a real universe seems to conflict with the approach of that pursuit as an act-in-context, the products and functional consequences of which are unique to the pursuer's history. Instead, pragmatic truth about what works is an enthusiastic and encompassing focus, and strict ontology is abandoned. In this way, *what is known* is not assumed to have implications as to *what is*, since knowing is, at least in part, unique to the knower's learning history interacting with the immediate contexts in which the knowing and all the behaviors involved in that knowing take place. The functional contextual therapist, like the functional contextual scientist, accepts their observations and experiences of their client, however systematic, in this same way: as a product of their own history and the immediate context provided by the client's behavior.

This perspective empowers the ACT therapist, who is working from strong functional contextual underpinnings to:

12. set aside attempts to assess, conceptualize, and treat in ways that are consistent with an objective ontological reality;
13. acknowledge the role that their own repertoire and learning history have in shaping that which they observe;
14. establish specific goals for their work as therapist at multiple levels (e.g., broadly, or by program, client, session, or moment);
15. develop and evaluate their behavior with regards to assessment, conceptualization, and treatment in terms of its effectiveness with respect to established goals across multiple levels.

Functional Contextualism's Truth Criterion: Implications of the Analytic Goal in ACT

Functional contextualism also goes one step further than Pepper's (1942) contextualism as a common epistemological stance in clarifying a specific analytic goal. In doing so, functional contextualism offers a more complete philosophy of science by providing a criterion by which the process and content of any analysis can be evaluated. The first article of the first issue of the *Journal of Contextual Behavioral Science* (Hayes et al., 2012, p. 4) clearly defines the purpose of this philosophical view: "The goal of functional contextualism is to predict-and-influence, with precision, scope, and depth, whole organisms interacting in and with a context considered historically and situationally."

Apart from the primary unit of analysis, what most distinguishes this goal from that of much of the rest of behavioral science is the emphasis on "prediction-and-influence" as a unified aim. Here, *prediction* refers to the understanding of relationships among behaviors and contexts such that descriptions of those relationships can be verified, while *influence* refers to contextual control as the standard for verification. Prediction goals would be satisfied simply through noting that behaviors and/or contexts co-occur. In contrast, influence goals would require that (1) contexts are included in the analysis, (2) the contexts noted are manipulable, and (3) manipulation of said contexts results in changes in the behaviors and/or relationships among them.

Whereas most behavioral sciences value influential applications of an analysis as potential *outcomes* of understanding, functional contextualism holds them as the *standard* by which understanding is evaluated. In this way, the complete analysis of act-in-context necessarily includes behavior(s) (including relationships among behaviors) as the dependent variable(s) and some aspect of context as the independent variable. For example, the description of a relationship among particular thoughts, feelings, and behaviors might be quite nuanced but would be a wholly incomplete analysis from a functional contextual perspective because it offers nothing actionable outside of the behavioral stream (i.e., how to influence these particular thoughts, feelings, and behaviors or their relationships to each other, which requires a change in the context in which the behavior occurs). For example, an attachment researcher might note that children who struggle to calm themselves when their parent departs and who reject their parent upon their return are likely to report dissatisfaction with relationships in adulthood. This does not speak, however, to the historical or immediate contexts that contributed to the emotional upset, the rejection, or the relationship satisfaction, nor to what shifts in context might change these behaviors or the relations among them.

Functional contextualism's broad analytic goal further specifies that prediction-and-influence should be accomplished with precision, scope, and depth. Precision generally refers to the number of alternative terms and theories that might be applied to explain an event. Thus, specifically with regards to prediction-and-influence, *precision* refers to the extent to which the analysis fosters effective action with respect to a specific instance. Scope generally refers to the range of events that particular terms and theories might be able to explain. Thus, specifically with regards to prediction-and-influence, *scope* refers to the breadth with which an analysis can be applied to foster effective action in a range of instances. Lastly, depth generally refers to the extent to which the terms and theories applied cohere with those accepted at other levels of analysis. Thus, specifically with regards to prediction-and-influence, *depth* refers to the extent to which the analysis fosters effective action across multiple levels of investigation and intervention.

This perspective empowers the ACT therapist working from strong functional contextual underpinnings to:

16. set aside as irrelevant characterizations about their clients, themselves, or the therapeutic relationship that predict but have no implications for action;
17. develop their therapy repertoires in terms of precision or the generation of specifically-effective aspects of intervention;
18. develop their therapy repertoires in terms of scope or the generation of broadly effective aspects of intervention;
19. scale the development of the precision of their therapy repertoires across varying levels of analysis (e.g., by moment, session, client, population, or format);
20. scale the development of the scope of their therapy repertoires across varying levels of analysis (e.g., across moments, clients, populations, or formats).

Functional Contextualism's Truth Criterion: Implications of Specifying Impact in ACT

CBS provides a further criterion for evaluating the effectiveness of contextual behavioral analyses across a range of contexts in terms of the *kind* of influence valued in the discipline. In fact, clarifying the impact valued by a scientific community may be particularly important to avoid

moral relativism, or even Machiavellianism (see Ruiz & Roche, 2007). The Association for Contextual Behavioral Science (Association for Contextual Behavioral Science, n.d.) offers vision, mission, and values statements, each of which could be applied to the pragmatic evaluation of the impact of any contextual behavioral analysis. With this, ACBS takes the first steps to create the social context needed to support adherence to philosophical and theoretical foundations in pursuit of a specific impact in the world. First, the vision of ACBS is "the alleviation of human suffering and the advancement of human well-being through research and practice grounded in contextual behavioral science" (ACBS, n.d.). As such, its members commit to evaluating the effectiveness of their work in terms not only of their specific analytic goals, but also the extent to which it contributes to alleviating suffering and advancing well-being.
Second, the mission of ACBS members is to

- support a dynamic interaction between basic and applied research;
- disseminate contextual behavioral science;
- continue to develop principles, theories, and practical applications grounded in empirical knowledge and guided by the best available scientific evidence;
- support all members who wish to participate in this work (ACBS, n.d.).

Third, ACBS declares a shared value of the community to be working "in a collegial, open, generous, self-critical, non-discriminatory, and mutually supportive way" (ACBS, n.d.). In other words, CBS specifies overarching impacts that characterize effective action or preferred influence. For example, CBS researchers and theoreticians might emphasize research studies with (1) clear practical implications over purely intellectual pursuits, (2) applicability to those most in need, and (3) easy disseminability. Further, all ACBS members, regardless of their profession, might allocate time and other resources to creating the context for other professionals to thrive. The organization's leadership creates contexts that support such efforts in many ways beyond simply establishing the vision, mission, and values. For example, the ACBS website includes a number of well-used repositories for research and practice protocols and other materials, an archive of past conference presentations, and a link for free access to the organization's flagship journal. In this way, at both the molar level of the organization and the molecular level of the individual contextual behavioral scientist, the ideal contextual behavioral analyses will be those that contribute both to the immediate goals of the analyst and to the above aims. Moreover, each activity of the contextual behavioral scientist or group of scientists can ultimately be practically evaluated in terms of such.

This perspective empowers the ACT therapist working from strong functional contextual underpinnings to:

21. develop their therapy repertoire specifically and professional behavior broadly in ways that typify and foster the vision, mission, and values of CBS;
22. create contexts that support other individuals behaving in ways that typify and foster the vision, mission, and values of CBS;
23. create contexts that support the ACBS and its subgroups behaving in ways that typify and foster the vision, mission, and values of CBS.

In this way, the ACT therapist is encouraged to apply the philosophical and theoretical underpinnings that characterize CBS beyond their specific therapy work to their broader professional repertoire. The emphasis on effective action, the selection of act-in-context as the primary unit of analysis, the dedication to a monistic conceptual account, the adoption of a functional epistemological and a-ontological stance, and commitment to prediction-and-influence all work to guide professional practices in such a way as to foster an end to human suffering and promote human well-being. For example, CBS practitioners, trainers, and administrators might build agency policies, procedures, and services that not only promote the interest of their direct stakeholders, but also allow for broader contributions to their local communities.

Conclusion

Both the development and dissemination of ACT have long been characterized by the specification of philosophical and theoretical underpinnings (Hayes, 2004). Today, these underpinnings define contextual behavioral science as the discipline of which ACT is a part. These CBS foundations have specific implications, not only for understanding ACT as an intervention approach, but also for defining and guiding effective implementation of ACT in each clinical (or other professional) situation a therapist faces.

Note

1. The phrase "functional relationship obtaining" uses "obtain" in its intransitive form, meaning to be in existence, in effect, or customary (obtaining, n.d.). This usage is typical when emphasizing functional relationships as common co-occurrences without implying additional assumptions about causation.

References

Association for Contextual Behavioral Science. (n.d.). *About ACBS.* Retrieved December 19, 2020, from https://contextualscience.org/acbs. Association for Contextual Behavioral Science.

Baer, D. M., Wolf, M. M., & Risley, T. R. (1968). Some current dimensions of applied behavior analysis. *Journal of Applied Behavior Analysis, 1*(1), 91.

Barnes, D., & Roche, B. (1994). Mechanistic ontology and contextualistic epistemology: A contradiction within behavior analysis. *The Behavior Analyst, 17*(1), 165.

Cook, J. M., Biyanova, T., Elhai, J., Schnurr, P. P., & Coyne, J. C. (2010). What do psychotherapists really do in practice? An Internet study of over 2,000 practitioners. *Psychotherapy: Theory, Research, Practice, Training, 47*(2), 260.

Dapretto, M., Davies, M. S., Pfeifer, J. H., Scott, A. A., Sigman, M., Bookheimer, S. Y., & Iacoboni, M. (2006). Understanding emotions in others: Mirror neuron dysfunction in children with autism spectrum disorders. *Nature Neuroscience, 9*(1), 28–30.

Delprato, D. J. (1993). Behavior analysis and SC Pepper's other mechanism. *The Behavior Analyst, 16*(1), 51.

Dougher, M. J. (Ed.). (2000). *Clinical behavior analysis.* Oakland, CA: Context Press/New Harbinger.

Hayes, L. J., & Fryling, M. J. (2019). Functional and descriptive contextualism. *Journal of Contextual Behavioral Science, 14*, 119–126.

Hayes, S. C. (1993). *Analytic goals and the varieties of scientific contextualism.* Oakland, CA: Context Press.

Hayes, S. C. (2004). Acceptance and commitment therapy, relational frame theory, and the third wave of behavioral and cognitive therapies. *Behavior Therapy, 35*(4), 639–665.

Hayes, S. C., Barnes-Holmes, D., & Roche, B. (Eds.). (2001). *Relational Frame Theory: A Post-Skinnerian Account of Human Language and Cognition.* New York: Springer Science & Business Media.

Hayes, S. C., Barnes-Holmes, D., & Wilson, K. G. (2012). Contextual behavioral science: Creating a science more adequate to the challenge of the human condition. *Journal of Contextual Behavioral Science, 1*(1–2), 1–16.

Hayes, S. C., Hayes, L. J., & Reese, H. W. (1988). Finding the philosophical core: A review of Stephen C. Pepper's world hypotheses: A study in evidence. *Journal of the Experimental Analysis of Behavior, 50*(1), 97.

Hayes, S. C., Hayes, L. J., Reese, H. W., & Sarbin, T. R. (Eds.). (1993). *Varieties of scientific contextualism.* Context Press.

Hayes, S. C., Strosahl, K. D., & Wilson, K. G. (1999). *Acceptance and commitment therapy: An experiential approach to behavior change.* Guilford Press.

Hayes, S. C., Strosahl, K. D., & Wilson, K. G. (2012). *Acceptance and commitment therapy: The process and practice of mindful change.* New York: Guilford press.

Kantor, J. R. (1958). *Interbehavioral psychology: A sample of scientific system construction.* Bloomington, IN: Principia Press.

Kohlenberg, R. J., Tsai, M., & Dougher, M. J. (1993). The dimensions of clinical behavior analysis. *The Behavior Analyst, 16*(2), 271–282.

Mason, K., Sripada, C. S., & Stich, S. (2010). The philosophy of psychology. *Routledge Companion to Twentieth-Century Philosophy.* London: Routledge.

Michael, J. (1982). Distinguishing between discriminative and motivational functions of stimuli. *Journal of the Experimental Analysis of Behavior, 37*(1), 149–155.
Morris, E. K. (1984). Interbehavioral psychology and radical behaviorism: Some similarities and differences. *The Behavior Analyst, 7*(2), 197–204.
Morris, E. K. (1988). Contextualism: The world view of behavior analysis. *Journal of Experimental Child Psychology, 46*(3), 289–323.
obtaining. (n.d.). *American Heritage® dictionary of the English language*. Retrieved September 29, 2020 from (5th ed.) (n.d.) https://www.thefreedictionary.com/obtaining.
Pepper, S. C. (1942). *World hypotheses: A study in evidence* (Vol. 31). Berkeley: University of California Press.
Reese, H. W. (1993). Contextualism and dialectical materialism. In S. C. Hayes, L. J. Hayes, H. W. Reese, & T. R. Sarbin (Eds.), *Varieties of scientific contextualism* (pp. 71–105). Context Press.
Ruiz, M. R., & Roche, B. (2007). Values and the scientific culture of behavior analysis. *The Behavior Analyst, 30*(1), 1–16.
Safran, J. D., & Messer, S. B. (1997). Psychotherapy integration: A postmodern critique. *Clinical Psychology: Science and Practice, 4*(2), 140–152.
Sandoz, E. K. (2020). Interbehavior as a clinical focus in CBS: A response to Hayes and Fryling (2019). *Journal of Contextual Behavioral Science, 18*, 273–275.
Shull, R. L., & Lawrence, P. S. (1993). Is contextualism productive?. *The Behavior Analyst, 16*(2), 241.
Skinner, B. F. (1974). *About Behaviorism*. New York: Random House.
Skinner, B. F. (1984). The operational analysis of psychological terms. *Behavioral and Brain Sciences, 7*(4), 547–553.
Wahler, R. G., & Fox, J. J. (1981). Setting events in applied behavior analysis: Toward a conceptual and methodological expansion. *Journal of Applied Behavior Analysis, 14*(3), 327–338.
Wilson, K. G. (2001). Some notes on theoretical constructs: Types and validation from a contextual behavioral perspective. *International Journal of Psychology and Psychological Therapy, 1*(2), 205–215.

CHAPTER

3

Primer on Basic Behavioral Principles

Thomas J. Waltz *and* Claudia Drossel

Abstract

Behavioral principles guided the initial development of acceptance and commitment therapy (ACT) and serve as the foundation for its flexible implementation. This article provides a broad introduction to the contextual approach to operant behavior, including behavioral principles, behavioral economics, and rule-governed behavior. Key applications of these relations include taking a constructional approach to building meaningful patterns of behavior that are supported by naturalistic contingencies outside of the therapeutic relationship, evaluating function-based hypotheses by monitoring response to treatment and other key variables, and occasionally systematically evaluating treatment outcomes using single-subject research designs. Examples used throughout the article help connect these foundational concepts to ACT practice. Behavioral principles support clinicians in taking a scientist-practitioner approach to ACT implementation and can support competent innovation while maintaining fidelity to the underlying functional contextual model.

Key Words: acceptance and commitment therapy, behavioral economics, behavioral principles, constructive approach, functional analysis, operant, rule-governed behavior, scientist-practitioner, verbal behavior

The difference between a scientist and a technician is that the technician knows how to do what he [sic] *has been taught to do while the scientist knows how to evaluate new information in order to devise and refine new techniques.*

(Ullmann, 1961, p. 120)

Behavioral Principles and the Scientist-Practitioner

Guidelines for doctoral-level training in cognitive-behavioral therapy distinguish the skill sets of scientist-practitioners from those of technicians (Klepac et al., 2012). These guidelines emphasize that trainees' understanding of behavioral principles is necessary to flexibly apply and individually tailor cognitive and behavioral therapies to the needs of diverse clients. A scientist-practitioner stance is achievable at multiple levels of training—at the master's level and across health professions—as long as behavioral principles are the foundations of providers' conceptualizations. Conversely, neither a doctoral education nor a specialization in clinical psychology guarantee the flexible problem solving of scientist-practitioners. With respect to cognitive-behavioral therapies, not all doctoral programs in clinical psychology offer sufficient training in behavioral principles to support the flexible application of acceptance and commitment therapy (ACT). From a dissemination perspective, insufficient training in behavioral principles represents a challenge for training whose goal is to prepare a wide variety of professionals to implement ACT flexibly and functionally. So far, a systematic approach to provide this training across the clinical professions has remained elusive.

To increase the accessibility of ACT to a diversely trained professional audience, the ACT community settled on using dissemination heuristics, often called middle-level terms, to guide novices without training in behavioral principles to adhere to the spirit of the treatment approach. Middle-level terms (acceptance, defusion, contact with the present moment, self-as-context, values, and committed action) are summarized under three response styles (open, centered, and engaged) and aim to serve as rules with heuristic value for practice (Hayes, Strosahl, & Wilson, 2012). These terms seek to facilitate the functional implementation of ACT independent from one's understanding of behavioral principles (Waltz & Hayes, 2010). While dissemination heuristics such as the hexaflex model (Hayes & Strosahl, 2004) or the matrix (Polk & Schoendorff, 2014) and the enumeration of techniques (e.g., Stoddard & Afari, 2014) can facilitate ACT implementation, they reflect a "just good enough" approach to introducing the ACT model to trainees and guiding implementation. Indeed, using middle-level terms as dissemination heuristics can be conceptualized as landmarks on the road to implementing ACT. Travelers who rely on landmarks, however, tend to get lost when situations change unexpectedly, as when clients do not behave as they ought per the manual, or when unanticipated external barriers show up (e.g., the client encounters resource-based barriers). Maneuvering under difficult conditions requires knowing more about one's whereabouts than certain landmarks. To navigate difficult conditions, it helps to know the general layout of the land and to access multiple wayfinding tools. Behavioral principles provide both the layout—in terms of theory—and the wayfinding tools—in terms of procedures. Understanding behavioral principles is thus particularly useful when a situation seems incalcitrant, indicative of unique, difficult, or complex circumstances that require problem solving within the scientific framework that underlies ACT. This article provides an introduction to behavioral principles from the contextual science perspective.

Most behavioral health professionals have at least some exposure to behavioral principles, but the depth and scope of that exposure as well as its alignment with a contextual science perspective can vary substantially. Indeed, most often behavior principles are introduced from a perspective that is inconsistent with contextual science. This inconsistency reflects the history of behaviorisms as a heterogeneous group of scientific approaches to behavior, emotion, and cognition (hereinafter summarized as "behavior"). "Instrumental" approaches to behavior spoke of stimuli, behavior, and consequences, but the philosophical assumptions they brought to their analytic units varied substantially (for a review, see Malone, 1990). To understand ACT, it is important to distinguish its unit of analysis (the act in context) from other behaviorisms that posit mediational mechanisms. Directly emerging from methodological behaviorisms, most of psychology takes a stimulus-mediator-response-consequence (S-M-R-C) approach to conceptualizing behavior. Life events occur, these events interact with some mediating internal processes (physiology, affect, and/or cognition),[1] and behaviors that result are measured and analyzed as evidence of these mediating processes. These processes are often conceptualized as participating in a linear mechanistic chain.

In contrast, ACT defines its subject matter as the act-in-context. This definition reflects its behavior-analytic roots, conceptualizing the unit of analysis as involving a dynamic interplay among antecedent, behavior, and consequence relations (A→[B⇆C]). In certain circumstances (*antecedent* context), some patterns of behavior are more (or less) likely to occur.

Moreover, the outcomes of these behavior patterns (*consequence* context) alter the frequency of those behavior patterns over time. While some temporality is present within an A-B-C analytic sequence, behavior is conceptualized within its context (i.e., coactive and reciprocal) rather than as a unidirectional element in a causal chain. This operant contingency as an analytic unit has profound implications when conceptualizing human behavior.

Even within the behavior-analytic community, heterogeneous philosophical assumptions may be brought to bear to explain behavioral principles (Hayes, 1978; Lee, 1987). As noted above when discussing the S-M-R-C model (e.g., Kanfer & Phillips, 1970), principles often are understood from a traditional methodological, linear, mechanistic chain approach that works well in some basic science contexts but can lack the contextual richness required to translate such principles to socially important patterns of behavior (Wilson, Bordieri, Flynn, Lucas, & Slater, 2011). A functional contextual approach to behavioral principles is more complicated, but it has fundamental implications for translating these principles into practice.

The Operant Contingency

The operant contingency is the behavior-analytic unit of analysis, defined by A-B-C relationships whose function emerges over time (Skinner, 1935). To fully understand these relationships, we first need to address the concepts of *functional relation* and *class*.

Functional Relations

Studying with Crozier (1892–1955), an associate professor in the Department of Physiology at Harvard University (Hoagland & Mitchell, 1956), Skinner learned to focus his work on parametric analyses of behavior under changing conditions and to use novel experimental designs to capture the behavior patterns of organisms over time (i.e., asking "what happens when . . . "; see also Sidman, 1960). When changing one variable reliably across systematic multiple observations leads to change in another variable, that interrelationship is measured and characterized as a functional relation. Through use of this approach, scientifically and practically meaningful patterns emerge from behavior–context relations that do not require any additional theorizing using mediational, hypothetical constructs.

Skinner's application of functional relations did away with hypothesizing mediating forces or agents as necessary for an analysis of behavior. A thorough parametric description of behavior–context relationships or patterns over time became the novel unit of analysis (Skinner, 1935). Measures of behavior-patterns-in-context rely on likelihood or frequency. Context and behavior are defined in relation to each other. Thus, an event is defined as a consequence of behavior if it changes the likelihood or frequency of that behavior over time, given that the event probabilistically depends on the occurrence of the behavior. Notice that this consequent event becomes more likely given the occurrence of behavior, but the consequence does not have to occur every time the behavior occurs.

Speaking in terms of functional relations instead of causes is countercultural. Our everyday ways of speaking overlap rather neatly with the S-M-R-C approach, that is, internal and stable attributions summarized by the mediating construct "M." We speak of "triggers" of M and invoke certain push–pull mechanisms for predictors of action, rather than uncertain likelihoods or frequencies distributed in time. In traditional methodological accounts, a stimulus exerts a causal force on one or more mediating processes (physiology, affect, cognition), which in turn exert a causal "triggering" force on behavior. Mechanistic metaphors (e.g., triggering events, overload, processing) impart a familiarity to S-M-R-C locutions used in everyday discourse. The mechanistic causal sequence implicit in the S-M-R-C approach gives speakers the sense of an explanation, as listeners can identify some hypothesized stable element that preceded the response in the casual chain. Functional relations are less satisfying: they lack the proximal stimulus, and uncertainty is inherent in a probabilistic account. The assumptions of a mechanistic approach suggest reasons or explanations for behavior that conflict with the contextual account of "act-in-context." Functional relations underlie ACT. They point to the circumstance that many of our stated reasons are not "causes" from a scientific perspective; that room for change persists even when a person says they are "triggered" or "cannot help" engaging in specific behaviors.

For example, take the statement "Bob succumbed to his cravings for alcohol after being laid off from work." Descriptively, Bob's drinking alcohol increased in both quantity and frequency after he was laid off from work. Here, changes in the frequency or quantity of Bob's alcohol consumption are attributed to "cravings," a mediational attribution. Within the S-M-R-C model, the situation is the unemployment (S), craving is the marker for a presumed neurobiological process (M), and drinking is the response (R), with many consequences in both the short and long term. In the mediational model as well as within lay communication, "craving" is the presumed proximal cause of drinking.

The contextual account points to the functional relationship between the situation conceptualized broadly (e.g., failures to find work, financial strain, interpersonal conflict) and alcohol consumption. It skips "cravings" as a cause of behavior and guides the client to notice the relationship between aspects of the situation and drinking. "Cravings" are acknowledged as reasons that clients may give for their drinking, but not as causes of drinking. When paying attention to the relationship between aspects of the situation and drinking, clients may notice that they drink without craving alcohol—that they habitually pour drinks or stop by the liquor store. Alternatively, to understand under what conditions Bob speaks of "cravings," he may start monitoring the contexts in which descriptions of cravings are most likely to be invoked. Again, to understand what is at issue when we speak of cravings, the operant account focuses on characterizing Bob's drinking or his report thereof as a function of contextual factors. Reasons such as cravings are more behavior to be accounted for within a contextual account, rather than a causal link in a mechanistic chain preceding drinking. Similarly, if Bob started taking a psychotropic medication (e.g., disulfiram) to curb substance use, the medication would become part of the context in which Bob's drinking occurs, and changes in drinking could be tracked in relation to this contextual change.

Importantly, descriptive functional relations characterize contextual variables that can be intervened upon and changed in some way. Clients and therapists collaboratively observe the relationship between variations in those variables and the behavior of interest. Thus, decreased availability of meaningful aspects of life independent of drinking (e.g., markers of social relationships such as status; hobbies or activities that are dependent upon a steady and generous income) may increase the relative likelihood that Bob will drink alcohol. Regardless of whether reports of alcohol cravings reflect a desire-for-pleasure narrative (e.g., I enjoy the buzz) or an escape-from-pain narrative (e.g., I can forget about my problems while drinking), a contextual account of Bob's report of cravings informs but does not replace a longitudinal contextual analysis of actual alcohol consumption and relevant aspects of the context. The distinction between functional relations and our more everyday ways of talking about causation will be revisited throughout the article.

BEHAVIOR–BEHAVIOR RELATIONS

The preceding discussion of alcohol cravings illustrates a key distinction between socially normative explanations for behavior on the one hand and explanations based on an operant analysis on the other. Unlike S-M-R-C explanations that give thoughts and feelings status as causal mediators within a mechanistic chain, an operant analysis conceptualizes these events as activities. Thoughts are not conceptualized as "things"; rather, speaking is viewed as behavior-in-context. Whether this behavior is public (i.e., talking aloud) or private (talking silently to oneself), saying or thinking are understood as behaviors in context. Similarly, emotions are not things, and our affective responses are analyzed in a way that does not differ from other behaviors. Whether behavior occurs in the context of high physiological arousal (e.g., rage) or not (e.g., disappointment), affective experiences and our descriptions thereof are behaviors to be understood in their context.

Behavior–behavior relations are problematic in an operant account not because they do not occur (they most certainly do), but because from a pragmatic philosophical perspective (see Sandoz & Fogle, this volume) variables given a causal status in operant relations need to be manipulable by contextual interventions (Hayes & Brownstein, 1986). Thus, when self-talk (e.g., I cannot stand this craving; I deserve a drink, given everything I've been through) and drinking alcohol co-occur, an operant analysis works to identify the manipulable contextual variables that ultimately influence both of these behaviors. In this respect an operant analysis is countercultural. Socially and in everyday parlance, thoughts and feelings are treated as default causes of behavior. In a behavior-analytic account, they lose the default causal status. When explaining everyday social relationships, treating thoughts and feelings as causes for behavior has heuristic value. Say-do-correspondence training and emotional expressive norms as part of our sociocultural conditioning allow us to use what people say to predict their behavior. If somebody tells us they are angry, we have a general sense of how they may behave in that situation. This predictive utility serves as the basis for treating thoughts and emotions colloquially as causes, without further analysis of what gave rise to them.

An operant technical analysis focuses on manipulable context–behavior relationships. This technical account takes on the added responsibility to influence and not just predict behavior patterns. A functional contextualist framework goes beyond behavior–behavior relations and identifies the contextual variables of which private events and public behavior patterns are a function. Furthermore, an operant analysis is concerned with patterns of behavior rather than instances (more on this below). Observations across time are necessary to observe the reliable relationship between variations in contextual variables and the behavior of interest. Again, to reiterate, meaningful aspects of life may have decreased as Bob's drinking increased; his relationships deteriorated, and he lost his job. This decrease makes drinking more likely. Concurrently, Bob reports that he "craves" or "wants" alcohol, communicating his preference of this outcome relative to other currently available alternatives in his postemployment social environment.

Classes of Behavior

The concept of class is fundamental to understanding operant contingencies. It is an extension of using functional relations to define contextual stimuli and behavior. As noted earlier, the unit of analysis is the act (or behavior) in context. Behavior is any activity that is demonstrated to have a functional relationship with contextual events (Skinner, 1935). Since behaviors vary from occurrence to occurrence, *classes of behavior are defined by similar functional relationships with a type of consequence over time.* Repeated observations are necessary to detect these behavior–consequence patterns. In therapy, for example, a client may engage in many different behaviors that function similarly. A client may avoid a topic or escape from the conversation by changing topics, stalling, or not answering questions, fidgeting, blowing their nose, or a host of other behaviors. Topographically very different, functionally these behaviors fall in the same class if, over time, they lead to the same outcome: The therapist gets distracted and discontinues their attempts to address a topic. The therapist's behavior, in turn, increases the probability that this class of behavior with its variations will persist in session or even increase in likelihood. Thus, the consequences change the likelihood of classes of behavior over time, as these behavior–consequence patterns repeat. Reliable behavior–consequence patterns are called *contingencies* to reflect the dynamic dependency between classes of behavior and consequences that goes beyond correlation, as they mutually affect each other. Functional context–behavior relations are inherently transactional within the A-B-C operant model (see also Linehan, 1993). Skinner's great innovation was to define behavior in terms of functional contingencies, directing scientist-practitioners to recognize that behaviors that look very different can be functionally similar via their shared consequences and that they are thus modifiable.

Curiosity is key to the contextual approach. Contingent behavior–consequence relationships emerge from activities and exploration over time, from "acting." They assume an active person. When thinking of children, we note that even a relatively simple activity, such as opening a bottle and then taking a drink, does not spontaneously emerge as a functional unit. A history of drinking from containers and opening containers will influence the acquisition of the skills involved in opening a bottle and taking a drink. Mechanically, one may twist or pry off the top of a bottle in a variety of ways, resulting in access to the beverage. While the range of topographies of these responses involves some creativity as a collective or class, they might be similar in the application of mechanical force to open the bottle, which in turn correlates with access to the beverage. However, asking someone else to open the bottle is also in the same class as these other behaviors if the request is followed by an open bottle and access to the beverage. The same functional relation spans requesting or manually opening the bottle via one consequence: access to the beverage is contingent upon the response. Uttering a sentence and using mechanical force fall into a single response class, defined by shared consequences that join these otherwise conceptually disparate behaviors as part of the same functional response class. In this sense, verbal behavior does not have default explanatory status and is treated analytically in the same way as any other behavior.

Operant accounts are careful not only with assigning verbal utterances default explanatory status, but also with speaking of internal motivators. Note that the above description made no mention of opening a bottle "in order to" get a drink. From an operant perspective, the bottle-opening class of behaviors all result in access to the beverage—this is a descriptive functional relation involving a class of behavior and a class of consequence (thus far emphasizing the B-C relations, of the A-B-C operant contingency). Language referring to intention, purpose, drive, or motivation—suggesting some type of inside-out causal chain or force—invokes mediating S-M-R-C-related explanatory conventions that might be useful in everyday interactions but unnecessarily distracts from focusing on contextual and modifiable factors if we were to troubleshoot a child's bottle-opening repertoire.

Response classes involve dynamic patterns of behavior–environment relationships rather than instances of behavior. Behavior–consequence functional relations can only be detected over time. When we are able to analyze a particular instance of behavior, especially for the first time, the behavior–environment relationships observed involve the uncertain and provisional application of behavioral principles as hypotheses. The analysis is provisional because functional relations can only be observed through analysis of patterns of behavior–environment relationships over time. As a result, much humility is brought to the analysis of instances. This stands in contrast to the assertive assumptions commonly made with the S-M-R-C model where the roles of stimuli and responses might be understood a priori.

Behavior within functional relations can occur at any temporal scale. Theoretically, at the molecular side of the spectrum, we can use neurophysiological equipment to observe the behavior of single neurons and their functional relationship with electrical stimulation of other neurons (Ishikawa, Matsumoto, Sakaguchi, Matsuki, & Ikegaya, 2014), unfolding across milliseconds. However, within therapist–client interactions the behavior of individual neurons is of little interest. Practically, physiological events and processes participate in functional relations to the extent they can participate in changeable relations with client behavior (see the field of behavioral pharmacology for examples, Winger & Woods, 2013). Similarly, appeals to unmodifiable brain structures for explanatory purposes point to a different level of analysis and are not useful in a practical operant account. The social impact of neurophysiological explanations among laypeople is distinct from their value in an operant analysis. If therapists do not directly measure impact on brain structures via the interventions they use, then the appeal to the neurophysiology is superfluous. Functional relations in an operant account reflect this type of pragmatism. In other words, the ACT therapist's specialty is behavior change in social contexts.

An analysis of behavior can involve observation of relatively discrete responses (e.g., flipping switches, waving hands, uttering single words) as well as collections of activities. To illustrate, a trip to the grocery store consists of several discrete behavior–environment relationships that influence elements of my travel (e.g., accelerating, braking, steering) and more macro relationships that influence that travel (e.g., prioritizing the expediency or quality of the scenery along the way). At another level, the response class of getting groceries may involve travel to one store rather than another because of the differential availability of preferred items, the ease of locating items in one store relative to another, or the opportunity to socialize with familiar staff while shopping. The number of actions that could potentially be enumerated in a larger pattern of behavior has no bearing on whether these actions constitute a potential response class. It is the functional relationship between the targeted activity pattern at a particular scale and its context that determines whether it is useful to speak of a behavior pattern as a meaningful unit.

Contingencies operating on behavior at different scales are also observed in language learning. When learning a language, some behavior–consequence contingencies focus on elementary elements: phonemes, morphemes, vocabulary, and letter and number identification. Additional behavior–consequence contingencies involve phrases, sentences, or topics. When responding at one level encounters problems (e.g., mispronouncing words), then the verbal community will return to a focus on behavior–consequence contingencies for elementary skills, such as the articulation of phonemes. Giving a speech, reciting a poem, telling a story, persuading, and negotiating involve even broader behavior–consequence contingencies regarding their impact on an audience (Hargie, 2017; Skinner, 1992).

The actual unit of analysis chosen for a particular situation is a practical matter. As clinicians, we often begin with a presenting problem (e.g., difficulties with interpersonal relationships), collect observations across multiple methods (e.g., intake interview, self-report or performance assessments, proxy reports), and generate a hypothesis about the response class in question (e.g., a response style that communicates indifference toward the listener). It is only when we change elements of a hypothesized behavior–consequence contingency that we can determine whether the unit of behavior selected for analysis is useful.

Finally, the focus on descriptive functional relations does not mean that all behavior–environment relationships must be publicly observable. For analytic purposes, private verbal behavior (i.e., verbal behavior that is inaccessible to others, such as thinking) is not different in kind from public behavior. It enters an operant account when a functional relationship takes place between private verbal behavior and other contextual events. The same holds for private stimuli such as physiological sensations: if a functional relationship between behavior and the private event is observed (e.g., headache pain, measured by disruption of ongoing behavior), an operant analysis of the act-in-context is possible.

Stimulus Classes

Just as response classes are defined in terms of their shared relationship with classes of consequences, classes of stimuli are defined in terms of their shared relationship with classes of behavior. As such, a stimulus is any event that has a functional relationship with behavior. A stimulus is not a *thing* that stands alone as a fundamental unit of the universe, detectable and independent from the behavior of an observer. *Classes of stimuli are defined by their functional relation with behavior.* This is a radical departure from relying on operational definitions to specify the "true" or "formal" physical features of stimuli that are conceptualized as being in the same category or class. Traditionally, operational definitions specify descriptive classes from measurable dimensions of stimuli, as defined by physics (e.g., color, size, shape). These descriptive classes reflect an observer's a priori assumptions about stimuli that ought to share a similar behavioral function because physics has defined their properties as similar. Skinner, in contrast, rejected this a priori assumption. He viewed operational definitions as a convention of the scientific community that reveals more about its verbal norms than about a "true" state of the world (Skinner, 1945). In an operant account, a stimulus class must demonstrate a shared functional relationship with classes of behavior over time. If a stimulus so conceived fails to set the occasion for a client's response (e.g., the child does not say "apple" in the presence of an apple but continues to say "ball"), then the "problem" lies within the contingencies that have been arranged over time: The contingencies failed to produce the intended functional stimulus class and more problem solving is necessary. Thus follows the assumption of a contextual approach that therapy can fail clients, but clients cannot fail in therapy. Again, curiosity is key, and barriers to progress are signs that more data are needed and that a reanalysis of functional classes may be indicated.

Classes of stimuli apply to consequences. Functional classes are defined by the impact of behavior; that is, they focus on the B-C relations of the A-B-C operant unit. A widely used illustration of the impact of behavior over time and the definition of a functional class involve the activities of children and their impact (for example, the ways caregivers provide access to social interactions contingent on these activities—child engagement followed by caregiver attention, B-C). In everyday parlance, we assume that child activities that are followed by caregiver attention that we deem "friendly" or "positive" will occur more reliably or increase in the future. We also assume that child activities followed by negative ("unfriendly") attention from caregivers will occur less reliably or decrease in the future. Here, caregiver attention deemed "positive" forms one class of consequences defined by their function (increase child behavior), while caregiver attention deemed "negative" forms a separate class of consequences, each having opposite effects on the future likelihood of the respective child response classes they are contingent upon. While this heuristic or topographical categorization of "positive" and "negative" may work some of the time, caregivers who seek professional consultation for child behavior problems often discover that these categorizations do not hold. They detect different relations via observation of acts-in-context. When the child "acts out," the caregiver provides attention presumed to be negative and corrective in order to reduce behavior viewed as problematic, yet the child's behavior persists or even increases over time. Here the functional relation between the child's behavior and the caregiver's "negative" attention has the functional relationship that is typically attributed when attention is deemed "positive." This example illustrates that it is useful to drop assumed "positive" and "negative" modifiers from our descriptions when they refer to heuristics of "friendly" or "unfriendly," "pleasant" or "unpleasant," and note that there is a functional relationship between the child's behavior and caregiver attention regardless of the type (or topography) of that attention. Caregiver activities that make up the consequences of a B-C functional relation can vary widely across many socially important dimensions (e.g., valence, intensity, warmth, developmental fit), and the common impact of activities on the child's behavior (for example, increasing or maintaining its occurrence) establishes them as a class of consequential events.

The Operant Contingency as the Fundamental Unit of Analysis

The preceding sections clarified how behavior classes and stimulus classes are defined in terms of functional relations. This is a significant departure from the conventional S-M-R-C explanatory framework that relies on causal chains, defines stimuli and responses in terms of their topographical features, and explains behavior in terms of mediating events. Yet, one more step is required in the operant account to make it fully contextual. Returning to earlier examples, we see that the B-C relations of opening a bottle and consuming a beverage, and child social engagement and caregiver attention do not occur in a vacuum. For an operant account to be complete, context needs to be brought into the analysis. Antecedent contexts are the situations in which B-C functional relations are more likely to be observed.

Revisiting the example of opening a bottle and drinking a beverage, we find that this B-C functional relation is more likely to occur in some antecedent contexts than in others. Histories, such as having ingested salt or exercised vigorously, or current circumstances, such as speaking loudly in a public forum or the physical presence of a bottled beverage, are examples of contextual variables that can influence the likelihood of opening a water bottle and drinking. Having done so in past situations increases the likelihood that such behavior will occur in similar circumstances in the future. The relationship between antecedents, behaviors, and potential consequence events completes the A-B-C operant unit.

As mentioned earlier, most of us find it challenging to focus on an operant contingency as a fundamental unit of analysis for client behavior. Because of our verbal histories, we may slip into a conventional account of client behavior that reflects everyday ways of understanding that are more consistent with the S-M-R-C account. The stance of uncertainty and curiosity to detect behavior-in-context patterns over time takes work. It is more effortful to characterize context and patterns of functional relations than it is to characterize instances. It requires more humility to observe context–behavior relationships over time and keep an open mind than to pronounce the function of stimuli or behavior based on a priori assumptions that permeate our culture. Utilizing the operant contingency as a unit of analysis is an act of intellectual discipline, and facility using this unit requires ongoing social interactions with a community of peers who share this analytic framework.

Antecedent Relations

The antecedent context for operant contingencies can be categorized along two broad dimensions: (1) motivating operations affect whether behavior–consequence contingencies are effective, and (2) discriminative stimuli are the conditions under which behavior–consequence contingencies are more or less likely. In addition to these two concepts, it is useful to contrast the antecedent with the consequence context, thereby highlighting how the environment changes when the consequence contingency is in effect.

MOTIVATING OPERATIONS

An operant analysis relies on motivating operations to provide a contextual account for the effectiveness of consequences. In an operant analysis, an event that functions as a "consequence" is not imbued with special a priori properties. Consequences gain their influence on behavior through environmental operations. They are established. Motivating or establishing operations are modifiable variables that are related to the effectiveness of stimuli, objects, or events as consequences (see also the previous example of salt ingestion increasing the likelihood of drinking liquids). When motivating operations are considered and modified, consequences become effective to increase (or decrease) the likelihood of the behavior they follow. For example, social isolation or deprivation during a pandemic lockdown tends to increase the effectiveness of in-person social contingencies. A person might go to great lengths to increase the frequency of social behaviors over time. Conversely, professional schedules filled with meetings and high-demand social interactions may decrease the effectiveness of social contingencies in maintaining social behavior. As with all operant constructs, motivating operations are defined relationally—by their actual impact. A wide variety of events can serve as motivating operations. In summary, motivating operations establish that an event following behavior will have a rate-altering effect on that behavior.

The procedures for establishing a particular motivating operation can involve exceptionally complicated learning histories. Consider advertising that models if–then (behavior–consequence) relationships. A drug maker markets a new drug for depression, Proloxil[2] (a fictitious product). Advertisements include sympathetic images of people who are initially presented as sad and socially isolated, struggling with daily life. Proloxil is introduced as a drug that "fixes the chemical imbalances[3] responsible for depression." The scene shifts, and the people who struggled are now smiling, greeted with open arms, and dancing with others. The advertisement is a contextual variable that establishes a relationship between obtaining and taking Proloxil and a wide range of socially relevant outcomes. It thereby may increase the effectiveness of the feedback loop between a consequence (e.g., social connectedness, belonging) and a class of behavior (e.g., drug-taking). As such, suggested response class activities (e.g., "ask a physician if Proloxil is right for you") become more likely.

ACT utilizes values clarification exercises as motivating operations. Explicitly stating long-term values that summarize or bundle a range of discrete meaningful outcomes, particularly in a social context (see Hayes et al., 1985 on social standard setting), increases the effectiveness of those outcomes to increase or maintain behavior. For example, stating one's values related to equity and social justice in session may increase the effectiveness of the feedback loop between a range of topographically dissimilar advocacy activities (i.e., values congruent behavior) and their consequences. Importantly, evaluating one's own behavior as being consistent with a values statement can serve as an important consequence that occurs concurrently with the other consequences accompanying the relevant behavior. Thus, motivating operations may work at different levels of analysis; in the case of values, they direct clients from the "instance" to "big picture" patterns.

Traditional conceptualizations of behavior, such as the S-M-R-C explanatory model, typically refer to organismic motivational states (M in the chain). Saying that someone is driven or motivated to fight for social justice appears explanatory. Drive and motivation as mediating constructs provide proximal reasons for why someone wrote a letter to an elected official, but these constructs do not tell us how to intervene—how to promote behaviors related to social justice with therapists and clients. We practically predict and influence behavior-in-context patterns through establishing operations, such as the wide range of in- and out-of-session activities that fall under values clarification. In this sense ACT is pragmatic and focuses on workability: What is effective for enhancing the consequential value of meaningful events? How do we help clients focus on larger patterns over time to inoculate them against life's everyday failures?

DISCRIMINATIVE STIMULUS

Some behavior–consequence contingencies are more likely in some circumstances than in others. We use the term *discriminative stimulus* to describe the larger context in which the behavior–consequence relationship is operative. Again, the role of a discriminative stimulus in increasing the likelihood of behavior is not due to any inherent properties of the stimulus but arises from the correlation between the presence of that stimulus and the differential effectiveness of the behavior–consequence contingency over time. The relevant learning history involves both positive exemplars (i.e., when the discriminative stimulus is present, the behavior–consequence relationship is more likely to be operative) and negative exemplars (i.e., when the discriminative stimulus is absent the behavior–consequence relationship is less likely to be operative).

Discrimination training characterizes the process that establishes a particular contextual stimulus or class of stimuli as predictive of specific behavior–consequence relationships. Social interactions are replete with examples of discrimination training. As speakers, we are more likely to be heard and understood when listeners are oriented to us (indicated, for example, by regular eye contact, leaning in of the upper body, body language and facial expressions that dynamically vary with the content of what the speaker says) than when listeners are distracted (e.g., looking at their phone, not varying body language, persistent flat or incongruent facial expressions). Communication skills training focuses on teaching clients to be heard by attending to listener cues for interest and engagement and by developing skills that increase the likelihood that listeners will engage.

Discrimination training typically involves the use of multiple exemplars because a predictive context involves a class of stimuli (e.g., stimuli reflecting social interest) rather than a discrete stimulus (e.g., red versus green traffic lights). For example, Azrin and Hayes (1984) trained college students to identify whether social engagement was mutual. The training was gendered in that men learned to attend to women's cues. Men watched multiple one-minute video examples that showed women's reactions within a conversation. The audio was muted so that the training could focus on the nonverbal aspects of the women's conversational behaviors. Men then rated women's interest on a 1 (strongly disinterested) to 7 (strongly interested) scale. First, the men received feedback on the accuracy of ratings rendered for 24 training videos. They then rated 20 additional videos, used for pre- and posttest assessments. Rating accuracy improved by 50%. Here, not easily described, complex, and varied nonverbal aspects of women's engagement in conversations were the discriminative stimuli (A) correlating with ratings (B) and feedback for their accuracy (C). There is a rich literature on how to conduct multiple exemplar training (Holth, 2017; Layng, 2019), and how to increase the likelihood that discrimination training in therapy sessions generalizes to everyday settings (Swan, Carper, & Kendall, 2015).

Events can also obtain their functional status as discriminative stimuli as part of larger, complex operant relationships and training histories (see Harte & Barnes-Holmes, this volume). In these circumstances, discriminative stimuli emerge when they have participated in indirect training histories of differential consequences for behavior according to experimenter-specified relations among stimulus classes (class x goes with class y, class x is larger than class y, opposite of, etc.). Notably, the function of emergent stimuli in an operant contingency is the same: they positively or negatively correlate with the availability of consequences. Yet, the history of operant relations involved in their obtaining that function is more complex.

Consequence Relations

Consequence relations are defined along two dimensions. The *functional dimension* indicates whether the consequence is followed by increases or decreases in the future rate of the behavior pattern the consequence was contingent upon (defined as reinforcement and punishment, respectively). The *procedural dimension* specifies whether the consequence is best characterized as something being added to (i.e., positive) or removed from the situation (i.e., negative).

REINFORCEMENT

A reinforcement contingency refers to behavior–consequence patterns that involve *increases* in the relevant response class under similar circumstances over time. A reinforcer is not a "reward" or some pleasant property imbued to a stimulus. In other words, vernacular judgments of "pleasant" or "unpleasant," "friendly" or "unfriendly," do not identify the rate-altering impact of consequences on behavior. A reinforcer is the class of events that serves as a consequence in a reinforcement contingency, and as such, reinforcers are defined by their participation in functional relations.

Positive reinforcement involves the response-contingent presentation of an object or event, resulting in an increased frequency of that response class. The relevant object or event is called a positive reinforcer by virtue of its observed role in this functional relation. For example, a middle-aged client may present to session and describe a history of verbal abuse during early childhood. During the session, the therapist offers simple and complex reflections of the client's narratives. If the client continues to talk about early childhood, then the therapist's reflections are likely serving as positive reinforcers for talking about early life experiences.

Negative reinforcement involves the response-contingent prevention, postponement, or removal of an object or event, resulting in an increased frequency of that response class. The relevant object or event is called a negative reinforcer by virtue of its observed role in this functional relation. Negative reinforcement is further distinguished by whether the event or object is currently present or is imminent. In escape contingencies, the response is made in the presence of the event. In avoidance contingencies, the response is made in the absence of the event and prevents or postpones its presentation.

An example of a potential escape contingency in therapy is the introduction of a between-session assignment. If the client redirects the conversation, comments upon feeling anxious, and the therapist responds with a mindfulness exercise, then escape from task may maintain the client's behavior. Similar situations in the future will reveal if this client's emotional disclosures function to remove demands (here, a between-session assignment). If the client reliably makes emotional disclosures when people (including the therapist) request the client interact with their agenda (e.g., between-session exercises, conversational topics concerning others), withdrawal of the demand is likely functioning as a negative reinforcer.

A second example of an avoidance contingency involves preventing the presentation of an event. Imagine a client presents with dissatisfaction in relationships. The client reports not getting their needs met and going out of their way to make sure that the relationship goes smoothly. At the beginning of each session, the client asks the therapist, "What do we have planned for today?" Demonstrating care and forethought, the therapist then describes the planned activities for the day based on the treatment plan and asks the client for input on the activities. The client agrees to the activities and the larger plan, and the session proceeds. Note that the therapist has not explicitly asked for the needs or concerns that the client wants to bring to the session agenda. Only by asking the client directly could the therapist notice the client's clinically significant difficulties in stating wants, needs, or concerns in relationships. By prompting the therapist's discussion of the agenda and acquiescing to it, the client has prevented "being put on the spot" and requesting attention to their needs or concerns. Potential patterns that lead to dissatisfaction in relationships are continued in the therapy context.

PUNISHMENT

A punishment contingency involves behavior–consequence patterns that involve *decreases* in the relevant response class under similar circumstances over time. Similar to reinforcers, punishers are not things or properties imbued to a stimulus. A punisher is a class of events that serves as a consequence in a rate-decreasing contingency, and as such punishers are defined by their participation in functional relations. Notably, to consider a decrease in the rate of behavior, something must be maintaining or increasing it. Thus, concurrent reinforcement contingency always maintains the relevant response class that is selected for a decrease.

Positive punishment involves the response-contingent presentation of an object or event, resulting in the decreased frequency of that response over time. The relevant object or event is called a positive punisher or a penalty by virtue of its role in this functional relation. Many exercises in ACT aim to reduce problematic behavior patterns (e.g., firmly believing one's thoughts). Therapist responses such as "Thank your mind for that thought" can function as positive punishers, decreasing the rate of similar verbal statements by the client over time. ACT- related psychoeducation clarifies the context for the therapist's application of punishment contingencies with the client. In this example, the therapist first explains that believing one's thoughts (such as "I am too depressed to do this") may lead to efforts to change these thoughts, and clients observe whether this change agenda is effective. With client consent, pointing out occasions in session when the client's thoughts function as barriers to effective action becomes part of the therapeutic mill. If a therapist has not provided a transparent rationale and collaborated with the client to illustrate the futility of the change agenda, responses such as "Thank your mind for that thought" may punish (i.e., decrease) the client's initiation of interactions with the therapist more generally. A top-down social hierarchical stance may also inadvertently emerge, lacking the collaborative, explorative, humble, and curious approach to thought–behavior relationships. Psychoeducation and the treatment rationale establish the therapeutic interaction as a discriminative stimulus (A) where client thought–action–fusion statements (B) will be challenged (C).

Negative punishment involves the response-contingent removal of an object or event, resulting in the decreased frequency of that response over time. The object or event that is removed might serve as a positive reinforcer in other circumstances. For this reason, the procedure can also be conceptualized as either a penalty or time-out from reinforcement (if the removal is temporary). Let us return to between-session assignments, this time as an example of a negative punishment contingency. If the client is actively engaged throughout the session, discussing relevant life events or participating in exercises, the client's engagement reinforces the therapist's behavior frequently and richly. If, at the end of the session and with the introduction of between-session assignments, the client decreases their engagement (e.g., checking their watch, becoming visibly restless, resorting to a passive response style), a reliable and conditional withdrawal of engagement may function as time-out from reinforcement for the therapist's behavior. If, over time, the therapist stops introducing between-session assignments, we can speak of the client's social withdrawal as a negative punisher.

EXTINCTION

Extinction involves the breaking of arranged behavior–consequence contingencies. When an extinction procedure is in place, behavior that was previously part of a reinforcement contingency will decrease over time, and behavior that was previously part of a punishment contingency will increase over time. Two procedures can be used to produce these rate-increasing or decreasing effects that are dependent on the baseline status quo. The *negative* procedure is most common and involves the omission of the consequence: Whenever the behavior occurs, the consequence (i.e., reinforcer or punisher) no longer follows.

The *positive* procedure involves presenting the consequence independent of the behavior of interest (noncontingent reinforcement; NCR). To facilitate implementation of noncontingent reinforcement and to make sure that clients are not deprived of reinforcers (e.g., therapist attention), novel behaviors are often chosen for intervention, which then produces the reinforcement that maintained the behavior deemed problematic. For example, through differential reinforcement of alternative behavior procedures (DRA) reinforcers never follow the target behavior (i.e., the behavior extinguishes) but rather follow specified alternative behaviors (replacement behaviors that now produce the consequence). In situations where specific alternative behaviors are difficult to pinpoint, a differential reinforcement of other behavior procedure (DRO) can be arranged: Now the consequence will be presented after any generally socially valid behavior that is different in kind from the original behavior.

While extinction procedures break behavior–consequence contingencies, the effects of reinforcement and punishment contingencies are not erased. If an extinction procedure is discontinued, and reinforcers or punishers again follow the target behavior, patterns that used to be maintained or decreased by these contingencies will return more quickly. In other words, histories of behavior-consequent relationships matter and influence the speed of acquisition and reacquisition.

Extinction and Positive Reinforcement

When a positive reinforcement contingency is discontinued (i.e., the negative procedure), it is common to see temporary increases in the frequency, intensity, or duration of the relevant behavior, as well as increased variability within the relevant response class. This phenomenon is called an *extinction burst*. When changes in physical or social environments result in discontinuations or breaks in contingent relationships between response class members and consequences, members of the response class that do not produce the usual impact occur less frequently over time, while those that continue to produce consequences become more likely. Responding with greater frequency, intensity, duration, or variability helps identify what response–consequence relationships are retained; this is how response classes are shaped by changing circumstances (e.g., some digital platforms may require swiping left to advance a page, as if turning a page in a book, while others may require swiping from the bottom of the screen upward to advance the page). If, however, an entire response class no longer participates in a positive reinforcement contingency, the general pattern of behavior will occur less frequently over time (e.g., dialing a rotary phone, which required rotating a wheel from a numbered start position to a fixed stop position).

When a positive reinforcement contingency is broken via the positive procedure, the consequence becomes available regardless of whether the response class occurs. The former consequence or outcome of behavior now occurs at other times, including prior to the behavior. As noted already, this procedure is useful for eliminating access to a consequence with high social impact via behavior that is not workable in the long run, or when extinction bursts may be dangerous (e.g., behavior escalates when consequences are withdrawn altogether). Extinction bursts are less likely when the formerly contingent consequences continue to be offered noncontingently, which are not in relation to any behavior that could be deemed problematic.

The transition of individuals to rehabilitative wards after complex, acute, and life-threatening medical illnesses provides an example for these types of extinction: Typically, the vital signs of patients on acute medical wards are monitored not only by machines but also by regular staff attention at timed intervals. As patients' health improves, they transition from an acute medical floor to a rehabilitative setting. This transition involves an abrupt change in environments, including the cessation of monitoring. Alone in their silent rooms for the first time, these patients' listening to the reassuring steady hum and beep of machines and interacting with nursing staff at high frequency throughout the day are being extinguished. In this situation, some patients will use the call button for reassurance and, if responses are not immediate, the intensity and frequency of their checking will escalate. This situation can be considered extinction with an extinction burst. Programmed attention and reassurance from staff offered noncontingently (i.e., checking on the patient initially, without the patient's use of the call button) can prevent patient worry and behavioral escalation.

Extinction and Negative Reinforcement

Extinction of escape contingencies involves the presence of the negative reinforcer despite relevant escape responding (i.e., safety behaviors stop working). A similar dynamic is at play for behavior that has a history of delaying or preventing the onset of a negative reinforcer.

Consider the following example in which a person's behavior occurs within the context of a negative reinforcement contingency. Ferster's (1973) model of depression suggested that reactions to profound loss, for example, of a spouse or a child, or of meaningful employment, typically solicit social supports, but that with time these supports shift toward "fixing" the irrevocable loss. For example, the person may hear that it is time to "get on with life," or "get over" the loss, or be goaded to "start anew." According to Ferster, social withdrawal results, avoiding well-intentioned yet coercive encouragement, with concurrent emergence of self-blame for not fulfilling social expectations. Such avoidance patterns are difficult to break, as consequences from the loss grow and narrow the person's alternatives as well as social feedback loops, until all of life is occupied with an agenda to change what one thinks or feels—and social relationships become even more improbable. Acceptance and willingness exercises in ACT are designed to break these cycles of withdrawal. They provide the skills to reenter social settings and encounter negative reinforcers without having to escape from them when doing so interferes with meaningful activities. Repeated exposure to escape contingencies is necessary for the relevant escape responding to decrease.

Acceptance and willingness exercises can be used to support engagement in meaningful activities even when negative reinforcers may be imminent. For both escape and avoidance extinction, interventions are similar to the differential reinforcement of alternative behavior (DRA) contingency arrangements, arranging support for tracking the positive reinforcement contingencies pertaining to overarching values while learning to ignore the immediate negative reinforcement contingencies.

Negatively reinforced behaviors raise another problem: Highly effective safety behaviors, when effective, prevent the negative reinforcer from occurring (i.e., the status quo is maintained). For this reason, it is difficult to detect whether negative reinforcement contingencies are still operative. In practice, preventing safety behaviors from occurring—also termed "response prevention"—provides opportunities to sample current contingencies when settings are safe. Decoupling thoughts from actions (i.e., "I have thought to check the lock" and not doing it as part of response prevention) assumes that the client's social and physical environments are safe and repetitive problem solving is not needed.

Extinction and Punishment

When punishment contingencies are discontinued, the effects of the related reinforcement contingencies that originally maintained the behavior might reemerge. As such, behavior typically increases in line with the reinforcement contingency. Therefore, ACT and other contextual therapies take a constructional approach to interventions. Programming to support clinically beneficial behavior patterns beyond the treatment setting will be described further in a later section of this article.

Key Dimensions of Consequence Relations

The immediacy, magnitude, and other dimensions of a consequence event impact its relative effectiveness.

IMMEDIACY

The acquisition and development of response classes occur more quickly when consequences are more immediate. All other things being equal, organisms will prefer immediate consequences to delayed consequences.

MAGNITUDE

Consequences that are greater in magnitude or intensity have a larger impact on the frequency of behavior than those of lesser magnitude. All other things being equal, organisms will prefer larger magnitude reinforcing consequences to smaller consequences. Larger magnitude punishment consequences decrease behavior more quickly than smaller magnitude consequences. Ethical use of punishment procedures specifies use of the minimum magnitude necessary to produce a therapeutic effect. Programmed ACT interactions involving punishment are typically verbal and of relatively low magnitude, yet sufficiently surprising to clients to disrupt social expectations (e.g., "So we can put that thought on another shovel you use to try to dig out of the hole"). Notably, decreasing the frequency of specific thoughts is not a therapeutic goal. In contrast, traditional cognitive therapy utilizes a wide range of punishment procedures, such as reframing, labeling specific content as irrational or dysfunctional, or thought stopping.

CONJUNCTIVE

Variability is the spice of life when it comes to consequences. Consequences whose immediacy and magnitude hinge on the quality or intensity of the behavior they follow have a much larger effect on behavior than consequences that do not systematically vary based on the quality or intensity of the contingent response. Operant contingencies with this type of dimensional feedback within the functional relation are exceptionally powerful. Earlier, we alluded to the dynamic variation in listener responses. The behavior of skilled public speakers varies contingent on their audience's responses, such that performances become shared experiences. Similarly, the sounds produced by a skilled musician go beyond the mechanical playing of the notes. Variation in the intensity and other qualitative features of the playing are responsible for the differential impact that skilled performance has on listeners.

SCHEDULES

Consequences are probabilistic in nature; they do not follow every response. We will review a few of the schedule arrangements below. While a comprehensive overview of behavior-consequent relations is beyond the scope of this article, note that the patterning of behavior–consequence relationships over time matters more in practice than do individual instances of behavior–consequence events.

When every instance of the behavior class is followed by a consequence event, reinforcement is said to be continuous. Continuous reinforcement is useful when a new behavior–consequence contingency is being established. For example, a client may have difficulties identifying specific, measurable, attainable, relevant, and timebound goals related to values (e.g., social justice). If descriptions occur only at the level of categorical abstractions related to the values (e.g., food security, affordable housing, living wages), values statements may not serve as antecedents to relevant action. Thus, the therapist may model and then differentially reinforce descriptions of concrete actions, as these are more likely to help the client track reinforcement contingencies outside of session (see the tracking section below).

In an intermittent reinforcement schedule, a consequence event follows the class of behavior intermittently. Intermittency can be based on number of responses (e.g., the number of requests made before a social partner acquiesces to a request, a variable ratio schedule) or on time (e.g., the work schedule at a place of employment is updated the third Friday of the month for the following month, and schedule requests can only be considered if submitted by that deadline, a fixed interval schedule). The more variable and lean an intermittent reinforcement schedule is, the more persistent the related patterns of behavior will be during an extinction procedure.

In rate-based reinforcement schedules, consequence events follow the class of behavior when the behavior is above, below, or within a particular criterion range for the behavior pattern. For example, individuals diagnosed with depression may speak at a slower than normal rate, often with long pauses. This depressed rate of speech can have a negative impact on social relationships. Social skills training can include explicit feedback on speech rate and pausing both in terms of descriptive praise (e.g., the therapist says I find it much easier to pay attention to what you have to say when you talk at that rate) and direct social response (e.g., the therapist systematically varies attentive body posture, eye contact, reflective listening with speech rate).

The DRA contingency introduced in the extinction section places target behaviors on extinction while reinforcing alternative behaviors. Many exercises in ACT involve this kind of arrangement (e.g., reinforcing the use of "and," extinguishing "but"). ACT draws attention to multiple contingencies (and, and, and . . .), converging and diverging. Examples are diverging contingencies on verbal behavior and other behavior (saying one thing and doing another); contingencies on values-related behaviors; and immediate contingencies on the same behaviors (values-consistent action in the short run). Similar to Linehan's dialectical approach (1993), noticing multiple, and sometimes even contradictory approach–avoidance, contingencies is part and parcel of the functional flexibility goals of the ACT model.

Behavioral Economics and Other Dynamic Relations

The key principles described earlier in this article have been investigated as models of decision making when multiple contingencies are operative. Much of our everyday behavior can be characterized as a never-ending succession of choices among diverse courses of action, each with different immediate and longer-term consequences, with certain or less certain consequences, and requiring differential effort. Within a behavioral economic framework, choice is not viewed as a spontaneous agentic act but as historically situated action that occurs relative to other behavior–consequence contingencies. These concepts maintain a focus on functional relationships for behavior patterns that are commonly attributed to personal or moral strengths or weaknesses.

Discounting

Consequences have their greatest impact on behavior when they are immediate and certain and require a mundane level of effort to access them. When a consequence is offered now or later, the immediate option is likely to be chosen. When a consequence is offered for sure or with some probability, the more certain option is likely to be chosen. Similarly, when a consequence can be obtained with moderate versus exceptional effort, the less effortful option is likely to be chosen. Delay, risk, and effort are aspects of concurrent reinforcement schedules that can change their relative impact ("discounting").

Most of life's interesting choices involve trade-offs among delay, risk, and effort. Do I open a bag of chips now, or do I prepare a healthy meal? When I feel hurt by a perceived slight, do I respond with anger (i.e., relatively certain interpersonal impact) or with vulnerability and conciliation (i.e., relatively less certain interpersonal impact)? Discounting research has quantified how increasing levels of delay, risk/uncertainty, and effort change the value of outcomes. This section will illustrate discounting by focusing on delay.

In choice paradigms, organisms choose between a large but delayed food delivery and a smaller but immediate food delivery across repeated choice trials that determine the value of reinforcers. Human operant research asks, "Would you rather receive $50 now or $100 one month from now?" If the answer is $100, the price of the immediate options titrates up, and the question is repeated until preference shifts from the delayed choice to the immediate choice (*point of indifference*). This point serves as an estimate of the immediate value of the outcome at a specific delay (one month). Then the choice assessment procedure is repeated across multiple delays (e.g., 1 day, 1 week, 6 months) and obtains indifference points for each delay. The obtained data are fit to quantitative models to allow prediction of choice patterns indicating self-control. Here, impulsive behavior has lost its traditional connotations of irrationality, carelessness, or thoughtlessness. Discounting is a relationship not unlike gravity or the circumstance that water flows downhill. Immediate consequences tend to impact behavior more than delayed outcomes, even if the immediate outcomes are relatively smaller. Self-control, in contrast, reflects a pattern of choosing larger delayed outcomes over smaller, more immediate outcomes.

Discounting models have been applied to individual participants as well as group-averaged data, as, for example, when comparing the curves of smokers with those of nonsmokers (Mitchell, 1999). While early research focused on delayed discounting of monetary outcomes, later research has looked at the discounting of substances of abuse (Coffey, Gudleski, Saladin, & Brady, 2003), food (Rasmussen, Lawyer, & Reilly, 2010), health (Chapman, 1996), social relationships (Belisle, Paliliunas, Vangsness, Dixon, & Stanley, 2020), and more. In general, discounting serves as a robust model for the functional relationship observed between a relative inconvenience (e.g., delay, risk/uncertainty, effort) and the effectiveness of associated outcomes in choice paradigms (Waltz & Follette, 2009).

Discounting research facilitates the understanding of ACT as an intervention: values work takes advantage of the circumstance that larger, bundled outcomes are a more likely choice—that is, they are discounted less steeply than comparatively smaller outcomes; and interventions can be used to minimize the impact of the inconveniences (e.g., delay, risk/uncertainty, effort), resulting in less discounting of larger outcomes. As noted earlier, many outcomes—delayed (e.g., graduation), probabilistic (e.g., health), and effortful (e.g., fitness)—tend to be highly preferred, yet discounted, when immediate, certain, and less effortful behavioral alternatives become available (e.g., engaging in social activities rather than studying; having French fries rather than salad as a side; or snoozing the alarm rather than getting up to work out). Social expectations are such that behavior "ought" to track remote or uncertain consequences, but in the absence of a robust, direct impact on behavior, such rules have limited credibility. Values clarification procedures facilitate rule stating and social standard setting. Additionally, these procedures identify potential bundles of reinforcers that are hypothesized to support behavior patterns consistent with a meaningful life. As such, values clarification exercises and the use of values to cluster behavior–outcome monitoring within multiple exemplar training can have an effect similar to that of increasing the value of the outcome in discounting models (for an example of values clarification and acceptance-based strategies, see Morrison, Madden, Odum, Friedel, & Twohig, 2014). Discrimination training for noticing actions that are consistent with values will increase the likelihood that individuals will be able to track these contingencies outside of the support of a therapeutic relationship. Consistent with a general behavior-analytic approach, it is important to establish patterns rather than instances of events when increasing the frequency of contacting positive reinforcement contingencies.

Committed action procedures further help clients identify situations where they might encounter delayed, probabilistic, and effortful consequences; monitor the relationship between their behavior patterns and these outcomes over time; and troubleshoot when necessary. For example, an individual whose social relationships have primarily involved shared substance use may have difficulties with social relationships that do not involve substance use. In addition to normalizing the discomfort and awkwardness that arises in novel social contexts, using acceptance as a distress tolerance technique, the client may rediscover old skills for meaningfully participating in substance-free social relationships. Successful life experiences of this sort are expected to decrease the discounting of substance-free social relationships. See Rung and colleagues (2018; 2019) for recent reviews on the types of interventions that have been demonstrated to influence discounting.

Matching Law

Choices come with the drawback that committing to one path of action may make another path unavailable, at least temporarily. We must prioritize how we allocate our time. In this sense, the occurrence of behavior patterns is influenced not only by the consequences this pattern encounters, but also practically by the consequences following all other behavior patterns. The matching law quantifies the relationship between two or more behavior patterns and their consequences. It states that the frequency of a behavior pattern, or the amount of time we spend engaging in that behavior pattern relative to other response options, is proportional to the frequency of reinforcement we encounter for that behavior pattern relative to all sources of reinforcement encountered. The matching law draws our attention to the fact that actually obtained reinforcement matters, not our conceptions of what ought to be reinforcing. Furthermore, the emphasis on relative rates of reinforcement directs scientist-practitioners to investigate the context in which the behavior of interest is occurring.

If the goal is to address deficits and increase behavior patterns, the matching law points to two contextual options. The first and most common approach is to increase the rate of reinforcement encountered for that behavior pattern (ACT, for example, uses committed action homework to bring clients into contact with reinforcement for values-congruent behavior patterns). The second contextual approach is to decrease access to reinforcement that is unrelated to or competes with behaviors targeted in ACT. Consider acceptance-based coping. For some clients, acceptance will involve a relatively new or infrequently used set of strategies, with more delayed consequences than escape or avoidance-based coping. Initially, acceptance-based coping may occur at a relatively low rate, reflecting the infrequent reinforcement this behavior has encountered, particularly relative to the reinforcement encountered for escape or avoidance-based coping. Creative hopelessness exercises in ACT are useful for highlighting past escape or avoidance-based coping responses and tagging them as futile. This type of discrimination training regarding the long-term effectiveness of these responses can decrease the use of these options by decreasing the relevant reinforcement they encounter (therapists investigate for each option; how did that work?). In short, decreasing access to problematic coping increases the relative reinforcement efficacy of consequences related to effective coping. The matching law also provides the experimental rationale for differential reinforcement. If the goal is to decrease a pattern of behavior without introducing a punishment contingency, then therapists can block access to reinforcement for that behavior pattern (extinction). Client in-session avoidance of difficult topics represents an opportunity for the therapist to block access to negative reinforcement (i.e., the therapist stays on topic). Best practices then also involve the therapist prompting and reinforcing client approximations to engage with the difficult topic, effectively increasing access to reinforcement for alternative behaviors.

The second and more contextual approach for decreasing a targeted behavior pattern is to increase access to extraneous reinforcement (i.e., enrich the availability of social reinforcers that are unrelated to the targeted behavior pattern). The entire ACT approach pivots on stepping away from symptom reduction and instead enriching available options in the client's life (values-oriented behavior). This constructional approach accords part and parcel with the matching law. In addition, ACT targets thought–action fusion, and many ACT exercises provide reinforcement for responding to the nonliteral aspects of language (e.g., semantic satiation exercise) and for noticing and describing thoughts without otherwise acting on them (e.g., mindfulness exercises).

Momentum

Factors that predict the conditions under which behavior will be more likely to persist when challenging circumstances arise (e.g., extinction, increased effort requirements) have been investigated in the behavioral momentum literature. This research area, considered a metaphorical extension of physics which defines momentum as mass times velocity, focuses on response rate and the total rate of reinforcement in a situation.

Response patterns that have a relatively high response rate are more likely to persist under challenging circumstances. Behavior patterns that have been acquired recently are more prone to disruption and occur at lower rates. Interventions that improve behavioral fluency (i.e., fast and accurate/situationally appropriate responding; Binder, 1996) are excellent tools for improving the likelihood that therapeutically relevant behavior patterns will occur both in and out of session. One of the defusion skills used in ACT, borrowed from mindfulness traditions, involves noticing private events (e.g., thoughts, including judgments and evaluations, memories, sensations, affect) and remaining at that point of perspective (i.e., just noticing) without taking action. The objective of this skill in ACT is to sensitize clients to the influence of private experiences by noticing and pausing. Practice needs to involve both elements, not just one or the other. Having attention shift away from the exercise or private events is essential for the skill to be repeated. This *notice and pause* skill interrupts automatic or impulsive behavior patterns aimed at managing private events. As noted in the discounting section above, delays often decrease the reinforcing effectiveness of outcomes. When pausing occurs, all possible outcomes become delayed, and under these altered circumstances, larger magnitude reinforcers (think of values) have a relatively higher competitive edge. In therapy, if observation is trained only briefly in a single experiential exercise and the rest of the session focuses on psychoeducation related to the importance of this skill, then the probability that the client will utilize this skill outside of the exercise or session is likely to be low. If, however, several opportunities to practice the skill in session occur and homework with engagement follows, then this *notice and pause* pattern will become increasingly fluent and become more likely to occur in challenging or clinically relevant situations.

The second determinant of behavioral momentum is the total rate of reinforcement in a situation. This has implications for how to implement reinforcement for new behaviors trained in therapy. Since reinforcement rate is often tied to response rate, fledgling behavior patterns that occur at a low rate are likely to encounter reinforcement in similar fashion. Supplementing the learning context with both task-specific reinforcers (e.g., descriptive praise) and social reinforcers for general engagement and putting forth effort all raise the total rate of reinforcement encountered in the situation. Since momentum is context-specific, it is important to train in ways that support generalization by increasing the similarity of the treatment context with the target context(s) and using supports as part of homework to facilitate generalization (see Swan et al., 2015).

The final insight gleaned from the behavioral momentum literature is that momentum is context-dependent. The importance for context-relevant training to support generalization has already been discussed. Contextual interventions can also decrease momentum by identifying situations in which behavior is ineffective. ACT activities that focus on assessing the workability of rules are a good example of this sort. Rules are very effective tools, and as such, rule-following as a behavior pattern has a lot of momentum. The introduction of workability as a metric helps clients identify situations in which rules are useful. Identifying situations where specific rules are experienced as not useful (i.e., suboptimal for encountering reinforcement) separates this context from those where the specific rules may be useful and from the usefulness of rule-governed behavior more generally.

The overall implications of the behavioral momentum research for ACT practitioners are that clients will benefit from treatment that focuses on the actual rehearsal of ACT-targeted skills to the point of fluency and through rich reinforcement. Reinforcement from the therapist's general encouragement for engagement and effort contributes to momentum as well as the reinforcers encountered directly from skills use. Programming for generalization is essential to ensure reinforcement and is encountered in a variety of contexts, particularly those similar to the contexts in which the client is likely to benefit from using the skills the most.

Basic Units of Analysis in Language

An operant account of language maintains its focus on functional relations and does not require any new principles that are discontinuous from those discussed in this article. An operant analysis of language focuses on how speakers and listeners dynamically interact with one another in mutually reinforcing ways (Skinner, 1992). This article concentrates on the basic units of analysis in language from an operant account. A later article in this handbook will focus on relational frame theory (RFT), which relies on the same principles to build the broader, nested operant relations that constitute RFT's analytic units (see Harte & Barnes-Holmes, this volume).

Language is fundamentally social, and words are tools of social influence. This section will briefly review three categories of verbal operants that focus on the behavior of the speaker and two types of rule-following that illustrate clinically relevant listener repertoires. While a comprehensive analysis of verbal behavior includes analyses of written and gestural forms of communication, this article will center on the spoken word for brevity.

Mands

Mands are statements that influence the behavior of listeners in ways that matter to the speaker. In this sense, they are tools for getting others to take some specific action. The label *mand* is derived from the words *command* and *demand*, but not all mands are commanding in construction or tone. Polite requests (e.g., please pass the salt) and questions (e.g., do you have the time?) are also mands. The consequences following the speaker's statement, observed across multiple occurrences, determines whether the statement in this context likely represents a mand. For example, imagine a family that watches the game show *Jeopardy* at 7:30 p.m. If someone in the family cries out, "it's 7:30," and subsequently another family member turns on the television, and this is observed on more than one occasion, then the utterance, "it's 7:30," likely functions as a mand for switching on the TV and gathering. Effective mands—regardless of their form—instruct listeners as to what to do and communicate that the listener's action matters to the speaker. When the listener takes meaningful action in relation to the speaker's utterance (e.g., switches on the TV), that consequence reinforces the speaker's mand. When the listener does not take action, then the speaker is less likely to make similar mands in the context of that listener in the future (i.e., manding extinguishes).

Motivating operations are part of the antecedent context for manding. For example, a client who is socially isolated may ask the therapist to engage in social interaction outside of the therapeutic context. As discussed earlier in the section Matching Law, rather than targeting the mand for reduction, addressing the motivating operation (social isolation) by collaborating to enrich the client's social context may be an appropriate response to the client's mand.

Manding often is of clinical interest because influencing the behavior of listeners in ways that matter to the speaker requires both reciprocity and skill (e.g., a focus of functional-analytic psychotherapy and also covered in interpersonal effectiveness skills of dialectical behavior therapy). In terms of reciprocity, shifting the unit of analysis to the behavior of the listener, the speaker's mand statement serves as an antecedent to the listener's effective response. The consequence for the listener's effective response is typically some expression of appreciation by the speaker (e.g., "thank you"). Social relationships that are maintained over time present many opportunities for speakers and listeners to alternate roles. Such alternations impact the quality of relationships.

Skillful manding includes both contextual sensitivity of the timing of the utterance (i.e., is this a situation where the listener is likely to respond favorably?) and the quality and clarity of the statement (i.e., does the listener clearly understand what specific actions are being requested?). Poorly timed or articulated mands might be aversive and negatively impact the likelihood of reciprocity in relationships. Individuals who have difficulty clearly communicating their needs in relationships may leave listeners feeling ineffective or unable to behave in ways that are meaningful to the speaker.

Tacts

Tacts are statements that direct the listener to attend to features of the environment. More specifically, speakers attend to events in the world, and tacting orients listeners to these events. Other than listening, no other action is necessary. The label " tact" derives from *contact* and indicates that tacting helps listeners to contact specific features of the world with regard to the speaker or the speaker's history. The consequences of tacting involve some shared form of understanding (i.e., the listener understands the speaker's behavior in context), or appreciation from listeners who are now able to behave effectively with regard to contingencies they have not encountered. The reinforcers for tacting include all ways in which people communicate shared understanding and appreciation. Antecedents are the discriminative events that set the occasion for tacting; they feature most prominently in analyses of tacting.

The types of stimulus relations and events that function as discriminative stimuli for tacting are broad. Bounded or tangible objects—living organisms, persons, things, events—are most easily recognized as discriminative stimuli, but not all discriminative stimuli are concrete.

Tacting of color, size, shape, or velocity brings the listener into contact with abstract dimensions of events, also categorized as a discriminative stimulus. Listeners also have histories that involve behaving with respect to "red" (e.g., stopping at a red light), and thus an identical history of reinforcement for uttering the word "red" to characterize the color of a specific object is not required. A functional similarity is necessary. Tacting is a class of behavior that brings the listener into contact with abstractions. Words such as poetry, music, disrespect, anxiety, stress, and grief occasion listener behavior with respect to complex verbal relations. Again, it is not necessary for the speaker and listener to have identical histories of reinforcement for uttering or writing the word "poetry" (e.g., having read the same poem), for the word "poetry" to occasion relevant behavior on the part of the listener. Similarly, it is not necessary for the speaker and listener to have identical histories uttering or hearing "anxiety," for the word "anxiety" to bring the listener into contact with relevant relations. In all cases, the relevant relations are not internal to the speaker, but being moved by poetry or imagining anxiety, they are functions of extended antecedent–behavior–consequence relations.

Skinner (1945, 1992) elaborated on how children acquire self-descriptions, such as "I have a tummy ache." To train tacting private events, parents—as members of the verbal community as large—rely on collateral information that is publicly observable (e.g., paleness, vomiting, holding one's midsection). An operant account of language emphasizes that neither the speaker who speaks of an event within the skin nor the listener may be guided by physiological stimuli. The latter may participate in the functional relation, but they may not. Practically, tacts help the listener come in contact with the broader conditions of the speaker's behavior that allow the listener to better predict what aspects of the current context may differentially impact the speaker (e.g., need for a restroom nearby in case of gastrointestinal difficulties; escape from loud noise or bright lights in the case of a headache). A similar abstract contact with operant contingencies occurs when speakers tact emotions. When a speaker says, "I am fearful," the listener contacts the present circumstances as correlating with negative outcomes. Tacts of emotions may orient the listener in a general way to the speaker's circumstances, placing the listener is in a better position to predict the speaker's behavior.

The accuracy of a speaker's tact is most apparent to the listener when both the speaker and the listener can directly observe the part of the world that serves as the discriminative stimulus for the speaker's tacting. Speakers can also tact events that are not directly observable to the listener. When a speaker reports on a historical event (e.g., a past social interaction), the speaker verbally re-creates features of the event that allow the listener to interact with the speaker in relation to that reported event. In any clinical work, tacting is a particularly important client repertoire, as clients are expected to tact recent and remote life events, and the therapist works with the client's descriptions of these behavior–environment relationships to set the agenda for therapy. When relevant events are not directly accessible to the listener, other contingencies must be expected to influence the content of the tact. Thus, any narrative of remote events can be expected to reflect multiple contingencies, including social desirability, embellishment, or understatement. As part of the therapeutic process, clients who have clinically significant difficulties tacting improve their skills, so that the discriminative stimuli that are influencing the behavior of the client (i.e., the speaker) can influence the behavior of the listener (i.e., therapist) more effectively. In session and between sessions, such skills training involves discrimination training, consisting of self-monitoring, observing behavior–environment relations and describing them.

Rule-Governed Behavior

While a functional analysis often distinguishes the listener's from the speaker's repertoire, people are both listeners and speakers. They also participate in multiple verbal communities, including idiosyncratic manding and tacting repertoires (e.g., professional versus personal lives; specific hobbies; childhood friends). Skinner (1992) spoke of multiple verbal selves, listener–speaker repertoires shaped by the different verbal communities, that then engage within one person. He later introduced rule-governed behavior to distinguish a broad category for behavior guided by verbal stimuli (e.g., instructions, rules, advice, admonitions) from behavior shaped by encountering the actual situation (Skinner, 1974). He pointed out that rule-governed behavior (e.g., pushing down piano keys by following instructions) could not be as skillful and artful as behavior shaped by features of the actual situation (e.g., the resulting sound). Skinner also noted that acquisition of complex repertoires often relied on rule-following until nuances of real-life consequences (here, tempo, discernible melodies) took over.

At the content level, rules are characterized as conditional "if . . . then" statements, specifying relations among events. They tell people about response options and their consequences. Rules are ubiquitous in daily life, and so are the practical and social consequences of rules that have become part of routines. Once contingency-shaped, they are on autopilot: performing wakeup routines, dressing, commuting, preparing meals, using electronic or digital technologies, participating in formal and informal relationships, managing finances, engaging in self-care, and so on. These repertoires have considerable momentum and, as behavior patterns that encounter high rates of reinforcement, they are relatively persistent under challenging circumstances. Rule-governed behavior is thus part and parcel of human strengths.

When rules are accurate, they help people behave more effectively more quickly. Of clinical interest, however, are situations in which adults implement rules that are ineffective or inaccurate, or have become obsolete. What does it take for the person to notice that the rule does not hold? Research has demonstrated that when initial instructions lead to success (such as a high score on a game), adults commonly are slow or fail to adjust their behavior when the rules of the game change, and the instruction no longer describes the prevailing contingencies. This suggests that in many cases, rule-following is disproportionally influenced by one's reinforcement history. To generate more flexible repertoires, a history of reinforcement of rule-following (socially desirable, yet sometimes leading to blind or uncritical adherence to strategies) might be amended by a reinforcement for effective tracking of contingencies (holding instructions lightly and testing them by sampling whether the conditions still hold).

Pliance

In the context of ACT, rule-governed behavior that is maintained by social reinforcement, with the behavior relatively insensitive to contingencies and not shaped by them, is called pliance. Adults have long histories of approval for adhering to rules and of sanctions for failing to adhere to rules. Rules maintain order and provide efficient means for societies to act collaboratively. Under ideal conditions, following rules produces good outcomes for the individual as well as groups and helps them to accomplish a wider arrange of actions effectively and collectively.

Because rules can be considered bridges to contacting outcomes (think of learning to play piano or acquiring other complex repertoires), many rules characterize if–then relationships related to relatively long-term outcomes. Values are the stuff of rules. On the other hand, rule-following is more strongly impacted by immediate social contingencies. As noted earlier, immediacy is a key dimension of consequent relations, and the strong social reinforcement history contributes to the likelihood that repertoires will persist when a rule may no longer be effective. While building flexibility, ACT also takes advantage of this circumstance by shaping rule-governed behavior related to values and banking that it will persist even when obstacles are encountered practically.

While rule-governed behavior can thus be advantageous, ACT builds flexibility by disrupting ineffective pliance repertoires, for example, through defusion exercises, so that clients can view their own verbal if–then conditional statements as curious artifacts rather than demands for action. As noted in the behavioral momentum section, discrimination training involving noticing when specific verbal statements are useful and when they are not can decrease the influence problematic or outdated rules have on current functioning, while building novel and effective rules related to long-term outcomes.

COUNTERPLIANCE

Counterpliance is defined as ignoring or behaving contrary to a rule statement. Notably, the listener's behavior is just as influenced by the rule, but the relation is "opposite" or "not" rather than "in accordance with." The listener's counterpliant response denies the speaker access to any consequences that commonly would reinforce the speaker's utterance. From the listener's perspective, the speaker's failure to follow through or enforce compliance may negatively reinforce counterpliance (e.g., by removing or reducing a threat posed by the speaker's behavior). When rule statements imply infringements on personal autonomy, responses that are likely to remove or reduce the likelihood of a speaker imposing such infringements will serve as negative reinforcers. These types of negative reinforcers can occur when the speaker and listener have very different reinforcers maintaining their behavior, when there is an asymmetry of interests, or when the social environment is coercive.

Ideally, rules enhance social relationships, with sufficient positive reinforcement-based reciprocity for counterpliant responses to infrequently occur. Clinically, problematic levels of counterpliance may occur if clients have histories of being coerced, abused, or exploited. The more frequently counterpliance encounters reinforcement, the greater the momentum and the likelihood that the repertoire is extended to functionally similar social relationships. The demands inherent in the therapist–client relationship may have sufficient similarities for the relationship dynamics to occasion client counterpliance, particularly when treatment-related rules are introduced. As momentum tends to be context-specific, therapists might emphasize their role as an ally and coach who supports the client in their goals, as opposed to the therapist with an agenda distinct from the client's. Motivational interviewing skills and values work can be effective tools for establishing the therapeutic relationship as one of positive collaboration. Similarly, the ACT therapeutic stance encourages clients to evaluate therapeutic instructions in relation to their own experience (i.e., experience separate from rules). This redirects the client from tracking interpersonal contingencies related to compliance and toward tracking other antecedent–behavior–consequence relationships that are likely to persist beyond the therapy room.

Tracking

As noted earlier, Skinner (1974) differentiated rule-governed and contingency-shaped behavior. Using the example of piano playing, instructions may ensure initial engagement, and then contingencies hone the skill. Tracking describes this shift to contingency-shaping. Rule-following behavior that is maintained by the rule's effectiveness in contacting the contingency described in the rule is called tracking. It can be useful to think of tracking as a skill that benefits from pliance (i.e., behavior consistent with a rule) but also involves tracking the dynamic interaction between behavior and the environment characterized in the rule. In this sense, the rule facilitates the listener's contact with relevant contingencies and the consequences that are directly encountered in that process are what maintain that behavior over time.

A good example of the pliance-tracking distinction can be observed when driving to an unfamiliar location using a navigation assistance program. Here, rules are given step-by-step, and the driver may reach their destination entirely by complying with the rules given by the navigation program. While pliance will get one to the destination, tracking would involve the driver attending to the landmarks along the route of travel (e.g., street order, buildings, other natural landmarks); when repeating the trip at a later time, they would be able to use those landmarks to guide their travel instead of requesting instructions from the navigation system.

Highly precise rules are useful when deviation from the rule may be dangerous or when the rule specifies contingencies that are very narrow in their applicability, as in highly technical applications. However, rules that are overly precise for their application (i.e., a much more variable range of behavior can be used to effectively contact the contingencies specified within the rule) can fail to bring listeners into contact with the range of contextual stimuli that will support the behavior pattern characterized in the rule. In this sense, overly specified rules can restrict the range of behavioral variability a listener exhibits when complying with the rule. As such, they may fail to dynamically respond to the needs of a particular situation.

Alternatively, imprecise or vague rules are less prescriptive and can increase the likelihood that the listener attends to the dynamic interactions between context and behavior specified in the rule. The listener's learning history will determine whether imprecise rules facilitate tracking or whether they serve as high-risk opportunities for failing to comply with the rule. In this sense, privilege begets more privilege. Listeners who have rich learning histories relevant to the range of antecedent context variables that can be tracked and who have breadth and variability in the relevant skills are more likely to vary their behaviors in dynamic ways that facilitate tracking a fuller range of scenarios in which they can effectively guide behavior. Conversely, listeners with relatively impoverished histories with respect to elements of the rule, or who have excessive punishment histories for failing to strictly comply with rules will be at greater risk for failing to track the contingencies specified by the rule.

Research has found that imprecise rules are better at facilitating contextually sensitive rule-following than precise rules. This serves as one of the underlying rationales for how values statements are used in ACT. Values statements are typically broad in scope. As rules, they generally focus on a domain of experience (e.g., work, family, community) and consequence categories that can only be contacted as part of a process or at a significant delay (e.g., contributing to a sense of purpose to fellow employees and value to customers, bringing safety and security to family, and helping all members of the community thrive).

When values statements serve as imprecise rule statements, a wide range of activities can occur that may be consistent with the value. While specific goals and actions subordinate to the value may be met with variable success, these efforts, being consistent with the value statement, can be sufficient to reinforce values-relevant action. Therapists are an important source of support for tracking this consistency and serve as a verbal community that elevates the value of such consistency as a reinforcer (i.e., motivating operation). Consistency as a verbal relation (see Harte & Barnes-Holmes, this volume) can be a useful and relatively immediate (and ongoing) source of reinforcement for valued behavior patterns for which other reinforcers are more delayed and probabilistic.

Self-Rules

As already noted, listening to what you say is an inevitable part of speaking. Just as speakers receive feedback on what they say from listeners (i.e., how what was said impacted the listener), speakers can respond to what they say as their own listener and adjust their behavior accordingly. For adults, this form of self-editing is a routine skill. Here a public didactic process establishes the skills and context for a self-didactic process.

A similar process occurs with regard to rule statements, with an individual serving both speaker and listener roles.

Augmentals

Augmentals are rule-related statements that alter the consequential effectiveness of events specified in contingencies. In this sense, these statements function as motivating operations. As noted in the motivating operations section above, values and values clarification exercises in ACT often serve this function in enhancing the types of events perceived to be consistent with values. As such, they may have increased reinforcing effectiveness for values-relevant behavior patterns.

Effective behavior change reinforces the therapist's work with clients. Committed action is much easier to achieve when motivating operations establish powerful reinforcers, when those reinforcers are available in the client's environment, and when the client has the relevant skills to access those reinforcers. Therapists identify augmental statements that can help their clients better identify and encounter meaningful reinforcers for committed action. It is important, however, for the therapist to ensure that they are taking a contextual approach to the client's life space, understand the multiple nested contingencies that may influence behavior, and address those needs as well. Attempts at leveraging behavior change exclusively through augmentals while ignoring skills deficits, resource deficits, and competing consequences fails to take advantage of the contextual account of behavior.

Key Applications of Basic Principles

The Constructional Approach to Behavior Change

Given peoples' histories and current circumstances, they are behaving exactly as they ought to behave. This is a fundamental assumption of the functional contextual perspective. Clinically relevant behaviors that are part of presenting problems are products of reinforcement contingencies and are maintained by reinforcement contingencies. These behaviors also come with costs. Amplifying the costs of these behaviors in therapy does nothing to alter the reinforcement contingencies that maintain the behavior. For this reason, a contextual approach to behavior change is constructional: the therapist works with the client to build increasingly effective behavior patterns that are in line with the client's goals and values, and these behavior patterns are ultimately supported by the positive reinforcement contingencies the client encounters in daily life.

The constructional approach comprises four core elements: identification of the target repertoires of interest (i.e., those needed to support treatment goals); identification of current skills, particularly those that are assets for treatment goals; identification of intermediate skill steps to transition from current skills to the target skills needed; and systems of support to aid in the acquisition of these skills as well as their maintenance outside of therapy (Goldiamond, 1974).

To identify what repertoires are needed for a client to consider therapy successful, we need to know how the client's life would differ at the end of treatment. In ACT, this process typically involves an exploration of values and goals subordinate to those values. If a client's values include being a warm and supportive partner, what skills do they need to have to flexibly enact this value in ways that the partner notices as supportive? The skills necessary for being supportive will differ for every dyad. Some types of support involve instrumental skills that need to be refined and maintained by their own reinforcement contingencies (e.g., managing finances, meal preparation). Other forms of support involve direct interpersonal interaction and tailored interpersonal skills training to help clients track the interpersonal support activities that positively impact their partner and the relationship (as opposed to rule following). To meet therapy goals, a transparent and collaborative approach is taken to characterize the repertoires involved.

Similarly, a transparent and collaborative assessment of the client's current repertoire in relation to therapy goals is taken. Focusing on strengths, what skills do the clients already demonstrate that are in line with their goals? In many areas of life, the problem is not that clients have profound skills deficits. Clients may have the relevant skills in their repertoire, but they have not encountered sufficient reinforcement to attain momentum under less-than-ideal circumstances. Similarly, the skills may be present but may still be awkward, and the client correctly identifies a lack of fluency and facility to adjust their skills effectively to the demands of new situations. "Knowing" how to do something is not the same as doing it, and doing something is not synonymous with behavior encountering positive reinforcement contingencies. When considering current strengths, it is important to focus on what the person does that directly encounters relevant reinforcement and thus is being supported by the client's environment.

In addition to current repertoire strengths, we also look at weaknesses: behaviors that have the potential to interfere with the target repertoire. In ACT, this typically involves addressing social settings in which thoughts and emotions are treated as barriers to effective action or as reasons for acting in ways that manage short-term concerns at the expense of longer-term values.

The third element of the constructional approach involves mapping out how the clinical work will incrementally support the client's current repertoire in moving toward the target repertoire. The developmental and experiential nature of this iterative process should be made clear to the client. For example, taking targeted time to practice observing private and public events builds a component skill set; later, observing and taking values-congruent action occur together.

The fourth element of the constructional approach involves an analysis of current and maintaining supports for the behaviors of interest. Well-meaning social supports generally treat thoughts and affect as reasons and causes, and accommodate behavior patterns that are contrary to the client's long-term best interests. Thus, it is important that social supports be aligned with client goals so that relevant behavior is supported. Clients may follow a rule (e.g., show care for my family by providing financial security) but not track its actual effects on others (i.e., do family members feel cared for in ways that matter to them?). Thus, it is important that values-congruent actions are monitored so that self-evaluation of their function over time can be an effective source of support.

One of the practice pitfalls in ACT is *talking about* doing ACT instead of doing ACT (Brock, Batten, Walser, & Robb, 2015). Exercises and homework in ACT help build skills and create opportunities for these skills to directly contact the reinforcement contingencies that are likely to maintain them outside of the therapeutic context. Additional reinforcement from the therapist for treatment-relevant engagement also can help support these new behavior patterns.

In the end, clinically meaningful behavior change can occur and persist only when it comes into regular contact with reinforcement that is available in the environment beyond the treatment setting. A thorough analysis of systems of support needed for target behaviors to be maintained should be conducted, and treatment planning should reflect the client's needs given the types of support available and the types of new support that may need to be built.

Functional Analysis

Functional analysis is "[t]he identification of important, controllable, causal functional relationships applicable to a specified set of target behaviors for an individual client" (Haynes & O'Brian, 1990, p. 654). The first step in facilitating it involves an assessment of the client's concerns, their related skills, and the context in which the client is operating. This information is then organized into an analysis of both the current and goal-related behavior patterns in terms of behavioral principles. This formulation is used to devise a function-based intervention, the intervention is implemented, and outcomes are monitored. If improvements are not observed, additional assessment is conducted to further inform or revise the function-based intervention. The updated treatment plan is then implemented, and outcomes are monitored. This process is repeated until client outcomes are achieved (Follette, Naugle, & Linnerooth, 2000). Functional analysis is considered a core framework for implementing cognitive-behavioral therapy (Drossel, Rummel, & Fisher, 2009; Klepac et al., 2012).

DESCRIPTIVE FUNCTIONAL ANALYSIS

A descriptive functional analysis is a conceptual analysis of the elements of the operant relations that constitute clinically relevant behavior patterns. A descriptive functional analysis is in this sense a working hypothesis, typically informed by client self-report, records review, and the therapist's observation of client behavior during sessions.

How the therapist organizes the information for a function-based case formulation can vary depending on the focus, for example, specific concerns versus multiple concurrent contextual variables. Figure 3.1 depicts a focused approach involving a descriptive analysis of a combat veteran presenting to treatment because their hypervigilant behavior patterns have had a negative impact on their ability to maintain employment. Here we can depict how the individual's history of military training and deployment resulted in vigilant monitoring of threats, with important and practical consequences for the client and members of their military unit. The antecedent side of the contingency diagram highlights the role of history and the potential role of rules and unfamiliar environments in increasing the likelihood of hypervigilance. The consequence side of the diagram highlights that momentary decreases in the perception of threat may negatively reinforce hypervigilant behaviors. The variables in this diagram point to interventions focused on flexible versus rigid rule-following and tolerating uncertainty. As a descriptive functional analysis, these relationships represent hypotheses, and the client's response to interventions based on these functional hypotheses serves as the basis for confidence in the analysis. If a positive response to intervention does not occur, the therapist uses direct observations of client behavior in the room as well as self-monitoring homework to update their functional hypotheses and the treatment plan. This process occurs iteratively until the client's treatment goals are met.

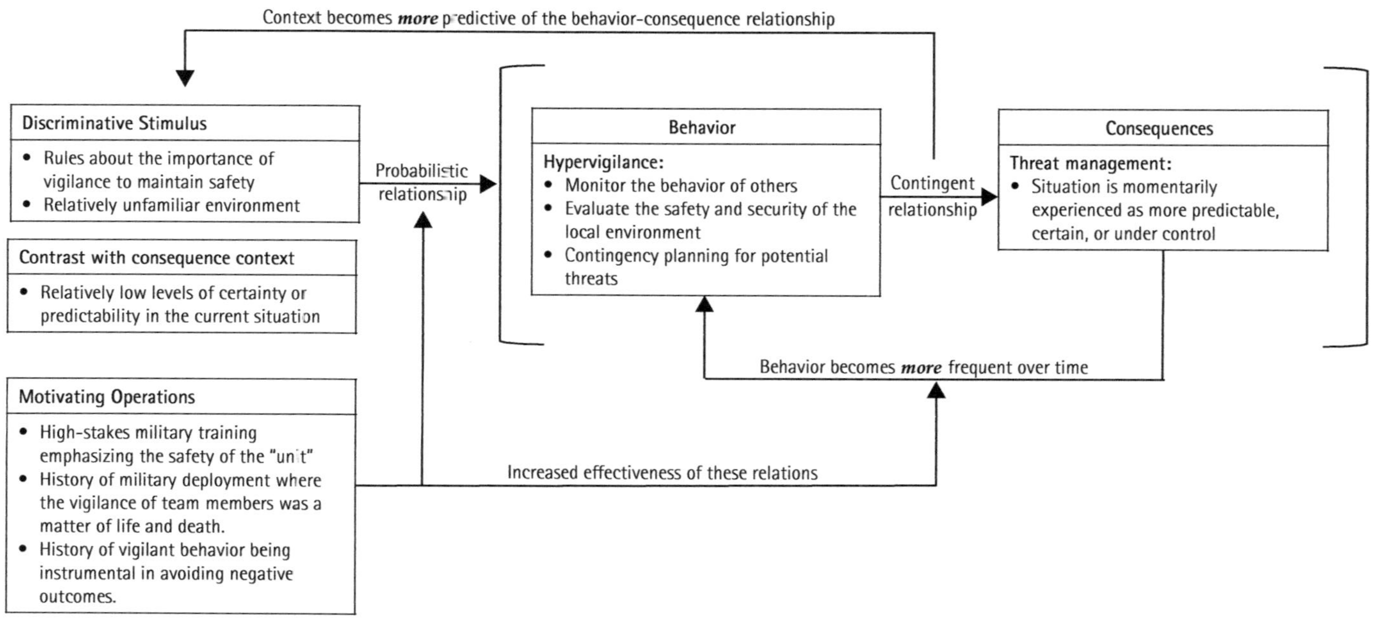

Figure 3.1. Contingency diagram for a hypervigilant veteran

Many factors contribute to a clinical presentation. Functional-analytic clinical case diagrams are tools for capturing the hypothesized relationships among multiple causal variables that are likely contributing to one or more clinical concerns (Haynes, O'Brian, & Kaholokula, 2011). These diagrams distinguish between changeable (circle) and relatively less changeable (diamond) causal variables. Behavioral concerns and their effects are depicted in rectangles. Interrelationships among the elements are depicted with one- or two-way arrows, and the thickness of the variable borders and arrows can be used to identify the perceived relative importance and strength of the relationships, respectively. Figure 3.2 depicts a functional-analytic clinical case diagram for the same veteran depicted in Figure 3.1. As with Figure 3.1, military history and vigilance-related rules are considered. In addition, other contextual variables are also considered that are hypothesized to have important causal relationships with hypervigilant behavior patterns. The veteran began using stimulants (e.g., coffee, expresso powder, caffeinated energy drinks) in the military during deployment and has continued to consume high levels of caffeine (e.g., two pots of coffee and a half dozen energy drinks daily). They do not sleep well and tend to doze off 30 to 90 minutes at a time rather than obtain a continuous bout of sleep overnight. After unrestful sleep, they address failures of sustained concentration by consuming more caffeine. Employment situations have been difficult because the client perceives their novel work environment as unpredictable, based on civilian employees not seeming to "take their jobs seriously." Workplace rules and expectations are treated with the same rigidity and diligence that characterized rules and job duties in the military.

Figure 3.2 serves as a succinct reminder of the complexity of the causal relations within the case formulation for this veteran. The diagram is a useful tool for the clinician and any

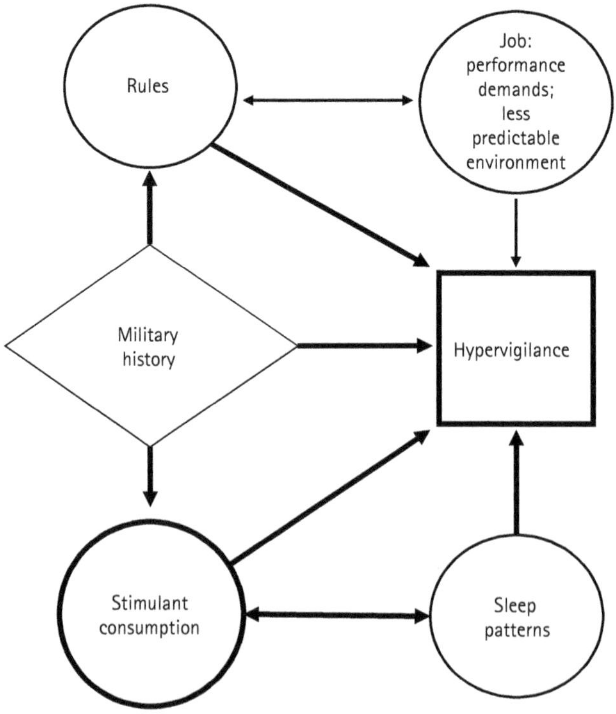

Figure 3.2. Functional-analytic clinical case diagram example

peers providing case consultation, and clients often find these diagrams useful for discussing treatment planning and sequencing. While this represents a more macro view of functional case formulation, any specific elements of the diagram can be broken down into a more focused contingency analysis like Figure 3.1.

EXPERIMENTAL FUNCTIONAL ANALYSIS

An experimental functional analysis begins with a descriptive functional analysis and uses behavior monitoring and the systematic introduction of intervention components to determine whether elements of the functional analysis indeed have the functions that were hypothesized. These formal evaluations of functions can occur in session (e.g., change in the rigid application of rules secondary to creative hopelessness focused exercises) or via client self-monitoring between sessions (e.g., caffeine consumption, instances of rigid rule-following and their context).

Experimental functional analysis has traditionally been conducted in clinical situations that could not identify clear antecedents or consequences for a clinically relevant behavior pattern. In these cases, specific antecedents or consequences are systematically introduced, while the relevant behavior patterns are being monitored to evaluate the specificity of the functional relationships involved. When these variables are interpersonal and can be replicated in the relationship between the client and therapist, a real-time experimental functional analysis can occur (e.g., the therapist systematically varies their social attentiveness, interrupts the client, or uses dismissive nonverbals while listening). Other variables may operate at a different time scale. Evaluating the antecedent effects of stimulants for the veteran in the previous example will take time, given the necessity of a caffeine taper to prevent adverse effects from acute withdrawal. During that time, the client could self-monitor their hypervigilance. During sessions, both the client and therapist could monitor behavioral indices of hypervigilance.

While a formal and systematic experimental functional analysis is less common in outpatient mental health settings (i.e., descriptive functional analyses alone often facilitate effective treatment planning), the approach can be invaluable when the therapist and client have difficulty determining whether specific antecedents or consequences have a functional relationship with clinically relevant behavior patterns and treatment fails to make progress. To obtain a better range of variables that may need to be explored in an experimental functional analysis, improved observation of the clinically relevant behavior patterns typically needs to occur. This may involve direct observation by the therapist in the relevant settings, obtaining proxy reports from other individuals in the client's life, enhanced self-monitoring (Korotitsch & Nelson-Gray, 1999), and structured analyses of chains of events that occur in the client's life related to the clinically relevant behavior patterns (Rizvi & Ritschel, 2014).

MEASUREMENT-BASED CARE

Formal confirmation of how behavior–context relations specifically function is not always necessary in routine care. Nevertheless, it is common for clinicians working from a functional-analytic framework to engage in measurement-based care by collecting data throughout treatment. Such a measurement may involve tracking problems, quality of life or functioning, mechanisms of change, and the quality of the working relationship between the therapist and client (Scott & Lewis, 2015). Measurement-based care is a valuable tool for obtaining converging evidence on whether client behaviors and their response to the interventions used grossly reflect the relationships described in the functional analyses informing the treatment plan.

An additional level of measurement-based care involves careful monitoring of the effects of interventions with single-case research designs (Hayes et al., 2019; Kazdin, 2021). Briefly, measurement is used to evaluate the effects of the systematic introduction of intervention components in ways that are compatible with routine care. Simple AB designs (A = baseline; B = treatment) are the most common in routine clinical care. Most interventions have multiple components or modules whose effects can be evaluated in a sequential fashion (i.e., multiple-baseline designs or additive treatment designs). There are several examples in the literature of single-case research designs using ACT with a variety of clinical presentations (e.g., Gould, Tarbox, & Coyne, 2018; Ruiz, Luciano, Flórez, Suárez-Falcón, & Cardona-Betancourt, 2020; Thompson, Twohig, & Luoma, 2021; Villatte et al., 2016).

Conclusion

Behavioral principles guided the initial development of ACT and serve as the foundation for its flexible implementation. To appreciate this foundation, a functional contextual understanding of the operant contingency as the fundamental unit of analysis was introduced, and key terms within this approach were characterized in terms of functional relations. In contrast with S-M-R-C analyses where the key elements are defined a priori and involve a linear causal sequence, operant A-B-C analyses involve relationally defined variables and dynamic feedback processes that can only be observed over time. Whether analysis of a clinical scenario involves a single behavior, two or more behaviors under systems of constraint, or the social contingencies involved in the use of language, operant functional relations can be used to characterize, predict, and influence clinically relevant behavior patterns. Key applications of these relations include taking a constructional approach to building meaningful patterns of behavior that are supported by naturalistic contingencies outside of the therapeutic relationship, evaluating function-based hypotheses by monitoring response to treatment and other key variables, and occasionally systematically evaluating treatment outcomes using single-subject research designs. Behavioral principles and the foundational tools for their application support clinicians in taking a scientist-practitioner approach to ACT implementation and can support competent innovation while maintaining fidelity to the underlying functional contextual model.

Notes

1. These internal processes are often termed *organismic*, or internal to the organism. *Organism* has often been used as a biological placeholder for both accumulated life experience and biological states. This terminology is used in the stimulus-organism-response-consequence model (S-O-R-C; Kanfer & Phillips, 1970).
2. A parody of a fictitious drug by this name and direct to consumer marketing practices used by the pharmaceutical industry to promote Zoloft® was made by person(s) affiliated with the now obsolete website astonishedhead.com. A repository of direct-to-consumer marketing videos and this parody can be found at https://www.antidepressantmarket.com/marketing.
3. This discredited claim, which initially was widely promoted by the pharmaceutical industry and has now been debunked, still persists in cultural explanations for mental health presentations.

References

Azrin, R. D., & Hayes, S. C. (1984). The discrimination of interest within a heterosexual interaction: Training, generalization, and effects on social skills. *Behavior Therapy, 15*(2), 173–184. https://doi.org/10.1016/S0005-7894(84)80018-0

Belisle, J., Paliliunas, D., Vangsness, L., Dixon, M. R., & Stanley, C. R. (2020). Social distance and delay exert multiple control over altruistic choices. *The Psychological Record, 70*(3), 445–457. https://doi.org/10.1007/s40732-020-00399-x

Binder, C. (1996). Behavioral fluency: Evolution of a new paradigm. *The Behavior Analyst, 19*(2), 163–197. https://doi.org/10.1007/BF03393163

Brock, M. J., Batten, S. V., Walser, R. D., & Robb, H. B. (2015). Recognizing common clinical mistakes in ACT: A quick analysis and call to awareness. *Journal of Contextual Behavioral Science, 4*(3), 139–143. https://doi.org/10.1016/j.jcbs.2014.11.003

Chapman, G. B. (1996). Temporal discounting and utility for health and money. *Journal of Experimental Psychology: Learning, Memory, and Cognition, 22*, 771–791.

Coffey, S. F., Gudleski, G. D., Saladin, M. E., & Brady, K. T. (2003). Impulsivity and rapid discounting of delayed hypothetical rewards in cocaine-dependent individuals. *Experimental and Clinical Psychopharmacology, 11*(1), 18–25. https://doi.org/10.1037/1064-1297.11.1.18

Drossel, C., Rummel, C., & Fisher, J. E. (2009). Assessment and cogntive behavior therapy: Functional analysis as key process. In W. T. O'Donohue & J. E. Fisher (Eds.), *General principles and empirically supported techniques of cognitive behavior therapy* (pp. 15–41). Hoboken, NJ: John Wiley & Sons.

Ferster, C. B. (1973). A functional analysis of depression. *American Psychologist, 28*(10), 857–870.

Follette, W. C., Naugle, A. E., & Linnerooth, P. J. N. (2000). Functional alternatives to traditional assessment and diagnosis. In M. J. Dougher (Ed.), *Clinical behavior analysis* (pp. 99–125). Oakland, CA: Context Press.

Goldiamond, I. (1974). Toward a constructional approach to social problems: Ethical and constitutional issues raised by applied behavior analysis. *Behaviorism, 2*(1), 1–84. https://www.jstor.org/stable/27758809

Gould, E. R., Tarbox, J., & Coyne, L. (2018). Evaluating the effects of acceptance and commitment training on the overt behavior of parents of children with autism. *Journal of Contextual Behavioral Science, 7*, 81–88. https://doi.org/10.1016/j.jcbs.2017.06.003

Hargie, O. (2017). *Skilled interpersonal communication: Research, theory, and practice* (6th ed.). London: Routledge.

Hayes, S. C. (1978). Theory and technology in behavior analysis. *The Behavior Analyst, 1*(1), 25–33. https://doi.org/10.1007/BF03392370

Hayes, S. C., & Brownstein, A. J. (1986). Mentalism, behavior-behavior relations, and a behavior-analytic view of the purposes of science. *The Behavior Analyst, 9*(2), 175–190. https://doi.org/10.1007/BF03391944

Hayes, S. C., Hofmann, S. G., Stanton, C. E., Carpenter, J. K., Sanford, B. T., Curtiss, J. E., & Ciarrochi, J. (2019). The role of the individual in the coming era of process-based therapy. *Behaviour Research and Therapy, 117*, 40–53. https://doi.org/10.1016/j.brat.2018.10.005

Hayes, S. C., Rosenfarb, I., Wulfert, E., Mint, E., Zettle, R. D., & Korn, Z. (1985). Self-reinforcement effects: An artfact of social standard setting? *Journal of Applied Behavior Analysis, 18*, 201–214. https://doi.org/10.1901/jaba.1985.18-201

Hayes, S. C., & Strosahl, K. D. (Eds.). (2004). *A practical guide to acceptance and commitment therapy.* New York: Springer.

Hayes, S. C., Strosahl, K. D., & Wilson, K. G. (2012). *Acceptance and commitment therapy: The process and practice of mindful change* (2nd ed.). New York: Guilford Press.

Haynes, S. N., & O'Brian, W. H. (1990). Functional analysis in behavior therapy. *Clinical Psychology Review, 10*(6), 649–668. https://doi.org/https://doi.org/10.1016/0272-7358(90)90074-K

Haynes, S. N., O'Brian, W. H., & Kaholokula, J. K. (2011). *Behavioral assessment and case formulation.* Hoboken, NJ: John Wiley & Sons.

Hoagland, H., & Mitchell, R. T. (1956). William John Crozier: 1892–1955. *American Journal of Psychology, 69*(1), 135–138. http://www.jstor.org/stable/1418136

Holth, P. (2017). Multiple exemplar training: Some strengths and limitations. *The Behavior Analyst, 40*, 225–241. https://doi.org/10.1007/s40614-017-0083-z

Ishikawa, D., Matsumoto, N., Sakaguchi, T., Matsuki, N., & Ikegaya, Y. (2014). Operant conditioning of synaptic and spiking activity patterns in single hippocampal neurons. *Journal of Neuroscience, 34*(14), 5044–5053. https://doi.org/10.1523/JNEUROSCI.5298-13.2014

Kanfer, F. H., & Phillips, J. S. (1970). *Learning foundations of behavior therapy.* New York: John Wiley & Sons.

Kazdin, A. E. (2021). *Single-case research designs: Methods for clinical and applied settings* (3rd, Ed.). New York: Oxford University Press.

Klepac, R. K., Ronan, G. F., Andrasik, F., Arnold, K. D., Belar, C. D., Berry, S. L., . . . Strauman, T. J. (2012). Guidelines for cognitive behavioral training within doctoral psychology programs in the United States: Report of the Inter-Organizational Task Force on Cognitive and Behavioral Psychology Doctoral Education. *Behavior Therapy, 43*(4), 687–697. https://doi.org/10.1016/j.beth.2012.05.002

Korotitsch, W. J., & Nelson-Gray, R. O. (1999). An overview of self-monitoring research in assessment and treatment. *Psychological Assessment, 11*(4), 415–425. https://doi.org/10.1037/1040-3590.11.4.415

Layng, T. V. J. (2019). Tutorial: Understanding concepts: Implications for behavior analysts and educators. *Perspectives on Behavior Science, 42*, 345–363. https://doi.org/10.1007/s40614-018-00188-6

Lee, V. L. (1987). Radical behaviorism and behavior analysis: A review of behaviour analysis and comtemporary psychology. *The Behavior Analyst, 10*, 95–101.
Linehan, M. (1993). *Cognitive-behavioral treatment of borderline personality disorder*. New York: Guilford Press.
Malone, J. C. (1990). *Theories of learning: A historical approach*. Middletown, CT: Wadsworth.
Mitchell, S. H. (1999). Measures of impulsivity in cigarette smokers and non-smokers. *Psychopharmacology, 146*(4), 455–464. https://doi.org/10.1007/PL00005491
Morrison, K. L., Madden, G. J., Odum, A. L., Friedel, J. E., & Twohig, M. P. (2014). Altering impulsive decision making with an acceptance-based procedure. *Behavior Therapy, 45*(5), 630–639. https://doi.org/10.1016/j.beth.2014.01.001
Polk, K. L., & Schoendorff, B. (Eds.). (2014). *The ACT Matrix: A new approach to building psychological flexibility across settings and populations*. Oakland, CA: New Harbinger.
Rasmussen, E. B., Lawyer, S. R., & Reilly, W. (2010). Percent body fat is related to delay and probability discounting for food in humans. *Behavioural Processes, 83*(1), 23–30. https://doi.org/10.1016/j.beproc.2009.09.001
Rizvi, S. L., & Ritschel, L. A. (2014). Mastering the art of chain analysis in dialectical behavior therapy. *Cognitive and Behavioral Practice, 21*(3), 335–349. https://doi.org/10.1016/j.cbpra.2013.09.002
Ruiz, F. J., Luciano, C., Flórez, C. L., Suárez-Falcón, J. C., & Cardona-Betancourt, V. (2020). A multiple-baseline evaluation of acceptance and commitment therapy focused on repetitive negative thinking for comorbid generalized anxiety disorder and depression. *Frontiers in Psychology, 11*, Article 356. https://doi.org/10.3389/fpsyg.2020.00356
Rung, J. M., & Madden, G. J. (2018). Experimental reductions of delay discounting and impulsive choice: A systematic review and meta-analysis. *Journal of Experimental Psychology: General, 147*(9), 1349–1381. https://doi.org/10.1037/xge0000462
Rung, J. M., Peck, S., Hinnenkamp, J. E., Preston, E., & Madden, G. J. (2019). Changing delay discounting and impulsive choice: Implications for addictions, prevention, and human health. *Perspectives on Behavior Science, 42*(3), 397–417. https://doi.org/10.1007/s40614-019-00200-7
Scott, K., & Lewis, C. C. (2015). Using measurement-based care to enhance any treatment. *Cognitive and Behavioral Practice, 22*(1), 49–59. https://doi.org/10.1016/j.cbpra.2014.01.010
Sidman, M. (1960). *Tactics of scientific research: Evaluating experimental data in psychology*. Boston, MA: Authors Cooperative.
Skinner, B. F. (1935). The generic nature of the concepts of stimulus and response. *Journal of General Psychology, 12*(1), 40–65. https://doi.org/10.1080/00221309.1935.9920087
Skinner, B. F. (1945). The operational analysis of psychological terms. *Psychological Review, 52*(2), 270–277. https://doi.org/10.1037/h0062535
Skinner, B. F. (1974). *About behaviorism*. Visalia, CA: Vintage Books.
Skinner, B. F. (1992). *Verbal behavior*. Boston: Copley Publishing Group.
Stoddard, J. A., & Afari, N. (2014). *The big book of ACT metaphors*. Oakland, CA: New Harbinger.
Swan, A. J., Carper, M. M., & Kendall, P. C. (2015). In pursuit of generalization: An updated review. *Behavior Therapy, 47*(5), 733–746. https://doi.org/10.1016/j.beth.2015.11.006
Thompson, B. L., Twohig, M. P., & Luoma, J. B. (2021). Psychological flexibility as shared process of change in acceptance and commitment therapy and exposure and response prevention for obsessive-compulsive disorder: A single case design study. *Behavior Therapy, 52*(2), 286–297. https://doi.org/10.1016/j.beth.2020.04.011
Ullmann, L. P. (1961). The clinician as behavioral scientist. *Journal of Clinical Psychology, 17*(2), 119–122.
Villatte, J. L., Vilardaga, R., Villatte, M., Plumb Vilardaga, J. C., Atkins, D. C., & Hayes, S. C. (2016). Acceptance and commitment therapy modules: Differential impact on treatment processes and outcomes. *Behaviour Research and Therapy, 77*, 52–61. https://doi.org/10.1016/j.brat.2015.12.001
Waltz, T. J., & Follette, W. C. (2009). Molar functional relations and clinical behavior analysis: implications for assessment and treatment. *The Behavior Analyst, 32*(1), 51–68.
Waltz, T. J., & Hayes, S. C. (2010). Acceptance and commitment therapy. In N. Kazantzis, M. A. Reinecke, & A. Freeman (Eds.), *Cogntive and behavioral theories in practice* (pp. 148–192). New York: Guilford Press.
Wilson, K. G., Bordieri, M. J., Flynn, M. K., Lucas, N. N., & Slater, R. M. (2011). Understanding acceptance and commitment therapy in context: A history of similarities and differences with other cognitive behavior therapies. In J. D. Herbert & E. M. Forman (Eds.), *Acceptance and mindfulness in cogntive behavior therapy: Understading and applying the new therapies* (pp. 233–263). Hoboken, NJ: John Wiley & Sons.
Winger, G., & Woods, J. H. (2013). Behavioral pharmacology. In G. J. Madden, W. V. Dube, T. D. Hackenberg, G. P. Hanley, & K. A. Lattal (Eds.), *APA handbook of behavior analysis, Vol. 1. Methods and principles* (pp. 547–567). American Psychological Association. https://doi.org/10.1037/13937-023

CHAPTER
4 A Primer on Relational Frame Theory

Colin Harte *and* Dermot Barnes-Holmes

Abstract
Both relational frame theory (RFT) and acceptance and commitment therapy (ACT) are based on the assumption that the evolution of human language (conceptualized as derived relational responding) creates the potential for a form of psychological suffering unique to the human species. Furthermore, it has often been argued that RFT provides the basic science foundation for ACT. Rather than dwell on these features of RFT, this article focuses on providing an up-to-date summary of the theory itself. Specifically, an historical and contemporary overview of RFT is presented, along with the details of recent ongoing efforts to advance the theory as a general behavior-analytic account of human language and cognition. In doing so, we provide a modern vision of how RFT may continue to connect with ACT in the years to come.

Key Words: relational frame theory, acceptance and commitment therapy, arbitrarily applicable relational responding, Hyper-Dimensional Multi-Level, relating, orienting, and evoking-motivating

Historically, relational frame theory (RFT; Hayes, Barnes-Holmes, et al., 2001) has been seen as providing the basic science foundation for acceptance and commitment therapy (ACT) by offering a detailed and empirically supported account of human language and cognition. The basic idea behind both RFT and ACT is that the evolution of human language, conceptualized as derived relational responding, has created the potential for a type of psychological suffering that is largely unique to humans. The purpose of this article is not to focus on how RFT accounts for human psychological suffering, but rather to provide an up-to-date summary of the theory itself. The general aim, therefore, is to help the reader contextualize and better understand any references made to RFT in other, more clinically focused articles of this volume.

Writings on RFT are numerous and widespread, with several hundred published empirical studies. The theory is over 30 years old, and its concepts appear to have stood the test of time, debate, and experimental scrutiny (e.g., see Hughes & Barnes-Holmes, 2016a, 2016b for recent reviews; see also Kissi et al., 2017). As a result, one may argue that RFT offers a relatively adequate, functional-analytic (behavioral) account of human language and cognition, while of course remaining very much a work in progress. In this text, we first cover the historical background of RFT within behavior analysis and its emergence as a behavioral theory of human language and cognition. We will then provide a detailed overview of the core concepts of RFT, in the context of what appear to be important recent developments in the theory, both empirically and conceptually. We also reflect briefly on how these recent advances may connect to clinically relevant issues within the ACT literature. We thus aim to present an overview of RFT and recent ongoing efforts to advance the theory, as an account of human language and cognition (Barnes-Holmes et al., 2016, 2017, 2018, 2020, 2021; Harte, Barnes-Holmes, Barnes-Holmes, & Kissi, 2020; Harte & Barnes-Holmes, 2021). Incorporating these recent advances and developments in RFT into this article provides readers with a modern vision of how RFT may continue to connect with ACT over the coming years.

Historical Background to the Emergence of RFT in Behavior Analysis

During the earlier part of the mid-20th century, behaviorism may have been seen as quite dominant, and indeed there is some substance to this view. Behaviorism, however, is a very broad term. One form of the concept, radical behaviorism—the form most closely associated with B. F. Skinner (1904–1990)—could be seen as surviving to this day, although paradoxically it is perhaps most closely associated with the demise of behavioral psychology. Specifically, it was Noam Chomsky's review (1959) of Skinner's book *Verbal Behaviour* (1957) that is often seen as marking the failure of behavior analysis to provide an adequate account of human language. While there may be some truth to this historical narrative, it fails to recognize the fact that Skinnerian behaviorism has indeed survived and continues to work on many features of human language and cognition.

Skinner (1957) made the first serious attempt within the school of radical behaviorism to develop an account of human language. Although Chomsky's review raised at least some legitimate concerns about Skinner's work, what is less well known is that almost 10 years later, Skinner proposed another concept that was directly relevant to the study of human language and cognition. Specifically, he suggested that human problem solving drew heavily on a type of behavior he referred to as rule-governed behavior or instructional control (1966). In doing so, Skinner recognized that verbally skilled humans frequently solved problems, not through direct contact with reinforcement contingencies that shaped appropriate behavior through trial and error, but through the selection of verbal statements about the world and how to interact with it. Thus, for example, a child could learn to avoid eating a toxic berry by following a rule provided by a caregiver rather than by having to eat the berry and experience sickness and risk even death. Skinner thus introduced the idea that a complete understanding of human psychology would require dealing with the extent to which human language created a type of learning pathway not shared with nonhuman animals.

Indeed, it was only 5 years later that another major figure in behavior analysis, Murray Sidman, reported an effect that highlighted another way in which human learning may differ dramatically from that of other animals (1971). At the time, Sidman was attempting to develop procedures for teaching basic reading skills to an individual with severe learning disabilities. Specifically, Sidman and colleagues taught the individual to match 20 spoken words to 20 pictures and to 20 printed words over more than 15 hours across 4 weeks. At the end of this time, and to the researchers' surprise, the individual spontaneously matched the 20 printed words to the pictures and vice versa in the absence of direct reinforcement for doing so. That is, reinforcing a subset of relational (reading) responses produced a number of emergent or unreinforced matching behaviors. Interestingly, these untaught or emergent matching or relating responses were discovered by Sidman and colleagues in the context of attempting to teach basic reading skills, and thus were clearly relevant to human language. Subsequently, the phenomenon that Sidman had revealed came to be known generally as the study of stimulus equivalence relations (see Sidman, 1994, for a book-length review of the early history of this research program).

The concept of the equivalence relation was refined over the following years, but it was not until the 1980s that a more rigorous and formalized account was presented (Sidman & Tailby, 1982; Sidman, 1986). Specifically, it was argued that the phenomenon comprised three formal properties, all shown in the absence of direct reinforcement: reflexivity, symmetry, and transitivity. Reflexivity required that each stimulus be conditionally related to itself (e.g., if A then A). In more concrete terms, given a picture of a dog, this picture will be chosen from an array containing a picture of the dog and other options (e.g., pictures of a cat and an apple). Symmetry required that the relation between stimuli be reversible (e.g., if A = B, then B = A). Or in more concrete terms, for example, if a child is presented with the written word "dog" and is taught to choose a picture of a dog, then the child should also readily choose the written word "dog" in the presence of the picture of the "dog."

Finally, transitivity required that a relation between two stimuli (e.g., A = B), combined with a relation between one of those stimuli and a novel stimulus (e.g., A = C), so that the relations B = C and C = B readily emerged. To again apply this example, imagine that, as in the earlier illustration, a child was presented with a picture of a dog and was taught to pick the written word "dog" as well as the written word "woof." Subsequently, the child may spontaneously match the written word "dog" with the word "woof" and the word "woof" with the written word "dog." When such a pattern of responses emerged, the participating stimuli were said to form an equivalence class or relation. Crucially, these emergent, untrained responses were demonstrated with relative ease in humans but were largely absent (or at best extremely weak) in nonhumans (e.g., Sidman et al., 1982; Dugdale & Lowe, 2000; see also Zentall et al., 2014, and related commentaries in Dougher et al., 2014, indicating that we still lack clear evidence that stimulus equivalence, as defined by Sidman, has been observed in nonhuman species).

The phenomenon of stimulus equivalence thus raised two key but related issues. First, it was difficult to explain the phenomenon in terms of direct reinforcement contingencies because previously unreinforced matching responses "emerged" during testing or probe trials. Second, there was an apparent link between stimulus equivalence and human language (because it was discovered when teaching basic reading skills, and nonhumans had failed to demonstrate clear evidence of equivalence responding). In attempting to reconcile these two issues, Sidman et al. (1982) suggested that equivalence may be a basic stimulus function unique to humans and thus provided an explanation for human language (or at least symbolic relations) itself. In contrast, other researchers suggested that human language, and in particular naming, provided the basis for stimulus equivalence (Horne & Lowe, 1996).

A third alternative explanation for the emergent properties of equivalence relations was proposed within an account that came to be known as relational frame theory (RFT). Specifically, Hayes (1991) argued that the relating behavior observed in emergent equivalence responding could be considered a class of generalized operant behavior (i.e., equivalence responding was essentially learned during early language acquisition, and thus equivalence and symbolic relations were functionally synonymous). Furthermore, Hayes argued that a wide variety of these classes of generalized operants were possible, and he referred to these as relational frames. In effect, during the course of early language learning, human children were taught to respond in accordance with relational frames, such as opposite, difference, and comparison (e.g., bigger versus smaller than), and thus a wide variety of derived relational responses should be possible. We will now turn to a description of the core concepts of RFT and its extension beyond stimulus equivalence as a basis for the complexities of human language and cognition.

RFT: Core Concepts and Technical Explanation

Just as Sidman had proposed that distinct properties were involved in the equivalence relation, RFT posits that three basic properties are involved in the relational frame: *mutual entailment*, *combinatorial entailment*, and the *transformation of stimulus functions*. Unlike the properties involved in stimulus equivalence, however, the properties involved in the relational frame are inherently more generic because they need to reflect the numerous different generalized patterns of derived stimulus relating that are possible from an RFT perspective (i.e., not just frames of coordination/equivalence but also those of opposition, comparison, difference, hierarchy, etc.). For example, the frame of opposition differs from coordination in that two opposite relations yield a derived relation of coordination, not opposite (e.g., "chilly" and "cold" are both opposite to hot, but they coordinate with each other). The frame of comparison includes many examples, but in the abstract may be represented using "more" and "less" signs (e.g., if A > B and B > C, then A > C and C < A). Comparison is also one of those frames that may yield "unspecified" relations when presented in abstract form. For example, if A > B and A > C, then the relation between B and C remains unspecified; B and C could be more or less than each other or indeed the same. Note, however, that according to RFT, correctly deriving that the relation between B and C remains unspecified is a "correct" derived response in this instance.

Other relational frames, such as hierarchy, are perhaps best considered to be complex relational networks rather than basic or simple frames. As such, a hierarchical network may involve containment, coordination, and difference. For example, the term *fruit* contains all fruits, but dividing fruits into "citrus" and "noncitrus" involves establishing one frame of *coordination* among all citrus fruits and a separate frame of coordination among all noncitrus fruits, and a frame of *difference* between the two categories. If you then divide the two categories (citrus and noncitrus) into hard- versus soft-skinned fruits, the resulting "frame" of hierarchy seems more like a network than a "basic" or simple frame composed of just three relata. That is, the superordinate category "fruit" is at the top of the hierarchy, with citrus and noncitrus at the next level down, and then below that level are the four categories citrus (hard- and soft-skinned) and noncitrus (hard- and soft-skinned).

The most basic or simplest relational network (or frame) is defined as a *generalized* (i.e., arbitrarily applicable) pattern of relational responding possessing the properties of mutual entailment, combinatorial entailment, and the transformation of stimulus functions. Mutual entailment is the most basic form of derived relational responding and marks the beginning of symbolic language development (Lipkens et al., 1993). It requires that the relation between two stimuli are related, bidrectionally, in a very specific way. For example, if A is more than B, then this relation mutually entails that B is less than A. In more concrete terms, if a child is taught that a car costs more than a bike, then the child may derive the idea (i.e., without further information, instruction, prompting or reinforcement) that a bike costs less than a car.

The second property, combinatorial entailment, refers to the novel relations that emerge among and between stimuli when three or more stimuli are related. For example, if A is the opposite to B (mutually entailing that B is the opposite to A) and B is the opposite to C (mutually entailing that C is the opposite to B), then the derived relations A is the same as C and C is the same as A may emerge. In more concrete terms, imagine a child is taught that "wrong" is the opposite of "right" and that "right" is the opposite of "mícheart" (Irish for wrong). Again, in the absence of further instruction or prompting or the like, the child may derive the notion that "mícheart" has the same meaning as (coordinated with) "wrong." As already noted, the terms *mutual* and *combinatorial* (entailment), rather than symmetry and transitivity, respectively, are used within RFT because the former (mutual and combinatorial entailment) are not bound or limited to derived relations in which the individual elements simply become substitutable or equivalent to each other.

The third and final core property of a relational frame (or basic network) is the transformation of stimulus functions; that is, the change in the functions of one stimulus participating in a frame, which results in spontaneous changes in the functions of other stimuli in the frame. Critically, these transformations of function occur in the absence of direct reinforcement, instruction, or prompting. This defining property of a relational frame thus highlights that symbolic relations in human language are involved in stimuli gaining, losing, or changing (i.e., transforming) their psychological properties. The distinction between relational entailment and the transformation of functions is critically important in RFT because it distinguishes between the act of relating stimuli in an "abstract sense" from the impact of that relating on the functions of those stimuli. Although not considered a core property within stimulus equivalence, a *transfer* of functions is recognized in stimulus equivalence research. The classic demonstration involves establishing an equivalence class composed of three or more stimuli (e.g., A = B = C = D), establishing a specific function for at least one of the stimuli (e.g., pairing A with an unpleasant taste or smell), and then observing that the other stimuli within the class also acquire that function in the absence of direct training (B and C and D acquire at least some of the unpleasant taste or smell functions).

The term *transformation* of function (rather than transfer) is employed within RFT because the functions of stimuli participating in relations other than equivalence/coordination do not transfer from one stimulus to another. Rather, the functions of the other stimuli in the frame are changed or *transformed* in accordance with the entailment properties. That is, the same function does not necessarily emerge among all participating stimuli within the frame; the nature of the transformation of stimulus functions depends on the specific relations involved (e.g., Dymond & Barnes, 1995). Imagine, for example, a situation in which a child has been bitten by a relatively small dog. The child later learns that a neighbor has just bought a very large dog. Based on the transformation of fear functions, in accordance with the frame of comparison (in this case, smaller/larger), it is possible that the neighbor's larger dog will evoke even greater fear and avoidance than the smaller dog that actually bit the child in the first place (see Dougher et al., 2007, for relevant experimental evidence).

In making a distinction between entailment and transformation of functions, RFT stipulates that these properties are under separate classes of contextual control. Specifically, entailment is determined by Crel contextual cues (i.e., controlling the type of relation), and the transformation of function is determined by Cfunc contextual cues (i.e., controlling the specific behavioral functions produced during the act of relating). Specifying these types of contextual control is essential in determining how entailment and transformation effects combine in any given instance of what RFT refers to as arbitrarily applicable relational responding (AARR). For example, if a friend told you that their new pet dog was called "Bongo," then the word "called" could function as a Crel for coordination (between the word "Bongo" and your friend's new pet dog). If your friend then says, "Bongo is really friendly," then the phrase "really friendly" may function as a Cfunc for actualizing some of the functions of a "friendly" dog (tail wagging, bouncy, safe, etc.). Of course, "tail wagging" and other phrases may also be *entailed* with the events to which they refer. However, in this example, we are highlighting their Cfunc properties to illustrate how RFT uses the defining properties of a frame (both Crel and Cfunc contextual control) to describe how verbal stimuli produce their effects in the natural environment of the wider verbal community.

We have just provided a description of the core properties of relational framing, which is seen as providing a behavioral unit of analysis for studying human language and cognition. On balance, RFT is not a "nativist" theory of language, in the sense that AARR is deemed to be learned behavior. That is, RFT aims to provide an explanation for establishing different classes of relational operants, or AARR, and their combination into increasingly complex networks of relations. For illustrative purposes, consider one of the most basic classes of AARR, naming. Young children may learn to point or look at a specific object upon hearing the name for that object, and they may also learn to produce the spoken name for the object. Across multiple exemplars of coordinating multiple objects and their names across many contexts, the operant class of coordination is established to the point that direct learning is no longer required in the presence of novel objects. That is, derived relating (coordination in this naming example) is established in the child's behavioral repertoire. For example, if the child is subsequently shown a novel object and is told its name, the child may subsequently name the object without having to be trained to do so. That is, once the generalized relational response of coordinating objects and their names is established, simply hearing the name for a novel object may "spontaneously" generate the appropriate naming response. Crucially, when this pattern of relational responding has been established, the generalized relational response may then be applied to any stimuli, given appropriate contextual cues (e.g., "this is a"). We will return to the important issue of learning histories involved in AARR in a later section.

According to an updated version of RFT, the ability to learn to AARR emerges from the evolution of highly cooperative behaviors within the human species (Hayes & Sanford, 2014). This updated version of RFT still maintains that AARR, for any given individual, involves years of increasingly complex interactions with the wider verbal community within which the individual resides. However, a more detailed treatment of the phylogenic and ontogenic origins of AARR is now emerging in the RFT literature (e.g., Hayes et al., 2017); we will incorporate these developments into this article.

RFT: The Role of Human Cooperation in the Evolution of AARR

As a behavioral account of human language and cognition, RFT traditionally focused on the learning experiences that occur within the lifetime of the individual. This focus is understandable because the theory has been driven by a pragmatic concern with predicting and influencing human language and cognition itself in clinical, educational, and wider social settings. On balance, it has always been recognized that the ability to acquire the relational operants identified by RFT, with relative ease, is likely to have emerged from a particular evolutionary history, but until recently work in this area has been limited (e.g., Hayes & Sanford, 2014; Wilson et al., 2014).

Wilson (2007) summarized human evolution as the "three C's": cognition, culture, and cooperation. While all three concepts were considered in early renditions of RFT, it appears that cooperation was somewhat underplayed, if not largely ignored. According to the first book-length treatment of RFT, Hayes, Barnes-Holmes, et al. (2001) suggested that mutual entailment (the bidirectional relational responding that may occur between two stimuli) in a listener could enhance or support avoidance of predators, even if entailment was not yet present as part of a vocal or speaking repertoire. In addition, it was argued that this small difference could generate a group of listeners who could then reinforce mutually entailed responses in a speaking/vocal repertoire. Upon reflection, this account relies heavily on the evolution of mutual entailment as an adaptation of cognition in listening responses and then spreads to speaking or vocal responses, thereby leading to increased social cooperation throughout the wider group or culture. In contrast to this account, Hayes and Sanford (2014) argued that it is more evolutionarily viable to assume that human cooperation was the primary driver in the evolution of mutual entailing, rather than the other way around. Indeed, as Hayes and Sanford point out, a wealth of empirical data support the argument that human cooperation was established by multilevel selection of cooperation itself because it provided advantages for human group competition, which occurred alongside the cultural suppression of individual selfishness.

From an RFT perspective, a critical feature of human cooperation involves pointing and grunting, for example, which provided humans with highly important behavioral skills, such as social referencing and joint attention. These skills, it is argued, increased the likelihood that more advanced forms of cooperation, involving the emission of specific vocal sounds, would be selected or reinforced, as is the case with young children. For example, if a young child orients to a caregiver and then toward a toy while emitting a vocal sound (e.g., "eh") and tries to reach for the toy, the caregiver may reinforce this cooperative act by giving the toy to the child. As Hayes and Sanford (2014) state: "The entire exchange will build cooperation, perspective taking, and joint attention as patterns that are maintained within the group because it is a functionally useful communication exchange. If we unpack this highly likely sequence it means that in the context of high levels of cooperation, and adequate skills in joint attention, social referencing, and perspective taking, any characteristic vocalization in the presence of a desired object would likely lead to reinforced instances of symmetry or mutual entailment" (p. 122).

According to an updated version of RFT, which focuses on cooperation as a key driver of derived relational responding itself (AARR), the critical behavioral history does not begin with speaking or even simply listening (in a manner that involves "understanding" what was said in a symbolic sense). Rather, it begins with mutually entailed orienting (Barnes-Holmes & Sivaraman, 2020), which we will argue is a key precursor for establishing AARR. A potential "marker" for this type of orienting, which appears to be unique to the human species, is bidirectional orienting, characterized by a child orienting (e.g., looking at) back and forth between a caregiver and an object or stimulus toward which the caregiver is oriented.[1] Mutually entailed orienting should therefore be seen as a type of transgenerational behavior (i.e., a class of behavior that stretches across ontogeny and phylogeny) and is selected by reinforcement contingencies operating within the lifetime of the individual. In this sense, an updated version of RFT seeks increased scope in terms of linking directly with a modern evolutionary science (e.g., Wilson et al., 2014), which argues that evolution operates at multiple levels (e.g., genetic, cellular, symbolic, and cultural). As noted above, therefore, the critical behavioral history for AARR does not begin with listening and speaking (with understanding). Rather, it starts with one of the most basic of human cooperative acts, that is, mutually entailed orienting. This act provides the infant with an opportunity to continue interacting with the caregiver as a dyad, which likely serves as a reinforcer for continuing to engage in such acts of cooperation (i.e., gradually creating a dynamical feedback loop between cooperation and AARR).

The critical importance of mutually entailed orienting cannot be underestimated because it allows caregivers to establish appetitive and aversive evoking functions for stimuli in the child's environment. Once a caregiver and an infant are engaging in mutually entailed orienting, the caregiver can then orient the child toward a particular stimulus and encourage the child to approach "safe" and avoid "dangerous" stimuli. Mutually entailed orienting may thus also involve establishing specific orienting and evoking functions for particular stimuli. For example, if a caregiver shouts loudly when the child approaches a dangerous stimulus (e.g., an insect with a powerful venom), that stimulus will likely acquire strong orienting and (aversive) evoking properties for the child. Furthermore, when an infant engages in mutually entailed orienting, even items that the caregiver is simply oriented toward, without issuing any sort of warning signal, may acquire relatively positive evoking (approach) functions for the infant. Thus, mutually entailed orienting is more accurately labeled mutually entailed orienting and evoking. As a listening repertoire develops, mutually entailing and evoking functions for particular stimuli become related, in an arbitrarily applicable manner, to specific sounds (i.e., words). Gradually, therefore, a new response unit involving relating, orienting, and evoking is established for the child. In an updated version of RFT, we refer to this response unit as the ROE (pronounced "row," which is an acronym for relating, orienting, and evoking); we will return to this conceptual unit of analysis later. At this point, however, it is important to understand that the term *mutually entailed* (orienting and evoking) serves to highlight that such cooperative acts occur in parallel with establishing a basic listener repertoire (e.g., a caregiver rarely engages a child in orienting and evoking without also emitting language-appropriate sounds, such as "Look, it's teddy," when orienting the child toward a toy teddy-bear).

We should emphasize that mutually entailed orienting/evoking are not simply new terms for mutual eye gaze, joint attention, and social referencing. The latter concepts have no "technical weight" within RFT itself, and thus by introducing these new concepts (mutually entailed orienting/evoking), an updated version of RFT seeks to establish explanatory depth. As already noted, the new concepts link the behavioral account of human language and cognition more directly to the evolution science argument that human cooperation drove, at least initially, the evolution of human language and cognition itself. In addition, the concepts of mutual eye gaze, joint attention, and social referencing are relatively topographical (e.g., all three behaviors involve mutual eye contact between two individuals). The term *mutually entailed orienting/evoking* aims to establish a functional-analytic-abstractive quality to the conceptual analysis of the behavioral topographies usually associated with the terms *joint attention* and *social referencing* (and *perspective-taking* more generally).

To appreciate the point being made here, imagine a dog owner trained his dog to fetch an object and bring it to him by pointing at it, or even by simply gazing at it and shouting "fetch." One might argue that this interaction was clearly cooperative and involved at least some element of joint attention (and perhaps even social referencing) because the dog and its owner both needed to attend to the same object for the dog to fetch it. In addition, a number of studies have shown that some dogs can follow human pointing to locations where food was hidden (e.g., Hare et al., 1998). According to an updated version of RFT, however, these interactions would not be defined as mutually entailed orienting for the dog, unless it was functioning as part of an ontogenic and phylogenic history for AARR for that animal. Or to put it another way, if the cooperative interaction is part of an evolutionary history that leads to the establishment of AARR (and ROEing) for the dog, then the dog could be considered as engaging in mutually entailed orienting; if there is little or no evidence of AARR in the dog's behavioral repertoire in the past (as a species) or in the future as an individual organism, then the term *mutually entailed orienting/evoking* should not be applied to the dog's behavior in this example of joint attention (or social referencing).

In emphasizing the importance of cooperation as a driver of AARR and introducing the concept of mutually entailed orienting, the potential origins of contextual control over the transformation of functions becomes apparent. When an infant engages in mutually entailed orienting, even items that are simply oriented toward by the caregiver, without issuing any sort of danger-warning signal, may become more valuable than other items in the environment and acquire relatively positive evoking (approach) functions for the infant. It is important to note that during the acts of cooperation involved in mutually entailed orienting/evoking, the caregiver does not necessarily become appetitive or aversive as a consequence of their reactions to the pleasurable and dangerous items in the environment. This may be the case at first—for example, if a child pulls away from or aggresses toward a caregiver when they shout at the child as a warning not to approach a dangerous object. However, an infant quickly learns to respond to the objects as being appetitive or aversive, and not to the caregiver. In effect, mutually entailed orienting and evoking between the caregiver and numerous stimuli serves to establish the caregiver as a stimulus that transforms the functions of novel stimuli and events in the environment while maintaining generally appetitive functions for the caregiver. In effect, a caregiver's actions or behaviors may transform the functions of a novel stimulus, but the caregiver appears to function as a context for limiting the transformation of functions to that stimulus.

This control (or limiting) over the transformation of functions could be seen as the basis for Cfunc control in RFT generally. This type of contextual control is seen in RFT as critical in selecting the specific functions that are transformed in any act of relating. For example, when an older child learns to relate the written word "chocolate" to actual chocolate they rarely attempt to eat the written word. Thus, it can be seen that the early cooperative acts involved in mutually entailed orienting and evoking in a sense provide the basis for the more sophisticated types of contextual control that are required as derived relational responding involving arbitrary stimuli is established in the child's listening and speaking repertoires.

As mutually entailed listening and speaking are established through ongoing interactions between the child and its caregivers, extended cooperation further facilitates the adaptation of the species by allowing for more complex adaptations of the functional units, such as combinatorial entailment. This increasing complexity in derived relational responding involves the use of symbols and the ability to problem-solve in the natural and social environment. According to this updated version of RFT, therefore, cooperation facilitates more useful forms of cognition rather than cognition producing more useful forms of cooperation, although it is important to appreciate that the relationship is likely nonlinear and dynamical (i.e., cooperation generates increasingly advanced cognition, which in turn feeds back into generating increasingly complex forms of cooperation).

The Relational Development of Increasingly Complex Patterns of AARR

Once the generic response unit of AARR (i.e., the ROE) is established, it allows for the evolution of increasingly complex relational responding inside the ROE, such as relational networking, the relating of relations (e.g., analogy and metaphor), and the relating of entire relational networks to other relational networks (e.g., extracting common themes from different narratives). An updated version of RFT has proposed a new multilevel framework for conceptualizing this increasing complexity in relational responding in terms of five levels of relational development: (1) mutually entailing, (2) combinatorial entailing, (3) relational networking, (4) relating relations, and (5) relating relational networks.

Before considering this framework in greater detail, it is important to consider the generic RFT explanation for establishing different classes of relational operants or AARR, known as relational frames, and their combination into increasingly complex networks of relations. Imagine, for example, that the wider verbal community directly reinforces a young child for pointing to or looking at a household pet such as a rabbit upon hearing the word "rabbit" and/or the rabbit's name (e.g., Roger). The child is also directly reinforced for producing other appropriate naming responses such as saying "rabbit" or "Roger" when this pet is observed, or in response to appropriate contextual cues such as "what is the rabbit's name?" or "what is this?" Across multiple exemplars of coordinating multiple other stimuli with their names in multiple other contexts, the operant class of coordination comes to be established, such that direct reinforcement is no longer required in the presence of novel stimuli. That is, derived coordination is established in the child's behavioral repertoire. For example, if the child is subsequently shown a picture of a kangaroo alongside the written word "kangaroo" and is told its name, upon being presented with a relevant picture or the word, the child may then say "That's a kangaroo!" in the absence of prompting or direct reinforcement. That is, once the generalized relational response of coordinating pictorial stimuli, spoken stimuli, and written words is established, directly reinforcing a subset of the relating behaviors "spontaneously" generates the complete set. Crucially, when this pattern of relational responding has been established, the generalized relational response may then be applied to any stimuli given appropriate contextual cues (e.g., "is").

In the same way that derived coordination responding was established above in the presence of appropriate contextual cues (Crel; e.g., "is a" to specify the relationship between a rabbit and "Roger"), other cues such as "smaller than" or "faster than" would be established across multiple exemplars to specify other patterns of relational frames. Across time, this generalized derived relational responding becomes arbitrarily applicable. The relating is not based solely on the physical or formal relations between and among the stimuli, but on additional contextual cues that determine the appropriate relational responses (again, in the absence of direct reinforcement).

For example, someone can abstractly say and understand that "a pig is bigger than a centipede" (which of course it is), despite the word "pig" being physically smaller and audibly shorter. Thus, the relationship between the two stimuli becomes arbitrarily applicable and is no longer determined by length or other physical characteristics. Subsequently, following a sufficient number of relevant exemplars to establish appropriate patterns of relational frames, you could be told that "A is bigger than B" and thus respond that "B must be smaller than A" without any knowledge of what A and B actually are.

Early research in RFT demonstrated a number of distinct patterns of AARR or relational frames. These patterns included: coordination (or sameness; e.g., Carr et al., 2000; Dunne et al., 2014; Luciano et al., 2007), distinction (or difference; e.g., Dunne et al., 2014; Roche & Barnes, 1997; Steele & Hayes, 1991), opposition (e.g., Barnes-Holmes et al., 2004; Dunne et al., 2014), comparison (e.g., Barnes-Holmes et al., 2004; Berens & Hayes, 2007; Dunne et al., 2014), temporality (e.g., O'Hora et al., 2004, 2005), hierarchy (e.g., Foody et al., 2013; Gil et al., 2012; Griffee & Dougher, 2002; Slattery & Stewart, 2014), and deictics (or perspective taking; e.g., Barnes-Holmes, 2001; McHugh et al., 2004, 2007). In addition, some early studies demonstrated the transformation of functions (as described previously) in accordance with specific relational frames (e.g., Dougher et al., 2007; Dymond & Barnes, 1995; Roche & Barnes, 1997). Furthermore, research demonstrated that relational framing could be shown with numerous experimental preparations, thus indicating that the phenomenon was not tied specifically to any particular experimental procedure. Finally, and indeed critically, empirical evidence emerged to support the argument that exposure to multiple exemplars appeared to be essential in establishing specific frames (e.g., Barnes-Holmes et al., 2004; Lipkens et al., 1993; Luciano et al., 2007). Thus, the argument that relational framing could be thought of as a generalized relational operant (i.e., established by appropriate multiple exemplars) gained considerable traction (see Barnes-Holmes & Barnes-Holmes, 2000; Healy et al., 2000).

COMPLEX RELATIONAL NETWORKING

According to RFT, the combination of relational frames into increasingly complex relational networks helps to explain scaling up to complex levels of human language and cognition, such as rule following and analogical reasoning. For RFT, a rule or instruction can be thought of as a network of relational frames, typically involving temporal and coordination relations accompanied by appropriate contextual cues that transform specific behavioral functions within the network (Barnes-Holmes et al., 2001). Take, for example, the instruction "If the alarm clock rings, then get out of bed." This simple rule involves frames of coordination between the words "alarm clock," "rings," and "get out of bed" and the physical alarm clock, the sound it makes when it rings, and the action of getting out of bed. The words "if" and "then" function here as contextual cues for establishing a temporal relation between the sound and the act of getting up (i.e., sound before getting up). Insofar as one actually gets up when the alarm clock rings, the functions of the sound itself have, in principle, been transformed by the network such that it now controls this specific behavior in this context. This conceptual analysis of rules as complex relational networks has also been successfully modeled in the lab (e.g., O'Hora et al., 2004, 2014). Excessive reliance on rules at the expense of contact with direct environmental contingencies has been at the core of the ACT explanation for human psychological suffering since the conception of the approach (Hayes et al., 1999). And while little experimental work has explored the complexities involved in excessive rule-following as derived relational networks, recent research has successfully begun to do so (see Harte, Barnes-Holmes, Barnes-Holmes, & Kissi, 2020). We will return to this discussion in a later section.

RELATING RELATIONS AND RELATING RELATIONAL NETWORKS

In scaling up in complexity again, RFT may readily explain other advanced levels of human language and cognition, such as metaphorical and analogical reasoning (Barnes et al., 1997). For example, consider the simple analogy "a hammer is to a mallet as a comb is to a brush." In this case, hammer and mallet are coordinated, as are comb and brush (via the cue "is to"). Furthermore, a coordination relation connects both of these coordination relations via the cue "as" (see Stewart & Barnes-Holmes, 2004, for a review of empirical work in this area). The example involves the relating of relations because the four relata (comb, brush, mallet, and hammer) do not "collapse" into a single relational network but involve relating one relation to another. In this sense, relating relations appears to involve responding relationally to one's own relational responding—that is, coordinating the hammer–mallet relational response with the comb–brush relational response. Critically, this level of relational responding likely involves deictic relational responding (see the next paragraph). At an even more advanced level of AARR, RFT proposes relating complex relational networks to other complex relational networks (Hayes, Gifford, et al., 2001). Empirical research in this area is somewhat limited (Ruiz & Luciano, 2011), but highly advanced verbal abilities such as complex problem solving and comparisons of extended narratives would likely involve this level of relating.

PERSPECTIVE-TAKING AND DEICTIC RELATIONS

A considerable body of conceptual and empirical research has been conducted on deictic relational responding in RFT, which is seen to be critical for the emergence of a verbal self, and perspective-taking. In an updated version of RFT, mutually entailed orienting would be seen as providing a critically important historical context for the gradual emergence of a verbal self. Specifically, it involves cooperation between two separate individuals—the infant and the caregiver—while the caregiver utters sounds (words) that later come to participate in arbitrary relations with the infant (e.g., the child's name), the caregiver (e.g., "Daddy"), and the stimulus they are orienting themselves toward (e.g., "teddy"). For example, a father might pick up a toy teddy, orient the child toward the teddy (i.e., hold the teddy in front of the child), and ask, "Would you like daddy to give you the teddy?" Initially, of course, the words in the question have no symbolic functions for the infant, but this example of mutually entailed orienting is a critical part of the history that serves to establish those symbolic functions across thousands of such cooperative episodes in the child's first months and years of life. As the words in these types of questions gradually acquire their appropriate symbolic functions, and the ROE as a generic response unit becomes established, deictic relating (see below) may then emerge.

For RFT, three core relations are involved in deictic relating (Barnes-Holmes, 2001): the interpersonal relation, I–You; the spatial relation, Here–There; and the temporal relation, Now–Then. These three types of relations combine into the basic or simplest deictic relational frame, which involves locating oneself in time and space relative to another individual. The core idea is that as children learn to respond in accordance with these deictic relations, they are essentially learning to relate the self to others in the context of particular times and spaces. For example, imagine a very young child being asked, "What did you have for breakfast at home this morning?" while they are eating lunch in a restaurant later that day with their family. If the child responds simply by referring to what, for example, their sister is currently eating, they may be corrected and told, "No, that's what your sister is now eating here. What did you eat earlier at home for breakfast?" Ongoing refinement of the three deictic relations in this way thus allows the child to respond appropriately to questions about their own behavior in relation to that of others, as it occurs in specific times and places (e.g., McHugh et al., 2004).

Deictic relational responding is viewed as being relatively advanced because it involves learning to respond to one's own relational responding. As noted previously, this level of relational responding is likely involved in relating relations, and certainly in relating entire relational networks to other relational networks. In simple terms, a child would find it difficult to relate two separate relational responses if they could not "locate" those relational responses in a specific time and space. Indeed, this basic argument was recently elaborated by Kavanagh et al. (2020) in their presentation of an RFT interpretation of the classic false belief perspective-taking task. We will return to this issue later.

A Hyperdimensional Multilevel Framework for Conceptualizing the Dynamics of AARR

Recall that an updated version of RFT proposes five key levels of behavioral development. In addition, the updated version of the theory emphasizes the dynamic nature of the relating activity that may occur along four dimensions, namely, coherence, complexity, derivation, and flexibility. Each level of the framework intersects with these four dimensions, thus yielding 20 units of analysis (see Figure 4.1; the reader should note that the figure also illustrates how the ROE fits into the framework).

Coherence refers to the extent to which a pattern of derived relational responding coheres or is consistent with previously established patterns of such responding. For instance, if an individual is told that a dog is smaller than a bear and is then told that a bear is larger than a dog, the second statement would likely be deemed coherent with the first. In this case, coherence would be high because the overall pattern ($A < B = B > A$) coheres with the manner in which such verbal relations have been established by the wider verbal community (e.g., there are few instances in which an English-speaking listener would reinforce, or not correct, the statement, "If A is bigger than B, then B is bigger than A").

Complexity refers to the level of detail or density of a particular pattern of derived relational responding. For example, a mutually entailed relation of coordination may be seen as less complex than a mutually entailed relation of comparison because the former involves only

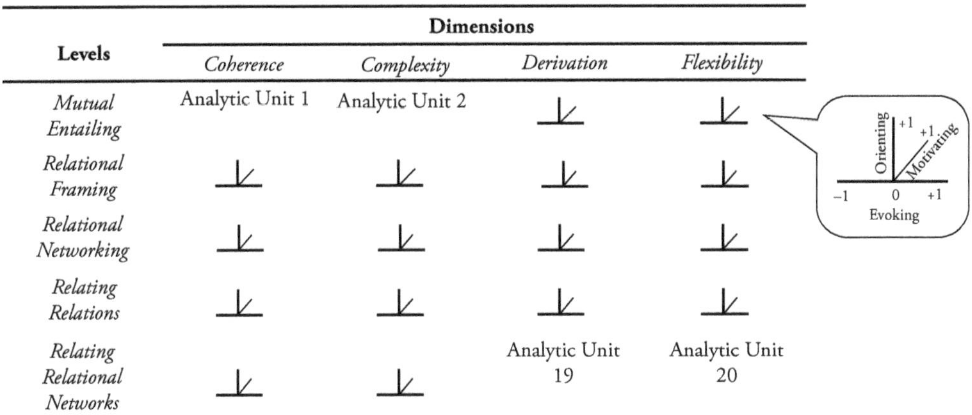

Figure 4.1. A visual representation of the Hyper-Dimensional, Multi-Level (HDML) framework

Note. 20 intersections between the five levels and four dimensions of arbitrarily applicable relational responding, combined with orienting and evoking functions, and motivating variables. Note that motivating is represented by a broken line because its impact is inferred based on changes in orienting and evoking functions. Overall, this figure aims to capture the dynamic nature of AARR (i.e., relating, orienting, evoking, and motivating; the ROE-M). Reprinted by permission from Springer Nature: Finn, M., Barnes-Holmes, D., & McEnteggart, C. (2018). Exploring the single-trial-type-dominance-effect on the IRAP: Developing a differential arbitrarily applicable relational responding effects (DAARRE) model. *The Psychological Record*, 68(1), 11–25. https://doi.org/10.1007/s40732-017-0262-z

one type of relation (e.g., if A is the same as B, then B is the same as A), whereas the latter involves two types (if A is larger than B, then B is smaller than A).

Derivation refers to the extent to which a particular pattern of derived relational responding has been "practiced" or emitted in the past. Each time a relation is derived, its derivation reduces because it acquires its own history that extends beyond the derivation that is made from the "baseline" relation. Imagine, for example, that an individual learns that bears are larger than dogs and thus derives that dogs are smaller than bears. The first time that the "a dog is smaller than a bear" relation is derived, it is derived "directly" from the "a bear is larger than a dog" baseline relation. However, as the individual subsequently continues to relate dogs as smaller than bears, that relational response gradually acquires its own history, rendering it less and less derived from the original baseline relation (irrespective of whether or not it is reinforced directly).

Flexibility refers to the extent to which a given instance of derived relational responding may be modified by current contextual variables. As a simple example, imagine a young child who is asked to respond with the wrong answer to the question, "Which is bigger, a bear or a dog?" The quicker the child responds with "dog," the more flexible the relational responding (see O'Toole & Barnes-Holmes, 2009). Of course, flexibility is always context-dependent, and thus if the child had been told previously not to give a wrong answer when asked to do so, it would be difficult to use the production of a correct or wrong answer as an indication of flexibility.

The levels of relational development and the dimensions along which they may vary were recently formalized within a Hyper-Dimensional Multi-Level (HDML; Barnes-Holmes et al., 2020) framework for conceptualizing and analyzing the dynamics involved in AARR (see Figure 4.1). As mentioned earlier, an updated version of RFT proposes that most, if not all, human psychological events involve the ROE. As an illustrative example, a mutually entailed relation (e.g., "hornets are dangerous") may be conceptualized as varying in coherence, complexity, derivation, and flexibility. In general terms, the relation between hornets and danger may be relatively high in coherence if the statement coheres with similar assertions (e.g., "a small number of hornet stings can kill"); relatively low in complexity if understanding the statement involves a limited number of other relational responses (e.g., the words "hornet" and "dangerous" are directly related to actual hornets and danger); relatively low in derivation (e.g., if similar statements have been heard many times in the past); and low in flexibility (e.g., if it is difficult to modify or "challenge" the perceived truth of the statement). Critically, this relational activity is seen to interact in a nonlinear and dynamical manner with the orienting and evoking functions of stimulating events for humans as they navigate their environments. For example, the statement ("hornets are dangerous") may increase orienting and (aversive) evoking functions for hornets if the statement is uttered just before entering an area where they are commonly found. This updated RFT framework for conceptualizing the dynamical interplay among relating, orienting, and evoking (i.e., ROEing) has been defined as hyperdimensional and multilevel (i.e., the HDML framework; Barnes-Holmes et al., 2020).[2]

A graphical representation of the HDML is presented in Figure 4.1. Each cell of the grid, which shows the intersection between the five levels and four dimensions, contains an inverted "T" with a third dashed line representing motivating variables. This symbol represents the orienting and evoking functions that may occur within each of the 20 functional-analytic abstractive units of relating. Conceptually, orienting is seen as lying on a continuum, on the vertical axis, from complete absence (0) to strongest orienting response possible (1). Evoking is seen as lying on a continuum, on the horizontal axis, from the strongest aversive response possible (–1) to the strongest appetitive response possible (+1), with 0 representing the absence of either an aversive or appetitive reaction. Again, it is important to emphasize the inseparable, interactive, and nonlinear nature of the relating, orienting, and evoking (ROEing) that the HDML aims to capture. Returning to the "hornets are dangerous" example above, let us imagine that you are shown some pictures of hornets and told that they are quite dangerous just before you enter a forest where they are commonly found (a relational event). As a result, orienting toward (or noticing) any insect that resembles a hornet and reacting aversively toward it may be more likely as you make your way through the forest. In contrast, imagine that you are provided with no warning about hornets before you enter the forest. You may be less likely to orient aversively toward a hornet, should you come across one, but you may still engage in some level of relating, such as emitting the simple self-generated rule (i.e., relational network), "That looks quite nasty, I'll keep my distance." In essence, the concept of the ROE is designed to capture the constant, dynamical, and nonlinear nature of the core unit of responding that characterizes human psychological events.

The current version of the HDML, as noted, includes an inverted "T" with a dashed line representing motivating variables. Strictly speaking, motivating variables are not generic response functions (similar to orienting and evoking), but rather constitute a ubiquitous property of all psychological events that impact upon the ROE itself. Hence, motivating is represented with the broken line, which is scaled from 0 to 1, indicating the putative strength of a variable(s) that impacts upon orienting and/or evoking functions in some specific manner. In this sense, the influence of motivating variables is always inferred through changes in measures of orienting and/or evoking functions. We have chosen to include motivating variables in this manner in light of a recent study (Gomes et al., 2020) that reported the impact of three different motivating conditions upon a measure that appears to be sensitive to orienting and evoking functions. The critical point is that the concept of the ROE remains largely unchanged. Nevertheless, the inclusion of a motivating variable indicates that motivating variables are always at play in codetermining the relative values of the orienting and evoking functions within each of the 20 units of analysis contained within the HDML framework. In recognizing the importance of motivating variables, the ROE acronym has been modified to ROE-M (pronounced "roam").

From an updated RFT perspective, the set of relational abilities and associated orienting and evoking functions contained within the ROE-M evolved into complex forms of communication and problem solving in only a few thousand years. Indeed, the ability to engage in ROE-Ming appears to be a defining characteristic of the human species and allows us to predict and influence our environment in increasingly sophisticated and powerful ways. From this perspective, once ROE-Ming evolves, the natural environment becomes thick and rich with stimuli that are symbolic, rather than direct-acting, as they appear to be for nonhuman species. For example, symbolic stimuli can be used to form new meanings and to construct new realities detached from direct experience (e.g., fiction, poetry, metaphor). As such, the transmission of behaviors from one individual to another and from one generation to the next is increased dramatically. This ultimately leads to greater variation in behavior and the potential for acquiring new behaviors that increase survival at multiple levels—individuals, groups, and species.

Updating RFT: Some Recent Empirical Advances

At this point, it seems important to consider some of the more recent empirical research that connects directly with the conceptual developments we have considered. To this end, we will briefly present research that focuses on (1) orienting functions, (2) evoking functions, (3) motivating variables, (4) relational networks (as rules), and (5) relating relational networks (in perspective-taking).

ORIENTING FUNCTIONS

The potential importance of recognizing the role of orienting functions in dealing with the dynamics of AARR first became apparent in Finn et al. (2018), a study using a procedure that had been developed to measure the relative strength or probability of AARR. This procedure, known as the implicit relational assessment procedure (IRAP), is a computer-based program that requires participants to respond quickly and accurately to specific stimuli deemed to be either consistent or inconsistent with participants' preexperimentally established learning histories. On each trial, participants are required to choose one of two response options (e.g., True or False), indicating the relation between the label (presented at the top of the screen) and target (presented in the center of the screen) stimulus. On some blocks of trials, participants are required to respond in a manner coherent with their preexperimental learning histories, while on other blocks they are required to respond in a manner incoherent with these histories. The general assumption that underpinned early IRAP research was that, all things being equal, relational responding should be quicker and more accurate across blocks of trials that require relational responding that is coherent with a participant's learning history than across blocks that require responding that does not cohere with that history. For example, an IRAP might present the word "flowers" or "insects" as label stimuli at the top of the screen, positive or negative adjectives as target stimuli in the center of the screen, and the response options True and False on the bottom left- and right-hand side of the screen. During some blocks of trials, participants would be required to respond in a history-consistent manner (i.e., choosing "True" on *Flowers-Positive* and *Insects-Negative* trials and "False" on *Flowers-Negative* and *Insects-Positive* trials), while on other blocks of trials the opposite response pattern would be required (e.g., responding "False" on a *Flowers-Positive* trial).

The typical IRAP may be conceptualized as comprising four separate types of trials involving a 2 x 2 crossover of the label and target stimuli. Following on from the pleasant-flowers example above, the trial types could be summarized as *Flowers-Pleasant, Flowers-Unpleasant, Insects-Pleasant,* and *Insects-Unpleasant.* The primary datum from the IRAP is response latency, measured in milliseconds, and is defined as the time that elapses from the onset of stimulus presentation on each trial to the emission of a correct response. As we have explained, the basic assumption was that participants would produce response biases in which the size of the IRAP effects (the difference score between latencies/accuracies on history-coherent versus history-incoherent trials) indicates the probability of responding in the natural environment. Thus, for example, one would expect an individual who "loved" flowers and "hated" insects to produce relatively large IRAP effects in the predicted direction.

Since the IRAP's development, many studies have demonstrated its utility in measuring response biases in a range of areas and domains such as age (e.g., Cullen et al., 2009), gender (e.g., Cartwright et al., 2017), race (e.g., Barnes-Holmes et al., 2010), religion (e.g., Hughes et al., 2017), and forensics (e.g., Dawson et al., 2009). The measure has also been used to predict racial group membership (Power et al., 2017) and parental smoking status (Cagney et al., 2017) over and above that of standard self-report measures. Finally, a meta-analysis of clinically related IRAP studies reported a relatively high level of predictive validity (Vahey et al., 2015).

A core assumption of early IRAP research was that responding would be faster and more accurate when the procedure required response patterns that were coherent with preexisting patterns of AARR than when it required patterns that were incoherent. Theoretically then, we could therefore assume that the IRAP effects for all four trial types should be roughly equal and in the same direction. However, this simple assumption did not always turn out to be the case (e.g., Finn et al., 2016; O'Shea et al., 2016). For instance, Finn et al. (2018) employed what they called a "shapes and colors" IRAP, and although all of the effects were generally in the predicted direction, the effect for the *color–color* trial type was significantly larger than that for the other three trial types (*color–shape, shape–color,* and *shape–shape*; see Figure 4.2). The smaller effect sizes for the *color–shape* and *shape–color* trial types could be explained by the fact

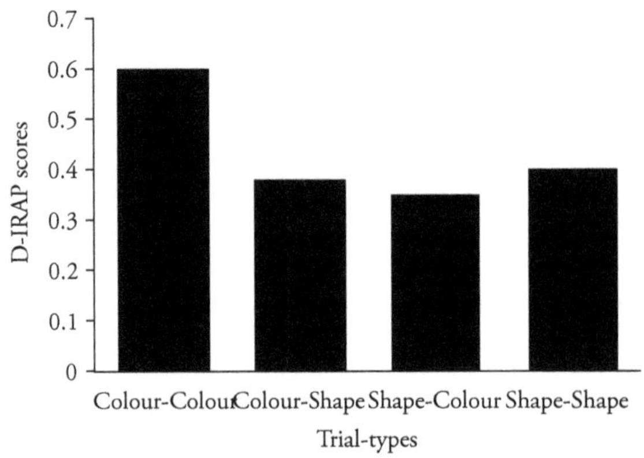

Figure 4.2 General pattern of trial-type effects produced by the Shapes-and-Colours IRAP

Note. In the Finn et al. (2018) study, participants were divided into two experimental groups based on experience with the IRAP (but this is not represented in the current figure). Reprinted by permission from Springer Nature: Barnes-Holmes, D., Barnes-Holmes, Y. & McEnteggart, C. (2020). Updating RFT (More Field than Frame) and Its Implications for Process-based Therapy. *The Psychological Record, 70,* 605–624. https://doi.org/10.1007/s40732-019-00372-3

that responding during history-coherent blocks of trials required choosing False rather than True. More specifically, if there was an inherent response bias toward confirming rather than disconfirming relations, then reduced effect sizes would be expected when False was the correct response option (i.e., for an incoherent relation, such *color–shape*). This explanation could not be used, however, to account for a larger effect for the *color–color* relative to the *shape–shape* trial type because they both involved responding "True" during history-coherent blocks. In grappling with an explanation for why this latter trial type difference emerged, the authors of the study (Keuleers et al., 2010) argued that the color words employed within the IRAP occurred with higher frequency in natural language relative to the shape words. As such, it was possible that the color words produced a stronger orienting response than their shape counterparts because the concept of color, and color words in general, were simply more salient than shapes for the average participant (because color words are used far more often in everyday discourse).

In developing a formal explanation for the differential trial-type effects, Finn et al. (2018) proposed the differential arbitrarily applicable relational responding effects (DAARRE) model (pronounced "dare"). According to this model, the differential trial-type effects may be explained by the extent to which the Cfunc and Crel properties of the stimuli contained within an IRAP cohere with specific properties of the response options across blocks of trials. Recall that, for RFT, each instance of relating occurs under two types of contextual control. One kind specifies the particular type of relation defining the relational response (Crel), and the other specifies the particular behavioral functions that are transformed in accordance with the response (Cfunc). The reader should also note that response options such as "True" and "False" are referred to as relational coherence indicators (RCIs) because they are often used to indicate the coherence or incoherence between the label and target stimuli that are presented within an IRAP (see Maloney & Barnes-Holmes, 2016, for a detailed treatment of RCIs). A visual representation of the basic DAARRE model, as it applies to the Shapes-and-Colours IRAP, is presented in Figure 4.3.

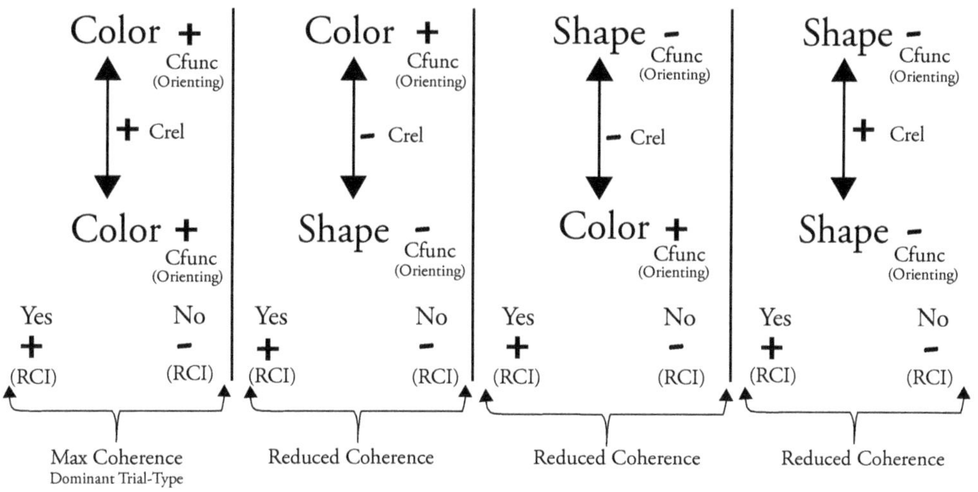

Figure 4.3 A DAARRE model analysis of the Shapes-and-Colours IRAP

Note. The "+" and "–" refer to the relative positivity of the transformation of function property (Cfunc) for each label and target stimulus, the entailment property between them (Crel), and the relational coherence indicator (RCI). Reprinted by permission from Springer Nature: Barnes-Holmes, D., Barnes-Holmes, Y. & McEnteggart, C. (2020). Updating RFT (More Field than Frame) and Its Implications for Process-based Therapy. *The Psychological Record*, 70, 605–624. https://doi.org/10.1007/s40732-019-00372-3

Three key sources of behavioral influence are highlighted: (1) the relation between the label and target stimuli (Crels); (2) the orienting functions of the label and target stimuli (Cfuncs); and (3) the coherence functions of the two RCIs (e.g., "True" and "False"). As mentioned above, the two critical trial types here were *color–color* and *shape–shape*. As can be readily observed, the Cfunc property for colors is labeled positive and the Cfunc property for shapes is labeled negative. This is in line with the suggestion that, based on differential frequencies in natural language, color-related stimuli likely possess stronger orienting functions relative to shape-related stimuli (the negative labeling for shapes should not be taken to specify a negative orienting function but simply an orienting function that is relatively weaker than that of colors). Relations between the label and target stimuli are labeled with plus or minus signs to indicate the extent to which they do or do not cohere, based on the participants' relevant history. Thus, the color–color relation is labeled with a plus sign (i.e., coherence), whereas the color–shape relation is labeled with a minus sign (i.e., incoherence). Finally, the two response options are similarly labeled to indicate their functions as either coherence or incoherence indicators. In the current example, "True" (+) would typically be used in natural language to indicate coherence and "False" (–) to indicate incoherence.

To appreciate the DAARRE model explanation for the differential trial-type effects, consider first the *color–color* trial type and note that all the Crel and Cfunc properties are labeled with plus signs. Additionally, the RCI that is deemed correct on history-coherent trials is also labeled with a plus sign; this is the only trial type that involves four plus signs. During history-coherent trials, therefore, this trial type may be considered maximally coherent.[3] By contrast, during incoherent trials, there is no coherence between the properties of the Crel, Cfuncs (all plus signs), and the required RCI (minus sign). According to the DAARRE model, this clear contrast in levels of coherence across blocks of trials results in a relatively large IRAP effect. Now consider the *shape–shape* trial type. During history-coherent trials, participants are required to choose the same RCI as is required for the *color–color* trial type, but here the property of the RCI (plus sign) does not cohere with the Cfunc properties of the label and target stimuli (both minus signs). During history-incoherent trials, however, the RCI coheres with the Cfunc properties but not with the Crel property (plus sign). Thus, the differences in coherence between history-coherent and history-incoherent trials across these two trial types are not equal (i.e., the difference is greater for the *color–color* trial type). Finally, as becomes apparent from inspecting Figure 4.3 for the remaining two trial types (*color–shape* and *shape–color*), the differences in coherence across history-coherent and history-incoherent blocks are reduced relative to the *color–color* trial type (two plus signs relative to four), thus again explaining, at least in part, the dominance of the *color–color* trial type over the other three. Subsequent studies have provided additional experimental support for this DAARRE model explanation in terms of orienting functions (see Experiment 3, Finn et al., 2018; Finn et al., 2019; Pinto et al., 2020).

EVOKING FUNCTIONS

The capacity for functions to transform across stimuli and evoke appetitive or aversive responses has long been recognized within RFT and behavior analysis more generally, particularly with regard to explaining the ubiquity of human psychological distress (e.g., Dougher et al., 2007; Luciano et al., 2013, 2014). However, fully appreciating the potential importance of the role of evoking functions in explaining the dynamics of AARR became particularly apparent in research reported by Leech and colleagues (2016, 2017). In both of these studies, participants responded on IRAPs that involved "cute" puppies or kittens versus aggressive-looking spiders as label stimuli, while target stimuli involved approach (e.g., "I can pick it up") versus avoidance ("I need to get away") descriptors. Response options were once again "True" and "False" RCIs.

The results of both studies were generally in accordance with what one might expect (i.e., positive response biases on the two pet trial types and a negative bias on one of the spider trial types). However, the response pattern on the *Spider-Approach* trial type was in the opposite direction to a commonsense prediction. Specifically, assuming that participants would not readily approach spiders in the natural environment, one would likely anticipate a negative response bias on the *Spider-Approach* trial type; counterintuitively, however, participants tended to press "True" more quickly than "False." On balance, this response bias did correlate significantly with participant performances on a behavioral task, which involved approaching a live spider. That is, the stronger the tendency to respond "True" more quickly than "False" (for *Spider-Approach*), the more likely participants were to approach an actual live spider. Thus, although the direction of the response pattern on this trial type may appear to be somewhat counterintuitive, it predicted *actual* behavior. How might we explain this outcome?

Conceptually, it is possible that two separate Cfunc properties (i.e., orienting and evoking) were involved in determining participants' responses. To appreciate this suggestion, consider the stimuli involved within the IRAP. First, the pictures of spiders could be seen as potentially dangerous or threatening stimuli and thus may likely possess strong orienting and aversive evoking functions, relative to the pet pictures. In contrast, the cute and cuddly-looking pet stimuli would likely possess relatively strong appetitive evoking functions (but perhaps relatively weaker orienting functions due to their lack of threat or danger). Additionally, the approach and avoidance descriptors may not possess orienting functions that differ dramatically from each other, but the evoking functions they possessed would differ (i.e., avoidance = aversive, approach = appetitive).

According to a DAARRE model interpretation, therefore, the orienting functions of spiders dominated over the evoking functions for participants relatively low in self-reported spider fear (i.e., because spiders were not particularly aversive or appetitive for these participants). In contrast, for participants who were relatively high in self-reported spider fear, the (aversive) evoking functions may have dominated over the orienting functions (because spiders were seen as highly threatening). If this was indeed the case, choosing "True" more quickly than "False" would be highly coherent for low-fear participants, but less so for the high-fear participants. (Participants were from a normative sample, and thus the relative differences in levels of spider fear would not be particularly extreme.) To fully appreciate this argument, consider the DAARRE interpretation of the *Spider-Approach* trial type illustrated in Figure 4.4.

This figure indicates that the Crel between spiders and approach is negative (i.e., most people would not report readily approaching spiders). Therefore, a correct response on history-coherent trial types would be "False." However, within the wider context of the IRAP, a relatively strong spider *orienting* function is likely established for the low spider fear participants, while a relatively strong aversive *evoking* function is likely established for the high spider fear participants. Thus, for the low-fear participants, the dominating Cfunc property for spiders (orienting) is positive, as is the Cfunc property for the approach descriptor (evoking), both of which cohere with the positive ("True") RCI. For the high-fear individuals, however, the dominating evoking Cfunc for spiders is negative but positive for the approach target stimulus. Thus, one of the Cfunc properties coheres with the positive "True" RCI, while the other coheres with the negative "False" RCI. If the foregoing (albeit post-hoc) interpretation is correct, it would explain why performance on this trial type appears to predict actual approach toward a live spider, although the overall direction of the effect is in a counterintuitive direction (i.e., the latter effect is explained by the fact that the sample was normative).

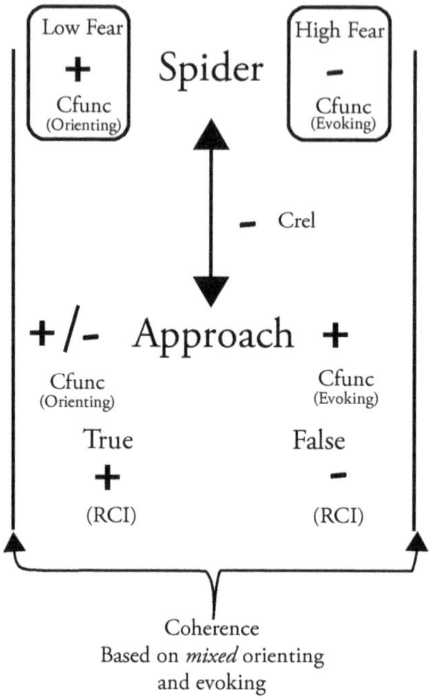

Figure 4.4 DAARRE model analysis of the Spider-Approach trial type for low and high spider fear participants

Note. The figure illustrates the Cfuncs that most likely dominate for individuals who are low (orienting; left-hand side) versus high (evoking; right-hand side) spider fear. The "+/–" symbol indicates the assumption that the orienting functions of the "approach" relative to the "avoidance" adjectives would not differ dramatically within this particular IRAP, but the evoking functions for "approach" would be positive relative to "avoidance."

ASSESSING THE CFUNC PROPERTIES OF THE LABEL STIMULI WITHIN AN IRAP

The preceding material on the DAARRE model draws heavily on the assumption that the Cfunc properties of the label and target stimuli play an important role in determining the types of effects observed with the IRAP. At the time of writing, however, direct experimental evidence for the impact of Cfunc properties for label and/or target stimuli was absent. That is, no published research had attempted to determine the impact of the Cfunc properties of, for example, the label stimuli independent of the target stimuli. However, very recent unpublished research has indicated that it is possible to examine the differential impact of the label stimuli (independently of the targets) using a modified IRAP combined with measures of neural activity (electroencephalograms [EEG]; Leech, 2020). Specifically, the research involved developing what is called a sequential IRAP in which the label stimulus on each trial is presented before the target stimulus. EEG signals are then recorded from the presentation of the label stimuli (i.e., before the target is presented). In Experiment 7 reported by Leech, pictures of pets and spiders were presented to participants. Critically, the difference in the EEG signals between pictures of pets and spiders interacted with laterality (i.e., whether the signal was recorded from the left or right side of the cortex) and whether the IRAP block required a history-coherent or history-incoherent response. This three-way interaction effect was observed within 300 ms of the label stimulus being presented on each trial (i.e., before the target stimulus was presented). In other words, it was possible to identify the impact of a Cfunc property for the label stimuli within an IRAP independently of the target stimuli.

Admittedly, this research is very new and will need to be replicated, but it does suggest that IRAP effects involve complex clusters of "interactants" that will require systematic analyses to better understand its functional-analytic properties and how it might be used to further explore human language and cognition within a behavior-analytic framework.

THE IMPACT OF MOTIVATING VARIABLES ON IRAP PERFORMANCES

As noted previously, the ROE acronym has been modified (the ROE-M) to highlight the ubiquity of motivating variables influencing orienting and evoking functions. Indeed, the important role of motivating variables has long been recognized in behavior analysis generally (e.g., Skinner, 1953, 1957; Michael, 1993, 2007), as well as in RFT with the concept of augmenting. On balance, augmenting is more specific to rule-governed behavior per se and could be considered a so-called middle-level term (see Harte & Barnes-Holmes, 2021, for an extended discussion). In any case, the impact of three different motivating conditions on an IRAP performance was recently reported in a study that used drops of pepper sauce to increase the size of appetitive functions for water-related stimuli presented within an IRAP (Gomes et al., 2020). Specifically, when two drops of pepper sauce were ingested by participants, the size of the IRAP effect for the "water-positive" trial type increased dramatically relative to that for a group of participants who did not ingest any pepper drops or ingested only a single drop of pepper. In effect, the evoking (appetitive) functions of the water stimuli appeared to increase when a motivating variable for access to water was manipulated. It therefore seems wise to assume that such motivating variables are part of the behavioral field of interactants that are always involved in determining the properties of any given instance of ROEing (hence ROE is more appropriately labeled ROE-M).

RELEVANCE TO ACT AND MIDDLE-LEVEL CONCEPTS

At this point, the DAARRE model interpretation of at least some IRAP effects could be seen as becoming so abstract that its connection to clinical psychology and human psychological suffering has been completely lost. On balance, we would argue that the effects and conceptual analyses we have considered here could be directly relevant to one or more of the well-known ACT-based middle-level terms (Barnes-Holmes et al., 2021). Let us consider the concept of defusion, for example. Perhaps the relative dominance of Cfunc over Crel properties, as measured within the IRAP, could provide a bottom-up approach to this middle-level concept. To appreciate this analysis, consider the pattern of trial-type effects illustrated in Figure 4.5 (left-hand side). As argued previously, the DAARRE model interpretation of this effect indicates that the Cfunc properties of the label, target, and RCIs strongly influence IRAP performance. Perhaps these differential trial-type effects could be seen as evidence for "fusion" with the Cfunc properties of the stimuli because they produce differential trial-type effects (i.e., the orienting and evoking functions of the stimuli partly determine the response patterns). In contrast, consider the right-hand side of Figure 4.5. In this case, all four IRAP trial-type effects are more or less even; critically, no trial type particularly dominates over the other. In this case, therefore, the Cfunc properties of the stimuli could be seen as having relatively limited impact on the IRAP performance. Or more informally, the Cfunc properties fail to create high levels of "fusion" because the participant is simply relating the stimuli (responding to their Crel properties) without being unduly influenced by their Cfunc properties. In principle, therefore, these two patterns of responding on the IRAP might provide a relatively precise experimental analysis of the distinction between fusion and defusion. Of course, this conceptual analysis is purely speculative and will require systematic experimental analysis.

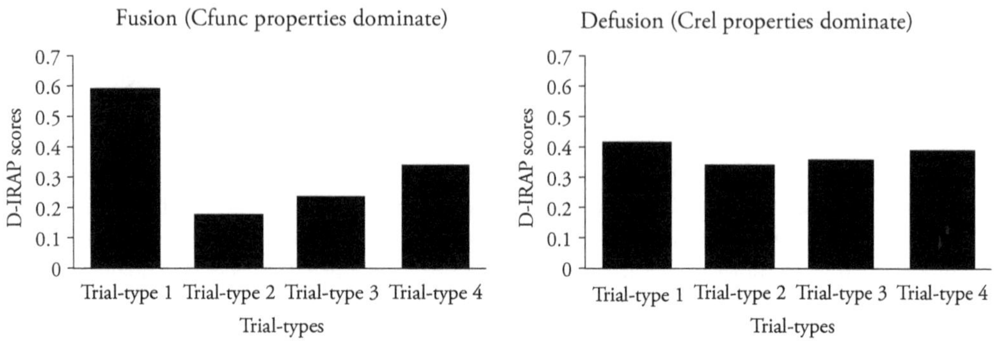

Figure 4.5 Hypothetical data illustrating the interpretation of differential trial-type effects on the IRAP

Note. On the left-hand panel, the Cfunc properties of the stimuli dominate over Crel properties, potentially modeling "fusion." On the right-hand panel, the Crel properties of the stimuli dominate over the Cfunc properties, potentially modeling "defusion."

RELATIONAL NETWORKS (AS RULES)

The importance of rule-governed behavior as a distinct feature of human language and cognition has long been acknowledged within RFT and behavior analysis more generally. In the 1970s and 1980s, a plethora of experimental research emerged exploring this concept and the extent to which rule governance led to insensitivity to direct contingencies of reinforcement (e.g., Lowe et al., 1983; Shimoff et al., 1986). Excessive rule-following has also been at the heart of ACT's conceptual understanding of human psychological suffering. The basic argument is that the human propensity to engage in rule-governed behavior undermines sensitivity to direct contingencies of reinforcement, and excessive rule-following in this regard is thus a critical feature in human psychological suffering (see Baruch et al., 2007; McAuliffe et al., 2014, for examples of experimental research exploring this suggestion in clinical samples; for a more recent review, see Kissi et al., 2020).

Within RFT, the conceptual analysis of rules as derived relational networks gained empirical support from two studies that successfully modeled rules as derived relational networks in the experimental lab (O'Hora et al., 2004, 2014). However, while the link between rule-following and AARR was clearly evident, other experimental research integrating these concepts was somewhat lacking until relatively recently (see Harte, Barnes-Holmes, Barnes-Holmes, & Kissi, 2020, for an extended discussion). Specifically, a series of studies have been published reporting on the impact of derived relations, varying across multiple dimensions within the HDML framework, on persistent rule-following (see also Monestes et al., 2017).

In an initial study, Harte et al. (2017) provided some participants with a direct rule, which did not involve responding in accordance with a derived relation generated within the experiment. That is, they were simply instructed to choose the *least like* comparison stimulus in a matching-to-sample (MTS) task (see below). In contrast, other participants were presented with the same instruction, but the phrase "least like" was replaced with a nonsense word that participated in a derived equivalence relation with that phrase. Or more informally, participants were required to treat the nonsense word as equivalent to the phrase "least like." The researchers sought to address the following critical question: Would there be any difference in persistent rule-following between these two groups of participants? For example, would participants who had been provided with a "direct" rule (one that did not require any derivation within the experiment) show higher levels of persistent rule-following than participants who were required to (partly) derive the meaning of the rule.

As noted, persistent rule-following was assessed by presenting participants with a MTS task. Each trial on the task involved presenting a sample shape at the top of the screen and three comparison shapes at the bottom of the screen, each varying in terms of their similarity to the sample shape (i.e., one shape was clearly the most like the sample shape; one shape was quite like the sample shape but with more variations; and one shape was completely different from the sample shape, with few or no overlapping similarities). The instruction or rule that participants received for responding on this task was initially consistent with feedback contingencies for responding on the task (i.e., the rule asked the participant to choose the least like comparison, and points were awarded to participants whenever they chose this comparison). After a certain number of MTS trials, however, the feedback contingencies were reversed, and now points were awarded for choosing the most similar comparison. The researchers took a number of measures of the extent to which participants persisted with following the rule or instruction, even though doing so ceased to produce points on the MTS task. In general, the results showed that participants who had been provided with a direct rule persisted for longer than those who were provided with a rule that required deriving a relation within the experiment—but only when they had at least 100 opportunities (Experiment 2) to follow the rule before the contingencies reversed.

In a subsequent study, Harte et al. (2018) explored the impact of level of derivation on rule persistence using a similar contingency switching MTS task (i.e., task contingencies initially supported the derived rule but later reversed). In this study, all rules provided to participants required a novel derivation within the experiment (i.e., there was no direct rule as in the previous study). In one condition, participants had many opportunities to make this novel derivation (low derivation), while in a second condition participants had relatively few opportunities (high derivation). This study also explored the impact of mutual and combinatorial entailment. That is, in one experiment, participants were required to derive that "least like" was equivalent to a nonsense word (i.e., A = B) many or few times, while in a second experiment, participants were required to derive that "least like" was equivalent to a nonsense word through a middle node (i.e., A = B = C), also many or few times. This relation was then inserted into the rule for responding on the contingency switching MTS task. In broad terms, the results indicated that lower-level derivation produced greater persistence in rule-following at both mutually and combinatorially entailed levels. That is, the more opportunities participants had to derive the rule, the more they persisted with rule-following when the MTS task contingencies no longer cohered with the rule.

In another two studies, researchers explored the impact of manipulating the coherence of the derived rule (Harte, Barnes-Holmes, Barnes-Holmes, McEnteggart, et al., 2020; Harte et al., 2021). The participants in these studies were again provided with rules that required a novel derivation within the experiment, but the coherence of these rules was manipulated through the provision or nonprovision of performance feedback for deriving the relations between the nonsense word and the key phrase "least like." Level of derivation was also manipulated but across studies. That is, within each experiment, all participants had the same number of opportunities to derive the relation, but across experiments they had relatively more or less opportunities (e.g., five blocks of training trials in one experiment versus only one block of training trials in another experiment). In other words, *within* each experiment, feedback was manipulated and level of derivation remained constant, but *across* each experiment, level of derivation varied. Results showed that feedback for deriving significantly impacted rule persistence within the experiments in which derivation was high (i.e., fewer opportunities to derive), but not when derivation was relatively low (i.e., more opportunities to derive). That is, it seemed that the less derived the rule became, the less impact feedback for deriving had on participants' MTS rule following. However, when the rule was relatively high in derivation, feedback significantly impacted MTS rule persistence.

The foregoing experimental analyses of rule persistence highlight what appear to be relatively subtle and complex effects. Specifically, the research has involved exploring the impact of coherence and derivation, for both mutually and combinatorially entailed relations (contained within a rule or network), on persistent rule-following. The findings indicate that persistent rule-following may be influenced by variables identified within the HDML framework. Thus there is a clear need to continue to explore the impact of these types of variables if persistent or excessive rule-following is to be better understood. Indeed, this work will be particularly important in advancing our understanding of how excessive or inflexible rule following plays a key role in human psychological suffering, as has been long argued in the ACT literature. For example, in providing a better understanding of the variables involved in persistent rule-following, in laboratory studies, it should be possible to develop increasingly sophisticated assessment and treatment models of human psychological suffering in which excessive rule-following is implicated (see Harte et al., 2017).

RELATING RELATIONAL NETWORKS (IN PERSPECTIVE-TAKING)

As noted earlier, the ability to perspective-take (i.e., through the deictic relations of I–You, Here–There and Now–Then) has been implicated in the development of the verbal self. Specifically, these relations are thought to be critical in developing the ability to locate oneself in time and space relative to others. While a considerable body of research on perspective-taking as deictic relational responding exists within RFT (e.g., Barnes-Holmes, 2001; McHugh et al., 2004, 2007), more complex conceptual analyses of this concept have only recently been offered. For example, Kavanagh et al. (2020) recently presented a conceptual analysis of a classic false belief perspective-taking task, wrought directly from the HDML. Although no experimental evidence is yet available to support this interpretation, it is presented here as an example of potential future RFT analyses. Hopefully, the apparent precision and specificity that the HDML may offer will be fully appreciated, particularly when one is attempting to articulate the relationship between experimental RFT analyses and high level, clinically relevant concepts such as perspective-taking.

A large body of research has emerged over the years, particularly within mainstream psychology, that has focused on different types of perspective-taking, emphasizing in particular children with a diagnosis of autism spectrum disorder (ASD; e.g., Boucher, 2012) and adults with specific disorders such as schizophrenia and borderline personality disorder (BPD; e.g., Németh et al., 2018). In broad terms, groups with these diagnostic labels tend to perform poorly on perspective-taking tasks such as false belief tasks relative to typical controls, but the literature indicates that performances vary widely depending on the nature of the tasks employed.

False belief refers to assumptions made about another person's false beliefs and/or another person's assumptions about beliefs held by a third party (Boucher, 2012). Perspective-taking tasks (e.g., the Sally-Anne test; the Deceptive Container task; the Unexpected Transfer task) aimed at assessing another person's false beliefs typically involve presenting a child, for example, with a scenario in which they are asked a question about a known false belief that differs from the child's own belief (e.g., that there is a glove in a box despite the child's belief that there is actually a scarf in the box). The second type of false belief, that involving another person's assumptions about beliefs, is typically assessed through presenting the child with a scenario involving a "change in location" element to determine whether they understand that someone can hold a false belief about someone else's belief. For example, this exercise can involve first telling the child that two people are given something to share (e.g., a chocolate bar) and that both then leave the item in a specific location (e.g., a cupboard). The child is then told that shortly afterward, one of the two people moved the item (e.g., to a rucksack). The child is next asked where the other person thinks the item is, the correct answer being in the original location (i.e., the cupboard). This second type of false belief is the focus of the conceptual functional analysis presented by Kavanagh et al. (2020), to which we now turn.

Kavanagh et al. (2020) first suggested that in order to respond successfully on a false belief task, which likely involves responding at the highest level of relational development (relating relational networks), a number of critical relational precursors would already need to be firmly established within the individual's behavioral repertoire. First, a number of basic relational frames (i.e., coordination, distinction, and temporality) would be required to be in place, therefore involving the first two levels of relational development as specified within the HDML framework (mutual entailment and relational framing). These basic patterns of relational responding would also need to be high in coherence (i.e., consistent with many other past and current instances of responding in accordance with these patterns), relatively high in complexity (i.e., subject to multiple sources of contextual control), low in derivation (i.e., have relatively extended histories), and low in flexibility (i.e., should persist in the absence of supporting contextual variables, such as reinforcement, and in contexts that could undermine such responding, such as "mild" punishment).

Second, Kavanagh et al. maintained that the three core deictic relations (I–You; Here–There; Now–Then) would also need to be firmly established within the individual's repertoire. They suggested that while these frames would naturally be located at the second level of relational development, if well established, they would likely also participate within larger relational networks. Responding in accordance with these relations would therefore additionally include this third level of relational development. Furthermore, as is the case for the frames of coordination, distinction, and temporality, the deictic frames would similarly need to be high in coherence and complexity, and low in levels of derivation and flexibility. Responding in accordance with these relations at these dimensional levels would likely be crucial in enabling the individual to "locate" relevant relational responses in a specific time and space.

Finally, Kavanagh et al. suggested that frames of causality (i.e., If–Then) would also be required, again at the first three levels of relational development with the same dimensional requirements specified above for the other relevant precursor frames. These If–Then frames would likely participate in complex relational networks with the deictic frames so that the individual could successfully derive such things as "if you and I both see something occur, then you and I both know that something has occurred." This type of derived relational responding would likely be essential, given the causal and temporal nature of the false belief task.

Assuming the relevant precursors are sufficiently established in the individual's history, Kavanagh and colleagues (2020) stated that the ability to understand and successfully engage with the false belief task likely involves both (1) relating relations and (2) relating entire relational networks to other entire relational networks. A graphical representation of the suggested relational responding involved in correctly identifying the unexpected location aspect of the classic false belief task is presented in Figure 4.6. The reader is first invited to examine the left-hand side of the figure. This indicates that, at Time 1, both the self and the other observe a hat being placed into a box. Based on this observation and the relational precursors just detailed, the self can conclude that both self and other know that the box contains a hat. The right-hand side of Figure 4.6 indicates that, at Time 2, the self observes the hat being replaced with a glove

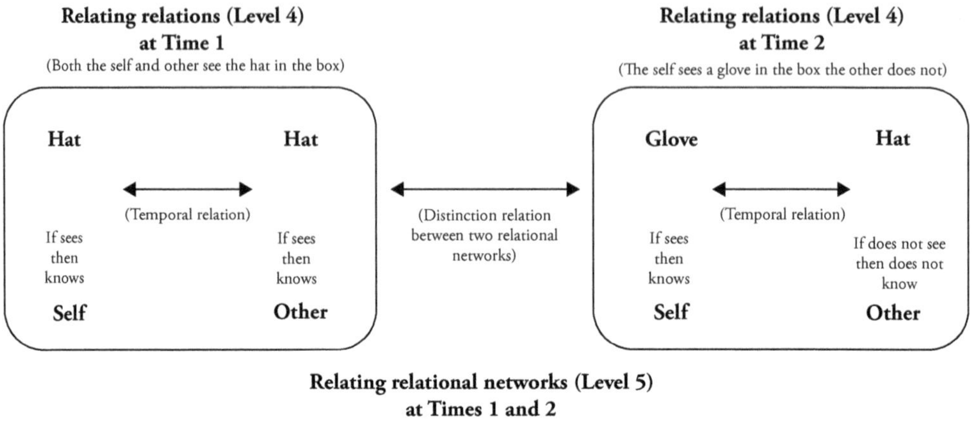

Figure 4.6 Visual representation of the functional analyses provided for responding correctly on a false belief task

when the other is not present to see this happen. Once again, based on this observation and the relational precursors described earlier, the self can conclude that only they know that there is now a glove, not a hat, in the box. The double-headed arrow linking both Times 1 and 2 indicates that correct responding requires that the self relate the two networks as distinct in terms of what each knows after Time 2. Crucially, if the self simply reported that the other does not know what is in the box after Time 2, that would indicate responding at the level of relating relations. If, however, the self reported that the other thinks that the box contains a hat, that would require the relating of relations at Time 2 to the relating of relations at Time 1. In other words, the self must understand that what the other thinks at Time 2 is still what they knew at Time 1. This would involve relating relational networks by relating relations to relating relations at a second point in time (a combination of the final two levels within the HDML).

The foregoing conceptual analysis, while speculative, reveals how complex even a relatively simple task like the false belief task appears to be and why young children often fail to complete the task successfully. The individual differences in levels of coherence, complexity, derivation, and flexibility among the relational precursors could also help to explain, at least in part, why the literature contains such wide variation in the ages at which false belief tasks can be solved correctly, and why performances vary widely depending on the variation of the task that is presented (see Kavanagh et al., 2020 for a recent review). Again, despite the speculative nature of this analysis in the absence of experimental testing, we present it here so that the reader can appreciate the potential precision offered by the HDML, as an example of cutting-edge RFT-based analyses of complex behaviors. The critical point, of course, is that such analyses might help applied researchers and practitioners alike to tackle deficits in perspective-taking when they are identified in specific clinical populations.

Concluding Comments

RFT, as a functional-analytic account of human language and cognition, has not simply stood still in the 20 years since publication of the seminal volume (Hayes, Barnes-Holmes et al., 2001). For example, recent advances have helped researchers to ask increasingly sophisticated questions, such as what is involved in a simple perspective-taking task, relationally speaking; what potential precursors are necessary for this type of relating; how can patterns of IRAP effects be used to interpret concepts such as fusion and defusion; what variables are important in excessive rule governance, and how are these variables relevant to human psychological suffering? Of course, the work outlined here has only begun to scratch the surface, and thus the recent conceptual and empirical work presented here should be seen as an ongoing work-in-progress.

In presenting these recent developments in RFT, we acknowledge the relatively rapid emergence of new RFT terms and concepts, including the DAARRE model, the HDML framework, the concept of mutually entailed orienting/evoking, and also the concept of the ROE-M. One could question the need for these new terms or concepts, or at least such a rapid pace of development. On balance, it is important to emphasize that these developments emerged directly from experimental research, and not solely from abstract theorizing. In time, alternative terms and concepts that allow for greater precision, scope, and depth may emerge, but that is exactly what we mean when we argue that RFT, and particularly the more recent empirical and conceptual developments, should be seen as a work in progress. Indeed, adopting this view seems as important now as ever in promoting RFT as a modern behavior-analytic account of human language and cognition, and in endeavoring to create "a science more adequate to the challenges of the human condition" (Hayes et al., 2012, p. 2).

Notes

1. Mutually entailed orienting obviously involves orienting responses, but these responses occur as part of a uniquely human cooperative act between two or more individuals. Orienting per se remains a relatively basic response to any event that functions as a stimulus (or roughly speaking is simply noticed). Indeed, strictly speaking, a stimulus cannot be defined as a stimulus without some orienting property. Thus, a young infant may show a startle response (and start to cry) if it hears a loud "unexpected" bang, but this may occur when the child is alone and thus is not engaging in what we are labeling mutually entailed orienting (because it is not part of a cooperative act). An important caveat, however, is that later we will refer to orienting as one of the core properties of a new generic unit of analysis that is emerging in an updated RFT. As such, orienting within this unit does not necessarily involve mutually entailed orienting, but the establishment of orienting "inside" the unit necessarily involved a history of mutually entailed orienting.
2. As discussed in note 1, the orienting property of the ROE does not necessarily involve mutually entailed orienting. Nevertheless, the ROE itself necessarily involved a history of mutually entailed orienting, and thus the orienting property of the ROE is necessarily determined, in a strictly functional-analytic sense, by a history of mutually entailed orienting.
3. The term *coherent* is being used here in a manner that is consistent with the general definition provided earlier (i.e., "the extent to which a pattern of derived relational responding [involving both Crel and Cfunc properties] coheres or is consistent with previously established patterns of such responding"). The term does *not*, therefore, apply simply to Crel properties (i.e., A = B coheres with B = A), but also applies to the Cfunc properties (including RCIs). In the context of the Shapes-and-Colours IRAP, the *color–color* trial type is considered maximally coherent because all of the critical responses during a history-coherent block involve relatively strong "confirmatory" responses. We are assuming here that most, if not all, participants would be subject to a general confirmation bias effect (e.g., Nickerson, 1998). For RFT such a bias is based on a history that involves a higher frequency of "confirming responses" for stimuli and events that are functionally similar (rather than functionally dissimilar). In principle, it would be possible to manipulate coherence within the current IRAP. Imagine, for example, if participants were exposed to a Shapes-and-Colours IRAP that presented the *shape–shape* trial type far more frequently, across numerous sessions, than the other three trial types. Given such a history, the pattern of Crel and Cfunc properties occurring for this trial type would likely increase in coherence (thus overriding the standard confirmation bias effect) because there would be greater functional overlap between the response pattern on this trial type and the dominant pattern observed during previous sessions for that IRAP. This all-embracing functional definition of coherence is required when the ROE-M is defined as the generic unit of analysis involving Crel *and* Cfunc properties (as codetermined by motivational variables).

References

Barnes, D., Hegarty, N., & Smeets, P. M. (1997). Relating equivalence relations to equivalence relations: A relational framing model of complex human functioning. *The Analysis of Verbal Behavior, 14*, 57–83. https://doi.org/10.1007/BF03392916

Barnes-Holmes, D., & Barnes-Holmes, Y. (2000). Explaining complex behaviour: Two perspectives on the concept of generalised operant classes. *The Psychological Record, 50*, 251–265. https://doi.org/10.1007/BF03395355

Barnes-Holmes, D., Barnes-Holmes, Y., Hussey, I., & Luciano, C. (2016). Relational frame theory: Finding its historical and philosophical roots and reflecting upon its future development: an introduction to part II. In R. D. Zettle, S. C. Hayes, D. Barnes-Holmes, & A. Biglan (Eds.), *The Wiley handbook of contextual behavioural science* (pp. 117–128). Wiley-Blackwell.

Barnes-Holmes, D., Barnes-Holmes, Y., Luciano, C., & McEnteggart, C. (2017). From IRAP and REC model to a multi-dimensional multi-level framework for analysing the dynamics of arbitrarily applicable relational responding. *Journal of Contextual Behavioural Science, 6*(4), 473–483. https://doi.org/10.1016/j.jcbs.2017.08.001

Barnes-Holmes, D., Barnes-Holmes, Y., & McEnteggart, C. (2020). Updating RFT (more field than frame) and its implications for process-based therapy. *The Psychological Record, 70*, 605–624. https://doi.org/10.1007/s40732-019-00372-3

Barnes-Holmes, D., Barnes-Holmes, Y., McEnteggart, C., & Harte, C. (2021). Back to the future with an updated version of RFT: More field than frame? *Perspectivas em Análise do Comportamento, 12*(1). https://doi.org/10.18761/PAC.2021.v12.RFT.03

Barnes-Holmes, D., Finn, M., McEnteggart, C., & Barnes-Holmes, Y. (2018). Derived stimulus relations and their role in a behaviour-analytic account of human language and cognition. *Perspectives on Behaviour Science, 41*(1), 155–173. https://doi.org/10.1007/s40614-017-0124-7

Barnes-Holmes, D., Murphy, A., Barnes-Holmes, Y., & Stewart, I. (2010). The implicit relational assessment procedure: Exploring the impact of private versus public contexts and the response latency criterion on pro-white and anti-black stereotyping among white Irish individuals. *The Psychological Record, 60*, 57–66. https://doi.org/10.1007/BF03395694

Barnes-Holmes, D., O'Hora, D., Roche, B., Hayes, S. C., Bissett, R. T., & Lyddy, F. (2001). Understanding and verbal regulation. In S. C. Hayes, D. Barnes-Holmes, & B. Roche (Eds.), *Relational frame theory: A post Skinnerian account of human language and cognition* (pp. 103–117). Plenum.

Barnes-Holmes, D., & Sivaraman, M. (2020, August 14). Updating RFT: Cooperation came first, the ROE as a unit of analysis, and engineering prosocial behaviour. https://science.abainternational.org/up-dating-rft-cooperation-came-first-the-roe-as-a-unit-of-analysis-and-engineering-prosocial-behavior/louise-mchughucd-ie

Barnes-Holmes, Y. (2001). *Analysing relational frames: Studying language and cognition in young children* (Unpublished doctoral thesis). National University of Ireland Maynooth.

Barnes-Holmes, Y., Barnes-Holmes, D., Smeets, P. M., Strand, P., & Friman, P. (2004). Establishing relational responding in accordance with more-than and less-than as generalized operant behavior in young children. *International Journal of Psychology and Psychological Therapy, 4*, 531–558.

Baruch, D. E., Kanter, J. W., Busch, A. M., Richardson, J. V., & Barnes-Holmes, D. (2007). The differential effect of instructions on dysphoric and nondysphoric persons. *The Psychological Record, 57*, 543–554. https://doi.org/10.1007/BF03395594

Berens, N. M., & Hayes, S. C. (2007). Arbitrarily applicable comparative relations: Experimental Evidence for relational operants. *Journal of Applied Behavior Analysis, 40*, 45–71. https://doi.org/10.1901/jaba.2007.7-06

Boucher, J. (2012). Putting theory of mind in its place: Psychological explanations of the socio-emotional-communicative impairments in autistic spectrum disorder. *Autism, 16*, 226–246. https://doi.org/10.1177/1362361311430403

Cagney, S., Harte, C., Barnes-Holmes, D., Barnes-Holmes, Y., & McEnteggart, C. (2017). Response biases on the IRAP for adults and adolescents with respect to smokers and nonsmokers: The impact of parental smoking status. *The Psychological Record, 67*(4), 473–483. https://doi.org/10.1007/s40732-017-0249-9

Carr, D., Wilkinson, K. M., Blackman, D., & McIlvane, W. J. (2000). Equivalence classes in individuals with minimal verbal repertoires. *Journal of the Experimental Analysis of Behavior, 74*, 101–115. https://doi.org/10.1901/jeab.2000.74-101

Cartwright, A., Hussey, I., Roche, B., Dunne, J., & Murphy, C. (2017). An investigation into the relationship between gender binary and occupational discrimination using the Implicit Relational Assessment Procedure. *The Psychological Record, 67*(1), 121–130. https://doi.org/10.1007/s40732-016-0212-1

Chomsky, N. (1959). A review of B. F. Skinner's *Verbal Behavior. Language. 35*(1), 26–58. https://doi.org/10.2307/411334

Cullen, C., Barnes-Holmes, D., Barnes-Holmes, Y., & Stewart, I. (2009). The implicit relational assessment procedure (IRAP) and the malleability of ageist attitudes. *The Psychological Record, 59*(4), 591–620. https://doi.org/10.1007/BF03395683

Dawson, D. L., Barnes-Holmes, D., Gresswell, D. M., Hart, A. J., & Gore, N. J. (2009). Assessing the implicit beliefs of sexual offenders using the implicit relational assessment procedure: A first study. *Sex Abuse, 21*(1), 57–75. https://doi.org/10.1177/1079063208326928.

Dougher, M. J., Hamilton, D., Fink, B., & Harrington, J. (2007). Transformation of the discriminative and eliciting functions of generalized relational stimuli. *Journal of the Experimental Analysis of Behaviour, 88*, 179–197. https://doi.org/10.1901/jeab.2007.45-05

Dougher, M. J., Twohig, M. P., & Madden, G. J. (Eds.). (2014). Stimulus-stimulus relations [Special Issue]. *Journal of the Experimental Analysis of Behaviour, 101*(1), 130–170.

Dugdale, N., & Lowe, C.F. (2000). Testing for symmetry in the conditional discriminations of language trained chimpanzees. *Journal of the Experimental Analysis of Behaviour, 73*, 5–22. https://doi.org/10.1901/jeab.2000.73-5.

Dunne, S., Foody, M., Barnes-Holmes, Y., Barnes-Holmes, D., & Murphy, C. (2014). Facilitating repertoires of coordination, opposition distinction, and comparison in young children with autism. *Behavioural Development Bulletin, 19*(2), 37–47. https://doi.org/10.1037/h0100576

Dymond, S., & Barnes, D. (1995). A transformation of self-discrimination response functions in accordance with the arbitrarily applicable relation of sameness, more-than, and less-than. *Journal of the Experimental Analysis of Behaviour, 64*, 163–184. https://doi.org/10.1901/jeab.1995.64-163

Finn, M., Barnes-Holmes, D., Hussey, I., & Graddy, J. (2016). Exploring the behavioral dynamics of the implicit relational assessment procedure: The impact of three types of introductory rules. *The Psychological Record, 66*(2), 309–321. https://doi.org/10.1007/s40732-016-0173-4

Finn, M., Barnes-Holmes, D., & McEnteggart, C. (2018). Exploring the single-trial-type-dominance-effect on the IRAP: Developing a differential arbitrarily applicable relational responding effects (DAARRE) model. *The Psychological Record, 68*(1), 11–25. https://doi.org/10.1007/s40732-017-0262-z

Finn, M., Barnes-Holmes, D., & McEnteggart, C. (2019). Predicting and influencing the single trial-type dominance effect. *The Psychological Record, 69*(3), 425–435. https://doi.org/10.1007/s40732-019-00347-4

Foody, M., Barnes-Holmes, Y., Barnes-Holmes, D., & Luciano, C. (2013). An empirical investigation of hierarchical versus distinction relations in a self-based ACT exercise. *International Journal of Psychology and Psychological Therapy, 13*(3), 373–388.

Gil, E., Luciano, C., Ruiz, F. J., & Valdivia-Salas, V. (2012). A preliminary demonstration of transformation of functions through hierarchical relations. *International Journal of Psychology and Psychological Therapy, 12*(1), 1–19.

Gomes, C., Perez, W., de Almeida, J., Ribeiro, A., de Rose, J., & Barnes-Holmes, D. (2020). Assessing a derived transformation of functions using the implicit relational assessment procedure under three motivative conditions. *The Psychological Record*, 69, 487–497. https://doi.org/10.1007/s40732-019-00353-6

Griffee, K., & Dougher, M. J. (2002). Contextual control of stimulus ategorization and stimulus equivalence in hierarchical ategorization. *Journal of the Experimental Analysis of Behaviour, 78*(3), 433–447. https://doi.org/10.1901/jeab.2002.78-433

Hare, B., Call, J., & Tomasello, M. (1998). Communication of food location between food and dog (*canis familaris*). *Evolution of Communication, 2*(1), 137–159. https://doi.org/10.1075/eoc.2.1.06har

Harte, C., & Barnes-Holmes, D. (2021). The status of rule-governed behaviour as pliance, tracking and augmenting within relational frame theory: Middle-level rather than technical terms. *The Psychological Record*. Advanced online publication. https://doi.org/10.1007/s40732-021-00458-x

Harte, C., Barnes-Holmes, D., Barnes-Holmes, Y., & Kissi, A. (2020). The study of rule governed behavior and derived stimulus relations: Bridging the gap. *Perspectives on Behavior Science, 43*, 361–385. https://doi.org/10.1007/s40614-020-00256-w

Harte, C., Barnes-Holmes, Y., Barnes-Holmes, D., & McEnteggart, C. (2017). Persistent rule-following in the face of reversed reinforcement contingencies: The differential impact of direct versus derived rules. *Behaviour Modification, 41*(6), 743–763. https://doi.org/10.1177/0145445517715871.

Harte, C., Barnes-Holmes, D., Barnes-Holmes, Y., & McEnteggart, C. (2018). The impact of high versus low levels of derivation for mutually and combinatorially entailed relations on persistent rule-following. *Behavioural Processes, 157*, 36–46. https://doi.org/10.1016/j.beproc.2018.08.005.

Harte, C., Barnes-Holmes, D., Barnes-Holmes, Y., & McEnteggart, C. (2021). Exploring the impact of coherence (through the presence versus absence of feedback) and levels of derivation on persistent rule-following. *Learning and Behavior, 49*, 222–239. https://doi.org/10.3758/s13420-020-00438-1

Harte, C., Barnes-Holmes, D., Barnes-Holmes, Y., McEnteggart, C., Gys, J., & Hassler, C. (2020). Exploring the potential impact of relational coherence on persistent rule-following: The first study. *Learning and Behavior, 48*, 373–391. https://doi.org/10.3758/s13420-019-00399-0

Hayes, S. C. (1991). A relational control theory of stimulus equivalence. In L. J. Hayes & P. N. Chase (Eds.), *Dialogues on verbal behavior* (pp. 19–40). Context Press.

Hayes, S. C., Barnes-Holmes, D., & Roche, B. (2001). *Relational frame theory: A post-Skinnerian account of human language and cognition.* Plenum.

Hayes, S.C., Barnes-Holmes, D., & Wilson, K. (2012). Contextual behavioural science: Creating a science more adequate to the challenge of the human condition. *Journal of Contextual Behavioural Science, 1*(1–2), 1–16. https://doi.org/10.1016/j.jcbs.2012.09.004

Hayes, S. C., Gifford, E. V., Townsend, R. C., Jr., & Barnes-Holmes, D. (2001). Thinking, problem-solving, and pragmatic verbal analysis. In S. C. Hayes, D. Barnes-Holmes, & B. Roche (Eds.), *Relational frame theory: A post Skinnerian account of human language and cognition* (pp. 87–101). Plenum.

Hayes, S. C., & Sanford, B. T. (2014). Cooperation came first: Evolution and human language and cognition. *Journal of the Experimental Analysis of Behaviour, 101*(1), 112–129. https://doi.org/10.1002/jeab.64

Hayes, S. C., Sanford, B. T., & Chin, F. T. (2017). Carrying the baton: Evolution science and contextual behavioural analysis of human language and cognition. *Journal of Contextual Behavioural Science, 6*(3), 314–328. https://doi.org/10.1016/j.jcbs.2017.01.002

Hayes, S. C., Strosahl, K., & Wilson, K.G. (1999). *Acceptance and commitment therapy: An experiential approach to behavior change*. Guilford Press.

Healy, O., Barnes-Holmes, D., & Smeets, P. M. (2000). Derived relational responding as generalised operant behaviour. *Journal of the Experimental Analysis of Behaviour, 74*(2), 207–227. https://doi.org/10.1901/jeab.2000.74-207.

Horne, P. J., & Lowe, C. F. (1996). On the origins of naming and other symbolic behaviour, *Journal of the Experimental Analysis of Behaviour, 65*, 185–241. https://doi.org/10.1901/jeab.1996.65-185

Hughes, S., & Barnes-Holmes, D. (2016a). Relational frame theory: The basic account. In R. D. Zettle, S. C. Hayes, D. Barnes-Holmes, & A. Biglan (Eds.), *The Wiley handbook of contextual behavioral science* (pp. 129–178). John Wiley & Sons.

Hughes, S., & Barnes-Holmes, D. (2016b). Relational frame theory: Implications for the study of human language and cognition. In R. D. Zettle, S. C. Hayes, D. Barnes-Holmes, & A. Biglan (Eds.), *The Wiley handbook of contextual behavioral science* (pp. 129–178). John Wiley & Sons.

Hughes, S., Barnes-Holmes, D., & Smyth, S. (2017). Implicit cross-community biases revisited: Evidence for ingroup favouritism in the absence of outgroup derogation in Northern Ireland. *The Psychological Record, 67*(1), 97–107. https://doi.org/10.1007/s40732-016-0210-3

Kavanagh, D., Barnes-Holmes, Y., & Barnes-Holmes, D. (2020). The study of perspective taking: Contributions from mainstream psychology and behaviour analysis. *The Psychological Record, 70*, 581–604. https://doi.org/10.1007/s40732-019-00356-3

Keuleers, E., Diependaele, K., & Brysbaert, M. (2010). Practice effects in large-scale visual word recognition studies: A lexical decision study on 14,000 Dutch mono- and disyllabic words and nonwords. *Frontiers in Psychology, 1*, 174. https://doi.org/10.3389/fpsyg.2010.00174.

Kissi, A., Harte, C., Hughes, S., De Houwer, J., & Crombez, G. (2020). The rule-based insensitivity effect: A systematic review. *Peer J, 8*, e9496. https://doi.org/10.7717/peerj.9496

Kissi, A., Hughes, S., Mertens, G., Barnes-Holmes, D., De Houwer, J., & Crombez, G. (2017). A systematic review of pliance, tracking, and augmenting. *Behaviour Modification, 41*(5), 683–707. https://doi.org/10.1177/0145445517693811

Leech, A. (2020). *Analyzing the functional independence of the derived transfer of fear and the derived transfer of avoidance responses* [Doctoral dissertation, Ghent University].

Leech, A., Barnes-Holmes, D., & Madden, L. (2016). The implicit relational assessment procedure (IRAP) as a measure of spider fear, avoidance, and approach. *The Psychological Record, 66*, 337–349. https://doi.org/10.1007/s40732-016-0176-1

Leech, A., Barnes-Holmes, D., & McEnteggart, C. (2017). Spider fear and avoidance: A preliminary study of the impact of two verbal rehearsal tasks on a behaviour–behaviour relation and its implications for an experimental analysis of defusion. *The Psychological Record, 67*, 387–398. https://doi.org/10.1007/s40732-017-0230-7

Lipkens, Hayes, S. C., & Hayes, L. J. (1993). Longitudinal study of derived stimulus relations in an infant. *Journal of Experimental Child Psychology, 56*, 201–239. https://doi.org/10.1006/jecp.1993.1032

Lowe, C. F., Beasty, A., & Bentall, R. P. (1983). The role of verbal behavior in human learning: Infant performance on fixed interval schedules. *Journal of the Experimental Analysis of Behaviour, 39*, 157–164. https://doi.org/10.1901/jeab.1983.39-157

Luciano, C., Gómez-Becerra, I., & Rodríguez-Valverde, M. (2007). The role of multiple-exemplar training and naming in establishing derived equivalence in an infant. *Journal of Experimental Analysis of Behaviour, 87*, 349–365. https://doi.org/10.1901/jeab.2007.08-06

Luciano, C., Valdivia-Salas, S., Ruiz, F. J., Rodríguez-Valverde, M., Barnes-Holmes, D., Dougher, M. J., Cabello, F., Sánchez, V., Barnes-Holmes, Y., & Gutierrez, O. (2013). Extinction of aversive conditioned fear: Does it alter avoidant responding? *Journal of Contextual Behavioural Science, 2*, 120–134. http://doi.org/10.1016/j.jcbs.2013.05.001

Luciano, C., Valdivia-Salas, S., Ruiz, F. J., Rodríguez-Valverde, M., Barnes-Holmes, D., Dougher, M. J., López-López, J. C., Barnes-Holmes, Y., & Gutierrez-Martínez, O. (2014). Effects of an acceptance/diffusion intervention on experimentally induced generalised avoidance: A laboratory demonstration. *Journal of the Experimental Analysis of Behaviour, 101*, 94–111. http://doi.org/10.1002/jeab.68

Maloney, E., & Barnes-Holmes, D. (2016). Exploring the behavioural dynamics of the implicit relational assessment procedure: The role of relational contextual cues versus relational coherence indicators as response options. *The Psychological Record, 66*, 395–403. http://doi.org/10.1007/s40732-016-0180-5

McAuliffe, D., Hughes, S., & Barnes-Holmes, D. (2014). The dark-side of rule governed behavior: An experimental analysis of problematic rule-following in an adolescent population with depressive symptomatology. *Behaviour Modification, 38*(4), 587–613. http://doi.org/10.1177/0145445514521630.

McHugh, L., Barnes-Holmes, Y., & Barnes-Holmes, D. (2004). Perspective-taking as relational responding: A developmental profile. *The Psychological Record, 54*, 115–144. http://doi.org/10.1007/BF03395465

McHugh, L., Barnes-Holmes, Y., Barnes-Holmes, D., Whelan, R., & Stewart, I. (2007). Knowing me, knowing you: deictic complexity in false-belief understanding. *The Psychological Record, 57*, 533–542. http://doi.org/10.1007/BF03395593

Micheal, J. (1993). Establishing operations. *The Behaviour Analyst, 16*(2), 191–206. http://doi.org/10.1007/BF03392623

Michael, J. (2007). Motivating operations. In O. J. Cooper, T. E. Heron, & W. L. Heward (Eds.), *Applied Behaviour Analysis* (2nd ed., pp. 374–391). Merrill Prentice Hall.

Monestes, J. L., Greville, W., & Hooper, N. (2017). Derived insensitivity: Rule-based insensitivity to contingencies propagates through equivalence. *Learning and Motivation, 59*, 55–63. http://doi.org/10.1016/j.lmot.2017.08.003

Németh, N., Mátrai, P., Hegyi, P., Czéh, B., Czopf, L., Hussain, A., Pammer, J., Imre Szabó, I., Solymár, M., Kiss, L., Hartmann, P., Szilágyi, A. L., Kiss, Z., & Simon, M. (2018). Theory of mind disturbances in borderline personality disorder: A meta-analysis. *Psychiatry Research, 270*, 143–153. https://doi.org/10.1016/j.psychres.2018.08.049

Nickerson, R. S. (1998). Confirmation bias: A ubiquitous phenomenon in many guises. *Review of General Psychology, 2*(2), 175–220. http://doi.org/10.1037/1089-2680.2.2.175

O'Hora, D., Barnes-Holmes, D., Roche, B., & Smeets, P. M. (2004). Derived relational networks and control by novel instructions: A possible model of generative verbal responding. *The Psychological Record, 54*, 437–460. http://doi.org/10.1007/BF03395484

O'Hora, D., Barnes-Holmes, D., & Stewart, I. (2014). Antecedent and consequential control of derived instruction-following. *Journal of the Experimental Analysis of Behaviour, 102*(1), 66–85. http://doi.org/10.1002/jeab.95.

O'Hora, D., Pelaez, M., Barnes-Holmes, D., & Amesty, L. (2005). Derived relational responding and human language: Evidence from the WAIS-III. *The Psychological Record, 55*, 155–174.

O'Shea, B. A., Watson, D. G., & Brown, G. (2016). Measuring implicit attitudes: A positive framing bias flaw in the implicit relational assessment procedure (IRAP). *Psychological Assessment, 28*(2), 159–170. http://doi.org/10.1037/pas0000172

O'Toole, C., & Barnes-Holmes, D. (2009). Three chronometric indices of relational responding as predictors of performance on a brief intelligence test: The importance of relational flexibility. *The Psychological Record, 59*, 119–132. http://doi.org/10.1007/BF03395652

Pinto, J. A. R., de Almeida, R. V., & Bortoloti, R. (2020). The stimulus' orienting function may play an important role in IRAP performance: Supportive evidence from an eye-tracking study of brands. *The Psychological Record, 70*, 257–266. http://doi.org/10.1007/s40732-020-00378-2

Power, P., Harte, C., Barnes-Holmes, D., Barnes-Holmes, Y. (2017). Exploring racial bias in a European country with a recent history of immigration of black Africans. *The Psychological Record, 65*, 365–375. http://doi.org/10.1007/s40732-017-0223-6

Roche, B., & Barnes, D. (1997). A transformation of respondently conditioned stimulus function in accordance with arbitrarily applicable relations. *Journal of the Experimental Analysis of Behaviour, 67*, 275–300. http://doi.org/10.1901/jeab.1997.67-275

Ruiz, F. J., & Luciano, C. (2011). Cross-domain analogies as relating derived relations among two separate relational networks. *Journal of the Experimental Analysis of Behaviour, 95*, 369–385. http://doi.org/10.1901/jeab.2011.95-369

Shimoff, E., Matthews, B. A., & Catania, A. C. (1986). Human operant performance: Sensitivity and pseudosensitivity to contingencies. *Journal of the Experimental Analysis of Behaviour, 46*, 149–157. http://doi.org/10.1901/jeab.1986.46-149

Sidman, M. (1971). Reading and auditory-visual equivalences. *Journal of Speech, Language, and Hearing Research, 14*, 5–13. http://doi.org/10.1044/jshr.1401.05

Sidman, M. (1986). Functional analysis of emergent verbal classes. In T. Thompson and M. E. Zeiler (Eds.), *Analysis and integration of behavioural units* (pp. 213–245). Laurence Erlbaum Associates.
Sidman, M. (1994). *Equivalence relations and behaviour: A research story*. Boston: Authors Cooperative.
Sidman, M., Rauzin, R., Lazar, R., Cunningham, S., Tailby, W., & Carrigan, P. (1982). A search for symmetry in the conditional discriminations of rhesus monkeys, baboons, and children. *Journal of the Experimental Analysis of Behaviour, 37*, 23–44. https://doi.org/10.1901/jeab.1982.37-23
Sidman, M., & Tailby, W. (1982). Conditional discrimination versus matching to sample: An expansion of the testing paradigm. *Journal of the Experimental Analysis of Behaviour, 37*, 5–22. https://doi.org/10.1901/jeab.1982.37-5
Skinner, B. F. (1953). *Science and human behaviour*. New York: Macmillan.
Skinner, B. F. (1957). *Verbal Behavior*. New York: Appelton-Century-Crofts.
Skinner, B. F. (1966). An operant analysis of problem solving. In B. Kleinmuntz (Ed.), *Problem-solving: Research, method, and theory* (pp. 225–257). John Wiley & Sons.
Slattery, B., & Stewart, I. (2014). Hierarchical classification as relational framing. *Journal of the Experimental Analysis of Behaviour, 101*(1), 61–75. https://doi.org/10.1002/jeab.63
Steele, D. L., & Hayes, S. C. (1991). Stimulus equivalence and arbitrarily applicable relational responding. *Journal of the Experimental Analysis of Behaviour, 56*, 519–555. https://doi.org/10.1901/jeab.1991.56-519.
Stewart, I., & Barnes-Holmes, D. (2004). Relational frame theory and analogical reasoning: Empirical investigations. *International Journal of Psychology and Psychological Therapy, 4*, 241–262.
Vahey, N., Nicholson, E., & Barnes-Holmes, D. (2015). A meta-analysis of criterion effects for the implicit relational assessment procedure (IRAP) in the clinical domain. *Journal of Behaviour Therapy and Experimental Psychiatry, 48*, 59–65. https://doi.org/10.1016/j.jbtep.2015.01.004.
Wilson, D. S. (2007). *Evolution for everyone: How Darwin's theory can change the way we think about our lives*. New York: Delacorte Press.
Wilson, D. S., Hayes, S. C., Biglan, A., & Embry, D. D. (2014). Evolving the future: toward a science of intentional change. *Behavioural and Brain Sciences, 37*(4), 395–416. https://doi.org/10.1017/S0140525X13001593
Zentall, T. R., Wasserman, E. A., & Urcuioli, P. J. (2014). Associative concept learning in animals. *Journal of the Experimental Analysis of Behaviour, 101*(1), 130–151. https://doi.org/10.1002/jeab.55

CHAPTER

5 Clinical Behavior Analysis and RFT: Conceptualizing Psychopathology and Its Treatment

Carmen Luciano, Niklas Törneke, *and* Francisco J. Ruiz

Abstract

Private events can have a dominant function in human behavior, especially with regard to the experience of self and selfing behavior. This article presents the building of selfing behavior throughout the early interactions of responding to others' behaviors and discusses the impact of learning to relate (i.e., learning human language). Special focus is on the significant impact of deictic and hierarchical framing in building self-contents, overaching abstract motivations, the abstraction of I, and the subsequent derivation of more self-contents. Also covered are the patterns of responding in coordination with one's own behavior (psychological inflexibility) and responding hierarchically (psychological flexibility); and hierarchical responding as the final common pathway for the many faces of therapeutic processes towards building psychological flexibility. Finally, the experimental evidence that has been signaling this path for years is summarized.

Key Words: self, selfing behaviors, private events, suffering, deictic framing, hierarchical framing

Introduction

On the night of November 27, 1994, the cruise ferry MS *Estonia* sank in the Baltic Sea on its way from Tallinn to Stockholm. There were 989 people on board; 852 people of whom died in the disaster. The rescue efforts were dramatic, given the rough weather. The wind was 15–20 meters per second, and the temperature in the water was around 10 degrees Celsius. The ship sank quickly and 137 survivors were rescued from rafts or directly from the cold water.

When survivors of the disaster describe their life experiences after the traumatic event, their testimonies confirm what we have learned from people who have had other life-threatening and extremely aversive experiences. Survivors report a variety of effects following a trauma, some of which seem more directly related to the events they have experienced. Memories of what happened and new situations of danger tend to trigger these memories and similar emotional responses. For instance, one person who survived the disaster of MS *Estonia* described a turbulent air flight and how she was brought back to the experience of that night on the Baltic Sea. Other experiences can seem a bit more surprising; for example, several years after the disaster, one person suddenly became very upset and anxious watching a dancing performance. Only after a while did she realize that the way the dancers moved their hands reminded her of the ways people had waved that night several years back, sitting in rafts on the stormy sea.

In these examples, the connection between the traumatic event and later happenings is pretty straightforward.

People continuously report one more thing after traumatic life events: they have to face their own, most commonly aversive reactions. A threat comes from within, so to speak. This is also true of specific memories or other more complex reactions. For example, it might be the experience of life lacking meaning. One relatively common testimony is a disabling sense of guilt that is not connected to a particular behavior during the catastrophic event but to the very fact that the person survived. In contrast, some people report an increased sense of meaning that they can use to redirect their life, even in the presence of painful memories.

Behavior Analysis and Private Responses

The starting point of the previous examples is an extreme, aversive event. In many ways, however, the aversive event only highlights what is true more generally; human beings interact not only with the outward environment but also with their own responses, including those that are only detectable by the person emitting them (e.g., emotions, sensations, and thoughts). Furthermore, this interaction occurs in the context of the particular history of interactions with the world. There is an environment "within the skin," to employ a term used by Skinner. This is central to the human experience; it has long been generally acknowledged within behavior analysis as the self. Skinner (1953) focused on this subject in several chapters of his book, *Science and Human Behavior*. He analyzed these phenomena, and how we tend to interact with them, under the heading of terms such as *self-control, self-knowledge, self-awareness,* or simply just *self.* His classical term for responses of this kind, which are only detectable for the person emitting them, is *private events*. Skinner's main argument in his analysis is that these phenomena should be understood as other behaviors and not as occurring in some other mental sphere that is traditionally called "the psyche." Skinner's approach to these topics was somewhat interpretative, however, and the influence of this behavior was part of an unknown path, even though prominent members of the behavior-analytic community have long argued for their relevance (Day, 1971; Ferster, 1972).

The Position of Clinical Behavior Analysis

Even though the theoretical position taken by modern models of therapy such as acceptance and commitment therapy (ACT), behavioral activation, functional-analytic psychotherapy, and dialectical behavior therapy (DBT) is firmly rooted in the behavior-analytic tradition, they share with psychotherapy the general assumption of the importance of private events for understanding and helping clients with psychological problems. The reason for this is in part practical and, in a way, the result of common sense. It is hard to imagine a dialogue with a person surviving a disaster like the one described at the start of this article and claiming that whatever the person remembers, feels, or thinks about the events is not relevant for therapy. The same is true for a more circumscribed problem, such as a specific phobic reaction (e.g., encountering a spider). Claiming that it is all about the spider and that what the person feels, thinks, or senses in the interaction with the spider is irrelevant is a hard position to take. The same goes for an everyday situation of meeting someone in the street and then recognizing the person as an old friend. The possible claim that the behavior we label "recognizing" is irrelevant for analyzing the subsequent behavior seems to miss something essential. Still, the behavior of recognizing could well be private in the Skinnerian sense—not detectable to anyone except for the person behaving that way.

At this point in our argument, it is essential to note that, although we claim that private events might have an important function for further behavior, we should not give these private behaviors a causal role in a mechanistic sense. Our claim rather is that they can have a function, even an important one, in a sequence of behavior. Consequently, private events often should be targeted, one way or another, in an effort to help the person to change in a personally desired direction. In taking this position, we start at the point where Skinner stopped because he lacked the scientific data now available to continue his analysis. The importance of private events for a behavior analysis of human behavior is not only to affirm the potentially relevant role of these events. It is to understand the context under which they are developed as well as what functions these kinds of events can have. Furthermore, it is yet another task to show how we can help people direct their lives the way they want to by using our analysis.

Analyzing the Function of Private Events with the Help of RFT

Basic, experimental science regarding human language and cognition has advanced since Skinner attempted to analyze these phenomena. One specific line of research that has retained the connection with the Skinnerian tradition of science is *relational frame theory* (RFT; Hayes, Barnes-Holmes, & Roche, 2001). The key element of the findings presented in RFT is that the basic unit of human language is a specific repertoire of relating that humans learn in early childhood. This acquired ability then has enormous effects on human behavior overall. Language-able humans will interact with the environment according to how they have learned to relate one phenomenon to another in very complex ways. Alternatively, in a more specific behavior-analytic terminology, stimuli can acquire function in a way that is different from what has been demonstrated for nonhuman animals due to the learned ability to relate in this particular way. The broad findings of RFT are covered in Hayes and colleagues (2001). At the same time, a few specific lines, findings, and conclusions from this research need to be discussed to perform a clinical analysis—first, a general conclusion.

Once a human has learned the particular type of relating that is at the core of language, in RFT termed *relational framing* or arbitrarily applicable relational responding, all human interaction with the environment is affected by this ability. Events of all kinds acquire particular meaning to humans; potentially everything a human encounters is symbolic due to the ability to frame relationally. However, the specific meaning is contextually controlled by the person's history and the present circumstances.

The characteristics of relational framing are not restricted to events in the physical environment. The same holds for events that are aspects of human behavior, or what the tradition of behavior analysis terms private events. Feelings, memories, thoughts, and bodily sensations are developed and acquire complex functions due to relational framing; thus, they influence behavior in critical ways. We can now go beyond the position where the reason for assuming the importance of private events for human functioning is common sense; it is also empirical. RFT provides us with the tools we need to analyze how private events develop and acquire such complex functions, how different ways of interacting with private responses develop and lead to behavioral traps, and how we can help clients to overcome such traps and redirect their lives. Making such an analysis requires that we go somewhat into depth with regard to how we learn to interact with our own responding and what type of behavior this is. Skinner referred to this phenomenological area as "the self." Because the self is not an object but a specific type of complex human behavior, we will use the term *selfing*.

The Behavior of Selfing

Selfing behavior is at the core of the human condition: it is a sophisticated, learned behavior that makes human beings conscious of themselves as acting organisms. We learn to respond to our own behavior, and thus we learn to make choices and be conscious of that behavior and all that follows. This type of responding might be effective or ineffective to our living, with ineffective responding being the source of psychological problems. Being so central, one of the most relevant lines of research from a behavior-analytic point of view is to identify the conditions under which we learn selfing behavior (e.g., emotions, thoughts, memories), as well as how this behavior becomes a source of functional control for subsequent behavior. Stated another way, thoughts and connected emotions influence subsequent responding. Again, this does not mean that one behavior is a formal cause for another behavior. However, private events acquire a functional role owing to a particular person's learning history. That is, the history in the present circumstances brings the function for the actual responding and the respective consequences. These events are then the whole behavioral universe at any given moment.

In this section, first, we will point to early behaviors that contribute to building the repertoire of selfing, especially the early conditions establishing that one behavior acquires functions for another. Second, we will discuss the impact of learning to relate and the transformation of antecedents and consequences. Third, we will point to how deictic and hierarchical responding account for the sophisticated selfing repertoire. Finally, we will emphasize how two functional classes of responding to one's own behavior are developed: one flexible and effective repertoire and the other inflexible and ineffective.

Early Building of Self-behaviors

As we know, human beings respond to the functions of present circumstances. The functions are generated from the phylogenetic background and the ontogenetic learning history of interactions with the physical and social systems. This is the whole. Consequently, the background of the selfing behaviors is the history with the verbal community. As Skinner (1974) pointed out, this means that others' behavior functions either as consequences or antecedents of the individual's response. This interplay between your own behavior and the behavior of others is central for learning the repertoire of being conscious of yourself as a unique human being and being in charge of your own actions. On this basis, the contingencies provided by the verbal community are also the context for learning private behavior. Even behavior that is not directly accessible to others is built on interactions with others (Skinner, 1945). So, the reaction of others to your responding becomes the main context for learning essential behaviors that characterize human beings, such as knowing who you are, what you want, where you are, what you are doing, why you are doing something, or even more, the *you* who realizes who is thinking, who is doing, who is giving reasons or noticing what happens because of some reason, and so on (Hayes, 1984). How does all this happen?

Early Interactions of Responding to Others' Behavior

The history of an individual begins within the inevitable interactions with others as the core context for development. The explicit contingencies under which we learn to respond to questions and instructions given by others are the key context for developing the motivations that will be central in our behavior. That is, at the same time the babies learn to name objects and events according to the behavior of others, they also learn to follow instructions under specific consequences, resulting in learning either to enjoy or to avoid those consequences. All of this is according to the cultural contingencies in the environment. For instance, the consequences might select responding based on the mediation of others or might select responding based on the natural consequences of the behavior. These two types of consequences are critical in forming the operants as classes of behavior that, later on, will be the basis on which to build our way of being in the world.

In this process, the children are asked for formulations about who, what, and why they do what they do, did, or will do; and they respond in the context of others prompting and reinforcing answers. Of course, the others behave according to the coherence given as a mirror of their own history. The opportunity to respond and the reinforcing consequences the others provide establish the repertoire needed for the child to develop the sophisticated selfing behavior. Then, the building of the different selfing behaviors is directly connected with the conditions provided by the others, either for following instructions and for deriving rules, and subsequently will control specific actions. These early contingencies of the multiple exemplar training (MET) will build functional classes that will become established under the meaning, interests, and values as higher-order or hierarchical motivational functions controlling the individual's own behavior.

More precisely, early on, the child is taught to follow instructions under the control of the consequences mediated by others (e.g., "Good that you are doing what I ask you to do. I am very glad and I will permit you to play outside."). When the MET of these behaviors is in place in a dominant way, then the children are taught to attend more to others' behaviors as the main source of motivation (whether positive or negative reinforcement) than to other consequences (e.g., the direct effect of their behavior beyond their parents's attention). However, it might happen that the children are taught to pay attention to what happens in the environment as a function of their behavior, that is, to look for the changes occurring because of their behavior (e.g., "Look, because you are wearing your coat, you are warm in this cold and windy day."). When MET of these behaviors is in place in a dominant way, the child's behavior becomes motivated for those natural consequences without the mediation of others' behavior, again, this being effective or ineffective depending on the context.

So, MET might result in (1) a pattern of responding, as a generalized operant selected under the consequences based on the mediation of others' behavior. This responding can be based on positive or negative reinforcement as receiving attention per se or receiving attention to achieve subsequent positive consequences or to escape/avoid from some aversive functions. MET might also result in (2) a pattern of responding, as a generalized operant selected under the natural consequences of responding, that is, according to how the physical and social world works, based on either positive or negative reinforcement. Moreover, the MET of these behaviors might form functional classes under the control of continuous or intermittent consequences. Even more, for a particular person, the contingencies in the MET might have established only one pattern of any of these two functional classes. In contrast, for another person, the contingencies in the MET might have developed functional classes appropriately contextualized to the survival contingencies in both the natural and the social worlds. An example of the latter case is to learn to respond under the control of the others' behavior in particular circumstances and under the control of the natural consequences of his behavior in other circumstances. However, this is not the only story. All that means that it is the individual that matters and, consequently, that the important thing to do is to check for the specific personal conditions.

While the child is learning to follow simple instructions and these functional classes are being built, the child is also learning to frame relationally under specific functions. Learning to frame relationally is a before–after point in the child's development. It is crossing the Rubicon, a crossing that will dress the previously learned functional classes with the coherent function attached to learning the behavior of arbitrarily applicable relational responding, a subject we now explore.

Learning to Relate and Derive Relations and Functions

According to RFT, relational framing underlies human language and cognition. Relational framing means relating two or more events based on arbitrarily established contextual cues (Hayes et al., 2001; Törneke, 2010) such as coordination ("is," "same as," "goes with," etc.), opposition ("opposite to," "is the contrary of"), distinction ("different from"), comparison ("more than," "less than"), spatial ("below," "above," "inside," "outside," etc.), hierarchy ("belongs to," "includes," "part of"), temporal ("before," "after"), causal ("if–then") and deictic (I–You, Here–There, Now–Then). All types of relational framing are generalized operant behaviors that are typically learned early in life through METs provided by the verbal community. Importantly, learning to relate this way permits deriving new relations without direct training, and the functions of one stimulus transform the functions of the stimuli related to it according to the specific type of relations. This core characteristic of relational framing accounts for the generativity of human behavior. Examples of the properties and types of relational framings are outlined in the following paragraphs (Hayes et al., 2001).

The various patterns of relational framing differ in relational complexity, so that some seem to develop before others do. For instance, after developing more complex repertoires of relational framing, Susan, our example child, shows more sophisticated behavior. For example, when learning to derive relations according to comparison, opposition, and deictic framing, she can understand her father saying, "Sweden is a cold country, but Spain is the opposite" by concluding that Spain is a hot country. Further, because of the learned opposite relation between being right and wrong, and being right as being intelligent and loved by others, when making a mistake, she begins to derive "Susan is silly and is not going to be loved." This derivation makes her feel sad and prompts the urge to respond correctly. Even more, she begins to count the number of times that she and her schoolmates Violet and Joe responded correctly to the math teacher's questions and derives, "I am smarter than Joe, but Violet is smarter than me, so Violet is the smartest one." According to this derivation, Susan feels confident and wants to compete against Joe in doing math but avoids competing against Violet.

RFT defines two forms of contextual control over relational framing. The first form is called *relational context* (C_{rel}) and specifies the type of relation established among the stimuli. The C_{rels} usually are some of the arbitrary relational cues presented above, such as "is," "same as," "is the opposite to," "more than," "less than," and "contains." The second form of contextual control is called *functional context* (C_{func}) and specifies what functions will be transformed in a given moment. Following the latter example, Violet, Joe, and Susan were related in a comparison regarding math skills. However, Susan has also learned that Joe is a very good soccer player, but Violet has no soccer skills. Thus, Susan has derived an opposite relation between Joe and Violet regarding soccer skills. However, when Susan's teacher asks her, "What teammate do you choose for your maths team?" the word "maths" works as the C_{func} to select Violet because she wants to win the competition. Alternatively, when asked to choose a teammate for a soccer competition, the word "soccer" works as the C_{func} to select Joe. Given these interactions, Susan is learning to derive with flexibility in relation to Violet, Joe, and herself.

Individuals differ in their opportunities for derived relational framing (Hayes et al., 2001; Luciano et al., 2009). In other words, a person might become more fluent deriving in a particular framing than others, with more or less contextual control as in Susan's above-mentioned examples. Each personal history is different, which implies that what might be a complex derivation for a person might be an easy one for another. Taking this consideration into account, we note that derived relational responding qualifies for a number of formal dimensions with different levels that have to be considered with caution because, in a functional-analytic perspective, individual history is what matters (Barnes-Holmes, Barnes-Holmes, Luciano, & McEnteggart, 2017). For instance, relational responding might show different levels of (1) derivation (e.g., only the first time a derived response is produced qualifies as a fully derived response because this derived response contacts to the contingencies connected to the history of derived responding. Moreover, when the derived response is further repeated, it strengthens the network to which they belong). At the same time, opportunities to derive form the fluency in relational responding (e.g., more in deictic I–You than in deictic I–Then–before or more in I–Then–before than I–Here–Now), (2) complexity (e.g., given A>B = C, deriving A is more than C is considered a more complex relational response than deriving A is the same as C given A = B = C; deriving relations among relations, as in analogies, is considered more complex than deriving relations in one network or group of stimuli relations); (3) flexibility (e.g., contrary to the example of Susan with Joe and Violet, it is when a network has not been sufficiently contextualized. Then, responding will not be sensitive to contextual changes, and the person showing such a network will not be easily adapted to the changes in contingencies, for instance).

Besides these formal dimensions (that might be used for filtering each particular history), derived relational responding shows a characteristic that is the very essence of this human ability: coherence. For Barnes-Holmes, Hayes, Dymond, and O'Hora (2002), "coherence or sense-making appears to function as powerful reinforcer for relational activity" (p. 70); for Hayes, Stroshal, and Wilson (2012) and Luciano (2017), coherence becomes the reinforcing context that envelops any instance of relational responding. Accordingly, coherence becomes a motivational context built across the opportunities to derive (Luciano et al., 2009), and it becomes the strength of derived relational responding. Thus, derived relational responding only occurs in the context of coherence, that is, according to the particular history of relational framing.

Consequently, all that verbal organisms do show the coherence of their relational history. Having said that, a person might show an incoherent response from our perspective, but it is coherent according to the individual's history. Even when the present circumstances let a person—Susan in our example—derive that "what is happening to me is not what it should be," or "I have been struggling and things are getting worse, I can not understand why, this is incoherent for me," none of these responses are incoherent with her over all relational responding. Quite the contrary, even when Susan says that something is incoherent, this is derived, or repeated, according to her particular coherent history of framing. That is, her history of relating permits her to frame what it should be occurring to her now as different—or opposite—to what is actually occurring to her. And because the former network is strength over the latter, according to her relational history, the former dominates and Susan derived thoughts and feelings as "it can not be that way and I am very disappointed."

In other words, the strength/domination of our relational history is the coherence of our relational history. It is the same thing as when we respond to what is inconsistent with our own coherent history by trying to uphold the very coherence. For instance, trying to convey the others or ourselves that "we are right and the others do not understand anything" as a way to recover the consistency and reducing the discomfort associated with contacting the inconsistency between what happens and the ideas/rules, as relating behavior, established in the own history. Thus, the coherence of derived relational responding is present in all the selfing behavior, as it is in any other relational responding. This is why coherence becomes a hierarchical function over any other characteristic or functions of relational responding (Luciano, 2017).

Deictic and Hierarchical as the Core Framings in Selfing Behavior

Deictic and hierarchical framing is at the core of most complex human behaviors. Both types of behaviors are essential for organizing coherent behavior overall, and they are needed for responding to others and the relation between different aspects of one's behavior. As a whole, flexible deictic and hierarchical relational framing likely facilitates problem-solving and interpersonal skills.

Deictic framing is learning to behave from different perspectives. Briefly stated, when the deictic framing repertoire is in place, the child can frame agent (I versus other), time (now versus then), and space (here versus there) from the unique I–here–now perspective. The social contingencies facilitating the distinction I–you are established early, and more complex contingencies are needed to establish I–now, I–before, I–after, I–here, I–there, and the respective combinations while learning to do it without losing the perspective of I–here–now (Barnes-Holmes, Hayes, & Dymond, 2001; Luciano, Valdivia, Cabello, & Hernández, 2009; Luciano, Gil-Luciano, Barbero, & Molina-Cobos, 2020).

Hierarchical framing is trained across many examples with different arrays of functional combinations so that different stimuli might be hierarchically organized—for instance, when the child is taught to respond to different stimuli (e.g., different cats, dogs, elephants, eagles) as belonging to a higher-order class based on sharing common functions (e.g., animals because of specific living functions). Hierarchical framing is perhaps the most sophisticated and flexible of the relational frames we can learn because of the flexibility to organize stimuli at different levels under different contextual functions. Social questions and contingencies are needed to establish the myriad flexible organizations of stimuli. Numerous kinds of hierarchical networks might be established, and they are essential to acquire flexibility in many different ways. As an illustration, imagine the many ways you can organize animals, minerals, stars, human beings, food, races, as well as organizations such as religions, political parties, countries, business, science, and even the taxonomic system of mental disorders, or the organization of a person's behaviors as types of personalities.

These latter examples are of special interest here. First, we will see how all framings partake in developing private events as thoughts/ideas/actions about ME and OTHERS. Next, we will see how the abstraction of ME functions as a continuity or common experience across multiple behaviors of the same individual. Following, we will describe the functional hierarchical organization of these behaviors. Finally, we will present two ways of responding (two functional classes) to these behaviors: (1) responding in coordination with the function of one's own behavior in a way that opposes other functions, resulting in limiting consequences to your life; and (2) responding hierarchically to one's own behavior, thereby integrating any other function of that behavior under the domination of another function, resulting in an adaptation to life.

DEICTIC AND HIERARCHICAL RESPONDING FOR DERIVING SELF-CONTENTS AND ESTABLISHING RELATIONAL FUNCTIONAL OPERANTS

As is true of other stimuli functions, human beings respond to ongoing private events according to their personal history and then contact the consequences of such responding. However, private events are not isolated phenomena, they are inevitably related to other private events in the person's history. Consequently, given always a particular history, in any present circumstance, an ongoing private event and its relations to other events, the response to its functions, and the consequences contacted are a single unit of behavior. Through MET, instances of such units become related based on their functional properties, and they form relational functional classes around the experience named I/ME, with deictic and hierarchical framing at the core.

Let's present several scenarios of possible early interactions with a small child, Mario, and the people around him. This example is in some ways extreme, but it is given to illustrate how relational framing can build overarching functional classes of behavior. The same principles of learning are assumed to be present in less extreme experiences.

Watch Mario as he cuts his hand with a blue knife. His mother cures the wound and blames him for what happened. She scolds him because he did not pay attention, and she compares his behavior to his father's, who died some time ago in a car accident. After this incident, Mario starts to avoid knives and other physically similar objects (e.g., scissors). He refuses to pick up such things and will not even open the kitchen drawer where spoons, forks, and knives are kept. His mother also insists that he should wait for her to help him do certain things and instructs him to be as careful as his intelligent brother. After hearing his mother's description of the event ("It's because you did not take care, you did that dangerous thing and you got hurt"), Mario derives contents such as: "There are many dangerous things," "I am hurt because I do not pay attention," "I have to avoid dangerous things and also my mother being mad at me." Then, this network is related to another network with opposite functions (i.e., "things that do not hurt"). For instance, Mario begins to approach objects with physical or arbitrary opposite functions in his history, such as feathers, and things with red color because he has learned that red is opposite to blue. Soon after, he refuses to use a mechanic escalator for the first time and is uncomfortable when any blue object is in his way. He also insists on crossing the street to avoid a hardware store. In all cases, "he is afraid to be hurt." His teacher and family, especially his mother, do not understand these behaviors. His mother says, "I'm tired of your inattentive and stupid actions," while his teacher tells Mario and the family that perhaps he has a brain problem. The point is that Mario has derived punishing functions based on very arbitrary relations. For instance, he was told that hardware stores have all kinds of metal things, and he knows that knives are made of metal. He also has read the written signal "Pay attention: Danger!" close to the mechanic escalators, and these words were related in Mario's history in coordination with being hurt. Finally, the deictic I–other repertoire permits Mario to derive more content about himself and the world around him, such as "I am different from the others," "My brain is different," "My mother does not want me close to her," or "I do not want to use escalators and prefer elevators."

At this point, Mario's fear of being hurt has been expanded based on stimulus generalization and symbolic generalization through relations of coordination, opposition, causality, deictic, and hierarchical framing. The result is a network of words, emotions, and actions coordinated under the function of avoidance (i.e., the fear of being hurt, the fear of dangerous things related to many actions named as "doing stupid things," and related to not taking care, disturbing others, and causing his mother to be mad at him). All of his "stupid reactions" have been related to "problems in the brain." At the same time, an additional network is formed, with thoughts, emotions, and actions based on opposite functions to danger and being hurt. In Mario's words, "being secure, escaping danger" is paramount. Further, more interactions can extend these relational functional operants by deriving more thoughts and actions that will acquire controlling functions. For instance, when his uncle says he needs to pay attention to learn biking, this becomes an aversive action. Therefore, he refuses to learn biking because he derives the idea that biking is as dangerous as entering hardware stores and mechanic escalators. Given the derived aversive and avoidance function of biking, Mario stays home and contacts the consequences of not being hurt, which is the opportunity to derive more self-content with aversive and avoidance functions (e.g., relating staying at home with the stable feeling of being secure and perhaps pleasing his mother). This is because his mother sometimes takes care of him even though, at other times, she rejects him without providing clear signals for

Mario to predict her reactions. This leaves him without cues to what would be better for him to do to impact the whole components of the networks. As we will explain later, deriving these thoughts and emotions and responding in coordination with the avoidance function they bring are coherent for Mario.

The story continues as Mario becomes more fluent in deictic framing and, thus, can elaborate new self-content by comparing himself to others (deictic I–other) and himself in different times/places (I–now, I–then; I–here, I–there) in conjunction with hierarchical framing where some elements belong to him and others belong to someone else. For instance, Mario, like his uncle, becomes a fan of the Barcelona soccer team (both are Barcelona fans, thus members in something that integrates them). Because this team is opposite to Real Madrid, Mario jumps with joy when Barcelona beats Real Madrid while shouting "We are winning," as he derives that his uncle and all the fans of Barcelona will be jumping. At the same time, he derives that his brother, who supports Real Madrid, will be angry.

Moreover, when watching a film in the school, Mario hears that "not taking any risk is a sign of cowardice" and that "cowardly people do not have fun." So, Mario derives that "he will not have fun," which makes him sad. Moreover, while watching other children having fun, Mario derives that they are brave, but he is different and alone. He wants to play with other children, but in one of the few attempts to play soccer, the coach puts him aside for not doing well, and he then escapes running away and crying. He derives that he is a coward and has no friends. So, he stays home alone to avoid being hurt. In addition, Mario's mother frequently asks Mario to be out of sight to avoid being mad at him; she tells him to behave like others, especially like his brother. So, Mario derives that he is silly instead of as intelligent as the others are and that he is a problem to his mother. This increases his feeling of being different and of being incapable of behaving like others.

Because of his fluency in temporal deictic and causality framing, Mario worries about the consequences of not having friends and being alone. Also, he thinks about being brave, being more like others, and behaving like others. So, Mario derives more self-content with aversive functions and is controlled by their avoidant functions that preclude contact with positive reinforcing functions. As Mario frequently engages in avoidance reactions, he is learning to repeat the previous derived content, increasing the strength of the coherence and making it (his self-contents) more rigid or inflexible.

Fortunately, in the middle of these interactions, Mario has had the opportunity to contact contingencies of positive reinforcement, mostly linked to activities with his uncle. For instance, he enjoys playing soccer, moving around in the field, tracking animals (especially birds), and playing and creating stories about animals. He also enjoys building different things with lego pieces. He often talks about enjoying these things and says that it is especially true in his uncle's company because he makes sure that nothing hurts him.

In conclusion, all these scenarios have been the occasions for Mario's framing in coordination, distinction, causality, comparison, opposition, conditionality, deictic, and hierarchical to derive thoughts and feelings (i.e. more derived contents that are attached to the already derived and now repeated), and to respond in coordination with the functions coming along with the derived behavior. Thus, as a consequence of Mario's daily interactions in the context of his relational history, two networks are on their way. More precisely, *two relational functional operants are being built.* On the one hand, there is the operant that dominates the scene: a relational functional operant involving many different stimuli, situations with thoughts and emotions showing up and actions, all connected to the function of avoidance (e.g., avoiding being hurt and bothering others and, consequently, approaching opposite functions as the reverse of this network). On the other hand, there is a weak relational functional operant that is being built based on all behaviors, mostly under positive reinforcement (e.g., the things he enjoys and that he is beginning to be identified with). However, the latter is not built only under appetitive functions of these actions but is also attached to avoiding social and physical risks when in the presence of his uncle. That is, the avoidance network, as a relational functional operant, is dominating Mario's daily interactions and is building a trap that is blocking other sources of functional control.

The behavioral units forming these relational functional classes are built of multiple relational framings with conditional and, mostly, deictic and hierarchical responding at the core; that is, all relational behavior should be in place. Importantly, here hierarchical framing is involved in more sophisticated behaviors, like the formation of abstract sources of motivations along with the functional establishment of ME and the functional organization of the contents connected to I. And yet, one more application of hierarchical framing sets the scene for responding effectively in the presence of whatever private behavior is fleeting in the moment of any circumstance. Let's explore these hierarchical applications, which would help Mario from being trapped in his own behavior.

HIERARCHICAL FRAMING IN THE ESTABLISHMENT OF OVERARCHING MOTIVATION

Technically speaking, hierarchical functional classes are built from the bottom up, based on common functions from specific actions. The actions at the bottom are arbitrarily connected to a more general and abstract function (going upward), which could also be connected to an even more abstract function. The most abstract function will control the whole network, since this characteristic defines the hierarchical function. That is, the hierarchical function will be the context for integrating elements with different functions, with all of them acquiring the top hierarchical function while keeping the differential functions. In this way, the individual history of interactions selecting the overarching/hierarchical functions will dominate responding even in the presence of other functions. On the one hand, when this is applied to one's behavior, the overarching/hierarchical function (e.g., an avoidance function) will control the functions of the different behaviors (e.g., thoughts, emotions, and actions) integrated into the hierarchical network (i.e., it should transform the functional properties of all these elements). On the other hand, the hierarchical functions should set the stage for additional derivations of more elements (e.g., more behavior) under their control. Let's illustrate this with the case of Mario.

Mario's interactions, primarily those with his uncle, have been opportunities for learning behaviors under positive reinforcement that ultimately will become hierarchical networks of private and public behaviors. Let's unpack how this could happen. Mario enjoys playing soccer as well as moving around in the field to learn about animals, especially birds. He also enjoys building bridges, villages, and castles with lego pieces, playing with the lego characters, and inventing stories with numbers. Even though these started as independent activities, they will eventually be connected and their functions will extend and be amplified beyond the early contingencies maintaining them. For instance, in the interactions with his uncle, a science teacher, Mario has learned to observe the characteristics of birds and other animals. He has also been told that he is becoming an explorer because he asks many questions as to how things work. While Mario plays with lego pieces and makes bridges, villages, and castles, his uncle tells him that he is very good at building and inventing things. His uncle also tells him that being an explorer and inventing things to resolve problems is what engineers do. This dialogue leads Mario to derive that he is like an engineer because he enjoys knowing about animals and building bridges and castles. Thus, "being like an engineer" becomes a hierarchical or overarching function that will control the functions of other behaviors (e.g., playing with lego pieces and observing birds) and will be the context for deriving more elements under its control. For instance, when Mario is told that engineers use math and the English language to resolve problems, his interest in math and English classes increases.

Let's now see an example of how the hierarchical function of "being like an engineer" can also be the context for deriving aversive functions. Imagine that Mario's mother does not understand his interest in being an engineer. Instead, she lets him know that engineers are intelligent and brave and do not say or do stupid things, as he does. Exacerbating the situation for Mario is his teacher's description of him as becoming "more impulsive" than before in math and English classes. The teacher tells Mario and his mother that he does this to claim attention and that he gets angry and runs away when making mistakes. At the end of the day, Mario feels sad because he will not be an engineer, and thinks he is a coward and cannot do many things. Unfortunately, these interactions actualize previous derived emotions and thoughts, which become the context for deriving more private events with aversive and avoidance functions. The main point is that these newly derived thoughts and emotions become the context for reducing Mario's interest in the activities he used to enjoy because the appetitive network is becoming connected to the avoidance network.

In summary, the hierarchical organization of valuing and establishing relational high-order or hierarchical reinforcers transforms the function of the many different actions integrated in the hierarchical network. This is an RFT conceptualization of values that is clinically very useful (e.g., Dahl, Lundgren, Plumb, & Stewart, 2009; Luciano, Valdivia-Salas, & Ruiz, 2012). The experimental analysis of the hierarchical transformation of functions is still on its way, though. It has been partly documented (e.g., bottom-up transformations of functions; Gil, Luciano, Ruiz, & Valdivia-Salas, 2012, 2014), although the complete picture (bottom-up and top-down) is still in its first steps (Callejón, 2020; Villarroel, Luciano, & Ruiz-Sánchez, 2021). Despite the need for further basic manipulations to demonstrate the hierarchical formation of values, a good number of studies in the last 15 years have shown the conditions under which the domination of a certain function over another is established. We will come back to these studies in the last section of this article. For now, let's look at some more implications of hierarchical framing that establish additional and more sophisticated self-behavior.

ABSTRACTION OF I/ME AND THE SUBSEQUENT DERIVATION OF MORE SELF-CONTENTS

Whatever behavior a person is exhibiting, there is a constant experience of ME, the one doing whatever is done. However, differentiating I as the context that is the doer as different from the thing done results from an arbitrary—socially mediated—learning process. As stated earlier, this is not an automatic process; rather, it depends on specific interactions with others, where deictic and hierarchical framing is learned.

From the very beginning of our interactions with others, the words **I** or **ME** are incorporated in hundreds of behaviors, all with their respective contingencies. However, these experiences are not sufficient conditions for discriminating or abstracting I from the behaviors done. The others' behavior, in particular ways, is needed to establish the arbitrary differentiation of the agent and the actions done (perhaps we should remember that we learn the so-called parts as arbitrary divisions because of convenience). That is, the child learns to abstract the differentiation. For instance, *from* Ieatbanana, Ieatapple, Idrinkwater, Idrinkmilk, Idrinkwater, Iwantplay, Iwantsleep *to* Ieat banana, Idrink apple, Iwant play, and lastly, *to* I eat, I want, I drink, and so on. This abstraction process leads to deriving the experience of I as the only context across all situations. Of course, all this occurs in the context of equivalent examples regarding the OTHER or YOU (Hayes, 1984; Kohlenberg & Tsai, 1991).

In other words, we are discriminating between the thing eaten and eating, or the thing being drunk and drinking and many others, as well as differentiating between the agent and the actions done; that is, the abstraction of I/ME through eating, drinking, feeling, seeing, and hearing are all the result of a learning process. This learning requires specific contextual cues provided by others. Questions such as what are you doing, who is doing it, who is doing that now, and there and then, etcetera, with clear and consistent contingencies are needed so that the child's responses become established in a consistent I across multiple opportunities. The context of the deictic I, in contrast to YOU, with the different combinations of I–YOU and Here–There and Now–Then are essential interactions to establish the hierarchical context of an I separated from actions in time and place. The deictic I establishes the conditions for the hierarchical abstraction of I/ME as a "locus" through many different responses in different times and places (see Barnes-Holmes et al., 2001; Hayes, 1984; Kohlenberg & Tsai, 1991; Luciano, Valdivia-Salas, Cabello et al., 2009; Skinner, 1945, 1953). Importantly, as Kohlenberg and Tsai (1991) suggested, when this discrimination process is lacking, the I that emerges is unstable and does not differentiate one's behavior and experience from those of the others.

Deictic framing across many exemplars generates the context for a hierarchical I as a basic experience. That is, responding to the question "who is doing X?", with "I am." "It is ME who is doing X." And when doing Z, it is ME who is doing Z. When feeling A, it is ME who is feeling, who is choosing, and so on. That way, ME/I is abstracted as a common function in all these instances. As a child becomes more fluent in multiple deictic framing, using the word "I" (or any other stimulus that should be used for the same purpose) leads to the derivation of myriad I-behaviors that were not connected previously but now become so. Accordingly, a hierarchical network is formed with functions coming from all the behaviors, including the initially derived behaviors. For instance, Mario's interactions with the questions of others establish the conditions for him to derive that "it is me who is not playing," "who has been beaten," "who is feeling alone," "who is bothering my mom," and so on. The derived relational behavior coming from these single deictic behaviors conjoint into a higher categorization, ME/I, summarizing the aversive and avoidance functions of single behaviors, as a deep feeling of being different, rejected, and alone.

Moreover, the different examples for avoiding being hurt to avoid risks, as well as discriminating the successful common avoidance effects across the different behaviors, is the context for deriving the functions of being a "safe person," as a higher-order category of "not taking risks," and with the emotional functions coming from all the avoidance behaviors. Importantly, having learned that "people who do not take risks are losers," Mario derives a more abstract thought and emotion of "me, a loser" that guides the derivation of additional self-behavior and extends the avoidance network, which strengthens its coherence. For instance, Mario rejects a school trip because he is told that it is necessary to be careful and pay attention to the teachers during the trip. Then, he derives that "the trip might be dangerous and to be a safe person you should not take a risk!" thereby increasing the strength of the coherence of his avoidance pattern. Moreover, because the only alternative conditions given to Mario are those that maintain the avoidance pattern, "the qualification as a safe person" is extended throughout the coming years. For instance, he might be invited to a party in his adolescent years, but he refuses to go in order to avoid the risk. Even later on, he might refuse a job because he feels he cannot do things by himself and needs help and support from others. Given these conditions and Mario's fluency in relational responding in deictic, causality and comparison, he will derive more general thoughts with the corresponding function. For instance, "I will never be normal as the others," "Nobody wants to be with me, I need to be out of view," and so on. To the extent that relational responding is reinforced, the person will develop greater fluency in deriving relations according to causality and comparison based on deictic framing. For instance, when Mario realizes that things are inconsistent with what he thought should be (i.e., when confronting problems), his primer reaction is to derive reasons based on his fluency in framing stimuli in causality and comparison based on deictic framings I–Other and I–Here, I–There. This way, Mario asks and responds to himself why things happened and compares himself at different times with others. Consequently, many thoughts are derived as reactions to the problems, thus becoming components of the functional relational operant as additional multiple exemplars. Needless to say, the relational avoidance operant is augmented with every single unit, and it strengthens according to the coherence established in Mario's life.

At the very end, Mario feels deeply different from others, a loser, unable to do many things, and living in an automatic way. Because he typically responds according to the avoidance functions of private events, Mario has multiplied that type of reaction to his world inside when contacting the world outside. Furthermore, he is encountering many limitations in his life and is deriving more fears and more suffering. In his middle twenties, Mario says that he feels like "a mouse escaping to the holes" most of the time. Generally speaking, he is deriving a metaphor as relating to networks. On the one side is the network with the causal relation established in Mario's experience with mice (e.g., "the mouse running away to the hole and escaping from the cat"). On the other side is his network of "running away from others' view and keep hidden to avoid being hurt and rejected." Given such a context, he derives more relations with the respective aversive functions as "he sees his life as a desert with nobody loving him, unable to do many things and not recognizing frequently who he is." In such a context, additional thoughts are derived as "no solution, nothing to be done, not being really alive, and not standing things being that way forever."

Importantly, *the self-contents* become frequently organized in *hierarchical networks*. The different groups of networks at the bottom gather into more abstract categories, with higher aversive or appetive functions (depending of the personal history) that finally derive at yet another more abstract level, all under the rubric of ME. That is, some private events might be concrete (e.g., "I failed the exam," "I have not gone to the party." "I cannot reach their attention"), with the specific function they bring according to a particular learning history, and become established at the bottom level of the hierarchy. Other verbal formulations are more abstract and connect the more concrete ones according to the particular person's history, which lastly is connected to the continuous experience of ME (e.g., "I do not do anything right," "I am a disaster." Moreover, they can go further up with increasing abstraction, and the higher up in the hierarchy, the more dominant/inclusive the function is, again, according to the person's history (e.g., "Nobody loves me," "I feel alone and empty"). Importantly, the functions integrated at all levels become connected to the continuous experience of ME with further derived responding (e.g., "What kind of person am I?", "I hate myself").

Recent research (Gil-Luciano, Calderón-Hurtado, Tovar, Sebastián-Sánchez, & Ruiz, 2019) has shown the frequent hierarchical organization of negative thoughts in most participants. They reported a higher aversive value in those thoughts that they have established at the top of the hierarchy compared to those at other levels. Beyond the clinical observations, this is congruent with the scarce available data on the hierarchical transformation of function. As indicated in the previous paragraph, research has shown the transformation of functions from the bottom to the top level of hierarchical networks (Gil et al., 2012, 2014). Furthermore, if a new function is given to the stimulus at the top of the hierarchy, it will be expanded to all the network members (top-down) (Callejón, 2020, and Villarroel et al., 2021). This means that when thoughts about oneself established during life, each with its specific functions, are organized in a hierarchical network, those at the top affect the meaning of all the hierarchy members.

Now, we will describe yet another application of hierarchical framing, perhaps the most complex one. As indicated in other sections of this article, we always respond to the stimulus functions in the present and we do so in the context of our personal history. Accordingly, when thoughts and emotions are derived, we may learn to choose the direction of our response *and what specific response to do*, but we cannot choose not to respond. The last portion of the second part of the article describes two patterns of responding to your behavior, with opposed functional focus, and, accordingly, different effects for the person and the whole community of individuals that establish what is meaningful in the respective culture.

TWO TYPES OF RESPONDING TO ONE'S OWN BEHAVIOR AS TWO RELATIONAL FUNCTIONAL OPERANTS

As described previously, human beings are constantly visited by emotions and thoughts that emerge in particular moments because of their personal history. These behaviors are brought with motivational and discriminative functions. The first and easiest way is to respond according to these functions, which generates reinforcing consequences accordingly that sooner or later will be transformed into suffering. This behavioral pattern is known as psychological inflexibility and is the relational operant dominating Mario's repertoire. The other, more complex way of responding to one's own behavior, named psychological flexibility, is characterized by responding to your own behavior under the control of meaningful personal motivations that should be established as a hierarchical function integrating any other present functions. Consequently, at least two functions need to be present, one that will become dominant (e.g., something to become meaningful for the person) over the other (e.g., fear, doubts). When responding to one function over other different functions, this function becomes an overarching function connected to I. This is the core of the repertoire of framing one's own behavior hierarchically. As stated previously, *this has to be specifically learned.*

Psychological Inflexibility as a Pattern of Responding in Coordination with One's Own Behavior

The pattern of psychological inflexibility is defined as a relational operant established by multiple exemplars of ***responding in coordination*** with the function of one's own behavior (Törneke, Luciano, Barnes-Holmes, & Bond, 2016). The most frequent function controlling this operant is responding to the avoidance functions that private events bring, as established in opposition to doing things in a meaningful direction. Although exemplars of this type of responding typically pay off in a short time in the context of avoidance, it does not consider what matters in each moment. Thus, this operant does not work in the long term because the result of the whole package of MET prevents contact with personally relevant contingencies. Consequently, when this operant dominates the person's repertory (e.g., it is the unique or most frequent operant), suffering and limitations will dominate life.

Let's think of Mario's history, where some appetitive functions that matter to him have been contextualized in opposition to specific private events. Consequently, when signals of fear, hurt, or disapproval surface, the avoidance function will dominate the scene. Then Mario will display different actions established in his inflexible operant along with his life (e.g., crying, running away, staying alone, complaining, and thinking about how to get away from all this). These actions are frequently effective in the context of avoidance but not in the context of the functions that, at the very end, matter to him. Accordingly, he is trapped, responding in coordination with avoidance functions based on the instructional control of rules inviting him to fight against certain emotions and thoughts. In other words, Mario displays a pattern of responding in which avoidance functions dominate in a never-ending cycle of avoidance that prevents contact with the contingencies that seem significant for Mario.

According to the conceptual and empirical research conducted, let's summarize the relational characteristics of this inflexible generalized functional class as an ineffective relational functional operant.

First, as is true of all functional classes, relational functional classes are operants, established *at the individual level and through multiple exemplar training (MET)*. Consequently, the repertoire of responding in coordination with one's own behavior is established in different ways across different persons, but all of them have that specific function.

Second, as an operant, topographical variability in the MET components for each person is key to building this repertoire. However, all behaviors are established in the context of a common function: responding in coordination to the avoidance function of private events. Then, the MET along the personal history shows variability in its components.

a. *Variability in the physical circumstance or stimuli that bring different functions as variability in private experiences*: the thoughts, feelings, and emotions are related in particular ways because of the specific history of relating (e.g., the rules established in the person's life).
b. *Variability in the different ways of reacting to the functions of such private events*: different reactions that are under a common function, say avoidance, based on the rules established in the person's life. For instance, avoidance behavior such as thinking over and over, consuming drugs, alcohol, crying, complaining, doing physical exercise, oversleeping, and so on. In turn, the consequences linked to the avoidance reactions are mostly negative reinforcement (the discomfort, fear, and pain are somehow alleviated) and all under the coherent reinforcing function of relational responding.
c. *Variability of exemplars controlled by the common function of avoidance*. There is typically a way of reacting to problematic private events. This is engaging in a cycle of "thinking and thinking" that does not solve the problems but occasions a motivational context for additional avoidance actions. This way of thinking, frequently known as rumination or repetitive negative thinking (Ehring & Watkins, 2008), is a pervasive, primer way of reaction that occurs according to the coherence of the relational history (Ruiz, Riaño-Hernández, Suárez-Falcón, & Luciano, 2016). In addition, the resulting thoughts and emotions of this relational activity show variability that depends on the particular fluency in relational framing when problematic private events are present. For instance, it might be given reasons as a function of comparing oneself in other times and places or with other persons, or it might be based on asking for/answers on causality and so on.
d. *Variability* in *motivation*, that is, in the *quality and the meaning of acting*. These motivative functions, which are frequently implicit or not well discriminated by the client, are not contacted because actions under its control are blocked by the domination of avoidance control based on relating aversive private events as opposed to valued actions. Consequently, the avoidance operant imprisons the person in his own behavior.

Third, as *coherence* is the hierarchical function that characterizes the history of relational responding, all the components of the operant, including the consequences of responding, are contextualized in the relational history that is brought to bear in any situation. This is why responding under the control of avoidance function makes sense even when it generates suffering in the context of higher-order or meaningful motivations (that are seen as opposed to the functions controlling avoidance). Once again, the reinforcing function of the coherence of relational history makes sense, perpetuating the pattern of responding.

Fourth, as an operant, this pattern of inflexibility is defined functionally and has been found to be transversal throughout most of the formally distinguished syndromes in mainstream psychopathology. Furthermore, it has been found transversal in many other areas where the human condition generates some level of suffering or discomfort in pursuing life. Note that the research evidence regarding these behavioral patterns is extensive in many respects (the reader will find some examples in the final part of this article).

Psychological Flexibility as a Pattern of Responding Hierarchically to One's Own Behavior

In the relational definition provided in Törneke et al. (2016), this pattern is seen as a functional class of responding characterized by framing one's own behavior in hierarchy with the deictic I. Put briefly, psychological flexibility is a relational functional operant of *framing one's own behavior hierarchically*.

What is needed to establish such a repertoire, at whatever age, is a MET of specific responding for learning to not respond directly to the functions showing up, being appetitive or aversive, and being aware of noticing them and responding in the inclusive context of another function—typically, a meaningful, higher-order, or abstract function based on positive reinforcement. Learning such an operant involves a complex process of becoming conscious of ME (deictic I), that is, of who is noticing the functions fleeting as well as of learning to make choices and responding under the control of that function that we would want to control our behavior. This way, when MET of this type of responding is in place, one function acquires a dominating hierarchical function over other functions. This is the case of Maria, who is having similar interactions with her family as Mario does in early childhood. However, she was moved to live with another family, who fortunately provided her with a motivational context based on positive reinforcement. In this new context, Maria learned to be willing to contact her avoidance rules and still acted according to those other functions. That way, Maria was able to build a consistent and transversal ME through effective ways of interacting with her private world. Rarely do we learn to fly with the winds of pain—of whatever form—without a systematic learning process that has promoted responding focused on a meaningful function and integrating—instead of escaping from—the pain in the way of acting under meaningful function.

Even Mario could have been quite a different person if he had been exposed to another history of interactions with others, a learning history that could have established an inclusive relational pattern of responding to his own behavior, as in the case of Maria. All in all, Mario is in a position to learn an effective relational operant, provided he is given the contextual conditions for learning a relational operant that will allow him to experience the contingencies available when choosing consciously to respond under the functions that might be developed as personal meaning. Said another way, if Mario is given conditions for effective interaction with his own behavior, then a hierarchical network—integrating different functions and actions under one dominating—will be established. That is, he can learn an effective repertoire consisting of integrating whatever functions show up, according to the networks established in his history, while having space to respond under the influence of the function most meaningful to him. That way, Mario will learn the flexibility repertoire, perhaps the most complex aspect of the legacy of our ancestors via the culture in which we are raised.

Before going there, let's note the characteristics of psychological flexibility as seen from the perspective of a relational operant as hierarchically responding to one's own behavior. Many key characteristics of the context, indicated previously regarding Maria's history, could remain the same except that the relational and functional contexts controlling the MET are radically different and, consequently, a different repertoire is established.

This repertoire is built through a deictic/hierarchical MET that connects the diversity of thoughts and emotions, and the functions they bring, to a diversity of actions all under the control of an inclusive function of other present functions to allow better adjustment to the personal meaning.

First, the type of deictic/hierarchical MET is defined by hierarchically responding to private events, of course, in the context of the deictic I. Each exemplar is a chosen act under the function connected to the hierarchical ME, noticing the act of inclusion/integration of the thoughts and emotions that come in the way. This means that each chosen act is done in the deictic I–Here and my thoughts/emotions in the deictic I–There, generating a space between these events and what really matters to me.

Second, variability in the MET is key to building this operant as any other one. It will be variability in the content or type of private events contextually depending on the present and historical contexts; variability in the personal meaning, although finally all connected to the experience of ME; variability in the actions chosen; and, consequently, variability in the formal consequences that finally will be transformed according to the personal meaning as the higher or hierarchical common function across multiple exemplars.

Third, as previously indicated, coherence is the reinforcing function for responding according to the relational history that is brought to bear in any situation and is transformed accordingly—in this case, in the common context of the actions chosen under the hierarchical function.

Fourth, the relational operant of responding hierarchically to one's own behavior is a behavioral pattern identified in many areas as an effective repertoire of psychological flexibility: from clinical to sport, business, and policy, from adults to adolescents and children. That is, it is transversal and seems to be the most effective way to interact with our condition as verbal humans.

When that type of MET has not been provided to a sufficient degree in the personal history, as in Mario's interactions, there is still a way to go: a repertoire needs to be learned. This is the process of therapy, a process of building a repertoire of flexibility in the context of the pervasive coherence where the dominant functions controlling the client's behavior are ruining the client's life. In basic terms, it is necessary to build a relational operant of responding hierarchically to one's own behaviors on the grounds of the pervasive relational operant of responding in coordination.

Clinical Strategies As MET to Build a Pattern of Hierarchical Responding to One's Own Behavior

Törneke et al. (2016) described three core strategies that are needed to build the pattern of psychological flexibility as responding to the ongoing private events in hierarchy with the deictic I: (1) Helping clients experientially contact their history of inflexible patterns; (2) helping clients build the ability to frame their private events in hierarchy with the deictic "I"; and (3) helping clients clarify and amplify hierarchical positive motivations and choosing actions linked to them. The three strategies constitute a whole package, and, consequently, all their movements are multiple exemplars that will help the client display the hierarchical response to their behavior. The following paragraphs focus, first, on the functional analysis as the basic strategy and, second, on different aspects of the whole process that conjoint to the final common pathway of hierarchical responding. Thus, this is a more technically precise way of describing what was described as three strategies in our earlier publications (Törneke et al., 2016; Törneke, 2017).

Functional Analysis as the Basic Strategy

Functional analysis is not a specific recipe but rather a functional perspective applied in different ways and for different aims. It can be applied to clinical work, basic or applied experiments, teaching, and many other types of action. From the very beginning, the ABC unit has been successful in altering or building operants: (A) the historical and present antecedents (motivational and discriminative functions in a particular moment), (B) the response to such functions, and (C) the consequences (as positive or negative contingencies of reinforcement). This functional unit of analysis is sufficiently flexible that it can also be used when the ABC is applied to the typical relational behavior of verbal human organisms. A threefold focus is needed to clarify these characteristics.

First, any present behavior results from a personal history and is exemplified mostly as an operant established, then, through a history of MET. When conducting a functional analysis, we look for the operant by examining the motivational and discriminative functions of antecedents, the different responses under such functions, and the common consequences that follow across different but functionally equivalent situations.

Second, when a verbal repertoire is in place, the functional analysis becomes a relational functional analysis (Luciano et al., 2020; Törneke, 2021). That is, the ABC now involves functions that have been established through relational responding, but functions nevertheless. So, we analyze relational motivational and discriminative functions of stimuli, the behavior that occurs under such functions, and its consequences, aware that these consequential functions are also established by relational responding. All this occurs in coherence with a particular relational history. Therefore, each examined behavioral unit (flexible or inflexible) will exemplify the client's typical thoughts, instructions, and emotions, their motivational and discriminative functions, the multiple behaviors that follow, and the consequences in both the short and long term.

Third, when performing a functional analysis as part of therapy, the goal is to generate the conditions *for the clients* to discriminate and experience their way of interacting (B) with their private events as the functional echoes of their relational personal history (A), and the overall effects of this responding (C). Alternatively, we can say that the goal is to help the clients become aware of their historical and present baggage and, given that, be confronted with "and then what?" In other words, the therapist helps the client to become aware of the historical and present sources of behavioral control in a way that opens the door to behavioral change.

One important point to stress is that fostering a flexible repertoire is not just talking about behavior but generating the conditions for the relevant functions of private events to be present, helping the client to notice them, and choosing the best response in such conditions.

Analyzing Interactions in the Moment

The function of the therapist's behavior is not in the therapist's behavior per se, but instead in the meaning (functions) for the client according to the client's relational history. Thus, the flexible relational functional class will be promoted through multiple exemplars, which must be understood in that context. This point connects directly to the earlier formulation of clinical behavior analysis (Dougher & Hayes, 2000; Ferster, 1974, Kohlenberg & Tsai, 1991). The critical point for the therapist is to be aware of the effects their own behavior produces in the interaction and rely on that analysis rather than on rigid rules about what might be the result of any action from their side. That is, the meaning (functions) of something is not in the physical properties of the stimulus, in the content of a particular sentence or a particular posture, but in the client's history. All this occurs, from the beginning to the end, through the functions that the client's behavior generates in the therapist's behavior and vice versa. So, the therapist needs to look for many different ways to adapt their behavior to the client's repertoire, thereby supporting the client's learning process in moving from responding in coordination to their own responding to responding hierarchically in the same context.

For instance, even as the therapist might start the first therapy session by asking the client for permission to question them about sensitive issues in their life and encouraging them to stop the therapist whenever they want to, the therapist should pay particular attention to the client's response to this basic therapist behavior. The therapist's intention, of course, is to establish a shared therapist–client context as a starting point for communication. The critical point here is that even such basic phrases, and other signals that the therapist might show, have to be functionally analyzed in the context of the client's responding. Accordingly, the therapist's continuous task is to explore how the client's behavior changes during the session.

All strategies the therapist uses to support the clients in their change process are played out in the interaction between the client's and the therapist's relational behaviors. This means that all types of relational responding will occur, as they probably are engaged in any kind of verbal interaction. To accomplish the MET needed to increase psychological flexibility, we will emphasize hierarchical responding as the most versatile and central repertoire to train. In the following section, we will thus describe the work centered around this training and also present different aspects of the process based on Torneke et al. (2016) and Luciano et al. (2020).

Helping Clients to Experience Their Problematic Strategy and Moving Towards the Alternative

The therapist's behavior focuses on generating a context of interaction that will increase the probability that the client will become aware of their inflexible behavioral pattern and how it relates to their current problematic experiences and ultimately to what is meaningful to them. In each process of discriminating one's own behavior, its problematic consequences on one hand and what is meaningful to oneself on the other, hierarchical framing of your own behavior is key. Consequently, the therapist tries to have the interaction move between the components of the inflexible repertoire to meaningful motivation (and vice versa) and constantly focus on the training of hierarchical framing of one's own responding. The different clinical interactions used to accomplish this objective can be summarized simply as: "What is the problem, what has been done to resolve it," and "what are the effects regarding who you want to be and to accomplish?" Questions and answers, exercises, and metaphors co-created with the client are used in this training.

As we continue to describe some clinical strategies the therapist can use, we want to caution the reader that the following is not presented as a list of items to be strictly followed. Rather, we intend it as only a guide to support the therapist in their efforts to make the interaction a learning experience for the client, so that new, flexible behavior emerges.

1. Helping the clients to (a) *differentiate the private events*, including their rules, as motivational and discriminative antecedents under which they respond in coordination, so that they start to (b) *differentiate hierarchically the one who is noticing and responding.*

Many types of interactions exemplify this strategy. For instance, the therapist reacts to our client (Paul's) different behaviors as follow:

"You say that when you are with people, as you are now, here, with me, you feel anxious . . . . How do you notice it, where in your body do you feel your anxiety . . . ? Are there other situations when you notice the visit of this feeling of anxiety?

"What thoughts come to you right now, feeling that anxiety in your chest?" Alternatively, "You say that you have the thought of being a disaster. What other thoughts are coming with disaster? What is your body feeling when these thoughts visit you?"

"There are many ways of feeling anxiety. In your case, can you tell where you notice the feeling of anxiety? Can you put your hand at the place in your body where you feel the anxiety? How is that? What kind of anxiety is it? Let's imagine that anxiety has a form and a color. What might it be? Let's think that you can touch it and you feel its temperature, how is that? Can you leave the anxiety in your chest for a while and put your attention somewhere else in your body? For example, can you move your attention to your right leg? Now you can move your attention back to your chest and notice you are back there . . . . Can you, once again, move your attention to any part of your body of your own choice? Do you notice that you can move your attention? (the client says yes). Let's notice that experience and stay with it for a moment . . . . Now, go back to notice the anxiety in your chest . . . . Notice that you are noticing what you are doing . . . Can you bring a picture of you when you are at home with that feeling in the chest? Any other picture of you when you are at work? Can you bring some more pictures of you when you were an adolescent in a moment at school? Whatever picture is OK . . . . Can you move your attention from one picture to the other? What about imagining yourself as a lighthouse that moves attention to different things occurring to you?"

If our client, Paul, has followed this interaction and there are signs that he is discriminating himself as the observer of his own responding, the therapist might continue with asking the client to imagine or draw out this experience on a piece of paper and share, pointing to different perceptions noticed, that he is the one who is moving and is noticing the lighthouse shifting the direction of the light.

"Although there are differences between us as humans, we all react to what we feel and think . . . . In your case, how do you react when your anxiety, sadness, loneliness, and worries about the future talk to you? You say that you do not want to feel that way, that you don't want to have the thoughts you have . . . . You say that you react in different ways to stop thinking and feeling these ways . . . . When you feel . . . you do . . . to avoid feeling worse . . . . When you feel . . . you do . . . And who is noticing it all? Who is noticing the feelings, the thoughts, what you do, who is noticing? (The client answers: "It is me, I guess . . . . "). Yes, so you are more than all the things you can notice with yourself in that sense. You are also the one noticing them; might you also realize being the noticer?"

2. Helping the client to potentiate the hierarchical experience of I/ME as the transversal functional context of my behavior.

Sooner or later, the therapist should help the client derive the hierarchical experience of ME as the permanent and hierarchical context of their own behavior. This is not only tacting the ME but also ensuring a common experience throughout all different behaviors, "of what I felt, what I am feeling now, and might be feeling if, of what I have done, am doing, and might do, of what I am thinking about the future, about the past, about my family, my country . . . . Over all this, I am experiencing or noticing the context of Me noticing and Me reacting to this unique experience.

"Let's put it this way, on a side, it is you feeling anxiety, and then you also are feeling sadness, it is also you feeling alone, and you feeling rejected . . . . It is you thinking that your mom is . . . and it is you seeing the past . . . and you seeing what it would be like if you were not feeling alone or rejected . . . it is you in all these situations. On another side, it is you as the observer of one aspect, you moving the attention to some other, then to one more, as if being a lighthouse moving the light from one place to another. Even more, there is an other orbit besides observing your thoughts and emotions. It is the orbit of you reacting to any of them, in one case, you did . . . in another, you did . . . now you are with me talking about this . . . . What do you see here? What do you notice?"

The therapist moves to help the client, Paul, derive the hierarchical I across many of his own behaviors to foster the hierarchical organization of his behaviors as different elements of his problematic strategy or repertoire, the one of responding in coordination. The therapist is using many different cues to that aim. In all cases, the therapist tries to train the experience of I–Here and behavior as I–There, and finally hierarchical framing in different domains.

3. Helping the client to give a common, hierarchical name to different private events.

One more example of hierarchical responding has the aim of helping the client to derive a common name for the multiple private events that have, through the personal history, acquired problematic functions. Putting the different events together is useful to support the discriminative process. Even if not all events have the same weight, they belong together as they share a common function, typically avoidance. For example, our client, Paul, might spontaneously name his thoughts and emotions as "alarms in the mind," or as "devils and angels in my head," or someone might describe his urges as "waves and storms in the sea." The therapist should be observant of these kinds of expressions, and when they seem to be helpful, should catch and use them. The therapist might also be the one introducing a metaphor. When Paul talks about worrying thoughts disturbing his sleep, for example, the therapist can say: "Yes, thoughts can be like irritating flies that keep you awake at night. You try to fight them, but they seem to be coming back and coming back." Let's say the client reacts to this description by saying: "Yes, there is a whole bunch of them, one worse than the other." Then the therapist can go on and co-develop the metaphor by, for example, asking the client to specify a couple of the worst "flies," perhaps giving them each particular names.

4. Helping the client to identify the different ways of responding connected to the same hierarchical function.

The same strategy of giving a common, perhaps metaphorical, name is used to help discriminate the different behaviors sharing the same function. This strategy can be applied to both inflexible and flexible classes of behavior. One important class that can be labeled this way is, of course, the different forms of experiential avoidance. For instance, the therapist might say, "When you have all these flies trouble you and block other things you want to do, what is your reaction? What do you do?" In this process, the therapist tries to help the client understand that different types of behavior are going in the same direction and have the same function. Perhaps all these different behaviors can be gathered together under the heading of "trying to strike the flies." In that way, the therapist can also help the client derive the relationships between the "flies" and the rules they carry with them, leading the client into problematic circles of avoidance, the effort of "trying to strike the flies."

It is particularly important to help the client, Paul, notice the quick, almost automatic, way he interacts with what turns up for him. These are the "self-evident," assumed "necessities of action" that constitute the motivational and discriminative functions the client tends to frame in coordination rather than hierarchically. These quick responses can be overt behavior, but they are also often ways of thinking and further elaborating about the problem experienced. The relational functional class of responding in coordination is frequently dominated by particular ways of thinking and thinking about the thoughts and discomfort that worry the client. When this is the case, the therapist should help the client derive the rule instructing these reactions. For instance, the therapist can help Paul identify the relation between the never-ending cascade of thoughts and emotions as, finally, the consequences of his efforts as indicated in the next point.

This way, the client will have the opportunity to notice that many different things they do are ways to escape or avoid aversive thoughts and emotions and that they all constitute the same strategy, providing the same problematic consequences.

5. Helping the client discriminate the causal relation between private events, responding under their control, and the short- and long-term effects.

The therapist can ask the client questions, helping them to discriminate the whole problematic pattern of certain private events, their functions, and the short- and long-term consequences of following such instructions or rules. This process can be described as the temporal relations of the sequence of events that should be discriminated as explicit causal relations. The therapist should assist the client in deriving cause–effect relationships across time between what they are looking for and the consequences they are pursuing, regarding the maintenance and expansion of the unwanted thoughts and emotions, as well as the persons they would like to be. First, these interactions aim for the client to contact the aversive functions provoked by responding in coordination as well as by projecting these aversive functions into the future according to the client's experience. Second, deriving the aversive functions will hopefully serve as motivation to contact higher reinforcing functions connected to them, that is, things that are of utmost importance to them in the long run. Of course, the process might go in the opposite direction, as when the interactions are first helping the clients to derive seeing themselves behaving in hierarchy with what is meaningful for them and, from such a context, seeing the aversive function of responding in coordination.

The therapist might point to the causal chain of events that the client, Paul, first described as separate events. The therapist can do so by saying, for example, "Let's look at this as if watching a film of you. You say that you are visited by anxiety and emptiness and then you have to do something to get rid of them. You say that you cannot pursue your life when those feelings and thoughts are visiting you. Is that correct? Moreover, I realize, being here with you, that these experiences are very uncomfortable. Furthermore, when these feelings and thoughts are present, then you do different things to stop them, the alarm, the flies (or whatever term is helpful)." If the client then seems to agree with the formulation (and it is very important for the therapist to evaluate whether that is so), the therapist can continue: "If you were not visited by these thoughts and feeling, would you be doing all these things?" Assuming that the client answers that they would not, then the causal relation is discriminated.

Once again, it might be useful to help the client formulate a metaphorical name for the I who is responding. It might be the driver, the captain of the boat, the boss, or something else. In addition to strengthening the experience of being capable of choosing what to do, it can help to connect to what is ultimately important to the client. For instance, what type of driver do you want to be: one who leaves the bus under the control to the flies or the alarms posed by the passengers, or the one who is in charge of the direction of the bus?

Once again, all types of relational behavior are present in this type of clinical dialogue, but hierarchical responding is "the final common pathway" in establishing clinical change.

6. Helping the client to integrate the most aversive private events into the hierarchical ME.

As indicated in the second part of this article, the networks established in the client's life are functionally coherent. They are built by deriving self-content and repeating them as well as the rest in the respective network. Any of the self-contents might have a relational discriminative function for more derived content. Helping the client to experience these networks, as the echoes of their personal history, seems to be a beneficial step in the process of integrating all and reacting to them.

For instance, when Paul is experiencing a very problematic thought, the therapist might help him give it a name (e.g., saying, "this seems to be a big one, doesn't it?"). Then, the therapist might invite the client to look for other thoughts that might be behind or around, even with most aversive functions. That is, on a side, the client is helped to give a name (perhaps the big thoughts for the most aversive ones, and the little ones for another with less aversive functions). On another side, the client is helped to take a distance from all of them, especially the big ones, and integrate them into themselves while moving forward. Typically, experiencing the emotional functions of the most fearful emotions and thoughts might be hard for the client because they are connected in some way to what is meaningful for the client. Consequently, this might be a key motivational context for helping the client to notice and integrate them and overcome the blocking effect.

7. The history in the present. Connecting private events hierarchically to the client's history.

Helping the client, Paul, identify causal relations between the most problematic and painful private events (thoughts and emotions) that he is experiencing now and episodes in his history seems to be an effective step in establishing a well-functioning hierarchical experience of self. This process is especially needed when the echoes of history prevent focusing on what matters. In such circumstances, the therapist should invite the client to go over them looking for moments, mainly those early in life, when these thoughts emerged. This will help the client integrate all the emotions involved and move forward.

The process of supporting the client in this work is in many ways similar to what has been described previously in this article. It typically adds dialogues and perhaps exercises where different key memories from the client's life are explored, and relational cues are provided for our client, Paul, to see himself from the perspective he had at the time of the event described. That perspective is then coordinated with the one experienced in the here and now by questions such as "Right here and now, can you notice that little child at that time? And can you notice that the one who was there and then is also YOU, being here with me?" This can be elaborated in many different ways, for example, by asking Paul to switch perspective, at one moment responding from the perspective of himself within the described event and in the next from the present situation. Moreover, as this is done, relational cues are provided for integrating the different perspectives as "ME."

Sometimes exposing a client to specific moments like these will cause very strong emotional responding. Therefore, the therapist should follow the client carefully, asking permission to continue or to stop. In the latter case, the therapist might later ask the client to go back and be willing to learn the repertoire of being the observer of the echoes of such episodes, and moving forward under meaningful functions, that is, as instances of hierarchical responding.

8. Helping the clients to experience the impact of the long-term and accumulative consequences of responding in coordination with their own behavior.

Under a previous heading (5), we discussed helping the client contact short-term and to some extent long-term consequences of their present, problematic behavior. We now want to place some extra focus on long-term consequences. As previously indicated, this is not merely discriminating a chain of events but deriving the causality between what the client is doing and the consequences in the long term. This matter should be examined in the context of what might be ultimately meaningful to the person.

The task is to help the client contact multiple examples of short-term consequences and ask the person to compare those consequences with the long-run effects. This question can be asked in the context of the life you want to live. Are you more or less tired now than you were at the onset of the problems? Do you experience yourself as stronger or weaker? In what way does the present strategy affect those disturbing thoughts and feelings? Compared to some time back?

The therapist might say: "Imagine yourself in a couple of years, continuing to do what you are doing now? What if you continue to fight the flies! What will your life look like? What about your dreams, your emotional situation, the sense in your body?"

This work will hopefully open the client to look in new directions. "What would it be like to be the captain of your own boat? In that case, where would you be heading? What kind of action performed now can take you in that direction?" If the client follows in the interaction, the therapist can ask: "How do you feel when looking at this? How does it sound to you?" Hopefully, the client will respond with curiosity, experiencing this possibility as something different. There might still be barriers, the uncertainty of what such possible actions imply. However, a possible way forward is present.

9. Helping to co-create a metaphor for the whole intervention model.

Using a metaphor that contains all the components we have discussed, ranging from responding in coordination with your own behavior to the alternative of responding hierarchically, has been found to be clinically and experimentally useful (Peña Vargas et al., submitted; Ruiz et al., 2016; Törneke, 2017). Metaphors can help the clients see the whole picture of their behaviors and open the horizon for a new way to act. For instance, some clients might say that their head is full of alarms or flies, or others might describe their life as an empty desert or, as our client Paul describes his situation, as running like a hamster in a wheel for years. The therapist might respond to these remarks by trying to co-create an overarching metaphor to help a client derive the components of both the problematic pattern and a possible new avenue. For instance, in responding to the description of Paul as being like a hamster, the therapist might make the following observations: "It seems that you do not like this sense of being like a hamster in a wheel. I see hamsters enjoying the wheel, but what about your experience of feeling as if being a hamster?"

In a dialogue based on the client's experience, all aspects of Paul's situation can be viewed through the lens of this metaphor. What occurs inside Paul that makes him jump into the wheel (examining private events and their functions as antecedents)? In what specific ways does he actually run, and how is he behaving inside the wheel (what actions are taken)? In addition, what is he obtaining when running in the wheel (asking for short-time consequences linked to the rules followed)? What things are important to the client, outside of the experience of being a hamster (asking for possible meaningful life patterns)? Or in the same direction: "If you could choose not to be a hamster, what type of animal would you like to be?" If Paul, for example, would respond that he would like to be a dolphin, being able to swim and jump in many different directions, then that metaphor can be used to explore the quality of the actions coordinated to being as a dolphin. If Paul should respond that "being a dolphin is being free," then the therapist should explore the possible alternative strategy and the possible consequences of acting with freedom.

10. Helping the client to potentiate the ability to frame private events in hierarchy.

We have emphasized the central repertoire of hierarchical framing of your own responding through this section of clinical intervention. Let us now add some directions to promote this behavior when the client does not show fluency in doing it. Like learning other abilities, MET to establish this behavior should include variability in the content but keep common relations. According to Luciano et al. (2011) and Luciano, Ruiz, Gil-Luciano, and Molina-Cobos (2021), hierarchical framing of your own behavior is connected to training deictic framing.

To help the client derive the deictic relation I–Here and their private events as I–There, MET might proceed from stimuli with neutral functions (e.g., the thoughts just emerging when looking at the glass, the lamp, or the window) to those stimuli with appetitive and mostly aversive/avoidance functions (e.g., the anxiety or the problematic thoughts). Several deictic and hierarchical relational cues should be used to encourage the response of observance and integration of thoughts or memories (e.g., "contemplating the thought as if you were contemplating a painting" or "writing it down on a post-it on the wall or writing on a balloon, if written in lower or uppercase letters"). In the case of emotions, the client might be helped to physicalize them, for instance, as if they were objects in some part of the body, and asking about what kind of object, what color if having a color, what size, what temperature and so on. In all cases, the aim is to promote a kind of distance and integration of private events as transitory events that one can observe without jumping into them and thereby ending up away from what matters. The training would encourage experimenting with the fact that one can observe one thought/emotion here, another one there, and so on. In this process, the therapist directs Paul's attention to the behavioral options connected to what might be meaningful for him, which would constitute a hierarchical response to overarching consequences for him.

One additional point in this process is to help the client, Paul, experience the very act of choosing behavior, the awareness of being the person who is doing the chosen act and connecting this experience to other acts and goals. That is, this process helps Paul derive the experience of himself hierarchically as "the I" who makes choices, who acts, who realizes that the quality of his acts is the central step in amplifying the relational operant of hierarchical framing of your own behavior. The final derivation promoted in the clarification and amplification of meaningful functions should be realizing that any private event is one aspect of oneself and that one is much more than any such single feeling and thought. What should be promoted is the experience of being a permanent transversal context of observation, having the ability to give space for whatever turns up on the private scene, as well as the experience of making choices as to what direction to take from there.

11. Helping to clarify and amplify the hierarchical function of meaningful directions.

In clinical situations, private events typically block the experience of appetitive motivation. Therefore, establishing such motivation as hierarchical and helping the client to act under such overarching functions is a critical aim. A key way for the therapist to increase the probability for this to happen is to help the client frame different actions and behavioral goals hierarchically, so that all of them become connected to what is experienced as ultimately important and meaningful.

This work involves interventions from the bottom of the hierarchy and upward and interactions moving from the top and downward (Luciano et al., 2021). As an illustration, imagine a client who has suddenly lost his wife soon after being retired from his work as a teacher. He summarizes his present situation as "the end of his life" and isolates himself from most activities outside his home. At the same time, as the therapist validates the client's loss, she might proceed by asking questions such as: "In your life together with your wife, what would you say were the most important things for you? What carried the deepest meaning, those feelings that were present when you were doing things together?" The same type of questions could be asked about his experience as a teacher. Through these questions, the therapist is looking for an overarching motivational function. Once something is made explicit, it can be used to move "downward" in the hierarchy, connecting it to specific acts and possible consequences in the present situation. So, for example, the therapist might continue: "So, this creativity and intimacy that you described from your earlier working situation when you were teaching your worst students, and you saw their faces when after a long way they achieved something, perhaps is there something that could be done now and that has something of the same feeling? Not so strong, perhaps, but still . . . .?" Alternatively, an exercise might be set up, bringing the client back to a typical appetitive situation from his experience as a teacher to see if he can contact some of this in imagery. Then, the therapist might ask: "If you could take that feeling, that sense of creativity and intimacy with your students and move it to some area of your life now, where do you want to bring it?" Also, the wife can be brought into the imagery, making her give him advice on how to live the kind of life they valued together.

A possible way for the therapist to move from the bottom of the hierarchy and upward would be to start in small events in the client's present life that seem to carry some meaning to the client. Perhaps the therapist notices something in some specific episode the client mentions. So, noticing something in the here and now, the therapist might focus on it saying: "I notice that this [something just mentioned] makes you look a bit interested" or: "There is a certain light in your eyes," or: "Something happens to you when you tell me about the phone call from your grandson. He seems to be important to you . . . . " All of these would be examples of moving from "the bottom up."

At the same time, as this work with building hierarchical functions of meaningful directions continues, the therapist needs to keep an eye on barriers that turn up in this very process. This is natural, as imagining alternative ways of acting to an extent is an analog of actually acting that way. Furthermore, that is a very difficult thing for the client to do in his situation. When this occurs, the therapist should make it explicit in the interaction and use it to go back to the other strategies already covered.

Finally, but not least, we point out the relevance of enveloping the clinical interactions hierarchically in a context of validation and comprehension.

Here we have pointed out some relevant aspects of the process that establish hierarchical responding through MET. We have emphasized that functional analysis is a continuous activity that permeates the therapeutic process, and we have described how it can be conducted with a focus on hierarchical responding, even when different aspects of the operant are worked with. This operant is defined by the hierarchical function of personal meanings that, in the end, envelop any single action. We have tried to make the basic relational processes somehow transparent, allowing the identification of the relational process involved in building a repertoire of flexibility in the context of the particular coherence defining the inflexibility repertoire, the repertoire dominating the scene when the therapy begins.

Empirical Evidence

This section presents relevant empirical evidence for the core aspects presented in this article.

Evidence of the Transformation of Eliciting and Avoidance Functions

A number of studies have demonstrated the transformation of eliciting and avoidance functions. Dougher, Augustson, Markham, Greenway, and Wulfert (1994) showed the transfer of respondent eliciting and extinction functions through equivalence relations, whereas Augustson and Dougher (1997) demonstrated the transfer of avoidance-evoking functions. These studies have been replicated and extended throughout the last two decades (e.g., Dougher, Hamilton, Fink, & Harrington, 2007; Dymond, Schlund, Roche, & Whelan, 2014; Luciano et al., 2014; Rodríguez-Valverde, Luciano, & Barnes-Holmes, 2009; Ruiz-Sánchez, Luciano, & Rodriguez, submitted).

Evidence of the Transformation of Functions through Hierarchical Relations

Gil et al. (2012, 2014) demonstrated the bottom-up transformation of functions through hierarchical networks that included relations of coordination and distinction. In addition, recent research has shown that class-inclusion responses can be trained through a nonarbitrary MET in autistic individuals (Zagrabska-Swiatkowska, Mulhern, Ming, Stewart, & McElwee, 2020). Finally, two very recent studies have systematically demonstrated contextual control in hierarchical responding at two levels (Callejón, 2020; Villarroel et al., 2021). These studies demonstrate first the top-down and bottom-up transformation of functions and, second, the domination of functions at the top over the other functions. These data are extraordinarily relevant as analogies of the formation of the selfing behaviors and the domination of some functions over others.

Evidence of the Hierarchical Organization of Self-contents

Some preliminary studies have shown that self-contents tend to be organized in hierarchical networks. For instance, Gil-Luciano and colleagues (2019) recruited 100 undergraduates who underwent several assessment phases, including a diagnostic interview, emotional symptoms and repetitive negative thinking (RNT), and a list of self-contents that usually serve as triggers for RNT. Participants selected the self-contents they usually experienced and rated how much they engaged in RNT. Subsequently, they were provided with three diagrams showing how these self-contents could be organized: Coordination, Comparison, and Hierarchy. Eighty percent of participants organized their self-contents in hierarchical networks.

Evidence of the Effects of Responding in Coordination to Behavioral Functions

Wide-ranging evidence exists that responding to eliminate painful private experiences (i.e., experiential avoidance) leads to increased suffering and prevents actions connected to hierarchical appetitive functions (i.e., values; Boulanger, Hayes, & Pistorello, 2010). In the experimental arena, Hayes et al. (1999) used the cold pressor task to compare the effect of a 90-minute acceptance protocol versus a control protocol. Participants who received the acceptance protocol kept the arm immersed in ice water significantly longer than participants receiving the protocol promoting discomfort control. Using electric shocks as aversive stimulation, Gutiérrez, Luciano, Rodríguez, and Fink (2004) compared the effect of 20-min acceptance-based versus control-based protocols, both in the context of a personal value. Participants who received the acceptance-based protocol showed significantly greater pain tolerance and lower pain believability (i.e., assessment of maximal discomfort while participants continued on task) than participants in the control condition. This study was replicated and extended in further studies (e.g., McMullen et al., 2008; Páez-Blarrina et al., 2008).

Evidence of Repetitive Negative Thinking as a Predominant Response in Coordination with Behavioral Functions

Robust experimental evidence has demonstrated that worry and rumination usually prolong and extend aversive functions (e.g., see reviews in Ehring & Watkins, 2008; Newman & Llera, 2011), and lead to other forms of experiential avoidance such as alcohol consumption, binge eating, self-injury, and suicidal behavior. Experimental analogs of such problematic responding has been done in Gil-Luciano et al. (submitted) in the context of more and less problematic thoughts.

Evidence of Hierarchically Framing of Ongoing Behavior as a Central Relational Process

In a preliminary study with at-risk adolescents, Luciano et al. (2011) analyzed the differential effect of two defusion protocols. The first protocol involved MET in framing ongoing private events through deictic framings (I–Here, My private events–There). The second protocol also added hierarchical framings and interactions to promote motivational functions to the verbal discrimination of private events (i.e., appetitive augmental functions). The results showed that the second protocol had a greater effect on reducing the frequency of problematic behaviors and psychological inflexibility at the 4-month follow-up. Some experimental analogs have replicated the results of the previous study with different dependent variables: experimentally induced emotional distress (Foody, Barnes-Holmes, Barnes-Holmes, & Luciano, 2013), tolerance on the cold pressor task and in the viewing of aversive films (Gil-Luciano, Ruiz, Valdivia-Salas, & Suárez-Falcón, 2017), and the performance in cognitive demanding tasks (López-López & Luciano, 2017). In conclusion, these studies suggest that including explicit hierarchical framings between the individual and their private events and providing the hierarchical context of regulatory functions to this discrimination enhance the efficacy of the MET in contrast to incorporating only deictic framing. To include only deictic framing is typical in many defusion exercises, whereas adding hierarchical framing is typical of a consistent intervention to promote the self-as-context linked to valued functions.

Two more complex and unpublished studies have produced advances over the previous research. Gil-Luciano, Tovar, Calderón-Hurtado, Sebastián, and Ruiz (submitted) tested the differential effect of two defusion protocols; one protocol consisted of MET in deictic framing, and the other consisted of MET in deictic and hierarchical framing plus motivational functions. These protocols were directed either to the hierarchical aversive self-content or to an aversive self-content in a low level of the hierarchy of self-contents. The results showed that the most complete protocol was more effective than the remaining combinations and a control condition in reducing the detrimental effects of a rumination–induction procedure. Finally, López-López (2016) tested the efficacy of four defusion protocols in improving performance on a cognitive demanding task (Protocol I: MET in deictic framing, Protocol II: MET in deictic + hierarchical framing, Protocol III: deictic + hierarchical framing + motivational functions, Protocol: deictic + hierarchical framing + motivational functions + hierarchically framing the chosen behavior). The results indicated that all the experimental protocols obtained a greater reduction in reported discomfort than the control condition. However, it was Protocol IV that obtained the greatest reduction in distress, and only Protocols III and IV significantly improved performance in the cognitive demanding task.

Evidence of Contacting Hierarchical Appetitive Functions as a Central Relational Process in ACT

Multiple experimental analogs have shown the effect of introducing a valued context in the protocols, either as the sole intervention strategy or as a multicomponent protocol (e.g., Gutiérrez et al., 2004; Hebert, Flynn, Wilson, & Kellum, 2021; Páez-Blarrina et al., 2008). Additionally, Luciano et al. (2010) found that aversive stimulation was rated as less intense when the discomfort was framed in a hierarchy advancing toward a valued direction (i.e., feeling discomfort and focusing on the task) than when it was framed in opposition.

Finally, only a few studies have analyzed the effect of protocols in the context of the transformation of functions as an experimental analog of the avoidance operant. For example, in Luciano et al. (2014), participants showed the acquisition of respondent eliciting and avoidance functions and their transference through equivalence classes. Afterward, the effect of a motivational protocol that established a conditional relation between approaching previously avoided stimuli and a general value was compared to a defusion protocol that included personally meaningful examples of approaching fear and a defusion exercise, including both deictic and hierarchical framings. The latter protocol eliminated the experimentally induced avoidance responding in all participants, even in the presence of respondent activation, whereas the former condition was effective in only 30% of participants. Lastly, Ruiz-Sánchez, Luciano, and Rodríguez-Valverde (submitted) measured the derived rules during the whole process and analyzed the effect of an if–then motivational protocol as keeping in the task and receiving a specific consequence, versus a hierarchical motivation protocol in which approaching previously avoided stimuli and receiving shock/noises were contextualized under personal meaning as a positive hierarchical reinforcer. The latter protocol was radically more effective than the former in all cases. Thus, this study shows that motivation based on positive hierarchical reinforcers produces almost complete suppression of avoidance behavior in contrast to reduced levels of suppression with only the if–then motivational protocol.

Evidence of the Components of Metaphors that Increase Their Therapeutic Effect

Some experimental analogs have been conducted regarding the relational processes involved in metaphors in the clinical setting. Sierra, Ruiz, Flórez, Riaño-Hernández, and Luciano (2016) found that participants who received metaphors, including common physical properties with the participants' pain, showed a higher increase in pain tolerance on a cold pressor task than participants who received the same metaphors but without common physical properties. These data were replicated by Criollo, Díaz-Muelle, Ruiz, and García-Martín (2018). All these results were in line with more basic studies conducted by Ruiz and Luciano (2015) regarding the effect of common physical properties in analogy aptness and derivation.

Peña-Vargas et al. (submitted) analyzed the effect on pain tolerance of metaphors that included hierarchical relations between the participants and their pain and/or amplified the long-term consequences of flexible and inflexible behavior. The results showed that the metaphor that included both components was significantly more effective. Lastly, Ramírez, Ruiz, Peña-Vargas, and Bernal (2021) analyzed the differential effects of presenting the metaphor by asking the individual to imagine being the protagonist of the story versus presenting the metaphor in the third person (Self vs. Other) and/or prompting the relational elaboration of the rules derived from the metaphor (Elaboration vs. No Elaboration). The results showed that including the components Self and Elaboration together significantly increased the participants' pain tolerance.

Efficacy of Brief Interventions Inspired by defining Psychological Flexibility as Hierarchically Framing of Ongoing Behavior

Some of the studies that have analyzed the effect of brief ACT protocols explicitly define many of the relational processes of psychological flexibility (Törneke et al., 2016). Ruiz et al. (2016) tested the efficacy of a one-session, repetitive-negative-thinking focused ACT protocol in a multiple-baseline design across 11 participants suffering from mild to moderate emotional disturbance. The results showed significant reductions in worry and rumination, emotional symptoms, experiential avoidance, cognitive fusion, and increased valued living in most participants. Ruiz et al. (2018) found very large effect sizes in bthe previous dependent variables when applying two sessions of a similar protocol to participants with moderate emotional disorders. These initial promising findings were followed by a randomized controlled trial comparing a previous two-session protocol against a waitlist control condition in participants with primary diagnoses of depression and/or generalized anxiety disorder. Again, a similar protocol produced large effect sizes and a high proportion of clinically significant changes (Ruiz et al., 2020).

Conclusion

This article invited the reader to travel across different sites concerning the development of human suffering and its treatment from a functional-analytic orientation. In this travel, we have used a boat under the title of hierarchical responding, a boat that has been used for several purposes.

To summarize, we have used hierarchical responding as the final common path to understand the many relevant aspects of selfing behaviors. Additionally, we have used hierarchical responding as the final common path to identify the many faces of the therapeutic process toward building a repertoire that will allow the clients to live a meaningful life. We are aware of the interpretative conceptualization involved in some parts of this article. At the same time, experimental evidence has been signaling this path for years. Still, a lot of extraordinary and creative work is still needed to open the many closed doors—including doors that we do not even know about. Perhaps the evolution of language has allowed us to learn such a highly flexible relational responding that we are now allowed to integrate the efforts of those who have preceded us, as well as to assimilate the many questions that we will leave behind. Perhaps this is why we often describe hierarchical responding as being at the top of our language abilities.

References

Augustson, E. M., & Dougher, M. J. (1997). The transfer of avoidance evoking functions through stimulus equivalence classes. *Journal of Behavior Therapy and Experimental Psychiatry, 28*, 181–191.

Barnes-Holmes, D., Barnes-Holmes, Y., Luciano, C., & McEnteggart, C. (2017). From the IRAP and REC model to a multi-dimensional multi-level framework for analyzing the dynamics of arbitrarily applicable relational responding. *Journal of Contextual Behavioral Science, 6*, 434–445.

Barnes-Holmes, D., Hayes, S. C., & Dymond, S. (2001). Self and self-directed rules. In S. C. Hayes, D. Barnes-Holmes, & B. Roche (Eds.), *Relational frame theory* (pp. 119–140). New York: Kluwer Academic.

Barnes-Holmes, D., Hayes, S. C., Dymond, S., & O'Hora, D. (2002). Multiple stimulus relations and the transformation of stimulus functions. In S. C. Hayes, D. Barnes-Holmes, & B. Roche (Eds.), *Relational frame theory* (pp. 51–71). New York: Kluwer Academic.

Boulanger, J. L., Hayes, S. C., & Pistorello, J. (2010). Experiential avoidance as a functional contextual concept. In A. M. Kring, & D. M. Sloan (Eds.), *Emotion regulation and psychopathology: A transdiagnostic approach to etiology and treatment* (pp. 107–136). New York: Guilford Press.

Callejón, Z (March 2020). *Training the hierarchical response* (Thesis defended). University of Almería.

Criollo, A. B., Díaz-Muelle, J. S., Ruiz, F. J., & García-Martín, M. B. (2018). Common physical properties improve metaphor effect even in the context of multiple exemplars. *The Psychological Record, 68*, 513–523.

Dahl, J., Lundgren, T., Plumb, J., & Stewart, I. (2009). *The art and science of valuing in psychotherapy: Helping clients discover, explore, and commit to valued action using Acceptance and Commitment Therapy*. Oakland, CA: New Harbinger.

Day, W. F. (1971). Humanistic psychology and contemporary behaviorism. *Humanist, 31*, 13–16.

Dougher, M. J., Augustson, E., Markham, M. R., Greenway, D. E., & Wulfert, E. (1994). The transfer of respondent eliciting and extinction functions through stimulus equivalence classes. *Journal of the Experimental Analysis of Behavior, 62*, 331–351.

Dougher, M. J., Hamilton, D., Fink, B., & Harrington, J. (2007). Transformation of the discriminative and eliciting functions of generalized relational stimuli. *Journal of the Experimental Analysis of Behavior, 88*, 179–197.

Dougher, M. J., & Hayes, S. C. (2000). Clinical behavior analysis. In M. J. Dougher (Ed.), *Clinical Behavior Analysis* (pp. 11–25). Reno, NV: Context Press.

Dymond, S., Schlund, M. W., Roche, B., & Whelan, R. (2014). The spread of fear: Symbolic generalization mediates graded threat-avoidance in specific phobia. *Quarterly Journal of Experimental Psychology, 67*, 247–259.

Ehring, T., & Watkins, E. R. (2008). Repetitive negative thinking as a transdiagnostic process. *International Journal of Cognitive Therapy, 1*, 192–205.

Ferster, C. B. (1972). An experimental analysis of clinical phenomena. *The Psychological Record, 22*, 1–16.

Ferster, C. B. (1974). Behavioral approaches to depression. In R. J. Friedman, & M. M. Katz (Eds.), *The psychology of depression: Contemporary theory and research* (pp. 29–53). Washington, DC: V. H. Winston.

Foody, M., Barnes-Holmes, Y., Barnes-Holmes, D., & Luciano, C. (2013). An empirical investigation of hierarchical versus distinction relations in a self-based ACT exercise. *International Journal of Psychology and Psychological Therapy, 13*, 373–388.

Gil, E., Luciano, C., Ruiz, F. J., & Valdivia-Salas, S. (2012). A preliminary demonstration of transformation of functions through hierarchical relations. *International Journal of Psychology and Psychological Therapy, 12*, 1–19.

Gil, E., Luciano, C., Ruiz, F. J., & Valdivia-Salas, S. (2014). Towards a functional analysis of hierarchical classification: A further experimental step. *International Journal of Psychology and Psychological Therapy, 14*, 137–153.

Gil-Luciano, B., Calderón-Hurtado, T., Tovar, D., Sebastián-Sánchez, B., & Ruiz, F. J. (2019). How are triggers for repetitive negative thinking organized? A relational frame analysis. *Psicothema, 31*, 53–59.

Gil-Luciano, B., Ruiz, F. J., Valdivia-Salas, S., & Suárez-Falcón, J. C. (2017). Promoting psychological flexibility on tolerance tasks: Framing behavior through deictic/hierarchical relations and specifying augmental functions. *The Psychological Record, 67*, 1–9.

Gutiérrez, O., Luciano, C., Rodríguez, M., & Fink, B. (2004). Comparison between an acceptance-based and a cognitive-control-based protocol for coping with pain. *Behavior Therapy, 35*, 767–783.

Hayes, S. C. (1984). Making sense of spirituality. *Behaviorism, 12*, 99–110.

Hayes, S. C., Barnes-Holmes, D., & Roche, B. (2001). *Relational frame theory*. New York: Kluwer Academic.

Hayes, S. C., Bissett, R., Korn, Z., Zettle, R. D., Rosenfarb, I., Cooper, L., & Grundt, A. (1999). The impact of acceptance versus control rationales on pain tolerance. *The Psychological Record, 49*, 33–47.

Hayes, S. C., Strosahl, K. D., & Wilson, K. G. (2012). *Acceptance and commitment therapy. The process and practice of mindful change*. New York: Guilford Press.

Hebert, E. R., Flynn, M. K., Wilson, K. G., & Kellum, K. K. (2021). Values intervention as an establishing operation for approach in the presence of aversive stimuli. *Journal of Contextual Behavioral Science*, 20, 144–154.

Kohlenberg R. J., & Tsai M. (1991). *Functional analytic psychotherapy: Creating intense and curative therapeutic relationships*. New York: Plenum Press.

López-López, J. C. (2016). *Experimental analysis of defusion and its impact on performance* (Doctoral dissertation), Universidad de Almería.

López-López, J. C., & Luciano, C. (2017). An experimental analysis of defusion interactions based on deictic and hierarchical framings and their impact on cognitive performance. *The Psychological Record, 67*, 485–497.

Luciano, C. (2017). The self and responding to the own's behavior. Implications of coherence and hierarchical framing. *International Journal of Psychology and Psychological Therapy, 17*, 3, 267–275.

Luciano, C., Gil-Luciano, B., Barbero, A., & Molina-Cobos, F. (2020). Perspective taking, empathy, and compassion. In M. Fryling, R. A. Rehfeldt, J. Tarbox, & L. J. Hayes (Eds), *Applied behavior analysis of language and cognition* (pp. 281–300). Oakland, CA: Context Press.

Luciano, C., Molina, F., Gutiérrez-Martínez, O., Barnes-Holmes, D., Valdivia-Salas, S., Cabello, F., . . . Wilson, K. G. (2010). The impact of acceptance-based versus avoidance-based protocols on discomfort. *Behavior Modification, 34*, 94–119.

Luciano, C., Ruiz, F. J., Gil-Luciano, B., & Molina-Cobos, F. J. (2021). Terapias contextuales. In E. Fonseca-Pedrero (Ed.), *Manual de tratamientos psicológicos. Adultos* (pp. 167–199). Madrid: Pirámide.

Luciano, C., Ruiz, F. J., Vizcaíno-Torres, R., Sánchez, V., Gutiérrez-Martínez, O., & López-López, J. C. (2011). A relational frame analysis of defusion interactions in Acceptance and Commitment Therapy. A preliminary and quasi-experimental study with at-risk adolescents. *International Journal of Psychology and Psychological Therapy, 11*, 165–182.

Luciano, C., Valdivia-Salas, S., Berens, N. M., Rodríguez-Valverde, M., Mañas, I. y Ruiz, F. J. (2009). Acquiring the earliest relational operants. Coordination, difference, opposition, comparison, and hierarchy. In R. A. Rehfeldt, & Y. Barnes-Holmes (Eds.), *Derived relational responding. Applications for learners with autism and other developmental disabilities* (pp. 149–170). Oakland, CA: New Harbinger.

Luciano, C., Valdivia-Salas, S., Cabello, F., & Hernández, M. (2009). Developing self-directed rules. In R. A. Rehfeldt, & Y. Barnes-Holmes (Eds.), *Derived relational responding. Applications for learners with autism and other developmental disabilities* (pp. 335–351). Oakland, CA: New Harbinger.

Luciano, C., Valdivia-Salas, S., & Ruiz, F. J. (2012). The self as the context for rule-governed behavior. In L. McHugh, & I. Stewart (Eds.) *The self and perspective taking: Research and applications* (pp. 143–160). Reno, NV: Context Press.

Luciano, C., Valdivia-Salas, S., Ruiz, F. J., Rodríguez-Valverde, M., Barnes-Holmes, D., Dougher, M. J., . . . Gutierrez-Martínez, O. (2014). Effects of an acceptance/defusion intervention on experimentally induced generalized avoidance: A laboratory demonstration. *Journal of the Experimental Analysis of Behavior, 101*, 94–111.

McMullen, J., Barnes-Holmes, D., Barnes-Holmes, Y., Stewart, I., Luciano, C., & Cochrane, A. (2008). Acceptance versus distraction: Brief instructions, metaphors and exercises in increasing tolerance for self-delivered electric shocks. *Behaviour Research and Therapy, 46*, 122–129.

Newman, M. G., & Llera, S. J. (2011). A novel theory of experiential avoidance in generalized anxiety disorder: A review and synthesis of research supporting a contrast avoidance model of worry. *Clinical Psychology Review, 31*, 371–382.

Páez-Blarrina, M., Luciano, C., Gutiérrez-Martínez, O., Valdivia, S., Ortega, J., & Rodríguez-Valverde, M. (2008). The role of values with personal examples in altering the functions of pain: Comparison between acceptance-based and cognitive-control-based protocols. *Behaviour Research and Therapy, 46*, 84–97.

Ramírez, E. S., Ruiz, F. J., Peña-Vargas, A., & Bernal, P. A. (2021). Empirical investigation of the verbal cues involved in delivering experiential metaphors. *International Journal of Environmental Research and Public Health, 18*(20), 10630.

Rodríguez-Valverde, M., Luciano, C., & Barnes-Holmes, D. (2009). Transfer of aversive respondent elicitation in accordance with equivalence relations. *Journal of the Experimental Analysis of Behavior, 92*, 85–111.

Ruiz, F. J., Flórez, C. L., García-Martín, M. B., Monroy-Cifuentes, A., Barreto-Montero, K., García-Beltrán, D. M., . . . Gil-Luciano, B. (2018). A multiple-baseline evaluation of a brief acceptance and commitment therapy protocol focused on repetitive negative thinking for moderate emotional disorders. *Journal of Contextual Behavioral Science, 9*, 1–14.

Ruiz, F. J., & Luciano, C. (2015). Common physical properties among relational networks improve analogy aptness. *Journal of the Experimental Analysis of Behavior, 103*, 498–510.

Ruiz, F. J., Peña-Vargas, A., Ramírez, E. S., Suárez-Falcón, J. C., García-Martín, M. B., García-Beltrán, D. M., . . . Sánchez, P. D. (2020). Efficacy of a two-session repetitive negative thinking-focused acceptance and commitment therapy (ACT) protocol for depression and generalized anxiety disorder: A randomized waitlist control trial. *Psychotherapy, 57*, 444–456.

Ruiz, F. J., Riaño-Hernández, D., Suárez-Falcón, J. C., & Luciano, C. (2016). Effect of a one-session ACT protocol in disrupting repetitive negative thinking. *International Journal of Psychology and Psychological Therapy, 16*, 213–233.

Sierra, M. A., Ruiz, F. J., Flórez, C. L., Riaño-Hernández, D., & Luciano, C. (2016). The role of common physical properties and augmental functions in metaphor effect. *International Journal of Psychology and Psychological Therapy, 16*, 265–279.

Skinner, B. F. (1945). The operational analysis of psychological terms. *Psychological Review, 52*, 270–276.

Skinner, B. F. (1953). *Science and human behavior*. New York: Macmillan.

Skinner B. F. (1974). *About behaviorism*. New York: Vintage Books.

Törneke, N. (2010). *Learning RFT. An introduction to relational frame theory and its clinical application*. Oakland, CA: New Harbinger.

Törneke, N. (2017). *Metaphor in practice: A professional's guide to using the science of language in psychotherapy*. Oakland, CA: New Harbinger.

Törneke, N. (2021). Clinical functional analysis and the process of change. *Perspectivas em Análise do Comportamento, 12*, 1–19.

Törneke, N., Luciano, C., Barnes-Holmes, Y., & Bond, F. W. (2016). RFT for clinical practice. In R. D. Zettle, S. C. Hayes, D. Barnes-Holmes, & A. Biglan (Eds.), *The Wiley handbook of contextual behavioral science* (pp. 254–272). New York: John Wiley.

Villarroel, J., Luciano, C., & Ruiz-Sánchez, L. J. (2021). *Experimental analysis of hierarchical responding*. Paper presented at ACBS Virtual World Conference.

Zagrabska-Swiatkowska, P., Mulhern, T., Ming, S., Stewart, I., & McElwee, J. (2020). Training class inclusion responding in individuals with autism: Further investigation. *Journal of Applied Behavior Analysis, 53*, 2067–2080.

SECTION 2

General ACT Methods

CHAPTER

6 An ACT Approach to Assessment, Case Conceptualization, and Treatment

Katrina M. Daigle, Mikala A. Grimaldi, Rebecca Schneider, *and* Lisa W. Coyne

Abstract

In comparison to a more traditional diagnostic-based assessment, the contextual behavioral science (CBS) approach focuses more broadly on the function of behaviors within a given context. A CBS assessment explores patterns of experiential avoidance and cognitive fusion, while the corresponding intervention encourages psychological flexibility and values-based action. Through recurrent assessment and case conceptualization, clinicians can assess and identify which ACT processes to target in treatment in order to shape psychological flexibility. Included in this article are a review of formal measurement and case formulation tools that support the assessment and treatment planning process, and a discussion of newer approaches to assessment, including application of clinical relational frame theory and evolutionary approaches.

Key Words: assessment, case conceptualization, treatment planning, acceptance and commitment therapy, contextual behavioral science, measurement, case formulation, functional analysis

The ACT Approach to Psychopathology

A Contextual Behavioral Model of Psychopathology

A contextual behavior science (CBS) approach to assessment seeks to understand behavior in context. That is, the role of the clinician is to evaluate how individuals get "stuck," explaining why they engage in behavior that leads to suffering, despite a strong desire to change. The culprit here is *psychological inflexibility*, which describes persistent avoidance of unwanted thoughts, feelings, or physical sensations that preclude their ability to engage in pursuits that matter to them. Stated another way, CBS assessment involves developing a functional understanding of the client's problems that will ultimately empower them to choose to engage in their own lives in a vital and meaningful way. CBS assessment can be considered *process-based* in that it employs idiographic functional analysis guided by empirically derived models such as acceptance and commitment therapy (ACT) and other third-wave cognitive behavior therapies that integrate a coherent set of change processes.

Because a CBS assessment approach is pragmatic, two core tenets are that (1) all behavior makes sense and (2) we cannot understand a behavior out of its context. The term *context* can be understood to mean the individual's external environment, as well as the "mental wallpaper" composed of their thoughts and feelings, as these extend over time and their learning history. In other words, an individual's context comprises the dynamic and potent constellation of derived relations that makes up their world.

If we do not understand why someone is behaving in a certain way, we simply do not have enough information. The job of the clinician, then, is to answer these questions: in what way does this individual's behavior work for them? What does it gain for them? What aversive experience does it remove? Clinicians gather information over time that illustrates, in essence, how a client's actions benefit them, and they consider this information in terms of the client's psychological flexibility. At the heart of this assessment approach is the understanding that the private events that trigger or consequence behavior arise from derived relational responding.

If behavior assessment viewed in this way seems a tall order, it is not: very simply put, a CBS approach is interested in understanding what behaviors a given individual is interested in changing, and the antecedents and consequences that regulate that behavior in a given context. It is interested in what matters to an individual; in what sorts of behaviors get in the way of pursuing that with vigor; and in what sorts of private events trigger those avoidance behaviors that divert that pursuit.

Traditional Diagnostic Approaches vs. Process-Based Assessment

CBS approaches arose, in part, in response to the wildly proliferating number of syndrome-based approaches. For clinicians in the field, application of such a variety of diagnosis-specific manuals, especially when comorbidity across disorder categories is the norm, proved unwieldy and unrealistic. It therefore made sense to move toward a more practical, flexible, and principles-based approach. Thus, CBS brings together a group of empirically derived theoretically coherent change processes that are functionally related to psychological well-being (Hayes, 2020). It is a flexible, bottom-up, principles-based approach that has resulted in a streamlined transdiagnostic way to look at assessment, case conceptualization, and treatment.

Given these characteristics, a CBS approach to assessing and intervening in behavior uses a somewhat broader lens than more traditional approaches to psychopathology. Rather than a narrow descriptive focus on categorization, diagnostic status, or symptom reduction, a CBS approach is interested in functional relationships between behavior and context. In general, CBS clinicians view psychopathology as rigid engagement in avoidance behavior in the presence of unwanted private events. Assessment, then, explores how and why individuals become "stuck" in these patterns of avoidance behavior, even when those patterns supersede engagement in valued action and lead to more suffering. Successful CBS interventions support individuals, as well as small and large groups, even cultures, to embody and enact their deepest values, consistently and flexibly, regardless of the presence or absence of adversity.

More traditional assessment approaches focus on a description of the individual's symptoms, with an interest in their reduction, within a diagnostic framework. The goal is to classify the client's problem, and get a sense of the intensity and severity of the problems. A CBS approach, in contrast, is tightly adherent to a behavior-analytic framework and is by nature transdiagnostic because it conceptualizes psychopathology in terms of psychological inflexibility across problem domains. Traditional approaches tend to be nomothetic—describing an individual's symptoms relative to similar peers—and thus do not tend to give a fine-grained idiographic, functional understanding of client behavior. Finally, more traditional approaches, though descriptive, do not necessarily answer the classic question of how to influence this individual, in this situation, given their learning history and therapeutic goals. Contextual behavioral assessment strives to meet clients where they are and to provide a clear-eyed, efficient way to shape greater psychological flexibility in ways that are meaningful to the client.

Treatment Targets/Goals of Contextual Behavioral Treatment

Two core processes are thought to underlie psychopathology across syndromes and are treatment targets: problematic *experiential avoidance* and *cognitive fusion*. Experiential avoidance, or unwillingness to experience private events, leads to rigid avoidance, insensitivity to context, and paradoxical intensification of those experiences. Cognitive fusion, the ability to experience thoughts as literal truths and conferred upon us by virtue of our languaging brain, can contribute to this avoidance. Said simply, our minds cannot always tell the difference between a thought tiger and an actual tiger; thus, we avoid thoughts about tigers with the same vigor as we might an actual tiger. CBS treatment seeks to increase psychological flexibility by changing one's relationship to unwanted private events. This is accomplished by addressing six processes: (1) present moment awareness/disconnection; (2) increasing acceptance and willingness to experience/avoidance; (3) defusion/fusion (transformation of function of cognitions—changing from "have to's" to choices); (4) self-as-context—acting from the present moment rather than having behavior organized by imagined futures or lingering memories of the past; (5) valuing (cultivating connection with things that truly matter) meaningful action whether or not in the presence of unwanted private events; and (6) committed action. Symptom reduction, for example, lessens anxiety or depression and often happens as a side effect; it is not an end goal in and of itself. Core here is reducing unnecessary and unworkable avoidance while increasing flexible, effective behavior. As flexible, values-driven behavior increases and individuals become more willing to experience painful private events as part of life, symptoms often naturally decrease. For example, as someone with OCD engages in previously avoided activities, they simultaneously reduce engagement in compulsions and compulsive avoidance, ultimately leading to a reduction in both obsessions and compulsions. Thus, CBS constitutes a whole-life approach.

This article will describe in detail CBS assessment as a process-based functional analysis of a client's behaviors within their context that is tightly linked to intervention planning. This analysis will be presented with an eye toward clinical and practical use. We will discuss case conceptualization to guide clinicians in how to assess and select ACT processes to use with a client to shape psychological flexibility. We will also describe a functional-analytic approach to assessment, inclusive of private events, consider that information in the context of ACT processes, and focus on an iterative case conceptualization and treatment planning that deepens over time and includes new information garnered during the process of treatment. We will emphasize individual therapy, although the underlying principles described can also be applied to other settings such as within groups, schools, or corporations. Finally, we will discuss newer approaches to assessment; specifically, application of clinical relational frame theory and evolutionary approaches.

Practical Issues in Process-Based Assessment

In ACT, the Hexaflex model suggests that the presence of the core processes at the level of the intervention, including assessment, promotes an effective therapeutic relationship. As such, the assessment process can be used as an initial intervention, wherein a clinician can start to provide psychoeducation and facilitate the change process. In this way, clinicians should be mindful of using ACT-consistent language throughout the assessment process and facilitate change by reframing a client's words in ACT-consistent ways from the beginning. For example, if a client reports "I can't do it," a clinician can reframe their statement by reflecting back, "You're having the thought that you can't do it, your mind is bossy isn't it?" By utilizing these skills and language, the clinician models ACT-consistent language that can initiate behavior change processes right from the initial assessment stage.

Assessing a client's history, presenting problems, goals, and behaviors as they relate to the core processes of psychological inflexibility and flexibility begins in the initial interview. This serves as a means of gathering information about what the client struggles with and in what contexts. Thus, it is important to understand the client's perspective on and conceptualization of the problem, and also to remain observant of antecedents and consequences of their behavior. Clinicians should gather information about the onset of the problem; contextual factors relating to that onset, and the way the problem impacts functioning and level of distress in major life domains—family, work, academics, and friendships. This information will guide the clinician's understanding of how client behaviors serve a function within a specific context, and have specific meanings, for each unique client. The data garnered from assessment, then, are used to evoke, reinforce, and shape client behaviors throughout treatment in order to increase psychological flexibility. Thus, it is critical to listen for the "story" the client has about the problem, as well as efforts to address the problem, and how they have worked or not worked, respectively

In the first order of business, the CBS assessment process gathers information about the client's "story" of their problem, with close attention to functional relationships. This data gathering involves not only listening to what the client says, but also careful observation. Patterns of avoidance often find their way into the therapy room in clients' verbal and nonverbal behavior. Clinicians should watch for subtle cues, such as shifts in tone or posture, variations in tone or rate of speech, or physical movements that may reflect a client's attitude toward difficult thoughts and feelings.

At the same time, clinicians should also be mindful of a perhaps equally important parallel process—and observe their own reactions to what the client says and does. Clinicians should attend to their own responses to the client; emotional, cognitive, and physiological data are useful as exemplars of how others perceive the client and of the effects of client behavior on others outside the session.

The clinician's awareness of and connection with their responses to the client often provide important information. For example, what does it mean if the clinician's attention begins to drift away as the client tells a story? Or what might it mean if the clinician is utterly moved by a client, even if the client speaks dispassionately about their experiences? Noticing these signals can provide clues about whether the client is connected to their experience or is simply storytelling, for example.

The clinician's persistent awareness and curiosity about such data are critical to process-based assessment, for they signal points at which clinicians might ask questions or gently direct the client's attention to their own experiences. It also supports the generation of hypotheses about client approach and avoidance behaviors in session that may be useful in illustrating patterns that extend elsewhere in the client's life. In essence, this approach constitutes what might be considered a "practice-based research" method. Finally, CBS has its greatest impact when clients are "in the room" and are in open, nonevaluative contact with their own emotions; and when they can develop a perspective on their own behavior, including the process of their thinking. Shaping these skills is to help clients become good observers of their own behavior. Thus, assessment nearly always involves intervention as well—gently bringing the client's attention to how the behavior works.

Often there is a disconnect between a client's "story" of the problem and the actual problem. Clients will create a narrative to describe their stuckness, and in this way, clinicians may be able to determine how the client's behavior "makes sense" to them. For example, a client might report that they cannot do well in school due to their diagnosis of attention deficit hyperactivity disorder (ADHD). There's an implicit assumption in this client's story: academic success is contingent on not having ADHD. This may suggest patterns of the client letting themselves off the hook if they are bored or understimulated, or if the ability to focus requires extra effort. Reframed in a psychological flexibility view, a clinician might conceptualize this scenario as the client being unwilling to experience boredom or frustration over the task at hand and engaging in a stream of other, more stimulating behaviors that allow a brief respite from this situation. Clinicians might consider this as a hypothesis and will look for similar patterns in the therapy room and other places in the client's life.

During this process, clinicians should be looking for patterns of rigidity and insensitivity to context. In our previous example, the belief "I cannot succeed in school because I have ADHD" may function as a "self-rule" that organizes the client's behavior in unhelpful ways. To buy into the notion that one "cannot" do something "unless" certain conditions are met is rigid and inflexible and is almost certainly *unworkable* for that client. When behavior becomes rule-governed, it is less sensitive to natural contingencies. When an individual's behavior complies with a rule, that is called *pliance:* a form of behavior that is under the control of socially mediated reinforcement for coordination with antecedent verbal stimuli (Zettle & Hayes, 1982). That is, behavior consistent with the rule is reinforced by virtue of being consistent with that rule: If I am anxious about giving a speech and expect that speech to go badly, I scan the environment for evidence of that poor performance. I might not notice positive comments or audience interest at all. Thus, clinicians might explore how and when the client's behavior is coordinated by that rule (i.e., consistent with their story) and assess for sensitivity to context. If their behavior fits the story, then it may be less "influenceable" by actual rather than verbally mediated contingencies (i.e., by their own self-talk).

A core intervention around client avoidance behavior that often begins during the assessment process is known as creative hopelessness. This intervention involves gathering information from the client about what they have done to fix the "problem" as they see it, the persistence of those efforts, and their results. This is done with gentle Socratic questioning and a nonevaluative stance. However, the clinician can guide client awareness to the *workability* of their behaviors—for example, whether certain behaviors result in avoidance of discomfort in the short term but are unhelpful or perhaps counterproductive in the long term. As such, this tool can help bring extended verbal consequences linked to what a person cares most about in life and how these actively influence behavioral responses in situations where avoidance is likely. In this way, clients begin to develop a more nuanced and distanced perspective on their behaviors and to understand that their function may not match their ideas or beliefs about how those behaviors work. For example, consider a client with obsessive-compulsive disorder who engages in cognitive rituals to neutralize the thought that they might harm a family member illustrated here:

THERAPIST: So, when you have the thought that harm might come to your partner, what do you do then?

CLIENT: I have to replace a bad thought with a good thought—so if there's an image of something terrible happening . . . I need to replace it with a positive thought that feels right.

THERAPIST: Tell me a little bit more about that. What is that like?

CLIENT: I need to focus on a thought that is something good, like that I associate with feeling a particular way, and I have to make sure that it's right—it has to feel right. If I have the wrong kind of thought, or it isn't right, then it's really scary, and I know it won't work.

THERAPIST: What do you mean "work"?

CLIENT: Oh, right. I mean I can't be sure that the bad thought won't happen. I mean, I know logically this doesn't make sense, but . . .

THERAPIST: That sounds really hard. Exhausting.

CLIENT: It is. Sometimes it takes hours to get it right. And I really can't do anything else until I get it right. And lately it's gotten harder and harder.

THERAPIST: How does *that* work in your life?

CLIENT: There have been days I've been late to work, or even called in sick. Sometimes I don't get out of bed at all.

THERAPIST: Does this impact your relationship with your partner?

CLIENT: She gets frustrated with me. But I can't really tell her what's going on. I mean, she knows I have OCD. But I couldn't possibly tell her what goes through my head.

THERAPIST: What is that like, experiencing those thoughts and images, and feeling like you have to keep them a secret?

CLIENT: (long pause) I wonder what kind of person thinks this stuff . . . . I mean, what does it mean that I think this way . . . and then I try to tell myself it's just OCD, but of course the doubt is there. And then I feel guilty because I'm struggling with how to be in a relationship if I might be a sociopath . . . .

THERAPIST: What do you do when that thought shows up, that you might be a sociopath?

CLIENT: I get terrified. And I go down a rabbit hole where I need to rehearse what I did that day, and check to see what I was feeling . . . like, what if I was rude and didn't feel remorseful or sad, or what if I actually *meant* to do something cruel, or unkind . . . so I need to check that . . .

THERAPIST: Let's just slow down a bit, and take a breath . . . that's it. Just breathe, nice and deep, for a moment . . . there's a lot here . . .

CLIENT: Yeah.

THERAPIST: What is it like telling me about all of this?

CLIENT: [pause] I guess I want you to tell me that I'm not a sociopath, that it's just OCD. And I want to find a way to get rid of these images.

THERAPIST: [pause] I'd like you to just slow down again, and see if you can get curious about that feeling of urgency, of wanting an answer . . . and breathe.

CLIENT: [breathing] Ok.

THERAPIST: As I'm listening to you describe what you do to avoid those images . . . how much time of your day is taken up by this?

CLIENT: Oh, hours, some days. It's easier if I'm busy, like when I'm at work. But downtime is terrible. So is nighttime, and it's really hard to fall asleep. Because I'm just working on making sure I *don't* have those thoughts.

THERAPIST: Wow. So my next question is, given all the effort, all the time you are spending on this, how well does it work? I mean, how successful are you at keeping those thoughts at bay?

CLIENT: Well, if I can get it right, it works.

THERAPIST: Let's slow down one more time. Just take a moment to notice all the time you are spending trying to manage or avoid these images . . . notice how long you've been working at this . . . and let's unpack that idea of keeping this at bay. Does all of this work do what you need it to do?

CLIENT: Well, I guess not . . . I'm still experiencing those images. I have good days and bad days. The relief is getting more and more fleeting. Sometimes it doesn't work at all. But that's why I'm here. To learn a better way to get rid of these images.

THERAPIST: So let me make sure I understand. All the effort you put in to avoid having bad, or the wrong thoughts . . . sounds like it feels really compelling and necessary in the moment . . . but basically, doesn't work the way it feels like it should? And you chose to come here to get help.

CLIENT: Yeah. So doesn't work so well, I guess.

THERAPIST: Ok. Right. So now that you are noticing that, what shows up for you?

CLIENT: [pause] I guess I feel pretty hopeless.

THERAPIST: Just see if you can breathe into that feeling for a moment . . . and just notice it . . . I can absolutely understand why you would feel that way . . . sometimes it's important to notice what isn't working before you can move forward. What if there might be some answers for you in this feeling of hopelessness?

CLIENT: This is a pretty dark place to be.

THERAPIST: Yes. And what if there's some really important information for you inside this space? Would you be willing to hang out here with me for a bit, to see what we might learn?

CLIENT: I'll try, I guess.

The client engages in many different avoidance behaviors beyond rituals. They report numerous cognitive rituals, including replacing a "bad" thought with a "good" thought, scanning for whether thoughts feel "right," mental rehearsal. There are also overt rituals such as seeking reassurance from the therapist. In addition, the client avoids going to work so as not to disrupt their mental rituals; they keep their thoughts secret from their partner, and they try to keep busy to avoid having these thoughts and images in the first place. Importantly, they are even approaching therapy (which should involve exposure and response prevention) as a control strategy. Because all these behaviors appear to have a similar purpose, namely, to avoid unpleasant private experiences, they can be conceptualized as a functional class. Consideration of client problems in this way, with close attention to functional relationships and including private events, suggests clear points of intervention, which we discuss in the next section.

Process-Based Assessment of Psychological Flexibility

From an ACT perspective, psychological flexibility is defined as "the ability to contact the present moment more fully as a conscious human being, and to change or persist in behavior when doing so serves valued ends" (Hayes et al., 2006, p. 7). Understanding the six core processes of inflexibility as they pertain to each specific client's presentation will help highlight the primary targets of intervention. In the ACT Hexaflex model, psychological flexibility consists of six core processes: *present moment awareness, acceptance, cognitive defusion, self-as-context, values,* and *committed action.* These skills increase the ability to consciously contact the present moment flexibly in various situations and adapt behavior to align with what one values (Hayes & Strosahl, 2004), thus allowing people to learn from what life has to teach them (i.e., contingencies). In contrast, psychological inflexibility consists of *inflexible attention, experiential avoidance, cognitive fusion, self-as-content, lack of contact with or clarity about values,* and *inaction impulsivity and avoidant persistence.* It is important to assess where clients may experience weakness or skills deficits in these areas, as these deficits suggest specific domains to target in treatment. This assessment is done by listening to what the client says and, of course, observing what the client does in session. Below are some descriptions of what clinicians might watch for to determine areas of vulnerability and behaviors that will help support psychological flexibility.

PRESENT MOMENT AWARENESS

The ability to stay in the present moment, connected with whatever thoughts, feelings, and physical sensations may arise, and to remain *aware* that one is in the present moment is foundational to all other skills implicit in psychological flexibility. This skill involves paying purposeful attention, at will, to one's experience in the moment. It also involves at least two discriminations: noticing when one drifts away or is pulled from the present moment into the future or the past, and noticing when one gets entangled with their thoughts and thus is unmoored from their sensory experience. The first of these discriminations can be considered "time travel," or at least, that is a simple and evocative way to describe it. The latter is critical to full engagement in trial-and-error learning: getting "hooked" by one's thoughts is emblematic of behavior under verbal control of a rule, which of course contributes to insensitivity to one's environment, and constrains an individual's ability to learn from *actual* contingencies in lieu of the mind's story of what is happening. From a behavior-analytic perspective, it's important to consider antecedents to these shifts into time traveling and to undermine them.

Client behaviors that suggest deficits in the ability or practice of staying in the present moment may include talking about their experience in a disconnected way, quickly moving from subject to subject, storytelling or problem solving, with little emphasis on what they are feeling, rigid description of concerns about the future or ruminations about the past, difficulty slowing down, an impoverished description of inner experience, a feeling of rushing through things or attachment to find an answer, and lack of curiosity about the present moment. Clinicians can also rely on their own internal barometers for observational data. For example, if clinicians feel disconnected from their clients, or unmoved by stories that seem well rehearsed, these tend to be clues that clients are having trouble staying put in the present moment. Often, clients are not aware of when they are in the present moment and when they are not—and that suggests a weakness in discrimination. One way to give clients some perspective on this particular deficit is to ask this question as an assessment tool: *If you thought about 100 percent of your time during a given day, what percent of time would you say that you are here, noticing what's happening right now only, rather than your mind thinking about the future, or mulling over the past?* When asked this question, most clients offer a relatively small percentage of time spent in the "here and now." This query is another example of assessment serving as an intervention: it is a prompt that evokes the desired behavior—slowing down, paying attention on purpose, with curiosity, about one' experience, and practicing discriminating between being in the present moment, or time traveling.

ACCEPTANCE

Acceptance involves the willingness to remain in contact with one's private events, including thoughts, feelings, and sensations. It also involves treating emotions as purveyors of useful information and as welcoming and entertaining them all, which Rumi described in his poem, "The Guest House." Nonacceptance involves attempts to avoid or mitigate these experiences in some way; it is emblematic of *experiential avoidance* and is present across disorder categories in some form or another. Most of us have been socialized to treat our negative emotions as though they are toxic. We are inured to the idea that they must be avoided, that we must ensure that they are not too intense, and that they do not last too long. It also involves an underlying assumption that too many, or too intense, emotions will break us. This language is embedded in most Western approaches to psychological well-being—at least those that are focused on emotion control or emotion management. Emotion regulation fits within a CBS approach when construed as the ability to engage in effective, flexible behavior in the presence of and remaining in contact with intense emotion (rather than functioning to reduce or avoid intense emotion). And this, in a sense, describes what clinicians might look for in session to reflect acceptance of private events. From a relational frame theory (RFT) perspective, clinicians might explore whether certain private experiences are in a frame of opposition with allowing, acceptance, or willingness. If this is the case, curiosity about these experiences is shaped such that transformation of function occurs: difficult private events evoke listening, opening, exploration, and acknowledgment.

Client behaviors that might reflect nonacceptance might include an impoverished emotional lexicon: when individuals spend a long time trying to avoid or numb the experience of negative emotions and thoughts, they may well also experience general suppression of awareness of positive emotions. The breadth and flexibility in their description of their emotional experience is narrow. For example, a depressed individual stuck in trying to avoid depression may describe *only* sadness, degrees of sadness, or low mood. On the one hand, these may be the dominant notes in session. On the other hand, clients may avoid expressing emotions at all—verbally, or by remaining guarded, or careful, in facial expressions. Paradoxically, an overfocus on unwanted private experiences often reflects a client's engagement in avoiding those experiences. One assessment tool that may also serve as a useful intervention is for the clinician to observe subtle shifts in client expression, pauses, changes in tone or rate of speech, sudden diversions to a different subject, the interjection of humor, or a lapse into quiet. Any of these reactions might hint that a client has had a painful thought or emotion. Clinicians might simply ask them to slow down at those moments and pose the following questions: *What just happened there? What did you notice? Can you make some room for that, breathe into it, and let me know?* Again, these questions evoke the desired behavior from one's client: turning their purposeful attention, in an expansive, curious, even welcoming way, to their private experience.

COGNITIVE DEFUSION

Detached awareness of the process of one's thinking, such that one can observe what sorts of thoughts or thinking may be helpful and what sorts are not, is a core feature of psychological flexibility. Cognitive fusion, though critical to our survival as humans, and essential to our everyday existence, can entangle us into treating our thoughts as enemies. They are not; however, when clients become hooked into efforts to suppress or avoid particular thoughts, paradoxically those same thoughts come to dominate their experience. One way to think of this involves *pliance,* meaning seeking coherence in one's experience by coordinating one's behavior with a self-rule. For example, a client with social anxiety about initiating conversation with others might engage in conversations with others and be hypervigilant for clues that others were negatively evaluating them. Their attention might be captured by this cue, at the expense of others—such as their conversation partners enjoying the chat, or demonstrating curiosity and asking them to say more, or expressing kindness. Fusion, then, reflects when an individual's behavior is under the control of a verbal rule and precludes their ability to *track,* or to observe the actual consequences of their behavior, in the world. From an RFT perspective, if an individual is fused, thoughts are in a frame of coordination with literal truth. Defusion, then, would be to derive a hierarchical relationship in which the client is more than their thoughts, for example.

This example provides some guidance on what clinicians might listen for or observe in session to detect weaknesses in observing their thoughts in a detached, accepting way. Clinicians can also look for client avoidance behavior in session, namely, talking about thoughts or other private events as "too hard," or "intolerable," changing the subject when the session strays into how clients may be feeling, even very verbal descriptions of their thoughts in session. In general, it may be the case that the more clients seek to make sense of, or explain, or justify, or describe their thoughts in what they may perceive as socially acceptable ways, the more reflective this may be of fusion and its fellow traveler, experiential avoidance. There is also a certain "stuckness" that suggests fusion—namely, explaining why they cannot move forward in their lives unless unwanted thoughts or emotions are removed or reduced. As clinicians assess this, it is helpful to shape how clients interact with their thoughts by using language such as "You are having the thought that . . . " rather than "You are thinking;" or "Your mind is telling you . . . " rather than "You believe . . . . " Again, these verbal prompts evoke a defused perspective on one's thoughts and support the client's ability to discriminate between thinking and becoming aware of one's process of thinking.

SELF-AS-CONTEXT/PERSPECTIVE-TAKING

Taking perspective on the self is at the heart of the ACT component self-as-context and involves two things: first, getting in contact with one's observing self as distinct from one's experiences; and second, cultivating the ability to notice the self as a *context* for one's experiences rather than buying into the story of who one is. Human language affords us the opportunity to extrapolate information and create stories about ourselves and others throughout time. As this overextension of language becomes steady over time, it may become unhelpful when conceptualized stories about oneself or others create stability in behavior with little flexibility. We can notice the process of observing oneself—for example, with mindful awareness of one's experiences in the present moment; and we can observe when stories about ourselves crop up based on our learning history—in much the same way we develop detached observation of thoughts.

From an RFT perspective, this perspective-taking capacity is developmental, shaped by social interactions over time, reinforcing relations like I–You, Here–There, and Now–Then. Skill in self-as-context, then, can be conceptualized as skill in taking perspective on one's experience such that it supports psychological flexibility. For example, a client who is experiencing self-doubt arising from a failed attempt at something important might get fused with the idea "I am a failure." A client with strong self-as-context skills might instead notice that thought arise, and take perspective on a moment of failure as just one experience, in a history of successes, failures, and everything in between. Additionally, that client might have the sense of observing their experience from a stable, safe vantage point from which to observe thoughts and experiences as they arise.

In order to assess self-as-context skills, clinicians can watch for attachment to calcified stories of who they are—their "conceptualized" selves. There may be an absence of self-awareness that while there is an unchanging, observing piece of ourselves, our moods, emotions, and ways of thinking change constantly as our context shifts and changes. Sometimes clients with weak perspective-taking skills have difficulty integrating novel or inconsistent information about themselves. Rather, they may get stuck in assimilating new information about themselves as confirmatory evidence of a conceptualized self. For example, consider an individual with agoraphobia who thinks of themselves as unable to tolerate a panic attack. When engaging in exposure and experiencing signs of panic, they might opt out, fused with the notion that those feelings are simply evidence that "it's just too hard." In contrast, a client who has skill in this area might be able to step back and notice those thoughts and feelings as they arise and remain on course in the exposure exercise. Similarly, clients can get fused with avoiding any evidence of a conceptualized self that they find unacceptable. For example, if an adolescent client is stuck on the idea that they are "a loser," they may avoid any risk that brings them in contact with that experience of who they are. This might involve opting out of social opportunities or perhaps excessive engagement in risk taking that might prove this idea of themselves untrue. Clinicians should listen for inflexibility in self-description, the ability to integrate new or discriminant information, and awareness of how moods, ways of thinking, and abilities and preferences change over time.

VALUING

Valuing involves awareness of and taking action toward those things we find meaningful and vital. Values are chosen qualities of being, meaning, and action in life that are evidenced in ongoing behavioral patterns. As such, values are considered the main motivator in the ACT treatment model (Barrett et al., 2019), which strives for individuals to flexibly engage in valued actions in order to live a meaningful life. The process of identifying and acting in conjunction with one's values is theoretically considered to be a core therapeutic mechanism of change within ACT (Hayes, 2004; Verplanken & Holland, 2002).

Values are freely chosen by an individual; they are not goals, but rather aspirations that can organize our behavior in helpful ways. From an RFT viewpoint, values are *motivative augmentals,* meaning that they are verbally constructed reinforcers that change the value of our behavior. Consider an individual who is experiencing depression and values being a good father. Even though taking any action might feel effortful and hopeless, he may be more willing to, for example, spend some time playing with his children daily because that is consistent with his notion of "being a good father." Moreover, the client's experience of play with his children will feel more reinforcing if he is connected to this value in the moment. From an RFT perspective, if this father's behavior is coordinated with his value, it will take on reinforcing psychological properties of that value.

In assessing valuing, clinicians should weigh two factors. First, they should assess whether an individual is aware of what they value and whether or not they may be able to articulate that value. If they encounter difficulty in this area, clients may feel confusion about what they care about, or perhaps may avoid thinking about it altogether. Clients can hold values in multiple domains and can have many different things that they value. Although values are individually chosen, personal preferences, individuals exist within a broader social and cultural context, and thus values are also inherently culturally-based. In order to facilitate a richer, more meaningful understanding of what matters to the client, clinicians must consider and appreciate this cultural impact on clients' values and on their ability to articulate these values.

A number of ACT tools are available to assist in assessing this impact, including the values card sort (Miller et al., 2001), values cards (Hayes & Ciarroch, 2015), and others. In terms of in-session behavior, clinicians should look for strong emotion, whether positive or negative, for that is frequently a signal for something the client cares about deeply. Earlier in this article, we mentioned the creative hopelessness exercise as a way to assess the function of client behavior. The flip side of this assessment tool is to get a sense of what the client has lost to their rigid attachment to avoidance of painful private events. In this sense of loss, clients may also find their values. Thus, clinicians should slow down and explore that sadness, or absence, with the client as a way of helping them to articulate what they most care about.

Once clients are able to connect with and articulate what they value, clinicians should assess how closely their behavior aligns with their values, as they have described. For example, if the father in the previous example values "being a good father" and consistently chooses to isolate and avoid interacting with his child in lieu of avoiding his own sense of discomfort or of being overwhelmed, that does not reflect valuing with integrity. Clinicians should be attentive to the function of client behavior: if clients engage in behavior in the service of avoiding painful private events, it is often at the expense of valuing. Similarly, if clients engage in behavior that "looks like" valuing (e.g., playing with one's child while feeling depressed) topographically, but the function of that behavior is to "get her to leave me alone for a while afterward," then that behavior is less about valuing and more about experiential avoidance. It is essential for clinicians to remain vigilant for how client behaviors function throughout the assessment process but especially in terms of valuing.

COMMITTED ACTION

Engaging in committed action is perhaps best described as making a promise to oneself to take an action, regardless of the presence of painful private experiences. This is essential to psychological flexibility in *action*. It is not just willingness to experience whatever challenging emotions and thoughts arise in the present moment—but it involves taking actions that may evoke these on purpose, if those actions are in the service of one's values. Committed actions get clients out of the therapy room chair and into their lives, one committed act at a time.

When assessing for the ability to engage in committed action, clinicians should note whether their clients have lost contact with their aspirations in life. This loss may result in inaction, impulsivity, and avoidant persistence that limit engagement in habitual values-based action. Clinicians should also note clients "talking the talk" without "walking the walk," and should listen for reasons explaining why this might be so. In terms of in-session and between-session behaviors, clinicians should assess whether clients who have stated their "commitment" to take a particular action outside of session have done so. With regard to an RFT lens, clinicians might assess what sorts of private events appear to be in opposition to engagement in committed action and to scaffold new derived relations in which committed action is coordinated with valuing, as well as those previously avoided experiences.

This ACT component is best assessed behaviorally, over time, with clinicians noting consistent engagement in committed action, and in the absence of this engagement, note what may have gotten in the way. It may also be able to assess *how* clients engage in committed action: is this action freely chosen, or do they bully or coerce themselves into acting, using self-deprecating talk? Truly committed action occurs with the intention of following one's values, rather than as a means to avoid or escape feeling like a failure, or as not good enough, or perhaps even to please one's clinician. This is another area where it may be especially important for clinicians to attend to the function of behavior.

Formal Measurement in Process-Based Assessment

A variety of assessment measures used in ACT provide clinicians with the ability to assess the core processes of psychological inflexibility and flexibility in a structured fashion. Importantly, these measures can be used to track progress over time and to gain insight into the client's view of improvements throughout treatment. The following section presents some examples of formal measurement tools used in process-based assessment to determine areas of client weakness or strength.

PRESENT MOMENT AWARENESS

The central focus in assessment of present moment awareness is gaining an understanding of the client's ability to flexibly and purposefully contact events in the present moment in a voluntary and focused way. There are various measures of present moment awareness, primarily measured as facets of mindfulness such as in the Five Facet Mindfulness Questionnaire (FFMQ; Baer et al., 2006), which has demonstrated its reliability and validity across clinical, community, and student samples. In youth, present moment awareness can be assessed using assessment tools such as the Child Acceptance and Mindfulness Measure (CAMM; Greco, Baer, & Smith, 2011), which has been validated in multiple independent samples. It is important to understand that the definition of mindfulness or present moment awareness may differ across measures, though in ACT, we aim to understand one's ability to attend to the current context regardless of aversive internal experiences.

ACCEPTANCE

Formal measures of acceptance and experiential avoidance are commonly used to inform case formulation and identify targets for treatment in ACT. In assessing acceptance processes, the main goal is to gain an understanding about the client's ability to embrace each experience in the moment, whether or not it is distressing and aversive. The most widely known measure is the Acceptance and Action Questionnaire (AAQ; Hayes et al., 2004) which has a strength in feasibility and predictability in predicting various forms of psychopathology. There are also various measures for youth, including the Avoidance and Fusion Questionnaire for Youth (Greco et al., 2008). However, it is important to note that across various measures of acceptance and experiential avoidance in the literature, there is a lack of consensus on the definition of acceptance.

DEFUSION

In assessing cognitive defusion processes, the main goal is to gain insight into examples of fused thought content and the impact of that content across various life domains. When assessing defusion processes, the goal is to understand the client's relationship with their thoughts rather than the content of the thoughts. It can be useful to inquire about the believability of a thought above and beyond its occurrence; thus, the majority of formal cognitive measures can be adapted to focus on one's relationship with a thought rather than the specific content of the thought. In addition, in recent years, measures that specifically aim to understand cognitive defusion have been developed, including the Cognitive Fusion Questionnaire (CFQ; Gillanders et al., 2014), which has been translated into several languages and been applied to specific conditions (e.g., CFQ-chronic illness; Trindade et al., 2018). The Avoidance and Fusion Questionnaire for Youth (Greco et al., 2008) represents the only validated measure of defusion in youth.

SELF-AS-CONTEXT/PERSPECTIVE-TAKING

Gaining insight into a client's ability to take perspective by observing the self as separate from their experiences and as a context for living experiences, rather than maintaining a rigid story of who one is throughout all contexts, is critical to assessing self-as-context in ACT. Throughout evaluation of this core process, clinicians aim to identify conceptualizations of oneself that are rigid, evaluative, and evocative and often dominate over all other forms of self-experience. Currently, few formal measures of self-as-context exist, but the Self as Context Scale (SACS; Zettle et al., 2018) and the Questionnaire on Self-Transcendence (QUEST; Fishbein et al., 2020) are two recently developed brief self-report inventories that may help guide clinical evaluation of self-as-context and perspective-taking ability in clients. Overall, the goal is to gain an understanding of the client's ability to see the "me/here/now" as different from the "me/there/then" perspective. The former perspective can also be elicited through less formal techniques such as role play, probing for what the client supposes others feel, applying metaphors and stories, among others.

VALUING

A central purpose of ACT is to help guide clients to act in ways consistent with what they care most about in life. Learning about the life one hopes to live is central to orienting and contextualizing treatment in ACT. There are various formal measures of values, such as the Valued Living Questionnaire (VLQ; Wilson et al., 2010), the Bull's Eye Values Survey (Lundgren et al., 2008), and the Valuing Questionnaire (VQ; Smout et al., 2014). Many of these formal tools can be used with youth, though values card sorts and worksheets (e.g., DNA-V My Valued Journey; Hayes & Ciarrochi, 2015) are often engaging ways to discuss and assess values with youth.

COMMITTED ACTION

In order to help clients build a life they love, ACT clinicians aim to guide clients toward committing to building ongoing patterns of values-consistent actions through consciously building larger patterns of values consistency. Within the ACT model, clients must have a sense of openness and centeredness, along with a clear sense of values in order to build a consistent behavioral repertoire of values-based actions. Therefore, in evaluating one's ability to build a life of vitality via committed action, an understanding of the client's ability to be open and centered, as well as their clarity of values, is the central goal of assessment in this domain. Formal measures of committed action are lacking, though some have recently been developed, such as the Engaged Living Scale (ELS; Trompetter et al., 2013), which assesses committed action state and trait characteristics and demonstrates good internal consistency and construct validity. Given the lack of formal measures, this domain can most simply be evaluated by noting consistent client engagement in values-based activities over time.

OVERALL PSYCHOLOGICAL FLEXIBILITY

The immediate purpose of ACT is to increase psychological flexibility, which is conceptually composed of the six core processes in the Hexaflex model and commonly assessed by self-report questionnaires such as the Acceptance and Action Questionnaire—II (AAQ-II; Bond et al., 2011), the Comprehensive Assessment of ACT Processes (CompACT; Francis et al., 2016), and the Multidimensional Psychological Flexibility Inventory (MPFI; Rolffs et al., 2016). The MPFI was validated on over 3000 participants across three studies and demonstrates good convergent and divergent validity, with an independently replicated factor structure.

Capturing the dimensionality of the Hexaflex model is an important feature of assessment measures in ACT. However, some debate has arisen over the utility of some of the widely used measures, such as the AAQ-II because its unidimensional model fails to capture the complexity of psychological flexibility and its underlying core processes. As a widely used measure, the construct validity of the AAQ-II has been scrutinized, as it may be an overall measure of psychological distress rather than inflexibility and experiential avoidance (Wolgast, 2014). In addition, the AAQ-II items differ in sensitivity to individual differences, indicating that changes on certain items may be more or less clinically meaningful, the total score depends more on certain items than others, and patient populations tend to respond more extremely than predicted, indicating a potential inflation or deflation of scores (Ong et al., 2019). These issues highlight common issues across measures in ACT. Assessment tools that provide a global understanding of psychological flexibility but neglect to capture the core processes in a multidimensional approach may lack clinical utility, as an understanding of how behaviors function within each core process is critical for case formulation and treatment planning.

Measures that capture quality of life and client functioning while capturing some multidimensionality of the Hexaflex model have high clinical utility in ACT. As an example, the VQ is a widely used tool that measures several valued domains of living via a two-factor model assessing progress in and obstruction to valued living (Smout et al., 2014). In attempts to capture each core process, some novel and promising multidimensional measures have been developed, including the CompACT, which encompasses three dimensions, openness to experience, behavioral awareness, and valued action (Francis et al., 2016), and the MPFI, which includes six dimensions from 12 subscales that map directly onto the six core processes in the Hexaflex model (Rolffs et al., 2016). In a recent study, Rogge and colleagues (2019) revealed more clinically meaningful patterns with measures that capture multiple dimensions of flexibility and inflexibility when compared to unidimensional measures. Further, they suggest that MPFI provides the most conceptually comprehensive scale to capture the dimensions of the Hexaflex model (Rogge et al., 2019). Although process-based measures in ACT are clinically useful in directly assessing the core processes, symptom-focused measures can provide additional information that may prove useful for case formulation.

Despite the push away from symptom-focused measures and treatment manuals aimed at alleviating psychological diagnoses in processed-based models, symptom-focused semistructured diagnostic instruments (e.g., Anxiety and related Disorders Interview Schedule for the DSM-5 (ADIS-5); Brown & Barlow, 2014) are supported in the ACT model. Symptom-focused tools can provide a fuller picture by highlighting information about a client's degree of challenges and functioning, as well as capture behaviors that a client may not otherwise think to mention that may be useful for conceptualization. For example, a comprehensive assessment may capture binge eating in a client who presents for trauma-related treatment, which the client may not mention because it was not the immediate reason for presenting to treatment, or it may have become such a typical part of their experience that they neglected to mention it. In this way, semistructured symptom-focused assessments can subsequently inform ways clients engage in experiential avoidance or other core processes. Finally, comprehensive symptom-focused measures may provide a common language or way of describing behaviors that clients may be more used to thinking about. As an example, it may be easier for clients to report that they feel sad and have difficulty sleeping rather than reporting the processes underlying the symptoms, such as challenges with present moment awareness (an underlying process of depressive symptoms).

Case Conceptualization: Key Approaches

Throughout the assessment, case formulation, and treatment processes in ACT, it is crucial for clinicians to ask themselves, "what function is this client's current behavior serving?" and continuously observe the client at several levels. Luoma and colleagues (2017) suggest that as an ACT clinician, one must actively practice tracking multiple levels of client communication in order to inform a comprehensive case formulation. The first level consists of the client's overt content, which simply involves taking the client's words at face value. Second, all behaviors observed within a session should be considered as a sample of the client's social behavior and can help provide insight into the client's everyday behaviors. A third observation considers behavior in terms of the therapeutic relationship, as what the client says and does could be relevant to the therapeutic relationship itself. Finally, at a fourth level of observation, a clinician should analyze themes in functional behaviors. Functional thinking across these levels throughout the assessment and treatment process will inform a case conceptualization that guides clinical answers to what interventions are useful for targeting which processes for what reasons in each specific client's case.

In ACT, understanding contextual information is a crucial component of case formulation that leads to a workable treatment plan for each unique client. As a result, it is important to consider several factors, such as the factors that may limit motivation to change or specific environmental barriers that may hinder treatment. Various contextual factors may decrease a client's motivation to change, such as thoughts about what may happen if challenging experiences were confronted, or lack of understanding regarding why change is important. Motivational barriers like these can be addressed in ACT by experiencing the costs of avoidant behaviors and increasing contact with values. It also is important to consider unique environmental barriers such as reinforcement for behaviors that cause psychological suffering (e.g., perfectionistic behavior, anorexic behavior) and lack of social support, which may influence a client's decision to move toward committed action. Regardless of the presence or absence of barriers mentioned, it is important to consider unique factors on the financial, social, familial, and cultural level that may act as barriers for change in each individual case.

Tools for Case Formulation

Clinicians can choose to formulate a client's case, with the ACT Hexaflex focusing on mindfulness and acceptance processes and commitment and behavior change processes, the three response styles of open/closed, aware/mindless, and engaged/disengaged, and use tools such as the ACT Matrix or DNA-V model, or they can take a more complex approach based in clinical RFT. Though the current literature seems to provide the most consistent support for the three-pillar model of psychological flexibility and inflexibility (Scott et al., 2016; Vowles et al., 2014), there are generally limited and inconclusive findings regarding which form best serves a thorough and effective case formulation (Christodoulou et al., 2019). Regardless of what clinicians choose, the message should be clear: the goal is to take a nonlinear, flexible stance to case conceptualization, emphasizing the function and workability of client behaviors in the service of what is important to them, within their context.

THE MATRIX

Various clinical tools exist that facilitate case formulation from an ACT perspective. One common and simplified tool, the ACT Matrix, facilitates conceptualization regarding the function and workability of a client's behavior with a collaborative stance (Polk & Schoendorff, 2014). The Matrix is a tool that reorganizes the six core processes of flexibility and prompts clinicians and clients alike to notice two differences: the differences between five senses experiencing and mental experiencing (e.g., thoughts, emotions), and the difference between moving toward values and moving away from internal sensations (e.g., anxiety). By focusing on four simple quadrants, the matrix provides a functional understanding of behavior, including what is difficult (i.e., psychological suffering) and important (i.e., values) for a client and what the client does to escape (i.e., experiential avoidance) or move toward what is important (i.e., committed action), while noticing the differences (i.e., present moment awareness) across different experiences (i.e., self-as-context). Within the Matrix, a clinician helps guide the client to clarify when behaviors are workable in the context of what they want most in life. Thus, the Matrix is a simple, yet powerful, tool that can be used to collaboratively formulate a case with a client, which leads to flexible and collaborative treatment planning organized by the client's priorities in treatment.

ACT ADVISOR

Understanding client experience within the six core processes is a beneficial approach to ACT case conceptualization, as this insight can guide a treatment plan that targets client weaknesses and builds upon strengths to foster psychological flexibility by facilitating behavior change and subsequent adaptive functioning. The ACT ADVISOR (developed by David Chantry) is a client assessment tool that requires the clinician and/or the client to rate each of the six core processes ranging from 0 to 10. In this model, individual ratings for the core processes, outlined using the acronym ACT ADVISOR (**A**cceptance; **C**ommitment & **T**aking action;

Attention to present; Defusion; Values Identification; Self as Observer; and Resulting psychological flexibility) can be summed to provide an overall cognitive flexibility score ranging from 0 to 60. A strength of the ACT ADVISOR tool is in its ability to reevaluate psychological flexibility through a rapid assessment of a client's perspective on their progress in therapy and clinically reevaluate flexibility using a quantifiable measure of change over time. The following case example illustrates the use of the ACT ADVISOR in ACT Case formulation and treatment planning.

CASE EXAMPLE OF ACT ADVISOR: EILEEN

Eileen is a 35-year-old married white cisgender woman, who presented to outpatient therapy for help with managing feelings of inadequacy and chronic worry primarily related to raising her 10-year-old daughter. She was observed to avoid eye contact with the clinician by looking down at her hands, which were constantly fidgeting throughout the evaluation. She spoke rapidly with slightly pressured speech, telling drawn-out stories about her daughter's challenging behavioral outbursts. The content of her speech was heavily focused on evaluations of herself as an inadequate and bad mother. For example, when describing a scenario in which her daughter threw a toy across the room because Eileen refused to let her sign up for social media, she described how she "just doesn't know what to do anymore" and repeatedly discussed how she is "incapable of being a good mom" to her daughter. Eileen described patterns of setting boundaries with her daughter and then going back on her word when her daughter put up a fight. She expressed feelings of inadequacy and her chronic worry related to how she was negatively impacting her daughter's adaptive development.

Eileen indicated that it was difficult for her to accept when her daughter was unhappy with her parenting decisions, to the point that she often gave in to her daughter's behavior. In addition, when her husband sets boundaries that caused their daughter to be unhappy, Eileen often would quickly jump in and negate the boundaries set by her husband. Afterward, these scenarios would leave her feeling inadequate as a mother and trigger worry about how she was "messing up" her daughter's future and her marriage. She described these categories of inadequacy and adequacy as having absolute properties, and she demonstrated little ability to attend to other factors that contributed to her parenting repertoire and her daughter's behavioral outcomes.

Eileen cares deeply about her family and about being a "good parent" who is there for her daughter and is a caring and supportive wife to her husband of 12 years. Her tone, posture, and affect slightly changed when she described her loved ones and what she hoped for in her family. She resisted acknowledging that her constant worry impacted her ability to connect with her family as she wished and to be the loving mother and partner she hoped to be. She struggled to identify ways in which she may have been successful in maintaining boundaries set with her daughter in the past.

The clinician completed the ACT Advisor ratings seen in the lower-right portion of Figure 6.1 (the ACT ADVISOR image and ratings). Eileen demonstrated various weaknesses, primarily related to cognitive fusion. Her fused content includes rigid, black-and-white evaluations of what she is like as a mother. When her daughter is unhappy, she actively attempts to avoid distressing thoughts and feelings about being a "bad parent" by giving her daughter what she wants. However, Eileen has a clear understanding of what she values most in life: being a loving and caring mother and partner. Her clear sense of values can be used to help her work on defusing from her current conceptions and increase her ability to accept challenging scenarios when they arise, in an effort to act in ways consistent with her values. ACT defusion strategies target the absolute nature of her fused thought content about adequacy as a mother and

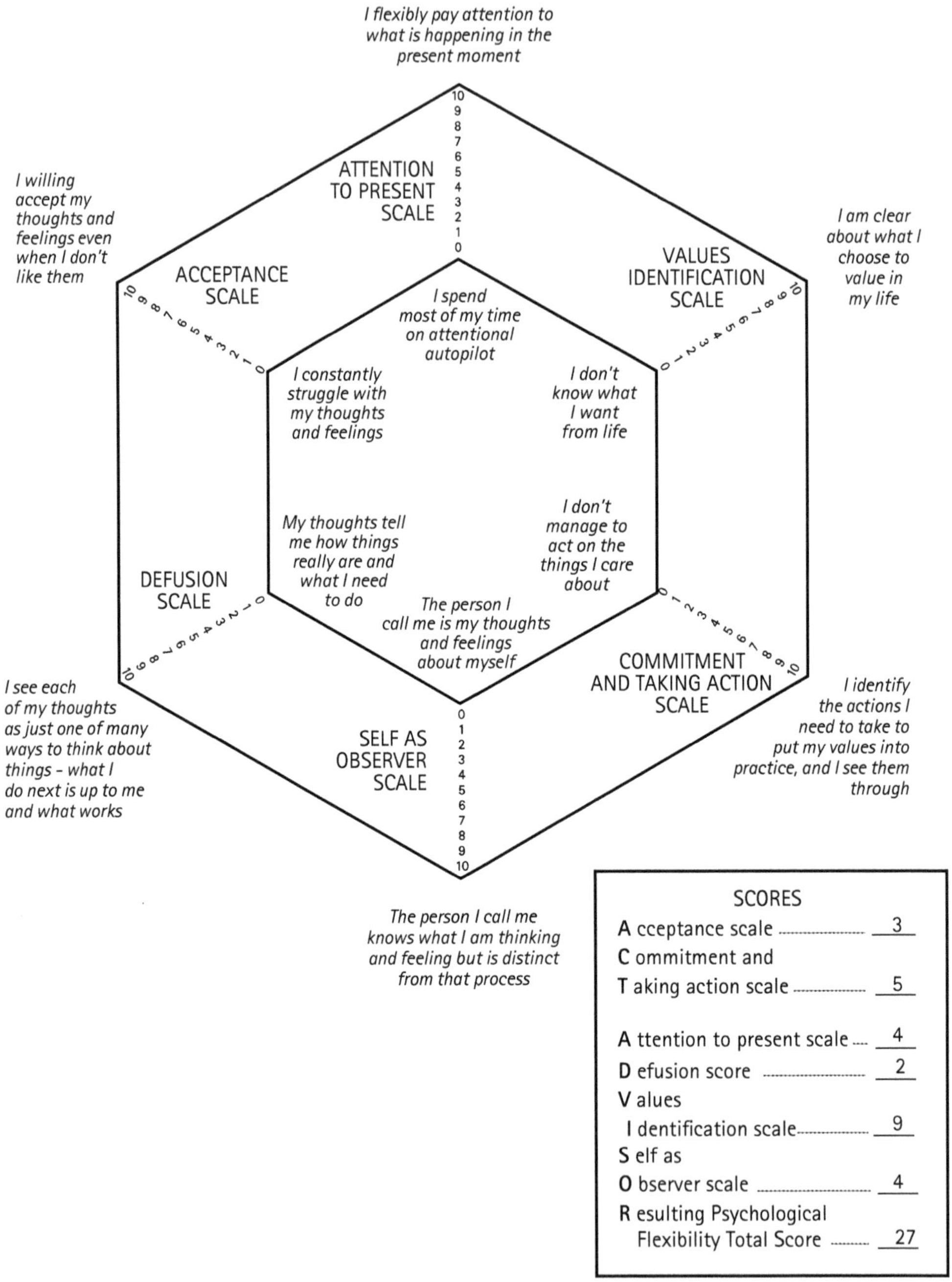

Figure 6.1. The use of the ACT ADVISOR to help track the psychological strengths and weaknesses of Eileen. Copyright by David Chantry. https://contextualscience.org/files/ACTADVISOR_0.pdf

supportive partner. She would likely also benefit from present moment awareness strategies to help her choose values-based actions when she finds herself in distressing scenarios with her daughter. Importantly, the ACT ADVISOR can be used to reevaluate Eileen's abilities in each of the domains throughout the progress of treatment and adjust treatment goals as needed.

DNA-V

The DNA-V (**D**iscoverer, **N**oticer, **A**dvisor, **V**alues) model is a useful tool in ACT case conceptualization which aims to increase flexibility and vitality in the lives of youth (Hayes & Ciarrochi, 2015). The DNA-V targets three classes of behavior: the Advisor, the Noticer, and the Discoverer. The Advisor highlights the use of language and relating to make sense of our worlds, without necessarily directly coming in contact with certain experiences. It is our "mind," the thinking part of our experience whose purpose is to detect threats and help us avoid them. The Noticer is a process that allows us to mindfully connect with our internal and external worlds via our five-senses experience, without evaluation or judgement. The Discoverer represents exploring and testing novel experiences in the world. Psychologically flexible use of this model entails shifting from one perspective to the others as best serves an individual. Importantly, Values are at the center of the model, and the Advisor, Noticer, and Discoverer provide means to engage in valued action and promote thriving and vitality. Importantly, the DNA-V model considers contextual factors that influence how we see ourselves (i.e., self-view) and others (i.e., social view) and takes a contextual approach in which the environment and DNA behavior reciprocally influence each other (Hayes & Ciarrochi, 2015).

Treatment Planning

Once treatment goals and objectives are identified through the lens of the core processes, identifying a plan of action can feel like a daunting task. ACT focuses on increasing flexibility, which is reflected in the treatment plan and administration of interventions. Although a clinician can flexibly move through the Hexaflex in treatment, ACT protocols follow two common structures: focus on what is getting in the client's way for change or focus on what values the client wants to move toward (Harris, 2019). When focusing on what is getting in the client's way, a clinician typically aims to increase contact with the present moment, cognitive defusion, acceptance, and awareness of self-as-context. This model is useful for clients who struggle to move toward valued ends. In contrast, focusing on which valued direction a client wants to move in is often a useful starting point for clients who lack values clarity. In this path, clinicians can help clarify values and set goals, create a plan of action, work on solving any problems that arise, and increase skills in order to work on exposure to private events. Importantly, however, all these processes are interconnected; therefore, it is expected that a clinician will address components regardless of the starting point in treatment.

Regardless of the treatment plan, values should be a central focus, as they are the basis of the therapeutic process that promotes positive change in client behaviors. As such, values are often seen as useful bookends to treatment. Initially, values can help give meaning to treatment, and therefore serve as a motivator. Toward the end of treatment, revisiting values once a client has increased clarity and is in more frequent contact with their values can help maintain gains.

Identifying where to start should be used as a loose guide in directing a clinician toward intervention selection. However, because ACT focuses on the workability of behaviors within each client's life, it is essential that a clinician maintain flexibility throughout the treatment rather than trying to rigidly adhere to a specific protocol. In efforts to tailor treatment to a client, understanding the learning history and current life context of each client is a useful tool to help guide the use of particular methods in ACT that may be used to target functional processes and ultimately increase psychological flexibility. Importantly, functional analysis helps select intervention on the purpose of client behavior rather than the form. Thus, focusing on the history that gave rise to a behavior, why it occurs in a particular context, and what maintains it, rather than getting wrapped up in the content of the behavior, is an essential skill for selecting interventions in ACT.

It is often useful to have a process goal in mind for planning each session. However, it is also important to flexibly attend and respond to when any of the core processes arise in session. Thus, it is important to continuously and fluidly move between treatment targets rather than "checking off the boxes" for targets. ACT clinicians should not have separate sessions focusing on one core process per session. Instead, it is more beneficial to flexibly revisit processes in multiple sessions and often address several processes within one session. This is reflected in ACT interventions, as many experiential exercises target multiple processes of the Hexaflex model. As an example, the passengers on the bus exercise (Hayes et al., 1999) addresses defusion (naming thoughts, creating passengers), acceptance (allowing each to be on the bus), values (identifying a valued direction), committed action (driving in a valued direction), self-as-context (passengers come and go, and throughout it all the client is still the bus driver), and mindfulness (awareness of the bus, passengers, values, and ability to flexibly shift attention). As such, a key component of treatment planning and implementation in ACT is in moving flexibly around the Hexaflex as a clinician to improve client flexibility.

Instead of looking for symptom reduction, search for increases in approach behavior in valued directions—mindful, meaningful risk, resilience and willingness to experience discomfort, to fail, to discover, and to engage in trial and error learning. Look for improved quality of life, whether or not a client is experiencing unwanted private events; increased engagement in valued action; or ability to self-direct. A transdiagnostic example includes engagement in valued activities (behavioral activation).

Conclusions and New Directions

Our field has historically taken a syndrome-based approach to assessment and treatment in which our task has been to identify symptoms, fit them within a diagnostic category, and choose a corresponding treatment protocol developed to target that diagnosis. This system has led to a proliferation of overlapping treatment manuals and an emphasis on symptom reduction over quality-of-life outcomes.

More recently, the field has shifted toward a transdiagnostic, process-based approach to assessment and treatment in order to identify the underlying treatment processes common across protocols and target these processes at an individual level. Rather than asking ourselves, "What treatment, by whom, is most effective for this individual with that specific problem, under which set of circumstances, and how does it come about?" (Paul, 1969, p. 44), the question is now, "What core biopsychosocial processes should be targeted with this client given this goal in this situation, and how can they most efficiently and effectively be changed?" (Hofmann & Hayes, 2019, p. 38).

In order to systematically identify these change processes and create an individualized treatment consisting of "intervention kernels" (Embry & Biglan, 2008), while maintaining scientific rigor and the ability to generalize idiographic data to the nomothetic level, an overarching structure needs to be in place. One recently proposed model suggests that an evolutionary-based conceptualization is well suited to capture the level of complexity associated with intraindividual processes while establishing a clear conceptual structure (Hayes et al., 2020). Evolutionary constructs such as variation, selection, and retention, within a given context, can be applied to any psychological process. These processes can be divided into several dimensions at the individual level (e.g., affective, cognitive, attentional, self, motivational, covert behavioral) nested within the physiological and social/cultural levels. For example, if a client presents to treatment and reports experiencing low mood and decreased interest and engagement in activities, one possible response would be to diagnose the client with major depressive disorder and deliver one of the associated treatment packages. Using the evolutionary framework, one could instead frame this problem as one with affective variation and motivational selection, and in response target the affective variation with pleasant events scheduling and the motivational selection with values work. This method allows for a process-based approach that can individualize treatment while maintaining a theoretical framework.

With regard to new assessment tools, thus far, the majority of publications have used nonbehavioral measures, especially self-report measures, as their primary assessment tool (Newsome et al., 2018). Self-report measures are quick, easy to administer, and affordable, and as such they are commonly employed in both research and clinical settings. More recently, however, there has been a call for more objective measures of behavior and a broader range of methods and approaches (Newsome et al., 2018). Behavioral measurement represents an important, yet thus far underutilized, tool for assessing behavioral change in an approach whose primary focus is behavior and the context in which it occurs.

Rather than just tracking subjective experience through self-report, studies are increasingly incorporating both subjective and objective outcome measures to track behavioral change in novel ways (Vilardaga & Vilardaga, 2019). For example, directly assessing a number of values-driven behaviors, duration of exposures completed, or time spent engaging in the target behavior (e.g., exercise, doctor's visits, mindfulness) provides an objective measurement of activity change that complements subjective experience. Utilizing ecological momentary assessment allows researchers to track target behaviors as they occur, while harnessing technology allows tracking of behaviors that might not otherwise be possible to obtain (e.g., time spent outside of the home, heart rate). Capitalizing on advances in technology and measurement in this manner allows for more accurate, reliable assessment that better captures the spirit of ACT.

Newer statistical and methodological approaches have enabled us to better capture the level of detail needed to systematically analyze data at the individual level, and technological advances have facilitated greater integration of contextual data into our conceptualization. Ecological momentary assessment (EMA) allows for frequent, real-time data collection within a natural setting, thus capturing moment-to-moment processes and better accounting for the impact of context. By using smartphones to record EMA data, we are able to capture objective information in the context in which it occurs (e.g., using electronically activated recorders to log time spent outside of the home, Metcalf & Dimidjian, 2020, or providing smartphone-based assessment prompts at set intervals). Ecological momentary interventions (EMI) use technology to provide tailored interventions in real time (e.g., providing in-the-moment skills coaching tailored to the context; Levin et al., 2019). Wearable devices can track physiological data, such as heart rate, in naturalistic settings. In addition, smartphone apps are increasingly being used to deliver treatment (e.g., Bricker et al., 2014) or as an adjunct to treatment (e.g., Levin et al., 2017), in order to expand our reach. Technology can also support traditional face-to-face sessions. For example, rather than using self-report measures to capture session-by-session information, it is now possible to more readily transcribe and code in-session behaviors, thus yielding richer information on the therapeutic process.

As advances in technological, statistical, and methodological approaches continue to develop, we will be increasingly able to cultivate a more nuanced understanding of the dynamic role of context for the individual within therapy. As a science that emphasizes behavior and context, ACT is well suited to lead the development of these novel assessment approaches. Institutional and community-level changes are needed to better support the implementation of behavioral assessment through training, resource sharing, and priority changes (Vilardaga & Vilardaga, 2019). In the future, ACT assessment will not just focus on subjective experience, but will be able to directly assess behavioral change within the context in which it occurs, thus expanding research and clinical work outside of the laboratory and therapy office to real-world settings.

References

Baer, R. A., Smith, G. T., Hopkins, J., Krietemeyer, J., & Toney, L. (2006). Using self-report assessment methods to explore facets of mindfulness. *Assessment, 13*(1), 27–45. https://doi.org/10.1177/1073191105283504

Barrett, K., O'Connor, M., & McHugh, L. (2019). A systematic review of values-based psychometric tools within acceptance and commitment therapy (ACT). *The Psychological Record, 69*(4), 457–485. https://doi.org/10.1007/s40732-019-00352-7

Bond, F. W., Hayes, S. C., Baer, R. A., Carpenter, K. M., Guenole, N., Orcutt, H. K., Waltz, T., & Zettle, R. D. (2011). Preliminary psychometric properties of the acceptance and action questionnaire – II: A revised measure of psychological inflexibility and experiential avoidance. *Behavior Therapy, 42*, 676–688.

Bricker, J. B., Mull, K. E., Kientz, J. A., Vilardaga, R., Mercer, L. D., Akioka, K. J., & Heffner, J. L. (2014). Randomized, controlled pilot trial of a smartphone app for smoking cessation using acceptance and commitment therapy. *Drug and Alcohol Dependence, 143*, 87–94. https://doi.org/10.1016/j.drugalcdep.2014.07.006

Brown, T. A., & Barlow, D. H. (2014). *Anxiety and related disorders interview schedule for DSM-5 (ADIS-5)*: Oxford University Press.

Christodoulou, A., Michaelides, M., & Karekla, M. (2019). Network analysis: A new psychometric approach to examine the underlying ACT model components. *Journal of Contextual Behavioral Science, 12*, 285–289. https://doi-org.ezp-prod1.hul.harvard.edu/10.1016/j.jcbs.2018.10.002

Embry, D. D., & Biglan, A. (2008). Evidence-based kernels: Fundamental units of behavioral influence. *Clinical Child and Family Psychology Review, 11*(3), 75–113. https://doi.org/10.1007/s10567-008-0036-x

Fishbein, J. N., Baer, R. A., Correll, J., & Arch, J. J. (2020). The Questionnaire on Self-Transcendence (QUEST): A measure of trait self-transcendence informed by contextual cognitive behavioral therapies. *Assessment*. https://doi.org/10.1177/1073191120980061

Francis, A. W., Dawson, D. L., & Golijani-Moghaddam, N. G. (2016). The development and validation of the comprehensive assessment of acceptance and commitment therapy processes (CompACT). *Journal of Contextual Behavioral Science, 5*, 134–145. https://doi.org/10.1016/j.jcbs.2016.05.003

Gillanders, D. T., Bolderston, H., Bond, F. W., Dempster, M., Flaxman, P. E., Campbell, L., Kerr, S., Tansey, L., Noel, P., Ferenbach, C., Masley, S., Roach, L., Lloyd, J., May, L., Clarke, S., & Remington, R. (2014). The development and initial validation of the Cognitive Fusion Questionnaire. *Behavior Therapy*, 45, 83–101. DOI: 10.1016/j.beth.2013.09.001

Greco, L. A., Baer, R. A., & Smith, G. T. (2011). Assessing mindfulness in children and adolescents: Development and validation of the Child and Adolescent Mindfulness Measure (CAMM). *Psychological Assessment, 23*(3), 606–614. https://doi.org/10.1037/a0022819

Greco, L. A., Lambert, W., & Baer, R. A. (2008). Psychological inflexibility in childhood and adolescence: Development and evaluation of the Avoidance and Fusion Questionnaire for Youth. *Psychological Assessment, 20*, 93–102.

Harris, R. (2019). *ACT made simple: An easy-to-read primer on acceptance and commitment therapy* (2nd ed.) New Harbinger Publications.

Hayes, L. L., & Ciarrochi, J., (2015). *The thriving adolescent: Using acceptance and commitment therapy and positive psychology to help teens manage emotions, achieve goals and build connection.* New Harbinger.

Hayes, S. (2004). Acceptance and commitment therapy, relational frame theory, and the third wave of behavioral and cognitive therapies. *Behavior Therapy, 35*(4), 639– 665.

Hayes S. C. (2020). Constructing a liberated and modern mind: Six pathways from pathology to euthymia. *World Psychiatry: Official Journal of the World Psychiatric Association (WPA), 19*(1), 51–52. https://doi.org/10.1002/wps.20715

Hayes, S. C., Hofmann, S. G., & Ciarrochi, J. (2020). A process-based approach to psychological diagnosis and treatment: The conceptual and treatment utility of an extended evolutionary meta model. *Clinical Psychology Review, 82*, 101908.

Hayes, S. C., Luoma, J. B., Bond, F. W., Masuda, A., & Lillis, J. (2006). Acceptance and commitment therapy: Model, processes and outcomes. *Behaviour Research and Therapy, 44*, 1–25. doi:10.1016/j.brat.2005.06.006

Hayes, S. C., & Strosahl, K. D. (2004). *A practical guide to acceptance and commitment therapy*. New York: Springer-Verlag.

Hayes, S. C., Strosahl, K., & Wilson, K.G. (1999). *Acceptance and commitment therapy: An experiential approach to behavior change*. Guilford Press.

Hayes, S. C., Strosahl, K. D., Wilson, K. G., Bissett, R. T., Pistorello, J., Toarmino, D., Polusny, M., A., Dykstra, T. A., Batten, S. V., Bergan, J., Stewart, S. H., Zvolensky, M. J., Eifert, G. H., Bond, F. W., Forsyth J. P., Karekla, M., & McCurry, S. M. (2004). Measuring experiential avoidance: A preliminary test of a working model. *The Psychological Record, 54*, 553–578.

Hofmann, S. G., & Hayes, S. C. (2019). The future of intervention science: Process-based therapy. *Clinical Psychological Science, 7*(1), 37–50. https://doi.org/10.1177/2167702618772296

Levin, M. E., Haeger, J., Pierce, B., & Cruz, R. A. (2017). Evaluating an adjunctive mobile app to enhance psychological flexibility in acceptance and commitment therapy. *Behavior Modification, 41*(6), 846–867. https://doi.org/10.1177/0145445517719661

Levin, M. E., Navarro, C., Cruz, R. A., & Haeger, J. (2019). Comparing in-the-moment skill coaching effects from tailored versus non-tailored acceptance and commitment therapy mobile apps in a non-clinical sample. *Cognitive Behaviour Therapy, 48*(3), 200–216. https://doi.org/10.1080/16506073.2018.1503706

Lundgren, J. D., Allison, K. C., O'Reardon, J. P., & Stunkard, A. J. (2008). A descriptive study of non-obese persons with night eating syndrome and a weight-matched comparison group. *Eating Behaviors, 9*, 343–351.

Luoma, J. B., Hayes, S. C., & Walser, R. D. (2017). *Learning ACT: An acceptance and commitment therapy skills training manual for therapists.* New Harbinger Publications.

Metcalf, C. A., & Dimidjian, S. (2020). In a mother's voice: Observing social-emotional aspects of postpartum daily life. *Journal of Family Psychology, 34*(3), 269–278. https://doi.org/10.1037/fam0000587

Miller, W., C'de Baca, J., Matthews, D., & Wilbourne, P. (2001). *Personal values card sort.* University of New Mexico.

Newsome, D., Newsome, K., Fuller, T., & Meyer, S. (2018). How contextual behavioral scientists measure and report about behavior: A review of JCBS. *Journal of Contextual Behavioral Science, 12.* 10.1016/j.jcbs.2018.11.005

Ong, C. W., Pierce, B. G., Woods, D. W., Twohig, M. P., & Levin, M. E. (2019). The acceptance and action questionnaire – II: An item response theory analysis. *Journal of Psychopathology and Behavioral Assessment, 41*, 123–134. https://doi.org/10.1007/s10862-018-9694-2

Paul, G. L. (1969). Behavior modification research: Design and tactics. In C. M. Franks (Ed.), *Behavior therapy: Appraisal and status* (pp. 29–62). McGraw-Hill.

Polk, K. L., & Schoendorf, B. (2014). *The ACT matrix: A new approach to building psychological flexibility across settings and populations.* New Harbinger Publications.

Rogge, R., Daks, J., Dubler, B., & Saint, K. (2019). It's all about the process: Examining the convergent validity, conceptual coverage, unique predictive validity, and clinical utility of ACT process measures. *Journal of Contextual Behavioral Science, 14.* doi:10.1016/j.jcbs.2019.10.001

Rolffs, J. L., Rogge, R. D., & Wilson, K. G. (2016). Disentangling components of flexibility via the Hexaflex model: Development and validation of the multidimensional psychological flexibility inventory (MPFI). *Assessment, 25*(4), 458–482. doi:10.1177/1073191116645905

Scott, W., McCracken, L. M., & Norton, S. (2016). A confirmatory factor analysis of facets of psychological flexibility in a sample of people seeking treatment for chronic pain. *Annals of Behavioral Medicine, 50*(2), 285–296. https://doi-org.ezp-prod1.hul.harvard.edu/10.1007/s12160-015-9752-x

Smout, M., Davies, M., Burns, N., & Christie, A. (2014). Development of the valuing questionnaire (VQ). *Journal of Contextual Behavioral Science, 3.* doi:10.1016/j.jcbs.2014.06.001

Trindade, I. A., Ferreira, C., & Pinto-Gouveia, J. (2018). Assessment of chronic illness-related cognitive fusion: Preliminary development and validation of a new scale with an IBD sample. *Journal of Clinical Psychology in Medical Settings, 25*(4), 356–366. https://doi.org/10.1007/s10880-017-9536-5

Trompetter, H. R., Ten Klooster, P. M., Schreurs, K., Fledderus, M., Westerhof, G. J., & Bohlmeijer, E. T. (2013). Measuring values and committed action with the Engaged Living Scale (ELS): Psychometric evaluation in a non-clinical sample and a chronic pain sample. *Psychological Assessment, 25*(4), 1235–1246. https://doi.org/10.1037/a0033813

Verplanken, B., & Holland, R. W. (2002). Motivated decision making: Effects of activation and self-centrality of values on choices and behavior. *Journal of Personality and Social Psychology, 82*(3), 434–447. https://doi.org/10.1037/0022-3514.82.3.434

Vilardaga, R., & Vilardaga, J. P. (2019). Marching our values forward: Progressing contextual behavioral science in line with its core epistemic assumptions. *Journal of Contextual Behavioral Science, 14*, 108–110.

Vowles, K. E., Sowden, G., & Ashworth, J. (2014). A comprehensive examination of the model underlying acceptance and commitment therapy for chronic pain. *Behavior Therapy, 45*(3), 390–401. https://doi-org.ezp-prod1.hul.harvard.edu/10.1016/j.beth.2013.12.009

Wilson, K. G., Sandoz, E. K., Kitchens, J., & Roberts, M. (2010). The valued living questionnaire: Defining and measuring valued action within a behavioral framework. *The Psychological Record, 60*, 249–272

Wolgast, M. (2014). What does the acceptance and action questionnaire (AAQ-II) really measure? *Behavior Therapy, 45*(6), 831–839. doi:10.1016/j.beth.2014.07.00

Zettle, R. D., Gird, S. R., Webster, B. K., Carrasquillo-Richardson, N., Swails, A., & Burdsal, C. A. (2018). The Self-as-Context Scale (SACS): Development and preliminary psychometric properties. *Journal of Contextual Behavioral Science, 10*, 64–74. https://doi.org/10.1016/j.jcbs.2018.08.010

Zettle. R. D., & Hayes, S. C. (1982). Rule governed behavior: A potential theoretical framework for cognitive therapy. In P. C. Kendall (Ed.), *Advances in Cognitive Behavioral Research and Therapy* (pp. 73–118). Academic.

CHAPTER 7

Psychological Flexibility

Clarissa W. Ong *and* Elizabeth H. Eustis

Abstract

Psychological flexibility is the ability to nonjudgmentally observe and be open to inner experiences in the present moment, while engaging in behaviors consistent with freely chosen values. A construct related to psychological flexibility is psychological inflexibility, which describes rigid responding to inner experiences, resulting in impulsivity or avoidance that interferes with meaningful action. Psychological inflexibility is posited as the key source of suffering in the acceptance and commitment therapy (ACT) model, and the central aim of ACT is to improve psychological flexibility. However, targeting psychological flexibility is complicated for several reasons: (1) it is difficult to measure with standardized instruments, (2) clinicians need to discern the idiographic function of behaviors to assess psychological flexibility, (3) clinicians themselves need to be able to practice and model psychological flexibility, and (4) cross-cultural research on the measurement of psychological flexibility is lacking. This article discusses these challenges and provides suggestions for future directions.

Key Words: psychological flexibility, psychological inflexibility, acceptance and commitment therapy, measurement, values

The acceptance and commitment therapy (ACT) psychological flexibility model consists of six subprocesses (described in detail elsewhere in this volume): acceptance, defusion, flexible attention to the present moment, self-as-context, values, and committed action (Hayes, Strosahl, et al., 2011). Psychological flexibility may also be represented by three processes in ACT and other contextual cognitive-behavioral therapies: (1) being open (acceptance, defusion); (2) being aware (present moment awareness, self-as-context); and (3) being active (values, committed action; Hayes, Villatte, et al., 2011).

General Concepts

Psychological Flexibility

Psychological flexibility is "the ability to contact the present moment more fully as a conscious human being, and to change or persist in behavior when doing so serves valued ends" (Hayes et al., 2006, p. 7). The overarching skill of psychological flexibility represents various combinations of the six subprocesses of change in ACT covered in earlier articles, such that being psychologically flexible generally entails *accepting* and *defusing* from difficult inner experiences as they show up *in the present moment*, recognizing that the *self is the context* for these inner experiences, in order to pursue personal *values* by *committing to actions* consistent with those values. Examples are being willing to experience anxiety (acceptance) as a collection of sensations, including chest tightness and muscle tension (defusion), and noticing these sensations as they occur (present moment awareness) in a space perceived as the self (self-as-context), while choosing to speak up in class (committed action) as a means to learning (value).

Psychological flexibility is couched in the premise that people have the innate ability to choose how to respond in the presence of difficult thoughts and feelings, even if they cannot control the thoughts and feelings themselves. In other words, in the framework of psychological flexibility, thoughts and feelings do not cause behaviors. Thus, a person practicing psychological flexibility can ride a roller-coaster when they feel fear, start homework when they feel unmotivated, and resist drinking when they feel the urge to drink. As opposed to only responding in prescribed ways to stimuli, psychological flexibility affords people the ability to respond in a variety of—usually more adaptive—ways to the same familiar stimuli.

Psychological Inflexibility

A construct closely related to psychological flexibility is psychological inflexibility. This refers to rigidly responding to internal experiences in ways that interfere with valued behaviors (Hayes, Strosahl, et al., 2011). In terms of the subprocesses, psychological inflexibility is characterized by *avoidance* of and *fusion* with difficult inner experiences that are perceived as comprising the *content of the self*, while being *disconnected from the present moment* and personal *values*, leading to *acting impulsively or failing to take action* toward values. Being psychologically inflexible may manifest as expending significant effort attempting to avoid anxiety (experiential avoidance), which is perceived as "bad" and "scary" (cognitive fusion) and a central part of who the person is (self-as-content), by worrying about possible future worst-case scenarios (fixation on the future) and choosing to self-isolate (inaction) despite caring about building relationships with loved ones (disconnection from values).

From an ACT perspective, one of the main sources of psychopathology is verbal abilities (i.e., language and cognition) gone awry, which happens when behavior is regulated by rigid verbal processes or rules rather than environmental contingencies (i.e., rule-governed behavior). Accordingly, verbal abilities can lead to context-insensitive responding (e.g., avoiding social situations even when they provide positive reinforcement), impeding a person's ability to act on their values in a given situation. Another source of psychological inflexibility is aversive control or being primarily motivated to avoid or escape aversive stimuli. Under aversive control, people are highly motivated to engage in experiential avoidance, limiting their response options in the presence of unpleasant thoughts and feelings.

For people who are psychologically inflexible, thoughts and feelings very much control behaviors and can have a ruinous effect on well-being. An example of psychological inflexibility in depression is following the rule that self-isolating when one is feeling down helps to alleviate suffering, even when direct experience belies the rule. Thus, psychological inflexibility leads to repeatedly responding in the same unhelpful ways (e.g., lashing out at people when feeling angry) despite those behaviors having deleterious consequences for the person. While all humans experience pain, psychological inflexibility is considered the root of unnecessary suffering because it produces responses to pain that only serve to amplify it.

Researchers have found that psychological flexibility and psychological inflexibility are related, yet distinct, processes rather than polar opposites of a single dimension (Rolffs et al., 2016), such that a person with low psychological inflexibility may not necessarily have high psychological flexibility. The literature in psychology provides other examples of related, yet distinct, processes that are not polar opposites, including psychopathology and flourishing, and negative and positive affect. For example, the absence of psychopathology does not mean an individual is flourishing, just as the absence of negative affect does not mean an individual is experiencing positive affect.

Acceptance and Commitment Therapy

The ultimate goal in ACT is to increase psychological flexibility, so this construct is central to its theoretical model. Because the target issue in the psychological flexibility model is rigid responding to stimuli as opposed to the stimuli themselves, the focus in ACT is not to change the *content* of the internal or verbal experience, but to alter the *function* of it by changing the way individuals relate to or interact with these experiences. This is accomplished by helping individuals develop a more open and flexible relationship with these verbal processes. For example, cognitive defusion can involve the skill of noticing thoughts and feelings while acting in ways that may seem contradictory to those thoughts and feelings like approaching anxiety or taking on a challenge when your mind says, "You can't do it." To practice psychological flexibility, one must be able and willing to notice verbal processes without automatically reacting to them and to base their behavioral decisions on what is personally important in a given situation.

Measuring Psychological (In)flexibility

Given that the main goal in ACT is to increase psychological flexibility, it is critical that measures of this construct are psychometrically sound. If psychological flexibility determines the efficacy of ACT and is poorly measured, we cannot determine if ACT works in the way it is hypothesized to work.

Self-Report Assessment

Psychological (in)flexibility is typically measured using self-report questionnaires.

ACCEPTANCE AND ACTION QUESTIONNAIRE—II (AAQ-II; BOND ET AL, 2011)

The most common measure of psychological inflexibility is the AAQ-II, a seven-item global self-report measure. Higher scores indicate higher levels of psychological inflexibility. The internal consistency and test–retest reliability of the AAQ-II is stronger than its original version (Hayes et al., 2004), which was historically developed to measure experiential avoidance. Preliminary research indicates that the AAQ-II has adequate internal consistency and validity (Bond et al., 2011; Fledderus et al., 2012). However, there are significant concerns with the discriminant validity of the AAQ-II (Tyndall et al., 2019): studies indicate that it may be a stronger measure of general negative affect or neuroticism (e.g., Rochefort et al., 2018; Wolgast, 2014) than inflexible responding to negative affect or distress. This limitation raises concerns that the AAQ-II does not capture the construct of psychological inflexibility. Furthermore, differential item functioning within the scale and response patterns across various samples have been reported (Ong, Pierce, et al., 2019), which means people with different profiles (e.g., clinical vs. nonclinical) may interpret and respond to items differently, rendering scores between sufficiently different populations incomparable.

In addition to the global AAQ-II, several context-specific versions of the AAQ focus on specific clinical presentations or populations, including acquired brain injury, adolescents, auditory hallucinations, body image, cancer, caregiving, chronic illness, chronic pain, diabetes, disordered eating, epilepsy, food craving, hearing loss, hoarding, infertility, irritable bowel syndrome, obsessions and compulsions, parenting, smoking, social anxiety, stigma, substance abuse, tinnitus, trichotillomania, university students, weight, and work (Galhardo et al., 2020; Krafft et al., 2019; Levin et al., 2019; Livheim et al., 2016; Ong, Lee, et al., 2019; Ong,

Whicker, et al., 2019). Context-specific versions of the AAQ appear to be more strongly associated with relevant outcomes for that population compared with the global AAQ-II (e.g., Houghton et al., 2014; Sandoz et al., 2013). Thus, researchers and clinicians should use context-specific versions of the AAQ if they are available. At the same time, although the majority of these AAQ variants have been found to have satisfactory preliminary psychometrics, additional research is needed. See Ong, Lee, et al. (2019) for a review of context-specific AAQ variants and other context-specific measures of psychological flexibility.

In addition to the AAQ-II, more recent self-report measures of psychological flexibility have been developed. These newer measures are all multidimensional.

COMPREHENSIVE ASSESSMENT OF ACCEPTANCE AND COMMITMENT THERAPY PROCESSES (COMPACT; FRANCIS ET AL, 2016)

The CompACT is a 23-item self-report measure that includes three subscales: openness to experience, behavioral awareness, and valued action; these subscales capture the six subprocesses of psychological flexibility. Given that one limitation of existing measures is their focus on only one or several processes at once, the authors aimed to develop a general measure of psychological flexibility that fully assessed this multidimensional construct. The CompACT was developed by selecting items from existing measures of psychological flexibility. Preliminary results indicate that the CompACT has excellent internal consistency and stronger discriminant validity than certain other measures of psychological flexibility (Francis et al., 2016; Ong et al., 2020).

MULTIDIMENSIONAL PSYCHOLOGICAL FLEXIBILITY INDEX (MPFI; ROLFFS ET AL, 2016)

The MPFI is a 60-item self-report measure that aims to assess all 12 dimensions of the ACT psychological flexibility/inflexibility or "hexaflex" model comprehensively and efficiently. To date, it is the only measure that assesses both psychological flexibility and inflexibility. Given that psychological flexibility and inflexibility appear to be related, yet distinct, constructs, it may be advantageous to measure both of these constructs and their processes within one measure. This measure yields a composite score for flexibility and inflexibility, as well as scores for each of the 12 processes. Preliminary results indicate that it has excellent internal consistency.

OPEN AND ENGAGED STATE QUESTIONNAIRE (OESQ; BENOY ET AL, 2019)

The OESQ is a four-item self-report measure that focuses on state-level behavior over the preceding seven days. Its development was informed by recommendations in the literature that measures of psychological flexibility should assess behaviors and use an approach that is contextually and temporally sensitive (Kashdan & Rottenberg, 2010; Wolgast, 2014). Preliminary results indicate that the OESQ has good internal consistency and stronger discriminatory validity from neuroticism than some other measures of psychological flexibility.

EVERYDAY PSYCHOLOGICAL INFLEXIBILITY CHECKLIST (EPIC; THOMPSON ET AL, 2019)

The EPIC is a seven-item self-report measure that consists of two factors: avoidance and behavioral rigidity. This scale was developed to examine psychological inflexibility broadly and, therefore, does not focus on psychopathology or use related language (i.e., no items reference pain, fear, or worry). While the majority of research on ACT and psychological flexibility has been in the context of mental and physical health symptoms and disorders, the model is applicable to human behavior broadly, and the EPIC provides a way to assess psychological inflexibility more generally. The authors suggest that it could be used in relation to important social concerns and injustices in society, including inequity, poverty, and climate change. Preliminary results indicate that the EPIC has acceptable internal consistency. More research is needed to explore the relationship between the EPIC and measures of prosocial behavior.

PERSONALIZED PSYCHOLOGICAL FLEXIBILITY INDEX (PPFI; KASHDAN ET AL, 2020)

The PPFI is a 15-item self-report measure on which individuals select one specific goal in their lives and answer questions based on that goal. Accordingly, it is more idiographic than previously discussed measures, and it is the only measure that links willingness to experience distress to the pursuit of a personally meaningful goal identified by the respondent. This is crucial because the ability to practice flexibility in the pursuit of personally meaningful actions is central to ACT. Preliminary results indicate that the PPFI has adequate/good internal consistency and stronger discriminant validity with unpleasant emotions compared to other measures of psychological flexibility.

Clinician-Administered Assessment

Clinicians can use several tools to assess psychological flexibility and track movement in flexibility over time, including the ACT ADVISOR, hexagon case formulation tools, and the Psy-Flex Planning Tool (Hayes, Strosahl, et al., 2011). Although these measures have not been published and psychometric data are unavailable, they may be useful to clinicians for assessing and tracking psychological flexibility and complement other assessments of psychological flexibility (Hayes, Strosahl, et al., 2011).

The ACT ADVISOR allows clinicians to rate client behavior on a scale from 1 to 10 on six scales that map on to the six subprocesses of psychological flexibility. The ACT ADVISOR is organized in the hexagonal diagram corresponding to the six subprocesses, providing a visual representation of level of psychological flexibility. There are multiple versions of the hexagon case formulation tools. These tools also include the six subprocesses of psychological flexibility arranged in a hexagon. They allow clinicians to rate clients from 0 to 10 on each process to identify and provide a visual representation of relative strengths and weaknesses. The Psy-Flex Planning Tool provides a succinct and visual summary of the six subprocesses of psychological flexibility for case formulation. In this tool, the psychological flexibility model is broken down into three components, each comprising two subprocesses: open (acceptance, defusion), centered (present moment, self-as-context), and engaged (values, committed action)

Psychological Flexibility in Therapy

A simplified definition of being psychologically flexible is varying responses to the same stimulus. Conceptualizing psychological flexibility in this way can make it easier to model and detect instances of psychological flexibility in therapy sessions. For instance, therapists can intentionally demonstrate different responses (e.g., noticing and sitting with, refocusing attention from) to a specific stimulus (e.g., anxiety, frustration) to model psychological flexibility. For clients, psychological flexibility is indicated by an expanded behavioral repertoire in the presence of previously life-constraining stimuli. For example, a client with obsessive-compulsive disorder (OCD) who used to eat snacks only with a napkin but who now eats them with their hands after washing them, after using hand sanitizer, or even without washing them, is showing more psychological flexibility because they are selecting from a *wider range of behaviors* when responding to the *same stimulus* of contamination fear and in the *same situation* of eating snacks. This functional framework illuminates the more nuanced aspects of psychological flexibility in practice, which are verbal content (language), the values criterion, homework, and idiographic assessment.

Example of ACT-Consistent Language

ACT therapists need to be mindful of how they use language to be fully consistent with the ACT model. Much of our language implies that there are good and bad inner experiences, which we *can* and *should* control. In particular, the problem-solving response is likely well entrenched in clients' (and therapists') repertoires. As such, therapists need to watch out for statements that reinforce these ideas, including those that:

1. label inner experiences as good or bad (e.g., "It's good that you're feeling less anxious"),
2. define the self in relation to thoughts and feelings (e.g., "I am anxious"),
3. imply we have control over thoughts and feelings (e.g., "Try not to think about that"),
4. imply that thoughts and feelings have power over behavior (e.g., "Only share if you feel comfortable sharing"),
5. encourage attempts to control thoughts and feelings (e.g., "See if you can make anxiety go down"), and
6. respond to the content of thoughts and feelings (e.g., trying to dispute the accuracy of thoughts).

Rather, therapists can demonstrate a stance that is more consistent with ACT by speaking in ways that actively promote flexible responding. This may include:

1. focusing on describing—rather than evaluating—thoughts and feelings (e.g., "It seems like your anxiety has decreased"),
2. relating thoughts and feelings as distinct from the self (e.g., "I am experiencing anxiety"),
3. commenting on the automaticity of thoughts and feelings (e.g., "How interesting that another one of those thoughts just showed up"),
4. framing choices in terms of willingness not comfort (e.g., "Share if you are willing to share"),
5. acknowledging the difficulty of regulating thoughts and feelings especially in the long term (e.g., "If you could get rid of your worries, wouldn't you have done that by now?"), and
6. responding to the function or effect of thoughts and feelings rather than their form (e.g., decreasing avoidance of anxiety over decreasing anxiety).

Therapists can also model psychological flexibility by responding to clients' experiences differently from how clients have responded historically. For example, if a client habitually argues with their thoughts, therapists can comment on client statements as "thoughts that show up" rather than get entangled with their content. Similarly, if a client often avoids feeling anxiety by changing the subject, therapists may choose to stay on topic and allow the anxiety to be present to show that a different way of responding is possible.

Example of Values Criterion

From an ACT perspective, values are used to shape clients' behavioral repertoires in that flexibility is useful only to the extent that it moves clients closer to self-determined values. In other words, variability is not useful in and of itself. Therefore, ACT therapists generally remind clients to select responses based on a values criterion: "Did responding in X way in Y situation move me closer to the life I want?" Flexible responding and a values criterion give clients the basic tools they need to test out different responses, learn from direct contingencies, and select behaviors that work based on context. The values criterion is important because it forms the basis for selection and retention of new behaviors. Without values to anchor these decisions, ACT may more closely resemble someone trying on clothes in a store without knowing what they want—the number of clothing items one tries on does not matter if they do not know what they are looking for.

Conversely, rigidity is not "bad" in and of itself; it is only "bad" when it prevents clients from pursuing the things that matter to them. There is undoubtedly a time and place when avoidance—either experiential or behavioral—serves personal values, and clients need to be able to discriminate those situations and select the appropriate response from their newly expanded behavioral repertoire. For example, it may be adaptive to be open to feelings of frustration when playing with our children but distract (a form of avoidance) from frustration when they are about people with whom we barely interact. Alternatively, while it may sometimes be adaptive to respond flexibly to frustration stemming from persistent microaggressions, it can similarly be adaptive to avoid situations that invariably expose us to those microaggressions in the first place to the extent that doing so is within our control—perhaps with reference to the value of self-preservation. Accepting and avoiding with reference to values is exactly consistent with the psychological flexibility model and, in fact, exemplifies it. After all, *always* choosing to be open to discomfort is a different type of rigidity.

Example of Homework

When assigning homework between sessions, therapists can choose to build on the skills practiced in session by explicitly framing homework in those terms. Because values are the metric against which flexibility is measured, it may be helpful to consistently ground homework in values. Thus, a complete homework assignment will likely include (1) a specific measurable action, (2) the value(s) with which it is consistent, and (3) the skill(s) targeted by the action. For example, for a client working on building relationships in the presence of social anxiety, their homework could be to (1) text at least a sentence to two people, (2) align with their value of connection, and (3) focus on making room for discomfort when it shows up during the exercise.

Research on Psychological (In)flexibility

Much evidence supports the centrality of psychological flexibility for meaningful living. It has been associated with positive indices such as job satisfaction, mental well-being, and treatment outcomes (Hayes et al., 2006; Kashdan & Rottenberg, 2010) and has been found to be a protective factor for physical and mental health outcomes in the presence of stress in the general population (Gloster et al., 2017). In contrast, psychological inflexibility is associated with a range of current and lifetime clinical presentations (e.g., anxiety disorders, depressive disorders) above and beyond psychological distress (Levin et al., 2014).

Also consistent with the psychological flexibility model is the fact that ACT-based interventions have been found to specifically shift psychological flexibility (Levin et al., 2012). Moreover, subprocesses have demonstrated the additive effects on outcomes, such that targeting combinations of subprocesses appears to have a larger effect than targeting subprocesses in isolation (Branstetter-Rost et al., 2009). At the same time, cognitive-behavioral therapy (CBT) has been found to improve psychological flexibility (Arch et al., 2012); hence, ACT may not uniquely impact psychological flexibility. In fact, by definition, any intervention that increases the range of responding to familiar stimuli (which includes most psychological therapies) necessarily targets psychological flexibility.

Evidence largely supports psychological flexibility as a mediator of outcomes in ACT, indicating that ACT affects outcomes by successfully targeting its hypothesized change process

(Stockton et al., 2019). This finding is especially consistent for mental health outcomes such as general psychological distress, but less so for physical health, patient functioning, and quality of life (Stockton et al., 2019).

The status of psychological flexibility as a moderator of treatment outcomes is unclear (e.g., Craske et al., 2014; Wolitzky-Taylor et al., 2012). For example, in one study on social anxiety disorder, participants in the CBT condition who reported lower psychological flexibility at baseline (AAQ-I) reported greater symptom improvement at 12-month follow-up, whereas this was not the case in the ACT condition (Craske et al., 2014). In another study with a mixed anxiety disorders sample, participants in the CBT condition with lower psychological flexibility at baseline (AAQ-I willingness subscale) did better at 12-month follow-up, while participants in the ACT condition with moderate baseline psychological flexibility did better at follow-up (Wolitzky-Taylor et al., 2012). Another study on clinical perfectionism found that lower baseline psychological inflexibility (AAQ-II) was associated with more improvement in quality of life, while higher baseline inflexibility was associated with more improvement in symptoms and distress (Ong, Barney, et al., 2019). Given inconsistent findings, it is unclear how baseline psychological flexibility influences treatment response. Rather, it is more likely that (1) moderation effects vary across outcomes and populations and (2) measurement methods influence results (most of these studies used different versions of the AAQ).

Challenges and Future Directions

The irony of defining psychological flexibility is that it is most readily understood as an amalgamation of six subprocesses or skills, when distinguishing among the subprocesses is only theoretically plausible. In actuality, the subprocesses necessarily entail each other to be fully realized. For example, it is nearly impossible to willingly experience intense sadness if one believes the sadness "must be avoided at all costs" (fusion) or to know what one's true values are if they are rigidly attached to concepts about who they are (self-as-content). Thus, part of the challenge of practicing psychological flexibility is that it requires learning multiple closely related skills adequately. Therefore, therapists may struggle with teaching psychological flexibility if clients are particularly stuck on a subprocess because that hinders learning of other subprocesses. For the most part, a significant level of clinical skill and ACT dexterity is needed to navigate these difficulties and to move clients along the journey of actualizing their values through practicing flexibility. Still, some evidence suggests that certain components may be selectively emphasized, depending on treatment goals. For example, focusing on values and committed action has been found to have greater effects on quality of life and valued action, whereas focusing on acceptance and defusion more positively impacts symptom severity (Villatte et al., 2016).

The complexity of psychological flexibility makes it a challenging construct to measure. For nomothetic measurement, there are five areas of consideration. First, as discussed previously, psychological flexibility refers to a multifaceted, contextually bound pattern of behaviors most accurately defined with reference to a person's history of responding. In other words, psychological flexibility looks different across people (topographically diverse) even if its function remains consistent (different responses to same stimuli with reference to values). The challenge then is to functionally assess levels of psychological flexibility with easily administered tools—typically self-report measures—that need to look the same for every respondent for the purpose of psychometric evaluation.

In theory, accurate measurement of psychological flexibility through self-report would require that the respondent first be able to identify their current patterns of responding, assess the amount of variability in those patterns vis-à-vis specific stimuli and previous responding, and evaluate how well those patterns align with their personal values. The unfeasibility of this task logically leads researchers and clinicians to devise methods to indirectly measure these concepts by simplifying questions as in the seven-item AAQ-II or by asking many questions as in the 60-item MPFI. The balance between risking poor validity due to brevity and burdening respondents with long surveys is difficult to navigate and forces a dichotomous choice between inaccurate assessment and ease of administration when it comes to assessing a construct as contextually bound as psychological flexibility.

Bridging the gap between these considerations requires innovative thinking and rigorous measure development. One method researchers have used is ecological momentary assessment or data collection in real time (e.g., responding to prompts from a phone app at random intervals during the day). For example, a study found that momentary psychological flexibility was associated with stress and well-being measured during the same narrow timeframe and that the relationship between momentary psychological flexibility and momentary well-being strengthened over the course of an ACT intervention (Grégoire et al., 2020). Findings like these that carry greater precision provide stronger support for the hypothesis that psychological flexibility is intimately associated with well-being. Nonetheless, further validation is needed to ascertain the advantages and disadvantages of this and other newer means of assessment.

Second, psychological flexibility can be measured as a state or "trait" (longer-term behavioral patterns), and researchers need to clarify which level of analysis they are interested in because this choice necessitates different forms of assessment. A state-level assessment is context-specific; it refers to how a person responds in a given circumstance. It is in this area that ecological momentary assessment is typically applied. There might also be variability in how flexibly one responds across contexts. For example, a person struggling with addiction might be able to display new responses in the presence of alcohol at home but not at a bar. In contrast, a trait-level assessment requires averaging of responses and conflation across settings to determine a person's overall psychological flexibility. These data also have different uses. A clinician might be more interested in state-level data to refine their case conceptualization and treatment planning, whereas a public health researcher might be more concerned about how generally being more psychologically flexible is associated with relevant outcomes.

Third, psychological flexibility must be clearly differentiated from distress, which is naturally correlated with, but theoretically distinct from, *responses to* distress. After all, the crux of psychological flexibility is that people can change their responses upon exposure to the same stimulus, necessarily weakening the relationship between distress and responses to it. Psychological flexibility with all its nuances is understandably a difficult construct to measure with just seven questions. Thus, it may not be surprising that the AAQ-II is susceptible to discriminant validity issues despite its other solid psychometric properties (Tyndall et al., 2019). This limitation is particularly salient given that the majority of ACT research has relied on the AAQ-II. Furthermore, measures of psychological flexibility generally seem to presume that responders understand there is a separation between inner experiences and behaviors—that thoughts and feelings do not cause behavior—and survey questions are phrased as such. However, this assumption may be untenable, creating a gap between how questions are intended to be answered and how they are actually answered, further obfuscating the meaning of survey responses.

Fourth, there is an ongoing discussion in the field as to whether measures of psychological flexibility effectively assess all six subprocesses within the psychological flexibility model, as some have been found to correlate more strongly with specific subprocesses versus others (Benoy et al., 2019; Francis et al., 2016). For example, the OESQ was found to be highly negatively correlated with cognitive fusion at posttreatment, but more moderately correlated with mindfulness in samples that included individuals who either met criteria for panic disorder and agoraphobia or were experiencing burnout. Researchers have posited that the items on the AAQ-II appear to be more focused on experiential avoidance/acceptance and cognitive fusion/defusion compared to the other subprocesses, and that there are fewer measures that assess other subprocesses, such as self-as-context (Francis et al., 2016). For example, the AAQ-II was found to have the greatest correlation with the CompACT subscale of openness to experience, compared to the other two subscales (behavioral awareness, and valued action) in a nonclinical sample (Francis et al., 2016). Additional research is needed in more populations (e.g., various clinical populations, nonclinical populations) to examine whether or not these results are replicated and to investigate these questions in other measures of psychological flexibility. Another area for future research is the relative importance of measuring each specific subprocess versus examining how measures may relate to the three broader processes that have been described recently as another way to capture the subprocesses of flexibility: being open (acceptance, defusion), aware (present moment awareness, self-as-context), and active (values, committed action; Hayes, Strosahl, et al., 2011).

Fifth, cultural considerations demand attention to the measurement invariance of psychological flexibility measures. The theory behind psychological flexibility hypothesizes that it is universal across humans and not specific to certain cultures. Accordingly, we need to be able to accurately measure this construct across cultures and languages without inadvertently privileging a dominant culture. Furthermore, many of the samples used in research on psychological flexibility to date have been predominately white, and psychometric data from these measures in samples with greater diversity with regard to race and other aspects of identity are needed (Flynn et al., 2016). Collecting data from various populations is critical to ensure that all experiences are represented in research and, specifically, to examine if there are important differences in how the construct of psychological flexibility is interpreted or experienced and if existing results generalize to more racially diverse samples. For example, at least one study to date has found that the AAQ-II was a significantly stronger predictor of symptom outcomes for participants who identified racially as white than those who identified as Asian or Latinx (Borgogna et al., 2020). Preliminary evidence suggests that the AAQ-II functions adequately as a cross-cultural assessment, though culturally informed adaptations would improve its psychometric quality (Borgogna et al., 2020). Similar tests are needed for other measures of psychological flexibility.

Finally, even if the previously mentioned nomothetic measurement concerns are addressed, as alluded to earlier, psychological flexibility is principally an idiographic construct because it is inextricable from context, which includes a person's biology, developmental history, current environment, interpersonal network, and societal mores. While nomothetic measurement helps with aggregate inferences, idiographic measurement is needed to understand how to improve and leverage psychological flexibility for the individual. This knowledge is particularly crucial for identifying precise links between treatment methods and psychological flexibility and supports the development of more targeted and, thereby, efficient interventions. Moreover, idiographic assessment is rooted in the premise that individual variability must be accounted for rather than controlled for in our clinical analyses, which is the cornerstone of personalized medicine. Hence, to conduct idiographic assessment and accurately track the function of clients' behaviors, therapists need to have an adequate grasp of how their clients perceive and interact with their environments; how psychological inflexibility shows up for one client may be different from how it manifests in another. As part of this understanding, therapists need to have a sense of what clients find aversive versus rewarding and how the valence of stimuli changes across contexts. Clearly, idiographic assessment requires greater effort than administering a self-report measure—which is why it provides the necessary data for refining treatment based on each client's unique presentation.

Another potential fruitful future direction is deeper investigation of the relationship between ACT and psychological flexibility. Why do CBT methods also shift psychological flexibility, and what are the implications of that for ACT as a therapeutic intervention? If other treatments move psychological flexibility, what is the exact procedure that is producing this change? Answers to these questions would clarify how to move psychological flexibility and facilitate refinement of ACT methods so that they can more precisely target psychological flexibility. Furthermore, the specific methods used in ACT to increase psychological flexibility need to be evidence-based for ACT to stand as an empirically grounded treatment. For instance, evidence must support use of acceptance specifically, not just general sustained exposure to a feared stimulus.

The practice of ACT might need to be revised as clinical researchers find methods to improve psychological flexibility more effectively than currently available techniques or find ways to effectively apply ACT to a wider range of presentations. As ACT currently stands, it is more helpful for certain conditions, such as chronic pain and anxiety, than others, such as posttraumatic stress disorder and borderline personality disorder. Reliable answers to these research questions are predicated on accurate measurement of psychological flexibility, which goes back to the assessment concerns outlined at the start of this section. Without trustworthy assessment, robust interpretations cannot be made from data, no matter how copious.

Conclusion

There is strong evidence that psychological flexibility has positive effects on well-being and functioning and that psychological inflexibility leads to maladaptive consequences. In addition, much research supports the effectiveness of ACT at targeting psychological flexibility and achieving positive treatment outcomes through improving psychological flexibility. Despite its conscientiously elaborated theoretical model, psychological flexibility faces challenges in clinical and scientific domains, primarily owing to its inherently idiographic, functional nature. Clinically, replicable and easily disseminated techniques to improve psychological flexibility effectively and efficiently need to be better identified. With respect to research, accurately measuring psychological flexibility is difficult, although newer measures appear to be improvements over older ones.

The tenets of clinical science beseech researchers and clinicians to use reliable and valid forms of assessment. This is in some ways a Sisyphean task as human variability and the complexity of psychological flexibility will likely continue to elude accurate measurement. At the same time, more effort needs to be made to account for its various facets: context sensitivity, idiosyncratic nature, relation to values, and cross-cultural expressions. With improved assessment and creative study designs, researchers will be better positioned to conduct granular analyses of this process of change, and clinicians will be better equipped to personalize their treatments. These developments are critical for ACT to grow as an empirically supported therapy and as a behavioral technology that has the express function of enhancing valued living.

References

Arch, J. J., Wolitzky-Taylor, K. B., Eifert, G. H., & Craske, M. G. (2012). Longitudinal treatment mediation of traditional cognitive behavioral therapy and acceptance and commitment therapy for anxiety disorders. *Behaviour Research Therapy, 50*(7–8), 469–478. https://doi.org/10.1016/j.brat.2012.04.007

Benoy, C., Knitter, B., Knellwolf, L., Doering, S., Klotsche, J., & Gloster, A. T. (2019). Assessing psychological flexibility: Validation of the Open and Engaged State Questionnaire. *Journal of Contextual Behavioral Science, 12*, 253–260. https://doi.org/10.1016/j.jcbs.2018.08.005

Bond, F. W., Hayes, S. C., Baer, R. A., Carpenter, K. M., Guenole, N., Orcutt, H. K., Waltz, T., & Zettle, R. D. (2011). Preliminary psychometric properties of the Acceptance and Action Questionnaire-II: A revised measure of psychological inflexibility and experiential avoidance. *Behavior Therapy, 42*(4), 676–688. https://doi.org/10.1016/j.beth.2011.03.007

Borgogna, N. C., McDermott, R. C., Berry, A., Lathan, E. C., & Gonzales, J. (2020). A multicultural examination of experiential avoidance: AAQ–II measurement comparisons across Asian American, Black, Latinx, Middle Eastern, and White college students. *Journal of Contextual Behavioral Science, 16*, 1–8. https://doi.org/10.1016/j.jcbs.2020.01.011

Branstetter-Rost, A., Cushing, C., & Douleh, T. (2009). Personal values and pain tolerance: Does a values intervention add to acceptance? *The Journal of Pain, 10*(8), 887–892. https://doi.org/10.1016/j.jpain.2009.01.001

Craske, M. G., Niles, A. N., Burklund, L. J., Wolitzky-Taylor, K. B., Vilardaga, J. C., Arch, J. J., Saxbe, D. E., & Lieberman, M. D. (2014). Randomized controlled trial of cognitive behavioral therapy and acceptance and commitment therapy for social phobia: Outcomes and moderators. *Journal of Consulting and Clinical Psychology, 82*(6), 1034–1048. https://doi.org/10.1037/a0037212

Fledderus, M., Oude Voshaar, M. A., Ten Klooster, P. M., & Bohlmeijer, E. T. (2012). Further evaluation of the psychometric properties of the Acceptance and Action Questionnaire-II. *Psychological Assessment, 24*(4), 925–936. https://doi.org/10.1037/a0028200

Flynn, M., Berkout, O., & Bordieri, M. (2016). Cultural considerations in the measurement of psychological flexibility: Initial validation of the Acceptance and Action Questionnaire–II among Hispanic individuals. *Behavior Analysis: Research and Practice*, 16. https://doi.org/10.1037/bar0000035

Francis, A. W., Dawson, D. L., & Golijani-Moghaddam, N. (2016). The development and validation of the Comprehensive assessment of Acceptance and Commitment Therapy processes (CompACT). *Journal of Contextual Behavioral Science, 5*(3), 134–145. https://doi.org/10.1016/j.jcbs.2016.05.003

Galhardo, A., Cunha, M., Monteiro, B., & Pinto-Gouveia, J. (2020). Assessing psychological inflexibility in infertility: The development and validation study of the Psychological Inflexibility Scale–Infertility (PIS-I). *Journal of Contextual Behavioral Science, 18*, 239–246. https://doi.org/10.1016/j.jcbs.2020.09.006

Gloster, A. T., Meyer, A. H., & Lieb, R. (2017). Psychological flexibility as a malleable public health target: Evidence from a representative sample. *Journal of Contextual Behavioral Science, 6*(2), 166–171. https://doi.org/10.1016/j.jcbs.2017.02.003

Grégoire, S., Chénier, C., Doucerain, M., Lachance, L., & Shankland, R. (2020). Ecological momentary assessment of stress, well-being, and psychological flexibility among college and university students during acceptance and commitment therapy. *Canadian Journal of Behavioural Science, 52*(3), 231–243. https://doi.org/10.1037/cbs0000175

Hayes, S. C., Luoma, J. B., Bond, F. W., Masuda, A., & Lillis, J. (2006). Acceptance and commitment therapy: Model, processes and outcomes. *Behaviour Research and Therapy, 44*(1), 1–25. https://doi.org/10.1016/j.brat.2005.06.006

Hayes, S. C., Strosahl, K. D., & Wilson, K. G. (2011). *Acceptance and Commitment Therapy, Second Edition: The process and practice of mindful change.* Guilford Press.

Hayes, S. C., Villatte, M., Levin, M., & Hildebrandt, M. (2011). Open, aware, and active: Contextual approaches as an emerging trend in the behavioral and cognitive therapies. *Annual Review of Clinical Psychology, 7*, 17.11–17.28. https://doi.org/0.1146/annurev-clinpsy-032210-104449

Hayes, S. C., Strosahl, K., Wilson, K. G., Bissett, R. T., Pistorello, J., Toarmino, D., Polusny, M. A., Dykstra, T. A., Batten, S. V., Bergan, J., Stewart, S. H., Zvolensky, M. J., Eifert, G. H., Bond, F. W., Forsyth, J. P., Karekla, M., & McCurry, S. M. (2004). Measuring experiential avoidance: A preliminary test of a working model. *The Psychological Record, 54*(4), 553–578. https://doi.org/10.1007/BF03395492

Houghton, D. C., Compton, S. N., Twohig, M. P., Saunders, S. M., Franklin, M. E., Neal-Barnett, A. M., Ely, L., Capriotti, M. R., & Woods, D. W. (2014). Measuring the role of psychological inflexibility in trichotillomania. *Psychiatry Research, 220*(1–2), 356–361. https://doi.org/10.1016/j.psychres.2014.08.003

Kashdan, T. B., Disabato, D. J., Goodman, F. R., Doorley, J. D., & McKnight, P. E. (2020). Understanding psychological flexibility: A multimethod exploration of pursuing valued goals despite the presence of distress. *Psychological Assessment, 32*(9), 829–850. https://doi.org/10.1037/pas0000834

Kashdan, T. B., & Rottenberg, J. (2010). Psychological flexibility as a fundamental aspect of health. *Clinical Psychology Review, 30*(7), 865–878. https://doi.org/10.1016/j.cpr.2010.03.001

Krafft, J., Ong, C. W., Twohig, M. P., & Levin, M. E. (2019). Assessing psychological inflexibility in hoarding: The Acceptance and Action Questionnaire for Hoarding (AAQH). *Journal of Contextual Behavioral Science, 12*, 234–242. https://doi.org/10.1016/j.jcbs.2018.08.003

Levin, M. E., Hildebrandt, M. J., Lillis, J., & Hayes, S. C. (2012). The impact of treatment components suggested by the psychological flexibility model: A meta-analysis of laboratory-based component studies. *Behavior Therapy, 43*(4), 741–756. https://doi.org/10.1016/j.beth.2012.05.003

Levin, M. E., Krafft, J., Pistorello, J., & Seeley, J. R. (2019). Assessing psychological inflexibility in university students: Development and validation of the Acceptance and Action Questionnaire for University Students (AAQ-US). *Journal of Contextual Behavioral Science, 12,* 199–206. https://doi.org/10.1016/j.jcbs.2018.03.004

Levin, M. E., MacLane, C., Daflos, S., Seeley, J. R., Hayes, S. C., Biglan, A., & Pistorello, J. (2014). Examining psychological inflexibility as a transdiagnostic process across psychological disorders. *Journal of Contextual Behavioral Science, 3,* 155–163. https://doi.org/10.1016/j.jcbs.2014.06.003

Livheim, F., Tengström, A., Bond, F. W., Andersson, G., Dahl, J., & Rosendahl, I. (2016). Psychometric properties of the Avoidance and Fusion Questionnaire for Youth: A psychological measure of psychological inflexibility in youth. *Journal of Contextual Behavioral Science, 5*(2), 103–110. https://doi.org/10.1016/j.jcbs.2016.04.001

Ong, C. W., Lee, E. B., Levin, M. E., & Twohig, M. P. (2019). A review of AAQ variants and other context-specific measures of psychological flexibility. *Journal of Contextual Behavioral Science, 12,* 329–346. https://doi.org/10.1016/j.jcbs.2019.02.007

Ong, C. W., Pierce, B. G., Petersen, J. M., Barney, J. L., Fruge, J. E., Levin, M. E., & Twohig, M. P. (2020). A psychometric comparison of psychological inflexibility measures: Discriminant validity and item performance. *Journal of Contextual Behavioral Science, 18,* 34–47. https://doi.org/10.1016/j.jcbs.2020.08.007

Ong, C. W., Pierce, B. G., Woods, D. W., Twohig, M. P., & Levin, M. E. (2019). The Acceptance and Action Questionnaire–II: An item response theory analysis. *Journal of Psychopathology and Behavioral Assessment, 41,* 123–134. https://doi.org/10.1007/s10862-018-9694-2

Ong, C. W., Whicker, J. J., Muñoz, K., & Twohig, M. P. (2019). Measuring psychological inflexibility in adult and child hearing loss. *International Journal of Audiology, 58*(10), 643–650. https://doi.org/10.1080/14992027.2019.1630759

Rochefort, C., Baldwin, A. S., & Chmielewski, M. (2018). Experiential avoidance: An examination of the construct validity of the AAQ-II and MEAQ. *Behavior Therapy, 49*(3), 435–449. https://doi.org/10.1016/j.beth.2017.08.008

Rolffs, J. L., Rogge, R. D., & Wilson, K. G. (2016). Disentangling components of flexibility via the hexaflex model: Development and validation of the Multidimensional Psychological Flexibility Inventory (MPFI). *Assessment, 25*(4), 458–482. https://doi.org/10.1177/1073191116645905

Sandoz, E. K., Wilson, K. G., Merwin, R. M., & Kellum, K. K. (2013). Assessment of body image flexibility: The Body Image-Acceptance and Action Questionnaire. *Journal of Contextual Behavioral Science, 2*(1–2), 39–48. https://doi.org/10.1016/j.jcbs.2013.03.002

Stockton, D., Kellett, S., Berrios, R., Sirois, F., Wilkinson, N., & Miles, G. (2019). Identifying the underlying mechanisms of change during acceptance and commitment therapy (ACT): A systematic review of contemporary mediation studies. *Behavioural and Cognitive Psychotherapy, 47*(3), 332–362. https://doi.org/10.1017/S1352465818000553

Thompson, M., Bond, F. W., & Lloyd, J. (2019). Preliminary psychometric properties of the Everyday Psychological Inflexibility Checklist. *Journal of Contextual Behavioral Science, 12,* 243–252. https://doi.org/10.1016/j.jcbs.2018.08.004

Tyndall, I., Waldeck, D., Pancani, L., Whelan, R., Roche, B., & Dawson, D. L. (2019). The Acceptance and Action Questionnaire-II (AAQ-II) as a measure of experiential avoidance: Concerns over discriminant validity. *Journal of Contextual Behavioral Science, 12,* 278–284. https://doi.org/10.1016/j.jcbs.2018.09.005

Villatte, J. L., Vilardaga, R., Villatte, M., Plumb Vilardaga, J. C., Atkins, D. C., & Hayes, S. C. (2016). Acceptance and commitment therapy modules: Differential impact on treatment processes and outcomes. *Behaviour Research and Therapy, 77,* 52–61. https://doi.org/0.1016/j.brat.2015.12.001

Wolgast, M. (2014). What does the Acceptance and Action Questionnaire (AAQ-II) really measure? *Behavior Therapy, 45,* 831–839. https://doi.org/10.1016/j.beth.2014.07.002

Wolitzky-Taylor, K. B., Arch, J. J., Rosenfield, D., & Craske, M. G. (2012). Moderators and non-specific predictors of treatment outcome for anxiety disorders: A comparison of cognitive behavioral therapy to acceptance and commitment therapy. *Journal of Consulting and Clinical Psychology, 80*(5), 786–799. https://doi.org/10.1037/a0029418

CHAPTER

8 Acceptance

Rhonda M. Merwin, Ashley A. Moskovich, Angela Pisoni, Sara Freeman, *and* Carly Onnink

Abstract

Acceptance refers to the active and aware embrace of unwanted private events. It is the cornerstone of acceptance and commitment therapy (ACT) interventions and is evoked whenever experiential avoidance interferes with valued living. This chapter provides a conceptual overview of acceptance, including the conditions that give rise to experiential avoidance and strategies to disrupt these ineffective behaviors and create a context for change. Included is a discussion of the use of functional assessment to identify targets for acceptance, and clinical interventions to evoke and reinforce acceptance or willingness in the presence of unwanted events and with progressively more challenging content. Also reviewed are current strategies to measure acceptance, which have relied heavily on self-report, but also include frequency counts, session coding, and longitudinal high-density measurement, such as in ecological momentary assessment. The article ends with a brief review of the empirical evidence for acceptance as a process of change in lab-based and outcome studies, as well as directions for future research.

Key Words: acceptance, experiential avoidance, process of change, creative hopelessness, shaping, functional assessment, willingness, clinically relevant behavior

Defining Acceptance

Acceptance refers to willingness to experience private events (thoughts, feelings, body sensations, urges, memories, etc.) without unnecessary attempts to change their form or frequency, or stated another way, acceptance is the open and aware embrace of private events occasioned by our history (Hayes et al., 2012). It is employed whenever experiential avoidance (EA) interferes with behaving flexibly, effectively, or consistently with deeply held personal values. While EA often involves attempts to avoid or control private events that are judged as negative or undesirable, it may also involve attempts to maintain pleasant experiences (or avoid experiencing their absence). Acceptance is applied to internal experiences rather than external circumstances, although individuals may benefit from accepting their emotional reactions to a situation in which they find themselves, or their inability to control a situation or another person's behavior.

Acceptance is distinguished from resignation, "giving up" or "giving in," and learned helplessness, which are more passive responses. This distinction is captured in the active language used to evoke acceptance, in which individuals are encouraged to *open up to*, *make space for*, or *welcome* unwanted thoughts/feelings. Acceptance is also distinguished from wanting or liking an experience and from emotional overattachment (i.e., fusing with emotion). Finally, it is distinguished from distress tolerance, which tends to be a less open and less flexible response, focused on the short-term goal of preventing impulsive actions that remove immediate pain but cause long-term harm. While acceptance is not the same as distress tolerance, distress tolerance may occur during the process of shaping acceptance. That is, an individual may first relinquish immediate and severe attempts to remove emotional pain (e.g., self-induced vomiting in an eating disorder case) by engaging in alternative behaviors that block the behavior (e.g., staying with people for 30 minutes after a meal). Later, the individual may allow discomfort with greater willingness and even actively approach situations with the potential for emotional pain if these situations are personally meaningful (e.g., eating out with friends as an act of social engagement). In this case, the aversive function of unwanted private events is changed, as openness to these experiences is coordinated with deeply held personal values. It is important to note, however, that actively approaching situations with the potential for emotional discomfort is not the same as engaging in behaviors that intentionally aim to *intensify* a painful emotional experience, which is often maladaptive and driven by avoidance and control.

In more basic analytic terms, acceptance is defined as "making contact with the automatic or direct stimulus functions of events, without acting to reduce or manipulate those functions, and without acting on the basis of their derived or verbal functions" (Hayes, 1994, pp. 30–31). This highlights the relevance of relational framing in the rejection of private events and the intersection between acceptance and defusion. That is, acceptance involves experiencing events directly, for what they are, rather than in relation to other events. For example, acceptance of the thought "I am worthless" would involve the open and aware embrace of this experience *as a thought*, that is, an internal experience cued in a particular context, stripped of its literal functions.

Acceptance involves secondary rather than primary change (i.e., a change in how an individual relates to their private events, rather than a change in the frequency or intensity of the events themselves). However, it is often associated with decreases in emotional distress, which is detectable by conventional symptom measures (e.g., Symptom Checklist-90 (SCL-90); Derogatis & Unger, 2010). Acceptance ultimately decreases emotional distress in several ways. First, when individuals relinquish attempts to suppress or avoid unwanted internal experiences, this decreases distress by circumventing paradoxical increases in these experiences that occur with intentional suppression (Wegner, 1994). It also decreases associated feelings of helplessness, guilt, or shame that may be experienced with repeated unsuccessful attempts to control private events. Second, with greater acceptance, individuals may experience fewer negative consequences associated with avoidant responses (e.g., lost relationships or relationship opportunities). Finally, as individuals begin to approach rather than avoid uncomfortable feelings, behavioral variability increases and provides opportunities for individuals to have new experiences that are rewarding or enhance life vitality.

Studies of ACT with psychosis provide a clear example of the difference between primary and secondary change. In these studies, participants do not report significant change in the intensity or frequency of hallucinations or delusions (the unwanted private events). However, they do report increased capacity to accept the presence of these experiences and take needed medications, resulting in lower rates of rehospitalization and decreased distress (e.g., Bach et al., 2012). Another example is chronic pain. Studies have found that ACT greatly improves functioning in chronic pain patients but has minimal impact on the frequency or intensity of pain itself (Feliu-Soler et al., 2018).

The Target of Acceptance Interventions: Experiential Avoidance

Acceptance is evoked whenever experiential avoidance (EA) interferes with behaving flexibly or effectively, given the demands of the situation, or consistently with deeply held personal values. EA is defined functionally and refers to a class of behavior aimed at changing the form or frequency of unwanted private events when doing so causes psychological harm (Hayes et al., 1996, 2006). EA is maintained by its more immediate benefits (e.g., alleviation of emotional discomfort) but has other unintended negative consequences in the short or long term, such as removing the individual from situations that are meaningful or could enhance life vitality or joy.

EA is associated with greater negative affect, stress, pain, and poor job performance (Hayes et al., 2006). EA has repeatedly been found to mediate the relationship between risk factors (e.g., trauma) and negative psychological outcomes (PTSD) (e.g., Orcutt et al., 2020). Moreover, ecological momentary assessment studies have found that higher levels of EA in daily life are associated with poorer outcomes (Merwin et al., 2015; Levin et al., 2018). EA is also a key feature of "syndromes" in the traditional diagnostic nomenclature. For example, social phobia is characterized by avoidance of anxiety-provoking social situations; panic disorder by avoidance of arousal or situations that generate arousal; and depression by withdrawal from daily life, which is experienced as intolerable. Considerable research also suggests that impulsive behaviors, such as self-harm, are often motivated by the desire to avoid or escape immediate emotional distress (Brereton & McGlinchey, 2020), and aberrant eating (e.g., restriction, binge eating) functions to manage feelings (e.g., Schaefer et al., 2020). And the list goes on. Even primarily cognitive activities, such as worry, may be understood as avoidance of negative emotions (Borkovec et al., 2004). There is also evidence that *the presence of* particular thoughts and feelings is insufficient to produce "syndromes," which may be determined by maladaptive responses to unwanted private events. For example, individuals in the general population report experiencing thoughts similar to those of individuals with obsessive-compulsive disorder (OCD; García-Soriano et al., 2011). However, OCD may be discriminated by attempts to avoid or escape these experiences (which may, in turn, paradoxically increase their intensity or frequency). Thus, while determining the function of behavior requires idiographic analyses, there are clearly data linking EA to problems in living across individuals and situations.

The fact that EA is defined functionally, rather than being based on the formal properties or topography of behavior, may simplify complex clinical presentations. For example, individuals with anorexia nervosa often also present with social phobia, generalized anxiety, or OCD (Jagielska & Kacperska, 2017). From a functional perspective, these diagnoses may be collectively conceptualized as a class of behaviors that function to reduce distress associated with social rejection or "doing something wrong" (i.e., making a mistake). Thus, while it may be necessary to prioritize one of these issues clinically (e.g., addressing restrictive eating first to restore basic cognitive-emotional faculties), it is not necessary to treat these as separate and distinct problems, sequentially or with different targeted treatment manuals. Instead, diverse behaviors such as restrictive eating, avoiding social situations, worry, or time-consuming rituals may be addressed as a functional class of experientially avoidant behavior.

A focus on function, rather than form, means that any action may function as EA, including behaviors that appear adaptive or desirable in form (e.g., compromising). However, the reverse is also true: actions that have the topography of avoidance and escape may not be EA. For example, while in one situation, removing oneself from a conflictual interpersonal exchange may be avoidance of discomfort associated with conflict; in another, removing oneself might be the more emotionally difficult, yet effective and value-guided response.

Determining whether actions are functionally EA requires that they are situated in the historical and situational context in which they occur, or by asking: *How is this behavior functioning for this individual at this time and in this situation?* EA is also indicated by the qualities of the action. EA behaviors, or behaviors that are maintained by immediate relief from emotional discomfort, rather than their ultimate effectiveness or consistency with personal values, are rigid or situationally insensitive; often signaled by use of absolutes (e.g., words such as "should," "must" or "have to").

Not all EA is problematic or interferes with life values. This may be particularly true if stressors are brief and infrequent. For example, many individuals seek distraction from the discomfort associated with a dental procedure or close their eyes during a gruesome movie scene. Such behaviors do not interfere with one's life functioning or valued living (e.g., experiencing a dental procedure or seeing a gruesome movie image is not typically meaningful or important) and thus would not be the target for intervention.

Theoretical Underpinnings of Experiential Avoidance (EA): The Human Condition

Avoidance and control are key to human survival. Problems arise in the overapplication of this response, or when this response is not under appropriate contextual control, that is, use of avoidance and control in situations where it is ultimately ineffective or even detrimental. This includes, for example, trying to avoid or control internal experiences (such as thoughts, feelings, and body sensations) that are simply the result of being a conscious human being, that is, an organism that reacts to its environment and has a history.

The conditions that give rise to and maintain EA are multileveled. Individuals' unique experiences of reinforcement have a central role (e.g., experience of relief following an avoidant response), as well as reinforcement from the individual's progressively larger communities or ecosystems. For example, different groups, subgroups, and cultures may have different emotional display rules (e.g., whether or not crying is viewed as "acceptable"). However, EA is also a natural outgrowth of the human capacity for language in which internal events (e.g., thoughts, images) "stand in" for actual events, and we derive relations among events in ways that increase suffering or generate emotional pain. More specifically, according to relational frame theory (Barnes-Holmes, Y., Hayes, S. C., Barnes-Holmes, D., & Roche, B., 2001), the basic behavioral process underlying language is arbitrarily applicable derived relational responding, or the ability to arbitrarily derive relationships among events and have the psychological functions of those events transformed in accordance with those relations. This has significant implications for behavior. Just considering tacting, in which there is a derived equivalence relation between a word (name or label) and the event it represents (e.g., the word "lemon" is equivalent to the oblong yellow fruit). In the appropriate context, there is no distinction between the words and the events to which they correspond. Rather, we experience them psychologically as the same thing (e.g., just thinking about a lemon can make our mouth pucker even though a lemon is not physically present). Thus, we can experience pain when we are thinking about painful events (e.g., remembering a loss or trauma), and pain that is not directly available in the current environment may be made present through language and relating. We derive not only equivalence relations, but also more/less (comparative/evaluative) and if/then (consequent) relations. As a result of our capacity to respond to one event in terms of another, even a very positive experience may become painful. For example, the individual may judge the experience as not as good as the last time, fear a time when this experience is gone, feel less deserving of the experience than other people, and the list goes on. In this way, humans can experience pain even when the external conditions would seem to support happiness and contentment. Under these circumstances, controlling thoughts and feelings themselves may be highly, if only temporarily, reinforced by the mitigation of immediate pain.

The Paradox of Intentional Control

Studies indicate that purposeful suppression of meaningful thoughts in high-valence contexts results in paradoxical increases in unwanted experiences (Wegner, 1994). Learning also works by addition, not subtraction. Studies show spontaneous recovery of conditioned responses (Quirk, 2002) and resurgence of derived relations after extinction (Doughty et al., 2011). Thus, while avoidance/suppression may alleviate immediate discomfort, the effect is usually temporary. Nothing is really eliminated, and thoughts and feelings that we have not experienced for a long time may reemerge given the relevant contextual cues. This experience may only exacerbate the problem, as the inability to permanently eliminate unwanted content is perceived as a personal failure and compels more desperate attempts to do something we "should" be able to do (but according to basic cognitive and behavioral science is ultimately impossible).

Acceptance work often starts with elucidating this unworkability and contacting the costs of experiential control (i.e., how EA has diminished the quality of life or interfered with other things that matter to the individual). This work continues with interventions that shape a greater capacity to allow a broad range of internal experience when doing so is aligned with deeply held, personal values.

Clinical Application—Methods

Acceptance consists of three components of work, which may be employed sequentially, but not necessarily so, and are often revisited:

- Identifying functional relationships (i.e., internal experiences that are unwanted and associated with avoidance/control)
- Disrupting the context of avoidance and control (i.e., interventions that allow the individual to contact a fuller range of their experience, including the ways in which avoidance or control is not working)
- Shaping an alternative response (i.e., acceptance or willingness in the service of deeply held, personal values)

Identifying Functional Relationships (Targets for Acceptance)

Clinical Interview

Through careful interviewing of the client's situation, the therapist identifies internal experiences that are unwanted and the breadth and depth of the avoidant repertoire, that is, the behaviors that the individual has engaged in so as to avoid or control internal experience. Interviewing may be facilitated by creating a historical timeline of the events that precipitated the problem behavior or that correspond with periods of remittance or exacerbation. This facilitates a more detailed exploration of setting events, or events that occasion the behavior, and how experience changed as a result.

> *T:* [probes antecedents] *It sounds like this started after you moved to a new school. What was that like for you? I wonder if you can tell me more about the thoughts and feelings that you were experiencing?*
> *T:* [probes behavioral response] *And then what did you do?*
> *T:* [probes consequences] *What was your experience after that?*
> *T:* [probes functionally equivalent behaviors] *What else has helped you feel that way?*

Diagnosis. Diagnosis is antithetical to ACT's nonpathogenic frame; however, it may be useful in identifying avoidance patterns (avoided events and avoidant repertoires). Diagnosis can help identify the internal experiences that are difficult for the individual, and the things that they have done to manage these experiences. For example, individuals who meet the criteria for panic disorder are often attempting to escape or avoid somatic correlates or constituents of fear (e.g., rapid heartbeat, sweating, sense of "doom"); individuals with generalized anxiety disorder may avoid uncertainty; and individuals with a depression diagnosis are likely to struggle with negative thoughts/feelings about the self, others, and the world (e.g., feelings of failure, low self-worth, hopelessness, and dread). Similarly, for individuals with alcohol abuse, drinking alcohol is likely the primary avoidance strategy, while for individuals with anorexia nervosa, the strategy is restricting food intake and so forth. Traditional diagnostic self-report measures, such as the SCL-90 (Derogatis & Unger, 2010) or Brief Symptom Inventory (BSI; Derogatis & Savitz, 1999), might be similarly useful in generating hypotheses regarding avoided events and avoidant repertoires.

Self-Monitoring and Chain Analyses

Self-monitoring diaries or worksheets and chain analyses conducted in session can also help identify functional relationships between internal experiences and behavior and enhance client self-awareness of avoidant patterns. These tools are particularly useful when clients present with greater awareness of one aspect of experience relative to another. For example, individuals might easily identify the internal experiences that are difficult for them (e.g., they may be aware that they feel anxious and do not want to feel this way), but they might not be able to identify behaviors that they engage in to avoid or control this experience, particularly if these behaviors are subtle or are justified in some other way (e.g., the client may manage anxiety by "preferring" to stay home or declining opportunities at work). Alternatively, individuals may easily report avoidant behaviors (e.g., alcohol abuse), but have limited awareness of the internal antecedents to the behaviors or the consequences that maintain them (e.g., decreased anxiety).

Self-monitoring diaries and chain analyses typically begin with the known element of the three-term contingency (**A**ntecedent, **B**ehavior, or **C**onsequence). Detailed analysis of the sequence of events identifies other elements (e.g., "What were you feeling right before you decided to drink last night? How did you feel after you drank?"). For many clients, this exercise is a practice in acceptance or willingness, as it requires contact with internal experiences preceding problem behaviors and awareness of the problem behaviors themselves, which may increase guilt or shame.

In-Session Behavior

Observation of in-session behavior can also help identify avoided events and avoidant repertoires. This includes, for example, observing when the individual who struggles with alcohol fantasizes about a drink or when the individual with anxiety worries or experiences a panic attack. It might also include other behaviors that are part of the functional class, as determined by idiographic analyses. These behaviors include, for example, an individual abruptly changing the topic, assuming a closed body posture or smiling inappropriately (while describing something painful). With permission, therapists can help clients notice these behaviors in session when they occur (e.g., "It seems like something happened there . . . you were talking freely about your emotions . . . and now you have shifted to problem-solving . . . do you notice that?) and explore emotional antecedents (e.g., "What were you thinking or feeling right before that happened?"). This line of inquiry can be approached as hypothesis testing (i.e., generating hypotheses about the factors that may be influencing the client's behavior). This activity also serves other purposes in treatment. Most important, it increases client self-awareness and provides an opportunity to shape acceptance in the moment.

Disrupting the Context of Avoidance and Control ("Creative Hopelessness")

Experiential avoidance has limited benefits. At its worst, it can have devastating consequences, as active attempts to avoid or control unwanted internal experiences lead to actions that are inconsistent with personal values or cause significant harm. Individuals can find themselves working to feel better, while putting other aspects of life on hold or moving away from things that are important to them in an effort to minimize painful thoughts and feelings. Creative hopelessness interventions disrupt the context of experiential control, setting the stage for acceptance. These interventions put individuals in contact with a fuller range of experience, such that they are not only experiencing the immediate, short-term benefits of EA, but are also contacting the ways in which control does not work and what it costs them with regard to personal values. This segment of work is referred to as *creative hopelessness* because it culminates to a perspective of *hopelessness* "that control can work" and prepares clients for a *creative* solution to pain (i.e., acceptance or willingness).

The therapist assumes a stance of compassionate curiosity as they help the client make experiential contact with the consequences of avoidance. For example, clients may experience that the relief provided by EA behaviors is short-lived and that emotional pain has increased rather than decreased over time. Clients may begin to notice that trying to avoid or control internal experience is exhausting or that avoidant behaviors detract from other things that matter to them or are even diametrically opposed to their personal values. For example, an individual struggling with social anxiety may initially feel better when they decline a social invitation; however, they may also observe that they later experience guilt or shame for avoiding the event and notice that avoidance directly interferes with values of friendship or intimacy. They might also notice that they are spending inordinate amounts of time planning how to avoid or escape social events, diminishing their quality of life, and that they are more, not less, anxious about the next social opportunity. Thus, while their behavior "works" in the short term or for limited goals (such as immediate relief from anxiety), it is simultaneously "unworkable" for a life well lived. Acceptance (or willingness) is then offered as an alternative to avoidance and control.

Creative hopelessness interventions can be delivered in varying degrees of depth and intensity, and for some clients already poised for change, they may not be necessary at all. Others clients may need to revisit creative hopelessness interventions throughout treatment, as avoidance or control reemerges in the face of new or more intense emotional pain.

Creative hopelessness interventions are varied and include metaphors and experiential exercises, as well as simple prompts that facilitate noticing consequences. Metaphors and experiential exercises help clients experience the automaticity of internal events (e.g., "Mary had a little _____"; Luoma et al., 2007) and how they defy intentional control (e.g., Chocolate cake exercise; Hayes, Strosahl, et al., 1999, Polygraph; Hayes et al., 2012), or how avoidance is effortful and diverts attention away from things that are personally important or meaningful (e.g., Joe the bum; Hayes, Strosahl, et al., 1999). Simple prompts invite clients to notice what else is happening when they engage in avoidant behavior (e.g., "When you were drinking, what were your kids doing?") or over time (e.g., "It sounds like when you drink excessively, you aren't able to be present and engaged with your family in the way that you would like to be . . . and that over time, you have also noticed that they have started to trust you less. Am I getting that right?").

Experiential exercises and metaphors are also used to introduce the concept of acceptance. These interventions highlight that while our natural instinct is to resist discomfort, it often causes more suffering (e.g., Chinese handcuffs; Hayes, Strosahl, et al., 1999, Quicksand;

Table 8.1. Interventions Referenced in Creative Hopelessness Section

	Function
Mary had a little ______ (Luoma et al., 2007)	Experience the automaticity of thoughts or thought content.
Chocolate cake exercise (Hayes, Strosahl, et al., 1999)	Experience that private events (e.g., thoughts) defy intentional control. Experience that intentional control may paradoxically increase the intensity or frequency of unwanted private events (e.g., thoughts).
Polygraph (Hayes et al., 2012)	Illustrate that private events (e.g., feelings) defy intentional control. Illustrates that intentional control may paradoxically increase the intensity or frequency of unwanted private events (e.g., feelings).
Chinese handcuffs (Hayes, Strosahl, et al., 1999)	Experience that while our instinct is to resist, resistance is ineffective or even counterproductive (tightens the grip). Experience a counterintuitive solution (pushing in).
Quicksand (Hayes, 2005)	Illustrate that while the instinct is to struggle, struggling is ineffective or even counterproductive (sinks you deeper) Experience a counterintuitive solution (spreading out; full contact).
Joe the bum (Hayes, Strosahl, et al., 1999)	Illustrate that one cannot be fully present and engaged in life if they must resist/avoid or control some experience. Suggests the possibility of allowing thoughts and feelings to be present as "guests in your home" while you live your life.
Act in a nutshell (clipboard exercise) (Harris, 2019)	Discriminate avoidance/control from acceptance/willingness. Experience that resistance is effortful. Experience the alternative response (allowing).
Tug-of-war with a monster (Hayes et al., 2012)	Discriminate avoidance/control from acceptance/willingness. Experience that resistance is effortful. Illustrate the alternative response (letting go).

Hayes, 2005). The solution, while counterintuitive, is to end the struggle with internal experience and instead invest energy in things that matter to us. Experiential exercises are also used to help clients discriminate avoidance and control from the action or choice of acceptance or willingness (e.g., ACT in a nutshell [clipboard exercise]; Harris, 2019, tug-of-war with a monster; Hayes et al., 2012). Table 8.1 outlines examples of creative hopelessness interventions and their therapeutic function.

Shaping Acceptance (or Willingness)

Acceptance interventions create a context of openness in which any and all thoughts and feelings are permitted. Practically, the therapist evokes a new response in the presence of an unwanted internal experience, reinforces successive approximations to a more open and receiving posture, and repeats this process. Over time, the clinical focus moves to generalizing acceptance to a variety of experiences or situations in the individual's life. The individual learns to discriminate when avoidance is and is not working, and when their personal values would be better served by acceptance or willingness. The ultimate aim is not to eliminate avoidance, but rather to bring it under contextual control, such that the client has a broad and flexible repertoire of behavior in the presence of unwanted thoughts/feelings.

Importantly, acceptance work requires the client's permission or informed consent. Similar to exposure treatment, approaching difficult or feared events should be freely chosen and never coerced. Client willingness to practice acceptance is facilitated by values or by both the client and the therapist being clear about how acceptance serves the client and their life. Acceptance interventions can be titrated to not exceed the client's capacity or willingness.

Behaviors that increasingly approximate acceptance can be reinforced either verbally or nonverbally. Reinforcement may include direct or indirect praise or increased warmth or engagement (e.g., leaning forward in one's chair). It might also include amplifying the positive consequences of the client practicing acceptance in their daily life to increase tracking (e.g., "It sounds like being willing to have anxiety allowed you to attend your best friend's graduation. What was that like for you?").

Acceptance interventions can vary widely (defined by their function, not their form) and may include any strategy that involves actively allowing internal experience as it is, or "without constriction, and without distorting, without judgment, without evaluating, without trying to keep it, and without trying to get rid of it" (Linehan, 1994, p. 80). This includes simply slowing down to notice or describe an internal experience (e.g., the presence of an uncomfortable thought/feeling) or label an emotion. It also includes experiential exercises such as making physical space for an internal experience (e.g., softening rather than tensing the body in the areas where the emotion is felt most strongly; allowing expression of an emotion on the face) or assuming a receiving posture (e.g., unclenching the fists, flipping the palms over as if to receive a gift), making an invitation ("Welcome feeling, it is OK for you to be here"), and metaphors that cue an existing behavioral repertoire of acceptance. Metaphors work by capitalizing on derived relational responding and the transfer of stimulus functions by situating an unwanted internal experience in a frame of coordination with people, places, or things that the individual has experience inviting (e.g., guests in home) or holding gently with kindness, compassion (e.g., baby), or appreciation (e.g., sunset, flowers blooming). Metaphors that match the clinical situation or the client's interests or experiences may have the potential for the greatest impact. Acceptance can also include any number of other unspecified interventions that facilitate the client interacting with an unwanted stimulus in new ways (anything other than avoidance or control). This may include interventions often used for defusion, such as singing an unwanted thought or describing a thought or feeling as an object.

Finally, because the therapist is similarly vulnerable to traps of avoidance and control, modeling openness is a powerful intervention tool. The therapist can model acceptance or willingness in interactions with the client with process-level comments about the experience in therapy ("I notice at this moment, I feel the urge to join you in trying to make that feeling go away . . . and I also know that you can have that feeling, that it is OK for that to be here . . . and that feeling and the ability to have it, might even be useful to you and allow you move in the direction of what is most important to you . . . ."), or less explicit communications about the acceptability of particular thoughts/feelings or emotional expressions (e.g., not describing emotions in evaluative terms or not responding to the absence of difficult feelings as "progress").

Table 8.2 provides some examples of acceptance interventions with clinical dialogue.

Skills Practice and Generalization

Skill generalization (generalizing skills from the therapy room to the natural environment) is a challenge in any therapy. Acceptance skill acquisition and generalization may be facilitated by homework. For example, clients may practice discriminating primary pain from the secondary suffering that one experiences when they judge, evaluate, or struggle with their thoughts/

Table 8.2. Interventions Referenced in Shaping Acceptance Section

Examples of Interventions to Shape Progressively Greater Acceptance—Willingness	
Interventions that Acknowledge or Allow Awareness of an Experience	
Slow and notice	**The therapist invites the client to slow down and notice the thoughts and feelings that might be present.** **Clinical context:** The client is narrating or story-telling in a disconnected manner. **Therapist:** "If it's OK with you, I'd like to invite you to slow down and notice your own experience . . . what is showing up for you right now . . . [thoughts, feelings, body sensations, urges, memories]"
Label	**The therapist invites the client to label their emotion.** **Clinical context:** The client is experiencing an emotion; however, they have not named the emotion. **Therapist:** "I wonder what you are feeling right now? If you could name it?"
Describe	**The therapist invites the client to describe their internal experience.** **Clinical context:** The client has named an emotion. **Therapist:** "I wonder if you can describe this feeling . . . where you feel that in your body . . . your chest, stomach . . . and the qualities o . . . it . . . [is heavy or light, a pit or . . .]
Interventions that Explicitly Evoke an Open Response	
Make an invitation	**The therapist encourages the client to invite a feeling to be present.** **Clinical context:** The client is experiencing sadness but is resisting the experience in their verbal and nonverbal behavior. **Therapist:** "What would it be like to open up to sadness . . . invite it in? Could you, in this moment extend an invitation to sadness, like a gentle "welcome, it is OK for you to be here . . . , " Maybe put a hand to your chest where you feel it, let it know that it doesn't have to go anywhere . . . you can hold it, receive it"
Make physical space	**The therapist encourages the client to make physical space for a feeling.** **Clinical context:** The client is experience anxiety in session, which in other situations, has prevented them from engaging in activities that they value. **Therapist:** "If you are willing . . . I would invite you to make space for anxiety, and that feeling in your stomach . . . maybe take a few slow, deep breaths . . . . See if you can send your breath to your belly, breathe air around that feeling, make some space for it . . . "
A receiving posture	**The therapist encourages the client to assume a receiving posture when a feeling is present.** **Clinical context:** The client is resisting feelings that are present but could inform decision making. **Therapist:** "It seems this is what is here now [feeling X]. I wonder if you would be willing to try something? To see what it is like to simply receive it? Like a gift? The gift of the present moment. Maybe there is something in there . . . of value to you? Like . . . that it might tell you something about what you care about, or what is important to you? If you are willing, rather than clinching fists, can you flip your palms over, allow your hands to be open and receiving?

(*continued*)

Table 8.2. *Continued*

Examples of Interventions to Shape Progressively Greater Acceptance—Willingness	
Allow expression	**The therapist invites the client to allow a fuller expression of an emotion they are experiencing.** **Clinical context:** Client's facial affect is incongruent to content. They are reporting a sad event but smiling. **Therapist:** "I can hear how painful that is for you. I also notice that it almost looks like you're smiling while you're talking about how sad you feel—can you feel that? I'd invite you to see if you can allow your face to soften and let your smile melt away . . . see if you can let your facial expression match what you're feeling inside."
Interventions that Use Metaphor to Cue Acceptance/Openness	
Guests	**Feelings (or other unwanted internal experiences) are put in a frame of coordination with guests in one's home to cue a welcoming response. This intervention also includes hierarchical relating (a self that is "bigger than" any particular thoughts/feeling).** **Clinical context:** The client has just expressed a painful or difficult feeling. **Therapist:** "I wonder what it would be like to have this feeling like a guest in your home that has come to visit. Just what is here now. Some guests are difficult . . . they smell bad or put their feet up on the table or stay too long . . . but you know how to welcome a guest in your home."
Baby	**Feelings (or other unwanted internal experiences) are put in a frame of coordination with a baby to cue a gentle, kind, compassionate response.** **Clinical context:** The client has just expressed a painful or difficult feeling. **Therapist:** "I wonder if you can hold that feeling as you would a baby . . . cradle it . . . in kindness or with love."
Sunset	**Feelings (or other unwanted internal experiences) are put in a frame of coordination with a sunset to cue appreciation.** **Clinical context:** The client has just expressed a complex and difficult emotion. **Therapist:** "It is like a sunset, there are places of deep blue, pink and orange . . . like can you look with me . . . . Without it needing to be different in some way. What if your feeling was a sunset . . . to notice and appreciate . . . instead of a problem to be solved?
Other Unspecified Interventions	
Interventions that facilitate interacting with unwanted thoughts/feelings in a new way	**The therapist invites the client to interact and stay with an unwanted thought/feeling.** **Clinical context:** The client has named that they are experiencing grief and has withdrawn. **Therapist:** "I hear you that you're noticing grief or loss right now . . . I wonder if we could just stay with this feeling for a little longer? Rather than shut down, I wonder if you could speak . . . give it voice . . . . "

Table 8.2. *Continued*	
Examples of Interventions to Shape Progressively Greater Acceptance—Willingness	
Interventions that Use Modeling	
Modeling openness	**The therapist models an open and receiving posture with respect to their own thoughts/feelings.** **Clinical context:** The therapeutic encounter continues to dead end without progress. **Therapist:** "I notice that I'm actually feeling stuck right now . . . and my mind is screaming "Do something!" . . . and this is what I have done before . . . I have gotten busy. Too busy!—as if it wasn't OK to have this experience. And I don't know that it has served us, or you and your values. I am going to commit to you to stop doing that, and instead make space for this feeling . . . .

feelings. Clients might also monitor the consequences of EA (or the alternative, acceptance/willingness), or practice specific exercises from the session with unwanted thoughts and feelings in daily life. They may also practice committed actions that, while meaningful, elicit unwanted thoughts/feelings. Mobile devices offer tools to easily practice and track acceptance in the home environment.

Acceptance and Other Psychological Flexibility Processes

ACT processes do not operate in isolation, and acceptance is facilitated by defusion, a transcendent sense of self and personal values. When individuals are able to experience thoughts as mental activity (rather than the literal events that they represent), they are more willing to have these experiences. Further, they are able to experience themselves as "more than" or "bigger than" any experience they might have, this decreases investment in the presence or absence of particular thoughts or feelings. Finally, when personal values are made salient, individuals may be more willing to experience discomfort because it is in service of other things that matter to them (i.e., it allows them to live with greater vitality or in line with their personal values). If the client is not progressing in acceptance work, it may suggest the need for greater engagement of these or other core processes.

Acceptance and Exposure and Response Prevention

Acceptance interventions may even formally look like exposure and response prevention (ExRP), which involves the individual coming into contact with aversive stimuli while intentionally inhibiting avoidance or escape responses. However, unlike traditional exposure, the goal of acceptance interventions is not decreased elicitation or arousal per se but rather a broad and flexible repertoire in the presence of an unwanted internal experiences. A deemphasis on the importance of habituation in exposure is consistent with emerging research on fear tolerance and inhibitory learning as the mechanism of change (Craske et al., 2014). Acceptance interventions may decouple the typical relationship between aversive internal experiences and overt actions, creating conditions for a broader array of behavioral responses, better matched to the demands of the situation and personal values (Levin et al., 2015). Unlike more traditional exposure paradigms, clients may be explicitly encouraged to interact with unwanted stimuli in as many diverse ways as possible, and flexibility may be tracked as the outcome of interest (rather than decreased distress).

Measuring Acceptance

Acceptance can be measured in a variety of ways, but multimodal assessment is preferred. Changes in acceptance can be tracked in session or across sessions. Strategies include monitoring clinically relevant behavior (e.g., frequency counts, coding systems), ecologically valid high-density longitudinal assessment, and more traditional self-report measures. Assessment may also include passive measurement of behavior using sensors and mobile devices.

Frequency Counts

The most straightforward and concrete indicator of increased acceptance may be a decrease in the client's avoidant behavior, although this may also be conceptualized as the clinical outcome. When avoidant behaviors are discrete, they may be operationalized and counted. For example, among individuals with eating and weight concerns, "body checking" may be identified as a target avoidant behavior and defined as pinching fat on the body, feeling the collarbone or hipbones, or measuring the wrist or thighs. It might also include topographically dissimilar behavior that serves a similar function, such as over-apologizing or reassurance seeking. Frequency of target behaviors may be tracked in session or between sessions using paper-and-pencil or electronic devices (e.g., smartphones). Between-session tracking may be particularly useful for behaviors that would not occur in session due to lack of opportunity. Examples in the area of eating disorders include restricting a meal (not eating at a designated meal time), self-inducing vomiting, or binge eating. It may also be possible to track alternative, approach behavior. Examples might include eating an adequate lunch or sharing feelings or opinions with an identified person or group. Frequencies can be graphed to reveal change over time (see Figure 8.1.)

Ratings—Coding Systems

Acceptance may also be indexed by session ratings or coding systems. There are many examples of ratings of coding systems for monitoring therapist fidelity to an intervention (e.g., O'Neill et al., 2019). However, similar strategies might also be used to rate client behavior and processes of change. Acceptance may be tracked with multiple dimensional items with anchors (see Table 8.3). Ratings are made by observing client verbal and nonverbal behaviors

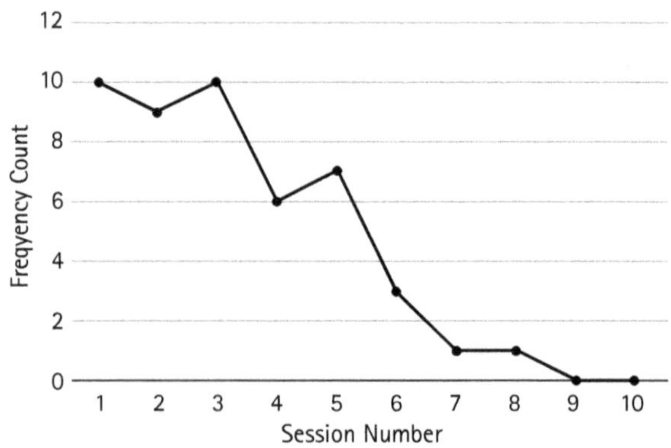

Figure 8.1. Frequency counts of target (avoidant) behavior by session.

Table 8.3. Example of session rating scale

Frequently judges or rejects their emotions	-3 -2 -1 0 1 2 3	Is receptive to their emotions; validates their feelings, treats them with respect
Actively suppresses feelings	-3 -2 -1 0 1 2 3	Allows feelings to be present and expresses them effectively
Avoids discussion that may generate strong feelings	-3 -2 -1 0 1 2 3	Approaches discussions that have emotional valance

in session. Consistency in ratings may be enhanced with client examples from idiographic analyses for scale anchors.

Acceptance can also be tracked in session with a simple Likert scale (e.g., 0 = low acceptance, 10 = high acceptance). Low acceptance may be indicated by denying emotion, clenching the jaw or holding back tears, or the opposite response: an inability to modulate or contain emotion. Low acceptance might also be indicated by a wide array of other behaviors that are rigid or situationally insensitive (as determined by the functional assessment), such as an inability to stay on a topic or excessively changing topics; a poverty of content or excessive content and detail; limited variability and intonation in speech or excessive intonation; constricted body posture (e.g., stiff, upright posture with arms and legs crossed, fixed averted gaze) or excessive movement (e.g., flailing, fidgeting); shutting down (no longer responding to prompts), among numerous other examples. High acceptance may be indicated by the ability to stay with emotional content and flexibly shift focus in accordance with the demands of the situation. It might also be indicated by interacting with unwanted thoughts and feelings in a variety of ways, access to a full range of emotions expressed without judgment, an open body posture, and good eye contact, among numerous other examples. Although it is possible to identify nomothetic indicators of acceptance, an idiographic approach is preferred (tracking the individual's unique expressions).

Behavioral Approach Tasks (BATs)

Behavioral approach tasks (BATs) may also be used to assess acceptance or willingness to come into contact with a specific target that elicits unwanted thoughts and feelings (Castagna et al., 2017). BATS are frequently used in exposure paradigms. In traditional paradigms, subjective units of distress (SUDS) are tracked as a marker of change. In an ACT frame, decreased distress might be a correlate but is less central, and the primary marker is increased ability to behave flexibly in the presence of an emotionally evocative stimulus.

Ecological Momentary Assessment

High-density longitudinal data collected in the natural environment is increasingly possible with mobile devices and other technology (e.g., sensors) and may capture processes of change, such as increased acceptance. Ecological momentary assessment (EMA) samples an individual's behavior and/or self-reported internal experience in near real time using random interval prompts or event-based recording (person-initiated report) and may have greater ecological validity than lab-based measures. EMA data collection might include repeated administration of an acceptance measure (such as the Acceptance and Action Questionnaire—II (AAQ-II; Bond et al., 2011) or single items. For example, individuals may be asked "Since the last prompt, how much did you try to distract or try to make negative thoughts and feelings go away?" (Levin et al., 2018, p. 160). Individuals may also be asked content-specific EA/

acceptance items in an EMA format, such as asking individuals with diabetes to rate their current "urge to avoid thinking about diabetes" (Merwin et al., 2015) or asking individuals with anxiety to rate the degree to which they tried to hide their anxiety, gave up things that mattered to them in order to control anxious thoughts and feelings, etc. (Kashdan et al., 2014).

Passive data collection might also be used to assess acceptance. It might include, for example, a daily step count for an individual avoiding exercise, or time spent on one's mobile phone for an individual who distracts with games or scrolling online.

Self-Report Measures

Self-report measures administered relatively infrequently is the most common strategy for assessment. Several self-report measures capture acceptance (or its inverse, EA), or the broader construct of psychological flexibility. There are also other multidimensional scales of emotion regulation, mindfulness, or other related constructs that include acceptance subscales. Table 8.4 summarizes self-report measures that capture acceptance and their primary advantages.

The Acceptance and Action Questionnaire (AAQ; Hayes et al., 2004; Bond et al., 2011) is the most commonly used measure in ACT. Originally described as a measure of EA (Hayes et al., 2004), the AAQ-II has since been conceptualized more broadly as a measure of psychological flexibility (Bond et al., 2011). However, the authors caution that this shift may be due to the emphasis placed on psychological flexibility during the maturation of the ACT model, rather than a reflection of the changes made to the original AAQ.

The first AAQ (Hayes et al., 2004) received criticisms of poor internal consistency and construct validity (Bond et al., 2011). Consequently, the AAQ-II revised the scale length and item wording and is reported to have acceptable to excellent internal consistency (Cronbach's alpha ranging from 0.78 to 0.93) and improved construct validity (McAndrews et al., 2019).

The AAQ-II has been adapted for the concerns of specific populations, including body image, obsessions and compulsions, and chronic illness. There are currently 28 or more content variants. Content variants of the AAQ appear to have greater sensitivity to change in clinical outcome studies, likely due to their face validity. Although content variants generally outperform the general AAQ (Ong et al., 2019), more research is needed to validate their psychometric properties.

State of the Evidence

Evidence from Lab-based Studies

Lab-based studies have been used to examine the effects of acceptance instructions on task persistence and distress during activities that involve manipulation of aversive states (such as anxiety, pain, negative affect, and intrusive thoughts). Pain (induced via the cold pressor task, loud noises, electrical stimulation, and other methods) and food and tobacco cravings are among the clinical areas that have been most well studied, likely due to the ease of measurement. Other studies have used methods such as carbon-dioxide-enriched air and public speaking tasks to elicit panic and anxiety, the Paced Auditory Serial Addition Task (PASAT) and mirror tracing to elicit frustration, targeted writing prompts to induce intrusive thoughts or body dissatisfaction, or emotional films and music to elicit sadness.

In this body of research, multiple ACT processes are engaged, rather than acceptance in isolation, which can be experimentally difficult and potentially not "real world." Results or experimental comparisons between these "acceptance strategies" and other more change-focused emotion regulation strategies like reappraisal and distraction have varied findings regarding their short-term effects. Many studies have focused on self-report frequency and intensity of internal experience (e.g., craving reduction) as the primary outcome, while

Table 8.4. Self-report measures assessing acceptance, or the inverse, nonacceptance/experiential avoidance

Questionnaire	Structure	Construct or Relevant Subscale	Number of Items in Scale (or Relevant Subscale)	Advantages—Disadvantages
Acceptance and Action Questionnaire II (AAQ-II) (Bond et al., 2011)	Single scale	Psychological flexibility	7	Widely used in ACT studies. Improved over the original AAQ (Bond et al., 2011). Content variants exist and are sensitive to change with intervention. Corresponds with clinical outcomes. Good test–retest reliability (Bond et al., 2011); Good to excellent internal consistency (Palladino et al., 2013; Scott et al., 2016). May correlate too highly with negative affect (Francis et al., 2016). May capture some aspects of psychological flexibility better than others.
Multidimensional Experiential Avoidance Questionnaire (MEAQ) (Gámez et al., 2011)	6 Subscales	Experiential avoidance	62	Multidimensional, capturing various forms of EA. Excellent convergent and discriminant validity, good internal consistency (Gamez et al., 2011). Research needed on test–retest reliability and sensitivity to change.
Brief Experiential Avoidance Questionnaire (BEAQ) (Gámez et al., 2014)	Single scale	Experiential avoidance	15	Brief measure relative to the MEAQ. High face validity—items are easy to read and understand. Strong construct validity, good internal consistency (Gámez et al., 2014). Research needed on test–retest reliability.
CompACT (Francis et al., 2016)	3 Subscales	Openness to experience and detachment from literality subscale	10	Designed to address the limitations of the AAQ-II. Differentiates ACT components of open, centered, engaged. High face validity—items are easy to read and understand and appear to differentiate the presence of thoughts/feelings from the response to them (Francis et al., 2016).

(continued)

Table 8.4. *Continued*

Questionnaire	Structure	Construct or Relevant Subscale	Number of Items in Scale (or Relevant Subscale)	Advantages—Disadvantages
Avoidance and Fusion for Youth Questionnaire (AFQ-Y) (Greco et al., 2008)	Single Scale	Experiential avoidance and cognitive fusion	17	Assesses psychological inflexibility specifically in children and adolescents. Excellent internal reliability (Greco et al., 2008)
Before Session Questionnaire (BSQ) (Forman et al., 2012)	Single scale	Acceptance vs change strategies	5	Designed for weekly administration to compare mechanisms of change in ACT and cognitive therapy (Forman et al., 2012). Research needed on psychometric properties.
PsyFlex (Firsching et al., 2018)	Single scale	Psychological flexibility	10	Captures all elements of psychological flexibility and as a state rather than a trait. More research is needed on psychometric properties.
Five Facet Mindfulness Questionnaire (FFMQ) (Baer et al., 2006)	5 Subscales	Mindfulness—Nonjudging subscale	8	Allows five components of mindfulness to be examined independently (observe, describe, act with awareness, nonjudge, nonreact). Acceptable reliability and validity for each subscale (Christopher et al., 2012)
15-Item Five Facet Mindfulness Questionnaire (FFMQ-15) (Baer et al., 2012)	5 Subscales	Mindfulness - Nonjudging subscale	3	Brief measure relative to the FFMQ. Good sensitivity to change, acceptable internal consistency for nonjudging subscale (Gu et al., 2016).
Philadelphia Mindfulness Scale (PHLMS) (Cardaciotto et al., 2008)	2 Subscales	Mindfulness—Nonjudgmental acceptance subscale	10	Conceptualizes mindfulness as two skills: present moment awareness and acceptance. Good internal consistency (Cardaciotto et al., 2008) Future research needed on test–retest reliability.
Kentucky Inventory of Mindfulness Skills (KIMS) (Baer et al., 2004)	4 Subscales	Mindfulness-Acceptance with nonjudgment subscale	9	Designed to assess four facets of mindfulness (observing, describing, acting with awareness, and accepting with nonjudgment). Good internal consistency, adequate to good test–retest reliability (Baer et al., 2004)

Difficulties in Emotion Regulation Scale (DERS) (Gratz & Roemer, 2004)	6 Subscales	Difficulties in Emotion Regulation—Nonacceptance Subscale	6	Assess component skills of emotion regulation individually, including the ability to be aware and accepting of one's emotional experience, which can be parsed from abilities or deficits in emotional clarity, etc. Significant body of literature on its use. Strong internal consistency, with the exception of the awareness subscale (Hallion et al., 2018). Good test–retest reliability; high internal consistency (Gratz & Roemer 2004).
State Difficulties in Emotion Regulation Scale (S-DERS) (Lavender et al., 2017)	4 Subscales	Difficulties in Emotion Regulation—Nonacceptance subscale	7	Brief version of the DERS modified to capture state of emotional dysregulation rather than trait. Good reliability; moderate correlation between S-DERS and original DERS (Lavender et al., 2017). Future research needed to test measure in clinical populations.
Affective Style Questionnaire (ASQ) (Hofmann & Kashdan, 2010)	3 Subscales	Emotion Regulation—Tolerating subscale	5	Trait-based measure designed to assess style of emotional coping. Acceptable internal consistency; high item validity; tolerating subscale is linked with emotional awareness (Hofmann & Kashdan, 2010).
Freiburg Mindfulness Inventory (FMI) (Buchheld et al., 2001)	Single scale	Openness to negative mind-states and nonjudgmental present moment observation	30	Designed for assessing individuals who are experienced meditators. Very good internal consistency (Buchheld et al., 2001).

others have examined behavioral outcomes and/or measures of the relationship to internal experiences.

In a meta-analysis, small to medium between-group effect sizes were found to favor ACT strategies with respect to pain tolerance, but no significant differences were observed between acceptance and other emotion regulation strategies with respect to pain intensity and negative affect (Kohl et al., 2012). Relatedly, several studies have found acceptance-based rationales to be superior to control-based rationales in decreasing believability of pain as a barrier to continuing the task (Hayes, Bissett, et al., 1999; Paez-Blarrina et al., 2008). In their review of the literature on smoking, Serfaty et al. (2018) reported that ACT-based strategies were associated with decreases in acute craving and negative affect when compared to inactive controls, but not cognitive control-based strategies.

In their meta-analysis of lab-based component studies, Levin et al. (2012) coded for psychological flexibility targeted outcomes, such as overt behavior and believability of thoughts, and "other outcomes" that are not theoretically specified (such as positive emotions, psychological arousal, attitudes, and motivation). They also examined the application of each ACT process separately. When all outcomes were included, they observed a small effect size for acceptance compared to inactive conditions (g = .32, 95% CI = –.03, .68). When only outcomes targeted by the psychological flexibility model were considered, a significant large effect size was observed favoring acceptance (g = .81, 95% CI = .45, 1.18). Larger effect sizes were also found for those interventions that included metaphors and experiential methods than for those that provided a rationale alone.

Other studies that discriminate the components of mindfulness have examined the impact of acceptance or willingness as a component process. Wang et al. (2019) reported significant increases in pain tolerance and pain endurance during a cold pressor task for participants trained in acceptance of pain or in a combination of acceptance and attention, but not for those who received only training in attention to pain. In the context of food craving, studies have found that the brief application of defusion or disidentification is associated with greater reductions in the intensity of craving and the consumption of craved food than the application of acceptance (Lacaille et al., 2014; Jenkins & Tapper, 2013).

Evidence from Ecological Momentary Assessment Studies

Studies that have used EMA methods to examine the impact of momentary acceptance have found that acceptance is associated with greater positive affect, lower negative affect, and greater engagement in value-guided behavior (Hershenberg et al., 2017; Levin et al., 2018; Vilardaga et al., 2013).

Evidence from Randomized Controlled Trials

In randomized controlled trials (RCTs) comparing ACT to waitlist or active control conditions, the preponderance of the evidence indicates that ACT increases psychological acceptance and improves outcomes of interest for a variety of clinical problems, including chronic pain (Feliu-Soler et al., 2018), eating and weight concerns (e.g., Fogelkvist et al., 2020), anxiety disorders (Bluett et al., 2014), and depression (Bai et al., 2020). A handful of studies have shown that baseline levels of acceptance moderate treatment effects (e.g., Levin et al., 2017).

A subset of RCTs have explicitly tested acceptance as a process of change and found that increases in acceptance (or decreases in EA) mediate treatment response. For example, increased acceptance has been shown to mediate improvements in depressive symptoms in veterans (Walser et al., 2015), individuals with comorbid alcohol use disorder (Petersen & Zettle, 2009), individuals experiencing depression following psychosis (Gumley et al., 2017), and weight loss in adults with obesity (e.g., Butryn et al., 2017). Acceptance has been found to mediate effects in in-person as well as web-based ACT interventions (e.g., Bricker et al., 2013). The number of studies that did not find mediation, however, is unknown. A few studies have examined mechanisms of change in ACT relative to CBT and have found that acceptance mediates effects specifically in ACT, suggesting unique processes of change (e.g., Forman et al., 2012).

Component—Dismantling Studies

A few recent studies have compared the efficacy of various components of the ACT model. Specifically, they compare the effect of openness (acceptance and defusion) to engagement (values and committed action) processes in online ACT interventions. Thus far, they indicate that the engaged components, as well as both components together, correspond with greater improvements in psychological functioning than the openness components alone (e.g., Levin et al, 2020). This finding appears to underscore the importance of contextualizing acceptance in the service of one's values. It might also suggest that acceptance and defusion are more difficult to deliver effectively online and that accordingly more research is needed.

Other Evidence

As previously noted, there is evidence of a correspondence between acceptance (or EA) and clinical endpoints in cross-sectional studies, case series, open trials, and nonrandomized controlled trials, among other study designs. There are also non-ACT studies showing that approach-based coping is prospectively associated with better functioning or outcomes, or mediates the relationship between a risk factor (e.g., trauma) and clinical outcome (e.g., onset of PTSD) (e.g., Orcutt et al., 2020).

Limitations in the Evidence Base and Future Directions for Research

Although there is considerable evidence for the efficacy of ACT relative to waitlist or nonactive control conditions with moderate to large effect sizes (Gloster et al., 2020), there continues to be significant limitations in the assessment of acceptance as a process of change. More studies need to assess acceptance at a higher rate of frequency and with greater scientific rigor. The assessment of acceptance also needs to be timed to capture dynamic change and predict outcomes.

Most notably, there is overreliance on self-report measures of acceptance, which might be attributed to the fact that acceptance is difficult to capture behaviorally while also discriminating from distress tolerance or related constructs (using the PASAT or other existing tasks). Thus, there is a need for innovations in behavioral measures. Brief measures that can be easily administered in the individual's natural environment, as well as strategies to assess change in acceptance in therapeutic encounters, also need to be further developed. Innovations might also include identifying biobehavioral markers of acceptance that can be captured with sensors or mobile devices.

References

Bach, P., Hayes, S. C., & Gallop, R. (2012). Long-term effects of brief acceptance and commitment therapy for psychosis. *Behavior Modification, 36*(2), 165–181. https://doi.org/10.1177/0145445511427193

Baer, R. A., Carmody, J., & Hunsinger, M. (2012). Weekly change in mindfulness and perceived stress in a mindfulness-based stress reduction program. *Journal of Clinical Psychology, 68*(7), 755–765. https://doi.org/10.1002/jclp.21865

Baer, R. A., Smith, G. T., & Allen, K. B. (2004). Assessment of mindfulness by self-report: The Kentucky Inventory of Mindfulness Skills. *Assessment, 11*(3), 191–206. https://doi.org/10.1177/1073191104268029

Baer, R. A., Smith, G. T., Hopkins, J., Krietemeyer, J., & Toney, L. (2006). Using self-report assessment methods to explore facets of mindfulness. *Assessment, 13*(1), 27–45. https://doi.org/10.1177/1073191105283504

Bai, Z., Luo, S., Zhang, L., Wu, S., & Chi, I. (2020). Acceptance and commitment therapy (ACT) to reduce depression: A systematic review and meta-analysis. *Journal of Affective Disorders, 260*, 728–737. https://doi.org/10.1016/j.jad.2019.09.040

Barnes-Holmes, Y., Hayes, S. C., Barnes-Holmes, D., & Roche, B (2001). Relational frame theory: A post-Skinnerian account of human language and cognition. *Advances in Child Development and Behavior, 28*, 101–138. https://doi.org/10.1016/s0065-2407(02)80063-5

Bluett, E. J., Homan, K. J., Morrison, K. L., Levin, M. E., & Twohig, M. P. (2014). Acceptance and commitment therapy for anxiety and OCD spectrum disorders: An empirical review. *Journal of Anxiety Disorders, 28*(6), 612–624. https://doi.org/10.1016/j.janxdis.2014.06.008

Bond, F. W., Hayes, S. C., Baer, R. A., Carpenter, K. M., Guenole, N., Orcutt, H. K., Waltz, T., & Zettle, R. D. (2011). Preliminary psychometric properties of the Acceptance and Action Questionnaire–II: A revised measure of psychological inflexibility and experiential avoidance. *Behavior Therapy, 42*(4), 676–688. https://doi.org/10.1016/j.beth.2011.03.007

Borkovec, T. D., Alcaine, O. M., & Behar, E. (2004). Avoidance theory of worry and generalized anxiety disorder. In R. G. Heimberg, C. L. Turk, & D. S. Mennin (Eds.), *Generalized anxiety disorder: Advances in research and practice* (pp. 77–108). Guilford Press.

Brereton, A., & McGlinchey, E. (2020). Self-harm, emotion regulation, and experiential avoidance: A systematic review. *Archives of Suicide Research, 24*(suppl.), 1–24. https://doi.org/10.1080/13811118.2018.1563575

Bricker, J., Wyszynski, C., Comstock, B., & Heffner, J. L. (2013). Pilot randomized controlled trial of web-based acceptance and commitment therapy for smoking cessation. *Nicotine and Tobacco Research, 15*(10), 1756–1764. https://doi.org/10.1093/ntr/ntt056

Buchheld, N., Grossman, P., & Walach, H. (2001). Measuring mindfulness in insight meditation (Vipassana) and meditation-based psychotherapy: The development of the Freiburg Mindfulness Inventory (FMI). *Journal for Meditation and Meditation Research, 1*(1), 11–34.

Butryn, M. L., Forman, E. M., Lowe, M. R., Gorin, A. A., Zhang, F., & Schaumberg, K. (2017). Efficacy of environmental and acceptance-based enhancements to behavioral weight loss treatment: The ENACT trial. *Obesity* (Silver Spring, MD), *25*(5), 866–872. http://dx.doi.org/10.1002/oby.21813

Cardaciotto, L., Herbert, J. D., Forman, E. M., Moitra, E., Farrow, V. (2008). The assessment of present-moment awareness and acceptance: The Philadelphia Mindfulness Scale. *Assessment, 15*(2), 204–223. https://doi.org/10.1177/1073191107311467

Castagna, P. J., Davis, T. E., & Lilly, M. E. (2017). The behavioral avoidance task with anxious youth: A review of procedures, properties, and criticisms. *Clinical Child and Family Psychology Review, 20*(2), 162–184. https://doi.org/10.1007/s10567-016-0220-3

Christopher, M. S., Neuser, N. J., Michael, P. G., & Baitmangalkar, A. (2012). Exploring the psychometric properties of the Five Facet Mindfulness Questionnaire. *Mindfulness, 3*(2), 124–131. https://doi.org/10.1007/s12671-011-0086-x

Craske, M. G., Treanor, M., Conway, C. C., Zbozinek, T., & Vervliet, B. (2014). Maximizing exposure therapy: An inhibitory learning approach. *Behaviour Research and Therapy, 58*, 10–23. https://doi.org/10.1016/j.brat.2014.04.006

Derogatis, L. R., & Savitz, K. L. (1999). The SCL-90-R, Brief Symptom Inventory, and Matching Clinical Rating Scales. In M. E. Maruish (Ed.), *The use of psychological testing for treatment planning and outcomes assessment* (pp. 679–724). Lawrence Erlbaum.

Derogatis, L. R., & Unger, R. (2010). Symptom Checklist-90-Revised. *The Corsini Encyclopedia of Psychology*, 1–2. https://doi.org/10.1002/9780470479216.corpsy0970

Doughty, A. H., Kastner, R. M., & Bismark, B. D. (2011). Resurgence of derived stimulus relations: Replication and extensions. *Behavioural Processes, 86*(1), 152–155. https://doi.org/10.1016/j.beproc.2010.08.006

Feliu-Soler, A., Montesinos, F., Gutiérrez-Martínez, O., Scott, W., McCracken, L. M., & Luciano, J. V. (2018). Current status of acceptance and commitment therapy for chronic pain: A narrative review. *Journal of Pain Research, 11*, 2145–2159. https://doi.org/10.2147/JPR.S144631

Firsching, V. J., Villanueva, J., Rinner, M., Benoy, C., Kuhweide, V., Brogli, S., Gloster, A. T. (2018). Measuring psychological flexibility in a context sensitive manner—development and preliminary psychometric properties of a short and accessible questionnaire. Poster session presented at the ACBS world conference 16, Montreal, Quebec, Canada.

Fogelkvist, M., Gustafsson, S. A., Kjellin, L., & Parling, T. (2020). Acceptance and commitment therapy to reduce eating disorder symptoms and body image problems in patients with residual eating disorder symptoms: A randomized controlled trial. *Body Image, 32*, 155–166. https://doi.org/10.1016/j.bodyim.2020.01.002

Forman, E. M., Chapman, J. E., Herbert, J. D., Goetter, E. M., Yuen, E. K., & Moitra, E. (2012). Using session-by-session measurement to compare mechanisms of action for acceptance and commitment therapy and cognitive therapy. *Behavior Therapy, 43*(2), 341–354. https://doi.org/10.1016/j.beth.2011.07.004

Francis, A. W., Dawson, D. L., & Golijani-Moghaddam, N. (2016). The development and validation of the Comprehensive Assessment of Acceptance and Commitment Therapy processes (CompACT). *Journal of Contextual Behavioral Science, 5*(3), 134–145. https://doi.org/10.1016/j.jcbs.2016.05.003

Gámez, W., Chmielewski, M., Kotov, R., Ruggero, C., Suzuki, N., & Watson, D. (2014). The Brief Experiential Avoidance Questionnaire: Development and initial validation. *Psychological assessment, 26*(1), 35–45. http://dx.doi.org/10.1037/a0034473

Gámez, W., Chmielewski, M., Kotov, R., Ruggero, C., & Watson, D. (2011). Development of a measure of experiential avoidance: The Multidimensional Experiential Avoidance Questionnaire. *Psychological Assessment, 23*(3), 692–713. https://doi.org/10.1037/a0023242

García-Soriano, G., Belloch, A., Morillo, C., & Clark, D. A. (2011). Symptom dimensions in obsessive–compulsive disorder: From normal cognitive intrusions to clinical obsessions. *Journal of Anxiety Disorders, 25*(4), 474–482. https://doi.org/10.1016/j.janxdis.2010.11.012

Gloster, A. T., Walder, N., Levin, M. E., Twohig, M. P., & Karekla, M. (2020). The empirical status of acceptance and commitment therapy: A review of meta-analyses. *Journal of Contextual and Behavioral Sciences, 18*, 181–192. https://doi.org/10.1016/j.jcbs.2020.09.009.

Gratz, K. L., & Roemer, L. (2004). Multidimensional assessment of emotion regulation and dysregulation: Development, factor structure, and initial validation of the Difficulties in Emotion Regulation Scale. *Journal of Psychopathology and Behavioral Assessment, 26*(1), 41–54. https://doi.org/10.1023/B:JOBA.0000007455.08539.94

Greco, L. A., Lambert, W., & Baer, R. A. (2008). Psychological inflexibility in childhood and adolescence: Development and evaluation of the Avoidance and Fusion Questionnaire for Youth. *Psychological Assessment, 20*(2), 93–102. https://doi.org/10.1037/1040-3590.20.2.93

Gu, J., Strauss, C., Crane, C., Barnhofer, T., Karl, A., Cavanagh, K., & Kuyken, W. (2016). Examining the factor structure of the 39-item and 15-item versions of the Five Facet Mindfulness Questionnaire before and after mindfulness-based cognitive therapy for people with recurrent depression. *Psychological Assessment, 28*(7), 791–802. http://dx.doi.org/10.1037/pas0000263

Gumley, A., White, R., Briggs, A., Ford, I., Barry, S., Stewart, C., Beedie, S., McTaggart, J., Clarke, C., MacLeod, R., Lidstone, E., Riveros, B. S., Young, R., &. McLeod, H. (2017). A parallel group randomised open blinded evaluation of Acceptance and Commitment Therapy for depression after psychosis: Pilot trial outcomes (ADAPT). *Schizophrenia Research, 183*, 143–150. https://doi.org/10.1016/j.schres.2016.11.026

Hallion, L. S., Steinman, S. A., Tolin, D. F., & Diefenbach, G. J. (2018). Psychometric properties of the Difficulties in Emotion Regulation Scale (DERS) and its short forms in adults with emotional disorders. *Frontiers in Psychology, 9*, Article 539. https://doi.org/10.3389/fpsyg.2018.00539

Harris, R. (2019). *ACT made simple: An easy-to-read primer on acceptance and commitment therapy*. New Harbinger Publications.

Hayes, S. C. (1994). Content, context, and the types of psychological acceptance. In S. C. Hayes, N. S., Jacobson, V. M. Follette, & M. J. Dougher (Eds.), *Acceptance and change: Content and context in psychotherapy* (pp. 13–32). Context Press.

Hayes, S. C. (2005). *Get out of your mind and into your life: The new acceptance and commitment therapy*. New Harbinger Publications.

Hayes, S. C., Bissett, R. T., Korn, Z., Zettle, R. D., Rosenfarb, I. S., Cooper, L. D., & Grundt, A. M. (1999). The impact of acceptance versus control rationales on pain tolerance. *The Psychological Record, 49*(1), 33–47. https://doi.org/10.1007/BF03395305

Hayes, S. C., Luoma, J. B., Bond, F. W., Masuda, A., & Lillis, J. (2006). Acceptance and commitment therapy: Model, processes and outcomes. *Behaviour research and therapy, 44*(1), 1–25. https://doi.org/10.1016/j.brat.2005.06.006

Hayes, S. C., Strosahl, K. D., & Wilson, K. G. (1999). *Acceptance and commitment therapy: An experiential approach to behavior change*. Guilford Press.

Hayes, S. C., Strosahl, K. D., & Wilson, K. G. (2012). *Acceptance and commitment therapy: The process and practice of mindful change*. Guilford Press.

Hayes, S. C., Strosahl, K., Wilson, K. G., Bissett, R. T., Pistorello, J., Toarmino, D., Polusny, M. A., Dykstra, T. A., Batten, S. V., Bergan, J., Stewart, S. H., Zvolensky, M. J., Eifert, G. H., Bond, F. W., Forsyth, J. P., Karekla, M. & McCurry, S. M. (2004). Measuring experiential avoidance: A preliminary test of a working model. *The Psychological Record, 54*(4), 553–578. https://doi.org/10.1007/BF03395492

Hayes, S. C., Wilson, K. G., Gifford, E. V., Follette, V. M., & Strosahl, K. (1996). Experiential avoidance and behavioral disorders: A functional dimensional approach to diagnosis and treatment. *Journal of Consulting and Clinical Psychology, 64*(6), 1152–1168. https://doi.org/10.1037/0022-006X.64.6.1152

Hershenberg, R., Mavandadi, S., Wright, E., & Thase, M. E. (2017). Anhedonia in the daily lives of depressed veterans: A pilot report on experiential avoidance as a moderator of emotional reactivity. *Journal of Affective Disorders, 208*, 414–417. https://doi.org/10.1016/j.jad.2016.10.011

Hofmann, S. G., & Kashdan, T. B. (2010). The affective style questionnaire: Development and psychometric properties. *Journal of Psychopathology and Behavioral Assessment, 32*(2), 255–263. https://doi.org/10.1007/s10862-009-9142-4

Jagielska, G., & Kacperska, I. (2017). Outcome, comorbidity and prognosis in anorexia nervosa. *Psychiatria Polska, 51*(2), 205–218. https://doi.org/10.12740/PP/64580

Jenkins, K., & Tapper, K. (2013). Effects of a brief cognitive defusion task on chocolate craving. *Appetite, 71*, 479. https://doi.org/10.1016/j.appet.2013.06.038

Kashdan, T. B., Goodman, F. R., Machell, K. A., Kleiman, E. M., Monfort, S. S., Ciarrochi, J., & Nezlek, J. B. (2014). A contextual approach to experiential avoidance and social anxiety: Evidence from an experimental interaction and daily interactions of people with social anxiety disorder. *Emotion, 14*(4), 769–781. https://doi.org/10.1037/a0035935 https://doi.org/10.1176/appi.ajp.161.12.2215

Kohl, A., Rief, W., & Glombiewski, J. A. (2012). How effective are acceptance strategies? A meta-analytic review of experimental results. *Journal of Behavior Therapy and Experimental Psychiatry, 43*(4), 988–1001. https://doi.org/10.1016/j.jbtep.2012.03.004

Lacaille, J., Ly, J., Zacchia, N., Bourkas, S., Glaser, E., & Knäuper, B. (2014). The effects of three mindfulness skills on chocolate cravings. *Appetite, 76*, 101–112. https://doi.org/10.1016/j.appet.2014.01.072

Lavender, J. M., Tull, M. T., DiLillo, D., Messman-Moore, T., & Gratz, K. L. (2017). Development and validation of a state-based measure of emotion dysregulation: The State Difficulties in Emotion Regulation Scale (S-DERS). *Assessment, 24*(2), 197–209. https://doi.org/10.1177/1073191115601218

Levin, M. E., Hildebrandt, M. J., Lillis, J., & Hayes, S. C. (2012). The impact of treatment components suggested by the psychological flexibility model: A meta-analysis of laboratory-based component studies. *Behavior Therapy, 43*(4), 741–756. https://doi.org/10.1016/j.beth.2012.05.003

Levin, M. E., Krafft, J., Hicks, E. T., Pierce, B., & Twohig, M. P. (2020). A randomized dismantling trial of the open and engaged components of acceptance and commitment therapy in an online intervention for distressed college students. *Behaviour Research and Therapy, 126*, 103557. https://doi.org/10.1016/j.brat.2020.103557

Levin, M. E., Krafft, J., Pierce, B., & Potts, S. (2018). When is experiential avoidance harmful in the moment? Examining global experiential avoidance as a moderator. *Journal of Behavior Therapy and Experimental Psychiatry, 61*, 158–163. https://doi.org/10.1016/j.jbtep.2018.07.005

Levin, M. E., Luoma, J. B., & Haeger, J. A. (2015). Decoupling as a mechanism of change in mindfulness and acceptance: A literature review. *Behavior Modification, 39*(6), 870–911. https://doi.org/10.1177/0145445515603707

Levin, M. E., Pierce, B., & Schoendorff, B. (2017). The acceptance and commitment therapy matrix mobile app: A pilot randomized trial on health behaviors. *Journal of Contextual Behavioral Science, 6*(3), 268–275. https://doi.org/10.1016/j.jcbs.2017.05.003

Linehan, M. M. (1994). Acceptance and change: The central dialectic in psychotherapy. *Acceptance and Change: Content and Context in Psychotherapy*, 73–86.

Luoma, J.B., Hayes, S. C., & Walser, R. D. (2007). *Learning ACT: An acceptance and commitment therapy skills-training manual for therapists.* New Harbinger Publications.

McAndrews, Z., Richardson, J., & Stopa, L. (2019). Psychometric properties of acceptance measures: A systematic review. *Journal of Contextual Behavioral Science, 12*, 261–277. https://doi.org/10.1016/j.jcbs.2018.08.006

Merwin, R. M., Dmitrieva, N. O., Honeycutt, L. K., Moskovich, A. A., Lane, J. D., Zucker, N. L., Surwit, R. S., Feinglos, M., & Kuo, J. (2015). Momentary predictors of insulin restriction among adults with type 1 diabetes and eating disorder symptomatology. *Diabetes Care, 38*(11), 2025–2032. https://doi.org/10.2337/dc15-0753

O'Neill, L., Latchford, G., McCracken, L. M., & Graham, C. D. (2019). The development of the Acceptance and Commitment Therapy Fidelity Measure (ACT-FM): A delphi study and field test. *Journal of Contextual Behavioral Science, 14*, 111–118. https://doi.org/10.1016/j.jcbs.2019.08.008

Ong, C. W., Lee, E. B., Levin, M. E., & Twohig, M. P. (2019). A review of AAQ variants and other context-specific measures of psychological flexibility. *Journal of Contextual Behavioral Science, 12*, 329–346. https://doi.org/10.1016/j.jcbs.2019.02.007

Orcutt, H. K., Reffi, A. N., & Ellis, R. A. (2020). Experiential avoidance and PTSD. In *Emotion in Posttraumatic Stress Disorder* (pp. 409–436). Academic Press. https://doi.org/10.1016/B978-012-816022-0.00014-4

Paez-Blarrina, M., Luciano, C., Gutiérrez-Martínez, O., Valdivia, S., Ortega, J., & Rodríguez-Valverde, M. (2008). The role of values with personal examples in altering the functions of pain: Comparison between acceptance-based and cognitive-control-based protocols. *Behaviour Research and Therapy, 46*(1), 84–97. https://doi.org/10.1016/j.brat.2007.10.008

Palladino, C. L., Ange, B., Richardson, D. S., Casillas, R., Decker, M., Gillies, R. A., House, A., Rollock, M., Salazar, W. H., Waller, J. L., Zeidan, R., & Stepleman, L. (2013). Measuring psychological flexibility in medical students and residents: A psychometric analysis. *Medical Education Online, 18*(1), 20932. https://doi.org/10.3402/meo.v18i0.20932 https://doi.org/10.1016/j.appet.2017.01.027

Petersen, C. L., & Zettle, R. D. (2009). Treating inpatients with comorbid depression and alcohol use disorders: A comparison of acceptance and commitment therapy versus treatment as usual. *The Psychological Record, 59*(4), 521–536. Gale General OneFile. https://doi.org/10.1007/BF03395679

Quirk, G. J. (2002). Memory for extinction of conditioned fear is long-lasting and persists following spontaneous recovery. *Learning and Memory, 9*(6), 402–407.

Schaefer, L. M., Smith, K. E., Anderson, L. M., Cao, L., Crosby, R. D., Engel, S. G., Crow, S. J., Peterson, C. B. & Wonderlich, S. A. (2020). The role of affect in the maintenance of binge-eating disorder: Evidence from an ecological momentary assessment study. *Journal of Abnormal Psychology, 129*(4), 387. https://doi.org/10.1037/abn0000517

Scott, W., McCracken, L. M., & Norton, S. (2016). A confirmatory factor analysis of facets of psychological flexibility in a sample of people seeking treatment for chronic pain. *Annals of Behavioral Medicine, 50*(2), 285–296. https://doi.org/10.1007/s12160-015-9752-x

Serfaty, S., Gale, G., Beadman, M., Froeliger, B., & Kamboj, S. K. (2018). Mindfulness, acceptance and defusion strategies in smokers: A systematic review of laboratory studies. *Mindfulness, 9*(1), 44–58. https://doi.org/10.1007/s12671-017-0767-1

Vilardaga, R., Hayes, S. C., Atkins, D. C., Bresee, C., & Kambiz, A. (2013). Comparing experiential acceptance and cognitive reappraisal as predictors of functional outcome in individuals with serious mental illness. *Behaviour Research and Therapy, 51*(8), 425–433. https://doi.org/10.1016/j.brat.2013.04.003

Walser, R. D., Garvert, D. W., Karlin, B. E., Trockel, M., Ryu, D. M., & Taylor, C. B. (2015). Effectiveness of acceptance and commitment therapy in treating depression and suicidal ideation in veterans. *Behaviour Research and Therapy, 74*, 25–31. https://doi.org/10.1016/j.brat.2015.08.012

Wang, Y., Qi, Z., Hofmann, S. G., Si, M., Liu, X., & Xu, W. (2019). Effect of acceptance versus attention on pain tolerance: Dissecting two components of mindfulness. *Mindfulness* 10, 1352–1359. https://doi.org/10.1007/s12671-019-1091-8

Wegner, D. M. (1994). Ironic processes of mental control. *Psychological Review, 101*(1), 34.

CHAPTER
9 Cognitive Defusion

Francisco J. Ruiz, Bárbara Gil-Luciano, *and* Miguel A. Segura-Vargas

Abstract

This article reviews the conceptualization and empirical evidence of the midlevel process called cognitive defusion. First, it presents examples of cognitive fusion and cognitive defusion definitions that are offered in acceptance and commitment therapy (ACT) manuals; discusses their relationships with other ACT midlevel processes; and offers a relational frame theory (RFT) conceptualization of these processes. Second, it describes the type of cognitive defusion exercises and discusses the basic processes involved in them. Third, it reviews the measurement of cognitive (de)fusion in the form of self-report instruments, behavioral measures, and assessment in the clinical session. Fourth, it reviews the research on cognitive (de)fusion separated in laboratory research, survey research, and the analysis of processes of change in clinical trials. Lastly, it discusses some challenges and future directions in conceptualizing and researching cognitive (de)fusion.

Key Words: cognitive defusion, acceptance and commitment therapy, relational frame theory, contextual behavioral science, self-as-context, psychological flexibility

Midlevel functional terms are higher-level functional abstractions that serve as shortcuts for applying basic principles to complex applied settings (Vilardaga, Hayes, Levin, & Muto, 2009). Acceptance and commitment therapy (ACT; Hayes, Strosahl, & Wilson, 1999; Wilson & Luciano, 2002) is usually presented in midlevel terms, with cognitive fusion and cognitive defusion being some of the most original and older concepts. This article provides a conceptual overview of them and the accompanying research. First, we define these constructs as usually presented in ACT, present the interrelationship with other midlevel ACT processes, and provide a relational frame theory (RFT) conceptualization. Second, we describe examples of clinical work with cognitive defusion and analyze some of the key processes involved. Third, we describe the instruments developed for measuring cognitive (de)fusion. Fourth, we review the empirical evidence regarding the efficacy of cognitive defusion exercises, component studies, survey research, and its role as a process of change in clinical interventions. Lastly, we suggest challenges and future research directions.

A Conceptual Overview of Cognitive Defusion

This section reviews the definitions of cognitive fusion and defusion; explores the interrelationship between these processes and the other processes of the *inhexaflex* and *hexaflex*; and provides an RFT conceptualization of these processes.

Definitions of Cognitive Fusion and Cognitive Defusion

In order to best understand cognitive defusion, it is necessary to explain the associated pathological process, cognitive fusion. Table 9.1 presents definitions of cognitive fusion as found in popular ACT writings.

According to the definitions presented previously, cognitive fusion has a metaphoric origin. In these terms, cognitive fusion involves the tendency of humans to get caught up in the content of their thinking as if this process and the world were one (e.g., Luoma, Hayes, & Walser, 2007). As such, individuals may respond to their thoughts as if they were literal truths, which is also known as "buying into" their thoughts (e.g., Bennett & Oliver, 2019; Dahl, Stewart, Martell, & Kaplan, 2014). In more technical terms, cognitive fusion involves the dominance of verbal functions over other direct and indirect psychological functions (Hayes & Strosahl, 2005; Wilson, 2009). Thus, cognitive fusion refers to behaving under the control of the ongoing transformation of functions without contacting alternative sources of stimulus control.

Cognitive fusion is a midlevel term, and as such, it has proven to have a high clinical utility but it also has the common problems that midlevel terms posit. For instance, cognitive fusion is simultaneously used to refer to an outcome, a process, and a general tendency (e.g., McEnteggart, Barnes-Holmes, Hussey, & Barnes-Holmes, 2015). Looking at the definitions

Table 9.1. Definitions of cognitive fusion in some ACT books

Definitions of cognitive fusion
Hayes and Strosahl (2005): "Human tendency to interact with events on the basis of their verbally ascribed functions rather than their direct functions, while being oblivious to the ongoing relational framing that establishes these functions. The event and one's thinking about it become so fused as to be inseparable and that creates the impression that verbal construal is not present at all" (p. 25). "Speaking technically, fusion is the dominance of particular verbal functions over other directly and indirectly available psychological functions" (p. 39).
Hayes, Strosahl, and Wilson (2012): "In a technical sense, cognitive fusion is a process by which verbal events exert strong stimulus control over responding, to the exclusion of other contextual variables. Phrased differently, fusion is a kind of verbal dominance in behavioral regulation" (p. 69).
Dahl et al. (2014): "In RFT terms, fusion could be understood to involve a transformation of functions such that people respond in accordance with the literal meaning of their relational framing (i.e., they 'buy into' their thoughts)" (p. 80).
Luoma et al. (2007): "In general terms, cognitive fusion refers to the tendency of human beings to get caught up in the content of what they are thinking so that it dominates over other useful sources of behavioral regulation . . . . The word fuse comes from a word that means 'to pour.' Metaphorically, it is as if the content of cognition and the world about which we are thinking are poured together until they are one, in much the same way that lemons, water, and sugar can together become lemonade" (p. 13).
Bennett and Oliver (2019): "The term fusion is a technical name for the process by which we respond to our thoughts as if they were literal truths. As with any ACT process, it is contextually dependent, which is to say that responding literally is not necessary problematic, but only so when it restricts or prevents actions towards values." (p. 74).
Wilson (2009): "Fusion is the process whereby certain verbal functions of events exert strong stimulus control over responding to the exclusion of other directly and indirectly available psychological functions" (pp. 54–55).

presented previously, we find that the term is generally used as an outcome behavior. In this regard, cognitive fusion could also be called fused behavior. It is also of note that it is common to eliminate the term *cognitive* and only use the word "fusion."

Table 9.2 presents some definitions of cognitive defusion commonly presented in ACT. In summary, "defusion" is an invented word that refers to undoing fusion. Metaphorically, cognitive defusion involves creating a space between the individual and their private events (e.g., Bennett & Oliver, 2019) or pulling the "person" apart from the "mind" (Hayes et al., 2012). This process allows the individual to contact and consider alternative behaviors, especially those linked to personal values and objectives.

In more technical terms, cognitive defusion involves being consciously aware of private events as ongoing relational processes to reduce their immediate verbal functions and contact other sources of stimulus control (Hayes et al., 2012; Luoma et al., 2007). Stated differently, cognitive defusion refers to seeing thought as thoughts, feelings as feelings, memories as memories, and physical sensations as physical sensations (Hayes & Strosahl, 2005). When perceiving these private events as they are, their immediate verbal functions are reduced. This process facilitates engaging in verbal activity that allows contacting values and the actions available in this context that advance toward values.

Table 9.2. Definitions of cognitive defusion in some ACT books

Definitions of cognitive defusion
Luoma et al. (2007): "Defusion is an invented word meaning to undo fusion, or 'de-fusion,' and refers to the process of creating nonliteral contexts in which language can be seen as an active, ongoing, relational process that is historical in nature and present in the current moment" (p. 18).
Hayes and Strosahl (2005): "Cognitive defusion works by changing the contexts that support detrimental functions that occur through relational learning so that the process of relating dominates over the results of that process . . . . As defusion skills are established, literal language itself is brought under better contextual control. Clinically, we want to teach clients to see thoughts as thoughts, feelings as feelings, memories as memories, and physical sensations as physical sensations. None of these private events are inherently toxic to human welfare when experienced for what they are" (p. 8).
Hayes, Strosahl, and Wilson (2012): "In their more elaborated forms featured in ACT, defusion involves learning to be consciously aware of one's thinking as it occurs" (p. 23). "In order to bring fusion under contextual control, ACT teaches clients how to separate ongoing cognitive process from its cognitive products. Metaphorically, this is tantamount to pulling the 'human' (the listener) apart from the 'mind' (the speaker)" (p. 24). "Defusion does not eliminate verbal meaning—it just reduces its automatic effect on behavior such that other sources of behavioral regulation can better participate in the moment" (p. 245).
Bennett and Oliver (2019): "When we are able to defuse, thoughts may still be true but they may also not be. We can relate to them less literally. They no longer require immediate attention and are less threatening. As space is created between ourselves and our thinking, there is the opportunity to consider other guides to behavior" (p. 75).
Dahl et al. (2014): "At its core, this is a process in which people come to experience thoughts as simply thoughts—as fleeting events that they need not directly respond to, challenge, or control." (p. 82).
Wilson (2009): "Defusion means making contact with verbal products as what they are, not as what they say they are" (p. 51).

The term *cognitive defusion* also demonstrates tremendous clinical utility. However, similar concerns regarding the limitations of midlevel terms apply. In this regard, the term is simultaneously referred to as a procedure, a process, and an outcome (Assaz, Roche, Kanter, & Oshiro, 2018). According to the definitions presented previously, it seems that cognitive defusion is most frequently used to refer to an outcome: a type of behavior that is not controlled by the immediate verbal functions of private events (i.e., defused behavior). As with cognitive fusion, the term *cognitive* is frequently omitted in favor of the word *defusion*.

Relationships with Other ACT Midlevel Processes

Cognitive fusion plays a central role in the psychological inflexibility model of psychopathology and behavioral ineffectiveness (Hayes & Strosahl, 2005). Cognitive fusion is also associated with the other midlevel processes. Briefly, fused behavior hinders present moment awareness and focuses individuals' behavior on unproductive verbalizations about themselves. Additionally, it usually leads to engagement in experiential avoidance strategies when experiencing private events with aversive functions. These detrimental effects of cognitive fusion make it difficult to contact values in the present moment and behave toward valued ends.

Cognitive defusion plays an essential role in the psychological flexibility model of mental health and behavioral effectiveness. Defusing from the immediate functions of private events might allow the individual to accept them, contact with self-as-context and values, and orient behavior toward the committed actions available in the present moment. Thus, developing defusion skills is often a crucial part of ACT. These skills are required to accept aversive private events and make the function of values symbolically present. The work on defusion is especially relevant in ACT when the client frequently experiences aversive private events. Metaphorically, developing defusion skills is a first step for the individual to stop acting under the control of aversive verbal functions and behave more wisely.

An RFT Conceptualization of Cognitive (De)fusion

This section provides a brief RFT analysis of the phenomena described by the midlevel terms *cognitive fusion* and *cognitive defusion*. According to Törneke et al. (2016), the core of psychopathology relies on how individuals respond to the functions of their behavior, which critically includes private events such as thoughts, memories, and emotions. Two types of functions are especially relevant in this context. First, private events have emotional functions that vary in the aversive-appetitive continuum. Second, private events usually have discriminative functions (e.g., approaching vs. avoidance functions). Emotional and discriminative functions are usually originated by derived relations and transformation of functions (see Harte & Barnes-Holmes, this volume, and Luciano, Törneke, & Ruiz, this volume).

Törneke et al. (2016) suggested that, from a functional point of view, there are two fundamental types of reaction to private events: (1) responding in coordination with their emotional and discriminative functions, and (2) framing them hierarchically with the deictic *I* and responding according to additional relational activity that specifies appetitive augmental functions.

The first type of reaction is more straightforward and will be the dominant one if a fluid and flexible repertoire of framing private events in hierarchy with the deictic *I* has not been developed. Responding in coordination implies behaving under the control of the immediate functions of private events. Importantly, when the private event has an aversive function, the individual will likely respond according to the discriminative functions of avoidance/escape. The specific form of the avoidance/escaping behavior displayed will depend on multiple factors, such as learning history, the availability of specific responses, and their potential behavioral cost.

Given our extreme fluency in derived relational responding, engaging in further relational responding about the coherence of the private event's content (e.g., worry/rumination) tends to become a predominant experiential avoidance strategy (Ruiz, Luciano, Flórez, Suárez-Falcón, & Cardona-Betancourt, 2020; Ruiz, Riaño-Hernández, Suárez-Falcón, & Luciano, 2016). This type of relational responding has especially counterproductive effects when carried out repeatedly. First, it usually generates the paradoxical effect of extending the negative affect because it focuses on aversive emotional content, which usually leads to other avoidance behaviors. Second, it increases the complexity of the relational networks involved in the thinking process and reduces their derivation and flexibility level (Ruiz, Luciano, et al., 2020). These counterproductive effects contribute significantly to repetition of the avoidance cycle and generate an inflexible behavior pattern that is negatively reinforced and hinders behaving under the control of abstract positive reinforcers.

The second way of reacting to one's behavior is more complex because it consists of framing it hierarchically with the deictic *I*. This implies deriving that ongoing private events are momentary experiences that occur in the context of a self that contains them and from where they can be experienced as a product of the learning history. Framing private events in hierarchy leads to reduced discriminative functions and the possibility of engaging in further relational responding that specifies appetitive augmental functions and behavior according to them. This way of responding is more flexible and makes it possible to develop a behavior pattern that is under the control of abstract positive reinforcers.

The pattern of behavior in which the individual responds in coordination with the discriminative functions of private events resembles the concept of psychological inflexibility in ACT. In contrast, the pattern of behavior consisting of framing private events in hierarchy with the deictic *I* and responding under the control of appetitive augmentals resembles the concept of psychological flexibility.

This RFT account does not map exactly onto the ACT midlevel processes (Törneke et al., 2016). However, the similarity between cognitive fusion and responding in coordination with private events' discriminative functions is straightforward. Also, there seems to be a high degree of similarity between cognitive defusion and hierarchically framing private events with the deictic *I*. In our view, the advantage of this RFT conceptualization is that it facilitates refining psychological interventions because the basic psychological processes are specified. The section dedicated to reviewing component studies on cognitive defusion will mention a series of studies prompted by this RFT conceptualization.

Clinical Examples of Cognitive Defusion and Processes of Change

Cognitive Defusion Exercises

Following Blackledge (2015), defusion exercises can be categorized into five types: (1) language conventions, (2) metaphors, (3) exercises that change language parameters, (4) exercises that promote distancing from private events, and (5) exercises that aim to undermine verbal rules and narratives. The therapist should establish an adequate context before introducing some defusion exercises because they might seem rather odd to clients and make them feel invalidated (e.g., Blackledge, 2015; Hayes et al., 2012; Wilson & Luciano, 2002).

Language conventions. Expressions highlighting the nature of private events are usually introduced in ACT. A typical example of these conventions is subtly identifying thoughts as thoughts or as products of the "mind." For instance, when clients make problematic verbalizations (e.g., "The breakup was only my fault."), the ACT therapist often uses expressions like “So, right now you are having the thought that it was your fault” or “Look what your mind is telling you. What a beautiful thought!” Another option that will create some distance between the clients and their private events is to talk with them in the third person (e.g., “What did Mark feel when he was at work?”; “It seems family relationships are very important for Beatriz”). The effect of these language conventions might not be very great, but introducing them during the therapy will prepare the client for more intensive work in defusion (Blackledge, 2015). Specifically, these language conventions establish frames of distinction and hierarchy between the clients and their private events.

Metaphors. The extensive use of metaphors is a hallmark of ACT. The metaphors can be used to promote defusion by objectifying private events as something different or included in the person (i.e., establishing a hierarchical relation between the client and their private events). A typical example is the “passengers on the bus” metaphor (Hayes et al., 1999). In this metaphor, distressing private events are presented as passengers on a bus the client is driving in a valued direction. Some of the passengers are annoying and verbalize the client’s aversive private events. The client has no control over what they say but can choose between driving the bus toward the valued direction or paying attention, fighting, or obeying them. The “passengers on the bus” metaphor has the advantage of targeting virtually all ACT processes at the same time: acceptance (the willingness of the bus driver to stay in contact with the passengers because this serves to advance in the valued direction), defusion (objectifying the challenging private events as the passengers), self-as-context (the bus contains all passengers), present moment awareness (the bus driver’s valued action is to focus on driving), values (the bus driver can choose their overall direction in life), and committed action (the bus driver can choose their immediate route to advance toward the overall life direction).

Changing language parameters. These exercises manipulate elements of the context that provide psychological functions to thoughts. These exercises aim to highlight the arbitrary nature of thoughts and present them as innocuous experiences (Blackledge, 2007; e.g., a thought can be seen as just a thought: a group of words ordered in a specific way that are pronounced with a specific tone, rate, and manner). Changing the contextual features associated with the functions of thoughts can alter their meaning and lead the client to experience them from a different perspective.

The most typical example of this type of exercise is the classic word-repetition exercise (Titchener, 1910). This exercise consists of continuously repeating a word for about half a minute or more. This provokes a profound change in the initial functions of the thought that are substituted by its perceptual, nonarbitrary functions. The exercise procedure usually involves presenting a brief rationale that highlights the arbitrary nature of thoughts. The client is invited to imagine a glass of milk and experience the functions of milk (e.g., it is white, creamy). Afterward, the client and the therapist quickly repeat the word “milk” until the functions of the word change momentarily. The same procedure is then applied to a distressing thought summarized in one word in order for the clients to realize the arbitrary nature of thoughts and to show that they can be experienced as transitory experiences in the context of a transcendet self.

Distancing exercises. These exercises locate private events at a spatial distance from oneself. The clients are then asked just to observe private events without judgment or without reacting to them, with the aim being to see thoughts as just thoughts, emotions as just emotions, and so on. A very typical exercise is the “leaves on a stream” exercise. There are different versions of this exercise in ACT texts. We will present a version of the exercise enriched with explicit hierarchical cues and questions to derive appetitive augmentals or regulatory functions (Luciano et al., 2011).

The exercise begins by inviting the clients to discriminate among ongoing private events or to recall some of the events experienced in difficult situations. They are asked to fully concentrate on one of these events, notice who was having them, and imagine them on a leaf in a tree that falls into a river. The clients are asked to notice that their event is now THERE while they are HERE observing it. The therapist asks the clients to suspend judgment (e.g., "Allow yourself not to judge the thought; just contemplate it much as you would contemplate a painting or a landscape") and focus on some nonarbitrary characteristics of the event (e.g., "See how many words the thought has and choose a color for the ink"). Subsequently, the therapist asks the clients to discriminate that the event is just a transitory experience they are having, its immediate discriminative functions and that they can choose just to observe this process (e.g., "Who is having this thought? What is it compelling you to do? Note that right now you are choosing just to observe it, that you have the capacity of choosing what to do"). Afterward, the therapist asks questions regarding the available ways of responding to the event (e.g., "What would happen right now if you let the thought be in charge? What would happen if you let this and other similar thoughts be in charge for another three months? Alternatively, what could you do that would imply that you are in charge? What would happen if you do that? What would happen if you respond to this and similar thoughts this way during the next three months?"). Lastly, the therapist invites the client to choose and discriminate that action (e.g., "What do you choose to do here and now? Note that you are the person who is choosing what to do, that you have the capacity to choose wisely the direction you want to take in your life. What would you achieve? How do you feel now, when noticing what you could achieve?).

Undermining verbal rules and narratives. Private events are often considered as causes of subsequent behavior. For instance, clients usually show fusion with reasons for behaving in a particular way without realizing that reasons are not causes; they are only verbalizations that arbitrarily became causes in the person's learning history. A typical defusion exercise used in this regard consists of asking the clients to think about not performing a particular action (e.g., "I will not take the pen on the table") and giving reasons for not doing so (e.g., "It is contaminated," "I will get stained with the ink"), while at the same time asking them to perform it. Then, the clients are asked to think and give reasons for performing the same action (e.g., "I will take the pen on the table," "I need it to write down something important") while also being asked not to perform it. The exercise aims to highlight the arbitrary connection between thoughts/reasons and actions. They also highlight the notion that clients can observe thoughts/reasons and choosing to behave according to other sources of stimulus control.

Processes Involved in Cognitive Defusion Exercises

Identifying the basic processes underlying the effect of defusion exercises is a complicated task, and research on this topic is still scarce (see the section "Variables Involved in the Effect of Defusion Exercises" later in this article). Blackledge (2007) suggested that defusion exercises seem to work by disrupting the context of literality. This effect is produced when the contextual conditions that provide meaning to thoughts via transformation of functions are displaced. A typical exercise would be the word-repetition exercise that alters the context in which aversive functions occur by focusing the client's attention on the thought's perceptual functions (e.g., the funny sound of the word).

Assaz et al. (2018) suggested that Blackledge's account neglected some learning processes. Central to their proposal is the idea that different learning processes can lead to similar outcomes: "Our main argument is that the reduction of transformation of function through verbal relations is an outcome that can be obtained through different basic behavioral processes" (p. 411). The authors provided analysis for different types of defusion exercises.

Regarding the exercises that focus on changing language parameters, Assaz et al. (2018) suggest that these exercises are mainly exposure procedures because the clients repeatedly contact private events without other associated stimulus until its verbally conditioned eliciting functions are reduced. Accordingly, the processes of change in this type of exercise could be the same as those involved in exposure: respondent extinction, counterconditioning, and inhibitory learning.

Defusion exercises that disrupt the link between thoughts and actions (e.g., see the exercise explained above about taking or not taking a pen when introducing the defusion exercises that aim to undermine verbal rules and narratives") would work through differential reinforcement. The rationale is that the alternative behaviors to the rigid responses caused by cognitive fusion will be reinforced somehow. This differential reinforcement implies that the thought becomes a discriminative stimulus for other responses.

Assaz et al. (2018) also suggest that some defusion exercises work because they show that thinking is not a coherent narrative depicting reality. Lastly, they suggest that distancing exercises such as the "leaves on a stream" work by locating thoughts at a spatial distance from oneself, which would result in a decrease in their functions.

Despite the merits of both proposals, we found at least one relevant omission and two areas where we disagree. The accounts omit the idea that teaching the clients to observe ongoing private events in a way that opens the door to other sources of stimulus control (i.e., framing private events in hierarchy with the deictic *I*; see the earlier section "An RFT Conceptualization of Cognitive (De)fusion") is a primary process involved in defusion exercises.

With this omission in mind, the first limitation is that the authors focus their attention on how defusion exercises may disrupt the transformation of functions. This seems to be true when one is practicing some defusion exercises in the therapy room (e.g., word-repetition exercise), but not when one is behaving outside. In everyday interactions, the extensive learning history in the context of literality will likely prevail over the brief defusion exercises practiced in the therapy room. Thus, "negative" thoughts will more likely elicit aversive functions automatically, and the client will have to respond to these functions in some way. It seems more likely that defusion exercises such as the word-repetition or distancing exercises teach clients to observe thoughts as transitory and arbitrary events. In this way, the thoughts used in the defusion practice (and others symbolically related to them) will probably acquire discriminative functions for framing them in hierarchy with the deictic *I*. This suggestion is in line with the following statement by Hayes et al. (2012): "Defusion does not eliminate verbal meaning—it just reduces its automatic effect on behavior such that other sources of behavioral regulation can better participate in the moment" (p. 245).

The second limitation is that we find that both conceptualizations fail to explore the temporal nature of the changes produced by defusion exercises. We will explain this point by commenting on some of Assaz et al.'s suggestions. These authors propose that the exercises that change language parameters (e.g., the word-repetition exercise) are exposure exercises that could work through respondent extinction, counterconditioning, or learning inhibition. Due to the procedure, it seems logical to think this way. However, it seems unlikely that these processes play a significant role in behavior change at the beginning of the therapy. Exposure techniques usually produce changes in behavior after several sessions. Following the idea presented in the previous paragraph, it seems more likely (and also more coherent with our clinical experience) that these exercises provide discriminative functions to frame these thoughts in hierarchy with the deictic *I*. The generation of these discriminative functions seems to be considerably faster than, for example, the respondent extinction that exposure techniques might provoke. Importantly, once the individual begins to frame aversive thoughts in hierarchy with the deictic *I*, instead of responding in coordination with their discriminative avoidance functions, respondent extinction will play a role in decreasing the emotional functions of the thoughts. In other words, it seems more likely that respondent extinction occurs after some practice in framing private events in hierarchy with the deictic *I*.

A similar rationale can be applied to the other processes suggested by Assaz et al. (2018). For instance, it is unlikely that defusion exercises will produce sufficient differential reinforcement of alternative responses (DRA) to overcome the clients' previous practice with avoidance responses. It seems more probable that DRA will occur after the client's practice in distancing from the predominant functions of private events. More importantly, when DRA is repeated due to framing private events in hierarchy, their predominant discriminative avoidance functions can be changed for other discriminative functions associated with the DRA process.

Our suggestion about the processes involved in defusion exercises highlights the role of hierarchically framing behavior with the deictic *I*. This analysis is derived from the RFT conceptualization presented previously that has produced some empirical analyses that will be presented later in this article. Further experimental analyses are needed to test if framing behavior in hierarchy is the predominant process of change of cognitive defusion exercises.

Measurement of Cognitive Defusion

Self-Report Instruments

Many self-report measures of cognitive defusion have been developed in the last decade. We will focus on those that were developed following the ACT conceptualization of these processes. Note, however, that other instruments have been developed for measuring related constructs such as decentering (Experiences Questionnaire-Decentering Scale—EQ-D; Fresco et al., 2007). Table 9.3 presents a summary of the cognitive (de)fusion instruments developed to date.

COGNITIVE FUSION QUESTIONNAIRE (CFQ; GILLANDERS ET AL, 2014)

The CFQ is the most widely used instrument to measure cognitive fusion as a trait and across contexts. It consists of seven items that are responded to on a 7-point Likert-type scale (7 = *always*; 1 = *never true*), with higher scores indicating a higher degree of cognitive fusion. The original validation study was conducted with a total sample of 1,800 participants (Gillanders et al., 2014). The CFQ demonstrated excellent internal consistency with Cronbach's alpha scores above.88 across samples, good test–retest reliability, a one-factor structure, discriminant validity, construct validity, and sensitivity to treatment effects.

The CFQ has been translated into several languages, including Spanish, French, German, Korean, Catalan, and Italian. These different versions of the questionnaire have shown similar psychometric properties to the original (i.e., excellent internal consistency and a one-factor structure) and overall convergent and concurrent validity (China, Hansen, Gillanders, & Benninghoven, 2018; Dionne et al., 2016; Kim & Cho, 2015; Oppo et al., 2019; Ruiz, Suárez-Falcón, Riaño-Hernández, & Gillanders, 2017; Solé et al., 2015).

A state version of the CFQ has also been developed (SCFQ; Bolderston, Gillanders, Turner, Taylor, & Coleman, 2019). The SCFQ items are very similar to the CFQ items, but they were rewritten to address fusion in the present moment. Additionally, the SCFQ instructions ask respondents to indicate how true each statement is for them at this moment. The SCFQ showed excellent internal consistency, a one-factor structure, stability over time, and sensitivity to short-term treatment effects. Accordingly, the SCFQ is especially well suited to be administered in laboratory-based studies implementing cognitive fusion inductions or analyzing the effect of brief defusion exercises or more general interventions.

Table 9.3. Summary of the self-report instruments designed to measure cognitive (de)fusion

Study	Instrument	N	N. Items	Scale	α	Factor Structure	Population	Items examples	Languages
Gillanders et al. (2014)	Cognitive Fusion Questionnaire (CFQ)	1800	7	7-point Likert-type scale (7 = *always*; 1 = *never true*)	.88	One-factor	Adults	"My thoughts cause me distress or emotional pain."	English German French Korean Italian Spanish
Bolderston et al. (2019)	State version of the Cognitive Fusion Questionnaire (SCFQ)	379	7	7-point Likert-type scale (7 = *always*; 1 = *never true*)	.95	One-factor	Adults	"I am very entangled in my thoughts."	English
Ferreira, Trindade, Duarte, & Pinto-Gouveia. (2015)	Cognitive Fusion Questionnaire—Body Image (CFQ-BI)	929	10	7-point Likert-type scale (7 = *always*; 1 = *never true*)	.96	One-factor	Adults	"I struggle with my thoughts related to my body or physical appearance."	English Portuguese
Trindade, Ferreira, & Pinto-Gouveia (2018a)	Cognitive Fusion Questionnaire-Chronic Illness (CFQ)	120	7	7-point Likert-type scale (7 = *always*; 1 = *never true*)	.97	One-factor	Adults	"I tend to get very entangled in my thoughts relating to my illness and/or symptoms."	English Portuguese
Duarte, Pinto-Gouveia, Ferreira, & Silva (2016)	Cognitive Fusion Questionnaire–Food Craving (CFQ-FC)	872	7	7-point Likert-type scale (7 = *always*; 1 = *never true*)	.94	One-factor	Adults	"My food-related thoughts cause me distress or emotional pain."	English Portuguese

(*continued*)

Table 9.3. *Continued*

Study	Instrument	N	N. Items	Scale	α	Factor Structure	Population	Items examples	Languages
Herzberg et al. (2012)	Believability of Anxious Feelings and Thoughts Questionnaire (BAFT)	935	16	7-point Likert-type scale (7 = *completely true*; 1 = *completely untrue*)	.95	A hierarchical factor with two or three lower-order factors	Adults	"I could lose control of myself when I feel anxious or afraid."	English Farsi Spanish
Forman et al. (2012a)	The Drexel Defusion Scale (DDS)	379	10	6-point Liker type scale (0 = *not at all*; 5 = *very much*)	.83-.80	One-factor	Adults	"Anxious thoughts. Things have not been going well at school or at your job, and work just keeps piling up. To what extent would you normally be able to defuse from anxious thoughts like "I'll never get this done."	English
Rolffs, Rogge, & Wilson (2016)	Multidimensional Psychological Flexibility Inventory (MPFI)	3040	60	6-point Likert-type scale (0 = *never*; 5 = *always*)	.88 (PF) .92 (PI)	Two higher-order factors	Adults	"It was very easy to get trapped into unwanted thoughts and feelings."	English Mandarin Japanese
Greco, Lambert, & Baer (2008)	Avoidance and Fusion Questionnaire for Youth (AFQ-Y)	1369	17	5-point Likert-type scale (4 = *very true*; 0 = *not at all true*)	.83	No conclusive results (one-factor)	Children and Adolescents	"My life won't be good until I feel happy," "My thoughts and feelings mess up my life"	English Persian Dutch Spanish Italian

The CFQ has also been adapted to specific contexts or disorders, including body image (Cognitive Fusion Questionnaire—Body Image, CFQ-BI; Ferreira et al. Pinto-Gouveia, 2015), chronic illness (Cognitive Fusion Questionnaire—Chronic Illness, CFQ-CI; Trindade, Barbosa, Ferreira, & Pinto-Gouveia, 2020; Trindade, Ferreira et al., 2018a), and food craving (Cognitive Fusion Questionnaire—Food Craving, CFQ-FC; Duarte et al. 2016). The validation studies have found similar psychometric properties to the original CFQ.

BELIEVABILITY OF ANXIOUS FEELINGS AND THOUGHTS QUESTIONNAIRE (BAFT; HERZBERG ET AL., 2012)

The BAFT is a 16-item questionnaire that measures cognitive fusion with anxious thoughts and feelings through a 7-point Likert-type scale (7 = *completely believable;* 1 = *not at all believable*). The initial validation study was conducted with a total sample of 935 participants, including undergraduates and highly anxious individuals (Herzberg et al., 2012). The BAFT showed excellent internal consistency (Cronbach's alpha of .90 to .91 across samples), a hierarchical factor structure with three lower-order factors and one hierarchical factor, convergent validity, and sensitivity to treatment effects. The BAFT has been translated into Spanish (Ruiz, Odriozola-González, & Suárez-Falcón, 2014) and Farsi (Mohammadipour & Ardehaee, 2016), showing similar psychometric properties to the original version.

DREXEL DEFUSION SCALE (DDS; FORMAN ET AL., 2012B)

The DDS is a 10-item self-report measure that evaluates the degree to which an individual defuses from unpleasant internal experiences through a 6-point Likert-type scale (0 = *not at all*; 5 = *very much*). The DDS defines defusion in its introduction to facilitate the participant's understanding of the concept. The initial validation study was conducted with a sample of 379 individuals, including undergraduates and clinical participants. The DDS showed good internal consistency (Cronbach's alpha from.80 to.83), a one-factor structure, and convergent and discriminant validity.

MULTIDIMENSIONAL PSYCHOLOGICAL FLEXIBILITY INVENTORY (MPFI; ROLFFS, ROGGE, & WILSON, 2016)

The MPFI is a 60-item self-report measure that evaluates psychological flexibility and inflexibility through a 6-point Likert-type scale (5 = *always*; 0 = *never*). The MPFI was designed to assess the six processes involved in psychological flexibility (i.e., acceptance, contact with the present moment, self as context, cognitive defusion, committed action, and values) and the six processes contained in psychological inflexibility (i.e., experiential avoidance, lack of contact with the present moment, self as content, fusion, inaction, and lack of contact with values). The validation study of the MPFI conducted with a total sample of 3,040 participants showed the expected factor structure with two higher-order factors that contained the six processes of psychological flexibility and inflexibility, respectively (Rolffs et al., 2016; Seidler, Stone, Clark, Koran, & Drake, 2020). The cognitive fusion and cognitive defusion subscales of the MPFI showed excellent internal consistency and convergent validity. The MPFI has been translated into Mandarin, simplified Mandarin, and Japanese (Lin, Rogge, & Swanson, 2020).

AVOIDANCE AND FUSION QUESTIONNAIRE—YOUTH (AFQ-Y; GRECO ET AL., 2008)

The AFQ-Y is a self-report measure of psychological inflexibility in children and adolescents. It consists of 17 items that are responded to on a 5-point Likert-type scale (4 = *very true*; 0 = *not at all true*). In the initial validation study, Greco et al. (2008) recruited a total sample of 1,369 children and adolescents. The AFQ-Y showed good internal consistency, a one-factor model, convergent, and construct validity. A short, 8-item version of the AFQ was also created (i.e., AFQ-8). Subsequent studies have found divergences regarding the factor structure of the AFQ, with some studies finding two factors: experiential avoidance and cognitive fusion (Livheim et al., 2016; Renshaw, 2018; Valdivia-Salas, Martín-Albo, Zaldivar, Lombas, & Jiménez, 2017). However, other studies have found that the one-factor model is adequate (Salazar et al., 2019; Schweiger et al., 2017; Simon & Verboon, 2016). Conversely, the AFQ-8 has consistently been shown to be a unidimensional measure across studies.

The AFQ-Y has been translated into several languages, including Spanish, Italian, Dutch, and Persian (García-Rubio et al., 2020; Salazar et al., 2019; Schweiger et al., 2017; Simon & Verboon, 2016; Valdivia-Salas et al., 2017). These adaptations have shown psychometric properties similar to the original version of the AFQ-Y.

Behavioral Measures

To our knowledge, no behavioral measures of cognitive (de)fusion have been developed. However, if we conceptualize cognitive fusion as responding in coordination to the transformed or actualized stimulus functions, inhibitory control tests could be seen as cognitive (de)fusion measures. This type of test asks participants to inhibit predominant behaviors and respond under the control of alternative stimulus functions. One of the most widely used inhibitory control tests is the Stroop Color and Word Test (SCWT; Stroop, 1935), in which participants are asked to name the ink color of words disregarding their meaning. For a proficient reader, reading is the predominant behavior response in the presence of words independently of their ink color. To obtain good performance in the SCWT, the participant has to inhibit the behavior of reading and only focus on the ink color's perceptual functions. In the traditional SCWT, the words that generate interference in the participant's performance are color names, which can be considered neutral stimuli. There are, however, a variety of Emotional Stroop Tasks (EST) that include stimuli with relevant functions (Williams, Mathews, & MacLeod, 1996). These versions of the Stroop Test might be used to measure cognitive fusion with words related to the client's problem (e.g., words related to anxiety, depression, fear).

The relationship between inhibitory control and cognitive (de)fusion has been addressed in only a few studies. For instance, Thomas and Bardeen (2020) found that inhibitory control moderated the relationship between cognitive fusion and anxiety. In another study, Pilecki and McKay (2012) found that participants in the defusion condition reacted slightly faster to the SCWT after being exposed to a negative emotion induction. Further research is needed to explore the suitability of inhibitory control tests as potential behavioral measures of cognitive (de)fusion.

Assessing Cognitive Defusion in the Clinical Session

To the best of our knowledge, there are no instruments that measure cognitive (de)fusion in clinical sessions. However, some verbal and nonverbal clues could indicate the degree of cognitive fusion that clients experience. For instance, Hayes et al. (2012) suggested that the most common examples are making repetitive statements, frequent comparisons, and constant evaluations that surpass objective descriptions. On some occasions, the client can also seem troubled, confused, or even exhibit signs of having "internal" arguments to decide what to do. The client may also attempt to justify their behavior and motivations. Lastly, cognitive fusion is also exemplified when the client perseveres in their beliefs without considering other perspectives. Blackledge (2015) suggests the following examples as potential cognitive fusion indicators: describing disturbing thoughts as absolute truths without considering other perspectives, an accelerated speech rate, and nonverbal behavior that matches the emotion and intensity of the client. It is also necessary to mention a couple of aspects that should be considered when assessing cognitive fusion in the clinical session. First, cognitive fusion varies among clients, and while a client might recognize some thoughts as just thoughts, they could be entangled with other thoughts. Second, cognitive fusion can also occur with positive thoughts, which can be as problematic as fusion with negative thoughts.

Hayes et al. (2012) mention that signs of progress include identifying when the thought process starts, categorizing thoughts as thoughts, and using a more descriptive discourse with fewer evaluations and comparisons. Blackledge (2015) mentioned additional examples, such as a relatively slower speech rate, using metaphors to describe internal experiences, utilizing less negative or positive emotional content in speech, separating oneself from one's thoughts, and acknowledging that thoughts are not equal to absolute truths.

Research on Cognitive Defusion

Component and Laboratory Research

We have identified approximately 40 experimental studies analyzing a wide array of cognitive defusion exercises. Because in some cases it is not easy to differentiate defusion from self-as-context exercises, we have judiciously included studies in this section. The dependent variables used across studies can be categorized in believability and emotional distress of private events and behavioral measures reflecting psychological flexibility. This section will differentiate studies that compared the relative efficacy of cognitive defusion interventions versus other strategies and studies that analyzed the variables involved in the effect of defusion exercises.

LABORATORY RESEARCH COMPARING COGNITIVE DEFUSION VERSUS OTHER STRATEGIES

Cognitive defusion has been shown to be more effective than inactive control and placebo conditions in increasing pain tolerance (Carrasquillo & Zettle, 2014), distress (Hinton & Gaynor, 2010) and decreasing thought believability (Prudenzi et al., 2019). Cognitive defusion conditions are also considered to be more efficacious than experiential avoidance (Hooper, Dack, Karekla, Niyazi, & McHugh, 2018), thought control (Gutiérrez, Luciano, Rodríguez, & Fink, 2004; Masuda, Hayes, Sackett, & Twohig, 2004; McMullen et al., 2008), thought suppression (Hooper, Sandoz, Ashton, Clarke, & McHugh, 2012), distraction (Hooper & McHugh, 2013; Mandavia et al., 2015; Masuda et al., 2004; Masuda, Feinstein, Wendell, & Sheehan, 2010; Masuda, Twohig, et al., 2010; Ritzert, Forsyth, Berghoff, Barnes-Holmes, & Nicholson, 2015), self-affirmations (Brandrick, Hooper, Roche, Kanter, & Tyndall, 2020), and general motivational protocols (Luciano et al., 2014). Schumacher, Kemps, and Tiggemann (2017, 2018) found that cognitive defusion was more efficacious than guided imagery in resisting food cravings in a general sample of women, but was equivalent in clinical samples of food cravers.

We have identified eight studies that compared the efficacy of cognitive defusion versus cognitive restructuring. The results showed equivalent efficacy in five of these studies (Barrera, Szafranski, Ratcliff, Garnaat, & Norton 2016; Beadman et al., 2015; Deacon, Fawzy, Lickel, & Wolitzky-Taylor, 2011; Donati et al., 2019; Yovel, Mor, & Shakarov, 2014). However, three studies showed that cognitive defusion was more efficacious than cognitive restructuring (Karekla et al., 2020; Larsson, Hooper, Osborne, Bennett, & McHugh, 2016; Moffitt, Brinkworth, Noakes, & Mohr, 2012). Two of these three studies tested the efficacy of the interventions in food cravings (Karekla et al., 2020; Moffitt et al., 2012). In conclusion, cognitive defusion interventions seem to be at least as efficacious as cognitive restructuring, and there is some evidence that they might be more effective in some contexts, such as resisting food cravings.

VARIABLES INVOLVED IN THE EFFECT OF DEFUSION EXERCISES

Component studies have been conducted with two types of cognitive defusion exercises: deliteralization and distancing. The studies analyzing deliteralization exercises have used the classic word-repetition technique (WRT; Titchener, 1910). Masuda et al. (2009) found that the reduction of emotional discomfort and thought believability was higher when a self-relevant negative thought was rapidly repeated during 20–30 seconds compared to smaller periods. Tyndall, Papworth, Roche, and Bennett (2017) compared three rates of the repetition of a negative thought: 0.5, 1, and 2 seconds. The rates of 0.5 and 1 seconds were more effective than the 2-second rate in reducing thought believability and emotional discomfort.

Following the RFT conceptualization presented, Luciano et al. (2011) differentiated the type of relational framings involved in distancing exercises for the first time. In a preliminary study with at-risk adolescents, the authors analyzed the differential effect of two defusion protocols: Defusion I and Defusion II. Defusion I involved framing ongoing behavior only through deictic framings (I–Here, Behavior–There). This perspective allows observing the ongoing private events with distance and without judging them. Defusion II added hierarchical framings and questions to promote regulatory functions to the verbal discrimination of private events. Hierarchical framings were added with the aim of deriving an explicit relation of inclusion between the individual and their private events. These interactions promoted the experience of the self as a consistent locus for all private events (e.g., "I am more than all my thoughts," "This thought is only a transitory experience I am having," etc.). The promotion of regulatory functions involved questions to explicitly derive appetitive augmentals that allow contacting with values and the actions in coordination with them at that moment. In other words, these interactions were directed to facilitate making a choice according to the individual's values. The results showed that Defusion II had a greater effect on reducing the frequency of problematic behaviors and psychological inflexibility at the 4-month follow-up.

The results of the previous study have been replicated in four experimental analogs. (1) Foody, Barnes-Holmes, Barnes-Holmes, and Luciano (2013) found that Defusion II (called "hierarchical self as context") was more efficacious in reducing experimentally induced emotional distress than Defusion I. Similarly, (2) Foody, Barnes-Holmes, Barnes-Holmes, Rai, and Luciano (2015) found that protocols that included framing ongoing private events through hierarchical relations were more efficacious than those that only introduced deictic relations. (3) Gil-Luciano, Ruiz, Valdivia-Salas, and Suárez-Falcón (2017) showed that the Defusion II protocol was more effective in promoting tolerance of discomfort induced by the cold-pressor task and aversive films than the Defusion I protocol and a control condition. These changes were produced in the absence of reductions in the discomfort experienced by the participants. Lastly, (4) López-López and Luciano (2017) replicated the previous findings in a cognitive demanding task that provoked discomfort—the Paced Auditory Serial Addition Task–Computerized (PASAT-C; Lejuez, Kahler, & Brown, 2003). Participants in the Defusion II protocol showed greater performance improvements than participants in Defusion I and the control condition. There was no difference between participants in Defusion I and the control condition. As in the previous study, the advantage of Defusion II was produced in the absence of significant reductions in discomfort compared to the other experimental conditions. These findings mean that Defusion II protocols affected the performance on behavioral tasks by modifying the discriminative functions of aversive private events, but not the emotional functions.

In conclusion, research is advancing in identifying some of the components of cognitive defusion exercises that maximize their effect. In the WRT, the empirical evidence indicates that it is important to repeat the negative thought for at least 20–30 seconds and a repetition rate of 0.5–1 seconds. The empirical evidence also shows that including explicit hierarchical framings between the individual and their private events, and providing regulatory functions to this discrimination, enhance the efficacy of typical distancing exercises, such as the "leaves on the stream" (Hayes et al., 1999). Although further research is needed to identify the relational processes involved in the efficacy of defusion exercises, the existing empirical evidence has the potential to improve the efficacy of these exercises and, consequently, ACT interventions.

Survey Research

Multiple studies have been conducted during the last decade showing the pernicious role of cognitive fusion. For instance, cognitive fusion has shown strong positive associations with depression and anxiety (Bardeen & Fergus, 2016; O'Loughlin, Bennett, & O'Hayer, 2020; Pinto-Gouveia, Dinis, Gregório, & Pinto, 2020; Sood & Newman-Taylor, 2020), posttraumatic stress disorder (Bardeen & Fergus, 2016; Basharpoor, Mowlaie, & Sarafrazi, 2020; Cox, Motl, Bakker, & Lunt, 2018; Russell, Bardeen, Clayson, Dolan, & Fergus, 2020), pain (Angarita-Osorio et al., 2020; Carvalho, Trindade, Gillanders, Pinto-Gouveia, & Castilho, 2019; Özkan, Zale, Ring, & Vranceanu, 2017), harmful body image beliefs (Melo, Oliveira, & Ferreira, 2019; Trindade & Ferreira, 2015; Trindade, Ferreira, et al., 2018a; Zucchelli, White, & Williamson, 2020), and eating disorders (Duarte & Pinto-Gouveia, 2017; Scardera, Sacco, Di Sante, & Booij, 2020).

Cognitive fusion has also been negatively correlated with values (Berghoff, Ritzert, & Forsyth, 2018) and life satisfaction (Flynn, Hernandez, Hebert, James, & Kusick, 2018; Ruiz et al., 2019). Fewer studies have been conducted analyzing the association of cognitive defusion with mental health and quality of life. However, as expected, cognitive defusion has shown negative correlations with emotional symptoms and positive correlations with values and quality of life (Forman et al., 2012b; Rolffs et al., 2016).

Some longitudinal studies have been conducted analyzing the role of cognitive fusion in exacerbating psychological and health symptoms. For instance, Carvalho et al. (2019) conducted a study with 86 women experiencing chronic pain to analyze if cognitive fusion predicted depressive symptomatology over 12 months. The results showed that cognitive fusion predicted depressive symptomatology at baseline and its changes during the 12 months of study. Cookson, Luzon, Newland, and Kingston (2020) conducted a longitudinal study over six weeks with a sample of 97 nonclinical participants to analyze whether experiential avoidance and cognitive fusion mediated the effect of worry, rumination, and stressful life events on emotional symptoms. The results showed that cognitive fusion independently mediated the association between the predictors and outcomes.

Ruiz and Odriozola-González (2017) found that cognitive fusion longitudinally mediated the relationship between negative metacognitive beliefs and anxiety and stress symptoms in a nonclinical sample of 106 participants over a lapse of 9 months. Lastly, Trindade, Ferreira, et al. (2018b) conducted a study with 116 patients with inflammatory bowel disease over 18 months. Cognitive fusion presented a negative correlation with psychological and physical health symptoms and influenced changes in these symptoms during the course of the study.

Process of Change in Clinical Interventions

Parallel to the development of cognitive (de)fusion measures, an increasing number of clinical trials have analyzed whether cognitive defusion worked as a process of change in ACT interventions; preliminary responses to this question support the role of cognitive defusion as an important process of change in ACT. For instance, cognitive defusion has acted as a mediator in participants with anxiety disorders (Arch, Wolitzky-Taylor, Eifert, & Craske, 2012), social anxiety (Krafft, Twohig, & Levin, 2020), residual depression symptoms (Østergaard, Lundgren, Zettle, Landrø, & Haaland, 2020), undergraduates with anxiety and depression (Forman et al., 2012a), distressed and nondistressed college students (Levin, Krafft, & Twohig, 2020; Morin, Grégoire, & Lachance, 2020), stressed parents of children with autism (Blackledge & Hayes, 2006; Fung, Lake, Steel, Bryce, & Lunsky, 2018), and tinnitus-related stress (Hesser, Westin, Hayes, & Andersson, 2009). It has also been shown to promote mental health in undergraduate students (Viskovich & Pakenham, 2020). Interestingly, some evidence also supports the role of cognitive defusion as a process of change in other therapies, including cognitive-behavioral therapy (Arch et al., 2012).

Challenges and Future Research Directions

Although cognitive defusion research has undeniably advanced, significant challenges remain and there are areas in which further work is needed.

Challenges and Future Directions for Research

We have identified five main limitations in the current research on cognitive defusion. First, behavioral measures of cognitive (de)fusion have not been developed. Developing this type of measure seems important to complement self-report measures and establish bridges with other literature (e.g., executive functioning). In this sense, we have suggested that inhibitory control tests such as the classical Stroop test and some of its variations might be analyzed as potential cognitive fusion measures. Second, although the advance in the measurement of cognitive (de)fusion through self-report is relevant, few attempts to develop measures appropriate for ecological momentary assessment (EMA) studies have been conducted. EMA studies have become increasingly popular, notably in the last years. They seem to be a promising tool to analyze the efficacy and processes of change of psychological interventions at the individual level due to the intensive measurement they involve.

Third, more component studies of the verbal processes involved in defusion exercises are needed. These studies are advancing in identifying some of these processes, but further refinements are needed. For instance, the studies analyzing distancing exercises have compared the effect of deictic framing (called Defusion I) versus deictic framing + hierarchical framing + cues to provide regulatory functions (called Defusion II). However, no published studies have analyzed, for example, the effect of separating hierarchical framing interactions from cues to provide regulatory functions (but see the unpublished doctoral thesis by López, 2016). Other combinations of these three components also deserve to be investigated, and additional components can be identified (e.g., hierarchically framing the displayed valued behavior after defusing from aversive private events; see López, 2016). Lastly, we recommend analyzing the effect of the verbal processes involved in defusion in behavioral measures resembling psychological flexibility because they are more similar to the aim of the defusion exercises in clinical interventions than measures of distress or believability.

Fourth, defusion exercises can be applied to all types of private events, such as thoughts, emotions, and memories. However, there is apparently no published empirical evidence regarding the potential differential effect of directing defusion exercises to different types of private events. Is it more efficacious to use defusion with aversive and personally relevant private events than neutral private events? The most closely related research in this regard is the study conducted by Gil-Luciano, Tovar, Calderón-Hurtado, Sebastián, and Ruiz (submitted) with triggers for repetitive negative thinking (RNT). Gil-Luciano, Calderón-Hurtado, Tovar, Sebastián, and Ruiz (2019) found that triggers for RNT (i.e., worry, rumination) are usually organized in hierarchical networks, with a hierarchical trigger symbolically containing other more concrete triggers. Gil-Luciano et al. (submitted) tested the differential effect of Defusion I and Defusion II interventions either directed to the hierarchical trigger or a trigger in a lower-level of the hierarchy. The results showed that the Defusion II protocol directed to the hierarchical trigger was more effective than the remaining combinations and a control condition in reducing the detrimental effects of a rumination-induction procedure. These results are consistent with the proposal made in RNT-focused ACT protocols for identifying the hierarchy of triggers for RNT and directing the clinical intervention to the hierarchical trigger (e.g., Ruiz, Luciano, et al., 2020; Ruiz et al., 2016; Ruiz, Peña-Vargas et al., 2020). The study by Gil-Luciano et al. (submitted) opens an interesting research line that deserves further empirical analysis.

Lastly, more studies analyzing the role of cognitive defusion as a process of change in ACT and other psychological therapies are needed. The empirical evidence to date supports the mediator role of cognitive defusion in the treatment effect of ACT. However, the number of studies is still small, and the mediation analyses have been conducted at a nomothetic level. Further studies might use EMA methodology to analyze the mediator role of cognitive defusion at the individual level.

Challenges and Future Directions for Clinical Work

Some relevant challenges for the clinical work in cognitive defusion deserve attention, three of which are as follows. First, a wide range of tools are available to promote cognitive defusion. However, it has not been established what type of exercises might be more effective or in which order they should be introduced. Are distancing exercises more effective than metaphors or deliteralization exercises? Is it better to begin the intervention in cognitive defusion with experiential exercises than with metaphors to avoid intellectualizing this process?

Second, some cognitive defusion exercises might be too abstract to be used with younger clients. Few studies have specified the appropriate exercises for different developmental levels. In this sense, the RFT conceptualization of psychological flexibility might help to specify the minimum verbal repertoire needed to use cognitive defusion exercises (e.g., Luciano, Valdivia-Salas, Cabello, & Hernández, 2009; Ruiz & Perete, 2015). In the case of the child or adolescent who does not have this minimum verbal repertoire, the relational framings involved might be first trained (Fryling, Rehfeldt, Tarbox, & Hayes, 2020).

Lastly, the research found in component studies of cognitive defusion should be transferred to the practitioner's work in order to improve the efficacy of ACT. Accordingly, ACT manuals and protocols should introduce these findings to enhance the connection between basic and applied research.

Conclusions

Cognitive defusion is one of the most studied ACT midlevel processes. The review conducted in this article indicates that (1) there is a growing number of self-report measures of cognitive (de)fusion, with the CFQ being the most analyzed; (2) cognitive defusion protocols have been shown to be more effective than most of the strategies with which they have been compared; (3) component studies have advanced in identifying some of the variables involved in the efficacy of deliteralization and distancing exercises; (4) multiple cross-sectional and longitudinal studies have shown the pernicious role of cognitive fusion and the adaptive role of cognitive defusion; and (5) reductions of cognitive fusion have been shown to mediate the effect of ACT and other forms of psychological interventions in clinical trials. Additional research is needed in areas such as measurement, component studies, mediation analyses, and practitioners' ability to adopt the findings from experimental evidence that might foster the effect of ACT.

References

Angarita-Osorio, N., Pérez-Aranda, A., Feliu-Soler, A., Andrés-Rodríguez, L., Borràs, X., Suso-Ribera, C., & Luciano, J. V. (2020). Patients with fibromyalgia reporting severe pain but low impact of the syndrome: Clinical and pain-related cognitive features. *Pain Practice: The Official Journal of World Institute of Pain, 20,* 255–261 https://doi.org/10.1111/papr.12847

Arch, J. J., Wolitzky-Taylor, K. B., Eifert, G. H., & Craske, M. G. (2012). Longitudinal treatment mediation of traditional cognitive behavioral therapy and acceptance and commitment therapy for anxiety disorders. *Behaviour Research and Therapy, 50,* 469–478.

Assaz, D. A., Roche, B., Kanter, J. W., & Oshiro, C. K. (2018). Cognitive defusion in acceptance and commitment therapy: What are the basic processes of change? *The Psychological Record, 68,* 405–418.

Bardeen, J. R., & Fergus, T. A. (2016). The interactive effect of cognitive fusion and experiential avoidance on anxiety, depression, stress and posttraumatic stress symptoms. *Journal of Contextual Behavioral Science, 5,* 1–6. https://doi.org/10.1016/j.jcbs.2016.02.002

Barrera, T. L., Szafranski, D. D., Ratcliff, C. G., Garnaat, S. L., & Norton, P. J. (2016). An experimental comparison of techniques: Cognitive defusion, cognitive restructuring, and in-vivo exposure for social anxiety. *Behavioural and Cognitive Psychotherapy, 44,* 249–254. https://doi.org/10.1017/S1352465814000630

Basharpoor, S., Mowlaie, M., & Sarafrazi, L. (2020). The relationships of distress tolerance, self-compassion to post-traumatic growth, the mediating role of cognitive fusion. *Journal of Aggression, Maltreatment and Trauma,* 1–12. https://doi.org/10.1080/10926771.2019.1711279

Beadman, M., Das, R. K., Freeman, T. P., Scragg, P., West, R., & Kamboj, S. K. (2015). A comparison of emotion regulation strategies in response to craving cognitions: Effects on smoking behaviour, craving and affect in dependent smokers. *Behaviour Research and Therapy, 69,* 29–39. https://doi.org/10.1016/j.brat.2015.03.013

Bennett, R., & Oliver, J. E. (2019). *Acceptance and commitment therapy: 100 key points and techniques.* London: Routledge.

Berghoff, C. R., Ritzert, T. R., & Forsyth, J. P. (2018). Value-guided action: Within-day and lagged relations of experiential avoidance, mindful awareness, and cognitive fusion in a nonclinical sample. *Journal of Contextual Behavioral Science, 10,* 19–23. https://doi.org/10.1016/j.jcbs.2018.07.005

Blackledge, J. T. (2007). Disrupting verbal processes: Cognitive defusion in acceptance and commitment therapy and other mindfulness-based psychotherapies. *The Psychological Record, 57,* 555–576.

Blackledge, J. T. (2015). *Cognitive defusion in practice: A clinician's guide to assessing, observing, and supporting change in your client.* Oakland, CA: New Harbinger Publications.

Blackledge, J. T., & Hayes, S. C. (2006). Using acceptance and commitment training in the support of parents of children diagnosed with autism. *Child and Family Behavior Therapy, 28,* 1–18. https://doi.org/10.1300/J019v28n01_01

Bolderston, H., Gillanders, D. T., Turner, G., Taylor, H. C., & Coleman, A. (2019). The initial validation of a state version of the Cognitive Fusion Questionnaire. *Journal of Contextual Behavioral Science, 12,* 207–215. https://doi.org/10.1016/j.jcbs.2018.04.002

Brandrick, C., Hooper, N., Roche, B., Kanter, J., & Tyndall, I. (2020). A comparison of ultra-brief cognitive defusion and positive affirmation interventions on the reduction of public speaking anxiety. *The Psychological Record,* 1–9. https://doi.org/10.1007/s40732-020-00432-z

Carrasquillo, N., & Zettle, R. D. (2014). Comparing a brief self-as-context exercise to control-based and attention placebo protocols for coping with induced pain. *The Psychological Record, 64,* 659–669. https://doi.org/10.1007/s40732-014-0074-3

Carvalho, S. A., Trindade, I. A., Gillanders, D., Pinto-Gouveia, J., & Castilho, P. (2019). Cognitive fusion and depressive symptoms in women with chronic pain: A longitudinal growth curve modelling study over 12 months. *Clinical Psychology and Psychotherapy, 26,* 616–625. https://doi.org/10.1002/cpp.2386

China, C., Hansen, L. B., Gillanders, D. T., & Benninghoven, D. (2018). Concept and validation of the German version of the Cognitive Fusion Questionnaire (CFQ-D). *Journal of Contextual Behavioral Science, 9,* 30–35. https://doi.org/10.1016/j.jcbs.2018.06.003

Cookson, C., Luzon, O., Newland, J., & Kingston, J. (2020). Examining the role of cognitive fusion and experiential avoidance in predicting anxiety and depression. *Psychology and Psychotherapy: Theory, Research and Practice, 93,* 456–473. https://doi.org/10.1111/papt.12233

Cox, D. W., Motl, T. C., Bakker, A. M., & Lunt, R. A. (2018). Cognitive fusion and post-trauma functioning in veterans: Examining the mediating roles of emotion dysregulation. *Journal of Contextual Behavioral Science, 8,* 1–7. https://doi.org/10.1016/j.jcbs.2018.02.002

Dahl, J., Stewart, I., Martell, C. R., & Kaplan, J. S. (2014). *ACT and RFT in relationships: Helping clients deepen intimacy and maintain healthy commitments using acceptance and commitment therapy and relational frame theory.* Oakland, CA: New Harbinger Publications.

Deacon, B. J., Fawzy, T. I., Lickel, J. J., & Wolitzky-Taylor, K. B. (2011). Cognitive defusion versus cognitive restructuring in the treatment of negative self-referential thoughts: An investigation of process and outcome. *Journal of Cognitive Psychotherapy, 25*, 218–232. https://doi.org/10.1891/0889-8391.25.3.218

Dionne, F., Gagnon, J., Balbinotti, M., Peixoto, E., Martel, M. E., Gillanders, D., & Monestès, J. L. (2016). "Buying into thoughts": Validation of a French translation of the Cognitive Fusion Questionnaire. *Canadian Journal of Behavioural Science/Revue canadienne des sciences du comportement, 48*(4), 278–285. https://doi.org/10.1037/cbs0000053

Donati, M. R., Masuda, A., Schaefer, L. W., Cohen, L. L., Tone, E. B., & Parrott, D. J. (2019). Laboratory analogue investigation of defusion and reappraisal strategies in the context of symbolically generalized avoidance. *Journal of the Experimental Analysis of Behavior, 112*, 225–241. https://doi.org/10.1002/jeab.550

Duarte, C., & Pinto-Gouveia, J. (2017). The impact of early shame memories in Binge Eating Disorder: The mediator effect of current body image shame and cognitive fusion. *Psychiatry Research, 258*, 511–517. https://doi.org/10.1016/j.psychres.2017.08.086

Duarte, C., Pinto-Gouveia, J., Ferreira, C., & Silva, B. (2016). Caught in the struggle with food craving: Development and validation of a new cognitive fusion measure. *Appetite, 101*, 146–155. https://doi.org/10.1016/j.appet.2016.03.004

Ferreira, C., Trindade, I. A., Duarte, C., & Pinto-Gouveia, J. (2015). Getting entangled with body image: Development and validation of a new measure. *Psychology and Psychotherapy: Theory, Research and Practice, 88*, 304–316. https://doi.org/10.1111/papt.12047

Flynn, M. K., Hernandez, J. O., Hebert, E. R., James, K. K., & Kusick, M. K. (2018). Cognitive fusion among hispanic college students: Further validation of the Cognitive Fusion Questionnaire. *Journal of Contextual Behavioral Science, 7*, 29–34. https://doi.org/10.1016/j.jcbs.2017.11.003

Foody, M., Barnes-Holmes, Y., Barnes-Holmes, D., & Luciano, C. (2013). An empirical investigation of hierarchical versus distinction relations in a self-based ACT exercise. *International Journal of Psychology and Psychological Therapy, 13*, 373–388.

Foody, M., Barnes-Holmes, Y., Barnes-Holmes, D., Rai, L., & Luciano, C. (2015). An empirical investigation of the role of self, hierarchy, and distinction in a common ACT exercise. *The Psychological Record, 65*, 231–243. https://doi.org/10.1007/s40732-014-0103-2

Forman, E. M., Chapman, J. E., Herbert, J. D., Goetter, E. M., Yuen, E. K., & Moitra, E. (2012a). Using session-by-session measurement to compare mechanisms of action for acceptance and commitment therapy and cognitive therapy. *Behavior Therapy, 43*, 341–354. https://doi.org/10.1016/j.beth.2011.07.004

Forman, E. M., Herbert, J. D., Juarascio, A. S., Yeomans, P. D., Zebell, J. A., Goetter, E. M., & Moitra, E. (2012b). The Drexel Defusion Scale: A new measure of experiential distancing. *Journal of Contextual Behavioral Science, 1*, 55–65. https://doi.org/10.1016/j.jcbs.2012.09.001

Fresco, D. M., Moore, M. T., van Dulmen, M. H., Segal, Z. V., Ma, S. H., Teasdale, J. D., & Williams, J. M. G. (2007). Initial psychometric properties of the experiences questionnaire: validation of a self-report measure of decentering. *Behavior Therapy, 38*, 234–246. https://doi.org/10.1016/j.beth.2006.08.003

Fryling, M., Rehfeldt, R. A., Tarbox, J., & Hayes, L. J. (Eds.). (2020). *Applied behavior analysis of language and cognition: Core concepts and principles for practitioners.* Oakland, CA: New Harbinger Publications.

Fung, K., Lake, J., Steel, L., Bryce, K., & Lunsky, Y. (2018). ACT processes in group intervention for mothers of children with autism spectrum disorder. *Journal of Autism and Developmental Disorders, 48*(8), 2740–2747. https://doi.org/10.1007/s10803-018-3525-x

García-Rubio, C., Lecuona, O., Blanco Donoso, L. M., Cantero-García, M., Paniagua, D., & Rodríguez-Carvajal, R. (2020). Spanish validation of the short-form of the Avoidance and Fusion Questionnaire (AFQ-Y8) with children and adolescents. *Psychological Assessment, 32*, e15–e27. https://doi.org/10.1037/pas0000801

Gil-Luciano, B., Calderón-Hurtado, T., Tovar, D., Sebastián, B., & Ruiz, F. J. (2019). How are triggers for repetitive negative thinking organized? A relational frame analysis. *Psicothema, 31*, 53–59.

Gil-Luciano, B., Ruiz, F. J., Valdivia-Salas, S., & Suárez-Falcon, J. C. (2017). Promoting psychological flexibility on tolerance tasks: Framing behavior through deictic/hierarchical relations and specifying augmental functions. *The Psychological Record, 67*, 1–10. https://doi.org/10.1007/s40732-016-0200-5

Gillanders, D. T., Bolderston, H., Bond, F. W., Dempster, M., Flaxman, P. E., Campbell, L., . . . Remington, B. (2014). The development and initial validation of the cognitive fusion questionnaire. *Behavior Therapy, 45*, 83–101. https://doi.org/10.1016/j.beth.2013.09.001

Greco, L. A., Lambert, W., & Baer, R. A. (2008). Psychological inflexibility in childhood and adolescence: Development and evaluation of the Avoidance and Fusion Questionnaire for Youth. *Psychological Assessment, 20*, 93–102. https://doi.org/10.1037/1040-3590.20.2.93

Gutiérrez, O., Luciano, C., Rodríguez, M., & Fink, B. C. (2004). Comparison between an acceptance-based and a cognitive-control-based protocol for coping with pain. *Behavior Therapy, 35*, 767–783.

Hayes, S. C., & Strosahl, K. D. (2005). *A practical guide to acceptance and commitment therapy.* New York: Springer.

Hayes, S. C., Strosahl, K. D., & Wilson, K. G. (1999). *Acceptance and commitment therapy. An experiential approach to behavior change.* New York: Guilford Press.

Hayes, S. C., Strosahl, K. D., & Wilson, K. G. (2012). *Acceptance and commitment therapy: The process and practice of mindful change.* New York: Guilford Press

Herzberg, K. N., Sheppard, S. C., Forsyth, J. P., Credé, M., Earleywine, M., & Eifert, G. H. (2012). The Believability of Anxious Feelings and Thoughts Questionnaire (BAFT): A psychometric evaluation of cognitive fusion in a nonclinical and highly anxious community sample. *Psychological Assessment, 24,* 877–891. https://doi.org/10.1037/a0027782

Hesser, H., Westin, V., Hayes, S. C., & Andersson, G. (2009). Clients' in-session acceptance and cognitive defusion behaviors in acceptance-based treatment of tinnitus distress. *Behaviour Research and Therapy, 47,* 523–528. https://doi.org/10.1016/j.brat.2009.02.002

Hinton, M., & Gaynor, S. (2010). Cognitive defusion for psychological distress, dysphoria, and low self-esteem: A randomized technique evaluation trial of vocalizing strategies. *International Journal of Behavioral and Consultation Therapy, 6,* 164–185. http://dx.doi.org/10.1037/h0100906

Hooper, N., Dack, C., Karekla, M., Niyazi, A., & McHugh, L. (2018). Cognitive defusion versus experiential avoidance in the reduction of smoking behaviour: An experimental and preliminary investigation. *Addiction Research and Theory, 26,* 414–420. https://doi.org/10.1080/16066359.2018.1434156

Hooper, N., & McHugh, L. (2013). Cognitive defusion versus thought distraction in the mitigation of learned helplessness. *The Psychological Record, 63,* 209–218. https://doi.org/10.11133/j.tpr.2013.63.1.016

Hooper, N., Sandoz, E. K., Ashton, J., Clarke, A., & McHugh, L. (2012). Comparing thought suppression and acceptance as coping techniques for food cravings. *Eating Behaviors, 1,* 62–64. https://doi.org/10.1016/j.eatbeh.2011.10.002

Karekla, M., Georgiou, N., Panayiotou, G., Sandoz, E. K., Kurz, A. S., & Constantinou, M. (2020). Cognitive restructuring vs. defusion: Impact on craving, healthy and unhealthy food intake. *Eating Behaviors, 37,* 101385. https://doi.org/10.1016/j.eatbeh.2020.101385

Kim, B. O., & Cho, S. (2015). Psychometric properties of a Korean version of the Cognitive Fusion Questionnaire. *Social Behavior and Personality: An International Journal, 43,* 1715–1723. https://doi.org/10.2224/sbp.2015.43.10.1715

Krafft, J., Twohig, M. P., & Levin, M. E. (2020). A randomized trial of acceptance and commitment therapy and traditional cognitive-behavioral therapy self-help books for social anxiety. *Cognitive Therapy and Research, 44.* 954–966. https://doi.org/10.1007/s10608-020-10114-3

Larsson, A., Hooper, N., Osborne, L. A., Bennett, P., & McHugh, L. (2016). Using brief cognitive restructuring and cognitive defusion techniques to cope with negative thoughts. *Behavior Modification, 40,* 452–482. https://doi.org/10.1177/0145445515621488

Lejuez, C. W., Kahler, C. W., & Brown, R. A. (2003). A modified computer version of the Paced Auditory Serial Addition Task (PASAT) as a laboratory-based stressor. *The Behavior Therapist, 26,* 290–293.

Levin, M. E., Krafft, J., & Twohig, M. P. (2020). Examining processes of change in an online acceptance and commitment therapy dismantling trial with distressed college students. *Journal of Contextual Behavioral Science, 17.* 10–16. https://doi.org/10.1016/j.jcbs.2020.05.001

Lin, Y. Y., Rogge, R. D., & Swanson, D. P. (2020). Cross-cultural flexibility: Validation of the traditional Mandarin, simplified Mandarin, and Japanese translations of the Multidimensional Psychological Flexibility Inventory. *Journal of Contextual Behavioral Science, 15,* 73–84. https://doi.org/10.1016/j.jcbs.2019.11.008

Livheim, F., Tengström, A., Bond, F. W., Andersson, G., Dahl, J., & Rosendahl, I. (2016). Psychometric properties of the Avoidance and Fusion Questionnaire for Youth: A psychological measure of psychological inflexibility in youth. *Journal of Contextual Behavioral Science, 5,* 103–110.

López, J. C. (2016). Experimental analysis of defusion and its impact on performance. Doctoral dissertation, Universidad de Almería (Spain).

López-López, J. C., & Luciano, C. (2017). An experimental analysis of defusion interactions based on deictic and hierarchical framings and their impact on cognitive performance. *The Psychological Record, 67,* 485–497. https://doi.org/10.1007/s40732-017-0250-3

Luciano, C., Ruiz, F. J., Torres, R. M. V., Martín, V. S., Martínez, O. G., & López, J. C. L. (2011). A relational frame analysis of defusion interactions in acceptance and commitment therapy. A preliminary and quasi-experimental study with at-risk adolescents. *International Journal of Psychology and Psychological Therapy, 11,* 165–182.

Luciano, C., Valdivia-Salas, S., Cabello, F., & Hernandez, M. (2009). Developing self-directed rules. In R. A. Rehfeldt & Y. Barnes-Holmes (Ed.), *Derived relational responding. Applications for learners with autism and other developmental disabilities* (pp. 335–352). Oakland, CA: Context Press.

Luciano, C., Valdivia-Salas, S., Ruiz, F. J., Rodríguez-Valverde, M., Barnes-Holmes, D., Dougher, M. J., . . . Gutierrez-Martínez, O. (2014). Effects of an acceptance/defusion intervention on experimentally

induced generalized avoidance: A laboratory demonstration. *Journal of the Experimental Analysis of Behavior, 101*, 94–111. https://doi.org/10.1002/jeab.68
Luoma, J. B., Hayes, S. C., & Walser, R. D. (2007). *Learning ACT: An acceptance and commitment therapy skills-training manual for therapists.* Oakland, CA: New Harbinger Publications.
Mandavia, A., Masuda, A., Moore, M., Mendoza, H., Donati, M. R., & Cohen, L. L. (2015). The application of a cognitive defusion technique to negative body image thoughts: A preliminary analogue investigation. *Journal of Contextual Behavioral Science, 4*, 86–95. https://doi.org/10.1016/j.jcbs.2015.02.003
Masuda, A., Feinstein, A. B., Wendell, J. W., & Sheehan, S. T. (2010). Cognitive defusion versus thought distraction: A clinical rationale, training, and experiential exercise in altering psychological impacts of negative self-referential thoughts. *Behavior Modification, 34*, 520–538. https://doi.org/10.1177/0145445510379632
Masuda, A., Hayes, S. C., Sackett, C. F., & Twohig, M. P. (2004). Cognitive defusion and self-relevant negative thoughts: Examining the impact of a ninety year old technique. *Behaviour Research and Therapy, 42*, 477–485. https://doi.org/10.1016/j.brat.2003.10.008
Masuda, A., Hayes, S. C., Twohig, M. P., Drossel, C., Lillis, J., & Washio, Y. (2009). A parametric study of cognitive defusion and the believability and discomfort of negative self-relevant thoughts. *Behavior Modification, 33*, 250–262. https://doi.org/10.1177/0145445508326259
Masuda, A., Twohig, M. P., Stormo, A. R., Feinstein, A. B., Chou, Y. Y., & Wendell, J. W. (2010). The effects of cognitive defusion and thought distraction on emotional discomfort and believability of negative self-referential thoughts. *Journal of Behavior Therapy and Experimental Psychiatry, 41*, 11–17. https://doi.org/10.1016/j.jbtep.2009.08.006
McEnteggart, C., Barnes-Holmes, Y., Hussey, I., & Barnes-Holmes, D. (2015). The ties between a basic science of language and cognition and clinical applications. *Current Opinion in Psychology, 2*, 56–59.
McMullen, J., Barnes-Holmes, D., Barnes-Holmes, Y., Stewart, I., Luciano, C., & Cochrane, A. (2008). Acceptance versus distraction: Brief instructions, metaphors and exercises in increasing tolerance for self-delivered electric shocks. *Behaviour Research and Therapy, 46*, 122–129.
Melo, D., Oliveira, S., & Ferreira, C. (2019). The link between external and internal shame and binge eating: The mediating role of body image-related shame and cognitive fusion. Eating and Weight Disorders-Studies on Anorexia, *Bulimia and Obesity*, 1–8. https://doi.org/10.1007/s40519-019-00811-8
Moffitt, R., Brinkworth, G., Noakes, M., & Mohr, P. (2012). A comparison of cognitive restructuring and cognitive defusion as strategies for resisting a craved food. *Psychology and Health, 27*, 74–90. https://doi.org/10.1080/08870446.2012.694436
Mohammadipour, M., & Ardehaee, F. N. (2016). A psychometric indices of the Farsi Version of the Believability of Anxious Feelings and Thoughts Questionnaire (BAFT). *International Journal of Mental Health and Addiction, 14*, 752–760. https://doi.org/10.1007/s11469-015-9624-4
Morin, L., Grégoire, S., & Lachance, L. (2020). Processes of change within acceptance and commitment therapy for university students: Preliminary evidence from a randomized controlled trial. *Journal of American College Health, 69*, 1–10. https://doi.org/10.1080/07448481.2019.1705828
O'Loughlin, C. M., Bennett, D. S., & O'Hayer, C. V. (2020). The nomological network of cognitive fusion among people living with HIV: Associations with rumination, shame, and depressive symptoms. *Journal of Contextual Behavioral Science, 15*, 245–252.
Oppo, A., Prevedini, A. B., Dell'Orco, F., Dordoni, P., Presti, G., Gillanders, D. T., & Moderato, P. (2019). Fusione e Defusione. Adattamento e proprietà psicometriche della versione italiana del Cognitive Fusion Questionnaire (I-CFQ). *Psicoterapia Cognitiva e Comportamentale , 25*. 53–73.
Østergaard, T., Lundgren, T., Zettle, R. D., Landrø, N. I., & Haaland, V. Ø. (2020). Psychological flexibility in depression relapse prevention: Processes of change and positive mental health in group-based ACT for residual symptoms. *Frontiers in Psychology, 11*, e528. https://doi.org/10.3389/fpsyg.2020.00528
Özkan, S., Zale, E. L., Ring, D., & Vranceanu, A. M. (2017). Associations between pain catastrophizing and cognitive fusion in relation to pain and upper extremity function among hand and upper extremity surgery patients. *Annals of Behavioral Medicine, 51*, 547–554. https://doi.org/10.1007/s12160-017-9877-1
Pilecki, B. C., & McKay, D. (2012). An experimental investigation of cognitive defusion. *The Psychological Record, 62*, 19–40.
Pinto-Gouveia, J., Dinis, A., Gregório, S., & Pinto, A. M. (2020). Concurrent effects of different psychological processes in the prediction of depressive symptoms—the role of cognitive fusion. *Current Psychology, 39*, 528–539. https://doi.org/10.1007/s12144-017-9767-5
Prudenzi, A., Rooney, B., Presti, G., Lombardo, M., Lombardo, D., Messina, C., & McHugh, L. (2019). Testing the effectiveness of virtual reality as a defusion technique for coping with unwanted thoughts. *Virtual Reality, 23*, 179–185. https://doi.org/10.1007/s10055-018-0372-1

Renshaw, T. L. (2018). Probing the relative psychometric validity of three measures of psychological inflexibility. *Journal of Contextual Behavioral Science, 7,* 47–54.

Ritzert, T. R., Forsyth, J. P., Berghoff, C. R., Barnes-Holmes, D., & Nicholson, E. (2015). The impact of a cognitive defusion intervention on behavioral and psychological flexibility: An experimental evaluation in a spider fearful nonclinical sample. *Journal of Contextual Behavioral Science, 4,* 112–120. https://doi.org/10.1016/j.jcbs.2015.04.001

Rolffs, J. L., Rogge, R. D., & Wilson, K. G. (2016). Disentangling components of flexibility via the hexaflex model: Development and validation of the Multidimensional Psychological Flexibility Inventory (MPFI). *Assessment, 25,* 458–482. https://doi.org/10.1177/1073191116645905

Ruiz, F. J., Luciano, C., Flórez, C. L., Suárez-Falcón, J. C., & Cardona-Betancourt, V. (2020). A multiple-baseline evaluation of RNT-focused acceptance and commitment therapy for comorbid generalized anxiety disorder and depression. *Frontiers in Psychology, 11,* 356.

Ruiz, F. J., & Odriozola-González, P. (2017). A longitudinal comparison of metacognitive therapy and acceptance and commitment therapy models of anxiety disorders. *Anales de Psicología, 33,* 7–17.

Ruiz, F., Odriozola-González, P., & Suárez-Falcón, J. (2014). The Spanish version of the Believability of Anxious Feelings and Thoughts Questionnaire. *Psicothema, 26,* 308–313. http://dx.doi.org/10.7334/psicothema2013.221

Ruiz, F. J., Peña-Vargas, A., Ramírez, E. S., Suárez-Falcón, J. C., García-Martín, M. B., García-Beltrán, D. M., . . . Sánchez, P. D. (2020). Efficacy of a two-session repetitive negative thinking-focused acceptance and commitment therapy (ACT) protocol for depression and generalized anxiety disorder: A randomized waitlist control trial. *Psychotherapy, 57,* 444–456.

Ruiz, F. J., & Perete, L. (2015). Application of a relational frame theory account of psychological flexibility in young children. *Psicothema, 27,* 114–119.

Ruiz, F. J., Riaño-Hernández, D., Suárez-Falcón, J. C., & Luciano, C. (2016). Effect of a one-session ACT protocol in disrupting repetitive negative thinking. *International Journal of Psychology and Psychological Therapy, 16,* 213–233.

Ruiz, F. J., Suárez-Falcón, J. C., Flórez, C. L., Odriozola-González, P., Tovar, D., López-González, S., & Baeza-Martín, R. (2019). Validity of the Satisfaction with Life Scale in Colombia and factorial equivalence with Spanish data. *Revista Latinoamericana de Psicología, 51,* 58–65. http://dx.doi.org/10.14349/rlp.2019.v51.n2.1

Ruiz, F. J., Suárez-Falcón, J. C., Riaño-Hernández, D., & Gillanders, D. (2017). Psychometric properties of the Cognitive Fusion Questionnaire in Colombia. *Revista Latinoamericana de Psicología, 49,* 80–87. http://dx.doi.org/10.1016/j.rlp.2016.09.006

Russell, L. H., Bardeen, J. R., Clayson, K. A., Dolan, S. L., & Fergus, T. A. (2020). The closed response style and post-traumatic stress: Examining the interaction between experiential avoidance and cognitive fusion among women experiencing sexual trauma. *Psychological Trauma: Theory, Research, Practice, and Policy, 12,* 627–634. https://doi.org/10.1037/tra0000580

Salazar, D. M., Ruiz, F. J., Suárez-Falcón, J. C., Barreto-Zambrano, M. L., Gómez-Barreto, M. P., & Flórez, C. L. (2019). Psychometric properties of the Avoidance and Fusion Questionnaire–Youth in Colombia. *Journal of Contextual Behavioral Science, 12,* 305–313. https://doi.org/10.1016/j.jcbs.2018.11.008

Scardera, S., Sacco, S., Di Sante, J., & Booij, L. (2020). Body image-related cognitive fusion and disordered eating: The role of self-compassion and sad mood. *Eating and Weight Disorders-Studies on Anorexia, Bulimia and Obesity,* 1–8. https://doi.org/10.1007/s40519-020-00868-w

Schumacher, S., Kemps, E., & Tiggemann, M. (2017). Acceptance- and imagery-based strategies can reduce chocolate cravings: A test of the elaborated-intrusion theory of desire. *Appetite, 113,* 63–70. https://doi.org/10.1016/j.appet.2017.02.012

Schumacher, S., Kemps, E., & Tiggemann, M. (2018). Cognitive defusion and guided imagery tasks reduce naturalistic food cravings and consumption: A field study. *Appetite, 127,* 393–399. https://doi.org/10.1016/j.appet.2018.05.018

Schweiger, M., Ristallo, A., Oppo, A., Pergolizzi, F., Presti, G., & Moderato, P. (2017). Ragazzi in lotta con emozioni e pensieri: la validazione della versione italiana dell'Avoidance and Fusion Questionnaire for Youth (I-AFQ-Y). *Psicoterapia Cognitiva e Comportamentale, 23,* 141–162.

Seidler, D., Stone, B., Clark, B. E., Koran, J., & Drake, C. E. (2020). Evaluating the factor structure of the Multidimensional Psychological Flexibility Inventory: An independent replication and extension. *Journal of Contextual Behavioral Science, 17,* 23–31. https://doi.org/10.1016/j.jcbs.2020.04.007

Simon, E., & Verboon, P. (2016). Psychological inflexibility and child anxiety. *Journal of Child and Family Studies, 25,* 3565–3573.

Solé, E., Racine, M., Castarlenas, E., de la Vega, R., Tomé-Pires, C., Jensen, M., & Miró, J. (2015). The Psychometric Properties of the Cognitive Fusion Questionnaire in Adolescents. *European Journal of Psychological Assessment, 32,* 181–186. https://doi.org/10.1027/1015-5759/a000244

Sood, M., & Newman-Taylor, K. (2020). Cognitive fusion mediates the impact of attachment imagery on paranoia and anxiety. *Cognitive Therapy and Research, 44*, 1–12. https://doi.org/10.1007/s10608-020-10127-y

Stroop, J. R. (1935). Studies of interference in serial verbal reactions. *Journal of Experimental Psychology, 18*, 643–662.

Thomas, K. N., & Bardeen, J. R. (2020). The buffering effect of attentional control on the relationship between cognitive fusion and anxiety. *Behaviour Research and Therapy, 132*, 103653.

Titchener, E. B. (1910). *A text-book of psychology*. New York: Macmillan.

Törneke, N., Luciano, C., Barnes-Holmes, Y., & Bond, F. W. (2016). RFT for clinical practice. In R. D. Zettle, S. C. Hayes, D. Barnes-Holmes, & A. Biglan (Eds.), *The Wiley Handbook of Contextual Behavioral Science* (pp. 254–272). New York: Wiley.

Trindade, I. A., Barbosa, R., Ferreira, C., & Pinto-Gouveia, J. (2020). Further validation of the Cognitive Fusion Questionnaire–Chronic Illness (CFQ-CI) in different health condition samples. *Journal of Contextual Behavioral Science, 16*, 45–48. https://doi.org/10.1016/j.jcbs.2020.03.004

Trindade, I. A., & Ferreira, C. (2015). Falling in the traps of your thoughts: The impact of body image-related cognitive fusion on inflexible eating. *Eating Behaviors, 19*, 49–52. https://doi.org/10.1016/j.eatbeh.2015.06.004

Trindade, I. A., Ferreira, C., & Pinto-Gouveia, J. (2018a). Assessment of chronic illness-related cognitive fusion: Preliminary development and validation of a new scale with an IBD sample. *Journal of Clinical Psychology in Medical Settings, 25*, 356–366. https://doi.org/10.1007/s10880-017-9536-5

Trindade, I. A., Ferreira, C., & Pinto-Gouveia, J. (2018b). The longitudinal effects of emotion regulation on physical and psychological health: A latent growth analysis exploring the role of cognitive fusion in inflammatory bowel disease. *British Journal of Health Psychology, 23*(1), 171–185.

Trindade, I. A., Marta-Simões, J., Ferreira, C., & Pinto-Gouveia, J. (2018). Chronic illness-related cognitive fusion explains the impact of body dissatisfaction and shame on depression symptoms in breast cancer patients. *Clinical Psychology and Psychotherapy, 25*, 886–893. https://doi.org/10.1002/cpp.2323

Tyndall, I., Papworth, R., Roche, B., & Bennett, M. (2017). Differential effects of word-repetition rate on cognitive defusion of believability and discomfort of negative self-referential thoughts postintervention and at one-month follow-up. *The Psychological Record, 67*, 377–386. https://doi.org/10.1007/s40732-017-0227-2

Valdivia-Salas, S., Martín-Albo, J., Zaldivar, P., Lombas, A. S., & Jiménez, T. I. (2017). Spanish validation of the Avoidance and Fusion Questionnaire for Youth (AFQ-Y). *Assessment, 24*, 919–931. https://doi.org/10.1177/1073191116632338

Vilardaga, R., Hayes, S. C., Levin, M. E., & Muto, T. (2009). Creating a strategy for progress: A contextual behavioral science approach. *The Behavior Analyst, 32*, 105–133.

Viskovich, S., & Pakenham, K. I. (2020). Randomized controlled trial of a web-based Acceptance and Commitment Therapy (ACT) program to promote mental health in university students. *Journal of Clinical Psychology, 76*, 929–951. https://doi.org/10.1002/jclp.22848

Williams, J. M. G., Mathews, A., & MacLeod, C. (1996). The emotional Stroop task and psychopathology. *Psychological Bulletin, 120*, 3–24.

Wilson, K. G. (2009). *Mindfulness for two: An acceptance and commitment therapy approach to mindfulness in psychotherapy*. Oakland, CA: New Harbinger Publications.

Wilson, K. G., & Luciano, M. C. (2002). *Terapia de aceptación y compromiso. Un tratamiento conductual orientado a los valores*. Madrid: Pirámide.

Yovel, I., Mor, N., & Shakarov, H. (2014). Examination of the core cognitive components of cognitive behavioral therapy and acceptance and commitment therapy: An analogue investigation. *Behavior Therapy, 45*, 482–494. https://doi.org/10.1016/j.beth.2014.02.007

Zucchelli, F., White, P., & Williamson, H. (2020). Experiential avoidance and cognitive fusion mediate the relationship between body evaluation and unhelpful body image coping strategies in individuals with visible differences. *Body Image, 32*, 121–127. https://doi.org/10.1016/j.bodyim.2019.12.002

CHAPTER

10 Present Moment Awareness

Matthew S. Herbert *and* Niloofar Afari

Abstract

Present moment awareness (PMA) is one of six interrelated processes that facilitate psychological flexibility within acceptance and commitment therapy (ACT). The process of PMA (1) brings deliberate attention to inner experiences such as thoughts, emotions, and physical sensations in the service of building psychological flexibility, and (2) increases the opportunity to come in contact with valued outer experiences. Thus, PMA can be considered a foundational process upon which other ACT processes rest, making it difficult to clearly distinguish PMA from the other ACT processes and study the unique impact of PMA in ACT interventions. This challenge is further complicated by inadequate measurement tools for PMA or mindfulness. The growing literature on the potential neurophysiological mechanisms of mindfulness in general suggests that this is a worthy area of study within ACT. Future studies should examine the potential benefits of formal mindfulness meditation practice in the context of ACT and capitalize on ecological momentary assessment and other technology to measure and support PMA and other ACT processes in real-world and real-time settings.

Key Words: mindfulness, meditation, private experience, ecological momentary assessment, acceptance and commitment therapy, present moment awareness, psychological flexibility

"Look past your thoughts, so you may drink the pure nectar of This Moment."

—*Rumi*

Humans possess the seemingly unique ability to be aware of their own responding in real time. Given that any clinical problem a client may face naturally unfolds in real time, strengthening present moment awareness (PMA) is key to promoting the alternative strategies being offered in acceptance and commitment therapy (ACT). However, the ultimate goal of intervention in ACT is psychological flexibility—the ability to stay open and fully present in the moment and to act guided by personal values. Thus, promoting awareness should serve a functional purpose and be reinforced based on evidence of workability.

Within ACT, PMA is defined as the focused, voluntary, and flexible orientation to present moment experiences (Hayes, Strosahl, & Wilson, 2012). In order to embrace what the present moment affords, some control over what and how experiences are attended to is needed. Being flexible is key because the present moment is constantly changing. What was once salient becomes trivial and vice versa. Sometimes, focusing attention on a particular task or stimulus will best serve goals; other times, broadening attention will be most effective. Another feature of PMA is being nonjudgmental. This trait should not be confused with approval and does not mean one should not have judgments or opinions. To clarify, consider that there is always an "is-ness" to any present moment experience. PMA is an acknowledgment of what is, akin to a landscape artist who paints what is there, without additions or modifications.

Contrasting the present moment with its opposite makes sense only from the perspective of language and cognition. The body has only existed, and will only exist, in the now. It was the evolution of human cognition that opened up the unique experience of maintaining representation of stimuli in their absence, and within that, the potential to reflect on past experience or conjure up a conceptualized future. So, does PMA mean you are not supposed to engage in past or future thought? Of course not. Reflecting and planning are extremely important, both within and outside of ACT. However, the assumption in ACT is that living a meaningful life entails a great deal of fully being here, not in the verbal past or future. This is the foundation of ACT.

The process of PMA in ACT, as well as in several other third-wave therapies, has its roots in ancient Eastern contemplative practices that are broadly known as mindfulness in the West. In this article, we will briefly review the history of mindfulness and differentiate PMA in ACT from the use of mindfulness practices in other third wave therapies. We will then take a deep dive to explicate how PMA relates to thoughts, emotions, and physical sensations, as well as to the other ACT processes. We also overview the limited clinical research on PMA as a process in ACT trials and provide a brief analysis of PMA from a relational frame theory (RFT) perspective. We next examine some of the research on neurophysiological correlates of mindfulness. Finally, we make broad clinical research recommendations that could facilitate both the understanding and the application of PMA within ACT. Our goal is to highlight some key conceptual and empirical underpinnings of PMA in order to provide insights into potential future directions to improve the health and well-being of clients.

Mindfulness Overview

The word "mindfulness" comes from the Pali word *sati*, which is typically translated as "memory," though there is much debate about the meaning of memory in this context as well as the translation itself (Dryden & Still, 2006). Mindfulness has roots in Buddhism but is also present in some form in many other cultures and traditions. Within Buddhism, mindfulness is one component of the eightfold path (more specifically "right mindfulness"), which is a framework to facilitate liberation from suffering (Bodhi, 2010). The eightfold path consists of three different types of training: wisdom (right view, right intention), ethics (right action, right speed, right livelihood), and meditation (right effort, right mindfulness, right concentration). Importantly, mindfulness was never separated or given additional weight relative to the other components of the eightfold path. Thus, just as PMA exists as one of six treatment processes that collectively facilitate psychological flexibility within ACT, within Buddhist traditions mindfulness operates akin to a treatment process that works synergistically with other practices within the tradition. This is not to say that ACT was derived from or is an extension of Buddhism (Hayes, 2002), but rather to draw a parallel that within Buddhism and ACT, mindfulness is not the outcome but rather one of several interrelated processes.

Mindfulness in Third Wave Therapies

Mindfulness gained acceptance as a clinical intervention with Jon Kabat-Zinn's stress reduction program, which would later become mindfulness-based stress reduction (MBSR; Kabat-Zinn, 1982). Kabat-Zinn was influenced by Buddhist meditation under the Vipassana and

Zen traditions (Chiesa & Malinowski, 2011) and was compelled to bring formal mindfulness meditation practice to the hospital setting. For obvious reasons, the religious connotations were kept to a minimum (Kabat-Zinn, 1982).

Notable therapies that are often labeled as mindfulness-based interventions include ACT, dialectical behavior therapy (DBT), MBSR, and mindfulness-based cognitive therapy (MBCT). These four approaches define and practice mindfulness in both similar and different ways. The conceptualization of mindfulness within ACT encompasses four core processes: PMA, defusion, acceptance, and self-as-context. Mindfulness is defined as "the defused, accepting, open contact with the present moment and the private events it contains as a conscious human being experientially distinct from the content being noticed" (Fletcher & Hayes, 2005, p. 322). The DBT definition of mindfulness is "the intentional process of observing, describing, and participating in reality nonjudgmentally, in the moment, and with effectiveness" (Hayes, Follette, & Linehan, 2004, p. 37). Perhaps the most commonly used definition and the one adopted by MBCT as well, is the one associated with MBSR: "paying attention in a particular way: on purpose, in the present moment, and nonjudgmentally" (Kabat-Zinn, 1994, p. 4).

Although several other definitions of mindfulness can be compared and contrasted, consensus will likely never be reached on either the definition of mindfulness or what it actually is. For example, mindfulness is often discussed as a state, an ongoing process, a technique, and/or an outcome. For the purposes of this article, a formal definition is not critical, as ACT specifies "mindfulness" as a collection of processes within the psychological flexibility model, and therefore mindfulness, however one chooses to define it, is evaluated with regard to workability.

Mindfulness in ACT and MBSR

ACT and MBSR conceptualize mindfulness in similar ways, and both share features of being transdiagnostic, widely studied interventions. These therapies highlight the wandering nature of the mind and teach clients to repeatedly return attention to present moment experiences without judgment. Acceptance is another commonality they share. In MBSR, acceptance is one of the core attitudinal factors taught to develop a formal mindfulness meditation practice and to cultivate mindfulness in daily activities (Kabat-Zinn, 2009). Further, MBSR emphasizes a willingness to fully experience the wealth of information of the present moment, whether negative, neutral, or positive, as well as the impermanence of all experiences (Kabat-Zinn, 2009). Similarly, ACT encourages the acceptance of private experiences as they are in the present moment, no matter the content, which promotes awareness and increases willingness to experience what exists. Defusion is an ACT-specific term, and therefore is not directly referred to in the MBSR approach. However, a similar concept is targeted. For example, through formal mindfulness meditation practice, Kabat-Zinn notes that one of the most profound learning experiences is the realization that one is not their thoughts (Kabat-Zinn, 2009). In ACT, defusion metaphors and experiential exercises are aimed to reduce the believability of thoughts, to see thoughts as thoughts, and to notice when one has entered a world of language and lost contact with the five-sense experience (Hayes et al., 2012). Finally, a transcendent sense of self is similarly emphasized in MBSR and ACT. With continued mindfulness practice, Kabat-Zinn refers to identifying with a transcendent experience of wholeness that is beyond one's problems, similar to self-as-context (Kabat-Zinn, 2009).

Formal and Informal Mindfulness Practice

From the standpoint of PMA, a key distinction between the treatment methods of ACT and other mindfulness-based interventions, including MBSR, lies in the centrality of formal mindfulness meditation practice. MBSR and MBCT rely heavily on formal practice as a primary treatment method. Participants are asked to practice for 45 minutes daily during a typical 8-week course, though shorter periods of practice have also been used with comparable outcomes (Reibel, Greeson, Brainard, & Rosenzweig, 2001). The primary meditation practices taught are sitting meditation, body scan, and Hatha yoga (Kabat-Zinn, 2009). Briefly, sitting meditation involves focusing on the sensations of breathing. When the mind wanders from the breath, the content is briefly noted, and then attention returns to the breath. Over time, practitioners are encouraged to let go of the focus on the breath and enter "choiceless awareness," described as being "completely open and receptive to whatever comes into the field of awareness, letting it all come and go" (Kabat-Zinn, 2009, p. 71).

Thus, formal mindfulness meditation entails being observant to all internal and external stimuli that arise during practice (e.g., thoughts, emotions, sounds, smells, sensations), unlike purely concentration-based meditations, where the nature of distraction is irrelevant (Baer, 2003). During the body scan, participants sweep through different body parts. Similar to sitting meditation, when attention wonders away from the body, the content may be briefly noted before returning attention to the body. The Hatha yoga practice includes several gentle to moderately difficult yoga poses.

ACT recognizes the benefits of formal mindfulness meditation practice and may encourage it. Therefore, many ACT protocols include contemplative practice such as the practices described previously. However, formal mindfulness meditation practice is not a primary treatment method in ACT (Hayes et al., 2012). Generally speaking, informal mindfulness practices are more heavily emphasized. DBT has taken a similar approach. DBT's developers initially incorporated formal practice into the approach, but after observing considerable distress and nonadherence among participants, chose to emphasize more accessible and understandable informal mindfulness skills (Welch, Rizvi, & Dimidjian, 2006).

Because of the way ACT conceptualizes mindfulness, any method that targets PMA, defusion, acceptance, or self-as-context can be said to be an informal mindfulness practice. For example, clients are often repeatedly asked to check in and observe what thoughts, emotions, and body sensations are showing up in the present moment. They may be asked to notice five-sense experiences and to describe how these differ from mentally constructed stimuli. Practices such as mindful eating, mindful walking, and mindful listening are often encouraged. Clients are asked to bring openness and curiosity into their daily activities, such as driving, brushing teeth, and doing dishes. More clinically relevant informal mindfulness practices are also utilized, for example, when clients are asked to bring the same openness and curiosity when experiencing cravings, entering into a social event, and having thoughts of suicide. Ultimately, the degree of formal and informal mindfulness practice within an ACT intervention will vary by therapist preference and client willingness. However, the utility of formal mindfulness meditation within ACT is an empirical question that has yet to be answered.

A Closer Look at Present Moment Awareness

In its simplest form, PMA means awareness of now. Broadly speaking, human awareness is a poorly understood phenomenon that is defined by either itself or other related terms such as consciousness, subjectivity, and selfhood (Farthing, 1992). At minimum, a certain level of arousal is required for awareness; an unconscious human, though alive, is most assuredly not aware. There is much debate, dating back at least to the nineteenth century, as to whether awareness and attention are distinct or inseparable processes (Wundt, 1874). Nonetheless, the development of awareness and attention processes is believed to be important for the benefits of mindfulness practice (Mikulas, 2011). Within ACT, the *process* of PMA brings flexible, yet deliberate, attention to one's experiences, whether outside or within the skin, as they happen (Wilson & DuFrene, 2009).

Inner and Outer Experiences

Inner experiences, also referred to as private experiences such as thoughts, emotions, and body sensations (Hayes et al., 2012), are often considered the root of problems in therapy. At times, the motivation for therapy lies in these problematic private experiences, or rather in the desire to control private experiences. Clients wish to no longer experience guilt, to rid themselves of anxious thoughts, to delete certain memories, or to be free of emotional or physical pain. ACT provides a useful framework for dealing with private experiences because the goal is not to get rid of them, but rather to *manage* private experiences better so that they do not control behavior.

Often paradoxical to client expectation, ACT advocates that these experiences be noticed without trying to change them, and there are good reasons to do so. Repeated experiences with problematic private experiences often lead to habitual avoidance responses. The individual with chronic pain forgoes activities because they "know" what will happen. This is what the mind does: it makes predictions based on past occurrences. Because it is impossible to remove learning histories, ACT argues that getting rid of such future projections is also impossible. Additionally, trying to control private experiences inherently consumes attention and further entangles the client with language processes. It is next to impossible to be fully present during meaningful activities when engaged in a private tug-of-war. Allowing problematic private experiences to be there will free up limited attentional resources.

In contrast to inner experiences which are often seen as problematic, events happening outside the skin are where most values live, such as spending quality time with friends and family, helping others, appreciating nature, enjoying a book or movie, working toward important goals, participating in meaningful tasks, and savoring leisure activities. While these outer experiences may consist of a certain degree of thinking, they mostly involve *doing*. One key importance of PMA methods applied in clinical practice is to promote awareness of outer experiences for the purpose of workability. The goal is not for clients to perseverate on maintaining awareness of inner or outer experiences of "I'm noticing this" and "now I'm noticing that," or to learn that living in the moment entails no conscious thought. Rather, PMA increases the opportunity to come in contact with these valued outer experiences.

Awareness and Thoughts

Thoughts are difficult to define, but for simplicity's sake they can be considered mental experiences that are not tied to here-and-now physical experiences. The ability to remember, evaluate, plan, organize, reason, compare, and fantasize is quite an impressive feat of human cognition and is no doubt responsible for the advancement of the species, as well as its suffering (Hayes et al., 2012). Also impressive is the ability, known as metacognition, to be aware of these cognitive processes as they are occurring (Flavell, 1979). Thoughts can often be significant barriers to psychological flexibility, for example, when linked to rule-governed behavior. Thus, PMA applied to thinking and its products deserves careful clinical consideration.

Bringing awareness to the process of thinking may be disruptive to the stream of thoughts, for example, when attempting to solve a math problem. However, that same level of disruption has clinical utility because PMA can create the necessary space to step back from thoughts. Consider rumination, a hallmark trait of many clinical conditions, including depression, anxiety, eating disorders, binge drinking, and self-harm (Nolen-Hoeksema, Wisco, & Lyubomirsky, 2008). Rumination is defined as "the mode of responding to distress that involves repetitively and passively focusing on symptoms of distress and on the possible causes and consequences of these symptoms" (Nolen-Hoeksema et al., 2008, p. 401). When ruminating, clients are not present. They are in a verbally constructed past or future attempting to understand or fix a problem, despite evidence that problems seldom get understood or fixed in this way. PMA helps clients notice this experience. This is the prerequisite first step: to be aware of what is going on. This space then provides the foundation for the other ACT processes to guide the client toward workable action.

This is not to say that PMA "fixes" thinking problems. We simply do not have tight control over what thoughts show up in the next moment. This is why a major focus of ACT is not getting rid of thinking, but rather changing one's relationship with thinking. Humans will *always* be interacting with thoughts throughout their lifespan. Therefore, one can only manage thoughts. With awareness, one can notice the act of thinking, choose how to respond to thoughts and other private experiences, and make choices based on values as opposed to impulse or habit.

Awareness and Emotions

It is natural to avoid stimuli that elicit negative emotions such as fear, anxiety, and shame and to seek out stimuli that generate positive emotions. Because aversive emotions will often present barriers to committed action, willingness to experience unwanted emotions in the service of values is a central feature of ACT. In this context, PMA becomes important in several ways. First, because emotions strongly influence approach and avoidance behaviors, they are so inherently tied to action that clients will often believe their actions are automatic. Anger is a fitting example, as states of intense anger can influence impulsive behavior with minimal awareness. However, with increased PMA, one can better observe antecedents of unworkable actions fueled by emotions. Second, emotional awareness can help identify choice-points to engage with values and not fall into the habit of avoidance. Unpleasant emotions often show up where values lie. For example, a father may avoid having a close relationship with his adult son because of the guilt he feels from being an absent parent. While the client may associate this guilt with the past (less of a concern in ACT), its presence is connected to a value (e.g., parenting) in the present; namely, that guilt is experienced because the value is important *now*. Third, PMA helps provide an experiential understanding of the ebb and flow of emotions. Emotions are temporally bound and do not last forever (Koole, 2009). This in itself can be very helpful for managing unpleasant emotions.

Awareness and Interoception

Interoception is a complex set of processes that can be broadly defined as the perception of internal bodily signals (Khalsa et al., 2018). Within the verbal human, this naturally entails the appraisal or *meaning* of internal bodily signals. Examples of interoceptive stimuli include heart rate, respiration, thermoregulation, muscle tension, hunger, fatigue, and pain. There is great interest in the overlap of interoception and emotion, cognition, decision making, and self-regulation, with some arguing that interoception is the foundation for conscious awareness itself (Craig, 2010).

Interoception is important within ACT for several reasons. First, many clinical conditions are associated with interoception dysfunction, including depression, anxiety, chronic pain, panic disorder, and substance use disorders (Khalsa et al., 2018). Second, orienting clients to attend to internal bodily states is often used in and out of session to promote PMA, as well as defusion, acceptance, and self-as-context. For example, if a client becomes highly distressed in session, the therapist may ask them where the emotion is currently being felt in the body or to notice the sensation of the breath, taking the client out of verbal-dominated experience. Third, the source of avoidance may be related to interoceptive avoidance, such as drinking to avoid withdrawal or staying at home to avoid experiencing elevated heart rate and chest pain. Thus, helping clients increase their willingness to experience unpleasant interoceptive stimuli may be key to promoting psychological flexibility.

It is important, however, to consider that individuals vary in interoceptive awareness and events that trigger heightened attention toward interoceptive signals. Although the literature is mixed, interoceptive awareness is often positively associated with anxiety (Domschke, Stevens, Pfleiderer, & Gerlach, 2010; Mallorquí-Bagué, Bulbena, Pailhez, Garfinkel, & Critchley, 2016) and negatively associated with depression (Khalsa & Lapidus, 2016; Pollatos, Traut-Mattausch, & Schandry, 2009). Thus, it is important to emphasize that within ACT, or therapy in general, the goal would not be to blindly increase interoception, but rather to consider the spectrum of interoceptive awareness during case conceptualization. For those lower on the spectrum, increasing awareness through various mindfulness strategies may be helpful. For those higher on the spectrum, decreasing awareness is often not possible. Once you are aware of something, making oneself unaware often does not work. In these instances, promoting defusion and acceptance may be helpful.

Awareness and Compassion

PMA entails an orientation of curiosity, kindness, openness, and acceptance toward each aspect of present moment experiences. This observing and nonjudgmental acknowledgment of what is, practiced over time, can engender a compassionate stance toward oneself and others (Neff & Dahm, 2015). Among evidence-based compassion training programs, including compassion cultivation training (Jazaieri et al., 2013), compassion-based cognitive therapy (Ash, Harrison, Pinto, DiClemente, & Negi, 2021), compassion-focused therapy (Gilbert, 2014), and mindful self-compassion (Neff & Germer, 2013), PMA lays the foundation for subsequent compassion practices and exercises. In order to address suffering, either in oneself or in others, it must first be noticed. Thus, PMA plays an important role in increasing compassion. While the goal of ACT is not cultivating compassion per se, at least one study has demonstrated that ACT can be successfully modified to focus on self-compassion (Yadavaia, Hayes, & Vilardaga, 2014).

Integration of Present Moment Awareness with Other ACT Processes

Most forms of psychotherapy attempt to promote awareness of experiences that were previously outside of awareness. Within ACT, this is similarly true, but with an emphasis on private experiences occurring in the present moment. Asking clients to specify what thoughts they are experiencing, where emotions are felt, and what bodily sensations are present is important for both client and therapist. For the client, labeling private experiences serves several useful functions. First, it promotes PMA. In order for the client to specify their internal world, they must first contact their internal world in the present. It also fuels other processes, particularly defusion and self-as-context. If one can notice these internal experiences, one cannot be the same thing as these internal experiences; through this noticing, one can recognize that they are the experiencer and not what is experienced. Perhaps most important, the practice of labeling private experiences, and the benefits of doing so, are intended to generalize beyond therapy. It is outside of therapy where the client lives their life and where valued actions are more readily available. For the therapist, it removes guess work as to what the client is experiencing and provides the kind of information needed for a functional analysis. A client telling the therapist, "I was just thinking about how upset my partner would be with me," provides rich historical and situational context and sheds light on the client's values. Thus, in a sense, all of the other ACT processes arise from PMA. If the present moment is all there is, how could this not be the case?

Defusion

Many instances of experiential avoidance are intertwined with the tendency to believe the literal content of thoughts; thus, cognitive defusion is one of the key processes of the ACT approach (Hayes et al., 2012). Being able to notice thoughts as thoughts (i.e., products of thinking), helps diminish the literality of these events. It allows for greater choice to act in ways that may violate the content of thoughts. Many PMA practices also enable the practice of defusion. Consider mindfully following the sensation of breathing. When ongoing thinking is noticed, it is released and attention is returned to the breath.

Acceptance

The behavior of acceptance, that is, allowing the presence of all positive and negative inner and outer experiences, is an alternative to experiential avoidance. PMA can help clients stay in contact with unpleasant internal experiences, and therefore it can clearly facilitate acceptance. However, because of the often long, complex histories associated with avoidance, the open and aware stance of acceptance can be overwhelming to some. When this is the case, the attention training embedded in PMA practices can offer different strategies. For example, many anxiety-related conditions are associated with a narrowing of attention, such as fixating on one body sensation or cognition. Intentionally noticing different elements of the internal experience (for example, through a grounding exercise to focus on the feeling in one's feet, or the external experience such as focusing on the sounds of a ticking clock or chirping birds in the environment) can loosen up attentional rigidity and allow for additional choices.

Self-as-Context

From an ACT perspective, the conscious experience of a self occurs through relational framing, specifically the I-here-now perspective (Torneke, 2010). I-here-now is the foundation not only for self-as-context, but also for the sense of self that is most central to PMA, self-as-process. This sense of self refers to the ongoing, observable aspects of ourselves occurring in the moment. However, unlike self-as-context, which refers to an unchangeable aspect of the self, self-as-process is always in flux. In essence, PMA infers change. You will only ever know I-here-now, but what you get when you contact I-here-now is different from any other I-here-now experience. In this way, it can be helpful to view PMA as a kind of constant update to the now. You will always return to the same perspective, but what you find will always be different. Sometime it will be slightly different, other times dramatically different.

Values

Core values are principles that guide action. In effect, values are the internalized and intrinsic motivations underlying effective action instead of responding to the short-term contingencies of the immediate context. Often, the learning histories and processes that have led to experiential avoidance make it difficult for one to recognize, acknowledge, or articulate the personal values that give their life meaning. Indeed, some clients are quite adamant that they either do not have personal values. Bringing focused attention, curiosity, and awareness through PMA can bring one's values into sharper focus; once identified, PMA can help one choose actions in accordance with these values.

Committed Action

Committed action is the purposeful behavior that moves one closer to values-consistent goals. PMA is important for choosing how to act, whether that be replacing a values-inconsistent behavior, like excessive drinking, or initiating a values-consistent behavior, like showing affection. Increasing awareness and attention in the present moment to behavior and its function for the client can activate the orientation and behavior change toward valued direction (Bailey, Ciarrochi, & Harris, 2014). PMA allows one to notice opportunities for behavioral choice; without PMA, one can fall back into habit.

Relational Frame Theory and Present Moment Awareness

The ACT approach is rooted in the principles of RFT, a modern behavioral theory of human language and cognition (Hayes et al., 2012). Based on behavior analytic principles, RFT proposes that the foundation of human language and cognition is relational responding and the emergence of derived stimulus relations (e.g., coordination) among stimuli established in the absence of direct training, and the alterations of stimulus function based on derived relations (Torneke, 2010). These features are believed to underlie the vastness of human cognition and the ability to reason and solve complex problems. A core assumption of ACT is that, while this ability has greatly served the species, language processes dominate over direct contingencies, such that responding often continues even when there is evidence of unworkability.

What makes matters particularly challenging for clients is that relational networks around psychological problems often have an extensive history. ACT purposely embraces the use of metaphors and exercises to circumvent these relational networks and increase the opportunity to stay in contact with and learn from direct contingencies. Further, exercises such as asking a client to establish a relationship between seemingly unrelated stimuli (e.g., "How are an eraser and an airplane similar?") allows an experiential understanding of derived stimulus relations and can help alter one's relationship with the process of thinking. Developing a healthy skepticism of thinking paves the way for defusion, which, in turn, paves the way for greater contact with the present moment.

A quote popularly attributed to B. F. Skinner, that "the major difference between rats and humans is that rats learn from experience," captures the essence of effective behavior entails. In order to learn from experience, one must remain in the present moment. Strengthening PMA skills can be helpful for not only bringing awareness to when unhelpful language processes are activated, but also leverage to stay in contact with the direct contingencies of behaving in the immediate internal and external environment. In effect, PMA can help humans be more like rats—better connected to the present moment and not so heavily influenced by inner experiences.

Assessment and Application of Present Moment Awareness in ACT Trials

It is difficult to clearly distinguish PMA from the other ACT processes. Defusing from thoughts, allowing unpleasant experiences to be without struggle, connecting with a transcendent sense of self, and committing to values-based actions all overlap with PMA. While this highlights the importance of PMA within ACT, it also makes studying the importance of PMA nearly impossible in controlled research settings. Indeed, recent dismantling trials have forgone any attempt to isolate PMA, focusing instead on examining the role of defusion, acceptance, committed action, and values (Levin, Krafft, & Twohig, 2020; Vilatte et al., 2016).

An additional challenge is the measurement of PMA. While one can choose from many measures of mindfulness, there is no "gold standard," and often these measures contain elements of acceptance, defusion, and/or self-as-context. Among available measures, the Mindful Attention and Awareness Scale (MAAS) appears to best approximate PMA. As the name suggests, this scale was developed to exclusively capture present moment attention and awareness and intentionally excluded attitudinal components, such as acceptance (Brown & Ryan, 2003). Like most mindfulness measures, however, the MAAS has been criticized on multiple fronts, including construct and convergent validity (Grossman, 2011). This presents significant limitations to the understanding of PMA within ACT. Until a reliable and valid measure can be isolated, if it can be, investigators will need to use a mindfulness measure of their choosing as a proxy for PMA. To aid in this decision, a list of common mindfulness measures and their characteristics is provided in Table 10.1.

Many ACT trials demonstrate significant improvements in various measures of mindfulness, yet there has been less convincing evidence that these improvements are an important mediator of treatment outcomes. Two pilot studies showed preliminary evidence of mindfulness as a mediator of treatment outcomes (Forman, Butryn, Hoffman, & Herbert, 2009; White et al., 2011). In a larger study (n = 168) that assessed individuals who completed an ACT-based interdisciplinary treatment for chronic pain, improvements in mindfulness as measured by the MAAS were associated with improvement in physical and psychosocial disability and pain-related anxiety; however, these associations became nonsignificant after accounting for other psychological flexibility processes (McCraken & Gutiérrez-Martínez, 2011). In an ACT-based intervention for social anxiety disorder, mindfulness and acceptance-based group therapy (MAGT), mindfulness was identified as a mechanism of change in reductions of social anxiety (Kocovski, Fleming, Hawley, Ho, & Antony, 2015). Interestingly, mindfulness was also a mechanism of change in the CBT comparison condition. Given the inherent limitations in measuring PMA and the existing scant literature, more research is needed to better examine the direct and indirect role of PMA in improving functional outcomes within ACT.

Research on Neurophysiological Correlates of Mindfulness

Because PMA is an element of mindfulness, we provide a brief overview of the physiological correlates of mindfulness more generally. Changes in the activity and structure of the anterior cingulate cortex, a region associated with attention, are most consistently linked to mindfulness practice (Chiesa & Serretti, 2010; Tang, Hölzel, & Posner, 2015). Reliable change is also observed in the default mode networks, which are implicated in self referential processing, as well as the insula and fronto-limbic networks, which are linked to self-awareness and emotion regulation processes, respectively (Tang et al., 2015). These findings fit well with theoretical and empirical accounts of the benefits of mindfulness practice in improving attention, body awareness, emotional regulation, and the perspective of self (Hölzel et al., 2011). Several studies demonstrate that these physiological correlates are associated with positive clinical outcomes, including reductions in depression and anxiety and improvements in resilience and alexithymia (Young et al., 2018).

There also is growing evidence that mindfulness practice has an impact on the immune and stress-regulatory systems. Meta-analyses in this area have linked mindfulness practice to reduced cortisol, blood pressure, heart rate, triglycerides and tumor-necrosis factor-alpha, decreased activity of inflammatory markers such as nuclear factor Kappa B and levels of C-reactive protein, and increased activity of the cell-mediated immune response (e.g., CD4 + T) and telomerase, which is protective against cellular aging mechanisms (Black & Slavich, 2016; Pascoe, Thompson, Jenkins, & Ski, 2017). The relationship between mindfulness and cardiovascular and autonomic system functioning also has received research interest. One popular assessment method is heart rate variability (HRV). HRV reflects the degree of parasympathetic

Table 10.1. Common Measures of Mindfulness

Measure	Reference	Subscales	General Info	Internal Consistency	Used in previous ACT trial? (Y/N)
Cognitive Affective Mindfulness Scale-Revised (CAMS-R)	Feldman, Hayes, Kumar, Greeson, & Laurenceau, 2007	1) Awareness 2) Attention 3) Present focus 4) Acceptance * The use of subscales is not recommended by the authors	12 items assessing awareness, attention, present-focus, and acceptance/nonjudgment of thoughts and feelings	Validated in nonclinical samples. Internal consistency: (Awareness: .42–.46; Attention: .79–.81; Present focus: .47–.53; Acceptance: .56–.66; Mindfulness (Total): .74–.77)	N
Five Facet Mindfulness Questionnaire (FFMQ)	Baer, Smith, Hopkins, Krietemeyer, & Toney., 2006	1) Observing 2) Describing 3) Acting with awareness 4) Nonjudging 5) Nonreactivity	39 items assessing five facets of mindfulness related to thoughts, emotions, experiences, and actions	Validated in nonclinical samples. Internal consistency (Observing:.83,Describing:.91,Acting with awareness: .87, Nonjudging: .87, Nonreactivity: .75)	Y
Freiburg Mindfulness Inventory (FMI)	Walach, Buchheld, Buttenmüller, Kleinknecht, & Schmidt, 2006	None	30 (long version) or 14 (short version) items assessing mindful presence, nonjudgmental acceptance, openness to experiences, and insight	Validated in clinical and nonclinical samples. Internal consistency (Long version: .87–.94; Short version: .79–.86)	Y
Kentucky Inventory of Mindfulness Skills (KIMS)	Baer, Smith, & Allen, 2004	1) Observing 2) Acting with awareness 3) Accepting without judgment 4) Describing	39 items assessing mindfulness skills used in daily life	Validated in clinical and nonclinical samples. Internal consistency (Observe: .85–.91, Describe: .84–.86, Acting with awareness: .76–.83, Accepting without judgment: .87)	Y
Mindful Attention Awareness Scale (MAAS)	Brown & Ryan, 2003	None	15 items assessing mindful awareness/attention	Validated in nonclinical samples. Internal consistency (.80–.87)	Y

Philadelphia Mindfulness Scale (PHLMS)	Cardaciotto, Herbert, Forman, Moitra, & Farrow, 2008	1) Awareness 2) Acceptance	20 items assessing awareness of thoughts, feelings, and body sensations, and experiential avoidance	Validated in clinical and nonclinical samples. Internal consistency (Awareness: .75–.86; Acceptance: .75–.91)	Y
Southampton Mindfulness Questionnaire (SMQ)	Chadwick et al., 2008	None	16 items assessing mindful awareness, attention to, acceptance, and nonreaction of distressing thoughts and images	Validated in clinical and nonclinical samples. Internal consistency (.82–.89)	Y
Toronto Mindfulness Scale (TMS)	Lau et al., 2006	1) Curiosity 2) Decentering	15 items assessing state (rather than trait) mindfulness	Validated in nonclinical samples. Internal consistency (Curiosity: .88; Decentering: .84)	Y

and sympathetic influence on heart rate, with higher levels indicating greater parasympathetic and less sympathetic activation. A 2018 systematic review and meta-analysis that included 17 studies of mind–body exercise programs like Tai Chi and yoga found small-to-moderate effects on HRV (Zou et al., 2018), while a 2019 systematic review and meta-analysis that included only four studies of mindfulness meditation-based programs found mixed and inconclusive effects (Radmark, Sidorchuk, Osika, & Niemi, 2019). Thus, more research is needed to examine the link between mindfulness practices and autonomic system functioning.

The growing body of literature on the potential neurophysiological mechanisms of mindfulness in general suggests the value of conducting related research within ACT. However, nearly all studies of ACT and its processes have remained focused on psychological outcomes such as behavioral, cognitive, and emotional functioning. Studies to examine the neurophysiological predictors of response or changes related to ACT processes, including PMA, would be useful in corroborating the clinical findings and validating change processes at multiple levels of understanding, including sociocultural, behavioral, psychological, neurobiological, physiological, and genetic levels (Hayes, Hoffmann, & Ciarrochi, 2020). Additionally, this multilevel approach to assessing predictors and outcomes of treatment can explicate both behavioral and biological targets for intervention, inform treatment choices, and help refine more precise interventions. Given that human behavior results from the interaction of psychological, biological, physiological, and sociocultural systems, it is ultimately this type of work where basic and behavioral research inform each other that has the greatest likelihood to determine what treatment works for whom under what conditions to reduce human suffering.

Clinical Research Directions

More work remains to be done to better understand and capitalize on the role of PMA in the context of ACT. In this section, we focus on three broad, overlapping research areas that may serve to advance the impact of PMA and other processes in ACT interventions.

Integration of Formal Mindfulness Practice within ACT

Surprisingly, very few ACT trials report on the degree of formal mindfulness meditation practice adherence, or assess the relationship between time spent in formal practice and treatment outcomes. Outside of ACT, meditation adherence is generally associated with positive outcomes. For example, a 2017 meta-analysis that included 1427 participants across 43 studies of MBSR or MBCT found a small but significant association between formal mindfulness meditation practice adherence and intervention outcome (Parsons, Crane, Parsons, Fjorback, & Kuyken, 2017). Nonetheless, there is much to learn about mindfulness meditation, how it should be practiced, and how it should be monitored. Given that therapy occurs, at best, during weekly one-hour sessions, mindfulness meditation practice outside the therapy session has great potential to assist the therapeutic process.

From the standpoint that formal mindfulness practice bolsters PMA and improves outcomes, it only seems logical that every client should undertake mindfulness meditation practice. However, it is not that simple. It is possible that formal mindfulness meditation practice could have a negative impact on the ultimate goal of psychological flexibility. For example, formal practice could itself be used as a form of experiential avoidance. Imagine a client that uses formal mindfulness practice solely to relax and distract from day-to-day living, the kind of living that ACT seeks to directly impact. Thus, it is important not to lose focus on the goal of formal mediation in ACT to increase psychological flexibility and ultimately functioning, and not to become an expert meditator.

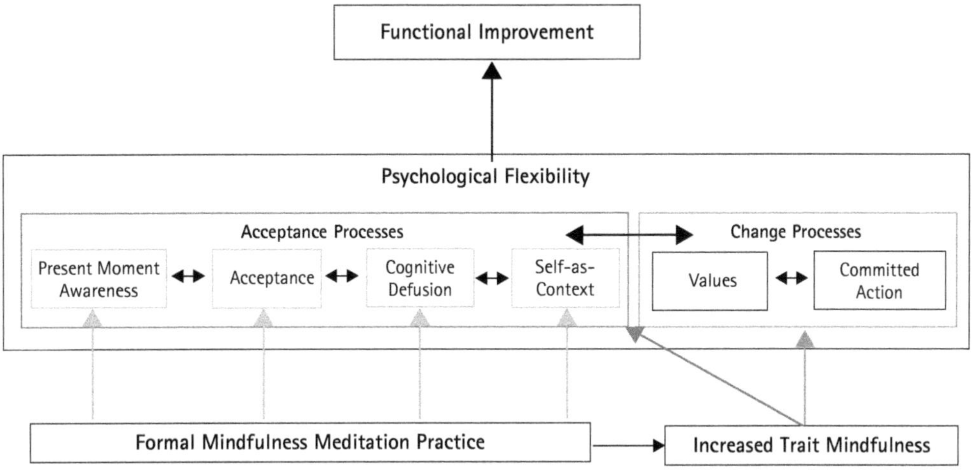

Figure 10.1. Conceptual model of benefits of integrating formal mindfulness meditation practice with ACT

Despite these potential pitfalls, examining the integration of formal mindfulness meditation practice within ACT may be fruitful as there is some empirical evidence that formal practice targets other mindfulness and acceptance processes of the psychological flexibility model. This includes not only PMA, but also acceptance (e.g., as measured by the Acceptance and Action Questionnaire-II; Arlt Mutch, Evans, & Wyka, 2020) and cognitive defusion (e.g., as measured by the Experiences Questionnaire; Hoge et al., 2015), as well as qualitative data supporting the development of an "observing self" during MBSR (Kerr, Josyula, & Littenberg, 2011). For those who practice mindfulness meditation, this is likely self-evident.

We also postulate that formal mindfulness meditation practice can increase trait mindfulness, or the predisposition to be mindful in daily life (Kiken, Garland, Bluth, Palsson, & Gaylord, 2015), which in turn, may maximize the reinforcing potential of meaningful life activities (i.e., committed action in the service of values-driven goals). Taken together, we propose a conceptual model in which formal mindfulness meditation practice directly and indirectly (via increased trait mindfulness) targets all psychological flexibility processes (depicted in Figure 10.1) to ultimately increase optimal functioning. The intention of these linkages is not to claim that practicing mindfulness meditation is practicing ACT, or vice versa, but rather to provide a testable rationale for mindfulness practice in the context of ACT. One of our own clinical trials is currently examining the impact of integrated formal mindfulness practice with ACT for chronic pain. We encourage other research to explicate the relationships with and value of formal mindfulness practice in ACT.

Real-World and Real-Time Measurement of Mindfulness

A 2015 meta-analysis of mindfulness-based programs found that 37 of 72 trials (51 percent) failed to demonstrate significant improvement in mindfulness (Visted, Vøllestad, Nielsen, & Nielsen, 2015). Given the challenges of measuring mindfulness as previously discussed, this finding must be reviewed with caution. One solution to move the field forward is to consider the method of measurement. Like other standard paper–pencil assessments, most mindfulness measures inquire about past behavior, typically over the previous week, which inherently suffers from recall bias. This is problematic for any construct measured in this way, but perhaps even more problematic for a construct like mindfulness.

Ecological momentary assessment (EMA) is one solution to improve the precision of measurement. EMA, also referred to as experience sampling, refers to the repeated sampling of behavior in real-world (ecological), real-time (momentary) settings. The benefits of these designs are a reduction in recall bias and an in-depth assessment of contextual variables that precede, co-occur, and follow a behavior of interest between and within individuals (Shiffman, Stone, & Hufford, 2008). A recent systematic review (Enkema, McClain, Bird, Halvorson, & Larimer, 2020) identified only eight studies that examined momentary mindfulness, suggesting the need for expanded research in this area. To provide one example of the nuances that EMA can provide, Gotink and colleagues (2016) found that momentary mindfulness predicted increased positive and decreased negative affect at the next assessment when analyzed within days. Interestingly, when examined across days, positive and negative affect the day before predicted decreased and increased momentary mindfulness at the next day, respectively. Further, two studies included in the review reported nonsignificant relationships between retrospective mindfulness and momentary mindfulness, providing additional concern over the standard paper–pencil assessment of mindfulness. By integrating EMA into future research, investigators will have additional tools to examine the utility of PMA and mindfulness within ACT trials.

EMA methods also can be used to improve the measurement of mindfulness practice. Most studies rely on weekly logs to measure practice, whereas some do not measure practice at all. The increasing popularity of mindfulness apps has enabled a more objective and preferable method of measuring practice by extrapolating time spent on the app. However, even this method has limitations. For instance, individuals may listen to the app while engaging in other activities or they may prefer to practice without the app. A multimodal approach may help improve the measurement of practice. For example, daily EMA prompts inquiring about the duration and characteristics of practice could be obtained along with objective app use to corroborate reports.

Just-in-Time Interventions

Just-in-time adaptive interventions are intended to offer clients tailored interventions in real-world, real-time settings. Similar to the benefits of using EMA for capturing data, just-in-time interventions hold promise to circumvent many of the challenges within the current model of weekly or less frequent therapy sessions. Clients live busy and complex lives, and it is nearly impossible to predict what type of future skill will best serve the client in future contexts. The just-in-time designs use mobile and sensing technologies to determine when and what type of intervention is needed. Within ACT, Levin, Navarro, Cruz, and Haeger (2019) demonstrated the utility of tailoring acceptance and defusion skills in a nonclinical sample based on responses to a check-in assessment on a mobile app. Although tailoring PMA and values skills was no more effective than randomly assigning these skills, additional research is needed to better understand when and how promoting just-in-time PMA exercises can influence psychological flexibility.

A wide-array of passive data can be collected to trigger just-in-time adaptive interventions. These include data that can be captured on smartphones (e.g., GPS), wearable technology (e.g., heart rate, physical activity), and household items (e.g., sensors on refrigerator doors). These interventions are constantly evolving with technology, and much remains to be learned. With the ability to capture more and more data and provide intervention based on present moment context, it is critical that appropriate health behavior change theories help steer the approach (Nahum-Shani et al., 2018). The psychological flexibility model provides useful guidance, yet ACT trials are still in the early stages of integrating EMA and just-in-time interventions. With well-thought-out designs, there is great potential to improve the understanding and application of PMA, as well as other processes, within ACT.

Conclusion

PMA is of critical importance to ACT and is the foundational process upon which other processes rest. Within our ability to be present and aware is our ability to stay open to inner and outer experiences while choosing to act on what matters. PMA is also the cornerstone of mindfulness-based interventions in which formal mindfulness meditation enhances awareness and improves clinical outcomes. The growing literature on the neurophysiological correlates of mindfulness also suggests multiple changes linked with the practice of mindfulness. However, much remains to be learned about the particular role of PMA in ACT and its potential direct and indirect effects on behavior change.

Undoubtedly, much debate will continue about what PMA exactly is, how to measure it, and how it should be practiced. From a research perspective, future studies should examine the potential benefits of formal mindfulness meditation practice in the context of ACT and capitalize on technology to measure and support PMA and other ACT processes in real-world and real-time settings. A multilevel approach that integrates basic (RFT and neurophysiological) and applied research can further elucidate change processes and help refine mindfulness strategies and ACT interventions to better address clients' needs. From a clinical standpoint, PMA allows us to see beyond the thoughts and emotions that bind us to our past or imagined future and to commit to behave in ways that are congruent with our deeply held values. That is as true for therapists as it is for clients—in fact, for all us. What may matter most is our own willingness to be fully present with our experiences and relationships, to be aware of our own reactions, judgments, and insights that show up, and to respond with openness and compassion.

References

Arlt Mutch, V. K., Evans, S., & Wyka, K. (2020). The role of acceptance in mood improvement during mindfulness-based stress reduction. *Journal of Clinical Psychology*, *77*(1), 7–19. https://doi.org/10.1002/jclp.23017

Ash, M., Harrison, T., Pinto, M., DiClemente, R., & Negi, L. T. (2021). A model for cognitively- based compassion training: Theoretical underpinnings and proposed mechanisms. *Social Theory and Health*, 19(1), 43–67. https://doi.org/10.1057/s41285-019-00124-y

Baer, R. A. (2003). Mindfulness training as a clinical intervention: A conceptual and empirical review. *Clinical Psychology: Science and Practice*, *10*(2), 125–143. https://doi.org/10.1093/clipsy.bpg015

Baer, R. A., Smith, G. T., & Allen, K. B. (2004). Assessment of mindfulness by self-report: The Kentucky Inventory of Mindfulness Skills. *Assessment*, *11*(3), 191–206. https://doi.org/10.1177/1073191104268029

Baer, R. A., Smith, G. T., Hopkins, J., Krietemeyer, J., & Toney, L. (2006). Using self-report assessment methods to explore facets of mindfulness. *Assessment*, *13*(1), 27–45. https://doi.org/10.1177/1073191105283504

Bailey, A., Ciarrochi, J., & Harris, R. (2014). *The weight escape: How to stop dieting and start living*. Boston: Shambhala Publications.

Black, D. S., & Slavich, G. M. (2016). Mindfulness meditation and the immune system: A systematic review of randomized controlled trials. *Annals of the New York Academy of Sciences*, *1373*(1), 13–24. https://doi.org/10.1111/nyas.12998

Bodhi, B. (2010). *The noble eightfold path: The way to the end of suffering*. Onalaska, WA: Buddhist Publication Society.

Brown, K. W., & Ryan, R. M. (2003). The benefits of being present: Mindfulness and its role in psychological well-being. *Journal of Personality and Social Psychology*, *84*(4), 822–848. https://doi.org/10.1037/0022-3514.84.4.822

Cardaciotto, L., Herbert, J. D., Forman, E. M., Moitra, E., & Farrow, V. (2008). The assessment of present-moment awareness and acceptance: The Philadelphia Mindfulness Scale. *Assessment*, *15*(2), 204–223. https://doi.org/10.1177/1073191107311467

Chadwick, P., Hember, M., Symes, J., Peters, E., Kuipers, E., & Dagnan, D. (2008). Responding mindfully to unpleasant thoughts and images: Reliability and validity of the Southampton mindfulness questionnaire (SMQ). *British Journal of Clinical Psychology, 47*(4), 451–455. https://doi.org/10.1348/014466508X314891

Chiesa, A., & Malinowski, P. (2011). Mindfulness-based approaches: Are they all the same? *Journal of Clinical Psychology, 67*(4), 404–424. https://doi.org/10.1002/jclp.20776

Chiesa, A., & Serretti, A. (2010). A systematic review of neurobiological and clinical features of mindfulness meditations. *Psychological Medicine, 40*(8), 1239–1252.http://doi:10.1017/S0033291709991747

Craig, A. D. (2010). The sentient self. *Brain Structure and Function, 214*, 563–577.https://doi.org/10.1007/s00429-010-0248-y

Domschke, K., Stevens, S., Pfleiderer, B., & Gerlach, A. L. (2010). Interoceptive sensitivity in anxiety and anxiety disorders: An overview and integration of neurobiological findings. *Clinical Psychology Review, 30*(1), 1–11. https://doi.org/10.1016/j.cpr.2009.08.008

Dryden, W., & Still, A. (2006). Historical aspects of mindfulness and self-acceptance in psychotherapy. *Journal of Rational-Emotive and Cognitive-Behavior Therapy, 24*(1), 3–28. https://doi.org/10.1007/s10942-006-0026-1

Enkema, M. C., McClain, L., Bird, E. R., Halvorson, M. A., & Larimer, M. E. (2020). Associations between mindfulness and mental health outcomes: A systematic review of ecological momentary assessment research. *Mindfulness, 11*, 2455–2469. https://doi.org/10.1007/s12671-020-01442-2

Farthing, G. W. (1992). *The psychology of consciousness.* Upper Saddle River, NJ: Prentice-Hall.

Feldman, G., Hayes, A., Kumar, S., Greeson, J., & Laurenceau, J. P. (2007). Mindfulness and emotion regulation: The development and initial validation of the Cognitive and Affective Mindfulness Scale-Revised (CAMS-R). *Journal of Psychopathology and Behavioral Assessment, 29*(3), 177–190. https://doi.org/10.1007/s10862-006-9035-8

Flavell, J. H. (1979). Metacognition and cognitive monitoring: A new area of cognitive– developmental inquiry. *American Psychologist, 34*(10), 906–911.https://doi.org/10.1037/0003-066X.34.10.906

Fletcher, L., & Hayes, S. C. (2005). Relational frame theory, acceptance and commitment therapy, and a functional analytic definition of mindfulness. *Journal of Rational-Emotive and Cognitive-Behavior Therapy, 23*(4), 315–336.https://doi.org/10.1007/s10942-005-0017-7

Forman, E. M., Butryn, M. L., Hoffman, K. L., & Herbert, J. D. (2009). An open trial of an acceptance-based behavioral intervention for weight loss. *Cognitive and Behavioral Practice, 16*(2), 223–235. https://doi.org/10.1016/j.cbpra.2008.09.005

Gilbert, P. (2014). The origins and nature of compassion focused therapy. *British Journal of Clinical Psychology, 53*(1), 6–41. https://doi.org/10.1111/bjc.12043

Gotink, R. A., Hermans, K. S., Geschwind, N., De Nooij, R., De Groot, W. T., & Speckens, A. E. (2016). Mindfulness and mood stimulate each other in an upward spiral: a mindful walking intervention using experience sampling. *Mindfulness, 7*(5), 1114–1122. https://doi.org/10.1007/s12671-016-0550-8

Grossman, P. (2011). Defining mindfulness by how poorly I think I pay attention during everyday awareness and other intractable problems for psychology's (re) invention of mindfulness: Comment on Brown et al. (2011). *Psychological Assessment, 23*(4), 1034–1040. https://doi.org/10.1037/a0022713

Hayes, S. C. (2002). Buddhism and acceptance and commitment therapy. *Cognitive and Behavioral Practice, 9*(1), 58–66. https://doi.org/10.1016/S1077-7229(02)80041-4

Hayes, S. C., Follette, V. M., & Linehan, M. (Eds.). (2004). *Mindfulness and acceptance: Expanding the cognitive-tradition.* New York: Guilford Press.

Hayes, S. C., Hoffmann, S. G., & Ciarrochi, J. (2020). Creating an alternative to syndromal diagnosis: Needed features of processes of change and the models that organize them. In S. C. Hayes and S. G. Hoffman (Eds.), *Beyond the DSM: Toward a process-based alternative for diagnosis and mental health treatment* (1–21). Oakland, CA: New Harbinger Publications.

Hayes, S. C., Strosahl, K. D., & Wilson, K. G. (2012). *Acceptance and commitment therapy, second edition: The process and practice of mindful change.* New York: Guilford Press.

Hoge, E. A., Bui, E., Goetter, E., Robinaugh, D. J., Ojserkis, R. A., Fresco, D. M., & Simon, N. M. (2015). Change in decentering mediates improvement in anxiety in mindfulness-based stress reduction for generalized anxiety disorder. *Cognitive Therapy and Research, 39*(2), 228–235. https://doi.org/10.1007/s10608-014-9646-4

Hölzel, B. K., Lazar, S. W., Gard, T., Schuman-Olivier, Z., Vago, D. R., & Ott, U. (2011). How does mindfulness meditation work? Proposing mechanisms of action from a conceptual and neural perspective. *Perspectives on Psychological Science, 6*(6), 537–559. https://doi.org/10.1177/1745691611419671

Jazaieri, H., Jinpa, G. T., McGonigal, K., Rosenberg, E. L., Finkelstein, J., Simon-Thomas, E., . . . Goldin, P. R. (2013). Enhancing compassion: A randomized controlled trial of a compassion cultivation training program. *Journal of Happiness Studies, 14*(4), 1113–1126. https://doi.org/10.1007/s10902-012-9373-z

Kabat-Zinn, J. (1982). An outpatient program in behavioral medicine for chronic pain patients based on the practice of mindfulness meditation: Theoretical considerations and preliminary results. *General Hospital Psychiatry*, *4*(1), 33–47. https://doi.org/10.1016/0163-8343(82)90026-3

Kabat-Zinn, J. (1994). *Wherever you go, there you are: Mindfulness meditation in everyday life.* New York: Hyperion.

Kabat-Zinn, J. (2009). *Full catastrophe living: Using the wisdom of your body and mind to face stress, pain, and illness.* New York: Delta.

Kerr, C. E., Josyula, K., & Littenberg, R. (2011). Developing an observing attitude: An analysis of meditation diaries in an MBSR clinical trial. *Clinical Psychology and Psychotherapy, 18*(1), 80–93. https://doi.org/10.1002/cpp.700

Khalsa, S. S., Adolphs, R., Cameron, O. G., Critchley, H. D., Davenport, P. W., Feinstein, J. S., . . . Meuret, A. E. (2018). Interoception and mental health: A roadmap. *Biological Psychiatry: Cognitive Neuroscience and Neuroimaging, 3*(6), 501–513. https://doi.org/10.1016/j.bpsc.2017.12.004

Khalsa, S. S., & Lapidus, R. C. (2016). Can interoception improve the pragmatic search for biomarkers in psychiatry? Frontiers in Psychiatry, *7*, 121. https://doi.org/10.3389/fpsyt.2016.00121

Kiken, L. G., Garland, E. L., Bluth, K., Palsson, O. S., & Gaylord, S. A. (2015). From a state to a trait: Trajectories of state mindfulness in meditation during intervention predict changes in trait mindfulness. *Personality and Individual differences*, 81, 41–46. https://doi.org/10.1016/j.paid.2014.12.044

Kocovski, N. L., Fleming, J. E., Hawley, L. L., Ho, M. H. R., & Antony, M. M. (2015). Mindfulness and acceptance-based group therapy and traditional cognitive behavioral group therapy for social anxiety disorder: Mechanisms of change. *Behaviour Research and Therapy, 70*, 11–22. https://doi.org/10.1016/j.brat.2015.04.005

Koole, S. L. (2009). The psychology of emotion regulation: An integrative review. *Cognition and Emotion, 23*(1), 4–41. https://doi.org/10.1080/02699930802619031

Lau, M. A., Bishop, S. R., Segal, Z. V., Buis, T., Anderson, N. D., Carlson, L., . . . Devins, G. (2006). The Toronto mindfulness scale: Development and validation. *Journal of Clinical Psychology, 62*(12), 1445–1467. https://doi.org/10.1002/jclp.20326

Levin, M. E., Krafft, J., & Twohig, M. P. (2020). Examining processes of change in an online acceptance and commitment therapy dismantling trial with distressed college students. *Journal of Contextual Behavioral Science, 17*, 10–16. https://doi.org/10.1016/j.jcbs.2020.05.001

Levin, M. E., Navarro, C., Cruz, R. A., & Haeger, J. (2019). Comparing in-the-moment skill coaching effects from tailored versus non-tailored acceptance and commitment therapy mobile apps in a non-clinical sample. *Cognitive Behaviour Therapy, 48*(3), 200–216. https://doi.org/10.1080/16506073.2018.1503706

Mallorquí-Bagué, N., Bulbena, A., Pailhez, G., Garfinkel, S. N., & Critchley, H. D. (2016). Mind-body interactions in anxiety and somatic symptoms. *Harvard Review of Psychiatry, 24*(1), 53–60. https://doi.org/10.1097/HRP.0000000000000085

McCracken, L. M., & Gutiérrez-Martínez, O. (2011). Processes of change in psychological flexibility in an interdisciplinary group-based treatment for chronic pain based on acceptance and commitment therapy. *Behaviour Research and Therapy, 49*(4), 267–274. https://doi.org/10.1016/j.brat.2011.02.004

Mikulas, W. L. (2011). Mindfulness: Significant common confusions. *Mindfulness, 2*(1), 1–7. https://doi.org/10.1007/s12671-010-0036-z

Nahum-Shani, I., Smith, S. N., Spring, B. J., Collins, L. M., Witkiewitz, K., Tewari, A., & Murphy, S. A. (2018). Just-in-time adaptive interventions (JITAIs) in mobile health: Key components and design principles for ongoing health behavior support. *Annals of Behavioral Medicine, 52*(6), 446–462. https://doi.org/10.1007/s12160-016-9830-8

Neff, K. D., & Dahm, K. A. (2015). Self-compassion: What it is, what it does, and how it relates to mindfulness. In M. Robinson, B. Meier and B. Ostafin (Eds.), *Handbook of mindfulness and self-regulation* (121–137). New York: Springer.

Neff, K. D., & Germer, C. K. (2013). A pilot study and randomized controlled trial of the mindful self-compassion program. *Journal of Clinical Psychology, 69*(1), 28–44.https://doi.org/10.1002/jclp.21923

Nolen-Hoeksema, S., Wisco, B. E., & Lyubomirsky, S. (2008). Rethinking rumination. *Perspective on Psychological Science, 3*(5), 400–424. https://doi.org/10.1111/j.1745-6924.2008.00088.x

Parsons, C. E., Crane, C., Parsons, L. J., Fjorback, L. O., & Kuyken, W. (2017). Home practice in mindfulness-based cognitive therapy and mindfulness-based stress reduction: A systematic review and meta-analysis of participants' mindfulness practice and its association with outcomes. *Behaviour Research and Therapy, 95*, 29–41. https://doi.org/10.1016/j.brat.2017.05.004

Pascoe, M. C., Thompson, D. R., Jenkins, Z. M., & Ski, C. F. (2017). Mindfulness mediates the physiological markers of stress: Systematic review and meta-analysis. *Journal of Psychiatric Research, 95*, 156–178. https://doi.org/10.1016/j.jpsychires.2017.08.004

Pollatos, O., Traut-Mattausch, E., & Schandry, R. (2009). Differential effects of anxiety and depression on interoceptive accuracy. *Depression and Anxiety, 26*(2), 167–173.https://doi.org/10.1002/da.20504

Rådmark, L., Sidorchuk, A., Osika, W., & Niemi, M. (2019). A systematic review and meta- analysis of the impact of mindfulness based interventions on heart rate variability and inflammatory markers. *Journal of Clinical Medicine, 8*(10), 1638.https://doi.org/10.3390/jcm8101638

Reibel, D. K., Greeson, J. M., Brainard, G. C., & Rosenzweig, S. (2001). Mindfulness-based stress reduction and health-related quality of life in a heterogeneous patient population. *General Hospital Psychiatry, 23*(4), 183–192. https://doi.org/10.1016/S0163-8343(01)00149-9

Shiffman, S., Stone, A. A., & Hufford, M. R. (2008). Ecological momentary assessment. *Annual Review of Clinical Psychology, 4*, 1–32. https://doi.org/10.1146/annurev.clinpsy.3.022806.091415

Tang, Y. Y., Hölzel, B. K., & Posner, M. I. (2015). The neuroscience of mindfulness meditation. *Nature Reviews Neuroscience, 16*(4), 213–225. https://doi.org/10.1038/nrn3916

Torneke, N. (2010). *Learning RFT: An introduction to relational frame theory and its clinical application.* Oakland, CA: New Harbinger Publications.

Villatte, J. L., Vilardaga, R., Villatte, M., Vilardaga, J. C. P., Atkins, D. C., & Hayes, S. C. (2016). Acceptance and commitment therapy modules: Differential impact on treatment processes and outcomes. *Behaviour Research and Therapy, 77*, 52–61. https://doi.org/10.1016/j.brat.2015.12.001

Visted, E., Vøllestad, J., Nielsen, M. B., & Nielsen, G. H. (2015). The impact of group-based mindfulness training on self-reported mindfulness: A systematic review and meta- analysis. *Mindfulness, 6*(3), 501–522. https://doi.org/10.1007/s12671-014-0283-5

Walach, H., Buchheld, N., Buttenmüller, V., Kleinknecht, N., & Schmidt, S. (2006). Measuring mindfulness—the Freiburg mindfulness inventory (FMI). *Personality and Individual Differences, 40*(8), 1543–1555. https://doi.org/10.1016/j.paid.2005.11.025

Welch, S. S., Rizvi, S., & Dimidjian, S. (2006). Mindfulness in dialectical behavior therapy (DBT) for borderline personality disorder. In R. A. Baer (Ed.), *Mindfulness-based treatment approaches: Clinician's guide to evidence base and applications* (117–139). Burlington, MA: Elsevier.

White, R., Gumley, A., McTaggart, J., Rattrie, L., McConville, D., Cleare, S., & Mitchell, G. (2011). A feasibility study of acceptance and commitment therapy for emotional dysfunction following psychosis. *Behaviour Research and Therapy, 49*(12), 901–907. https://doi.org/10.1016/j.brat.2011.09.003

Wilson, K. G., & Dufrene, T. (2009). *Mindfulness for two: An acceptance and commitment therapy approach to mindfulness in psychotherapy.* Oakland, CA: New Harbinger.

Wundt, W. (1874). *Grundzüge der Physiologischen Psychologie. 3 Bände.* Leipzig: Engelmann.

Yadavaia, J. E., Hayes, S. C., & Vilardaga, R. (2014). Using acceptance and commitment therapy to increase self-compassion: A randomized controlled trial. *Journal of Contextual Behavioral Science, 3*(4), 248–257. https://doi.org/10.1016/j.jcbs.2014.09.002

Young, K. S., van der Velden, A. M., Craske, M. G., Pallesen, K. J., Fjorback, L., Roepstorff, A., & Parsons, C. E. (2018). The impact of mindfulness-based interventions on brain activity: A systematic review of functional magnetic resonance imaging studies. *Neuroscience and Biobehavioral Reviews, 84*, 424–433. https://doi.org/10.1016/j.neubiorev.2017.08.003

Zou, L., Sasaki, J. E., Wei, G. X., Huang, T., Yeung, A. S., Neto, O. B., . . . Hui, S. S. C. (2018). Effects of mind–body exercises (Tai Chi/Yoga) on heart rate variability parameters and perceived stress: A systematic review with meta-analysis of randomized controlled trials. *Journal of Clinical Medicine, 7*(11), 404. https://doi.org/10.3390/jcm7110404

CHAPTER 11

Self-as-Context

Louise McHugh *and* Alison Stapleton

Abstract
The ability to understand ourselves and take others' perspectives is fundamental to the development of our sense of self. This article explores self-as-context, an acceptance and commitment therapy process that fosters a healthy sense of self and flexible perspective-taking. The discussion begins with a conceptual overview of self-as-context, highlighting its relevance to psychological well-being and its relation to both relational frame theory and traditional behavior-analytic principles. Also provided here are clinical descriptions of the process of change involved in developing a self-as-context repertoire and the means of assessing self-as-context, as well as a synthesis of the research that has been done on self-as-context to date. Finally, future directions for research and practice with this process of change are described.

Key Words: self-as-context, perspective-taking, relational frame theory, selfing, self, psychological flexibility, acceptance and commitment therapy

"I'm a waste of space. I am not even worth my own time and effort. I don't do anything that matters and when I do try to do things I mess them up anyway. I don't actually matter to anyone in my life. I am just a burden who causes others to suffer. I cannot stand myself. The world would be a much better place if I was not in it."

—*Adapted from an ACT realplay in a training context.*

Our view of our self and who we are has a huge impact on the life we live. As practitioners and/or researchers interested in human behavior, we cannot ignore issues to do with the self, as every person has a sense of self. From an acceptance and commitment therapy (ACT) perspective, how we view and relate to our self is often limited and fails to capture much of who we are. Often, we view our self as being a collection of labels, evaluations, descriptions, and experiences. However, these are not stable parts of our self, and inflexibility with our view in this regard is highly problematic. For an example, see the excerpt from a therapy session presented at the beginning of this article. Rather than viewing ourselves as literally this content, stepping back and viewing our self as the container or observer promotes better long-term outcomes. Self-as-context is one of the six core processes of ACT and refers to this container view. Specifically, self-as-context is the perspective from which our self content and moment-to-moment ongoing experiences of self are observed.

In this article we provide a conceptual overview of self-as-context, focusing on how it applies to improving psychological problems and its relation to relational frame theory (RFT) and traditional behavior-analytic principles. In addition, we describe the means to measure self-as-context, clinical descriptions of the process of change involved in developing a self-as-context repertoire, and research on self-as-context to date. Finally, we explore future directions for research and practice with this process of change.

Developing a Self-ing Repertoire

A sense of self originates in learning to discriminate one's own and others' behavior. Children learn to relate to their own behavior as different from that of others by learning three key "deictic" or "perspective" relations: I versus YOU; HERE versus THERE; and NOW versus THEN. They learn to respond appropriately to questions such as "What are YOU doing HERE?, What am I doing NOW?, What was I doing THEN?" and so on. They also learn that whenever they are asked about their own behavior, they always answer from the point of view of I, HERE, and NOW. They learn that this perspective is consistent and different from that of others. For example, if you ask one author about their behavior, they will always answer from the position of I, HERE, and NOW in response to your question asked by YOU, THERE (where you are), and THEN (when you asked—a few seconds ago). "I" is always from this perspective here, not from someone else's perspective there. A sense of self is therefore abstracted through learning to talk about one's perspective in relation to other perspectives. As we relationally frame more and more of our own behavior (e.g., "I feel scared") and compare it with that of others ("I am more scared than you"), we begin to have a concept of self ("I am an anxious person"). As the child grows into an adult, these repertoires of framing one's behavior in relation to that of others becomes increasingly fluent. As a sense of self develops, so too does the ability to understand that others have desires, beliefs, and wishes. From the contextual behavioral science (CBS) perspective, relational framing underpins the development of empathy, a sophisticated sense of self, and transcendence (McHugh et al., 2019).

From the CBS point of view, there are three functionally different self-repertoires: (1) self-as-content; (2) self-as-process; and (3) self-as-context (Hayes, 1995; see Table 11.1). Before describing these three self-repertoires, it is important to note a terminological issue. In contrast to mainstream traditional approaches, CBS defines the self as an action (i.e., responding to

Table 11.1 A summary of the self-repertoires in accordance with contextual behavioral science

Self-Repertoire	Definition	Example	Therapeutic Question Prompts
Self-as-content	Stories, evaluations, and descriptions about "I"	"I am boring" "I am not enough" "I am a failure"	"List things about yourself? How do you describe yourself? What descriptions of yourself limit you?"
Self-as-process	Ongoing knowing self/ current experience	"I am currently having the thought that I am 'not enough' and feeling anxiety."	"What were you feeling then? And what are you feeling now?"
Self-as-context	Flexible perspective-taking	"I notice that my thoughts and feelings are part of me but I am more than these parts. I am the witness of all my experiences across my life."	"Who is noticing? Notice you are having the thought that you are not good enough. Who is having that thought??

one's own responding) and not as an entity. Hence, it is arguably more appropriate within our approach to use the term *self-ing* (i.e., as a verb) rather than *the self* (i.e., as a noun) for the phenomenon in which we are interested. Sometimes it seems more appropriate, and less confusing, to refer to the self as a "product" of the action of self-ing, rather than to refer to the action itself, and thus at times in this article the term *self* is used as well.

Self-as-Content

Self-as-content consists of all the labels, evaluations, and descriptions that people construct about themselves and their histories over time (e.g., "I am bad at writing book chapters, I am only pretty with make-up, I am shy in public"). As soon as verbal humans become self-aware, they begin to interpret, explain, evaluate, predict, and rationalize their behaviors. They strive to organize their descriptions and evaluations of personal histories and tendencies into a consistent presentation of a "self" that generally persists across time and situations. For example, someone might describe themselves as a kind person based on a noticed behavior pattern over time whereby they frequently give compassionate advice, time, or assistance to other people. This description which they might use to portray themselves to others is coherent in that it groups together functionally similar instances of behavior consistent with the concept of kindness as they have learned it.

Self-as-content includes every verbally known aspect of life that integrates self-knowledge of one′s current and historical feelings, sensations, preferences, abilities, thoughts, interactions, learning, and the like—in fact, all of one's conscious experiences. It is also multilayered because contingencies support different depths of self-knowledge in different contexts. For example, a person might explain a given instance of behavior to their boss in a different way than they would explain it to their therapist. Also, the way they might present themselves or even think of themselves might be very different with different people (e.g., friends, family, work colleagues) based on differences in their history with different individuals.

Self-evaluations are always made here and now about current (HERE and NOW) and noncurrent (THERE and THEN) behaviors. However, people rarely attend to the process of interpreting and evaluating as it happens in the present moment—in other words, to the fact that this process is itself an act of relational framing. Difficulties can occur when the products of relational framing (e.g., thoughts, judgments, comparisons, beliefs) are responded to as objectively true and as inherent aspects of the real world. When such responding (e.g., believing thoughts such as "I am worthless") results in dysfunctional or maladaptive behavioral outcomes (e.g., experiential avoidance), this is referred to in ACT as cognitive fusion (see Ruiz, Gil-Luciano, & Segura-Vargas, this volume, for more discussion of cognitive fusion).

One particularly important aspect of self-as-content is the issue of coherence that is built into language and how it impacts the sense of self. Language is useful because it allows people to predict and influence the behavior of others as well as to alter their environment in certain ways (e.g., problem solving). However, in order for it to work in this way, there must be a certain level of coherence between the formulations themselves as well as between what people say and what they actually do. Society trains children to be coherent and consistent in their use of language from the moment they first begin to speak. For example, imagine a young boy sees a dog for the first time and says that he is scared of the dog. As he gets more curious, he approaches the dog and says he loves it. An adult might laugh at the child's incoherent responding, unintentionally punishing the child for flexibility in favor of coherence. People are directly trained to provide consistent responses. So, any changes in preferences or opinions are often met with aversive stimuli (e.g., people laughing at us).

Coherence becomes associated with social reinforcement (e.g., we get praise for working things out, for being right), while lack of coherence becomes associated with social punishment (e.g., we get directly punished or perhaps are even ridiculed). Cognitive fusion and coherence can be problematic when self-evaluations (e.g., "I'm selfish") come to appear as historically rooted and unchangeable (e.g., "I've learned to be selfish because I've never had anyone else have my back"). People's stories may become rigid and ossified and no longer mere descriptions of past behavior, and rather also become guides of future behavior in directions that maintain the story's coherence (e.g., "Because I'm selfish, people often end up not liking me, even in intimate relationships. On the other hand, what can I do? You can't teach an old dog new tricks! So maybe it's best that I continue to look out for myself as much as possible because, ultimately, I'm not going to get on with people anyway"). This may result in the person ignoring or discounting contradictory evidence (e.g., "Yes, I was kind and generous in that specific case, but it suited me to act that way at that time"), selectively attending to and amplifying confirmatory evidence (e.g., "As a result of thinking only of myself, I've let people down time and time again"), and acting in ways that are consistent with their story about who they are and how they came to be that way.

Conceptualized self-stories can lay a trap in that they can appear to explain the causes of a person's past behavior. A person might say things like: "I failed that exam because I'm stupid" or "I didn't get out of bed today because I'm depressed." This kind of reasoning, though common, can create a self-amplifying feedback loop where one seems to lose the ability to change what one does because what a person does is who they are and who they are is what they have done in their past. This implies that the only way to change the future is to change the past, which is impossible. Thus, this line of thinking can effectively lock a person into a verbal cage of their own making. Coherence-based fusion with a conceptualized self may thereby maintain dysfunctional patterns of behavior.

Self-as-Process

Humans are behaving organisms that live and change with time. As humans interact with their environment, they respond both overtly and covertly in response to their ongoing experiences. Self-as-process is the ongoing verbal discrimination of the psychological events that are experienced as they occur. Statements that reflect the self as a process of knowing typically begin with phrases such as "I feel . . . , I think . . . , I wonder . . . ." The self-as-process feeds the self-as-content (e.g., in order to know that "I am a depressed person," I must first know that I frequently feel sad and have low energy across many contexts) and is also necessary to contact a sense of the transcendent self or self-as-context because a self-monitoring repertoire is required to observe the observer.

Self-as-process is extremely useful in behavioral regulation for the socio-verbal community as well as for the individual. With regard to the socio-verbal community, it allows other members of the verbal community to predict a person's behavior without knowledge of that person's learning history. For example, if an individual says that they feel anger toward another, then this may allow other people to predict how they might act toward that person in particular contexts. Self-as-process is also a critical guide for the individuals themselves. In order to respond effectively to one's own responding, one must first be aware of the response and its impact. For example, understanding and responding to thoughts and feelings about other people's behaviors in a fluid and flexible manner are critical in the context of establishing and maintaining personal relationships.

Self-rules would also be much less effective without self-as-process. Verbal humans produce vast numbers of self-directed rules that guide their behavior. Some are simple and trivial (e.g., "I should take a left turn at the shop"), while others are complex and profound (e.g., "I must do something meaningful with my life"). However, the effect of self-rules is undoubtedly significant. Self-rules are relevant with respect to both self-as-content as well as self-as-process. In regard to self-as-content, for example, a person may prescribe a rule for themselves based on their self-concept (e.g., "I won't bother applying to university because I'm not intelligent enough to get accepted"). Nevertheless, self-rules produced on the basis of self-as-process are particularly important because they can guide behavior in an ongoing way in potentially important life situations. Such rules might include the appropriate way to act with regard to particular feelings in particular contexts (e.g., feelings of anxiety that might arise in an important situation such as a job interview) and might be relatively useful (e.g., "anticipate and accept such feelings as they arise while continuing to perform as needed") or potentially disadvantageous (e.g., "avoid such feelings at all costs, including if possible by avoiding situations where they typically arise").

Threats to development of a self-as-process include inadequate training by the verbal community, such as when awareness and expression of emotions, thoughts, and sensations are punished, ignored, denied, or contradicted. This is frequently observed in the case of child neglect or abuse. A neglected child may not learn to accurately describe sets of emotions and sensations they experience as "hunger" or "boredom" or "fatigue" if there is no one to ask questions and teach to label these experiences in a way that allows them and others to respond to these experiences effectively. Similarly, a child who experiences pain and fear at the hands of a parent and is met with the response "Mommy/ Daddy loves you and would never do anything to hurt you" may not learn to accurately predict or describe their psychological experience.

An individual can also have weak self-knowledge as the result of experiential avoidance, particularly if they try to avoid or escape difficult internal experiences (i.e., thoughts, feelings, and physical sensations). Self-knowledge of aversive events is itself aversive, which means that humans cannot successfully avoid or escape pain in the long term. Because they cannot escape their own psychological experience, instead they often attempt to avoid the awareness of the experience (e.g., "I don't know how I'm feeling. I feel nothing at all."). Chronic experiential avoidance of this nature results in difficulties in observing and describing thoughts, emotions, and sensations, which are characteristic of such psychological disorders as depression, post-traumatic stress disorder, and borderline personality disorder, and have obvious implications for the self.

Other difficulties linked to deficits in the self-as-process repertoire include an inability to persist in or change focus (e.g., attention disorders, obsessive self-focus leading to phobic anxiety), the dominance of a conceptualized past and future whereby the present moment is lost to worry and rumination (e.g., anxiety and depression), and the dominance of judgments and their relevance to self (e.g., narcissism, depression, anxiety, personality disorders).

Self-as-Context

Self-as-context is the stable perspective from which all self-relevant processes can be seen, including problematic self-labeling as well as helpful self-based values (i.e., life directions that are meaningful to the individual). Self-as-context is used to help clients disentangle themselves from their descriptions and evaluations. Self-as-context involves the clients seeing themselves as the thinkers, not their thoughts, and to be the feelers, not their feelings. Self-as-context is the invariant in all perspective discriminations (i.e., HERE and NOW). It can be thought of as a transcendence of psychological content that allows acceptance of that content. In the CBS literature, Hayes (2011, as cited in Moran et al., 2018, p. 57) defines self-as-context as:

> the coming together and flexible social extension of a cluster of deictic relations (especially I/here/now) that enable observation and description from a perspective or point of view. Self-as-context

enables or facilitates many different experiences, including theory of mind, empathy, compassion, self-compassion, acceptance, defusion, and a transcendent sense of self.

Self-as-context is a complex process, requiring deictic, distinction, hierarchy, and temporal frames. Essentially, self-as-context requires I–here–now noticing that "I am distinct from my internal experiences," that "I am the container of these experiences," and that, "unlike these internal experiences, the part of me that notices them is stable, continuous, and unchanging over time." Simply put, self-as-context involves noticing the perspective of I, HERE, and NOW where one is looking from rather than just being the thoughts, feelings, or sensations that one is currently experiencing. In that sense, self-as-context involves flexible perspective-taking. Flexible perspective-taking underpins many psychological processes such as empathy (e.g., "I here now notice your pain"), compassion (e.g., "I here now notice your pain and respond with kindness"), and defusion ("I here now am having the thought that I am not good enough").

As self-as-context is an abstraction from the content of verbal responding, it is "contentless" and thus constant, stable, and unchanging from the time it first emerged (i.e., you will always be the observer observing from I, HERE, and NOW). Self-as-context is a product of verbal responding that applies to everything that a person has ever done, it incorporates both the nonverbal self (as a behavioral stream resulting from direct psychological processes) as well as the verbal self (as both object and process of knowledge gained through language) and has thus been described as providing the experiential link between nonverbal and verbal self-knowledge.

Self-as-context in the narrow sense has sometimes been referred to as the transcendent self because it is difficult to describe or contact verbally despite being a product of language. It cannot be experienced as an object because experiencing it would necessitate adopting a perspective on it that was not one's own perspective, which is impossible! Hence, it is not thing-like and thus can be described as limitless, unchanging, and ever present. For these reasons, it is often linked with spiritual and religious concepts and experiences. The appearance of these connotations of the self-as-context in the CBS literature has sometimes led people to think of this concept as relatively ethereal and perhaps out of the range of normal experience. This is true to the extent that even though these phenomena are an apotheosis of the process of deictic framing, they do not define the process. Furthermore, understanding the self-as-context as a core feature of deictic framing that facilitates a sense of self is important for an individual, even if they rarely or never experience phenomena such as those just mentioned. At the same time, they are potentially important and powerful experiences that should be developed and promoted. For example, increasing levels of deliberate reflexive engagement with one's behavior (i.e., self-as-process) may strengthen the self-as-context repertoire and make core experiences (such as those aforementioned) more likely.

Self-as-context, especially in the narrower "pure perspective" sense, has important implications for how humans experience and regulate psychological pain because this sense of self is not threatened by aversive content in the way that the conceptualized or knowing selves can be. It allows a person to confront deep emotional pain and facilitates willingness, compassion, and intimacy. Self-as-context assists with defusion, particularly from the conceptualized self, and also fosters acceptance. Self-as-context is powerful clinically, enabling clients to view their experiences from a safe place while also providing a sense of stability amidst the constant chaotic changing of the other selves.

A weak self-as-context repertoire results in a variety of social and psychological problems, including an unstable identity or sense of self (as seen, for example, in borderline personality and dissociative disorders), fear of annihilation in the face of aversive private experiences, difficulties with intimacy or connecting with others, social anhedonia, stigma or objectification of others, and a lack of empathy or self-compassion.

How to Facilitate Self-as-Context

A suite of metaphors and exercises are available to train self-as-context in the ACT literature. Two key tools widely used to illustrate self-as-context to clients in applied settings are the Classroom Metaphor (Stoddard & Afari, 2014) and the Observer Exercise.

The Classroom Metaphor

> Imagine a classroom full of students. Some of them are "problem" students who talk back to the teacher, stick gum under the desks, and send text messages when the teacher isn't looking. Some are "good" students who pay attention, get good grades, and suck up to the teacher. Some are "average" students who sit at their desks and go relatively unnoticed. Then there's the teacher at the front of the room who evaluates all the students, telling the problem students to pipe down, pay attention, and be good, and praising the good students and putting gold stars on their papers . . . . So perhaps you aren't the students or the teacher—the thoughts, feelings, or evaluations—but the classroom—the vessel that simply contains those experiences.
>
> *(Stoddard & Afari, 2014, p. 120)*

Stoddard and Afari's (2014) Classroom Metaphor was designed to illustrate that clients are more than their internal experiences. The rowdy, unruly students represent the client's negative thoughts, feelings, and physical sensations (internal experiences), while the good and average students represent their positive and neutral internal experiences, respectively. The teacher at the head of the classroom represents how the client evaluates and engages with their internal experiences. When people are operating from a self-as-content framework, they are like the teacher evaluating students; trying to tell the rowdy students to pipe down and awarding the good students gold stars. However, in doing this, people often fail to notice that they are more than the students or the evaluations, that there is another part to this metaphor; the classroom. While the classroom is in close contact with the students, it is also distinct from them. It is the container holding them, expansive and stable across time.

The Classroom Metaphor is a useful clinical tool to facilitate a perspective shift from self-as-content to self-as-context. It can be easily adapted (e.g., team, coach, field of play; client, therapist, therapy room), allowing clinicians to ground the metaphor in a context that is relevant to their particular client, enhancing saliency.

The Observer Exercise

The Observer Exercise (Hayes et al., 1999b) was designed to begin to establish a sense of self that exists in the present and to provide a context for cognitive defusion. In this exercise, the client's attention is directed to different domains with which people can become overidentified. It creates a psychological state in which there is a sense of transcendence and continuity; a stance that is self-aware of the content but not defined by it. The Observer Exercise helps the client become aware that they are present in this space at this moment and that they are the one noticing. The typical format of the exercise involves inviting the client to bring a number of past memories from their lives (e.g., three) to their awareness. As each memory is brought to mind, explicit cues such as "Who notices this?" are introduced to illustrate the observer perspective. Before exploring the memories with the client, the therapist grounds the client in the present by guiding them to direct their attention inward. This can involve instructions on how to sit and to close the eyes or find a spot to focus their gaze and to direct their attention on the five senses or bodily experiences such as the breath, sitting in a chair, feeling their feet on the floor or their arms on the armrest or on their lap. Once the client is grounded, a number of memories can be explored. An example of how to guide the client to notice the observer perspective for a past memory is as follows:

> I want you to remember something that happened last summer. Raise your finger when you have an image in your mind. Good. Now just look around that image. Remember all the things that were happening then. Remember the sights . . . the sounds . . . your feelings . . . and as you do that, see if you can notice that you were there, then noticing what you were noticing. See if you can catch the person behind your eyes who saw, and heard, and felt. You were there then and you are here now. I'm not asking you to believe this. I'm not making a logical point. I am just asking you to note the experience of being aware and check and see if it isn't so that in some deep sense the you that is here now was there then. The person aware of what you are aware of is here now and was there then. See if you can notice the essential continuity—in some deep sense, at the level of experience, not of belief, you have been you your whole life.
> *(Adapted from Hayes et al., 1999b, p. 193)*

Other metaphors such as the Chessboard (Hayes et al., 1999b), the Sky and the Weather (Harris, 2019), and the Stage Show (Harris, 2019) are also useful clinical tools. Each of these metaphors features stimuli that can be used to illustrate appetitive/ aversive internal experiences (i.e., chess pieces; clouds; actors and props) and expansive stable containers representing the self-as-context perspective (i.e., the chessboard; the sky; the stage/theater).

When using metaphors to enhance self-as-context, it is important to ensure that clients are not attempting to use self-as-context as a means to avoid unwanted internal experiences. For example, when exploring The Stage Show Metaphor, a client who expresses a desire to wait in the lobby for the duration of parts of the show that represent negatively evaluated internal experiences may be attempting to engage in experiential avoidance. It is important to emphasize that self-as-context is our noticing self that allows us to contact unwanted internal experiences in a nonthreatening way, and not divorce them entirely.

The previous exercises are extremely useful clinical tools. However, it is important to stress that practitioners must know which processes they are trying to target when promoting self-as-context or broad flexible perspective taking repertoires. The section that follows presents the key repertoires that a practitioner needs to focus on to promote flexible self-ing (Villatte et al., 2015). Put simply, any exercises that promote an ongoing reflective process of awareness, perspective-taking, self as the container of experiences, and the interactive nature of self as action are exercises that will facilitate self-as-context. One key issue is that a balance must be found between stability in the self and variability in the behavioral repertoire. That is, variability and stability often seem to be opposing processes. The sections that follow will illustrate how to promote both in tandem. Specifically, to develop flexible self-ing, the practitioner needs to focus specifically on how they can target: (1) I as Various; (2) I as Perspective; (3) I as Container; and (4) I as Flexible. Each of these will be presented in more detail.

I as Various

In order to find variability in the process of awareness, the practitioner can stabilize the client's perspective so that they can see the fluctuation of experiences across time. This involves stopping and noticing. It can be achieved through a number of ways such as: long-term meditative practice; repeatedly directing the client's attention to the present while helping them to notice the changes in experiences (e.g., "How do you feel now? And now? And now?"); or getting the client to notice changes in perspective (e.g., recall different situations and moments of their life). Techniques that illustrate variability in the process of awareness will focus on either variability in the client's experiences or variability in the client's views over time.

NOTICING THE VARIABILITY OF EXPERIENCES

When clients indicate in therapy that they are constantly having one particular feeling or thought that seems to subsume all other experiences (e.g., "I am disliked by everyone"), helping them stop and find the variability in the process of awareness is useful. Regular mindfulness practice can help clients to notice the variability of their experiences. In applied contexts, the practitioner can also point to how experiences vary in session. For example, if a client states that they are constantly having a certain feeling (e.g., anxiety) or thought (e.g., "I am stupid"), the practitioner can ask the client, "Is that feeling showing up here now?" As the session progresses, the therapist can again ask the client, "And what are you feeling now?" Over time, checking in with the client about their current feelings or thoughts will help the client see that their experiences vary even within the timeframe of their sessions.

NOTICING MULTIPLE VIEWS

In addition to demonstrating that experiences vary, the therapist can also help the client by varying views. Clients overlook variability when fused. In order to do this, the therapist can get the client to remember different situations and moments of their life when things were experienced differently. For example, if a client mentions a certain view they hold about themselves, such as "I am unstable," the therapist can help the client look at different times when they may hold other views about themselves: "Is this always the case? Is there ever a time when you don't see yourself as unstable?" By exploring different views of themselves ("How did you see yourself before you were diagnosed? How did you view yourself when you were promoted at work?"), the therapist helps the client see that the one view that seems to override all others is just one view and that the view they hold of themselves varies.

I as Perspective

In the last section, we stressed the importance of noticing variability of experience to broaden the client's sense of self. However, the practitioner's attempt to highlight the variability of experience can also disrupt the client's sense of self. After all, if the client is not just their experiences, then what is stable across time? Finding stability in a sense of perspective involves noticing the common perspective across experiences (e.g., notice who is noticing thoughts, sensations, and feelings across a variety of experiences) and noticing the common perspective across points of view (e.g., notice who is noticing the experiences of you today, yesterday, in a year's time). In order to start to notice the fluctuations in experience across time, the practitioner needs to help the client to notice that there is something stable across time about them too. There is someone who has noticed all their experiences. What is stable is not their experiences (these vary) but rather the perspective from which these experiences are contacted. In order to help clients to gain this sense of stability while noticing variability, it is important to identify this sense of perspective, which is sometimes referred to as the "observer" perspective. The therapist can help the client to develop this observer perspective by helping them notice perspective-taking across experiences and perspective-taking across points of view.

NOTICING PERSPECTIVE-TAKING ACROSS EXPERIENCES

Experiences are different across times (e.g., today, last year), places, and perspectives, but the noticer is the same. The practitioner can help the client notice who is observing their experiences of today, yesterday, or a year's time. In order to do this, the therapist can get the client to notice different views they have held about themselves across different activities. For example, if a client says "I am a loser," the practitioner can point out that this is a view they hold by saying, for example, "You are thinking of yourself as a loser right now." Next, they can look to other times in the client's life by asking, "How did you think about yourself when you were a student at university,? Or when you won the marathon?" This approach helps by pointing to the fact that across all views the client holds about themselves (i.e., how they conceptualize themselves), there is a stable part that has noticed all these views (e.g., "What is the part of you that has noticed all these views?").

NOTICING PERSPECTIVE-TAKING ACROSS POINTS OF VIEW

From an ACT perspective, practitioners can also help clients to notice that there is a common perspective across points of view. To help the client develop this stable sense of self (i.e., the observer of all their experiences), practitioners can help them notice different points of view they have held/will hold about themselves. For example, if a client comes to session saying that they are "pathetic," the therapist can extend this limited self-conceptualization by looking at whether this view is/was/will be the view they hold as they look across different views (e.g., "What was your view of yourself before your marriage broke down," and "What would it be in a year if you met someone new?"). Then the practitioner can emphasize the stable perspective that notices all clients' views about themselves across time (e.g., now, when they were married, in a year's time). This will help the client become aware of the ongoing stable part of themselves that is unchanging across time.

I as Container

The first two steps of developing a flexible sense of self emphasize the importance of helping clients notice the variability in their experiences and developing perspective-taking skills to foster a broad sense of self that is stable across time (e.g., the unchanging noticer or observer). However, as verbal organisms, people are always navigating in the sea of language. Coherence is built into human language. Helping clients find coherence in context is an important part of developing a flexible self repertoire. This involves facilitating the development of a more contextual sense of self that brings together the experiences and stability in the sense of perspective of these experiences into a coherent network based on hierarchical relations. That is, there is an "I" that contains all of my thoughts, feelings, sensations, and memories across time that is at the top of a hierarchy, and all these experiences are just parts of that "I."

Viewing the self hierarchically as a context of all experiences allows awareness of experiential processes and perspective-taking. This hierarchical dimension of self is targeted by a number of self-as-context exercises and metaphors in ACT such as the Classroom Metaphor discussed earlier (i.e., you are not the students or the teacher; you are the classroom holding them). Exercises such as these are designed to illustrate that there is a distinction between the self and psychological experiences and also that a hierarchical relation exists between experiences and self as the context of all of them. This perspective is useful because when the self is at the top of the hierarchy, then even when things within a lower level of the hierarchy change (e.g., descriptions, evaluations, thoughts about self), our self still remains intact at the top level of the hierarchy. Of course, it is important not to build the hierarchical sense of self as just another story about the self (i.e., another self-concept); rather, the therapist first wants to help the client gain a broader awareness of experiences and sense of perspective. Once this awareness has been established, a new, functionally coherent sense of self-ing is possible that is broad and flexible. Exercises that emphasize coherence in context will target a hierarchical dimension of self and a distinction between the self and the client's experiences.

EMPHASIZING THE DISTINCTION BETWEEN THE SELF AND THE EXPERIENCES

Noticing coherence in context involves helping a client to notice when coherence is unworkable. Emphasizing the distinction between the client's self and their experiences shifts the focus of the client's self-labels, judgments, and evaluations to their actions. Practitioners can help clients to relate to their self-labels, judgments, and evaluations as distinct from their "self" (e.g., "You are not your evaluations"). When a client is fused with self-judgments and evaluations, these become part of their self-concept. The difficulty for clients is that, when this occurs, the self-concept can become the target for change when self-judgments and evaluations are negative or unwanted. For example, if a client evaluates themselves as unworthy, they may think that somehow they need to change being unworthy rather than noticing that this is an evaluation they hold about themselves. When emphasizing the distinction between the self and experiences, the practitioner is helping the client change their perspective from viewing themselves as their experiences to seeing themselves as distinct from their experiences.

EMPHASIZING THE OBSERVER AS A HIERARCHICAL DIMENSION OF SELF

A number of techniques can be employed to help foster a hierarchical (observer) sense of self. There is a distinction between relating to the self hierarchically versus as the same as one's experiences. In order to emphasize the hierarchical dimension of self (e.g., self-as-context), the practitioner can help the client to formulate their experiences as something they *have* rather than something they *are*.

I as Flexible

When facilitating clients to develop self-as-context, one issue that cannot be ignored is responsibility. At times, clients can take too much responsibility for their actions and be overly self-critical, whereas at other times clients might see themselves as being completely out of control of their life and their choices. Of course, these are not mutually exclusive attitudes, given that someone might take too much responsibility and be overly self-critical while also seeing themselves as being out of control. In fact, someone who is too focused on needing to be in control might be someone who perceives themselves as being out of control. From the ACT perspective, what is most important is that the client sees that they are not solely responsible but that they are able to respond. A simple intervention that may help with this distinction is to point out to the client that the word "responsibility" combines two words, "response" and "ability," or ability to respond (Hayes et al., 2012).

NOTICING THE IMPACT OF THE CONTEXT

The first way in which the practitioner can develop responsibility in the interaction is by helping the client become aware of the influence of contextual variables on their actions (e.g., "Given your history, it is not surprising that you made these choices"). To do this, the therapist can ask questions about a variety of current and past elements that may contribute to the client's ineffective action. For example: "Can you think of things that characterized that day that might have led you to acting this way?"; "If you were me right now, how would you view this situation?"; "Given your history, how could it be any other way?" This approach can help the client see that they are not to blame for the current situation they are in.

NOTICING THE IMPACT OF BEHAVIORS

In order to empower clients, the practitioner can direct the client's attention to: (1) the impact of their actions on the contextual variables: for example, "Now with this knowledge, what can you do that is in line with what matters to you," and (2) the impact of the client's influence: for example, "When you study, how does that impact your grades and/or your relationship with your parents?" This can help the client to see that they do have the ability to respond in ways that are useful in bringing them toward meaningful life directions. Table 11.2 summarizes the targets that promote self-as-context.

Measuring Self-as-Context

Measurement is an important issue to consider when looking at processes of change. Measures allow us to track clients' repertoires pre-, during, and postintervention, helping to determine whether interventions are required or effective. Measures available to assess self-as-context include three quantitative measures (Jeffcoat, 2015; Yu et al., 2016; Zettle et al., 2018) and one qualitative coding framework (Atkins & Styles, 2016). See Table 11.3 for a summary of these measures and an overview of published peer-reviewed empirical support for their psychometric properties. Since the writing of this chapter, another measure called the Questionnaire on Self-Transcendence (QUEST; Fishbein et al., 2020) has been released and validated as a measure of self-transcendence.

Table 11.2 A summary of targets and respective ways to promote self-as-context

Major Target	Specific Target	Prompts
I as Various	Noticing the variability of experiences	"How do you feel now? And now? And now?"
	Noticing multiple views	"Remember different situations and moments of your life."
I as Perspective	Noticing perspective-taking across experiences	"Who is noticing thoughts, sensations, and feelings across a variety of experiences."
	Noticing perspective-taking across points of view	"Notice who is noticing the experiences of you today, yesterday, in a year's time."
I as Container	Emphasizing the distinction between the self and the experiences	Help the client to separate experience from action.
	Emphasizing the observer as a hierarchical dimension of self	Help the client to notice they are the container of all their experiences.
I as Flexible	Promoting awareness of the influence of contextual variables on actions	"Given your history, it is not surprising that you made these choices." (i.e., you are not to blame)
	Promoting awareness of the impact of actions on the contextual variables	"Now with this knowledge what can you do which is in line with what matters to you?"

Table 11.3 Summary of self-as-context measures and samples they have been employed with			
Measure	Aspect of Self-as-Context	Published Peer-Reviewed Empirical Support	Sample
Three-Dimensional Reno Inventory of Self Perspective (3D-RISP; Jeffcoat, 2015)	Entanglement (fusion with self-content), centering (grounding), and transcendence	Internal consistency (Gallego et al., 2020) Brazilian adaptation (Peixoto et al., 2019)	College students College students
Self-Experiences Questionnaire (SEQ; Yu et al., 2016)	Distinction from internal experiences and observing self	Internal consistency, construct validity, and predictive validity (Yu et al., 2016) Internal consistency and construct validity (Yu et al., 2017a, 2017b) Internal consistency (Zettle et al., 2018) Internal consistency (Moran & McHugh, 2019)	Adults with chronic pain Adults with chronic pain College students Young adults
Self as Context Scale (SACS; Zettle et al., 2018)	Centering (grounding) and transcending (observing self)	Internal consistency, test–retest reliability, concurrent validity, discriminant validity, incremental validity, known groups validity (Zettle et al., 2018) Internal consistency (Moran et al., 2018)	College students; Adults receiving psychotherapy Adolescents
The Functional Self-Discrimination Measure (FSDM; Atkins & Styles, 2016)	Distinction from internal experiences and hierarchy between self and private events for the self (SX) and others (OX)	Feasibility, interrater reliability (Atkins & Styles, 2016) Interrater reliability (Styles & Atkins, 2018) Interrater reliability (García-Zambrano et al., 2019) Interrater reliability (Moran & McHugh, 2020)	Adults working in a law firm or hospital Adults in a range of organizational settings Adults with disabilities Adolescents

The 3-Dimensional Reno Inventory of Self-Perspective

The 3-Dimensional Reno Inventory of Self-Perspective (3D-RISP; Jeffcoat, 2015) is a 13-item self-report measure of the self that consists of three subscales: (1) entanglement (fusion with self-content; "*Negative thoughts are harmful to me*"); (2) centering (the ability to remain grounded; "*Even as my emotions rise and fall, I tend to remain grounded*"); and (3) transcendence (hierarchical self; "*No matter how great the pain is, there is a place inside that remains unchanged as long as I live*"). Items are rated on a seven-point scale (1 = never, 7 = always), with higher scores indicating greater self-perspective skills and lesser fusion with self-content. Jeffcoat (2015) found that the 3D-RISP had good internal consistency (α = .86 in a sample of 646 college students; α = .79 in a sample of 543 members of the general population) and construct validity in two large samples. Further support for the reliability of the 3D-RISP comes from Gallego et al. (2020), who found good internal consistency (α = .88) for the total measure in a sample of college students. In terms of cross-cultural validity, Peixoto et al. (2019) observed good psychometric properties (measurement invariance between genders, scale reliability, and construct validity) for a Brazilian version of the RISP.

The Self-Experiences Questionnaire

The Self-Experiences Questionnaire (SEQ; Yu et al., 2016) is a 15-item self-report measure of a "contextual self" that consists of two subscales: (1) self-as-distinction (defusion from self content; *"I am able to separate myself from my thoughts and feelings"*), and (2) self-as-observer ("*I can observe experiences in my body and mind as events that come and go*"). Items are rated on a seven-point scale (*0 = never true, 6 = always true*), with higher scores indicating greater perception of the self as distinct from self content and a greater tendency to be the observer of one's internal experiences (i.e., greater self-as-context). In a sample of 528 adults with chronic pain, Yu et al. (2016) evidenced the factor structure of the SEQ, further finding support for the measure's construct validity, predictive validity, and internal consistency (α = .9). The psychometric properties of the SEQ, specifically internal consistency and construct validity, were further supported by Moran and McHugh (2019), Yu et al. (2017a, 2017b), and Zettle et al. (2018) in samples of adolescents, adults with chronic pain, and college students, respectively.

The Self as Context Scale

The Self as Context Scale (SACS; Zettle et al., 2018) is a 10-item self-report measure consisting of two subscales: centering (fusion with self content; "*I am able to notice my changing thoughts without getting caught up in them*") and transcending (observer self; "*Even though there have been many changes in my life, I'm aware of a part of me that has witnessed it all*"). Items are rated on a seven-point scale (*1 = strongly disagree, 7 = strongly agree*), with higher scores indicating greater defusion from self content and a greater tendency to notice the observer perspective. In a large sample of college students, across a series of six studies, Zettle et al. (2018) evidenced the factor structure of the SACS, further finding support for the measure's concurrent, discriminant, incremental, and known-groups validity, internal consistency, and test–retest reliability. The internal consistency of the SACS measure was further supported by Moran et al. (2018) in a sample of adolescents (α = .819).

The Functional Self-Discrimination Measure

The Functional Self-Discrimination Measure (FSDM; Atkins & Styles, 2016) is an RFT-informed functional assessment measure that examines occurrences of self and other discriminations in qualitative responses using a coding framework. This measure recognizes two types of self-as-context: self-as-distinction (defusion from self content: "*Shame is only a feeling*") and hierarchical self (acknowledgment that private events are contained within the self: "*I'm the space in which my thoughts and feelings happen*"). It is important to note that the latter of these is exceptionally rare in natural language and that the FSDM functions only as a proxy for self-as-context because, as a concept, self-as-context is highly experiential and defined by the absence of content. The FSDM has been employed in a range of contexts, from adults in organizational and academic settings (Atkins & Styles, 2016; Styles & Atkins, 2018) to adults with disabilities receiving services from a rehabilitation center (García-Zambrano et al., 2019), to people experiencing homelessness (Murthy et al., 2021), and to adolescents (Moran & McHugh, 2020). Overall, while each study reported good interrater reliability, the consensus is that codes for self-as-context (particularly those for the hierarchical self) may require further finetuning in order to sufficiently capture self-as-context in natural language while also distinguishing it from defusion.

Existing Research

Several different types of studies examine self-as-context in accordance with the CBS approach to the self. Four categories of emergent research support are: (1) correlational data, (2) qualitative research, (3) quantitative research with a self-as-context process measure, and (4) quantitative research assessing self-as-context interventions. See Table 11.4 for a summary of the key findings from these research bodies.

Correlational Data

There are seven published peer-reviewed studies that examine the relationships between self-as-context and other psychologically relevant variables. The first of these studies, by Yu et al. (2016), developed and assessed the psychometric properties of the SEQ in a sample of adults (n = 528) attending a pain management service. SEQ total scores were positively correlated with pain acceptance, decentering, and committed action, and were also negatively correlated with depression, pain interference, and functional impairment in work.

Table 11.4 A summary of findings from studies examining self-as-context in accordance with contextual behavioral science

Study Type	Overall Summary of Findings
Correlational data	Self-as-context is positively correlated with pain acceptance, decentering, committed action, spirituality, well-being, mindfulness, psychological flexibility, self-as-process, and less rigid self-as-content repertoires. Self-as-context is negatively correlated with pain-related interference, functional impairment in work, depression, stress, experiential avoidance, suicidal thinking, psychological inflexibility, neuroticism, and depression-related interference.
Qualitative research	Data are mixed regarding the relationships between self-as-context (SX) and well-being, distress, and psychological flexibility. While there is strong evidence that SX combined with values-oriented self-rules and perspective-taking significantly predicts well-being in general population adults, it is unclear whether these findings extend to diverse populations. SX codes, particularly hierarchical self codes, are rare and likely need to be refined.
Quantitative research with a self-as-context process measure	Self-as-context (as measured by the SEQ) improved following ACT, with these improvements maintained at 9-month follow-up. Changes in SEQ scores significantly predicted changes in pain-related interference, functional impairment in work, and depression.
Quantitative research assessing self-as-context interventions	In the research laboratory, self-as-context beneficially impacts tolerance of aversive stimuli, task performance, and experience of completing a self-criticism task. Outside the laboratory, self-as-context beneficially impacts adolescents' problematic behaviors, impulsivity, psychological inflexibility, depressive/ anxious thoughts, and mindfulness. Self-as-hierarchy may be superior to self-as-distinction for these purposes.

Using the SEQ, the second correlational study by Yu et al. (2017a) examined the role of self-as-context in functioning in a sample of adults with fibromyalgia (n = 298). SEQ total scores were positively correlated with pain acceptance and negatively correlated with pain-related interference, functional impairment in work, depression, and depression-related interference. After controlling for pain, SEQ scores were statistically significant predictors of pain-related interference, functional impairment in work, and depression, but not depression-related interference.

Employing the SEQ, the third correlational study by McCracken et al. (2018) examined the relationships between suicidal thinking and components of psychological flexibility in a sample of adults attending treatment for chronic pain (n = 424). SEQ total scores displayed a small, statistically significant negative correlation with suicidal thinking. In contrast to acceptance and committed action, neither SEQ total scores nor defusion were unique predictors of suicidal thinking.

In the fourth correlational study, Moran and McHugh (2019) examined SEQ scores in relation to distress in a sample of young adults (n = 102) while controlling for gender and deictic ability. Dependent variables were depression, anxiety, stress, experiential avoidance, deictic ability, and gender. Scores of the SEQ self-as-observer subscale were negatively correlated with depression, stress, and experiential avoidance. Other than a strong positive correlation with the self-as-observer subscale, the self-as-distinction subscale was not statistically significantly related to any variable.

In developing and assessing the psychometric properties of the SACS, Zettle et al. (2018) conducted a series of six studies using a large sample of college students. In addition to being strongly positively correlated with SEQ total scores, SACS total scores were positively correlated with spirituality, well-being, and mindfulness, and negatively correlated with psychological inflexibility, neuroticism, and distress.

Using the SACS, in a sample of adolescents (n = 176), the sixth correlational study by Moran et al. (2018) examined relationships between the three selves and mental health. SACS total scores were moderately negatively correlated with scores on depression, anxiety, and stress (Depression, Anxiety and Stress Scale; DASS-21 total scores). Higher SACS total scores were also related to greater self-as-process and less rigid self-as-content repertoires.

Employing the 3D-RISP, the seventh correlational study by Gallego et al. (2020) examined public speaking anxiety among college students (n = 106). While no statistically significant correlation was found between public speaking anxiety and the transcendence subscale, higher levels of public speaking anxiety were moderately correlated with higher levels of entanglement and lower levels of centering. 3D-RISP total scores were also strongly positively correlated with psychological flexibility.

Qualitative Research

To date, five studies have employed the FSDM. Two of these studies used the measure with adults in organizational and academic settings (Atkins & Styles, 2016; Styles & Atkins, 2018), while the remainder used the FSDM with more diverse samples, specifically adults with disabilities (García-Zambrano et al., 2019), adolescents (Moran & McHugh, 2020), and people experiencing homelessness (Murthy et al., 2021).

As part of an evaluation of a coaching program at a law firm and a hospital, Atkins and Styles (2016) conducted semistructured interviews over the phone (n = 29) ranging from 35 to 60 minutes in duration. During these interviews, participants were prompted to talk about their lived experience, exploring perceived antecedents and consequences of their responses to situations. Overall, findings revealed that self-as-context (SX) displayed small positive correlations with well-being and significantly predicted depression when controlling for values-oriented self-rules (VOR). A combination of VOR+SX better predicted well-being than VOR alone, predicting approximately 25% of variance in some well-being measures. Finally, even when controlling for well-being at baseline, the occurrence of VOR + SX was a reliable predictor of well-being 12 months later.

In a subsequent replication with a new sample (10 adults with a tertiary qualification who were interviewed for an average of 44 minutes three to four times, three to five days apart), Styles and Atkins (2018) found that VOR, SX, and VOR + SX were statistically significantly positively correlated with psychological flexibility and all included measures of well-being. SX displayed a strong positive correlation with OX (i.e., taking the perspective of an other; other-as-context). While SX and OX alone were not sufficient predictors of well-being, they displayed significant negative correlations with control-oriented self-rules, with the combination of VOR + SX + OX strongly significantly predicting well-being.

García-Zambrano et al. (2019) examined the effects of a defusion plus perspective-taking protocol on the occurrence of SX codes with a sample of 20 individuals (10 assigned to a control group), with disabilities receiving services from a rehabilitation center. Interviews averaged 9 minutes in duration. Overall, seven participants who received the protocol demonstrated an increase in the occurrence of SX codes, while one displayed a decrease in rate. In terms of the control group, two participants demonstrated an increase in the occurrence of SX codes, while four demonstrated a decrease in rate. However, these differences between groups at posttest were not statistically significant.

In an analysis of adolescents' textual responses (n = 76) to prompts requiring them to discuss a time they felt a particular emotion, Moran and McHugh (2020) found no occurrences of hierarchical self codes. As such, in this study, SX codes referred only to instances of self-as-distinction. Overall, no statistically significant correlations were observed between SX and depression, anxiety, stress, well-being, or experiential avoidance, highlighting a need to further refine SX codes.

Using semistructured interviews (ranging from 40 to 78 minutes in duration) with people experiencing homelessness, Murthy et al. (2021) replicated Moran and McHugh's (2020) finding regarding a dearth of hierarchical self codes. Unlike the results of previous research, no statistically significant correlations were observed between SX and VOR or between SX and OX. Further diverging from earlier research was the finding that SX codes were moderately positively correlated with shame and psychological inflexibility, with no statistically significant correlation observed between SX and well-being. In this study, instances of SX were often related to substance misuse and as such may have been more closely linked to dissociation than to transcendence. Nonetheless, Murthy et al. concluded that SX codes should be further refined.

Quantitative Research with a Self-as-Context Process Measure

In an uncontrolled longitudinal study with a sample of adults (n = 412) with chronic pain, Yu et al. (2017b) examined changes in self-as-context (as measured by the SEQ) following approximately 22 hours of ACT, further testing if SEQ scores were associated with changes in other outcome measures. Participants completed process (SEQ and pain acceptance) and outcome (pain intensity, pain-related interference, functional impairment in work, and depression) measures at three points in time (preintervention, postintervention, and at 9-month follow-up). Overall, scores on all process and outcome measures improved postintervention, with improvements maintained at follow-up. Changes in SEQ scores significantly predicted changes in pain-related interference, functional impairment in work, and depression. Finally, participants who worsened posttreatment (i.e., participants whose raw change scores for outcome measures did not improve by half a standard deviation) differed from those who improved, showing a decline in SEQ scores from baseline to posttreatment.

Quantitative Research Assessing Self-as-Context Interventions

A number of published peer-reviewed empirical studies have examined the impact of self-as-context interventions on myriad outcome variables. Using a pre-post design, in the research laboratory, studies have examined the impact of a self-as-context intervention on participants' tolerance of aversive stimuli (i.e., cold-pressor task and 90-second aversive film clip), task performance, and experience (i.e., affect, discomfort, anxiety, and distress) post generating a negative self-referential thought (e.g., Carrasquillo & Zettle, 2014; Foody et al., 2013; Foody et al., 2015; Gil-Luciano et al., 2017; Hayes et al., 1999a; López-López & Luciano, 2017). Although an exhaustive overview of this research is beyond the scope of this article, we will present a brief overview of key studies. For a complete systematic review, readers are directed to Godbee and Kangas (2019).

With regard to tolerance of aversive stimuli, experimenters measured the length of time that participants endured the stimuli (i.e., held their hand in the cold water or continued to watch an aversive film), in addition to participants' self-reported pain, discomfort, and sensation intensity (Carrasquillo & Zettle, 2014; Gil-Luciano et al., 2017; Hayes et al., 1999a). Each study employed a control group for comparison against the group receiving a self-as-context intervention. In these studies conducted with college students and adult samples, the self-as-context interventions focused on the observing self (Carrasquillo & Zettle, 2014), a combination of the hierarchical self and self-as-distinction (Gil-Luciano et al., 2017), and self-as-distinction (Hayes et al., 1999a). While Gil-Luciano et al. (2017) and Hayes et al. (1999a) found that self-as-context interventions were associated with greater tolerance (but not reduced self-reported pain) than were control protocols, Carrasquillo and Zettle (2014) found that a generic self-as-context intervention was functionally equivalent to an attention-placebo condition in terms of its impact on tolerance (study 1). Carrasquillo and Zettle (2014) reported a stronger effect of the self-as-context intervention when it was tailored to the participants' context (i.e., the experience of pain), highlighting the importance of tailoring self-as-context interventions for the individual.

Regarding task performance, in a sample of undergraduates (n = 42), López-López and Luciano (2017) found that a self-as-distinction plus self-as-hierarchy intervention significantly increased participants' performance on a discomfort-inducing task (i.e., greater frequency of correct responses and productivity scores) relative to a self-as-distinction or control protocol. Furthermore, for participants in the control condition, greater discomfort at posttest was related to lower task performance. However, this relationship was not observed for participants receiving either self-as-context protocols, further evidencing that self-as-context promotes a beneficial perspective shift.

Saunders et al. (2013) observed a similar effect of self-as-context on task performance. In a sample of college students (n = 100), Saunders et al. compared the impact of an observing self-intervention versus an unfocused attention control on a memory task that required participants to recall self-referent behaviors that were either socially desirable or undesirable. Only the self-as-context protocol increased recall. Saunders et al. (2013) concluded that self-as-context decreased the extent to which participants engaged in experiential avoidance of socially undesirable self-referent behaviors (i.e., perceived negative self-as-content), facilitating superior retrieval.

Finally, in a recent study with a sample of older adults (n = 59) who were primed with negative stereotypes about aging, Hashimoto et al. (2020) found that a self-as-context intervention (observing self plus a rapid word repetition defusion exercise) improved performance on a Block Design task from the Wechsler Adult Intelligence Scale-III. Simply put, self-as-context appeared to prevent older adults' task performance from being impaired by behavioral assimilation to age stereotypes. Older adults assigned to an attention-placebo control did not display this "inoculation" effect. However, fusion with a conceptualized self did not moderate the effect. Hashimoto et al. (2020) suggest that the function of ageing stereotypes may have been transformed independently of participants' psychological flexibility and call for future research to further explore this suggestion.

Regarding the experience of generating negative self-referential thoughts, in college student samples (n = 44 and n = 59), Foody et al. (2013, 2015) compared the impact of self-as-distinction and self-as-hierarchy interventions. Foody et al. (2013) found that self-as-hierarchy but not self-as-distinction resulted in a decrease in discomfort and anxiety following the self-criticism task, with self-as-hierarchy further resulting in decreases in stress, whereas self-as-distinction resulted in an increase in stress. Diverging from this result, despite employing a similar methodology, Foody et al. (2015) found negligible differences between self-as-hierarchy and self-as-distinction protocols on discomfort and anxiety. However, self-as-hierarchy was superior to self-as-distinction in beneficially impacting stress.

Beyond these laboratory-based studies, Luciano et al. (2011) examined the impact of self-as-distinction and self-as-hierarchy protocols on impulsivity, psychological inflexibility, depressive/ anxious thoughts, and mindfulness in a sample of adolescents displaying problematic behaviors. Adolescents (categorized as low and high risk) attended four 60-minute weekly sessions where they received the protocols in an experiential-computerized format. Low-risk participants received either the self-as-distinction (n = 4) or the self-as-hierarchy (n = 5) protocol, while high-risk participants only received the self-as-hierarchy protocol (n = 6). For low-risk participants, self-as-hierarchy had a greater effect than self-as-distinction on all measures. For high-risk participants, while there was no significant change in psychological inflexibility, self-as-hierarchy resulted in increases in mindfulness and a reduction in problematic behaviors. Overall, self-as-context appeared to beneficially impact problematic behaviors, impulsivity, psychological inflexibility, depressive/ anxious thoughts, and mindfulness.

Future Directions

Self-as-context is a powerful tool that provides clients with a safe place from which to explore their experiences. The potentiality for clients to attempt to use self-as-context as a mechanism to engage in experiential avoidance is worth further exploration (e.g., if a client mentions escaping to the lobby during the Stage Show Metaphor). It is important to remember that function trumps topography, so clinicians must explore seemingly avoidant tactics to gain insight into the functions for that specific client.

Given that self-as-context is a complex process that includes myriad relational frames (i.e., deictic, distinction, hierarchy, and temporal frames), enhancing ACT interventions via clinical RFT is a viable future direction (see Villatte, 2020, for more on enhancing ACT via clinical RFT). While clinical RFT has its challenges, it brings precision, fluidity, and flexibility to the therapeutic process. As a field, we must make RFT accessible rather than burdensome, while also maintaining its functional contextual underpinning. Above all else, when presenting self-as-context, it is important to remain grounded in the philosophy and principles underlying CBS.

While work on self-as-context has increased over the last number of years, much still remains to be done. For example, there is a serious need to explore the kinds of metaphors used to present self-as-context to clients, whether tailoring metaphors to enhance salience impacts on comprehensibility and whether experiential or didactic delivery results in better outcomes. This is particularly important for self-as-context because people can find it confusing initially (e.g., Dalrymple et al., 2020).

In addition, there is a need to explore means of measuring self-as-context. While existing self-report measures and qualitative coding frameworks can tap into self-as-context, ecological momentary assessment, behavioral measures, and single-item indicators of self-as-context would undoubtedly be useful in clinical and experimental contexts. Given that self-as-context is essentially a fluid perspective-taking repertoire that allows us to relate to stimuli in a variety of ways (i.e., with self-as-context the behavioral repertoire is not dominated by one perspective), recent empirical work on deictics may offer insights into developing such measures (e.g., Montoya-Rodriguez et al., 2017).

Concluding Remarks

The present article provides a tour of the CBS approach to the self, with a particular focus on self-as-context. It began with the development of self-ing and the three functionally different self-repertoires. From here, the article focused on ways to facilitate self-as-context via metaphors and exercises (e.g., the Classroom and the Observer), in addition to the key repertoires that a practitioner must focus on to promote flexible self-ing. Also described are means of assessing self-repertoires and existing research on self-as-context in accordance with CBS.

The most important relationship people can have is the one with themselves. If we can foster a flexible sense of self-as-context within ourselves and our clients/ participants/ fellow humans, then we can create profound change AND discover within ourselves a safe place from which to view this change. This work aims to move us all from self-as-content to self-as-context, for example, from the client quote at the beginning of the chapter to a broader more flexible sense of self:

> *I, here, now am noticing that I am distinct from my internal experiences. There is more to me than my thought that "I am a waste of space." There is more to me than my thought that "the world would be a much better place if I was not in it." I am the container of these experiences and, unlike these experiences, unlike these thoughts and feelings, the "me" that is noticing and having them is continuous and unchanging. I can hold these experiences without allowing them alone to define who I am.*

References

Atkins, P., & Styles, R. (2016). Measuring self and rules in what people say: Exploring whether self-discrimination predicts long-term wellbeing. *Journal of Contextual Behavioural Science, 5*(2), 71–79. https://doi.org/10.1016/j.jcbs.2016.05.001

Carrasquillo, N., & Zettle, R. D. (2014). Comparing a brief self-as-context exercise to control-based and attention placebo protocols for coping with induced pain. *The Psychological Record, 64*, 659–669. https://doi.org/10.1007/s40732-014-0074-3

Dalrymple, K. L., D'Avanzato, C., & Morgan, T. (2020). Implementing ACT in a partial hospitalization program. In M. E. Levin, M. P. Twohig, & J. Krafft (Eds.), *Innovations in acceptance and commitment therapy: Clinical advancements and applications in ACT* (pp. 188–202). New Harbinger Publications.

Fishbein, J. N., Baer, R. A., Correll, J., & Arch, J. J. (2020). The Questionnaire on Self-Transcendence (QUEST): A measure of trait self-transcendence informed by contextual cognitive behavioral therapies. *Assessment*, In press. https://doi.org/10.1177/1073191120980061.

Foody, M., Barnes-Holmes, Y., Barnes-Holmes, D., & Luciano, C. (2013). An empirical investigation of hierarchical versus distinction relations in a self-based ACT exercise. *International Journal of Psychology and Psychological Therapy, 13*, 373–388.

Foody, M., Barnes-Holmes, Y., Barnes-Holmes, D., Rai, L., & Luciano, C. (2015). An empirical investigation of the role of self, hierarchy and distinction in a common ACT exercise. *The Psychological Record, 65*, 231–243. https://doi.org/10.1007/s40732-014-0103-2

Gallego, A., McHugh, L., Villatte, M., & Lappalainen, R. (2020). Examining the relationship between public speaking anxiety, distress tolerance and psychological flexibility. *Journal of Contextual Behavioral Science, 16*, 128–133. https://doi.org/10.1016/j.jcbs.2020.04.003

García-Zambrano, S., Rehfeldt, R. A., Hertel, I. P., & Boehmert, R. (2019). Effects of deictic framing and defusion on the development of self-as-context in individuals with disabilities. *Journal of Contextual Behavioral Science, 12*, 55–58. https://doi.org/10.1016/j.jcbs.2019.01.007

Gil-Luciano, B., Ruiz, F. J., Valdivia-Salas, S., & Suárez-Falcón, J. C. (2017). Promoting psychological flexibility on tolerance tasks: Framing behavior through deictic/hierarchical relations and specifying augmental functions. *The Psychological Record, 67*, 1–9. https://doi.org/10.1007/s40732-016-0200-5

Godbee, M., & Kangas, M. (2019). The relationship between flexible perspective taking and emotional well-being: A systematic review of the "self-as-context" component of acceptance and commitment therapy. *Behavior Therapy, 51*(6), 917–932. https://doi.org/10.1016/j.beth.2019.12.010

Harris, R. (2019). *ACT made simple: An easy-to-read primer on acceptance and commitment therapy* (2nd ed.). New Harbinger Publications.

Hashimoto, K., Muto, T., Spencer, S. D., & Masuda, A. (2020). Mitigating behavioral assimilation to age stereotypes: A preliminary analogue investigation of a contextual behavioral science approach. *Journal of Contextual Behavioral Science, 18*, 48–52. https://doi.org/10.1016/j.jcbs.2020.08.006

Hayes, S. C. (1995). Knowing selves. *The Behaviour Therapist, 18*, 94–96.

Hayes, S. C., Bissett, R. T., Korn, Z., Zettle, R. D., Rosenfarb, I. S., Cooper, L. D., & Grundt, A. (1999a). The impact of acceptance versus control rationales on pain tolerance. *The Psychological Record, 49*, 33–47. https://doi.org/10.1007/BF03395305.

Hayes, S. C., Strosahl, K. D., & Wilson, K. G. (1999b). *Acceptance and commitment therapy: An experiential approach to behavior change*. Guilford Press.

Hayes, S. C., Strosahl, K. D., & Wilson, K. G. (2012). *Acceptance and commitment therapy: The process and practice of mindful change* (2nd ed.). Guilford Press.

Jeffcoat, T. (2015). *Development of the Reno Inventory of Self-Perspective (RISP): Measuring self in the ACT model* [Unpublished Doctoral thesis, University of Reno].

López-López, J. C., & Luciano, C. (2017). An experimental analysis of defusion interactions based on deictic and hierarchical framings and their impact on cognitive performance. *The Psychological Record, 67*, 485–497. https://doi.org/10.1007/s40732-017-0250-3

Luciano, C., Ruiz, F. J., Vizcaíno Torres, R., Sánchez Martín, V., Gutiérrez Martínez, O., & López López, J. C. (2011). A relational frame analysis of defusion interactions in acceptance and commitment therapy: A preliminary and quasiexperimental study with at-risk adolescents. *International Journal of Psychology and Psychological Therapy, 11*, 165–182.

McCracken, L., Patel, S., & Scott, W. (2018). The role of psychological flexibility in relation to suicidal thinking in chronic pain. *European Journal of Pain, 22*(10), 1774–1781. https://doi.org/10.1002/ejp.1273

McHugh, L., Stewart, I., & Almada, P. (2019). *A contextual behavioral guide to the self: Theory and practice*. New Harbinger Publications.

Montoya-Rodriguez, M. M., Molina, F. J., & McHugh, L. (2017). A review of relational frame theory research into deictic relational responding. *The Psychological Record, 67*(4), 569–579. https://doi.org/10.1007/s40732-016-0216-x

Moran, O., Almada, P., & McHugh, L. (2018). An investigation into the relationship between the three selves (self-as-content, self-as-process and self-as-context) and mental health in adolescents. *Journal of Contextual Behavioral Science, 7*, 55–62. https://doi.org/10.1016/j.jcbs.2018.01.002

Moran, O., & McHugh, L. (2019). Patterns of relational responding and a healthy self in older adolescents. *Journal of Contextual Behavioral Science, 12*, 74–80. https://doi.org/10.1016/j.jcbs.2019.02.002

Moran, O., & McHugh, L. (2020). Measuring occurrences of self and other discriminations in relation to mental health in adolescent textual responses. *Journal of Contextual Behavioral Science, 15*, 253–263. https://doi.org/10.1016/j.jcbs.2020.01.010

Murthy, V., Stapleton, A., & McHugh, L. (2021). Self and rules in a sample of adults experiencing homelessness: Relationships to shame, well-being, and psychological inflexibility. *Journal of Contextual Behavioral Science*. https://doi.org/10.1016/j.jcbs.2021.06.003

Peixoto, E. M., Gagnon, J., & Jeffcoat, T. R. (2019). Reno Inventory of Self-Perspective RISP: Cross-cultural adaptation and validity evidence. *Psico-USF, 24*(2), 233–244. https://doi.org/10.1590/1413-82712019240202

Saunders, J., Barawi, K., & McHugh, L. (2013). Mindfulness increases recall of self-threatening information. *Consciousness and Cognition, 22*(4), 1375–1383. https://doi.org/10.1016/j.concog.2013.09.001

Stoddard, J. A., & Afari, N. (2014). *The Big Book of ACT Metaphors: A practitioner's guide to experiential exercises and metaphors in acceptance and commitment therapy.* New Harbinger Publications.

Styles, R. G., & Atkins, P. W. (2018). Measuring perceptions of self and others in what people say: A replication and extension of the functional self-discrimination measure. *Journal of Contextual Behavioral Science, 9,* 45–52. https://doi.org/10.1016/j.jcbs.2018.06.005

Villatte, M. (2020). Using clinical RFT to enhance ACT interventions: The example of values work. In M. E. Levin, M. P. Twohig, & J. Krafft (Eds.), *Innovations in acceptance and commitment therapy: Clinical advancements and applications in ACT.* (pp. 30–40). New Harbinger Publications.

Villatte, M., Villatte, J. L., & Hayes, S. C. (2015). *Mastering the clinical conversation: Language as intervention.* Guilford Press.

Yu, L., McCracken, L., & Norton, S. (2016). The Self Experiences Questionnaire (SEQ): Preliminary analyses for a measure of self in people with chronic pain. *Journal of Contextual Behavioural Science, 5*(3), 127–133. https://doi.org/10.1016/j.jcbs.2016.07.006

Yu, L., Norton, S., Almarzooqi, S., & McCracken, L. M. (2017a). Preliminary investigation of self-as-context in people with fibromyalgia. *British Journal of Pain, 11,* 134–143. https://doi.org/10.1177/2049463717708962

Yu, L., Norton, S., & McCracken, L. M. (2017b). Change in "self-as-context" ("perspective-taking") occurs in acceptance and commitment therapy for people with chronic pain and is associated with improved functioning. *Journal of Pain, 18,* 664–672. https://doi.org/10.1016/j.jpain.2017.01.005

Zettle, R. D., Gird, S., Webster, B., Carrasquillo-Richardson, N., Swails, J., & Burdsal, C. (2018). The self-as-context scale: Development and preliminary psychometric properties. *Journal of Contextual Behavioural Science, 10,* 64–74. https://doi.org/10.1016/j.jcbs.2018.08.010

CHAPTER
12

Values in Acceptance and Commitment Therapy

Jenna LeJeune *and* Jason Luoma

Abstract
While the concept of values has been present in behavioral traditions dating back to Skinner, the analysis of the role of values in modern contextual behavioral science (CBS) in relation to motivation has greatly expanded over the past 30 years. In particular, values are important in a modern understanding of the role of human language in modifying how reinforcement occurs. In this article we outline values work as a foundational component of acceptance and commitment therapy (ACT) and analyze values through a CBS and relational frame theory lens. Included are an extensive review of the empirical literature on the role of values in ACT and a discussion of values measures commonly used in CBS research and clinical practice. Finally, we offer recommendations for the next steps needed to expand our understanding of this essential process.

Key Words: values, acceptance and commitment therapy, relational frame theory, contextual behavioral science, research, therapy, meaning, motivation, measures

Issues of meaning, purpose, values, and living a quality life are central to nearly all psychotherapy traditions, even if only implicitly. The concept of values has been present in behavioral traditions dating back to Skinner, who viewed values as an important source of reinforcement: "any list of values," he wrote, "is a list of reinforcers—conditioned or otherwise" (Rogers & Skinner, 1956, p. 1064). The role of values in modern behavioral approaches to motivation has greatly expanded over the past 30 years as researchers and theoreticians have attempted to more thoroughly understand the role of human language in modifying how reinforcement occurs. Concurrently, the so-called third wave of cognitive-behavioral therapy (CBT), arose and new forms of CBT, including acceptance and commitment therapy (ACT; Hayes et al., 2012), moved away from a more exclusive focus on symptom reduction toward a more central focus on flexible and adaptive responding, with values as a guide for that action (Hayes, 2004).

While many approaches address values and meaning in some capacity, working explicitly with values is a foundational component of ACT. According to Hayes (2004), chosen values are a "necessary component of a meaningful life and indeed a meaningful course of therapy" (p. 647). In ACT, the primary goal of therapy is to facilitate an individual's ability to choose what they want their life to be in the service of goal and then help them organize their behavior such that it serves those ends in a consistent, holistic, and sustainable way. In ACT, values define what is considered workable and effective for an individual, and ultimately, all of the other psychological flexibility processes are important only to the extent to which they facilitate valued living. In this article, we provide a conceptual and theoretical overview of values and the values process from an ACT perspective. We also review some of the values measures most commonly used in ACT research and clinical practice. Finally, we review some of the empirical data related to the way values are defined in ACT and offer recommendations for the next steps needed to expand our understanding of this essential process.

Conceptual Overview

Defining Values

This article focuses on a contextual behavioral science (CBS), and specifically ACT, perspective of values. CBS focuses on understanding the behavior of organisms in a context, defined historically and situationally. Thus, while we use the term *values*, a more accurate term might be *valuing*, as it highlights that the term *values* points to a particular form of verbal behavior. Although a more technical framework for understanding values can be found in the literature on relational frame theory (RFT; Hayes et al., 2001), the theory of language and cognition linked to ACT, in this chapter we will largely use the middle-level terms of the psychological flexibility model (Hayes et al., 2012) and the more common terms from behavior analysis.

Perhaps the most commonly cited and comprehensive definition of values from this perspective is that "values are freely chosen, verbally constructed consequences of ongoing, dynamic, evolving patterns of activity, which establish predominant reinforcers for that activity that are intrinsic in engagement in the valued behavioral pattern itself" (Wilson & Dufrene, 2009, p. 64). This definition is not meant to make an ontological claim that this is what values *are*, but instead to present a strategic explication of values intended to guide science and practice. This article considers each element of this definition.

VALUES ARE FREELY CHOSEN

Values, from an ACT perspective, have a quality of personal ownership, meaning that the individual has the subjective experience of choosing for themselves the principles they want to guide their behavior (Hayes et al., 2012). Values are by definition not selected based dominantly on aversive control or pliance, that is, behavior that follows relatively fixed, socially mediated rules. Another way to say this is that values are not dominantly based out of, constructed, or serving goals of avoidance or escape from pain or based on the expectations of others. The idea that values are freely chosen is not meant to imply an ontological claim of free will or behavior divorced from history or context, but instead points to the experience of choice that tends to occur when the selection between behaviors is relatively free from aversive control. Framing values as a choice also has strategic advantages in that it can help foster novel behavior that is less constricted by people's histories and personal narratives.

VALUES ARE VERBALLY CONSTRUCTED

Values are verbally constructed and thus dependent on language. Their psychological functions depend on behavioral principles of language (emerging from RFT) that incorporate but also go beyond older conceptions of operant or classical conditioning (Hayes et al., 2001). Unlike nonverbal animals, human behavior can be influenced by contingencies that are incredibly distanced in time or that may even not occur within their lifetimes (Wilson et al., 2010a). As such, values are able to influence behavior even if the individual has never had any direct contact with the events described (da Silva Ferreira et al., 2019). For example, a person may choose to attend protests in the service of building a society that is just and free, even if they have never personally experienced a just and free society.

VALUES ARE ONGOING, DYNAMIC, EVOLVING PATTERNS OF ACTIVITY

Values are behavior—they are constructed through language by humans. To talk about values as discovered, innate, or "true" apart from human action and intention, may be potentially useful clinically at times but is not coherent with ACT theory. These complex patterns of activity we call "values" are evolving and dynamic in the sense that the behavior changes across time as the individual is exposed to various experiences. Values are dynamic in that the expression of a value will vary from situation to situation. For example, a father might value being a loving and involved parent, but this will look different when the child is 3 months old versus an adult. In addition, the father's understanding of this value and their expression of the value will change from situation to situation and will evolve over time as the relationship matures, learning takes place, and different aspects of the value are articulated. Values are described as ongoing in that they refer to patterns of action that are constructed by an individual and can be seen in the larger patterns of behavior over time. Values are distinct from goals in that goals can be achieved and have an end. Values are also not found in any action itself (e.g., exercising, praying, or buying flowers for one's partner) but in the overarching purpose of the behavior (e.g., healthy living, expansive connection, or lovingly caring). Values are also not fleeting feelings or thoughts, but instead can be observed over time by seeing the larger pattern of purposes in someone's life.

VALUES ESTABLISH PREDOMINANT REINFORCERS INTRINSIC IN ENGAGEMENT IN THE VALUED BEHAVIORAL PATTERN ITSELF

Values are variables that maintain or reinforce particular ways of behaving (da Silva Ferreira et al., 2019). Values can establish certain events as reinforcing or heighten the reinforcement from already reinforcing events (Hayes & Wilson, 1993), thereby affecting the behavior emitted. Alternatively, we may state that values are verbal statements that serve to make certain consequences even more motivating (Dahl et al., 2009).

Values are intrinsic in the sense that it is the engagement in the valued behavior itself that is reinforcing, not other events that are extrinsic to the behavior and its natural consequences. For example, the reinforcement for someone whose behavior is guided by a values-based intention to be a loving brother does not come from the praise that is received by parents for acting in such a way, but from the very behavior of being loving toward one's sibling. At least part of the strength of this reinforcement comes from the coherence between the ongoing construction of what it means to be a brother and their behavior toward said brother. For example, this value could continue to reinforce behavior connected to being a loving brother even after the brother has died, for example by supporting his surviving child. In contrast to aversive control linked to negative reinforcement, which may decrease intrinsic motivation (Elliot & Harackiewicz, 1996), values strengthen motivation linked to positive reinforcement.

Functions of Values in ACT

VALUES GUIDE TREATMENT TARGETS

Values are at the heart of any ACT-based treatment plan and guide whatever success is achieved in therapy. "Values work [in ACT] establishes the primary purpose of therapy to be increasing the client's active contact with whatever is most important to him or her" (Sandoz & Anderson, 2015, p. 60). Inflexible behavioral repertoires, such as cognitive fusion and experiential avoidance, are key treatment targets in ACT only to the extent to which they interfere with values-consistent living.

Although from an ACT perspective, increased valued living is the ultimate therapeutic goal, many clients present to therapy with the primary goal of reducing suffering. Much of their behavior, just as it is for most humans, is likely oriented around experiential avoidance, that is, attempts to avoid, minimize, escape, or ameliorate internal difficult private experiences (e.g., thoughts, memories, feelings, sensations). People who are depressed are likely to orient much of their behavior around trying to feel less depressed. People who are anxious focus much of their energy on having less anticipatory anxiety or avoiding stimuli that trigger fear. Values provide an alternate guide for behavior that is larger than avoidance or escape, situating painful internal experiences in the context of more encompassing life goals, and through that, facilitate acceptance. While decreases in suffering are not the main point of ACT, empirically, evidence exists that not only is values-based action negatively correlated with subjective suffering, but values-based action frequently *precedes* changes in suffering (Gloster et al., 2017). Thus, it appears that when a person is supported in contacting and engaging with their values, their distress tends to reduce over time, not that reductions in distress precede valued living.

VALUES PROVIDE MOTIVATION AND SUSTAIN BEHAVIOR

In addition to directing treatment interventions, values provide motivation for the hard work of therapy and the hard work of living (Wilson & Murrell, 2004). When clients are able to experience the sense of free choice that is present when values guide behavior as opposed to behavior that is under aversive control or dominated by pliance, it is likely that these behaviors will be more sustained over time, persisting even in times of difficulty or when barriers are present. For example, values work is used as a method to increase motivation to engage in exposure-type interventions in which people confront fear or other difficult emotions (Wilson & Murrell, 2004; Thompson et al., 2013). From an ACT perspective that is grounded in values, exposure is framed as a way to develop the ability to make room for painful events so that those painful events do not deflect from a well-lived life.

From an RFT perspective, values are augmentals in that they are verbal stimuli that change the reinforcing value of particular consequences (Leigland, 2005; Plumb et al., 2009). RFT suggests that identifying and connecting with one's values serves as formative or motivative augmenting. They temporarily bring an individual into contact with potential verbal sources of reinforcement, thereby increasing the likelihood that the individual will choose to behave in line with their values (Hayes et al., 2001).

Additionally, RFT describes how language-able humans seek to maintain coherence in their verbal relational networks. Thus, declaring a value to be personally important may increase the likelihood that engaging in behavior consistent with that value will be intrinsically reinforced due to coherence with the value (Hayes et al., 2001). In contrast, incoherence between stated values and behaviors is likely to create dissonance and distress and therefore will be less likely to persist (Freijy & Kothe, 2013).

VALUES PROVIDE A LARGER AND MORE CONSISTENT SENSE OF MEANING AND DIRECTION IN LIFE

Values function, in part, to help establish a consistent and overarching direction in life. Avoidance and escape focus on moving away from that which one does not want to experience. In contrast, values are constructive in that they involve moving toward a particular direction over time or building up a particular quality in life by engaging in increasingly expanding patterns of behavior that serve those ends.

The process of valuing creates meaning. "Meaning is constructed in moments when we are connected with what matters" (LeJeune & Luoma, 2019, p. 21). Values provide a kind of verbal glue that links present moment actions to purposes and meanings that are larger than this moment, perhaps even larger than the individual themselves. The sense that one's behavior serves a larger purpose can elevate a person beyond themselves and bring a richness to life that is lacking when one is solely focused on the concrete events occurring in the present.

Values can provide a more consistent sense of direction than fleeting thoughts and feelings. Feelings and thoughts are constantly changing, but values, at least at their more abstract levels, tend to be relatively consistent over time (Luoma et al., 2017). Similarly, values string together actions and goals into a larger verbal tapestry, providing a sense of consistency in the face of changing life situations, circumstances, and relationships. Clarity as to what is most important can serve as a guide for action across a range of situations and through many hardships. Values can serve as a kind of lighthouse amidst the psychological storms that are frequent in life (Luoma et al., 2017).

VALUES ENABLE FLEXIBILITY IN THE SELECTION OF GOALS

While many therapy approaches help clients identify goals, in ACT, goal setting is secondary to and dependent on values construction. Goals are selected because they are directly linked to values the client has chosen to make important. Values are the direction, and the goals are markers that provide more proximal guides for behavior and allow the individual to track whether they are still moving in that direction. Prioritizing values over goals enables the individual to be less rigidly attached to a particular goal if that goal becomes unworkable in a given context, thereby facilitating behavioral flexibility. For example, a more consistent connection to an overarching value around healthy living may enable more adaptive behavior change in response to a disabling injury compared to attachment to a particular physical activity that is no longer available because of the injury.

Values Measures

While numerous values measures are used in other frameworks, this section focuses on only those measures relating to values specifically based on an ACT or CBS framework. The three values measures cited most often in the ACT empirical literature are the Valued Living Questionnaire (VLQ; Wilson et al., 2010b), the Bull's Eye Values Survey (BEVS; Lundgren et al., 2012), and the Valuing Questionnaire (VQ; Smout et al., 2014). A more general overview of other ACT values measures is presented in Table 12.1. Comprehensive reviews of values measures can also be found in reviews by Barrett et al. (2019) and Reilly et al. (2019).

Valued Living Questionnaire

DESCRIPTION AND APPLICATION OF THE VLQ

The VLQ (Wilson et al., 2010b) is the most widely utilized ACT values measure in research (Reilly et al., 2019). It is a 20-item self-report measure consisting of 10 valued domains on which individuals provide a rating for how important that particular domain is to them (importance) and how consistent they feel their behavior has been with their values in the domain (consistency). A valued living composite score is calculated by multiplying importance and consistency scores for each domain and summing the scores, and is recommended as the primary score of interest (Reilly et al., 2019).

The VLQ has been adapted for specific populations and behaviors including dementia caregivers (Romero-Moreno et al., 2016), bereaved college students (Davis et al., 2016), adolescents (Swain et al., 2015), alcohol use (Miller et al., 2016), and Malaysian young adults at risk of developing psychosis (Berry et al., 2019). A revised version called the VLQ-2 was published in a book (Wilson & Dufrene, 2009) for clinical use but does not appear to have been studied psychometrically. The VLQ-2 identifies 12 valued domains rated across six

Table 12.1 ACT Values Measures

Measure	Reference	Domains[1]	Importance rating[2]	Consistency rating[3]	Written narrative[4]	Perceived barriers[5]	Values motives[6]
Bull's Eye Values Survey (BEVS)	Lundgren et al., 2012	Y	N	Y	Y	Y	N
Chronic Pain Values Inventory (CPVI)	McCracken & Yang, 2006	Y	Y	Y	N	N	N
Daily Valuing Tracking Form (DVTF)	LeJeune & Luoma, 2019	N	N	Y	Y	N	N
Engaged Living Scale (ELS)	Trompetter et al., 2013	N	N	Y	N	Y	N
Novel Values Questionnaire (NVQ)	Grégoire et al., 2018	N	Y	Y	N	N	N
Personal Values Questionnaire (PVQ)	Blackledge & Ciarocchi, 2006	Y	Y	Y	Y	N	Y
Personalized Psychological Flexibility Index (PPFI)	Kashdan et al., 2020	N	N	Y	N	N	N
Survey of Guiding Principles (SGP)	Ciarrochi & Bailey, 2008	Y	Y	Y	N	N	Y
Valued Time and Difficulty Questionnaire (VTDQ)	Wiggs & Drake, 2016	Y	Y	Y	N	Y	N
Values Tracker (VT)	Pielech et al., 2016	N	N	Y	N	N	N
Valued Living Questionnaire (VLQ)	Wilson, Sandoz, Kitchens, et al., 2010b	Y	Y	Y	N	N	N
Valued Living Questionnaire-2 (VLQ-2)	Wilson and DuFrene, 2009	Y	Y	Y	N	Y	N

Valued Living Scale (VLS)	Jensen et al., 2015	Y	Y	Y	N	N	N
Values for Physical Activity Questionnaire (VPAQ)	Clemens et al., 2020	Y	Y	Y	Y	Y	Y
Values of Younger Ages Scale (VOYAGE)	Ishizu et al., 2020	N	N	Y	N	Y	N
Values Wheel	Barrett et al., 2020	N	Y	Y	N	N	N
Valuing Questionnaire (VQ)	Smout et al., 2014	N	N	Y	N	Y	N

1. Does the scale distinguish between different valued domains?

2. Does the scale assess how important a respondent feels a particular value/domain to be?

3. Does the scale assess the extent to which a respondent believes their behaviors are consistent with their stated values?

4. Is there an opportunity for the respondent to provide a written narrative of their values?

5. Does the scale assess the respondent's perceived level of barriers to living out their values?

6. Does the scale allow for the respondent to indicate why they hold a particular value to be important (e.g., intrinsic versus extrinsic motives)?

dimensions: possibility, current importance, overall importance, action, satisfaction with level of action, and concern.

PSYCHOMETRICS OF THE VLQ

In their original psychometric investigation in an undergraduate sample ($n = 253$), Wilson et al. (2010b) reported generally adequate internal consistency (importance scale $\alpha = 0.77$, consistency scale $\alpha = 0.75$, composite score $\alpha = 0.77$) and test–retest reliability (importance scale $r = 0.90$, consistency scale $r = 0.58$, composite score $r = 0.75$). Subsequent studies have also shown satisfactory to excellent internal reliability estimates for the VLQ composite scores, ranging from $\alpha = 0.71$ (Pakenham, 2015; Stafford-Brown & Pakenham, 2012) to $\alpha = 0.91$ (VanBuskirk et al., 2011) and the importance scale, ranging from $\alpha = 0.71$ (Swain et al., 2015) to $\alpha = 0.93$ (Juncos et al., 2017). However, the consistency scale has been somewhat less internally consistent, with Cronbach's alphas ranging from poor, $\alpha = 0.60$ (Juncos et al., 2017) to good $\alpha = 0.89$ (Wetterneck et al., 2013). Convergent validity evidence is based on modest but statistically significant correlations of the VLQ composite score with measures of experiential avoidance, anxiety, depression, relationship difficulties, general psychopathology, and overall mental health functioning (Wilson et al., 2010b). Finally, although the VLQ was originally normed on a predominantly white population, subsequent studies have demonstrated sound psychometrics for Black samples as well (Graham et al., 2015; Miller & Orsillo, 2020; VanBuskirk et al., 2011). Overall, a recent review of values measures (Reilly et al., 2019) judged the VLQ to have moderately good psychometric quality based on their measures of the VLQ's content validity, internal consistency, and construct validity.

Bull's Eye Values Survey

DESCRIPTION AND APPLICATION OF THE BEVS

The BEVS (Lundgren et al., 2012) is one of the most widely used and broadly applicable ACT-based values measures. Relatively brief and easy to use, the BEVS is also one of the few values measures that includes respondent's qualitative description of their values. This self-report measure utilizes a visual depiction of a bull's eye or target divided into four quadrants—labeled work/education, leisure, personal growth, and relationships. Respondents are asked to write a brief values statement for each domain based on the following instructions: "What are the qualities that you would like to get out of each area and what are your expectations from these areas of your life?" They then place an "X" on the target to represent their distance from the "bull's eye" in how consistently they are living that stated value (i.e., the consistency score). Respondents then record barriers they believe are interfering with their ability to live their stated values within each domain and rate how much each barrier is impeding them (i.e., the persistence score). Finally, they are asked to write a "valued action plan" and a specific action step for each domain.

Although the BEVS is used in research and clinical settings, its methodological quality suggests more support for its use as a clinical assessment and clinical intervention tool than for its use in empirical research (Reilly et al., 2019). Because it relies on relatively simple visual cues (a depiction of a bull's eye/target) that respondents interact with, the BEVS can be easily used across individuals from a wide range of ages, cognitive abilities, and cultures. Low values consistency ratings can be used to identify high-value treatment targets. In addition, changes across time can be used to track client perceptions of change in values-based action.

PSYCHOMETRICS OF THE BEVS

Lundgren et al. (2012) report supportive evidence for content validity, convergent validity, and divergent validity in two samples: 27 South African adults with epilepsy and 181 Swedish undergraduates. Measurements at three time points demonstrated adequate to good test–retest reliability for both the attainment (r = .70–.85) and the persistence scores (r = .71–.90). Modest correlations with measures of overall life satisfaction and experiential avoidance were reported for the attainment and persistence scores, demonstrating some convergent validity for the BEVS. No evidence for structural validity was provided in these initial validation studies. In general, subsequent studies using the BEVS have not reported internal reliability (Lundgren et al., 2008, Murrell & Kapadia, 2011, Tyrberg et al., 2016), though Villatte et al. (2016) reported a Cronbach's alpha score of α = 0.95 for the BEVS consistency subscale in their study of 15 adults seeking outpatient mental health services. Based on their criteria for its level of demonstrated content validity, internal consistency, and construct validity, Reilly et al. (2019) concluded that there is a "slight lack of evidence for the methodological quality of the BEVS for empirical ACT research" (p. 298).

The Valuing Questionnaire

DESCRIPTION AND APPLICATION OF THE VQ

The VQ (Smout et al., 2014) is a self-report scale with 10 statements rated according to how true they are of the respondent's behavior. Unlike the VLQ or the BEVS, the VQ does not attempt to assess or differentiate values based on discrete-valued domains. Rather, it measures general consistency in living in line with values in all areas of life. It was specifically designed to allow clinicians to track client progress on a regular basis. Exploratory and confirmatory factor analysis conducted during measurement development identified two subscales: a progress scale, which reflects enactment of values and "clear awareness of what is personally important and perseverance" (Smout et al., 2014, p. 166), and an obstruction subscale, which measures impairment in valued living "due to avoidance of unwanted experience and distraction from values by inattention to values or attention to other psychological experiences" (Smout et al., 2014, p. 166). Confirmatory factor analysis has supported the identification of these two subscales (Carvalho et al., 2018).

PSYCHOMETRICS OF THE VQ

Initial validation studies (Smout et al., 2014) conducted using an undergraduate sample (n = 630) and adult outpatients (n = 285) demonstrated good internal consistency (progress scale α = 0.89, obstruction scale α = 0.87). Convergent validity evidence was found in correlations between both the VQ progress and VQ obstruction scales and measures of depression, anxiety, positive affect, negative affect, mindfulness, psychological flexibility, and overall life satisfaction. In general, these correlations are higher than those reported for either the VLQ or the BEVS, suggesting that the VQ may have superior convergent validity (Smout et al., 2014). Subsequent studies have demonstrated poor to good internal consistency for the progress subscale, ranging from α = 0.61 (Levin et al., 2018) to α = 0.89 (Levin et al., 2016) and satisfactory to good on the obstruction score, ranging from α = 0.76 (Rickardsson et al., 2019) to α = 0.88 (Christie et al., 2016). A study utilizing a population in Sierra Leone reported a Cronbach's alpha of α = 0.39 for the full-scale VQ, though the authors noted that this was likely because several of the items on the VQ did not translate well into Sierra Leonean culture (Stewart et al., 2016). Studies on the psychometrics of the VQ, with the exception of Stewart et al. (2016), have involved predominantly (80% or more) white participants, suggesting more study with diverse samples is needed. Of the eight ACT values measures evaluated by Reilly et al. (2019), the VQ was rated the highest in terms of psychometric quality, with the VQ receiving passing scores on all eight measures of content validity, internal consistency, and construct validity.

Values-Focused Clinical Interventions

Values work within ACT focuses on increasing the ability to choose what ways of living (i.e., values) would result in a sense of meaning, purpose, or integrity and as well as on helping to organize actions into increasingly expanding patterns of behavior that serves those ends (LeJeune & Luoma, 2019). While the extent to which values are explicitly targeted in ACT will vary depending on the clinical context, values provide the foundation for any ACT-based therapy as values are ultimately the "why" in ACT (Luoma et al., 2017). As values are fundamental to treatment planning in ACT, the concept of values is typically introduced very early in therapy, often as part of the informed consent and intake process. For example, a brief values measure might be included in the initial assessment. An ACT therapist might orient the client toward values early in therapy by saying something like the following:

> "I've heard quite a bit about your struggles with depression and our work will definitely include identifying strategies to address those. And yet, a meaningful life is more than just the absence of depression. So, we also need to be able to take a step back to get a bigger picture of your life and ensure that ultimately our work is about helping you create a well-lived, meaningful life, whatever that would be for you personally. The word we use for that in ACT is 'values' and we'll talk more about that as we go along. But since this is at the heart of what our work will ultimately be about, I wanted to introduce you to this idea of values right from the start."

Thus, treatment planning from an ACT perspective includes not only identifying presenting problems, but also looking at the bigger picture of the client's life and the context in which those difficulties are situated (LeJeune & Luoma, 2019). Bringing values into the early stages of treatment allows for that broader perspective and can help motivate and increase willingness to engage in therapeutic tasks (Katz et al., 2016).

Although values are frequently introduced early on in ACT clinical interventions, it is not uncommon that after this initial introduction and possibly a more cursory assessment of values is done, the therapy focus may shift more toward other psychological flexibility processes (e.g., defusion or acceptance repertoires), returning to do more extensive values assessment and exploration after psychological flexibility is strengthened. Thus, like other flexibility processes, values work in ACT is not typically confined to discrete periods but rather is returned to again and again, woven in across the course of therapy. Depending on the depth and breadth of the clinical work, values work may include encouraging clients to articulate and publicly commit to their values, helping track current behaviors and assess those for consistency or inconsistency with stated values, and helping the client learn to distinguish between more outcome-oriented goals and values that are more focused on the process of living (Luoma et al., 2017).

One commonly used ACT-based values intervention is a values card sort (Hayes & Ciarrochi, 2015; LeJeune & Luoma, 2019). In this exercise, clients are presented with a set of cards on which are written values statements or words. Clients are asked to sort the cards into categories—for example, those that are most important, moderately important, and least important to them. When sorting the cards, clients are encouraged to approach the exercise from a place of choice rather than avoidance, with instructions such as "What would you want to make important in your life if you were totally free to choose?" or "Imagine that all your suffering has ended and that you have no more problems. What would you still find meaningful and worthwhile?" (LeJeune & Luoma, 2019, p. 62). Often used during the initial stages of values exploration, this exercise is not intended to be a means for clients to definitively identify or choose values, but rather as a tool to allow them to gain experience with choosing in relation to values.

Various values assessment measures that lead clients to reflect on and write about their values, such as in the Personal Values Questionnaire (Blackledge & Ciarrocchi, 2006) or the BEVS (Lundgren et al., 2012), can also be used. Other common values exercises lead clients through eyes-closed visualizations, such as imagining attending their own funeral or retirement party. One such visual exercise is the Sweet Spot exercise (Wilson & Dufrene, 2009) wherein clients are guided to explore past examples of valued living. Through facilitating shifts in temporal, spatial, and/or interpersonal relational frames, this exercise allows clients to contact the contingencies of living out those values in the there-and-then in a way that can shape their current behavior.

While engaging in values-based action is most often conceptualized as the committed action process in ACT, which is outlined elsewhere in this volume, experimenting with values-based action can also be incorporated into values construction and exploration interventions. For example, in values prototyping exercises (LeJeune & Luoma, 2019), clients engage in values exploration specifically through engaging in values-based activity. Values prototyping is an iterative process in which therapist and client develop prototypes together that the client then enacts in order to help explore values and gather information about what values they may choose to commit to.

Research Overview

Values processes focus on identifying, articulating, and contacting what matters to clients whereas committed action processes focus on putting values into action. Most of the existing research relating to values does not distinguish between these two processes, and partially, as a consequence, the research on values processes is relatively underdeveloped compared to other flexibility processes.

Values Consistency

The largest body of research relates to self-reports of how successful people feel they have been in putting their values into action, which we refer to using the rubric "values consistency." Most of the research is either correlational in nature or measures changes in values consistency in response to intervention.

CORRELATIONAL STUDIES

Cross-sectional studies have shown that values consistency is robustly associated with a variety of measures of healthy functioning. Greater values consistency has been associated with greater well-being and lower cancer-related distress among cancer patients (Ciarrochi et al., 2010), lower burnout among addiction counselors (Vilardaga et al., 2011), well-being and life-satisfaction in a general treatment sample (Barrett et al., 2020), resilience, satisfaction with life, and depression in college students (Ceary et al., 2019), lower rates of suicidal ideation among veterans (Bahraini et al., 2013) and those receiving care on inpatient units (Roush et al., 2018), higher quality of life among those diagnosed with generalized anxiety disorder (GAD; Michelson et al., 2011), and lower symptom severity among those diagnosed with obsessive-compulsive disorder (OCD; Wetterneck et al., 2013). Stapleton et al. (2020) reported a complex set of findings wherein values-consistent living was associated with some indices of physical health, but not others in their college student sample.

Living in a manner consistent with one's values may also buffer the effects of various stressors. In college students, values consistency moderated the negative impact of stressful life events on resilience, such that, at high levels of valued living, had little impact on self-reported resilience (Ceary et al., 2019). In African American university students, engagement in valued action moderated the relationship between experiences with racist events and anxious and depressive symptoms, such that when valued living was high, experiences with racism were not significantly associated with symptoms (Graham et al., 2015). In a sample of racial/ethnic minority graduate students, higher values-based living was predictive of lower depression, anxiety, and stress over and above the negative impacts of low perceived belongingness and racism-related stressors (Miller & Orsillo, 2020). In a trauma-exposed sample, values consistency predicted lower functional impairment, lower posttraumatic stress, and lower depression (Donahue et al., 2017). In the same study, values consistency also moderated the relationship between posttraumatic symptoms and functional impairment such that the link between these two variables was weakened as valued living increased. Values processes also appeared to mitigate the impact of COVID-19 related stress in Italian adults (Pakenham et al., 2020). Finally, values consistency was associated with higher self-reported resiliency among bereaved college students (Murrell et al., 2017).

CHANGES IN VALUES CONSISTENCY DUE TO INTERVENTION

Values consistency has been shown to increase following ACT and acceptance-based clinical interventions targeting treatment-resistant panic disorder (Wersebe et al., 2017), long-term chronic illness (Brassington et al., 2016), major depression with psychotic features (Gaudiano et al., 2012), GAD (Michelson et al., 2011), and social anxiety disorder (Dalrymple & Herbert, 2007; Kocovski et al., 2013). Similar findings related to values consistency have also been demonstrated in nonclinical ACT and acceptance-based interventions, including targeting student overall well-being (Danitz et al., 2016; Firestone et al., 2019; Grégoire et al., 2018); high-weight individuals experiencing weight stigma (Levin et al., 2018); and stress in psychology trainees (Stafford-Brown & Pakenham, 2012), high-weight women (Wallin et al., 2018), and professionals assisting people with developmental disabilities (Castro et al., 2016). Other studies of ACT interventions for gamblers (Dixon et al., 2016), college students (Levin et al., 2016), nongovernmental workers in Sierra Leone (Stewart et al., 2016), anxious college students (Swain et al., 2015), and smokers (O'Connor et al., 2020) did not show a posttreatment difference on overall values consistency compared to controls. Similarly, a DVD-based ACT intervention did not increase values consistency related to physical exercise (Moffitt & Mohr, 2015).

In a few studies, improvements in values consistency have been associated with improved outcomes, for example, during ACT-based therapy for chronic pain (Foote et al., 2015; McCracken & Yang, 2006; Vowles & McCracken, 2008; Vowles et al., 2011), GAD (Hayes et al., 2010), and depression in veterans (Bramwell & Richardson, 2018). In a large sample of adults receiving outpatient CBT (n = 3687), increases in values-based action significantly explained life satisfaction ratings at end of treatment, even after controlling for symptom reduction (Hoyer et al., 2020), suggesting values consistency may be important outside ACT. College students who participated in an online intervention and engaged in more values writing showed a greater reduction in depression postintervention (Danitz et al., 2016; Sagon et al., 2018). Among at-risk college students, educational values consistency at postintervention predicted subsequent grade point average (Sandoz et al., 2017). Finally, in the only mediational data we were able to find, two studies showed that values consistency and persistence in the face of barriers at least partially mediated outcomes of an ACT-based intervention for epilepsy (Lundgren et al., 2006; 2008).

Values Importance

A handful of cross-sectional studies suggest that reporting a range of strongly held values may be associated with better functioning. For example, among parentally bereaved college students, those who had lower overall values importance ratings reported greater bereavement-related distress as compared to those who placed more importance overall on their values (Murrell et al., 2017). Bahraini et al. (2013) found that values importance was associated with lower odds of suicidal ideation in a sample of veterans. In a study of college students, values importance predicted self-reported resilience even after values consistency was controlled for, suggesting it may carry additional explanatory value beyond values consistency (Ceary et al., 2019). Similarly, Ciarrochi et al. (2010) found that values importance was linked to reported success in associated domains, though the study failed to find a relationship between values importance and well-being.

In contrast to the fairly consistent findings from cross-sectional studies, findings relating to change in values importance are more inconsistent. For example, Bramwell and Richardson (2018) showed that an overall increase in rated importance of values during treatment was not related to improved depression or distress in a small (n = 38) outpatient sample of veterans. Hoyer et al. (2020) found that values importance decreased slightly during treatment in a large CBT sample (n = 3687). Values importance around health also decreased following a DVD-based ACT intervention for exercise promotion (Moffit & Mohr, 2015). Finally, overall values importance did not increase as the result of a smoking cessation smartphone app based on ACT (O'Connor et al., 2020).

Effects of Briefly Writing about Important Values

A number of studies have examined the effects of briefly reflecting on values through writing. Much of this literature is linked to a paradigm called "values affirmation" in which people write about important values before engaging in various tasks. These studies suggest that reflecting on values can sometimes alter subsequent behavior and emotional responses. However, the pattern of results from the values affirmation literature is complex. In addition, it is most frequently framed in terms of self-affirmation theory (Sherman & Cohen, 2006), which may not be consistent with ACT theory. For example, in their meta-analysis of the values affirmation interventions within self-affirmation theory, Epton et al. (2015) suggest that values affirmation tasks function by "bolstering or restoring a perception of oneself as adaptively and morally adequate" (p. 187). Next we review some of the key findings related to values affirmation tasks that are more consistent with an ACT theoretical perspective.

Several studies show that values writing can increase values-consistent behavior. For example, Engle and Follette (2018) showed that people who were assigned to write about values related to giving were more likely to donate to a charity compared to people assigned to a control condition. Writing about values held to be highly important has also been shown to predict increased physical activity and positive attitudes toward physical activity among university students (Cooke et al., 2014). Values affirmation writing also resulted in more weight loss and lower body mass index (BMI) after 2 months among college women compared to a control condition (Logel & Cohen, 2011). In their meta-analysis that included 41 studies, Epton et al. (2015) concluded that there is a consistent, though small, positive impact of values affirmation interventions on health-related behavior change.

Some authors have concluded that reflecting on important values may reduce defensiveness and increase receptivity to potentially self-threatening information, at least in part due to creating a sense of self-transcendence (Crocker et al., 2008). For example, students who engaged in values writing tasks, compared to a control task, exhibited significantly lower rates of state paranoia when exposed to a paranoia-induction task (Evans et al., 2019; Kingston & Ellett, 2014). Harris and Napper (2005) found that among students whose alcohol consumption placed them in a "high-risk" category, those who were asked to write about their important values were better able to imagine themselves developing cancer in response to cancer-related information and reported greater intent to reduce alcohol consumption in response to alcohol-related information as compared to high-risk participants who did not engage in the values affirmation task. The authors interpreted their findings as an example of incorporating new information due to lower levels of defensive responding. Data from neuroimaging studies show activation of the ventromedial prefrontal cortex during exposure to potentially threatening health information following a values affirmation task (Falk et al., 2015). The authors of this paper concluded that this result supports the idea that values affirmation tasks may facilitate peoples' ability to see self-relevance and personal importance in what would otherwise be experienced as threat-inducing information.

Reflecting on important values may also buffer some forms of stress. College students who were asked to respond to questions about values that they held to be of high personal importance evidenced lower physiological stress response during a subsequent high-stress task than control participants who were asked questions about low-importance values (Creswell et al., 2005). In a study with undergraduates, Gregg et al. (2014) found that participants who completed the BEVS, compared to a control task, showed decreased cortisol (a measure of stress) in response to an acute social stressor. In a sample of 14 African American students, a values-writing exercise, compared to a control task, decreased distress in response to a racism-related stimulus (West et al., 2013). However, Czech et al. (2011) found that values writing did not reduce anticipatory stress to a speech task, and Berghoff et al. (2018) failed to show that adding a values-writing task to mindfulness meditation online training had a significant impact on participants' levels of anxiety.

Some evidence also suggests that reflecting on one's values may change behavior in relation to stigma and prejudice, perhaps through reducing threat responding. African American middle schoolers who wrote about deeply held personal values as opposed to low-importance values significantly improved academic performance and reduced the academic achievement gap between white and Black students (Cohen et al., 2006); these findings were generally maintained at 2-year follow-up (Cohen et al., 2009). Participating in two very brief values writing tasks reduced the gender achievement gap between men and women in an undergraduate physics course (Miyake et al., 2010). A similar study of values affirmation tasks given to seventh graders in the United States showed that the task did not influence white or Asian student outcomes but did have a small but statistically significant positive impact on overall grade point average for Black and Latinx students' overall grade point average, though not other measures of academic achievement (Borman et al., 2016). These findings suggest that values affirmation tasks may have differential impact on those who are more vulnerable to stereotype threat, but large-scale replication attempts have failed to demonstrate any positive impact of values affirmation tasks on stereotype threat. Hanselman et al. (2017) have called the earlier findings into question. Some findings have even been negative, with Burgess et al. (2014) reporting that Black patients, presenting to a health care setting, who participated in a brief values affirmation intervention displayed lower performance and social self-esteem than Black patients in a control condition.

Values and Other ACT Processes of Change

The ACT model holds that effective therapeutic work around values depends on other psychological flexibility processes (LeJeune & Luoma, 2019). For example, cognitive fusion impedes effective values exploration because people can get derailed by rigid judgments about values choices. Experiential avoidance can impede the exploration and construction of values because reflecting on values can often be painful due to lack of behavioral consistency. A lack of present moment focuses means that values work will be lifeless talk about some abstract future and not relevant to here-and-now choices. Values work without flexible perspective-taking is constricting because people get caught up in stories linked to their conceptualized self, thereby limiting what is possible for them. Psychological inflexibility can also interfere with putting values into action, with research showing a negative relationship between experiential avoidance and engagement in values-based action (Michelson et al., 2011; Smout et al., 2014; Wilson et al., 2010b).

Two studies have used dismantling designs to examine the effects of delivering the open (defusion and acceptance) components versus the engaged (values and committed action) components of ACT. One study randomized 181 distressed college students to an online intervention focusing the open processes, engaged processes, a combination intervention (full ACT intervention), or a waitlist control (Levin et al., 2020). The conditions that included values components (i.e., the engaged and full conditions) resulted in greater reliable clinical change than the open condition and greater improvement in positive mental health than the waitlist condition. This suggests that the inclusion of values and committed action added something beyond acceptance and defusion processes on their own. The second study used a randomized, nonconcurrent multiple baselines across participants design with 15 clients with elevated distress and compared open versus engaged treatment modules (Villatte et al., 2016). The open modules resulted in greater session-by-session improvements and larger reductions in symptom severity, whereas the engaged modules produced greater changes in value-based behavior and greater quality-of-life improvements.

We found three studies that examined the effects of values combined with an acceptance rationale compared to control conditions. First, a study of 99 college students found that adding a values component to an acceptance intervention resulted in higher pain tolerance to a cold pressor task compared to an acceptance-only or control condition (Branstetter-Rost et al., 2009). Two other studies examined the importance of acceptance versus control rationales when combined with values. Páez-Blarrina et al. (2008 a, b) randomly assigned 90 undergraduates to a pain acceptance plus values condition, a pain reduction plus values condition, or a control condition that did not include values. Participants in the acceptance condition demonstrated significantly higher levels of pain tolerance and lower levels of pain believability than either the pain reduction or the no-values control condition. These findings were largely replicated in a similar study (Páez-Blarrina et al., 2008a, b). These studies suggest that acceptance and values may work together to promote positive behavioral change. Relatively little research has examined the links between values and other psychological flexibility processes. Research on mindfulness has shown that values can account for the relationship between mindfulness and well-being (Christie et al., 2016), suggesting that valuing processes may be part of the pathway between mindfulness and psychological well-being found in the larger literature.

Finally, a study of university students showed that an online values intervention combined with goal setting (i.e., committed action) was able to increase subsequent grade point average compared to goal setting alone or waitlist conditions (Chase et al., 2013). Overall, more research is needed on how values interventions might interact with other ACT processes beyond acceptance.

Challenges and Future Directions

Despite the explosion of ACT-focused research in recent years, the values process in ACT has received less empirical attention than some of the other processes (Vowles et al., 2009). As opposed to studying the process of constructing, articulating, and contacting values, most studies focus on values consistency (i.e., behaving in line with stated values), which is more closely related to the committed action process in ACT.

One of the biggest barriers to such empirical exploration of the values process is measurement. Values define a rich, multifaceted area of behavior within the psychological flexibility model, making it extremely difficult to come up with comprehensive, yet usable, measures that address the idiographic nature of values and factors related to cultural, linguistic, cognitive, and developmental contexts. A recent qualitative study involving 11 ACT experts reported that "all experts agreed that sufficient measures to assess the valuing process have not yet been developed" (Barney et al., 2019, p. 229). Specifically, Barney et al.'s report finds that existing ACT values measures tend to oversimplify the valuing process and do not recognize or otherwise measure the individualized nature of values (Barney et al., 2019). Indeed, nearly all existing values measures focus on either measuring the importance of different valued domains and/or action within various valued domains. To date, little research has been done on the *quality* of the action within those domains, which is a fundamental aspect of the valuing process in ACT. Furthermore, few if any existing measures assess a person's contact with values or a sense of meaningfulness, vitality, choice, or other specific appetitive qualities that are theoretically part of engaging in a values-consistent behavior (Barney et al., 2019). As these are all essential elements of the concept of values from the ACT perspective, the failure of existing measures to capture these is a significant limitation. An exception is the Multidimensional Psychological Flexibility Inventory, which has separate subscales that assess values processes as distinct from commitment processes and focuses on qualities such as contact, connection, prioritizing what is important, and having a sense of direction in life (Rolffs et al., 2018). In their review of the recommendations made by ACT-focused values experts, Barney et al. (2019) identified three primary recommendations for future values measure development: (1) that future measures need to be more comprehensive and multimodal, (2) that values measures also assess an individual's direct momentary experience while they are engaging in values-based action, and (3) that future values measures allow for more individualized responses that can reflect the highly personal and rich nature of values.

Many studies only report one parameter that provides an overall assessment of values-related behavior, showing the need for more multimodal and granular assessment. Often, this parameter combines variables that would seemingly relate to values and committed action processes, for example, through composite scores that combine importance and consistency ratings (Ceary et al., 2019; Donahue et al., 2017; Graham et al., 2015; Michelson et al., 2011; Miller & Orsillo, 2020; Wetterneck et al., 2013). For example, the VLQ (Wilson et al., 2010b) and the Values Wheel (O'Connor et al., 2019; Barrett et al., 2020) calculate composite scores by multiplying the scores from the values importance and consistency subscales in order to get an overall rating of valued living. This likely conceals important differences in that a person who has low-consistency ratings and high importance ratings will have a composite score similar to that of people with high-consistency ratings and low importance, but it seems doubtful that these scores point to comparable behavioral repertoires. This also means that it is unclear to what extent outcomes are more associated with values processes, as potentially reflected in varying levels of importance scores, or commitment processes, as potentially reflected in higher consistency scores.

A few studies illustrate why more multimodal, idiographic, and granular assessments of values and values-related behaving are needed. For example, the presence of values clarity can be psychometrically distinguished from lack of contact with values (Rolffs et al., 2018). Other studies have shown that people report more discrepancy between behavior and values in nonsocial versus social domains (Wersebe et al., 2017; Villanueva et al., 2020). A study of drinkers found that when alcohol use was aligned with important values, this was associated with increased heavy drinking in college students (Miller et al., 2016). Research on goal-related striving (Steger et al., 2013) that uses idiographic measures of valued goals and assessments of success in achieving those goals might also inform future research. This was the strategy used in the newly developed Personalized Psychological Flexibility Index (Kashdan et al., 2020). Examples of qualitative studies include one of people with chronic pain, which found they differentiated between valued domains (Casey et al., 2020), and another qualitative study described how people responded to a values workshop (Fitzpatrick et al., 2016).

Research on values would also benefit from moving beyond more traditional self-report assessments taken at just one or two points in time. For example, intensive longitudinal designs such as ecological momentary assessment (EMA) could obtain reports of behavior closer in time to the actual behavior and generally have a stronger ability to examine intraindividual variation over time and between contexts. Furthermore, mixed-methods approaches that combine qualitative and quantitative approaches might be useful in researching how to quantify what it means to have values clarity, defined as the extent to which people know what values apply in a given context and their ability to contact them to guide action. Experimental designs are needed to explore concepts such as "contacting" values and how this affects motivation, perhaps in experiments offering choices over various forms of reinforcement.

Also noticeable is the lack of data related to values importance ratings, despite many studies including measures that assess that dimension. For example, the VLQ (Wilson et al., 2010b) includes two subscales (importance and consistency), but most papers only report results from the composite rating. This makes it difficult to assess the strength of findings related to values importance, perhaps due to a file drawer problem wherein null findings are underreported. We recommend that researchers report analyses related to all measures of values included in studies, even if results are not statistically significant, as suggested by open science advocates (Nelson et al., 2018). Also, some measures of values importance appear to suffer from ceiling effects, with a general skew toward domains being rated highly important (e.g., Murrell et al., 2017); therefore better assessments of values importance may be needed.

Different data-analytic approaches that go beyond assessments of mean values at the group level, such as those assessing the importance of variability itself, would also be potentially beneficial. For example, researchers might examine not just total scores across valued domains, but whether variation within and between domains or within and between values-related behaviors is related to outcomes. An example of this approach is the literature on emotion differentiation, which shows that within-subjects variability in responding to emotion terms predicts better outcomes in some situations (Smidt & Suvak, 2015).

Finally, many of the projects reviewed suffer from relatively small sample sizes, which is likely to result in wide variation in parameter estimates and increase the problem of file drawer effects where nonsignificant findings are simply not reported. Thus, in general, this literature would benefit from larger replication studies.

Conclusion

Humans' yearning to live lives of meaning and purpose is fundamental to what separates our species from nonhuman animals. We propose that ACT, with its roots in behavior analysis, its rich understanding of human language and cognition offered by RFT, and its grounding in a functional contextual perspective, has something unique to offer when it comes to our exploration of the topic of values.

Within a psychological flexibility framework, values are a rich, multifaceted category of verbal behavior. In this article, we reviewed the growing empirical support for the importance of considering these complex patterns of activity in therapy and the potential of valued action in creating profound impacts on quality of life and suffering. Yet much more research is needed to further our empirical and clinical understanding of values. In particular, researchers could benefit from further differentiating between activities involved in values construction and contact (e.g., values exploration and articulation, contacting values through writing, choosing valued directions) versus those activities of values-based committed action. Measures need to be refined to better capture the ongoing, evolving pattern of behavior we call values, and more rigorous methodological designs need to be utilized. Clinical interventions need to be honed so that values are brought to life in the therapy room and clients are able to contact the intrinsically reinforcing properties of values. ACT offers the opportunity to explore issues of values, meaning, and purpose, not merely as existential or philosophical constructs, but rather as the subject of rigorous scientific inquiry. In doing so, ACT can further refine our ability to measure, predict, and influence these elements that are so fundamental to what it means to be human and to be able to live a well-lived human life.

References

Bahraini, N. H., Devore, M. D., Monteith, L. L., Forster, J. E., Bensen, S., & Brenner, L. A. (2013). The role of value importance and success in understanding suicidal ideation among veterans. *Journal of Contextual Behavioral Science, 2*(1–2), 31–38. https://doi.org/10.1016/j.jcbs.2013.03.001

Barney, J. L., Lillis, J., Haynos, A. F., Forman, E., & Juarascio, A. S. (2019). Assessing the valuing process in acceptance and commitment therapy: Experts' review of the current status and recommendations for future measure development. *Journal of Contextual Behavioral Science, 12*, 225–233. https://doi.org/10.1016/j.jcbs.2018.08.002

Barrett, K., O'Connor, M., & McHugh, L. (2019). A systematic review of values-based psychometric tools within acceptance and commitment therapy (ACT). *The Psychological Record, 69*(4), 457–485. https://doi.org/10.1007/s40732-019-00352-7

Barrett, K., O'Connor, M., & McHugh, L. (2020). Investigating the psychometric properties of the Values Wheel with a clinical cohort: A preliminary validation study. *Journal of Contextual Behavioral Science, 15*, 210–218. https://doi.org/10.1016/j.jcbs.2019.12.009

Berghoff, C. R., Forsyth, J. P., Ritzert, T. R., Eifert, G. H., & Anderson, D. A. (2018). Evaluation of the contribution of values clarification to a brief mindfulness meditation intervention for anxiety. *Journal of Clinical Psychology, 74*(9), 1387–1402. https://doi.org/10.1002/jclp.22610

Berry, C., Othman, E., Tan, J. C., Gee, B., Byrne, R. E., Hodgekins, J., Michelson, D., Ng, A. L. O., Marsh, N. V., Coker, S., & Fowler, D. (2019). Assessing social recovery of vulnerable youth in global mental health settings: A pilot study of clinical research tools in Malaysia. *BMC Psychiatry, 19*(1), 1–13. https://doi.org/10.1186/s12888-019-2164-x

Blackledge, J., & Ciarrochi, J. (2006). *Social values survey.* Unpublished manuscript, University of Wollongong, Wollongong.

Borman, G. D., Grigg, J., & Hanselman, P. (2016). An effort to close achievement gaps at scale through self-affirmation. *Educational Evaluation and Policy Analysis, 38*(1), 21–42. https://doi.org/10.3102/0162373715581709

Bramwell, K., & Richardson, T. (2018). Improvements in depression and mental health after acceptance and commitment therapy are related to changes in defusion and values-based action. *Journal of Contemporary Psychotherapy, 48*(1), 9–14. https://doi.org/10.1007/s10879-017-9367-6

Branstetter-Rost, A., Cushing, C., & Douleh, T. (2009). Personal values and pain tolerance: Does a values intervention add to acceptance? *The Journal of Pain, 10*(8), 887–892. https://doi.org/10.1016/j.jpain.2009.01.001

Brassington, L., Ferreira, N. B., Yates, S., Fearn, J., Lanza, P., Kemp, K., & Gillanders, D. (2016). Better living with illness: A transdiagnostic acceptance and commitment therapy group intervention for chronic physical illness. *Journal of Contextual Behavioral Science, 5*(4), 208–214. https://doi.org/10.1016/j.jcbs.2016.09.001

Burgess, D. J., Taylor, B. C., Phelan, S., Spoont, M., van Ryn, M., Hausmann, L. R., Do, T., & Gordon, H. S. (2014). A brief self-affirmation study to improve the experience of minority patients. *Applied Psychology: Health and Well-Being, 6*(2), 135–150. https://doi.org/10.1111/aphw.12015

Carvalho, S. A., Palmeira, L., Pinto-Gouveia, J., Gillanders, D., & Castilho, P. (2018). The utility of the valuing questionnaire in chronic pain. *Journal of Contextual Behavioral Science, 9*, 21–29. https://doi.org/10.1016/j.jcbs.2018.06.002

Casey, M. B., Murphy, D., Neary, R., Wade, C., Hearty, C., & Doody, C. (2020). Individuals perspectives related to acceptance, values and mindfulness following participation in an acceptance-based pain management programme. *Journal of Contextual Behavioral Science, 16*, 96–102. https://doi.org/10.1016/j.jcbs.2020.03.005

Castro, M., Rehfeldt, R. A., & Root, W. B. (2016). On the role of values clarification and committed actions in enhancing the engagement of direct care workers with clients with severe developmental disorders. *Journal of Contextual Behavioral Science, 5*(4), 201–207. https://doi.org/10.1016/j.jcbs.2016.09.003

Ceary, C. D., Donahue, J. J., & Shaffer, K. (2019). The strength of pursuing your values: Valued living as a path to resilience among college students. *Stress and Health, 35*(4), 532–541. https://doi.org/10.1002/smi.2886

Chase, J. A., Houmanfar, R., Hayes, S. C., Ward, T. A., Vilardaga, J. P., & Follette, V. (2013). Values are not just goals: Online ACT-based values training adds to goal setting in improving undergraduate college student performance. *Journal of Contextual Behavioral Science, 2*(3–4), 79–84. https://doi.org/10.1016/j.jcbs.2013.08.002

Christie, A. M., Atkins, P. W. B., & Donald, J. N. (2016). The meaning and doing of mindfulness: The role of values in the link between mindfulness and well-being. *Mindfulness, 8*(2), 368–378. https://doi.org/10.1007/s12671-016-0606-9

Ciarrochi, J., & Bailey, A. (2008*). A CBT practitioners guide to ACT: How to bridge the gap between cognitive behavioural therapy and acceptance and commitment therapy*. New Harbinger Publications.

Ciarrochi, J., Fisher, D., & Lane, L. (2010). The link between value motives, value success, and well-being among people diagnosed with cancer. *Psycho-Oncology, 20*(11), 1184–1192. https://doi.org/10.1002/pon.1832

Clemens, K. S., Tull, M. T., Murray, A. B., Boardley, D., Tipton, J., & Geers, A. L. (2020). Examination of the relationship between affect, values, and physical activity among cancer survivors. *Journal of Contextual Behavioral Science, 18*, 68–74. https://doi.org/10.1016/j.jcbs.2020.08.010

Cohen, G. L., Garcia, J., Apfel, N., & Master, A. (2006). Reducing the racial achievement gap: A social-psychological intervention. *Science, 313*(5791), 1307–1310. https://doi.org/10.1126/science.1128317

Cohen, G. L., Garcia, J., Purdie-Vaugns, V., Apfel, N., & Brzustoski, P. (2009). Recursive processes in self-affirmation: Intervening to close the minority achievement gap. *Science, 324*, 400–403. https://doi.org/10.1126/science.1170769

Cooke, R., Trebaczyk, H., Harris, P., & Wright, A. J. (2014). Self-affirmation promotes physical activity. *Journal of Sport and Exercise Psychology, 36*(2), 217–223. https://doi.org/10.1123/jsep.2013-0041

Creswell, J. D., Welch, W. T., Taylor, S. E., Sherman, D. K., Gruenewald, T. L., & Mann, T. (2005). Affirmation of personal values buffers neuroendocrine and psychological stress responses. *Psychological Science, 16*(11), 846–851. https://doi.org/10.1111/j.1467-9280.2005.01624.x

Crocker, J., Niiya, Y., & Mischkowski, D. (2008). Why does writing about important values reduce defensiveness? Self-affirmation and the role of positive other-directed feelings. *Psychological Science, 19*(7), 740–747. https://doi.org/10.1111/j.1467-9280.2008.02150.x

Czech, S. J., Katz, A. M., & Orsillo, S. M. (2011). The effect of values affirmation on psychological stress. *Cognitive Behaviour Therapy, 40*(4), 304–312. https://doi.org/10.1080/16506073.2011.585347

da Silva Ferreira, T. A., Simões, A. S., Ferreira, A. R., & dos Santos, B. O. S. (2019). What are values in clinical behavior analysis? *Perspectives on Behavior Science, 43*(1), 177–188. https://doi.org/10.1007/s40614-019-00219-w

Dahl, J. C., Plumb, J. C., Stewart, I., & Lundgren, T. (2009). *The art and science of valuing in psychotherapy: Helping clients discover, explore, and commit to valued action using acceptance and commitment therapy* (1st ed.). New Harbinger Publications.

Dalrymple, K. L., & Herbert, J. D. (2007). Acceptance and commitment therapy for generalized social anxiety disorder: A pilot study. *Behavior Modification, 31*(5), 543–568. https://doi.org/10.1177/0145445507302037

Danitz, S. B., Suvak, M. K., & Orsillo, S. M. (2016). The mindful way through the semester: Evaluating the impact of integrating an acceptance-based behavioral program into a first-year experience course for undergraduates. *Behavior Therapy, 47*(4), 487–499. https://doi.org/10.1016/j.beth.2016.03.002

Davis, E. L., Deane, F. P., & Lyons, G. C. (2016). Prediction of individual differences in adjustment to loss: Acceptance and valued-living as critical appraisal and coping strengths. *Death Studies, 40*(4), 211–222. https://doi.org/10.1080/07481187.2015.1122677

Dixon, M. R., Wilson, A. N., & Habib, R. (2016). Neurological evidence of acceptance and commitment therapy effectiveness in college-age gamblers. *Journal of Contextual Behavioral Science, 5*(2), 80–88. https://doi.org/10.1016/j.jcbs.2016.04.004

Donahue, J. J., Huggins, J., & Marrow, T. (2017). Posttraumatic stress symptom severity and functional impairment in a trauma-exposed sample: A preliminary examination into the moderating role of valued living. *Journal of Contextual Behavioral Science, 6*(1), 13–20. https://doi.org/10.1016/j.jcbs.2017.01.003

Elliot, A. J., & Harackiewicz, J. M. (1996). Approach and avoidance achievement goals and intrinsic motivation: A mediational analysis. *Journal of Personality and Social Psychology, 70*(3), 461–475. https://doi.org/10.1037/0022-3514.70.3.461

Engle, J. L., & Follette, V. M. (2018). An experimental comparison of two acceptance and commitment therapy (ACT) values exercises to increase values-oriented behavior. *Journal of Contextual Behavioral Science, 10*, 31–40. https://doi.org/10.1016/j.jcbs.2018.08.001

Epton, T., Harris, P. R., Kane, R., van Koningsbruggen, G. M., & Sheeran, P. (2015). The impact of self-affirmation on health-behavior change: A meta-analysis. *Health Psychology, 34*(3), 187–196. https://doi.org/10.1037/hea0000116

Evans, N., Ellett, L., Carpenter, R., & Kingston, J. (2019). Immediate and short term effects of values-based interventions on paranoia. *Journal of Behavior Therapy and Experimental Psychiatry, 65*, 101500. https://doi.org/10.1016/j.jbtep.2019.101500

Falk, E. B., O'Donnell, M. B., Cascio, C. N., Tinney, F., Kang, Y., Lieberman, M. D., Taylor, S. E., An, L., Resnicow, K., & Strecher, V. J. (2015). Self-affirmation alters the brain's response to health messages and subsequent behavior change. *Proceedings of the National Academy of Sciences, 112*(7), 1977–1982. https://doi.org/10.1073/pnas.1500247112

Firestone, J., Cardaciotto, L., Levin, M. E., Goldbacher, E., Vernig, P., & Gambrel, L. E. (2019). A web-based self-guided program to promote valued-living in college students: A pilot study. *Journal of Contextual Behavioral Science, 12*, 29–38. https://doi.org/10.1016/j.jcbs.2019.01.004

Fitzpatrick, M., Henson, A., Grumet, R., Poolokasingham, G., Foa, C., Comeau, T., & Prendergast, C. (2016). Challenge, focus, inspiration and support: Processes of values clarification and congruence. *Journal of Contextual Behavioral Science, 5*(1), 7–15. https://doi.org/10.1016/j.jcbs.2016.02.001

Foote, H. W., Hamer, J. D., Roland, M. M., Landy, S. R., & Smitherman, T. A. (2015). Psychological flexibility in migraine: A study of pain acceptance and values-based action. *Cephalalgia, 36*(4), 317–324. https://doi.org/10.1177/0333102415590238

Freijy, T., & Kothe, E. J. (2013). Dissonance-based interventions for health behaviour change: A systematic review. *British Journal of Health Psychology, 18*(2), 310–337. https://doi.org/10.1111/bjhp.12035

Gaudiano, B. A., Nowlan, K., Brown, L. A., Epstein-Lubow, G., & Miller, I. W. (2012). An open trial of a new acceptance-based behavioral treatment for major depression with psychotic features. *Behavior Modification, 37*(3), 324–355. https://doi.org/10.1177/0145445512465173

Gloster, A. T., Klotsche, J., Ciarrochi, J., Eifert, G., Sonntag, R., Wittchen, H. U., & Hoyer, J. (2017). Increasing valued behaviors precedes reduction in suffering: Findings from a randomized controlled trial using ACT. *Behaviour Research and Therapy, 91*, 64–71. https://doi.org/10.1016/j.brat.2017.01.013

Graham, J. R., West, L., & Roemer, L. (2015). A preliminary exploration of the moderating role of valued living in the relationships between racist experiences and anxious and depressive symptoms. *Journal of Contextual Behavioral Science, 4*(1), 48–55. https://doi.org/10.1016/j.jcbs.2014.11.001

Gregg, J. A., Namekata, M. S., Louie, W. A., & Chancellor-Freeland, C. (2014). Impact of values clarification on cortisol reactivity to an acute stressor. *Journal of Contextual Behavioral Science, 3*(4), 299–304. https://doi.org/10.1016/j.jcbs.2014.08.002

Grégoire, S., Lachance, L., Bouffard, T., & Dionne, F. (2018). The use of acceptance and commitment therapy to promote mental health and school engagement in university students: A multisite randomized controlled trial. *Behavior Therapy, 49*(3), 360–372. https://doi.org/10.1016/j.beth.2017.10.003

Hanselman, P., Rozek, C. S., Grigg, J., & Borman, G. D. (2017). New evidence on self-affirmation effects and theorized sources of heterogeneity from large-scale replications. *Journal of educational psychology, 109*(3), 405–425. https://doi.org/10.1037/edu0000141

Harris, P. R., & Napper, L. (2005). Self-affirmation and the biased processing of threatening health-risk information. *Personality and Social Psychology Bulletin, 31*(9), 1250–1263. https://doi.org/10.1177/0146167205274694

Hayes, L. L., & Ciarrochi, J. V. (2015). *The thriving adolescent: Using acceptance and commitment therapy and positive psychology to help teens manage emotions, achieve goals, and build connection*. New Harbinger Publications.

Hayes, S. A., Orsillo, S. M., & Roemer, L. (2010). Changes in proposed mechanisms of action during an acceptance-based behavior therapy for generalized anxiety disorder. *Behaviour Research and Therapy, 48*(3), 238–245. https://doi.org/10.1016/j.brat.2009.11.006

Hayes, S. C. (2004). Acceptance and commitment therapy, relational frame theory, and the third wave of behavioral and cognitive therapies. *Behavior Therapy, 35*(4), 639–665.

Hayes, S. C., Barnes-Holmes, D., & Roche, B. (2001). *Relational frame theory: A post-Skinnerian account of human language and cognition.* Kluwer Academic/Plenum Publishers.

Hayes, S. C., Strosahl, K. D., & Wilson, K. G. (2012). *Acceptance and commitment therapy: The process and practice of mindful change* (2nd ed.). Guilford Press.

Hayes, S. C., & Wilson, K. G. (1993). Some applied implications of a contemporary behavior-analytic account of verbal events. *The Behavior Analyst, 16*(2), 283–301. https://doi.org/10.1007/bf03392637

Hoyer, J., Čolić, J., Grübler, G., & Gloster, A. T. (2020). Valued living before and after CBT. *Journal of Contemporary Psychotherapy, 50*(1), 37–45. https://doi.org/10.1007/s10879-019-09430-x

Ishizu, K., Ohtsuki, T., Shimoda, Y., & Takahashi, F. (2020). Bon Voyage: Developing a scale for measuring value among younger populations and examining its reliability and validity. *Journal of Contextual Behavioral Science, 15*, 153–161. https://doi.org/10.1016/j.jcbs.2019.12.007

Jensen, M. P., Vowles, K. E., Johnson, L. E., & Gertz, K. J. (2015). Living well with pain: Development and preliminary evaluation of the Valued Living Scale. *Pain Medicine, 16*(11), 2109–2120. https://doi.org/10.1111/pme.12802

Juncos, D. G., Heinrichs, G. A., Towle, P., Duffy, K., Grand, S. M., Morgan, M. C., Smith, J. D., & Kalkus, E. (2017). Acceptance and commitment therapy for the treatment of music performance anxiety: A pilot study with student vocalists. *Frontiers in Psychology, 8*(986), 1–16. https://doi.org/10.3389/fpsyg.2017.00986

Kashdan, T. B., Disabato, D. J., Goodman, F. R., Doorley, J. D., & McKnight, P. E. (2020). Understanding psychological flexibility: A multimethod exploration of pursuing valued goals despite the presence of distress. *Psychological Assessment,* 32(9), 829–850. https://doi.org/10.1037/pas0000834

Katz, B. A., Catane, S., & Yovel, I. (2016). Pushed by symptoms, pulled by values: Promotion goals increase motivation in therapeutic tasks. *Behavior Therapy, 47*(2), 239–247. https://doi.org/10.1016/j.beth.2015.11.002

Kingston, J., & Ellett, L. (2014). Self-affirmation and nonclinical paranoia. *Journal of Behavior Therapy and Experimental Psychiatry, 45*(4), 502–505. https://doi.org/10.1016/j.jbtep.2014.07.004

Kocovski, N. L., Fleming, J. E., Hawley, L. L., Huta, V., & Antony, M. M. (2013). Mindfulness and acceptance-based group therapy versus traditional cognitive behavioral group therapy for social anxiety disorder: A randomized controlled trial. *Behavior Research and Therapy, 51*(12), 889–898. https://doi.org/10.1016/j.brat.2013.10.007

Leigland, S. (2005). Variables of which values are a function. *The Behavior Analyst, 28*(2), 133–142. https://doi.org/10.1007/bf03392109

LeJeune, J., & Luoma, J. (2019). *Values in therapy: A clinician's guide to helping clients explore values, increase psychological flexibility, and a more meaningful life.* New Harbinger Publications.

Levin, M. E., Haeger, J. A., Pierce, B. G., & Twohig, M. P. (2016). Web-based acceptance and commitment therapy for mental health problems in college students: A randomized controlled trial. *Behavior Modification, 41*(1), 141–162. https://doi.org/10.1177/0145445516659645

Levin, M. E., Krafft, J., Hicks, E. T., Pierce, B., & Twohig, M. P. (2020). A randomized dismantling trial of the open and engaged components of acceptance and commitment therapy in an online intervention for distressed college students. *Behaviour Research and Therapy, 126*, 103557. https://doi.org/10.1016/j.brat.2020.103557

Levin, M. E., Potts, S., Haeger, J., & Lillis, J. (2018). Delivering acceptance and commitment therapy for weight self-stigma through guided self-help: Results from an open pilot trial. *Cognitive and Behavioral Practice, 25*(1), 87–104. https://doi.org/10.1016/j.cbpra.2017.02.002

Logel, C., & Cohen, G. L. (2011). The role of the self in physical health: Testing the effect of a values-affirmation intervention on weight loss. *Psychological Science, 23*(1), 53–55. https://doi.org/10.1177/0956797611421936

Lundgren, T., Dahl, J., & Hayes, S. C. (2008). Evaluation of mediators of change in the treatment of epilepsy with acceptance and commitment therapy. *Journal of Behavioral Medicine, 31*(3), 225–235. https://doi.org/10.1007/s10865-008-9151-x

Lundgren, T., Dahl, J., Melin, L., & Kies, B. (2006). Evaluation of acceptance and commitment therapy for drug refractory epilepsy: A randomized controlled trial in South Africa—A pilot study. *Epilepsia, 47*(12), 2173–2179. https://doi.org/10.1111/j.1528-1167.2006.00892.x

Lundgren, T., Luoma, J. B., Dahl, J., Strosahl, K., & Melin, L. (2012). The Bull's-Eye Values Survey: A psychometric evaluation. *Cognitive and Behavioral Practice, 19*(4), 518–526. https://doi.org/10.1016/j.cbpra.2012.01.004

Luoma, J. B., Hayes, S. C., & Walser, R. D. (2017). Learning ACT: *An acceptance and commitment therapy skills-training manual for therapists* (2nd ed.). New Harbinger Publications.

McCracken, L. M., & Yang, S. Y. (2006). The role of values in a contextual cognitive-behavioral approach to chronic pain. *Pain, 123*(1–2), 137–145. https://doi.org/10.1016/j.pain.2006.02.021

Michelson, S. E., Lee, J. K., Orsillo, S. M., & Roemer, L. (2011). The role of values-consistent behavior in generalized anxiety disorder. *Depression and Anxiety, 28*(5), 358–366. https://doi.org/10.1002/da.20793

Miller, A. N., & Orsillo, S. M. (2020). Values, acceptance, and belongingness in graduate school: Perspectives from underrepresented minority students. *Journal of Contextual Behavioral Science, 15*, 197–206. https://doi.org/10.1016/j.jcbs.2020.01.002

Miller, M. B., Meier, E., Lombardi, N., Leavens, E. L., Grant, D. M., & Leffingwell, T. R. (2016). The Valued Living Questionnaire for Alcohol Use: Measuring value-behavior discrepancy in college student drinking. *Psychological Assessment, 28*(9), 1051–1060. https://doi.org/10.1037/pas0000235

Miyake, A., Kost-Smith, L. E., Finkelstein, N. D., Pollock, S. J., Cohen, G. L., & Ito, T. A. (2010). Reducing the gender achievement gap in college science: A classroom study of values affirmation. *Science, 330*(6008), 1234–1237. https://doi.org/10.1126/science.1195996

Moffitt, R., & Mohr, P. (2015). The efficacy of a self-managed acceptance and commitment therapy intervention DVD for physical activity initiation. *British Journal of Health Psychology, 20*(1), 115–129. https://doi.org/10.1111/bjhp.12098

Murrell, A. R., Jackson, R., Lester, E. G., & Hulsey, T. (2017). Psychological flexibility and resilience in parentally bereaved college students. *OMEGA: Journal of Death and Dying, 76*(3), 207–226. https://doi.org/10.1177/0030222817693154

Murrell, A. R., & Kapadia, V. (2011). Brief report on experiential avoidance and valuing in at-risk adolescents. *Behavioral Development Bulletin, 17*(1), 38–42.

Nelson, L. D., Simmons, J., & Simonsohn, U. (2018). Psychology's renaissance. *Annual Review of Psychology, 69*, 511–534.

O'Connor, M., Tennyson, A., Timmons, M., & McHugh, L. (2019). The development and preliminary psychometric properties of the Values Wheel. *Journal of Contextual Behavioral Science, 12*, 39–46. https://doi.org/10.1016/j.jcbs.2019.01.005

O'Connor, M., Whelan, R., Bricker, J., & McHugh, L. (2020). Randomized controlled trial of a smartphone application as an adjunct to acceptance and commitment therapy for smoking cessation. *Behavior Therapy, 51*(1), 162–177. https://doi.org/10.1016/j.beth.2019.06.003

Páez-Blarrina, M., Luciano, C., Gutiérrez-Martínez, O., Valdivia, S., Ortega, J., & Rodríguez-Valverde, M. (2008a). The role of values with personal examples in altering the functions of pain: Comparison between acceptance-based and cognitive-control-based protocols. *Behaviour Research and Therapy, 46*(1), 84–97. https://doi.org/10.1016/j.brat.2007.10.008

Páez-Blarrina, M., Luciano, C., Gutiérrez-Martínez, O., Valdivia, S., Rodríguez-Valverde, M., & Ortega, J. (2008b). Coping with pain in the motivational context of values: Comparison between an acceptance-based and a cognitive control-based protocol. *Behavior Modification, 32*(3), 403–422. https://doi.org/10.1177/0145445507309029

Pakenham, K. I. (2015). Investigation of the utility of the acceptance and commitment therapy (ACT) framework for fostering self-care in clinical psychology trainees. *Training and Education in Professional Psychology, 9*(2), 144–152. https://doi.org/10.1037/tep0000074

Pakenham, K. I., Landi, G., Boccolini, G., Furlani, A., Grandi, S., & Tossani, E. (2020). The moderating roles of psychological flexibility and inflexibility on the mental health impacts of COVID-19 pandemic and lockdown in Italy. *Journal of Contextual Behavioral Science, 17*, 109–118. https://doi.org/10.1016/j.jcbs.2020.07.003

Pielech, M., Bailey, R. W., McEntee, M. L., Ashworth, J., Levell, J., Sowden, G., & Vowles, K. E. (2016). Preliminary evaluation of the values tracker: A two-item measure of engagement in valued activities in those with chronic pain. *Behavior Modification, 40*(1–2), 239–256. https://doi.org/10.1177/0145445515616911

Plumb, J. C., Stewart, I., Dahl, J., & Lundgren, T. (2009). In search of meaning: Values in modern clinical behavior analysis. *The Behavior Analyst, 32*(1), 85–103. https://doi.org/10.1007/bf03392177

Reilly, E. D., Ritzert, T. R., Scoglio, A. A., Mote, J., Fukuda, S. D., Ahern, M. E., & Kelly, M. M. (2019). A systematic review of values measures in acceptance and commitment therapy research. *Journal of Contextual Behavioral Science, 12*, 290–304. https://doi.org/10.1016/j.jcbs.2018.10.004

Rickardsson, J., Zetterqvist, V., Kemani, M. K., Holmström, L., Andersson, E., & Wicksell, R. K. (2019). Assessing values—Psychometric properties of the Swedish version of the Valuing Questionnaire in adults with chronic pain. *Journal of Contextual Behavioral Science, 14*, 40–49. https://doi.org/10.1016/j.jcbs.2019.08.009

Rogers, C. R., & Skinner, B. F. (1956). Some issues concerning the control of human behavior: A symposium. *Science, 124*, 1057–1066. https://doi.org/10.1126/science.124.3231.1057.

Rolffs, J. L., Rogge, R. D., & Wilson, K. G. (2018). Disentangling components of flexibility via the hexaflex model: Development and validation of the Multidimensional Psychological Flexibility Inventory (MPFI). *Assessment, 25*(4), 458–482. https://doi.org/10.1177/1073191116645905

Romero-Moreno, R., Gallego-Alberto, L., Márquez-González, M., & Losada, A. (2016). Psychometric properties of the Valued Living Questionnaire adapted to dementia caregiving. *Aging and Mental Health, 21*(9), 983–990. https://doi.org/10.1080/13607863.2016.1191055

Roush, J. F., Cukrowicz, K. C., Mitchell, S. M., Brown, S. L., & Seymour, N. E. (2018). Valued living, life fulfillment, and suicide ideation among psychiatric inpatients: The mediating role of thwarted interpersonal needs. *Journal of Contextual Behavioral Science, 7*, 8–14. https://doi.org/10.1016/j.jcbs.2017.11.001

Sagon, A. L., Danitz, S. B., Suvak, M. K., & Orsillo, S. M. (2018). The Mindful Way through the semester: Evaluating the feasibility of delivering an acceptance-based behavioral program online. *Journal of Contextual Behavioral Science, 9*, 36–44. https://doi.org/10.1016/j.jcbs.2018.06.004

Sandoz, E. K., & Anderson, R. S. (2015). Building awareness, openness, and action: Values work in behavior therapy. *The Behavior Therapist, 38*(3), 60–69.

Sandoz, E. K., Kellum, K. K., & Wilson, K. G. (2017). Feasibility and preliminary effectiveness of acceptance and commitment training for academic success of at-risk college students from low income families. *Journal of Contextual Behavioral Science, 6*(1), 71–79. https://doi.org/10.1016/j.jcbs.2017.01.001

Sherman, D. K., & Cohen, G. L. (2006). The psychology of self-defense: Self-affirmation theory. *Advances in Experimental Social Psychology, 38*, 183–242. https://doi.org/10.1016/S0065-2601(06)38004-5

Smidt, K. E., & Suvak, M. K. (2015). A brief, but nuanced, review of emotional granularity and emotion differentiation research. *Current Opinion in Psychology, 3*, 48–51. https://doi.org/10.1016/j.copsyc.2015.02.007

Smout, M., Davies, M., Burns, N., & Christie, A. (2014). Development of the Valuing Questionnaire (VQ). *Journal of Contextual Behavioral Science, 3*(3), 164–172. https://doi.org/10.1016/j.jcbs.2014.06.001

Stafford-Brown, J., & Pakenham, K. I. (2012). The effectiveness of an ACT informed intervention for managing stress and improving therapist qualities in clinical psychology trainees. *Journal of Clinical Psychology, 68*(6), 592–613. https://doi.org/10.1002/jclp.21844

Stapleton, A., O'Connor, M., Feerick, E., Kerr, J., & McHugh, L. (2020). Testing the relationship between health values consistent living and health-related behavior. *Journal of Contextual Behavioral Science, 17*, 17–22. https://doi.org/10.1016/j.jcbs.2020.05.002

Steger, M., Sheline, K., Merriman, L., & Kashdan, T. (2013). Using the science of meaning to invigorate values-congruent, purpose-driven action. *Mindfulness, acceptance, and positive psychology: The seven foundations of well-being* (pp. 240–266). New Harbinger Publications.

Stewart, C., White, R. G., Ebert, B., Mays, I., Nardozzi, J., & Bockarie, H. (2016). A preliminary evaluation of acceptance and commitment therapy (ACT) training in Sierra Leone. *Journal of Contextual Behavioral Science, 5*(1), 16–22. https://doi.org/10.1016/j.jcbs.2016.01.001

Swain, J., Hancock, K., Hainsworth, C., & Bowman, J. (2015). Mechanisms of change: Exploratory outcomes from a randomised controlled trial of acceptance and commitment therapy for anxious adolescents. *Journal of Contextual Behavioral Science, 4*(1), 56–67. https://doi.org/10.1016/j.jcbs.2014.09.001

Thompson, B. L., Luoma, J. B., & LeJeune, J. T. (2013). Using acceptance and commitment therapy to guide exposure-based interventions for posttraumatic stress disorder. *Journal of Contemporary Psychotherapy, 43*(3), 133–140. https://doi.org/10.1007/s10879-013-9233-0

Trompetter, H. R., Ten Klooster, P. M., Schreurs, K. M., Fledderus, M., Westerhof, G. J., & Bohlmeijer, E. T. (2013). Measuring values and committed action with the Engaged Living Scale (ELS): psychometric evaluation in a nonclinical sample and a chronic pain sample. *Psychological Assessment, 25*(4), 1235–1246. https://doi.org/10.1037/a0033813

Tyrberg, M. J., Carlbring, P., & Lundgren, T. (2016). Brief acceptance and commitment therapy for psychotic inpatients: A randomized controlled feasibility trial in Sweden. *Nordic Psychology, 69*, 110–125. https://doi.org/10.1080/19012276.2016.1198271.

VanBuskirk, K., West, L., Malcarne, V., Afari, N., Liu, L., Petkus, A., & Wetherell, J. L. (2011). Confirmatory factor analysis of the Valued Living Questionnaire in a Black American sample: Implications for cognitive research and practice. *Cognitive Therapy and Research, 36*(6), 796–805. https://doi.org/10.1007/s10608-011-9405-8

Vilardaga, R., Luoma, J. B., Hayes, S. C., Pistorello, J., Levin, M. E., Hildebrandt, M. J., Kohlenberg, B., Roget, N. A., & Bond, F. (2011). Burnout among the addiction counseling workforce: The differential roles of mindfulness and values-based processes and work-site factors. *Journal of Substance Abuse Treatment, 40*(4), 323–335. https://doi.org/10.1016/j.jsat.2010.11.015

Villanueva, J., Meyer, A. H., Rinner, M. T. B., Block, V. J., Benoy, C., Brogli, S., Karekla, M., Walter, M., & Gloster, A. T. (2020). The everyday lives of in- and outpatients when beginning therapy: The importance of

values-consistent behavior. *International Journal of Clinical and Health Psychology, 20*(2), 91–99. https://doi.org/10.1016/j.ijchp.2020.02.002
Villatte, J. L., Vilardaga, R., Villatte, M., Vilardaga, J. C. P., Atkins, D. C., & Hayes, S. C. (2016). Acceptance and commitment therapy modules: Differential impact on treatment processes and outcomes. *Behaviour Research and Therapy, 77*, 52–61. https://doi.org/10.1016/j.brat.2015.12.001
Vowles, K. E., & McCracken, L. M. (2008). Acceptance and values-based action in chronic pain: A study of treatment effectiveness and process. *Journal of Consulting and Clinical Psychology, 76*(3), 397–407. https://doi.org/10.1037/0022-006x.76.3.397
Vowles, K. E., McCracken, L. M., & O'Brien, J. Z. (2011). Acceptance and values-based action in chronic pain: A three-year follow-up analysis of treatment effectiveness and process. *Behaviour Research and Therapy, 49*(11), 748–755. https://doi.org/10.1016/j.brat.2011.08.002
Vowles, K. E., Wetherell, J. L., & Sorrell, J. T. (2009). Targeting acceptance, mindfulness, and values-based action in chronic pain: Findings of two preliminary trials of an outpatient group-based intervention. *Cognitive and Behavioral Practice, 16*(1), 49–58. https://doi.org/10.1016/j.cbpra.2008.08.001
Wallin, E., Parling, T., Weineland, S., & Dahl, J. (2018). Acceptance and commitment therapy to promote value attainment among individuals with overweight: A multiple baseline evaluation. *Journal of Contextual Behavioral Science, 10*, 41–49. https://doi.org/10.1016/j.jcbs.2018.08.007
Wersebe, H., Lieb, R., Meyer, A. H., Hoyer, J., Wittchen, H. U., & Gloster, A. T. (2017). Changes of valued behaviors and functioning during an acceptance and commitment therapy intervention. *Journal of Contextual Behavioral Science, 6*(1), 63–70. https://doi.org/10.1016/j.jcbs.2016.11.005
West, L. M., Graham, J. R., & Roemer, L. (2013). Functioning in the face of racism: Preliminary findings on the buffering role of values clarification in a Black American sample. *Journal of Contextual Behavioral Science, 2*(1–2), 1–8. https://doi.org/10.1016/j.jcbs.2013.03.003
Wetterneck, C. T., Lee, E. B., Smith, A. H., & Hart, J. M. (2013). Courage, self-compassion, and values in obsessive-compulsive disorder. *Journal of Contextual Behavioral Science, 2*(3–4), 68–73. https://doi.org/10.1016/j.jcbs.2013.09.002
Wiggs, K. A., & Drake, C. E. (2016). Building psychological flexibility to mitigate adjustment disorder: Assessing treatment progress with a measure of treatment processes. *Clinical Case Studies, 15*(1), 18–34. https://doi.org/10.1177/1534650115585387
Wilson, K. G., & DuFrene, T. (2009). *Mindfulness for Two: An acceptance and commitment therapy approach to mindfulness in psychotherapy*. New Harbinger Publications.
Wilson, K. G., & Murrell, A. R. (2004). Values work in acceptance and commitment therapy. Mindfulness and acceptance: Expanding the cognitive-behavioral tradition. In S. C. Hayes, V. M. Follette, & Linehan, M. M. (Eds), *Mindfulness and acceptance: Expanding the cognitive-behavioral tradition* (pp. 120–151). Guilford Press.
Wilson, K., Sandoz, E. K., Flynn, M. K., Slater, R. M., & DuFrene, T. (2010a). Understanding, assessing, and treating values processes in mindfulness-and acceptance-based therapies. In R. A. Baer (Ed.), *Assessing mindfulness and acceptance processes in clients: Illuminating the theory and practice of change* (pp. 77–106). New Harbinger Publications.
Wilson, K. G., Sandoz, E. K., Kitchens, J., & Roberts, M. (2010b). The Valued Living Questionnaire: Defining and measuring valued action within a behavioral framework. *The Psychological Record, 60*(2), 249–272. https://doi.org/10.1007/bf03395706

CHAPTER

13 Committed Action

Lance M. McCracken

Abstract

Committed action is a fundamentally important facet of psychological flexibility and acceptance and commitment therapy (ACT). This article introduces committed action, reviews how definitions of it have evolved over time, presents a current definition, and summarizes current evidence. While the term itself has not always garnered great attention either in the clinic or in research, any research in behavioral activation and goal setting will directly relate to processes of committed action. Research explicitly into "committed action" is finally underway, beginning 14 years after publication of the first book on ACT. This was enabled by the appearance of adequate self-report measures of the process. A critical appraisal of the research around committed action shows that not all purported measures of committed action reflect this process with equal fidelity, and some fail to reflect key features. Nonetheless, evidence so far demonstrates that committed action from within the frame of psychological flexibility can be assessed in a theoretically consistent fashion. Measures of it correlate with measures of functioning and change when targeted with appropriate treatment methods; these changes in turn correlate with improvements in key clinical outcomes. These results, taken together with evidence from behavioral activation and goal-setting methods, provide substantial and growing evidence that committed action constitutes an evidence-based process of behavior change. It is recommended that methods to assess and promote this process continue to be developed and that they be included in future treatments.

Key Words: psychological flexibility, hexaflex, goal setting, behavior change, values, therapy component

The second main word in acceptance and commitment therapy (ACT) is commitment, not defusion, awareness, self, or values. Even though abbreviations such as ADT, AST, and AVT have a nice sound, they were not chosen. ACT is a good word. So, ought we to take any further meaning from this "C" word other than a way to produce a good abbreviation for a therapy, one that creates a suitable meaning when spoken as a word? When the second edition of the ACT book came out, the chapter on committed action explained that the word behind the "C" expresses "the fundamental importance that ACT places upon behavioral change" and moreover, "if a client does not change his or her behavior, then all of our efforts working on defusion-acceptance, present moment-self-as-perspective, and values are for naught" (Hayes, Strosahl, & Wilson, 2012, p. 328), and that certainly sounds right.

To understand the word "commitment" in the context of ACT, one might look at how it and related words are commonly used. This is a useful exercise because any use of terms such as *committed action* will conjure up a range of meanings. In fact, "commit" is commonly used in different ways and can mean "to carry into action deliberately" or "to pledge or assign to some particular course or use," among other meanings (Merriam-Webster, n.d.). For any native English speaker, a committed action can be a *done* action that is perpetrated or accomplished. At the same time, there will be a sense that "commitment" means to promise or pledge that one will do a certain thing and keep doing it, not as just an act but as a "course" of action. A committed relationship is one that a person promises to stick with, "forsaking all others," and other commitments. For example, a pledge of allegiance to a symbol of one's country seems to carry that same kind of promise. In this context, there is a distinction about committed actions that are *done* versus actions that are *promised.* There is nothing particularly problematic here with respect to ACT or contextual behavioral science, except possibly a lack of precision. All that one can say so far is that the dictionary does not fully help us understand the meaning of "committed action" in ACT.

Committed Action in ACT, 1999–2020

In the first book on ACT, Chapter 9 is titled "Willingness and Commitment: Putting ACT into Action" (Hayes, Strosahl, & Wilson, 1999). The closest thing to a definition of committed action that appears in that chapter is as follows: "Commitment involves the description of valued behavior that one is going to produce and the subsequent production of that behavior under the control of this self-rule" and later, "If the behavior is successful in producing valued outcomes, the temporary insensitivity produced by overt commitment will allow those contingencies to be contacted" (Hayes et al., 1999, p. 237). This is really interesting because it seems to emphasize the actual making of a pledge or promise as part of committed action. It frames committed action as a pattern of "make a verbal commitment and keep the commitment," the latter part here meaning to act on it. In addition, it makes committed action at the outset a kind of verbal behavior, a kind of rule-governed behavior, which seemingly we might understand mostly as "tracking."

In the 1999 version of the ACT book, the term *commitment* appears in both a chapter title name and the index but *committed action* does not. The entry in the index is called "Commitment phase" to be exact, and there it headlines 12 related topics. Looking back more than 20 years, we notice one other thing: how much "willingness" was featured in early descriptions as part of what we now call committed action (Hayes et al., 1999). One gets an impression that committed action is little more than the action part of acceptance. When we read the chapters from the first and second editions of the book on ACT side by side, we detect some shifts. In the 2012 edition, Chapter 12 is simply called "Committed Action" (Hayes et al., 2012). The index carries no entry for "commitment" and the term *committed action,* which does appear, is a marker for 32 separate related topics. This could reflect merely differences in the process of indexing terms or differences in emphasis and distinctions in meaning that emerged from the authors.

Thirteen years after the first descriptions of commitment or committed action appeared, the explicit emphasis on making a verbal commitment and keeping it is not detectible in the second edition of the primary text on ACT. Also, there is less exclusive partnering of committed action with willingness, and a more equal partnering across the other facets of psychological flexibility (PF). This includes present focused awareness: "One of the major misunderstandings about commitment is that it often seems like a promise made about the future . . . in fact, commitment is not really about the future at all . . . commitment occurs in the very moment a person takes a step in one of two directions." (Hayes et al., 2012, p. 328). Later, this is elaborated: "in ACT, committed action is a values-based action that occurs at a particular moment in time and that is deliberately linked to creating a pattern of action that serves the value" (p. 328). And further, "the very moment one sees a divergence between actions and a value, and chooses again to act to embody and grow the value, that very action is a committed action" (p. 329). Again, the notion of making and keeping a promise or pledge is apparently absent in the newer description of committed action. If one had to add another feature, it is that it operates in an interactive fashion with *all* other facets of PF.

More recently, committed action was defined as "action that is guided by goals and values, is persistent, in that it can incorporate setbacks or discomfort and continue, and flexible, in that it can stop when it is unsuccessful" (McCracken, Chilcot, & Norton, 2015, p. 678). This definition includes echoes of the definition presented in the first edition of the ACT book, minus the aspect of an actual verbal commitment. It does not, unfortunately, include the aspect emphasized in the 2012 edition, that being the connection between committed action as part of a process of building larger patterns of values-based action. What follows is a summary of features of committed action from the available sources reviewed, a kind of state of the art and current clinical definition of the term. To summarize the key features of committed action and suggest a current definition would be to say that committed action is values-based action that is intentionally linked to a growing, continuing, and integrating pattern of values-based action and includes a mutual relationship with each of the other processes of psychological flexibility. A feature of committed action is that it is "growing" or progressive. It typically begins with small steps that build into larger and more stable patterns of behavior. The "continuing" quality requires that it explicitly include contact with potential barriers to continued action, including failure experiences, unwanted emotions, or pain; it persists, and it is repeated. In a similar sense, the purpose is not necessarily in the immediate outcome, the events encountered directly following the act itself, but in the overall direction served. The "integrating" quality means it activates behavioral selection and retention mechanisms. With committed action, behavior can be shaped, reinforced, and generalized, or not, through the results that have been produced. Ideally, through this process, effective and resilient behavior patterns emerge that may produce increasing success in the future. One might be tempted to see committed action as the outcome of the other processes of PF, but it is probably not ideal to frame it this way. Rather, it is as much the means for reaching outcome as any of the other processes, not the end point of a series of processes delivered.

Evidence from Experimental Studies

Committed action is a values-based act, in the moment, that is connected to an extended pattern of behavior. One might expect that it could be difficult to produce this quality in a laboratory setting, although in truth it probably need be no more difficult than values-based action in general. After all, a person ought to be able to choose and engage in a small values-based action framed in relation to a larger pattern of behavior over time, and should even be able to choose and engage in it again in the lab. At the same time, the entire pattern need not occur in the lab. Regardless of this reasoning, it is not clear that there have been any previous lab-based studies of committed action per se, at least none or few that were precisely labeled as such.

In a systematic review and meta-analysis of experimental laboratory studies of components defined within the PF model, 66 studies were identified (Levin, Hildebrandt, Lillis, & Hayes, 2012). None of these studies focused on committed action, but there is a particular reason why. Studies of committed action alone, including studies of behavioral methods, such as goal-setting, contingency management, or behavioral activation, were excluded from this review because the literature on these topics is very large and well established (Levin et al., 2012), and presumably does not need review in the same way that the other facets do.

It has been suggested that experimental evidence for the role of committed action in relation to psychological outcomes can be found in experimental studies of goal-setting and behavioral activation (BA), for example. With regard to goal-setting, while goal-setting can be entirely consistent with committed action as a method, it does not necessarily incorporate all of the features of committed action discussed here. Goals as commonly defined are meant to be desirable or relevant, but this may not be the same thing as saying they are values-based. Also, a goal is something that is doable and "completable," and it is not necessarily a part of a growing pattern of behavior. Having said that, note that committed action is a skill that can be used as a tool, such as during therapy, or after therapy when one recognizes that they are stuck or are not succeeding as they want to do. Technically, it seems, one could apply committed action and then stop consciously and intentionally applying it when one succeeds or reaches the goal from doing so. With these points in mind, evidence for goal-setting speaks to a part of what can be done, or methods that apply, under the umbrella of committed action.

Goal-setting is in fact widely considered as an effective and key element in helping people change their behavior. In a systematic review and meta-analysis including 155 studies and 384 effect sizes in 16,523 people, goal setting was seen to produce a small, positive, unique effect on behavior ($d = .34$; Epton, Currie, & Armitage, 2017). The goals typically included cognitive or sports performances, 49 percent and 22 percent, respectively. Control groups were typically given the instruction to "do your best." Most of the participants, 77 percent were university students, and goal achievement was assessed over a mean follow-up period of 2.1 weeks after the goal-setting intervention. Increased goal difficulty was significantly associated with goal success, as were goals that were set publicly, set face to face rather than online, and group goals. Interestingly, a measure of commitment has been employed in some of the studies, including 74 of the effect sizes. This measure, which actually focuses on strength of commitment, was taken after the goal was set and before it was acted on, and this was associated with a smaller effect of goal-setting on behavior (Epton et al., 2017). This kind of effect was also observed in a very small number of studies that manipulated goal commitment. In the case of assessment of commitment, it was thought that the smaller effect was due to participants realizing that their actual commitment to the goal was low, and as a result, less effort was applied. In the case of manipulated commitment, it was thought that an actual positive effect was probably hidden by most of the goals included, which were too easy. The expectation is that strength of commitment is only able to exert an impact in the case of difficult goals (Epton et al., 2017).

One intention of committed action is to create patterns of behavior that reflect values, are in a sense inherently positively reinforcing, and meet reinforcing contingencies when the person engages in them. This focus, essentially on contact and engagement with response contingent positive reinforcement, means that committed action overlaps considerably with BA. This also means that evidence for BA will apply to a degree to committed action. As with goal-setting, it seems everything in the processes and methods of BA is able to fit within the frame of committed action. BA includes self-monitoring and activity scheduling for the purpose of increasing overt behavior, again, with the further purpose of making contact with personally relevant positive reinforcers in the settings of a person's daily life (Lejuez, Hopko, Acierno, Daughters, & Pagoto, 2011). As with goal-setting, BA has not necessarily included value clarification in the past, although relevance and desirability might appear to be assumed within the concept of reinforcement itself. BA also includes preventing patterns of avoidance, such as patterns of avoidance entailed in rumination that can block awareness, and is entirely consistent with committed action and psychological flexibility in general. The essential breaking down of behavior patterns into smaller manageable steps and gradually shaping larger longer term patterns from there form a direct parallel to committed action.

A recent systematic review and meta-analysis of BA included 28 studies (*n* = 1853; Stein, Carl, Cuijpers, Karyotaki, & Smits, 2020). Beyond focusing on effects on depression as is customarily done, these authors also examined effects on anxiety and activation itself, finding that BA outperformed inactive control conditions for improvements in these with large effect sizes, *g* = .83, small effect sizes, *g* = .37, and medium ones, *g* = .64, for depression, anxiety, and activation, respectively. Effect sizes for BA in comparison to active control conditions were not significant. This analysis also aimed to determine the moderating effect of including discussion of values in BA. Based on 19 studies, the effect size for the subgroup with the discussion of values was *g* = .86, while the effect for the subgroup without discussion of values was *g* = .82, which does not constitute a significant difference (Stein et al., 2020).

Measures of Committed Action

For many years, there were no specific measures of psychological flexibility processes except for the Acceptance and Action Questionnaire (AAQ; Hayes et al., 2004), its subsequent revisions, such as the AAQ-II, and variants from the same family designed to include specific experiences or populations. The Chronic Pain Acceptance Questionnaire (CPAQ; McCracken, 1998) was an early example of these measures. An interesting point about the early measures, even though the AAQ came to be called a measure of PF and later inflexibility, is that they never clearly included committed action as we understand it today. Even when the AAQ included 49 items, including versions circulated around 2003, none of the items, as far as one could tell, were ideally framed to reflect committed action. Two items that appeared closest to the process were, "I can set a course in my life and stick to it, even if I have doubts," and "If I promise to do something, I'll do it, even if I later don't feel like it." In fact, many of the items reflect a similar format: "I (relevant or important action) even if (potential barrier)." In this sense, they are true to the name of the measure, acceptance + action. They represent hybrid items, a combination of two processes. None of the items reflect a sense of performing small actions as part of a continuing and growing pattern of values-based action.

Committed Action Questionnaire

The first published instrument specifically intended to measure committed action within the psychological flexibility model was the Committed Action Questionnaire (CAQ; McCracken, 2013). It took a long time to arrive, appearing 14 years after the first book on ACT. The first version of this measure included 18 items derived from a pool of 24. It was developed based on data from participants in a specialty chronic pain service in the UK (*n* = 216). Part of the motivation for creating the CAQ was the need to remedy the absence of a measure of this important facet of PF. The other motivation was to provide an alternative conceptualization to a commonly applied approach to activity management in chronic pain, namely, "pacing." Pacing as a concept tends to be applied just as it seems it would be: a way to create and maintain activity that is active but does not increase pain significantly and stays within the limits of a person's level of energy or stamina. One problem associated with pacing that might seem immediately obvious is how to apply the term in treatment without creating behavior patterns that function mainly as avoidance, as it will generally include pain or fatigue as guiding influences.

Positively keyed items of the CAQ included "I am able to persist with a course of action after experiencing difficulties"; "when a goal is difficult to reach, I am able to take small steps to reach it"; and "I am able to incorporate discouraging experiences into the process of pursuing my long term plans." Clearly, these items include acceptance elements, and the previously noted action + acceptance format, consistent with the earliest conceptualizations of "willingness and commitment" (Hayes et al., 1999). You could say they reflect committed action, particularly in the context of challenges to that action. Examples of negatively keyed items include: "I act impulsively when under pressure," "I get stuck doing the same thing over and over even if I am not successful," and "If I make a commitment and later fail to reach it, I then drop the commitment." In the original development study, the CAQ demonstrated a Cronbach's alpha of .91, and the total score correlated significantly with acceptance of pain, $r = .49$, and with depression, social and mental health, vitality and general health, $r = -.57$, .40, .58, .33, and .37, respectively. Its correlation with physical functioning, based on the SF-36, was smaller, $r = .20$. Also, in regression, for all outcomes with the exception of physical functioning, the CAQ total score accounted for significant variance independent of pain intensity and acceptance of pain (McCracken, 2013; see also Bailey, Vowles, Witkiewitz, Sowden, & Ashworth, 2016).

As data accumulated on the CAQ, it became possible to develop a shorter version. An 8-item version appeared in 2015 (McCracken et al., 2015). As is true of the original CAQ, the shorter version retained an equal number of positively and negatively keyed items. Beyond what was done with the CAQ, the CAQ-8 was a product of confirmatory factor analysis and Mokken scaling analysis, to check the assumption of monotonicity in item responses. The scale analyses demonstrated that the items can be appropriately used to derive a summary score. The alpha reliability for the total scale was .87, and the correlation of the short version with the longer version was $r = .96$. In correlation analyses, generally speaking, the CAQ-8 performed nearly identically to the CAQ. There is naturally a loss of item content and information in the shorter version, but based on results in the development study, the two instruments appear to be substantially equivalent (McCracken et al., 2015).

The CAQ has been translated from the original English and validated in Swedish (Åkerblom, Perrin, Rivano-Fischer, & McCracken, 2016), French (Gagnon, Dionne, Balbinotti, & Monestès, 2017), Spanish (Galán et al., 2019), and German (Terhorst, Baumeister, McCracken, & Lin, 2020). It has also been demonstrated that the items from the CAQ-8 form separate factors in modeling multiple components of PF/inflexibility in confirmatory factor analysis, factors that nonetheless also fit within an overall general factor mainly dominated by acceptance (Scott, McCracken, & Norton, 2016).

Engaged Living Scale

Following the CAQ to publication by just 3 short months, the Engaged Living Scale (ELS; Trompetter et al., 2013) appeared. It was intended to pick up values-based action, or "valued-living" as the authors refer to it, and committed action, defined as "undertaking actions and performing behaviors that are congruent with chosen values, even when barriers or obstacles are encountered" (p. 1237). There was also an additional facet incorporated in the item generation phase. This was called "evaluation" and was referred to as "the evaluation of the outcome of fulfillment of living in accordance with values and performing committed actions" (p. 1237). The development of the measure employed undergraduate students, their parents and grandparents, and people with chronic pain as participants. Sixteen items were retained from an initial pool of 31 and a two-factor structure was confirmed, with the two parts of the measure called Valued Living and Life Fulfillment. The subscale and total scores showed good internal consistency (alpha), .86 for both subscales and.90 for the total scale. Construct validity was supported in correlations of the total scale score with PF/inflexibility, $r = .51$, psychological well-being, $r = .35$ to .64, and mental health, $r = .49$.

An important point is what one sees in looking at the final item content of the ELS. At least one item matches the definition of committed action provided by the authors: "I make choices based on my values, even if it is stressful." Two other items approach this pattern of behavior by reflecting an absence of barriers to action: "My emotions don't hold me back from doing what's important to me," and "Nothing can stop me from doing something that's important to me." In addition, two items more or less reflect values-based action generally: "I live the way I always intended to live," and "I make time for the things that I consider important." This analysis so far leaves 11 items remaining. Eight of the remaining items include either the phrase "I know . . . " or "I believe . . . ," four items each. For the remaining three, the main action in the item is "have," "am," and "feel." Based on this analysis of content, the ELS appears mainly to assess knowledge of values and belief about following values and perhaps little actual committed action as such, at least not directly. This is not to say it is not a measure of committed action, or is not related to committed action; it simply does not address the process, as it says here, in a direct way.

Subsequent to the introduction of the 16-item ELS, a nine-item version also appeared, based on a Portuguese translation from the Dutch and derived within a sample of university students (Trinidade, Ferreira, Pinto-Gouveia, & Nooren, 2016). The 16-item and 9-item versions performed adequately in internal consistency, factor structure, and correlations with related variables, and the two different versions performed similarly in this regard. From a perspective of committed action, the 9-item version seems essentially similar to the 16-item version.

CompACT

In an attempt to avoid the limitations of measures focused on limited numbers of PF processes or focused on particular problem contexts, recent attempts to assess committed action have fit it within a wider focus across the facets of PF. One of these efforts produced what is called the Comprehensive Assessment of Acceptance and Commitment Therapy processes or the CompACT (Francis, Dawson, & Golijani-Moghaddam, 2016). The development of the CompACT included Delphi consensus methods and item analyses, along with factor analysis. These methods yielded a 23-item measure from an initial item pool of 106 taken from 11 available ACT process measures, including the CAQ-8. A three-factor solution emerged from these items, reflecting openness to experience, behavioral awareness, and valued action, and three subscales were named accordingly. The eight-item valued action subscale in particular demonstrated predictable significant correlations with depression, anxiety, and stress, and with physical and mental health, more so for mental than physical health.

Once again looking at item content, one sees a dominance of values-based action items, which is by no means inconsistent with committed action. Interestingly, the item with the highest factor loading was, "My values are really reflected in my behavior." Another typical item with a high loading was, "I can identify the things that matter to me in life and pursue them." Three of the items on the face of them clearly reflect committed action: "I am able to follow my long-term plans including times when the progress is slow," selected originally from the CAQ-8; "I can keep going with something when it's important to me"; and "I undertake things that are meaningful to me, even when I find it hard to do so," once again the familiar acceptance + action format. Overall then, while the CompACT includes some item content that is relevant to committed action, it is not able to provide a separate and complete reflection of just this process as it now stands.

Multidimensional Psychological Flexibility Inventory

The next in line multidimensional measure of PF is the aptly named Multidimensional Psychological Flexibility Inventory (MPFI; Rolffs, Rogge, & Wilson, 2018). Its development was similarly motivated as the CompACT: to make a single comprehensive measure of PF, and bring clarity and order where the field was otherwise characterized by many measures of limited breadth. The development work for this measure included $n = 3040$ participants in three studies. The starting point for gathering data included an item pool of 494 items, gathered as for the CompACT, from 22 existing measures of PF or mindfulness. These were supplemented with an additional 84 items written by the authors to "diversify the item pool." From that point, items were administered and selected empirically with factor analysis, 12 dimensions were distinguished, 74 additional items were written, and 288 items were submitted to analyses based on Item Response Theory (IRT). Sixty items emerged from these analyses: five items each for each facet of PF and psychological inflexibility. The authors argue, based on exploratory and confirmatory factor analysis, that the MPFI items form two higher-order factors, global flexibility and inflexibility, each including six five-item factors reflecting specific underlying dimensions, consistent with the PF model. The authors present convincing evidence for convergent and discriminant validity, based on adults in the United States recruited from university students and online research recruitment sites.

Relevant to the topic of the present text are two dedicated subscales in the MPFI, one of which addresses committed action and the other "inaction." All items are keyed consistently with the subscale title. Three of the committed action items take the form "Even when . . . [potential barrier], I . . . [action]." Here the barriers are "stumbled," "times got tough," and "life got stressful and hectic." The actions so to speak were "didn't quit," "take steps toward what I value," and "worked toward things that were important." The other two items take the form "I didn't let . . . [potential barrier] . . . " with the barriers being "setbacks" and "own fears and doubt" and the actions they might slow or stop being "taking action toward what I really want in life" and "taking action toward my goals." All of the inaction items represent statements of barriers, including thoughts, feelings, or negative experiences, leading to an absence, or stopping, of action. It is perhaps no surprise that there is no action in the inaction items, except for the action of the events in relation to behavior. Once again, committed action here is focused more on continuing values-based action in the face of potential barriers than on aspects of committed action that include building extended, growing patterns of values-based action.

A relevant development in relation to the MPFI is that the factor structure has been replicated independently, albeit in an undergraduate sample (Seidler, Stone, Clark, Koran, & Drake, 2020). Anyone who has conducted factor analysis in the context of instrument development will know this is no small feat. Sixty items and 12 factors, where the expectation will be that the behavior patterns included will substantially overlap, present a real challenge in confirmatory factor analysis. Worth adding too is the finding that the factor structure of a short form of the measure, including just two items per facet, was also confirmed. This is important, as 60 items might represent a significant burden for respondents, particularly for repeated use.

Finally, in a recent notable study that included the MPFI, the moderating roles of PF and inflexibility on the mental health impacts of COVID-19 were studied (Pakenham et al., 2020). In this study, 1035 adults in Italy completed measures of 12 lockdown risk factors, including lockdown duration, family infection by COVID-19, domestic violence, and unhealthy lifestyle, summarized as a "lockdown index," and three mental health outcomes, including peritraumatic distress, anxiety, and depression. In regression path analyses, after controlling for demographic variables, global PF and four facets, including committed action, were shown to "mitigate" the detrimental impacts of the COVID-19 risk factors on the mental health outcomes. In addition to showing the role of committed action in a particular, current, pandemic context, the study shows the successful use of the MPFI in complex modeling analyses. In summary, then, while they represent a somewhat narrow response set from within the whole class of committed action-related behavior, the items from the MPFI can be regarded as reflecting a well-validated and usefully short measure of committed action, and it appears distinguishable from the other five facets of PF within this measure. There is also an added benefit from this measure in a separate inaction subscale embedded within a higher-order global inflexibility factor. The fact that the PF and inflexibility parts of this measure together yield 12 factors that are so far replicable is a significant step forward in the assessment of PF.

Other Relevant Measures

While committed action might not be highlighted in the name or descriptions, there are other measures that carry some content like committed action. Among these measures is the Multidimensional Experiential Avoidance Questionnaire (MEAQ; Gámez, Chmielewski, Kotov, Ruggero, & Watson, 2011). The subscales labeled procrastination, including a sense of putting off things that are needed but unpleasant, and distress endurance, including willingness to suffer for things that matter, appear to be directly applicable to the behavior pattern of committed action. Once again, particularly with the distress endurance items, a familiar pattern appears: what is being called "action + acceptance" where a behavior related to an important purpose is available and is done in the presence of a potential barrier.

When it came time to make a better measure of psychological flexibility, the authors of one recent effort laid out their essential definition: "the pursuit of valued goals despite the presence of distress" (Kashdan, Disabato, Goodman, Doorley, & McKnight, 2020). The measure they created was called the Personalized Psychological Flexibility Index (PPFI). Once again, a distinct specific committed action scale did not emerge from their scale development analyses. Instead, they produced a 15-item measure with three scales: avoidance, acceptance, and harnessing. Clearly, there are items in the avoidance scale that reflect what will be recognized from the context of other committed action measures, content that directly reflects the absence of committed action, "When I feel stressed pursuing this goals, I give it up," and "When I feel discouraged, I let my commitments for this goal slide."

Finally, there is another example of a measure, one that explicitly includes committed action, and it deserves mention, if for no other reason than the context in which it was designed to be used, *in* sessions of ACT or CBT (Probst et al., 2020). The authors called their measure the Acceptance and Commitment Therapy Session Questionnaire (ACT-SQ), and they referred to it as assessing the "in-session realization" of the six core components of ACT in the patient's view. The six items of the measure formed a single factor based on a sample of 87 patients treated by nine ACT therapists. All items included the stem "The last . . . psychotherapy session(s) helped me . . . ," and the committed action item included "to act in daily life according to what is important to me in my life and what gives orientation to my life." As a point of comparison, the values item included " . . . to recognize what is important to me in my life and what gives orientation to my life."

Evidence for Committed Action as Process in ACT

Committed action was featured in a systematic review of mediation studies of ACT (Stockton et al., 2018). In the review, the authors identified 12 clinical trials of ACT compared with another active treatment that included mediation analyses published between 2006 and 2015. In general, it was concluded that mediation results were consistent with the PF model, however, that studies were of limited quality and focused only on a limited number of processes. Four out of five studies reportedly demonstrated that PF was a mechanism of change for mental health outcomes, and the same number for acceptance in relation to the same outcome domains. Lesser numbers of studies provided support for the other individual facets of PF. Two of the studies included reportedly showed evidence that committed action was a mechanism of change during ACT and cognitive therapy/conventional cognitive-behavioral therapy (CBT). However, on further examination, it was not clear that either of these studies properly assessed committed action. In a study by Forman et al. (2012), a comparison of ACT and cognitive therapy in a university clinic ($n = 174$), a measure called the Before Session Questionnaire was developed and used. It included seven items, reflecting symptom severity, progress toward goals, and five potential mediator items, one reportedly being committed action. The item designed to assess committed action was adapted from the AAQ and included "my anxiety, depression, and other distress." with responses ranging from "Does not prevent me from doing anything of importance . . . " to "Prevents me from doing many important things." This content is mixed, not purely like committed action as defined here, but more like acceptance, willingness, or avoidance. In the other study, by Hesser, Zetterqvist Westin, and Andersson (2014), comparing internet-delivered ACT with CBT for tinnitus ($n = 67$), the measure of committed action was a subscale of a measure based on another measure of acceptance of chronic pain (McCracken, Vowles, & Eccleston, 2004). In the original measure, the subscale used here was designed to reflect taking action in the presence of a potential avoidance-promoting experience, again the action part of acceptance. So, there is some confounding here of two processes, seemingly leaving it an unclear test of outcomes being mediated by committed action.

More recently, several studies have shown that ACT-based treatments may produce significant effects on committed action as assessed by validated measures of this facet. Possibly the first demonstration of a relationship between delivery of an ACT-based treatment and change on a validated measure of committed action was in the context of a specialized interdisciplinary treatment for complex chronic pain in the UK (Scott, Hann, & McCracken, 2016). This study included 384 consecutive participants who provided data before and after treatment, and 214 of these who provided data at a nine-month follow-up appointment. Treatment was residentially based and lasted four weeks. The aim of the study was to investigate change in facets of PF and their relations with outcomes. According to the results, each of three assessed facets of PF changed significantly from pre- to posttreatment and from pretreatment to follow-up. The changes in committed action, as measured by the CAQ, were small, immediately posttreatment and at follow-up, $d = .34$ and $d = .20$. Correlations between change in committed action and changes posttreatment in physical functioning, social functioning, and depression, were $r = .27$, $r = .37$, and $r = -.41$, respectively. At follow-up these were marginally higher, at $r = .30$, $r = .44$, and $r = -.46$. All of these were significant at $p < .001$. In regression analyses controlling for pain severity, which also included measures of change in acceptance and cognitive defusion, change in committed action contributed significantly to prediction in improvement in depression, but not to prediction of the other outcomes.

The treatment effects in relation to committed action from a context of specialty chronic pain treatment were replicated twice in independent cohorts. The first study included 252 adults with chronic pain who participated in the same treatment at later dates (Daly-Eichenhardt, Scott, Howard-Jones, Nicolaou, & McCracken, 2016). This study focused on sleep-related outcomes. In the analyses, change in committed action was shown to correlate with improvements in insomnia severity, sleep interference, and sleep efficiency in bivariate analyses but not in multivariate analyses where other facts of PF were also included. The second study included 354 adults with chronic pain, again at the same center (Yu, Scott, & McCracken, 2020). The effect on committed action posttreatment was once again in the small range, $d = .18$. As before, change in committed action was correlated with change in outcomes, this time including pain interference, work and social adjustment, depression, and fatigue, $r = -.31$, $r = -.29$, $r = -.40$, and $r = -.36$, respectively, all $p < .001$. This time in multiple regression analyses that included control for change in pain, acceptance, and cognitive fusion, change in committed action significantly predicted change in fatigue severity, the primary focus of the study.

An additional demonstration of committed action in the context of ACT appeared in a feasibility RCT of an online version of ACT for chronic pain in the UK (Scott, Guildford, Daly-Eichenhardt, & McCracken, 2018), in the same center as the other cohort studies previously described. In this study, 61 participants were randomized to either online ACT plus specialty medical treatment or the specialty medical treatment alone. Once again small effects were observed for committed action at 3 months and 9 months posttreatment, $d = .26$ and $d = .42$. This was a brief treatment, including just eight core sessions delivered online, over a period of 5 weeks. Most of the content was delivered by video and audio, and the total combined video and audio time was 208 minutes, 3 hours 45 minutes total, or about 26 minutes per session of content delivery time.

Summary and Recommendations

An assessment of the literature on committed action as represented in the context of PF and ACT shows first that the action or engagement in committed action is critical to the completeness of the model and to the treatment's capacity to achieve its intended goals (e.g., Levin, Krafft, Hicks, Pierce, & Twohig, 2020). As stated at the opening of this article, in the absence of the behavior change element included in committed action, the contributions of all other parts of ACT in people's lives remain unrealized. Second, the history of committed action has been marked by some conceptual confusion, which in turn has led to related difficulties, particularly in assessment methods. Resolving this confusion and difficulty may improve research and the clinical methods associated with this process.

ACT might have been better called acceptance and committed-action therapy, but it is probably too late to effect a name change. Use of the term *commitment*, emphasized somewhat in the key first text (Hayes et al., 1999), may have emphasized the pledge or promise part of the concept and deemphasized the quality of the action part. In addition, there was a discernible tendency to blend committed action with willingness or acceptance at that same point in the past, which seems to have created a lingering effect. This acting with willingness quality has been the tone of committed action since the start, to the detriment perhaps of the quality of a connection to progressively growing wider patterns of persistent values-based action. Committed actions will need willingness some of the time, but clearly not just that.

Some of the quibbling described here regarding items in available instruments might seem like the concerns of some kind of obsessive content purist. Nonetheless, it seems like a good rule of thumb in assessment to look specifically at the behavior described in the items that make up the instruments we employ. Do the items predominantly assess the frequency of knowing, believing, potential barriers exerting or not exerting an effect? Or do they assess the respondent's *values-based action*, and/or action that also has a connection to larger and persistent patterns? The recycling of previously developed items into the newer generation of multidimensional measures only perpetuates this impurity—call it lack of precision if you like. A key recommendation here is that future instrument developers heed this call for measures of committed action in the future to reflect these points, that they represent actions, not just in knowing or believing, but in interaction with direct contingencies in the world, with a connection to building patterns of behavior. These patterns may start as "make a commitment and keep a commitment" and then grow, supported in tandem by the commitment and these contingencies. We are still vetting the full PF model as a clinical tool. Making sure that all the facets are measurable, distinguishable elements, and coherent within themselves will be important to this task.

Committed action has not been the biggest, baddest, or hottest part of PF; rather, its most appealing parts have been acceptance, defusion, values, or self-as-context, if you dare. Committed action has had this "been there, done that" quality. Even previous reviews of evidence that could have included it based the work on previous reviews of goal-setting and behavioral activation. Some, relying on their experience and perhaps the data, may believe that this neglect is unwarranted and comes at a cost. The number one recommendation of this article is that researchers and clinicians focus greater attention on understanding, assessing, and applying methods that will enhance committed action in treatments where people need to benefit.

References

Åkerblom, S., Perrin, S., Rivano Fischer, M., & McCracken, L. M. (2016). A validation and generality study of the Committed Action Questionnaire in a Swedish sample with chronic pain. *International Journal of Behavioral Medicine, 23*, 260–270.

Bailey, R. W., Vowles, K. E., Witkiewitz, K., Sowden, G., & Ashworth, J. (2016). Examining committed action in chronic pain: Further validation and clinical utility of the Committed Action Questionnaire. *Journal of Pain, 17*, 1095–1104.

Daly-Eichenhardt, A., Scott, W., Howard-Jones, M., Nicolaou, T., & McCracken, L. M. (2016). Changes in sleep problems and psychological flexibility following interdisciplinary acceptance and commitment therapy for chronic pain: An observational cohort study. *Frontiers in Psychology, 7*, 1326.

Epton, T., Currie, S., & Armitage, C. J. (2017). Unique effects of setting goals on behavior change: Systemic review and meta-analysis. *Journal of Consulting and Clinical Psychology, 85*, 1182–1198.

Forman, E. M., Chapman, J. E., Herbert, J. D., Goetter, E. M., Yuen, E. K., & Moitra, E. (2012). Using session-by-session measurement to compare mechanisms of action for acceptance and commitment therapy and cognitive therapy. *Behavior Therapy, 43*, 341–354.

Francis A. W., Dawson, D. L., & Golijani-Moghaddam, N. (2016). The development and validation of the Comprehensive assessment of Acceptance and Commitment Therapy processes (CompACT). *Journal of Contextual Behavioral Science, 5*(3), 134–145.

Gagnon, J., Dionne, F., Balbinotti, M., * Montetès, J. (2017). Dimensionality and validity of the Committed Action Questionnaire (CAQ-8) in a chronic pain and university student population. *Journal of Contextual Behavioral Science, 6*, 252–260.

Galán, S., Roy, R., Solé, E., racine, M., de la Vega, R., Jensen, M. P., & Miró, J. (2019). Committed action, disability and perceived health in individuals with fibromyalgia. *Behavioral Medicine, 45*, 62–69.

Gámez, W., Chmielewski, M., Kotov, R., Ruggero, C., & Watson, D. (2011). Development of a measure of experiential avoidance: The Multidimensional Experiential Avoidance Questionnaire. *Psychological Assessment, 23*, 692–713.

Hayes, S. C., Strosahl, K. D., & Wilson, K. G. (1999). *Acceptance and commitment therapy: An experiential approach to behavior change*. London: Guildford Press.

Hayes, S. C., Strosahl, K. D., & Wilson, K. G. (2012). *Acceptance and comment therapy: The process and practice of mindful change* (second edition). London: Guildford Press.

Hayes, S. C., Strosahl, K. D., Wilson, K. G., Bissett, R. T., Pistorello, J., Toarmino, D., . . . McCurry, S. M. (2004). Measuring experiential avoidance: A preliminary test of a working model. *The Psychological Record, 54*, 553–578.

Hesser, H., Westin, V. Z., & Andersson, G. (2014). Acceptance as a mediator in internet-delivered acceptance and commitment therapy and cognitive behavior therapy for tinnitus. *Journal of Behavioral Medicine, 37*, 756–767.

Kashdan, T. B., Disabato, D. J., Goodman, F. R., Doorley, J. D., & McKnight, P. E. (2020). Understanding psychological flexibility: A multimethod exploration of pursuing valued-goals despite the presence of distress. *Psychological Assessment, 32*, 829–850.

Lejuez, C. W., Hopko, D. R., Acierno, R., Daughters, S. B., & Pagoto, S. L. (2011). Ten year revision of the brief behavioral activation treatment for depression: Revised treatment manual. *Behavior Modification, 35*, 111–161.

Levin, M. E., Hildebrandt, M. J., Lillis, J., & Hayes, S. C. (2012). The impact of treatment components suggested by the psychological flexibility model: A meta-analysis of laboratory-based component studies. *Behavior Therapy, 43*, 741–756.

Levin, M. E., Krafft, J., Hicks, E. T., Pierce, B., & Twohig, M. P. (2020). A randomized dismantling trial of the open and engaged components acceptance and commitment therapy in an online intervention of distress college students. *Behaviour Research and Therapy, 126*, 103557.
McCracken, L. M. (1998). Learning to live with the pain: Acceptance of pain predicts adjustment in persons with chronic pain. *Pain, 74*, 21–27.
McCracken, L. M. (2013). Committed action: An application of the psychological flexibility model to activity patterns in chronic pain. *Journal of Pain, 14*, 828–835.
McCracken, L. M., Chilcot, J., & Norton, S. (2015). Further development in the assessment of psychological flexibility: A shortened Committed Action Questionnaire (CAQ-8). *European Journal of Pain, 19*, 677–685.
McCracken, L. M., Vowles, K. E., & Eccleston, C. (2004). Acceptance of chronic pain: Component analysis and a revised assessment method. *Pain, 107*, 159–166.
Merriam-Webster. (n.d.) "Commit." *Merriam-Webster.com Dictionary*, https://www.merriam-webster.com/dictionary/commit. Accessed October 11, 2020.
Pakenham, K. I., Lani, G., Boccolini, G., Furlani, A., Grandi, S., & Tossani, E. (2020). The moderating roles of psychological flexibility and inflexibility on the mental health impacts of COVID-19 pandemic and lockdown in Italy. *Journal of Contextual Behavioral Science, 17*, 109–118.
Probst, T., Mühlberger, A., Kühner, J., Eifert, G. H., Pieh, C., Hackbarth, T., & Mander, J. (2020). Development and initial validation of a brief questionnaire on the patients' view of the in-session realization of the six core components of acceptance and commitment therapy. *Clinical Psychology in Europe, 2*, e3115, https://doi.org/10.32872/cpe.v2i3.3115
Rolffs, J. L., Rogge, R. D., & Wilson, K. G. (2018). Disentangling components of flexibility via the hexaflex model: Development and validation of the Multidimensional Psychological Flexibility Inventory (MPFI). *Assessment, 25*, 458–482.
Scott, W., Guildford, B., Daly-Eichenhardt, A., & McCracken, L. M. (2018). Feasibility randomized-controlled trial of online Acceptance and Commitment Therapy for patients with complex chronic pain in the United Kingdom. *European Journal of Pain, 22*, 1473–1484.
Scott, W., Hann, K. E. J., & McCracken, L. M. (2016). A comprehensive examination of change in psychological flexibility following acceptance and commitment therapy for chronic pain. *Journal of Contemporary Psychotherapy, 46*, 139–148.
Scott, W., McCracken, L. M., & Norton, S. (2016). A confirmatory factor analysis of facets of psychological flexibility in a sample of people seeking treatment for chronic pain. *Annals of Behavioral Medicine, 50*, 285–296.
Seidler, D., Stone, B., Clark, B. E., Koran, J., & Drake, C. E. (2020). Evaluating the factor structure of the Multidimensional Psychological Flexibility Inventory: An independent replication and extension. *Journal of Contextual Behavioral Science, 17*, 23–31.
Stein, A. T., Carl, E., Cuijpers, P., Karyotaki, E., & Smits, J. A. J. (2020). Looking beyond depression: A meta-analysis of the effect of behavioral activation on depression, anxiety, and activation. *Psychological Medicine, 51*(9), 1491–1504. http://doi.org/10.1017/S0033291720000239
Stockton, D., Kellett, S., Berrios, R., Sirois, F., Wilkinson, N., & Miles, G. (2018). Identifying the underlying mechanisms of change during acceptance and commitment therapy (ACT): A systematic review of contemporary mediation studies. *Behavioural and Cognitive Psychotherapy, 47*, 332–362.
Terhorst, Y., Baumeister, H., McCracken, L. M., & Lin, J. (2020). Further development in the assessment of psychological flexibility: Validation of the German committed action questionnaire. *Health and Quality of Life Outcomes, 18*, 260.
Trinidad, I. A., Ferreira, C., Pinto-Gouveia, J., & Noreen, L. (2016). Clarity of personal values and committed action: Development of a shorter Engaged Living Scale. *Journal of Psychopathology and Behavioral Assessment, 38*, 258–265.
Trompetter, H. R., ven Klooster, P. M., Schreurs, K. M. G., Fledderus, M., Westerhof, G. J., & Bohlmeijer, E. T. (2013). Measuring values and committed action with the Engaged Living Scale (ELS); Psychometric evaluation in a nonclinical sample and a chronic pain sample. *Psychological Assessment, 25*, 1235–1246.
Yu, L., Scott, W., & McCracken, L. M. (2020). Change in fatigue in acceptance and commitment therapy-based treatment for chronic pain and its association with enhanced psychological flexibility. *European Journal of Pain, 24*, 234–247.

SECTION 3

Specific Applications of ACT

CHAPTER 14

Depression

Jacqueline A-Tjak *and* Louise Hayes

Abstract

Depressive disorders most commonly refer to either dysthymia, a persistent or chronic form of mild depression, or major depressive disorder. The two primary symptom clusters are depressed mood and loss of interest/pleasure. Comorbid conditions account for the largest portion of the adverse impact of depression. One of the most influential and researched treatments for this disorder is cognitive-behavioral therapy (CBT). This therapy is often the therapy of choice, with about two-thirds of those suffering from depression benefiting from it. Of growing importance in the treatment of depression is acceptance and commitment therapy (ACT), which has been shown to be as efficacious as CBT. The ACT model consists of six interrelated processes: experiential avoidance, fusion, attachment to a conceptualized self, loss of contact with the present moment, loss of contact with values, and lack of valued action. The body of research on depression and its purported mechanisms can inform the ACT model of psychological flexibility and inflexibility and could influence ACT treatment. The paradox of treating it as a diagnostic category can be addressed via a transdiagnostic perspective.

Key Words: depression, acceptance and commitment therapy, efficacy, psychological flexibility, psychological inflexibility, mechanisms of change, transdiagnostic, epidemiology

Introduction

The word "depressed" is widely used. In daily life, it can signify an instance of low mood. In psychiatry, it is broadly used to cover mental states ranging from dysthymia to several kinds of mood disorders—including bipolar disorders, consisting of manic and depressive episodes separated by periods of normal mood. Depressive disorders most commonly refer to either dysthymia, a persistent or chronic form of mild depression, or major depressive disorder (MDD). According to the *Diagnostic and Statistical Manual of Mental Disorders* (5th ed.; DSM–5; American Psychiatric Association, 2013), MDD is either of two primary symptom clusters: depressed mood or loss of interest/pleasure. Five or more symptoms need to be present for at least 2 weeks, and symptoms must represent a change from previous functioning. Other symptoms include appetite and sleep disturbance, behavioral unrest or retardation, tiredness, feelings of guilt or worthlessness, problems with concentration and indecisiveness, and suicidal ideation. The symptoms should cause clinically significant distress or impairment in social, occupational, or other important areas of functioning.

Two different conceptualizations of depression influence theory and research (Phillips, Hine, & Thorsteinsson, 2010). The first is a dimensional perspective, where depression is seen as a continuum, and those suffering from depression are viewed as differing only in valence and intensity of depression. In this continuum perspective, it is hypothesized that similar effects of therapy will be observed with or without a formal diagnosis. The second perspective is a categorical viewpoint. It posits that clinically depressed individuals possess qualitatively different characteristics, such as cognitions, from nondepressed individuals. Therefore, from a categorical perspective, different effects should be found in clinical compared to nonclinical studies.

The Impact of Depression

More than 264 million people of all ages suffer from depression (WHO; 2021). This number may even be higher if research in postconflict countries is considered (Hoppen & Morina, 2019). Country-specific estimates can be accessed at Global Health Data Exchange. The global burden of depression has been increasing over time, particularly in lower-income countries (WHO, 2021). Poverty, unemployment, life events (e.g., death of a loved one or a relationship dissolution), physical illness, and problems caused by alcohol and drug use increase the risk of becoming depressed. Depressive disorders are also ranked as the single largest contributor to nonfatal health loss worldwide.

Comorbid conditions seem to account for the largest portion of the adverse impact of depression, both with other mental disorders and with chronic health conditions, cardiac problems, and smoking (Gotlib, Joormann, & Foland-Ross, 2014). Comorbidity of MDD with other mental disorders is high, with approximately 75 percent of people suffering from MDD in the United States (Richards, 2011) and meeting the criteria for one or more current comorbid mental disorders. MDD with comorbidity has significantly poorer psychosocial functioning and recovery rates over 12 months when compared to those with no comorbidity. Interestingly, Buhk, Schadegg, Dixon, and Tull (2020) found severity in generalized anxiety disorder (GAD) is associated with increased emotional avoidance, which, in turn, was associated with greater severity of depression symptoms. This finding suggests that psychological inflexibility processes may contribute to comorbidity.

Depression impacts the quality of interpersonal relationships (Gotlib et al., 2014). For example, the divorce rate is higher among depressed than among nondepressed individuals. Loneliness, defined as the experience of subjective social isolation and the lack of meaningful interactions, seems to affect depression (Erzen & Çikrikci, 2018). However, relationships that promote confiding in others and meeting with family and friends can also play a protective role. In a large study, Choi et al. (2020) found several relationship factors were associated with developing depression. In this study, the protective effects of social connection were visible even for individuals at higher risk for depression due to genetic vulnerability or trauma early in life.

The suffering experienced by people with depression is not confined to their own lives. Children of depressed parents, ranging in age from infancy through adolescence, have a three- to five-fold higher risk of becoming depressed themselves than children of parents without psychiatric problems (Gotlib et al., 2014). Even after 30 years, the devastating effects of parental depression are visible via an elevated risk for depression, morbidity, and mortality (Weissman et al., 2016).

Depression is occurring at increasingly younger ages (Gotlib et al., 2014). MDD affects 8–20 percent of all youth (Henje Blom et al., 2014). Youth with early-onset depression can have pervasive dysfunction throughout their lives and are at higher risk of future psychiatric morbidity in adulthood (Gotlib et al., 2014). If left untreated, with time depressive disorders in the younger years can be increasingly challenging to treat (Cox et al., 2014).

Between 20 and 50 percent of the people who become depressed for the first time recover and, with or without treatment, will not suffer from another episode (Boland & Keller, 2009;

Eaton et al., 2008). However, even with treatment, depression can become recurrent or chronic (Bockting, Hollon, Jarrett, Kuyken, & Dobson, 2015). Although more psychological therapies have become available since the 1970s, the 12-month population prevalence rates have not dropped (Ormel, Kessler, & Schoevers, 2019), making depression a chronic, lifelong illness for many. Previous episodes of depression and residual depressive symptoms predict increased rates of depressive relapse and recurrence (Bockting et al., 2015). In a prospective study during 23 years of follow-up after treatment, Eaton and colleagues (2008) found that for 15 percent of people treated for depression, no remission was reached, and MDD recurred for 35 percent of those treated. With antidepressants (ADs) and no psychological treatment, these numbers are higher, and when ADs are discontinued, the risk of relapse increases (Conradi, Bos, Kamphuis, & de Jonge, 2017).

Psychological Treatment for Depression

One of the most influential and researched treatments for depression is cognitive-behavioral therapy (CBT; Beck, Rush, Shaw, & Emery, 1979). The original model for this therapy focused on changing the content of thoughts based on the assumption that maladaptive cognitions contribute to the onset and maintenance of depression. Clients learn to question how realistic and helpful their thoughts are, and they form new conclusions about their thoughts (Hofmann, Asnaani, Vonk, Sawyer, & Fang, 2012). Later, a shortened version of behavioral activation (BA; Lewinsohn, Munoz, Youngren, & Zeiss, 1986) was added to Beck et al.'s model (1979). This model assumes that depressive behavior is a consequence of insufficient and inadequate positive reinforcement. Low positive reinforcement leads to a decrease in the level of activity a person displays, and subsequently, positive reinforcement further decreases, resulting in a downward spiral. In BA, clients learn to make functional analyses of their behavior patterns and change their behavioral repertoire to gain more positive reinforcement. The CBT model can contain a third component of social skills training, where clients practice skills to communicate their boundaries, emotions, and needs.

CBT for depression is often recommended as the therapy of choice, and about two-thirds of those suffering from depression benefit from it (Cuijpers et al., 2014). It lowers the chance of relapse by nearly a quarter compared to treatment as usual (Clarke, Mayo-Wilson, Kenny, & Pilling, 2015). Other, less well-researched psychological treatments for depression seem to be equally efficacious as CBT, or the differences are small and clinically not relevant (Barth et al., 2013). Cuijpers and Gentili (2017) conclude that the effects of psychological interventions are comparable to those of pharmacological treatment and likely last longer.

Ideally, therapists are expected to be able to predict who will benefit most from which therapy. Yet, even researchers find complexity and slow progress in this area, with many factors to consider. Research on treatment outcomes shows that those who experienced a substantial reduction of symptoms in the first 10 weeks of CBT treatment (i.e., early responders) showed less depressive symptomatology at the end of treatment (Schlagert & Hiller, 2017). Similar outcomes for several other forms of psychological and pharmacological treatment have also been found (Beard & Delgadillo, 2019); early responders were at least four times more likely to attain positive treatment outcomes.

A Different Perspective

Depression as Adaptation

So far, depression has been discussed as a disorder with dimensional or categorical properties; however, depression can alternatively be seen as an aversive yet adaptive response to context (Syme & Hagen, 2020). This reframe would shed a different light on the high prevalence rates, the apparent rise in depression rates, and the small progress made in detecting biological and genetic causes. MDD has relatively low heritability, which suggests that environmental factors play a more influential role. A normal reaction to contextual adversity may turn into a seemingly inescapable cycle of suffering, even when depression is not seen as an illness or disorder. Therefore, it seems crucial to understand how a response considered as adaptive results in chronic dysfunction.

Psychological Inflexibility and Depression

Acceptance and commitment therapy (ACT) is a functional contextual approach to human behavior where depression is considered a signal of ineffective patterns of living or psychological inflexibility (PI; Zettle & Hayes, 2002). PI refers to getting stuck inside our thoughts or feelings, and being unable to take action until our thoughts and feelings are "right." Conversely, psychological flexibility (PF) is the ability to approach life's challenges and persist in what we care about even if we have difficult thoughts or feelings. Environmental contexts are important, and efforts should be made to change problematic factors such as abusive relationships, poverty, and unemployment. However, to empower such change and valued action more broadly, ACT focuses on the *verbal* contexts that link mood, thought, and behavior. Western culture is a highly verbal context that views depression as problematic because it must be *eliminated* before more effective living is possible. From an ACT point of view, it is the tight link between mood and thought on the one hand and overt behavior on the other that needs to be loosened by changing contextual control—mood or thought itself does not have to be changed directly. The model assumes that all people can and will get trapped in human psychological processes because searching for danger and problems is part of our evolutionary adaptation. ACT assumes that all humans will get caught up in repetitive, narrow cognitions and overt behaviors that lack vitality and meaning. PF is about being able to see this trap and release oneself, whereas PI is staying in the trap. The PI trap often leads to depressive symptoms, diminished functioning, and increased suffering. The ACT model for PI consists of six interrelated processes: experiential avoidance (EA), fusion, attachment to a conceptualized self, loss of contact with the present moment, loss of contact with values, and lack of valued action (S. C. Hayes, Strosahl, & Wilson, 2012). Within these six processes, different functions of PI can be discriminated that are likely connected with depressive symptoms and diagnosable depression.

EXPERIENTIAL AVOIDANCE

Within ACT, depression is often regarded as a "secondary emotion" that appears in reaction to another emotional reaction, such as dysphoria or sadness (Zettle, 2016). Through experiential avoidance (EA), the "normal pain" of emotions that are part of life accumulates into a depressive mood, which is "added pain"—pain resulting from trying to control primary emotions. The outcome of this vicious circle of controlling emotions, cognitions, and mood is that clients may feel depressed about feeling depressed. EA can lead to loss of (values-based) positive reinforcement and social connection and may interfere with helpful emotional processing (e.g., mourning after loss). Findings from several studies (e.g., Maitland, 2020) show that engaging in high EA may lead individuals to be less likely to participate in relationship-building behaviors, resulting in diminished perceived social support and feelings of loneliness.

Research consistently shows that depressed people are more likely to use avoidant coping styles and less likely to employ problem-solving coping techniques than people with no depressive symptoms (Zettle & Hayes, 2002). An avoidant coping style is both a risk factor and a predictor of exacerbation and continuation of mood disorders. Furthermore, it is related to poor responsivity to treatment. This underscores the importance of addressing avoidant coping styles in treatment. Although all kinds of ineffective coping styles can function as EA, it is notable that thought suppression, rumination, and reason-giving may particularly relate to depression.

Experimental analyses have shown that both subclinically and clinically depressed populations have reported the use of thought suppression, apparently based on the assumption that suppression is effective in eliminating depressing thoughts (Zettle & Hayes, 2002). However, thought suppression is ineffective and leads to a rise in intrusive thoughts and an increase in depressed mood. Research shows that depressed people use dysphoric thoughts as distracters instead of neutral or positive thoughts, leading to a vicious circle between dysphoric mood and thought suppression (Zettle, 2016). Suppression is linked to rumination. Thought suppression tends to make unwanted thoughts return (Wenzlaff & Wegner, 2000), and rumination can be seen as a way to suppress unwanted thoughts or feelings (Liverant, Kamholz, Sloan, & Brown, 2011).

Rumination, generally speaking, consists of excessive, perseverative thinking about problems and associated negative feelings, usually with an orientation to the past and the self. People may ruminate to solve a discrepancy between the social pressure to feel happy and lack of happiness (Karabati, Ensari, & Fiorentino, 2019). Rumination has been defined in several ways (Papageorgiou & Wells, 2004). It is related to the onset, persistence, exacerbation, and relapse of depression (e.g., Nolen-Hoeksema, 2004), depending on what definition is used. Nolen-Hoeksema describes (emotion-focused) rumination as "repetitively focusing on the fact that one is depressed; on one's symptoms of depression; and on the causes, meanings, and consequences of depressive symptoms" (Nolen-Hoeksema, 1991, p 569). Stress-reactive rumination (Spasojević, Alloy, Abramson, Maccoon, & Robinson, 2008) is rumination that occurs in response to negative mood, negative life events, or both, and is thought to occur prior to the onset of depressed mood. Thus, emotion-focused rumination is a response to depressed mood itself, whereas stress-reactive rumination is a response to life stress. Longitudinal research shows that rumination predicts the onset of a subsequent major depressive episode in nondepressed people and a relapse of depression in previously depressed persons (Spinhoven et al., 2018). Liverant et al. (2011) found that individuals who frequently use rumination are also more likely to rely on other forms of emotional suppression.

There is some circumstantial evidence for PI and PF's role in rumination and its link to depression. Michalak, Hölz, and Teismann (2011) report a significant decrease in rumination during a course in mindfulness-based cognitive therapy (MBCT). This corresponds with the ACT model, in which rumination is seen as part of the processes of EA, fusion, and loss of contact with the present moment. The psychologically flexible processes of acceptance, defusion, contact with the present moment, and self-as-context are all considered mindfulness skills and may decrease rumination. Competitive memory training is another treatment that overlaps with ACT processes in that it trains people to vividly remember instances of being indifferent (defused) or adopting an attitude of acceptance toward worrisome or emotionally charged situations, which has also been shown effective at reducing depressive rumination (Ekkers et al., 2011). A study by Bakker, Cox, Hubley, and Owens (2019) indicated that higher self-compassion levels were associated with lower depressive symptoms through rumination, experiential avoidance, and acceptance, while cognitive reappraisal did not mediate the relation. These findings underscore the importance of addressing rumination in the treatment of depression. There is also some evidence that a specific focus on rumination in therapy is effective for ACT (Ruiz, Luciano, Flórez, Suárez-Falcón, & Cardona-Betancourt, 2020; Ruiz, Peña-Vargas, et al., 2020).

Reason-giving refers to attempts to find the reasons why one is depressed to get rid of the depression (Zettle & Hayes, 2002). Often, private events or previous life events are seen as causes. However, attempts to alter such events may contribute to PI and the continuation of depression because past events *cannot* be changed. The verbal-social community and clients themselves frequently believe the causes must be changed to overcome depression (Zettle & Hayes, 2002). Research shows that those depressed clients who can offer "good" reasons for their depressed behavior tend to be both more depressed posttreatment and more challenging to treat than other depressive clients (Addis & Jacobson, 1996). Thus, to make treatment work, it is important to address the believability of reasons for depression.

Avoidance extends beyond emotions and cognitions to imagery such as intrusive images of past events or imagined future events. Imagery in depression may include scenes of childhood physical or sexual assault, humiliation, failure, or loss. Once again, suppression is the culprit, with imagery suppression strengthening intrusions. Research shows that during depressive episodes, intrusive memories of childhood trauma may present themselves, and higher levels of intrusions are associated with more severe depression (Kuyken & Brewin, 1994). Depressed individuals show higher levels of avoidance of intrusive memories when compared to never-depressed individuals. Avoidance of such memories is associated with more overgeneral memory (Holmes, Blackwell, Burnett Heyes, Renner, & Raes, 2016), which is an inability to retrieve specific memories from one's autobiographical memory. Overgeneral memory is associated with difficulties with problem solving and rumination, among other key factors believed to maintain depression.

FUSION

Fusion refers to how language and cognition dominate behavioral regulation. Without adequate awareness, thoughts and beliefs drive behavior and obscure a broader perspective of one's experience. Fusion is seen as especially problematic when cognitions get in the way of valued living. The owner of the fused cognitions may not be conscious of their influence. For instance, a person may be convinced that they are boring and therefore not participate in conversations with their colleagues without realizing their beliefs about why they do not participate.

Several forms of fusion may be especially related to depression, specifically reason-giving, evaluating, and storytelling (Zettle, 2016). Reason-giving was already discussed as a form of EA; however, the ACT model processes are interrelated, and behaviors such as reason-giving can serve several functions or be part of several ACT processes. It is not difficult to see that when people start to search for reasons for their depression, the reasons that they come up with can influence their subsequent behavior. For instance, when a person believes they are depressed because other people are making their lives miserable, they may not see ways to improve their situation. Rumination and thought suppression fuel fusion by putting thoughts center stage. Both impair the ability to process (negative) information (e.g., Compare, Zarbo, Shonin, Van Gordon, & Marconi, 2014). Furthermore, research shows that focusing on thought content may sometimes worsen rather than decrease rumination (Ekkers et al., 2011).

People are expected to be able to tell their life stories in everyday living and in therapy. The skill of storytelling can reflect flexibility when people can tell different stories about themselves depending on the context. However, when people suffer from depression, especially when it is chronic, their story is often that of being a victim and they relate reasons for depression with autobiographical facts that have no other possible outcome beyond being depressed (Zettle, 2016). Their story can therefore become impregnable. They no longer see that it has been constructed and that it can therefore be reconstructed with a different outcome.

Lastly, evaluations can become problematic when they are taken to be descriptions (Zettle & Hayes, 2002). In the example given previously, the person may think that they can be described as boring (I am boring) and not see that "boring" is an evaluative concept. Daily language is full of such evaluations that pass as descriptors, such as when we speak of negative thoughts or emotions. Evaluating emotions as "negative" may function as a signal to stay away or get rid of those emotions.

ATTACHMENT TO A CONCEPTUALIZED SELF

In CBT for depression (e.g., Beck et al., 1979), attention is paid to negative core beliefs about oneself. When negative beliefs are present and influence mood, therapists will help the client alter their beliefs. However, in ACT, these self-beliefs are not seen as problematic; rather, fusion with self-conceptualizations is hypothesized to be the issue (S. C. Hayes et al., 2012). These conceptualizations are experienced as negative and unwanted, and they drive EA. When depression endures, it can develop into an identity, "I am my depression," further enhancing PI. Clients can start to see themselves as damaged and beyond repair (Zettle, 2016). Depressive self-conceptualizations are associated with perfectionism and self-criticism.

Clients may think of themselves as "not good enough" or another unwanted self-evaluation and try to compensate by meeting excessively high standards. They may believe that only if they meet those standards will people accept them. This belief may feed into meticulously monitoring one's accomplishments and criticizing oneself for not meeting the set standards. This may lead to perceiving others as demanding perfection, concern over mistakes and doubts about one's actions, and habitual self-criticism (M. M. Smith et al., 2016). It interferes with functioning and/or causes the individual significant distress. Clinical perfectionism is a risk and maintenance factor in depression, among other pathologies (Ong et al., 2019). However, perfectionism is not inherently problematic (Ong et al., 2019), such as when one strives for high standards and experiences distress when these standards are not met. When people set their standards in flexible ways and adjust them to their contexts, it can work well. It becomes inflexible when people set standards that must be reached, no matter what.

Self-criticism is characterized by negative self-judgment and self-evaluation in response to perceived failure. The goal of self-criticism often is to feel better about oneself by behaving according to certain standards, but when the standards are excessive, people may feel worse. The self-evaluations they try to avoid are affirmed, and they may identify with being a failure. Self-criticism is associated with several emotions, especially contempt and disgust for the self (Ehret, Joormann, & Berking, 2015). Research suggests that self-critical individuals are at risk for developing, maintaining, and experiencing relapse in depressive episodes, when they also have strong negative emotions directed towards the self, and an inability to cope with these emotions adequately.

LOSS OF CONTACT WITH THE PRESENT MOMENT

Although people with depression often focus on the past, they can also be preoccupied with the future (Zettle, 2016). This preoccupation limits their ability to respond in a psychologically flexible manner to what happens in the here and now. They can lack attentional control, which gets in the way of valued living in the moment. Thinking about the past or future excessively can lead to a loss of pleasure and enjoyment, which is one of the core symptoms of depression. Furthermore, attention to ourselves and our surroundings is vital in helping us choose how to behave; for instance, seeing how others perceive one's behavior. This leads to self-knowledge, such as knowledge about how one impacts the world. A lack of attention and subsequent self-knowledge can lead to learned helplessness or to other ineffective behavior.

When a person cannot accept frustration and other unwanted negative experiences, attentional capacity and decision-making capabilities are narrowed (Kashdan & Rottenberg, 2010). Rumination can also inhibit contact with the present moment and diminish the capacity to find possible solutions (Zettle, 2016).

LOSS OF CONTACT WITH VALUES

Imagery plays an important part in contacting values. Research supports higher levels of imagery in daily life as significantly associated with better momentary mood and more positive affect (Slofstra et al., 2018). Imagery enables people to remember the past, as well as simulate and preexperience the future. It is important for decision making, for it allows fantasizing about possible (rewarding) events in the future or contacting memories of valuable events in the past. Furthermore, mental imagery of future behaviors has been shown to increase the chances of adopting the behavior (Holmes et al., 2016). For example, when people are depressed, they may find it hard to generate a vivid future—or past-oriented mental images—and they'll struggle to generate imagery of a specific memory (Holmes et al., 2016). Often, their memories are overgeneralized, which is negatively associated with problem-solving skills. However, Holmes and colleagues (2016) also suggest that depressed individuals can generate vivid positive imagery if given appropriate guidance. It is important to use concrete events with much sensory detail when retrieving a (positive) image. This concerns visual information as well as sound, touch, and other sensory information. Research further indicates that depression is associated with a tendency to recall memories from an observer perspective, perhaps linking to a reduction in vividness and associated emotion (Holmes et al., 2016). People contact their values, for instance, by bringing back memories of significant events or by fantasizing about possible futures. When no specific memories of meaningful events or images of a meaningful future are available, people may lose their awareness of values. Subsequently, values may fail to guide behavior, and important reinforcement may be missed.

Recently, some interest has been expressed in the role of (low levels of) positive emotions (anhedonia) and depression. Several prospective studies show that self-reported anhedonia predicts worse longitudinal symptoms of MDD (Craske, Meuret, Ritz, Treanor, & Dour, 2016). Depressed individuals show less attention to positive stimuli. Further, low positive affect predicts the onset of MDD. When someone is already depressed, the lack of positive emotions is a substantial predictor of suicide and suicidal ideation. There is evidence that individuals who are depressed show neural deficits in reward processing. Although the data are correlational, research outcomes suggest that a treatment specifically targeting reward anticipation, reward learning, and reward consumption could positively influence depression (Craske et al., 2016). This suggestion makes sense, considering BA and ACT's effectiveness specifically, where increased contact with values leads to more positive reinforcement and rewards, increasing positive emotions such as enjoyment and fulfillment.

LACK OF VALUED ACTION

Lower levels of pleasurable and task-oriented activities result in a loss of positive reinforcement. From an ACT perspective, it is not the change in levels of pleasurable and task-oriented activities that has this effect, but the extent to which such a change reduces valued living (Zettle, 2016). Value-congruent behavior is reinforcing when people see the correspondence between their behavior and the values they hold. When being aware that one's values are connected to one's behavior, reinforcement becomes intrinsic to the behavior. People with high levels of discrepancies between stated values and current behavior are more likely to show higher levels of pretreatment depression (Plumb, Stewart, Dahl, & Lundgrun, 2017) and lower levels of well-being (Villanueva et al., 2020). Research has found that the probability of subsequent values-consistent behavior increased when judged as more important or embedded in a social context (Villanueva et al., 2020).

Fusion with certain thoughts can get in the way of valued action. For instance, people may think that there is no use in trying, that they will fail and prove their unworthiness, that they cannot stand the emotional or physical pain that comes with the activity, or that they lack energy (or something else) to get into action. Another barrier that is associated with fusion clients insisting on being right before they can start acting to improve their lives. Often, this concerns some wrongdoing by others that must be admitted and made right again. People may invest in finding evidence of being right and self-stories of being a victim at the cost of valued living (Zettle, 2007).

SUMMARY OF PI AND DEPRESSION

Figure 14.1 summarizes different ways PI may lead to depression. Some people may only display some aspects, whereas others may show many, if not all, aspects of these pathways. The summary is not meant to be exhaustive. All pathways have to be seen from the client's current life context. Certain learning histories may set people up for excessive use of experiential avoidance. Others may have learning histories that have created memories they want to avoid or that make them prone to emotions they find hard to bear. Problematic reinforcement concerns lack of contact with values and lack of values action. It may result from a history of being punished for having dreams and ambitions or not being stimulated to fantasize over attractive possible futures. People may be reinforced to attain goals that are not satisfying in the long run, or they may follow rules that do not lead to meaningful outcomes. They may have become dependent on reinforcers that stop being available when circumstances change. Problematic reinforcement, dysphoria, unwanted emotions and memories, and experiential avoidance may enhance each other's impact.

PI may be associated with a learning history of seeking coherence in the content of thoughts, combined with messages that define people as "not good enough" in some form, or with messages about why they are depressed, or the conviction that being right is more important than living a valued life. Experiential avoidance and fusion limit adequate attention to the experience of one's inner world and the outside world. All parts of this figure may influence each other and build a more coherent and narrowing learning history, resulting in depression.

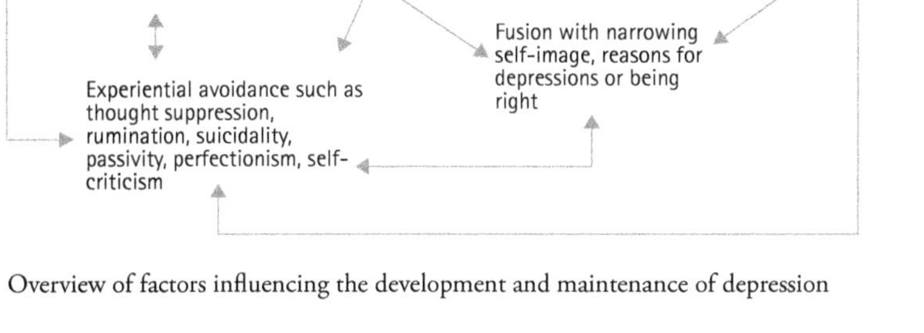

Figure 14.1 Overview of factors influencing the development and maintenance of depression

Some evidence supports the moderating and mediating role of PI on depression. This type of research looks at the influence of PI on the occurrence and level of depressive symptoms without any treatment involved. Bardeen and Fergus (2016) found evidence that individuals with high cognitive fusion and high EA experienced more psychological distress. They showed that the relationship between EA and measures on anxiety, depression, stress, and posttraumatic stress symptoms became increasingly stronger with more cognitive fusion. Peltz, Rogge, Bodenlos, Newman Kingery, and Pigeon (2020) found undergraduates' sleep disturbance to be a significant predictor of their depressive symptoms and suicidal ideation through changes in their levels of PI. Following their systematic review, S. C. Hayes, Luoma, Bond, Masuda, and Lillis (2006) concluded that PI accounts for 16–28 percent of the observed variance concerning various mental health indicators generally used in research. Another meta-analysis of 20 correlational studies similarly found strong correlations between PI and symptoms of depression and anxiety (Ruiz, 2010).

There are also some indications that PF (the converse to PI) acts as a protective factor of mental and physical health. In a preliminary study, Trindade, Mendes, and Ferreira (2020) found that higher PF was protective for depression symptomatology, particularly for those who experienced higher levels of learned helplessness. In a correlational study, Gloster, Meyer, and Lieb (2017) noted that PF moderated the relation between daily stress and various mental health indicators (e.g., life satisfaction, emotional well-being) and physical health indicators (e.g., frequency of medical consultations). The more PF people reported, the weaker the relationship between risk factors such as daily stress and problems with physical health, psychological health, and well-being.

Promoting Psychological Flexibility with Depression

ACT for depression can be delivered individually (e.g., A-Tjak, Morina, Topper, & Emmelkamp, 2018), in groups (e.g., Zettle & Hayes, 1986), as a guided self-help intervention (e.g., Fledderus, Bohlmeijer, Fox, Schreurs, & Spinhoven, 2013), and as a web-based intervention (e.g., Pots et al., 2016). Several protocols are available (e.g., Zettle, 2007). However, it is best delivered when tailored to the specific needs of clients (and therapists).

Working with ACT for depression, starting with clarification of values helps set an agenda of hope. A glimpse of a life worth living can encourage a client to open up to the ACT approach. However, not all clients can state their values, hopes, dreams, or needs clearly enough at the start of treatment. Fusion with self-beliefs or entanglement in avoidance behavior may interfere with contacting (precursors of) values. Another common way to start an ACT treatment is to create awareness of the hopelessness of the control agenda, which is also known as creative hopelessness. For some clients with depression, this may indeed be a good starting point. Other clients may need time to build a solid therapeutic relationship. Otherwise, the message of creative hopelessness may be understood as if the client or life itself is hopeless.

Furthermore, it is essential to know the core of the client's avoidance for creative hopelessness to fall into place. Self-beliefs may be the incentive for experiential avoidance. If so, exposing the control agenda may leave the client in a trap of knowing what not to do but not changing their behavior. In this case, the therapist should first take time to explore self-beliefs and how they interact with unhelpful behavior, and then carefully help the client to defuse these beliefs. Patience is needed when fusion is high. Training in mindfulness skills is a good way to start the treatment, if clients are open to it. Reluctance may be reduced by explaining that these skills are helping the client to steer their attention toward making better behavioral choices. Committed action could be introduced early in treatment to get out of a loop of inactivity, lack of reinforcement, and declining motivation for action. At the beginning of treatment, small, doable steps are paramount for the client to experience success and breach learned helplessness. They can be aimed at health-promoting behaviors known to influence mood, such as physical movement. Along the way, internal barriers like emotions and thoughts can be addressed by teaching acceptance and defusion skills.

When people have already been diagnosed with depression and may identify with it, it is important to address the ACT stance on depression, framing depression as an outcome of ineffective living patterns. The ACT therapist may convey the idea that depression does not have to go away before valued living is possible. The therapist could start a conversation on EA and investigate whether there are specific emotions, thoughts, or memories they have problems facing. This may be difficult for clients when they are not aware of what is avoided and how it occurs. The therapist could use insights into the dynamics of depression, as described previously, to improve understanding of the nature of EA and the private experiences involved. When the client finds it discomforting to approach private experiences, therapist and client might first want to focus on what valued living would look like. An image of how life might become more meaningful could motivate the hard work of facing difficult inner experiences.

Trying to achieve a state of continuous happiness may contribute to rumination (Karabati et al., 2019), and so a focus on values may be a more psychologically flexible alternative. It appears that social domains are judged as having more value than nonsocial domains. Furthermore, social connection is a protective factor for depression. For parents, their relationship with their children can be an important target of committed action. This will help the parents to be emotionally available during challenging times, thereby preventing their offspring from becoming depressed. Therefore, a focus on values in the social domain is paramount. When people suffering from depression find it hard to determine their values, it may help to choose actions that are focused on important social contexts as well as positive social emotions such as gratitude, compassion, love, or appreciation of beauty (S. C. Hayes, 2013). This may shift the focus from what is experienced as negative to more fulfilling and uplifting experiences that elicit positive emotions.

Both acceptance and committed action might require taking small steps that are manageable and that will allow for perceived control. For instance, when someone fears being overwhelmed by emotions, we may work to bring them in contact with emotions while also titrating the time and extent, so that they are not overwhelmed. For example, shifting between emotions and neutral physical sensations or sensory input could be helpful.

Having the sense of a self that contains one's emotions and inner sensations may produce a sense of control as clients engage in acceptance and committed action. The self might be likened to a river in which water flows through just as emotions flow through. Although the water never stays the same, the river can be sensed as a constant presence that encompasses *all* the water, no matter how much or in what form. In relational frame theory (RFT), the theoretical foundation underpinning ACT, this view is called self-as-hierarchy, a more specified part of self-as-context. It allows for observing one's behavior and inner experiences, and it facilitates other ACT processes. Greater awareness that the self is a context is related to lower depression (Moran & McHugh, 2019).

When people are stuck and give themselves content labels such as depressed, helpless, failed, or damaged beyond repair, it may be necessary to bring some distance to their sense of self. This may be done through basic defusion exercises that give the individual an understanding of how language and cognition may create a verbal prison. Working directly on loosening a rigid self-image may be too frightening, for it may feel denigrating or disrespectful, and individuals may not be aware of certain limiting self-images. In these instances, clients must be helped to know themselves before a self-image can be defused. For instance, one could start by exploring several situations in which a client felt stuck. Focusing on thoughts that arose in those situations may reveal a pattern that points to a fused, restrictive self-image. Another approach is to look at the clients' action in search of a common theme across situations. For instance, when clients act aggressively if someone points out a mistake, a theme may be that clients think they are perceived as being a failure. Becoming aware of when this theme shows up in daily life could be the first step in instigating defusion.

Self-compassion, that is, relating with kindness to oneself in times of suffering or failure, may also be useful for self-critical people (e.g., Gilbert, 2010). In ACT, self-compassion involves acceptance and defusion of self-aspects, and it can be seen as a way of valuing one's well-being. It appears to be a robust protective factor against depressive symptoms, with strong empirical support for a negative association between self-compassion and depressive symptoms found in cross-sectional and longitudinal studies (Bakker et al., 2019). Asking clients to see themselves as a young child struggling with strong feelings, self-criticism, or a difficult self-image often awakens compassionate feelings, which can be re-directed to the current version of that child, who the client now is. When clients are a parent, the unconditional love they feel for their child, if present, may be transferred to themselves. Gestures such as putting a hand on one's chest may foster self-compassion. Self-compassion may evoke hurt about not being seen and accepted before. If so, it is helpful to create space for this hurt.

Behaviors such as perfectionism and self-criticism focus on outcomes, and ACT therapists aim to turn to the *process* of acting on values. Some research findings suggest that reflecting on personal values can keep neuroendocrine and psychological responses to stress at low levels (Creswell et al., 2005). For example, laboratory experiments show that people can endure more distress when they relate it to values (e.g., B. M. Smith et al., 2019). People writing about highly rated values report greater feelings of love, connectedness, empathy, and giving compared to those writing about a low-rated value (Crocker, Niiya, & Mischkowski, 2008). Also, a focus on values is related to well-being (positive mental health). Thus, a focus on values can be helpful in the treatment of depression by lowering stress responses, enhancing acceptance, and stimulating positive emotions and well-being.

It is essential to create awareness that committed action may not always lead to positive emotions. People can learn to shift their focus from deficits in their behaviors to seeing which behaviors are already in line with their values. Working on committed actions may also involve imagery about a possible future in which values are lived. It may generate positive emotions or fear. Experiencing all emotions is needed. Mental rehearsal of future behaviors may support committed action and strengthen problem-solving skills (Holmes et al., 2016). Keinonen and Lappalainen (2020) found that competence and adherence in ACT played a role in early change and may be associated with favorable outcomes for treatment in depression. Specifically, the more frequently and extensively the therapists addressed committed action during their intervention, the larger the overall changes in depression and psychological flexibility.

Some forms of behavioral activation (BA; e.g., Addis & Martell, 2004) are highly compatible with an ACT approach. People learn to see the relationship between their activities and mood (self-knowledge, present moment). They are urged not to seek reasons for depression (defusion) but instead try out new behaviors (committed action) and look for the lived consequences of these activities (present moment). ACT therapists may want to bring in values to connect with new activities and meaning as an important consequence, even when this does not lift one's mood in the short term. The important focus of BA is on small steps toward behavioral change, which is very helpful for people who have become inactive and find it hard to become active again.

Research on Outcome and Processes of Change in Act

How Effective Is ACT for Depression?

To date, about 50 randomized controlled studies have been done on depression using ACT. In a review of meta-analyses, Gloster, Walder, Levin, Twohig, and Karekla (2020) found nine meta-analyses that reported the effects of ACT for depression. Six meta-analyses presented with significant small- to medium-effect sizes (ES) favoring ACT (range of ES $g = .24\text{– } .76$) compared to active (all active psychological interventions except CBT) and inactive (e.g., waitlist, placebo) conditions. A meta-analysis not included in this review was from Bai, Luo, Zhang, Wu, and Chi (2019). These authors analyzed 18 randomized controlled trials (RCT) using ACT for depression. Studies were included from nine different countries, with a total of 1,088 participants. Four studies had high methodological quality, whereas the remaining fourteen studies were rated as being of moderate quality. These authors found that ACT was effective mainly for clients with mild depression, they saw less evidence for those with moderate or severe depression. However, Walser et al. (2015) found ACT to be effective for 647 veterans with moderate to severe depression in the context of its naturalistic implementation within a large health care system. A randomized controlled trial found that ACT and CBT were similarly effective for people suffering from depressive and other mental disorders treated in a psychiatric ward (Samaan et al., 2020). In this study, 177 inpatients in a psychiatric ward were included and assigned to either ACT ($n = 83$) or CBT ($n = 94$) group intervention. Except for Ruiz (2012), no reviews or meta-analyses have found a difference in efficacy between CBT and ACT (e.g., A-Tjak et al., 2015; Öst, 2014).

Some preliminary evidence shows that ACT may also effectively treat adults over 60 years of age (Bunyathikan, Soonthornchaiya, & Charernboon, 2020; Davison, Eppingstall, Runci, & O'Connor, 2017). Bunyathikan and colleagues compared routine nursing care with an ACT program, with 30 patients diagnosed with major depressive disorder in each condition. The ACT program led to significantly fewer depressive symptoms compared to the control condition. Davidson, Eppingstall, Runci, and O'Connor (2017) included 41 patients age 63 to 97 years living in long-term care. After a 12-session ACT intervention implemented by trainee psychology therapists, scores on depression measures were significantly lower than the waitlist control.

Preliminary evidence also shows the effectiveness of ACT for depression in youths. An Australian study among 66 adolescents screened for psychosocial problems in school settings showed significant reductions in depressive symptoms with a large effect and significant reductions in psychological inflexibility with a medium effect compared to a control group who received standard care (Livheim et al., 2015). The ACT intervention was an eight-session manualized group program. In a prevention sample, 243 adolescents age 15–16 years were randomly assigned to three groups; two groups received an ACT-based online intervention, including support via WhatsApp, with or without two face-to-face meetings. In both active treatment groups, adolescents' depressive symptoms decreased, and life satisfaction increased among those who had completed more than half of the program (Lappalainen et al., 2021). A pilot study compared ACT with treatment as usual (TAU) for 30 adolescents, with 73.6 percent in the clinical range for depression (L. Hayes, Boyd, & Sewell, 2011). At posttreatment on measures of depression, participants in the ACT condition showed significantly greater improvement statistically, and 58 percent showed clinically reliable change in favor of ACT. Outcomes from 3-month follow-up data suggest that improvement increased in magnitude. Measures of global functioning also showed statistically significant improvement for ACT.

As comorbid problems often co-occur with depression, there may be an added benefit of transdiagnostic treatments, as they may also be effective for comorbid disorders. A systematic review and meta-analysis of transdiagnostic psychological treatments by Newby, McKinnon, Kuyken, Gilbody, and Dalgleish (2015) found preliminary evidence that transdiagnostic treatments may be superior for reducing depression. Newby and colleagues found that transdiagnostic treatments have a large effect on both depression and anxiety symptoms in studies targeting both outcomes. Effect sizes were larger for depression than for anxiety. Several examples of studies on ACT have been applied to depression and to some comorbid disorders. For instance, Dalrymple et al. (2014) developed and pilot-tested an integrated acceptance-based behavioral treatment for depression and comorbid social anxiety disorder. Results for 38 participants showed significant improvement in symptoms and functioning, from pre- to post-treatment, and high satisfaction with the treatment. White et al. (2011) randomized 27 participants with psychosis to either 10 sessions of ACT plus TAU or TAU alone. Results showed that a significantly greater proportion of the ACT group was not depressed at follow-up, and showed a greater reduction in negative symptoms. Furthermore, this group had significantly fewer crisis contacts over the study.

Low-cost interventions may decrease the possibility of developing major depressive episodes for people with risk factors, such as low mood at subclinical levels. ACT has been shown to be effective as an early intervention in groups (Bohlmeijer et al., 2011). In this RCT, adults with mild to moderate depressive symptomatology were randomly assigned to the ACT intervention (n = 49) or a waiting list (n = 44). There was a statistically significant reduction in depressive symptomatology in the ACT group compared to the waitlist (Cohen's d = .60). Reductions were maintained at the 3-month follow-up. Significant reductions in anxiety and fatigue were also observed, which further adds to the evidence that ACT is a beneficial transdiagnostic approach.

ACT has also been applied as self-help with extensive or minimal e-mail support (Fledderus et al., 2013; Fledderus, Bohlmeijer, Pieterse, & Schreurs, 2012) and as a web-based intervention (Brown, Glendenning, Hoon, & John, 2016; Pots et al., 2016). Pots and colleagues (2016) randomized 82 adults with depressive symptoms to ACT, 67 to expressive writing, and 87 to a waiting-list control. They found significant reductions in depressive symptoms following the ACT intervention, compared with the control group (Cohen's d = 0.56) and the expressive writing intervention (d = 0.36). The effects were sustained at 6-month and 12-month follow-up. In a systematic review and meta-analysis of online interventions, Brown et al. (2016) included 10 studies. They found good adherence to study protocols and completion, suggesting that ACT delivered online is highly acceptable for people with various mental health problems, as well as the general public. Jeffcoat and Hayes (2012) reported that ACT delivered via a self-help book had significant preventive and ameliorative effects on depression relative to a waitlist with educational workers. The effectiveness of self-help for depression, guided by a mental health worker and having less intensity than traditional psychological therapy, has been demonstrated convincingly (Van Straten, Hill, Richards, & Cuijpers, 2015). Mental health apps could also play a role in prevention or as an addition to treatment, but the research behind it is emerging. A recent review of mental health apps (Marshall, Dunstan, & Bartik, 2020) found 293 apps offering some form of treatment for anxiety and/or depression. Of 162 apps that claimed to use a theoretical framework, only 6.2 percent had published evidence for their efficacy. Five apps made use of ACT, none of which had published research behind it.

Finally, ACT for depression seems to be applicable across different countries and cultures. This therapy has been found effective for depression in studies conducted across many countries, including Australia, Canada, China, Finland, Iran, the Netherlands, Spain, Sweden, the United Kingdom, and the United States.

Processes of Change

Research has focused on how ACT processes mediate outcomes from the first RCT on ACT for depression (Zettle & Hayes, 1986). S. C. Hayes et al. (2006) reanalyzed the data from this study and found that greater changes in the believability of depressogenic thoughts mediated the outcomes achieved by ACT in the study by Zettle and Hayes (1986). The data of two out of three conditions from a study by Zettle and Rains (1989) were reanalyzed by Zettle, Rains, and Hayes (2011). The Cognitive Therapy (CT) condition included 13 women experiencing moderate to severe depression, while the ACT condition included 12 women. Treatment was delivered in a group format. ACT produced greater reductions in levels of self-reported depression using an intent-to-treat analysis. Posttreatment levels of cognitive defusion mediated this effect at follow-up. Neither the occurrence of depressogenic thoughts nor dysfunctional attitudes mediated treatment outcomes.

Forman and colleagues (2012) included 174 clients with anxiety or depression and randomly assigned them to receive ACT or CT. Presumed mediators and outcomes were assessed before each session. Using hierarchical linear modeling, the authors found that acceptance, willingness, and defusion predicted outcomes in subsequent ACT sessions for people suffering from anxiety or depression. While increased acceptance was more influential for ACT, willingness and defusion also mediated change in CBT. Increased use of cognitive and affective *change* strategies mediated change in CBT more than in ACT.

Bramwell and Richardson (2018) conducted a repeated measures design analyzing data from a pre-post open trial design, with 33 clients receiving individual ACT treatment. The authors found a relationship between depression outcomes, decreased defusion, and increased values-based action. These findings are in line with Vowles and McCracken (2008), showing that increases in acceptance and values-based action were significantly related to lower levels of depression for people suffering from chronic pain. A-Tjak, Morina, Topper, and Emmelkamp (2021) analyzed five treatment intervals (e.g., sessions 1 to 6) with structural equation modeling. They found that changes during a treatment interval in dysfunctional attitudes and decentering (used to represent defusion) were related to symptom levels at the end of that interval for both CBT and ACT. In contrast, changes in experiential avoidance were significantly associated with symptom levels in the ACT condition only. Of note, the studies by Forman et al. (2012) and A-Tjak et al. (2021) fulfilled the criterion of three or more assessment points during the treatment phase, as stated by Lemmens, Müller, Arntz, and Huibers (2016) as necessary to measure potential mediators of behavior change.

Challenges and Future Directions for Research and Clinical Work

The treatment of depression through ACT and its processes has been researched at many levels and phases, such as in non- and subclinical populations, as prevention, for people of different ages suffering from depression with or without comorbidity, across different cultures, and through different modes of delivery, such as face-to-face treatment, self-help online, or with books or apps and combinations of these modes. Studies and meta-analyses overall find ACT to be effective and do not find a difference in efficacy between ACT and the best researched therapy today, CBT.

Although there are more than 50 RCTs on depression, most focus on depressive symptoms without a formal diagnosis of depression. Evidence for the efficacy of ACT for depressed youth or elderly people is scarce. Treatment of persistent depression, such as chronic or recurrent depression with ACT is also scant. This is not surprising, considering that ACT focuses more on processes than on diagnostic categories. From a functional contextual perspective, depression is dimensional (Phillips et al., 2010), or rather, psychopathology in the form of PI is dimensional. The ACT model does not change at its core, whether treatment is aimed at people of different ages, different cultures, or different phases or levels of intensity of depression, different diagnoses, or other psychological problems.

Of more interest to the ACT researcher and therapist than a diagnosis are the historical and situational contexts of a person suffering from depression and what processes need to be moved to relieve that suffering. Therapists can adjust treatment to the specific needs of people only when they have sufficient information on relevant idiographic contextual variables and processes. RCTs focusing on symptom improvement as an outcome are not in line with the functional contextual underpinnings of ACT. RCTs often focus on protocolled treatments such as CBT. These treatments are effective, but they are not for everyone.

Furthermore, research on the long-term effects of psychological treatment for depression is limited and often focuses on depressive symptoms; how people fare with comorbid problems and quality of life is often not considered. To comply with the demands of an RCT, ACT is often protocolized (e.g., A-Tjak et al., 2018); however, in clinical practice, therapists are encouraged to apply ACT by following the idiographic needs of clients.

Few studies have compared transdiagnostic approaches, such as ACT, head to head with diagnostic approaches (Newby et al., 2015). Studies that compare a treatment based on a diagnosis with a transdiagnostic approach may shed light on the question of whether there is added value in diagnosing someone with depression. Yet, studies like that are challenging to execute. Even when therapists focus on transdiagnostic features, they will adjust their work to the client's specific context and needs. Depressive symptoms may be part of that context. Alternatively, when the diagnosis of depression is given priority, therapists will still work with the ACT processes, which are purportedly transdiagnostic. Thus, there may not be a clear divide between a transdiagnostic approach and a diagnostic approach, forcing researchers to differentiate the treatment conditions artificially.

Nevertheless, as comorbid conditions may account for the largest portion of the adverse impact of depression, a transdiagnostic approach has specific benefits compared to an approach that focuses on single diagnostic categories. A transdiagnostic approach can positively impact several problems simultaneously. The six PF processes apply to all kinds of psychological problems, and the generalization of skills learned may lead to favorable outcomes regarding comorbidity. In fact, in the ACT model, comorbidity is not distinct from depression; instead, clients are seen holistically, with flexible and inflexible behaviors. More research is needed to study the purported benefits of a transdiagnostic approach.

The current evidence on mechanisms of change does not decisively answer the question of which treatment should be used with each specific client. However, insights from research into depression and its causes, processes, and consequences can inform therapists to focus on specific forms of PI that often show up for people suffering from depression (e.g., rumination, reason-giving, suppression, behavioral avoidance). These insights can help therapists to decide how to stimulate PF.

There is a lack of precise prognostic determinants to match clients to treatments (Van Straten et al., 2015). This means that neither clients nor therapists can decide beforehand whether ACT is a good treatment option. To date, only a few studies have examined true moderators of outcome, specifically comparing different treatments. The statistical power of most existing trials is too limited to generate the interactions that reveal moderation (Huibers et al., 2015). For clinicians to use predictors, studies need to consider predictors or moderators in relation to each other. DeRubeis and colleagues (2014) introduced a new treatment selection method that combines multiple predictors and moderators in a statistical model, called the

Personalized Advantage Index (PAI). The PAI identifies the treatment that is predicted to be more efficacious for each individual and provides the magnitude of advantage.

The ACT model is based on the assumption that the six processes of PI and PF interact. Research into mechanisms of change supports the ACT model broadly but is still in its infancy due to the complexity of the subject. Furthermore, the research is mostly correlational, often with insufficient power, which means that causal inferences cannot be made. Research aimed at analyzing those processes or other mediators in relation to each other will do more justice to the complexity of human behavior and behavior change. Mediational analysis should focus more on the interactive and nonlinear nature of change processes. RCTs can play a role in this type of research, but so can single-subject, basic, applied, and experimental analog methods. Collecting enough data for adequate statistical power may be facilitated by mobile technologies, which make it possible to measure repeatedly, in real time, and in the natural environment of participants (S. C. Hayes et al., 2021).

Conclusive Remarks

RCTs may be needed to further substantiate the efficacy of ACT for depression, especially for youth and the elderly, and for MDD and persistent depression. Valued living and well-being should be part of outcome research, and processes of change should be part of the design, with adequate measurement. The methodology needs sufficient quality to infer causal relations and study of several different change processes and associations. One way this can be done is to compare treatments that supposedly rely on different processes. However, basic, applied, and experimental analog research methods can improve our understanding of processes of change just as much.

In line with the functional contextual underpinning of ACT, future research should make a greater effort to emphasize contextual and functional aspects of depression. RCTs often bring those aspects under control, locking out important information. Intraindividual variability is an important part of understanding processes of change, for which idiographic approaches that focus on person-specific investigations of functional relationships between context and behavior are more appropriate. This calls for a shift to methods with intensive longitudinal designs that include large numbers of observations within an individual over time, such as single-case experimental designs, with appropriate measurement instruments.

References

A-Tjak, J. G. L., Davis, M. L., Morina, N., Powers, M. B., Smits, J. A., & Emmelkamp, P. M. G. (2015). A meta-analysis of the efficacy of acceptance and commitment therapy for clinically relevant mental and physical health problems. *Psychotherapy and Psychosomatics, 84*, 30–36. doi:10.1159/000365764

A-Tjak, J. G. L., Morina, N., Topper, M., & Emmelkamp, P. M. (2021). One year follow-up and mediation in cognitive behavioral therapy and acceptance and commitment therapy for adult depression. *BMC Psychiatry, 21*, 41. doi: 10.1186/s12888-020-03020-1

A-Tjak, J. G. L., Morina, N., Topper, M., & Emmelkamp, P. M. G. (2018). A randomized-controlled trial in routine clinical practice comparing acceptance and commitment therapy with cognitive behavioral therapy in the treatment of major depressive disorder. *Psychotherapy and Psychosomatics, 87*, 154–163. doi:10.1159/000486807

Addis, M. E., & Jacobson, N. S. (1996). Reasons for depression and the process and outcome of cognitive-behavioral psychotherapies. *Journal of Consulting and Clinical Psychology, 64*, 1417–1424.

Addis, M. E., & Martell, C. (2004). *Overcoming depression one step at a time: The new behavioral activation approach to getting your life back*. Oakland, CA: New Harbinger Publications.

American Psychological Association. (2013). *Diagnostic and statistical manual of mental disorders* (5th ed.). Washington, DC: American Psychological Association.

Bai, Z., Luo, S., Zhang, L., Wu, S., & Chi, I. (2019). Acceptance and commitment therapy (ACT) to reduce depression: A systematic review and meta-analysis. *Journal of Affective Disorders, 260*, 728–737. doi:10.1016/j.jad.2019.09.040

Bakker, A. M., Cox, D. W., Hubley, A. M., & Owens, R. L. (2019). Emotion regulation as a mediator of self-compassion and depressive symptoms in recurrent depression. *Mindfulness, 10,* 1169–1180. doi:10.1007/s12671-018-1072-3

Bardeen, J. R., & Fergus, T. A. (2016). The interactive effect of cognitive fusion and experiential avoidance on anxiety, depression, stress and posttraumatic stress symptoms. *Journal of Contextual Behavioral Science, 5,* 1–6. doi:10.1016/j.jcbs.2016.02.002

Barth, J., Munder, T., Gerger, H., Nüesch, E., Trelle, S., Znoj, H., . . . Cuijpers, P. (2013). Comparative efficacy of seven psychotherapeutic interventions for patients with depression: A network meta-analysis. *PLoS Med, 10*(5), e1001454. doi:10.1371/journal.pmed.1001454

Beard, J. I., & Delgadillo, J. (2019). Early response to psychological therapy as a predictor of depression and anxiety treatment outcomes: A systematic review and meta-analysis. *Depression and Anxiety, 36*(9), 866–878. doi:10.1002/da.22931

Beck, A. T., Rush, J., Shaw, B. F., & Emery, G. (1979). *Cognitive therapy of depression.* New York: Guilford Press.

Bockting, C. L. H., Hollon, S. D., Jarrett, R. B., Kuyken, W., & Dobson, K. (2015). A lifetime approach to major depressive disorder: The contributions of psychological interventions in preventing relapse and recurrence. *Clinical Psychology Review, 41,* 16–26. doi:10.1016/j.cpr.2015.02.003

Bohlmeijer, E. T., Fledderus, M., Rokx, T. A. J. J., & Pieterse, M. E. (2011). Efficacy of an early intervention based on acceptance and commitment therapy for adults with depressive symptomatology: Evaluation in a randomized controlled trial. *Behaviour Research and Therapy, 49*(1), 62–67. doi:10.1016/j.brat.2010.10.003

Boland, R. J., & Keller, M. B. (2009). Course and outcome of depression. In I. H. Gotlib & C. L. Hammen (Eds.), *Handbook of depression* (2nd ed., pp. 23–43). New York: Guilford Press.

Bramwell, K., & Richardson, T. (2018). Improvements in depression and mental health after acceptance and commitment therapy are related to changes in defusion and values-based action. *Journal of Contemporary Psychotherapy, 48,* 9–14. doi:10.1007/s10879-017-9367-6

Brown, M., Glendenning, A., Hoon, A. E., & John, A. (2016). Effectiveness of web-delivered acceptance and commitment therapy in relation to mental health and well-being: A systematic review and meta-analysis. *Journal of Medical Internet Research, 18*(8), 1–14. doi:10.2196/jmir.6200

Buhk, A. H., Schadegg, M. J., Dixon, L. J., & Tull, M. T. (2020). Investigating the role of negative and positive emotional avoidance in the relation between generalized anxiety disorder and depression symptom severity. *Journal of Contextual Behavioral Science, 16,* 103–108. doi:10.1016/j.jcbs.2020.03.006

Bunyathikan, T., Soonthornchaiya, R., & Charernboon, T. (2020). The effects of an acceptance and commitment therapy program on the depressive symptoms of elderly patients with major depressive disorder. *Journal of Psychiatric Nursing and Mental Health, 34*(2), 118–131.

Choi, K. W., Stein, M. B., Nishimi, K. M., Ge, T., Coleman, J. R. I., Chen, C. Y., . . . Smoller, J. W. (2020). An exposure-wide and mendelian randomization approach to identifying modifiable factors for the prevention of depression. *American Journal of Psychiatry, 177*(10), 944–954. doi:10.1176/appi.ajp.2020.19111158

Clarke, K., Mayo-Wilson, E., Kenny, J., & Pilling, S. (2015). Can non-pharmacological interventions prevent relapse in adults who have recovered from depression? A systematic review and meta-analysis of randomised controlled trials. *Clinical Psychology Review, 39,* 58–70.

Compare, A., Zarbo, C., Shonin, E., Van Gordon, W., & Marconi, C. (2014). Emotional regulation and depression: A potential mediator between heart and mind. *Cardiovascular Psychiatry and Neurology, 324374,* 1–10. doi:10.1155/2014/324374

Conradi, H. J., Bos, E. H., Kamphuis, J. H., & de Jonge, P. (2017). The ten-year course of depression in primary care and long-term effects of psychoeducation, psychiatric consultation and cognitive behavioral therapy. *Journal of Affective Disorders, 217,* 174–182. doi:10.1016/j.jad.2017.03.064

Cox, G. R., Callahan, P., Churchill, R., Hunot, V., Merry, S. N., Parker, A. G., & Hetrick, S. E. (2014). Psychological therapies versus antidepressant medication, alone and in combination for depression in children and adolescents. *Cochrane Database of Systematic Reviews, 11.* doi:10.1002/14651858.CD008324

Craske, M. G., Meuret, A. E., Ritz, T., Treanor, M., & Dour, H. J. (2016). Treatment for anhedonia: A neuroscience driven approach. *Depression and Anxiety, 33,* 927–938. doi:10.1002/da.22490

Creswell, J. D., Welch, W. T., Taylor, S. E., Sherman, D. K., Gruenewald, T. L., & Mann, T. (2005). Affirmation of personal values buffers neuroendocrine and psychological stress responses. *Psychological Science, 16*(11), 846–851. doi:10.1111/j.1467-9280.2005.01624.x

Crocker, J., Niiya, Y., & Mischkowski, D. (2008). Why does writing about values reduce defensiveness? Self-affirmation and the role of positive other-directed feelings. *Psychological Science, 19,* 740–747. doi:10.1111/j.1467-9280.2008.02150.x

Cuijpers, P., & Gentili, C. (2017). Psychological treatments are as effective as pharmacotherapies in the treatment of adult depression: a summary from randomized clinical trials and neuroscience evidence. *Research in Psychotherapy: Psychopathology, Process and Outcome, 20*(2), 147–152. doi:10.4081/ripppo.2017.284

Cuijpers, P., Karyotaki, E., Weitz, E., Andersson, G., Hollon, S. D., & Van Straten, A. (2014). The effects of psychotherapies for major depression in adults on remission, recovery and improvement: a meta-analysis. *Journal of Affective Disorders, 159,* 118–126. doi:10.1016/j.jad.2014.02.026

Dalrymple, K. L., Morgan, T. A., Lipschitz, J. M., Martinez, J. H., Tepe, E., & Zimmerman, M. (2014). An integrated acceptance-based behavioral approach for depression with social anxiety: Preliminary results. *Behavior Modification, 39,* 1–33. doi:10.1177/0145445513518422

Davison, T. E., Eppingstall, B., Runci, S., & O'Connor, D. W. (2017). A pilot trial of acceptance and commitment therapy for symptoms of depression and anxiety in older adults residing in long-term care facilities. *Aging and Mental Health, 21,* 766–773. doi:10.1080/13607863.2016.1156051

DeRubeis, R. J., Cohen, Z. D., Forand, N. R., Fournier, J. C., Gelfand, L. A., & Lorenzo-Luaces, L. (2014). The Personalized Advantage Index: Translating research on prediction into individualized treatment recommendations. A demonstration. *PLOS One, 9,* e83875. doi:10.1371/journal.pone.0083875

Eaton, W. W., Shao, H., Nestadt, G., Lee, H. B., Bienvenu, O. J., & Zandi, P. (2008). Population-based study of first onset and chronicity in major depressive disorder. *Archives of General Psychiatry, 65*(5), 513–520. doi:10.1001/archpsyc.65.5.513

Ehret, A. M., Joormann, J., & Berking, M. (2015). Examining risk and resilience factors for depression: The role of self-criticism and self-compassion. *Cognition and Emotion, 29*(8), 1496–1504. doi:10.1080/02699931.2014.992394

Ekkers, W. D. J., Korrelboom, K. W., Huijbrechts, I. P. A. M., Smits, N., Cuijpers, P., & Van der Gaag, M. (2011). Competitive memory training for treating depression and rumination in depressed older adults: A randomized controlled trial. *Behaviour Research and Therapy, 49*(10), 588–596. doi:10.1016/j.brat.2011.05.010

Erzen, E., & Çikrikci, Ö. (2018). The effect of loneliness on depression: A meta-analysis. *International Journal of Social Psychiatry, 64*(5), 427–435. doi:10.1177/0020764018776349

Fledderus, M., Bohlmeijer, E. T., Fox, G. J. A., Schreurs, K. M. G., & Spinhoven, P. (2013). The role of psychological flexibility in a self-help acceptance and commitment therapy intervention for psychological distress in a randomized controlled trial. *Behaviour Research and Therapy, 51*(3), 142–151. doi:10.1016/j.brat.2012.11.007

Fledderus, M., Bohlmeijer, E. T., Pieterse, M. E., & Schreurs, K. M. G. (2012). Acceptance and commitment therapy as guided self-help for psychological distress and positive mental health: A randomized controlled trial. *Psychological Medicine, 42*(3), 485–495. doi:10.1017/S0033291711001206

Forman, E. M., Chapman, J. E., Herbert, J. D., Goetter, E. M., Yuen, E. K., & Moitra, E. (2012). Using session-by-session measurement to compare mechanisms of action for acceptance and commitment therapy and cognitive therapy. *Behavior Therapy, 43,* 341–354.

Gilbert, P. (2010). *The compassionate mind.* London: Constable.

Gloster, A. T., Meyer, A. H., & Lieb, R. (2017). Psychological flexibility as a malleable public health target: Evidence from a representative sample. *Journal of Contextual Behavioral Science, 6*(2), 166–171. doi:10.1016/j.jcbs.2017.02.003

Gloster, A. T., Walder, N., Levin, M. E., Twohig, M. P., & Karekla, M. (2020). The empirical status of acceptance and commitment therapy: A review of meta-analyses. *Journal of Contextual Behavioral Science, 18,* 181–192. doi:10.1016/j.jcbs.2020.09.009

Gotlib, I. H., Joormann, J., & Foland-Ross, L. C. (2014). Understanding familial risk for depression: A 25-year perspective. *Perspectives on Psychological Science, 9*(1), 94–108. doi:10.1177/1745691613513469

Hayes, L., Boyd, C. P., & Sewell, J. (2011). Acceptance and commitment therapy for the treatment of adolescent depression: A pilot study in a psychiatric outpatient setting. *Mindfulness, 2,* 86–94. doi:10.1007/s12671-011-0046-5

Hayes, S. C. (2013). The genuine conversation. In T. B. Kashdan & J. Ciarrochi (Eds.), *Mindfulness, acceptance and positive psychology.* Oakland, CA: Context Press.

Hayes, S. C., Luoma, J. B., Bond, F. W., Masuda, A., & Lillis, J. (2006). Acceptance and commitment therapy: Model, processes and outcomes. *Behaviour Research and Therapy, 44*(1), 1–25. doi:10.1016/j.brat.2005.06.006

Hayes, S. C., Merwin, R. M., McHugh, L., Emily Sandoz, E., A-Tjak, J. G. L., Ruiz, F. J., . . . McCracken, L. M. (2021). Report of the ACBS Task Force on the strategies and tactics of contextual behavioral science research. *Journal of Contextual Behavioral Science, 20,* 172–183.

Hayes, S. C., Strosahl, K. D., & Wilson, K. G. (2012). *Acceptance and commitment rherapy. The process and practice of mindful change.* New York: Guilford Press.

Henje Blom, E., Duncan, L. G. H., T. C., Connolly, C. G., LeWinn, K. Z., Chesney, M., Hecht, F. M., & Yang, T. T. (2014). The development of an RDoC-based treatment program for adolescent depression: "Training for Awareness, Resilience, and Action" (TARA) *Frontiers in Human Neuroscience, 8,* 630. doi:10.3389/fnhum.2014.00630

Hofmann, S. G., Asnaani, A., Vonk, I. J., Sawyer, A. T., & Fang, A. (2012). The efficacy of cognitive behavioral therapy: A review of meta-analyses. *Cognitive Therapy and Research, 36*(5), 427–440. doi:10.1007/s10608-012-9476-1

Holmes, E. A., Blackwell, S. E., Burnett Heyes, S., Renner, F., & Raes, F. (2016). Mental imagery in depression: Phenomenology, potential mechanisms, and treatment implications. *Annual Review of Clinical Psychology, 12*, 249–280. doi:10.1146/annurev-clinpsy-021815-092925

Hoppen, T. H., & Morina, N. (2019). The prevalence of PTSD and major depression in the global population of adult war survivors: A meta-analytically informed estimate in absolute numbers. *European Journal of Psychotraumatology, 10*(1), 1578637. doi:10.1080/20008198.2019.1578637

Huibers, M. J. H., Cohen, Z. D., Lemmens, L. H. J. M., Arntz, A., Peeters, F. P. M. L., Cuijpers, P., & DeRubeis, R. J. (2015). Predicting optimal outcomes in cognitive therapy or interpersonal psychotherapy for depressed individuals using the personalized advantage index approach. *PLOS One, 10*(11), e 0140771. doi:10.1371/journal.pone.0140771

Jeffcoat, T., & Hayes, S. C. (2012). A randomized trial of ACT bibliotherapy on the mental health of K-12 teachers and staff. *Behaviour Research and Therapy, 50*(9), 571–579. doi:10.1016/j.brat.2012.05.008

Karabati, S., Ensari, N., & Fiorentino, D. (2019). Job Satisfaction, rumination, and subjective well-being: A moderated mediational model. *Journal of Happiness Studies, 20*, 251–268. doi:10.1007/s10902-017-9947-x

Kashdan, T. B., & Rottenberg, J. (2010). Psychological flexibility as a fundamental aspect of health. *Clinical Psychology Review, 30*(7), 865–878. doi:10.1016/j.cpr.2010.03.001

Keinonen, K., & Lappalainen, R. (2020). Competence and adherence in an acceptance and values-based intervention: Effects on treatment outcome and early changes in depression. *Journal of Contextual Behavioral Science, 17*, 159–165. doi:10.1016/j.jcbs.2020.07.007

Kuyken, W., & Brewin, C. R. (1994). Intrusive memories of childhood abuse during depressive episodes. *Behaviour Research and Therapy, 32*, 525–528.

Lappalainen, R., Lappalainen, P., Puolakanaho, A., Hirvonen, R., Eklund, K., Ahonen, T., . . . Kiuru, N. (2021). The Youth Compass—the effectiveness of an online acceptance and commitment therapy program to promote adolescent mental health: A randomized controlled trial. *Journal of Contextual Behavioral Science, 20*, 1–12. doi:10.1016/j.jcbs.2021.01.007.

Lemmens, L. H. J. M., Müller, V. N. L. S., Arntz, A., & Huibers, M. J. H. (2016). Mechanisms of change in psychotherapy for depression: An empirical update and evaluation of research aimed at identifying psychological mediators. *Clinical Psychology Review, 50*, 95–107. doi:10.1016/j.cpr.2016.09.004

Lewinsohn, P. M., Munoz, R. F., Youngren, M. A., & Zeiss, A. M. (1986). *Control your depression*. Englewood Cliffs, NJ: Prentice Hall.

Liverant, G. I., Kamholz, B. W., Sloan, D. S., & Brown, T. A. (2011). Rumination in clinical depression: A type of emotional suppression? *Cognitive Therapy Research, 35*, 253–265. doi:10.1007/s10608-010-9304-4

Livheim, F., Hayes, L., Ghaderi, A., Magnusdottir, T., Högfeldt, A., Rowse, J., . . . Tengström, A. (2015). The effectiveness of acceptance and commitment therapy for adolescent mental health: Swedish and Australian pilot outcomes. *Journal of Child and Family Studies, 24*, 1016–1030. doi:10.1007/s10826-014-9912-9

Maitland, D. W. M. (2020). Experiential avoidance and fear of intimacy: A contextual behavioral account of loneliness and resulting psychopathology symptoms. *Journal of Contextual Behavioral Science, 18*, 193–200. doi:10.1016/j.jcbs.2020.10.002

Marshall, J. M., Dunstan, D. A., & Bartik, W. (2020). Apps with maps—Anxiety and depression mobile apps with evidence-based frameworks: systematic search of major app stores. *JMIR Mental Health, 7*(6), e16525. doi:10.2196/16525

Michalak, J., Hölz, A., & Teismann, T. (2011). Rumination as a predictor of relapse in mindfulness-based cognitive therapy for depression. *Psychology and Psychotherapy: Theory, Research and Practice, 84*, 230–236. doi:10.1348/147608310X520166

Moran, O., & McHugh, L. (2019). Patterns of relational responding and a healthy self in older adolescents. *Journal of Contextual Behavioral Science, 12*, 74–80. doi:10.1016/j.jcbs.2019.02.002

Newby, J. M., McKinnon, A., Kuyken, W., Gilbody, S., & Dalgleish, T. (2015). Systematic review and meta-analysis of transdiagnostic psychological treatments for anxiety and depressive disorders in adulthood. *Clinical Psychology Review, 40*, 91–110. doi:10.1016/j.cpr.2015.06.002

Nolen-Hoeksema, S. (1991). Responses to depression and their effects on the duration of depressive episodes. *Journal of Abnormal Psychology, 100*(4), 569–582. doi:10.1037/0021-843X.100.4.569

Nolen-Hoeksema, S. (2004). The response styles theory. In C. Papageorgiou & A. Wells (Eds.), *Depressive rumination: Nature, theory and treatment* (pp. 107–124). doi:10.1002/9780470713853.ch6

Ong, C. W., Lee, E. B., Krafft, J., Terry, C. L., Barrett, T. S., Levin, M. E., & Twohig, M. P. (2019). A randomized controlled trial of acceptance and commitment therapy for clinical perfectionism. *Journal of Obsessive-Compulsive and Related Disorders, 22*, 100444. doi:10.1016/j.jocrd.2019.100444

Ormel, J., Kessler, R. C., & Schoevers, R. (2019). Depression: More treatment but no drop in prevalence: How effective is treatment? And can we do better? *Current Opinion in Psychiatry, 32*(4), 348–354. doi:10.1097/YCO.0000000000000505

Öst, L. G. (2014). The efficacy of acceptance and commitment therapy: An updated systematic review and meta-analysis. *Behavioral Research Therapy, 61*, 105–121. doi:10.1016/j.brat.2014.07.018

Papageorgiou, C., & Wells, A. (2004). Nature, functions, and beliefs about depressive rumination. In C. Papageorgiou & A. Wells (Eds.), *Depressive rumination: Nature, theory and treatment* (pp. 3–20). Chichester: John Wiley & Sons. doi:10.1002/9780470713853.ch1

Peltz, J. S., Rogge, R. D., Bodenlos, J. S., Newman Kingery, J., & Pigeon, W. R. (2020). Changes in psychological inflexibility as a potential mediator of longitudinal links between college students' sleep problems and depressive symptoms. *Journal of Contextual Behavioral Science, 15*, 110–122. doi:10.1016/j.jcbs.2019.12.003

Phillips, W. J., Hine, D. W., & Thorsteinsson, E. B. (2010). Implicit cognition and depression: A meta-analysis. *Clinical Psychology Review, 30*(6), 691–709. doi:10.1016/j.cpr.2010.05.002

Plumb, J. C., Stewart, I., Dahl, J., & Lundgrun, T. (2017). In search of meaning: Values in modern clinical behavior analysis. *The Behavior Analyst, 32*, 85–103. doi:10.1007/BF03392177

Pots, W., Fledderus, M., Meulenbeek, P., Ten Klooster, P., Schreurs, K. M. G., & Bohlmeijer, E. T. (2016). Acceptance and commitment therapy as a web-based intervention for depressive symptoms: Randomised controlled trial. *British Journal of Psychiatry, 208*(1), 69–77. doi:10.1192/bjp.bp.114.146068

Richards, D. (2011). Prevalence and clinical course of depression: A review. *Clinical Psychology Review, 31*, 1117–1125. doi:10.1016/j.cpr.2011.07.004

Ruiz, F. J. (2010). A review of acceptance and commitment therapy (act) empirical evidence: Correlational, experimental psychopathology, component and outcome studies. *International Journal of Psychology and Psychological Therapy, 10*(1), 125–162.

Ruiz, F. J. (2012). Acceptance and commitment therapy versus traditional cognitive behavioral therapy: A systematic review and meta-analysis of current empirical evidence. *International Journal of Psychology and Psychological Therapy, 12*(3), 333–357.

Ruiz, F. J., Luciano, C., Flórez, C. L., Suárez-Falcón, J. C., & Cardona-Betancourt, V. (2020). A multiple-baseline evaluation of acceptance and commitment therapy focused on repetitive negative thinking for comorbid generalized anxiety disorder and depression. *Frontiers in Psychology, 11*, 356. doi:10.3389/fpsyg.2020.00356

Ruiz, F. J., Peña-Vargas, A., Ramírez, E. S., Suárez-Falcón, J. C., García-Martín, M. B., García-Beltrán, D. M., . . . Sánchez, P. D. (2020). Efficacy of a two-session repetitive negative thinking-focused acceptance and commitment therapy (ACT) protocol for depression and generalized anxiety disorder: A randomized waitlist control trial. *Psychotherapy (Chic), 57*(3), 444–456. doi:10.1037/pst0000273

Samaan, M., Diefenbacher, A., Schade, C., Dambacher, C., Pontow, I. M., Kenneth Pakenham, K., & Fydrich, T. (2020). A clinical effectiveness trial comparing ACT and CBT for inpatients with depressive and mixed mental disorders. *Psychotherapy Research, 31*(3), 372–385. doi:10.1080/10503307.2020.1802080

Schlagert, H. S., & Hiller, W. (2017). The predictive value of early response in patients with depressive disorders. *Psychotherapy Research, 27*(4), 488–500. doi:10.1080/10503307.2015.1119329

Slofstra, C., Nauta, M. H., Holmes, E. A., Bos, E. H., Wichers, M., Batalas, N., . . . Bockting, C. L. H. (2018). Exploring the relation between visual mental imagery and affect in the daily life of previously depressed and never depressed individuals. *Cognition and Emotion, 32*(5), 1131–1138. doi:10.1080/02699931.2017.1365047

Smith, B. M., Villatte, J. L., Ong, C. W., Butcher, G. M., Twohig, M. P., Levin, M. E., & Hayes, S. C. (2019). The influence of a personal values intervention on cold pressor-induced distress tolerance. *Behavior Modification, 43*(5), 688–710. doi:10.1177/0145445518782402

Smith, M. M., Sherry, S. B., Rnic, K., Saklofske, D. H., Enns, M., & Gralnick, T. (2016). Are Perfectionism Dimensions Vulnerability Factors for Depressive Symptoms After Controlling for Neuroticism? A Meta-analysis of 10 Longitudinal Studies. *European Journal of Personality, 30*, 201–212. doi:10.1002/per.205

Spasojević, J., Alloy, L. B., Abramson, L. Y., Maccoon, D., & Robinson, M. S. (2008). Reactive rumination: outcomes, mechanisms, and developmental antecedents. In C. Papageorgiou & A. Wells (Eds.), *Depressive rumination: Nature, theory and treatment* (pp. 43–58). Chichester: John Wiley & Sons. doi:10.1002/9780470713853.ch3

Spinhoven, P., Klein, N., Kennis, M., Cramer, A. O. J., Siegle, G., Cuijpers, P., . . . Bockting, C. L. H. (2018). The effects of cognitive-behavior therapy for depression on repetitive negative thinking: A meta-analysis. *Behaviour Research and Therapy, 106*, 71–85. doi:10.1016/j.brat.2018.04.002

Syme, K. L., & Hagen, E. H. (2020). Mental health is biological health: Why tackling "diseases of the mind" is an imperative for biological anthropology in the 21st century. *Yearbook Physical Anthropology, 171*, 87–117. doi:10.1002/ajpa.23965

Trindade, I. A., Mendes, A. L., & Ferreira, N. B. (2020). The moderating effect of psychological flexibility on the link between learned helplessness and depression symptomatology: A preliminary study. *Journal of Contextual Behavioral Science, 15*, 68–72. doi:10.1016/j.jcbs.2019.12.001

Van Straten, A., Hill, J., Richards, D., & Cuijpers, P. (2015). Stepped care treatment delivery for depression: A systematic review and meta-analysis. *Psychological Medicine, 45*(2), 231–246. doi:10.1017/S0033291714000701

Villanueva, J., Meyer, A. H., Rinner, M. T. B., Block, V. J., Benoy, C., Brogli, S., . . . Gloster, A. T. (2020). The everyday lives of in- and outpatients when beginning therapy: The importance of values-consistent behavior. *International Journal of Clinical and Health Psychology, 20*(2), 91–99. doi:10.1016/j.ijchp.2020.02.002

Vowles, K. E., & McCracken, L. M. (2008). Acceptance and values-based action in chronic pain: A study of treatment effectiveness and process. *Journal of Consulting and Clinical Psychology, 76*(3), 397–407. doi:10.1037/0022-006X.76.3.397

Walser, R. D., Garvert, D. W., Karlin, B. E., Trockel, M., Ryu, D. M., & Taylor, C. B. (2015). Effectiveness of acceptance and commitment therapy in treating depression and suicidal ideation in Veterans. *Behaviour Research and Therapy, 74*, 25–31. doi:10.1016/j.brat.2015.08.012

Weissman, M. M., Wickramaratne, P. J., Gameroff, M. J., Warner, V., Pilowsky, D. J., Kohad, R. G., . . . Talati, A. (2016). Offspring of depressed parents: 30 years later. *American Journal of Psychiatry, 173*(10), 1024–1032. doi:10.1176/appi.ajp.2016.15101327

Wenzlaff, R. M., & Wegner, D. M. (2000). Thought suppression. *Annual Review of Psychology, 51*, 59–91.

White, R. G., Gumley, A. I., McTaggart, J., Rattrie, L., McConville, D., Cleare, S., & Mitchell, G. (2011). A feasibility study of acceptance and commitment therapy for emotional dysfunction following psychosis. *Behaviour Research and Therapy, 49*(12), 901–907. doi:10.1016/j.brat.2011.09.003

World Health Organization (2021). *Depression and Other common mental disorders: Global health estimates.* Retrieved from: https://www.who.int/news-room/fact-sheets/detail/depression2021-01-11

Zettle, R. D. (2007). *ACT for depression. A clinician's guide to using acceptance and commitment therapy in treating depression.* Oakland, CA: New Harbinger Publications.

Zettle, R. D. (2016). Acceptance and commitment theory of depression. In A. Wells & P. L. Fisher (Eds.), *Treating depression: MCT, CBT and third wave therapies* (pp. 169–193). Malden, MA: Wiley Blackwell.

Zettle, R. D., & Hayes, S. C. (1986). Dysfunctional control by client verbal behavior: The context of reason giving. *Analysis of Verbal Behavior, 4*, 30–38.

Zettle, R. D., & Hayes, S. C. (2002). Brief ACT treatment of depression. In F. W. Bond & W. Dryden (Eds.), *Handbook of brief cognitive behaviour therapy* (pp. 35–54). Chichester: John Wiley & Sons. doi:10.1002/9780470713020.ch3

Zettle, R. D., & Rains, J. C. (1989). Group cognitive and contextual therapies in treatment of depression. *Journal of Clinical Psychology, 45*(438–445).

Zettle, R. D., Rains, J. C., & Hayes, S. C. (2011). Processes of change in acceptance and commitment therapy and cognitive therapy for depression: A mediation reanalysis of Zettle and Rains. *Behavior Modification, 35*(3), 265–283. doi:10.1177/0145445511398344

CHAPTER

15 ACT for Anxiety and Trauma-Related Disorders

Brooke M. Smith, Gregory S. Smith, *and* Ellen J. Bluett

Abstract

Anxiety and trauma-related disorders are described in terms of maladaptive response patterns that largely consist of avoidance of various threat cues. Following an introduction to the classes of disorders and primary behavioral processes that maintain them, the authors briefly review traditional conceptualizations of etiology and associated treatments, followed by a theoretical rationale that underscores acceptance and commitment therapy (ACT) as a conceptually sound and comprehensive treatment for these disorders. An overview of empirical research supporting the efficacy of ACT for these disorders is then provided, followed by clinical considerations and examples of implementation as they relate to specific disorders within the overarching classes. Lastly, the authors discuss limitations in the extant literature and provide recommendations for future research, including a shift to a more process-based approach of conceptualization and treatment of these classes of disorders.

Key Words: anxiety disorders, trauma-related disorders, avoidance, threat cues, maladaptive behavior, fear, generalized anxiety, social anxiety, posttraumatic stress

An Overview of Anxiety and Trauma-Related Disorders

Origins of Anxiety and Trauma-Related Disorders

Defensive behaviors, or an organism's set of responses to potentially dangerous situations, are adaptive behaviors critical to the survival of our own and other species. When faced with a threatening situation, defensive behaviors protect an individual from present or future harm. This protection usually involves the activation of the autonomic nervous system and the body's fight-or-flight response. The fight-or-flight response involves physiological changes, such as increased respiration and heart rates, dilated pupils, and tensed muscles, that prepare the body for physical exertion and for response to the perceived threat (Gunnar & Quevedo, 2007). In some cases, individuals experience a decrease in blood pressure and faint in the presence of certain stimuli (e.g., the sight of blood), which may serve the adaptive function of mitigating blood loss during physical trauma. In still other cases, tonic immobility, or the body's innate freeze response, may dominate (Barlow, 2004). Cognitive changes also occur during threatening situations. Increased vigilance allows potential threats to be detected more quickly. When a threat is detected, attention automatically shifts to the perceived threat and potential modes of escape, attention narrows, and extraneous stimuli are ignored (Huijding et al., 2011). Finally, at an overt behavioral level, the individual is compelled to take actions geared toward escaping the threat—fighting or fleeing—or toward avoiding future threat. Avoidance behavior can be either active, when a person takes specific actions to avoid a threatening stimulus or situation (e.g., taking a different route to work to avoid going through a certain neighborhood), or passive, when a person avoids a potentially threatening situation through nonaction (e.g., choosing not to take a walk in the woods so as not to encounter dangerous animals).

Species-typical defensive reactions are innate and occur in the absence of learning, while operant behaviors occur due to their history of reinforcement by consequences. However, all defensive behaviors can be conditioned or occasioned by stimuli in the environment with which there is a history of pairing, reinforcement, or verbal learning. The learned ability to respond to potentially dangerous situations allows preparation for and avoidance of danger before an individual actually encounters harm. For example, if a person has the unfortunate experience of being involved in a car accident, cars may become conditioned stimuli that elicit physiological arousal (e.g., increased heart rate), defensive reflexes (e.g., startle response), and goal-directed defensive actions (e.g., avoidance). If these conditioned responses prevent the individual from exposure to dangerous situations related to car accidents in the future, for example, by increasing the likelihood of wearing a seatbelt or avoiding speeding, such behaviors are of obvious adaptive benefit. However, when defensive behaviors become excessive (i.e., out of proportion to the actual level of threat) and persistent (i.e., habitual and insensitive to naturally occurring contingencies), interfering with an individual's ability to function well in life, they are considered maladaptive. It is these maladaptive defensive behaviors that characterize anxiety and trauma-related disorders.

Description of Anxiety and Trauma-Related Disorders

CLASSIFICATION

While the various anxiety and trauma-related disorders all focus on maladaptive responses to perceived threat, the disorders differ as to the focus or nature of the perceived threat, that is, the threat cues (or fear stimuli) that elicit or evoke maladaptive defensive behavior. The *Diagnostic and Statistical Manual of Mental Disorders, Fifth Edition* (*DSM-5*; American Psychiatric Association, 2013) classifies anxiety and trauma-related disorders based on these topographical differences; the value of doing so is questionable, however, given that such differences may be seen as trivial. More important than the topographical differences between the disorders are their functional similarities. Each anxiety disorder is characterized by excessive experiences of subjective fear and anxiety, various maladaptive defensive behaviors, similar functions of these behaviors (e.g., escape and avoidance), and the same core mechanisms, or processes, of change (Abramowitz & Blakey, 2020). The anxiety and trauma-related disorders can therefore be considered various manifestations of the same underlying functional processes, with different combinations of defensive behaviors occurring in different disorders, each with its own unique threat cues.

The *DSM-5* (American Psychiatric Association, 2013) describes the following major anxiety disorders: separation anxiety disorder, selective mutism, specific phobia, social anxiety disorder (SAD), panic disorder (PD), agoraphobia, and generalized anxiety disorder (GAD). Trauma-related disorders, including posttraumatic stress disorder (PTSD) and acute stress disorder (ASD), were included among anxiety disorders in the *DSM-IV-TR*, the *DSM-5*'s predecessor. In *DSM-5*, they now occupy their own category: trauma and stressor-related disorders. Because of the former categorical scheme, much of the research prior to the 2013 publication of *DSM-5* placed these disorders in the same class. In the present article, we include trauma-related disorders, along with illness anxiety disorder (IAD), which is classified under somatic symptom disorders in the *DSM-5* because they share functional similarities with other anxiety disorders. However, we do not include separation anxiety disorder or selective mutism, as these disorders are much more common in children (American Psychiatric Association, 2013) and are covered in another article of this volume.

EPIDEMIOLOGY

As a class, anxiety and trauma-related disorders are the most prevalent psychological disorders in the world (Kessler et al., 2007). Those who meet the criteria for an anxiety disorder experience a significantly lower quality of life than those who do not (Olatunji et al., 2007). Furthermore, anxiety disorders tend to develop earlier than other common psychological disorders and are more prevalent in younger populations (Remes et al., 2016). Because they are often not treated until adulthood, they may represent a potential risk factor for the development of secondary psychological disorders (Christiana et al., 2000). Comorbidity is high among the anxiety disorders and between anxiety and other disorder classes (particularly mood and substance use disorders), and it is strongly related to severity: comorbidity predicts poorer clinical course and a greater likelihood of recurrence (Bruce et al., 2005). A prospective naturalistic study found that probabilities of recovery over 12 years were lowest for social phobia (SAD in *DSM-5*), at 0.37, followed by PD with agoraphobia (0.48), GAD (0.58), and PD without agoraphobia (0.82; Bruce et al., 2005). The difference in recovery rates for PD with and without agoraphobia suggests that the presence of persistent avoidance negatively affects the long-term outcome of the disorder. Not only are recovery rates generally low in the anxiety disorders, recurrence rates tend to be high, with probabilities ranging from 0.45 for GAD to 0.58 for PD with agoraphobia (Bruce et al., 2005).

SYMPTOMS AND CLINICAL PRESENTATION

Specific Phobia

Threat cues in specific phobias include any specific object or situation (the phobic stimulus) that elicits disproportionate levels of fear, anxiety, or avoidance. Any stimulus has the potential to be a phobic stimulus, so the number of different specific phobias are, in theory, unlimited. A phobic stimulus may be an animal (e.g., snakes, dogs, insects), natural environment (e.g., heights, water), blood-injection-injury (e.g., needles, blood), situational (e.g., airplanes, small spaces), and other (e.g., vomit, clowns). The phobic stimulus (or stimuli, if more than one phobia) consistently elicits excessive fear or anxiety that is disproportionate to the actual danger it poses, and the individual either engages in active avoidance of the stimulus or tolerates it with intense distress (American Psychiatric Association, 2013).

Social Anxiety Disorder

SAD is characterized by excessive fear or anxiety (usually involving embarrassment) about social situations, which may include interacting with other people (e.g., conversing), being observed by others (e.g., eating in public), or situations in which the individual must perform in front of others (e.g., public speaking). As with specific phobia, those with SAD either avoid or endure social situations with intense distress. Individuals with SAD are hypervigilant about disapproval from others, perceiving others as overly critical of them. This may result in divided attentional resources, actually causing people with SAD to perform poorly, thus reinforcing their beliefs (Heimberg & Magee, 2014).

Panic Disorder

Panic attacks are discrete episodes in which an abrupt surge of intense fear and physiological arousal reaches a peak within a few minutes. During these episodes, at least 4 of 13 potential physiological and cognitive symptoms are present (American Psychiatric Association, 2013). The experience of a panic attack is not in itself sufficient for a diagnosis of PD. In order to meet the criteria for PD, at least two attacks must be unexpected, with a month or more of persistent worry about having additional attacks or a maladaptive change in behavior due to the attacks. Although at least some attacks in PD are unexpected (i.e., they occur in the absence of a predictable external threat cue), physiological arousal itself can become conditioned to elicit fear. Thus, the threat cues in PD are often internal bodily sensations (e.g., racing heart, sweating) and the thoughts (e.g., "I'm having a heart attack") and emotions (e.g., extreme distress) that accompany them. These misperceptions of one's own physiological arousal, along with attempts to downregulate these reactions, result in an escalation of these same defensive reactions (Craske & Barlow, 2014). Thus, PD epitomizes the "vicious cycle" of fear in which one's own threat responding leads to a perception of threat (e.g., "I'm having a heart attack"), which further amplifies threat responding and the subjective experience of panic (Barlow, 2004). PD is often thought of as a disorder largely involving "fear of fear."

Agoraphobia

Agoraphobia is characterized by excessive and persistent fear or anxiety about at least two of five situations: using public transportation, being in open spaces, being in enclosed spaces, being in a crowd (or standing in line), and being outside one's home without a companion, though other situations may also be included. Individuals fear and avoid these situations because of the possibility that panic or other embarrassing symptoms (e.g., vomiting, losing bowel control) may occur and escape or help might not be available. Severity of agoraphobia can range on a continuum from mild (e.g., feeling fearful when driving to work but doing so anyway) to moderate (e.g., only leaving the home with a companion) to severe (e.g., unable to leave the home entirely; Craske & Barlow, 2014). Approximately one-third of individuals with agoraphobia fall on the severe end of the continuum (American Psychiatric Association, 2013) and experience significant functional impairment as a result.

Generalized Anxiety Disorder

The defining feature of GAD, and that which makes it a unique anxiety disorder, is the presence of excessive *generalized* anxiety and worry. That is, while the other anxiety disorders are associated with specific classes of stimuli that elicit maladaptive threat responses, GAD is characterized by persistent worry that is not specific to any circumscribed stimulus class or situation but, rather, occurs across multiple domains of life. Although worry and anxiety are both focused on the future, worry is more cognitive, while anxiety is more of an emotional experience.

One theory of GAD proposes that worry functions as avoidance behavior in the form of problem solving for potentially negative future situations (Borkovec et al., 1983). Another more recent theory, based on relational frame theory (RFT), proposes that, as a form of *repetitive negative thinking* (Wong et al., 2019), worry functions as experiential avoidance. Worry then paradoxically prolongs and helps to maintain negative affect and physiological arousal in GAD. Because worry is an ineffective strategy to reduce aversive states, individuals turn to more overt maladaptive avoidance behaviors that are also attempts at experiential avoidance, ultimately leading to an inflexible and narrow behavioral repertoire that is disconnected from personal values (Ruiz et al., 2020).

Posttraumatic Stress Disorder and Acute Stress Disorder

PTSD and ASD are unique among psychological disorders in that their diagnoses require the experience of one or more "criterion A" traumatic events, or an event in which an individual is exposed, either firsthand or through the experience of a close friend or family member, to actual or threatened death, serious injury, or sexual violence. PTSD and ASD differ in the amount of time symptoms have been present following the traumatic event (a minimum of 1 month for PTSD and 3 days to 1 month for ASD) and the number and type of symptoms required. Symptoms include emotional and cognitive intrusions, avoidance of trauma-related stimuli, persistent negative mood or cognition, and changes in mood and reactivity (American Psychiatric Association, 2013). The threat stimuli in ASD and PTSD, either stimuli in the external environment (e.g., crowds, loud noises) or cognitive or emotional experiences (e.g., memories, shame), are related to the traumatic event.

Illness Anxiety Disorder

IAD is characterized by high levels of anxiety about and preoccupation with getting or having a serious illness. Actual somatic symptoms are either not present or they are mild and not indicative of disease or illness. Threat cues can include bodily sensations that individuals believe may indicate illness, or external health-related cues (e.g., doctors, hospitals). Maladaptive behavior in response to these cues involves excessive health-related behavior, such as attending medical appointments, researching symptoms, or avoidance of health-related stimuli. Individuals often have a high degree of health care utilization, frequently attending medical appointments in order to confirm their beliefs about the presence of illness; others do the opposite and avoid medical appointments out of a concern that their fears will be confirmed (Scarella et al., 2019).

Theoretical Rationale for ACT

Cognitive-behavioral therapy (CBT) is generally considered the gold standard treatment for anxiety disorders, and, as a component of CBT, exposure therapy is a central feature of treatment (Arch & Craske, 2009). Treatment including exposure generally outperforms treatment that does not include it (Carpenter et al., 2018). Exposure therapy consists of systematically confronting and engaging with objectively safe situations or stimuli that provoke fear and defensive behavior, while refraining from avoidance or coping behaviors that reduce fear (Abramowitz et al., 2019). Exposures can be conducted with external stimuli in the environment (in vivo exposure), internal physiological sensations (interoceptive exposure), thoughts and memories (imaginal exposure), through writing (narrative exposure), or with the assistance of virtual reality devices (virtual reality exposure). In terms of disorders, the largest effects are observed in exposure therapy for PTSD, specific phobia, and panic disorders (Abramowitz et al., 2019; van Dis et al., 2019). Regardless of whether exposure is included, GAD consistently shows smaller effects following CBT than the other anxiety disorders (Olatunji et al., 2010). This may be due to the diffuse nature of anxiety and worry in GAD, making exposure less straightforward. Also, the response prevention component of exposure therapy is harder to enact when it must occur cognitively. Accordingly, CBT for GAD tends to utilize exposure components less frequently, focusing more on cognitive and emotion regulation aspects of the disorder (Cuijpers et al., 2014).

Traditionally, theories of exposure therapy have focused on decreases in fear as the mechanism responsible for behavioral change. This treatment model is predicated on the assumption that conscious fear and associated physiological arousal cause other symptoms of the disorder (e.g., avoidance) and, therefore, in order to decrease symptoms, fear and arousal must be reduced or eliminated. At the same time, an apparent lack of theoretical attention has been paid within this tradition to the actual avoidance responses themselves, which are the primary behavioral symptoms in question. Knowledge of basic behavioral principles gives reason to question the effectiveness of a treatment approach based primarily on fear reduction. Of foremost concern is the well-documented fact that extinguished "fear" (often measured as Pavlovian responding) can recover under a variety of conditions, including the mere passage of time (spontaneous recovery; Quirk, 2002), changes in context from that in which extinction originally occurred (renewal; Bouton, 2002), and reexposure to the unconditioned stimulus (reinstatement; Haaker et al., 2014). If symptom reduction is predicated on elimination of Pavlovian responses, and we know that Pavlovian responding can recover under a wide set of circumstances, many of which may be unavoidable, then we may expect maintenance of treatment gains to be lacking and relapse to be frequent, which the data appear to bear out.

Similarly, recent findings on the relationship between fear and avoidance behavior call into question the conceptualization of fear-reduction models. For example, recent research does not support the assumption of a unidirectional causal relationship from "fear" to avoidance (Pittig et al., 2020). Instead, studies have shown that avoidance can persist despite fear reduction (Rodriguez-Romaguera et al., 2016), the availability of an avoidance response in the absence of fear can increase fear (Vervliet & Indekeu, 2015; Xia et al., 2019), and continuing to engage in avoidance responding after an aversive stimulus has been removed can interfere with fear extinction (Lovibond et al., 2009) and increase fear of a safety stimulus (Engelhard et al., 2015). Based on this evidence, it would appear that the relationship between fear and avoidance is more complex than has traditionally been assumed.

In addition to avoidance, other operant processes are involved in successful treatment of anxiety and trauma. It could be argued that the purpose of any therapy is to increase client functioning and to help clients live more meaningful lives. Psychosocial functioning involves a variety of operant approach behaviors—for example, showing up to one's job on time, studying, completing household tasks, maintaining an exercise regimen, and fulfilling social and familial roles. As Craske and colleagues have stated, "the success of an exposure treatment may be measured most accurately by the increase in approach than by the decrease in fear" (2018, p. 7). Accordingly, decreases in distress do not necessarily lead to more engagement in valued areas of life (Gloster et al., 2017). However, experimental research has shown that when positively reinforced behaviors compete with avoidance responding, avoidance decreases and approach increases, despite fear levels remaining unchanged. Once the aversive stimulus is removed, these approach behaviors actually facilitate fear extinction (Pittig, 2019; Pittig & Dehler, 2019). In other words, targeting operant avoidance and approach behaviors in combination may lead to more engagement in meaningful life activities and have the secondary benefit of actually decreasing fear.

From the perspective of these behavioral processes, we argue that ACT is particularly well suited to address anxiety and trauma-related disorders. ACT focuses on living a valued life with greater quality, even in the face of difficult and unpleasant experiences such as those associated with anxiety and trauma. That is, ACT is largely concerned with increasing operant approach behavior that is meaningful to the individual because of its relationship to personally stated values.

Targeting Maladaptive Defensive Behavior with ACT

We have suggested that ACT can target the core behavioral processes operating to maintain various patterns of pathological behavior regardless of the specific threat cues or behavioral topographies associated with any one anxiety or trauma-related disorder. In the following section, we briefly describe how each ACT process of change, organized into three pillars (Hayes et al., 2012), may be used during treatment to target the adaptive and maladaptive behavioral processes involved in the treatment of anxiety and trauma, thus informing a transdiagnostic or process-based approach to therapy.

Open: Acceptance and Cognitive Defusion

One way ACT promotes improved psychological functioning in the face of unwanted emotional and physiological arousal is to increase acceptance of these experiences—in other words, willingness to have the experience instead of engaging in behaviors to escape or change it (i.e., experiential avoidance). Unpleasant conditioned arousal, which may be difficult to extinguish (and may likely recover even if temporarily extinguished), is likely to evoke operant avoidance behavior in order to reduce or remove the aversive sensations (Smith et al., 2020). Avoidance behavior of this sort (i.e., experiential avoidance) has been shown to contribute to distress and impaired functioning when it overgeneralizes to situations that do not pose legitimate physical threats (Kashdan et al., 2014). Because individuals cannot control and therefore eliminate these unwanted experiences, the focus of the ACT model is not to attempt to eliminate them but, rather, to promote healthy, values-driven behavior in the presence of them. Willingness to experience unpleasant internal experiences in this way constitutes a form of approach behavior.

Many anxiety and trauma-related disorders have notable maladaptive components related to thinking and language which can exert substantial control over behavior. Acceptance and cognitive defusion play important roles in reducing rigid control of behavior by language. Not only is it beneficial to see thoughts for the behavior (and not reality) that they are, but it is also important to understand that certain thought content will likely be evoked in certain circumstances and there is generally no way to prevent this from occurring. Uncontrollable worry in GAD is one example. If one can accept the fact that worry will undoubtedly arise under specific conditions, then one can give up fruitless and tiring attempts to control worry and actually disrupt the aversive worry spiral. Willingness to have whatever thought content may arise, and a focus on not becoming entangled with those thoughts (i.e., defusion), can open up the range of possible responses available to the person in that context and allow for one's attention and intention toward specified, values-aligned behaviors (i.e., committed actions).

Behavior motivated by cognitions such as overestimation of the likelihood of danger in specific phobia, misinterpretation of arousal-related body sensations in PD, misperception of benign bodily sensations in IAD, repetitive negative thinking in SAD and GAD, various distorted cognitions in PTSD, and imagined negative consequences of panic in agoraphobia are all examples of thoughts that can evoke experiential avoidance from clients. Shifting one's perspective from buying into the content of a thought ("This pain in my stomach is surely cancer") to seeing the process of thinking for what it is—a form of behavior that is difficult to control, much like physiological arousal—can create new possibilities for responding in the presence of those thoughts, thus expanding one's behavioral repertoire. As with acceptance, this opens up the possibility of pursuing values-based behaviors that may have seemed impossible before.

Centered: Self-As-Context and Present Moment Awareness

Another aspect of language is the development of problematic self-concepts that can underlie much of psychopathology. Self-as-content, the opposite of self-as-context, can be understood as cognitive fusion with unhelpful self-concepts (McHugh et al., 2019). When cognitive fusion with stories and rules about one's identity dominate behavior, it can limit the variety of responses available to an individual across circumstances. Self-as-context work focuses on defusing from self-narratives and recognizing that verbally constructed stories about the self, like any thoughts, come and go, while the observer of those thoughts remains unchanged and is not defined by any one of them. This process reduces the rigid control of behavior by self-narratives and allows for greater behavioral flexibility across a variety of situations. One example of a common self-narrative in the anxiety and trauma-related disorders is event centrality, or the perception of a traumatic or stressful event as a central component of one's identity. Event centrality has been identified as a potential risk factor for PTSD and is associated with severity of PTSD symptoms (Gehrt et al., 2018). As shown by Boals and Murrell (2016), an ACT intervention emphasizing the self-as-context process led to decreases in PTSD symptoms; event centrality significantly mediated this effect, thus pointing to its potentially important role in ACT treatment for trauma.

Present moment awareness is another key ACT process in the treatment of anxiety and trauma-related disorders. Present moment awareness is a kind of touchstone process in the ACT model, which facilitates one's ability to implement other ACT-based skills in the service of valued living. In the case of conditioned threat reactions, awareness of when unpleasant physiological arousal is occurring and its role in motivating escape behavior can serve a discriminative function for engaging in psychologically flexible behavior instead. This desired chain of behavior is more likely to emerge when one is able to notice the occurrence and influence of bodily sensations in the moment and thus alter the typical maladaptive patterns of behavior. Conversely, if one is not aware of the influence of unpleasant internal events on behavior in the moment, it increases the likelihood that long-established patterns of avoidance will be evoked before one is able to implement newly acquired adaptive skills. Present moment awareness therefore facilitates the use of other ACT processes and skills (see Smith et al., 2020 for more detailed discussion).

Engaged: Values and Committed Action

An important component of the ACT model is its focus on quality of life and meaningful psychosocial functioning, exemplified by values and values-aligned committed actions. The work done in ACT to target the maladaptive behaviors described above is not aimed at reducing those behaviors simply for the sake of reducing them, nor does it focus on eliminating behavior in a vacuum. Rather, it is done to allow for other classes of behavior associated with meaningful areas of life to emerge in their place. This is where the role of values in the ACT model is critical.

Values are verbally constructed statements that serve to guide patterns of behavior by relating an individual's day-to-day choices to meaningful areas and ways of living. As such, values help define treatment goals, guide in-session exercises such as exposures or behavioral commitments, and motivate change by creating a greater context and purpose for continuing the hard work of overcoming difficult experiences and applying the skills acquired in treatment. Often, the areas of life in which individuals experience the most anxiety and maladaptive threat reactions are those areas that are most meaningful to them. When clients get in touch with values, the importance of change and the cost of continuing to live life in the manner that brought them into therapy becomes clear. They are thus more likely to engage in behaviors that are aligned with values, that is, committed actions. Committed actions are used to identify and set attainable behavioral goals in the direction of valued living.

In therapy, arranging contingencies such that committed actions produce planned reinforcement (e.g., "rewards" for completing homework exercises) can help increase the frequency of values-based behavior and strengthen such behavior, especially if that behavior is not likely to contact naturally occurring sources of reinforcement. Even in the absence of such reinforcement, the fact that committed action is based on values means that engaging in committed actions can be reinforcing through verbal processes alone, given their relation to values statements (e.g., Smith et al., 2018). This potential should not be overlooked in the therapeutic context. Consistently highlighting the relationship between committed actions and values may help provide sufficient reinforcement to maintain committed actions when other reinforcement is lacking. This is important because when newly practiced adaptive behaviors that are meant to replace maladaptive behaviors experience a decrease or elimination of reinforcement (i.e., extinction), the maladaptive behavior often returns—an operant phenomenon known as resurgence, which in this context would be considered treatment relapse (Smith et al., 2017). Contact with values has the potential to mitigate disruptions in reinforcement, thus mitigating relapse.

In terms of ACT processes that are most directly related to maladaptive operant avoidance responses, committed action, which involves behavioral strategies such as task analyses, goal setting, and reinforcement, is central. Exposure techniques fall within this category and are fully consistent with ACT's underlying theory, even if they are not consistently included in ACT treatment manuals for anxiety. Considering that avoidance of certain stimulus events or situations is a primary maladaptive behavior in many anxiety and trauma-related disorders, decreasing the avoidance response through exposure, in which the individual refrains from engaging in avoidance or escape (i.e., response prevention), serves to disrupt the avoidance response. Connecting exposure exercises to values (choosing exposure exercises that are values-based behaviors) provides additional reinforcement for the difficult work of engaging in previously avoided activities.

Evidence Supporting ACT for Anxiety and Trauma-Related Disorders

Review of ACT for Anxiety

Evidence of the efficacy of ACT for the treatment of anxiety and anxiety disorders has increased in the last decade, with a number of meta-analyses now available to compare ACT to controls and other active treatments. In 2014, Bluett and colleagues conducted a systematic review of all outcome data of ACT for anxiety and obsessive-compulsive-spectrum disorders in the extant literature to that point. Nine studies were included in a preliminary meta-analysis ($n = 404$). Of these, two RCTs compared ACT against waitlist controls, and large effects favoring ACT were observed in both (Hedge's $g = 4.22$ and 1.07, $ps < .05$). For the seven studies that compared ACT to an established manualized treatment (e.g., CBT), there was no significant effect size difference on primary outcomes (Hedge's $g = .02$, 95% CI = $-.24, .27$, $z = .13$, $p = .89$, $k = 7$) or process of change measures (Hedge's $g = .12$, 95% CI = $-17, .41$; $z = .83$, $p = .41$, $k = 5$). The authors noted that their preliminary meta-analysis was lacking in terms of sample size, number of studies, and homogeneity across studies. Up to that point, there had been only two RCTs of ACT for GAD and four RCTs of ACT for heterogeneous anxiety. No RCTs had evaluated ACT for other anxiety disorders or for trauma-related disorders.

One year later, in a larger meta-analysis comparing the efficacy of ACT with CBT and control conditions (treatment as usual, waitlist control, psychological placebo), A-Tjak and colleagues (2015) combined anxiety and depression outcomes into a subset of eight RCTs ($n = 378$). With regard to anxiety and depression in particular, they found that ACT was superior to control conditions (Hedge's $g = 0.37$, $SE = 0.17$, 95% CI = 0.04, 0.70, $p = .030$). Hacker and colleagues (2016) also meta-analyzed ACT for anxiety and depression outcomes. They included any study that used a randomized controlled design and a manualized ACT treatment, thereby not limiting studies to those that examined anxiety disorders specifically or in which anxiety was the primary treatment target. This resulted in 28 studies that reported anxiety outcomes. They also used two distinct analytical approaches: cumulative meta-analysis (CMA) and sequential meta-analysis (SMA). The more traditional meta-analytic approach

(CMA) found large, significant effects in pre-post reduction of anxiety for ACT versus controls ($d = .95, p < .001, k = 28$), indicating sufficient evidence for the efficacy of ACT for the treatment of anxiety. Based on the more novel SMA approach, however, the authors determined that the existing literature did not provide enough studies to properly power the analytical approach for group comparisons, again highlighting the need for more research of this sort. Despite this finding, the SMA did still uncover moderate pre-post effects for ACT for anxiety; the effect was amplified when anxiety was the primary treatment target.

In the context of increasingly popular self-help treatment approaches, four recent meta-analyses have examined ACT delivered via computer, smartphone app, or book. Brown and colleagues (2016) conducted a meta-analysis of the effects of internet-delivered ACT. Of the 10 total studies, seven included measures of anxiety, though no study specifically targeted anxiety disorders. In this subset, the authors found a significant effect favoring ACT compared to control conditions, with the size of the effect just failing to meet the threshold to be considered small (Hedge's $g = 0.18, p < .03, k = 7$). Linardon and colleagues (2019) conducted a meta-analysis on ACT-based smartphone interventions, which showed significant effect sizes for generalized anxiety symptoms (Hedge's $g = .30$, 95% CI = 0.11, 0.49, $p < .001$). However, when compared to smartphone interventions that were not ACT-based, the differences were not statistically significant. French and colleagues (2017) meta-analyzed 13 studies of self-help ACT, including delivery via book and computer (i.e., internet, smartphone app, DVD, e-book). Ten studies included measures of anxiety, but again, no study specifically targeted anxiety or trauma-related disorders. In this subset ($n = 1824$), a significant small effect favoring ACT over control conditions was observed (Hedge's $g = 0.35$, 95% CI = 0.09, 0.60, $p = .008$). Finally, Thompson and colleagues (2021) reviewed 25 studies that delivered ACT via the internet (iACT). Compared to controls, iACT showed significant small effects for anxiety measures (Hedge's $g = 0.24$, $SE = 0.045$, 95% CI = 0.16, 0.33, $p < .001$), with 53 percent of studies resulting in clinically significant reductions in anxiety. Thus, evidence suggests that self-help ACT is effective for anxiety.

Recently, Gloster and colleagues (2020) reviewed the meta-analytic evidence for ACT, identifying 20 meta-analyses representing 133 individual studies and 12,477 participants, spanning 32 years (from 1986 to 2018). They found that ACT is broadly efficacious across conditions. Eleven meta-analyses specifically focused on ACT for anxiety disorders. The mean effect size observed was small (Hedge's $g = 0.24$), with six meta-analyses reporting significant effect sizes favoring ACT and one reporting a nonsignificant effect favoring active comparison conditions. Effect sizes were larger when ACT was compared to inactive controls and smaller when compared to active controls. ACT resulted in small to medium effect sizes in terms of functional outcomes (quality of life, well-being, functioning, disability), which are the primary treatment targets of ACT (as opposed to symptom reduction). Small to large effects were also observed for psychological flexibility, providing evidence that ACT achieves its effects through its core theorized process of change. Overall, research evidence supports ACT as an efficacious treatment for anxiety disorders and anxiety outcomes for in-person and self-help, including online, formats.

Review of ACT for Trauma-Related Disorders

In contrast to anxiety disorders, the evidence for ACT in the treatment of trauma-related disorders is still in its infancy. In 2017, Bean and colleagues reviewed the extant data on ACT for trauma. At the time, the literature consisted of only two RCTs and a handful of case studies and series. The first study was a semi-randomized trial comparing ACT plus treatment as usual (TAU) to TAU in 63 participants with elevated PTSD symptoms (Boals & Murrell, 2016).

TAU consisted of various cognitive-behavioral therapies, with some exposure components, in a community outreach center. The ACT condition consisted of four weekly ACT sessions in addition to TAU. It emphasized the self-as-context process of ACT as a means of targeting event centrality, or the degree to which an individual identifies with a traumatic event. The authors observed a significant effect of treatment condition, favoring ACT, on pre-post measures of PTSD symptoms, depression, and event centrality. Event centrality significantly mediated the relationship between condition and PTSD symptoms, providing supportive evidence for the role of a theorized ACT process in the treatment of PTSD (Boals & Murrell, 2016). The second study compared treatment with ACT to a present-centered therapy control condition for 160 veterans with symptoms of general distress, 82% of which had a PTSD diagnosis (Lang et al., 2017). Both conditions received 12, 1-hour sessions, and neither condition utilized exposure or instructed participants to directly focus on trauma. In intent-to-treat analyses, both groups experienced equivalent pre- to posttreatment improvements in general distress and functioning (effect sizes were medium to large), with no between-group differences. On secondary outcomes, the ACT group experienced more improvement in insomnia compared to the control group (Lang et al., 2017).

Since the Bean and colleagues (2017) review, only one controlled treatment efficacy study has been published. Muscara and colleagues (2020) compared an ACT-based group intervention (the Take a Breath program) to a waitlist control in the treatment of PTSD symptoms. Participants were parents whose children had recently been diagnosed with a sudden-onset life-threatening illness or injury (n = 81). The ACT condition received five 90-minute weekly sessions and a 3-week booster session delivered via online videoconferencing. Following treatment, the ACT condition showed significantly larger decreases in PTSD symptoms and improvements in their subjective experiences of their child's illness.

Recently, two noncontrolled effectiveness trials of ACT have been completed in military samples. Meyer and colleagues (2018) conducted an open pilot trial of a 12-week outpatient ACT program for co-occurring PTSD and alcohol use disorder (AUD) among 43 veterans. Participants received weekly individual psychotherapy sessions with daily mindfulness and values-consistent behavioral assignments. Although one session focused on mindful awareness of emotions related to participants' index trauma, the program did not include explicit exposure exercises. Two-thirds of the participants completed the program. Results indicated medium to large reductions in PTSD, alcohol-related, and depressive symptoms at posttreatment, with maintenance at 3-month follow-up. Quality of life increased at posttreatment, with a medium effect, and was maintained at follow-up. Functional disability and suicidal ideation were not significantly different at posttreatment, but both became significant by follow-up, with small effects. Finally, experiential avoidance, but not psychological inflexibility, decreased at posttreatment, and reductions in these processes of change were related to symptom change on most measures.

Ramirez and colleagues (2021) recently published the results of an open effectiveness trial in the treatment of 311 active-duty service members who had previously not responded to evidence-based outpatient PTSD treatment. The intensive outpatient program combined elements of prolonged exposure therapy (PE) with ACT over the course of 6 weeks and consisted of 12 hours of group therapy and two sessions of individual therapy (60–90 minutes each) per week. Voluntary dropout was low (3.9 percent). Using intent-to-treat analyses, all measures showed significant change from pretreatment to posttreatment. Effect sizes were large for PTSD symptoms, medium for anxiety, and small for depression. Participants also significantly increased functioning, with a medium effect, and valued living, with a small effect.

Importantly, large and significant changes were concurrently observed for ACT processes of change.

In summary, two noncontrolled effectiveness trials have shown promising results for ACT with PTSD in traditionally difficult to treat military populations (co-occurring PTSD and AUD and PTSD treatment nonresponders). In addition, three randomized controlled trials of ACT for trauma have shown mixed results, with two of the three showing favorable outcomes for ACT. The one study that showed equivalent change in ACT and the control condition utilized an active treatment control, did not include exposure, and did not focus directly on trauma. Given that exposure is generally considered an important component of CBT treatment for PTSD, including exposure and directly focusing on trauma may also be an important component of treatment in ACT for trauma. Regardless, research in this area is still in its nascent stages, and much more research is needed before conclusions can be drawn regarding the efficacy of ACT for trauma-related disorders.

Clinical Applications of ACT for Anxiety

While a comprehensive application of ACT for each anxiety disorder would likely be redundant given the similarities between disorders described earlier, we will share clinical scenarios related to the treatment of three representative disorders to demonstrate how the processes of psychological flexibility can be applied for different clinical presentations of anxiety and trauma. In order to give readers a sense of the range of treatment applications, we selected disorders with varying clinical presentations—PD, GAD, and PTSD—for which the treatment approaches would likely vary. Through the clinical examples, we demonstrate that ACT processes do not function in isolation. Rather, each process works interdependently with other ACT processes to promote psychologically flexible behavior. For example, committed action is, by definition, defined by values. Therefore, we cannot incorporate committed action into treatment without also clarifying and evoking client-specific values. Consistently engaging in committed action will likely necessitate the use of acceptance and defusion skills, as unwanted internal experiences arise during the course of the valued activity. Given that exposure therapy is fundamental in the treatment of most anxiety and trauma-related disorders, we first provide a model for ACT-based exposures.

ACT-Based Exposures

Exposure is considered an essential component of the successful treatment of most disorders that involve maladaptive threat responding. From an ACT perspective, exposure is undertaken as an instance of committed action and an opportunity to practice acceptance of unwanted internal experiences without attempting to escape or otherwise control them (Twohig et al., 2015). In vivo exposures consist of choosing meaningful values-based activities that the client may otherwise avoid and encouraging the client to engage with them while being willing to experience unwanted thoughts, sensations, and emotions. As previously discussed, the focus of exposure within ACT is not on reducing the frequency, intensity or duration of the fear response, but rather on engaging in committed actions that are aligned with personal values regardless of the presence or absence of distress. In ACT, exposures are pursued as a means to practice acceptance of unwanted internal experiences, to strengthen approach behaviors, to engage in response flexibility, and to increase values-based living.

Values are at the heart of exposure exercises in ACT. Self-identified values provide a rationale for engaging in exposure and serve as reinforcement for increasing values-based living (Twohig et al., 2015). For example, exposure hierarchies are created based on activities that are meaningful to the individual rather than on how much distress or anxiety they might evoke (as is done in traditional CBT-based exposure). In each session, the client selects the exposure exercise instead of following the hierarchy in a linear fashion. This gives the client additional opportunities to make behavioral choices in the service of their values. For example, a client with a specific phobia of dogs may avoid going to the park with his family for fear of encountering a dog. If we assume that spending time with his family is a values-based activity, in vivo exposure could involve going to the park with his family while practicing acceptance of physiological and emotional threat responses that arise.

In ACT, exposure exercises are tailored to increase each client's opportunities for psychological flexibility. Therefore, the six core processes of change (organized into three pillars) are woven into exposures based on the client's unique presentation of psychological inflexibility. During exposure, little Socratic questioning takes place, and there is no solicitation for a client's level of subjective units of distress (i.e., SUDS). Rather, the therapist queries about how open or willing the client is toward their internal and external experiences in the moment. The therapist might utilize a metaphor or encourage willingness for the sake of reconnecting with self-identified values. Again, the focus of the exposure session is not on the strength or severity of the internal experience but, rather, on how open the client is to that experience (Twohig et al., 2015). Exposure exercises are encouraged both in and between sessions as opportunities to practice willingness, defusion, and committed actions.

ACT and Panic

Individuals who meet the criteria for panic disorder (PD) have developed maladaptive threat reactions to their own physiological sensations and the thoughts and feelings with which they are correlated. Attempts to downregulate these experiences lead to further arousal and a positive feedback loop of increasing panic. Attempts at downregulation of the panic-related sensations, thoughts, and feelings are a form of experiential avoidance of the body's innate threat response. ACT encourages clients to function in the presence of panic-related inner experiences, rather than engaging in attempts to control, alter, or eliminate them, in order to participate in values-driven behaviors (Meuret et al., 2012).

During an ACT session for panic, a therapist might use a metaphor that allows the client to see that their attempt to control their panic-related experiences, while normal, is counterproductive. For example, the therapist might equate trying to fall in love on command with trying to "turn off" or control panic-related inner experiences. This metaphor helps the client to recognize how unreasonable it is to try to control panic-related inner experiences, just as trying to force oneself to fall in love would be ineffective and counterproductive. They may realize that the desire to regulate panic responses (e.g., shortness of breath, rapid heart rate, tightness in chest) actually results in more panic sensations.

To break this counterproductive cycle, a client might be asked to engage in interoceptive exposures as a way to practice acceptance of unwanted panic sensations. Interoceptive exposures could include breathing through a straw for 2 minutes or running up a flight of stairs to intentionally induce shortness of breath and rapid heart rate. During the exposure, the client would be encouraged to maintain a curious and open stance toward their breathlessness and pounding heart. The therapist might ask the client: "How willing are you to have this experience (0–100)?" "How open are you to your heart beating quickly?" "Are you digging your heels in and waiting until this is over?" Based on the client's responses, the therapist could encourage acceptance, defusion, or connection to core values to increase the client's willingness to stay with the exposure. Over time, the client begins to recognize that the more often they approach the uncomfortable stimuli (e.g., shortness of breath, rapid heart rate), the more they can have panic sensations as an occasional part of their lives.

Clients with panic often present rigid interpretations of panic-related inner experiences. For example, a client with panic might notice a gentle pressure in their chest and have the thought, "I must be having a heart attack." This initial response would likely evoke additional thoughts such as "I can't handle this" and "I am going to die," resulting in the development of a panic attack. Defusion techniques can help the client disentangle from this behavior. Through experiential exercises, a client would learn that their shortness of breath is not really a threat, but, rather, it is the labeling and negative evaluation in response to shortness of breath that creates the problem.

Threat responses can also become conditioned to environmental cues or situations that have previously been paired with panic attacks (e.g., elevators, crowds). Verbal processes, such as cognitive fusion, also serve to strengthen the aversive aspects of the situation (e.g., "It would be really bad to have a panic attack here because . . . "). As a result, avoidance of these cues and of situations in which panic attacks may occur can become so excessive that individuals avoid entire categories of activities or, in extreme cases, avoid leaving their homes altogether—the hallmark of extreme agoraphobia. This passive avoidance reinforces fear and anxiety about panic. Therefore, in ACT, a client is encouraged to reflect on their personal values and on how avoidance behaviors (e.g., staying at home, minimizing physical activity) are in direct competition with those values. For example, if a client stated that being present for their child was one of their core values, the therapist and client might discuss what that looks like on a day-to-day basis. If the client stated, "attending my kid's soccer game," the therapist and client could collaboratively create daily in vivo exposures that would facilitate leaving the house, with the eventual goal of the parent attending their child's soccer game.

ACT and Trauma

For individuals experiencing posttraumatic stress, life becomes about minimizing or managing intrusive memories and nightmares, avoiding trauma-related stimuli, coping with guilt and shame, and living in a hyperaroused state. Given the amount of effort allocated to managing symptoms of traumatic stress, it is common for individuals experiencing trauma-related disorders to feel disconnected from their core values. An initial session for the treatment of traumatic stress might begin with exploring and identifying personal values. To do so, the client might engage in a values card-sorting exercise or write a brief speech about what they hope someone might say about them at their retirement party. Through values work, clients develop motivation to engage in exposure exercises and create a broader context for trauma-focused work beyond symptom reduction (B. L. Thompson et al., 2013).

Avoidance is at the core of posttraumatic stress and is often the most dominant symptom (B. L. Thompson et al., 2013). Exposure exercises may be used to reduce avoidance and increase approach behaviors. Prior to engaging in trauma-related exposures, it is helpful to introduce the concept of willingness. When teaching acceptance to trauma survivors, the term *willingness* is often used instead of acceptance because it highlights the element of choice when practicing acceptance and engaging in exposures (B. L. Thompson et al., 2013). Once willingness has been practiced in session, imaginal exposures to the traumatic memory can be implemented. Imaginal exposures consist of the client recalling and describing the traumatic memory in order to create new learning and ultimately toleration/acceptance of the fear memory. From an ACT framework, imaginal exposures are presented as an opportunity to practice willingness to come into contact with painful thoughts, memories, and emotions (Ramirez et al., 2021). It is critical to connect the approach behavior (e.g., recitation of the trauma memory) to previously identified values. For example, the therapist might remind the client, "Remember why you are doing this. The discomfort you are feeling is so you can have a closer relationship with your children." In doing so, clients are likely to experience greater willingness to engage with this often difficult exercise.

Attachment to the conceptualized self, that is, being fused with the thoughts and stories of "who I am," is common in the context of posttraumatic stress. Trauma survivors often label themselves in the context of their traumatic experience. For example, a war veteran who witnessed the death of a civilian might be haunted by the belief that they should have intervened or rescued the individual. This narrative becomes the foundation for additional beliefs about one's self such as "I am a horrible person" or "I am a coward." To encourage an alternative perspective, the therapist might guide the client through a mindfulness exercise, such as the Constant Observer (Forsyth & Eifert, 2016), during which a client would be asked to imagine a series of memories (e.g., their very first day of school, their first date) and then asked to recall what they were thinking, feeling, and sensing during that event. The therapist would reflect to the client that, at each event, there was the same person behind their eyes who saw, heard, and had thoughts about the events. This constant perspective is known as the "observer self." Through such exercises, clients learn that there is a stable perspective that transcends their different life experiences, from which they watch or observe all that is occurring, and that cannot be defined by one experience or thought in time. In our example, the war veteran would learn to recognize the observer self, ultimately creating space between them and the thoughts around which they have formed their identity and allowing them to unhook their behavior from being rigidly controlled by this identity story.

ACT and Generalized Anxiety

Generalized anxiety is characterized by excessive and uncontrollable worry, perseveration, and the physical tension that results from chronic worry. Individuals who experience uncontrollable worry are often fused with thoughts about what "could happen," resulting in their living in fear of the future. Clients experiencing generalized anxiety often describe an impending sense of doom or feeling as though something awful might happen. To prevent a possible negative future event, they attempt to manage their anxiety through avoidance and future problem solving (i.e., worry), further digging them into the mire of worry and negative affect associated with the imagined future events. Clients also engage in overt active and passive avoidance behavior, which narrows their behavioral repertoire and disconnects them from values (Ruiz et al., 2020).

Clarifying values and contacting the cost of staying stuck in a cycle of worry and avoidance are important pieces of treatment. The left and center pillar processes (acceptance, defusion, present moment awareness, and self-as-context) provide the client with the necessary skills to be able to get out of their heads and engage in meaningful actions, even in the presence of relentless worry. To increase client awareness, centering exercises may be practiced in session to bring attention to the here and now. For example, the therapist might facilitate a guided mindfulness exercise at the beginning of each session to orient the client to the present moment. Verbal prompts provided during the exercise can help the client observe the process of thinking (e.g., "Notice that your thoughts are moving by like a rushing river—watch the river") as opposed to getting caught in the content of individual thoughts. This type of exercise also involves stepping back and seeing thoughts from a larger, more stable, perspective.

Although exposures are not always used in traditional treatment for generalized anxiety, in ACT, a client might be encouraged to engage in daily in vivo exposures to connect with the things that are most important in their life and disconnect from the cycle of avoidance. Exposure would also provide an opportunity during the client's day-to-day life to practice acceptance and cognitive defusion with regard to worry. Whether the clinician chooses to utilize exposures during treatment will depend on the client's particular presentation. Unlike the case with other anxiety and trauma-related issues, presentations of generalized anxiety may not lend themselves as easily to exposures per se. Rather, values-aligned committed actions may be used to provide opportunities for the client to apply and practice the skills they have learned in therapy. The classic Passengers on the Bus metaphor is often useful for clients with generalized anxiety to acknowledge that worried thoughts will likely persist, despite the client's efforts to control them, but that the client can still choose to engage in valued behavior. That is, they can drive their bus in whatever direction they choose, even with loud and sometimes scary thoughts (passengers) telling them otherwise.

Challenges and Future Directions

Research on ACT for anxiety and trauma-related disorders has come a long way in the last decade. Nevertheless, important areas for future work remain. For one, there is a notable lack of research examining the efficacy of ACT for trauma-related disorders. In particular, studies investigating which ACT treatment components are necessary for client response to treatment are important. For example, studies investigating the efficacy of ACT for different trauma presentations and various client populations is needed. Additional questions include determining which ACT treatment components are necessary for improved outcome. For example, is it necessary for treatment to focus directly on traumatic experiences? Relevant to trauma and anxiety disorders are the questions of whether, to what degree, and for which clinical presentations is exposure an integral component of treatment. Because ACT is a transdiagnostic treatment, exposure is not necessarily considered an essential part of the ACT model. Studies of anxiety and trauma disorders have varied in the extent to which exposure has been included in treatment protocols. It remains an open question as to whether exposure embedded within a broader ACT treatment model can produce better outcomes than ACT without exposure and whether this would hold only in certain circumstances (e.g., is it more important to include exposure in treatment for trauma-related pathology relative to generalized anxiety).

Similarly, it is important that researchers gain a better understanding of the various ways in which maladaptive and adaptive behaviors interact in a given client to promote and impede functioning. Some of the behaviors and change processes described previously have been thoroughly researched over many decades (e.g., Pavlovian threat reactions and extinction learning; Craske et al., 2012). However, others, such as the complex relationship between Pavlovian threat reactions and avoidance, and the interaction of language and cognition with these processes, have received far less attention. A better understanding of each of these behaviors and their interactions is essential to gain a complete picture of the maladaptive patterns of responding in which they participate.

A process-based approach to therapy (PBT; Hofmann & Hayes, 2019) is beginning to gain traction in the field. ACT is an early example of PBT due to its theoretical and empirical links with psychological flexibility and the processes of change that comprise it (Levin et al., 2012; Ong et al., 2020). In order to put a process-based approach to ACT into practice with regard to anxiety and trauma-related disorders, we first must identify the maladaptive defensive behaviors and processes that we, as clinicians, hypothesize play a primary role in impacting and maintaining the client's problems. Once we have identified behavioral targets, which occurs in collaboration with the client as part of functional case conceptualization and treatment planning, we assess each behavior or process in an idiographic manner. This assessment may be accomplished through use of standardized measures, 0–100 scales (e.g., "on a scale of 0–100, how much did you try to push away your anxiety today?", "on a scale of 0–100, how much did you move in the direction of your values today?"), or technology such as ecological momentary assessment (EMA; Shiffman et al., 2008). Ideally, we would assess behavior frequently in order to track behavior as it changes, confirming or disconfirming hypothesized functional relations, identifying new functional relations, and tracking progress through treatment. Finally, we use these data to adjust treatment as necessary to meet the client's treatment goals (Ong et al., 2020).

As PBT is a relatively new approach to clinical care, many details still need to be worked out. For example, which idiographic behavioral patterns, when identified, would suggest the use of which treatment procedures? Are there circumstances in which we would not use exposure for an anxiety or trauma-related disorder? Perhaps exposure continues to be a key component of treatment, with idiographic analyses informing how or when exposure is implemented or whether it is used in conjunction with other procedures. Despite these questions, we believe a process-based approach, especially in the context of functionally similar anxiety and trauma-related disorders, has much to offer above the current paradigm of manualized protocols for topographically defined syndromes. A move toward PBT promises increased treatment precision, efficiency, and, potentially, efficacy.

In order to further process-based research, appropriate idiographic measures will have to be developed to capture and evaluate movement in different processes with the needed level of sensitivity. This challenge is not specific to anxiety and trauma-related disorders, but it does apply to a process-based approach to treatment in general, as does the need to continue development of appropriate analytical tools (e.g., network analyses) to further this research agenda (Hofmann et al., 2020). In addition, more outcome measures related to adaptive functioning and quality of life need to be included, going beyond the typical outcome measures that focus on symptom reduction, in order to better align with the overarching philosophy of ACT and CBS.

Conclusion

Anxiety and trauma-related disorders pose substantial difficulties for those who experience them. ACT is particularly well suited to address the current state of treatment in this area, in which response, attrition, and recurrence rates continue to limit the effectiveness of treatment and in which there is a notable disconnect between current evidence-based treatments and their underlying theories. Research suggests that standard ACT in manualized form is efficacious for the treatment of anxiety disorders, though more research will be needed before it is determined whether the same can be said for trauma. However, given the functional similarities between the various anxiety and trauma-related disorders, we recommend moving toward a more process-oriented approach to implementing ACT, utilizing ACT's existing evidence-based processes and procedures to target the maladaptive defensive behaviors that maintain this class of disorders. It is our hope that this work continues to progress and move in an innovative direction that best supports our clients in building full and meaningful lives.

AcknowledgmentThe authors would like to acknowledge Alexander J. Twohy for his help with the literature review for this article.

References

Abramowitz, J. S., & Blakey, S. M. (Eds.). (2020). *Clinical handbook of fear and anxiety: Maintenance processes and treatment mechanisms*. American Psychological Association.

Abramowitz, J. S., Deacon, B. J., & Whiteside, S. P. H. (2019). *Exposure therapy for anxiety* (2nd ed.). Guilford Press.

American Psychiatric Association. (2013). *Diagnostic and statistical manual of mental disorders (DSM-5®)* (5th ed.). American Psychiatric Publishing.

Arch, J. J., & Craske, M. G. (2009). First-line treatment: A critical appraisal of cognitive behavioral therapy developments and alternatives. *Psychiatric Clinics of North America, 32*(3), 525–547. https://doi.org/10.1016/j.psc.2009.05.001

A-Tjak, J. G. L., Davis, M. L., Morina, N., Powers, M. B., Smits, J. A. J., & Emmelkamp, P. M. G. (2015). A meta-analysis of the efficacy of acceptance and commitment therapy for clinically relevant mental and physical health problems. *Psychotherapy and Psychosomatics, 84*(1), 30–36. https://doi.org/10.1159/000365764

Barlow, D. H. (2004). *Anxiety and its disorders: The nature and treatment of anxiety and panic* (2nd ed.). Guilford Press.

Bean, R. C., Ong, C. W., Lee, J., & Twohig, M. P. (2017). Acceptance and commitment therapy for PTSD and trauma: An empirical review. *The Behavior Therapist, 40*(4), 145–149.

Bluett, E. J., Homan, K. J., Morrison, K. L., Levin, M. E., & Twohig, M. P. (2014). Acceptance and commitment therapy for anxiety and OCD spectrum disorders: An empirical review. *Journal of Anxiety Disorders, 28*(6), 612–624. https://doi.org/10.1016/j.janxdis.2014.06.008

Boals, A., & Murrell, A. R. (2016). I am > trauma: Experimentally reducing event centrality and PTSD symptoms in a clinical trial. *Journal of Loss and Trauma, 21*(6), 471–483. https://doi.org/10.1080/15325024.2015.1117930

Borkovec, T. D., Robinson, E., Pruzinsky, T., & DePree, J. A. (1983). Preliminary exploration of worry: Some characteristics and processes. *Behaviour Research and Therapy, 21*(1), 9–16. https://doi.org/10.1016/0005-7967(83)90121-3

Bouton, M. E. (2002). Context, ambiguity, and unlearning: Sources of relapse after behavioral extinction. *Biological Psychiatry, 52*, 976–986. https://doi.org/10.1016/S0006-3223(02)01546-9

Brown, M., Glendenning, A., Hoon, A. E., & John, A. (2016). Effectiveness of web-delivered acceptance and commitment therapy in relation to mental health and well-being: A systematic review and meta-analysis. *Journal of Medical Internet Research, 18*(8), e221. https://doi.org/10.2196/jmir.6200

Bruce, S. E., Yonkers, K. A., Otto, M. W., Eisen, J. L., Weisberg, R. B., Pagano, M., Shea, M. T., & Keller, M. B. (2005). Influence of psychiatric comorbidity on recovery and recurrence in generalized anxiety disorder, social phobia, and panic disorder: A 12-year prospective study. *American Journal of Psychiatry, 162*(6), 1179–1187. https://doi.org/10.1176/appi.ajp.162.6.1179

Carpenter, J. K., Andrews, L. A., Witcraft, S. M., Powers, M. B., Smits, J. A. J., & Hofmann, S. G. (2018). Cognitive behavioral therapy for anxiety and related disorders: A meta-analysis of randomized placebo-controlled trials. *Depression and Anxiety, 35*(6), 502–514. https://doi.org/10.1002/da.22728

Christiana, J. M., Gilman, S. E., Guardino, M., Mickelson, K., Morselli, P. L., Olfson, M., & Kessler, R. C. (2000). Duration between onset and time of obtaining initial treatment among people with anxiety and mood disorders: An international survey of members of mental health patient advocate groups. *Psychological Medicine, 30*(3), 693–703.

Craske, M. G., & Barlow, D. H. (2014). Panic disorder and agoraphobia. In D. H. Barlow (Ed.), *Clinical handbook of psychological disorders* (5th ed., pp. 1–61). Guilford Press.

Craske, M. G., Liao, B., & Vervliet, B. (2012). Role of inhibition in exposure therapy. *Journal of Experimental Psychopathology, 3*(3), 322–345. https://doi.org/10.5127/jep.026511

Cuijpers, P., Sijbrandij, M., Koole, S., Huibers, M., Berking, M., & Andersson, G. (2014). Psychological treatment of generalized anxiety disorder: A meta-analysis. *Clinical Psychology Review, 34*(2), 130–140. https://doi.org/10.1016/j.cpr.2014.01.002

Engelhard, I. M., van Uijen, S. L., van Seters, N., & Velu, N. (2015). The effects of safety behavior directed towards a safety cue on perceptions of threat. *Behavior Therapy, 46*(5), 604–610. https://doi.org/10.1016/j.beth.2014.12.006

Forsyth, J. P., & Eifert, G. H. (2016). *The mindfulness and acceptance workbook for anxiety: A guide to breaking free from anxiety, phobias and worry using acceptance and commitment therapy* (2nd edition). New Harbinger Publications.

French, K., Golijani-Moghaddam, N., & Schröder, T. (2017). What is the evidence for the efficacy of self-help acceptance and commitment therapy? A systematic review and meta-analysis. *Journal of Contextual Behavioral Science, 6*(4), 360–374. https://doi.org/10.1016/j.jcbs.2017.08.002

Gehrt, T. B., Berntsen, D., Hoyle, R. H., & Rubin, D. C. (2018). Psychological and clinical correlates of the Centrality of Event Scale: A systematic review. *Clinical Psychology Review, 65*, 57–80. https://doi.org/10.1016/j.cpr.2018.07.006

Gloster, A. T., Klotsche, J., Ciarrochi, J., Eifert, G., Sonntag, R., Wittchen, H.-U., & Hoyer, J. (2017). Increasing valued behaviors precedes reduction in suffering: Findings from a randomized controlled trial using ACT. *Behavior Research and Therapy, 91*, 64–71. https://doi.org/10.1016/j.brat.2017.01.013

Gloster, A. T., Walder, N., Levin, M., Twohig, M., & Karekla, M. (2020). The empirical status of acceptance and commitment therapy: A review of meta-analyses. *Journal of Contextual Behavioral Science, 18*, 181–192. S2212144720301940. https://doi.org/10.1016/j.jcbs.2020.09.009

Gunnar, M., & Quevedo, K. (2007). The neurobiology of stress and development. *Annual Review of Psychology, 58*(1), 145–173. https://doi.org/10.1146/annurev.psych.58.110405.085605

Haaker, J., Golkar, A., Hermans, D., & Lonsdorf, T. B. (2014). A review on human reinstatement studies: An overview and methodological challenges. *Learning and Memory, 21*(9), 424–440. https://doi.org/10.1101/lm.036053.114

Hacker, T., Stone, P., & MacBeth, A. (2016). Acceptance and commitment therapy—Do we know enough? Cumulative and sequential meta-analyses of randomized controlled trials. *Journal of Affective Disorders, 190*, 551–565. https://doi.org/10.1016/j.jad.2015.10.053

Hayes, S. C., Strosahl, K. D., & Wilson, K. G. (2012). *Acceptance and commitment therapy: The process and practice of mindful change* (2nd ed.). Guilford Press.

Heimberg, R. G., & Magee, L. (2014). Social anxiety disorder. In D. H. Barlow (Ed.), *Clinical handbook of psychological disorders* (5th ed., pp. 114–154). Guilford Press.

Hofmann, S. G., Curtiss, J. E., & Hayes, S. C. (2020). Beyond linear mediation: Toward a dynamic network approach to study treatment processes. *Clinical Psychology Review, 76*, 101824. https://doi.org/10.1016/j.cpr.2020.101824

Hofmann, S. G., & Hayes, S. C. (2019). The future of intervention science: Process-based therapy. *Clinical Psychological Science, 7*(1), 37–50. https://doi.org/10.1177/2167702618772296

Huijding, J., Mayer, B., Koster, E. H. W., & Muris, P. (2011). To look or not to look: An eye movement study of hypervigilance during change detection in high and low spider fearful students. *Emotion, 11*(3), 666–674. https://doi.org/10.1037/a0022996

Kashdan, T. B., Goodman, F. R., Machell, K. A., Kleiman, E. M., Monfort, S. S., Ciarrochi, J., & Nezlek, J. B. (2014). A contextual approach to experiential avoidance and social anxiety: Evidence from an experimental interaction and daily interactions of people with social anxiety disorder. *Emotion, 14*(4), 769–781. https://doi.org/10.1037/a0035935

Kessler, R. C., Angermeyer, M., Anthony, J. C., de Graaf, R., Demyttenaere, K., Gasquet, I., De Girolamo, G., Gluzman, S., Gureje, O., Haro, J. M., Kawakami, N., Karam, A., Evinson, D., Medina Mora, M. E., Browne, M. A. O., Posada-Villa, J., Stein, D. J., Adley Tsang, C. H., Aguilar-Gaxiola, S., . . . & Ustun, T. B. (2007). Lifetime prevalence and age-of-onset distributions of mental disorders in the World Health Organization's World Mental Health Survey Initiative. *World Psychiatry, 6*, 168–176.

Lang, A. J., Schnurr, P. P., Jain, S., He, F., Walser, R. D., Bolton, E., Benedek, D. M., Norman, S. B., Sylvers, P., Flashman, L., Strauss, J., Raman, R., & Chard, K. M. (2017). Randomized controlled trial of acceptance and commitment therapy for distress and impairment in OEF/OIF/OND veterans. *Psychological Trauma: Theory, Research, Practice, and Policy, 9*(Suppl. 1), 74–84. https://doi.org/10.1037/tra0000127

Levin, M. E., Hildebrandt, M. J., Lillis, J., & Hayes, S. C. (2012). The impact of treatment components suggested by the psychological flexibility model: A meta-analysis of laboratory-based component studies. *Behavior Therapy, 43*(4), 741–756. https://doi.org/10.1016/j.beth.2012.05.003

Linardon, J., Cuijpers, P., Carlbring, P., Messer, M., & Fuller-Tyszkiewicz, M. (2019). The efficacy of app-supported smartphone interventions for mental health problems: A meta-analysis of randomized controlled trials. *World Psychiatry, 18*(3), 325–336. https://doi.org/10.1002/wps.20673

Lovibond, P. F., Mitchell, C. J., Minard, E., Brady, A., & Menzies, R. G. (2009). Safety behaviours preserve threat beliefs: Protection from extinction of human fear conditioning by an avoidance response. *Behaviour Research and Therapy, 47*(8), 716–720. https://doi.org/10.1016/j.brat.2009.04.013

McHugh, L., Stewart, I., & Almada, P. (2019). *A contextual behavioral guide to the self: Theory and practice.* Context Press.

Meuret, A. E., Twohig, M. P., Rosenfield, D., Hayes, S. C., & Craske, M. G. (2012). Brief acceptance and commitment therapy and exposure for panic disorder: A pilot study. *Cognitive and Behavioral Practice, 19*(4), 606–618. https://doi.org/10.1016/j.cbpra.2012.05.004

Meyer, E. C., Walser, R., Hermann, B., Bash, H., DeBeer, B. B., Morissette, Kimbrel, N. A., Kwok, O., Batten, S. V., & Schnurr, P. P. (2018). Acceptance and commitment therapy for co-occurring posttraumatic stress disorder and alcohol use disorders in veterans: Pilot treatment outcomes. *Journal of Traumatic Stress, 31*(5), 781–789. https://doi.org/10.1002/jts.22322

Muscara, F., McCarthy, M. C., Rayner, M., Nicholson, J. M., Dimovski, A., McMillan, L., Hearps, S. J. C., Yamada, J., Burke, K., Walser, R., & Anderson, V. A. (2020). Effect of a videoconference-based online group intervention for traumatic stress in parents of children with life-threatening Illness: A randomized clinical trial. *JAMA Network Open, 3*(7), e208507. https://doi.org/10.1001/jamanetworkopen.2020.8507

Olatunji, B. O., Cisler, J. M., & Deacon, B. J. (2010). Efficacy of cognitive behavioral therapy for anxiety disorders: A review of meta-analytic findings. *Psychiatric Clinics of North America, 33*(3), 557–577. https://doi.org/10.1016/j.psc.2010.04.002

Olatunji, B. O., Cisler, J. M., & Tolin, D. F. (2007). Quality of life in the anxiety disorders: A meta-analytic review. *Clinical Psychology Review, 27*(5), 572–581. https://doi.org/10.1016/j.cpr.2007.01.015

Ong, C. W., Levin, M. E., & Twohig, M. P. (2020). Beyond acceptance and commitment therapy: Process-based therapy. *The Psychological Record, 70*(4), 637–648. https://doi.org/10.1007/s40732-020-00397-z

Pittig, A. (2019). Incentive-based extinction of safety behaviors: Positive outcomes competing with aversive outcomes trigger fear-opposite action to prevent protection from fear extinction. *Behaviour Research and Therapy, 121*, 103463. https://doi.org/10.1016/j.brat.2019.103463

Pittig, A., & Dehler, J. (2019). Same fear responses, less avoidance: Rewards competing with aversive outcomes do not buffer fear acquisition, but attenuate avoidance to accelerate subsequent fear extinction. *Behaviour Research and Therapy, 112*, 1–11. https://doi.org/10.1016/j.brat.2018.11.003

Pittig, A., Wong, A. H. K., Glück, V. M., & Boschet, J. M. (2020). Avoidance and its bi-directional relationship with conditioned fear: Mechanisms, moderators, and clinical implications. *Behaviour Research and Therapy, 126*, 103550. https://doi.org/10.1016/j.brat.2020.103550

Quirk, G. J. (2002). Memory for extinction of conditioned fear is long-lasting and persists following spontaneous recovery. *Learning and Memory, 9*(6), 402–407. https://doi.org/10.1101/lm.49602

Ramirez, M. W., Woodworth, C. A., Evans, W. R., Grace, G. A., Schobitz, R. P., Villarreal, S. A., Howells, C. J., Gissendanner, R. D., Katko, N. J., Jones, K. N., McCabe, A. E., & Terrell, D. J. (2021). A trauma-focused intensive outpatient program integrating elements of exposure therapy with acceptance and commitment therapy: Program development and initial outcomes. *Journal of Contextual Behavioral Science, 21*, 66–72. https://doi.org/10.1016/j.jcbs.2021.06.002

Remes, O., Brayne, C., van der Linde, R., & Lafortune, L. (2016). A systematic review of reviews on the prevalence of anxiety disorders in adult populations. *Brain and Behavior, 6*(7), e00497. https://doi.org/10.1002/brb3.497

Rodriguez-Romaguera, J., Greenberg, B. D., Rasmussen, S. A., & Quirk, G. J. (2016). An avoidance-based rodent model of exposure with response prevention therapy for obsessive-compulsive disorder. *Biological Psychiatry, 80*(7), 534–540. https://doi.org/10.1016/j.biopsych.2016.02.012

Ruiz, F. J., Peña-Vargas, A., Ramírez, E. S., Suárez-Falcón, J. C., García-Martín, M. B., García-Beltrán, D. M., Henao, Á. M., Monroy-Cifuentes, A., & Sánchez, P. D. (2020). Efficacy of a two-session repetitive negative thinking-focused acceptance and commitment therapy (ACT) protocol for depression and generalized anxiety disorder: A randomized waitlist control trial. *Psychotherapy, 57*(3), 444–456. https://doi.org/10.1037/pst0000273

Scarella, T. M., Boland, R. J., & Barsky, A. J. (2019). Illness anxiety disorder: Psychopathology, epidemiology, clinical characteristics, and treatment. *Psychosomatic Medicine, 81*(5), 398–407. https://doi.org/10.1097/PSY.0000000000000691

Shiffman, S., Stone, A. A., & Hufford, M. R. (2008). Ecological momentary assessment. *Annual Review of Clinical Psychology, 4*(1), 1–32. https://doi.org/10.1146/annurev.clinpsy.3.022806.091415

Smith, B. M., Smith, G. S., & Dymond, S. (2020). Relapse of anxiety-related fear and avoidance: Conceptual analysis of treatment with acceptance and commitment therapy. *Journal of the Experimental Analysis of Behavior, 113*(1), 87–104. https://doi.org/10.1002/jeab.573

Smith, B. M., Smith, G. S., Shahan, T. A., Madden, G. J., & Twohig, M. P. (2017). Effects of differential rates of alternative reinforcement on resurgence of human behavior. *Journal of the Experimental Analysis of Behavior, 107*(1), 191–202. https://doi.org/10.1002/jeab.241

Smith, B. M., Villatte, J. L., Ong, C. W., Butcher, G. M., Twohig, M. P., Levin, M. E., & Hayes, S. C. (2018). The influence of a personal values intervention on cold pressor-induced distress tolerance. *Behavior Modification, 43*(5), 688–710. https://doi.org/10.1177/0145445518782402

Thompson, B. L., Luoma, J. B., & LeJeune, J. T. (2013). Using acceptance and commitment therapy to guide exposure-based interventions for posttraumatic stress disorder. *Journal of Contemporary Psychotherapy, 43*(3), 133–140. https://doi.org/10.1007/s10879-013-9233-0

Thompson, E. M., Destree, L., Albertella, L., & Fontenelle, L. F. (2021). Internet-based acceptance and commitment therapy: A transdiagnostic systematic review and meta-analysis for mental health outcomes. *Behavior Therapy, 52*(2), 492–507. https://doi.org/10.1016/j.beth.2020.07.002

Twohig, M. P., Abramowitz, J., Bluett, E. J., Fabricant, L. E., Jacoby, R. J., Morrison, K. L., Reuman, L., & Smith, B. M. (2015). Exposure therapy for OCD from an acceptance and commitment therapy (ACT) framework. *Journal of Obsessive-Compulsive and Related Disorders, 6*, 167–173. https://doi.org/10.1016/j.jocrd.2014.12.007

van Dis, E. A. M., van Veen, S. C., Hagenaars, M. A., Batelaan, N. M., Bockting, C. L. H., van den Heuvel, R. M., Cuijpers, P., & Engelhard, I. M. (2019). Long-term outcomes of cognitive behavioral therapy for anxiety-related disorders: A systematic review and meta-analysis. *JAMA Psychiatry, 77*(3), 265–273. https://doi.org/10.1001/jamapsychiatry.2019.3986

Vervliet, B., & Indekeu, E. (2015). Low-cost avoidance behaviors are resistant to fear extinction in humans. *Frontiers in Behavioral Neuroscience, 9*(184), 351. https://doi.org/10.3389/fnbeh.2015.00351

Wong, Q. J. J., McEvoy, P. M., & Rapee, R. M. (2019). Repetitive thinking in social anxiety disorder: Are anticipatory processing and post-event processing facets of an underlying unidimensional construct? *Behavior Therapy, 50*(3), 571–581. https://doi.org/10.1016/j.beth.2018.09.004

Xia, W., Eyolfson, E., Lloyd, K., Vervliet, B., & Dymond, S. (2019). Living in fear: Low-cost avoidance maintains low-level threat. *Journal of Behavior Therapy and Experimental Psychiatry, 62*, 57–64. https://doi.org/10.1016/j.jbtep.2018.09.001

CHAPTER

16 Obsessive Compulsive and Related Disorders

Eric B. Lee, Myles Arendtson, *and* Andy Wall

Abstract

Obsessive compulsive disorder (OCD) and related disorders share many functional components and are often comorbid with one another. Acceptance and commitment therapy (ACT) for OCD and related disorders is described and is situated as a version of cognitive-behavioral therapy. Also described are the key psychological inflexibility measures for each of these disorders and the outcomes work with OCD and related disorders. Research supports ACT and ACT plus exposure therapy for OCD, and ACT plus habit reversal as a treatment for trichotillomania. The work in skin picking, hoarding disorder, and BDD is limited but is growing. Finally, guidance on the integration of ACT with exposure exercises and habit reversal, as well as future directions for work in this area, are presented.

Key Words: acceptance and commitment therapy, obsessive-compulsive disorder, hoarding disorder, trichotillomania, skin picking, body dysmorphic disorder, treatment, psychological flexibility

Introduction

Obsessive-compulsive and related disorders are part of a broad array of problem behaviors and disorders categorized in the *Diagnostic and Statistical Manual of Mental Disorders*, Fifth Edition (American Psychiatric Association, 2013). While varying topographically to a significant degree, they share many functional components and are often comorbid with one another. Moreover, psychological flexibility appears to often play a significant role in the maintenance of these problems and has proved to be a viable treatment target. As a transdiagnostic, process-based treatment, ACT is well suited to target the heterogeneous functional components of obsessive-compulsive and related disorders. Examples of these components include obsessive thoughts (i.e., unwanted intrusive thoughts, impulses, or mental imagery), compulsive behaviors (i.e., repetitious behaviors perceived as necessary in a given moment), excessive acquisition of objects and fear of discarding them, tension, stress, preoccupations with personal physical traits and subsequent excessive behaviors (e.g., hairpulling, checking), and general experiences that do not feel "just right." Furthermore, ACT has demonstrated an ability to integrate effectively with well-established components of behavior therapy such as habit reversal training and exposure. ACT could potentially enhance the potency and/or acceptability of these gold standard techniques with some clients.

While much research is still needed in this topic area, the evidence for ACT as an effective treatment for obsessive-compulsive and related disorders is quickly accumulating. This article will focus on the theoretical implications of ACT, current evidence for ACT as a treatment, and considerations and recommendations for using ACT to treat obsessive-compulsive and related disorders as defined by the *DSM-5*. This includes obsessive-compulsive disorder, body dysmorphic disorder, trichotillomania, excoriation disorder, and hoarding disorder.

Obsessive-Compulsive Disorder

Obsessive-compulsive disorder (OCD) is characterized by obsessive thoughts and compulsive behaviors. It is estimated that the lifetime prevalence of OCD in the general population is 1–3% (Ruscio et al., 2010). The typical age of onset is 20 years and, without treatment, tends to run a chronic course with symptoms fluctuating throughout an individual's lifetime, often causing significant debilitation (Subramaniam et al., 2013). Engaging in compulsions is time consuming and tiring, and interferes with daily functioning to a significant degree. On average, individuals with OCD experience a diminished quality of life compared to the general population with regard to psychological well-being, self-esteem, functioning at school, work performance, enjoyment of leisure activities, and the expression of religion. These impacts extend to lower average incomes and fewer academic achievements, as well higher rates of unemployment and dependence on social security than the general population (Norberg et al., 2008). Furthermore, OCD can have detrimental effects on social relationships, as family and loved ones are often negatively impacted by associated distress and dissatisfaction, as well as being compelled to accommodate compulsive behaviors (Norberg et al., 2008).

The relationship between obsessive thinking and compulsive behaviors is symbiotic in nature, with compulsive acts legitimizing obsessions as something to be feared and avoided and compulsive acts as increasingly necessary strategies of avoidance. Persistent intrusive thoughts, urges, or images typically involve themes of contamination, order and symmetry, responsibility for harm coming to others, and/or violent sexual or immoral thoughts (Abramowitz, 2006). Obsessions are involuntary and unwanted, and cause intense anxiety and fear. In most cases, individuals respond to obsessions with compulsive behavior in an attempt to ignore, suppress, neutralize, or distract from the associated distress. Compulsions are repetitive actions that, like obsessions, can vary significantly in form as either overt behaviors (e.g., handwashing, ordering, checking) or covert mental acts (e.g., counting, repeating words/phrases, praying; Subramaniam et al., 2013).

From an ACT perspective, compulsions, in any form, can functionally be described as experiential avoidance or an unwillingness to openly make space for internal events (i.e., obsessions). Furthermore, obsessions are often related to feared experiences or outcomes that are incongruous with one's perceived self or values and are thus likely to be fused with thoughts such as "this is dangerous" or "this is too risky to ignore." This process can lead to compulsions becoming a habitual rule that is followed ostensibly in order to prevent the occurrence of catastrophic or unwanted events. Over time, this experientially avoidant behavior simply becomes a short-term inconvenience that unfortunately comes at the cost of long-term well-being. The level of insight into these processes and these costs among those with OCD varies and can be an important treatment consideration, with some recognizing the improbability of the feared events occurring and others being steadfast in their beliefs that their compulsions are necessary (Cherian et al., 2012). Other treatment considerations relevant to ACT are OCD's association with inaccurate or dysfunctional beliefs, overestimation of the importance of thoughts, the need to control thoughts, overestimating threat, and an intolerance for uncertainty (Abramowitz, 2006). ACT's focus on acceptance or willingness of these cognitive components of OCD can offer a fresh perspective and foster an open and compassionate, rather than a combative or submissive, relationship with these experiences.

Body-Focused Repetitive Behaviors

Excoriation (skin-picking disorder) and trichotillomania (hairpulling disorder) are types of body-focused repetitive behaviors. Other relevant types of behaviors such as nail, cheek, lip, or tongue picking and biting are not recognized in the *DSM-5*. It is estimated that excoriation and trichotillomania each affect approximately 1–3% of the general population across the lifetime, with approximately three-quarters being female (Grant et al., 2020). These diagnoses are often accompanied by other comorbidities, including depression, OCD, and other body-focused repetitive behaviors. Individuals often hide the affected areas, avoid public spaces, or choose not to engage in certain activities (e.g., swimming) due to feelings of shame or embarrassment. This avoidance can reduce quality of life and is associated with social and occupational impairment. Moreover, the long-term effects of these repetitive behaviors can damage the affected zones, causing scars, loss of hair, and infection.

Excoriation is characterized by damage to the skin caused by excessive picking. Fingernails or tools such as tweezers are used, agitating healthy or irregular skin conditions such as scabs, acne, and callouses and often not allowing full healing. Individuals who engage in these behaviors tend to obsess about the condition of their skin and the damage associated with picking. For example, they may obsess about having smooth skin or reducing imperfections. Trichotillomania is characterized by excessive pulling out of hair. Fingers or tools are used to remove hair from various regions of one's body—most commonly hair on the head or face—often leading to noticeable hair loss. Hairpulling can occur as a habitual soothing behavior that is engaged in when the individual is distracted or preoccupied, or as an intentional behavior that is performed to reduce distress, feelings of tension, or "not-just-right" experiences.

Excoriation disorder, trichotillomania, and other types of body-focused repetitive behaviors are generally understood to be functionally similar to one another, meaning that the overt picking or pulling serves the same purpose of reducing stress, urges, or other unwanted internal experiences. Most people who engage in body-focused repetitive behaviors also engage in more mindless or automatic behaviors that are generally soothing, but not to explicitly reduce unwanted internal events. Both types of behaviors, focused and automatic, are captured well by ACT's model of psychological flexibility. ACT's process-based approach allows for the flexibility to target processes relevant to a given context and person. For example, people often engage in automatic repetitive behaviors at specific times and locations and can learn to practice present moment awareness skills in those contexts to help increase awareness and reduce problem behavior. Similarly, environments known for focused repetitive behaviors can be modified with reminders of values to encourage practice of acceptance strategies.

Hoarding Disorder

Hoarding is characterized by a strong aversion to the act of discarding possessions. Although estimates vary, approximately 2–4% of people meet the criteria for hoarding disorder of their lifetime (Postlethwaite et al., 2019). Hoarding generally involves the compulsive acquisition and accumulation of items, often in an attempt to reduce or avoid unwanted internal experiences. These items are saved regardless of value or available space to store them, to the extent that it impedes functioning. Significant value is placed on possessions—even the most mundane of items (e.g., empty paint cans, weather-damaged clothing, batteries without charge)—exacerbating the distress associated with discarding possessions. Hoarding can impair daily living activities such as hygiene maintenance, cooking, and sleeping, and can cause significant distress within familial relationships. Moreover, it can also put individuals and families at risk for myriad health and safety concerns (e.g., fire, falling, and unsanitary living conditions).

Hoarding is generally considered a complex and difficult problem behavior to treat. Insight into hoarding behavior can vary significantly from person to person. Lack of insight could be related to overidentification with labels and self-narratives that promote less functional behaviors. For example, someone might overidentify as a "frugal" or "thrifty" person who "is never wasteful." This may result in strict rule-following and saving or accumulating behaviors that are unhelpful and lead to long-term suffering. Some may not experience apparent anxiety or distress but may instead have difficulties with relationships, work, or other types of valued action due to a lack of psychological flexibility and fusion with their conceptualized self. Treatment refusal and dropout are common and consistent predictors of poor outcomes (Frost et al., 2010; Steketee & Frost, 2003). It is estimated that individuals with hoarding disorder may have more difficulty in complying with treatment protocols than those with other obsessive-compulsive and related disorders (Mataix-Cols et al., 2002). Poor insight, dependent personality traits, and psychological inflexibility are potential contributors to noncompliance (Wheaton et al., 2011).

ACT's focus on valued action may have an impact on some of these treatment difficulties. Often, those with hoarding behavior have so strongly prioritized their strict adherence to their thought content and rules that they no longer have the energy or resources to engage in actions that are truly meaningful to them and that might foster long-term well-being. Relationships, hobbies, careers, and more wither over time as one continually deals with unwanted internal experiences in the short term. Values exploration has the potential to help people attach meaning and purpose to otherwise difficult behaviors. For example, if the value of "being a loving grandmother" is identified for a client, the act of discarding items in a family room in order to have a place for her grandchildren to play can shift from "unthinkable, because I need to save those" to "my mind tells me I can't and I am still choosing to get rid of this because I care about my grandchildren." Because it has generally been difficult to treat, hoarding interventions require further exploration and study. More personalized, process-focused interventions such as ACT might be valuable as the field works to identify better methods to treat this difficult problem.

Body Dysmorphic Disorder

Body dysmorphic disorder is characterized by a preoccupation with imagined or slight defects in appearance (Phillips et al., 2006). This preoccupation can be related to multiple body areas, such as muscles, weight, hair, and face. Additionally, body dysmorphic disorder involves repetitive behaviors or mental acts in response to and in relation to concerns about physical appearance. Although the flaws in appearance are slight or unobservable to others, individuals with body dysmorphic disorder commonly report feeling ashamed of them and how excessively focused they are on their appearance (Phillips et al., 2006). Despite its relatively low research prominence, body dysmorphic disorder is somewhat common, affecting approximately 2 percent of adults in the United States at a given time (Veale et al., 2016). It is associated with poor quality of life and low levels of functioning among various domains, including occupational, educational, and social functioning, as well as life satisfaction (Phillips et al., 2006).

In theory, ACT appears to be well suited to treat body dysmorphic disorder. Although current research is very limited, body dysmorphic disorder has been associated with higher levels of experiential avoidance than the general population, and treatment has been shown to increase psychological flexibility for those diagnosed with the disorder (Linde et al., 2015; Wilson et al., 2014), indicating potential for ACT as a viable treatment. People experiencing body dysmorphia experience frequent, unwanted thoughts and often appear to be highly fused with thoughts related to their self-concept. Furthermore, these thoughts are often accompanied with a sense of urgency to check on or fix perceived imperfections. In a similar manner as other obsessive-compulsive and related disorders, processes related to fostering psychological flexibility have potential to enhance treatment. For example, learning to slow down in the presence of persistent thoughts and to make space between those thoughts and actions could help clients better engage in meaningful, values-consistent behaviors. Further research is sorely needed to examine these possibilities and assess the value of ACT as a treatment for body dysmorphic disorder.

Cognitive-Behavioral Therapy and Exposure and Response Prevention

Cognitive-behavioral therapy (CBT) is the most widely used treatment for obsessive-compulsive and related disorders. More specifically for OCD, the CBT intervention considered to be the first-line treatment is exposure and response prevention. Exposure consists of repeated, systematic confrontation with external and internal anxiety-provoking stimuli, usually with the help of a clinician (Berman et al., 2017). This confrontation usually takes place following the development of a fear hierarchy, which is a ranked list of the situations that are feared and/or avoided (Foa et al., 2012). In traditional exposure and response prevention, exposure starts at the lower end of the hierarchy and the client works their way up gradually as they become more comfortable confronting their fear (Foa et al., 2012). The cues utilized for this purpose can either be in vivo, meaning the stimuli are confronted in real life, or imagined. Following exposure, the client refrains from performing their safety behavior or ritual that would normally provide them with momentary relief. The clinician and client repeat this process, provoking the feared obsession using exposure and then preventing safety behaviors, until the client is able to habituate to the anxiety. The rationale behind this treatment is that when individuals engage in compulsions in order to avoid feeling anxiety or fear, a context is created wherein obsessive thoughts become more believable and thus more frightening, resulting in compulsive behavior becoming more likely in the presence of these thoughts. Because they do not allow themselves the opportunity to learn that their obsessions may be irrational or exaggerated, the cycle of OCD is maintained and the likelihood that their maladaptive behavior will continue increases. By instead helping the client learn to experience and tolerate anxiety, they discover that there is no need to engage in compulsions.

Exposure and response prevention has developed strong empirical support over the years and is regarded as an effective treatment for OCD. A review of cognitive-behavioral therapy treatment outcomes reported a posttreatment response rate of 43.3 percent for OCD and 35.6 percent at follow-up (Loerinc et al., 2015). Moreover, dropout rates are approximately 16 percent in exposure and response prevention treatment trials and while treatment refusal rates are unknown, it is likely a treatment barrier for some (Ong et al., 2016). While traditional exposure and response prevention has been one of psychology's biggest successes, the field continues to have substantial interest in how to improve the acceptability and effectiveness of the technology.

Acceptance and Commitment Therapy

From an ACT perspective, the presence of obsessions is not inherently problematic and treatment tends to be somewhat deemphasized (Smith et al., 2017). Instead, ACT tends to conceptualize individuals by how they respond to the presence of obsessions and how they function in their lives. To accomplish this, ACT utilizes its six core processes to build psychological flexibility and help individuals understand and interact with their inner experiences in a different way. By doing so, the hope is that people will orient toward their values and more effectively use the time and energy spent on compulsions and avoidance with meaningful action.

ACT conceptualizes OCD as the repetitive adherence to rigid rules that do not ultimately foster valued action and well-being. A rule is a verbal statement that specifies a cause-and-effect relationship, such as "if this happens, then this will happen." Although rule-governed behavior is often helpful, obeying rules in the context of OCD is time-consuming and harmful to an individual's well-being. Following these rules prevents individuals from having the opportunity to directly experience how the world realistically functions (Smith et al., 2017). Without the chance to learn from these experiences, their behavior continues to be based on their inaccurate and inflexible verbal rules. When treating obsessive-compulsive and related disorders, a major focus of ACT is to foster recognition of these rules and to practice intentionally disobeying them in values-consistent ways.

ACT places more emphasis on living according to personal values than on obsession reduction, and it also focuses more on acquiring new, flexible behavioral repertoires than on habituation to anxiety. Values in the context of ACT are instrumental in motivating individuals to behave in ways that allow them to live a more fulfilling life. When values are poorly understood or not easily identified, a major focus of treatment will be determining what areas of life are important and clarifying how obsessions may be interfering with living in ways that are consistent with those values. A focus on values might be particularly useful in addressing concerns with treatment dropout, motivation, and refusal, for values provide a strong rationale for being exposed to feared situations and resisting the urge to engage in safety behaviors or rituals. The "wallowing in the swamp" metaphor used in ACT aptly illustrates this concept, as the client is encouraged to confront and intentionally lean into their distressing inner experiences (i.e., walk through the swamp) in order to move toward their values that lie on the other side. Placing focus on moving toward valued actions over reducing anxiety can better motivate individuals to engage in exposure and response prevention despite the associated short-term distress, as they have an understanding of how the exercise can have a profound and beneficial impact on their lives in the long term.

A key feature of ACT is its approach to coping with internal experiences that emphasizes acceptance or willingness. Often, people enter therapy understandably seeking strategies and techniques to take control of, change, or eliminate their obsessive thoughts, urges, or other related inner experiences. Paradoxically, trying to control or reduce these inner experiences tends to increase their frequency, require significant effort, and at best provide only short-term relief. For this reason, it can be helpful to explore past attempts and strategies used to control inner experiences and to evaluate the long-term effectiveness of these strategies. Over time, people can begin to recognize that their efforts to control (e.g., compulsions, avoidance, suppression) have only led to long-term suffering, diminished quality of life, and overall worsening of their condition. They instead tend to focus on altering the relationship with these unwanted experiences rather than attempting to alter the experiences themselves. The goal of therapy then shifts from changing the presence of the obsessions or urges to changing the overt behaviors in the presence of unwanted experiences such that compulsions are reduced and valued action is increased.

Measures for ACT and Obsessive-Compulsive and Related Disorders

A critical variable of interest for ACT, regardless of the specific psychopathology, is psychological flexibility. A widely used measure of this construct for clinical and research purposes is the Acceptance and Action Questionnaire (AAQ-II; Bond et al., 2011). In addition to the original measure, which is used as a generic measure of psychological flexibility, domain-specific AAQs have been developed that are meant to assess psychological flexibility in the context of particular problem behaviors, including OCD, trichotillomania, hoarding, and body dysmorphia.

These specific measures appear to generally be more sensitive to detecting psychological flexibility in their respective domains (Ong et al., 2019). Multiple context-specific measures of psychological flexibility relevant to obsessive-compulsive and related disorders are available. When working with OCD, trichotillomania, or hoarding, these should be considered instead of, or in addition to, the AAQ-II.

The Acceptance and Action Questionnaire for Obsessions and Compulsions (AAQ-OC; Jacoby et al., 2018) measures psychological flexibility in response to unwanted intrusive thoughts. More specifically, it assesses willingness to experience these thoughts without attempting to control or eliminate them; the ability to distance oneself from their content; and valued engagement while in their presence. The measure was developed using a nonclinical, predominantly white, undergraduate sample. The 13-item questionnaire consists of two factors: Valued Action, which measures impairments with valued action in the presence of intrusive thoughts, and Willingness, which measures the acceptance/willingness of obsessions and attempts to control intrusions. The internal consistency of the AAQ-OC is good (α = 0.93, Valued Action: α = 0.92, Willingness: α = 0.82). It displays good convergent validity with moderate to strong correlations with measures of OC symptoms and cognitions (Dimensional Obsessive-Compulsive Scale, and the White Bear Suppression Inventory) and good discriminant validity with weak correlations with depression and social anxiety symptoms (Depression Anxiety and Stress Scale and the Brief Fear of Negative Evaluation Scale). Finally, the AAQ-OC demonstrated partial incremental validity, predicting responsibility for harm and unacceptable thoughts, but not contamination or symmetry obsessive-compulsive symptoms above and beyond the AAQ-II. A Persian version of the AAQ-OC has also been developed and has demonstrated good initial psychometric properties (Soltani et al., 2020).

The Acceptance and Action Questionnaire-Trichotillomania (AAQ-TTM) measures psychological flexibility in the context of urges to engage in hairpulling (Houghton et al., 2014). The measure was developed using a treatment-seeking sample of individuals with trichotillomania. The nine-item questionnaire consists of two factors: *Control*, which measures urges management strategies and attitudes toward urges, and *Interference*, which measures general functioning related to hairpulling. The internal consistency of the AAQ-TTM is satisfactory to good (α = 0.84, Control: α = 0.66, Interference: α = 0.90). It displays good convergent validity with moderate correlations with the AAQ-II and measures of hairpulling severity and focused pulling behavior (Massachusetts General Hospital Hairpulling Scale, Milwaukee Inventory of Subtypes of Trichotillomania-Adult Version [focused subscale], and the NIMH Trichotillomania Scale) and good discriminant validity with weak correlations with automatic pulling behavior (the Milwaukee Inventory of Subtypes of Trichotillomania [automatic subscale], which is consistent with the ACT theory of trichotillomania. Finally, the AAQ-TTM was more strongly correlated with symptoms of trichotillomania and less strongly correlated with general psychopathology than the AAQ-II. This finding suggests that the AAQ-TTM more effectively measures psychological flexibility related to trichotillomania-specific cognitions and affect.

The Acceptance and Action Questionnaire for Hoarding (AAQH) measures psychological flexibility in the context of hoarding behavior (Krafft et al., 2019). The measure was developed using a predominantly white, female, undergraduate sample with elevated hoarding symptoms. The 14-item questionnaire consists of two factors: *Saving*, which measures psychological flexibility related to discarding, and *Acquisition*, which is related to acquiring and possessing belongings. The internal consistency of the AAQH is adequate to good (α = 0.90, Saving: α = 0.89, Acquisition: α = 0.84). It displays good convergent and divergent validity with measures of psychological inflexibility, hoarding symptoms, symptoms of other psychological disorders, and life satisfaction. The AAQH does not appear to measure general distress or psychopathology and is more relevant to hoarding specific symptomatology. Furthermore, the AAQH demonstrated incremental validity, predicting additional variance in hoarding symptoms above and beyond the AAQ-II.

The Body Image Psychological Inflexibility Scale (BIPIS) measures body image disturbance and body dysmorphia (Callaghan et al., 2015). It is important to note that body dysmorphia symptomatology includes body preoccupations with diverse body areas other than obesity or weight-related distress. This means that measures like the Body Image Acceptance and Action Questionnaire and the Acceptance and Action Questionnaire for Weight Related Distress are less appropriate for measuring these types of problems. The measure was developed using three ethnically diverse undergraduate samples with a range of body image disturbance symptoms. The 16-item questionnaire consists of a single factor that measures psychological flexibility specific to body image disturbance. The BIPIS displays good internal consistency ($\alpha = 0.93$) and good convergent and divergent validity with measures of overall inflexibility, general psychological distress, body avoidance, and body image disturbance. The BIPIS has also demonstrated incremental validity, predicting body image disturbance above and beyond the AAQ-II. Finally, this measure has demonstrated good test–retest reliability over a one-month period ($r = .90$).

Empirical Support for ACT and Obsessive-Compulsive and Related Disorders

Obsessive-Compulsive Disorder

Of the obsessive-compulsive and related disorders, OCD has received the most research attention. Most early research intentionally excluded in-session exposure and response procedures from treatment protocols in order to examine the effects of ACT alone. These studies were composed of case studies and multiple baseline across participant designs (Armstrong et al., 2013; Barney et al., 2017; Dehlin et al., 2013; Izadi et al., 2012; Twohig et al., 2006a; Twohig et al., 2010b; Vakili et al., 2014). They demonstrated preliminary evidence of ACT as a standalone treatment for reducing OCD symptom severity across age ranges.

Three randomized controlled trials of ACT were also conducted with active control conditions that included the use of selective serotonin reuptake inhibitors (SSRIs), and progressive muscle relaxation. First, a randomized controlled trial in Iran of 75 adults with OCD compared ACT ($n = 25$), SSRI ($n = 25$), and combined ACT + SSRI ($n = 25$) groups and found significant large treatment effects for all groups through follow-up (Baghooli et al., 2014). However, OCD symptom reductions were greatest in the ACT group (within-group $d = 3.08$) and combination group (within-group $d = 3.30$), with no significant between-group difference. Second, another randomized controlled trial in Iran of 32 adults with OCD compared ACT ($n = 10$), SSRI ($n = 11$), and combined ACT + SSRI ($n = 11$) groups (Vakili et al., 2014). Large significant differences in OCD symptom reduction from pre- to posttreatment were demonstrated between the ACT versus SSRI ($d = 1.14$) and ACT + SSRI versus SSRI ($d = 1.28$) comparisons, both in ACT's favor. There were no significant differences between the ACT and ACT + SSRI groups. Third, a randomized controlled trial in the United States of 79 adults with OCD compared eight sessions ACT ($n = 41$) or progressive relaxation training (PRT; $n = 38$), with no in-session exposures (Twohig et al., 2010a). Participants in the ACT and PRT conditions showed significant reductions in OCD symptoms from pre- to posttreatment, with ACT demonstrating larger effects compared to PRT at posttreatment ($d = 0.77$) and 3-month follow-up ($d = 1.10$).

Two recent trials examined the efficacy of ACT for OCD by implementing it in a group format without in-session exposure exercises. The first trial examined the impact of group ACT on individuals at an optimal dose of SSRI, with continued SSRI management (Rohani et al., 2018). Both ACT + SSRI (n = 23) and SSRI (n =23) conditions demonstrated similar significant within-group reductions in self-reported OCD, depression, and rumination symptoms from pre- to posttreatment that were further improved at a 16-week follow-up (Cohen's *ds* for OCD = 2.19 and 1.90, respectively). However, improvements were significantly greater at a 16-week follow-up in the ACT + SSRI condition (between-group d = 1.53). The second trial concerning the impact of group ACT compared ACT + SSRI (n = 22), CBT + SSRI (n = 22), and SSRI only (n = 25) conditions for adolescents in Iran (Shabani et al., 2019). The ACT + SSRI and CBT + SSRI conditions demonstrated significant OCD symptom reductions at posttreatment (Hedges' g = 1.72 and 2.22, respectively) and 3-month follow-up (g = 1.04 and 1.07, respectively). Both conditions outperformed the SSRIs alone condition, which demonstrated small to medium effects at posttreatment (g = 0.25) and follow-up (g = 0.57). Of note, the study measured ACT-relevant processes of change and demonstrated significantly greater improvements in psychological flexibility, valued living, and mindfulness in the ACT + SSRI condition than the CBT + SSRI and SSRI conditions over the course of treatment and through follow-up. Significant within-group differences were found for the ACT + SSRI and CBT + SSRI conditions from pre- to posttreatment for psychological flexibility (g = 1.73 and 1.20, respectively), with the CBT + SSRI condition maintaining these improvements from posttreatment to follow-up and the ACT + SSRI condition making further significant gains over the same period (g = .66). The SSRI only condition demonstrated nonsignificant changes from pre- to posttreatment and small, significant improvement from posttreatment to follow-up (g = .69). Measures of valued living and mindfulness both saw significant improvement from pre- to posttreatment in the ACT-SSRI condition (*gs* = 1.33 and 1.17, respectively). At follow-up, these improvements continued for mindfulness (g = 1.08) and were maintained for valued living. Participants in the CBT + SSRI and SSRI only conditions reported nonsignificant results from pre- to posttreatment as well as from posttreatment to follow-up.

A recent, large randomized controlled trial of 58 participants with OCD incorporated ACT into traditional exposure and response prevention protocols in order examine whether ACT might enhance more traditional CBT methods and potentially increase the acceptability of, and adherence to, exposure (Twohig et al., 2018). The trial compared exposure and response prevention (ERP; n = 28) to exposure and response prevention plus ACT (ACT + ERP; n = 30). Both the ERP and ACT + ERP conditions demonstrated similarly large, significant reductions in OCD severity (g = 2.50 and 2.67, respectively) at posttreatment that were maintained at a 6-month follow-up. Moreover, psychological flexibility and obsessive beliefs process measures saw similar significant changes in both groups (ERP g = .62 and 1.09, respectively; ERP + ACT g = .66 and .73). The study underscored that ACT and exposure and response prevention share similar processes of change, requiring further research to examine differential effectiveness based on client characteristics. Further analysis found that comorbid anxiety, comorbid depression, and psychological inflexibility were clinically meaningful moderators of outcome in the ACT + ERP condition compared to the ERP only condition (Ong et al., 2018).

Of all the obsessive-compulsive and related disorders, OCD has received the most ACT-specific research attention. Overall, across seven single-subject designs and seven randomized trials, ACT alone or combined with more traditional CBT methods appears to be largely similar to gold standard exposure and response prevention. While more study is clearly needed,

ACT can generally be considered a strong treatment option for adolescents and adults when provided in individual or group formats.

Body-Focused Repetitive Behaviors (Trichotillomania and Excoriation Disorder)

Research supporting ACT for body-focused repetitive behaviors is modest but promising. An early ACT multiple baseline trial including five participants did not combine ACT with traditional habit-reversal or CBT techniques to treat excoriation (Twohig et al., 2006a). Results showed that symptoms were meaningfully reduced for all participants at posttreatment (66%, 95%, 96%, 97%, and 100% reductions in picking at posttreatment); however, these improvements were not fully maintained at follow-up (28%, 35%, 41%, 100%, *decreases* and a 42% *increase* in picking from pretreatment to follow-up). Four participants also demonstrated reductions in experiential avoidance (29 to 59% reductions), with treatment benefits being maintained at follow-up (15 to 63%, reductions).

Most other ACT trials incorporated traditional behavioral methods, namely, habit reversal training. These studies included three multiple baseline trials and three randomized controlled trials. The first trial was a multiple baseline design across six participants testing the feasibility of combining ACT and habit reversal training to treat adults with trichotillomania (Twohig & Woods, 2004). Four of the six participants demonstrated large reductions in hairpulling at posttreatment (67%, 67%, 70%, 100% reductions in severity scores) and three of those maintained treatment gains at a 3-month follow-up (59%, 73%, and 100% reductions in severity scores from pretreatment). A second trial, a small study (n = 5) of ACT plus habit reversal training, examined the effects of sequencing treatment components and found similar significant reductions in symptom severity for all participants at posttreatment (Flessner et al., 2008). A third multiple baseline study of five participants with trichotillomania found similar positive results for ACT plus habit reversal training (Crosby et al., 2012). The severity of hairpulling symptoms were reduced for all participants at posttreatment (28%, 36%, 37%, 43%, and 66% reductions). At a 3-month follow-up, two participants had maintained their gain, two had partially maintained gains, and one had returned to pretreatment levels of severity.

Randomized controlled trials further expanded the evidence for use of ACT for trichotillomania. The first was a trial of 25 participants with trichotillomania that compared ACT plus habit reversal training (n =12) to a waitlist control condition (n = 13; Woods et al., 2006). Sixty-six percent of participants in the treatment group demonstrated clinically significant reductions in hairpulling severity compared to 8 percent in the waitlist group. Moreover, participants in the ACT plus habit reversal condition demonstrated significant reductions in anxiety, depression, and psychological inflexibility. A second trial included 25 adults and adolescents with trichotillomania and compared ACT alone (n = 15) to a waitlist (n = 10; Lee et al., 2018a). Participants in the ACT condition demonstrated 77 percent decreases in self-reported daily hairs pulled and 24 percent decreases in psychological inflexibility compared to 10 percent and 2 percent decreases in the waitlist condition, respectively. A third trial included 22 adults with trichotillomania and tested the feasibility of providing ACT plus habit reversal training using telehealth (Lee et al., 2018b). Participants in the ACT plus habit reversal training condition demonstrated 39 percent reductions in hairpulling severity, on average. Sixty percent of participants achieved clinically significant reductions posttreatment, and 37 percent met the criteria for clinical improvement at a 3-month follow-up.

Of the body-focused repetitive behaviors, trichotillomania has received the vast majority of research attention. Because of the functional similarities of these problems, the research findings for trichotillomania likely generalize to excoriation disorder and other types of body-focused repetitive behaviors. In summary, it appears that ACT is a suitable treatment for body-focused repetitive behaviors, producing outcomes similar to traditional habit reversal training procedures alone. Further research is needed to further increase effectiveness and to better maintain treatment gains following treatment.

Hoarding Disorder

Despite its potential in the area, little research has been done on ACT for hoarding disorder. Theorized processes that might contribute to the maintenance of hoarding disorder are well suited to ACT, including overestimation of threat from emotions, anxiety sensitivity, distress intolerance, and intolerance of uncertainty, that are associated with hoarding (Oglesby et al., 2013; Timpano et al., 2009). Moreover, psychological flexibility appears to play a role in maintaining hoarding symptoms in clinical and nonclinical samples (Fernández de la Cruz et al., 2013) and could potentially mediate the relationship between distress and hoarding symptoms (Ong et al., 2018). More recently, Ong et al. (2020) found that acceptance training did not contribute to hoarding symptom reduction beyond a psychoeducation condition in a nonclinical sample of 47 college students with elevated hoarding symptoms.

To date, no randomized controlled clinical trials have examined ACT as a treatment for hoarding disorder; however, initial findings in single cases, single-subject designs, and findings from OCD trials that included hoarding show some promise. A single case presented with hoarding symptoms in a multiple baseline trial for OCD. Over the eight-session trial, the participants demonstrated significant hoarding symptom improvement that was maintained at a 3-month follow-up (Twohig et al., 2006b). In a recent multiple-baseline design, a 10-session protocol of ACT for hoarding disorder was tested (Ong et al., 2021). Six adults with hoarding disorder were placed in two multiple baseline designs. All participants reported a decrease in hoarding disorder, self-reported clutter, depression, and functional impairment. Using clinically significant change analyses, 60 percent of the sample showed reliable clinically significant change. Another OCD trial that compared ACT to progressive relaxation training included 79 participants with varying OCD symptomology (Twohig et al., 2010a). Of those participants, 25 (9 in the ACT group, 16 in the relaxation group) presented with hoarding symptoms. The authors did not break down treatment findings by symptom subtype. Yet their findings demonstrated significant improvement in the ACT condition compared to the relaxation condition at posttreatment ($d = 0.77$) and follow-up ($d = 0.62$), providing some evidence for ACT's potential to help individuals with hoarding as well as a direction for future research.

Overall, any type of treatment studies for hoarding in general are severely lacking, and the evidence for ACT as a treatment for hoarding disorder is quite limited. While in theory, ACT appears to be a potentially useful treatment for hoarding, further study is needed to understand the role it might have in improving this class of behaviors.

Body Dysmorphic Disorder

Like hoarding disorder, body dysmorphic disorder has received limited research attention in general and with regard to ACT. Similarly, ACT appears to conceptually be a good fit for body dysmorphic disorder, for it has been shown to be associated with experiential avoidance compared to healthy controls (Wilson et al., 2014). Two studies have provided preliminary evidence for ACT as a viable treatment of body dysmorphic disorder. First, a trial of 12-week, group, acceptance-based exposure therapy for 21 participants who met criteria for body dysmorphic disorder demonstrated promising results (Linde et al., 2015). At posttreatment, 68 percent of participants showed clinically significant improvement in body dysmorphic symptoms ($d = 1.93$) as well as significant improvements in psychological flexibility and quality of life, with treatment gains being maintained at a 6-month follow-up. Second, a recent multiple baseline trial across six participants meeting the criteria for body dysmorphic disorder found that ACT significantly reduced worry and interpersonal problems, and improved quality of life in all participants (Dehbaneh, 2018). From pretreatment through a 3-month follow-up, on average, worry decreased by 55.5 percent, interpersonal problems decreased by 59.7 percent, and physical, psychological, social, and environmental quality of life domains increased by 55.1, 50.4, 43.1, and 56.9 percent, respectively. Unfortunately, body dysmorphic symptom data were not gathered, but the results indicate overall improvement. Although the existing evidence for ACT is promising, further research is needed in this area.

Traditional CBT Technology from an ACT Perspective

While built on a theoretical foundation that differs from traditional cognitive-behavioral therapies, ACT is still comfortably at home under the broad umbrella of CBT. From its functional contextual perspective, ACT can harness proven cognitive-behavioral methods while reframing their ultimate goals to better align with fostering psychological flexibility and valued action. The following are examples of treatment technology applicable to obsessive-compulsive and related disorders that combine traditional cognitive behavioral techniques with ACT theory and processes.

Exposure

Exposure is a foundational treatment technology for anxiety and obsessive-compulsive and related problems. Exposure to distress-provoking stimuli—no matter the content—without the use of compulsions, reassurance, safety behaviors, or other distress-reducing behaviors fosters new learning through the development of new relations of distressing stimuli in novel contexts. Traditional models of exposure have emphasized habituation of fear or distress as the primary goal of treatment. However, newer conceptualizations of the process of exposure, such as inhibitory learning and acceptance-based models like ACT, have deemphasized fear reduction in favor of new learning development and valued action in the midst of distressing or fearful situations (Craske et al., 2014; Twohig et al., 2015). Due to this shift in emphasis, exposures from an ACT perspective do not place client focus on the distress in a traditional manner. Rating scales such as subjective units of distress (SUDS) are rarely used in ACT because they tend to focus the client on the *amount* of distress rather than on its *quality and experience*. Focusing on the quantity can have the implicit influence of defining a level of distress that might be "too much" for the client to handle and can show that it is important to monitor and control their distress level rather than simply make space for distress as it naturally ebbs and flows. From this perspective, there is nothing about obsessions that is inherently problematic; rather, it is how one relates and responds to obsessions that truly matters.

For example, during exposure to a feared stimulus, the client will be asked to notice and describe the internal experiences that their mind labels as distress, observing them in a spirit of curiosity. These descriptions of "distress" or "anxiety" would include specific somatic features (e.g., increased heart rate, neck tension, clammy hands) and cognitions (e.g., "I am scared," "this is too much," "I am going to die"). As the client becomes more skilled at observing their internal experiences, they can go one step further and practice observing the process of observing. Eventually, they might learn to say something like, "I am noticing myself feel my heart rate increasing and the muscles in my neck tightening. I am having the thought 'I am scared and going to die.' My mind labels these experiences 'anxiety'." This technique serves as a way for clients to learn new ways of relating to their fear and distress that can empower valued action even when experiencing distress (i.e., psychological flexibility). These skills can then be further generalized and expanded upon through practice in novel contexts with a variety of feared stimuli.

The deemphasis of subjective ratings of distress naturally changes the process of creating a fear hierarchy. Traditionally, fear hierarchies include a list of feared stimuli and situations that would provoke fear arranged in order of perceived difficulty/distress. In ACT, fear hierarchies tend to be eschewed in favor of a list of avoided behaviors and situations that relate to the client's values. For example, instead of asking, "what are you afraid of?" a therapist might ask, "what are you missing out on that is important to you?" and "what gets in the way of living the kind of life you want to live?" Thus, the fear hierarchy becomes a sort of valued living hierarchy—a list of meaningful actions that, in order to be achieved, will require contact with feared stimuli.

We can illustrate this difference using the classic "passengers on the bus" metaphor in which internal experiences are conceptualized as passengers on a bus and who are often unruly, obnoxious, or downright frightening. You, the driver, are in charge of choosing the destination and can easily fall into the trap of being persuaded or bullied by the passengers to choose their preferred destinations instead. From a traditional CBT exposure and response prevention perspective, your fear hierarchy would consist of a list of specific passengers that you would confront in order to learn that they are not as frightening as you once perceived. While this approach can certainly be helpful, from an ACT perspective, it emphasizes the passengers in favor of the destination. Essentially, traditional exposure and response prevention can lead to an expectation that passengers must be taken care of before driving can fully occur; thus, you may spend more time being pulled over fighting passengers than actually driving. In ACT, the hierarchy would consist of a list of destinations where you would like to drive the bus and emphasize the act of driving, with or without unwanted passengers. Ultimately, both methods will involve driving practice and learning to cope with passengers; however, ACT emphasizes driving and movement toward meaningful action first and foremost.

This is not to say that ACT deemphasizes exposure as a treatment technology. In fact, exposure can be thought of as a core technique in the pursuit of fostering greater psychological flexibility. What better way could there be to develop psychological flexibility—the ability to openly and willingly make space for difficult internal experiences while intentionally engaging in valued actions? From an ACT perspective, exposure is one of the best tools available to teach the behavior of psychological flexibility.

Habit Reversal Training

Habit reversal training is a behavioral procedure commonly used to treat habitual or repetitive problem behaviors. It has received considerable research support and is highly applicable to body-focused repetitive behaviors such as trichotillomania, excoriation, or any other problem habitual behavior (Azrin & Nunn, 1973). Three components are generally included in habit reversal training procedures: awareness training, competing response training, and social support training (Azrin & Nunn, 1973). ACT can play a role in enhancing and potentially increasing acceptability and adherence to these procedures that, though simple in concept, can be difficult for individuals to implement effectively.

Habit reversal training was designed to target overt problem behaviors. In its basic form, it can fail to account for and target the difficult internal states that occur when using competing responses. Researchers have long been aware of this shortcoming and have subsequently supplemented habit reversal training and competing responses with cognitive-behavioral approaches intended to target these internal states. This supplement has included traditional cognitive-behavioral therapy (Lerner et al., 1998), dialectical behavior therapy (Keuthen et al.,

2012), metacognitive therapy (Shareh, 2017), and ACT (Twohig & Woods, 2004). Of these therapies, ACT has received the most research attention, including a habit reversal training plus ACT treatment manual that has demonstrated effectiveness in multiple trials (Woods & Twohig, 2008). The awareness training and competing response training components of habit reversal training are especially amenable to being built upon and enhanced by ACT.

Awareness Training

Awareness training is a foundational procedure for treating unwanted repetitive behaviors because they are so often automatically maintained and occur outside of one's awareness. The training involves recollection and in-the-moment practice to recognize contexts in which the problem behavior occurs. This training then allows for the employment of interventions to reduce the behavior. People often struggle to recognize their own problem behavior in the moment, let alone identify their internal antecedent experiences that lead to the behavior. ACT's present moment awareness process can enhance awareness training with exercises to develop these skills. Conceptualizing present moment awareness as a behavior—a skill to be learned—can empower people who often feel overwhelmed when asked to notice seemingly illusory experiences. Practicing present moment awareness in contexts where problem behavior occurs can enhance the exercise. This practice can be done by having someone verbalize internal experiences while touching their hair or skin, while in front of a mirror, or while sitting in a chair where the behavior often occurs. Awareness of these experiences is paramount to successful treatment and can take time. However, the insight gained from this newly learned behavior can enhance the creative hopelessness process and help people better recognize the function of their pulling behaviors as short-term attempts to control unwanted internal experiences.

Competing Response Training

Competing response training involves the replacement of a problem behavior with another simple behavior such as clenching fists or toes. The new competing response may be designed to be incompatible with the problem behavior, although it does not necessarily have to be (Woods et al., 1999). People are instructed to use their competing response anytime they notice an urge to engage in the problem behavior or have caught themselves already engaging in the behavior, thus eliminating or reducing the frequency of the problem behavior. At first glance, one might think the approach to be overly simplistic or even patronizing, similar to telling someone to "just stop worrying and think of something else." However, intentionally exercising and building a new behavioral repertoire in response to longstanding internal experiences can lead to meaningful behavioral change. Developing this skill can be very difficult though, when stressors, anxieties, and urges persist and even worsen as one engages in competing responses. This makes adherence and buy-in difficult for many.

When supplemented with ACT, competing response training can be reframed from tolerance and endurance to openness and willingness; that is, from "control your urges, push through the discomfort" to "let's get to know your urges a bit better. What if you invited them to sit with you for a while?" This shift in perspective is similar to an ACT approach to exposures. It fosters the development of new relationships with old internal experiences. Aligning the use of competing responses with values can further enhance their meaning and purpose. Over time relationships with urges, obsessions, or anxiety can shift from being driven by fear to being a reminder of goals and purpose. From a relational frame theory perspective, this shift is a result of a transformation of stimulus function. Internal stimuli that once triggered fear, avoidance, and problem behaviors can instead remind one of their values and motivate them to take action—in this case, in the form of a competing response—toward actions that will ultimately reduce suffering and improve quality of life.

Future Directions

Behaviors associated with obsessive-compulsive and related disorders are generally maintained by a verbal system that supports actions completed to regulate internal experiences. Problem behaviors that include avoidance, compulsions, or other repetitive behaviors pay an ostensibly small fee for what turns out to be only short-term relief from unwanted obsessions, urges, or anxieties. The results are significant; long-term suffering and reduction in meaningful behavior and quality of life. ACT processes are poised to help people make the shift from short-term relief at great cost to long-term purpose and meaning for the price of open and willing contact with all of their human experience. ACT has potential to reframe and ease the burden of exposure and other difficult behavioral exercises—and it could help shift the treatment perspective from symptom reduction to valued living and engagement. The promise of ACT for treating these problem behaviors is indeed significant; however, much empirical work is needed to claim these promises.

With regard to hoarding disorder and body dysmorphic disorder, research support is lacking generally for psychotherapies as a whole and specifically for ACT. These topics would benefit from any well-implemented ACT research, including studies focused on descriptive associations, treatment outcomes, and processes of change. Fear of discarding items and obsessive thoughts about one's body image appear to have, at the very least, some association with psychological inflexibility and would likely benefit from ACT's treatment model. Furthermore, these problems tend to be somewhat treatment resistant and difficult to adequately target. Thus, a process-focused, individualized, contextually sensitive approach like ACT should be further considered and researched to further our understanding and treatment of these problem behaviors.

In the areas of OCD and body-focused repetitive behaviors, the research provides a compelling argument for the use of ACT with regard to overall treatment outcome. Multiple randomized controlled trials on these topics have demonstrated ACT's efficacy with regard to reducing symptoms and enhancing psychological flexibility. However, outside of a couple of instances, little is known about differences in treatment processes between ACT and traditional cognitive-behavioral therapy. What processes are leading to changes, and for whom are these changes most significant? Moreover, do some people or certain symptom presentations respond better to ACT or to specific treatment processes? Greater emphasis is now needed on processes of change, potential moderators of treatment outcome, and personalized treatment tailored to ideographic symptom presentations. Furthermore, while perhaps pragmatically necessary in order to receive research funding and recognition in the broader psychological community, ACT research on obsessive-compulsive and related disorders has largely focused on treatment outcome vis-à-vis symptom reduction. It is time for ACT researchers to make more deliberate efforts to target and measure changes in outcome that are theoretically consistent with the treatment model. This effort might include measures of functioning, behavioral outcome, quality of life, more specific measures of psychological flexibility, or personalized measures of psychological flexibility that are contextually sensitive, such as the Personalized Psychological Flexibility Index (Kashdan et al., 2020).

The future of process-based treatments like ACT for obsessive-compulsive and related disorders is bright. Obsessions, urges, and similar unwanted internal experiences compel a call to fight—a charge to control or solve undesired human experiences that ultimately only leads to despair and loss. ACT has demonstrated broad efficacy in these areas, and much important work remains to be done to further reduce the suffering caused by these problems and, more importantly, to increase meaning and purpose in life that has been lost due to the fight.

References

Abramowitz, J. S. (2006). The psychological treatment of obsessive-compulsive disorder. *Canadian Journal of Psychiatry, 51*(7), 10.

American Psychiatric Association. (2013). *Diagnostic and statistical manual of mental disorders* (5th ed.). https://doi.org/10.1176/appi.books.9780890425596

Armstrong, A. B., Morrison, K. L., & Twohig, M. P. (2013). A preliminary investigation of acceptance and commitment therapy for adolescent obsessive-compulsive disorder. *Journal of Cognitive Psychotherapy, 27*(2), 175–190. https://doi.org/10.1891/0889-8391.27.2.175

Azrin, N. H., & Nunn, R. G. (1973). Habit-reversal: A method of eliminating nervous habits and tics. *Behaviour Research and Therapy, 11*(4), 619–628. https://doi.org/10.1016/0005-7967(73)90119-8

Baghooli, H., Dolatshahi, B., Mohammadkhani, P., Moshtagh, N., & Naziri, G. (2014). Effectiveness of acceptance and commitment therapy in reduction of severity symptoms of patients with obsessive-compulsive disorder. *Advances in Environmental Biology*, 2519–2525. https://doi.org/10.17795/ijpbs845

Barney, J. Y., Field, C. E., Morrison, K. L., & Twohig, M. P. (2017). Treatment of pediatric obsessive compulsive disorder utilizing parent-facilitated acceptance and commitment therapy: Act for pediatric OCD. *Psychology in the Schools, 54*(1), 88–100. https://doi.org/10.1002/pits.21984

Berman, N. C., Schwartz, R., & Park, J. (2017). Psychological models and treatments of OCD for adults. In J. S. Abramowitz, D. McKay, & E. A. Storch (Eds.), *The Wiley handbook of Obsessive Compulsive Disorders* (1st ed., pp. 223–243). John Wiley. https://doi.org/10.1002/9781118890233.ch12

Bond, F. W., Hayes, S. C., Baer, R. A., Carpenter, K. M., Guenole, N., Orcutt, H. K., Waltz, T., & Zettle, R. D. (2011). Preliminary psychometric properties of the Acceptance and Action Questionnaire-II: A revised measure of psychological inflexibility and experiential avoidance. *Behavior Therapy, 42*(4), 676–688. https://doi.org/10.1016/j.beth.2011.03.007

Callaghan, G. M., Duenas, J. A., Nadeau, S. E., Darrow, S. M., Van der Merwe, J., & Misko, J. (2012). An empirical model of body image disturbance using behavioral principles found in functional analytic psychotherapy and acceptance and commitment therapy. *International Journal of Behavioral Consultation and Therapy, 7*(2–3), 16–24. https://doi.org/10.1037/h0100932

Callaghan, Glenn M., Sandoz, E. K., Darrow, S. M., & Feeney, T. K. (2015). The Body Image Psychological Inflexibility Scale: Development and psychometric properties. *Psychiatry Research, 226*(1), 45–52. https://doi.org/10.1016/j.psychres.2014.11.039

Cherian, A. V., Narayanaswamy, J. C., Srinivasaraju, R., Viswanath, B., Math, S. B., Kandavel, T., & Reddy, Y. C. J. (2012). Does insight have specific correlation with symptom dimensions in OCD? *Journal of Affective Disorders, 138*(3), 352–359. https://doi.org/10.1016/j.jad.2012.01.017

Craske, M. G., Treanor, M., Conway, C. C., Zbozinek, T., & Vervliet, B. (2014). Maximizing exposure therapy: An inhibitory learning approach. *Behaviour Research and Therapy, 58*, 10–23. https://doi.org/10.1016/j.brat.2014.04.006

Crosby, J. M., Dehlin, J. P., Mitchell, P. R., & Twohig, M. P. (2012). Acceptance and commitment therapy and habit reversal training for the treatment of trichotillomania. *Cognitive and Behavioral Practice, 19*(4), 595–605. https://doi.org/10.1016/j.cbpra.2012.02.002

Dehbaneh, M. A. (2018). Effectiveness of acceptance and commitment therapy in improving interpersonal problems, quality of life, and worry in patients with body dysmorphic disorder. *Electronic Journal of General Medicine, 16*(1), em105. https://doi.org/10.29333/ejgm/93468

Dehlin, J. P., Morrison, K. L., & Twohig, M. P. (2013). Acceptance and commitment therapy as a treatment for scrupulosity in obsessive compulsive disorder. *Behavior Modification, 37*(3), 409–430. https://doi.org/10.1177/0145445512475134

Fernández de la Cruz, L., Landau, D., Iervolino, A. C., Santo, S., Pertusa, A., Singh, S., & Mataix-Cols, D. (2013). Experiential avoidance and emotion regulation difficulties in hoarding disorder. *Journal of Anxiety Disorders, 27*(2), 204–209. https://doi.org/10.1016/j.janxdis.2013.01.004

Flessner, C. A., Busch, A. M., Heideman, P. W., & Woods, D. W. (2008). Acceptance-enhanced behavior therapy (AEBT) for trichotillomania and chronic skin picking: Exploring the effects of component sequencing. *Behavior Modification, 32*(5), 579–594. https://doi.org/10.1177/0145445507313800

Foa, E. B., Yadin, E., & Lichner, T. K. (2012). *Exposure and response (ritual) prevention for obsessive compulsive disorder: Therapist guide.* Oxford University Press.

Frost, R. O., Tolin, D. F., & Maltby, N. (2010). Insight-related challenges in the treatment of hoarding. *Cognitive and Behavioral Practice, 17*(4), 404–413.

Grant, J. E., Dougherty, D. D., & Chamberlain, S. R. (2020). Prevalence, gender correlates, and co-morbidity of trichotillomania. *Psychiatry Research, 288*, 112948.

Houghton, D. C., Compton, S. N., Twohig, M. P., Saunders, S. M., Franklin, M. E., Neal-Barnett, A. M., Ely, L., Capriotti, M. R., & Woods, D. W. (2014). Measuring the role of psychological inflexibility in trichotillomania. *Psychiatry Research, 220*(1–2), 356–361. https://doi.org/10.1016/j.psychres.2014.08.003

Izadi, R., Asgari, K., Neshatdust, H., & Abedi, M. R. (2012). The effect of acceptance and commitment therapy on the frequency and severity of symptoms of obsessive compulsive disorder. *Zahedan Journal of Research in Medical Sciences, 14*(10), 107–112.

Jacoby, R. J., Abramowitz, J. S., Buchholz, J., Reuman, L., & Blakey, S. M. (2018). Experiential avoidance in the context of obsessions: Development and validation of the Acceptance and Action Questionnaire for Obsessions and Compulsions. *Journal of Obsessive-Compulsive and Related Disorders, 19*, 34–43. https://doi.org/10.1016/j.jocrd.2018.07.003

Kashdan, T. B., Disabato, D. J., Goodman, F. R., Doorley, J. D., & McKnight, P. E. (2020). Understanding psychological flexibility: A multimethod exploration of pursuing valued goals despite the presence of distress. *Psychological Assessment, 32*(9), 829.

Keuthen, N. J., Rothbaum, B. O., Fama, J., Altenburger, E., Falkenstein, M. J., Sprich, S. E., Kearns, M., Meunier, S., Jenike, M. A., & Welch, S. S. (2012). DBT-enhanced cognitive-behavioral treatment for trichotillomania: A randomized controlled trial. *Journal of Behavioral Addictions, 1*(3), 106–114.

Krafft, J., Ong, C. W., Twohig, M. P., & Levin, M. E. (2019). Assessing psychological inflexibility in hoarding: The Acceptance and Action Questionnaire for Hoarding (AAQH). *Journal of Contextual Behavioral Science, 12*, 234–242. https://doi.org/10.1016/j.jcbs.2018.08.003

Lee, E. B., Haeger, J. A., Levin, M. E., Ong, C. W., & Twohig, M. P. (2018b). Telepsychotherapy for trichotillomania: A randomized controlled trial of ACT enhanced behavior therapy. *Journal of Obsessive-Compulsive and Related Disorders, 18*, 106–115. https://doi.org/10.1016/j.jocrd.2018.04.003

Lee, E. B., Homan, K. J., Morrison, K. L., Ong, C. W., Levin, M. E., & Twohig, M. P. (2018a). Acceptance and commitment therapy for trichotillomania: A randomized controlled trial of adults and adolescents. *Behavior Modification, 44*(1), 70–91.

Lerner, J., Franklin, M. E., Meadows, E. A., Hembree, E., & Foa, E. B. (1998). Effectiveness of a cognitive behavioral treatment program for trichotillomania: An uncontrolled evaluation. *Behavior Therapy, 29*(1), 157–171. https://doi.org/10.1016/S0005-7894(98)80036-1

Linde, J., Rück, C., Bjureberg, J., Ivanov, V. Z., Djurfeldt, D. R., & Ramnerö, J. (2015). Acceptance-based exposure therapy for body dysmorphic disorder: A pilot study. *Behavior Therapy, 46*(4), 423–431. https://doi.org/10.1016/j.beth.2015.05.002

Loerinc, A. G., Meuret, A. E., Twohig, M. P., Rosenfield, D., Bluett, E. J., & Craske, M. G. (2015). Response rates for CBT for anxiety disorders: Need for standardized criteria. *Clinical Psychology Review, 42*, 72–82. https://doi.org/10.1016/j.cpr.2015.08.004

Mataix-Cols, D., Marks, I. M., Greist, J. H., Kobak, K. A., & Baer, L. (2002). Obsessive-compulsive symptom dimensions as predictors of compliance with and response to behaviour therapy: results from a controlled trial. *Psychotherapy and Psychosomatics, 71*(5), 255–262. https://doi.org/10.1159/000064812

Norberg, M. M., Calamari, J. E., Cohen, R. J., & Riemann, B. C. (2008). Quality of life in obsessive-compulsive disorder: An evaluation of impairment and a preliminary analysis of the ameliorating effects of treatment. *Depression and Anxiety, 25*(3), 248–259. https://doi.org/10.1002/da.20298

Oglesby, M. E., Medley, A. N., Norr, A. M., Capron, D. W., Korte, K. J., & Schmidt, N. B. (2013). Intolerance of uncertainty as a vulnerability factor for hoarding behaviors. *Journal of Affective Disorders, 145*(2), 227–231. https://doi.org/10.1016/j.jad.2012.08.003

Ong, C. W., Krafft, J., Levin, M. E., & Twohig, M. P. (2018). An examination of the role of psychological inflexibility in hoarding using multiple mediator models. *Journal of Cognitive Psychotherapy, 32*(2), 97–111. https://doi.org/10.1891/0889-8391.32.2.97

Ong, C. W., Krafft, J., Panoussi, F., Petersen, J. M., Levin, M. E., & Twohig, M. P. (2021). In-person and online-delivered acceptance and commitment therapy for hoarding disorder: A multiple baseline study. *Journal of Contextual Behavioral Science, 20*, 108–117.

Ong, Clarissa W., Clyde, J. W., Bluett, E. J., Levin, M. E., & Twohig, M. P. (2016). Dropout rates in exposure with response prevention for obsessive-compulsive disorder: What do the data really say? *Journal of Anxiety Disorders, 40*, 8–17. https://doi.org/10.1016/j.janxdis.2016.03.006

Ong, Clarissa W., Krafft, J., Levin, M. E., & Twohig, M. P. (2020). Comparing effects of acceptance training and psychoeducation on hoarding symptoms. *Journal of Obsessive-Compulsive and Related Disorders, 25*, 100521. https://doi.org/10.1016/j.jocrd.2020.100521

Ong, Clarissa W., Lee, E. B., Levin, M. E., & Twohig, M. P. (2019). A review of AAQ variants and other context-specific measures of psychological flexibility. *Journal of Contextual Behavioral Science, 12,* 329–346. https://doi.org/10.1016/j.jcbs.2019.02.007

Phillips, K. A., Menard, W., Fay, C., & Pagano, M. E. (2006). Psychosocial functioning and quality of life in body dysmorphic disorder. *Comprehensive Psychiatry, 46*(4), 254–260.

Postlethwaite, A., Kellett, S., & Mataix-Cols, D. (2019). Prevalence of hoarding disorder: A systematic review and meta-analysis. *Journal of Affective Disorders, 256,* 309–316.

Rohani, F., Rasouli-Azad, M., Twohig, M. P., Ghoreishi, F. S., Lee, E. B., & Akbari, H. (2018). Preliminary test of group acceptance and commitment therapy on obsessive-compulsive disorder for patients on optimal dose of selective serotonin reuptake inhibitors. *Journal of Obsessive-Compulsive and Related Disorders, 16,* 8–13. https://doi.org/10.1016/j.jocrd.2017.10.002

Ruscio, A. M., Stein, D. J., Chiu, W. T., & Kessler, R. C. (2010). The epidemiology of obsessive-compulsive disorder in the National Comorbidity Survey Replication. *Molecular Psychiatry, 15*(1), 53–63. https://doi.org/10.1038/mp.2008.94

Shabani, M. J., Mohsenabadi, H., Omidi, A., Lee, E. B., Twohig, M. P., Ahmadvand, A., & Zanjani, Z. (2019). An Iranian study of group acceptance and commitment therapy versus group cognitive behavioral therapy for adolescents with obsessive-compulsive disorder on an optimal dose of selective serotonin reuptake inhibitors. *Journal of Obsessive-Compulsive and Related Disorders, 22,* 100440. https://doi.org/10.1016/j.jocrd.2019.04.003

Shareh, H. (2017). A preliminary investigation of metacognitive therapy and habit reversal as a treatment for trichotillomania. *Behavioural and Cognitive Psychotherapy, 46*(1), 1–20. https://doi.org/10.1017/S1352465817000546

Smith, B. M., Bluett, E. J., Lee, E. B., & Twohig, M. P. (2017). Acceptance and commitment therapy for OCD. In J. S. Abramowitz, D. McKay, & E. A. Storch (Eds.), *The Wiley handbook of obsessive compulsive disorders* (1st ed., pp. 596–613). John Wiley. https://doi.org/10.1002/9781118890233.ch33

Soltani, E., Ghanizadeh, A., Dastgheib, S. A., Wong, Q. J. J., & Jaafari, N. (2020). Psychometric properties of the Persian version of the acceptance and Action Questionnaire for obsessions and compulsions (AAQ-OC). *Journal of Obsessive-Compulsive and Related Disorders, 27,* 100582. https://doi.org/10.1016/j.jocrd.2020.100582

Steketee, G., & Frost, R. O. (2003). Compulsive hoarding: Current status of the research. *Clinical Psychology Review, 23*(7), 905–927. https://doi.org/10.1016/j.cpr.2003.08.002

Subramaniam, M., Soh, P., Vaingankar, J. A., Picco, L., & Chong, S. A. (2013). Quality of life in obsessive-compulsive disorder: Impact of the disorder and of treatment. *CNS Drugs, 27*(5), 367–383. https://doi.org/10.1007/s40263-013-0056-z

Timpano, K. R., Buckner, J. D., Richey, J. A., Murphy, D. L., & Schmidt, N. B. (2009). Exploration of anxiety sensitivity and distress tolerance as vulnerability factors for hoarding behaviors. *Depression and Anxiety, 26*(4), 343–353. https://doi.org/10.1002/da.20469

Twohig, M. P., Abramowitz, J. S., Bluett, E. J., Fabricant, L. E., Jacoby, R. J., Morrison, K. L., Reuman, L., & Smith, B. M. (2015). Exposure therapy for OCD from an acceptance and commitment therapy (ACT) framework. *Journal of Obsessive-Compulsive and Related Disorders, 6,* 167–173. https://doi.org/10.1016/j.jocrd.2014.12.007

Twohig, M. P., Abramowitz, J. S., Smith, B. M., Fabricant, L. E., Jacoby, R. J., Morrison, K. L., Bluett, E. J., Reuman, L., Blakey, S. M., & Lederman, T. (2018). Adding acceptance and commitment therapy to exposure and response prevention for obsessive-compulsive disorder: A randomized controlled trial. *Behaviour Research and Therapy, 108,* 1–9.

Twohig, M. P., Hayes, S. C., & Masuda, A. (2006a). A preliminary investigation of acceptance and commitment therapy as a treatment for chronic skin picking. *Behaviour Research and Therapy, 44*(10), 1513–1522. https://doi.org/10.1016/j.brat.2005.10.002

Twohig, M. P., Hayes, S. C., & Masuda, A. (2006b). Increasing willingness to experience obsessions: Acceptance and commitment therapy as a treatment for obsessive-compulsive disorder. *Behavior Therapy, 37*(1), 3–13. https://doi.org/10.1016/j.beth.2005.02.001

Twohig, M. P., Hayes, S. C., Plumb, J. C., Pruitt, L. D., Collins, A. B., Hazlett-Stevens, H., & Woidneck, M. R. (2010a). A randomized clinical trial of acceptance and commitment therapy versus progressive relaxation training for obsessive-compulsive disorder. *Journal of Consulting and Clinical Psychology, 78*(5), 705–716. https://doi.org/10.1037/a0020508

Twohig, M. P., Whittal, M. L., Cox, J. M., & Gunter, R. (2010b). An initial investigation into the processes of change in ACT, CT, and ERP for OCD. *International Journal of Behavioral Consultation and Therapy, 6*(1), 67–83. https://doi.org/10.1037/h0100898

Twohig, M. P., & Woods, D. W. (2004). A preliminary investigation of acceptance and commitment therapy and habit reversal as a treatment for trichotillomania. *Behavior Therapy, 35*(4), 803–820. https://doi.org/10.1016/S0005-7894(04)80021-2

Vakili, Y., Gharraee, B., Habibi, M., Lavasani, F., & Rasoolian, M. (2014). The comparison of acceptance and commitment therapy with selective serotonin reuptake inhibitors in the treatment of obsessive-compulsive disorder. *Zahedan Journal of Research in Medical Sciences, 16*, 10–14. https://doi.org/10.17795/ijpbs845

Veale, D., Gledhill, L. J., Christodoulou, P., & Hodsoll, J. (2016). Body dysmorphic disorder in different settings: A systematic review and estimated weighted prevalence. *Body Image, 18*, 168–186.

Wheaton, M. G., Abramowitz, J. S., Franklin, J. C., Berman, N. C., & Fabricant, L. E. (2011). Experiential avoidance and saving cognitions in the prediction of hoarding symptoms. *Cognitive Therapy and Research, 35*(6), 511–516. https://doi.org/10.1007/s10608-010-9338-7

Wilson, A. C., Wilhelm, S., & Hartmann, A. S. (2014). Experiential avoidance in body dysmorphic disorder. *Body Image, 11*(4), 380–383. https://doi.org/10.1016/j.bodyim.2014.06.006

Woods, D. W., Murray, L. K., Fuqua, R. W., Seif, T. A., Boyer, L. J., & Siah, A. (1999). Comparing the effectiveness of similar and dissimilar competing responses in evaluating the habit reversal treatment for oral–digital habits in children. *Journal of Behavior Therapy and Experimental Psychiatry, 30*(4), 289–300. https://doi.org/10.1901/jaba.2001.34-517

Woods, D. W., & Twohig, M. P. (2008). *Trichotillomania: An ACT-enhanced behavior therapy approach therapist guide.* Oxford University Press.

Woods, D. W., Wetterneck, C. T., & Flessner, C. A. (2006). A controlled evaluation of acceptance and commitment therapy plus habit reversal for trichotillomania. *Behaviour Research and Therapy, 44*(5), 639–656. https://doi.org/10.1016/j.brat.2005.05.006

CHAPTER 17

ACT for Eating Disorders

Adrienne Juarascio, Paakhi Srivastava, Christina R. Felonis, *and* Olivia B. Wons

Abstract
Existing cognitive and behavioral treatments for eating disorders leave substantial room for improvement, with recent systematic reviews and meta-analyses finding that 40–50 percent of patients with binge-eating disorder and nearly 70 percent of patients with bulimia nervosa remain at least partially symptomatic after a full course of cognitive-behavioral therapy (CBT). In an effort to improve outcomes, a growing number of researchers have begun to evaluate the use of mindfulness and acceptance-based behavioral treatments such as acceptance and commitment therapy (ACT) for this population. Cross-sectional and longitudinal research supports the theory that ACT processes such as experiential avoidance, cognitive fusion, and low-values clarity commonly occur within eating disorder populations, which suggests that treatment approaches that target these processes could be beneficial. Although the research on ACT and ACT-informed treatments for eating disorders remains nascent, preliminary evidence supports the potential efficacy of this treatment approach and suggests that ACT may be facilitating treatment outcomes through its hypothesized mechanisms. This article reviews the existing evidence of ACT and ACT-informed treatments for eating disorders and discusses future directions for research.

Key Words: eating disorders, binge-eating, bulimia nervosa, anorexia nervosa, loss of control eating

Clinical Significance of Eating Disorders

Eating disorders (EDs) are considered critical public health issues and are associated with significant negative physical and psychosocial consequences (APA, 2000; Hudson, Hiripi, Pope, & Kessler, 2007). According to a recent study, as many as 3.7 million Americans will have a lifetime bulimia nervosa (BN) or binge-eating disorder (BED) diagnosis (Udo & Grilo, 2018) and as many as 42.2 million Americans will experience clinically significant binge-eating (Mitchison, Touyz, González-Chica, Stocks, & Hay, 2017). Binge-eating is associated with a number of poor health and psychosocial consequences, including poor health-related quality of life (Mitchison, Hay, Slewa-Younan, & Mond, 2012), days of lost productivity (Mond & Hay, 2007), depression (Roberto, Grilo, Masheb, & White, 2010), and increased use and costs of health services (Roberto et al., 2010). Anorexia nervosa (AN) is one of the most severe psychiatric illnesses due to the life-threatening medical complications that can arise in individuals who fail to maintain a healthy body (Moskowitz & Weiselberg, 2017; Whitelaw, Lee, Gilbertson, & Sawyer, 2018). Because of the high costs associated with hospitalization and the need for intensive and often long-term treatment, AN has one of the highest treatment costs of any psychiatric disorder (Agh et al., 2016; Guarda et al., 2017). For example, the annual costs of untreated or undertreated AN have recently been estimated to be nearly $2.6 billion (Bode, Gotz von Olenhusen, Wunsch, Kliem, & Kroger, 2017). These results clearly highlight the large psychological, economic, and societal burden of EDs.

Cognitive-Behavioral Therapy for Eating Disorders

Cognitive-behavioral therapy (CBT), including an enhanced transdiagnostic version, is the current frontline treatment approach for both BN and BED (NICE, 2017; Wilson, 2005). CBT is based on the premise that rigid dietary restriction (i.e., deliberate attempts to drastically reduce the overall amount of food eaten or the types of food eaten, with the intention of influencing one's shape or weight) leaves patients in a state of deprivation that increases vulnerability to binge-eating episodes (Fairburn, Cooper, & Shafran, 2003). In an effort to combat potential weight gain after a binge-eating episode, patients often engage in compensatory behaviors (e.g., in BN: self-induced vomiting, laxative use) and/or resume dietary restriction (in both BN and BED), perpetuating a cycle of disordered eating behavior (Cooper, Wells, & Todd, 2004). To reduce dietary restriction, CBT requires patients to change their eating behavior outside of binge episodes in three key ways: (1) schedule eating episodes at regular intervals throughout the day, with a goal of eating three meals and one to two snacks per day, (2) eat a sufficient amount of food at each meal or snack to prevent acute hunger, and (3) eat a sufficient range of food, including foods the patient may fear eating (e.g., desserts, carbohydrates), to reduce feelings of deprivation. Changing eating behaviors in these three ways reduces several types of dietary restriction (e.g., delayed eating, caloric restriction, and hedonic restriction, respectively) that increase vulnerability to binge-eating episodes. Once dietary restriction is reduced, any remaining binge episodes are targeted by skills designed to help patients better identify and cope with internal (e.g., body image dissatisfaction) and external (e.g., presence of palatable foods) triggers for residual binge episodes.

Although CBT can be an effective treatment for many individuals, recent systematic reviews and meta-analyses have found that 40–50 percent of patients with BED (Peat et al., 2017) and nearly 70 percent of patients with BN (Linardon, 2018) fail to achieve remission after a full course of CBT. CBT is even less effective for AN, where there remains no effective evidence-based outpatient treatment for adult patients (Watson & Bulik, 2013).

Why CBT for Eating Disorders Produces Sub-Par Results

The primary behavioral components of CBT focus on changing restrictive or chaotic eating behaviors that maintain binge-eating episodes. However, given that overvaluation of weight and shape is a hallmark feature of eating disorders (Fairburn et al., 2008), the behavior change recommended in CBT often provokes considerable distress as patients fear that any reductions in dietary restriction will lead to weight gain. The inherent distress associated with reducing dietary restriction in patients with EDs often means that compliance with the behavioral components of CBT is poor (Hay, Bacaltchuk, Stefano, & Kashyap, 2009; Shah, Passi, Bryson, & Agras, 2005). Thus, despite the strong behavioral focus of CBT, many patients are not able to successfully manage the distressing internal experiences that will inevitably occur as they begin to change their behaviors and continue to engage in high levels of restrictive eating. The ability to succeed in treatment such as CBT requires an adequate capacity for self-regulation (i.e., the ability to control one's behavior—in the face of attentional, motivational, emotional, and cognitive challenges—so as to align with the pursuit of long-term goals; Nielsen et al., 2018). A robust body of literature suggests that individuals with EDs commonly experience deficits in several facets of self-regulation (Lavender et al., 2015; Stice, 2002; Baumeister & Heatherton, 1996). Of note, while individuals with BN and BED on average experience deficits in self-regulation, there is considerable variability across the patient population. This variability may partially explain why some patients are able to successfully comply with the behavioral components of CBT and experience positive outcomes from this treatment approach.

Mindfulness and Acceptance-Based Treatments for Eating Disorders

Within the past two decades, mindfulness- and acceptance-based treatments (MABTs) have emerged as an alternative to traditional CBTs for a variety of psychological disorders (Haynos, Forman, Butryn, & Lillis, 2016; Kahl, Winter, & Schweiger, 2012). MABTs integrate behavioral treatment with a set of psychological strategies designed to enhance self-regulation, such as mindful awareness, distress tolerance, emotion modulation, and values-based decision making. All of these strategies are hypothesized to enhance self-regulation capacity (Forman & Butryn, 2015; Shapiro, Carlson, Astin, & Freedman, 2006; Zimmerman, 2000; Baumeister, Heatherton, & Tice, 1994). MABTs have increasingly become one of the most frequently used treatments in clinical practice for EDs (Linardon, Fairburn, Fitzsimmons-Craft, Wilfley, & Brennan, 2017). For example, in one recent study, patients with an eating disorder were more likely to report that their therapist used mindfulness techniques (77%) than CBT techniques such as food monitoring records (53%) or weekly in-session weigh-ins (39%; Cowdrey & Waller, 2015). While numerous MABT modalities have been tested and have shown promise for EDs, the remainder of this text will focus specifically on a close examination of ACT as a treatment approach for EDs.

Rational and Conceptual Model of ACT for Eating Disorders

Experiential Avoidance/Acceptance

Experiential avoidance refers to the inability to allow an internal experience to be what it is without trying to control, reduce, or escape it (Hayes, Strosahl, & Wilson, 2012). Consistent with this definition, EDs are frequently conceptualized as disorders of control. Specifically, individuals continuously strive to maintain control over their shape, weight, and eating behavior (Orsillo & Batten, 2002; Fairburn, Shafran, & Cooper, 1999). Additionally, they may strive to control their ED-specific and broad internal experiences, including thoughts, feelings, physical sensations, and urges (Merwin & Wilson, 2009). In fact, ED behaviors can be construed as coping mechanisms developed to temporarily avoid distressing internal experiences in an attempt to control them (Hayes & Pankey, 2002; Keyser et al., 2009; Leehr et al., 2015). By becoming hyperfocused on tangible concerns like their body and eating behavior, individuals with EDs may be attempting to avoid other distressing internal experiences that are outside of their control such as feelings of imperfection, rejection, and failure (Hayes & Pankey, 2002; Keyser et al., 2009; Leehr et al., 2015). For example, research has indicated that restrictive eating promotes an intense focus on the body instead of other sources of internal distress such as low interpersonal self-efficacy and perfectionistic tendencies (Cain, Bardone-Cone, Abramson, Vohs, & Joiner, 2010; Lavender et al., 2016). Similarly, binge-eating facilitates escaping momentary negative emotions, including guilt, sadness, fear, and hostility (Berg et al., 2013; Schaefer et al., 2020). Compensatory behaviors function similarly by facilitating the avoidance of distressing internal experiences associated with binge-eating such as fear of gaining weight or being out of control (Orsillo & Batten, 2002).

Experiential avoidance is one of the most widely studied ACT components among individuals with EDs. A substantial literature base supports a high degree of experiential avoidance within this population. Specifically, individuals with AN, BN, and BED report higher levels of experiential avoidance compared to healthy controls (HCs; Mallorquí-Bagué et al., 2018). Across these diagnoses, experiential avoidance has been found to be positively associated with global eating pathology as measured through the Eating Disorder Examination (EDE; Cooper & Fairburn, 1987; Prefit, Cândea, & Szentagotai-Tătar, 2019). It has also been shown to predict both restrictive eating (Merwin, Zucker, Lacy, & Elliott, 2010) and binge-eating (Lillis, Hayes, & Levin, 2011). The high degree of experiential avoidance observed within this population indicates that individuals with EDs may benefit from developing acceptance toward their internal experiences instead of relying on ED behaviors (e.g., restrictive eating) to control or avoid them.

Cognitive Fusion/Defusion

The high degree of experiential avoidance observed in individuals with EDs may be partly due to their tendency to be fused with their distressing internal experiences. Individuals with EDs have been found to be fused with a variety of ED-related internal experiences, including subjective dietary rules, food cravings, and urges to eat (Duarte, Ferreira, Pinto-Gouveia, Trindade, & Martinho, 2017; Duarte, Pinto-Gouveia, Ferreira, & Silva, 2016). Fusing with these internal experiences results in individuals automatically engaging in ED behaviors to temporarily reduce their internal suffering without considering the long-term social, physical, and psychological consequences of their actions (Manlick, Manlick, et al., 2013). For example, fusing with a food craving may lead to automatically consuming that food to temporarily alleviate the distress associated with the craving, despite the feelings of guilt that may arise afterward.

Furthermore, research indicates that individuals with EDs are particularly fused with cognitions surrounding their shape and weight. Among the general population, shape- and weight-related cognitive fusion has been shown to be positively associated with global eating pathology (Ferreira, Trindade, Duarte, & Pinto-Gouveia, 2015). Additionally, compared to HC, individuals with AN, BN, and BED report higher levels of fusing with three types of weight and shape-related cognitions: (1) thinking about a forbidden food makes weight gain more likely, (2) thinking about a forbidden food increases the feeling of fatness, and (3) thinking about a forbidden food is morally equivalent to consuming it (Wyssen et al., 2018). In all three cases, individuals may rely on the cognition alone to guide their behavior instead of taking the entirety of their experience into account. For example, if individuals rely exclusively on the cognition "thinking about a forbidden food makes weight gain more likely," they may be more likely to engage in weight-control behaviors such as purging to compensate for it. Similar research has found that weight- and shape-related cognitive fusion mediate the relationship between weight and shape concern and global eating pathology (Ferreira, Palmeira, & Trindade, 2014). This suggests that gaining psychological distance from internal experiences may be a key intervention point for individuals with EDs.

Conceptualized Past and Feared Future/Contact with the Present Moment

Individuals with EDs tend to be unaware of the entirety of their present experience (e.g., social, physical, and psychological; Hayes et al., 2012) when making eating-related decisions. This may be partly due to their evaluation of the present moment based on rumination over the past or concern for the future. For example, individuals with EDs may avoid eating specific foods they enjoy because in the past being hyperfocused on those foods led to a binge-eating episode. Similarly, they may engage in compensatory behaviors following a binge-eating episode because of being fixated on the idea that they might gain weight.

Being mindful of one's present experience may be particularly challenging for individuals with AN, BN, and BED as they have shown deficits in their ability to recognize and be aware of their emotions (Mallorquí-Bagué et al., 2018; Westwood, Kerr-Gaffney, Stahl, & Tchanturia, 2017) and physical sensations (Brown et al., 2017). Across these diagnoses, the inability to recognize and be aware of emotions has been found to be positively associated with global eating pathology (Prefit et al., 2019). It may be that this inability makes it challenging for individuals with EDs to gain distance from their emotions. Combined, these inabilities may lead to the perception of all emotions as scary, thereby contributing to engagement in ED behaviors in an attempt to suppress or avoid these emotions instead of nonjudgmentally observing them (Fink, Anestis, Selby, & Joiner, 2010).

Not surprisingly, research indicates that individuals with EDs also show a lack of awareness surrounding their eating habits, which has been found to be positively associated with binge-eating frequency and body mass index (Pintado-Cucarella & Rodríguez-Salgado, 2016). To address this lack of awareness, various mindful eating interventions have been developed in recent years that encourage patients to be mindful of all aspects of the eating experience, including cues impacting food choice, qualities of the food being consumed, and eating-related internal experiences (Monroe, 2015). Individuals with EDs may therefore benefit greatly from increasing their recognition and nonjudgmental awareness of eating-specific as well as broad internal experiences.

Attachment to the Conceptualized Self/Self-as-Context

In ACT, self-as-context is conceptualized as a distinct aspect of consciousness that can observe changing contexts and internal experiences. Attachment to the conceptualized self or self-as-content can alternatively be conceptualized as a state of consciousness where beliefs and observations are fused to the sense of self and where individuals perceive themselves as the content of their experiences. Individuals with EDs are often attached to their ED and view the ED as "who they are as a person", which can be conceptualized through a self-as-content perspective (Juarascio et al., 2013b). The attachment to an ED identity cultivates a maladaptive constructed view of the self, such that individuals with an ED struggle to objectively observe disorder-consistent thoughts and feelings (e.g., weight and shape concerns, fears around eating) and instead view these thoughts and feelings as part of who they are (Juarascio et al., 2013b; Manlick, Cochran, & Koon, 2013). This self-as-content tendency leads these individuals to conceptualize their self-image based on the thoughts and feelings that drive their disordered eating behaviors (Manlick et al., 2013). This high level of attachment to the ED identity can interfere with treatment as individuals may be highly ambivalent about "giving up" the ED identity. In fact, some researchers have argued that AN is a disorder of self-as-context deficits and that this alone may be the basis of eating disorder psychopathology (Amianto, Northoff, Abbate Daga, Fassino, & Tasca, 2016).

To date, relatively limited research exists on the direct relationship between self-as-content and eating disorders symptoms and behaviors. The majority of the research to date has focused on the link between ED symptoms and attachment to the ED as a source of identity. For example, one study has shown that individuals who do not have a clear sense of their identity tend to focus on external sources (i.e., shape, weight) for defining themselves (Bardone-Cone, Thompson, & Miller, 2020). Additionally, low self-esteem and identity exploration, especially during adolescence and emerging adulthood, are factors that are highly correlated with eating disorder symptomatology (Corning & Heibel, 2016; Gonidakis, Lemonoudi, Charila, & Varsou, 2018). Extant literature primarily focuses on how attachment to the ED identity manifests in AN. However, a few research studies suggest that some individuals with BN may also experience attachment to an ED identity. For example, one study found that individuals with BN include physical constructs like body appearance and attitudes toward the body as part of their identity at much higher rates than healthy controls (Dada, Izu, Montebruno, Grau, & Feixas, 2017).

Lack of Values Clarity/Values

For many individuals with an ED, values (i.e., verbally constructed, global, desired and chosen life directions; Dahl, Luciano, & Wilson, 2005) are often unformulated and vaguely held, which reduces their ability to serve as a momentary guide for behavioral choices. Individuals with EDs have been found to fear valuing less tangible things (e.g., building better relationships versus reaching a certain weight) and/or things that are difficult to achieve (e.g., achievement at work; Merwin & Wilson, 2009). Instead, certain disorder-specific values (e.g., overvaluation of weight and shape or control over eating) can be so prominent that they limit access to and awareness of other important life values. For example, across ED diagnoses, importance and overvaluation of shape and weight have been shown to predict and maintain ED symptoms (Duarte, Ferreira, & Pinto-Gouveia, 2016). Overvaluation of weight and shape can be particularly challenging to treat in individuals with EDs because of the ego-syntonic nature of the illness and attachment to the conceptualized self-described previously. A strong values imbalance as a result of attachment to an ED identity and poor values clarity in other life domains can hinder motivation for treatment and maintain ED symptoms (Bardone-Cone et al., 2020; Manlick et al., 2013). An underlying assumption about values is that they are finite; that is, there is a limit to what can be encapsulated in an individual's value base. Thus, the overvaluation of weight and shape that occurs in EDs necessitates that there is less "room" for other valued domains, further sustaining a strong values imbalance.

Inaction, Impulsivity, or Avoidance/Committed Action

As noted earlier, the ability to succeed in most behavioral treatment approaches requires an adequate capacity for self-regulation (Nielsen et al., 2018). Yet a large body of literature suggests that individuals with EDs commonly experience deficits in several facets of self-regulation. Emotion dysregulation has been implicated in the onset and maintenance of EDs, with binge-eating often being conceptualized as a maladaptive self-regulatory strategy (Baumeister & Heatherton, 1996; Lavender et al., 2015; Stice, 2002). A number of ecological momentary assessment studies have examined momentary affect surrounding ED behavior in BN and BED, showing that negative affect increases prior to and decreases after binge-eating (Smyth et al., 2007). Such studies have provided strong support for affect regulation theories, which posit binge-eating functions to escape from or regulate negative affective states. Similarly, a recent meta-analysis (Wu et al., 2013) found that individuals with BN and BED have worse inhibitory control compared to healthy controls. These findings are consistent with the "resource depletion" theory of binge-eating, which suggests that when some individuals are under emotional distress, they devote resources to regulate/escape from negative affect and therefore have fewer "top-down" cognitive resources available (Loth et al., 2016). Collectively, these deficits in self-regulation can maintain ED symptoms and contribute to poor ability to engage in committed action, a requirement for successful behavioral treatment approaches.

Psychological Inflexibility/Flexibility

As indicated through the six processes of experiential avoidance, cognitive fusion, conceptualized past and feared future, attachment to the conceptualized self, lack of values clarity, and inaction, impulsivity, or avoidance, individuals with EDs tend to experience broad and ED-specific psychological inflexibility (i.e., inability to contact the present moment and internal experiences while continuing or changing behavior according to one's values; Hayes et al., 2012). Individuals with AN, BN, and BED report higher levels of psychological inflexibility broadly and with their food and exercise compared to HCs (Dahlgren, Hage, Wonderlich, & Stedal, 2019). Additionally, psychological inflexibility broadly and with urges and cravings have been found to be positively associated with shape and weight concerns, restrictive eating, and binge-eating severity (Sarno, 2020; White, 2018). It may be, for example, that individuals low in psychological flexibility narrowly focus on experiencing an urge and engage in binge-eating instead of an alternative, values-consistent behavior (e.g., calling a friend).

Within this population, an emphasis has been placed on the contribution of body image-related psychological inflexibility to ED symptomatology. In individuals with AN and BN, being psychologically inflexible with their body image (e.g., avoiding distressing thoughts about their body, prioritizing a certain weight or shape over other life domains) has been found to be positively associated with eating and weight concerns (Bluett et al., 2016). Furthermore, body image-related psychological inflexibility has been shown to be positively associated with binge-eating severity (Paola, Sérgio, Margareth da Silva, & José, 2017). Collectively, these findings suggest that the multifaceted construct of psychological inflexibility may be a key treatment target for individuals with EDs.

Empirical Evidence of ACT for EDs

ACT has a growing empirical base, demonstrating its efficacy for treating EDs. Typically, treatments for EDs that have been informed by ACT integrate one or more ACT skills within a more traditional behavioral treatment program for EDs that also provides specific dietary recommendations designed to address dietary restriction and binge-eating/purging. As a result, a vast majority of treatment research has evaluated ACT-informed treatments (i.e., behavioral treatments that include one or more ACT components and not the full ACT model), which limits our ability to understand the efficacy of a full ACT treatment approach for EDs. Additionally, within the past two decades, many of these ACT-informed treatments have also included other psychological strategies (such as mindful eating training or emotion modulation) from other third-wave treatment approaches such as mindfulness-based eating awareness training (Kristeller & Wolever, 2010) and dialectical behavior therapy (DBT; Linehan, Bohus, & Lynch, 2007). Although, emerging research shows the promise of these third-wave treatments for EDs (Godfrey, Gallo, & Afari, 2015; Katterman Kleinman, Hood, Nackers, & Corsica 2014; Linardon et al., 2017), because the treatment packages evaluated in these studies often include skills from several third-wave treatments, it is difficult to parse the independent treatment effects of ACT-specific skills on clinical outcomes. As such, we chose to review the evidence for full ACT treatments and ACT-informed treatments together to allow for a more comprehensive literature base to review. In the following section, we review the literature on clinical outcomes, process variables, mechanisms of action, and predictor/moderators of ACT and ACT-informed treatments for EDs.

Outcomes from ACT and ACT-informed Treatments for ED

In total, 15 studies have evaluated the efficacy of ACT in treating EDs. Two studies have utilized formal ACT (Berman, Boutelle, & Crow, 2009; Parling , Cernvall, Ramklint, Holmgren, & Ghaderi, 2016), and the rest have utilized an ACT-informed treatment.

Of the 15 studies, 5 utilized a sample of individuals with AN (Berman et al., 2009; Parling et al., 2016; Timko, Zucker, Herbert, Rodriguez, & Merwin, 2015; Wildes, Marcus, Cheng, McCabe, & Gaskill, Marcus, 2011; Wildes et al., 2014), one utilized a sample of individuals with BN or subthreshold BN (Strandskov et al., 2017), three utilized a sample of individuals with BED (Evans, Murray, Muratore, Lantz, & Juarascio, 2019; Hill, Masuda, Melcher, Morgan, & Twohig, 2015; Juarascio, Manasse, Schumacher, Espel, & Forman, 2017), two utilized transdiagnostic ED samples (Fogelkvist, Gustafsson, Kjellin, & Parling, 2020; Juarascio et al., 2013a), and the remaining three utilized a sample of subthreshold EDs (Hill, Schaefer,

Spencer, & Masuda, 2020; Juarascio, Forman, & Herbert, 2010; Pearson, Follette, & Hayes, 2012). Notably, only four studies conducted a fully randomized clinical trial (Fogelkvist et al., 2020; Juarascio et al., 2010; Parling et al., 2016; Strandskov et al., 2017), whereas the others utilized either a case series (Berman et al., 2009; Evans et al., 2019; Hill et al., 2015; Hill et al., 2020; Wildes & Marcus, 2011) or nonrandomized groups/open trial design (Juarascio et al., 2017; Juarascio et al., 2013a, 2015; Pearson et al., 2012; Timko et al., 2015; Wildes et al., 2014). Regarding treatment delivery, eight studies delivered an individual, face-to-face ACT protocol (Berman et al., 2009; Hill et al., 2015, 2020; Juarascio et al., 2010; Parling et al., 2016; Timko et al., 2015; Wildes & Marcus, 2011; Wildes et al., 2014); one delivered an internet-based intervention supported by clinician feedback (Strandskov et al., 2017); one delivered brief workshop intervention (Pearson et al., 2012); and the remainder delivered a group-based intervention model (Evans et al., 2019; Fogelkvist et al., 2020; Juarascio et al., 2013a, 2015, 2017).

OUTCOMES FOR AN

Several case series and open trials have suggested that ACT produces symptom improvement in individuals with AN (Berman et al., 2009; Timko et al., 2015; Wildes & Marcus, 2011; Wildes et al., 2014). Results from case series (Wildes & Marcus, 2011) and an open trial (Wildes et al., 2014) evaluating emotion acceptance behavior treatment (EABT, a treatment focused on increasing experiential acceptance of emotions) for AN showed that adults with AN restored weight to a healthy range and recovered from eating pathology from pre- to posttreatment. These gains were maintained at 6-month follow-up. An open trial of preliminary evaluation of an acceptance-based separated family treatment (ASFT) for adolescents (n = 47 families) showed that nearly two-thirds of adolescents achieved full or partial remission from eating disorder symptoms and reached expected body weight at posttreatment (Timko et al., 2015). A randomized controlled trial (RCT) demonstrated that although ACT did not outperform treatment as usual (TAU) among individuals with AN (n = 43, ACT = 24, TAU = 19), the odds ratio (OR) indicated that participants receiving ACT were nonsignificantly more likely to gain weight and show improvements in eating pathology at posttreatment (OR = 2.50 [95% CI: 0.3–16.1]) and 6-month follow-up compared to those receiving TAU (OR = 1.50 [95% CI: 0.2–9.4]; Parling et al., 2016). Furthermore, participants receiving ACT had significantly greater reductions in shape and weight concerns from pre- to posttreatment and at 5-year follow-up, and improved quality of life and self-esteem from pre- to posttreatment and at 2-year follow-up compared to those receiving TAU (Parling et al., 2016). Another study that included individuals with AN (in addition to other diagnoses) (n = 140, ACT = 66, TAU = 74) found that individuals with AN receiving weekly group-based ACT treatment in a residential setting experienced greater improvements in ED symptoms and lower relapse rates at 6-month follow-up compared to TAU (Juarascio et al., 2013a).

OUTCOMES FOR BN

Evidence for ACT in treating BN is nascent but promising. A trial evaluating the efficacy of an internet-based ACT intervention supported by clinician feedback for BN or subthreshold BN (n = 92, ACT = 46, waitlist = 46) demonstrated that compared to a waitlist control condition, ACT produced small to moderate effect-size improvements (d = 0.35–0.64) in eating pathology and shape and weight concerns from pre- to posttreatment (Strandskov et al., 2017). In the same study described previously for AN where a weekly group-based ACT treatment in a residential setting was compared to TAU, individuals with BN spectrum disorders (in addition to other diagnoses) (n = 140, ACT = 66, TAU = 74) also experienced greater improvements in ED symptoms compared to TAU (Juarascio et al., 2013a).

OUTCOMES FOR BED

Numerous case series and open trials examining acceptance-based behavioral treatment (ABBT, an ACT-informed treatment approach that also contains some emotion-focused content drawn from DBT) for individuals with BED demonstrate clinically significant reductions in eating pathology from pre- to posttreatment (Evans et al., 2019; Hill et al., 2015; Juarascio et al., 2017) and at 3-month follow-up (Juarascio et al., 2017). ABBT for BED has also been shown to improve depression and quality of life (Evans et al., 2019; Juarascio et al., 2017).

OUTCOMES FOR OTHER ED POPULATIONS

Finally, ACT has shown promise in the treatment of subthreshold and residual ED symptoms. For example, a case series demonstrated that compassion-focused acceptance-based treatment reduced ED symptoms and body dissatisfaction in an adult sample with restrictive eating and problematic body checking (Hill et al., 2020). Another study demonstrated the preliminary efficacy of a one-day ACT brief workshop for women with body dissatisfaction (n = 73, ACT = 39, Waitlist = 34) in producing significant reductions in body-related anxiety compared to the waitlist control condition at posttreatment (Pearson et al., 2012). In a RCT comparing ACT with CBT for the treatment of subthreshold EDs (n = 55, ACT = 27, CBT = 28), individuals receiving ACT had greater reductions in ED pathology than those receiving CBT (Juarascio et al., 2010). A recent study showed moderate effect-size improvements (d = 0.57–0.64) in eating pathology, shape and weight concerns, and body dissatisfaction in a transdiagnostic sample of individuals with residual ED symptoms (n = 99, ACT = 52, TAU = 47) who received group-based ACT after completing a day treatment program compared to TAU (Fogelkvist et al., 2020). Taken together, these findings suggest that ACT is an effective therapy for EDs.

CAVEATS IN INTERPRETING OUTCOME RESULTS

While the results of ACT for EDs are promising, it is important to note that the existing literature base contains numerous limitations that reduce our ability to synthesize results. Most of the trials included in the review were either open trials or small pilot RCTs comparing to a waitlist control, TAU, or a minimally active treatment condition. To date, there has still been no adequately powered noninferiority trial RCT of ACT versus CBT for full threshold EDs. The absence of this trial limits our ability to determine with confidence that ACT can be an effective treatment alternative to CBT. Adding to the difficulties in interpretation has been the wide variation in how the body of research as a whole has been implemented (e.g., length, frequency, and number of sessions; group vs. individual) and in what specific components of ACT were included in the treatment tested. Thus, although initial results are promising, more research is clearly needed to fully understand the impact of ACT on ED symptoms.

Effects on Psychological Flexibility Processes

The most researched process variables in studies to date have been psychological flexibility (n = 4), including studies that examined body image flexibility (n = 3; Berman et al., 2009; Hill et al., 2015; Hill et al., 2020) and flexibility surrounding food-specific internal experiences (n = 1; Juarascio et al., 2015). Other mechanisms of action include experiential acceptance (n = 4; Juarascio et al., 2017; Juarascio et al., 2013a; Pearson et al., 2012; Timko et al., 2015), willingness (n = 1; Juarascio et al., 2013a), mindful awareness (n = 1; Fogelkvist et al.,

2020); emotional regulation (n = 3; Evans et al., 2019; Juarascio et al., 2013a, 2017), cognitive defusion (n = 1; Juarascio et al., 2015), negative urgency (n = 1; Juarascio et al., 2017), and dysfunctional thinking (n = 1; Juarascio et al., 2013a). Across all studies, significant improvements in all process variables at end of treatment have been observed. For example, two publications from the same study demonstrated improvements in psychological flexibility surrounding both general and food-specific internal experiences, willingness, cognitive defusion, and access to emotional regulation strategies from pre- to posttreatment following group-based ACT treatment for AN and BN in a residential treatment center (Juarascio et al., 2013a, 2017). A recent study showed clinically significant improvements at the end of treatment in body image flexibility and increases in behaviors aligned with valued life domains outside of the ED (e.g., active social engagements to move in the direction of values related to interpersonal relationships instead of social withdrawal because of thoughts of "appearing heavy or bloated"; Hill et al., 2020). Another study with individuals reporting residual ED symptoms demonstrated medium effect-size improvements over time in mindful awareness for individuals receiving ACT compared to those receiving TAU (d = 0.56; Fogelkvist et al., 2020).

Mechanisms of Action

A growing body of literature has also provided preliminary evidence for the role of ACT process variables as driving therapeutic change in ED pathology. Only one study to date has tested whether improvements in process variables temporally precede and predict reductions in ED symptoms (i.e., test of formal mediation). Juarascio and colleagues (2013a) observed that willingness to experience distress significantly mediated the effects of treatment condition on global ED pathology. This study found that willingness trended toward greater improvements within the ACT condition compared to TAU, and willingness significantly predicted lower global ED pathology scores at end of treatment across both treatment conditions. Six other studies examined change in both process variables and ED pathology from pre- to posttreatment and assessed whether change in process variables predicted change in ED pathology (i.e., "proxy" mediation). These studies have shown that pre- to posttreatment improvements in body image flexibility (Berman et al., 2009; Hill et al., 2015, 2020), emotional regulation abilities (Evans et al., 2019; Juarascio et al., 2017), experiential acceptance (Pearson et al., 2012; Timko et al., 2015), and mindful awareness (Fogelkvist et al., 2020) corresponded to pre- to posttreatment reductions in ED symptoms during ACT or ACT-informed treatments. In another study, Juarascio and colleagues (2015) found that increases in cognitive defusion abilities were significantly associated with increases in ED- related quality of life at posttreatment.

Predictors/Moderators

Only four studies to date have examined predictors or moderators of outcomes from ACT treatments for EDs. Two studies demonstrated that greater body image psychological flexibility at pretreatment longitudinally predicts improvements in eating disorders, mental health, and overall quality of life from residential treatments, including ACT for eating disorders (Bluett et al., 2016; Lee, Ong, Twohig, Lensegrav-Benson, & Quakenbush-Roberts, 2018). One study showed that greater severity of ED pathology at baseline demonstrated greater trend-level improvements in ED symptomatology following TAU + ACT treatment compared to TAU only (Juarascio et al., 2013a). Another study demonstrated that elevated levels of negative urgency at baseline were significantly associated with smaller reductions in binge frequency and global ED pathology following a 10-weekly ACT-based group treatment compared to those with low levels of negative urgency at baseline (Manasse et al., 2016). These findings suggest that ACT may be well suited to treat individuals who present with greater severity of EDs and that body image psychological flexibility and negative urgency might be an additional modifiable target for ACT.

Summary

Extant research provides preliminary support for ACT in treating EDs, and for the underlying therapeutic model targeting psychological flexibility. However, lack of systematic research precludes us from drawing firm conclusions that ACT is an effective treatment for EDs. Further research is warranted to extend previous findings and examine the effectiveness of this approach for EDs.

Treating EDs from an ACT Perspective

Behavioral Treatment for Eating Disorders

Given the strong evidence that treatment outcomes for individuals with EDs (particularly for disorders characterized by binge-eating) benefits from the behavioral components of traditional CBT for EDs, ACT-based treatments for ED's should start with these key behavioral components as a foundation of treatment (Fairburn et al., 2008). These include (1) self-monitoring of food intake and eating disorder symptoms, (2) regular eating (defined as scheduling eating episodes at regular intervals throughout the day, with a goal of never going longer than four waking hours in between planned eating episodes and eating three meals and one to two snacks each day), and (3) reducing dietary restraint (defined as both eating a sufficient amount of food at each meal or snack to prevent acute hunger and eating a sufficient range of food, including foods the patient may fear eating to reduce feelings of deprivation). Below we provide additional information on each of these BT techniques.

SELF-MONITORING OF FOOD INTAKE AND EATING DISORDER SYMPTOMS

Self-monitoring refers to daily tracking of meals and snacks, eating disorder symptoms (including binge episodes and compensatory behaviors), and relevant situational factors accompanying eating episodes. Patients will track the mealtime, type of food and drink consumed (but not caloric content), location where the food or drink was consumed, and whether the episode constituted a binge for each meal and snack. Patients are instructed to record this information accurately and in real-time (i.e., as soon as possible following the eating episode or behavior). Patients problem-solve barriers to self-monitoring with their clinician throughout treatment. Self-monitoring is an essential component of behavioral eating disorder treatment as it provides information about daily eating behaviors and eating disorder symptoms and identifies potential areas for intervention. Self-monitoring does not aim to change the patient's pattern of eating, although it may facilitate interventions related to regular eating and reducing dietary restraint.

REGULAR EATING

Regular eating involves eating meals or snacks every 3 to 4 hours, with the goal of consuming three meals and two snacks per day. Patients are instructed to avoid eating between scheduled meal and snack times, to not skip meals or snacks, to know in advance roughly what and when they will next eat, and to not compensate for eating (i.e., via purging). Since hunger and fullness cues are often dysregulated as a result of dietary restriction and binge-eating, patients are asked to follow their planned eating schedule regardless of feelings of hunger or fullness. In addition, patients are encouraged to formalize eating (e.g., sitting down at a table), portion out food onto the serving dish before eating, focus on their eating (e.g., not combine it with a distracting activity like television), avoid "picking" at food (e.g., while cooking), and attempt to slow their eating (e.g., put down cutlery between bites).

REDUCING DIETARY RESTRAINT

Reducing dietary restraint involves (1) eating a sufficient amount of food at each meal or snack to prevent acute hunger and eliminate caloric restriction and (2) eating a sufficient range of food, including foods the patient may fear eating to reduce feelings of deprivation. Reducing caloric restriction consists of psychoeducation regarding the dangers of caloric restriction and healthy weight ranges, identifying the pros and cons (both current and future) of increasing intake, identifying implications for change, maintaining motivation, involving friends and family, and problem-solving difficulties with increasing intake (e.g., feelings of fullness, fear of weight gain). Patients are not instructed to count calories or given pre-set caloric guidelines to follow for meals, but instead are instructed to base portion sizes on what others around them are eating. In session, therapists will also provide guidance on appropriate portion sizes and will encourage patients to increase portion sizes if self-monitoring logs indicate the patient may be consuming too little food at each meal or snack. Eating a sufficient range of foods (including feared foods) is primarily conducted through behavioral experimentation. Patients identify a specific rule and what is motivating it (e.g., not eating carbohydrates out of fear that it will turn into a binge episode); explore what they believe will be the consequences of breaking the rule (e.g., binge-eating); devise an experiment to test out their hypothesized consequences (e.g., eating bread at dinner with a friend in the assigned week and planning a distracting activity afterward); and analyze the implications of the experiment (e.g., did binge-eating occur?) as well as the advantages of breaking the rule (e.g., the patient enjoyed eating bread, t he patient was able to eat the same food as a friend).

Using ACT to Facilitate Behavior Change

ACT techniques can be used to enhance the ability to engage in the difficult work of behavioral treatments for EDs. Below we describe the application of three ACT components (present moment awareness, acceptance/defusion, and values) to the treatment of EDs with a focus on how these ACT components can be used to facilitate behavior change.

PRESENT MOMENT AWARENESS

Present moment awareness is presumed to improve adherence to the behavioral recommendations of treatment by increasing an individual's attunement with internal cues and sensations that are typically nonconscious and thus govern eating decisions. Individuals can be encouraged to build a present-focused attentional state that emphasizes observing and experiencing rather than evaluating and changing internal experiences (thoughts, emotions, and urges, as well as hunger, fullness, and other physical sensations). Patients should be taught how to identify and label internal experiences in detail to enhance their ability to fully describe the entirety of their present moment experience. Skills such as gentle attention shifting can be taught to help the patient redirect their attention to objective descriptions of the present moment when they are experiencing future-oriented worries, ruminations about the past, or judgments/evaluations of their current experiences.

For patients with an ED, there should be a particular focus on the application of present moment awareness to eating specifically, with the goal of increasing momentary awareness of both hunger and satiety cues and other internal experiences that could drive eating behavior (e.g. eating due to boredom or stress). Patients with EDs can often approach eating-related behaviors in habitual or impulsive ways, and increasing mindful awareness will help the patient to make more mindful decisions about eating behaviors. Increasing patients' present moment awareness can thus be conceptualized as one method to help patients acquire and utilize the behavioral treatment skills effective in treating eating disorders. Treatment may focus on helping the patient learn how to tune into, and accurately perceive, label, assess, and distinguish internal experience (e.g., fullness; true hunger vs hedonic hunger), which will allow them to make behavioral choices consistent with recovery from an eating disorder. For example, patients may be instructed to engage in a brief mindful awareness check-in before, in the middle, and after each meal and to record hunger and satiety signals as part of traditional self-monitoring to begin to refine awareness of internal experiences during eating.

ACCEPTANCE AND DEFUSION

During treatment, patients can be taught a range of skills that will facilitate an ability to tolerate distressing thoughts, feelings, and sensations that have previously been maintaining eating disorder behaviors. For example, a strong focus of acceptance work is on learning that uncomfortable internal experiences such as hunger or fullness, urges to binge, sadness, and anxiety, and a range of other internal experiences are an inherent part of the human experience that cannot be fully controlled or avoided. Instead, patients will need to learn how to accept the inevitability of distressing thoughts and feelings without letting these thoughts and feelings control behaviors. For most patients, behavioral treatment recommendations around regular eating and reducing dietary restraint will inevitably increase worries about weight gain or fears of losing control over eating. A key aspect of treatment will be learning to engage in these treatment recommendations even while having these fears. Patients can be taught how to "uncouple" internal experiences such as thoughts, feelings, and urges from behaviors by learning to choose behaviors that are inconsistent with whatever internal experience they may be undergoing using traditional defusion exercises. For example, patients can be taught to separate ED thoughts (e.g., a thought such as "I need to restrict my eating so I don't gain weight") from ED behaviors (e.g., eating fewer calories than needed to sustain body weight) and recognize that while ED thoughts may be inevitable during the early stages of treatment, patients do have control over their behavioral decisions in response to these thoughts. Acceptance and defusion work is presented as methods that can help promote a state of willingness such that individuals are able to engage in the type of behaviors needed to recover from an eating disorder, even when doing so is uncomfortable or scary.

VALUES

For many patients with an ED, values are often unformulated and vaguely held, which reduces their ability to serve as a momentary guide for behavioral choices. Even when patients may have some awareness of their values, the behaviors they are engaging in to move toward those values are often ineffective. For example, this often takes the form of engaging in disordered eating behaviors that the patient perceives as values-consistent (e.g., purging or restricting eating in an effort to lose weight so that they are more "attractive") but that are ineffective ways to pursue the connected value (e.g., finding a loving and supportive romantic relationship). Additionally, certain disorder-specific "values" (e.g., overvaluation of weight and shape, overvaluation of control over eating) can be so prominent that they may limit access to and awareness of other important life values. While these ED "values" are often not true values, they can be perceived as such by patients and reinforce problematic engagement in disordered eating behaviors.

Treatment can focus on helping patients identify the values that are most important to them (values clarity), learn how to make decisions regarding eating that are values-consistent, and begin building a life that is overall aligned with their values. This work is hypothesized to facilitate change in ED behaviors via both an indirect and direct pathway. The indirect pathway focuses on enhancing motivation to change ED symptoms by assisting the patient in developing a valued, meaningful, and fulfilling life outside of their ED. Consistent with this notion, treatment aims to alter patients' valuation system by clarifying any "values" that are wrapped up in their eating disorder (e.g., overvaluation of weight and shape or control over eating, perfectionism or achievement-oriented values [if problematic]) and identifying the deeper and more fundamental value that underlies these eating disorder "values." Once the patient's values are better clarified, treatment will focus on increasing behaviors consistent with these newly identified valued directions (e.g., building close and meaningful interpersonal relationships, finding a career path that is personally satisfying). If individuals can begin to live more consistently with their deepest and most fundamental values, the improvements in quality of life may make disordered eating behaviors feel less appealing or necessary. As part of this indirect pathway, patients should also be encouraged to think about the ways that continued engagement in their ED makes it nearly impossible to fully pursue their other goals and values (e.g., how rigid dietary restriction/failure to maintain a healthy body weight interferes with social activities and relationships, how waiting to feel comfortable with your body size or shape before engaging in certain behaviors limits the ability to start engaging in values-consistent behaviors now).

The direct pathway focuses on momentary use of values-based decision-making skills during times when an individual is experiencing an urge to engage in ED symptoms. Patients can be taught to recognize when they are having a desire to engage in a disordered eating behavior and use this desire as a sign that they should be using their values-based decision-making skills. This skill involves (1) bringing values to mind in the moment of decision making, (2) recognizing that this moment is a decision point where they have the ability to make a decision that will either move them closer to their values or further away from them, and (3) striving to consistently make decisions that move them closer to their values. In the vast majority of situations relevant to an ED decision, the behavioral action that would move a patient closer to their most fundamental values will be consistent with the behavioral treatment recommendations.

Future Directions and Conclusions

As reviewed previously, substantial evidence supports the position that psychological inflexibility processes predict the maintenance of ED pathology. However, most of the research supporting these psychological processes as maintenance factors for ED pathology is based on self-report findings. Considering the multifaceted nature of these constructs, it would be beneficial for future research to examine how they contribute to ED pathology using alternative assessment paradigms such as behavioral coding and neurocognitive assessments. Additionally, the majority of the research to date has focused on cross-sectional assessment of ACT constructs within individuals already experiencing ED pathology, minimizing the degree to which we can understand how these constructs may contribute to risk for developing an ED.

While the results of ACT as a treatment for EDs are promising, many unanswered questions remain. To date, most of the ACT trials for EDs are either open trials or small pilot RCTs that are compared to a waitlist control or treatment as usual. As of now, there remains no RCT comparing ACT to CBT for EDs, thereby limiting our ability to understand how outcomes from an ACT treatment approach may compare to the current gold standard treatment. Adding to the difficulties in interpretation, the body of research as a whole has widely varied in how it was implemented (e.g., length, frequency, and number of sessions; group vs. individual) and whether the treatment was a full ACT protocol or an ACT-informed treatment approach that may have also utilized treatment techniques from other third-wave CBTs such as DBT. There is a clear need to understand the impact of individual ACT or other third-wave components on clinical outcomes to allow us to determine which components are most impactful for this population. Ideally, future research may benefit from using innovative treatment designs such as the Multiphase Optimization Strategy (MOST; i.e., a comprehensive, engineering-inspired framework for optimizing and evaluating multicomponent behavioral interventions (Collins et al., 2011; Collins, Murphy, Nair, & Strecher, 2005; Dziak & Nahum-Shani, 2016; Penn State Methodology Center, 2016) to identify the independent and synergistic efficacy of individual treatment components. Lastly, while ACT may be working through its intended mechanisms, the research on mechanisms of action and moderators of treatment outcome remains in its infancy.

In summary, ACT for EDs continues be a promising intervention approach worthy of additional study. Given the frequency with which ACT is employed in clinical practice for EDs (Cowdrey & Waller, 2015), additional research on this approach would allow us to confirm the efficacy of ACT and determine mechanisms of action and predictors/moderators of treatment outcome.

References

Agh, T., Kovacs, G., Supina, D., Pawaskar, M., Herman, B. K., Voko, Z., & Sheehan, D. V. (2016). A systematic review of the health-related quality of life and economic burdens of anorexia nervosa, bulimia nervosa, and binge eating disorder. *Eating and Weight Disorders, 21*(3), 353–364. doi:10.1007/s40519-016-0264-x

American Psychological Association. (2000). *Diagnostic and statistical manual of mental disorders*. Washington, DC: American Psychiatric Association.

Amianto, F., Northoff, G., Abbate Daga, G., Fassino, S., & Tasca, G. A. (2016). Is anorexia nervosa a disorder of the self? A psychological approach. *Frontiers in Psychology, 7*, 849.

Bardone-Cone, A. M., Thompson, K. A., & Miller, A. J. (2020). The self and eating disorders. *Journal of Personality, 88*(1), 59–75.

Baumeister, R. F., & Heatherton, T. (1996). Self-regulation failure: An overview. *Psychological Inquiry, 7*(1), 1–15.

Baumeister, R. F., Heatherton, T. F., & Tice, D. M. (1994). *Losing control: How and why people fail at self-regulation*: New York: Academic Press.

Berg, K. C., Crosby, R. D., Cao, L., Peterson, C. B., Engel, S. G., Mitchell, J. E., & Wonderlich, S. A. (2013). Facets of negative affect prior to and following binge-only, purge-only, and binge/purge events in women with bulimia nervosa. *Journal of Abnormal Psychology, 122*(1), 111–118. doi:10.1037/a0029703

Berman, M., Boutelle, K., & Crow, S. J. (2009). A case series investigating acceptance and commitment therapy as a treatment for previously treated, unremitted patients with anorexia nervosa. *European Eating Disorders Review: The Professional Journal of the Eating Disorders Association, 17*(6), 426–434.

Bluett, E. J., Lee, E. B., Simone, M., Lockhart, G., Twohig, M. P., Lensegrav-Benson, T., & Quakenbush-Roberts, B. (2016). The role of body image psychological flexibility on the treatment of eating disorders in a residential facility. *Eating Behaviors, 23*, 150–155. doi:10.1016/j.eatbeh.2016.10.002

Bode, K., Gotz von Olenhusen, N. M., Wunsch, E. M., Kliem, S., & Kroger, C. (2017). Population-based cost-offset analyses for disorder-specific treatment of anorexia nervosa and bulimia nervosa in Germany. *International Journal of Eating Disorders, 50*(3), 239–249. doi:10.1002/eat.22686

Brown, T. A., Berner, L. A., Jones, M. D., Reilly, E. E., Cusack, A., Anderson, L. K., & Wierenga, C. E. (2017). Psychometric evaluation and norms for the Multidimensional Assessment of Interoceptive Awareness (MAIA) in a clinical eating disorders sample. *European Eating Disorders Review, 25*(5), 411–416. doi:10.1002/erv.2532

Cain, A. S., Bardone-Cone, A. M., Abramson, L. Y., Vohs, K. D., & Joiner, T. E. (2010). Prospectively predicting dietary restraint: The role of interpersonal self-efficacy, weight/shape self-efficacy, and interpersonal stress. *International Journal of Eating Disorders, 43*(6), 505–512. doi:10.1002/eat.20740

Collins, L. M., Baker, T. B., Mermelstein, R. J., Piper, M. E., Jorenby, D. E., Smith, S. S., . . . Fiore, M. C. (2011). The multiphase optimization strategy for engineering effective tobacco use interventions. *Annals of Behavioral Medicine, 41*(2), 208–226.

Collins, L. M., Murphy, S. A., Nair, V. N., & Strecher, V. J. (2005). A strategy for optimizing and evaluating behavioral interventions. *Annals of Behavioral Medicine, 30*(1), 65–73.

Cooper, M. J., Wells, A., & Todd, G. (2004). A cognitive model of bulimia nervosa. *British Journal of Clinical Psychology, 43*(1), 1–16.

Cooper, Z., & Fairburn, C. (1987). The eating disorder examination: A semi-structured interview for the assessment of the specific psychopathology of eating disorders. *International Journal of Eating Disorders, 6*(1), 1–8. doi:10.1002/1098–108x(198701)6:1<1::Aid-eat2260060102>3.0.Co;2–9

Corning, A. F., & Heibel, H. D. (2016). Re-thinking eating disorder prevention: The case for prioritizing the promotion of healthy identity development. *Eating Disorders, 24*(1), 106–113.

Cowdrey, N. D., & Waller, G. (2015). Are we really delivering evidence-based treatments for eating disorders? How eating-disordered patients describe their experience of cognitive behavioral therapy. *Behaviour Research and Therapy, 75*, 72–77.

Dada, G., Izu, S., Montebruno, C., Grau, A., & Feixas, G. (2017). Content analysis of the construction of self and others in women with bulimia nervosa. *Frontiers in Psychology, 8, 1-8.* doi:10.3389/fpsyg.2017.00480

Dahl, J., Luciano, C., & Wilson, K. (2005). *Acceptance and commitment therapy for chronic pain.* Oakland, CA: New Harbinger Publications.

Dahlgren, C. L., Hage, T. W., Wonderlich, J. A., & Stedal, K. (2019). General and eating disorder specific flexibility: Development and validation of the Eating Disorder Flexibility Index (EDFLIX) questionnaire. *Frontiers in Psychology, 10*, 1–14. doi:10.3389/fpsyg.2019.00663

Duarte, C., Ferreira, C., & Pinto-Gouveia, J. (2016). At the core of eating disorders: Overvaluation, social rank, self-criticism and shame in anorexia, bulimia and binge eating disorder. *Comprehensive Psychiatry, 66*, 123–131. doi:https://doi.org/10.1016/j.comppsych.2016.01.003

Duarte, C., Ferreira, C., Pinto-Gouveia, J., Trindade, I. A., & Martinho, A. (2017). What makes dietary restraint problematic? Development and validation of the Inflexible Eating Questionnaire. *Appetite, 114*, 146–154. doi:10.1016/j.appet.2017.03.034

Duarte, C., Pinto-Gouveia, J., Ferreira, C., & Silva, B. (2016). Caught in the struggle with food craving: Development and validation of a new cognitive fusion measure. *Appetite, 101*, 146–155. doi:10.1016/j.appet.2016.03.004

Dziak, J. J., & Nahum-Shani, I. (2016). Three-level modeling for factorial experiments with experimentally induced clustering. University Park, PA: The Methodology Center, Penn State.

Evans, B. C., Murray, H. B., Muratore, A. F., Lantz, E. L., & Juarascio, A. S. (2019). Developing an acceptance-based behavioral weight loss treatment for individuals with binge eating pathology: A preliminary proof of concept study and clinical case series. *Cognitive and Behavioral Practice, 26*(2), 395–410.

Fairburn, C. G., Cooper, Z., & Shafran, R. (2003). Cognitive behaviour therapy for eating disorders: A "transdiagnostic" theory and treatment. *Behaviour Research and Therapy, 41*(5), 509–528.

Fairburn, C. G., Cooper, Z., Shafran, R., Bohn, K., Hawker, D., Murphy, R., & Straebler, S. (2008). Enhanced cognitive behavior therapy for eating disorders: The core protocol. *Cognitive Behavior Therapy and Eating Disorders*, 47–193.

Fairburn, C. G., Shafran, R., & Cooper, Z. (1999). A cognitive behavioural theory of anorexia nervosa. *Behaviour Research and Therapy, 37*(1), 1–13. doi:10.1016/S0005–7967(98)00102–8

Ferreira, C., Palmeira, L., & Trindade, I. A. (2014). Turning eating psychopathology risk factors into action. The pervasive effect of body image-related cognitive fusion. *Appetite, 80*, 137–142. doi:10.1016/j.appet.2014.05.019

Ferreira, C., Trindade, I. A., Duarte, C., & Pinto-Gouveia, J. (2015). Getting entangled with body image: Development and validation of a new measure. *Psychology and Psychotherapy: Theory, Research and Practice, 88*(3), 304–316. doi:10.1111/papt.12047

Fink, E. L., Anestis, M. D., Selby, E. A., & Joiner, T. E. (2010). Negative urgency fully mediates the relationship between alexithymia and dysregulated behaviours. *Personality and Mental Health, 4*(4), 284–293. doi:10.1002/pmh.138

Fogelkvist, M., Gustafsson, S. A., Kjellin, L., & Parling, T. (2020). Acceptance and commitment therapy to reduce eating disorder symptoms and body image problems in patients with residual eating disorder symptoms: A randomized controlled trial. *Body image, 32*, 155–166.

Forman, E. M., & Butryn, M. L. (2015). A new look at the science of weight control: how acceptance and commitment strategies can address the challenge of self-regulation. *Appetite, 84*, 171–180.

Godfrey, K. M., Gallo, L. C., & Afari, N. (2015). Mindfulness-based interventions for binge eating: a systematic review and meta-analysis. *Journal of Behavioral Medicine, 38*(2), 348–362.

Gonidakis, F., Lemonoudi, M., Charila, D., & Varsou, E. (2018). A study on the interplay between emerging adulthood and eating disorder symptomatology in young adults. *Eating and Weight Disorders-Studies on Anorexia, Bulimia and Obesity, 23*(6), 797–805.

Guarda, A. S., Schreyer, C. C., Fischer, L. K., Hansen, J. L., Coughlin, J. W., Kaminsky, M. J., . . . Redgrave, G. W. (2017). Intensive treatment for adults with anorexia nervosa: The cost of weight restoration. *International Journal of Eating Disorders, 50*(3), 302–306. doi:10.1002/eat.22668
Hay, P., Bacaltchuk, J., Stefano, S., & Kashyap, P. (2009). Psychological treatments for bulimia nervosa and binging. *Cochrane Database Systematic Review, 4*, CD000562.
Hayes, S. C., & Pankey, J. (2002). Experiential avoidance, cognitive fusion, and an ACT approach to anorexia nervosa. *Cognitive and Behavioral Practice, 9*(3), 243–247. doi:10.1016/S1077–7229(02)80055–4
Hayes, S. C., Strosahl, K. D., & Wilson, K. G. (2012). *Acceptance and commitment therapy: The process and practice of mindful change* (2nd ed.). New York: Guilford Press.
Haynos, A. F., Forman, E. M., Butryn, M. L., & Lillis, J. (2016). *Mindfulness and acceptance for treating eating disorders and weight concerns: Evidence-based interventions.* Oakland, CA: New Harbinger Publications.
Hill, M. L., Masuda, A., Melcher, H., Morgan, J. R., & Twohig, M. P. (2015). Acceptance and commitment therapy for women diagnosed with binge eating disorder: A case-series study. *Cognitive and Behavioral Practice, 22*(3), 367–378.
Hill, M. L., Schaefer, L. W., Spencer, S. D., & Masuda, A. (2020). Compassion-focused acceptance and commitment therapy for women with restrictive eating and problematic body-checking: A multiple baseline across participants study. *Journal of Contextual Behavioral Science, 16*, 144–152.
Hudson, J. I., Hiripi, E., Pope Jr, H. G., & Kessler, R. C. (2007). The prevalence and correlates of eating disorders in the National Comorbidity Survey Replication. *Biological Psychiatry, 61*(3), 348–358.
Juarascio, A. S., Forman, E. M., & Herbert, J. D. (2010). Acceptance and commitment therapy versus cognitive therapy for the treatment of comorbid eating pathology. *Behavior Modification, 34*(2), 175–190.
Juarascio, A. S., Manasse, S. M., Schumacher, L., Espel, H., & Forman, E. M. (2017). Developing an acceptance-based behavioral treatment for binge eating disorder: Rationale and challenges. *Cognitive and Behavioral Practice, 24*(1), 1–13.
Juarascio, A. S., Schumacher, L. M., Shaw, J., Forman, E. M., & Herbert, J. D. (2015). Acceptance-based treatment and quality of life among patients with an eating disorder. *Journal of Contextual Behavioral Science, 4*(1), 42–47.
Juarascio, A. S., Shaw, J., Forman, E., Timko, C. A., Herbert, J., Butryn, M., . . . Lowe, M. (2013a). Acceptance and commitment therapy as a novel treatment for eating disorders: An initial test of efficacy and mediation. *Behavior Modification, 37*(4), 459–489.
Juarascio, A. S., Shaw, J., Forman, E. M., Timko, C. A., Herbert, J. D., Butryn, M. L., & Lowe, M. (2013b). Acceptance and commitment therapy for eating disorders: Clinical applications of a group treatment. *Journal of Contextual Behavioral Science, 2*(3-4), 85–94.
Kahl, K. G., Winter, L., & Schweiger, U. (2012). The third wave of cognitive behavioural therapies: What is new and what is effective? *Current Opinion in Psychiatry, 25*(6), 522–528. doi:10.1097/YCO.0b013e328358e531
Katterman, S. N., Kleinman, B. M., Hood, M. M., Nackers, L. M., & Corsica, J. A. (2014). Mindfulness meditation as an intervention for binge eating, emotional eating, and weight loss: A systematic review. *Eating Behaviors, 15*(2), 197–204.
Keyser, J., Sharma, P., Pastelak, N., Wirth-Granlund, L., Testa, C., & Alloy, L. (2009). Do emotional avoidance and fear of emotions relate to disordered eating in undergraduate females. Paper presented at the Association for Behavioral and Cognitive Therapies, New York, NY.
Kristeller, J. L., & Wolever, R. Q. (2010). Mindfulness-based eating awareness training for treating binge eating disorder: The conceptual foundation. *Eating Disorders, 19*(1), 49–61.
Lavender, J. M., Mason, T. B., Utzinger, L. M., Wonderlich, S. A., Crosby, R. D., Engel, S. G., . . . Peterson, C. B. (2016). Examining affect and perfectionism in relation to eating disorder symptoms among women with anorexia nervosa. *Psychiatry Research, 241*, 267–272. doi:10.1016/j.psychres.2016.04.122
Lavender, J. M., Wonderlich, S. A., Engel, S. G., Gordon, K. H., Kaye, W. H., & Mitchell, J. E. (2015). Dimensions of emotion dysregulation in anorexia nervosa and bulimia nervosa: A conceptual review of the empirical literature. *Clinical Psychology Review, 40*, 111–122.
Lee, E. B., Ong, C. W., Twohig, M. P., Lensegrav-Benson, T., & Quakenbush-Roberts, B. (2018). Increasing body image flexibility in a residential eating disorder facility: Correlates with symptom improvement. *Eating Disorders, 26*(2), 185–199.
Leehr, E. J., Krohmer, K., Schag, K., Dresler, T., Zipfel, S., & Giel, K. E. (2015). Emotion regulation model in binge eating disorder and obesity: A systematic review. *Neuroscience and Biobehavioral Reviews, 49*, 125–134. doi:10.1016/j.neubiorev.2014.12.008
Lillis, J., Hayes, S. C., & Levin, M. E. (2011). Binge eating and weight control: The role of experiential avoidance. *Behavior Modification, 35*(3), 252–264. doi:10.1177/0145445510397178

Linardon, J. (2018). Meta-analysis of the effects of cognitive-behavioral therapy on the core eating disorder maintaining mechanisms: Implications for mechanisms of therapeutic change. *Cognitive Behaviour Therapy, 47*(2), 107–125.

Linardon, J., Fairburn, C. G., Fitzsimmons-Craft, E. E., Wilfley, D. E., & Brennan, L. (2017). The empirical status of the third-wave behaviour therapies for the treatment of eating disorders: A systematic review. *Clinical Psychology Review, 58*, 125–140.

Linehan, M. M., Bohus, M., & Lynch, T. R. (2007). Dialectical behavior therapy for pervasive emotion dysregulation. *Handbook of Emotion Regulation, 1*, 581–605.

Loth, K. A., Goldschmidt, A. B., Wonderlich, S. A., Lavender, J. M., Neumark-Sztainer, D., & Vohs, K. D. (2016). Could the resource depletion model of self-control help the field to better understand momentary processes that lead to binge eating? *International Journal of Eating Disorders, 49*(11), 998–1001. doi:10.1002/eat.22641

Mallorquí-Bagué, N., Vintró-Alcaraz, C., Sánchez, I., Riesco, N., Agüera, Z., Granero, R., . . . Fernández-Aranda, F. (2018). Emotion regulation as a transdiagnostic feature among eating disorders: Cross-sectional and longitudinal approach. *European Eating Disorders Review, 26*(1), 53–61. doi:10.1002/erv.2570

Manasse, S. M., Espel, H. M., Schumacher, L. M., Kerrigan, S. G., Zhang, F., Forman, E. M., & Juarascio, A. S. (2016). Does impulsivity predict outcome in treatment for binge eating disorder? A multimodal investigation. *Appetite, 105*, 172–179.

Manlick, C. F., Cochran, S. V., & Koon, J. (2013). Acceptance and commitment therapy for eating disorders: Rationale and literature review. *Journal of Contemporary Psychotherapy, 43*(2), 115–122.

Merwin, R. M., & Wilson, K. G. (2009). Understanding and treating eating disorders: An ACT perspective. *Acceptance and commitment therapy: Contemporary theory, research, and practice*, 87–117. Bowens Hills, Australia: Australian Academic Press.

Merwin, R. M., Zucker, N. L., Lacy, J. L., & Elliott, C. A. (2010). Interoceptive awareness in eating disorders: Distinguishing lack of clarity from non-acceptance of internal experience. *Cognition and Emotion, 24*(5), 892–902. doi:10.1080/02699930902985845

Mitchison, D., Hay, P., Slewa-Younan, S., & Mond, J. (2012). Time trends in population prevalence of eating disorder behaviors and their relationship to quality of life. *PloS One, 7*(11), e48450.

Mitchison, D., Touyz, S., González-Chica, D. A., Stocks, N., & Hay, P. (2017). How abnormal is binge eating? 18-Year time trends in population prevalence and burden. *Acta Psychiatrica Scandinavica, 136*(2), 147–155.

Mond, J. M., & Hay, P. J. (2007). Functional impairment associated with bulimic behaviors in a community sample of men and women. *International Journal of Eating Disorders, 40*(5), 391–398.

Monroe, J. T. (2015). Mindful eating: Principles and practice. *American Journal of Lifestyle Medicine, 9*(3), 217–220. doi:10.1177/1559827615569682

Moskowitz, L., & Weiselberg, E. (2017). Anorexia nervosa/Atypical anorexia nervosa. *Current Problems in Pediatric Adolescent Health Care, 47*(4), 70–84. doi:10.1016/j.cppeds.2017.02.003

National Guidance Alliance (UK). (2017). *E ating disorders: Recognition and treatment*. National Institute for Health and Care Excellence (NICE).

Nielsen, L., Riddle, M., King, J. W., Aklin, W. M., Chen, W., Clark, D., . . . Ferrer, R. (2018). The NIH Science of Behavior Change Program: Transforming the science through a focus on mechanisms of change. *Behaviour Research and Therapy, 101*, 3–11.

Orsillo, S. M., & Batten, S. V. (2002). ACT as treatment of a disorder of excessive control: Anorexia. *Cognitive and Behavioral Practice, 9*(3), 253–259. doi:10.1016/S1077-7229(02)80057-8

Paola, L.-S., Sérgio, A. C., Margareth da Silva, O., & José, P.-G. (2017). Body-Image Acceptance and Action Questionnaire: Its deleterious influence on binge eating and psychometric validation. *International Journal of Clinical and Health Psychology, 17*(2), 151–160. doi:10.1016/j-ijchp.2017.03.001

Parling, T., Cernvall, M., Ramklint, M., Holmgren, S., & Ghaderi, A. (2016). A randomised trial of acceptance and commitment therapy for anorexia nervosa after daycare treatment, including five-year follow-up. *BMC Psychiatry, 16*(1), 272.

Pearson, A. N., Follette, V. M., & Hayes, S. C. (2012). A pilot study of acceptance and commitment therapy as a workshop intervention for body dissatisfaction and disordered eating attitudes. *Cognitive and Behavioral Practice, 19*(1), 181–197.

Peat, C. M., Berkman, N. D., Lohr, K. N., Brownley, K. A., Bann, C. M., Cullen, K., . . . Bulik, C. M. (2017). Comparative effectiveness of treatments for binge-eating disorder: Systematic review and network meta-analysis. *European Eating Disorders Review, 25*(5), 317–328.

Penn State Methodology Center. (2016). Optimizing behavioral interventions. Retrieved from https://www.methodology.psu.edu/research-and-rigor/

Pintado-Cucarella, S., & Rodríguez-Salgado, P. (2016). Mindful eating and its relationship with body mass index, binge eating, anxiety and negative affect. *Journal of Behavior, Health & Social Issues, 8*(2), 19–24. doi:10.1016/j.jbhsi.2016.11.003
Prefit, A.-B., Cândea, D. M., & Szentagotai-Tătar, A. (2019). Emotion regulation across eating pathology: A meta-analysis. *Appetite, 143*, 104438. doi:10.1016/j.appet.2019.104438
Roberto, C. A., Grilo, C. M., Masheb, R. M., & White, M. A. (2010). Binge eating, purging, or both: eating disorder psychopathology findings from an internet community survey. *International Journal of Eating Disorders, 43*(8), 724–731.
Sarno, M. (2020). *Valued living and psychological inflexibility as predictors of binge eating behavior* (Order No. 28087365) [Doctoral dissertation, Alliant International University]. ProQuest Dissertations & Theses Global.
Schaefer, L. M., Smith, K. E., Anderson, L. M., Cao, L., Crosby, R. D., Engel, S. G., . . . Wonderlich, S. A. (2020). The role of affect in the maintenance of binge-eating disorder: Evidence from an ecological momentary assessment study. *Journal of Abnormal Psychology, 129*(4), 387–396. doi:10.1037/abn0000517
Shah, N., Passi, V., Bryson, S., & Agras, W. S. (2005). Patterns of eating and abstinence in women treated for bulimia nervosa. *International Journal of Eating Disorders, 38*(4), 330–334.
Shapiro, S. L., Carlson, L. E., Astin, J. A., & Freedman, B. (2006). Mechanisms of mindfulness. *Journal of Clinical Psychology, 62*(3), 373–386.
Smyth, J. M., Wonderlich, S. A., Heron, K. E., Sliwinski, M. J., Crosby, R. D., Mitchell, J. E., & Engel, S. G. (2007). Daily and momentary mood and stress are associated with binge eating and vomiting in bulimia nervosa patients in the natural environment. *Journal of Consulting and Clinical Psychology, 75*(4), 629–638. doi:10.1037/0022-006X.75.4.629
Stice, E. (2002). Risk and maintenance factors for eating pathology: A meta-analytic review. *Psychological Bulletin, 128*(5), 825–848.
Strandskov, S. W., Ghaderi, A., Andersson, H., Parmskog, N., Hjort, E., Wärn, A. S., . . . Andersson, G. (2017). Effects of tailored and ACT-influenced internet-based CBT for eating disorders and the relation between knowledge acquisition and outcome: A randomized controlled trial. *Behavior Therapy, 48*(5), 624–637.
Timko, C. A., Zucker, N. L., Herbert, J. D., Rodriguez, D., & Merwin, R. M. (2015). An open trial of Acceptance-based Separated Family Treatment (ASFT) for adolescents with anorexia nervosa. *Behaviour Research and Therapy, 69*, 63–74.
Udo, T., & Grilo, C. M. (2018). Prevalence and correlates of DSM-5–defined eating disorders in a nationally representative sample of US adults. *Biological Psychiatry, 84*(5), 345–354.
Watson, H. J., & Bulik, C. M. (2013). Update on the treatment of anorexia nervosa: review of clinical trials, practice guidelines and emerging interventions. *Psychological Medicine, 43*(12), 2477–2500. doi:10.1017/S0033291712002620
Westwood, H., Kerr-Gaffney, J., Stahl, D., & Tchanturia, K. (2017). Alexithymia in eating disorders: Systematic review and meta-analyses of studies using the Toronto Alexithymia Scale. *Journal of Psychosomatic Research, 99*, 66–81. doi:10.1016/j.jpsychores.2017.06.007
White, Z. L. (2018). *Self-concealment, psychological flexibility, and severity of eating disorders* (Order No. 10975158) (Doctoral dissertation). Columbia University. ProQuest Dissertations & Theses Global.
Whitelaw, M., Lee, K. J., Gilbertson, H., & Sawyer, S. M. (2018). Predictors of complications in anorexia nervosa and atypical anorexia nervosa: Degree of underweight or extent and recency of weight loss? *Journal of Adolescent Health, 63*(6), 717–723. doi:10.1016/j.jadohealth.2018.08.019
Wildes, J. E., & Marcus, M. D. (2011). Development of emotion acceptance behavior therapy for anorexia nervosa: A case series. *International Journal of Eating Disorders, 44*(5), 421–427.
Wildes, J. E., Marcus, M. D., Cheng, Y., McCabe, E. B., & Gaskill, J. A. (2014). Emotion acceptance behavior therapy for anorexia nervosa: A pilot study. *International Journal of Eating Disorders, 47*(8), 870–873.
Wilson, G. T. (2005). Psychological treatment of eating disorders. *Annual Review of Clinical Psychology, 1*, 439–465.
Wu, M., Giel, K. E., Skunde, M., Schag, K., Rudofsky, G., de Zwaan, M., . . . Friederich, H. C. (2013). Inhibitory control and decision making under risk in bulimia nervosa and binge-eating disorder. *International Journal of Eating Disorders, 46*(7), 721–728.
Wyssen, A., Debbeler, Luka J., Meyer, A. H., Coelho, J. S., Humbel, N., Schuck, K., . . . Munsch, S. (2018). Relevance of the Thought–Shape Fusion Trait Questionnaire for healthy women and women presenting symptoms of eating disorders and mixed mental disorders. *Clinical Psychology and Psychotherapy, 25*(4), 601–607. doi:10.1002/cpp.2186
Zimmerman, B. J. (2000). Attaining self-regulation: A social cognitive perspective. In M. Boekaerts, P. R. Pintrich, & M. Zeidner (Eds.), *Handbook of self-regulation* (pp. 13–39). San Diego, CA: Academic Press.

CHAPTER

18 Health Promotion and Weight Management for Obesity

Jason Lillis *and* Dayna Lee-Baggley

Abstract

Obesity is prevalent and carries substantial individual and societal-level consequences, including increased mortality and high health care costs. Obesity is best viewed as a chronic disease that requires both individual and system-level interventions that take into account a multitude of contributing factors. Acceptance and commitment therapy (ACT) principles and strategies can play a role in the treatment of individuals with obesity primarily by addressing barriers to healthy behavior change by teaching values, acceptance, defusion, and mindfulness skills. Interventions incorporating these ACT methods have shown improved obesity management outcomes relative to current gold standard behavioral treatments, and ACT can be considered evidence for use in this area. However, behavioral treatments in general are limited in terms of reach and effectiveness, and system- and environmental-level interventions will be required to meaningfully address obesity worldwide. Future research on ACT and other contextual therapeutic approaches should focus on addressing these system-level factors in order to support already well-developed individual-level interventions.

Key Words: obesity, weight management, health promotion, stigma, acceptance-based behavior therapy, mindfulness, psychological flexibility

Obesity is a prevalent, detrimental, and costly disease. Global studies indicate that 38 percent of the world population meet criteria for overweight and 13 percent meet criteria for obesity based on the body mass index (BMI; World Health Organization, 2020). In the United States, statistics for 2017–2018 showed that 42.4 percent of American adults met the criteria for obesity (Hales, Carroll, Fryar, & Odgen, 2020). Obesity is associated with significant health complications, including increased mortality rates from cancer and increased risk of a number of other diseases such as cardiovascular disease, neurological disease, and psychiatric conditions, as well as reduced quality of life (Calle, Thun, Petrelli, Rodriguez, & Heath, 1999; Catenacci, Hill, & Wyatt, 2009; Lauby-Secretan et al., 2016; Luppino et al., 2010; Wang et al., 2011; Whitlock et al., 2009). Obesity is also associated with substantial annual health care costs, which are estimated to be more than two trillion US dollars globally, including costs for disability and lost productivity (Tremmel, Gerdtham, Nilsson, & Saha, 2017).

Definition of Obesity

Obesity is most commonly defined through the body mass index (BMI), which is a calculation of weight versus height (kg/m^2). "Normal" weight is defined as BMI ≥18 kg/m^2 and <25 kg/m^2, "overweight" as BMI ≥25 kg/m^2, and "obesity" as BMI ≥30 kg/m^2. Furthermore, "obesity" can be classified as Class 1 (BMI of 30– <35), Class 2 (BMI of 35–<40), or Class 3 (BMI of 40 or higher).

However, there are limitations in using BMI as a classification for obesity. First, studies show that BMI is not the best predictor of health (Canning, Brown, Wharton, Sharma, & Kuk, 2015; Padwal, Pajewski, Allison, & Sharma, 2011). For example, many elite athletes are classified as overweight or obese because the BMI makes no distinction between muscle mass and adipose. Thus, the definition overemphasizes the importance of weight. Second, this definition does not define obesity explicitly as a chronic condition, which likely contributes to the fact that the multifaceted nature of obesity is deemphasized or at times outright ignored in favor of the perspective that obesity is a matter of behavioral self-regulation failure. In fact, scientific advancements in biology and neuroscience have revealed that a multitude of factors influence weight.

Factors Impacting Weight

THE ROLE OF EVOLUTIONARY AND PHYSIOLOGICAL FACTORS IN OBESITY

Evolutionary science highlights that excess weight is not a disorder. Starving to death has always been a major threat to the human species and continues to be: approximately 9 million people die of hunger every year, and countless more just barely escape this worst case outcome. As a result of this ongoing threat, evolution has shaped humans to have a number of systems to prevent starving to death. For example, research shows that food smells better and tastes better a year after weight loss (Dulloo, Jacquet, & Girardier, 1996; Tremblay, Royer, Chaput, & Doucet, 2013), which would be a highly adaptive way to promote weight gain and prevent starvation after weight loss. Additionally, through a process known as metabolic adaptation (Bliss & Whiteside, 2018; Mebel, Wong, Dong, & Borgland, 2012; Muller, Enderle, & Bosy-Westphal, 2016; Rosenbaum & Leibel, 2010), metabolism slows down after weight loss and tends to stay slowed down even when weight is regained (Fothergill et al., 2016).

THE ROLE OF THE BRAIN IN OBESITY

Humans do not eat simply for fuel, and complex neural patterns and functions are implicated in weight that are outside of conscious control. There are three main systems in the brain (homeostatic, hedonic, and executive functioning) that impact obesity by influencing weight, eating, cravings, and satiety (Wharton et al., 2020).

Newer studies have demonstrated the way in which brain structures and functions may predispose people to obesity and are altered as a result of living with obesity. For example, after people lose weight, the mesolimbic system is more easily activated in response to food cues (Lau & Wharton, 2020). Experientially, this means that people with obesity are experiencing more intense cravings in response to food cues than people without obesity. Furthermore, genetic studies demonstrate that a complex combination of genes influence obesity (e.g., over 40 genetic regions; Fall, Mendelson, & Speliotes, 2017). Concordance rates for the heritability of body mass range from 50 to 80 percent, which (on the upper end) are comparable to the heritability of height (Thornton, Mazzeo, & Bulik, 2011). Overall, scientific findings demonstrate that the contributors of obesity are multifactorial and not simply related to individual choice in eating and exercise.

THE ROLE OF THE ENVIRONMENT IN OBESITY

Most individuals in wealthier nations live in an obesogenic environment, which is characterized by factors that are barriers to achieving a healthy weight (Kirk, Penney, & McHugh,

2010). These can include aspects of the physical environment (e.g., accessibility and availability of physical activity, neighborhood walkability, sedentary lifestyles, exposure to food advertisements, and automotive use), economic environment (e.g., neighborhood socioeconomic status, food insecurity), political microenvironment (e.g., any "rule" that is imposed on individuals, from workplace policies regarding break times or cafeteria menus to household rules for children regarding TV time), sociocultural microenvironment (e.g., social support, body weight norms), and the macroenvironment (e.g., media, food production and manufacturing, food marketing, urban/rural development, transportation and the health system). Consistent with the notion that obesity is multifactorial, obesity rates will not be meaningfully impacted by focusing only on individual-level interventions. The individual struggling to manage weight must recognize that we all live in an environment that not only undermines healthy choices but often fosters unhealthy choices.

THE ROLE OF WEIGHT BIAS, STIGMA, AND DISCRIMINATION IN OBESITY

Weight bias refers to having negative attitudes toward people with obesity and can take the forms of explicit bias (overt negative attitudes), implicit bias (unconscious negative attitudes), or internalized bias (individuals living with obesity holding negative attitudes about themselves; Kirk, Ramos, Alberga, & Russell-Mayhew, 2020). Common negative attitudes toward people living with obesity include assumptions that people with obesity are lazy, unmotivated, lack self-discipline, or are noncompliant (Puhl & Brownell, 2001; Puhl & Heuer, 2009). Studies show that internalized weight bias is associated with behaviors detrimental to weight management, such as exercise avoidance and binge eating (Puhl & Heuer, 2010). Weight stigma refers to manifestations of weight bias. Examples include health care providers who don't offer weight-related treatment to people with obesity because they assume they will be noncompliant with medical advice and lower rates of job attainment and college admission acceptance for individuals with obesity. Weight bias and stigma are prevalent and have been documented in the general population as well as in specific populations such as teachers, employers, and health care providers (Cameron, 2016; Pearl, 2018; Rudolph, Wells, Weller, & Baltes, 2009; Teachman & Brownell, 2001).

Weight bias, stigma, and discrimination clearly have a detrimental impact on individuals living with obesity, including mental illness, body image, perceived stress, substance use, health behaviors, morbidity and mortality, social support, and economic consequences (Kirk et al., 2020; Puhl & Heuer, 2010). Furthermore, theory and research demonstrate how weight bias, stigma, and discrimination may impact weight management directly. Tomiyama (2014) described the Cycle Obesity/Weight-Based Stigma (COBWEBS) model, which details the behavioral, emotional, and physiological mechanisms through which experiencing weight bias can cause weight gain in a vicious cycle, including through changes in eating behavior and increases in cortisol. A review of the literature showed that weight stigma is directly related to physiological and psychological health outcomes, including weight gain, diabetes risk, cortisol levels, eating disturbances, depressive symptoms, anxiety, self-esteem, body image, and psychological distress in individuals living with obesity (Wu & Berry, 2018). Another study showed that even internalized weight stigma can impact cortisol response in individuals with obesity (Jung, Bae, Kratzsch, Riedel-Heller, & Luck-Sikorski, 2020). Finally, Daly, Sutin, & Robinson (2019) showed that both weight and perceived weight discrimination predicted increases in physiological dysregulation in a 4-year longitudinal study. These studies show that weight bias, stigma, and discrimination impact not only mental health and health behaviors but also physiological mechanisms that contribute to weight gain. This is additional evidence that obesity is best understood as a chronic, multifaceted disease.

A Revised Definition of "Obesity"

A revised definition of obesity has been offered to address the limitations of the current definition of obesity (Wharton et al., 2020). For example, the most recent clinical guidelines for obesity management from Obesity Canada define obesity as "excess weight causing medical or psychological complications" (Wharton et al., 2020). This definition addresses the issue that weight (or BMI) is not the best indicator of health (Canning et al., 2015; Padwal et al., 2011), and therefore weight alone should not define the medical condition of obesity. For example, it is possible for people to have excess weight that is not defined as obesity because it is not causing medical or psychological complications. This definition therefore allows a distinction between "large bodies" and a medical condition requiring medical intervention. This definition removes some of the stigma of excess weight while allowing for treatment when excess weight starts to create health problems. In addition, this definition highlights the idea that obesity management should focus on health and well-being and not simply weight loss (Kuk et al., 2011; Osunlana et al., 2015).

TREATING OBESITY AS A CHRONIC DISEASE

When obesity is defined in this way, it should also be managed as a chronic disease (Wharton et al., 2020). One significant implication of such a definition is that obesity must be continuously managed over time. There is no "cure" for obesity, and there is no "diet" that will result in long-term changes once the intervention has ended. For comparison, a physician would never treat diabetes for only 6 weeks and then be surprised when blood sugars are out of control one year later. In every other chronic disease (e.g., diabetes, heart disease, cancer), a variety of medical interventions are available, including medications and surgeries to manage the illness. In no other chronic disease is lifestyle change viewed as the only intervention. Consistent with other chronic diseases, obesity should be managed with a variety of medical interventions, including anti-obesity medication and bariatric surgery when appropriate.

THE PILLAR MODEL OF OBESITY MANAGEMENT

This view of obesity as a chronic disease is captured in the new obesity management guidelines by Obesity Canada (Wharton et al., 2020). These guidelines move beyond the traditional pyramid model of interventions. The pyramid model is often portrayed as one in which lifestyle changes form the base of the pyramid and treatments are escalated to medication if lifestyle changes "fail" and then are escalated to surgery. It is well documented that most individuals relying solely on lifestyle changes do not maintain long-term weight loss (Wing & Phelan, 2005). However, rather than seeing the intervention as failing the patient, it has been traditionally viewed as the patient having failed the intervention. Instead, the new obesity guidelines present a pillar model of obesity management. Lifestyle change is necessary, but most often it is not a sufficient treatment on its own. Lifestyle changes must be supported by one or multiple pillars. The pillars include medication, surgery, and psychological treatment. Psychological interventions therefore play a major part in managing obesity as a chronic disease.

Psychological interventions for weight take one of two main forms. One addresses lifestyle-based changes and works primarily at behavior change related to diet and exercise habits (e.g., counting calories, weighing oneself frequently, setting goals, problem solving). The second form includes more psychological aspects that are designed to target health, well-being, thoughts, and emotions in addition to any behavior change. Acceptance and commitment is an example of this latter form, and it most often focuses on whole health and well-being in the context of weight influencing intervention.

ACT for Overweight and Obesity Theoretical Overview

ACT interventions for overweight and obesity can be broadly organized under the goal of facilitating healthy behavior change, most often including reduced intake of unhealthy foods, increased healthfulness of dietary choices, and increased physical activity, both in structured and daily activity form. To date, these interventions have almost exclusively been delivered in group-based, in-person formats. Length of intervention varies widely and is often influenced by the degree of integration with standard behavioral intervention. For example, one model is to deliver ACT after initial weight loss intervention (additive model), and that could be delivered in a single 1-day workshop or in three to five sessions over 3–6 months. This format would focus almost exclusively on ACT-based processes in support of previously learned behavior skills (e.g., teaching defusion skills to address thoughts that interfere with exercising). Alternatively, a fully integrated protocol might combine ACT methods with standard behavioral therapy over the course of a 6–12 month, weekly to biweekly intervention structure. This kind of approach would "switch" between elements of both, for example, providing nutrition education followed by acceptance methods to help tolerate food cravings.

ACT interventions typically have a strong emphasis on behavior change and on tracking healthy behaviors, not unlike traditional behavioral approaches. However, the role of weight and weight tracking in ACT treatment varies considerably across applications—from one end of the spectrum emphasizing weight loss as a primary outcome to the other end explicitly discouraging focus on weight, as well as gradations in between. When implementing ACT in this area, it is important to fully clarify and articulate the role of weight in your intervention.

We lean toward deemphasizing weight as a primary focus of intervention for several reasons. First, as explained previously, weight can be influenced, but it cannot be fully controlled. Thus, goal weights, and more importantly the use of goal weights as arbiters of lifestyle change "success," are inherently problematic and can obscure the importance of the health and well-being benefits of behavior change. Weight is not a behavior, and ACT is a technology designed to facilitate behavior change. Thus, it is more theoretically consistent and clinically useful to define the outcomes of interest as the healthy behaviors desired.

The second reason to consider a deemphasis on weight is the potential problems posed by the weight loss agenda itself. The goal of weight loss, at its core, can be an agenda of inflexibility and avoidance. For example, a person may cite the desire to "feel better about myself," pointing to a primary function of changing internal experiences in the form of negative thoughts/self-judgments ("I'm weak, worthless"), feelings (shame, guilt, disgust, lack of confidence), and assumed perceptions from others ("They find me unattractive, incapable, lazy, gross"). Given what is known about experiential avoidance and psychological inflexibility, a weight loss agenda emphasizing the scale and focused on changing internal experiences, from an ACT perspective, is less likely to lead to long-term healthy behavior change as compared to an agenda focused on behavior change consistent with one's values.

In addition, it is important to consider the message being delivered by encouraging a primary focus on weight and internal change motivation. We are likely fostering (or at least reinforcing) an avoidance agenda if we emphasize the scale and encourage motivation based on "feeling better" (emotional change), "having more confidence" (cognitive change), or "fitting into my bathing suit" (i.e., avoiding my own self-criticism and co-occurring emotion). An avoidance-based agenda may work in the short term, but evidence suggests that it may be ineffective in the long term. Individuals may find that they did not lose "enough" weight to "fix" their thoughts and feelings, or that they lost the weight and still find themselves struggling to change thoughts and feelings. Therefore, we believe that ACT intervention for overweight and obesity needs to take some measure of undermining avoidance-based sources of motivation and narrow focus on weight as the primary outcome.

Of course, it can be difficult to undermine the weight loss agenda, and extreme attempts to do so risk alienating clients, who will most often maintain *some* focus on weight throughout and after treatment regardless. Accordingly, it can be more helpful to promote an "additional" agenda focused on behavior change linked to values, with an emphasis on tracking behavior changes (e.g., health behaviors in the service of moving toward a meaningful, purposeful life), moving the scale to the periphery in terms of clinical focus, as opposed to repeatedly challenging the importance of weight. For example, we might say that successfully managing weight is a side effect of healthy living. This is similar to other ACT interventions that focus on the control agenda around "getting rid" of "negative" feelings such as anxiety. The ACT treatment does not focus on reducing anxiety, but a well-established "side effect" is the reduction of anxiety (i.e., numerous randomly controlled trials indicate ACT interventions for anxiety result in clinically significant reductions in anxiety; Swain, Hancock, Hainsworth, & Bowman, 2013).

Therefore, one of the organizing themes of ACT for overweight and obesity is that healthy living—that is, eating healthy foods in sensible proportions, avoiding unhealthy eating choices, being physically active, and tracking your health behaviors—is a values-based choice that aligns with and empowers living consistent with core personal values. Healthy behaviors are viewed in the context of what deeply matters to the individual, and steps are taken in treatment to clarify the link between healthy behaviors and values-consistent living. The following are examples of how to align healthy behaviors with values:

- Healthy habits can lead to increased energy, stamina, mobility, functionality, or longevity, which enable participation in desired activities (taking hiking vacations, playing tennis with a partner, joining a fitness activity-oriented group, walking with a friend) or allows for attending and fully participating in significant events (weddings, birthdays, anniversaries).
- Healthy habits may contribute to reduced physical discomfort, improved sleep, better concentration/awareness/connection to the present moment, and subjective mood improvements, which may allow one to improve the quality of interaction with others, whether that be increased patience with children, better listening, and validation with family members, or greater intimacy-seeking behavior with one's partner.
- Healthy habits may directly represent the value of taking care of one's self and others by improving one's physical status, devoting time to caring for one's self, and setting a positive health example for loved ones.

Clarifying values and linking healthy behaviors to values help address the inherent problem of short-term versus long-term motivation in health promotion. Positive health status is a diffuse and future-oriented outcome, making it difficult for use in sustaining healthy lifestyle motivation in most individuals who have not experienced serious threats to their health. The short-term reinforcement of highly palatable food and sedentary behavior is powerful, and easily accessible. Initial weight loss efforts are buoyed by rapid, tangible treatment gains (reduced weight, clothing size changes, energy/mobility improvements, and social comments from others). However, these benefits are reduced or eliminated over time. Continuing to engage in healthy behaviors can be experienced as increasingly effortful and tedious, and it requires forgoing short-term pleasure. This is likely part of the reason that individuals tend to regain lost weight, as the short-term pull to seek pleasure or comfort is no longer matched or offset by other short- to medium-term benefits for engaging in healthy behaviors.

One advantage of aligning day-to-day healthy lifestyle with core personal values is that this link can bring moment-to-moment satisfaction to healthy behaviors that typically do not provide short-term satisfaction or reinforcement. Counting calories to "meet a prescribed goal" might be acceptable when weight loss is apparent, but motivation to count calories is much less likely after plateauing, let alone gaining weight. Alternatively, if counting calories is about "being a more present, loving, patient partner and mother," then one can access an ongoing sense of meaning, purpose, and satisfaction in this typically mundane, effortful behavior.

As is the case with traditional weight methods, self-monitoring has a central role in ACT for overweight and obesity, with modified targets. The ultimate goal of self-monitoring in ACT applied here is to track the presence of healthy behaviors that have been explicitly linked to a broader context of core personal values, as well as unhealthy behaviors considered to be health- and core-value inconsistent. This places the emphasis squarely on behavior in control of the individual and fosters connection with the big picture role these healthy habits play in the individual's life. The emphasis is on behaviors as opposed to weight. Tracking weight is permissible (although, again, the degree of emphasis on weight varies considerably across ACT interventions) in the context of increasing healthy behaviors consistent with one's core values. Change in weight is information that can be utilized to track and improve engagement in healthy behaviors. Thus, the role of tracking weight is explicitly discussed and clarified. Tracking calorie intake and activity level is more central to ACT interventions, as these targets reflect behavioral choices and can directly guide behavior-change efforts. Values engagement, more broadly speaking (as opposed to just related to health targets), can also be a self-monitoring target.

Another important aspect of ACT for overweight and obesity intervention is the greater emphasis on the function of behavior than on its topography. For example, if an individual did not exercise in the past week, a traditional behavioral approach would engage in problem-solving interventions. The interventionist might brainstorm alternative times to exercise (before work, during lunch break), identify strategies to prepare in advance for physical activity (keep your walking shoes in the car, take your gym clothes to work), or intervene on time management (schedule the exercise in your calendar, set reminders).

In ACT, the interventionist might instead try to look at the functions of not exercising. Did exercising allow the individual to avoid unpleasant physical sensations associated with exercise? Did it reduce the possibility of fears of judgments from others whom they might encounter while exercising? Did the alternative behaviors (e.g., watching TV) provide some comfort or relief from unwanted feeling states (e.g., stress, fatigue, boredom)? Was the client aware of the vital connections between regular exercise and their goals and core values to the point where appropriate motivation was present? From an ACT perspective, it is important to understand the function of the behavior (in this case exercise avoidance) in order to identify which ACT process to target (e.g., defusion, acceptance, values).

Another important theme in ACT for overweight and obesity intervention is "doing what works." Thus, problem solving, or virtually any traditional behavior technique (e.g., goal setting, stimulus control), can be utilized in treatment. Usually, some distinction is made about applying change efforts where they are helpful (e.g., aspects of behavior and manipulable parts of their environment), while letting go of change efforts in areas where it is unhelpful (e.g., thoughts, feelings, bodily sensations). This allows for using strategies such as changing the time of day for exercising or removing desired foods (e.g., ice cream) from the home, or looking at restaurant menus in advance of a family outing in order to select a lower calorie item. These strategies sometimes work, but they also can be limited when underlying issues of a cognitive and emotional control agenda go unidentified or unaddressed.

Table 18.1. ACT Conceptual Model for Common Barriers to Healthy Behaviors

Barrier	ACT Conceptualization
Lack of motivation	Lack of congruence between healthy behaviors and core values; that is, no awareness of the link between healthy behaviors and empowering values-consistent living and/or inadequate ability to contact awareness of this link when needed.
Unrestrained eating/ food cravings	Eating functions to relieve individual of an unwanted physiological (hunger, pain, discomfort) or emotional state (e.g., deprivation, sadness, anxiety, stress, boredom) and/or is driven by producing a short-term desired physiological or emotional state (comfort, pleasure, excitement, happiness).
Excuses, self-critical thoughts, permissive thoughts	Fusion with thoughts. Excuses are experienced as literally true, and thus healthy behaviors are not seen as possible in such a context. Self-criticism is experienced as threatening and requiring change efforts to combat threats to psychological and emotional well-being and also contribute to demotivation. Permissive thoughts (e.g., "Just one won't hurt" or "I deserve this") are bought into and frequently conceptualized as acts of self-care.
Mindless behavior in general, and mindless eating specifically	Lack of mindfulness. Awareness of behavioral choices is a necessary precursor to sustained healthy habits. Mindfulness of present cognitions and emotional and physiological states is necessary to implement ACT-based skills to prevent unhealthy, short-term, cognitive, emotional, and physiological change-oriented behavioral patterns.

An emphasis on "doing what works" requires agreement between client and practitioner about to what end. Thus, the organizing treatment goal is of paramount importance. Ideally, an ACT intervention encourages clients to "do what works" in facilitating the initiation and persistence with healthy eating and activity habits contributing toward a more value-consistent life. The strategies utilized are therefore judged on their ability to increase or sustain engagement in healthy behaviors (as opposed to weight change or cognitive/emotional change). See Table 18.1 for examples of how ACT conceptualizes barriers to healthy behavior change.

Acceptance, defusion, and mindfulness are therefore typically presented as skills to help enable patients to take effective action ("do what works"), and they can be tailored to the specific needs of the individual. Acceptance strategies have been targeted most often at hunger, cravings, and emotions linked with overeating, such as stress. There can be a strong link between having a food craving and immediately satisfying that craving, regardless of whether the satisfaction is fleeting or if psychological (guilt, shame) or physical consequences (feeling sick, tired) happened soon after. Similarly, individuals often seek pleasurable foods to soothe negative emotions, like stress from a bad day at work, or sadness from a relationship problem. Acceptance strategies aim to increase openness to, and embracing of, these unwanted experiences for the purpose of meeting health goals consistent with one's values.

Defusion strategies target thoughts that serve as barriers to consistent engagement in healthy behaviors consistent with one's values. Although almost any thought could potentially function as a barrier to someone, it is common for permissive thoughts (e.g., "One won't hurt!" "You deserve this." "You can do that tomorrow") to be reported as problematic. Defusion strategies aim to help patients contact the familiar and repetitive nature of these thoughts, undermine their literality or believability, identify their role in overeating and sedentary behavioral patterns, and ultimately help build a more "distanced" perspective from which to observe these thoughts while simultaneously being able to choose healthy behavioral options that run counter to them.

The role of mindfulness can vary more widely in ACT treatments for obesity. Some protocols include formal mindfulness training and/or specific training in mindful eating methods. The focus here is on building general mindfulness skills that can function to slow down the automatic nature of food choice and eating. Other approaches may employ more "practical" mindfulness training in the form of recalling values narratives and values-based goals in difficult situations (a mindful awareness focus), or possibly target the recognition of behavioral choices made throughout the day, sometimes referred to as "choice points." In this case, the focus is aimed at consistent awareness of a key concept or skill (e.g., remembering your values, or "seeing" the choice) but typically does not include formal contemplative practice. This latter method can involve technology-based reminders and writing as training tools.

Overall, ACT uses familiar processes—values, acceptance, defusion, mindfulness—tailored to issues related to obesity management for the purpose of facilitating or fostering adherence to healthy behavior changes.

Evidence

Evidence for using ACT in this area can be evaluated in a variety of ways. We chose to review the following: (1) general efficacy for using ACT in weight management, (2) evidence that ACT can be delivered in different formats, and, (3) process-based evidence. We note that this review is not systematic, but rather selective to illustrate the types of studies and general evidence in each area.

Efficacy Support for Using ACT for Weight Management

A series of treatment development and efficacy studies have been completed by Drs. Forman, Butryn, and colleagues at Drexel University. Their group developed an acceptance-based treatment (ABT) that integrates techniques from ACT (with an emphasis on mindfulness and acceptance processes) with strategies from standard behavioral treatment (SBT) for weight loss (e.g., goal setting, self-monitoring, environmental control). The first study was an open trial of a 12-week ABT intervention in which participants showed a mean weight loss of 6.6 percent at 3 months (posttreatment) and 9.6 percent at 9 months (Forman, Butryn, Hoffman, & Herbert, 2009). This compares favorably to gold standard behavioral weight loss intervention, which averages about 7 percent weight loss between 9 and 12 months (Butryn, Webb, & Wadden, 2011).

In a medium-sized randomized controlled trial, 128 participants with overweight or obesity were assigned to 40 weeks of ABT or SBT (Forman et al., 2013). Results showed greater weight loss for ABT compared to SBT at posttreatment (13.17% vs 7.54%) and 6 months after treatment ended (10.98% vs 4.83%). There was evidence supporting the proposition that ABT was more potent when delivered by experts and when received by participants with greater baseline depression symptomatology and higher reactivity to food cues.

In a large randomized controlled trial, 190 participants with overweight or obesity were assigned to ABT or SBT and received 25 sessions of intervention over one year (Forman et al., 2016). ABT participants had greater weight loss at posttreatment (12 months) as compared to SBT (13.3% vs. 9.8%). In addition, ABT had a greater proportion of participants who lost and maintained at least a 10% weight loss by month 12 (64% vs 49%).

Another series of studies have been conducted by Lillis, Wing, and colleagues at the Alpert Brown Medical School. Similar to the Drexel studies, ACT methods were integrated with standard behavioral methods to develop an acceptance-based behavioral intervention

(ABBI). The initial test was an open trial of ABBI in a 24-week protocol (Niemeier, Leahey, Reed, Brown, & Wing, 2012). Participants (n = 21) high on internal disinhibition (eating in response to thoughts and emotions) were targeted and included in the study because on average they tend to have poorer outcomes in SBT (Niemeier, Phelan, Fava, & Wing, 2007). Results showed a mean weight loss of 12 kg at posttreatment, which is well above typical weight loss over the same timeframe for individuals with high internal disinhibition. Weight loss was maintained (12.1 kg) when assessed 3 months later (Niemeier et al., 2012).

In a follow-up RCT, ABBI was compared to SBT for 162 adults with overweight or obesity who reported high internal disinhibition at baseline (Lillis et al., 2016). Participants received 32 sessions over the course of 12 months, and the final assessment was given at 24 months after baseline. Although there were no differences between groups at posttreatment, at 24 months ACT had mean weight loss of –4.1 percent compared to –2.4 percent for SBT, primarily because ACT participants regained significantly less weight on average after treatment was discontinued (4.6 kg vs 7.1 kg, respectively).

Given previous results, another RCT was conducted using ACT methods to target weight loss maintenance. In this trial, 188 participants received an online, 12-week weight loss intervention, and those who lost ≥5 percent (n = 102) were then randomly assigned to a one-time, 5-hour workshop based on ACT, Self-Regulation (SR), or no workshop (Control), with limited email follow-up (Lillis & Wing, 2019). ACT showed greater overall 24-month weight loss when compared to Control (–7.18% vs –1.15%) and greater weight loss than SR among those with the highest initial weight losses.

Taken together, the studies reviewed here, along with a number of small studies with similar intervention approaches and outcomes, suggest that the use of ACT methods for weight management (1) do not impede weight loss efforts and (2) have the potential to greatly improve weight loss outcomes when compared to current gold standard traditional behavioral approaches in both short and long timeframes.

Alternative Formats for ACT Intervention Delivery

Given the high prevalence of overweight and obesity, there is a need for more scalable options for treatment. Increasingly, studies have examined whether nontraditional formats beyond face-to-face therapy are effective for ACT interventions related to weight. Various alternative delivery formats have been examined, including one-time workshops, mobile apps, and self-help.

Lillis, Hayes, Bunting, and Masuda (2009) examined the outcomes of a randomized one-time, 5-hour ACT workshop vs waitlist control. This workshop was not specifically designed to impact weight but rather health behaviors and weight-stigma issues. At 3-month follow-up, a significantly higher proportion of the ACT participants had maintained or lost weight and showed significant improvements in quality of life and reductions in psychological distress and self-stigma as compared to the control group. Tapper and colleagues (2009) examined a randomized one-time, 2-hour ACT workshop compared to a no-treatment control group for women who were already trying to lose weight. Within the ACT group, participants who reported applying the principles in the workshop showed a significant decrease of 2.3 kg 6 months later when compared to those who reported never applying them. and overall ACT participants engaged in significantly more physical activity following the intervention as compared to participants in the control condition.

Levin, Potts, Haeger, and Lillis (2018) conducted an open trial of guided self-help (self-help with phone coaching). Results indicated that participants reported high engagement and satisfaction rates. Results also showed significant improvements over time on self-reported weight self-stigma, eating behaviors, weight-related health behaviors, quality of life and depression. Although the treatment groups also demonstrated weight loss at posttest, it was not maintained at 3-month follow up. Potts, Krafft and Levin (2020) conducted a randomized controlled trial of this same self-help treatment that included randomization to self-help book plus phone coaching, self-help book plus email prompts, and waitlist condition. Both treatment conditions showed high self-reported ratings of satisfaction and engagement as well as improvements in self-stigma compared to the waitlist groups. The phone coaching condition also showed improvements in eating behaviors and general physical activity, but neither treatment conditions showed changes in weight. Levin et al. (2021) conducted a randomized trial of online guided self-help ACT intervention (online self-help program with phone coaching) with nutritional education or waitlist. Compared to the waitlist control, online guided self-help showed improvements on healthy eating, self-reported weight, mental health, weight self-stigma, and psychological inflexibility but not self-reported physical activity.

Levin, Pierce, and Schoendorff (2017) examined the effectiveness of an ACT-based mobile app compared to a waitlist on weight-related health behaviors. They found that the app had an impact on weight-related health behaviors for those who adhered to the app, with several effects being significant or trending toward significance. Jarvela-Reijonen and colleagues (2018) conducted a randomized controlled trial examining ACT for eating behavior and diet using face-to-face contact versus a mobile app versus control. Both ACT interventions showed some effects on aspects of eating behaviors (e.g., mindful eating) but not dietary choices. The authors highlighted the notion that some type of human interaction may be beneficial when using technology for delivery, and they also pointed to the need for nutritional education.

Overall, these studies suggest that ACT interventions for weight using different formats beyond face-to-face can have a meaningful impact on a variety of health and psychological measures. However, the results are inconsistent regarding which outcomes show improvements, and improvements in objectively measured health behaviors and/or weight are not consistently observed across studies. Furthermore, most authors suggest some form of human interaction, such as phone coaching, may be necessary to show improvements in mobile or self-help formats. However, given the prevalence of overweight and obesity, scalable options for delivery are needed; these studies suggest that alternative formats are viable options.

Process-Based Evidence: How Does It Work?

A range of process variables have been examined in ACT studies for weight. Two randomized clinical trials found evidence of mediation for food-related psychological acceptance on the impact of ACT on weight loss (Forman et al., 2013, 2016). ACT has also been found to work through the mechanisms of weight-related experiential avoidance (Lillis et al., 2009), autonomous motivation (Forman et al., 2016), and values-consistent behavior change (Lillis et al., 2016).

Levin et al. (2018) demonstrated that psychological inflexibility and valued action were both processes that changed in a guided self-help open trial. although they did not test any mediational tests of these processes. Potts et al. (2020) also found changes in psychological inflexibility compared to waitlist control during a guided self-help randomized trial. Levin and colleagues (2021) tested mediational analyses on the impact of weight-related psychological inflexibility as a mediator of outcomes at posttreatment in a randomized trial of online guided self-help intervention for diet and physical activity in individuals with overweight or obesity. They found significant mediational effects of psychological inflexibility on uncontrolled eating, emotional eating, weight self-stigma, and general mental health but not dietary recall, dietary choice, or self-reported weight.

Some studies have found that, while ACT produced significant change in theoretically identified mechanisms, significant changes were observed in SBT conditions as well, and thus mediation was not demonstrated. For example, Lillis and colleagues failed to find between-group differences in weight-related experiential avoidance change comparing ACT to SBT in two studies (Lillis et al., 2016; Lillis et al., in press). Possible explanations for these finding include the need for more sensitive measurement in this area, treatment potency, or the possibility that standard weight loss may genuinely move ACT processes. Further study is needed to provide clarity.

Challenges and Future Directions

From a clinical perspective, implementing ACT for obesity management presents a number of challenges. Patients generally have expectations that obesity management services will be similar to general medical treatment services and less akin to psychotherapy. As such, experiential exercises and more personally focused content of the sessions can run counter to expectations. This situation can be a welcome surprise for some but off-putting to others. Setting expectations for what will be asked of patients and providing informed consent for an alternative, more vulnerable approach are both important.

As mentioned previously, the provider will face difficulties undermining the weight on the scale as the sole arbiter of success. The challenge is to gently undermine weight as the primary outcome of interest, while building a foundation of values clarification and awareness as an alternative stream of access to reinforcement for engaging in healthy behaviors. The key is to link healthy behaviors to values-based domains, narratives, and outcomes of interest.

From a research perspective, it is important to continue to produce high-quality research and secure continued interest from funding agencies, which has been somewhat limited to date. A key issue is process of change. High-quality studies, which could be short in duration, are needed to establish the mechanisms by which ACT methods produce improved obesity management outcomes. For example, currently no study shows a direct link between change in psychological flexibility and improved adherence to prescribed eating or physical activity behaviors, which in turn produce changes in weight. These kinds of mediator/mechanism links need to be established in order to (1) better understand the impact of ACT in this area and (2) help refine interventions to focus on active elements to improve potency.

Another significant issue is who can be trained to deliver ACT or ACT-enhanced interventions for obesity. Previous research has shown that experts can produce better outcomes (Forman et al., 2013), while other successful studies have utilized mostly PhD-level interventionists, typically with prior experience in ACT (e.g., Lillis et al., 2016). Training and implementation innovations will be required for ACT-based interventions to have any meaningful reach. In addition, optimal dosing, timing, and treatment matching-related issues remain largely open questions.

By far the biggest challenge in the field of obesity, however, is the undeniable fact that meaningful population improvements will require large-scale changes to environment and culture. Psychology as a discipline has a strong bias toward "fixing" the individual and ignoring the micro- and macro-level environments in which the individual operates (Kirk et al., 2014). This bias of focusing on the individual is best captured by the commonly heard phrase "if you just believe in your dreams, anything is possible." This serves to emphasize the role of the individual for their lack of success, while ignoring the systematic ways that culture, resources, laws, and institutions support some individuals and hinder others. For example, people of color are often not given the same opportunities as their white counterparts and are instead exposed to systemic barriers to achievement and progress (Crosby, Bromley, & Saxe, 1980).

However, if we "blame" the individual, citing the role of characterological factors above all other factors, the systems and institutions that benefit the privileged are ignored and the status quo is maintained.

This bias of focusing on individual, characterological factors is also evident in obesity management (Kirk et al., 2020). Interventions are primarily focused on the individual changing their own behavior. The environment is addressed only as it pertains to arranging one's own home (e.g., what foods to stock and keep away). However, there is ample evidence that public policy is crucial for facilitating population-level behavior-change efforts. Smoking is an example of behavior-change programs. When laws were introduced banning smoking indoors, taxing tobacco products, and limiting marketing practices, smoking behavior and deaths due to smoking decreased drastically (Hopkins et al., 2001). A variety of public policy changes will likely be needed to stall and reverse the upward trends of obesity worldwide, including possibly marketing regulation (specifically related to ads for children), banning unhealthy foods in schools, allowing lawsuits against food companies, subsidizing healthy food production while taxing unhealthy foods, and a variety of city development and zoning law changes to promote physical activity for both leisure and travel. Until public policies impact such macro-level systems, we will not make a significant dent in obesity rates.

ACT has the potential to address environmental, system-level issues more than other psychological interventions because its theory and interventions include a focus on contextual change. However, ACT interventions rarely target institutional or system-level variables, and to our knowledge they have not yet done so in the area of obesity. Thus, an important future direction for obesity management is to better understand the macro-level environmental impacts on obesity and policy-level changes that could address these issues. Psychological and contextually based interventions can contribute to these efforts by developing evidence-based practices for influencing policymakers and promoting public health messages that result in change.

One of the key systemic issues to address is weight bias in the health care system and in health care providers. There is well-documented evidence that health care providers exhibit weight bias and weight stigma (Flint, Oliver, & Copeland, 2017). Further evidence of systemic bias can be found in the lack of billing codes that physicians can use for obesity treatment; the existence of medical clinics that do not offer appropriate equipment (e.g., waiting room chairs, scales, blood pressure cuffs) for larger bodies; and the failure of insurance companies to pay for anti-obesity medication, among others. A meaningful direction for ACT interventions is to create treatments that address weight bias and stigma in health care providers and the health care system. Some of these interventions may be individual-level interventions for health care providers for them to better understand implicit bias, increase their own awareness, and move toward value-based behavior in terms of treating people with obesity with appropriate compassion and respect. Similar interventions related to racial discrimination have been developed and could serve as a model for these interventions (Kanter et al., 2020).

Higher-level interventions that address system-level problems also need to be developed. These may take the form of interventions for teams, leaders, organizational policymakers, or law change advocacy. ACT can contribute to interventions that help groups change their behaviors or move toward shared purposes. The ProSocial ACT Matrix provides a framework for such group-level interventions (Atkins, Wilson, & Hayes, 2019). Furthermore, the research literature on ACT for the workplace that addresses system-level interventions such as workplace policies or leadership practices may form a guide for the development of such interventions (see Flaxman, Prudenzi, & Zernerova, this volume).

Previous studies have demonstrated that ACT can effectively address weight management issues. Future studies need to move beyond individual-level change to address micro- and macro-level influences to truly impact obesity rates. ACT can play a meaningful role in such interventions and draw upon work already conducted in other domains (e.g., racial discrimination, leadership, and organizational change).

Conclusion

Obesity is a multifaceted problem that continues to increase in prevalence worldwide. ACT has been applied to the treatment of obesity, has general support for improving weight management outcomes, can be applied in a variety of formats and contact schedules, and mostly demonstrates the theoretically consistent process of change. However, obesity intervention in general and ACT specifically have largely ignored the fact that addressing obesity very likely will require (1) acknowledging obesity as a chronic medical disease requiring integrated medical treatment, and (2) intervening on systemic and environmental factors that continue to promote obesity. Future research on ACT and other contextual therapeutic approaches should focus on addressing these system-level factors in order to support already well-developed individual-level interventions.

References

Atkins, P. W. B., Wilson, D. S., & Hayes, S. C. (2019). *Prosocial: Using evolutionary science to build productive, equitable, and collaborative groups.* Oakland, CA: Context Press.

Bliss, E. S., & Whiteside, E. (2018). The gut-brain axis, the human gut microbiota and their integration in the development of obesity. *Frontiers in Physiology, 9.* doi:10.3389/fphys.2018.00900

Butryn, M. L., Webb, V., & Wadden, T. A. (2011). Behavioral treatment of obesity. *Psychiatric Clinics of North America, 34*(4), 841–+. doi:10.1016/j.psc.2011.08.006

Calle, E. E., Thun, M. J., Petrelli, J. M., Rodriguez, C., & Heath, C. W. (1999). Body-mass index and mortality in a prospective cohort of US adults. *New England Journal of Medicine, 341*(15), 1097–1105. doi:10.1056/nejm199910073411501

Cameron, E. (2016). Challenging "Size matters" messages: An exploration of the experiences of critical obesity scholars in higher education. *Canadian Journal of Higher Education, 46*(2), 111–126.

Canning, K. L., Brown, R. E., Wharton, S., Sharma, A. M., & Kuk, J. L. (2015). Edmonton obesity staging system prevalence and association with weight loss in a publicly funded referral-based obesity clinic. *Journal of Obesity, 3.* doi:10.1155/2015/619734

Catenacci, V. A., Hill, J. O., & Wyatt, H. R. (2009). The obesity epidemic. *Clinics in Chest Medicine, 30*(3), 415–+ . doi:10.1016/j.ccm.2009.05.001

Crosby, F., Bromley, S., & Saxe, L. (1980). Recent unobtrusive studies of black and white discrimination and prejudice—a literature review. *Psychological Bulletin, 87*(3), 546–563. doi:10.1037/0033-2909.87.3.546

Daly, M., Sutin, A. R., & Robinson, E. (2019). Perceived weight discrimination mediates the prospective association between obesity and physiological dysregulation: evidence from a population-based cohort. *Psychological Science, 30*(7), 1030–1039. doi:10.1177/0956797619849440

Dulloo, A. G., Jacquet, J., & Girardier, L. (1996). Autoregulation of body composition during weight recovery in human: The Minnesota Experiment revisited. *International Journal of Obesity, 20*(5), 393–405.

Fall, T., Mendelson, M., & Speliotes, E. K. (2017). Recent advances in human genetics and epigenetics of adiposity: Pathway to precision medicine? *Gastroenterology, 152*(7), 1695–1706. doi:10.1053/j.gastro.2017.01.054

Flint, S. W., Oliver, E. J., & Copeland, R. J. (2017). Editorial: Obesity stigma in healthcare: impacts on policy, practice, and patients. *Frontiers in Psychology, 8,* Article 2149. doi:10.3389/fpsyg.2017.02149

Forman, E. M., Butryn, M. L., Hoffman, K. L., & Herbert, J. D. (2009). An open trial of an acceptance-based behavioral intervention for weight loss. *Cognitive and Behavioral Practice, 16,* 223–235.

Forman, E. M., Butryn, M. L., Juarascio, A. S., Bradley, L. E., Lowe, M. R., Herbert, J. D., & Shaw, J. A. (2013). The Mind Your Health Project: A randomized controlled trial of an innovative behavioral treatment for obesity. *Obesity, 21*(6), 1119–1126. doi:10.1002/oby.20169

Forman, E. M., Butryn, M. L., Manasse, S. M., Crosby, R. D., Goldstein, S. P., Wyckoff, E. P., & Thomas, J. G. (2016). Acceptance-based versus standard behavioral treatment for obesity: Results from the mind your health randomized controlled trial. *Obesity, 24*(10), 2050–2056. doi:10.1002/oby.21601

Fothergill, E., Guo, J. E., Howard, L., Kerns, J. C., Knuth, N. D., Brychta, R., . . . Hall, K. D. (2016). Persistent metabolic adaptation 6 years after "The Biggest Loser" competition. *Obesity, 24*(8), 1612–1619. doi:10.1002/oby.21538
Hales, C. M., Carroll, M. D., Fryar, C. D., Odgen, C. L. (2020). *Prevalence of obesity and severe obesity among adults: United States, 2017–2018*. Hyattsville, MD: National Center for Health Statistics (Data Brief No. 360).
Hopkins, D. P., Briss, P. A., Ricard, C. J., Husten, C. G., Carande-Rulis, V. G., Fielding, J. E., . . . Task Force Community, P. (2001). Reviews of evidence regarding interventions to reduce tobacco use and exposure ao environmental tobacco smoke. *American Journal of Preventive Medicine, 20*(2), 16–66. doi:10.1016/s0749-3797(00)00297-x
Jarvela-Reijonen, E., Karhunen, L., Sairanen, E., Muotka, J., Lindroos, S., Laitinen, J., . . . Kolehmainen, M. (2018). The effects of acceptance and commitment therapy on eating behavior and diet delivered through face-to-face contact and a mobile app: a randomized controlled trial. *International Journal of Behavioral Nutrition and Physical Activity, 15*(1), 22. doi:10.1186/s12966-018-0654-8
Jung, F. U., Bae, Y. J., Kratzsch, J., Riedel-Heller, S. G., & Luck-Sikorski, C. (2020). Internalized weight bias and cortisol reactivity to social stress. *Cognitive Affective and Behavioral Neuroscience, 20*(1), 49–58. doi:10.3758/s13415-019-00750-y
Kanter, J. W., Rosen, D. C., Manbeck, K. E., Branstetter, H. M. L., Kuczynski, A. M., Corey, M. D., . . . Williams, M. T. (2020). Addressing microaggressions in racially charged patient-provider interactions: A pilot randomized trial. *BMC Medical Education, 20*(1). doi:10.1186/s12909-020-02004-9
Kirk, S. F. L., Penney, T. L., & McHugh, T. L. F. (2010). Characterizing the obesogenic environment: The state of the evidence with directions for future research. *Obesity Reviews, 11*(2), 109–117. doi:10.1111/j.1467-789X.2009.00611.x
Kirk, S. F. L, Price, S. L, Penney, T. L, Rehman, L., Lyons, R. F., Piccinini-Vallis, H., . . . Aston, M. (2014). Blame, shame, and lack of support: A multilevel study on obesity management. *Qualitative Health Research, 24*(6), 790–800. doi:10.1177/1049732314529667
Kirk, S. F. L., Ramos, S. X., Alberga, A. S., & Russell-Mayhew, S. (2020). *Reducing weight bias in obesity management, practice, and policy*. Edmonton, Canada: University of Alberta. Retrieved from https://obesitycanada.ca/guidelines/weightbias/.
Kuk, J. L., Ardern, C. I., Church, T. S., Sharma, A. M., Padwal, R., Sui, X. M., & Blair, S. N. (2011). Edmonton obesity staging system: association with weight history and mortality risk. *Applied Physiology Nutrition and Metabolism, 36*(4), 570–576. doi:10.1139/h11-058
Lau, D. C. W., & Wharton, S. (2020) *Canadian Adult Obesity Clinical Practice Guidelines: The Science of Obesity*, pp. 1–7. Retrieved from https://obesitycanada.ca/guidelines/science. Accessed on May 1, 2022.
Lauby-Secretan, B., Scoccianti, C., Loomis, D., Grosse, Y., Bianchini, F., Straif, K., & Int Agcy Res Canc, H. (2016). Body Fatness and cancer—Viewpoint of the IARC Working Group. *New England Journal of Medicine, 375*(8), 794–798. doi:10.1056/NEJMsr1606602
Levin, M. E., Petersen, J. M., Durward, C., Bingeman, B., Davis, E., Nelson, C., & Cromwell, S. (2021). A randomized controlled trial of online acceptance and commitment therapy to improve diet and physical activity among adults who are overweight/obese. *Translational Behavioral Medicine, 11*, 1216–1225.
Levin, M. E., Pierce, B., & Schoendorff, B. (2017). The acceptance and commitment therapy matrix mobile app: A pilot randomized trial on health behaviors. *Journal of Contextual Behavioral Science, 6*(3), 268–275. doi:10.1016/j.jcbs.2017.05.003
Levin, M. E., Potts, S., Haeger, J., & Lillis, J. (2018). Delivering acceptance and commitment therapy for weight self-stigma through guided self-help: results from an open pilot trial. *Cognitive and Behavioral Practice, 25*(1), 87–104.
Lillis, J., Hayes, S. C., Bunting, K., & Masuda, A. (2009). Teaching acceptance and mindfulness to improve the lives of the obese: A preliminary test of a theoretical model. *Annals of Behavioral Medicine, 37*, 58–69.
Lillis, J., Niemeier, H. M., Thomas, J. G., Unick, J., Ross, K. M., Leahey, T. M., . . . Wing, R. R. (2016). A randomized trial of an acceptance-based behavioral intervention for weight loss in people with high internal disinhibition. *Obesity, 24*(12), 2509–2514. doi:10.1002/oby.21680
Lillis, J., & Wing, R. R. (2019). *Using novel behavioral interventions to improve long-term weight loss: A randomized trial comparing acceptance and commitment therapy and self-regulation for weight loss treatment seeking adults with overweight and obesity*. Paper presented at the Annual meeting of the Association for Contextual Behavioral Science, Dublin, Ireland.
Luppino, F. S., de Wit, L. M., Bouvy, P. F., Stijnen, T., Cuijpers, P., Penninx, B., & Zitman, F. G. (2010). Overweight, obesity, and depression: A systematic review and meta-analysis of longitudinal studies. *Archives of General Psychiatry, 67*(3), 220–229. doi:10.1001/archgenpsychiatry.2010.2
Mebel, D. M., Wong, J. C. Y., Dong, Y. F. J., & Borgland, S. L. (2012). Insulin in the ventral tegmental area reduces hedonic feeding and suppresses dopamine concentration via increased reuptake. *European Journal of Neuroscience, 36*(3), 2336–2346. doi:10.1111/j.1460-9568.2012.08168.x

Muller, M. J., Enderle, J., & Bosy-Westphal, A. (2016). Changes in energy expenditure with weight gain and weight loss in humans. *Current Obesity Reports, 5*(4), 413–423. doi:10.1007/s13679-016-0237-4
Niemeier, H. M., Leahey, T., Reed, K. P., Brown, R. A., & Wing, R. R. (2012). An acceptance-based behavioral intervention for weight loss: A pilot study. *Behavior Therapy, 43*(2), 427–435.
Niemeier, H. M., Phelan, S., Fava, J. L., & Wing, R. R. (2007). Internal disinhibition predicts weight regain following weight loss and weight loss maintenance. *Obesity, 15*, 2485–2494.
Osunlana, A. M., Asselin, J., Anderson, R., Ogunleye, A. A., Cave, A., Sharma, A. M., & Campbell-Scherer, D. L. (2015). 5As Team obesity intervention in primary care: development and evaluation of shared decision-making weight management tools. *Clinical Obesity, 5*(4), 219–225. doi:10.1111/cob.12105
Padwal, R. S., Pajewski, N. M., Allison, D. B., & Sharma, A. M. (2011). Using the Edmonton obesity staging system to predict mortality in a population-representative cohort of people with overweight and obesity. *Canadian Medical Association Journal, 183*(14), E1059–E1066. doi:10.1503/cmaj.110387
Pearl, R. L. (2018). Weight bias and stigma: Public health Implications and structural solutions. *Social Issues and Policy Review, 12*(1), 146–182. doi:10.1111/sipr.12043
Potts, S., Krafft, J., & Levin, M. E. (2020). A pilot randomized controlled trial of acceptance and commitment therapy guided self-help for overweight and obese adults high in weight self-stigma. *Behavior Modification, 46*, 178–201. doi:10.1177/0145445520975112
Puhl, R., & Brownell, K. D. (2001). Bias, discrimination, and obesity. *Obesity Research, 9*(12), 788–805.
Puhl, R., & Heuer, C. A. (2009). The stigma of obesity: A review and update. *Obesity, 17*, 941–964.
Puhl, R. M., & Heuer, C. A. (2010). Obesity stigma: Important considerations for public health. *American Journal of Public Health, 100*(6), 1019–1028. doi:10.2105/ajph.2009.159491
Rosenbaum, M., & Leibel, R. L. (2010). Adaptive thermogenesis in humans. *International Journal of Obesity, 34*, S47–S55. doi:10.1038/ijo.2010.184
Rudolph, C. W., Wells, C. L., Weller, M. D., & Baltes, B. B. (2009). A meta-analysis of empirical studies of weight-based bias in the workplace. *Journal of Vocational Behavior, 74*(1), 1–10. doi:10.1016/j.jvb.2008.09.008
Swain, J., Hancock, K., Hainsworth, C., & Bowman, J. (2013). Acceptance and commitment therapy in the treatment of anxiety: A systematic review. *Clinical Psychology Review, 33*(8), 965–978. doi:10.1016/j.cpr.2013.07.002
Tapper, K., Shaw, C., Ilsley, J., Hill, A. J., Bond, F. W., & Moore, L. (2009). Exploratory randomised controlled trial of a mindfulness-based weight loss intervention for women. *Appetite, 52*, 396–404.
Teachman, B. A., & Brownell, K. D. (2001). Implicit anti-fat bias among health professionals: is anyone immune? *International Journal of Obesity, 25*(10), 1525–1531.
Thornton, L. M., Mazzeo, S. E., & Bulik, C. M. (2011). The heritability of eating disorders: methods and current findings. *Current Topics in Behavioral Neuroscience, 6*, 141–156.
Tomiyama, A. J. (2014). Weight stigma is stressful. A review of evidence for the Cyclic Obesity/Weight-Based Stigma model. *Appetite, 82*, 8–15. doi:10.1016/j.appet.2014.06.108
Tremblay, A., Royer, M. M., Chaput, J. P., & Doucet, E. (2013). Adaptive thermogenesis can make a difference in the ability of obese individuals to lose body weight. *International Journal of Obesity, 37*(6), 759–764. doi:10.1038/ijo.2012.124
Tremmel, M., Gerdtham, U. G., Nilsson, P. M., & Saha, S. (2017). Economic burden of obesity: A systematic literature review. *International Journal of Environmental Research and Public Health, 14*(4), 435. doi:10.3390/ijerph14040435
Wang, C., Jackson, G., Jones, T. H., Matsumoto, A. M., Nehra, A., Perelman, M. A., . . . Cunningham, G. (2011). Low testosterone associated with obesity and the metabolic syndrome contributes to sexual dysfunction and cardiovascular disease risk in men with type 2 diabetes. *Diabetes Care, 34*(7), 1669–1675. doi:10.2337/dc10-2339
Wharton, S., Lau, D. C. W., Vallis, M., Sharma, A. M., Biertho, L., Campbell-Scherer, D., . . . Wicklum, S. (2020). Obesity in adults: A clinical practice guideline. *Canadian Medical Association Journal, 192*(31), E875–E891. doi:10.1503/cmaj.191707
Whitlock, G., Lewington, S., Sherliker, P., Clarke, R., Emberson, J., Halsey, J., . . . ARIC, P. S. C. C. (2009). Body-mass index and cause-specific mortality in 900 000 adults: collaborative analyses of 57 prospective studies. *Lancet, 373*(9669), 1083–1096. doi:10.1016/s0140-6736(09)60318-4
Wing, R. R., & Phelan, S. (2005). Long-term weight loss maintenance. *American Journal of Clinical Nutrition, 82*(1), 222S–225S.
World Health Organization. (2020). *Obesity and overweight: Fact sheet.* Geneva, Switzerland: World Health Organization. Retrieved from https://www.who.int/news-room/fact-sheets/detail/obesity-and-overweight.
Wu, Y. K., & Berry, D. C. (2018). Impact of weight stigma on physiological and psychological health outcomes for overweight and obese adults: A systematic review. *Journal of Advanced Nursing, 74*(5), 1030–1042. doi:10.1111/jan.13511

CHAPTER

19 Acceptance and Commitment Training in the Workplace

Paul E. Flaxman, Arianna Prudenzi, *and* Lucie Zernerova

Abstract

Over the past two decades, the workplace has become an important context for delivering acceptance and commitment therapy (ACT) interventions. This article summarizes the evidence that has accumulated on worksite ACT-based training programs. Although these programs have been shown to be effective in improving employees' general mental health, their effects on job burnout and overall psychological flexibility have been less consistent. The authors respond to calls to provide clearer conceptualization of ACT's hypothesized influence on people's work-related well-being by considering the functions of psychological flexibility from the perspective of resource-based theories of job characteristics, burnout, and work engagement. The article highlights opportunities for further workplace research and practice, including: exploring the predictive influence of psychological flexibility on the effects of job demands and job resources; the use of multidimensional measures of flexibility to investigate specific subprocesses of change in worksite ACT interventions; and the potential of cultivating flexibility as part of other organizational initiatives.

Key Words: Acceptance and commitment training, workplace interventions, employee well-being, work-related stress, job burnout, work engagement

Introduction

Twenty years have passed since Frank Bond and David Bunce published the first controlled trial of an acceptance and commitment therapy (ACT) intervention that was delivered to employees in the workplace (Bond & Bunce, 2000). They adapted one of ACT's earlier treatment protocols into a brief (three-session) psychological skills training program (Bond & Hayes, 2002). When compared to a work stress management intervention and a waitlist control group, the ACT program was found to be effective in reducing the common symptoms of psychological distress over a 6-month evaluation period. Moreover, the beneficial effects of the ACT intervention on mental health were found to be mediated via an increase in employees' willingness to experience undesirable thoughts and feelings (indicated by changes in an initial version of the Acceptance and Action Questionnaire [AAQ]).

During the ensuing period, there has been a slow yet steady stream of research evaluating ACT interventions in workplace settings, and there has also been a concomitant strand of correlational research investigating the predictive influence of psychological flexibility on various markers of employees' mental health and work-related functioning (e.g., Bond & Bunce, 2003; Bond et al., 2013; Kopperud et al., 2021; Vilardaga et al., 2011). Another thriving area of research examines ACT's utility within occupational rehabilitation programs (e.g., Aasdahl et al., 2018; Finnes et al., 2017). Emerging organizational applications include ACT for coaching (e.g., Hill & Oliver, 2018), team-level, leader, and organizational flexibility (e.g., Bond et al., 2016; Gascoyne, 2019), and applying prosocial principles to work groups (Atkins et al., 2019). These varied and ongoing activities demonstrate that the workplace has become an important arena for conveying contextual behavioral science (CBS) and ACT principles to general (working) populations.

In the present article, we discuss ACT-based skills training programs that are designed primarily to improve employees' psychological health. Such programs have typically adopted a delivery format similar to that used by Bond and Bunce (2000), offering ACT-based training over a small number of sessions to groups of employees (Prudenzi et al., 2021a; Rudaz et al., 2017). ACT principles and skills have also been successfully imparted to employees using online platforms, smartphone apps, and bibliotherapy formats (e.g., Hofer et al., 2018; Jeffcoat & Hayes, 2012; Ly et al., 2014).

We focus on the reported effects of these employee-focused ACT programs for three reasons. First, among the various applications of ACT in the workplace, these programs have attracted the most research attention, with a new group of controlled trials appearing in the past few years (e.g., Habibian et al., 2018; Hofer et al., 2018; Kinnunen et al., 2020; Prudenzi et al., 2022; Puolakanaho et al., 2020; Waters et al., 2018). Second, despite supportive outcome findings, uncertainty remains surrounding the efficacy of these programs for reducing job burnout and improving employees' overall psychological flexibility (Gloster et al., 2020; Prudenzi et al., 2021a; Reeve et al., 2018). Third, we sense that the field is on the cusp of a new generation of research, which can capitalize on the availability of multidimensional measures of psychological flexibility to investigate more specific subprocesses of change (e.g., Francis et al., 2016; Kashdan et al., 2020; Rogge & Daks, 2021; Rolffs et al., 2018). Accordingly, this seems an opportune moment to gather the evidence and practical knowledge that have accumulated around ACT-based training programs delivered in workplace settings.

This article is structured as follows. In the next section, we summarize the primary findings of recent reviews of the relevant intervention research literature, which have evaluated the effectiveness of worksite ACT programs for reducing distress, alleviating burnout, enhancing job performance, and improving employees' psychological flexibility. In the section following this summary, we respond to calls for greater conceptual clarity surrounding ACT's potential utility for reducing work-related stress and burnout (Reeve et al., 2018; Rudaz et al., 2017). Specifically, we consider the advantages of viewing the workplace functions of psychological flexibility (and its subprocesses) through the lens of prominent *resource-based* theories of job characteristics, burnout, and work engagement. In the final sections, we provide an overview of the practical features of these programs, including variations in training delivery format and program content, before offering a set of suggestions to help guide the next generation of research on ACT-based training for working populations.

Summary of Evidence Surrounding ACT-Based Training in Workplace Settings

Prior to presenting a theoretical rationale for promoting psychological flexibility in the workplace, we offer a summary of outcomes and psychological flexibility subprocesses that have been targeted by ACT-based training for various occupational groups. For this purpose, we utilized the results reported in five reviews of the relevant workplace intervention research literature: Reeve et al.'s (2018) systematic review and meta-analysis of ACT-based training for direct care staff in mental health and intellectual disability settings; Rudaz et al.'s (2017) systematic review, which examined the effects of workplace ACT programs for mental health professionals and trainees; Archer's (2018) broader narrative synthesis of research investigating ACT's efficacy in a range of occupational settings; Prudenzi et al.'s (2021a) meta-analysis of ACT in group format for health care professionals; and Towey-Swift et al.'s (2022) systematic review and narrative synthesis of ACT for staff burnout. Taken together, the findings of these reviews provide good coverage of ACT-based training programs that have been empirically evaluated in workplace settings over the past two decades. Based on the patterns of findings reported across these reviews, we generated five evidence statements.

Evidence statement 1: ACT-Based Training in the Workplace Reduces Symptoms of Psychological Distress, Particularly among Employees with Higher Baseline Distress

The extant body of outcome evidence provides the strongest support for ACT's effectiveness in improving employees' general mental health (specifically reducing common symptoms of psychological stress and distress). This beneficial impact of ACT programs is most pronounced and reliable among employees who begin the intervention with an elevated level of psychological distress (Archer, 2018; Reeve et al., 2018). Because many workplace studies do not exclude employees with lower distress, this latter finding has emerged from studies that analyzed change among subgroups of participants with different levels of baseline distress (e.g., Brinkborg et al., 2011; Flaxman & Bond, 2010a; Reeve et al., 2018).

The validity of this first evidence statement is enhanced by the fact that numerous studies adopted the same outcome measure to assess change in employee distress: the *general health questionnaire* (GHQ). All studies reviewed by Reeve et al. (2018) included the GHQ (typically the GHQ-12) as one of the outcome measures, as did 9 of 14 studies reviewed by Archer (2018). This measure is useful for workplace settings—and congruent with ACT's transdiagnostic philosophy—because it captures various common manifestations of psychological ill-health, including anxiety-related difficulties, depressed mood, social withdrawal, reduced problem-solving effectiveness, and lack of self-confidence.

The importance of this first element of ACT's evidence base should not be underestimated. Across national and workforce surveys conducted in various industrialized countries, estimates suggest that around one in six employees may be experiencing a common mental health problem at any one time (Parsonage & Saini, 2017). Moreover, a large proportion of the financial burden of mental health problems is attributed to lost productivity among psychologically distressed or exhausted workers (Goetzel et al., 2018; Lerner et al., 2018; Parsonage & Saini, 2017). As a result, there is pressure to increase the accessibility of evidence-based psychological interventions in the workplace, given that only a small percentage of distressed employees seek or gain access to individual psychotherapy (Goetzel et al., 2018; Lerner et al., 2018). ACT is useful as a worksite mental health promotion program because of its brief and skills-based approach, transdiagnostic philosophy, potential benefits beyond reducing stress symptoms (e.g., self-awareness, values-based living, flourishing), and suitability for delivery in group and self-help formats (Biglan et al., 2008; Flaxman et al., 2013).

Evidence Statement 2: ACT-Based Training Has Inconsistent Effects on Job Burnout

Within this same body of research are examples of studies that have detected the salutary effects of ACT programs in reducing the burnout syndrome (i.e., exhaustion and depersonalization; e.g., Hayes et al., 2004; Kinnunen et al., 2020; Lloyd et al., 2013). In their systematic review, Towey-Swift et al. (2022) reported that nine out of fourteen controlled trials showed a statistically significant effect of ACT over control conditions on at least some burnout subscales. However, other studies have failed to find reductions in core components of burnout following an ACT program (e.g., Bethay et al., 2013; Clarke et al., 2015; Habibian et al., 2018). In their meta-analysis of ACT's influence on emotional exhaustion (the most commonly measured aspect of burnout), Reeve et al. (2018) found no pooled effect in favor of ACT compared to control conditions, neither at postintervention nor at follow-up (with follow-up periods ranging from 6 weeks to 6 months among the reviewed studies). Reeve and colleagues concluded that this strand of research requires a clearer theoretical account of why ACT might be expected to reduce employee burnout.

From a methodological standpoint, it is noteworthy that nearly all studies testing ACT's effect on burnout have utilized the Maslach Burnout Inventory (MBI; Maslach et al., 1996). This is not surprising, as the MBI remains the most well-known and widely used measure of this construct. Nonetheless, the MBI's response format spans a broader timeframe when compared to other distress measures commonly included in these ACT studies (such as the perceived stress scale or GHQ-12), in that the timeframe for reporting burnout symptom frequency on the MBI ranges from a few times a year (or less) through to every day (Schonfeld et al., 2019). Given that controlled evaluations of ACT studies might span a few months, it is worth considering the MBI's sensitivity for detecting change over modest time periods, especially if study samples include subgroups of employees who were experiencing infrequent burnout symptoms prior to the intervention (Reeve et al., 2018). Consistent with this observation, Prudenzi et al.'s (2021a) meta-analysis combined burnout measures with other measures of work-related distress and found a pooled effect in favor of ACT over control conditions only at follow-up and not at postintervention (suggesting ACT's influence on people's work-related functioning may take some time to emerge).

Evidence Statement 3: ACT-Based Training Elicits Improvements on Self-Rated Indicators of Job Performance

Because researchers (and reviewers) have focused primarily on examining ACT's impact on employees' stress, distress, and burnout, less attention has been paid to change on measures of work-related performance that have been included in a subset of worksite intervention studies (Archer, 2018; Prudenzi et al., 2021a). Synthesizing ACT's influence on job performance is challenging, as a range of different measures have been used reflecting the context of each study. Yet, when adopting a broad classification of the performance-oriented measures, the evidence indicates that ACT-based training often enhances people's (self-rated) effectiveness at work.

In his review, Archer (2018) noted that ACT significantly and positively impacted performance in all intervention studies that assessed such outcomes. Markers of work-related effectiveness have most often been included in ACT studies involving psychologists, therapists, and direct care staff. Among these studies, ACT has been shown to improve counseling self-efficacy (Pakenham, 2015), perceived quality of the therapeutic relationship (Clarke et al., 2015; Stafford-Brown & Pakenham, 2012), attitudes toward clients (Hayes et al., 2004), and utilization of evidence-based treatments as part of therapeutic practice (Varra et al., 2008). Outside of counseling and psychotherapeutic settings, ACT has been found to improve teaching-related efficacy among special education staff (Biglan et al., 2013) and innovation potential among employees working in the media (Bond & Bunce, 2000).

Attendance at ACT programs has also been linked to improved scores on the MBI's *professional accomplishment* dimension. This subscale captures people's sense of competence and achievement at work, particularly in terms of having a positive influence on others and supporting the recipients of one's service. While this group of findings arguably holds relevance for ACT's impact on burnout, the MBI's professional accomplishment dimension has been psychometrically and conceptually distinguished from the other MBI dimensions, which are usually considered the core features of burnout syndrome (i.e., exhaustion and depersonalization; de Beer & Bianchi, 2019). In their review of ACT's effect on burnout among mental health professionals, Rudaz et al. (2017) found significant improvements in three out of four studies that included this performance-oriented subscale, two of which demonstrated significantly greater improvement in professional accomplishment among ACT participants relative to control conditions. Towey-Swift et al.'s (2022) more recent review suggests that ACT's positive influence on personal accomplishment is seen primarily among staff in therapeutic roles.

Evidence Statement 4: ACT-Based Training Has Mixed Effects on Overall Psychological Flexibility

In assessments of psychological flexibility, most evaluations of worksite ACT programs have utilized the AAQ or AAQ-II (Archer, 2018; Prudenzi et al., 2021a; Reeve et al., 2018; Towey-Swift et al., 2022). The literature reviews display lack of agreement on the robustness of ACT's effects on employees' overall or global flexibility. Rudaz et al. (2017) and Archer (2018) concluded that employees' psychological flexibility tends to improve following ACT-based training, whereas two meta-analyses found no significant pooled effect in favor of ACT over control conditions (Prudenzi et al., 2021a; Reeve et al., 2018). Although this statement might raise questions about the efficacy of ACT in the workplace, it is important to note that uncertain effects of worksite ACT programs on employees' flexibility have been attributed to the traditional overreliance on the AAQ and AAQ-II (Reeve et al., 2018; Towey-Swift et al., 2022) or were derived from subsuming a range of different ACT process measures within a single psychological flexibility outcome cluster (Gloster et al., 2020; Prudenzi et al., 2021a). The picture looks considerably more encouraging when we venture beyond overall flexibility to consider studies that examined the influence of worksite ACT programs on more specific markers of the hexaflex model's subprocesses.

Evidence Statement 5: ACT-Based Training Elicits Improvements on Mindfulness and Acceptance Subprocesses of Psychological Flexibility

Various scales have been utilized to explore change on flexibility's subprocesses in response to worksite ACT programs, including ACT-specific measures (e.g., values or fusion questionnaires) and prominent mindfulness inventories, such as the Mindfulness Attention and Awareness Scale (MAAS; Brown & Ryan, 2003) and the Five-Facet Mindfulness Questionnaire (FFMQ; Baer et al., 2006). Studies administering such measures have revealed particularly strong support for cognitive defusion as an influential process activated by a range of worksite ACT programs. Defusion has been assessed via scales that assess believability in unhelpful (e.g., depressogenic or burnout-related) cognitions, the FFMQ's nonreactivity subscale, and the Cognitive Fusion Questionnaire (CFQ; Gillanders et al., 2014). A group of worksite ACT studies observed tangible improvements in defusion, even when there were no concurrent reductions in the frequency with which employees were reporting negative or unhelpful psychological content (e.g., Bethay et al., 2013; Varra et al., 2008; Waters et al., 2018). Moreover, in some cases, ACT's beneficial effects on employees' mental health and/or work-related functioning were uniquely mediated via defusion, while controlling for the influence of other pertinent variables, such as frequency of negative cognitions, other mindfulness skills, or global psychological (in)flexibility (e.g., Varra et al., 2008; Waters et al., 2018).

There is also reliable evidence supporting the premise that ACT programs increase employees' willingness to experience difficult thoughts and emotions. This assertion is based on demonstrations of favorable patterns of change on specific markers of experiential acceptance (e.g., the FFMQ's nonjudging subscale, and the White Bear Thought Suppression Inventory). Interestingly, the findings suggest that worksite ACT programs can have a "delayed" effect on employees' acceptance skills, with improvements on this subprocess sometimes observed only at follow-up time points (rather than immediately after an ACT program; Hofer et al., 2018; McConachie et al., 2014). In addition, some results suggest that the cultivation of acceptance becomes particularly influential in explaining the longer-term effects of worksite programs on employees' psychological health (Frögéli et al., 2019; Kinnunen et al., 2020).

Taking a broad view across the mindfulness measures, we find support for the notion that worksite ACT programs increase employees' present moment awareness. The findings reveal variation across different indicators of this subprocess. For instance, in some studies, workplace ACT programs have exhibited weak effects on employees' inattentiveness and distraction, as captured by the FFMQ's acting with awareness subscale. Nonetheless, the same (and other) studies found significant improvements among ACT participants on a separate marker of present moment awareness: the FFMQ's observing facet (Biglan et al., 2013; Pakenham, 2015; Waters et al., 2018). Changes on this mindfulness facet indicate that ACT increases employees' bodily awareness, awareness of thoughts and feelings, and capacity for contacting the present moment via the five senses. It is encouraging that relatively brief ACT programs have been shown to cultivate this type of mindful awareness alongside increased acceptance/defusion, given that this particular combination of skills is considered important for improving emotional health (Lindsay & Creswell, 2017; Waters et al., 2018). These findings deserve mention, for observing items have recently been integrated into an expanded multidimensional measure of psychological flexibility's subprocesses (Rogge & Daks, 2021).

Finally, there is surprisingly little support for the contention that ACT programs improve employees' mental health (in part) by improving their valuing skills. The currently weak evidence is likely due to the small number of published worksite intervention studies that included values questionnaires (e.g., Biglan et al., 2013; Stafford-Brown & Pakenham, 2012). We consider this a promising avenue for future evaluations of ACT programs, given the increased availability of measures that capture values-based behavioral activation subprocesses (e.g., Francis et al., 2016; Rogge & Daks, 2021; Rolffs et al., 2018; Smout et al., 2014).

Section Summary

The evidence accumulated over the past two decades supports the use of ACT-based training in the workplace for reducing the symptoms of psychological stress and distress in various occupational groups. A smaller, yet promising, strand of evidence suggests that the same programs elicit improvements in employees' self-reported effectiveness at work. Despite some promising findings, there is less conclusive evidence that these programs reliably reduce job burnout or increase employees' overall psychological flexibility.

When discussing the less consistent findings, the cited reviews highlighted a need to go beyond overall psychological flexibility to examine the impact of worksite ACT programs on flexibility's subprocesses. As summarized earlier (see Evidence Statement 5), a convincing body of research demonstrates the efficacy of ACT-based training for targeting acceptance and mindfulness skills (specifically acceptance, defusion, and mindful awareness). The reviews also identified a need for clearer conceptualization of ACT's influence on people's work-related functioning (such as job burnout), which accounts for the well-established influence of work environment variables (e.g., workload, supervisory support, performance feedback, and job control; Reeve et al., 2018; Rudaz et al., 2017). In the next section, we address this issue by considering the hypothesized workplace functions of psychological flexibility through the lens of resource-based theories of employee well-being.

Viewing Psychological Flexibility from the Perspective of Resource-Based Theories of Work Stress, Job Burnout, and Work Engagement

ACT interventions are often delivered in group format in workplace settings to help improve employees' general psychological health. Thus, ACT's workplace applications share similarities with ACT in groups for common mental health conditions, such as moderate levels of anxiety and/or depression (e.g., Bohlmeijer et al., 2011). Accordingly, the underlying theoretical rationale for therapeutically oriented worksite programs is similar in many respects to ACT delivered in other community and health promotion settings.

To understand why ACT might be useful beyond improving *general* mental health in the workplace, it is informative to consider theoretical models that are designed to explain why certain job and personal characteristics are associated with work stress, motivation, burnout, and performance-related outcomes. In this section, we view psychological flexibility from the standpoint of three interrelated theoretical approaches: the goal-related context-sensitivity hypothesis (e.g., Bond et al., 2006); the conservation of resources (COR) theory of job burnout (e.g., Shirom, 2003); and the job demands-resources (JD-R) theory (e.g., Bakker & Demerouti, 2017). These theories exhibit a useful degree of overlap, as they all offer resource-based conceptualizations of employees' (work-related) psychological health and behavioral effectiveness.

The Goal-Related Context-Sensitivity Hypothesis (Bond et al., 2006)

Bond et al. (2006) developed the concept of *goal-related context sensitivity* to integrate the features of psychological flexibility that are theorized to influence employees' mental health, awareness, and utilization of job resources, and (performance-related) behavior at work. This model is based on the following assumptions. First, due to their greater willingness to experience discomforting inner experiences, psychologically flexible employees are expected to be less inclined to expend their finite attentional and energy resources on controlling, overanalyzing, or avoiding negative thoughts (e.g., self-doubt), feelings (e.g., anxiety), and sensations (e.g., trembling). As a result, these individuals should have greater cognitive and energy resources available that can instead be oriented toward recognizing opportunities for goal-related and values-congruent behavior unfolding at work. Moreover, because they are less likely to avoid goal-relevant or personally valued actions, situations, or conversations that elicit undesirable psychological content, psychologically flexible employees are theorized to have a wider range of options for responding effectively to such opportunities (Bond et al., 2006, 2013). In this way, flexibility is hypothesized to be associated with an improved capacity for noticing and harnessing aspects of the work environment that can protect (and potentially improve) well-being, work engagement, and job performance (Bond et al., 2006).

A small group of studies has supported these propositions, particularly by demonstrating functional links between psychological flexibility and *job control*, which is considered an important job resource in most work design models (e.g., Bakker & Demerouti, 2017; Häusser et al., 2010). Job control refers to how much "say" employees have over when and how they complete work tasks, their level of autonomy or freedom at work, and their opportunities to participate in decision-making. Job control can manifest in relatively simple issues, such as when one can take breaks during the working day, through to being consulted on, and closely involved in, the design and implementation of organizational changes that affect one's job.

Two longitudinal studies of financial customer service workers in the UK found that psychological flexibility (assessed by the AAQ) interacted with job control to predict mental health and objectively measured performance (computer input errors) over a 1-year assessment period (Bond & Bunce, 2003), as well as the ability to learn a new computer software program

(Bond & Flaxman, 2006). Specifically, the positive influences of job control on mental health, performance, and learning outcomes were significantly enhanced among employees with higher flexibility. Another study examined the role of psychological flexibility in employees' experiences of a work reorganization intervention that was designed to increase job control (Bond et al., 2008). In this quasi-experimental study, a participatory work redesign intervention led to general increases in job control, improved mental health, and reduced absence rates among customer service employees of a financial organization. These intervention effects were significantly moderated by employees' psychological flexibility. Compared to their less flexible counterparts, workers with greater flexibility perceived higher levels of job control as a result of the work reorganization process. They were apparently also better able to harness the increased opportunities for control to improve their work-related functioning and general mental health.

These empirical demonstrations of *synergistic* effects between flexibility and job control are important to the wider field of work and organizational psychology, where there have been calls to increase knowledge about the individual characteristics and self-regulation strategies that help to maximize the benefits of job resources (Van Veldhoven et al., 2020). From a practical viewpoint, these findings suggest that work redesign intervention outcomes could be enhanced by also implementing worksite programs that increase employees' psychological flexibility.

Conservation of Resources Theory (Hobfoll, 1989)

Conservation of resources (COR) theory underpins research on a range of work and organizational psychology topics, especially burnout and employee recovery from work-related effort during nonwork time (e.g., Gorgievski & Hobfoll, 2008; Westman et al., 2004). This widely applicable motivation and stress theory is based on the premise that humans possess a natural instinct to protect, retain, and build valued resources. Resources include objects (e.g., a salary, a home), life conditions (e.g., a satisfying job, supportive relationships), personal characteristics (e.g., personality traits, adaptive coping skills), and energies (e.g., emotional, cognitive, and physical energy). Stress is expected to arise under three conditions: when a person perceives a threat to valued resources (i.e., anticipation of resource loss); when resources are actually lost; or when investment of resources fails to "pay off" in terms of preventing further resource loss or facilitating resource gain (Hobfoll, 1989). The theory asserts that resource loss is disproportionally more salient than resource gain, and it highlights the risk of resource "loss spirals," which can gather speed and strength in the face of chronic stressors if resources continue to be depleted.

The COR conceptualization of job burnout is based on these theoretical principles, and focuses primarily on employees' *energetic* resources (Shirom, 2003). To elaborate, employees are likely to experience gradual erosion of their physical, cognitive, motivational, and emotional energies as they expend effort meeting the demands of work and coping with job stressors. Periodic recovery opportunities—such as evenings and weekends—can help interrupt the cycle of work-related energy depletion, replenish depleted resources, and enable employees to invest energy in valued nonwork resources, such as leisure activities and meaningful relationships with family or friends (Bennett et al., 2018; Westman et al., 2004). However, some experiences can impair recovery from work-related effort, including excessive overtime working, and/or entanglement in worry and rumination about work issues during nonwork time (Geurts & Sonnentag, 2006).

To provide an example of the theorized cyclical energy resource loss process, imagine an office-based employee (we'll call her "Maria"), who is already feeling very busy at work.

With little explanation, she is rather bluntly informed by a senior manager that she must now take on additional job demands. To ensure that she can successfully meet the newly imposed demands, while maintaining her usual level of performance, Maria begins working during evenings and on some weekends. As a result, she is less able to replenish the energetic resources that have been depleted during the working week. Even when she is not working, Maria frequently drifts off into worrying about whether she'll end up falling short of expectations; the worry is affecting her sleep quality. Because of reduced recovery time, Maria begins each new working week in a suboptimal state, which means she must invest compensatory effort just to perform her usual tasks, further increasing her sense of fatigue and perception of work overload. To make matters worse, the reluctant investment of time and energy in evening and weekend working has created tension with her family, resulting in additional worry about undermining a valued nonwork resource. If such conditions are prolonged, an energy resource loss cycle may attract momentum, so that the ability to recover from work-related effort becomes progressively more elusive. Sustained over time, such experiences might culminate in burnout, which COR theory conceptualizes as an affective "end-state" characterized by overdepletion of cognitive, physical, and emotional energies (Shirom, 2003).

The same COR principles underpin the inverted process of resource *gain spirals*. People who possess greater resources are generally considered more capable of orchestrating further resource gai, and less vulnerable to becoming caught up in problematic cycles of resource loss. Although resource gains are considered less salient than (actual or anticipated) losses, they can nonetheless unfold in a positive cyclical pattern with energy enhancement (Gorgievski & Hobfoll, 2008).

To illustrate, let's imagine a different scenario for Maria. In scenario two, Maria's senior manager invites her for a one-to-one lunch meeting, where the manager explains the reasons behind a major change that is about to impact the whole department (it has to do with implementation of a new computer system), resulting in an immediate need to increase everyone's responsibilities and change their ways of working. The manager expects there to be an increase in workload, at least over the next 3 months, while the new system is implemented. Maria is asked if she has any initial ideas for how this might best be managed in relation to her own work. The manager lists a number of specific project tasks that need to be completed and asks Maria whether she has a preference for working on any of those. Maria requests to be involved in gathering feedback on people's day-to-day experiences with the new IT system and to take the lead in collating this feedback into a usability report. The manager seems pleased with Maria's choice and explains how this part of the project provides a great fit with Maria's talent for putting people at ease and the level of trust she has across the department. In response to this unexpected feedback, Maria feels energized and recognized by the manager. Maria finds herself viewing the imminent technological changes (and increased workload) with some trepidation, but also with a fresh sense of personal interest and determination to be successful in this new aspect of her job role. When she returns home that evening, Maria tells her partner about the meeting, revealing her sense of trepidation, excitement, and opportunity; Maria's partner tells her to "go for it," and they begin discussing how they might alternate their family responsibilities to enable Maria to put in some overtime during this period.

In the workplace, this type of resource-based energetic gain spiral is theorized to facilitate higher levels of *work engagement*, which is an affective-motivational state characterized by vigor, absorption, and dedication in one's work. In sum, COR theory recognizes two processes, with cycles of energy resource investment and depletion in the face of chronic job stress (without sufficient gain or replenishment) leading to burnout, and positive cycles of energetic resource gain fostering work engagement (Gorgievski & Hobfoll, 2008).

COR theory has yet to be widely utilized in workplace studies of ACT or psychological flexibility (see Kopperud et al., 2021 for a recent exception). Nonetheless, we outline its main principles here for the following reasons. First, this theory has become a prominent model of job burnout, so it is an obvious candidate for addressing the conceptual uncertainty surrounding ACT's suitability for reducing burnout syndrome (Reeve et al., 2018). Second, COR scholars have recognized the importance of individual characteristics and coping strategies that are conceptually related to psychological flexibility, including cognitive and emotional flexibility and tolerance for failure (Gorgievski & Hobfoll, 2008). Finally, as we discuss next, COR principles have informed the influential job demands-resources (JD-R) theory, which has begun to be adopted by researchers investigating the influence of psychological flexibility on job burnout and work engagement.

3.3. The Job Demands-Resources Theory (Bakker & Demerouti, 2017)

The job demands-resources (JD-R) theory integrates COR principles to help explain how work design characteristics—categorized broadly as job demands and job resources—lead to employee outcomes such as burnout, engagement, and job performance. Job demands include time pressure, workload, role conflict, and emotionally demanding interactions with clients or customers. Examples of job resources can be seen in Maria's second scenario, and they include autonomy in one's work (i.e., job control), constructive performance feedback, social support, opportunities for growth and professional/personal development, and a high-quality relationship with one's supervisor (Bakker & Demerouti, 2017).

The theory is organized around two parallel processes that elicit different outcomes: (1) a *health-impairment* process linking high job demands to burnout and (2) a *motivational* process linking availability of job resources to increased work engagement. One of the theory's propositions is that job demands are most strongly correlated with burnout, while job resources are most strongly related to engagement and that the availability of job resources can help buffer (i.e., moderate) the relationship between high job demands and burnout (Bakker & Demerouti, 2017). For example, note that in both of Maria's scenarios, the demands and pressures will remain high. In the second scenario, however, the increased demands would (in theory) be less likely to raise the risk of burnout and give the protective influence of key job resources (such as participation in decision making, and a supportive relationship with the manager).

Employees are not expected to be passive recipients of the job demands and resources that management happens to impose on them, but ideally they have the potential to engage in *job crafting* behaviors. For instance, an employee might ask for additional feedback, request clarification on strategic priorities to reduce role ambiguity, or proactively seek out the types of projects and activities that have potential to increase personal growth, learning, and meaning derived from work (Bakker & Demerouti, 2017).

It is also important to note that job demands are not considered universally problematic and that job resources are not universally beneficial. A distinction is made between *hindrance* job demands, which represent constraints on an employee's ability to achieve valued work goals (e.g., role conflict or excessive work overload); and *challenge* job demands, which have energy costs but also the potential to foster personal growth and skill development (e.g., time pressure, increased responsibility). Similarly, the benefits of job resources are expected to be contingent upon contextual factors (e.g., whether the available resources are useful for managing the specific job demands) and employees' personal characteristics (Van Veldhoven et al., 2020).

Most relevant to our current purpose, the JD-R theoretical framework accommodates the influence of individual characteristics (or *personal resources*) on the health impairment and motivational pathways. Personal resources can include various traits, states, and coping repertoires that affect how employees appraise work events, their responses when encountering stressors, and propensity for progressing toward goals in the face of challenge and adversity (van den Heuvel et al., 2010).

An emerging body of research has investigated the role of psychological flexibility as a personal resource within this theoretical framework. Biron and van Veldhoven (2012) argued that psychological flexibility meets the functional conditions for personal resources as posited by JD-R theory: (1) it aids in achieving work goals; (2) it reduces the physiological and psychological costs of high job demands; and (3) it stimulates personal growth, learning, and development. Biron and van Veldhoven employed a daily diary method to investigate whether psychological flexibility (assessed with the AAQ) influenced the strategies of service sector workers for managing the emotional labor demands of their work. They found that psychological flexibility significantly reduced the detrimental impact of day-level work demands on day-level emotional exhaustion, lending support to the JD-R proposition on the moderating (buffering) role of personal resources in the health impairment process (also see Onwezen et al., 2014).

Given the concerns surrounding the AAQ and AAQ-II as measures of overall flexibility (e.g., Wolgast, 2014), it is worth noting that similar patterns of findings have emerged when other flexibility scales have been adopted (e.g., Boatemaa et al., 2019; Kopperud et al., 2021; Novaes et al., 2018; Prudenzi et al., 2021b; Ruiz & Odriozola-Gonzalez, 2017; Vilardaga et al., 2011). For example, Novaes et al. (2018) utilized JD-R theory to investigate the functions of work-related psychological flexibility (using the Work-related Acceptance and Action Questionnaire [WAAQ]; Bond et al., 2013) among a large sample of employees (n = 4867) in Brazil. Consistent with JD-R assumptions, psychological flexibility significantly attenuated the detrimental influence of work overload on job satisfaction and negative affect. Also, consistent with the hypothesized role of personal resources in the motivational pathway, they found that psychological flexibility strengthened the functional relationship between job autonomy and work-related positive affect.

Section Summary

There is a useful alignment between resource-based theories of workplace well-being and ACT's model of psychological flexibility. In simple terms, integrating these theories allows us to account for employees' responses to their internal and external contexts (and the interrelations between them). Internal context refers to people's private experiences (e.g., one's thoughts and emotions that arise in response to the demands of work), whereas external context refers particularly to psychosocial features of the working environment (e.g., workload, job control, and supervisory support).

As we have outlined in this section, a common trend runs through both the CBS and occupational health literatures regarding conceptualizing synergistic influences between people's responses to these internal and external contexts. In the CBS field, such synergy is evident in Frank Bond's model of *organizational* flexibility, which delineates various ways that the functions of psychologically flexible subprocesses might manifest (and be cultivated) at an organizational level (see Bond et al., 2016). Similarly, in the occupational health literature, JD-R theory has recently been expanded to clarify how high job strain can (over time) lead to burnout by (1) triggering the use of maladaptive self-regulation strategies (such as avoidance and coping inflexibility) and (2) impairing employees' propensity to use more adaptive self-regulation strategies (such as recovery and job crafting; see Bakker & de Vries, 2021). These multilevel theoretical models create opportunities for research into the roles of psychological flexibility and its subprocesses for reducing the harmful impacts of job stressors and for enhancing the personal and organizational benefits gained through effective leadership and motivating job characteristics.

The cross-sectional, longitudinal, dyadic, and daily survey research cited in this section shows an encouraging consistency, despite being conducted across different countries, involving people from a range of occupations, and using different measures of job demands, job resources, and psychological flexibility. Taken together, this group of studies suggests that employees with higher flexibility possess a cognitive-behavioral repertoire that enables them to find the daily demands of work less exhausting; remain effective even in the face of very high job demands; notice and take advantage of positive aspects of the work design environment; and gain a degree of protection from stress and burnout.

Beyond the theoretical utility, there is a powerful *practical* argument for testing the influence of psychological flexibility and its subprocess within work design frameworks, such as the JD-R model. Unlike more stable individual characteristics that also meet the criteria for personal resources (e.g., adaptive personality traits), psychological flexibility is conceptualized as a malleable and skills-based capacity that can be targeted for improvement via ACT's well-established intervention technology. This could, in turn, elevate the profile of ACT in the workplace as a viable approach for strengthening employees' and leaders' ability to manage job demands and capitalize on job resources and enhancing responses to work redesign, work-life balance, and job crafting interventions.

Content and Format of ACT-Based Training Programs

There is considerable variability in the way that ACT has been adapted for delivery in workplace settings. This is evident in terms of (1) the wide range of program durations and delivery formats, and (2) the nature and sequencing of the specific strategies deployed (e.g., whether the training involves minimal or extensive practice in formal mindfulness meditation). In this section, we provide an overview of these practical features, drawing from the worksite ACT interventions that have been subject to empirical evaluation.

Delivery Format

Among the interventions delivered in person to groups of employees, ACT-based training has been administered over 3 x 3 hour sessions (Bond & Bunce, 2000; Flaxman & Bond, 2010a), 4 x 3 hour sessions (Brinkborg et al., 2011; Stafford-Brown & Pakenham, 2012), 6 x 2 hour sessions (Frögéli, et al., 2016), 8 x 2 hour sessions (Kinnunen et al., 2020; Puolakanaho et al., 2020), two full days of training (Clarke et al., 2015; Gaupp et al., 2020), and in a one-day workshop format (Hayes et al., 2004; Varra et al., 2008; Waters et al., 2018), in some cases supplemented by an additional half-day session a few weeks later (McConachie et al., 2014; Noone & Hastings, 2009, 2010). Until recently, there have been few indications that duration or number of training sessions has a strong influence on outcomes achieved (Archer, 2018). However, Prudenzi et al.'s (2021a) recent meta-analysis suggests that longer ACT programs may produce larger improvements in employees' general mental health.

Time commitment can be a salient issue for practitioners and organizations when considering offering ACT programs to staff during working hours. Where possible, delivering ACT over a series of weekly sessions remains attractive from a skills progression point of view. Yet the multiple-session format could represent a barrier in some organizations (e.g., where staff cannot be easily or repeatedly released during work time for training attendance). Hence, evidence that ACT has the potential to be delivered effectively in various formats may increase its perceived suitability across different workplace settings.

The amount of contact time required may be contingent upon the aims and ethos of the program. If the aim is to improve general mental health among employees who are experiencing (or at risk of) clinically relevant burnout or distress, we would usually suggest a requirement of around 8 to 10 hours of contact time (e.g., 3 x 3 hour sessions or 4 x 2 hour sessions) to ensure skills transfer. Ideally, this would involve a sequence of sessions so that skills can be practiced between sessions, and any challenges or concerns can be elicited, validated, and discussed. However, if the aim is to deliver ACT to help more general employee groups learn how to clarify personal values and increase values-based action in their work and personal lives, then more focused and briefer ACT interventions may be suitable (Archer, 2018). Unfortunately, we do not yet have sufficient evidence to communicate to practitioners that one delivery format is superior to any other, or how much ACT training is likely to be enough to elicit durable improvements in employees' psychological well-being and/or behavioral effectiveness.

Workplace implementation challenges are influencing interest in the potential of web-based, smartphone apps and other self-help methods for imparting ACT skills to working populations (Hofer et al., 2018; Kaipainen et al., 2017; Ly et al., 2014; Petersen et al., 2021). As Hofer et al. (2018) noted, employees' ability to access an ACT program has traditionally been "at the mercy of good fortune" (p. 190), according to whether they happen to work for an organization that offers (in-person) ACT-based training to staff. Most of the published evidence has been obtained from staff working in health care, education, and government settings, presumably because these are the types of organizations with links to ACT practitioners and researchers. Hofer and colleagues reached a more diverse range of employees (at least in terms of occupation) by administering ACT via a self-help book and online platform.

Despite advantages in terms of convenience, reduced costs, and accessibility, it should be noted that technology-administered methods omit group processes that are harnessed by trainers when ACT is delivered "live" to groups of staff (e.g., to support the normalization of undesirable psychological content or to facilitate group role plays of ACT metaphors). Whether such variations in delivery format influence ACT's effects on employees' psychological flexibility or its subprocesses is a question ready to be addressed by the next generation of intervention research.

Workplace ACT Program Content

Despite sharing some common features, exercises, and metaphors, rarely do two workplace ACT programs have exactly the same content or sequence of techniques. Although this technical heterogeneity might pose a challenge for study replication, and when synthesizing this strand of ACT research, it is congruent with the CBS movement's emphasis on processes over protocols. From a practical perspective, ACT's technical flexibility enables a useful degree of tailoring of workplace program content to the organizational context, intervention aims, or occupational group.

While perusing the reported content of workplace programs, we identified five broad categories of the ACT-based training protocol delivered to employees over the past 20 years. There is plenty of overlap between the protocols, given that they are all explicitly based on ACT's principles and practices. Nonetheless, we organize them into five groups to (1) provide readers with an overview of groups of studies that examined the effects of relatively similar program content (or that were at least inspired by the same ACT protocols), and (2) communicate the different ways that ACT's messages and skills have been imparted to employees, depending on context and intervention aims.

A first group of studies evaluated in-person interventions that were based on, or explicitly adapted from, Frank Bond's original translation of ACT into a three-session skills training program for the workplace (Bond, 2005; Bond & Bunce, 2000; Bond & Hayes, 2002). Ensuing collaborations between Bond, Flaxman, and Lloyd led to various modifications of this approach, extended its application to staff in other organizations, and produced further studies demonstrating ACT's effectiveness for improving employees' mental health (Flaxman & Bond, 2006, 2010a, 2010b, 2010c; Lloyd et al., 2013, 2017). In Sweden, Fredrik Livheim and his colleagues also adapted Bond's protocol into a widely applicable stress management intervention, which has been shown to reduce stress among social workers (Brinkborg et al., 2011) and informed an effective ACT intervention for trainee nurses (Frögéli et al., 2016, 2019).

These earlier workplace protocols have continued to evolve, integrating innovations in ACT practice and responding to feedback from participants and trainers. Bond's training approach informed a subsequent ACT protocol that is explicitly organized around the experiential links between mindfulness and valuing skills (Flaxman et al., 2013). This protocol was more recently further modified into a four-session training program that is organized around open, aware, and active skills, and that utilizes an adaptation of the ACT matrix (Flaxman et al., 2019). Similarly, Livheim's protocol developed into a structured mindfulness and acceptance program, which has been widely disseminated to working populations using a train-the-trainer approach (Livheim et al., 2018).

A second group of studies tailored Bond's training approach specifically for staff working in intellectual disability settings. A number of these studies evaluated variants of a protocol described by Noone and Hastings (2009, 2010). In this occupational setting, the training has often been delivered in a full-day workshop followed by another (e.g., half-day) workshop a few weeks later. The training cultivates ACT's processes in relation to specific challenges arising from supporting clients with intellectual disabilities (e.g., Bethay et al., 2013; McConachie et al., 2014).

A third group of studies evaluated ACT workshops and courses for clinical psychology trainees, therapists, and counselors (e.g., Hayes et al., 2004; Luoma & Viladarga, 2013; Pakenham, 2015; Stafford-Brown & Pakenham, 2012; Varra et al., 2008). This set of studies evaluated various formats, ranging from one-day workshops to a 12-week ACT course embedded within a postgraduate curriculum. Despite this variation, these therapist-focused interventions tend to be characterized by their pursuit of concurrent personal and professional aims: (1) improving therapists' psychological flexibility and well-being (e.g., reducing burnout), *while at the same time* (2) developing therapists' ACT knowledge and capacity to use ACT with their clients and/or (3) enhancing therapeutic practice (e.g., by improving the therapeutic alliance or increasing willingness to adopt evidence-based practice). As a result, some of these programs include a greater number of ACT practices and metaphors compared to other worksite applications, and in some cases provide opportunities for participants to practice ACT-based case conceptualization and therapeutic stance (e.g., Pakenham, 2015). The underlying ethos of such programs is that therapists need to develop psychological flexibility in their own lives before applying ACT with clients (Luoma & Vilardaga, 2013).

A fourth group of studies evaluated the effects of embedding ACT's principles and practices within the structured (8-week) mindfulness training framework developed by Williams and Penman (2011; Kinnunen et al., 2020; Puolakanaho et al., 2020). This type of program retains the main mindfulness meditation practices (i.e., body scan, mindfulness of breath, sounds and thoughts meditation) and introduces values exercises in each session, with participants invited to engage in values-based actions as part of the daily home practices. Accordingly,

Kinnunen et al. (2020) describe this as a mindfulness, acceptance, and values-based intervention approach.

The final group of researched protocols falls within the self-help category of ACT for working populations. This includes structured bibliotherapy interventions administered to employees using ACT self-help books (e.g., Jeffcoat & Hayes, 2012; Hofer et al., 2018), and ACT-based smartphone applications for employees and managers (Ly et al., 2014).

Section Summary

This overview of the format and technical composition of workplace programs leads us to the following observations. First, almost all studies have examined "full" ACT programs, in that the protocols impart a combination of mindfulness and acceptance and values-based behavioral activation skills. There have been few published dismantling or component-focused studies in this area (see Engle & Follette, 2018 for an exception). Among the full ACT programs, the sequence of training practices can vary. For example, some protocols introduce values exercises from the outset (e.g., Flaxman et al., 2013, 2019), while others introduce values after initial work on presenting acceptance as the alternative to internal control (e.g., Bond & Hayes, 2002; Frögéli et al., 2016).

Second, some protocols include other psychoeducational and skills components in addition to widely recognizable ACT practices. For instance, Frögéli's intervention included psychoeducation on the human stress response, work-life balance, sleep, and exercise, and utilized role plays for developing communication and assertiveness skills. Similarly, Bethay et al.'s (2013) program for intellectual disability staff included a session dedicated to integrating ACT skills with applied behavioral analysis. Rather than treating these "additional" components as separate from ACT's (sub)processes, in practice they are likely to be harnessed in the service of cultivating psychological flexibility (Archer, 2018; Hayes et al., 2004).

Our third observation concerns the extent to which the training content is oriented toward work-related topics and applications. That is, some programs invite employees to reflect on stress-related issues relevant to their job role, while others have more generic ACT content (i.e., they cultivate ACT skills without placing particular emphasis on work over other areas of life). The degree to which the content is work-related or generic (or both) likely depends on whether ACT is delivered to a homogeneous occupational group, in which participants share similar job characteristics and stressors (e.g., Bethay et al., 2013; Noone & Hastings, 2009). If the program is being delivered to a diverse group of participants (in terms of job role), a more generic ACT program may be called for.

Anecdotally, when delivering ACT to improve mental health among diverse staff in large organizations (e.g., a hospital), we tend to *deemphasize* the notion that the program is about dealing with job-related stress. Instead, we present the intervention as an opportunity to learn a set of psychological and behavioral skills that can help us relate more effectively to "the human condition." We have sensed that this messaging sometimes helps to sidestep initial (and understandable) cynicism among some attendees, for instance, that the training is being implemented "by management" to improve performance, reduce absence costs, or tackle staff unrest about unpopular organizational initiatives. In settings where these do not appear to be the reasons for offering the intervention, our intention is to communicate to participants that the ACT program is a personal resource "for you," with encouragement throughout to utilize the skills in all areas of life.

Similar observations can be found in the wider occupational health psychology literature, where interventions that are implemented for "performance reasons" may have little impact on employees' psychological health when compared to interventions that are dedicated to promoting staff well-being (Nielsen & Randall, 2013). We are not presenting these alternatives as "right" and "wrong" ways of implementing ACT-based training in the workplace. Indeed, in some cases, ACT skills will be imparted explicitly in the service of enhancing performance and other organizational outcomes (e.g., as part of leadership training or coaching initiatives; Archer, 2018). We highlight these issues to reiterate the value of being sensitive to context, aims, and audience when designing and offering such programs.

Our final program-level observation concerns the experience of trainers who deliver ACT programs to working populations. Workplace programs have been delivered by highly experienced ACT therapists (e.g., Varra et al., 2008), by relative novices, students, or trainee psychologists (e.g., Brinkborg et al., 2011; Frögéli et al., 2016), and by pairing novices with more experienced therapists. Brinkborg et al. (2011) tested whether therapist experience impacted the effects of ACT-based training delivered to social workers and found no differences in outcome between staff groups trained by masters-level students (who had been trained to deliver ACT) and groups trained by licensed psychologists. They concluded that this type of ACT skills training has the potential to be delivered effectively by relatively inexperienced psychologists.

Train-the-trainer initiatives are increasing the reach of ACT-based programs to working populations. Such initiatives involve transferring ACT delivery knowledge and skills to in-house practitioners, so that organizations do not always have to rely on external (and potentially expensive) trainers. Livheim has been particularly successful in transferring ACT delivery expertise to a considerable number of practitioners (Flaxman et al., 2013; Livheim et al., 2018). In the UK, Flaxman and colleagues have transferred delivery expertise to numerous staff support teams, particularly in health care settings, who have then successfully cascaded ACT-based training to staff within their own organizations (Jennings et al., 2017; Waters et al., 2018).

Similar to the way that ACT is delivered to trainee psychologists and therapists (e.g., Pakenham, 2015), train-the-trainer initiatives benefit from including: experiential and conceptual elements; opportunities for co-facilitation with more experienced ACT practitioners (with observation and feedback); sufficient time for new practitioners to apply ACT in their own lives; and preparation for the types of challenges that can arise in workplace training program (e.g., how to respond should a participant become visibly upset while engaging in an ACT exercise, or when group conversations keep veering away from the training to organizational-level issues). Comprehensive and well-designed train-the-trainer programs should help to extend the reach of ACT to a greater range of organizations and staff groups, while ensuring the training continues to be cascaded in a safe, effective, and ACT-consistent way.

Future Directions

In this penultimate section, we highlight potentially fruitful avenues for future research on these programs. Rather than looking too far into the future, we bring our focus to a set of recommendations that we sense are achievable now, pending some modest improvements to study design. Our intention is to motivate and guide the next generation of ACT researchers interested in applying and evaluating ACT-based skills training among working populations.

The Next Generation of Randomized Controlled Trials of Workplace ACT Programs

There are examples of well-designed RCTs evaluating ACT-based training for employees (e.g., Bond & Bunce, 2000; Brinkborg et al., 2011; Frögéli, et al., 2016, 2019; Hofer et al., 2018; Puolakanaho et al., 2020). However, reviewers have suggested that the overall methodological quality of the workplace ACT literature needs to be improved (Prudenzi et al., 2021a; Reeve et al., 2018; Towey-Swift et al., 2022). The reviewers discussed specific recommendations for improving trial quality ratings, and we will not repeat them all here. Instead, we offer the following suggestions to help guide future research on the utility of these programs.

Our first and most obvious recommendation is for researchers in this field to utilize the recently developed multidimensional measures of psychological flexibility (e.g., Francis et al., 2016; Kashdan et al., 2020; Rogge & Daks, 2021; Rolffs et al., 2018). The adoption of such measures has clear potential to enhance knowledge about the most influential subprocesses of change when ACT is applied with working populations, while also providing guidance to intervention designers seeking to maximize the efficiency and impact of these programs. Alongside the multidimensional measures, the field would benefit from additional studies examining effects on (and through) *work-related* psychological flexibility (i.e., using the WAAQ; Bond et al., 2013). In contrast to the AAQ-II (which is strongly related to distress outcomes), the WAAQ has exhibited stronger associations with work engagement and other performance-oriented outcomes (Ruiz & Odriozola-González, 2017; Xu et al., 2018). Although there exists a growing body of promising correlational research using the WAAQ, few intervention studies examine the degree to which cultivating flexibility specifically in the work domain contributes to the positive effects of ACT-based training.

Second, when selecting outcome variables, we recommend the routine inclusion of positive markers of employees' general and job-related well-being. Reflecting a broader shift in the well-being literature, there have been calls for researchers to go beyond assessing employees' affective state to capture *eudaimonic* aspects of well-being (e.g., sense of meaning and purpose, interpersonal connection, personal growth, and self-acceptance; Bartels et al., 2019). Given that ACT explicitly targets such experiences, ACT interventions seem pertinent to this trend. However, because researchers tend to prioritize distress measures, this potential is yet to be fully realized (Archer, 2018; Prudenzi et al., 2021a). We therefore recommend that more traditional outcome measures (e.g., burnout and perceived stress) are supplemented with measures of (for example) work engagement, subjective vitality, meaning and purpose in one's work, and other indicators of psychosocial flourishing. If these sorts of experiences are found to be reliably cultivated via ACT-based training, it could result in these programs reaching a greater proportion of the workforce, beyond employees who attend (or are recruited) because they are looking to address symptoms of burnout or distress.

Third, we recommend increasing the number of measurement occasions and (where possible) extending the controlled follow-up period beyond 3 months. For example, whereas many studies in this area include a maximum of three time points (i.e., pre-, post-, follow-up), researchers could consider administering measures to ACT (and control) participants every month for several months. This type of design may help to reveal whether some subprocesses are strengthened sooner than others and would support more widespread application of data-analytic approaches for modeling longitudinal change processes (e.g., latent growth modeling). Moreover, increasing the number and frequency time points would support more rigorous testing of mediators of change (Stockton et al., 2019).

Fourth, this field would benefit from additional comparisons of ACT-based training programs with active intervention conditions. ACT has generally performed well against various control conditions (Prudenzi et al., 2021a; Towey-Swift et al., 2022). However, there is a need for further research comparing ACT to other established psychological interventions applied in the workplace, such as CBT-based stress management/resilience training, psychological capital interventions, or mindfulness-based programs (e.g., MBSR). It is not necessarily about proving ACT is superior, but rather about investigating whether subprocesses of change are specific to ACT or are equally targeted by other approaches (Flaxman & Bond, 2010b;

Stockton et al., 2019). Comparative research could also take the form of dismantling studies of ACT among working populations, to compare the efficacy of individual ACT elements (or modules) with one another and with whole programs (Petersen et al., 2021).

Fifth, most reviews of this literature recommend going beyond self-report measures to include organizational outcomes, such as sickness absence rates, patient safety (in health care settings), or supervisory performance ratings. Such data can enable researchers to estimate cost-effectiveness and return on investment (Finnes et al., 2017). Given a point made earlier, it may be important to consider what is communicated to potential participants if a research team is asking permission to access absence or performance records (in that it might communicate that the program is not about staff well-being but about the bottom line). Nonetheless, demonstrating effects on objective organizational outcomes, perhaps achieved via improvements in staff well-being, would represent powerful evidence of ACT's utility in workplace settings.

Sixth, in terms of demographics, female participants working in the public sector (e.g., health care, social work, and educational) organizations have been overrepresented in workplace ACT intervention research. Accordingly, it would be useful to see additional studies evaluating ACT's applications in different (e.g., corporate or manufacturing) industry settings, along with investigations of whether male employees in some settings might be less inclined to volunteer for this type of training. Although much of the research has been conducted in Western countries, there are recent examples of ACT being delivered to frontline staff groups in other parts of the world, including Sierra Leone, Uganda, and Iran. We hope to see further evaluations of ACT for staff groups in a wider range of countries, along with accounts of any cultural-specific adaptations to the training content and research measures.

Finally, there is scope for further research focusing on the influence of baseline characteristics on the effectiveness of ACT in the workplace. This area of research is prone to a "dilution" effect in that workplace studies may include participants who are psychologically healthy alongside those who enter the training with moderate or higher levels of distress (Brinkborg et al., 2011; Flaxman & Bond, 2010a). More recent studies have addressed this issue at the design stage by only including participants who are scoring above a predefined threshold on burnout or stress measures (e.g., Hofer et al., 2018; Puolakanaho et al., 2020). However, this keeps the focus on ACT as a primarily therapeutic intervention, without considering whether a different pattern may be found on other markers of employee well-being or behavioral change.

Other Evaluation Methods

Although the RCT remains the most influential design for intervention evaluation, it is important to acknowledge that maintaining a (potentially untreated) control group of employees for several weeks or months is not always possible in workplace settings (Nielsen & Miraglia, 2017; Waters et al., 2018). It is therefore worth considering alternative designs that can generate valuable data on people's experiences of ACT-based training. For instance, Reeve et al. (2021) recently adopted a single-case experimental design, varying the sequence of ACT modules across different individuals. They were able to address a number of empirical questions, including the degree to which ACT modules reduced burnout and increased work engagement, and the extent to which change in these outcomes was associated with improvements in values-based behavior. Analyzing data obtained from this type of study is not an easy option but demonstrates how detailed exploration of workplace interventions can be performed even in the absence of a large sample or control group.

Another option is to utilize a higher density of measurement of both outcomes and processes (e.g., across several work days) to capture patterns of change unfolding immediately after an ACT intervention. We have most often seen this type of design used in the workplace mindfulness literature (e.g., Hülsheger et al., 2015). It seems particularly well suited to examining proximal changes elicited by relatively brief (e.g., self-help) applications of ACT for employees.

Even in the absence of a control group, researchers can track change in ways that offer more precise information on the subprocesses that are targeted when ACT is applied in the workplace. For example, brief versions of subprocess measures could be administered to employees on a weekly basis (e.g., once per week), capturing a period during and after implementation of ACT-based training, ideally for a period of several consecutive weeks. Such data can reveal trajectories of change in discrete subprocesses, and change in subprocesses could in turn be associated with outcome change. This type of design is more common in the clinical literature (based on data collected from clients in each consecutive session), but it holds untapped potential for enhancing our understanding of the effects of worksite ACT interventions.

Finally, we have focused on quantitative methods, but there is clearly scope for further qualitative (and mixed methods) research on these workplace programs (e.g., Wardley et al., 2014). Qualitative investigations could address a wide range of research questions by gathering ACT participants' accounts of (for example) what they sense has changed in how they respond to challenges at work and home, which aspects of the training had most impact (and why), and any concerns related to participating in the program. Such data is likely to provide a valuable source of information on the active ingredients of change, while also offering more practical insights, such as what it is like to attend this type of training alongside colleagues.

Implementation and Ethical Considerations

A broader ethical issue surrounds the use of ACT-based training to improve the psychological health and well-being of employees. The training programs we have focused on are classified as "individual-focused" interventions in the occupational health literature (Bunce, 1997). That is, they seek to provide employees with personal skills and resources that will help them respond more effectively/healthily to work and life stressors, as well as to any difficult thoughts and emotions that may arise. The onus is on changing the individual employee, and not the organization, management style or work design. Yet, as we know from decades of research, potent sources of stress may reside in the psychosocial work environment, including excessive job demands coupled with a lack of job control (i.e., job strain), inadequate workplace support, organizational injustice, and a chronic imbalance between effort and rewards (Sara et al., 2018). Most ACT programs are not designed to address these risk factors, so that participants may complete an ACT intervention only to return to an unhealthy work environment.

We do not raise this issue to undermine the use of ACT in workplace settings. In our experience, individual-focused ACT programs are very popular among the workforces that receive them, and interest is often spread via word-of-mouth from colleagues who have already attended. However, it pays to be mindful about these background factors, which may be influencing attendance at an ACT program, and may be discussed by participants during the sessions.

It is usually recommended that organizations adopt a comprehensive staff well-being strategy, with a combination of initiatives functioning at primary, secondary and tertiary levels of prevention (Flaxman & Bond, 2010a). Primary interventions typically involve work redesign and/or modifications to the management of work, for example, to increase employees' level of autonomy and control over how to meet their job demands and/or to improve supervisory support. When delivered to employees with relatively modest levels of distress (but who may be at risk of developing a common mental health problem), ACT would be deemed to operate at a secondary level of prevention. But ACT can also have a tertiary-level impact, due to its well-established therapeutic benefits for those already experiencing elevated distress (Brinkborg et al., 2011; Flaxman & Bond, 2010a; Kinnunen et al., 2020; Waters et al., 2018).

These considerations also highlight the potential benefits of integrating ACT's principles and processes with other organizational initiatives. This might involve: providing individual-oriented ACT skills training as a natural adjunct to interventions designed to increase organizational flexibility (Bond et al., 2016; Gascoyne, 2019); embedding the cultivation of ACT's subprocesses within mainstream learning and development curricula, such as leadership and coaching programs (Archer, 2018; Pingo et al., 2019); or adopting an ACT-based approach when designing and delivering work redesign, job crafting, and recovery-promoting interventions. In this way, ACT can become more seamlessly positioned within a multilevel approach to workplace health and well-being.

Conclusion

In view of the intervention research that has accumulated over the past 20 years, it seems appropriate to conclude that ACT has been successfully translated into accessible, popular, diverse, and effective training programs suitable for workplace settings. The evidence most clearly supports the use of ACT-based training as part of worksite mental health promotion, given multiple demonstrations of program efficacy in reducing the common symptoms of psychological stress and distress.

Thus far, only a relatively modest literature has sought to conceptualize and test the utility of integrating psychological flexibility within established theories of workplace well-being, such as JD-R theory. Thus, we hope to see further longitudinal, daily survey, dyadic (leader-employee), and experiential sampling studies exploring the functions of psychological flexibility as a personal resource (or self-regulation repertoire) within work design frameworks. Moreover, the recent development of various multidimensional measures provides tools for conducting closer examinations of the specific skills that are cultivated when ACT is translated into staff training interventions.

We narrowed our focus to review the increasingly popular ACT-based training programs, which have tended to be therapeutically oriented, in that they seek to improve employees' mental health. Nonetheless, we have also touched upon numerous avenues for implementing and evaluating other theoretically consistent workplace applications, including the promotion of organizational flexibility, and cultivating employees' and leaders' psychological flexibility as part of other workplace initiatives. Collectively, these traditional and innovative applications hold considerable promise for extending the reach of CBS and ACT programs to increasingly greater proportions of the global workforce.

References

Aasdahl, L., Pape, K., Vasseljen, O., Johnsen, R., Gismervik, S., Halsteinli, V., Fleten, N., Nielsen, C. V., & Fimland, M. S. (2018). Effect of inpatient multicomponent occupational rehabilitation versus less comprehensive outpatient rehabilitation on sickness absence in persons with musculoskeletal- or mental health disorders: A randomized clinical trial. *Journal of Occupational Rehabilitation, 28*(1), 170–179. https://doi.org/10.1007/s10926-017-9708-z

Archer, R. (2018). The impact of a focused acceptance and commitment training workplace intervention: Is less, less? [Unpublished doctoral thesis, Kingston Business School]. https://eprints.kingston.ac.uk/id/eprint/43020/

Atkins, P. W.B., Wilson, D. S., & Hayes, S. C. (2019). *Prosocial: Using evolutionary science to build productive equitable and collaborative groups.* Context Press.

Baer, R. A., Smith, G. T., Hopkins, J., Krietemeyer, J., & Toney, L. (2006). Using self-report assessment methods to explore facets of mindfulness. *Assessment, 13*, 27–45. doi: 10.1177/1073191105283504.

Bakker, A. B., & Demerouti, E. (2017). Job demands–resources theory: Taking stock and looking forward. *Journal of Occupational Health Psychology, 22*(3), 273–285. https://doi.org/10.1037/ocp0000056

Bakker, A. B., & de Vries, J. D. (2021). Job demands—Resources theory and self-regulation: new explanations and remedies for job burnout. *Anxiety, Stress, and Coping*, *34*(1), 1–21. https://doi.org/10.1080/10615806.2020.1797695

Bartels, A. L., Peterson, S. J., & Reina, C. S. (2019). Understanding well-being at work: Development and validation of the eudaimonic workplace well-being scale. *PloS One*, *14*(4), e0215957. https://doi.org/10.1371/journal.pone.0215957

Bennett, A. A., Bakker, A. B., & Field, J. G. (2018). Recovery from work-related effort: A meta-analysis. *Journal of Organizational Behavior*, *39*, 262–275. https://doi.org/10.1002/job.2217

Bethay, J. S., Wilson, K. G., Schnetzer, L. W., Nassar, S. L., & Bordieri, M. J. (2013). A controlled pilot evaluation of acceptance and commitment training for intellectual disability staff. *Mindfulness*, *4*, 113–121.

Biglan, A., Hayes, S. C., & Pistorello, J. (2008). Acceptance and commitment: Implications for prevention science. *Prevention Science*, *9*, 139–152.

Biglan, A., Layton, G., Jones, L. B., Hankins, F. M., & Rusby, J. C. (2013). The value of workshops on psychological flexibility for early childhood special education staff. *Topics in Early Childhood Special Education*, *32*(4), 196–210.

Biron, M., & van Veldhoven, M. (2012). Emotional labour in service work: Psychological flexibility and emotion regulation. *Human Relations*, *65*(10), 1259–1282. https://doi.org/10.1177/0018726712447832

Boatemaa, M. A., Oppong Asante, K., & Agyemang, C. B. (2019). The moderating role of psychological flexibility in the relationship between organizational commitment, workaholism, job security, and corporate entrepreneurship among information technology workers in Accra, Ghana. *SAGE Open*. https://doi.org/10.1177/2158244019871063

Bohlmeijer, E. T., Fledderus, M., Rokx, T. A., & Pieterse, M. E. (2011). Efficacy of an early intervention based on acceptance and commitment therapy for adults with depressive symptomatology: Evaluation in a randomized controlled trial. *Behaviour Research and Therapy*, *49*(1), 62–67. https://doi.org/10.1016/j.brat.2010.10.003

Bond, F. W. (2005). ACT for Stress. In S. C. Hayes & K. D. Strosahl (Eds.), *A practical guide to acceptance and commitment therapy* (pp. 275–293). Springer Science + Business Media.

Bond, F. W., & Bunce, D. (2000). Mediators of change in emotion-focused and problem-focused worksite stress management interventions. *Journal of Occupational Health Psychology*, *5*(1), 156–163. https://doi.org/10.1037/1076-8998.5.1.156

Bond, F. W., & Bunce, D. (2003). The role of acceptance and job control in mental health, job satisfaction, and work performance. *Journal of Applied Psychology*, *88*(6), 1057–1067. https://doi.org/10.1037/0021-9010.88.6.1057

Bond, F. W., & Flaxman, P. E. (2006). The ability of psychological flexibility and job control to predict learning, job performance, and mental health. *Journal of Organizational Behavior Management*, *26*(1-2), 113–130. https://doi.org/10.1300/J075v26n01_05

Bond, F. W., Flaxman, P. E., & Bunce, D. (2008). The influence of psychological flexibility on work redesign: Mediated moderation of a work reorganization intervention. *Journal of Applied Psychology*, *93*(3), 645–654. https://doi.org/10.1037/0021-9010.93.3.645

Bond, F. W., & Hayes, S. C. (2002). ACT at work. In F. W. Bond & W. Dryden (Eds.), *Handbook of brief cognitive behaviour therapy* (pp. 117–140). Chichester, UK: John Wiley.

Bond, F. W., Hayes, S. C., & Barnes-Holmes, D. (2006). Psychological flexibility, ACT, and organizational behavior. *Journal of Organizational Behavior Management*, *26*, 25–54.

Bond, F. W., Lloyd, J., Flaxman, P. E., & Archer, R. (2016). *Psychological flexibility and ACT at work*. In R. D. Zettle, S. C. Hayes, D. Barnes-Holmes, & A. Biglan (Eds.), *The Wiley handbook of contextual behavioral science* (pp. 459–482). Hoboken, NJ: Wiley Blackwell.

Bond, F. W., Lloyd, J., & Guenole, N. (2013). The work-related acceptance and action questionnaire: Initial psychometric findings and their implications for measuring psychological flexibility in specific contexts. *Journal of Occupational and Organizational Psychology*, *86*(3), 331–347.

Brinkborg, H., Michanek, J., Hesser, H., & Berglund, G. (2011). Acceptance and commitment therapy for the treatment of stress among social workers: A randomized controlled trial. *Behaviour Research and Therapy*, *49*, 389–398. doi: 10.1016/j.brat.2011.03.

Brown, K. W., & Ryan, R. M. (2003). The benefits of being present: Mindfulness and its role in psychological well-being. *Journal of Personality and Social Psychology*, *84*(4), 822–848. https://doi.org/10.1037/0022-3514.84.4.822

Bunce, D. (1997). What factors are associated with the outcome of individual-focused worksite stress management interventions? *Journal of Occupational and Organizational Psychology*, *70*(1), 1–17. https://doi.org/10.1111/j.2044-8325.1997.tb00627.x

Clarke, S., Taylor, G., Lancaster, J., & Remington, B. (2015). Acceptance and commitment therapy-based self-management versus psychoeducation training for staff caring for clients with a personality disorder: A randomized controlled trial. *Journal of Personality Disorders 29*, 163–176.

de Beer, L. T., & Bianchi, R. (2019). Confirmatory factor analysis of the Maslach Burnout Inventory: A Bayesian structural equation modeling approach. *European Journal of Psychological Assessment, 35*(2), 217–224. https://doi.org/10.1027/1015-5759/a000392

Engle, J. L., & Follette, V. M. (2018). An experimental comparison of two acceptance and commitment therapy (ACT) values exercises to increase values-oriented behavior. *Journal of Contextual Behavioral Science, 10*, 31–40. https://doi.org/10.1016/j.jcbs.2018.08.001

Finnes, A., Enebrink, P., Sampaio, F., Sorjonen, K., Dahl, J., Ghaderi, A., Nager, A., & Feldman, I. (2017). Cost-effectiveness of acceptance and commitment therapy and a workplace intervention for employees on sickness absence due to mental disorders. *Journal of Occupational and Environmental Medicine, 59*(12), 1211–1220. https://doi.org/10.1097/JOM.0000000000001156

Flaxman, P. E., & Bond, F. W. (2006). Acceptance and commitment therapy in the workplace. In R. A. Baer (Ed.) *Mindfulness-based treatment approaches* (pp. 377–402). Elsevier.

Flaxman, P. E., & Bond, F. W. (2010a). Worksite stress management training: Moderated effects and clinical significance. *Journal of Occupational Health Psychology, 15*(4), 347–358. https://doi.org/10.1037/a0020522

Flaxman, P. E., & Bond, F. W. (2010b). A randomised worksite comparison of acceptance and commitment therapy and stress inoculation training. *Behaviour Research and Therapy, 48*(8), 816–820. https://doi.org/10.1016/j.brat.2010.05.004

Flaxman, P. E., & Bond, F. W. (2010c). Acceptance and commitment training: Promoting psychological flexibility in the workplace. In R. A. Baer (Ed.), *Assessing mindfulness and acceptance processes in clients: Illuminating the theory and practice of change* (pp. 281–308). New Harbinger Publications.

Flaxman, P. E., Bond, F. W., & Livheim, F. (2013). *The mindful and effective employee: An acceptance and commitment therapy training manual for improving well-being and performance.* New Harbinger Publications.

Flaxman, P. E., McIntosh, R., & Oliver, J. (2019). *Acceptance and commitment training or workplace settings: Summary overview for trainers.* Unpublished ACT training handout, University of London.

Francis, A. W., Dawson, D. L., & Golijani-Moghaddam, N. (2016). The development and validation of the comprehensive assessment of acceptance and commitment therapy processes (CompACT). *Journal of Contextual Behavioral Science, 5*(3), 134–145. https://doi.org/10.1016/j.jcbs.2016.05.003

Frögéli, E., Djordjevic, A., Rudman, A., Livheim, F., & Gustavsson, P. (2016). A randomized controlled pilot trial of acceptance and commitment therapy (ACT) for preventing stress-related ill-health among future nurses. *Anxiety, Stress and Coping, 29*(2), 202–218. doi: 10.1080/10615806.2015.

Frögéli, E., Rudman, A., & Gustavsson, P. (2019). Preventing stress-related ill health among future nurses: Effects over 3 years. *International Journal of Stress Management, 26*(3), 272–286. https://doi.org/10.1037/str0000110

Gascoyne, A. C. (2019). The development and validation of a measure of organisational flexibility. [Unpublished doctoral thesis, University of London].

Gaupp, R., Walter, M., Bader, K., Benoy, C., & Lang, U. E. (2020). A two-day acceptance and commitment therapy (ACT) workshop increases presence and work functioning in healthcare workers. *Frontiers in Psychiatry, 11*, 861. https://doi.org/10.3389/fpsyt.2020.00861

Geurts, S. A. E., & Sonnentag, S. (2006). Recovery as an explanatory mechanism in the relation between acute stress reactions and chronic health impairment. *Scandinavian Journal of Work, Environment and Health, 32*, 482–492.

Gillanders, D. T., Bolderston, H., Bond, F. W., Dempster, M., Flaxman, P. E., Campbell, L., Kerr, S., Tansey, L., Noel, P., Ferenbach, C., Masley, S., Roach, L., Lloyd, J., May, L., Clarke, S., & Remington, B. (2014). The development and initial validation of the cognitive fusion questionnaire. *Behavior Therapy, 45*(1), 83–101. https://doi.org/10.1016/j.beth.2013.09.001

Gloster, A. T., Walder, N., Levin, M., Twohig, M., & Karekla, M. (2020). The empirical status of acceptance and commitment therapy: A review of meta-analyses. *Journal of Contextual Behavioral Science, 18*, 181–192. https://doi.org/10.1016/j.jcbs.2020.09.009

Goetzel, R. Z., Roemer, E. C., Holingue, C., Fallin, M. D., McCleary, K., Eaton, W., Agnew, J., Azocar, F., Ballard, D., Bartlett, J., Braga, M., Conway, H., Crighton, K. A., Frank, R., Jinnett, K., Keller-Greene, D., Rauch, S. M., Safeer, R., Saporito, D. Mattingly, C. R. (2018). Mental health in the workplace: A call to action proceedings from the mental health in the workplace-public health summit. *Journal of Occupational and Environmental Medicine, 60*(4), 322–330. https://doi.org/10.1097/JOM.0000000000001271

Gorgievski, M., & Hobfoll, S. (2008). Work can burn us out or fire us up: Conservation of resources in burnout and engagement. In J. R. B. Halbesleben (Ed.), *Handbook of stress and burnout in health care* (pp. 7–22). Nova Science Publishers.

Habibian, Z., Sadri, Z., & Nazmiyeh, H. (2018). Effects of group acceptance and commitment therapy-based training on job stress and burnout among pediatric oncology and special diseases nurses. *Iranian Journal of Pediatric Hematology and Oncology, 8*(2), 118–125.

Häusser, J. A., Mojzisch, A., Niesel, M., & Schulz-Hardt, S. (2010). Ten years on: A review of recent research on the job demand-control (-support) model and psychological well-being. *Work and Stress*, *24*(1), 1–35. https://doi.org/10.1080/02678371003683747

Hayes, S. C., Bissett, R., Roget, N., Padilla, M., Kohlenberg, B. S., Fisher, G., Masuda, A., Pistorello, J., Rye, A. K., Berry, K., & Niccolls, R. (2004). The impact of acceptance and commitment training and multicultural training on the stigmatizing attitudes and professional burnout of substance abuse counselors. *Behavior Therapy*, *35*, 821–835. https://doi.org/10.1016/S0005-7894(04)80022-4

Hill, J., & Oliver, J. (2018). *Acceptance and commitment coaching: Distinctive features*. London: Routledge.

Hobfoll, S. E. (1989). Conservation of resources: A new attempt at conceptualizing stress. *American Psychologist*, *44*(3), 513–524. https://doi.org/10.1037/0003-066X.44.3.513

Hofer, P. D., Waadt, M., Aschwanden, R., Milidou, M., Acker, J., Meyer, A. H., Lieb, R., & Gloster, A. T. (2018). Self-help for stress and burnout without therapist contact: An online randomised controlled trial. *Work and Stress*, *32*(2), 189–208. https://doi.org/10.1080/02678373.2017.1402389

Hülsheger, U. R., Feinholdt, A., & Nubold, A. (2015). A low-dose mindfulness intervention and recovery from work: Effects on psychological detachment, sleep quality, and sleep duration. *Journal of Occupational and Organizational Psychology*, *88*(3), 464–489. doi: 10.1111/joop.12115.

Jeffcoat, T., & Hayes, S. C. (2012). A randomized trial of ACT bibliotherapy on the mental health of K-12 teachers and staff. *Behaviour Research and Therapy*, *50*(9), 571–579. https://doi.org/10.1016/j.brat.2012.05.008

Jennings, T., Flaxman, P., Egdell, K., Pestell, S., Whipday, E., & Herbert, A. (2017). A resilience training programme to improve nurses' mental health. *Nursing Times*, *13*(10), 22–26. https://www.nursingtimes.net/roles/nurse-educators/a-resilience-training-programme-to-improve-nurses-mental-health-18-09-2017/

Kaipainen, K., Välkkynen, P., & Kilkku, N. (2017). Applicability of acceptance and commitment therapy-based mobile app in depression nursing. *Translational Behavioral Medicine*, *7*(2), 242–253. https://doi.org/10.1007/s13142-016-0451-3

Kashdan, T. B., Disabato, D. J., Goodman, F. R., Doorley, J. D., & McKnight, P. E. (2020). Understanding psychological flexibility: A multimethod exploration of pursuing valued goals despite the presence of distress. *Psychological Assessment*, *32*(9), 829–850. https://doi.org/10.1037/pas0000834

Kinnunen, S. M., Puolakanaho, A., Mäkikangas, A., Tolvanen, A., & Lappalainen, R. (2020). Does a mindfulness-, acceptance-, and value-based intervention for burnout have long-term effects on different levels of subjective well-being? *International Journal of Stress Management*, *27*(1), 82–87. https://doi.org/10.1037/str0000132

Kopperud, K. H., Buch, R., & Skogen, C. (2021). Work overload and leader–member exchange: The moderating role of psychological flexibility. *Journal of General Management*, *46*(3), 173–184. https://doi.org/10.1177/0306307020942905

Lerner, D., Lyson, M., Sandberg, E., & Rogers, W. H. (2018). *The high cost of mental disorders: Facts for employers*. One Mind at Work. Retrieved from https://onemindatwork.org/wp-content/uploads/2018/12/Updated-OMI-White-Paper-R18.pdf

Lindsay, E. K., & Creswell, J. D. (2017). Mechanisms of mindfulness training: Monitor and acceptance theory (MAT). *Clinical Psychology Review*, *51*, 48–59. doi: 10.1016/j.cpr.2016.10.011

Livheim, F., Bond, F. W., Ek, D., & Hedensjo, B. (2018) *The mindfulness and acceptance workbook for stress reduction: Using acceptance and commitment therapy to manage stress, build resilience, and create the life you want*. New Harbinger Publications.

Lloyd, J., Bond, F. W., & Flaxman, P. E. (2013). The value of psychological flexibility: Examining psychological mechanisms underpinning a cognitive behavioural therapy intervention for burnout. *Work and Stress*, *27*, 181–199. doi: 10.1080/02678373.2013.782157.

Lloyd, J., Bond, F. W., & Flaxman, P. E. (2017). Work-related self-efficacy as a moderator of the impact of a worksite stress management training intervention: Intrinsic work motivation as a higher order condition of effect. *Journal of Occupational Health Psychology*, *22*(1), 115–127. https://doi.org/10.1037/ocp0000026

Luoma, J. B., & Vilardaga, J. P. (2013). Improving therapist psychological flexibility while training acceptance and commitment therapy: A pilot study. *Cognitive Behaviour Therapy*, *42*(1), 1–8. https://doi.org/10.1080/16506073.2012.701662

Ly, K. H., Asplund, K., Andersson, G. (2014). Stress management for middle managers via an acceptance and commitment-based smartphone application: A randomized controlled trial. *Internet Interventions*, *1*(3), 95–101. doi: 10.1016/j.invent.2014.06.003.

Maslach, C., Jackson, S. E., & Leiter, M. P. (Eds.). (1996). *Maslach Burnout Inventory Manual* (3rd ed.). Consulting Psychologists Press.

McConachie, D. A. J., McKenzie, K., Morris, P. G., & Walley, R. M. (2014). Acceptance and mindfulness-based stress management for support staff caring for individuals with intellectual disabilities. *Research in Developmental Disabilities*, *35*, 1216–1227.

Nielsen, K., and Miraglia, M. (2017). What works for whom in which circumstances? On the need to move beyond the "what works?" question in organizational intervention. *Human Relations, 70*(1), 40–62. https://doi.org/10.1177/0018726716670226

Nielsen, K., & Randall, R. (2013). Opening the black box: Presenting a model for evaluating organizational-level interventions. *European Journal of Work and Organizational Psychology, 22,* 601–617. https://doi.org/10.1080/1359432X.2012.690556

Noone, S. J., & Hastings, R. P. (2009). Building psychological resilience in support staff caring for people with intellectual disabilities: Pilot evaluation of an acceptance-based intervention. *Journal of Intellectual Disabilities, 13,* 43–53. doi: 10.1177/1744629509103519.

Noone, S. J., & Hastings, R. P. (2010). Using acceptance and mindfulness-based workshops with support staff caring for adults with intellectual disabilities. *Mindfulness, 1,* 67–73. doi: 10.1007/s12671-010-0007-4

Novaes, V. P., Ferreira, M. C., & Valentini, F. (2018). Psychological flexibility as a moderator of the relationships between job demands and resources and occupational well-being. *The Spanish Journal of Psychology, 21,* E11. https://doi.org/10.1017/sjp.2018.14

Onwezen, M. C., van Veldhoven, M. J. P. M., & Biron, M. (2014). The role of psychological flexibility in the demands–exhaustion–performance relationship. *European Journal of Work and Organizational Psychology, 23*(2), 163–176. https://doi.org/10.1080/1359432X.2012.742242

Pakenham, K. I. (2015). Effects of acceptance and commitment therapy (ACT) training on clinical psychology trainee stress, therapist skills and attributes, and ACT processes. *Clinical Psychology and Psychotherapy, 22*(6), 647–655. https://doi.org/10.1002/cpp.1924

Parsonage, M., & Saini, G. (2017). *Mental health at work: The business costs ten years on.* Centre for Mental Health.

Petersen, J. M., Krafft, J., Twohig, M. P., & Levin, M. E. (2021). Evaluating the open and engaged components of acceptance and commitment therapy in an online self-guided website: Results from a pilot trial. *Behavior Modification, 45*(3), 480–501. https://doi.org/10.1177/0145445519878668

Pingo, J. C., Dixon, M. R., & Paliliunas, D. (2019). Intervention enhancing effects of acceptance and commitment training on performance feedback for direct support professional work performance, stress, and job satisfaction. *Behavior Analysis in Practice, 13*(1), 1–10. https://doi.org/10.1007/s40617-019-00333-w

Prudenzi, A., Graham, C. D., Clancy, F., Hill, D., Driscoll, R. O., Day, F., & O'Connor, D. B. (2021a). Group-based acceptance and commitment therapy interventions for improving general distress and work-related distress in healthcare professionals: A systematic review and meta-analysis. *Journal of Affective Disorders, 295,* 192–202. Available at: https://doi.org/10.1016/j.jad.2021.07.084

Prudenzi, A., Graham, C. D., Flaxman, P. E., & O'Connor, D. B. (2021b). Wellbeing, burnout, and safe practice among healthcare professionals: predictive influences of mindfulness, values, and self-compassion. *Psychology, Health and Medicine,* 1–14. Advance online publication. https://doi.org/10.1080/13548506.2021.1898651

Prudenzi, A., Graham, C. D., Flaxman, P. E., Wilding, S., Day, F., & O'Connor, D. B. (2022). A workplace Acceptance and Commitment Therapy (ACT) intervention for improving healthcare staff psychological distress: A randomised controlled trial. *PloS One, 17*(4), e0266357. https://doi.org/10.1371/journal.pone.0266357

Puolakanaho, A., Tolvanen, A., Kinnunen, S. M., & Lappalainen, R. (2020). A psychological flexibility-based intervention for burnout: A randomized controlled trial. *Journal of Contextual Behavioral Science, 15,* 52–67. doi:10.1016/j.jcbs.2019.11.007

Reeve, A., Moghaddam, N., Tickle, A., & Young, D. (2021). A brief acceptance and commitment intervention for work-related stress and burnout amongst frontline homelessness staff: A single case experimental design series. *Clinical Psychology and Psychotherapy, 28*(5), 1001–1019. https://doi.org/10.1002/cpp.2555

Reeve, A., Tickle, A., and Moghaddam, N. (2018). Are acceptance and commitment therapy-based interventions effective for reducing burnout in direct-care staff? A systematic review and meta-analysis. *Mental Health Review Journal, 23*(3), 131–155. https://doi.org/10.1108/MHRJ-11-2017-0052

Rogge, R. D., & Daks, J. S. (2021). Embracing the Intricacies of the path toward mindfulness: Broadening our conceptualization of the process of cultivating mindfulness in day-to-day life by developing the Unified Flexibility and Mindfulness Model. *Mindfulness, 12,* 701–721. https://doi.org/10.1007/s12671-020-01537-w

Rolffs, J. L., Rogge, R. D., & Wilson, K. G. (2018). Disentangling components of flexibility via the hexaflex model: Development and validation of the multidimensional psychological flexibility inventory (MPFI). *Assessment, 25*(4), 458–482. https://doi.org/10.1177/1073191116645905

Rudaz, M., Twohig, M. P., Ong, C. W. & Levin, M. E. (2017). Mindfulness and acceptance-based trainings for fostering self-care and reducing stress in mental health professionals: A systematic review. *Journal of Contextual Behavioral Science, 6,* 380–390. doi:10.1016/j.jcbs.2017.10.001

Ruiz, F. J., & Odriozola-González, P. (2017). The predictive and moderating role of psychological flexibility in the development of job burnout. *Universitas Psychologica, 16*(4), 1–8. https://doi.org/10.11144/Javeriana.upsy16-4.pmrp
Sara, J. D., Prasad, M., Eleid, M. F., Zhang, M., Widmer, R. J., & Lerman, A. (2018). Association between work-related stress and coronary heart disease: A review of prospective studies through the job strain, effort-reward balance, and organizational justice models. *Journal of the American Heart Association, 7*(9), e008073. https://doi.org/10.1161/JAHA.117.008073
Schonfeld, I. S., Verkuilen, J., & Bianchi, R. (2019). Inquiry into the correlation between burnout and depression. *Journal of Occupational Health Psychology, 24*(6), 603–616. https://doi.org/10.1037/ocp0000151
Shirom, A. (2003). Job-related burnout: A review. In J. C. Quick & L. E. Tetrick (Eds.), *Handbook of occupational health psychology* (pp. 245–264). American Psychological Association. https://doi.org/10.1037/10474-012
Smout, M., Davies, M., Burns, N., & Christie, A. (2014). Development of the Valuing Questionnaire (VQ). *Journal of Contextual Behavioral Science, 3*(3), 164–172. https://doi.org/10.1016/j.jcbs.2014.06.001
Stafford-Brown, J., & Pakenham, K. I. (2012). The effectiveness of an ACT informed intervention for managing stress and improving therapist qualities in clinical psychology trainees. *Journal of Clinical Psychology, 68*(6), 592–613. https://doi.org/10.1002/jclp.21844
Stockton, D., Kellett, S., Berrios, R., Sirois, F., Wilkinson, N., & Miles, G. (2019). Identifying the underlying mechanisms of change during acceptance and commitment therapy (ACT): A systematic review of contemporary mediation Studies. *Behavioural and Cognitive Psychotherapy, 47*(3), 332–362. https://doi.org/10.1017/S1352465818000553
Towey-Swift, K. D., Lauvrud, C., & Whittington, R. (2022). Acceptance and Commitment Therapy (ACT) for professional staff burnout: A systematic review and narrative synthesis of controlled trials. *Journal of Mental Health*, 1–13. Advance online publication. https://doi.org/10.1080/09638237.2021.2022628
van den Heuvel, M., Demerouti, E., Bakker, A. B., & Schaufeli, W. B. (2010). Personal resources and work engagement in the face of change. In J. Houdmont & S. Leka (Eds.), *Contemporary Occupational Health Psychology* (pp. 124–150). Wiley-Blackwell. https://doi.org/10.1002/9780470661550.ch7
Van Veldhoven, M., Van den Broeck, A., Daniels, K., Bakker, A. B., Tavares, S. M., & Ogbonnaya, C. (2020). Challenging the universality of job resources: Why, when, and for whom are they beneficial? *Applied Psychology, 69*(1), 5–29. https://doi.org/10.1111/apps.12211
Varra, A. A., Hayes, S. C., Roget, N., & Fisher, G. (2008). A randomized control trial examining the effect of acceptance and commitment training on clinician willingness to use evidence-based pharmacotherapy. *Journal of Consulting and Clinical Psychology, 76*, 449–458. https://doi.org/10.1037/0022-006X.76.3.449
Vilardaga, R., Luoma, J. B., Hayes, S. C., Pistorello, J., Levin, M. E., Hildebrandt, M. J., Kohlenberg, B., Roget, N. A., & Bond, F. W. (2011). Burnout among the addiction counseling workforce: The differential roles of mindfulness and values-based processes and work-site factors. *Journal of Substance Abuse Treatment, 40*, 323–335. https://doi.org/10.1016/j.jsat.2010.11.015
Wardley, M. N., Flaxman, P. E., Willig, C., & Gillanders, D. (2014). "Feel the Feeling": Psychological practitioners' experience of acceptance and commitment therapy well-being training in the workplace. *Journal of Health Psychology, 21*(8), 1536–1547. https://doi.org/10.1177/1359105314557977
Waters, C. S., Frude, N., Flaxman, P. E., & Boyd, J. (2018). Acceptance and commitment therapy (ACT) for clinically distressed health care workers: Waitlist-controlled evaluation of an ACT workshop in a routine practice setting. *British Journal of Clinical Psychology, 57*(1), 82–98. https://doi.org/10.1111/bjc.12155
Westman, M., Hobfoll, S., Chen, S., Davidson, R., & Lasky, S. (2004). Organizational stress through the lens of conservation of resources (COR) theory. In P. Perrewé & D. Ganster (Eds.), *Research in occupational stress and well-being*, vol. 5. (pp. 167–220). JAI Press/Elsevier Science.
Williams, M., & Penman, D. (2011). *Mindfulness: A practical guide to finding peace in a frantic world.* Piatkus.
Wolgast M. (2014). What does the Acceptance and Action Questionnaire (AAQ-II) really measure?. *Behavior Therapy, 45*(6), 831–839. https://doi.org/10.1016/j.beth.2014.07.002
Xu, X., Liu, X., Ou, M., Xie, C., & Chen, Y. (2018). Psychological flexibility of nurses in a cancer hospital: Preliminary validation of a Chinese version of the Work-related Acceptance and Action Questionnaire. *Asia-Pacific Journal of Oncology Nursing, 5*(1), 83–90. https://doi.org/10.4103/apjon.apjon_62_17

CHAPTER

20 Acceptance and Commitment Therapy for Chronic Pain

Karlyn A. Edwards *and* Kevin E. Vowles

Abstract

Chronic pain, defined as pain that persists for 3 months or longer, is a common and costly health care concern. Psychological approaches to the treatment of chronic pain have a longstanding and robust evidence base of positive effectiveness. This article briefly reviews the history of these approaches and focuses on acceptance and commitment therapy (ACT) for chronic pain, one of the most distinctive examples of the recently developed treatment approaches. ACT's theoretical model as it pertains to chronic pain is outlined, as is the evidence base regarding its measures, methods, treatment outcomes, and mechanisms. The article concludes with a discussion of key clinical issues and the identification of key avenues for future development.

Key Words: acceptance and commitment therapy, chronic pain, psychological approaches, behavioral medicine, clinical health psychology

Introduction

Pain is a common and complex experience that occurs in both human and nonhuman species. It is an unpleasant sensory and emotional experience that serves as a signal for potential or actual bodily harm (Raja et al., 2020). While unpleasant, pain serves an important role in survival. It can be thought of as an alarm system that draws the organism's attention to harmful stimuli to foster efficient responses in order to avoid damage, address injuries, and escape from harm.

In humans, pain is uniquely complex because its impact and intensity are influenced by verbal and nonverbal communication, social context, and environmental setting, which play an important role in the detection, severity, and impact of the pain experience (Walters & Williams, 2019). Thus, pain can be viewed as an important experience with an adaptive function. Despite its largely adaptive role in survival, however, pain can also have deleterious effects on physical, psychological, and social well-being, particularly when it persists over the longer term.

Duration is an important diagnostic indicator that informs the impact and consequences of pain; it can also help guide treatment selection. Generally, pain duration can be divided into two categories: acute and chronic. Typically, acute pain has been defined as pain that lasts less than 3 months. Further, the severity of acute pain is generally proportional to the severity of injury, although this is not always the case. For example, cramps, headaches, and muscle soreness do not typically involve detectable levels of tissue damage, although they can be associated with significant discomfort. While acute pain can be associated with significant disruptions in functioning, this disruption typically resolves with time and healing (Vasseljen et al., 2013).

In contrast, chronic pain lasts 3 months or longer. While chronic pain can develop following an injury, it can also occur without a clear etiology. In either case, chronic pain is distinctive in that it persists over the longer term despite the passage of time, occurrence of healing, and interventions targeting pain reduction (Loeser & Melzack, 1999; Nicholas et al., 2019). Further, chronic pain is associated with equally persistent impairments in physical, psychological, and social functioning (Nicholas et al., 2019). Importantly, the adaptive "alarm" aspect of acute pain is diminished or absent in chronic pain. For instance, in cases of acute pain, decreases in the "alarm's" intensity (i.e., pain reduction) can be used as a signal to resume normal activity. In chronic pain, however, this alarm system becomes less effective and loses its ability to discriminate between dangerous and innocuous signals, as pain is always present. Essentially, the alarm is always on, and its sound rarely diminishes, which can lead to long-term, and at times indefinite, absence of normal activity.

Chronic pain is a prevalent and disabling condition worldwide. A recent survey across 195 countries found that chronic low back pain ranked among the 20 most prevalent conditions and was the leading cause of disability for men and women (James et al., 2018). In the United States, one in five people report having a chronic pain condition, and experience poorer global functioning and higher health care utilization as compared to their chronic pain-free counterparts (Dahlhamer et al., 2018; Von Korff et al., 2005). Chronic pain accounts for significant annual health care expenditures and lost work productivity, and remarkably it is more costly than individual costs associated with heart disease, cancer, and diabetes (Gaskin & Richard, 2012).

These high costs can, at least in part, be attributed to the fact that many of the available medical treatments for pain provide minimal, if any, long-term relief for chronic pain. For instance, while opioid medications can provide short-term pain reduction for some, prolonged use can result in tolerance, increased pain (e.g., hyperalgesia), and increased risk for overdose and death (Els et al., 2017; Higgins et al., 2019). Nonopioid medications and topical ointments are also frequently used, although these similarly only show evidence of mild short-term pain reduction (Chou et al., 2017). Injections, implantable devices, and surgery rarely provide sustained pain relief and can risk worsening pain and poor functioning (Grider et al., 2016; Kaye et al., 2015; Yavin et al., 2017). Taken together, there has yet to be a treatment that can reliably eliminate pain in those with chronic pain, and the ongoing pursuit of more invasive medical procedures can potentially worsen pain, mental health, and pain-related disability (Azevedo et al., 2013). One implication of the previous evidence is that chronic pain is likely to persist over the longer term for many (Andersson, 2004; Elliott et al., 2002).

While pain may persist, improved functioning and quality of life is possible. Behavioral and psychological treatments are particularly well suited for achieving these improvements within a context of continued pain (Jensen & Turk, 2014). To understand the role of psychological treatments in the context of chronic pain, it is important to highlight the distinction between the *sensation* of pain and one's *response* to pain. The physical location, temporal pattern, and descriptive qualities make up the sensation of pain. For example, it can occur in the low back, have persisted for months or years in that location, and may be unpredictable in its intensity. Conversely, responses to pain encompass the emotions, thoughts, and behaviors that follow pain perception. These responses commonly include emotions such as frustration or helplessness, cognitions such as catastrophic thinking about pain, and actions such as diminished physical and social activity. All psychological treatments aim to intervene in varying aspects of the patient's response to pain (e.g., thoughts, emotions, actions) in order to improve physical, psychological, and social functioning in the context of ongoing pain (Kerns et al., 2011).

The present article has three specific objectives. First, it will review the history of psychological treatments for chronic pain through its three "waves": the initial operant model approaches, the "second-wave" cognitive-behavioral treatments, and the contextual and functional "third-wave" approaches. Changes in the understanding and treatment of chronic pain over the past 60 years will be highlighted. Second, the article will provide an in-depth overview of a distinctive example of a third-wave approach to chronic pain, that of acceptance and commitment therapy (ACT; Hayes et al., 2012). Following a brief overview of the ACT model as it relates to chronic pain, key measures will be described. The outcome literature concerning ACT for chronic pain will also be highlighted, including an analysis of treatment mechanisms and important areas for further research. Third and finally, the article will highlight a number of key clinical issues specific to the treatment of chronic pain.

A Historical Account of Psychological Models for Chronic Pain

Historically, our understanding of pain has been shaped by cultural influences, as well as developments in science, technology, and medicine. For example, in the 1600s pain was viewed as an integral part of the healing process and an unavoidable aspect of the human experience (Shealy & Cady, 2002). With the development of general anesthesia and morphine in the 1800s, pain was later understood as a symptom of underlying injury or disease (Fordyce, 1973). This recognition led to increased use of biomedical treatments for pain, such as surgeries, injections, and medications. Concerns regarding the aggressive treatment of pain became apparent, however, during the Second World War as returning soldiers presented with persistent pain that did not respond to medical interventions and in some cases reported worsening pain as a result of such treatments (Deyo & Mirza, 2009). During the ensuing decades, research into the mechanisms and treatment of pain increased significantly, which importantly included the study of how psychological principles impact pain perception.

Melzack and Wall (1965) developed the first widely publicized theory that integrated psychosocial and biological mechanisms of pain perception. This theory, termed the gate control theory of pain, posited that sensations detected throughout the peripheral nervous system were quickly passed on to the brain where the pain's intensity could be modulated based on several factors, including attention, interpretation, memory, situational factors, cognition, and emotion. This work was transformative for the field as it marked a shift from a predominantly biomedical approach to a more holistic and integrative approach to our understanding of pain and its treatment. Specifically, it highlighted the critical role of psychological factors in the experience of pain, and provided a rationale for a multifaceted biopsychosocial approach to pain treatment that included psychosocial interventions.

The First Wave: An Operant Model

The operant model, based on operant conditioning principles developed by Skinner (1938) and colleagues, encompasses the first wave of psychological treatments used in the treatment of chronic pain. The operant model proposes that behavior is occasioned and shaped through its interaction with the environment. Fordyce and colleagues were among the first to apply these principles to patients with chronic pain, which subsequently marked the beginning of behavioral treatment of chronic pain (Fordyce et al., 1968). Specifically, Fordyce described patients as emitting "pain behaviors" that helped communicate their experience of pain to others (e.g., limping, scowling, moaning). Crucially, as was the case with other contingent relations, behaviors could increase in frequency if positively or negatively reinforced (e.g., affection, reduction in responsibilities) or decrease in frequency if positively or negatively punished or if contingent reinforcement was removed (i.e., extinction). These same principles were also applied to "well behaviors" or actions that maintain active and healthy lifestyles. Fordyce and colleagues argued that pain behaviors were adaptive in the context of an acute injury, but they could become maladaptive among those with chronic pain by promoting inactivity, disability, and pain. Therefore, the operant model of treatment focused on identifying relevant patient pain behavior, and used a graded approach to increase well behaviors and decrease pain behaviors (Fordyce, 1973).

Operant pain treatment provided several novel advances. Most importantly, it was probably the first pain treatment to target patient behavior as a means of treating chronic pain. Since its inception, operant pain treatment has demonstrated effectiveness in reducing reports of pain, improving physical functioning, and decreasing psychological distress (Henschke et al., 2010). Although a recent systematic review found that randomized controlled trials (RCTs) of operant therapy provided generally low-quality evidence, there was an effect on pain, disability, and distress compared to active control treatments (Williams et al., 2020).

Further, the operant model provided strong evidence supporting the inclusion of patient functioning as a meaningful treatment outcome. Prior pain treatments had focused on reduction in pain intensity as the principal criterion of treatment success. Emotional and physical functioning, in addition to pain intensity and the patient's impression of global improvement, have now been adopted by the Initiative on Methods, Measurement, and Pain Assessment in Clinical Trials (IMMPACT) to form the four core recommended outcome measures in chronic pain clinical trials (Dworkin et al., 2005). Lastly, the operant model laid the groundwork for the development and dissemination of interdisciplinary pain treatment programs, which enlist a team of medical and psychological providers to treat patients with chronic pain. Interdisciplinary treatment has now been widely adopted as the gold standard for pain management and is more cost effective than medical management alone; psychological models have served as the foundational model for these approaches from the very beginning (Gatchel et al., 2014).

Second Wave: A Cognitive-Behavioral Model

Operant treatments for pain were criticized for their perceived lack of inclusion of cognitive processes and their relation to overt behavior (Bandura, 1969). These concerns were also prominent more broadly in psychology during the 1970s and contributed to the development of the cognitive-behavioral model, which has been referred to as the "second" wave of psychological treatments for chronic pain. Cognitive models of behavior often rely on information processing theory, which posits that individuals can consciously process information about internal and external stimuli. Our thoughts, interpretations, and beliefs about such stimuli then directly influence or alter emotional, physiological, and behavioral responses.

Cognitive therapy for depression was one of the first widely disseminated cognitive treatments that aimed to change irrational and maladaptive thoughts and beliefs to be more adaptive and rational. It was efficacious in improving depressive symptoms and overall functioning (Dobson, 1989). Soon after, clinicians began incorporating both cognitive and operant techniques into their treatments marking the birth of cognitive-behavioral therapy (CBT). Modern CBT interventions typically utilize both cognitive evaluation techniques to address maladaptive beliefs and thoughts in addition to graded behavioral approaches to improve engagement in healthy lifestyle activities, later referred to as coping skills training in the treatment of chronic pain (Turner et al., 2000). CBT has demonstrated efficacy across a variety of psychiatric and chronic physical health conditions (Butler et al., 2006). However, despite a unified model, CBT interventions vary widely in the specific techniques used, making it difficult to compare findings across clinicians, studies, and psychiatric conditions (Gatchel et al., 2007; Morley, 2011).

In 1983, a book-length treatment of the cognitive-behavioral model as applied to the conceptualization and treatment of chronic pain was published (Turk et al., 1983). Specifically, this model posited that maladaptive thoughts and beliefs about pain exacerbated pain-related distress and disability. Thought content that encompassed negative evaluations of one's ability to cope with painful stimuli, as well as exaggerated appraisals of painful stimuli as uncontrollable, persistent, and threatening, were identified as an important treatment target (Sullivan et al., 1995). These maladaptive thoughts and beliefs were termed *pain catastrophizing* and were found to be reliably associated with worse pain-related distress and poorer physical, psychological, and social functioning (Edwards et al., 2016). CBT interventions for chronic pain, which also vary in specific techniques used, typically include cognitive (re)evaluation techniques to address pain catastrophizing thoughts and coping skills training. Commonly targeted pain coping skills included relaxation strategies, physical activity, and engagement in enjoyable activities. The current research literature suggests that CBT for chronic pain produces small to medium effects on pain intensity, pain catastrophizing, and mood, with small effects on pain-related disability and activity interference (Ehde et al., 2014). Overall, the second wave of psychological pain management treatments highlighted the importance of integrating cognitive content into psychological pain treatments and further expanded research on effective pain coping skills (Jensen et al., 1991). Cognitive treatments were also embedded alongside behavioral treatments within interdisciplinary pain clinics, which continue to be the gold standard of care for chronic pain (Gatchel et al., 2014).

Third Wave: A Contextual Cognitive-Behavioral Model

While the CBT model flourished in the field of psychology and was found to have generally supportive evidence, a number of critical concerns were later raised about the empirical evidence supporting the underlying model, as well as the lack of a standardized protocol and specific techniques used across interventions. When cognitive therapy was developed, it distinguished itself from other therapies by identifying cognitive change as the primary mechanism underlying all treatment-related change (Hofmann et al., 2013). However, critiques were raised about whether there was sufficient empirical evidence to suggest that cognitive change was a *necessary* component of successful treatment (Hayes, 2004). Additionally, given the integration of behavioral techniques into CBT interventions, it was postulated that other therapeutic mechanisms could be accounting for such change. In response, a review of component research on CBT interventions for depression and anxiety found that cognitive change components did not appear to provide any added benefit to behavioral intervention components, and that changes in cognition did not appear to mediate symptomatic improvement over the course of treatment (Longmore & Worrell, 2007). While there was a level of disagreement with Longmore and Worrell's (2007) conclusions (e.g., Hofmann, 2008), their conclusions are supported in the chronic pain literature (Smeets et al., 2006; Vowles et al., 2007).

The third wave of psychological pain management treatments, which principally encompasses ACT, continued to build from the foundation of operant models and developments in the cognitive-behavioral models. First, in many ways, third-wave treatments are firmly grounded in operant models. Treatment success, for example, is defined as changes in behavior that align with one's personal values and goals, a definition that is clearly compatible with Fordyce's (1973) well behavior. Moreover, the third-wave models define behavior in terms of its function, not solely its form, which allows for understanding the processes that maintain behavior across settings and over time (Hayes et al., 2006).

Like cognitive approaches, third-wave treatments also take the role of cognition and human language into account with regard to the experience of human suffering. However, in contrast to cognitive treatments, the third-wave approaches also focus on fostering an open and nonstruggling interaction with negative thoughts and emotions (rather than actively changing them), which is paired with skills to build engagement in personally meaningful areas of life. These third-wave models have been referred to as contextual in that they encompass operant and cognitive models, as well as a broader context of history, situation, and ongoing response patterns (Hayes et al., 2013; McCracken, 2005). It has been argued that these contextual models are particularly well suited to the problems inherent in chronic pain, including its persistence, durable negative effects on physical and emotional functioning, and the need to alter *responses* to these experiences when it does not seem possible to alter the experiences themselves.

Acceptance and Commitment Therapy for Chronic Pain

An Overview

As noted earlier in this volume, psychological flexibility/inflexibility lies at the core of the ACT model and its model of human behavior (see Ong & Eustis, this volume). Psychological inflexibility is theorized to occur when cognitive, emotional, and sensory processes disrupt engagement in functional patterns of behavior and promote dysfunctional patterns of behavior despite experiencing negative consequences (Hayes et al., 2001). Psychological flexibility is theorized to occur when one can persist with and change behavior to align with personally meaningful values while also being open and willing to experience physical sensations, emotions, and thoughts. Six core processes are posited to underlie psychological flexibility: acceptance, being present, cognitive defusion, selfas-context, values, and committed action. Each core process exists on a continuum and also has a counterpart that can be described in terms of psychological inflexibility. All core processes are seen as interrelated, and an analysis of one necessitates the analysis of others (Hayes et al., 2006).

In the context of chronic pain, psychological flexibility allows an individual to adaptably respond to the experience of pain and associated aversive experiences in a way that minimizes needless suffering and maximizes options for behavior that align with one's values. Conversely, psychological inflexibility encompasses unsuccessful efforts to escape or control pain and associated aversive experiences leading to increased suffering and reduced options for values-based behavior. For example, psychological inflexibility might arise as a persistent pursuit of ineffective medical treatments as a means to avoid or control pain, even when these interventions result in harmful side effects and losses in important areas of life. Treatment would aim to alter one's response to pain by increasing willingness to experience it fully, in the moment, and increase engagement in values-directed behavior that contributes to a fuller and more meaningful life, even with pain. This would be done through engagement of the six core processes, each of which serves an important role in how one responds adaptively to pain.

ACCEPTANCE

Acceptance is the nonjudgmental embracing of one's experience, including physical sensations, emotions, and thoughts, without ineffective attempts to change or alter them. Experiential avoidance, in contrast to acceptance, is described as efforts to avoid, control, or change one's experience. In chronic pain, experiential avoidance is often characterized by persistent and harmful efforts to reduce or eliminate pain, such as unsafe use of medications, physical inactivity, and reduced engagement in social roles, which can negatively impact health and well-being. Acceptance instead focuses on allowing oneself to feel pain fully (and other distressing aspects of their experience) without engaging in control or avoidance strategies.

BEING PRESENT

Cultivating a nonjudgmental, present moment focused awareness is a foundational aspect of ACT. Incorporating aspects of mindfulness, being present allows one to fully and nonjudgmentally contact all parts of their present moment experience (thoughts, emotions, physical sensations, and actions) and notice when their mind is drifting to the past or future. Among those with chronic pain, being present often means untangling the sensation of pain from their judgments, predictions, and stories about pain. For example, a patient may notice a painful sensation and think, "Here we go again, another bad pain day," prompting further judgments, predictions, and fears about pain leading to spending the day in bed. Being present means still noticing the same painful sensation and initial thought, but also noticing the mind wandering to the future, bringing attention back to the present moment, and *choosing* a response that aligns with their values.

COGNITIVE DEFUSION

Cognitive defusion is the ability to observe and detach from thoughts without altering their frequency or form in order to increase possible options for behavior. Cognitive fusion, in contrast, is an attachment to thoughts as being believable and "true," thereby limiting options for behavior. For example, a patient might think, "I always have to push through the pain" which, if believed, limits behavior to persisting with unsafe physical activity, further contributing to greater disability over time. A cognitively defused stance might involve noticing this thought and the urges that follow, and reducing attachment to the thought and its intended outcome. This process can diminish the influence of cognitions on behavior and increase the possibility for other options.

SELF-AS-CONTEXT

Self-as-context means separating the self from one's experience. There is a self, and there are experiences that the self is having; these are not the same. The self, when seen as the observer, has no attachment or investment in the quality or quantity of experiences that occur. In contrast, self-as-content means inflating the self to be synonymous with the content of one's experience. A patient with chronic pain might say to themselves, "I am a failure, I am a chronic pain patient," or "My pain won't let me do anything." Self-as-content would foster actions that align with these statements, such as withdrawing from important areas of life and overutilizing health care. In a self-as-context approach, these thoughts still occur, although they do not define the self or actions that follow.

VALUES

Values are important areas of life that bring meaning, purpose, and direction. Values cannot ever be accomplished, but they are directions that can guide behavior from moment to moment in a fashion that can be rewarding when in direct contact with the present moment. For patients with chronic pain, engagement in valued areas of life are often diminished as behavior quickly becomes controlled by desires to remove or reduce pain and associated distress (e.g., canceling plans with friends due to a flare-up of pain). A central tenet of ACT is helping people with pain engage in more valued activities within a context of continued pain and discomfort.

COMMITTED ACTION

A pattern of behavior that is flexible, persistent, and aligned with one's values characterizes committed action. It can be promoted through use of short- and long-term goals, and learning and applying relevant skills to move toward stated goals. In contrast, inaction or persistent action, despite significant consequences, can promote ineffective and inflexible behavior. In chronic pain, inaction is a common response to persistent pain and can place engagement in important areas of life on hold indefinitely. Additionally, behavior may persist in an unhelpful and damaging way, such as pushing through pain despite greater disability over time. Committed action would foster flexible and more effective patterns of behavior, such as introducing small incremental goals to slowly increase activity engagement or slowing down the pace of each task to promote sustained long-term engagement.

Measures

It is recommended that four key domains be assessed when examining treatment efficacy and effectiveness in chronic pain: (1) pain, which includes its intensity and interference, (2) physical functioning, (3) emotional and psychosocial functioning, and (4) the patient's rating of overall improvement and satisfaction with treatment (Dworkin et al., 2005). In relation to ACT, it is also important to assess how pain interferes with valued activity, acceptance, mindfulness, psychological flexibility, and use of pain-coping strategies. A handful of measures based on the ACT model are used in chronic pain populations; these are described in the paragraphs that follow. A number of other commonly used general ACT measures are reviewed in earlier articles of this book; their use in chronic pain samples will be briefly described here as it is relevant to our later discussion of ACT treatment outcomes and mechanisms in chronic pain samples.

CHRONIC PAIN ACCEPTANCE QUESTIONNAIRE (CPAQ)

The CPAQ measures acceptance of pain or how one reacts and adapts to pain. It was originally developed in an unpublished dissertation and had a total of 34 items (Geiser, 1992). The measure was later revised using factor analysis and included 24 items and two subscales. Pain Willingness assesses the degree to which one can experience pain without engaging in attempts to control or avoid it. Activity Engagement assesses the degree to which one engages in activities with pain present (McCracken et al., 2004). This factor structure has been supported in further studies (Vowles et al., 2008; Wicksell et al., 2009), and each subscale has been reliably related to pain-related disability and distress (Reneman et al., 2010). The CPAQ has been shown to mediate treatment outcomes, such as changes in disability, anxiety, depression, and health care utilization (Cederberg et al., 2016; Vowles, Witkiewitz, et al., 2014). Two briefer CPAQ measures have also been developed: an eight-item measure called the CPAQ-8 (Fish et al., 2010), and a two-item measure called the CPAQ-2 (Vowles, Kruger, et al., 2020).

PSYCHOLOGICAL INFLEXIBILITY IN PAIN SCALE (PIPS)

The PIPS measures psychological inflexibility in patients with chronic pain. It is a 12-item measure that has two subscales, cognitive fusion and avoidance of pain (Wicksell et al., 2008). The two-factor structure has been supported across multiple chronic pain samples and is significantly related to measures of depression, anxiety, pain-related functioning, and mindfulness in a theoretically consistent manner (Trompetter et al., 2014; Wicksell et al., 2008, 2010). The PIPS has also mediated treatment outcomes among a large sample of whiplash injury-related pain (Wicksell et al., 2010).

CHRONIC PAIN VALUES INVENTORY (CPVI)

The CPVI measures engagement in valued living by assessing the importance and perceived success of engaging in six domains: family, intimate relations, friends, work, health, and growth/learning (McCracken & Yang, 2006). The measure yields three scores, an average importance score, an average success score, and an average discrepancy score between importance and success. The values success score is associated with emotional and physical functioning, pain acceptance, and pain-related distress (Vowles et al., 2011; Vowles, Witkiewitz, et al., 2014). Both the values success score and the discrepancy score have demonstrated sensitivity to ACT interventions and have been shown to improve over the course of treatment (Vowles et al., 2011, 2019; Vowles & McCracken, 2008).

VALUED LIVING SCALE (VLS)

The VLS is a 24-item measure that assesses the importance, success, and confidence in achieving value-related goals across eight domains: physically healthy, feeling emotionally healthy, productivity, parenting, spirituality, spousal/ partner relationships, friendships, and community citizenship. The measure was intended to guide treatment targets, such that valued goals that were rated high in importance, but low in confidence and success, could be targeted by clinicians (Jensen et al., 2015). The VLS has two subscales, Health and Productivity and Social and Relational Activities, which have been confirmed in two separate samples. Both subscale scores were significantly associated with pain intensity, pain interference, and depression (Jensen et al., 2015, 2019). It has not been evaluated longitudinally or in the context of an ACT treatment study.

VALUES TRACKER (VT)

The VT is a brief two-item measure that assesses engagement in valued activity, and it was designed to track change from session to session. It was evaluated in a large sample of patients with chronic pain, and a sum score across the two items was found to be significantly associated with pain-related functioning, even after controlling for pain intensity and pain-related distress (Pielech et al., 2016). Change in the VT over the course of a 4-week interdisciplinary ACT treatment was associated with change in psychosocial functioning at posttreatment, but not at3-month follow-up (Vowles et al., 2019).

BRIEF PAIN COPING INVENTORY (BPCI)

The BPCI assesses a range of responses to pain and includes both acceptance-based coping strategies and typical CBT-based strategies, such as exercise, relaxation, and positive self-statements. In its original form, it had 18 items (McCracken et al., 2005); however, it was later revised and expanded to include additional broader coping patterns of psychological flexibility. The revised version was named the BPCI-2 and had 19 items with two subscales, psychological flexibility and pain management strategies (McCracken & Vowles, 2007). Both subscales of the BPCI-2 were predictive of pain-related distress and anxiety, depression, physical and psychosocial disability, and medical visits (McCracken & Vowles, 2007; Vowles, Sowden, et al., 2014).

OTHER RELEVANT MEASURES OF ACT

In addition to these measures, five other commonly used ACT and mindfulness measures have been examined in chronic pain samples. First, the Acceptance and Action Questionnaire-II (AAQ-II; Bond et al., 2011) assesses general psychological acceptance, and its one-factor structure was confirmed in a chronic pain sample. It was significantly related to patient functioning measures, and change in the AAQ-II over the course of ACT treatment was associated with improved patient outcomes (McCracken & Zhao-O'Brien, 2010; Scott et al., 2017).

Second, the Committed Action Questionnaire (CAQ; McCracken, 2013) is a measure of behavioral patterns in line with valued life directions. Its two-factor structure has been confirmed in chronic pain samples, and is associated with several health-related functioning measures (Bailey et al., 2016; McCracken, 2013).

Third, the Mindful Attention and Awareness Scale (MAAS; Brown & Ryan, 2003) assesses mindful behavior. Its validity and reliability have been supported in a chronic pain sample, but there was incomplete support of a single-factor model (McCracken & Thompson, 2009). Further studies have shown the MAAS to be uniquely related to pain-related anxiety and overall patient functioning (McCracken et al., 2007). It was also shown to moderate the relation between pain intensity and pain catastrophizing (Schütze et al., 2010).

Fourth, the Five Facet Mindfulness Questionnaire (FFMQ; Baer et al., 2008) assesses five component skills of mindfulness. While its psychometric properties have not been studied in a chronic pain sample, it has demonstrated associations with pain intensity, pain interference, and depression among those with chronic pain (Elvery et al., 2017).

Finally, the Self-Compassion Scale (SCS; Neff, 2003) measures kindness, understanding, and compassion towards oneself along with other aspects of mindfulness. Its psychometric properties have not been studied in a chronic pain sample. However, the SCS is related to several physical and psychological functioning measures and mediates some aspects of ACT treatment outcomes among those with chronic pain (Edwards et al., 2019; Vowles, Sowden, et al., 2014)

Treatment Outcomes

Studies examining the efficacy of ACT in chronic pain populations has grown significantly since it was first developed. Therefore, this section will focus on systematic review and meta-analytic findings of treatment outcomes. Most recently, Hughes and colleagues (2017) conducted a systematic review and meta-analysis of ACT for chronic pain which included 11 randomized control trials (RCTs) totaling a combined sample size of 863. Assessment time points included posttreatment as well as 3- and 6-month follow-up. All studies were of adults with chronic pain and spanned across several settings, including primary care, specialized pain care, and community health clinics. Across the eight studies that examined ACT in comparison to a control condition, ACT produced medium to large effect sizes on measures of pain acceptance and psychological flexibility at posttreatment and 3-month follow-up. At 6-month follow-up, a large effect size favoring ACT was observed on measures of pain acceptance, and a single study favored ACT on measures of psychological flexibility. These findings are in line with the theorized ACT model and provide evidence that ACT, in comparison to control conditions, targets its intended processes among those with chronic pain (Hughes et al., 2017). These findings are also in line with previous systematic reviews and meta-analytic findings that found ACT to produce similar effect sizes in pain acceptance and psychological flexibility measures as compared to control conditions (Cavanagh et al., 2014; Hann & McCracken, 2014).

On measures of functioning, depression, and anxiety, ACT produced small to medium effect sizes at posttreatment. Effect sizes were sustained at 3 months for measures of functioning and depression, although there was insufficient evidence of an effect for measures of anxiety. By 6 months, there was insufficient evidence of an effect across all functioning, depression, and anxiety measures. In addition, ACT did not produce any effect on quality of life or pain intensity measures at any time point (Hughes et al., 2017). These findings are inconsistent with previous systematic review and meta-analytic findings, which have found small to large effects of ACT on measures of depression, anxiety, and general emotional distress at posttreatment and 2- to 6-month follow-up. Small effects were also observed on measures of pain intensity, quality of life, physical functioning, and disability favoring ACT at posttreatment and 2- to 6-month follow up (Hann & McCracken, 2014; Veehof et al., 2016). The disparate effect estimates, particularly at follow-up time points, is likely due to several factors.

First, while all comparator conditions were deemed inactive, differences in effect sizes may be reflecting variation in control conditions. In particular, some studies used medical treatment as usual as the comparator, which is known to vary by study setting. Second, the clinical heterogeneity across studies, such as intervention delivery, intensity, duration, and setting, is also impacting effect estimates. For example, in a subgroup analysis of the Hughes and colleagues review, therapist-delivered ACT (excluding guided self-help) as compared to control conditions revealed medium to large effects across all outcomes favoring ACT at posttreatment and 3-month follow-up, with the exception of quality of life (Hughes et al., 2017). Based on this finding, it is possible that ACT delivered through a self-help format does not produce sustained improvements among those with chronic pain. Prior work has demonstrated that acceptance and mindfulness self-help interventions produce small to medium effects on measures of anxiety and depression across a wide range of presenting physical and mental health concerns (Cavanagh et al., 2014). However, effect sizes were only estimated at posttreatment, and no follow-up time points were analyzed. More research on the long-term effectiveness of self-help ACT interventions among those with chronic pain is needed. Despite this lack, overall meta-analytic findings suggest that, in comparison to inactive treatments, ACT is generally efficacious among those with chronic pain and produces improvements in pain acceptance, psychological flexibility, and physical and mental health.

When compared to active treatments, ACT produced small to large effect sizes on measures of psychological flexibility, pain acceptance, functioning, depression, and anxiety at posttreatment and follow-up time points, in comparison to applied relaxation and expressive writing (Hughes et al., 2017). In comparison to CBT and mindfulness-based interventions, ACT was not more beneficial on treatment outcomes (Hann & McCracken, 2014; Hughes et al., 2017; Veehof et al., 2016). One exception was noted in which ACT produced a higher mean effect on depression and anxiety measures as compared to mindfulness-based interventions comprised mostly of mindfulness-based stress reduction protocols (MSBR; Veehof et al., 2016). Additionally, when paired with brief motivational interviewing, ACT and CBT were equally efficacious in promoting pain acceptance and reducing depressive symptoms and substance use, specifically in primary care settings (Barrett & Chang, 2016).

Treatment Mechanisms

In 2010, the National Institutes of Health (NIH) initiated a science of behavior change program that seeks to identify unified mechanisms of behavior change across a wide range of health disease outcomes. Mechanisms of behavior change are modifiable treatment targets that play a role in initiating or maintaining behavior change (Nielsen et al., 2018). Within ACT, the six core processes (acceptance, defusion, present moment awareness, self as context, values, and committed action) are theorized to be mechanisms of psychological flexibility, which in turn, produce effective and sustained behavior change in important areas of life. Psychological flexibility and the six core processes that compose it, are theorized to be transdiagnostic mechanisms relevant to all human conditions meeting NIH's stated goals for behavioral research. Among those with chronic pain, several studies have examined the six core processes and their relation to treatment outcomes using mediation analyses and structural equation modeling (SEM).

Changes in each of the six core processes have been shown to mediate treatment outcomes. Acceptance has emerged as one of the strongest mediators among those with chronic pain and has evidence of mediating changes in physical functioning, psychological functioning, depression, and anxiety (Baranoff et al., 2016; Cederberg et al., 2016; Lin et al., 2018; McCracken & Gutiérrez-Martínez, 2011; Vowles, Witkiewitz, et al., 2014). Among experimental pain studies, meta-analytic findings show acceptance strategies to be superior to other emotional regulation strategies, such as suppression, distraction, and reappraisal, for increasing pain tolerance (Kohl et al., 2012). Similarly, use of pain control strategies, such as pain medications or resting, has been shown to be a unique predictor of higher disability, depression, and anxiety (McCracken, Vowles, et al., 2007). Changes in self-as-context, over and above changes in pain acceptance, have also mediated treatment outcomes and are most strongly associated with changes in depression. This suggests that gaining distance from one's experience may be most impactful upon emotional functioning. It has also been found that, among individuals who worsened after treatment, a worsening in self-as-context (or rather an increase in self-as-content) was observed (Yu et al., 2017). Changes in mindfulness and cognitive defusion have also mediated treatment outcomes, with stronger effects observed in mental health outcomes (Edwards, 2019; McCracken et al., 2014; Wicksell et al., 2010). Together, acceptance, mindfulness, defusion, and self-as-context processes are particularly notable and useful in chronic pain because they likely foster a "decoupling"' between the *sensation* and experience of pain from the *response* to pain, increasing possible options for behavioral responses that align with one's values and goals (Levin et al., 2015). Aspects of decoupling can also foster a willingness to contact uncomfortable experiences, including pain, rather than struggle to try and control them.

Values-based action is also a key mediator of treatment outcomes. When examined with pain acceptance, it typically accounts for the second highest amount of variance in treatment outcomes and mediates outcomes up to 3 years following treatment (Vowles et al., 2011). More engagement in values-based activity within treatment is also associated with concurrent improvement in psychosocial functioning (Vowles et al., 2019). Interestingly, some findings suggest that changes in acceptance are more strongly associated with changes in functioning from pre- to posttreatment, while changes in values-based action are more strongly associated with changes in functioning from pretreatment through long-term follow up. This suggests that changes in acceptance may facilitate engagement in values-based action and also highlights the importance of committed action in sustaining engagement in values-based action following the end of treatment (Trompetter et al., 2013; Vowles & McCracken, 2008).

To date, only four studies have examined four or more processes in relation to treatment outcomes among individuals with chronic pain. First, using cross-sectional data (n = 274), Vowles, Sowden, et al. (2014) conducted an exploratory factor analysis of several measures of psychological flexibility and functioning measures, and used SEM to examine the relation between factors of psychological flexibility and functioning. Measures of psychological flexibility included psychological flexibility in coping, pain acceptance, values-based action, and self-compassion. While self-compassion itself is not a theorized process of ACT, the measure has six subscales that overlap with several core ACT processes, including present moment awareness, self-as-context, and defusion (Hayes et al., 2013). Three psychological flexibility factors emerged. These factors appeared to be consistent with prior work that has described the six core processes more succinctly as three pairs of response styles: open (defusion/acceptance), centered (present moment awareness/self-as-context), and engaged (values/committed action; Hayes et al., 2012). SEM analyses revealed that higher scores on the open, centered, and engaged factors were significantly related to lower pain intensity, emotional distress, and disability (Vowles, Sowden, et al., 2014).

Second, Vowles, Witkiewitz, et al. (2014) examined how changes in several core processes over the course of a 4-week ACT-based interdisciplinary program were related to measures of functioning at posttreatment and 3-month follow-up (*n* = 117). Measures of pain acceptance, psychological flexibility coping, self-compassion, and values-based action were used as mediators. Findings suggested that all four process measures mediated treatment outcomes consistent with the theoretical model of ACT, such that improvements in each process were significantly related to improvements in physical disability, psychological disability, depression, pain-related anxiety, medical visits, and number of classes of analgesics. Notably, changes in pain acceptance and self-compassion were the strongest overall mediators (Vowles, Witkiewitz, et al., 2014). These findings further support the proposed "decoupling" processes (acceptance, mindfulness, defusion, self-as-context) as being particularly important in fostering psychological flexibility among those with chronic pain (Levin et al., 2015).

Third, Scott et al. (2016) examined how four ACT processes changed over the course of a 4-week ACT-based interdisciplinary program (*n* = 384). Pain acceptance, defusion, self-as-context, and committed action were collected at pre- and posttreatment, as well as 9 months following treatment. Hierarchical multiple regressions examined the shared and unique contributions of change in each process to changes in treatment outcomes from pre- to posttreatment and pre- to 9-month follow-up. Overall, change in pain acceptance uniquely predicted change in all treatment outcomes from pre- to posttreatment, which included physical and social functioning, depression, and pain intensity. Interestingly, from pre- to 9-month follow-up, pain acceptance uniquely predicted change in only pain intensity and social functioning. These findings are in alignment with prior work suggesting that acceptance is most impactful on changes during treatment. Similarly, changes in committed action uniquely predicted change in depression and physical functioning from pre- to 9-month follow-up. However, there was less effect from pre- to posttreatment outcomes, suggesting that committed action and values-based action are more important in sustaining behavior change after treatment (Vowles & McCracken, 2008). Lastly, change in cognitive fusion uniquely predicted change in social functioning and depression across both assessment time periods, and change in self-as-context was not uniquely associated with change in any treatment outcome. The authors suggest that the lack of findings in self-as-context may signal greater overlap between these processes than theorized, or the measures themselves may not adequately capture distinct aspects of each process (Scott et al., 2016).

Fourth, Scott et al. (2017) conducted a similar study examining the same treatment processes within a small sample (*n* = 60) of those aged 65 years and older who also completed a 2- or 4-week interdisciplinary ACT program. Hierarchical multiple regressions were used to examine the shared and unique contributions of change in each process to changes in treatment outcomes from pre- to posttreatment, and pre- to 9-month follow-up. Among this older-aged sample, only change in acceptance and committed action were associated with improvements in treatment outcomes. Improvements in acceptance uniquely contributed to improvements in social functioning from pre- to posttreatment and improvements in depression from pre- to 9-month follow-up. Additionally, improvements in committed action uniquely predicted improvements in mental health and depression from pre- to posttreatment (Scott et al., 2017). These findings diverge somewhat from the previous study findings, such that changes in defusion as well as self-as-context processes were not associated with changes in treatment outcome. However, the findings do support acceptance and committed action as important processes among older adults with chronic pain.

Areas for Future Research

Taken together, these findings provide robust evidence for the efficacy of ACT in promoting improved functioning during and following treatment among those with chronic pain. Preliminary evidence also shows that the six theorized processes mediate treatment outcomes. However, research on the ACT model in chronic pain populations is in its infancy, and many gaps remain. First, certainly more studies examining the full comprehensive model of ACT are needed to support its continued use in chronic pain populations. Many of the studies described previously in this article lack inclusion of demographically diverse patients, and the bulk of the studies have been conducted within similar treatment programs and clinics. It is imperative that, given ACT's theorized transdiagnostic model, the six processes of behavior change are applicable and useful among diverse patients and settings. If not, then appropriate modifications must be made. For example, further studies may provide more robust support for the open, centered, and engaged model adaptation that collapses the six processes into three response styles (Hayes et al., 2012). This parsimonious model may well reduce theoretical and statistical overlap and may be more easily translated into clinical practice.

Second, in order to better capture the distinct aspects of each process, further measurement, development, refinement, and testing of the psychometric properties of process measures are sorely needed among chronic pain samples. Recent findings suggest that current process measures evidence potential overlap, signaling a lack of measurement precision and questionable validity and reliability. To date, only the psychometric properties of the CPAQ and CPVI have been systematically examined across studies. Although these reviews found some support for their validity and reliability across studies, neither measure met multiple important validity and reliability criteria (Barrett et al., 2019; Reneman et al., 2010). In order to study the full, comprehensive ACT model, it is key that the measurements used to examine each process have improved precision and support for their validity and reliability across diverse samples.

Third, to better characterize change in the core processes, proximal measurements of these constructs are also likely to be useful in gaining a better understanding of the interrelations between each process and in characterizing patterns of change over time. For example, studies should utilize ecological momentary assessment or daily dairy methods to better contextualize these processes in real time rather than through retrospective self-report. These methods are in line with the philosophical underpinnings of ACT that stem from functional contextualism. This approach characterizes behavior as an ongoing act in context, such that a behavior cannot be fully understood unless it is analyzed within the environment in which it occurred (Hayes et al., 2006). Proximal ecological assessment of these processes will be particularly important among those with chronic pain to better understand the ongoing interrelations between pain, behavior, and environment. In addition, characterizing patterns of change within each process will also improve our understanding of the interrelations between each core process and their specific roles in fostering sustained treatment outcomes. Findings may also highlight needed adaptations to treatment delivery and implementation practices to foster improved outcomes.

Lastly, in addition to identifying mechanisms of behavior change, NIH research programs have also called for efforts to improve precision medicine (Collins & Varmus, 2015). Within the behavioral and social sciences, this effort entails identifying important patient and environmental characteristics that might influence mechanisms of behavior change and overall treatment response (Hekler et al., 2020). Some work has been done in identifying treatment response to psychological treatment broadly within chronic pain (McCracken & Turk, 2002), and specifically to CBT for chronic pain (Broderick et al., 2016). Little work has been done to identify predictors for treatment response related to ACT among those with chronic pain.

One recent study found no baseline characteristics to moderate treatment response (Vowles, Sowden, et al., 2019), while another found that age moderated treatment response to ACT and CBT. For example, younger adults were more likely to respond to CBT and older adults more likely to respond to ACT (Wetherell et al., 2016). Further research in this area would foster a more effective, individualized, implementable intervention across all patient populations and health care settings.

Clinical Issues Specific to Chronic Pain

Although it is important to review and acknowledge the empirical basis of ACT, this therapy is, at its core, a clinical endeavor— the interaction between treatment provider and treatment recipient. Therefore, it is important to review a handful of key clinical issues specific to the practice of ACT among those with chronic pain. First, we discuss how patient experiences with providers and pain treatments shape their current patterns of behavior. Second, we discuss the use and efficacy of unidisciplinary and interdisciplinary ACT among those with chronic pain. Finally, the efficacy and application of ACT among those with chronic pain and opioid misuse will also be highlighted, given the growing prevalence rate of these co-occurring conditions.

Patient's Pain History

Before beginning treatment of a patient, it is important to consider the experiences that have led them to treatment. For those with chronic pain, it is particularly important to consider their prior experiences with health care providers and pain treatments which have undoubtedly shaped their presentation to treatment. First, at the provider level, patients may have had negative experiences in which they were marginalized, stigmatized, or not listened to. Perhaps they came away with messages that pain was all in their head, that they were exaggerating their pain, or they may have been labeled as drug-seeking when they inquired about opioid medications. Maybe they felt that their provider was not doing enough or was withholding a potentially helpful treatment. Prior work has specifically shown that patient-provider communication can directly and indirectly impact patients' rating of pain intensity, pain interference, satisfaction with treatment, and compliance with recommendations (Hirsh et al., 2005; Ruben et al., 2018). Additionally, black, indigenous, and people of color (BIPOC), as well as those with limited English proficiency, have substantially more experiences of marginalization and discrimination, receive worse quality health care, and have lower satisfaction with pain care (Tait & Chibnall, 2014). These experiences likely impact the patient's experience of pain and their engagement in treatment. It is important to consider how these interactions may shape their interaction with future providers and their expectations for treatment.

For some patients, the continued search for a fix to pain has probably led to a long list of medical treatments that have provided little, if any, long-term relief. These and other experiences have likely reinforced the message that treatment is determined to have "worked" based on its ability to reduce pain. This message can be problematic and can lead to a potentially endless struggle for pain reduction at the cost of valued areas of life. There continues to be debate in the field about whether pain reduction is a necessary component of improved functioning. In the ACT literature, meta-analytic findings suggest that ACT has minimal impact on pain intensity. This report is somewhat expected given that ACT does not explicitly target this variable. However, more importantly, recent work has shown that reduction in pain intensity and pain-related distress is not necessary to achieve improved functioning outcomes (Vowles et al., 2017). Additionally, improvements in values-based action and disability over the course of treatment and any following treatment have been shown to be unrelated to changes in pain intensity (Vowles, Fink, et al., 2014; Vowles, Sowden, et al., 2019). These findings suggest that sustained engagement in values-based action is possible, even without pain reduction. While this message is certainly at odds with medicalized pain treatments, it can, at the very least, broaden the criteria by which treatment success is determined.

Unidisciplinary versus Interdisciplinary ACT Treatment

The studies reviewed earlier in this article included ACT interventions that were delivered either in a unidisciplinary format or as part of an interdisciplinary program. These treatment formats differ significantly from each other. Namely, unidisciplinary ACT is typically delivered in a more standard outpatient format, consisting of weekly sessions lasting 1–2 hours delivered by a mental health clinician. Interdisciplinary ACT is delivered in a higher intensity format consisting of programming that spans 6–8 hours a day for 2–4 weeks. Within interdisciplinary programs, only about 1–2 hours a day are spent receiving mental health services, while the other hours are devoted to physical therapy, occupational therapy, group-based exercise (i.e., Tai Chi or Yoga), and medical appointments. All providers are trained to deliver their component of treatment within an ACT framework. Given these stark differences in treatment format, a comparative meta-analysis was recently conducted to better understand the differential effectiveness of unidisciplinary and interdisciplinary ACT on functioning outcomes. Overall, treatment effects were larger for interdisciplinary ACT for three of six outcomes—physical disability, psychosocial impact, and depression. Unidisciplinary and interdisciplinary ACT had equivalent outcomes for pain-related anxiety, pain intensity, and pain acceptance (Vowles, Pielech, et al., 2020). Overall, these findings suggest that, for those with chronic pain, the incorporation of other disciplines outside of mental health may be more effective in reducing the impact of pain on physical and emotional functioning. For example, engagement in physical therapy may facilitate willingness to have pain in the service of valued activity. Importantly, gains in these areas were also sustained at follow-up, suggesting that skills learned in the treatment setting were also generalized into their home environment.

Opioid Misuse

It is estimated that 21–29 percent of patients with chronic pain misuse opioids and 8–12 percent use opioids in a harmful manner consistent with opioid use disorder (OUD; Vowles et al., 2015). Chronic pain is also among the most frequently co-occurring diagnoses among those with OUD, with estimates ranging from 49 to 64 percent (Hser et al., 2017; Wollschlaeger et al., 2017). Given that a substantial proportion of those with chronic pain also report opioid misuse, it is important to understand the efficacy of psychological treatments for chronic pain among this subpopulation. A recent systematic review of psychological treatments aimed at reducing opioid misuse among those with chronic pain found that only two of five interventions produced improvements in opioid use at posttreatment and follow-up, and only one intervention produced improvements in both opioid use and pain-related outcomes (Eccleston et al., 2017). Therapeutic interactive voice response (TIVR), which is an automated, telephone-based tool for maintenance enhancement, was delivered following group CBT for chronic pain and was found to improve opioid use and pain-related outcomes (Naylor et al., 2008, 2010). More recently, an integrated ACT and mindfulness-based relapse prevention (MBRP) group treatment was tested among a small sample (n = 32) of veterans, which also produced improvements in opioid use, pain interference, and pain behavior (Vowles, Witkiewitz, et al., 2019). These findings provide preliminary support for the use of ACT, with added mindfulness components, among those with chronic pain and opioid misuse. Further examination of the efficacy of the integrated ACT and MBRP intervention is currently being studied in a large multisite clinical trial among veterans with chronic pain and opioid misuse who are also maintained on buprenorphine.

Conclusions

Chronic pain is a prevalent condition that can cause significant impacts in functioning and impede overall quality of life. To date, although there is no medical treatment that can reliably eliminate chronic pain, psychological therapies are available that provide an avenue toward restoring function and quality of life. ACT was developed from past behavioral and cognitive psychological interventions and incorporates new theoretical and practical advances as well. Most importantly, ACT aims to increase psychological flexibility, or the ability to contact one's direct moment experience and engage in sustained values-based action. In the treatment of chronic pain, there is good empirical evidence to support ACT's efficacy in promoting functioning via its six theorized processes. Further research is still needed to help refine our understanding of how the processes change over time and their impact over longer term follow-up periods. There are also important clinical considerations regarding the application of ACT in chronic pain populations, specifically related to the patient's pain history, treatment delivery, and presence of opioid misuse. Overall, ACT for chronic pain is an efficacious treatment that can provide a path toward improved functioning and a better, full life, even with ongoing pain.

References

Andersson, H. I. (2004). The course of non-malignant chronic pain: A 12-year follow-up of a cohort from the general population. *European Journal of Pain, 8*, 47–53. https://doi.org/10.1016/S1090-3801(03)00064-8

Azevedo, L. F., Costa-Pereira, A., Mendonça, L., Dias, C. C., & Castro-Lopes, J. M. (2013). Chronic pain and health services utilization: Is there overuse of diagnostic tests and inequalities in nonpharmacologic treatment methods utilization? *Medical Care, 51*(10), 859–869. https://doi.org/10.1097/MLR.0b013e3182a53e4e

Baer, R. A., Smith, G. T., Lykins, E., Button, D., Krietemeyer, J., Sauer, S., Walsh, E., Duggan, D., & Williams, J. M. G. (2008). Construct validity of the five facet mindfulness questionnaire in meditating and nonmeditating samples. *Assessment, 15*(3), 329–342. https://doi.org/10.1177/1073191107313003

Bailey, R. W., Vowles, K. E., Witkiewitz, K., Sowden, G., & Ashworth, J. (2016). Examining committed action in chronic pain: Further validation and clinical utility of the Committed Action Questionnaire. *Journal of Pain, 17*(10), 1095–1104. https://doi.org/10.1016/j.jpain.2016.06.011

Bandura, A. (1969). *Principles of behavior modification.* Rinehart & Winston.

Baranoff, J. A., Hanrahan, S. J., Burke, A. L. J., & Connor, J. P. (2016). Changes in acceptance in a low-Intensity, group-based acceptance and commitment therapy (ACT) chronic pain intervention. *International Journal of Behavioral Medicine, 23*(1), 30–38. https://doi.org/10.1007/s12529-015-9496-9

Barrett, K., O'Connor, M., & McHugh, L. (2019). A systematic review of values-based psychometric tools within acceptance and commitment therapy (ACT). *Psychological Record, 69*(4), 457–485. https://doi.org/10.1007/s40732-019-00352-7

Barrett, Kathleen, & Chang, Y.-P. (2016). Behavioral interventions targeting chronic pain, depression, and substance use disorder in primary care. *Journal of Nursing Scholarship, 48*(4), 345–353. https://doi.org/10.1111/jnu.12213

Bond, F. W., Hayes, S. C., Baer, R. A., Carpenter, K. M., Guenole, N., Orcutt, H. K., Waltz, T., & Zettle, R. D. (2011). Preliminary psychometric properties of the Acceptance and Action Questionnaire-II: A revised measure of psychological inflexibility and experiential avoidance. *Behavior Therapy, 42*(4), 676–688. https://doi.org/10.1016/j.beth.2011.03.007

Broderick, J. E., Keefe, F. J., Schneider, S., Junghaenel, D. U., Bruckenthal, P., Schwartz, J. E., Kaell, A. T., Caldwell, D. S., McKee, D., & Gould, E. (2016). Cognitive behavioral therapy for chronic pain is effective, but for whom? *Pain, 157*(9), 2115–2123. https://doi.org/10.1097/j.pain.0000000000000626

Brown, K. W., & Ryan, R. M. (2003). The benefits of being present: Mindfulness and its role in psychological well-being. *Journal of Personality and Social Psychology, 84*(4), 822–848. https://doi.org/10.1037/0022-3514.84.4.822

Butler, A. C., Chapman, J. E., Forman, E. M., & Beck, A. T. (2006). The empirical status of cognitive-behavioral therapy: A review of meta-analyses. *Clinical Psychology Review, 26*(1), 17–31. https://doi.org/10.1016/j.cpr.2005.07.003

Cavanagh, K., Strauss, C., Forder, L., & Jones, F. (2014). Can mindfulness and acceptance be learnt by self-help?: A systematic review and meta-analysis of mindfulness and acceptance-based self-help interventions. *Clinical Psychology Review, 34*(2), 118–129. https://doi.org/10.1016/j.cpr.2014.01.001

Cederberg, J. T., Cernvall, M., Dahl, J. A., von Essen, L., & Ljungman, G. (2016). Acceptance as a mediator for change in Acceptance and commitment therapy for persons with chronic pain? *International Journal of Behavioral Medicine, 23*(1), 21–29. https://doi.org/10.1007/s12529-015-9494-y

Chou, R., Deyo, R., Friedly, J., Skelly, A., Weimer, M., Fu, R., Dana, T., Kraegel, P., Griffin, J., & Grusing, S. (2017). Systemic pharmacologic therapies for low back pain: A systematic review for an American College of Physicians clinical practice guideline. *Annals of Internal Medicine, 166*(7), 480–492. https://doi.org/10.7326/M16-2458

Collins, F. S., & Varmus, H. (2015). A new initiative on precision medicine. *New England Journal of Medicine, 372*(9), 793–795. https://doi.org/10.1056/NEJMp1500523

Dahlhamer, J., Lucas, J., Zelaya, C., Nahin, R., Mackey, S., DeBar, L., Kerns, R., Von Korff, M., Porter, L., & Helmick, C. (2018). Prevalence of chronic pain and high-impact chronic pain among adults—United States, 2016. *MMWR. Morbidity and Mortality Weekly Report, 67*(36), 1001–1006. https://doi.org/10.15585/mmwr.mm6736a2

Deyo, R. A., & Mirza, S. K. (2009). The case for restraint in spinal surgery: Does quality management have a role to play? *European Spine Journal, 18*(Suppl. 3), 331–337. https://doi.org/10.1007/s00586-009-0908-x

Dobson, K. S. (1989). A meta-analysis of the efficacy of cognitive therapy for depression. *Journal of Consulting and Clinical Psychology, 57*(3), 414–419. https://doi.org/10.1037/0022-006x.57.3.414

Dworkin, R. H., Turk, D. C., Farrar, J. T., Haythornthwaite, J. A., Jensen, M. P., Katz, N. P., Kerns, R. D., Stucki, G. Allen, R. R., Bellamy, N., Carr, D. B., Chandler, J., Cowan, P., Dionne, R., Galer, B. S., Hertz, S., Jadad, A. R., Kramer, L. D., Manning, D. C., Martin, S.& Witter, J. (2005). Core outcome measures for chronic pain clinical trials: IMMPACT recommendations. *Pain, 113*(1–2), 9–19. https://doi.org/10.1016/j.pain.2004.09.012

Eccleston, C., Fisher, E., Thomas, K., Hearn, L., Derry, S., Stannard, C., Knaggs, R., & Moore, R. A. (2017). Interventions for the reduction of prescribed opioid use in chronic non-cancer pain. *Cochrane Database of Systematic Reviews, 11*, 1–33. https://doi.org/http://dx.doi.org/10.1002/14651858.CD010323

Edwards, D. J. (2019). Age, pain intensity, values-discrepancy, and mindfulness as predictors for mental health and cognitive fusion: Hierarchical regressions with mediation analysis. *Frontiers in Psychology, 10*, 1–11. https://doi.org/10.3389/fpsyg.2019.00517

Edwards, K. A., Pielech, M., Hickman, J., Ashworth, J., Sowden, G., & Vowles, K. E. (2019). The relation of self-compassion to functioning among adults with chronic pain. *European Journal of Pain, 23*, 1538–1547. https://doi.org/10.1002/ejp.1429

Edwards, R. R., Dworkin, R. H., Sullivan, M. D., Turk, D. C., & Wasan, A. D. (2016). The role of psychosocial processes in the development and maintenance of chronic pain disorders. *Journal of Pain, 17*(9), T70–T92. https://doi.org/10.1016/j.jpain.2016.01.001

Ehde, D. M., Dillworth, T. M., & Turner, J. A. (2014). Cognitive-behavioral therapy for individuals with chronic pain: Efficacy, innovations, and directions for research. *American Psychologist, 69*(2), 153–166. https://doi.org/10.1037/a0035747

Elliott, A. M., Smith, B. H., Hannaford, P. C., Smith, W. C., & Chambers, W. A. (2002). The course of chronic pain in the community: Results of a 4-year follow-up study. *Pain, 99*, 299–307. https://doi.org/10.1016/S0304-3959(02)00138-0

Els, C., Jackson, T., Kunyk, D., Lappi, V., Sonnenberg, B., Hagtvedt, R., Sharma, S., Kolahdooz, F., & Straube, S. (2017). Adverse events associated with medium- and longer-term use of opioids for chronic non-cancer pain: An overview of *Cochrane Reviews*. *Cochrane Database of Systematic Reviews, 10*, 1–46. https://doi.org/10.1002/14651858.CD012509

Elvery, N., Jensen, M. P., Ehde, D. M., & Day, M. A. (2017). Pain catastrophizing, mindfulness, and pain acceptance. *Clinical Journal of Pain, 33*(6), 485–495. https://doi.org/10.1097/AJP.0000000000000430

Fish, R. A., Mcguire, B., Hogan, M., Morrison, T. G., & Stewart, I. (2010). Validation of the Chronic Pain Acceptance Questionnaire (CPAQ) in an internet sample and development and preliminary validation of the CPAQ-8. *Pain, 149*(3), 435–443. https://doi.org/10.1016/j.pain.2009.12.016

Fordyce, W. E. (1973). An operant conditioning method for managing chronic pain. *Postgraduate Medicine, 53*(6), 123–128. https://doi.org/10.1080/00325481.1973.11713462

Fordyce, W. E., Fowler, R. S., & Delateur, B. J. (1968). An application of behavior modification technique to a problem of chronic pain. *Behavior Research and Therapy, 6*, 105–107. https://doi.org/10.1016/0005-7967(68)90048-x

Gaskin, D. J., & Richard, P. (2012). The economic costs of pain in the United States. *Journal of Pain, 13*(8), 715–724. https://doi.org/10.1016/j.jpain.2012.03.009

Gatchel, R. J., McGeary, D. D., McGeary, C. A., & Lippe, B. (2014). Interdisciplinary chronic pain management. *American Psychologist, 69*(2), 119–130. https://doi.org/10.1037/a0035514

Gatchel, R. J., Peng, Y. B., Peters, M. L., Fuchs, P. N., & Turk, D. C. (2007). The biopsychosocial approach to chronic pain: Scientific advances and future directions. *Psychological Bulletin, 133*(4), 581–624. https://doi.org/10.1037/0033-2909.133.4.581

Geiser, D. (1992). *A comparison of acceptance- focused and control-focused psychological treatments in a chronic pain treatment center* [Unpublished doctoral dissertation, University of Nevada].

Grider, J., Manchikanti, L., Carayannopoulos, A., Sharma, M. L., Balog, C. C., Harned, M. E., Grami, V., Justiz, R., Nouri, K. H., Hayek, S. M., Vallejo, R., & Christo, P. J. (2016). Effectiveness of spinal cord stimulation in chronic spinal pain: A systematic review. *Pain Physician, 19*(1), E33–E54.

Hann, K. E. J., & McCracken, L. M. (2014). A systematic review of randomized controlled trials of Acceptance and commitment therapy for adults with chronic pain: Outcome domains, design quality, and efficacy. *Journal of Contextual Behavioral Science, 3*(4), 217–227. https://doi.org/10.1016/j.jcbs.2014.10.001

Hayes, S. C. (2004). Acceptance and Commitment therapy and the new behavior therapies: Mindfulness, acceptance, and relationship. In S. C. Hayes, V. M. Follette, & M. M. Linehan (Eds.), *Mindfulness and acceptance: Expanding the cognitive-behavioral tradition* (pp. 1–29). Guildford Press.

Hayes, S. C., Barnes-Holmes, D., & Roche, B. (2001). *Relational frame theory: A post skinnerian account of human language and cognition.* Kluwer Academic.

Hayes, S. C., Levin, M. E., Plumb-Vilardaga, J., Villatte, J. L., & Pistorello, J. (2013). Acceptance and commitment therapy and contextual behavioral science: Examining the progress of a distinctive model of behavioral and cognitive therapy. *Behavior Therapy, 44*, 180–198. https://doi.org/10.1016/j.beth.2009.08.002

Hayes, S. C., Luoma, J. B., Bond, F. W., Masuda, A., & Lillis, J. (2006). Acceptance and commitment therapy: model, processes and outcomes. *Behavior Research and Therapy, 44*(1), 1–25. https://doi.org/10.1016/j.brat.2005.06.006

Hayes, S. C., Strosahl, K. D., & Wilson, K. G. (2012). *Acceptance and commitment therapy: The process and practice of mindful change* (2nd ed.). Guilford Press.

Hekler, E., Tiro, J. A., Hunter, C. M., & Nebeker, C. (2020). Precision health: The role of the social and behavioral sciences in advancing the vision. *Annals of Behavioral Medicine, 54*(11), 805–826. https://doi.org/10.1093/abm/kaaa018

Henschke, N., Rwjg, O., Mw, V. T., Jws, V., Morley, S., Wjj, A., & Cj, M. (2010). Behavioural treatment for chronic low-back pain (Review). *Cochrane Database of Systematic Reviews, 7*, 1–98. https://doi.org/10.1002/14651858.CD002014

Higgins, C., Smith, B. H., & Matthews, K. (2019). Evidence of opioid-induced hyperalgesia in clinical populations after chronic opioid exposure: A systematic review and meta-analysis. *British Journal of Anaesthesia, 122*(6), e114–e126. https://doi.org/10.1016/j.bja.2018.09.019

Hirsh, A. T., Atchison, J. W., Berger, J. J., Waxenberg, L. B., Lafayette-Lucey, A., Bulcourf, B. B., & Robinson, M. E. (2005). Patient satisfaction with treatment for chronic pain: Predictors and relationship to compliance. *Clinical Journal of Pain, 21*(4), 302–310. https://doi.org/10.1097/01.ajp.0000113057.92184.90

Hofmann, S. G. (2008). Common misconceptions about cognitive mediation of treatment change: A commentary to Longmore and Worrell (2007). *Clinical Psychology Review, 28*(1), 67–70. https://doi.org/10.1016/j.cpr.2007.03.003

Hofmann, S. G., Asmundson, G. J. G., & Beck, A. T. (2013). The science of cognitive therapy. *Behavior Therapy, 44*, 199–212.

Hser, Y. I., Mooney, L. J., Saxon, A. J., Miotto, K., Bell, D. S., & Huang, D. (2017). Chronic pain among patients with opioid use disorder: Results from electronic health records data. *Journal of Substance Abuse Treatment, 77*, 26–30. https://doi.org/10.1016/j.jsat.2017.03.006

Hughes, L. S., Clark, J., Colclough, J. A., Dale, E., & McMillan, D. (2017). Acceptance and commitment therapy (ACT) for chronic pain: A systematic review and meta-analyses. *Clinical Journal of Pain, 33*(6), 552–568. https://doi.org/10.1097/AJP.0000000000000425

James, S. L., Abate, D., Abate, K. H., Abay, S. M., Abbafati, C., Abbasi, N., Abbastabar, H., Abd-Allah, F., Abdela, J., Abdelalim, A., Abdollahpour, I., Abdulkader, R. S., Abebe, Z., Abera, S. F., Abil, O. Z., Abraha, H. N., Abu-Raddad, L. J., Abu-Rmeileh, N. M. E., Accrombessi, M. M. K., et al. (2018). Global, regional, and national incidence, prevalence, and years lived with disability for 354 diseases and injuries for 195 countries and territories, 1990–2017: A systematic analysis for the Global Burden of Disease Study 2017. *The Lancet, 392*(10159), 1789–1858. https://doi.org/10.1016/S0140-6736(18)32279-7

Jensen, M. P., Devlin, H. C., Vowles, K. E., & Molton, I. R. (2019). Assessing perceived success in valued living in individuals with long-term physical health conditions. *Journal of Aging and Health, 31*(10S), 195S–213S. https://doi.org/10.1177/0898264319861006

Jensen, M. P., & Turk, D. C. (2014). Contributions of psychology to the understanding and treatment of people with chronic pain: Why it matters to ALL psychologists. *American Psychologist, 69*, 105–118. https://doi.org/10.1037/a0035641

Jensen, M. P., Turner, J. A., Romano, J. M., & Karoly, P. (1991). Coping with chronic pain: A critical review of the literature. *Pain, 47*(3), 249–283.

Jensen, M. P., Vowles, K. E., Johnson, L. E., & Gertz, K. J. (2015). Living well with pain: Development and preliminary evaluation of the Valued Living Scale. *Pain Medicine, 16*(11), 2109–2120. https://doi.org/10.1111/pme.12802

Kaye, A. D., Manchikanti, L., Abdi, S., Atluri, S., Bakshi, S., Benyamin, R., Boswell, M. V., Buenaventura, R., Candido, K. D., Cordner, H. J., Datta, S., Doulatram, G., Gharibo, C. G., Grami, V., Gupta, S., Jha, S., Kaplan, E. D., Malla, Y., Mann, D. P., Nampiaparampil, D. E. & Hirsch, J. A. (2015). Efficacy of epidural injections in managing chronic spinal pain: A best evidence synthesis. *Pain Physician, 18*(6), E939–E1004. https://doi.org/10.36076/ppj.2015/18/E939

Kerns, R. D., Sellinger, J., & Goodin, B. R. (2011). Psychological treatment of chronic pain. *Annual Review of Clinical Psychology, 7*, 411–434. https://doi.org/10.1146/annurev-clinpsy-090310-120430

Kohl, A., Rief, W., & Glombiewski, J. A. (2012). How effective are acceptance strategies? A meta-analytic review of experimental results. *Journal of Behavior Therapy and Experimental Psychiatry, 43*(4), 988–1001. https://doi.org/10.1016/j.jbtep.2012.03.004

Levin, M. E., Luoma, J. B., & Haeger, J. A. (2015). Decoupling as a mechanism of change in mindfulness and acceptance: A literature review. *Behavior Modification, 39*(6), 870–911. https://doi.org/10.1177/0145445515603707

Lin, J., Klatt, L. I., McCracken, L. M., & Baumeister, H. (2018). Psychological flexibility mediates the effect of an online-based acceptance and commitment therapy for chronic pain: An investigation of change processes. *Pain, 159*(4), 663–672. https://doi.org/10.1097/j.pain.0000000000001134

Loeser, J. D., & Melzack, R. (1999). Pain: An overview. *The Lancet, 353*(9164), 1607–1609. https://doi.org/10.1016/S0140-6736(99)01311-2

Longmore, R. J., & Worrell, M. (2007). Do we need to challenge thoughts in cognitive behavior therapy? *Clinical Psychology Review, 27*(2), 173–187. https://doi.org/10.1016/j.cpr.2006.08.001

McCracken, L. M. (2005). *Contextual cognitive-behavioral therapy for chronic pain.* IASP Press.

McCracken, L. M. (2013). Committed action: An application of the psychological flexibility model to activity patterns in chronic pain. *Journal of Pain, 14*(8), 828–835.

McCracken, Lance M., Barker, E., & Chilcot, J. (2014). Decentering, rumination, cognitive defusion, and psychological flexibility in people with chronic pain. *Journal of Behavioral Medicine, 37*(6), 1215–1225. https://doi.org/10.1007/s10865-014-9570-9

McCracken, Lance M., Eccleston, C., & Bell, L. (2005). Clinical assessment of behavioral coping responses: Preliminary results from a brief inventory. *European Journal of Pain, 9*(1), 69–78. https://doi.org/10.1016/j.ejpain.2004.04.005

McCracken, Lance M., Gauntlett-Gilbert, J., & Vowles, K. E. (2007). The role of mindfulness in a contextual cognitive-behavioral analysis of chronic pain-related suffering and disability. *Pain, 131*(1–2), 63–69. https://doi.org/10.1016/j.pain.2006.12.013

McCracken, Lance M., & Gutiérrez-Martínez, O. (2011). Processes of change in psychological flexibility in an interdisciplinary group-based treatment for chronic pain based on acceptance and commitment therapy. *Behavior Research and Therapy, 49*(4), 267–274. https://doi.org/10.1016/j.brat.2011.02.004

McCracken, Lance M., & Thompson, M. (2009). Components of mindfulness in patients with chronic pain. *Journal of Psychopathology and Behavioral Assessment, 31*(2), 75–82. https://doi.org/10.1007/s10862-008-9099-8

McCracken, Lance M., & Turk, D. C. (2002). Behavioral and cognitive-behavioral treatment for chronic pain. *Spine, 27*(22), 2564–2573. https://doi.org/10.1097/00007632-200211150-00033

McCracken, Lance M., & Vowles, K. E. (2007). Psychological flexibility and traditional pain management strategies in relation to patient functioning with chronic pain: An examination of a revised instrument. *Journal of Pain, 8*(9), 700–707. https://doi.org/10.1016/j.jpain.2007.04.008

McCracken, Lance M., Vowles, K. E., & Eccleston, C. (2004). Acceptance of chronic pain: Component analysis and a revised assessment method. *Pain, 107*(1–2), 159–166. https://doi.org/10.1016/j.pain.2003.10.012

McCracken, Lance M., Vowles, K. E., & Gauntlett-Gilbert, J. (2007). A prospective investigation of acceptance and control-oriented coping with chronic pain. *Journal of Behavioral Medicine, 30*(4), 339–349. https://doi.org/10.1007/s10865-007-9104-9

McCracken, Lance M., & Yang, S. Y. (2006). The role of values in a contextual cognitive-behavioral approach to chronic pain. *Pain, 123*(1–2), 137–145. https://doi.org/10.1016/j.pain.2006.02.021

McCracken, Lance M., & Zhao-O'Brien, J. (2010). General psychological acceptance and chronic pain: There is more to accept than the pain itself. *European Journal of Pain, 14*(2), 170–175. https://doi.org/10.1016/j.ejpain.2009.03.004
Melzack, R., & Wall, P. D. (1965). Pain mechanisms: A new theory. *Science, 150*, 971–979.
Morley, S. (2011). Efficacy and effectiveness of cognitive behaviour therapy for chronic pain: Progress and some challenges. *Pain, 152*, S99–S106. https://doi.org/10.1016/j.pain.2010.10.042
Naylor, M. R., Keefe, F. J., Brigidi, B., Naud, S., & Helzer, J. (2008). Therapeutic interactive voice response for chronic pain reduction and relapse prevention. *Pain, 134*(3), 335–345. https://doi.org/10.1038/mp.2011.182.doi
Naylor, M. R., Naud, S., Keefe, F. J., & Helzer, J. (2010). Therapeutic inveractive voice response (TIVR) to reduce analgesic medication use for chronic pain management. *Journal of Pain, 11*(12), 1410–1419. https://doi.org/10.1038/mp.2011.182.doi
Neff, K. (2003). Self-compassion: An alternative conceptualization of a healthy attitude toward oneself. *Self and Identity, 2*, 85–101. https://doi.org/10.1080/15298860390129863
Nicholas, M. K., Costa, D. S. J., Blanchard, M., Tardif, H., Asghari, A., & Blyth, F. M. (2019). Normative data for common pain measures in chronic pain clinic populations. *Pain, 160*(5), 1156–1165. https://doi.org/10.1097/j.pain.0000000000001496
Nielsen, L., Riddle, M., King, J. W., Team, C. I., Aklin, W. M., Chen, W., Clark, D., Collier, E., Czajkowski, S., Esposito, L., Ferrer, R., Green, P., Hunter, C., Kehl, K., King, R., Onken, L., Simmons, J. M., Stoeckel, L., Stoney, C., Tully, L. & Weber, W. (2018). The NIH Science of Behavior Change Program: Transforming the science through a focus on mechanisms of change. *Behavior Research and Therapy, 101*, 3–11. https://doi.org/10.1016/j.brat.2017.07.002.The
Pielech, M., Bailey, R. W., Mcentee, M. L., Ashworth, J., Levell, J., Sowden, G., & Vowles, K. E. (2016). Preliminary evaluation of the Values Tracker: A two-item measure of engagement in valued activities in those with chronic pain. *Behavior Modification, 40*(1–2), 239–256. https://doi.org/10.1177/0145445515616911
Raja, S. N., Carr, D. B., Cohen, M., Finnerup, N. B., Flor, H., Gibson, S., Keefe, F. J., Mogil, J. S., Ringkamp, M., Sluka, K. A., Song, X., Stevens, B., Sullivan, M. D., Tutelman, P. R., Ushida, T. & Vader, K. (2020). The revised International Association for the Study of Pain definition of pain: Concepts, challenges, and compromises. *Pain, 161*(9), 1976–1982. https://doi.org/10.1097/j.pain.0000000000001939
Reneman, M. F., Dijkstra, A., Geertzen, J. H. B., & Dijkstra, P. U. (2010). Psychometric properties of Chronic Pain Acceptance Questionnaires: A systematic review. *European Journal of Pain, 14*(5), 457–465. https://doi.org/10.1016/j.ejpain.2009.08.003
Ruben, M. A., Meterko, M., & Bokhour, B. G. (2018). Do patient perceptions of provider communication relate to experiences of physical pain? *Patient Education and Counseling, 101*(2), 209–213. https://doi.org/10.1016/j.pec.2017.08.002
Schütze, R., Rees, C., Preece, M., & Schütze, M. (2010). Low mindfulness predicts pain catastrophizing in a fear-avoidance model of chronic pain. *Pain, 148*(1), 120–127. https://doi.org/10.1016/j.pain.2009.10.030
Scott, W., Daly, A., Yu, L., & McCracken, L. M. (2017). Treatment of chronic pain for adults 65 and over: Analyses of outcomes and changes in psychological flexibility following interdisciplinary acceptance and commitment therapy (ACT). *Pain Medicine, 18*(2), 252–264. https://doi.org/10.1093/pm/pnw073
Scott, W., Hann, K. E. J., & McCracken, L. M. (2016). A comprehensive examination of changes in psychological flexibility following Acceptance and commitment therapy for chronic pain. *Journal of Contemporary Psychotherapy, 46*(3), 139–148. https://doi.org/10.1007/s10879-016-9328-5
Shealy, C. N., & Cady, R. K. (2002). Historical perspective of pain management. In W. S. Weiner (Ed.), *Pain management: A practical guide for clinicians* (6th ed., pp. 9–16). CRC Press.
Skinner, B. F. (1938). *The behavior of organisms: An experimental analysis*. Appleton-Century Company.
Smeets, R. J. E. M., Vlaeyen, J. W. S., Kester, A. D. M., & Knottnerus, J. A. (2006). Reduction of pain catastrophizing mediates the outcome of both physical and cognitive-behavioral treatment in chronic low back pain. *Journal of Pain, 7*(4), 261–271. https://doi.org/10.1016/j.jpain.2005.10.011
Sullivan, M. J. L., Bishop, S. R., & Pivik, J. (1995). The pain catastrophising scale. *Psychological Assessment, 7*(4), 524–532. https://doi.org/10.1016/s1836-9553(10)70047-3
Tait, R. C., & Chibnall, J. T. (2014). Racial/ethnic disparities in the assessment and treatment of pain: Psychosocial perspectives. *The American Psychologist, 69*(2), 131–141. https://doi.org/10.1037/a0035204
Trompetter, H. R., Bohlmeijer, E. T., Baalen, B. Van, Kleen, M., Köke, A., Reneman, M., & Schreurs, K. M. G. (2014). The Psychological Inflexibility in Pain Scale (PIPS) exploration of psychometric properties in a heterogeneous chronic pain sample. *European Journal of Psychological Assessment, 30*(4), 289–295. https://doi.org/10.1027/1015-5759/a000191

Trompetter, H. R., Ten Klooster, P. M., Schreurs, K. M. G., Fledderus, M., Westerhof, G. J., & Bohlmeijer, E. T. (2013). Measuring values and committed action with the Engaged Living Scale (ELS): Psychometric evaluation in a nonclinical sample and a chronic pain sample. *Psychological Assessment, 25*(4), 1235–1246. https://doi.org/10.1037/a0033813

Turk, D. C., Meichenbaum, D., & Genest, M. (1983). *Pain and behavioral medicine: A cognitive-behavioral perspective.* Guilford Press.

Turner, J. A., Jensen, M. P., & Romano, J. M. (2000). Do beliefs, coping, and catastrophizing independently predict functioning in patients with chronic pain? *Pain, 85*(1–2), 115–125. https://doi.org/10.1016/S0304-3959(99)00259-6

Vasseljen, O., Woodhouse, A., Bjørngaard, J. H., & Leivseth, L. (2013). Natural course of acute neck and low back pain in the general population: The HUNT study. *Pain, 154*(8), 1237–1244. https://doi.org/10.1016/j.pain.2013.03.032

Veehof, M. M., Trompetter, H. R., Bohlmeijer, E. T., & Schreurs, K. M. G. (2016). Acceptance- and mindfulness-based interventions for the treatment of chronic pain: A meta-analytic review. *Cognitive Behavior Therapy, 45*(1), 5–31. https://doi.org/10.1080/16506073.2015.1098724

Von Korff, M., Crane, P., Lane, M., Miglioretti, D. L., Simon, G., Saunders, K., Stang, P., Brandenburg, N., & Kessler, R. (2005). Chronic spinal pain and physical-mental comorbidity in the United States: Results from the National Comorbidity Survey replication. *Pain, 113*(3), 331–339. https://doi.org/10.1016/j.pain.2004.11.010

Vowles, K. E., Fink, B. C., & Cohen, L. L. (2014). Acceptance and commitment therapy for chronic pain: A diary study of treatment process in relation to reliable change in disability. *Journal of Contextual Behavioral Science, 3*(2), 74–80. https://doi.org/10.1016/j.jcbs.2014.04.003

Vowles, K. E., Kruger, E. S., Bailey, R. W., Sowden, G., Hickman, J., & Mccracken, L. M. (2020). Initial evaluation of the Chronic Pain Acceptance Questionnaire – 2. *European Jounal of Pain*, August, 2027–2036. https://doi.org/10.1002/ejp.1650

Vowles, K. E., & McCracken, L. M. (2008). Acceptance and values-based action in chronic pain: A study of treatment effectiveness and process. *Journal of Consulting and Clinical Psychology, 76*(3), 397–407. https://doi.org/10.1037/0022-006X.76.3.397

Vowles, K. E., McCracken, L. M., & Eccleston, C. (2007). Processes of change in treatment for chronic pain: The contributions of pain, acceptance, and catastrophizing. *European Journal of Pain, 11*(7), 779–787. https://doi.org/10.1016/j.ejpain.2006.12.007

Vowles, K. E., McCracken, L. M., McLeod, C., & Eccleston, C. (2008). The Chronic Pain Acceptance Questionnaire: Confirmatory factor analysis and identification of patient subgroups. *Pain, 140*(2), 284–291. https://doi.org/10.1016/j.pain.2008.08.012

Vowles, K. E., McCracken, L. M., & O'Brien, J. Z. (2011). Acceptance and values-based action in chronic pain: A three-year follow-up analysis of treatment effectiveness and process. *Behavior Research and Therapy, 49*, 748–755. https://doi.org/10.1016/j.brat.2011.08.002

Vowles, K. E., McEntee, M. L., Julnes, P. S., Frohe, T., Ney, J. P., & van der Goes, D. N. (2015). Rates of opioid misuse, abuse, and addiction in chronic pain: A systematic review and data synthesis. *Pain, 156*(4), 569–576. https://doi.org/10.1097/01.j.pain.0000460357.01998.f1

Vowles, K. E., Pielech, M., Edwards, K. A., McEntee, M. L., & Bailey, R. W. (2020). A comparative meta-analysis of unidisciplinary psychology and interdisciplinary treatment outcomes following acceptance and commitment therapy for adults with chronic pain. *Journal of Pain, 21*(5–6), 529–545. https://doi.org/10.1016/j.jpain.2019.10.004

Vowles, K. E., Sowden, G., & Ashworth, J. (2014). A comprehensive examination of the model underlying acceptance and commitment therapy for chronic pain. *Behavior Therapy, 45*, 390–401. https://doi.org/10.1016/j.beth.2013.12.009

Vowles, K. E., Sowden, G., Hickman, J., & Ashworth, J. (2019). An analysis of within-treatment change trajectories in valued activity in relation to treatment outcomes following interdisciplinary acceptance and commitment therapy for adults with chronic pain. *Behavior Research and Therapy, 115*, 46–54. https://doi.org/https://doi.org/10.1016/j.brat.2018.10.012

Vowles, K. E., Witkiewitz, K., Cusack, K. J., Gilliam, W. P., Cardon, K. E., Bowen, S., Edwards, K. A., McEntee, M. L. & Bailey, R. W. (2019). Integrated behavioral treatment for Veterans with co-morbid chronic pain and hazardous opioid use: A randomized controlled pilot trial. *Journal of Pain*, 21(7–8), 798–807. https://doi.org/10.1016/j.jpain.2019.11.007

Vowles, K. E., Witkiewitz, K., Levell, J., Sowden, G., & Ashworth, J. (2017). Are reductions in pain intensity and pain-related distress necessary? An analysis of within-treatment change trajectories in relation to improved functioning following interdisciplinary acceptance and commitment therapy for adults with chronic pain. *Journal of Consulting and Clinical Psychology, 85*(2), 87–98. https://doi.org/10.1037/ccp0000159

Vowles, K. E., Witkiewitz, K., Sowden, G., & Ashworth, J. (2014). Acceptance and commitment therapy for chronic pain: Evidence of mediation and clinically significant change following an abbreviated interdisciplinary program of rehabilitation. *Journal of Pain, 15*(1), 101–113. https://doi.org/10.1016/j.jpain.2013.10.002

Walters, E. T., & Williams, A. C. (2019). Evolution of mechanisms and behaviour important for pain. *Philosophical Transactions of the Royal Society B, 374*, 1–4. https://doi.org/10.1098/rstb.2019.0275

Wetherell, J. L., Petkus, A. J., Alonso-Fernandez, M., Bower, E. S., Steiner, A. R. W., & Afari, N. (2016). Age moderates response to acceptance and commitment therapy vs. cognitive behavioral therapy for chronic pain. *International Journal of Geriatric Psychiatry, 31*(3), 302–308. https://doi.org/10.1002/gps.4330

Wicksell, R. K., Lekander, M., Sorjonen, K., & Olsson, G. L. (2010). The Psychological Inflexibility in Pain Scale (PIPS)—Statistical properties and model fit of an instrument to assess change processes in pain related disability. *European Journal of Pain, 14*(7), 771.e1–771.e14. https://doi.org/10.1016/j.ejpain.2009.11.015

Wicksell, R. K., Olsson, G. L., & Melin, L. (2009). The Chronic Pain Acceptance Questionnaire (CPAQ)—Further validation including a confirmatory factor analysis and a comparison with the Tampa Scale of Kinesiophobia. *European Journal of Pain, 13*(7), 760–768. https://doi.org/10.1016/j.ejpain.2008.09.003

Wicksell, R. K., Reno, J., Bond, F. W., & Melin, L. (2008). Avoidance and cognitive fusion—Central components in pain related disability? Development and preliminary validation of the Psychological Inflexibility in Pain Scale (PIPS). *European Jounal of Pain, 12*, 491–500. https://doi.org/10.1016/j.ejpain.2007.08.003

Williams, A. C. D. C., Fisher, E., Hearn, L., & Eccleston, C. (2020). Psychological therapies for the management of chronic pain (excluding headache) in adults. *Cochrane Database of Systematic Reviews, 8*, 1–98. https://doi.org/10.1002/14651858.CD007407.pub4

Wollschlaeger, B. A., Willson, T. M., Montejano, L. B., Ronquest, N. A., & Nadipelli, V. R. (2017). Characteristics and treatment patterns of US commercially insured and Medicaid patients with opioid dependence or abuse. *Journal of Opioid Management, 13*(4), 207–220. https://doi.org/10.5055/jom.2017.0389

Yavin, D., Casha, S., Wiebe, S., Feasby, T. E., Clark, C., Isaacs, A., Holroyd-Leduc, J., Hurlbert, R. J., Quan, H., Nataraj, A., Sutherland, G. R. & Whitmore, R. G. (2017). Lumbar fusion for degenerative disease: A systematic review and meta-analysis. *Clinical Neurosurgery, 80*(5), 701–715. https://doi.org/10.1093/neuros/nyw162

Yu, L., Norton, S., & McCracken, L. M. (2017). Change in "self-as-context" ("perspective-taking") occurs in Acceptance and commitment therapy for people with chronic pain and is associated with improved functioning. *Journal of Pain, 18*(6), 664–672. https://doi.org/https://doi.org/10.1016/j.jpain.2017.01.005

CHAPTER

21 ACT for Chronic Health Conditions

Lilian Dindo, Julia R. Van Liew, *and* Joanna J. Arch

Abstract

Chronic health conditions are the leading cause of disability, reduced quality of life, and death. For 20 percent of these patients, clinical anxiety and depression exacerbate existing disease. Despite the high prevalence of comorbidity, existing treatments and service delivery approaches largely reflect fragmented, disease-specific care. Traditional psychological interventions are often unfeasible or unappealing. Transdiagnostic, process-based, and flexibly delivered, acceptance and commitment therapy (ACT) can meet the heterogeneous needs and treatment preferences of patients with physical, mental health, behavioral, and co-occurring difficulties. ACT directly addresses behavioral avoidance, a common problem in behavioral medicine. It attends to the values and goals of patients and teaches skills to flexibly pursue values despite obstacles, including those presented by serious chronic disease. ACT has been effectively implemented in hospital settings and primary care and specialty care clinics. A rapidly evolving literature supports the preliminary feasibility, acceptability, and efficacy of brief ACT treatments, including those in medical care settings. This therapy has been associated with improved medical, mental health, and behavioral outcomes, as well as overall functioning and quality of life. As medicine increasingly recognizes the importance of mental health, well-being, and health behavior change, ACT's transdiagnostic, process-based approach and flexible delivery options ideally position it to address behavioral health care needs in diverse medical populations.

Key Words: chronic disease, behavioral medicine, transdiagnostic treatment, acceptance and commitment therapy, comorbidity

An Overview of Chronic Health Conditions and Distress

Chronic health conditions (CHC) are broadly defined as conditions that last one year or more and require ongoing medical attention, limit activities of daily living, or both. In the United States, an estimated 60 percent of individuals live with at least one CHC (Hartzler, Castle, Lewis, & Zakaria, 2020), and 40 percent manage two or more of them. By 2030, an estimated 171 million Americans will be living with multiple CHCs (Gerard, 2010). CHCs are the leading cause of long-term disability, hospitalization, reduced quality of life, and death in the United States (Raghupathi & Raghupathi, 2018). In fact, two-thirds of all deaths are caused by one or more of the following five chronic diseases: heart disease, cancer, stroke, chronic obstructive pulmonary disease, and diabetes. In addition to this extensive human cost, CHCs account for approximately 75 percent of all health care expenditures. In total, treatment for chronic diseases coupled with illness-driven productivity losses cost the U.S. economy more than $1 trillion annually (Waters & Graf, 2018).

Long-term management of CHCs can be challenging for patients and their health care providers, with patient behavior representing a central component of successful management of these conditions (Holman & Lorig, 2000). Unlike treatment for acute illnesses, CHCs typically entail multiple patient self-management behaviors such as engagement in at-home tasks (e.g., physical therapy exercises), complex medication or treatment regimens (e.g., daily medication administration, dialysis or chemotherapy sessions), symptom monitoring (e.g., tracking vital signs or insulin levels), and regular appointments with a team of providers (Grady & Gough, 2014). Moreover, CHCs may necessitate difficult health behavior changes such as smoking cessation, dietary changes or disease-specific dietary restrictions, exercise, or weight loss. Patients are called upon to engage in sustained behavioral self-management of their condition, while simultaneously dealing with the condition's symptoms, treatment side effects, and illness-related changes in functioning, quality of life, valued activities, or roles.

For 30 percent of patients with CHC, clinical anxiety or depression co-occur with their illness (Evans et al., 2005; Merikangas et al., 2007). For some individuals, distress may begin after a major illness-related event such as initial diagnosis, prominent disease progression, or functional decline. Others find that, over time spent living with a CHC, isolation increases, frustration with the illness and symptom burden mounts, and the possibility of living rich and rewarding lives seems ever more remote, thus increasing the possibility of significant depression and/or anxiety.

Importantly, the association between CHCs and distress is complex and bidirectional (Evans et al., 2005). Chronic distress can weaken the immune system and increase the inflammatory response through mind–body pathways including psychoneuroimmunology and endocrine pathways (Segerstrom & Miller, 2004). This can place individuals at higher risk for developing a CHC in the first place or can exacerbate an existing condition. Moreover, significant distress also influences the onset or trajectory of CHCs through its impact on behavioral factors such as engagement in health behaviors (e.g., smoking, sedentary lifestyle), disease self-management, and treatment adherence (DiMatteo, Lepper, & Croghan, 2000). For example, patients with depression are three times less likely than nondepressed patients to adhere to medical treatment recommendations (DiMatteo et al., 2000). Finally, CHCs and mental distress may also share common risk factors for development such as childhood adversity, chronic stress, and social determinants of health (Goodell, Druss, & Walker, 2011).

Broadly, co-occurring mental distress and CHCs are associated with more severe medical pathology, elevated symptom burden, poorer prognosis, poorer treatment adherence, higher functional impairment, decreased length and quality of life, and higher health care utilization and costs compared to those with only a CHC (Arnow et al., 2006; Celano & Huffman, 2011; Lowe et al., 2008). The comorbidity of mental distress and CHCs thus magnifies the existing challenges faced by patients and health care providers in managing CHCs (Evans et al., 2005). Behavioral medicine approaches, which consider the biological, psychological, and behavioral causes and effects of medical disease, aim to leverage this synergy to improve adjustment to CHCs and to promote health-related behavior change and other health outcomes (Engel, 1977). This includes reducing mental distress related to coping with CHCs and understanding and modifying health behaviors that can influence the course of disease.

Even absent the co-occurrence of clinically significant levels of anxiety or depression, the diagnosis and management of a CHC naturally provokes a broad range of personal life changes. These common and collective patient experiences occurring across CHCs will be referenced in more detail later in this article, but they broadly include experiences such as coping with the diagnosis; coping with the disease and its treatment; dealing with stigma and changes in one's sense of self; adapting to changing roles and narrowing of focus; and considering death and dying. Thus, to some extent, all individuals with CHCs necessarily experience some degree of illness-related coping and behavioral or lifestyle modification as a natural part of their illness experience. Further, many will experience illness-related emotional distress and decline in quality of life that are consequential and yet may not be categorized as a specific mental health diagnosis. Thus, while some individuals develop full-blown anxiety or mood disorders following disease diagnosis (Arch, Genung, et al., 2020), other forms of distress fall outside the scope of the *Diagnostic and Statistical Manual of Mental Disorders*, Fifth Edition (*DSM-5*) clinical conditions but nonetheless emerge as important illness sequelae (Katon, 2004). Without attention to these common personal experiences related to living with a CHC, such experiences can negatively impact an individual's well-being and/or engagement with their medical care (Katon, 2011).

In this article, we will identify personal and structural factors that influence patient adjustment to chronic illness. We will then describe how acceptance and commitment therapy (ACT) offers a valuable model for addressing many of the needs of both patients and health care systems. After reviewing relevant research literature for ACT in this population, we illustrate how the ACT processes apply to common transdiagnostic features of living with CHCs as well as to specific illness populations. We identify current challenges and future opportunities in this area and conclude by offering implications for research and practice.

Personal Factors Influencing Coping with Chronic Health Conditions

Patients with CHCs commonly face unwanted and uncomfortable internal experiences associated with both the illness and/or the treatment (e.g., fatigue, pain, shortness of breath), as well as with the associated psychological distress (e.g., anxiety, shame). The way individuals cope with a CHC and the associated stress appears to have important long-term effects on health and well-being (Spleen, Lengerich, Camacho, & Vanderpool, 2014). A patient's adaptation may be influenced by the nature of the health condition itself and the psychosocial context in which it occurs, with variability in patient response both within and across health conditions. Some individuals demonstrate resilience, in which they persist in the face of adversity and, when needed, accept circumstances that cannot be changed (Bonanno, 2004). Others struggle more in response to these challenges, often responding with maladaptive coping strategies.

To cope with anxiety, fatigue, and other difficulties common in CHCs, patients may turn to maladaptive coping strategies that offer short-term relief but have detrimental long-term effects. Behavioral, emotional, and cognitive avoidant coping strategies, such as avoidance of important activities, distraction techniques, mental disengagement, and denial, are predictive of negative results in patients with CHCs, including lower motivation to attend appointments and poorer health outcomes (Carver et al., 1993; Hofmann & Hay, 2018). For example, if patients are strongly avoidant due to disease stigma or anxiety, they may choose to forgo important health behaviors such as attending clinic visits. They may also turn to harmful behaviors to cope, such as drug or alcohol use. A patient with a CHC may avoid going out with friends due to fear of experiencing more fatigue, drink alcohol to avoid the experience of anxiety or emotional distress, avoid going to a doctor's appointment because it is reminder that they have a chronic condition, or avoid intimacy due to shame (Dijkstra & Homan, 2016).

Although these avoidance strategies lead to short-term relief of internal discomfort associated with physical symptoms and/or difficult emotional experiences (e.g., fatigue, anxiety, and shame), they do not effectively solve the problem in the long run. In fact, they maintain or worsen the problem, can have negative long-term health consequences, and ultimately have severe costs to quality of life and functioning (Moos & Schaefer, 1993). For example, the regular use of alcohol to reduce anxiety can lead to long-term addiction problems and difficulties with work and family. Over time, avoidance provoked by fatigue can lead to physical deconditioning. Avoidance of social activity over extended periods leads to social isolation and fewer meaningful relationships. Ultimately, this can serve as a pathway for the development of depression and anxiety through decreased values-driven appetitive behavior and interpersonal connection, increased hypersensitivity to illness cues, and narrowing of one's sense of purpose and meaning to focus on the illness. Figure 21.1 illustrates this process of avoidance coping with a general unwanted internal experience and with specific applications for unwanted physical and emotional experiences of fatigue and anxiety, respectively.

Overall, patients who use avoidance as an attempt to ignore, distract, or escape from the physical symptoms, stigma, or stresses of living with a CHC are at risk for feeling worse about their illness, experiencing a worsened psychological state and, potentially, poorer retention in medical services (Carver et al., 1993; Holtforth, 2008). Importantly, avoidance coping is a modifiable factor for patients with CHCs, and building more adaptive coping strategies can increase resilience and improve health outcomes. For example, engagement in important and meaningful activities, even in the presence of illness, is associated with better health outcomes (McCracken & Yang, 2006; Viane, Crombez, Eccleston, Devulder, & De Corte, 2004; Vowles et al., 2007).

Structural Factors Influencing Coping with Chronic Health Conditions

There is a mismatch between the frequent co-occurrence of distress in patients with CHCs and a health care delivery system in which care for these interrelated experiences is treated as separate. Although patients with CHCs frequently exhibit psychological distress, existing treatments and service delivery approaches largely reflect fragmented, disease-specific care rather than integrated, whole-person approaches (Mohr et al., 2006). Most patients with CHCs frequently visit their health care specialists, often establishing a close relationship with these providers. As mental health services are rarely embedded or co-located within such specialty medical settings, providers are left to refer distressed patients to a mental health provider in a separate clinic (Backenstrass et al., 2006). Unfortunately, such referrals typically receive suboptimal follow-up. The burden is placed on the patient to make an appointment with the mental health clinic and attend numerous sessions in a separate location that may be inconvenient and stigmatizing to the patient (Pietrzak, Johnson, Goldstein, Malley, & Southwick, 2009). Additional limiting factors for seeking traditional mental health services may include not seeing oneself as having problems that could be addressed by behavioral means, strong chronic illness identity or identification as a medical patient, and mental health stigma (Bell et al., 2011). Practical barriers may include time constraints, financial cost, limited access to mental health services, long and costly travel to treatment facilities, and competing priorities (e.g., work and family demands).

Even when patients with CHCs successfully present to a mental health clinic, treatment adherence is a common problem. Patients living with CHCs that require ongoing management and frequent medical care may be even more likely to find it difficult to regularly attend appointments given the time, energy, and expense already invested in medical care for their illness. Traditional mental health interventions—for example, 12 sessions of individual outpatient psychotherapy at an outpatient mental health clinic—are typically not seen as feasible or appealing to patients with CHCs for this array of reasons (Robinson & Strosahl, 2009).

In fact, because high attrition rates are a known problem in psychotherapy in general, some have argued that the term *gold standard* evidence-based treatment must be reserved for

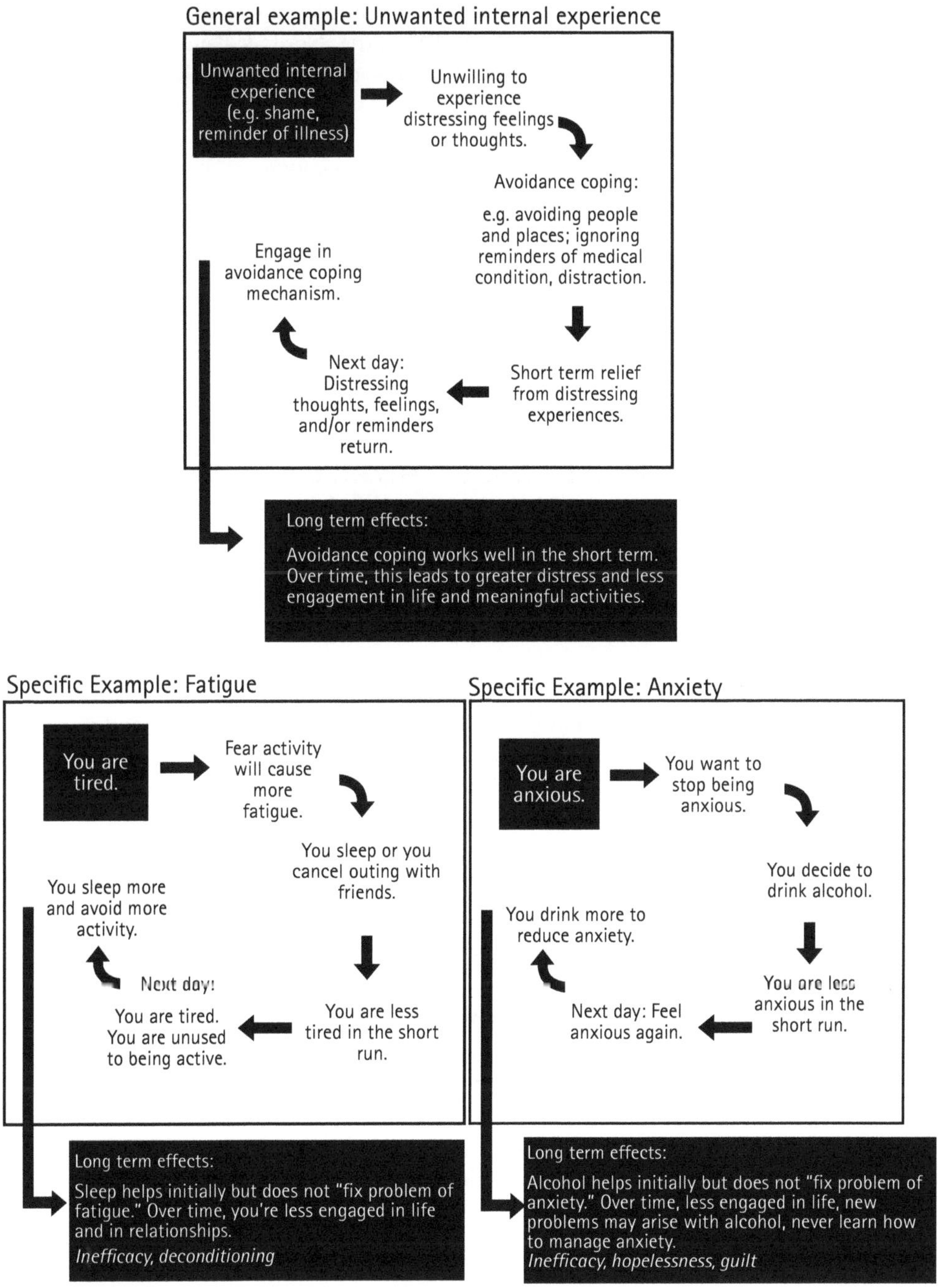

Figure 21.1 Avoidance coping with unwanted internal experiences.

interventions that show not only positive effects in randomized controlled trials, but also feasibility and strong retention rates in typical clinical settings (Najavits, 2015). Embedding behavioral health interventions within medical settings is an effective way to provide broad access and comprehensive care for the behavioral aspects of medical conditions and mental health problems. Such systems-based approaches can result in improved overall outcomes for both medical and mental health problems (Goodrich, Kilbourne, Nord, & Bauer, 2013; Robinson & Strosahl, 2009). The Agency for Healthcare Research and Quality considers integration of mental health care into health care as one of three key priority areas for patients with CHCs (LeRoy, Bayliss, & Domino, 2014).

This diversity of personal and structural problems encountered among patients with CHCs calls for a transdiagnostic, flexibly delivered psychotherapeutic approach that can be readily integrated in diverse health care settings and that focuses on targeting adaptive coping strategies that address both unwanted physical symptoms of the illness as well as the associated emotional distress. ACT is well suited for addressing both these individual and structural factors influencing adjustment to CHC. It can adapt to the needs, preferences, and utilization practices of patients in diverse clinical settings as well as to the settings themselves, including offering opportunities for brief treatment courses, integrated service delivery, and broad applicability to a range of emotional and physical experiences.

ACT is Well Suited to Meet Patient and Health Care Systems Needs

Core features of the ACT approach address the personal and structural needs of patients with CHCs. The following features make ACT particularly appropriate for meeting the diverse needs of patients with CHC. ACT is transdiagnostic, ACT addresses avoidance, ACT focuses on values, ACT is acceptance-based, ACT is workability-focused, and ACT is flexibly delivered to meet implementation needs. These features are summarized in Table 21.1.

ACT is Transdiagnostic

ACT is a transdiagnostic intervention that aims to promote greater resilience and flexibility in the face of life's challenges. It was designed as a general intervention model with relevance across diverse personal and behavioral experiences. Given the broad range of patient problems

Table 21.1 ACT Features Addressing the Personal and Structural Needs of CHC

Transdiagnostic	The varied emotional and physical health problems encountered in behavioral medicine are diverse and sometimes not even diagnosable.
Addresses Avoidance Directly	Many problematic behaviors in behavioral medicine contexts arise from pervasive avoidance, which ACT targets directly.
Values-Based	ACT helps refocus patients on how health-related behaviors fit with their values. This may undermine "resistance" and increase or sustain motivation to change.
Acceptance-Based	In behavioral medicine, patients' bodies may experience permanent changes. Helping patients to accept these changes can free up energy to focus on who and what they value.
Workability-Focused	Living well with a long-term condition involves developing awareness of the impact of behavioral choices on outcomes. ACT strengthens nonjudgmental identification of "unworkable" behavioral patterns and facilitates behavior changes that are "workable" and aligned with long-term valued ends.
Flexible Delivery Format	Behavioral medicine typically does not allow for the weekly session format of most therapies. ACT can be flexibly delivered in brief form and embedded into medical settings.

encountered in medical settings, encompassing both challenging physical and emotional experiences associated with the CHC, it is valuable to draw upon such a unified model in conceptualizing and addressing these problems. The same ACT processes can be used across various illness populations to address content related to the multidimensional physical and emotional challenges of living with the CHC, and this transdiagnostic approach fits patients regardless of the specific type or number of medical or psychological conditions. Moreover, it can be applied for patients who may not "fit" into specific psychological diagnostic categories but are nonetheless experiencing difficulties adjusting to a chronic disease. This can include social and occupational functioning and/or significant distress, including subclinical or subsyndromal problems (Arch, Genung, et al., 2020; Voigt et al., 2017). A transdiagnostic approach also decreases training burden and cost, as training in one approach can address a multitude of problems.

ACT Addresses Avoidance

Many problematic behaviors among patients with CHCs arise from pervasive avoidance, which ACT directly targets. As noted earlier, if patients rigidly avoid uncomfortable internal experiences (e.g., difficult thoughts and feelings) or locations that trigger such states (e.g., hospitals), they may turn to maladaptive health behaviors (e.g., not keeping appointments, not taking their prescribed medication, drinking or eating too much) in order to cope (Hayes, Wilson, Gifford, Follette, & Strosahl, 1996). ACT provides a model for understanding and evaluating forms of avoidance that can lead to problems and helps patients overcome avoidance with the skills of acceptance, defusion, mindfulness, perspective taking, and committed action toward valued domains. These ACT skills can be flexibly applied to address avoidance in any domain of living, including CHCs.

ACT Focuses on Values

ACT emphasizes the pursuit of valued life areas and directions, such as intimate relationships, meaningful work, and personal growth, even in the presence of distressing physical symptoms and emotional sequelae of the CHC. Focused attention on what matters most (e.g., family, friends, community) provides patients with the motivation to make difficult choices because they are consistent with a richer and more meaningful life. In medical settings, ACT helps refocus patients on how health-related behaviors align with their values. Within ACT, health is viewed as a means to valued ends. That is, patients are encouraged to think about "why" they may want to engage in activities that promote their health and to consider: What is health in the service of? Connecting self-care to a patient's values in turn may undermine "resistance" and increase or sustain motivation to engage in lifestyle changes or adhere to treatment (Hayes, Strosahl, & Wilson, 2012).

ACT Is Acceptance-Based

ACT's foundational conceptualization of painful emotional experiences (e.g., disappointment, loss, fear, sadness) as inevitable features of human life rather than experiences to be avoided or suppressed can be broadened to encompass the uncomfortable physical health symptoms of the CHC. Often patients with chronic illness experience permanent changes to their bodies or bodily functions. ACT emphasizes active acceptance of what cannot be fully changed and a reorientation toward what *can* be changed or influenced, namely, our own behavior and the choices we make in our lives. Given that CHCs often present patients with realities that cannot be changed or fully influenced—such as physical changes and disabilities, incurable conditions, pain, fatigue, and other symptoms that fail to respond well to medication—an intervention that emphasizes active acceptance and flexible responsiveness seems particularly well suited to meeting the needs of patients with CHCs. In contrast to other treatment approaches that are more explicitly focused on symptom reduction or elimination, ACT's acceptance-based approach is particularly relevant to individuals living with the realities of a long-term CHC, who face an array of physical and emotional challenges that elude full control throughout the course of an extended illness.

Of note, acceptance is not equivalent to "liking" or "approving" of a disease or illness. It is the acknowledgment that struggling with something that is unchangeable or uncontrollable adds suffering and reduces vitality. Helping patients to let go of that struggle can free up energy to focus on who and what they value. For example, one of us worked with a cancer survivor who spent significant time and energy worried about her hair loss and obsessed over why her newly growing hair looked different after chemotherapy than her old hair. Through working on acceptance, this patient managed to reduce the struggle against her internal experience with her illness and focus more on engaging with her valued activities and relationships. Acceptance of difficult internal experiences and reengaging in life in meaningful ways (rather than resorting to avoidance) often lead to improvements in quality of life, mood, and functioning (Hayes et al., 2012).

ACT Is Workability-Focused

Key to the ACT model is "workability," whereby patients are encouraged to examine the "workability" of their behaviors and recognize whether those behaviors are "working" in terms of effectively solving the problem and moving one toward valued ends. This focus on long-term valued living and building a meaningful life despite challenges contrasts with the short-term reinforcement of avoidance-based coping. Workability and an emphasis on long-term valued living provide a particularly beneficial framework for living with the ongoing challenges of a long-term health condition. It can also help the patient develop greater awareness of the impact of behavioral choices on outcomes. For example, a patient may be asked if their use of alcohol to cope with health-related anxiety is working in the long run, in terms of solving the problem of anxiety. Further, the patient may be guided through examining the long-term costs in valued life areas associated with using this strategy. Importantly, nonjudgmental identification of "unworkable" behavioral patterns motivated by short-term symptom relief helps to facilitate behavior changes that are aligned with long-term valued ends (Hayes et al., 2012).

ACT Is Flexibly Delivered to Meet Implementation Needs

As noted previously, structural factors limit the applicability of the standard weekly therapy session format to the particular needs of patients with CHCs and the realities of health care systems. ACT has shown great flexibility in terms of delivery format and integration potential within the often fast-paced, time-limited context of medical practice. Flexibility in delivery format and duration allows focus to be placed on how best to package and deliver the intervention to meet the needs of the patient population and treatment setting, ensure treatment adherence, and increase successful dissemination. For example, Kirk Strosahl and Patricia Robinson have pioneered the integration of brief, time-limited ACT sessions into primary care medical practices with good success (Robinson & Strosahl, 2009). Lilian Dindo and colleagues have developed and piloted one-day ACT workshops aimed at improving mental health and functioning outcomes among patients with co-occurring migraine and co-occurring depression, among distressed patients at risk for cardiovascular disease, among patients undergoing surgery, and among patients with inflammatory bowel disease (Dindo, Van Liew, & Arch, 2017; Dindo, Weinrib, & Marchman, 2019). Joanna Arch and colleagues have developed blended or hybrid ACT interventions for advanced cancer patients, which alternate in-person group sessions with online modules and daily check-ins completed independently between group sessions (Arch, Fishbein, et al., 2020). Together, these approaches point toward ACT's ability to help patients within resource-limited medical contexts as well as within serious disease contexts that present barriers to extended face-to-face interventions.

EMBEDDING INTO MEDICAL SETTINGS

Many of the personal and structural barriers to providing mental health care to patients with CHCs can be addressed by embedding behavioral health interventions into existing primary or specialty medical care settings. As discussed, most patients with CHC frequently visit these clinical settings and have established relationships with these treatment teams. The benefits of integrating medical and mental health care include improved care coordination between treating providers, lessened patient burden, reduced stigma, and improved access to mental health services. Offering integrated care that holistically addresses these co-occurring conditions is often more acceptable to patients and demonstrates the equal importance of care for physical and mental health symptoms. Finally, embedding mental health services in medical settings may offer the unique opportunity for patients with the same CHC to connect through group-based services in these settings. Such condition-specific groups can reduce common illness-related experiences such as stigma, isolation, and feeling misunderstood by others.

ONE-DAY WORKSHOPS

A one-day workshop is another valuable approach for working with patients with CHCs. To begin, offering a "workshop" format rather than "therapy" is more approachable for patients for whom seeking mental health care is associated with stigma. A workshop is also better suited for primary or specialty care settings where patients often present with different expectations than patients explicitly seeking mental health care. Most patients with CHC make multiple visits to primary care annually (U.S. Department of Health and Human Services, 2017). Thus, embedding a "workshop" within a primary care setting can be a valuable way to improve access to behavioral health services and reduce the effects of stigma.

A one-day workshop ensures treatment adherence and completion. A meta-analysis of 125 studies on outpatient psychotherapy found that 50 percent of patients drop out of treatment prematurely and nearly 40 percent terminate treatment after the first or second visit (Wierzbicki & Pekanik, 1986; Wierzbicki & Pekanik, 1993). Such high dropout levels are problematic because patients continue to experience symptoms and thus may increase health care utilization in other ways. An effective intervention that can be completed in one day (6–7 hours) would address these problems while providing patients with more contact time than is routinely available in outpatient settings. As such, it provides an attractive alternative to the regularly prescribed weekly psychotherapy treatments. A one-day workshop is also more accessible and feasible than weekly treatments, particularly for patients who live in rural communities (Arcury et al., 2005; Cully, Jameson, Phillips, Kunik, & Fortney, 2010). Compared with urban Americans, rural residents tend to be in poorer health and face more difficulty accessing health services (Arcury et al., 2005).

Dindo and colleagues have developed 1-day (5–6 hours) ACT workshops for patients at risk for cardiac disease; with inflammatory bowel disease; polytrauma (mild traumatic brain injury, chronic pain, and psychopathology); migraine; and undergoing orthopedic surgery and therefore are at risk for developing chronic pain and prolonged opioid abuse. Across all studies we teamed up with a corresponding medical specialist (e.g., neurologist, gastrointestinal physician, orthopedic surgeon) and tailored the intervention to meet the needs of the specific patient population. We embedded the workshop within the relevant specialty clinic, and all patients who attended the workshop completed it. We also obtained promising preliminary effects on functioning, physical symptom severity, and symptoms of distress (Dindo et al., 2017).

BLENDED INTERVENTIONS

Blended, hybrid, or multimodal interventions integrate "multiple methods of information delivery into a single learning system" (Cucciare, Weingardt, & Villafranca, 2008, p. 299). For example, a single intervention might include both in-person and online components. Compared to fully in-person interventions, blended approaches offer a higher intervention dose while requiring fewer provider resources by leveraging other learning modalities. Compared to *entirely online* interventions in behavioral medicine populations with no provider contact, which typically show high attrition or do not impact the targeted outcomes (e.g., Hong, Pena-Purcell, & Ory, 2012), blended approaches that include some provider contact have been shown to result in lower attrition and better mental health outcomes (Baumeister, Reichler, Munzinger, & Lin, 2014). Multiple ACT interventions have used blended approaches (e.g., Jarvela-Reijonen et al., 2018; Pedersen et al., 2019), one of which we highlight next.

Arch and colleagues (2020) developed a blended intervention for adults with metastatic cancer experiencing significant anxiety or depression symptoms. The original intervention consisted of four face-to-face groups sessions that alternated with online modules and check-ins completed independently between the group sessions. One advantage of this blended format is that the group helped to hold patients accountable for completing the online modules at home between group sessions. Though automated reminders were sent, group members knew they would need to report what they learned from the online modules to one another and group leaders each week, creating a peer- and provider-based accountability structure. In a pilot study (Arch, Fishbein, et al., 2020), despite dealing with often intensive and debilitating treatment for metastatic cancer, participants completed an average of 3.25 of the four group sessions (SD = 0.68) and 2.92 of the three online modules (SD = 0.28), plus three online check-ins per week throughout the intervention, suggesting the feasibility and acceptability of the online components. Thus, this blended approach significantly increased the intervention dose beyond the group sessions without relying on additional provider resources. A fully powered randomized trial is currently underway.

In summary, CHCs often present numerous complex and enduring obstacles to pursuing life values, prompting avoidance-based coping in patients. Both personal and structural factors influence the way patients with CHC cope with their illness. Thus, to successfully help patients with CHC, an intervention would ideally (1) be transdiagnostic (i.e., apply to more than one condition, encompassing physical and emotional experiences); (2) target avoidance-based coping; (3) build on the patient's values and goals to motivate them to make difficult decisions; (4) be nonstigmatizing; and (5) be delivered efficiently and flexibly alongside medical care. ACT is a strong match in each of these areas and thus is well equipped to help patients skillfully cope with CHCs. As a comprehensive and flexibly delivered treatment model, ACT helps to motivate and maintain health behavior change as well as to identify, evaluate, and address obstacles to such change.

Evidence Supporting ACT for Chronic Health Conditions

Accumulating evidence suggests that ACT is helpful both in promoting health behavior change and in enhancing adaptive coping and reducing distress among those with medical disease—the primary areas addressed by behavioral medicine. A comprehensive review of this literature is beyond the scope of this article. Instead, we first provide a broad overview of the ACT reviews and meta-analyses that include studies of CHCs, followed by a more detailed review of literature in two of the most common and debilitating CHCs—cancer and heart disease, and finally, we provide a brief overview of the ACT research in patients with diabetes and multiple sclerosis—two areas that have several ACT randomized controlled trials (RCTs).

Overview of ACT Research across CHCs

As of November 2020, there were over 400 published RCTs on ACT. A recent meta-analytic review of 20 meta-analyses of ACT (Gloster, Walder, Levin, Twohig, & Karekla, 2020), based on 133 studies and over 12,000 participants, concluded that ACT is efficacious for a broad range of clients, including those with mental health (e.g., depression, anxiety, psychosis, substance abuse, eating disorders), medical (e.g., chronic pain, cancer, epilepsy, diabetes), behavioral (e.g., smoking, weight loss), and other issues (e.g., stigma, parenting, human prejudice). ACT was nonsignificantly different from established "gold standard" interventions such as cognitive-behavioral therapy and superior to other active conditions (e.g., treatment as usual) or inactive controls (e.g., waitlist). Variability exists across meta-analyses with regard to the magnitude and significance of effect sizes for ACT, with generally medium effect sizes compared with treatment as usual, but with larger effect sizes compared with waitlist control.

A 2016 systematic review of ACT across many chronic disease and long-term health conditions (e.g., HIV, cancer, epilepsy) included eight RCTs, four pre-/post-designs, and six case studies. Outcomes included quality of life, symptom control, distress, and coping processes across these diseases/conditions. Results were promising for areas including parenting of children with long-term conditions, control of seizures in epilepsy, psychological flexibility, and possibly disease self-management. The authors caution, however, that more high-quality research is needed to show that ACT is a well-established intervention for chronic disease and long-term health conditions (Graham, Gouick, Krahe, & Gillanders, 2016).

A meta-analysis of the efficacy of ACT for clinically significant mental or physical health conditions, which included 39 RCTs and nearly 2000 patients, concluded that ACT is more effective than treatment as usual or placebo (effect size = 0.57) and as effective as established psychotherapeutic interventions for anxiety, depression, addiction, and somatic health problems (A-Tjak et al., 2015). Of the 39 studies included in the meta-analysis, 15 were for "somatic health problems" and included RCTs of patients with CHCs such as diabetes, tinnitus, fibromyalgia, chronic headache, cancer, and chronic pain. In a subanalysis of these 15 studies with a total of 683 participants, ACT was superior to control conditions with an effect size of 0.58 on the primary outcome measures.

Given that CHCs often present patients with physical changes and symptoms that cannot be changed or fully influenced, an intervention that enhances quality of life or satisfaction even in the presence of symptoms is particularly important. Indeed, many ACT treatment trials examine the impact of ACT on well-being and life satisfaction. A recent systematic review and meta-analysis of RCTs examined the impact of ACT on subjective well-being in adults with various physical and mental health issues (Stenhoff, Steadman, Nevitt, Benson, & White, 2020). The review included 11 studies with a total of 357 international participants, entailing individual and group formats, guided self-help interventions and online studies, and active comparisons and control comparisons. Of the 11 studies reviewed, 6 recruited patients with chronic health conditions and 4 included individuals with distress and/or depression. Overall, the ACT interventions improved subjective well-being in clinical (e.g., women with multiple sclerosis [MS] recruited from MS society, patients who had experienced a stroke recruited from stroke clinics) and nonclinical (e.g., individuals with chronic pain recruited from the general population) populations. The A-Tjak meta-analysis referenced previously also conducted subanalyses on secondary outcomes of life satisfaction/quality-of-life measures. Included in their analyses were 19 studies and 931 participants. Results similarly found that, CT was superior to control conditions on life satisfaction across pooled time and types of disorders (effect size = 0.37).

Research examining the impact of ACT interventions on a range of specific CHC populations is growing rapidly and includes patients with cancer, heart disease, diabetes, multiple sclerosis, epilepsy, tinnitus, migraines and other headaches, HIV, irritable bowel syndrome, inflammatory bowel disease, kidney disease, stroke survivors, patients undergoing major surgeries, traumatic brain injury, chronic fatigue syndrome, lupus, tuberculosis, and others. Among these populations, the most studied have been cancer (over 15 RCTs), diabetes (at least 5 RCTs and several more uncontrolled trials), and multiple sclerosis (at least 6 RCTs and several more uncontrolled trials). Literature on these conditions will be briefly reviewed here, as well as cardiovascular disease as another of the most common CHCs. At this time, one to three ACT treatment trials in each of the remaining CHC populations have been studied, with most having fewer than 40 participants and inactive control conditions. With few exceptions (e.g., migraine study with n = 104; inflammatory bowel disease study with n = 122), most of these studies are pilot trials with a small number of participants and inactive control conditions, precluding robust empirical understanding of the potential role of ACT in a broader array of CHCs. Enhancing the methodological rigor of studies and including larger sample sizes, active comparators, and standardized measures of well-being will strengthen our understanding of the role of ACT in cultivating the well-being of patients living with CHCs (Stenhoff et al., 2020).

Specific Review of ACT for Cancer

In terms of ACT treatment trials for specific chronic illness populations, cancer has the largest literature base. In one review, Gonzales et al. (2019) examined the usefulness of ACT among oncological patients. Across 19 studies, the authors concluded that ACT resulted in improved emotional health, quality of life, and psychological flexibility among patients with cancer.

A systematic review of ACT in adult cancer survivors, which included 13 studies and over 500 patients, concluded that ACT significantly reduced distress and fear of cancer recurrence and improved quality of life and psychological flexibility (Mathew, Doorenbos, Jang, & Hershberger, 2020). The authors recommended increased attention to other troubling symptoms among cancer survivors (e.g., pain and insomnia) and enhanced rigor of future studies (e.g., blinding, random assignment). They also suggested that embedding ACT into a comprehensive posttreatment survivorship program may improve the well-being of patients.

In addition to studies examining the impact of ACT interventions in oncological patients, several large studies have been published examining relations between ACT processes (or similar constructs) and a range of symptoms. For example, one large cross-sectional study of hematological cancer survivors (n = 922) found acceptance to be negatively associated with fatigue and cognitive impairment (Kuba et al., 2019). In fact, a recent meta-analysis found acceptance of cancer to be a mediator for distress tolerance and depression in cancer patients (Secinti, Tometich, Johns, & Mosher, 2019). Another meta-analysis found that emotional avoidance is related to elevated levels of psychological distress among cancer survivors (Baziliansky & Cohen, 2020).

In a 3-month longitudinal study of 178 patients with cancer, a strong relationship was found between meaning and purpose at baseline and lower levels of demoralization and depression at follow-up. These results suggest that values-focused interventions may enhance the well-being of patients with cancer (Vehling et al., 2011). Among 75 patients with breast cancer, illness-related cognitive fusion (e.g., body dissatisfaction, shame) was associated with depressive symptoms. The impact of shame on depressed mood was significantly explained by chronic illness-related cognitive fusion. These findings suggest that body image and chronic illness shame can lead to breast cancer patients' depression symptoms and that chronic illness-related cognitive fusion plays a central role in these relationships (Trindade, Marta-Simoes, Ferreira, & Pinto-Gouveia, 2018a). In a group of 82 breast cancer patients, avoidance was related to depressive symptoms, and part of this effect was explained by lower committed actions (Trindade, Marta-Simoes, Ferreira, & Pinto-Gouveia, 2018b). Jointly, these studies suggest that enhancing acceptance, committed action, values, and defusion in psychotherapeutic interventions could improve the mental health and quality of life of patients with cancer.

Specific Review of ACT for Cardiovascular Disease

A leading cause of death and disability in the United States is heart failure, and this is an emerging area for ACT and other acceptance/mindfulness based-treatment trials research. Although not focused on ACT specifically, a recent meta-analysis, including 16 studies with 1476 patients, addressed mindfulness-based interventions for adults with cardiovascular disease who had experienced a cardiac event (Scott-Sheldon et al., 2020). Examined treatments included MBSR, MBCT, and mindfulness meditation, with only one study including ACT components. All studies had a comparison condition and assessed psychological or physiological (e.g., systolic or diastolic blood pressure) outcomes. Compared to controls, participants who received a mindfulness-based intervention reported greater improvements in psychological outcomes (i.e., anxiety, depression, distress, and perceived stress) with moderate effect sizes (d = 0.49–0.64) and greater reductions in systolic blood pressure (effect size d = 0.89).

Currently, many small pilot studies have examined the impact of ACT on patients with cardiovascular disease or patients who are significantly at risk for cardiovascular disease.

For example, a recent quasi-experimental study of 45 patients with cardiovascular disease who were referred to cardiac rehabilitation compared ACT (eight one-hour sessions), Guided Mental Imagery (GMI; 10, 45-minute sessions), and no-treatment (Shahabi, Asgari, & Makvandi, 2020). Both ACT and GMI resulted in greater resilience at the one-month follow-up compared to the control condition. In addition, ACT outperformed GMI in resilience (Shahabi et al., 2020). A study of 30 cardiovascular patients with a history of myocardial infarction or open-heart surgery in the previous month were randomly assigned to ACT plus rehabilitation or to rehabilitation only (Abdollahi et al., 2020). Postintervention, patients in the ACT group exhibited significantly greater improvements in physical symptoms, anxiety and depression, social functioning, hopefulness, and meaning in life (Abdollahi et al., 2020). A longer follow-up period, the inclusion of process measures, and more information about the intervention would have strengthened this study. A series of small ACT treatment trials (approximately n = 30/per trial) conducted in Iran with patients with cardiovascular disease found promising preliminary findings on anger (Kheyran-Alnesa, Mirzaian, & Yar-Ali, 2018), resilience, and quality of life (Mohamadi, Mirzaian, & Dousti, 2019), marital conflicts (Khaneiee, Jazayeri, Bahrami, Montazeri, & Etemadi, 2019), emotion regulation (Sheibani, Sheibani, Amreei, & Masrour, 2019), and illness perception (Khosroshahi, Mirzaian, & Hasanzadeh, 2019).

Dindo et al. (2015) randomly assigned patients with cardiovascular risk factors (e.g., hypertension, dyslipidemia, diabetes) and clinically significant anxiety or depression to a one-day ACT plus Illness Management workshop (ACT-IM; n = 26) or to treatment as usual (TAU; n = 14). At the 6-month follow-up, participants in the ACT-IM condition exhibited significantly greater improvements in depressive and anxiety symptoms. They also exhibited significant improvements in quality-of-life domains. Importantly, the effects of the ACT-IM intervention on depression at 6 months were mediated by improvement in psychological flexibility.

In a study examining the effects of acceptance-oriented versus evaluative emotional processing on cardiovascular habituation and recovery, 81 participants were randomly assigned to write about an ongoing stressful experience while either evaluating the appropriateness of their emotional response, attending to their emotions in an accepting way, or describing the objective details of the experience. Results indicated that writing about emotions in an accepting manner resulted in more efficient heart rate habituation compared to writing about emotions in an evaluative way. These results suggested that evaluating one's emotional responses may have negative consequences for cardiovascular health (Low, Stanton, & Bower, 2008).

Brief Review of ACT for Type 2 Diabetes and Multiple Sclerosis

Type 2 Diabetes. The first study utilizing the 1-day ACT workshop approach enrolled 81 patients with type 2 diabetes (Gregg, Callaghan, Hayes, & Glenn-Lawson, 2007). Patients were randomized to either 7 hours of diabetes education (n = 38) or 4 hours of education plus 3 hours of ACT (n = 43). Three months after the intervention, patients who received the combined intervention exhibited lower blood glucose levels (effect size = 0.35), better diabetes self-care (effect size = 0.68), and higher levels of diabetes-related acceptance (effect size = 0.78). Notably, acceptance and improved self-care behaviors mediated the relationship between group assignment and blood glucose. Since this successful RCT in 2007, several RCTs have been conducted for patients with type 2 diabetes. In one RCT, 106 patients were randomly assigned to education alone (n = 53) or to education plus group-based ACT (n = 53) over a period of 10 sessions. At 3-month follow-up, the ACT group reported better diabetes self-care and levels of HbA1C (Hemoglobin A1c, a measure of glycemic control; Shayeghian, Hassanabadl, Aguilar-Vafale, Amiri, & Ali Besharat, 2016). In another RCT, 118 patients were randomly assigned to a nurse-led education workshop, nurse-led education plus ACT workshop, or usual care (Whitehead et al., 2017). At 6-month follow-up, HbA1c increased in the control group and decreased in both intervention groups, but this change was statistically significant only in the education group. The participants in this study had suffered from type 2 diabetes for an average of 10 years. Several other studies enrolling 50 participants or fewer have also been done and generally favor ACT for diabetes management outcomes and coping.

Multiple Sclerosis: ACT Research in Patients with MS in an Emergent Area. The largest ACT pilot RCT in MS included 39 patients, examined both qualitative and quantitative outcomes, and compared ACT to relaxation (each condition had seven weekly group sessions). Results suggested that participants favored the ACT condition qualitatively, but there were no significant differences in quantitative physical and mental outcomes (Giovannetti et al., 2020). The remaining RCTs in this area have generally found positive effects of ACT on the well-being and functioning of patients with MS. However, sample sizes were small (no more than 30 participants per study), and several compared ACT to no treatment (e.g., Yazdanbakhsh et al., 2016). The few studies that compared ACT to another active condition (e.g., ACT versus logotherapy in 30 women with MS) found similar effects across the active conditions (Azimi, Hoseini, Najafi, & Rafieenia, 2018). Overall, much remains to be studied in the area of MS.

Application of ACT Processes to Patients with Chronic Health Conditions

In this section, we describe the six ACT hexaflex processes and how they apply to the experiences of patients with CHC. We first illustrate application of these processes across the common and collective experiences of patients with CHC in order to demonstrate the broad relevance of hexaflex processes across aspects of illness adjustment. Then, we apply the hexaflex more specifically to the contexts of cancer and heart disease as two of the most common, debilitating CHCs for which ACT has been applied.

The ACT approach posits that significant human suffering is due to a lack of behavioral flexibility and effectiveness, which emerges from experiential avoidance, cognitive entanglement, difficulty with perspective-taking, loss of contact with the present, and failure to take needed behavioral steps in accord with core values. Powerful alternatives are available in the ACT model through the skills of acceptance, cognitive distancing, perspective-taking, mindfulness, values, and committed action. Although the content of an ACT intervention would naturally differ across conditions and individual patients, these identified ACT processes can help us understand and address common and diverse problems and symptoms among patients with CHCs.

As noted previously, despite significant variability in patient experiences, there are indeed some overarching frequent patient experiences across CHCs. Table 21.2 identifies several of these common experiences faced by patients with CHCs and components of the ACT hexaflex related to these experiences.

The hexaflex processes aim to cultivate greater psychological flexibility, which has been defined as "the ability to contact the present moment more fully as a conscious human being and to either change or persist when doing so serves valued ends" (Hayes, Luoma, Bond, Masuda, & Lillis, 2006, p. 7). Based on the hexaflex model of ACT, Table 21.3 more specifically illustrates forms that psychological inflexibility and flexibility can take in two common CHCs: cancer and heart disease. This directly illustrates how core ACT processes can be applied to understand common patient experiences within different diseases.

Acceptance. Chronic diseases such as heart disease and cancer typically offer many physical and psychosocial challenges for patients and their families. Thus, it is not surprising that some patients and families might respond some or all of the time with experiential avoidance—pushing away or avoiding the challenging thoughts, beliefs, fears, images, and bodily sensations associated with the illness and the contexts that engender them. This response can take many forms, including denying the severity or implications of the illness and the loss and grief it entails, as well as the examples outlined in Table 21.3. Actively accepting the disease often includes acknowledging its severity, symptoms, and treatment, and engaging in one's care in accordance with one's values. For example, in advanced cancer, this might include the willingness to acknowledge that one has a serious disease and perhaps, if appropriate, accept that the disease can be managed to varying degrees but ultimately is incurable. This acknowledgment is one that only a minority of patients with advanced cancer currently make (Weeks et al., 2012). In heart disease, this acknowledgment might involve accepting that one will need to monitor vital signs and take medications indefinitely. In all cases, active acceptance ideally paves the way toward directing one's current and future care and health behaviors toward choices that are aligned with one's core values.

Defusion. Individuals facing chronic disease, like all individuals, can be readily triggered and "hooked" by rigid beliefs, rules, stories, fantasies, and thoughts that dominate behavioral choices. In addition to the examples of cognitive fusion illustrated in Table 21.3, common examples include the following: "I must never show weakness," pretending that everything is fine and refusing to discuss challenging aspects of the illness under rigid rules such as "out of sight, out of mind" or beliefs such as "I can't possibly face this" or admit one's feelings

Table 21.2 Common Patient Experiences across Chronic Health Conditions

Patient Experience	Related Hexaflex Processes
Coping with a diagnosis	
• Loss of control over one's body and life • Uncertainty and worry about the future • Altered sense of meaning and purpose • Changing relationship with religion or spirituality • Grief and loss over life changes • Guilt and regret over life experiences	• Experiential avoidance of unpleasant thoughts, emotions, memories • Lack of values clarity • Dominance of conceptualized past or feared future
Coping with the disease and its treatment	
• Painful or unpleasant symptoms of the disease • Making difficult treatment decisions • Adherence to complex medical treatment regimens and lifestyle restrictions • Health behavior changes • Side effects of treatments • Burden and sacrifice of treatments (e.g., financial and time investment)	• Experiential avoidance of difficulty symptoms or side effects • Lack of values clarity • Inaction, or avoidant persistence
Dealing with stigma and change in sense of self	
• Self-stigma of being a person with this diagnosis • Stigma of this diagnosis imposed by or perceived from others • Impact of stigma on connecting with others	• Cognitive fusion • Attachment to the conceptualized self
Changing roles	
• Changes in relationships with family and friends • Sense of isolation • Changes in relationship to one's own body, body image, and sexuality • Changes in ability to maintain work or other roles • Increased reliance on others	• Cognitive fusion • Attachment to the conceptualized self • Lack of values • Dominance of conceptualized past or feared future
Narrowing of focus	
• Shifting priorities • Giving up on goals and dreams rather than flexibly adapting them • Increased time spent on illness and management • Decreased time or functional ability to pursue values • Viewing life in terms of the disease and being a person with the disease	• Cognitive fusion • Attachment to the conceptualized self • Lack of values • Dominance of conceptualized past or feared future • Inaction, or avoidant persistence
Death and dying	
• Sense of a foreshortened future • Awareness of one's own mortality • Balancing quality of life and length of life • Processing life experiences and legacy • Unfinished business • Existential issues	• Experiential avoidance of unpleasant thoughts, emotions, memories, physical symptoms • Lack of values • Dominance of conceptualized past or feared future • Cognitive fusion

Table 21.3 Examples of how the core ACT processes may apply to two common chronic health conditions

Psychological Inflexibility	Psychological Flexibility
Experiential Avoidance—escaping from, avoiding, or trying to control, unpleasant experiences such as difficult symptoms or side effects, thoughts, emotions, memories, and body sensations Heart disease: Patient won't take medication because doing so reminds him he has a chronic disease. Feels overwhelmed by the tasks, so just says "forget it." Cancer: Patient isolates and avoids socializing with family or friends; spends most days at home or in bed so others don't see her sick or ask about her health.	**Acceptance**—becoming more willing to experience whatever thoughts, emotions, memories, and body sensations that show up when moving in a valued direction Heart disease: Patient takes medication and exercises, even though it initially causes distress and anxiety. Cancer: Patient engages with family and friends directly, despite concern about how others will respond to her changed appearance and worries about the questions she'll receive.
Cognitive Fusion—being "hooked" by thoughts, rules, beliefs, and stories and letting them determine what you do in your life, even when they are not helpful in terms of moving you in the direction of your values and goals Heart disease: Patient believes he is worthless and just "old, fat, and useless." Cancer: Patient believes she looks ugly; that things will never be the same as before cancer; that cancer has alienated her from others and stolen all she enjoys.	**Defusion**—stepping back from the thoughts, images, memories, and body sensations that pose as barriers, and noticing them as thoughts, images, memories, and body sensations that need not determine what one does. Heart disease: Patient recognizes that he has automatic thoughts that "hook him" and often lead him to behave in ways that reinforce these thoughts. Begins to notice these "as thoughts" that need to be obeyed. Cancer: Patient notices and names the worry and fear that show up whenever she leaves the house, responds by compassionately allowing the worries to be there without allowing them to dominate her behavior, and goes out to meet her friends.
Dominance of Conceptualized Past or Feared Future—being preoccupied by past or future events and experiences; unaware of one's own ongoing experience Heart disease: Patient constantly worries about health and dying; also worries about his children and whether he will be around for them. Cancer: Patient is obsessed with what she has done in the past to cause this disease and what the future might bring in terms of her illness.	**Contact with the Present Moment**—being aware of your immediate experience right here and right now rather than being preoccupied with past and future events and experiences. Heart disease: Patient is getting better at noticing when he is lost in his mind and disconnected from the present moment. He is learning how to bring his attention back to the present moment when he is with his children. Cancer: Patient starts to accept the uncertainty that she will never know what caused her cancer or what the future holds. She opens up to engaging more fully with family, friends, and her health care team in the present.

(*continued*)

Table 21.3 *Continued*	
Attachment to Conceptualized Self—being "hooked" to stories of who we are; "the story of me"; unable to step back from self-conceptualizations and see them for what they are Heart disease: Patient is attached to the idea that he is now a "sick person" that got here because of his failures, and that his life is now all about the illness. Cancer: Patient feels her appearance lowers her self-worth; believes she must return to pre-cancer activity levels or else she has failed.	**Self-as-Context**—taking the perspective of the observing self to notice one's ongoing experiences, including noticing limiting self-stories. Heart disease: Patient begins to appreciate that he is not just a patient with heart disease. He is also a parent, a friend, a spouse, and a colleague. He can still be involved in many parts of his life. Cancer: Patient begins to accept that cancer recovery takes time. She mourns her losses, noticing the narrow ways she defined herself and the many forms of connection still available to her. She starts to define her roles in more flexible ways.
Lack of Values Clarity—not knowing what matters; doing what you're "supposed" to do; or avoiding the feelings of vulnerability you get when you think about values Heart disease: Patient is narrowly focused on his illness and has been disengaged from life since he was diagnosed with diabetes and high blood pressure. Cancer: Patient is so thrown by her cancer diagnosis that cancer and the possibility of dying is all she thinks about. She disconnects from sources of meaning and connection, and her life becomes very narrow.	**Values**—clarifying and strengthening connection to what really matters; values are what you choose to care about; choosing in this moment to care about something Heart disease: Patient connects with the importance of being present and providing for his children and wife, as well as contributing to his community. Cancer: Patient clarifies her core values of being a loving wife, mother, and friend and engaging with her religious community.
Inaction, Impulsivity, or Avoidant Persistence—being unwilling to do what it takes to pursue a valued life; doing what's easy or less difficult in the moment, rather than what will be more difficult but more meaningful Heart disease: Patient doesn't exercise or take his medications and stops spending quality time with his children. He is living on automatic pilot from day to day. Cancer: Patient stops going out with friends or taking calls from concerned family members; stops attending religious services.	**Committed Action**—engaging in the actual behavior that our values require; returning to a pattern of valued living when you find yourself moving away; "the gentle turn back" Heart disease: Patient chooses to take his medications and to exercise so that he can be healthier for his family. He consciously chooses to attend more family gatherings. Cancer: Patient reinvests in caring for her children, spending time with her husband, attending religious services, and engaging with her community.

about it. For family members and patients alike, these rigid beliefs and thoughts can impede seeking much-needed help in managing the effects of chronic disease. We also commonly encounter beliefs based on the theme of "I can't allow any negative thoughts in, or it will make me sicker." These beliefs lead to chronic repression and denial of the full range of experience with the illness and to forced attempts at total positivity. Using cognitive defusion skills to unhook oneself from rigid rules and beliefs can free up much-needed energy to engage in vital life activities and self-care. This is particularly important when managing chronic diseases that are often associated with enduring fatigue (Bower, 2005; MacAllister & Krupp, 2005), a condition that, in our experience, is worsened by efforts to constantly push away unacceptable thoughts and feelings.

Present Moment Focus. If one is dominated by coping with a chronic illness, particularly an illness with a perceived poor prognosis, it would make sense to be dominated by a feared future or to be obsessed with what one could have done differently to prevent the illness. Thus, ACT's emphasis on contacting the present moment can be particularly helpful, yet challenging, in these contexts. Table 21.3 illustrates the importance of cultivating mindful attention and grounding in the present, as well as practicing mindful acceptance toward past actions and the future uncertainty posed by chronic disease. These skills can help individuals skillfully deal with past- and future-focused regret, guilt, and fear in a way that ultimately refocuses them on what they can do in the present.

Self-as-Context. Present moment focus intersects with self-as-context, the reverse of which is attachment to a conceptualized self. Given the numerous changes that chronic illness can make in the body and its functioning, it is understandable that many individuals with CHC face a dual challenge. First, they have been labeled with a serious disease, which can radically shift their identity and generate so much fear and uncertainty that focusing on other sources of identity becomes difficult (Mathieson & Stam, 1995). Reinforcing this notion is the fact that they are often treated as "patients" by medical providers, whom they now see more frequently. Second, they understandably remain attached to the physical, mental, and role functioning and appearance they had prior to the onset of illness, particularly when illness diagnosis is sudden and treatment is intensive. They notice the sometimes sudden and dramatic discrepancies between who they seemed then and who they seem to be now. Mindfully stepping back and observing the moment-by-moment flow of experience, cultivating a transcendent sense of self, and flexibly maintaining identities and connections beyond the disease itself—self-as-context processes—can help to counter narrowing forms of self-identity that can keep individuals stuck in a single, rigid, and limited identity.

Values and Committed Action. Finally, values and committed action are core processes not only for coping with challenging emotions and thoughts that CHC can trigger, but also for clarifying motivation and committing to health behavior changes that might be needed to manage the illness and improve its trajectory. Thus, as illustrated, in Table 21.3, connecting with core values and committing to align one's actions with those values can help individuals with CHC to move toward taking charge of their current and future care, including adhering to medication and treatment regimens, initiating and maintaining healthy behavior changes such as smoking cessation (Bricker, Watson, Mull, Sullivan, & Heffner, 2020) or weight loss (Forman et al., 2016), and engaging in advance care planning (Arch, Fishbein, et al., 2020). That is, individuals can begin to explore, communicate, and document their values, goals, and preferences for future medical care if they become unable to clearly communicate them for themselves. When conducting committed action work with individuals facing chronic illness, we emphasize the need for significant flexibility in actualizing values within challenging contexts that may include physical or mental limitations related to ongoing functional declines, financial limitations given mounting medical bills, and discrepancies between patients and family members in facing and communicating about the illness. Given these challenges, we also highlight a strong orientation toward self-compassion.

For example, in a recent trial for anxious cancer survivors (Arch et al., in press), individuals committed each week to doing a small, concrete-valued action, recorded barriers to or facilitators of this action, and then asked themselves: "No matter what happened, how can I cultivate compassion for myself?" As participants tended to be self-critical about cancer treatment recovery time and their limited physical and mental energy, group sessions discussed how to treat oneself with kindness when they were unable to meet weekly valued action commitments. For most participants, self-kindness seemed to offer a new, flexible form of perspective-taking. The trial study also emphasized a sense of shared or common humanity throughout the intervention, a key component of Neff's (2003) conceptualization of self-compassion, which appeared to facilitate acceptance and defusion. Future studies could test these relationships directly.

Challenges and Future Directions

Challenges

One of the enduring frontiers in this work remains how to best integrate behavioral interventions such as ACT into routine care in medical settings. The skillsets of mental health professionals prepare them to effectively collaborate and even lead interdisciplinary teams. However, integration into medical settings is an adjustment for many practitioners and requires increased flexibility and acculturation to medical settings. Doing these interventions in a medical setting requires the cooperation of the relevant specialty area and particularly strong support from physicians to refer patients and encourage them to attend. We have found that it can take some persistence to find the right medical partner, but, once a match is made, it is a highly rewarding experience for all parties. This work also requires that the mental health profession have a general understanding of the medical condition at hand and the associated behavioral challenges. Such information can be obtained quite effectively from a specialist with up-to-date knowledge of the medical condition or from scientific resources or continuing education opportunities. The therapist can digest the information and make it more user-friendly for patients. Providing basic illness education can help enhance the ACT work; and ACT work can enhance commitment to engaging in illness management. For example, keeping the value of family front and center often provides the motivation needed to engage in a difficult endeavor because the patient wants to be healthier for their family.

When conducting ACT interventions, it is important to ideally work in a principle-based manner rather than depend entirely on a protocol that tells you exactly what to do and when to do it. Techniques and procedures need to be selected and adapted spontaneously and flexibly to fit the needs of the moment, so therapists need a full bag of tricks and a willingness to improvise. Therapists need to be skilled in engaging patients in the work and motivating them to enhance their health behaviors in the service of living a more fulfilling life.

Future Directions

The research to date on the role of ACT in medical conditions is encouraging and merits further study. It is still unclear if the entire ACT treatment package is needed to improve medical outcomes or if specific ACT principles would be sufficient for change. Related to this issue is the question of whether we still don't know if specific ACT principles should be highlighted more for particular clinical problems or patients. For example, focusing on the acceptance/mindfulness processes of ACT may be particularly valuable in conditions associated with unavoidable pain such as migraine or surgical recovery. In contrast, emphasizing committed action and values-based behavior may be more critical for medical conditions that require significant self-management such as diabetes and cardiovascular disease. Some of these questions can be explored further with dismantling studies and with more explicit assessments of mediators and moderators of change. Understanding the specific mechanisms or processes that mediate clinical improvement in outcomes will allow us to optimize our intervention by emphasizing the components responsible for change and eliminating nonactive ingredients.

An outstanding question also remains about the added value of an ACT intervention, over and above a supportive and illness education/management intervention. An intervention focused on providing support and illness education (only) requires less training and fewer resources than an ACT or another active therapy such as CBT. A recent study of patients with migraine showed that support plus illness education (group workshop) led to improvements in mental health and functioning. At the same time, the ACT intervention led to greater reduction in anxiety and depression (Dindo et al., 2020). More work is needed to gain a better understanding of which patients benefit from support or education only and which need more active coping skills.

The duration and frequency of ACT treatment trials vary significantly. More research is needed to answer the questions of how much is enough? Which patients benefit from brief approaches and which patients need more? Relatedly, when an ACT treatment fails to achieve the expected or hoped-for results, we need to better understand what led to this failure. What patient factors influence outcomes? And what therapist factors are needed for success? Few studies have begun to explore such questions. For example, in a trial examining the impact of a one-day intervention on postsurgical pain and opioid use among at-risk patients (by virtue of having significant distress or pain), those who had complications following surgery did not benefit from the intervention as much as those without complications. It is possible that patients experiencing surgical complications require added support or booster sessions (Dindo et al., 2018).

The way health care providers deliver care is changing rapidly to adapt to technological advances and patient preferences. To expand the scope and reach of ACT interventions, we will need to adapt ACT protocols to a telehealth format. Telehealth interventions can reach and enhance care delivery for isolated (e.g., rural) and vulnerable or functionally impaired populations. Telehealth platforms allow providers and patients to share information through screen sharing and offer a provider a unique view of the patient's physical space. However, it is challenging to modify the usual in-person ACT interventions and exercises for an online format in a way that yields new and creative ways to connect with patients and communicate the ACT concepts virtually. In order to align with changes in the medical field, however, implementation of ACT-consistent telehealth will be essential. We have begun to test one-day ACT group workshops in a virtual format. It is yet to be seen if the power of this approach can be harnessed through a digital medium.

Additionally, smartphone applications and other mobile health approaches are increasingly considered part of a broader public health approach to care. Based on principles and interventions of evidence-based psychotherapies, such applications ("apps") may be intended either as a treatment adjunct (i.e., used in conjunction with traditional therapy) or as a standalone disease self-management platform. For example, the Department of Veterans Affairs and the Department of Defense have a collection of apps that anyone (including the general public) can download and use at no charge; these apps are based on evidence-based interventions such as ACT, CBT, CBT for insomnia, mindfulness, and prolonged exposure therapy. Although empirical analysis of the ACT treatment adjunct app in particular is lacking, systematic reviews of these collections of apps are promising (Gould et al., 2019; Owen et al., 2018). Treatment-companion apps are well received by clinicians, who perceive improved patient engagement in treatment protocols and possibly enhanced outcomes. Self-management apps are popular and well-received among patients, yet efficacy evidence is more limited. In the ACT literature, apps have primarily been used for health behavior change such as smoking cessation, with favorable outcomes for smoking quit rates and reduction rates (Bricker et al., 2017). Apps or other mobile health platforms such as text messaging interventions may be best utilized in blended treatment approaches to ensure provider oversight of their use. In this manner, they may be able to augment care or assist with relapse prevention. It is important to consider that health platforms may expand access and autonomy for some patients, such as those who cannot easily attend frequent in-person appointments, yet may present new challenges for others, such as older adults with less familiarity with the technology.

In order for psychological interventions to truly be considered a success, they need to be (1) effective and (2) disseminated. The early success of ACT interventions embedded in medical contexts is encouraging. We hope fellow practitioners can continue to widen the scope of practice settings as a means of reducing suffering and increasing valued living in behaviorally underserved medical populations. Future research should assess the cost effectiveness of such integrated approaches, which are anticipated to promote improved symptomatic and functional outcomes among comorbid patients at lower costs.

Broader dissemination of ACT principles in medical settings may also be approached through training allied members of an interdisciplinary health care team in select ACT interventions or ACT theory-informed interventions that are particularly suited to their clinical context. In particular, values and committed action represent high-impact ACT processes given their direct application to health care system priority areas of clinician and patient-shared decision making and patient-centered care. While discussion of values has long been part of palliative care to inform end-of-life preferences and goals of care, the call is increasingly being made to shift these conversations upstream in disease processes and to contextualize chronic disease treatment decision making in what matters most to patients (Bayliss et al., 2014). In this manner, disease management shifts from being the explicit goal to serving as one of several means to patient-identified valued actions, with potential to influence patient engagement and adherence and promote improved health and quality of life (Tinetti & Fried, 2004; Tinetti, Naik, & Dodson, 2016). While clearly distinct from delivering comprehensive ACT psychotherapy, flexible integration of select ACT concepts can expand the reach of ACT into behavioral medicine through shifting the way that chronic disease management is conceptualized by patients and health care teams. Emerging evidence in our work in this area among older adults with multiple CHCs suggests that eliciting patients' values and translating them into specific health outcome goals is clinically feasible for health care teams. Patients work with a trained member of the health care team to identify their primary goals based on what matters most to them (i.e., values) and to specify what they are willing (or unwilling) to do to achieve those outcomes (i.e., their health care preferences). The results of these discussions are shared with the patient's clinicians and are used to align health care decisions with patient priorities (Naik et al., 2018). Initial results suggest that this process is associated with decreases in treatment burden and unwanted health care and increases in care aligned with patients' priorities (Tinetti et al., 2019; Naik et al., 2018). Thus, training frontline staff (e.g., social workers) to elicit patient values and training physicians to integrate values-based goals into treatment decision making can lead to important outcomes for patients. These interventions also demonstrate the benefits of ACT-informed values discussions among patients without comorbid mental health diagnoses, further supporting the transdiagnostic application of ACT processes to medical symptom management.

Conclusion

Medical conditions influence and are influenced by mental health symptoms. Despite the high prevalence of comorbidity, existing treatments and service delivery approaches largely reflect fragmented, disease-specific care. Integrated transdiagnostic treatment for comorbid physical and mental health symptoms is an increasingly valued approach for improving whole-person patient health and quality of life. For example, the Agency for Healthcare Research and Quality recently identified inclusion of mental health treatment into health care as one of three key priorities for future research on patients with multiple chronic conditions (LeRoy et al., 2014). Further, a panel of comorbidity experts recently identified understanding contextual factors, such as patients' relationships, values, and goals, as a vital paradigm shift in the treatment of patients with multiple chronic conditions (Bayliss et al., 2014).

ACT is a transdiagnostic treatment model that meets each of these recent calls for more inclusive, tailored, and whole-person-centered health care. As a process-based and flexibly delivered approach, ACT represents a promising way to meet the heterogeneous needs and treatment preferences of patients with a broad range of problems, including medical, mental health, behavioral, and co-occurring physical and mental health symptoms. ACT directly addresses behavioral avoidance, a common problem in behavioral medicine. ACT attends to the values and goals of patients and teaches skills to flexibly pursue life values in spite of obstacles that arise, including the many obstacles presented by serious chronic disease. ACT has been effectively implemented in hospital settings, primary care clinics, and specialty care clinics. A rapidly evolving literature supports the preliminary feasibility, acceptability, and efficacy of brief ACT treatments, including those embedded in existing medical care settings. ACT interventions have been associated with improvements in medical, mental health, and behavioral outcomes, as well as overall functioning and quality of life. As medicine continues to recognize the centrality of mental health, well-being, and health behavior change to its overall mission, ACT's transdiagnostic, process-based approach and ability for flexible delivery ideally position it to address behavioral health care needs in diverse medical populations. This is an exciting time for ACT in behavioral medicine.

References

A-Tjak, J., Davis, M. L., Morina, N., Powers, M. B., Smits, J. A., & Emmelkamp, P. M. (2015). A meta-analysis of the efficacy of acceptance and commitment therapy for clinically relevant mental and physical health problems. *Psychotherapy and Psychosomatics, 84*(1), 30–36. doi:10.1159/000365764

Abdollahi, S. M., Rafiepoor, A., & Sabet, M. (2020). The effectiveness of acceptance and commitment therapy on mental health, hopefulness and meaningfulness in people with cardiovascular disease. *Iranian Journal of Health Psychology, 3*(1), 61–70.

Arch, J. J., Fishbein, J. N., Ferris, M. C., Mitchell, J. L., Levin, M. E., Slivjak, E. T., . . . Kutner, J. S. (2020). Acceptability, feasibility, and efficacy potential of a multimodal acceptance and commitment therapy intervention to address psychosocial and advance care planning needs among anxious and depressed adults with metastatic cancer. *Journal of Palliative Medicine, 23*(10), 1380–1385. doi:10.1089/jpm.2019.0398

Arch, J. J., Genung, S. R., Ferris, M. C., Kirk, A., Slivjak, E. T., Fishbein, J. N., . . . Stanton, A. L. (2020). Presence and predictors of anxiety disorder onset following cancer diagnosis among anxious cancer survivors. *Support Care Cancer, 28*(9), 4425–4433. doi:10.1007/s00520-020-05297-0

Arch, J. J., Mitchell, J. L., Genung, S. R., Judd, C. M., Andorsky, D. J., Bricker, J. B., & Stanton, A. L. (in press). Randomized trial of an acceptance and commitment therapy intervention for anxious cancer survivors in community clinics: Outcomes and moderators. *Journal of Consulting and Clinical Psychology, 89*(4), 327–340. doi:10.1037/ccp0000630

Arcury, T. A., Gesler, W. M., Preisser, J. S., Sherman, J., Spencer, J., & Perin, J. (2005). The effects of geography and spatial behavior on health care utilization among the residents of a rural region. *Health Service Research, 40*(1), 135–155. doi:10.1111/j.1475-6773.2005.00346.x

Arnow, B. A., Hunkeler, E. M., Blasey, C. M., Lee, J., Constantino, M. J., Fireman, B., . . . Hayward, C. (2006). Comorbid depression, chronic pain, and disability in primary care. *Psychosom Med, 68*(2), 262–268. doi:10.1097/01.psy.0000204851.15499.fc

Azimi, A., Hoseini, S. M., Najafi, M. & Rafieenia, P. (2018). A comparative study on effectiveness of acceptance and commitment therapy and logotherapy on symptoms of depression, anxiety and stress of women suffering relapsing remitting multiple sclerosis: A randomized controlled trial study. *Koomesh, 20*(4), 612–619.

Backenstrass, M., Joest, K., Frank, A., Hingmann, S., Mundt, C., & Kronmuller, K. T. (2006). Preferences for treatment in primary care: A comparison of nondepressive, subsyndromal and major depressive patients. *General Hospital Psychiatry, 28*(2), 178–180. doi:10.1016/j.genhosppsych.2005.10.001

Baumeister, H., Reichler, L., Munzinger, M., & Lin, J. (2014). The impact of guidance on Internet-based mental health interventions—A systematic review. *Internet Interventions, 1*(4), 205–215.

Bayliss, E. A., Bonds, D. E., Boyd, C. M., Davis, M. M., Finke, B., Fox, M. H., . . . Stange, K. C. (2014). Understanding the context of health for persons with multiple chronic conditions: Moving from what is the matter to what matters. *Annals of Family Medicine, 12*(3), 260–269. doi:10.1370/afm.1643

Baziliansky, S., & Cohen, M. (2020). Emotion regulation and psychological distress in cancer survivors: A systematic review and meta-analysis. *Stress and Health, 37*(1), 3–18. doi:10.1002/smi.2972

Bell, R. A., Franks, P., Duberstein, P. R., Epstein, R. M., Feldman, M. D., Fernandez y Garcia, E., & Kravitz, R. L. (2011). Suffering in silence: Reasons for not disclosing depression in primary care. *Annals of Family Medicine, 9*(5), 439–446. doi:10.1370/afm.1277

Bonanno, G. A. (2004). Loss, trauma, and human resilience: Have we underestimated the human capacity to thrive after extremely aversive events? *American Psychology, 59*(1), 20–28. doi:10.1037/0003-066X.59.1.20

Bower, J. E. (2005). Prevalence and causes of fatigue after cancer treatment: The next generation of research. *Journal of Clinical Oncology, 23*(33), 8280–8282. doi:10.1200/JCO.2005.08.008

Bricker, J. B., Copeland, W., Mull, K. E., Zeng, E. Y., Watson, N. L., Akioka, K. J., & Heffner, J. L. (2017). Single-arm trial of the second version of an acceptance and commitment therapy smartphone application for smoking cessation. *Drug Alcohol Dependency, 170,* 37–42. doi:10.1016/j.drugalcdep.2016.10.029

Bricker, J. B., Watson, N. L., Mull, K. E., Sullivan, B. M., & Heffner, J. L. (2020). Efficacy of smartphone applications for smoking cessation: A randomized clinical trial. *JAMA Internal Medicine, 180*(11), 1472–1480. doi:10.1001/jamainternmed.2020.4055

Carver, C. S., Pozo, C., Harris, S. D., Noriega, V., Scheier, M. F., Robinson, D. S., . . . Clark, K. C. (1993). How coping mediates the effect of optimism on distress: A study of women with early stage breast cancer. *Journal of Personality and Social Psychologyl, 65*(2), 375–390. doi:10.1037//0022-3514.65.2.375

Celano, C. M., & Huffman, J. C. (2011). Depression and cardiac disease: A review. *Cardiology Review, 19*(3), 130–142. doi:10.1097/CRD.0b013e31820e8106

Cucciare, M. A., Weingardt, K. R., & Villafranca, S. (2008). Using blended learning to implement evidence-based psychotherapies. *Clinical Psychology: Science and Practice, 15*(4), 299–307.

Cully, J. A., Jameson, J. P., Phillips, L. L., Kunik, M. E., & Fortney, J. C. (2010). Use of psychotherapy by rural and urban veterans. *Journal of Rural Health, 26*(3), 225–233. doi:10.1111/j.1748-0361.2010.00294.x

Dijkstra, M. T., & Homan, A. C. (2016). Engaging in rather than disengaging from stress: effective coping and perceived control. *Frontiers in Psychology, 7,* 1415. doi:10.3389/fpsyg.2016.01415

DiMatteo, M. R., Lepper, H. S., & Croghan, T. W. (2000). Depression is a risk factor for noncompliance with medical treatment: meta-analysis of the effects of anxiety and depression on patient adherence. *Archives of Internal Medicine, 160*(14), 2101–2107.

Dindo, L., Marchman, J., Gindes, H., & Fiedorowicz, J. (2015). A brief behavioral intervention targeting mental health risk factors for vascular disease: A pilot study. *Psychotherapy and Psychosomatics, 84*(3), 183–185. doi:10.1159/000371495

Dindo, L. N., Recober, A., Calarge, C. A., Zimmerman, B. M., Weinrib, A., Marchman, J. N., & Turvey, C. (2020). One-day acceptance and commitment therapy compared to support for depressed migraine patients: A randomized clinical trial. *Neurotherapeutics, 17*(2), 743–753. doi:10.1007/s13311-019-00818-0

Dindo, L., Van Liew, J. R., & Arch, J. J. (2017). Acceptance and commitment therapy: A transdiagnostic behavioral intervention for mental health and medical conditions. *Neurotherapeutics, 14*(3), 546–553. doi:10.1007/s13311-017-0521-3

Dindo, L., Weinrib, A., & Marchman, J. (2019). One-day ACT workshops for patients with chronic health problems and associated emotional disorders. In M. E. Levin, M. P. Twohig, & J. Krafft (Eds.), *Innovations in ACT* (pp. 203–220). Oakland, CA: New Harbinger Publications.

Dindo, L., Zimmerman, M. B., Hadlandsmyth, K., StMarie, B., Embree, J., Marchman, J., . . . Rakel, B. (2018). Acceptance and commitment therapy for prevention of chronic postsurgical pain and opioid use in at-risk veterans: A pilot randomized controlled study. *Journal of Pain, 19*(10), 1211–1221. doi:10.1016/j.jpain.2018.04.016

Engel, G. L. (1977). The need for a new medical model: A challenge for biomedicine. *Science, 196*(4286), 129–136. doi:10.1126/science.847460

Evans, D. L., Charney, D. S., Lewis, L., Golden, R. N., Gorman, J. M., Krishnan, K. R., . . . Valvo, W. J. (2005). Mood disorders in the medically ill: Scientific review and recommendations. *Biological Psychiatry, 58*(3), 175–189. doi:10.1016/j.biopsych.2005.05.001

Forman, E. M., Butryn, M. L., Manasse, S. M., Crosby, R. D., Goldstein, S. P., Wyckoff, E. P., & Thomas, J. G. (2016). Acceptance-based versus standard behavioral treatment for obesity: Results from the mind your health randomized controlled trial. *Obesity* (Silver Spring), *24*(10), 2050–2056. doi:10.1002/oby.21601

Gerard, F. A. (2010). *Chronic care: Making the case for ongoing care.* Robert Wood Johnson Foundation.

Giovannetti, A. M., Quintas, R., Tramacere, I., Giordano, A., Confalonieri, P., Uccelli, M. M., . . . Pakenham, K. I. (2020). A resilience group training program for people with multiple sclerosis: Results of a pilot single-blind randomized controlled trial and nested qualitative study. *PLoS One, 15*(4): e0231380.

Gloster, A. T., Walder, N., Levin, M., Twohig, M., & Karekla, M. (2020). The empirical status of acceptance and commitment therapy: A review of meta-analyses. *Journal of Contextual Behavioral Science, 18,* 181–192.

Gonzalez-Fernandez, S., & Fernandez-Rodriguez, C. (2019). Acceptance and commitment therapy in cancer: Review of applications and findings. *Behavioral Medicine, 45*(3), 255–269. doi:10.1080/08964289.2018.1452713

Goodell, S., Druss, B. G., & Walker, E. R. (2011). *The Synthesis Project Report: Mental disorders and medical comorbidity.*Retrieved from Robert Wood Johnson Foundation.

Goodrich, D. E., Kilbourne, A. M., Nord, K. M., & Bauer, M. S. (2013). Mental health collaborative care and its role in primary care settings. *Current Psychiatry Reports, 15*(8), 383. doi:10.1007/s11920-013-0383-2

Gould, C. E., Kok, B. C., Ma, V. K., Zapata, A. M. L., Owen, J. E., & Kuhn, E. (2019). Veterans affairs and the Department of Defense mental health apps: A systematic literature review. *Psychol Services, 16*(2), 196–207. doi:10.1037/ser0000289

Grady, P. A., & Gough, L. L. (2014). Self-management: A comprehensive approach to management of chronic conditions. *American Journal of Public Health, 104*(8), e25–31. doi:10.2105/AJPH.2014.302041

Graham, C. D., Gouick, J., Krahe, C., & Gillanders, D. (2016). A systematic review of the use of acceptance and commitment therapy (ACT) in chronic disease and long-term conditions. *Clinical Psychological Review, 46,* 46–58. doi:10.1016/j.cpr.2016.04.009

Gregg, J. A., Callaghan, G. M., Hayes, S. C., & Glenn-Lawson, J. L. (2007). Improving diabetes self-management through acceptance, mindfulness, and values: A randomized controlled trial. *Journal of Consulting and Clinical Psychology, 75*(2): 336–343.

Hartzler, M. L., Castle, L., Lewis, C., & Zakaria, L. (2020). A functional approach to the chronic disease epidemic. *American Journal of Health-System Pharmacy, 77*(8), 668–672. doi:10.1093/ajhp/zxaa032

Hayes, S., Luoma, J., Bond, F., Masuda, A., & Lillis, J. (2006). Acceptance and commitment therapy: Model, process and outcomes. *Behaviour Research and Therapy, 44,* 1–25. doi:10.1016/j.brat.2005.06.006

Hayes, S., Strosahl, K., & Wilson, K. (2012). *Acceptance and commitment therapy: The process and practice of mindful change.* (2nd ed.). New York: Guilford Press.

Hayes, S. C., Wilson, K. W., Gifford, E. V., Follette, V. M., & Strosahl, K. (1996). Experiential avoidance and behavioral disorders: A functional dimensional approach to diagnosis and treatment. *Journal of Consulting and Clinical Psychology, 64*(6), 1152–1168.

Hofmann, S. G., & Hay, A. C. (2018). Rethinking avoidance: Toward a balanced approach to avoidance in treating anxiety disorders. *Journal of Anxiety Disorders, 55,* 14–21. doi:10.1016/j.janxdis.2018.03.004

Holman, H., & Lorig, K. (2000). Patients as partners in managing chronic disease. Partnership is a prerequisite for effective and efficient health care. *British Medical Journal 320* (7234), 526–527. doi:10.1136/bmj.320.7234.526

Holtforth, M. G. (2008). Avoidance motivation in psychological problems and psychotherapy. *Psychotherapy Research, 18*(2), 147–159. doi:10.1080/10503300701765849

Hong, Y., Pena-Purcell, N. C., & Ory, M. G. (2012). Outcomes of online support and resources for cancer survivors: A systematic literature review. *Patient Education and Counseling, 86*(3), 288–296. doi:10.1016/j.pec.2011.06.014

Jarvela-Reijonen, E., Karhunen, L., Sairanen, E., Muotka, J., Lindroos, S., Laitinen, J., . . . Kolehmainen, M. (2018). The effects of acceptance and commitment therapy on eating behavior and diet delivered through face-to-face contact and a mobile app: A randomized controlled trial. *International Journal of Behavioral Nutrition and Physical Activity, 15*(1), 22. doi:10.1186/s12966-018-0654-8

Katon, W. J. (2004). The many faces of depression in primary care. *Journal of General Internal Medicine, 19*(8), 893–895. doi:10.1111/j.1525-1497.2004.40601.x

Katon, W. J. (2011). Epidemiology and treatment of depression in patients with chronic medical illness. *Dialogues in Clinical Neuroscience, 13*(1), 7–23.

Khaneiee, D., Jazayeri, R., Bahrami, F., Montazeri, N., & Etemadi, O. (2019). Investigating the effectiveness of acceptance and commitment therapy (ACT) on marital conflicts of coronary artery bypass patients. *Quarterly of Clinical Psychology Studies, 9*(33), 91–103.

Kheyran-Alnesa, M., Mirzaian, B., & Yar-Ali, D. (2018). The effectiveness of acceptance and commitment-based therapy on anger, anxiety and hostility for heart surgery patients. *Journal of Biochemical Technology, 9*(4), 43.

Khosroshahi, H., Mirzaian, B., & Hasanzadeh, R. (2019). Acceptance and commitment therapy on illness perception in patients with coronary heart disease. *Middle Eastern Journal of Disability Studies, 9*, 85.

Kuba, K., Weissflog, G., Gotze, H., Garcia-Torres, F., Mehnert, A., & Esser, P. (2019). The relationship between acceptance, fatigue, and subjective cognitive impairment in hematologic cancer survivors. *International Journal of Clinical Health Psychology, 19*(2), 97–106. doi:10.1016/j.ijchp.2018.12.001

LeRoy, L., Bayliss, E., & Domino, M. (2014). The Agency for Healthcare Research and Quality. Multiple chronic conditions research network. *Medical Care, 52*, S15–S22.

Low, C. A., Stanton, A. L., & Bower, J. E. (2008). Effects of acceptance-oriented versus evaluative emotional processing on heart rate recovery and habituation. *Emotion, 8*(3), 419–424. doi:10.1037/1528-3542.8.3.419

Lowe, B., Spitzer, R. L., Williams, J. B., Mussell, M., Schellberg, D., & Kroenke, K. (2008). Depression, anxiety and somatization in primary care: Syndrome overlap and functional impairment. *General Hospital Psychiatry, 30*(3), 191–199. doi:10.1016/j.genhosppsych.2008.01.001

MacAllister, W. S., & Krupp, L. B. (2005). Multiple sclerosis-related fatigue. *Physical Medicine and Rehabil Clinics of North America, 16*(2), 483–502. doi:10.1016/j.pmr.2005.01.014

Mathew, A., Doorenbos, A. Z., Jang, M. K., & Hershberger, P. E. (2020). Acceptance and commitment therapy in adult cancer survivors: A systematic review and conceptual model. *Journal of Cancer Survivorship, 15*(3), 427–451. doi:10.1007/s11764-020-00938-z

Mathieson, C., & Stam, H. (1995). Renegotiating identity: Cancer narratives. *Sociology of Health and Illness, 17*, 283–306. doi:10.1111/1467-9566.ep10933316

McCracken, L. M., & Yang, S. Y. (2006). The role of values in a contextual cognitive-behavioral approach to chronic pain. *Pain, 123*(1-2), 137–145. doi:10.1016/j.pain.2006.02.021

Merikangas, K. R., Ames, M., Cui, L., Stang, P. E., Ustun, T. B., Von Korff, M., & Kessler, R. C. (2007). The impact of comorbidity of mental and physical conditions on role disability in the US adult household population. *Archives of General Psychiatry, 64*(10), 1180–1188. doi:10.1001/archpsyc.64.10.1180

Mohamadi, K. A., Mirzaian, B., & Dousti, Y. A. (2019). Effectiveness of acceptance and commitment therapy on the quality of life and resiliency in cardiac surgery patients. *Tabari Biomedical Student Research Journal, 1*, 9–15.

Mohr, D. C., Hart, S. L., Howard, I., Julian, L., Vella, L., Catledge, C., & Feldman, M. D. (2006). Barriers to psychotherapy among depressed and nondepressed primary care patients. *Annals of Behavioral Medicine, 32*(3), 254–258. doi:10.1207/s15324796abm3203_12

Moos, R. H., & Schaefer, J. A. (1993). Coping resources and processes: current concepts and measures. In B. S. Goldberger L (Ed.), *Handbook of stress: Theoretical and clinical aspects* (Vol. 2nd ed, pp. 234–257). New York: Free Press.

Naik, A. D., Dindo, L. N., Van Liew, J. R., Hundt, N. E., Vo, L., Hernandez-Bigos, K., . . . Tinetti, M. E. (2018). Development of a clinically feasible process for identifying individual health priorities. *Journal of the American Griatric Society, 66*(10), 1872–1879. doi:10.1111/jgs.15437

Najavits, L. M. (2015). The problem of dropout from "gold standard" PTSD therapies. *F1000Prime Reports, 7*, 43. doi:10.12703/P7-43

Neff, K. D. (2003). Self-compassion: An alternative conceptualization of a healthy attitude toward oneself. *Self and identity, 2*(2), 85–101. doi: 10.1080/15298860309032

Owen, J. E., Kuhn, E., Jaworski, B. K., McGee-Vincent, P., Juhasz, K., Hoffman, J. E., & Rosen, C. (2018). VA mobile apps for PTSD and related problems: Public health resources for veterans and those who care for them. *Mhealth, 4*, 28. doi:10.21037/mhealth.2018.05.07

Pedersen, H. F., Agger, J. L., Frostholm, L., Jensen, J. S., Ornbol, E., Fink, P., & Schroder, A. (2019). Acceptance and commitment group therapy for patients with multiple functional somatic syndromes: A three-armed trial comparing ACT in a brief and extended version with enhanced care. *Psychological Medicine, 49*(6), 1005–1014. doi:10.1017/S0033291718001666

Pietrzak, R. H., Johnson, D. C., Goldstein, M. B., Malley, J. C., & Southwick, S. M. (2009). Perceived stigma and barriers to mental health care utilization among OEF-OIF veterans. *Psychiatric Services, 60*(8), 1118–1122. doi:10.1176/ps.2009.60.8.1118

Raghupathi, W., & Raghupathi, V. (2018). An empirical study of chronic diseases in the United States: A Visual analytics approach. *International Journal of Environmental Research and Public Health, 15*(3), 431–455. doi:10.3390/ijerph15030431

Robinson, P. J., & Strosahl, K. D. (2009). Behavioral health consultation and primary care: lessons learned. *Journal of Clinical Psychology in Medical Settings, 16*(1), 58–71. doi:10.1007/s10880-009-9145-z

Scott-Sheldon, L. A. J., Gathright, E. C., Donahue, M. L., Balletto, B., Feulner, M. M., DeCosta, J., . . . Salmoirago-Blotcher, E. (2020). Mindfulness-based interventions for adults with cardiovascular disease: A systematic review and meta-analysis. *Annals of Behavioral Medicine, 54*(1), 67–73. doi:10.1093/abm/kaz020

Secinti, E., Tometich, D. B., Johns, S. A., & Mosher, C. E. (2019). The relationship between acceptance of cancer and distress: A meta-analytic review. *Clinical Psychology Review, 71*, 27–38. doi:10.1016/j.cpr.2019.05.001

Segerstrom, S. C., & Miller, G. E. (2004). Psychological stress and the human immune system: A meta-analytic study of 30 years of inquiry. *Psychological Bulletin, 130*(4), 601–630. doi:10.1037/0033-2909.130.4.601

Shahabi, A., Asgari, P., & Makvandi, B. (2020)., (2020). Comparison of the effectiveness of acceptance and commitment therapy (ACT) and guided imagery on the resilience of cardiac disease patients referring to the heart rehabilitation department. *The Horizon of Medical Sciences, 26*(3), 276–297.

Shayeghian, Z., Hassanabadl, H., Aguilar-Vafale, M. E., Amiri, P., & Ali Besharat, M. (2016). A randomized controlled trial of acceptance and commitment therapy for type 2 diabetes management: The moderating role of coping styles." *PLoS One* 11 (12): e0166599.

Sheibani, H., Sheibani, K. A., Amreei, N. N., & Masrour, M. J. (2019). An investigation of the effects of the acceptance and commitment therapy in groups on the cognitive strategies of emotion regulation and self-control in coronary heart disease patients. *Journal of Medicine and Life*(12), 361–367.

Spleen, A. M., Lengerich, E. J., Camacho, F. T., & Vanderpool, R. C. (2014). Health care avoidance among rural populations: Results from a nationally representative survey. *Journal of Rural Health, 30*(1), 79–88. doi:10.1111/jrh.12032

Stenhoff, A., Steadman, L., Nevitt, S., Benson, L., & White, R. (2020). Acceptance and commitment therapy and subjective wellbeing: A systematic review and meta-analyses of randomised controlled trials in adults. *Journal of Contextual Behavioral Science, 18*, 256–272. doi:10.1016/j.jcbs.2020.08.008

Tinetti, M. E., & Fried, T. (2004). The end of the disease era. *American Journal of Medicine, 116*(3), 179–185. doi:10.1016/j.amjmed.2003.09.031

Tinetti, M. E., Naik, A. D., Dindo, L., Costello, D. M., Esterson, J., Geda, M., . . . Blaum, C. (2019). Association of patient priorities-aligned decision-making with patient outcomes and ambulatory health care burden among older adults with multiple chronic conditions: A nonrandomized clinical trial. *JAMA Internal Medicine, 179*(12), 1688–1697. doi:10.1001/jamainternmed.2019.4235

Tinetti, M. E., Naik, A. D., & Dodson, J. A. (2016). Moving from disease-centered to patient goals-directed care for patients with multiple chronic conditions: Patient value-based care. *JAMA Cardiology, 1*(1), 9–10. doi:10.1001/jamacardio.2015.0248

Trindade, I. A., Marta-Simoes, J., Ferreira, C., & Pinto-Gouveia, J. (2018a). Chronic illness-related cognitive fusion explains the impact of body dissatisfaction and shame on depression symptoms in breast cancer patients. *Clinical Psychology and Psychotherapy, 25*(6), 886–893. doi:10.1002/cpp.2323

Trindade, I. A., Marta-Simoes, J., Ferreira, C., & Pinto-Gouveia, J. (2018b). Developments on committed action: Validity of the CAQ-8 and analysis of committed action's role in depressive symptomatology in breast cancer patients and healthy individuals. *Clinical Psychology and Psychotherapy, 25*(1), e42–e50. doi:10.1002/cpp.2125

U.S. Department of Health and Human Services. Agency for Healthcare Research and Quality. (Accessed December 14, 2017.). Medical Expenditure Panel Survey (MEPS). https://meps.ahrq.gov/mepsweb/.

Vehling, S., Lehmann, C., Oechsle, K., Bokemeyer, C., Krull, A., Koch, U., & Mehnert, A. (2011). Global meaning and meaning-related life attitudes: Exploring their role in predicting depression, anxiety, and demoralization in cancer patients. *Support Care Cancer, 19*(4), 513–520. doi:10.1007/s00520-010-0845-6

Viane, I., Crombez, G., Eccleston, C., Devulder, J., & De Corte, W. (2004). Acceptance of the unpleasant reality of chronic pain: Effects upon attention to pain and engagement with daily activities. *Pain, 112*(3), 282–288. doi:10.1016/j.pain.2004.09.008

Voigt, V., Neufeld, F., Kaste, J., Buhner, M., Sckopke, P., Wuerstlein, R., . . . Hermelink, K. (2017). Clinically assessed posttraumatic stress in patients with breast cancer during the first year after diagnosis in the prospective, longitudinal, controlled COGNICARES study. *Psychooncology, 26*(1), 74–80. doi:10.1002/pon.4102

Vowles, K. E., McNeil, D. W., Gross, R. T., McDaniel, M. L., Mouse, A., Bates, M., . . . McCall, C. (2007). Effects of pain acceptance and pain control strategies on physical impairment in individuals with chronic low back pain. *Behavioral Therapy, 38*(4), 412–425. doi:10.1016/j.beth.2007.02.001

Waters, H., & Graf, M. (2018). The costs of chronic disease in the U.S.: Executive Summary. Milken Institute, Santa Monica, CA.

Weeks, J. C., Catalano, P. J., Cronin, A., Finkelman, M. D., Mack, J. W., Keating, N. L., & Schrag, D. (2012). Patients' expectations about effects of chemotherapy for advanced cancer. *New England Journal of Medicine, 367*(17), 1616–1625. doi:10.1056/NEJMoa1204410

Whitehead, L. C., Crowe, M. T., Carter, J. D., Maskill, V. R., Carlyle, D., Bugge, C., & Frampton, C. M. A. (2017). A nurse-led education and cognitive behaviour therapy-based intervention among adults with uncontrolled type 2 diabetes: A randomised controlled trial. *Journal of Evaluation in Clinical Practice*, *23*, 821–829.

Wierzbicki, M., & Pekanik, G. (1986). The relationship between expected and actual psychotherapy treatment duration. *Psychotherapy (Chic)*, *23*, 532–534.

Wierzbicki, M., & Pekanik, G. (1993). A meta-analysis of psychotherapy dropout. *Professional Psychological Research*, *24*, 190–195.

Yazdanbakhsh, K., Kaboudi, M., Roghanchi, M., Dehghan, F., & Nooripour, R. (2016). The effectiveness of acceptance and commitment therapy on psychological adaptation in women with MS. *Journal of Fundamental and Applied Sciences*, 8, 2767–2777.

CHAPTER

22 Acceptance and Commitment Therapy for Substance Use

Maria Stavrinaki, Megan Kelly, *and* Maria Karekla

Abstract

Global incidence for legal and illegal substance abuse is increasing, with marginalized groups and adolescents bearing the brunt. Substance use disorders (SUDs) are linked with serious and enduring physical health consequences, persistent psychological problems, criminality, homelessness, unemployment, and diminished educational opportunities. The issue of SUD prevention and treatment is therefore considered to be of the utmost importance worldwide. Current evidence-based treatments, though effective, present with mediocre abstinence rates, leaving room for improvement in the treatment of these conditions. Newer cognitive-behavioral therapy (CBT) approaches, such as acceptance and commitment therapy (ACT), acknowledge the inevitability of attempting to control internal states, which has been shown to ameliorate abstinence rates. ACT cultivates psychological flexibility, experiential acceptance, distress tolerance, and behavior change, with the aim of living a more fulfilled, valued life. More specifically, ACT for SUDs openly aims to increase awareness of contextual and internal substance cues, while simultaneously identifying and following personally relevant, valued directions. The evidence in support of ACT, in the context of SUDs, as well as the specifics of how to apply openness, awareness, and valued activity in treatment, are detailed in this article.

Key Words: substance use disorders, acceptance and commitment therapy, psychological flexibility, experiential avoidance, distress tolerance, targeted practice

The Impact of Substance Use Disorders

According to the World Drug Report (WDR), global use of legal (alcohol, tobacco) and illegal substances (e.g., opiates, cocaine, cannabis, amphetamine-type stimulants, and new psychoactive substances [NPS]) is on the rise (WDR, 2020). Global incidence of illegal substances increased by 30% in the last decade, while over 35 million people currently suffer from substance use disorders (SUDs; WDR, 2020). Marginalized groups and adolescents seem to be responsible for the brunt of this increase (WDR, 2020). The National Survey on Drug Use and Health in the United States shows that SUDs tend to develop in late adolescence and have an average duration of 30 years, with a lifetime prevalence of 24.8% (NSDUH, 2012). SUDs are associated with serious and enduring physical health consequences, persistent psychological problems, criminality, homelessness, unemployment, and diminished educational opportunities (NSDUH, 2012). Not surprisingly, people with SUDs rate their quality of life as very low (Whiteford, Ferrari, Degenhardt, Feigin, & Vos, 2015). In view of this information, SUD prevention and treatment is of utmost importance worldwide (NSDUH, 2012; WDR, 2020).

Evidence-Based Treatment for Substance Use Disorders

SUDs are heterogeneous in their underlying causes, clinical presentation, and features and domains of functioning. A multilevel and multimodal approach to assessment and treatment is thus required (Gloster & Karekla, 2020). Ideally, SUDs should be managed via a flexible stepped care and integrative model in which treatment intensity is adjusted based on the individual and their unique circumstances (Bruneau et al., 2018). Such an approach involves first a complete assessment and functional analysis of the individual's problems, where focus is on treatment of intoxication and withdrawal syndromes and development of an individualized treatment plan that will address any comorbid psychiatric or other problems (APA, 2016). Generally, treatment aims to achieve abstinence or reduction in use, with decreases in the frequency and severity of relapse, while at the same time improving psychosocial functioning in individuals with SUDs (APA, 2016).

Medication and adjunctive nonpharmacological psychosocial therapy are currently recommended as first-line, evidence-based treatment options for people with SUDs (APA, 2018; Bruneau et al., 2018; VA/DoD, 2015). Various international guidelines suggest a range of psychosocial interventions: motivational enhancement therapy (MET; utilizing principles of motivational interviewing), cognitive-behavioral therapy (CBT; focusing on the thoughts, emotions, and behaviors related to use and ways to manage urges and use triggers), medical management (MM; providing education and strategies to support abstinence and medication adherence), contingency management, and behavioral couples therapy for drug-specific problems (APA, 2016, 2018; NICE, 2016; RANZCP, 2016). Community-based peer support groups such as 12-step programs (e.g., Alcoholics Anonymous [AA] and Narcotics Anonymous [NA] groups) are also recommended with demonstrated aid in achieving long-term remission, yet not replacing formal treatment (APA, 2016).

Despite high prevalence, societal cost, and available treatments, SUDs remain generally undertreated, with less than 10% of individuals diagnosed receiving any treatment and few receiving any evidence-based treatment (APA, 2018). Although considered effective, current evidence-based treatments are hindered by small effect sizes and mediocre abstinence rates ranging from 40 to 80% within the first year after treatment and approximately 20% return to their pretreatment levels of use within the same year (Menon & Kandasamy, 2018). The presence of comorbid conditions, particularly medical and psychiatric disorders (e.g., heart disease, depression, anxiety, posttraumatic stress disorder, psychosis), as well as social challenges (e.g., poverty, homelessness, stigma, and shame), increase the complexity of SUDs and its treatment. These comorbidities can partly explain why so many people suffer lapses and relapses soon after treatment (Stotts & Northrup, 2015). The frequency of psychiatric disorders among people with SUDs is extremely high, ranging between 47 and 100% for common mental health problems such as anxiety and depression (Kingston, Marrel, & Mills, 2017). Additionally, medical multimorbidity (e.g., ≥ 2 concurrent chronic conditions) among individuals with SUDs is high; 17.4% of patients report at least two chronic conditions (Han, Termine, Moore, Sherman, & Palamar, 2018). Individuals exhibiting multimorbidity tend to present with low income, smoking history, and comorbid mental health problems, and they often are suffering from financial, legal, or housing instability (Han et al., 2018).

Another significant reason why SUDs interventions show low abstinence rates and high postintervention relapse (Otto, O'Cleirigh, & Pollak, 2007; Priddy et al., 2018) relates to the suboptimal handling of internal (i.e., interoceptive) cues in treatment (e.g., thoughts, emotions, and somatic sensations). Avoiding, trying to control, or suppressing internal drug cues such as negative or positive thoughts and emotions, drug cravings, and somatic withdrawal symptoms (a common practice of many evidence-based interventions for SUDs) leads, paradoxically, to an increase in these internal cues (Bowen, Witkiewitz, Dillworth, & Marlatt, 2007; Priddy et al., 2018). An early retrospective study on people with opioid use disorder found that interoceptive cues accounted for the majority of reasons for relapse: 32% of those who relapsed stated that they did so due to their wish to regulate negative emotions, 32% as a means of dealing with negative somatic symptoms (e.g., somatic pain in relation to an accident), 16% due to somatic sensations similar to withdrawal (e.g., getting the flu, feeling sick), and 5% owing to positive emotions (e.g., celebrating a birthday, wedding, job success; Chaney, Roszell & Cummings, 1982). In addition, laboratory-induced negative emotional states, as well as naturally occurring negative emotions, were found to enhance drug craving, which in turn could result in relapse (e.g., Karekla, Panayiotou, & Collins, 2017). This research suggests that use of a control of internal states (thoughts, emotions, cravings) agenda as a treatment goal makes potential failure and relapse more likely. Individuals will not be able to apply such control techniques long term, for their natural internal states will inevitably return. The reemergence of these states leaves the individual experiencing feelings of inadequacy, fatigue, and frustration over their reappearance and ultimately places them in similar emotional states as those the person was previously trying to eliminate by using substances.

Newer CBT approaches like acceptance and commitment therapy (ACT) are adopting a perspective that acknowledges the inevitability of efforts to control internal states as part of the human experience. ACT alternatively works to cultivate psychological flexibility, propagate experiential acceptance, distress tolerance and behavior change, with the aim of living a more fulfilling and valued life.

Acceptance and Commitment Therapy for SUD Treatment

In SUDs, ACT (Hayes, Strosahl, & Wilson, 2011) aims to help individuals become more aware of contextual and internal drug cues (e.g., external reminders, rigid cognitive responding, or craving) without judging, analyzing, or reacting to their literal content, while concurrently choosing to behave in healthier alternative ways consistent with their values. This process is hypothesized to weaken, and eventually disrupt, the habitual response to use substances while helping to reshape or build new goal-directed associations (Luoma, Kohlenberg, Hayes, & Fletcher, 2012; Witkiewitz, Lustyk, & Bowen, 2013).

A central target of ACT is experiential avoidance (EA), a transdiagnostic variable known to influence the etiology and maintenance of SUDs. EA is characterized by an unwillingness to approach distressing or negative internal events (Lejuez, Paulson, Daughters, Bornovalova, & Zvolensky, 2006). Several studies have demonstrated that EA functions as a behavioral diathesis and a risk factor for psychopathology. For example, EA exacerbates aversive emotional reactions in individuals with no known history of psychopathology (Feldner, Zvolensky, Eifert, & Spira, 2003). People exhibiting greater EA display higher levels of distress and lower quality of life (Feldner et al., 2003; Karekla, Forsyth, & Kelly, 2004; Karekla & Panayiotou, 2011). It has also been shown to predict drinking for both coping and enhancement purposes (Stewart, Zvolensky, & Eifert, 2002); people who drink to cope as opposed to having a good time are more likely to develop problem drinking behavior (Cooper, 1994). Moreover, individuals with more severe SUD symptomatology display higher EA scores (Luoma, Drake, Kohlenberg, & Hayes, 2011). Alternatively, lower levels of EA or demonstrating flexibility toward one's psychological content is found to interrupt the negative spiral of emotional dysregulation that can eventuate in drug use, lapse, and relapse (Hayes & Levin, 2012). While a person's negative emotional state is a known reason for relapse (Marlatt & Donovan, 2005), those who are more experientially avoidant of negative life events are even more likely to relapse (Westrup, 2001).

EA is a specific target of ACT, which aims to cultivate an accepting stance toward all emotions as a means of achieving well-being.

EA overlaps significantly with other well-established predictors of SUDs such as anxiety sensitivity, otherwise known as the "fear of fear" (e.g., Lejuez et al., 2008; Zvolensky, Vujanovic, Bernstein, & Leyro, 2010). Studies have shown that people with high anxiety sensitivity are at increased risk for becoming dependent on depressants (Conrod, Pihl, Stewart, & Dongier, 2000) and that anxiety sensitivity is predictive of the frequency of drug and alcohol use (DeHaas, Calamari, & Bair, 2002). ACT for substance use specifically targets anxiety sensitivity variables through acceptance of all internal states as parts of the human experience and redirecting actions to functional values-consistent venues. Similarly, EA overlaps with distress tolerance, or one's perceived ability to experience and endure negative emotional states (Simons & Gaher, 2005), which has been linked to an increased probability of drug addictions (Buckner, Keough, & Schmidt, 2007; Carleton et al., 2012; Daughters et al., 2005; Richards, Daughters, Bornovalova, Brown, & Lejuez, 2011) and quantity of alcohol use and alcohol-related problems (Lejuez et al., 2008; Stewart, Zvolensky, & Eifert, 2001; Zvolensky et al., 2009). Zvolensky et al. (2009) found that higher distress tolerance scores are significantly and negatively related to both "conformity" and "coping motives." In other words, people who can tolerate emotional states are less likely to use cannabis to fit in or to cope compared to those with low tolerance of their emotional states. A few studies suggest that distress tolerance, anxiety sensitivity, and EA measure very similar constructs (Schmidt, Buckner, & Keough, 2007a; Schmidt, Richey, Cromer, & Buckner, 2007b), sharing at least 20% variance, depending on the population or drug type being examined (Zvolensky et al., 2009). As such, these psychological vulnerability factors can be encompassed within the ACT work on how to approach internal states that contribute to drug use and are addressed via the cultivation of psychological flexibility (Hayes et al., 2011).

Another key ACT target relevant to SUDs is cognitive fusion, the inflexible focus on the content of thoughts. The role of cognitions and their relation to drug use is especially evident in SUDs (Marlatt & Donovan, 2005). Research suggests that a person's beliefs about the usefulness of drug taking for emotional relief is a strong predictor of SUD severity and relapse rates (Miller, Westerberg, Harris, & Tonigan, 1996). Worry, rumination, and craving have also been shown to shift people's attention away from the present moment, leading to loss of control over drug cues, known as the autopilot state (Goldman, Brown, Christiansen, & Smith, 1991). For example, a preoccupation with or rigid attention to past and future events can result in a deterioration in awareness of internal events (e.g., thoughts and feelings). This preoccupation diminishes one's mental resources, which might otherwise be helpful in gaining distance, a nonjudgmental perspective, or clarity in a difficult situation; leaving one exposed to impulsive, or destructive behavior, as is the case in substance use. Furthermore, the elaborated intrusion theory of craving proposes that preoccupation with (vs. flexible attention in) the present moment, not just past and future events, can be just as problematic. Elaborating or dwelling on intrusive drug urges can be gratifying in the moment, while at the same time, trigger feelings of deprivation, exasperating anticipation and resulting in an increase in drug use (Kavanagh, Andrade, & May, 2005). ACT specifically aims to change how a person relates to their internal experiences and propagates a more flexible and defused approach to thoughts and cravings so that the existence of substance-related thoughts does not lead to use behaviors.

Fusion with a cognitive interpretation of the self (coined as self-as-content) is another component of the ACT model for SUDs treatment (Luoma et al., 2007). Inflexible self-as-content patterns often result in people with SUDs acting out self-stigma or self-fulfilling prophecies as a way to remain consistent with their negative labels or self-concepts (Luoma et al., 2012).

For example, the label can elicit feelings of despair such as "I'm an addict, I can't control my use so why even bother trying." Self-stigma in substance-using populations is linked to delays in seeking treatment, lower self-efficacy to quit using, and lower quality of life (Luoma et al., 2012). Although counterintuitive, positive self-concepts can function in equally problematic ways, with self-labels of being strong and self-sufficient leading to reluctance in seeking help or taking sufficient steps to avoid temptations (Lindgren, Foster, Westgate, & Neighbors, 2013a; Lindgren et al., 2013b). ACT explains that this inflexibility and fusion with the content of thoughts (whether positive or negative) is what becomes problematic, rather than the mere presence of negative or positive thoughts themselves. ACT fosters the idea of self-as-context, of regarding oneself as being more than all the things they struggle with, including feelings and thoughts. Taking this self-as-context perspective frees the person from self-defeating behaviors. Instead, it helps them move toward values-based actions that are in accordance with the kind of person they would like to be.

Another key component targeted in ACT for SUDs is values confusion and disengagement (Hayes & Strosahl, 2004). Individuals with SUDs may utilize emotional coping mechanisms known as traumatic deflection or a disengagement from their valued path as a way to avoid pain (Hayes & Strosahl, 2004). This is because SUD clients often have deep-rooted, longstanding problems associated with living in volatile or traumatic environments (e.g., neglect, sexual abuse, violence, severe emotional abuse). In such conditions, goals or valued life directions are frequently abandoned, ignored, or paired with disappointment and/or pain. Pain avoidance is therefore seen as a form of experiential avoidance (a defense mechanism) that is manifested by a generalized lack of values or values disengagement (Hayes & Strosahl, 2004). Alternatively, again for similar reasons, individuals with SUDs engage in "pliance" or reliance on other people's expectations of right and wrong, a behavior that often results in lack of clarity or confusion regarding their values (Hayes & Strosahl, 2004). The presence of a clear and personalized valued path can, in contrast, provide a powerful motivator for sustained changes to substance use. This is because values are abstract, evolving patterns of behavior that provide meaning, purpose, and vitality to people's lives through reinforcement (Wilson, Sandoz, Kitchens, & Roberts, 2010). These naturally occurring, inexhaustible reinforcers compete with drug use and are key to the treatment of addiction (Plumb, Stewart, Dahl, & Lundgren, 2009). This is especially relevant given that many evidence-based treatment modalities, which use artificial reinforcers to modify substance use behavior, lose their effect over time (Prendergast, Podus, Finney, Greenwell, & Roll, 2006; Roozen et al., 2004). For example, establishing an environment that encourages abstinence through values-based action has been shown to reduce alcohol consumption (Heffner, Eifert, Parker, Hernandez, & Sperry, 2003). Other research also suggests that living a valued life may moderate impulses to drink or use drugs (Roos, Kirouac, Pearson, Fink, & Witkiewitz, 2015).

To date, addiction treatment options have focused on reducing exposure to situations and triggers for substance use, a strategy that, at best, can offer only partial success in abstinence (Woodward, 2017). This is because situations that have not previously related to drug use have the capacity to provoke cravings and lead to relapse (Woodward, 2017). Research on exposure to drug cues has been inconsistent; longer-term outcomes have shown the reemergence of previously extinguished functions, particularly in different contexts. With this in mind, acceptance seems to be a promising alternative to methods seeking to eliminate triggers or cue-elicited cravings (Conklin & Tiffany, 2002). Acceptance or psychological flexibility promoted by ACT is especially relevant when psychological triggers to drink or use drugs are unavoidable or cannot be eliminated using exposure (Woodward, 2017). In this light, mindful acceptance of the present moment has been shown to both break the urge to drink and eliminate actual drinking behavior—an effect that has been shown to be partially mediated by reduction in thought suppression (Bowen et al., 2007; Ostafin & Marlatt, 2008).

Mindfulness refers to a specific mental state that is achieved through awareness of the present moment, peacefully acknowledging, and accepting one's feelings, thoughts, and bodily sensations (Hasenkamp & Barsalou, 2012). It is a therapeutic technique intended to further reduce the risk of relapse by helping clients deal with some of the psychological discomfort present when experiencing withdrawal or cravings (Hasenkamp et al., 2012). Mindfulness utilized within ACT aims to give individuals with SUDs an increased awareness of present moment experiences and the "space" to engage in valued or prosocial behavior in the face of emotional, cognitive, and physical drug cues (Bowen et al., 2014).

More generally, ACT for SUDs aims to promote psychological flexibility by helping people become more aware and accepting of their present experiences whether they are judged as good or bad (e.g., feelings of excitement/grief, cravings/urges, withdrawal), as well as achieve more clarity or contact with their personal values (Hayes et al., 2011). In summary, ACT for SUDs systematically targets the three pillars of psychological flexibility. First, it focuses on openness to experience, the changing of one's relationship to thoughts, memories, and emotions, rather than trying to change the form or frequency of these internal events. ACT for SUDs targets openness to experience through techniques such as defusion, acceptance, and self-as-context. Reducing attachment to thoughts, emotions, physical sensations, or indeed the conceptualized self by increasing access to an alternative *context* has been shown to help people with SUDs observe discomfort from afar and achieve an alternative, more objective perspective (Wilson & Byrd, 2004). Second, awareness of experience, the flexible mindful attention to experiences in the here-and-now, is also targeted in ACT for SUDs. The third pillar includes active engagement in life as seen through motivation to change, valued-living, behavioral activation, and purposeful action (Hayes et al., 2011). Committed action skills training (e.g., refusal, communication, and problem-solving skills) can bring about greater, more successful valued actions, while making room for psychological triggers that function as barriers to living a purposeful life.

Evidence in Support of ACT for SUDs

The empirical evidence for the effectiveness of ACT as a treatment for SUDs is growing (Cavicchioli, Movalli, & Maffei, 2018). ACT is efficacious, with significant reductions in substance use from pre- to posttreatment, for a variety of substances (Lanza, Garcia, Lamelas, & González-Menéndez, 2014). A recent review of meta-analytic evidence underscored ACT's efficacy for SUDs as compared to other active interventions (e.g., CBT) with small, controlled effect sizes (Gloster, Walder, Levin, Twohig, & Karekla, 2020). ACT for SUDS was found to be superior to the outcome of 63.3–67.4% of individuals undergoing other active interventions (Gloster et al., 2020).

There is limited evidence for some specific substances, and thus more research is needed. For example, in the case of cannabis, preliminary but controlled evidence, using a sample of only three people, suggests that ACT can help individuals reduce their use up to 3 months follow-up (Twohig, Shoenberger, & Hayes, 2007). This study used a combination of self-report and biological samples to confirm complete abstinence postintervention; 3-month follow-ups showed abstinence maintenance in one case, while the other two showed reduction from their baseline cannabis use (Twohig et al., 2007). Additionally, participants saw improved mental health outcomes (on depression and anxiety scales), lowered EA, and improved withdrawal symptoms, which were maintained at follow-up (Twohig et al., 2007).

With regard to opioid use, several studies have shown promising results (Stotts, Masuda, & Wilson, 2009; Stotts et al., 2012; Lanza et al., 2014). More specifically, Stotts el al. (2012) randomized participants to receive either drug counseling or ACT in a methadone reduction program. Both groups received weekly 50-minute sessions for 6 months, with equal success on most drug-specific outcomes except for abstinence (36.7 vs. 19.2%) and anxiety specific measurements, both of which favored ACT (Stotts et al., 2012). In a second study on outpatient methadone detoxification for 50 incarcerated women, results favored ACT over both CBT and a control group (González-Menéndez, Fernándeza, Rodríguez, & Villagráa, 2014). More specifically, while the results favored CBT for reducing anxiety sensitivity at posttreatment, results at 6-month follow-up showed ACT to be more effective than CBT in reducing drug use (43.8 vs. 26.7%, respectively) and improving mental health (26.4 vs. 19.4%, respectively).

Limited evidence exists for cocaine use, with two studies showing promise for ACT (Schmitz et al., 2018; Stotts et al., 2014). A breakdown of the effectiveness of a contingency management (CM) intervention for people who use cocaine demonstrated that those who were nonresponsive to treatment had significantly higher baseline levels of avoidance and behavioral inflexibility in the context of distressing cocaine-related thoughts, feelings, and physical sensations (Stotts et al., 2014). This result suggests that ACT, in combination with CM, may further increase abstinence in cocaine users. Along similar lines, Schmitz et al. (2018) also suggest that initial CM effectiveness can be improved when ACT is integrated into treatment.

Several studies lend support to ACT for use with methamphetamine use problems (Arjmand et al., 2019; Bahrami & Asghari, 2017; Smout, Hayes, Atkins, Klausen, & Duguid, 2010). In a randomized, controlled trial (RCT) examining differences between a group of 104 methamphetamine users who received either ACT or CBT, no significant differences in treatment attendance and methamphetamine-related outcomes were found between the two groups (Smout et al., 2010). Methamphetamine use and severity, as well as health and social consequences improved over time in both groups. However, methodological problems should lend caution to the conclusions of this study, with attrition reaching 70% at 12 weeks and 86 percent at 24 weeks postentry, leaving the study underpowered to detect true differences (Smout et al., 2012).

More research on ACT can be found for alcohol use problems. A laboratory study found that mindful acceptance of internal cues weakened the relationship between automatic urges to drink alcohol and hazardous drinking (Ostafin & Marlatt, 2008). Additionally, single-case design study outcomes supported ACT for alcohol use disorder (AUD; Heffner et al., 2003; Luciano, Gómez, Hernández, & Cabello, 2001). Intervention studies and systematic reviews also lend support to ACT for alcohol use, with one study suggesting that ACT fares better than no treatment and treatments of minimal efficacy, and is comparable to other evidence-based psychosocial treatments for AUDs (Byrne et al., 2019). Similarly, two studies support the use of ACT for alcohol use and comorbid disorders (Meyer et al., 2018; Petersen & Zettle, 2010). The first, an uncontrolled pilot study (Meyer et al., 2018), examined ACT for comorbid AUD and PTSD in veterans, with therapy completers reporting significant reductions in both clinician-assessed and self-reported PTSD symptoms, along with improvements in quality of life, functional ability, and mental well-being at posttreatment and 3-month follow-up. Importantly, individuals experiencing suicidal ideation presented with significant reductions by follow-up; results were found to align with the ACT theoretical model, with more between-session mindfulness practice resulting in reductions in experiential avoidance (Meyer et al., 2018). Further, in a study of individuals who were involuntarily committed for treatment of comorbid alcohol use disorder and depression, both ACT and 12-step (i.e., treatment as usual [TAU]) approaches resulted in equivalent and significant reductions in depression levels. However, participants randomly assigned to receive ACT needed a briefer, smaller dose intervention to meet criteria for discharge compared to their TAU counterparts (i.e., ACT produced equivalent results more efficiently than TAU). Again, as expected, an analysis of the therapeutic process indicated that a decrease in experiential avoidance in the ACT group contributed to its potentially superior therapeutic effect (Petersen & Zettle, 2010).

In the case of polysubstance use, a RCT study compared the effectiveness of ACT versus CBT in incarcerated women with polydrug use (González-Menéndez et al., 2014). Over several time points in an 18-month period, there were equal reductions in drug use, anxiety sensitivity levels, and avoidance in both conditions. Especially interesting was the reduction in mental health comorbidities observed only among ACT participants, with ACT faring significantly better than CBT in maintaining abstinence rates at the 18-month follow-up period (González-Menéndez et al., 2014). In a different study of individuals abusing multiple substances along with opioid use disorder, ACT was compared to 12-step and care-as-usual/methadone maintenance (Hayes et al., 2004). For this study, both ACT and the 12-step approach were associated with less objectively verified drug use compared to methadone maintenance, and 23 percent fewer ACT participants reported drug use relative to the 12-step approach at follow-up. Overall, ACT appears to be efficacious for use with individuals with polysubstance use (Hayes, Pankey, Gifford, Batten, & Quiñones, 2002; Shorey et al., 2018; Wilson, Schnetzer, Flynn, & Kurz, 2012).

An innovative area of ACT research for SUDs is in applying ACT to address shame and self-stigma. For example, in a study of a 28-day residential treatment center, shame and stigma were targeted. ACT participants were more than twice as likely to remain abstinent, use drug/alcohol treatment facilities at higher rates, and report less internalized shame at 4-month follow-up relative to participants who received treatment as usual (Luoma et al., 2012). It is especially encouraging for ACT because the intervention utilized in this study was less intensive and consisted of three 2-hour group sessions within a one-week period as compared to TAU.

ACT for SUDs has thus been applied in a variety of settings and specific population groups (e.g., prisons, methadone clinics, residential, outpatient treatment centers, women, and veterans), while targeting a range of additional mental health comorbidities with very encouraging outcomes (González-Menéndez et al., 2014; Lanza et al., 2014; Petersen & Zettle, 2010; Stotts & Northrup, 2015; Weinrib et al., 2017). Bringing all evidence together, ACT demonstrates posttreatment abstinence, which persists at follow-ups (Stotts & Northrup, 2015). A recent meta-analysis found a small to medium effect-size difference in favor of ACT over other active treatment approaches (Lee, An, Levin, & Twohig, 2015). Further, when paralleled with first-line treatments such as CBT, the literature generally favors ACT (Stotts & Northrup, 2015). However, some outcome studies showed equivalent outcomes for ACT and CBT at posttreatment for polysubstance use (Wilson et al., 2012; Wilson, Hayes, & Byrd, 2000). ACT has accumulated empirical support for a wide range of behavioral and psychological problems, including SUDs of various kinds (Gloster et al., 2020). ACT for SUDs can effectively address internal/interoceptive cues, which is often responsible for substance initiation, maintenance, and relapse.

The Application of ACT for SUDs

Several ACT-based treatment protocols for SUDs focus on a variety of problem areas, including protocols specific for outpatients (Smout et al., 2010; Woodward, 2017), adolescents (Thurstone, Hull, Timmerman, & Emrick, 2017), shame and stigma (Luoma et al., 2012), veterans, and severe inpatient use (Hayes et al., 2004; Turner, Welches, & Conti, 2013). These protocols, in addition to presenting how to work with SUDs from an ACT approach, demonstrate its combination with relapse prevention, motivational interviewing, and contingency management skills. Some ACT protocols are available as books (e.g., DuFrene & Wilson, 2012), while others can be downloaded from the Association for Contextual Behavioral Science website (ACBS; https://contextualscience.org/treatment_protocol_and_manuals accessed 09/2020).

Some general ACT-based SUDs treatment guidelines can be extracted from these protocols and are outlined here. ACT for SUDs can be conducted individually or in a group format over several sessions (e.g., 15 sessions; Woodward, 2017). Additional modes of delivery have also been examined and are available. These include self-help/bibliotherapy and digital interventions with various degrees of therapist involvement, depending on the severity and substance of choice (Stavrinaki & Karekla, 2019).

Overall, five key points should be addressed when doing ACT with SUDs, which can be approached in any order, depending on the person's individual needs and wants. These points include (1) functional analysis of the problem (i.e., to help people consider the function of substance use and assess its workability for themselves in both the short and long term); (2) openness to internal experiences, which helps people identify avoided psychological content that triggers substance use and acceptance of all internal states; (3) awareness of experience (e.g., practice giving flexible attention to experiences in the here-and-now, experiencing thoughts of the past and future from a here-and-now perspective, and discriminating between being on "autopilot" and being "mindfully aware"); (4) compassionate observation (i.e., practice relating to the observer self and developing a more compassionate relationship toward oneself), and finally; (5) active engagement in life by encouraging free choice in values, helping to clarify valued directions and working toward them, to use values as a compass to evaluate drinking/drug use and other strategies used to control unwanted thoughts and emotions, and to help people tolerate slips and translate them into committed action (Woodward, 2017).

Prior to beginning ACT, a thorough functional analysis is carried out in which the therapist and the client investigate the function substances play in the life of the person and explore the purpose it has for the client's life. Through this case conceptualization, the different areas that ACT theorizes will contribute to psychopathology (experiential avoidance, cognitive fusion, lack of present moment awareness, self as content, lack of values clarity, and impulsive or nonvalues directed behaving) are explored as to how they relate to rigidity in behaving (i.e., substance use). The functional analysis guides the therapist in their decision on where to begin with therapy. For some individuals (especially if motivation to make changes is an issue), the therapist may choose to begin with values clarification. For other persons, experiential avoidance may be the most salient problem area that contributes to substance use, and thus, therapy will begin by working on acceptance and cognitive defusion skills. In this article, we present examples of the different areas that illustrate the ACT approach. However, we emphasize that these are not sequential—therapy can start from any point in the ACT model, and different ACT processes can be worked on simultaneously within each session based on the functional analysis, needs, and readiness of the client.

One of ACT's main goals for SUDs is to develop openness to internal experiences rather than try to change these experiences through the use of substances. Openness is promoted by altering one's association to their personalized interoceptive cues by learning to experience or observe them for what they are (e.g., thoughts, emotions, somatic sensations, memories). This introduces "distance" from them and allows the person to function in their life in the presence of distressing thoughts and emotions. To illustrate the futility of old ways of behaving (i.e., substance use) as emotional and thought control strategies, a technique called creative hopelessness is utilized, along with discussing the various short- and long-term consequences of substance use (Turner et al., 2013). Various exercises exist related to the concepts of acceptance and cognitive defusion; they are employed to provide the client with tools used to adopt an "open" response style (Woodward, 2017). ACT metaphors and exercises help the person learn to open up and change how they relate to internal events (e.g., "Monsters on the Bus," "Tug of War with a Monster," and "Leaves on a Stream"; see Stoddard & Afari, 2014 for detailed presentations of these metaphors).

Furthermore, clients are taught to become more aware of personalized interoceptive as well as external substance cues responsible for lapses and relapses (Thurstone et al., 2017). As is the case with CBT relapse prevention manuals, clients can be introduced to the concept of *Seemingly Irrelevant Decisions* (also known as *Apparently Irrelevant Decisions*) that predate a lapse or a full-blown relapse (Woodward, 2017). Characteristically, a series of mini, seemingly irrelevant choices, justified as inconsequential in the eyes of the client, eventually set up a situation that can later either unnoticeably lead to a relapse or be used as an excuse to justify a relapse. Clients are helped to get out of the "automatic pilot" mode of listening to their inner dialogue and become more in tune with their choices and actions through increased present moment awareness achieved via mindfulness, self-compassion, and self-as-context exercises. For example, the "Torch in the Dark" is a self-as-context metaphor in which the light from a torch represents mindful attention of internal or external drug triggers (e.g., cravings, physical sensations related to withdrawal or being in risky situations such as feeling lonely, driving by a pub, running into your ex-dealer) and circumstantially illuminates objects in a dark room. What is of importance in this metaphor is that the source of illumination always comes from the same source: that of the observing self, which remains unchanged and distanced from all triggers. Other useful metaphors include "Loving Kindness Meditation," and "Chessboard Metaphor" (see Stoddard & Afari, 2014 for more metaphors).

Self-defeating behaviors, such as substance use, are often perpetuated by rigid beliefs about the self or unchangeable life stories, such as criticizing or blaming oneself for having certain qualities, past behaviors, or feeling victimized (Woodward, 2017). Clients can be encouraged to work on their identity and on how they relate to their life story. For example, helping clients recognize that they are more than just "addicts/people who use substance users" or victims of their past, and that instead they are human beings with many different qualities and abilities for behaving, learning, evolving, growing and so on. This viewpoint can be fostered through self-as-context and self-compassion exercises. Dealing with environmental or contextual triggers is also important, and ACT incorporates techniques with demonstrated effectiveness for dealing with them. Refusal skills, communication skills, assertiveness training, social skills, and the like, are also included as needed in protocols of ACT for SUDs, as they constitute opportunities to practice new responses to being offered a drink or drugs or aid in gaining increased support from family and friends (Witkiewitz, Donnovan, & Hartzler, 2012).

Ultimately, the aim of ACT is "psychologically flexible behaving and active engagement in life" achieved through clarifying values and utilizing what is important for the person as a motivator for behavior change (Hayes et al., 2011). Valued-living, behavioral activation, and purposeful action are instigated through various techniques, exercises, and metaphors (e.g., "Skiing Metaphor," "the Path up the Mountain metaphor," "the values bullseye exercise," "the Sweet-Spot exercise," and "the Game of Life"). An important therapeutic target here would be to facilitate the understanding that it is not always the destination but the journey that is of importance. The skiing metaphor describes this well, with the idea being that if someone kept taking you down to the bottom of a ski run with a helicopter every time you got to the top, it would be frustrating because even though the outcome goal is to get to the bottom, what really matters is the process of how you get down, by skiing. Skiing gives you a chance to experience the whole process, to feel the cold air against your skin, to feel the energy in your body rising as you move down the slope, to experience the thrill of coordinating your legs and arms, and to sense the rise in your heartbeat and the change in your breathing. All these exhilarating experiences are missed if you do not take the skiing journey down the mountain. Similarly, while an aim in therapy might be to remain abstinent, a pill curing you of all cravings would deprive you of all the skills building needed for prolonged abstinence (e.g., going through the motions of acknowledging and accepting your cravings while creating a safe space between yourself and your internal cues).

Furthermore, impulsivity or the urgency to achieve things quickly, is a key etiological and maintenance factor attributed to SUDs (Poulton & Hester, 2020), which should be targeted as frequently and as thoroughly as possible in therapy. Mindfulness exercises aimed at slowing down and being present in the moment are key processes throughout ACT for SUDs protocols. Further, the "path up the mountain" metaphor highlights what is wrong with monitoring only "snapshots" of life as opposed to the "big picture" (i.e., noticing the twists and turns, circling around, or perhaps even the downward slopes of your path up the mountain instead of your overall, steady, and continuous progress to reach your goal).

Similar to motivational interviewing, values-based exercises serve to "develop discrepancy" between what the person wants and how they are presently living their life, setting the stage for committing to make a change (quit use) in the service of living a values-filled life (Turner et al., 2013). Clients learn to recognize obstacles to valued living (internal and external) and exercise their values-based choices when faced with dilemmas that can drive them back to use. Problem-solving external barriers and defusing from interoceptive ones, such as unwanted thoughts, emotions, urges, and sensations, are encouraged, along with having action plans available when a pivotal situation arises.

Taken together, ACT for SUDs encompasses all the aspects of traditional ACT protocols, while combining them with skills and components identified by the literature as essential for the treatment of individuals with SUDs, such as relapse prevention, motivational interviewing, and contingency management skills (Hayes et al., 2011).

Future Research Directions

While studies on ACT for SUDs are still being amassed, preliminary evidence indicates much promise. Studies of ACT for SUDs have shown reduction in substance use regardless of the substance addressed, as well as reductions in cravings, avoidance-based coping strategies, anxiety and depressive symptoms, negative affectivity, and posttraumatic symptoms (Cavicchioli, Movallia, & Maffei, 2018; Chiesa & Serretti, 2014; Li, Howard, Garland, McGovern, & Lazar, 2017; Zgierska et al., 2009). ACT's functional contextualistic approach aids in tackling comorbid disorders via identification of transdiagnostic elements as well as disorder-specific treatment components that can commonly address various psychological disorders (Ii et al., 2019).

Although ACT for SUDs is promising, there is still a need for larger, adequately powered outcome studies, as well as more studies to inform precise mechanisms responsible for behavior change in substance-abusing populations. Future research should also focus on more comprehensively addressing comorbidities such as personality and impulsivity-related factors through ACT processes such as values and present moment awareness (Mohi, Deane, Bailey, Mooney-Reh, & Ciaglia, 2018; Korponay et al., 2019). In an effort to personalize treatment, future work could address differentiating qualities of individuals with SUDs in a more targeted fashion (e.g., presence of self-stigma; Luoma & Platt, 2015; Wong et al., 2019). Additionally, treatment could be personalized according to an individual's addiction severity scores, their drugs of choice, as well as drug-specific vulnerability factors such as anxiety sensitivity and distress tolerance. Examinations of the differential effectiveness of various ACT-based components for specific drug types, severities, or populations may be useful with these gaps in the literature. Future studies need to expand this work on how to make interventions more personalized to the needs and context of each specific person with their set of circumstances.

Substance use disorders are characterized by a chronic and relapsing nature, and novel treatment modalities to deliver or augment ACT may prove helpful in this regard. Text messages (Stotts, Northrup, & Norwood, 2013), telephone and audio-assisted self-help programs (Stavrinaki & Karekla, 2019), and computer/web-based programs (Bricker, Wyszynski, Comstock, & Heffner, 2013; Bricker et al., 2014 ; Karekla et al., 2020) are a few promising examples. Future work can examine different types of innovative treatment methodologies to deliver or expand ACT either as a stand-alone intervention or an add on to already existing interventions. Beyond treatment, the need for more individualized and accurate assessments for people who use substances has also been highlighted (Carpenter, Martinez, Vadhan, Barnes-Holmes, & Nunes, 2012; Callaghan, 2017; Gloster & Karekla, 2020).

Development and use of new ACT and substance-specific, valid measurements (e.g., Acceptance and Action Questionnaire-Substance Abuse; Luoma et al., 2011) are vital to successfully address and understand the effectiveness of ACT as well as the specific processes of change that are at work when conducting interventions. Implicit measurement of substance-related variables may add to existing self-report measures (Thush et al., 2007). This is especially relevant given that explicit measures have several limitations, including sensitivity to contextual and social effects (Barnes-Holmes, Barnes-Holmes, Stewart, & Boles, 2010), response biases (Latkin, Edwards, Davey-Rothwell, & Tobin, 2017) as well as limited access to complicated mental processes (Nisbett & Wilson, 1977). Within the substance use literature, drug-taking behavior is understood as being partly induced through automatic processes that act outside of conscious control (Wiers & Stacy, 2006). Implicit measures are therefore particularly appropriate when assessing people who use substances (Wiers & Stacy, 2006). A relatively new implicit measure, the implicit relational assessment procedure (IRAP), has many benefits compared to its predecessors, including validity, reliability, specificity, immunity from "fakability," as well as a theoretically sound background (Drake, Seymour, & Habib, 2016; Golijani-Moghaddam, Hart, & Dawson, 2013). Three studies—on alcohol, cocaine, and a group of multidrug users—have examined implicit drug-related attitudes using the IRAP (Carpenter et al., 2012; Callaghan, 2017; Stavrinaki & Karekla, 2019). Biases identified by the IRAP have been shown to be malleable using appropriate exemplar training (AET; Cullen, Barnes-Holmes, Barnes-Holmes, & Stewart, 2009). These lines of inquiry of course need more research within a functional contextualistic framework to decipher their impact upon improving assessment and treatment for SUDs. Furthermore, from an ACT perspective, discomfort, believability, and avoidance of private events are functional processes, and they should be studied within the context of ongoing stimulus-behavior relations (Masuda, Feinstein, Wendell, & Sheehan, 2010). Self-report type methods do not assess these processes directly when they occur; therefore, the development of behavioral methodology or implicit assessment, that captures the function of self-referential thoughts seems extremely important in future studies. Overall, multilevel and multimodal assessments (Gloster & Karekla, 2020) may more accurately and timely identify mechanisms that lead to SUDs and intervene via both prevention and intervention methods to achieve our goals of better serving those who seek our services to achieve a dependence-free life, increased well-being, and decreased suffering.

Conclusion

In this article, we reviewed the evidence for the ACT approach to treatment of SUDs. Use of ACT for SUDs has shown much promise, with some outcome studies demonstrating greater abstinence as well as lower dropout and relapse levels in favor of ACT when compared to other effective treatment options (Cavicchioli et al., 2018; Lee et al., 2015; Stavrinaki & Karekla, 2019). Furthermore, ACT for SUDs could successfully address the interoceptive cues that are often responsible for substance initiation, maintenance, and relapse (Otto et al., 2007; Priddy et al., 2018). Moreover, key transdiagnostic and vulnerability factors attributed to SUDs (e.g., psychological inflexibility and distress tolerance) are well addressed in this approach (Lejuez et al., 2008; Stavrinaki & Karekla, 2019). Future research could further develop improvements in the assessment and personalization of substance use treatment.

References

American Psychiatric Association. (2016). The American Psychiatric Association practice guidelines for the psychiatric evaluation of adults (3rd Edition). *American Journal of Psychiatry, 173*(5), 543–546. doi: 10.1176/appi.ajp.2015.1720501.

American Psychiatric Association. (2018). *Practice guideline for the pharmacological treatment of patients with alcohol use disorder*. Washington, DC: American Psychiatric Association. doi/pdf/10.1176/appi.books.9781615371969.

Bahrami, S., & Asghari, F. (2017). A controlled trial of acceptance and commitment therapy for addiction severity in methamphetamine users: Preliminary study. *Archives of Psychiatry and Psychotherapy, 2*, 49–55.

Barnes-Holmes, D., Barnes-Holmes, Y., Stewart, I., & Boles, S. (2010). A sketch of the implicit relational assessment procedure (IRAP) and the relational elaboration and coherence (REC) model. *The Psychological Record, 60*(3), 10.

Bowen, S., Witkiewitz, K., Clifasefi, S. L., Grow, J., Chawla, N., Hsu, S. H., . . . & Larimer, M. E. (2014). Relative efficacy of mindfulness-based relapse prevention, standard relapse prevention, and treatment as usual for substance use disorders: A randomized clinical trial. *JAMA Psychiatry, 71*(5), 547–556.

Bowen, S., Witkiewitz, K., Dillworth, T. M., & Marlatt, G. A. (2007). The role of thought suppression in the relationship between mindfulness meditation and alcohol use. *Addictive Behaviors. 32*, 2324–2328.

Bricker, J. B., Mull, K. E., Kientz, J. A., Vilardaga, R., Mercer, L. D., Akioka, K. J., & Heffner, J. L. (2014). Randomized, controlled pilot trial of a smartphone app for smoking cessation using acceptance and commitment therapy. *Drug Alcohol Dependency, 143*, 87–94.

Bricker, J., Wyszynski, C., Comstock, B., & Heffner, J. L. (2013). Pilot randomized controlled trial of web-based acceptance and commitment therapy for smoking cessation. *Nicotine Tobacco Research, 15*,1756–1764.

Bruneau, J., Ahamad, K., Goyer, M. È., Poulin, G., Selby, P., Fischer, B., . . . & Wood, E. (2018). Management of opioid use disorders: A national clinical practice guideline. *CNAJ, 190*(9), E247–E257.

Buckner, J. D., Keough, M. E., & Schmidt, N. B. (2007). Problematic alcohol and cannabis use among young adults: The roles of depression and discomfort and distress tolerance. *Addictive Behaviours, 32*(9), 1957–1963.

Byrne, S. P., Haber, P., Baillie, A., Costa, D. S. J., Fogliati, V., & Morley, K (2019). Systematic reviews of mindfulness and acceptance and commitment therapy for alcohol use disorder: Should we be using third wave therapies? *Alcohol and Alcoholism, 54*(2), 159–166.

Callaghan, R. (2017). IRAP attitudes and alcohol. Unpublished doctorate thesis. Maynooth University.

Carleton, R. N., Mulvogue, M. K., Thibodeau, M. A., McCabe, R. E., Antony, M. M., & Asmundson, G. J. G. (2012). Increasingly certain about uncertainty: intolerance of uncertainty across anxiety and depression. *Journal of Anxiety Disorders, 26*, 468–479.

Carpenter, K. M., Martinez, D., Vadhan, N. P., Barnes-Holmes, D., & Nunes, E. V. (2012). Measures of attentional bias and relational responding are associated with behavioral treatment outcome for cocaine dependence. *American Journal of Drug and Alcohol Abuse, 38*(2), 146–154.

Cavicchioli, M., Movalli, M., & Maffei, C (2018). The clinical efficacy of mindfulness-based treatments for alcohol and drugs use disorders: A meta-analytic review of randomized and nonrandomized controlled trials. *European Addiction Research, 24*(3), 137–162.

Chaney, E. F., Roszell, D. K., & Cummings, C. (1982). Relapse in opiate addicts: A behavioral analysis. *Addictive Behaviours, 7*(3), 291–297.

Chiesa, A., & Serretti, A. (2014). Are mindfulness-based interventions effective for substance use disorders? A systematic review of the evidence. *Substance Use Misuse, 49*(5), 492–512.

Conklin, C. A., & Tiffany, S. T. (2002). Applying extinction research and theory to cue-exposure addiction treatments. *Addiction, 97*(2), 155–167. doi: 10.1046/j.1360-0443.2002.00014.x. PMID: 11860387
Conrod, P. J., Pihl, R. O., Stewart, S. H., & Dongier, M. (2000). Validation of a system of classifying female substance abusers on the basis of personality and motivational risk factors for substance abuse. *Psychology of Addictive Behaviors, 14,* 243–256.
Cooper, M. L. (1994) Motivations for alcohol use among adolescents: Development and validation of a four-factor model. *Psychological Assessment, 6,* 117–128.
Cullen, C., Barnes-Holmes, D., Barnes-Holmes, Y., & Stewart, I. (2009). The implicit relational assessment procedure (IRAP) and the malleability of ageist attitudes. *The Psychological Record, 59*(4), 6.
Daughters, S. B., Lejuez, C. W., Bornovalova, M. A., Kahler, C. W., Strong, D. R., & Brown, R. A. (2005). Distress tolerance as a predictor of early treatment dropout in a residential substance abuse treatment facility. *Journal of Abnormal.Psychology,114,* 729–734.
DeHaas, R. A. B., Calamari, J. E., & Bair, J. P. (2002). Anxiety sensitivity and the situational antecedents to drug and alcohol use: An evaluation of anxiety patients with substance use disorders. *Cognitive Therapy and Research. 26,* 335–353.
Drake, C. E., Seymour, K. H., & Habib, R. (2016) Testing the IRAP: Exploring the reliability and fakability of an idiographic approach to interpersonal attitudes. *Psychological Record, 66,* 153–163.
DuFrene, T., & Wilson, K. (2012). *The wisdom to know the difference: An acceptance and commitment therapy workbook for overcoming substance abuse.* Oakland, CA: New Harbinger Publications.
Feldner, M. T., Zvolensky, M. J., Eifert, G. H., & Spira, A. P. (2003). Emotional avoidance: An experimental test of individual differences and response suppression using biological challenge. *Behavior Research and Therapy, 41,* 401–411
Gloster, A. T., & Karekla, M. (2020). A multi-level, multi-method approach to testing and refining intervention targets. In S.G. Hoffman & S. Hayes (Eds.), *Beyond the DSM* (pp. 226–249). Oakland, CA: Context Press/New Harbinger Publications.
Gloster, A. T., Walder, N., Levin, M. E., Twohig, M. P., & Karekla, M. (2020). The empirical status of acceptance and commitment therapy: A review of metaanalyses. *Journal of Contextual Behavioural Science, 18,* 181–192.
Goldman, M. S., Brown, S. A., Christiansen, B. A., & Smith, G. T. (1991). Alcoholism and memory: Broadening the scope of alcohol-expectancy research. *Psychological Bulletin, 110*(1), 137.
Golijani-Moghaddam, N., Hart, A., & Dawson, D. L. (2013). The implicit relational assessment procedure: Emerging reliability and validity data. *Journal of Contextual Behavioral Science,* 2 (3–4), 105–119. http://dx.doi.org/10.1016/j.jcbs.2013.05.002
González-Menéndez, A., Fernándeza, P., Rodríguez, F., & Villagráa, P. (2014). Long-term outcomes of acceptance and commitment therapy in drug-dependent female inmates: A randomized controlled trial. *International Journal of Clinical and Health Psychology, 14*(1), 18–27.
Han, B. H., Termine, D. J., Moore, A. A., Sherman, S. E., & Palamar, J. J. (2018). Medical multimorbidity and drug use among adults in the United States. *Preventive Medicine Reports, 12,* 214–219. https://doi.org/10.1016/j.pmedr.2018.10.007
Hasenkamp, W., & Barsalou, L. W. (2012). Effects of meditation experience on functional connectivity of distributed brain networks. *Frontiers in Human Neuroscience, 6,* 38.
Hayes, S. C., & Levin, M. E. (2012). Contextual cognitive behavior therapies for addictive behaviors. In S. C. Hayes & M. E. Levin (Eds.), Mindfulness and acceptance for addictive behaviors: Applying contextual CBT to substance abuse and behavioral addictions (pp. 1–26). Oakland, CA: New Harbinger Publications.
Hayes, S. C., Pankey, J., Gifford, E. V., Batten, S., & Quiñones, R. (2002) Acceptance and commitment therapy in the treatment of experiential avoidance disorders. In T. Patterson (Ed.), Comprehensive handbook of psychotherapy, Volume 2: *Cognitive / behavioral / functional approaches* (pp. 319–351). New York: John Wiley.
Hayes, S. C., & Strosahl, K. D. (Eds.). (2004). *A practical guide to acceptance and commitment therapy.* New York: Springer-Verlag.
Hayes S. C., Strosahl K. D., & Wilson K. G. (2011). *Acceptance and commitment therapy: The process and practice of mindful change.* New York: Guilford Press.
Hayes, S. C., Wilson, K. G., Gifford, E. V., Bissett, R., Piasecki, M., Batten, S. V., . . . Gregg, J. (2004). A preliminary trial of twelve-step facilitation and acceptance and commitment therapy with polysubstance-abusing methadone-maintained opiate addicts. *Behavior Therapy, 35*(4), 667–688.
Heffner, M., Eifert, G. H., Parker, B. T., Hernandez, D. H., & Sperry, J. A. (2003) Valued directions: Acceptance and commitment therapy in the treatment of, alcohol dependence. *Cognitive and Behavioral Practice, 10*(4), 378–383,

Ii, T., Sato, H., Watanabe, N., Kondo, M., Masuda, A., Hayes, S. C., & Akechi, T. (2019). Psychological flexibility-based interventions versus first-line psychosocial interventions for substance use disorders: Systematic review and meta-analyses of randomized controlled trials. *Journal of Contextual Behavioral Science, 13*, 109–120.

Karekla, M., Forsyth, J. P., & Kelly, M. M. (2004). Emotional avoidance and panicogenic responding to a biological challenge procedure. *Behavior Therapy, 35*(4), 725–746.

Karekla, M., Georgiou, N., Panayiotou, G. P., Sandoz, E., Kurz, S., & Constantinou, M. (2020). Cognitive restructuring vs. defusion: Impact on craving, healthy and unhealthy food intake. *Eating Behaviors, 37*. https://doi.org/10.1016/j.eatbeh.2020. 101385.

Karekla, M., & Panayiotou, G. P (2011). Coping and experiential avoidance: Unique or overlapping constructs? *Journal of Behavior Therapy and Experimental Psychiatry, 42*(2), 163–170.

Karekla, M., Panayiotou, G., & Collins, B. N. (2017). Predictors of urge to smoke under stressful conditions: An experimental investigation utilizing the PASAT-C task to induce negative affect in smokers. *Psychology of Addictive Behaviors, 31*(7), 735–743, DOI: 10.1037/adb0000309.

Kavanagh, D. J., Andrade, J., & May, J. (2005). Imaginary relish and exquisite torture: The elaborated intrusion theory of desire. *Psychological Review, 112*(2), 446.

Kingston, R. E. F., Marel, C., & Mills, K. L (2017). A systematic review of the prevalence of comorbid mental health disorders in people presenting for substance use treatment in Australia. *Drug Alcohol Review, 36*, 527–539.

Korponay, C., Dentico, D., Kral, T. R. A. Ly, M., Kruis, A., Davis, K. Davidson, R. (2019). The effect of mindfulness meditation on impulsivity and its neurobiological correlates in healthy adults. *Scientific Reports, 9*, 11963 https://doi.org/10.1038/s41598-019-47662-y

Lanza, P. V., Garcia, P. F., Lamelas, F. R., & González-Menéndez, A. (2014). Acceptance and commitment therapy versus cognitive behavioral therapy in the treatment of substance use disorder with incarcerated women. *Journal of Clinical Psychology, 70*(7), 644–657.

Latkin, C., Edwards, C., Davey-Rothwell, M. A., & Tobin, K. E (2017). The relationship between social desirability bias and self-reports of health, substance use, and social network factors among urban substance users in Baltimore, Maryland. *Addictive Behaviors. 73*, 133–136.

Lee, E. B., An, W., Levin, M. E., & Twohig, M. P. (2015). An initial meta-analysis of acceptance and commitment therapy for treating substance use disorders. *Drug and Alcohol Dependence, 155*, 1–7.

Lejuez, C. W., Paulson, A., Daughters, S. B., Bornovalova, M. A., & Zvolensky, M. J. (2006). The association between heroin use and anxiety sensitivity among inner-city individuals in residential drug use treatment. *Behaviour Research and Therapy, 44*, 667–677.

Lejuez, C. W., Zvolensky, M. J., Daughters, S. B., Bornovalova, M. A., Paulson, A. Tull, M., . . . Otto, M. W. (2008). Anxiety sensitivity: A unique predictor of dropout among inner-city heroin and crack/cocaine users in residential substance use treatment. *Behaviour Research and Therapy, 7*, 811–818.

Li, W., Howard, M. O., Garland, E. L., McGovern, P., & Lazar, M. (2017). Mindfulness treatment for substance misuse: A systematic review and meta-analysis. *Journal of Substance Abuse Treatment, 75*, 62–96.

Lindgren, K. P., Foster, D. W., Westgate, E. C., & Neighbors, C. (2013a). Implicit drinking identity: Drinker+ me associations predict college student drinking consistently. *Addictive Behaviors, 38*(5), 2163–2166.

Lindgren, K. P., Neighbors, C., Teachman, B. A., Wiers, R. W., Westgate, E., & Greenwald, A. G. (2013b). I drink therefore I am: Validating alcohol-related implicit association tests. *Psychology of Addictive Behaviors, 27*(1), 1.

Luciano, M. C., Gómez, S., Hernández, M., & Cabello, F. (2001). Alcoholismo, evitación experiencial y Terapia de Aceptación y Compromiso (ACT). *Análisis y Modificación de Conducta, 27*(113), 333–371.

Luoma, J., Drake, C. E., Kohlenberg, B. S., & Hayes, S. C. (2011). Substance abuse and psychological flexibility: The development of a new measure. *Addiction Research and Theory, 19*, 3–13.

Luoma, J. B., Kohlenberg, B. S., Hayes, S. C., & Fletcher, L. (2012). Slow and steady wins the race: A randomized clinical trial of acceptance and commitment therapy targeting shame in substance use disorders. *Journal of Consulting and Clinical Psychology, 80*(1), 43–53.

Luoma, J., & Platt, M. G. (2015). Shame, self-criticism, self-stigma, and compassion in acceptance and commitment therapy. *Current Opinion in Psychology, 2*, 97–101.

Luoma, J. B., Twohig, M. P., Waltz, T., Hayes, S. C., Roget, N., Padilla, M., & Fisher, G. (2007). An investigation of stigma in individuals receiving treatment for substance abuse. *Addictive Behaviors, 32*(7), 1331–1346.

Marlatt, G. A., & Donovan, D. M. (Eds.). (2005). *Relapse prevention: Maintenance strategies in the treatment of addictive behaviors* (2nd ed.). New York: Guilford Press.

Masuda, A., Feinstein, A. B., Wendell, J. W., & Sheehan, S. T. (2010). Cognitive defusion versus thought distraction: A clinical rationale, training, and experiential exercise in altering psychological impact of negative self-referential thoughts. *Behavior Modification, 34*, 520–538.

Menon, J., & Kandasamy, A. (2018). Relapse prevention. *Indian Journal of Psychiatry, 60*(Suppl. l4), S473–S478. https://doi.org/10.4103/psychiatry.IndianJPsychiatry_36_18

Meyer, E. C., Walser, R., Hermann, B., La Bash, H., DeBeer, B. B., Morissette, S. B., & Schnurr, P. P. (2018). Acceptance and commitment therapy for co-occurring posttraumatic stress disorder and alcohol use disorders in veterans: Pilot treatment outcomes. *Journal of Traumatic Stress, 31*(5), 781–789.

Miller, W. R., Westerberg, V. S., Harris, R. J., & Tonigan, J. S. (1996). What predicts relapse? Prospective testing of antecedent models. *Addiction, 91*(12s1), 155–172.

Mohi, S. R., Deane, F. P., Bailey, A., Mooney-Reh, D., & Ciaglia, D. (2018). An exploration of values among consumers seeking treatment for borderline personality disorder. *Borderline Personality Disorder and Emotion Dysregulation, 5*(*1*), 1–10.

National Survey on Drug Use and Health. (2012). Summary of National Findings, NSDUH Series H-46, HHS Publication No. (SMA) 13-4795. Rockville, MD: Substance Abuse and Mental Health Services Administration.

NICE. (2016). Drug misuse in over 16s: Psychosocial interventions. Clinical guideline [CG51]. https://www.nice.org.uk/guidance/cg51/chapter/1-Guidance#general-considerations

Nisbett, R. E., & Wilson, T. D. (1977). Telling more than we can know: Verbal reports on mental processes. *Psychological Review, 84*(3), 231–259. https://doi.org/10.1037/0033-295X.84.3.231

Ostafin, B. D., & Marlatt, G. A. (2008). Surfing the urge: Experiential acceptance moderates the relation between automatic alcohol motivation and hazardous drinking. *Journal of Social and Clinical Psychology, 27*(4), 404–418.

Otto, M. W., O'Cleirigh, C. M., & Pollak, M. H. (2007). Attending to emotional cues for drug use: Bridging the gap between clinic and home behaviour. *NIDA Science and Practice Perspectives, 3*(2), 48–55.

Petersen, C. L., & Zettle, R. (2010) Treating inpatients with comorbid depression and alcohol use disorders: A comparison of acceptance and commitment therapy versus treatment as usual *The Psychological Record, 59*, 521–536.

Plumb, J. C., Stewart, I., Dahl, J., & Lundgren, T. (2009). In search of meaning: values in modern clinical behavior analysis. *The Behavior Analyst, 32*(1), 85–103. https://doi.org/10.1007/BF03392177

Poulton, A., & Hester, R. (2020). Transition to substance use disorders: Impulsivity for reward and learning from reward, *Social Cognitive and Affective Neuroscience, 15*(10), 1182–1191,

Prendergast, M., Podus, D., Finney, J., Greenwell, L, & Roll, J. (2006). Contingency management for treatment of substance use disorders: A meta-analysis. *Addiction*, 101(11):1546–1560. doi: 10.1111/j.1360-0443.2006.01581.x. PMID: 17034434

Priddy, S. E., Howard, M. O., Hanley, A. W., Riquino, M. R., Friberg-Felsted, K., & Garland, E. L. (2018). Mindfulness meditation in the treatment of substance use disorders and preventing future relapse: Neurocognitive mechanisms and clinical implications. *Substance Abuse and Rehabilitation, 9*, 103–114. https://doi.org/10.2147/SAR.S145201

The Royal Australian and New Zealand College of Psychiatrist (RANZCP). (2016). website(https://www.ranzcp.org/news-policy/news-archive/news-archive-2016)

Richards, J. M., Daughters, S. B., Bornovalova, M. A., Brown, R. A., & Lejuez, C. W. (2011). Substance use disorders. In M. J. Zvolensky, A. Bernstein, & A. Vujanovic, *Distress tolerance: Theory, research, and clinical applications* (pp. 171–197). New York: Guilford Press.

Roos, C. R., Kirouac, M., Pearson, M. R., Fink, B. C., & Witkiewitz, K. (2015). Examining temptation to drink from an existential perspective: Associations among temptation, purpose in life, and drinking outcomes. *Psychology of Addictive Behaviors: Journal of the Society of Psychologists in Addictive Behaviors, 29*(3), 716–724. https://doi.org/10.1037/adb0000063

Roozen, H. G., Boulogne, J. J., van Tulder, M. W., van den Brink, W., De Jong, C. A., Kerkhof, A. J. A systematic review of the effectiveness of the community reinforcement approach in alcohol, cocaine and opioid addiction. (2004). *Drug Alcohol Dependency, 74*(1), 1–13. doi: 10.1016/j.drugalcdep.2003.12.006. PMID: 15072802.

Schmidt, N. B., Buckner, J. D., & Keough, M. E. (2007a). Anxiety sensitivity as a prospective predictor of alcohol use disorders. *Behavior Modification, 31*(2), 202–219.

Schmidt, N. B., Richey, J. A., Cromer, K. R., & Buckner, J. D. (2007b). Discomfort intolerance: Evaluation of a potential risk factor for anxiety psychopathology. *Behavior Therapy, 38*(3), 247–255.

Schmitz, J. M., Stotts, A. L., Vujanovic, A. A., Weaver, M. F., Yoon, J. H., Vincent, J., & Green, C. E. (2018). A sequential multiple assignment randomized trial for cocaine cessation and relapse prevention: Tailoring treatment to the individual. *Contemporary Clinical Trials, 65*, 109–115. https://doi.org/10.1016/j.cct.2017.12.015

Shorey, R. C., Haynes, E., Brem, M., Florimbio, A. R., Grigorian, H., & Stuart, G. L. (2018). Marijuana use is associated with intimate partner violence perpetration among men arrested for domestic violence. *Translational Issues in Psychological Science, 4*(1), 108–118. https://doi.org/10.1037/tps0000140

Simons, J. S., & Gaher, R. M. (2005). The Distress Tolerance Scale: Development and validation of a self-report measure. *Motivation and Emotion, 29*(2), 83–102.

Smout, M. F., Hayes, L., Atkins, P., Klausen, J., & Duguid, J. E (2012). The empirically supported status of acceptance and commitment therapy: An update. *Clinical Psychologist, 16* (3), 97–109.
Smout, M. F., Longo, M., Harrison, S., Minniti, R., Wickes, W., & White, J. M. (2010). Psychosocial treatment for methamphetamine use disorders: A preliminary randomized controlled trial of cognitive behavior therapy and acceptance and commitment therapy. *Substance Abuse, 31,* 98–107.
Stavrinaki, M., & Karekla, M. (2019). Internal cues and drug dependency: Cognitive reappraisal and cognitive defusion as potential processes of change. PhD thesis, University of Cyprus.
Stewart, S. H., Zvolensky, M. J., & Efiert, G. H. (2001). Negative-reinforcement drinking motives mediate the relation between anxiety sensitivity and increased drinking behavior. *Personality and Individual Differences, 31*(2), 157–171.
Stewart, S. H., Zvolensky, M. J., & Eifert, G. H. (2002). The relations of anxiety sensitivity, experiential avoidance, and alexithymic coping to young adults' motivations for drinking. *Behavior Modification, 26*(2), 274–296.
Stoddard, J. A., & Afari, N. (2014). The Big Book of ACT metaphors: A practitioner's guide to experiential exercises and metaphors in acceptance and commitment therapy. Oakland, CA: New Harbinger Publications.
Stotts, A. L., Green, C., Masuda, A., Grabowski, J., Wilson, K., Northrup, T. F., . . . Schmitz, J. M. (2012). A stage I pilot study of acceptance and commitment therapy for methadone detoxification. *Drug and Alcohol Dependence, 125*(3), 215–222.
Stotts, A. L., Masuda, A., & Wilson, K. (2009). Using acceptance and commitment therapy during methadone dose reduction: Rationale, treatment description, and a case report. *Cognitive and Behavioral Practice, 16*(2), 205–213.,
Stotts, A. L., & Northrup, T. F. (2015). The promise of third-wave behavioral therapies in the treatment of substance use disorders. *Current Opinion in Psychology, 1,* 75–81.
Stotts, A., Northrup, T., & Norwood, W. (2013). Initial pilot test of a group-texting intervention to sustain opioid abstinence following residential detoxification and treatment. *Journal of Addictive Behaviors, Therapy and Rehabilitation, 8,* 2.
Stotts, A. L., Vujanovic, A., Heads, A., Suchting, R., Green, C. E., & Schmitz, J. M. (2014). The role of avoidance and inflexibility in characterizing response to contingency management for cocaine use disorders: A secondary profile analysis. *Psychology of Addictive Behaviors, 29*(2), 408–413.
Thurstone, C., Hull, M., Timmerman, J., & Emrick, C. (2017). Development of a motivational interviewing/acceptance and commitment therapy model for adolescent substance use treatment. *Journal of Contextual Behavioral Science, 6*(4), 375–379.
Thush, C., Wiers, R. W., Ames, S. L., Grenard, J., Sussman, S., & Stacy, A. W. (2007). Apples and oranges? Comparing indirect measures of alcohol-related cognition predicting alcohol use in at-risk adolescents. *Psychology of Addictive Behaviors, 21,* 587–591.
Turner, N., Welches, P., & Conti, S. (2013). *Mindfulness-based sobriety: A clinician's guide for addiction recovery using relapse prevention therapy acceptance and commitment therapy.* Oakland, CA: New Harbinger Publications.
Twohig, M. P., Shoenberger, D., & Hayes, S. C. (2007). A preliminary investigation of acceptance and commitment therapy as a treatment for marijuana dependence in adults. *Journal of Applied Behavior Analysis, 40*(4), 619–632.
Veterans Affairs/Department of Defense. (2015). Clinical practice guideline for the management of substance use disorders (version 3). https://www.healthquality.va.gov/guidelines/MH/sud/VADoDSUDCPGRevised22216.pdf
Wong, P. C., Hsieh, Y. P., Ng, H. H., Kong, S. F., Chan, L. K., Yeung, T., . . . Fung, X. C. C. (2019). Investigating the self-stigma and quality of life for overweight/obese children in Hong Kong: A preliminary study. *Child Indicators Research, 12,* 1065–1082. https://doi.org/10.1007/s12187-018-9573-0
World Drug Report. (2020). United Nations publication, Sales No. E. 20. XI.
Weinrib, A. Z., Azam, M. A., Birnie, K. A., Burns, L. C., Clarke, H., & Katz, J. (2017). The psychology of chronic post-surgical pain: New frontiers in risk factor identification, prevention and management. *British Journal of Pain, 11*(4), 169–177.
Westrup, D. A. (2001). Experiential avoidance and alcohol dependence relapse. *Dissertation Abstracts International: Section B: The Sciences and Engineering, 62*(1-B), 568.
Whiteford, H. A., Ferrari, A. J., Degenhardt, L., Feigin, V., & Vos, T. (2015). The global burden of mental, neurological and substance use disorders: an analysis from the Global Burden of Disease Study 2010. *PloS one, 10*(2), e0116820.
Wiers, R. W., & Stacy, A. W. (2006). Implicit cognition and addiction. *Current Directions in Psychological Science, 15*(6), 292–296.

Wilson, K. G., & Byrd, M. R. (2004). Acceptance and commitment therapy for substance abuse and dependence. In S. C. Hayes & K. Strosahl (Eds.), *A practical guide to acceptance and commitment therapy* (pp. 153–184). New York: Springer Press.
Wilson, K. G., Hayes, S. C., & Byrd, M. R (2000). Exploring compatibilities between acceptance and commitment therapy and 12-step treatment for substance abuse. *Journal of Rational-Emotive and Cognitive-Behavior Therapy, 18*(4), 209–234.
Wilson, K. G., Sandoz, E. K., Kitchens, J., & Roberts, M. (2010). The Valued Living Questionnaire: Defining and measuring valued action within a behavioral framework. *The Psychological Record, 60,* 249–272.
Wilson, K. G., Schnetzer, L. W., Flynn, M. K., & Kurz, S. A. (2012). *Acceptance and commitment therapy for addiction.* Oakland, CA: Context Press.
Witkiewitz, K., Donovan, D. M., & Hartzler, B. (2012). Drink refusal training as part of a combined behavioral intervention: Effectiveness and mechanisms of change. *Journal of Consulting and Clinical Psychology, 80*(3): 440–449.
Witkiewitz, K., Lustyk, M., & Bowen, S. (2013). Retraining the addicted brain: A review of hypothesized neurobiological mechanisms of mindfulness-based relapse prevention. *Psychology of Addictive Behaviors: Journal of the Society of Psychologists in Addictive Behaviors, 27*(2), 351–365. https://doi.org/10.1037/a0029258
Woodward, L. (2017). Act on your recovery: A 15 session group work manual. Unpublished. ACBS website https://contextualscience.org/
Zgierska, A., Rabago, D., Chawla, N., Kushner, K., Koehler, R., & Marlatt, A. (2009). Mindfulness meditation for substance use disorders: A systematic review. *Substance Abuse; 30,* 266–294.
Zvolensky, M. J., Marshall, E. C., Johnson, K., Hogan, J., Bernstein, A., & Bonn-Miller, M. O. (2009). Relations between anxiety sensitivity, distress tolerance, and fear reactivity to bodily sensations to coping and conformity marijuana use motives among young adult marijuana users. *Experimental and Clinical Psychopharmacology, 17*(1), 31.
Zvolensky, M. J., Vujanovic, A. A., Bernstein, A., & Leyro, T. (2010). Distress tolerance: Theory, measurement, and relations to psychopathology. *Current Directions in Psychological Science, 19*(6), 406–410.

CHAPTER

23 Acceptance and Commitment Therapy for Smoking Cessation

Jonathan B. Bricker

Abstract

This article summarizes the theory, clinical methods, evidence, and mechanisms of action for the application of acceptance and commitment therapy (ACT) to tobacco smoking cessation. Following an overview of the relational frame theory underlying the ACT cessation interventions and contrasts between ACT and standard behavioral clinical practice guideline cessation interventions, a session-by-session clinical summary is presented for the delivery of an ACT cessation intervention. The evidence reviewed from the 15 randomized clinical trials published to date (total $N = 6991$) shows that ACT is a strong alternative to standard behavioral therapies when delivered in traditional modalities (e.g., group) and is particularly efficacious as a smartphone-delivered cessation intervention (e.g., iCanQuit smartphone app). Acceptance of cravings is an important mechanism of action. Future directions include next generations of digital delivery, such as conversational agents (i.e., "chatbots").

Key Words: acceptance and commitment therapy, relational frame theory, smoking cessation, digital interventions, clinical protocol, evidence, acceptance of cravings, chatbots

Globally, tobacco smoking is now the second leading cause of early death and disability (GBD 2015 Risk Factors Collaborators, 2016), accounting for over one in ten deaths (GBD 2015 Tobacco Collaborators, 2017). Standard smoking cessation behavioral interventions follow the U.S. Clinical Practice Guidelines (USCPG; Fiore et al., 2008). The USCPG have these behavioral components: tracking smoking status, assisting in quit planning and setting a quit date, advice on Food and Drug Administration-approved pharmacotherapy for smoking cessation, motivational interviewing, cognitive-behavioral skills to prevent relapse, and skills for identifying and eliciting social support for quitting (Abroms et al., 2011, 2013; Fiore et al., 2000, 2008). Multiple meta-analyses of USCPG behavioral interventions report modest weighted-average 12-month outcomes of 6% to 25% smoking cessation rates, depending on the delivery modality (Civljak et al., Car, 2010; Fiore et al., 2008; Graham et al., 2011; Hutton et al., 2011; Lancaster & Stead, 2017; Shahab & McEwen, 2009; Silagy et al., 2004; Stead et al., 2006, 2013, 2017; Webb, 2009; Whittaker et al., 2012). These success rates are generally higher than the 4% success rate from quitting smoking on one's own (Fiore et al., 2008), but there is a lot of room for improvement.

To improve on the modest success rates of USCPG interventions, since 2004, a total of 15 randomized clinical trials have been published that compare acceptance and commitment therapy (ACT) to USCPG interventions for tobacco smoking cessation. In the context of smoking cessation, acceptance means noticing and not acting on physical cravings (e.g., urges to smoke), emotions (e.g., sadness that cues smoking), and thoughts (e.g., thoughts that cue smoking). Commitment means expressing what is deeply important and meaningful to a person—that is, one's values—to guide specific plans of action (e.g., setting a quit date).

ACT is based on relational frame theory (RFT; Hayes et al., 2001). RFT posits that overt environmental, cognitive, physiological, and emotional stimuli can become related to one another in every imaginable way. For example, smokers may have a powerful urge to smoke during their first visit to a nonsmoking bar due to a history of connections between bars where they used to enjoy smoking; the word "smoking," an urge to smoke, and the like. An innovative principle of RFT is that trying to control or eliminate these relations creates a paradox: new relations are formed that interfere with behavior change. For example, distraction from an urge becomes related with more urges, impeding quitting smoking. Therapeutically, RFT suggests the innovative approach of creating new relations that support valued behavior change. For example, a person with the thought "I need to smoke to feel better" could add the thought: "I care about my health, so I won't act upon this thought." RFT suggests that a person's thoughts do not necessarily reflect that person's intrinsic characteristics. Instead, RFT suggests that a person notice thoughts as just thoughts while choosing actions consistent with what the person cares about (e.g., living a healthy life). RFT principles are supported in basic science experiments, and these principles guide ACT therapeutic techniques (Hayes et al., 2013).

Both ACT and the USCPG focus on teaching skills to cope with urges to smoke. However, the philosophy and content of those skills follow fundamentally different paradigms. Unlike the USCPG, ACT does not focus on changing the content of thoughts (e.g., replacing an inaccurate thought with an accurate thought) but rather one's *relationship* to them via active awareness and observation of thoughts (Hayes et al., 2006). ACT's first key innovation is a focus on increasing a person's willingness to experience urges to smoke (Gifford et al., 2004; Hernandez-Lopez et al., 2009). In contrast, the USCPG use problem-solving skills to avoid and control urges to smoke (Fiore et al., 2008; Perkins et al., 2008). ACT's second key innovation is promoting value-driven behavior change (Gifford et al., 2004; Hayes et al., 1999; Hernandez-Lopez et al., 2009; Luoma et al., 2007), whereas the USCPG promote reason-driven behavior change (Fiore et al., 2008; Perkins et al., 2008). For the change approach, ACT teaches skills primarily through metaphors and experiential exercises (Gifford et al., 2004; Hernandez-Lopez et al., 2009; Luoma et al., 2007), whereas the USCPG teach skills primarily through logical and literal explanation (Fiore et al., 2000; Perkins et al., 2008). In ACT, metaphors and experiential exercises help people step back from literal thought, feeling, and urges. Finally, ACT differs from mindfulness-based therapies in that (1) being mindful is only one of numerous ACT strategies for increasing willingness to experience urges and (2) ACT focuses on values (Herbert & Forman, 2011). The differences between ACT and the USCPG are further elaborated in Table 23.1.

Clinician Delivery of ACT for Smoking Cessation

To apply and adapt ACT concepts for cigarette smoking cessation, our research team has developed a clinician's intervention manual that has been continuously refined over the years (Bricker et al., 2010; Bricker, Bush, et al., 2014; McClure et al., 2020). Our manual is a five-session (30 minutes for Session One; 15–20 minutes for Sessions Two to Five) intervention that can be delivered either as a stand-alone treatment or as adjunct to an ongoing ACT-based treatment for other behaviors. Session One focuses on values, acceptance, and committed action. Specifically, the clinician will elicit the core values that guide a patient's plan to quit

Table 23.1 Differences between ACT and USCPG for smoking cessation

Conceptual Level	*ACT*	*USCPG*
Theoretical Basis	***Relational Frame Theory:*** *Overt environmental, cognitive, physiological, and emotional stimuli can be related to one another—and thereby take on each other's qualities and functions—in every imaginable way: (Example: seeing an actual cigarette↔ thought "urge" ↔ physical urge↔ smoking a cigarette). Trying to control these processes just adds new relations and interferes with behavior change (Example: distraction from an urge ↔ more urges). In contrast, increasing willingness to experience (and not change) these processes increases value-guided behavior change (Hayes et al., 2001).*	***Information Processing Theories:*** *The mind processes information through the application of mental rules/strategies that guide behavior. Applying Illogical rules/strategies leads to dysfunctional behavior. (Example: Applying the illogical belief that "smoking controls stress" will lead one to smoke.) In contrast, applying logical rules/strategies leads to more effective information processing and functional behavior (Newell, 1990).*
Clinical Level	***ACT***	***USCPG***
General approach to intervening on urges, emotions, and thoughts that cue smoking	***Acceptance****: Openness to experience urges, emotions, and thoughts as they are and without any intent that they change (e.g.,* ***no*** *desire that urge reduces). Example: Asking: "How willing are you to have, and not try to change, your urges to smoke?" (Gifford et al., 2004; Luoma et al., 2007)*	***Avoidance:*** *Actively trying not to experience urges, emotions, and thoughts with the intent that that they change (e.g., desire for urge to reduce). Example: Asking: "How can you avoid or control your urges to smoke?" (Perkins et al., 2008, p. 74).*
Specific approach to intervening on urges and emotions that cue smoking	***Being Present****: Being fully aware of the present moment with openness. Nonjudgmental description of experiences in the present moment. Example: while holding an unlit cigarette, take one minute to describe out loud its color, length, texture, smell. Describe urges and emotions (Gifford et al., 2004; Luoma et al., 2007).*	***Urge/Emotion Coping Skills****: A broad set of strategies designed to manage or control urges and emotions that cue smoking. Examples: avoiding places where you often smoke; engaging in a distracting activity (e.g., crossword puzzle); keeping hands active (e.g., gripping a stress ball; Perkins et al., 2008, p. 81).*
Specific approach to intervening on thoughts that cue smoking	***Cognitive Defusion****: Seeing thoughts, self-judgments, images, and memories as just words and pictures. Allowing them to come and go without trying to control or avoid them. Example: For a thought that often cues smoking (e.g., "I want to smoke."), reduce it to one key word (e.g. "smoke") and then say the word out loud repeatedly for 30 seconds, while not smoking (Gifford et al., 2004; Luoma et al., 2007).*	***Cognitive Restructuring:*** *Changing the content of one's unrealistic/ irrational beliefs and/or replacing them with realistic/rational beliefs. Example: Change the thought "Smoking is how I cope with things" with this response: "Smoking does nothing to help a smoker cope, other than relieving withdrawal" (Perkins et al., 2008, p. 41).*

(*continued*)

Table 23.1 *Continued*

Conceptual Level	*ACT*	*USCPG*
Specific approach to increase motivation to quit smoking	***Values:*** *Chosen life directions that guide actions. Values require no reasoning. Valuing is a process, not a life goal achieved or an outcome. Examples: "What really matters to you?; How would you like to build your personal relationships?" (Gifford et al., 2004; Luoma et al., 2007).*	***Reasons to Change:*** *The specific expectations one would have for when a behavior has changed. Examining the advantages and disadvantages of a behavior change. Examples: Listing expected benefits of quitting smoking; Listing all of the reasons for quitting and for not quitting smoking (Perkins et al., 2008, pp. 49–50).*

smoking. This would include asking questions, including "What makes quitting smoking now important to you?"; "If you were not smoking, how would you be spending your time?" Broadly, the areas of life that often guide a patient's quitting smoking are issues of health and relationships. The clinician invites the patient to keep these answers in mind as they work on quitting smoking and will remind them whenever the patient is struggling with cravings or has a lapse. Shifting to acceptance, the clinician focuses on enhancing willingness to notice triggers to smoke for the sake of values. This would include asking: "How willing are you to have and not act on your urges to smoke cigarettes?" and "Would you be willing to not act on your cravings, for sake of ________ (e.g., your family or your health)?" For patients struggling with willingness, clinicians focus on past valued actions in the face of extreme personal challenges: "Have you done something really important that was hard to do?" Finally, Session One ends with a plan to take committed action, which may include setting a quit date (ideally within the next 2 weeks or before the third session); planning to take any FDA-approved medications for stopping smoking; and tracking to triggers to smoke cigarettes. Medications are framed as a short-term method for coping with cravings and withdrawal, while the patient is learning ACT skills as a long-term method for responding to these sensations and preventing relapse.

Session Two focuses on the ACT processes of being present and committed action. Following a brief session bridge and review of progress since Session One, the clinician introduces the concept of being present and then illustrates it with a Stop and Breathe exercise. With eyes closed, the patient is invited to take slow, deep breaths in and out, and then to notice sensations, thoughts, and emotions for about 5 minutes. In the debrief, the clinician advises the patient to practice Stop and Breathe at least three times a day while having an urge to smoke. Next, the clinician presents an acronym for remembering key concepts of the program: B.R.E.A.K.S.: B = brake (stop!), R = read what's inside (how does it feel inside?), E = expand (breathe in and out), A = allow everything (the situation and your experience), K = know what's important to you, and S = step it forward (take a step in your important direction). Finally, the session wraps up with a committed action plan that includes practicing Stop and Breathe, following the B.R.E.A.K.S. acronym, and using FDA-approved quit smoking medications. If the quit date is set to occur within the next week, the next session should be timed for several days after the quit date as a measure to help prevent relapse.

Session Three focuses on cognitive defusion and committed action. Following a brief session bridge and review of progress since Session Two, the clinician introduces the concept of defusion and illustrates it with an exercise. Given the seemingly automatic nature of smoking behavior, patients are sometimes unaware of the thoughts they have before or during smoking. In these cases, the clinician can provide common examples such as "I need a break, "I want a cigarette," or "I am going to fail at quitting smoking." Recording the thoughts the patient is having during an urge to smoke is often a useful strategy for becoming more aware of these thoughts. The most common exercise used in our program for defusing from thoughts is "I am Having the Thought," which involves rating the strength of the thought (e.g., 0 to 10 scale), then adding and saying aloud several times the phrase, "I am having the thought that . . . " and finally re-rating the thought to observe any changes in the strength of the thought. Finally, the session shifts to a committed action plan that includes plans for taking quit smoking medications, daily practice of "I am Having the Thought," and practice of any exercises from previous sessions.

Session Four focuses on self-compassionate perspective-taking and committed action. Following a brief session bridge and review of progress since Session Three, the clinician frames self-compassionate perspective-taking simply as an exercise for dealing with stress—a common trigger for smoking. The exercise called "Puppy Exercise" asks the patient to imagine finding a cute little puppy that is stressed and how the patient would respond (e.g., by comforting it). And then the clinician asks: "You wouldn't give the puppy a cigarette, would you?" Following a pause, the perspective shifts to how the patients treats themselves when they are stressed. Instead of smoking when stressed, patients could remember the stressed puppy and consider alternative ways of responding, including taking a moment, resting, or reaching out to a friend. The session then closes with a committed action plan that is similar to the prior session.

Session Five focuses on acceptance and values. Following a brief session bridge and review of progress since Session Four, the clinician reviews the core acceptance message of the program: practicing letting go of urges will help you stay quit for life. Relatedly, the clinician states that "you are not your urges," emphasizing the defusion from people's self-identification with sensations, thoughts, and emotions that trigger smoking, and instead seeing them as internal and changing experiences they have. Shifting to values, the clinician elicits from the patient what matters most about quitting smoking and how that aspect has served as an inspiration to persist even in the face of challenges. Reflecting on the entire program, the clinician presents six summary words: be aware, be willing, and be inspired. Specifically, be aware of your triggers to smoke, be willing to have these triggers, and be inspired by your values.

Efficacy

Published randomized clinical trials comparing ACT with USCPG behavioral interventions have been conducted in four modalities of delivery: group therapy, telephone coaching, website, and smartphone application. This section briefly reviews the efficacy of ACT in each of these modalities.

Group Therapy

There are numerous barriers to accessing group-delivered intervention for smoking cessation interventions. These barriers include little or no insurance reimbursement and lack of patient demand (Husten, 2010). Nonetheless, group therapy for smoking cessation will likely remain available in some limited form for the foreseeable future (Stead et al., 2017). The first trials of group-delivered (or group plus individual sessions) ACT were pilot studies that, by design, had important methodological limitations, including small sample sizes, quasi-experimental designs, lack of a behavioral intervention control arms (e.g., comparison was medications only), and exclusion of people with substance use and psychiatric comorbidities (Brown et al., 2013, 2018; Gifford et al., 2004, 2011; Hernandez-Lopez et al., 2009). These trials motivated a full-scale randomized trial of group-delivered ACT that compared five weekly 90-minute sessions of ACT to five weekly 90-minute sessions of group-delivered UCSPG skills therapy in a sample of 450 adults smoking at least 10 cigarettes per day (McClure et al., 2020). In both treatment arms, participants received 8 weeks of nicotine replacement therapy. Master's level therapists delivered the interventions with a high level of adherence to their respective interventions (i.e., 4.9 out of 5 in each arm). Smoking cessation rates did not differ between study arms at the main outcome of no smoking in the past 30 days (i.e., 30-day point prevalence abstinence) at the 12-month follow-up (13.8% for ACT vs. 18.1% for USCPG; OR [odds ratio] = .68 (95% CI [confidence interval]: .35 to 1.27)). Collectively, the current evidence base from randomized trials suggests that group-delivered ACT is a reasonable alternative to group-delivered USCPG intervention for smoking cessation.

Telephone Coaching

Smoking cessation hotlines, commonly known as "quitlines" (QLs), are a critical component of the broad public health approach to global tobacco control (Fiore et al., 2000, 2008). In the United States alone, quitlines reach over 350,000 smokers each year (Consortium, 2017). However, they have a modest average success rate of 14% (range 8–20%) at 12-month follow-up (Fiore et al., 2008; Matkin et al., 2019).

With the aim of improving the success rates of quitlines, a pilot randomized trial (n =121) compared telephone therapist-delivered ACT to telephone therapist-delivered USCPG intervention, with both interventions offering five sessions (30 minutes for Call 1; 15 minutes for Calls 2–5; (Bricker, Bush, et al., 2014). Adults smoking at least 10 cigarettes per day received a standard 2-week course of nicotine patch or gum (participant's choice)—consistent with pharmacotherapy practices of the state quitline from where participants were recruited. This pilot trial showed promising results: the intent-to-treat 30-day point prevalence abstinence rates at 6 months postrandomization were 31% in ACT versus 22% in USCPG (OR = 1.5, 95% CI = 0.7–3.4). These results motivated a full-scale randomized trial, which is now underway (ClinicalTrials.gov ID: NCT02421991).

Website

Globally, millions of people who smoke use websites to help them quit smoking (Borrelli et al., 2015). Randomized clinical trials of websites for smoking cessation have poor outcome data follow-up rates (e.g., 34% at 12-month follow-up [range: 11–72%]). The weighted average 12-month 30-day point prevalence cessation rate for previous web-delivered intervention trials was 9% (range: 7–17%; Graham et al., 2016; Taylor et al., 2017).

Two randomized trials have compared web-delivered ACT to web-delivered USCPG for smoking cessation. The first was a pilot randomized trial of 222 U.S. adults smoking at least five cigarettes per day, comparing the ACT-based WebQuit.org website with the U.S. National Cancer Institute's USCGP-based Smokefree.gov website (Bricker et al., 2013). No medication was provided in either treatment group. The results showed that the ACT treatment group had over double the fraction of participants quitting smoking (23% vs. 10%; OR = 3.05; 95% CI = 1.01–9.32). These results motivated a second study: a full-scale randomized trial comparing WebQuit.org with Smokefree.gov in a sample of 2637 adults smokers (at least five cigarettes per day) recruited from all 50 U.S. states (Bricker et al., 2017). Like the pilot trial, no medication was provided in either group. The 12-month outcome data follow-up rate was 88% (2309/2637). The 30-day point prevalence abstinence rates at the 12-month follow-up were 24% (278/1141) for WebQuit.org and 26% (305/1168) for Smokefree.gov (OR = 0.91; 95% CI = 0.76, 1.10). The difference in observed quit rates between the two trials was potentially due to the study design of the pilot (Bricker et al., 2013) versus the full-scale trial (Bricker et al., 2017): the pilot trial had a lower outcome data retention rate (54% vs. 88%), smaller sample size (222 vs. 2637), and shorter follow-up period (3 months vs. 12 months; Bricker et al., 2013). With a quit rate that is over two times higher than the average quit rate of web-delivered interventions (9% vs. 24%), together the two trials suggest that web-delivered ACT, in particular WebQuit, is a helpful option for people seeking online help for quitting smoking.

Smartphone

Smartphone applications for quitting smoking have a high population-level reach (Whittaker et al., 2019). To date, approximately 500 English-language smoking cessation applications have been downloaded an estimated total of 33 million times.[1] In the United States, as of 2019, 81% of all adults owned smartphones—up from 35% in 2011 (Pew Research Center, 2019). Despite their ubiquity, there has been very little evidence for the efficacy of these smartphone applications, with the 2019 *Cochrane Review* showing that the five included randomized trials had 6-month follow-up quit smoking rates ranging from 4 to 8% (Whittaker et al., 2019).

Two randomized trials have compared smartphone-delivered ACT to smartphone-delivered USCPG for smoking cessation. The first was a pilot randomized trial of 196 U.S. adults smoking at least five cigarettes per day, comparing the ACT-based application SmartQuit with the U.S. National Cancer Institute's USCGP-based QuitGuide application (Bricker, Mull, et al., 2014). No medication was provided in either treatment group. On the primary outcome of 30-day point prevalence abstinence at 2 months postrandomization, the quit rates were 13% in SmartQuit versus 8% in QuitGuide (OR = 2.7; 95% CI = 0.8–10.3). The second was a full-scale randomized trial comparing the ACT-based application called iCanQuit with QuitGuide in a sample of 2415 adults smokers (at least five cigarettes per day) recruited from all 50 U.S. states (Bricker et al., 2020). No medication was provided in either group. The 12-month follow-up outcome data retention rate was 87.2% (2107/2415). For the primary outcome of 30-day point prevalence at the 12-month follow-up, iCanQuit participants had 1.49 times higher odds of quitting smoking as compared to QuitGuide participants [28.2% (293/1040) abstinent versus 21.1% (225/1067) abstinent; OR = 1.49; 95% CI = 1.22, 1.83]. Effect sizes were very similar and statistically significant for all secondary outcomes such as cessation of all tobacco products, including e-cigarettes/vaping (OR range: 1.26–2.20). This trial provides strong evidence that, relative to a USCPG-based smartphone application, an ACT-based smartphone application was more efficacious for quitting cigarette smoking and thus can be an impactful treatment choice.

Mechanisms

Eleven randomized trials provide an evidence base for the mediating role of acceptance of internal triggers (e.g., cravings) in smoking cessation. Of the eleven trials, eight showed either formal statistical mediation or higher levels of acceptance of internal triggers to smoke in the ACT intervention arm (Bricker et al., 2013, 2017; Bricker, Bush, et al., 2014; Bricker, Mull, et al., 2014; Brown et al., 2013; Gifford et al., 2004, 2011; Vilardaga et al., 2019). In all eight trials, ACT showed more favorable smoking cessation outcomes than the USCPG comparison intervention. By contrast, the remaining three trials showed no evidence of mediation or higher acceptance of internal triggers in the ACT arm, and the cessation outcomes were similar in both arms—even though overall increases in acceptance of internal triggers predicted higher odds of smoking cessation (Brown et al., 2018; McClure et al., 2020; O'Connor et al., 2020).

Together, these results have three implications: (1) increases in acceptance of internal triggers may be an important theoretical pathway of smoking cessation, (2) ACT interventions that have higher levels of acceptance of internal triggers than comparison interventions yield higher cessation rates; (2) ACT interventions that have similar levels of acceptance of internal triggers relative to comparison interventions yield similar cessation rates. This latter implication may explain why the remaining three trials found similar cessation rates for ACT and the USCPG comparison interventions. For ACT intervention design, this body of evidence suggests that the critical role of creating components can impact acceptance of internal triggers to smoke.

Future Research Directions

Three directions for future research on ACT for smoking cessation are recommended: special populations, new digital technologies, and dissemination/implementation.

With regard to special populations, there is an emerging literature on the development and testing of ACT smoking cessation interventions for populations of smokers who have the highest smoking rates and/or the lowest quit rates. To date, five pilot randomized trials have examined the initial efficacy of ACT for these special populations of smokers: early lapsers, young adults, people with serious mental disorders, and cancer patients. Early lapsers are smokers who have not been able to achieve at least 72 hours of abstinence from a quit attempt, a phenomenon that is believed to be due to an inability to tolerate distress—mainly the stress of nicotine withdrawal. Therefore, a group plus individual therapy (9 × 2-hour group and 6 × 50-minute individual sessions) treatment that compared combined gradual exposure to withdrawal-related distress with ACT skills training to standard behavioral therapy, with both arms providing 8 weeks of nicotine patch, was piloted in a randomized trial of 49 early relapsers (Brown et al., 2013). Results showed that the main effect of treatment condition was promising but not statistically significant in the 4- to 16-week follow-up period (OR = 1.83; 95% CI = 0.46–7.34). With regard to young adult smokers—who have the highest smoking rates of any age group—a study of 84 university student smokers compared a six-session avatar-led ACT intervention with a waitlist control, finding highly promising but not statistically significant differences at end of treatment (OR = 3.10; 95% CI: .92 to 10.41; Karekla et al., 2020). Regarding individuals with serious mental illness (e.g., bipolar disorder), who have high smoking rates, a pilot randomized trial (n = 62) compared a smartphone-delivered ACT intervention tailored to this population to QuitGuide, finding highly promising but not statistically significant differences in quit rates at the 16 week follow-up (OR = 3.86; 95% CI: .41 to 36; Vilardaga et al., 2019). A pilot randomized trial (n = 51) comparing WebQuit tailored to bipolar smokers to Smokefree.gov found, in both arms, identical quit rates at 4-week posttreatment follow-up (8%; OR = .96; 95% CI: .12, 7.57; Heffner et al., 2019). Finally, cancer patients who smoke, up to 80% of whom continue to smoke after diagnosis, were recruited into a pilot randomized trial (n = 59) comparing a smartphone-delivered ACT intervention tailored to cancer patients to QuitGuide, finding highly promising quit rates at the 8-week follow-up (OR = 5.16; 95% CI: .71, 37.29; Bricker et al., 2019). As part of the continued pilot research, future work can focus on human-centered design (Giacomin, 2014; Matheson et al., 2015) methods to adapt and refine the ACT interventions for these special populations, in order to ensure that they fit their specific needs. Protocol-driven user interviews, focus groups, and diary studies are some examples of user-centered design methods for learning how these adapted interventions can address population-specific needs, including cognitive and visual impairments and technological literacy. Once developed, full-scale trials of ACT interventions for all of these special populations are needed or are already underway (e.g., ClinicalTrials.gov ID: NCT04409236).

Newer digital technologies hold promise for future research in delivering smoking cessation interventions, including those that follow an ACT behavior change model. One technology provides a therapeutic conversation to address the problem of low patient engagement that commonly affects digital behavioral interventions (Szinay et al., 2020). Advances in machine learning, natural language processing, and cloud computing are now making it possible to create and widely disseminate conversational agents (CAs), which are computer-powered digital coaches designed to form long-term social-emotional connections with users through conversations (Gardiner et al., 2017; Provoost et al., 2017). CAs can increase engagement through an informal therapeutic conversational style, with interactions tailored to users' unique barriers to quitting. CAs are supportive, empathic, reflectively listen, provide personalized responses, and offer advice appropriately timed to the user's needs (Bickmore et al., 2016; King et al., 2017). CAs only require a text response to operate, thereby making them ideal for all smokers, including those with low technology literacy (King et al., 2017). In addition to mobile telephones, CAs can be deployed on a smartphone app, website, or social media platforms (e.g., Facebook). To date, there are six published randomized trials of CA for behavior change, with all showing high user engagement and promising short-term effects on the target outcome behavior (Bickmore, Schulman, et al., 2013; Bickmore, Silliman, et al., 2013; Edwards et al., 2013; Fitzpatrick et al. 2017; Gardiner et al., 2017; Provoost et al., 2017; Watson et al., 2012). The therapeutic qualities of a CA make it well suited for development and testing as an ACT intervention for smoking cessation, with the fundamental shift forward being human-like conversational abilities found in a skilled therapist.

A final future direction of ACT for smoking cessation research is in dissemination and implementation. This area of research can test methods for (1) health care systems to adopt ACT interventions for smoking cessation; (2) training and supervising clinicians to provide ACT interventions for smoking cessation; (3) evaluating the cost-effectiveness of these interventions; and (4) maximizing population-level reach of ACT smoking cessation interventions at the lowest possible cost. A major challenge for adopting new interventions is the lack of resources for training and ongoing supervision. For example, for a health care system to adopt an ACT intervention for smoking cessation, it needs to train its clinical staff in the intervention and then provide ongoing supervision for maintaining fidelity. Automated systems, databases, and tracking systems would likely need to be updated for this implementation. Payers of these services (e.g., insurance companies, government agencies) have to decide whether the added benefit of ACT was worth the added time and resources of implementing the intervention. These types of implementation challenges present research questions that can be addressed via transdisciplinary collaborations between ACT researchers, health economists, and health care policy researchers. In general, such transdisciplinary collaborations are needed to allow ACT smoking cessation research to move forward, given that smoking has a pervasive impact across the health care system.

Summary

Fifteen published randomized trials include a total of 6991 participants showing that ACT is a mature area of smoking cessation research. The full-scale trials show that group-delivered and website-delivered ACT are strong alternatives to USCPG standard behavioral interventions for smoking cessation delivered in these same modalities. Smartphone-delivered ACT is efficacious and may have a high public health impact if broadly disseminated. There is consistent evidence that ACT interventions are mediated through acceptance of internal triggers (e.g., cravings) to smoke. Future research on special populations of smokers, newer digital technologies, and dissemination/implementation is now needed.

Note

1. April 2020 analysis by SensorTower.com of all English-language cigarette smoking cessation applications on the Google Play and Apple App Store downloaded to smartphone devices.

References

Abroms, L. C., Lee Westmaas, J., Bontemps-Jones, J., Ramani, R., & Mellerson, J. (2013). A content analysis of popular smartphone apps for smoking cessation. *American Journal of Preventive Medicine, 45*(6), 732–736. doi:10.1016/j.amepre.2013.07.008

Abroms, L. C., Padmanabhan, N., Thaweethai, L., & Phillips, T. (2011). iPhone apps for smoking cessation: a content analysis. *American Journal of Preventive Medicine, 40*(3), 279–285. doi:10.1016/j.amepre.2010.10.032

Bickmore, T. W., Schulman, D., & Sidner, C. (2013). Automated interventions for multiple health behaviors using conversational agents. Patient education and counseling. *Patient Education and Counseling, 92*(2), 142–148. doi:10.1016/j.pec.2013.05.011

Bickmore, T. W., Silliman, R. A., Nelson, K., Cheng, D. M., Winter, M., Henault, L., & Paasche-Orlow, M. K. (2013). A randomized controlled trial of an automated exercise coach for older adults. *Journal of the American Geriatric Society, 61*(10), 1676–1683. doi:10.1111/jgs.12449

Bickmore, T. W., Utami, D., Matsuyama, R., & Paasche-Orlow, M. K. (2016). Improving access to online health information with conversational agents: A randomized controlled experiment. *Journal of Medical Internet Research, 18*(1), e1. doi:10.2196/jmir.5239

Borrelli, B., Bartlett, Y. K., Tooley, E., Armitage, C. J., & Wearden, A. (2015). Prevalence and frequency of mHealth and eHealth use among US and UK smokers and differences by motivation to quit. *Journal of Medical Internet Research, 17*(7), e164. doi:10.2196/jmir.4420.

Bricker, J., Wyszynski, C., Comstock, B., & Heffner, J. L. (2013). Pilot randomized controlled trial of web-based acceptance and commitment therapy for smoking cessation. *Nicotine and Tobacco Research: Official Journal of the Society for Research on Nicotine and Tobacco, 15*(10), 1756–1764. doi:10.1093/ntr/ntt056

Bricker, J. B., Bush, T., Zbikowski, S. M., Mercer, L. D., & Heffner, J. L. (2014). Randomized trial of telephone-delivered acceptance and commitment therapy versus cognitive behavioral therapy for smoking cessation: A pilot study. *Nicotine Tobacco Research, 16*(11), 1446–1454. doi:10.1093/ntr/ntu102

Bricker, J. B., Mann, S. L., Marek, P. M., Liu, J., & Peterson, A. V. (2010). Telephone-delivered acceptance and commitment therapy for adult smoking cessation: A feasibility study. *Nicotine and Tobacco Research, 12*(4), 454–458. doi:10.1093/ntr/ntq002

Bricker, J. B., Mull, K. E., Kientz, J. A., Vilardaga, R., Mercer, L. D., Akioka, K. J., & Heffner, J. L. (2014). Randomized, controlled pilot trial of a smartphone app for smoking cessation using acceptance and commitment therapy. *Drug and Alcohol Dependence, 143*, 87–94. doi:10.1016/j.drugalcdep.2014.07.006

Bricker, J. B., Mull, K. E., McClure, J. B., Watson, N. L., & Heffner, J. L. (2017). Improving quit rates of web-delivered interventions for smoking cessation: Full-scale randomized trial of WebQuit.org versus Smokefree.gov. *Addiction, 113*(5), 914–923. doi:10.1111/add.14127

Bricker, J. B., Mull, K. E., Sullivan, B. M., & Heffner, J. L. (2020). Efficacy of smartphone applications for smoking cessation: A randomized clinical trial. *Journal of the American Medical Association: Internal Medicine, 180*(11), 1472–1480.

Bricker, J. B., Sulllivan, B., Watson, N. L., Heffner, J. L., Mull, K. E., Kwon, D., Westmaas, J. L., & Ostroff, J. (2019). Smartphone app designed to help cancer patients stop smoking: Results from a pilot randomized trial on feasibility, acceptability, and effectiveness. *Journal of Medical Internet Research: Formative Research, 4*(1), e16652.

Brown, R. A., Palm Reed, K. M., Bloom, E. L., Minami, H., Strong, D. R., Lejuez, C. W., Zvolensky, M. J., & Hayes, S. C. (2018). A randomized controlled trial of distress tolerance treatment for smoking cessation. *Psychology of Addictive Behaviors, 32*(4), 389–400. doi:10.1037/adb0000372

Brown, R. A., Reed, K. M., Bloom, E. L., Minami, H., Strong, D. R., Lejuez, C. W., Kahler, C. W., Zvolensky, M. J., Gifford, E. V., & Hayes, S. C. (2013). Development and preliminary randomized controlled trial of a distress tolerance treatment for smokers with a history of early lapse. *Nicotine and Tobacco Research, 15*(12), 2005–2015. doi:10.1093/ntr/ntt093

Center, P. R. (2019). Internet/Broadband Fact Sheet. Retrieved from https://www.pewinternet.org/fact-sheet/internet-broadband.

Civljak, M., Sheikh, A., Stead, L. F., & Car, J. (2010). Internet-based interventions for smoking cessation. *Cochrane Database of Systematic Reviews* (9), CD007078. doi:10.1002/14651858.CD007078.pub3

Consortium, N. A. Q. (2017). Results from the 2017 NAQC Annual Survey of Quitlines. Retrieved from http://www.naquitline.org/?page=2017Survey

Edwards, R. A., Bickmore, T., Jenkins, L., Foley, M., & Manjourides, J. (2013). Use of an interactive computer agent to support breastfeeding. *Maternal and Child Health Journal, 17*(10), 1961–1968. doi:10.1007/s10995-013-1222-0

Fiore, M. C., Bailey, W. C., Cohen, S. J., Dorfman, S. F., Goldstein, M. G., Gritz, E. R., et al. (2000). *Treating tobacco use and dependence. Clinical practice guideline.* U.S. Department of Health and Human Services. Public Health Service.

Fiore, M. C., Jaén, C. R., Baker, T. B., Bailey, W. C., Benowitz, N. L., Curry, S. J., et al. (2008). Treating tobacco use and dependence: 2008 update. In *Clinical Practice Guideline.* U.S. Department of Health and Human Services, Public Health Service.

Fitzpatrick, K. K., Darcy, A., & Vierhile, M. (2017). Delivering cognitive behavior therapy to young adults with symptoms of depression and anxiety using a fully automated conversational agent (Woebot): A randomized controlled trial. *JMIR Mental Health, 4*(2), e19. doi:10.2196/mental.7785

Gardiner, P. M., McCue, K. D., Negash, L. M., Cheng, T., White, L. F., Yinusa-Nyahkoon, L., Jack, B. W., & Bickmore, T. W. (2017). Engaging women with an embodied conversational agent to deliver mindfulness and lifestyle recommendations: A feasibility randomized control trial. *Patient Education and Counseling, 100*(9), 1720–1729. doi:10.1016/j.pec.2017.04.015

GBD 2015 Risk Factors Collaborators. (2016). Global, regional, and national comparative risk assessment of 79 behavioural, environmental and occupational, and metabolic risks or clusters of risks, 1990–2015: A systematic analysis for the Global Burden of Disease Study 2015. *Lancet, 388*(10053), 1659–1724. doi:10.1016/s0140-6736(16)31679-8

GBD 2015 Tobacco Collaborators. (2017). Smoking prevalence and attributable disease burden in 195 countries and territories, 1990–2015: A systematic analysis from the Global Burden of Disease Study 2015. *Lancet, 389*(10082), 1885–1906. doi:10.1016/s0140-6736(17)30819-x

Giacomin, J. (2014). What is human centered design?. *The Design Journal, 17*(4), 606–623.

Gifford, E. V., Kohlenberg, B. S., Hayes, S. C., Antonuccio, D. O., Piasecki, M. M., Rasmussen-Hall, M. L., Palm, K. M. (2004). Acceptance-based treatment for smoking cessation. *Behavior Therapy, 35*, 689–705. doi:10.1016/S0005-7894(04)80015-7

Gifford, E. V., Kohlenberg, B. S., Hayes, S. C., Pierson, H. M., Piasecki, M. P., Antonuccio, D. O., & Palm, K. M. (2011). Does acceptance and relationship focused behavior therapy contribute to bupropion outcomes? A randomized controlled trial of functional analytic psychotherapy and acceptance and commitment therapy for smoking cessation. *Behavior Therapy, 42*(4), 700–715. doi:10.1016/j.beth.2011.03.002

Graham, A. L., Carpenter, K. M., Cha, S., Cole, S., Jacobs, M. A., Raskob, M., & Cole-Lewis, H. (2016). Systematic review and meta-analysis of Internet interventions for smoking cessation among adults. *Substance Abuse and Rehabilitation, 7*, 55–69. doi:10.2147/sar.s101660

Graham, A. L., Cobb, N. K., Papandonatos, G. D., Moreno, J. L., Kang, H., Tinkelman, D. G., Bock, B. C., Niaura, R. S., & Abrams, D. B. (2011). A randomized trial of Internet and telephone treatment for smoking cessation. *Archives of Internal Medicine, 171*(1), 46–53. doi:10.1001/archinternmed.2010.451

Hayes, S. C., Barnes-Holmes, D., & Roche, B. (2001). *Relational frame theory: A post-Skinnerian account of human language and cognition.* Plenum Press.

Hayes, S. C., Levin, M. E., Plumb-Vilardaga, J., Villatte, J. L., & Pistorello, J. (2013). Acceptance and commitment therapy and contextual behavioral science: Examining the progress of a distinctive model of behavioral and cognitive therapy. *Behavior Therapy, 44*(2), 180–198. doi:10.1016/j.beth.2009.08.002

Hayes, S. C., Luoma, J. B., Bond, F. W., Masuda, A., & Lillis, J. (2006). Acceptance and commitment therapy: Model, processes and outcomes. *Behaviour Research and Therapy, 44*(1), 1–25. doi:10.1016/j.brat.2005.06.006

Hayes, S. C., Strosahl, K. D., & Wilson, K. G. (1999). *Acceptance and commitment therapy: An experimental approach to behavior change.* Guilford Press.

Heffner, J. L., Kelly, M. M., Waxmonsky, J., Mattocks, K., Serfozo, E., Bricker, J. B., Mull, K. E., Watson, N. L., & Ostacher, M. (2019). Pilot randomized controlled trial of web-delivered acceptance and commitment therapy versus Smokefree.gov for smokers with bipolar disorder. *Nicotine and Tobacco Research, 22*(9), 1543–1552. doi:10.1093/ntr/ntz242

Herbert, J. D., & Forman, E. M. (ed.). (2011). *Acceptance and mindfulness in cognitive behavior therapy.* John Wiley & Sons.

Hernandez-Lopez, M., Luciano, M. C., Bricker, J. B., Roales-Nieto, J. G., & Montesinos, F. (2009). Acceptance and commitment therapy for smoking cessation: A preliminary study of its effectiveness in comparison with cognitive behavioral therapy. *Psychology of Addictive Behaviors, 23*(4), 723–730. doi:10.1037/a0017632

Husten, C. G. (2010). A Call for ACTTION: Increasing access to tobacco-use treatment in our nation. *American Journal of Preventive Medicine, 38*(3 Suppl.), S414–417. doi:10.1016/j.amepre.2009.12.006

Hutton, H. E., Wilson, L. M., Apelberg, B. J., Tang, E. A., Odelola, O., Bass, E. B., & Chander, G. (2011). A systematic review of randomized controlled trials: Web-based interventions for smoking cessation among adolescents, college students, and adults. *Nicotine and Tobacco Research, 13*(4), 227–238. doi:10.1093/ntr/ntq252

Karekla, M., Savvides, S. N., & Gloster, A. (2020). An Avatar-led intervention promotes smoking cessation in young adults: A pilot randomized clinical trial. *Annals of Behavioral Medicine, 54*(10), 747–760. doi:10.1093/abm/kaaa013

King, A. C., Campero, I., Sheats, J. L., Castro Sweet, C. M., Garcia, D., Chazaro, A., Blanco, G., Hauser, M., Fierros, F., Ahn, D. K., Diaz, J., Done, M., Fernandez, J., & Bickmore, T. (2017). Testing the comparative effects of physical activity advice by humans vs. computers in underserved populations: The COMPASS trial design, methods, and baseline characteristics. *Contemporary Clinical Trials, 61*, 115–125. doi:10.1016/j.cct.2017.07.020

Lancaster, T., & Stead, L. F. (2017). Individual behavioural counselling for smoking cessation. *Cochrane Database of Systematic Reviews, 3*(3), Cd001292. doi:10.1002/14651858.CD001292.pub3

Luoma, J. B., Hayes, S. C., & Walser, R. D. (2007). *Learning ACT: An acceptance and commitment therapy skills training manual for therapists.* New Harbinger.

Matheson, G. O., Pacione, C., Shultz, R. K., & Klügl, M. (2015). Leveraging human-centered design in chronic disease prevention. *American Journal of Preventive Medicine, 48*(4), 472–479.

Matkin, W., Ordóñez-Mena, J. M., & Hartmann-Boyce, J. (2019). Telephone counselling for smoking cessation. *Cochrane Database of Systematic Reviews, 5*(5), Cd002850. doi:10.1002/14651858.CD002850.pub4

McClure, J. B., Bricker, J., Mull, K., & Heffner, J. L. (2020). Comparative effectiveness of group-delivered acceptance and commitment therapy versus cognitive behavioral therapy for smoking cessation: A randomized controlled trial. *Nicotine and Tobacco Research, 22*(3), 354–362. doi:10.1093/ntr/nty268

Newell, A. (1990). *Unified theories of cognition.* Harvard University Press.

O'Connor, M., Whelan, R., Bricker, J., & McHugh, L. (2020). Randomized controlled trial of a smartphone application as an adjunct to acceptance and commitment therapy for smoking cessation. *Behavior Therapy, 51*(1), 162–177. doi:10.1016/j.beth.2019.06.003

Perkins, K. A., Conklin, C. A., & Levine, M. D. (2008). *Cognitive-behavioral therapy for smoking cessation: A practical guide to the most effective treatments.* Routledge.

Provoost, S., Lau, H. M., Ruwaard, J., & Riper, H. (2017). Embodied conversational agents in clinical psychology: A scoping review. *Journal of Medical Internet Research, 19*(5), e151. doi:10.2196/jmir.6553

Shahab, L., & McEwen, A. (2009). Online support for smoking cessation: A systematic review of the literature. *Addiction, 104*(11), 1792–1804. doi:10.1111/j.1360-0443.2009.02710.x

Silagy, C., Lancaster, T., Stead, L., Mant, D., & Fowler, G. (2004). Nicotine replacement therapy for smoking cessation. *Cochrane Database of Systematic Reviews* (3), CD000146. doi:10.1002/14651858.CD000146.pub2

Stead, L. F., Carroll, A. J., & Lancaster, T. (2017). Group behaviour therapy programmes for smoking cessation. *Cochrane Database of Systematic Reviews, 3*(3), Cd001007. doi:10.1002/14651858.CD001007.pub3

Stead, L. F., Hartmann-Boyce, J., Perera, R., & Lancaster, T. (2013). Telephone counselling for smoking cessation. *Cochrane Database of Systematic Reviews, 8*, CD002850. doi:10.1002/14651858.CD002850.pub3

Stead, L. F., Perera, R., & Lancaster, T. (2006). Telephone counselling for smoking cessation. *Cochrane Database of Systematic Reviews, 3*, CD002850. doi:10.1002/14651858.CD002850.pub2

Szinay, D., Jones, A., Chadborn, T., Brown, J., & Naughton, F. (2020). Influences on the uptake of and engagement with health and well-being smartphone apps: systematic review. *Journal of Medical Internet Research, 22*(5), e17572. doi:10.2196/17572.PMID: 32348255

Taylor, G. M. J., Dalili, M. N., Semwal, M., Civljak, M., Sheikh, A., & Car, J. (2017). Internet-based interventions for smoking cessation. *Cochrane Database of Systematic Reviews, 9*, Cd007078. doi:10.1002/14651858.CD007078.pub5

Vilardaga, R., Rizo, J., Palenski, P., Mannelli, P., Oliver, J. A., & McClernon, F. J. (2019). Pilot randomized controlled trial of a novel smoking cessation app designed for individuals with co-occurring tobacco dependence and serious mental illness. *Nicotine and Tobacco Research, 23*(2), 411. doi:10.1093/ntr/ntz202

Watson, A., Bickmore, T., Cange, A., Kulshreshtha, A., & Kvedar, J. (2012). An internet-based virtual coach to promote physical activity adherence in overweight adults: randomized controlled trial. *Journal of Medical Internet Research, 14*(1), e1. doi:10.2196/jmir.1629

Webb, T. L. (2009). Commentary on Shahab and McEwen (2009): Understanding and preventing attrition in online smoking cessation interventions: A self-regulatory perspective. *Addiction, 104*(11), 1801806. doi:10.1111/j.1360-0443.2009.02751.x

Whittaker, R., McRobbie, H., Bullen, C., Borland, R., Rodgers, A., & Gu, Y. (2012). Mobile phone-based interventions for smoking cessation. *Cochrane Database of Systematic Reviews, 11*, CD006611. doi:10.1002/14651858.CD006611.pub3

Whittaker, R., McRobbie, H., Bullen, C., Rodgers, A., Gu, Y., & Dobson, R. (2019). Mobile phone text messaging and app-based interventions for smoking cessation. *Cochrane Database of Systematic Reviews, 10*, Cd006611. doi:10.1002/14651858.CD006611.pub5

CHAPTER

24 ACT for the Treatment of Psychosis and Schizophrenia-Spectrum Disorders

Brandon A. Gaudiano *and* Stacy Ellenberg

Abstract

Acceptance and commitment therapy for psychosis (ACTp) is supported by a number of randomized controlled trials documenting that the treatment is safe and efficacious for patients with psychosis and a range of schizophrenia-spectrum disorders. These initial clinical trials show that ACTp produces improvements in psychotic symptoms, depression, functioning, and quality of life in both inpatient and outpatient samples, and has been delivered in group and individual formats. In particular, several studies have documented the ability of ACTp to reduce rehospitalization rates at follow-up. Initial work also supports ACT-consistent processes of change in terms of the treatment's potential mechanisms of action. Future research is needed to further specify mediators and moderators of effects, and to confirm the effects of ACTp in larger samples when implemented in real-world practice settings.

Key Words: psychosis, schizophrenia, severe mental illness, rehospitalization, acceptance, mindfulness, empirically supported therapies

Background

Schizophrenia ranks as one of the top 10 causes of disability across the globe consistently year after year (First, Williams, Karg, & Spitzer, 2015; Harvey, Strassnig, & Silberstein, 2019). Positive symptoms (hallucinations, delusions, disorganization) and negative symptoms (anhedonia, avolition, alogia, affective flattening, asociality) define psychotic and schizophrenia-spectrum disorders (SZ). With a prevalence rate of 0.33–0.64 percent of the global population (Moreno-Küstner, Martin, & Pastor, 2018), SZ remains a heterogeneous diagnosis, and what we call "schizophrenia" may actually constitute a collection of separate mental disorders with varying courses, onsets, and biological and environmental origins (Jablensky, 2010).

The etiology of SZ is poorly understood and is associated with a number of genetic and environmental risk factors, including male sex, immigrant status, social isolation, trauma in childhood, viruses, and factors during pregnancy, such as placental health and immune status (Kendler & O'Donovan, 2014; Stilo & Murray, 2019). While the heritability and genetic vulnerability for SZ is considered high, specific genetic markers have not been reliably identified in the pathogenesis of the illness (Van Os, Linscott, Myin-Germeys, Delespaul, & Krabbendam, 2009). Heterogeneity in onset and course of illness poses significant limitations related to the identification of a reliable or clinically meaningful phenotypic profile (Kendler

& O'Donovan, 2014). Cognitive limitations are documented to occur in individuals with SZ during childhood, suggesting the potential presence of a developmental component to SZ (First et al., 2015). Individuals with SZ consistently demonstrate deficits in cognitive functioning such as problems with working memory, insight, social skills, social cognition, and theory of mind (First et al., 2015; Fulford, Campellone, & Gard, 2018). Information processing and reasoning deficits in SZ include attentional and "jumping-to-conclusion" biases (Mander & Kingdon, 2015), which impede the person's ability to exert control over perceptions and emotional experiences (Green, Horan, & Lee, 2015).

Typically onsetting in late adolescent or early adult years, one-third of individuals with schizophrenia will have an ongoing, chronic, and deleterious course of illness over time (First et al., 2015). However, one-third will experience full remission and will return to a state free of psychotic symptomatology, and the remaining third will experience a combination of the two, never fully remitting and experiencing intermittent psychosis throughout the lifetime. In higher socioeconomic status (SES) societies, lower SES individuals have an elevated risk of developing SZ (Luo et al., 2019). Black Americans are more than three times as likely to be diagnosed with schizophrenia as compared to white Americans, with bias in diagnosis or variation in expression of symptomatology being a more likely explanation than an actual difference in prevalence (Eack, Bahorik, Newhill, Neighbors, & Davis, 2012).

In SZ, comorbid substance and mental disorders, medical conditions, frequent rehospitalizations, bullying and stigma, and cognitive limitations are among a few of the ongoing difficulties that lead to functional impairment and disability. Panic disorder, obsessive-compulsive disorder, substance use disorders, affective illnesses, and sleep disorders are highly comorbid problems among individuals with SZ (Barnes, Mutsatsa, Hutton, Watt, & Joyce, 2006; Braga, Petrides, & Figueira, 2004; Kaskie, Graziano, & Ferrarelli, 2017). The prevalence rates for physical disease and illnesses such as HIV infection, osteoporosis, cardiovascular disease, diabetes, polydipsia, as well as conditions including altered pain sensitivity and obesity, are significantly higher for individuals with SZ as compared to the general population (Leucht, Burkard, Henderson, Maj, & Sartorius, 2007). The mortality rate for individuals with SZ is twice that of individuals in the general population (Harris & Barraclough, 1998), a rate worsening by the decade (Saha, Chant, & McGrath, 2007). Nearly 5–6 percent of individuals with SZ die as a result of suicide, and 20 percent endorse a history of suicide attempt (First et al., 2015).

Stigma is commonly reported by individuals with SZ: nearly half (40 percent) of individuals with SZ report having experienced high levels of stigmatization by others (Brohan, Elgie, Sartorius, Thornicroft, & Group, 2010; Valery & Prouteau, 2020). Some have described the experience of stigma alone as a "second illness" accompanying SZ due to ongoing shame, bullying, and the disabling limits imposed upon them by family, friends, health care providers, the media, and society as a whole (Schulze & Angermeyer, 2003; Valery & Prouteau, 2020). Stigma extends into the domain of the medical profession, with numerous studies revealing that individuals with SZ are unfairly denied medical procedures, in comparison to the general population (e.g., Lawrence, D'Arcy, Holman, Jablensky, & Hobbs, 2003; Leucht et al., 2007).

Additionally, structural and economic barriers such as transportation problems, unstable housing, and poverty severely limit access to health care for individuals with SZ (De Hert et al., 2011). Individuals with SZ have lower marriage and employment rates than the general population (First et al., 2015) and experience difficulties achieving other activities of daily living, with 70–90 percent reporting vocational and residential difficulties (Harvey et al., 2019). Despite these challenges, individuals with SZ report valuing social, occupational, educational, and personal goals (Shumway et al., 2003), and are capable of experiencing consummatory pleasure much like the general population (Fulford et al., 2018).

SZ was ranked as one of the top 20 most costly conditions under U.S. Medicare in 2013, with annual hospital costs alone amounting to $1.2 billion USD (Torio & Moore, 2006). Inpatient hospitalizations are common for individuals with SZ, representing an estimated 121.9 of every 100,000 patients hospitalized for all physical and psychiatric reasons in 2012 (Heslin & Weiss, 2015). Hospitalizations occur when an individual is no longer capable of functioning independently, the individual's or others' safety is not ensured, medication changes are needed, or symptom worsening occurs (Lilja & Hellzén, 2008). Within one month, 13.4% of discharged inpatients with SZ become rehospitalized; 38.9 percent are readmitted within one year (Hudson, 2019). Productivity losses in individuals with SZ were estimated at $155.7 billion, with inpatient hospitalizations accounting for $15.2 billion of this estimate (Cloutier et al., 2016). Furthermore, suicidality spikes upon discharge from an inpatient hospitalization (Qin & Nordentoft, 2005). Suicidal ideation and history of inpatient hospitalizations constitute the most robust predictors of rehospitalization (Beard et al., 2016; Lorine et al., 2015).

Antipsychotic medications may be effective in targeting positive symptoms (hallucinations and delusions) but fail to adequately address negative symptoms (Leucht, Arbter, Engel, Kissling, & Davis, 2009) and quality of life (Leucht, Arbter, Engel, Kissling, & Davis, 2009). Thus, the provision of medication alone is typically insufficient for treating SZ, highlighting the need for psychosocial and behavioral interventions designed to promote overall functional improvement and recovery.

Rationale for Using ACT to Treat Psychosis

Acceptance and commitment therapy for psychosis (ACTp) is based on an overarching philosophy of functional contextualism, which focuses on a pragmatic truth criterion and is interested in prediction and influence of behavior, taking into account the entire person, their external and internal context, and their history (Hayes, Levin, Plumb-Vilardaga, Villatte, & Pistorello, 2013). Psychopathology is theorized to develop from arbitrary verbal rules in which language and cognition are associated with each other through "relational frames," as specified in relational frame theory (Hughes & Barnes-Holmes, 2016). Based on this account, arbitrary rules that become associated with internal stimuli (e.g., thoughts, sensations, and emotions) over time through normal learning and language processes transform the function of these stimuli so that people can experience them as either benign or malicious. In ACTp, phenomena such as auditory hallucinations and delusional thoughts are conceptualized as manifestations of these same language–environment interactions that are similar in their development to other symptoms such as depression or anxiety (Gaudiano, 2015). Indeed, voice hearing and forms of paranoid ideation are present in the general, non-help-seeking population and are not pathognomonic of schizophrenia (Powers, Kelley, & Corlett, 2017). For example, sensations of threat provoked during certain ambiguous or unfamiliar situations may become associated over time through relational framing processes with elaborate paranoid delusions as the person attempts to explain and manage these sensations. Through treatment, when these same stimuli can be experienced for what they are at a more basic or fundamental level again (e.g., thoughts as thoughts, feeling as feelings), an individual can open up and let go of them without the unnecessary avoidance or struggle that usually causes impairment.

Experiential Avoidance

In addition, ACTp takes into account the full context in which a behavior occurs—the environment in which it is situated, its antecedents and consequences, as well as the personal history of the individual—to determine the function of that behavior. Often, an unhealthy or maladaptive behavior serves an individual temporarily through operant processes by allowing that person to avoid or escape the possibility of rejection, failure, distress, and the like, through a phenomenon called experiential avoidance (EA). For example, individuals may experience a derogatory auditory hallucination (e.g., a voice saying "You're worthless") which has been internalized over time because others have often told them this hurtful message when the person was growing up. The more ruminative and preoccupied that patients become with their internalized negative thoughts, the more these thoughts over time will tend to be experienced as external voices separate from their sense of personal self through habitual EA processes. Individuals may try to distract themselves when they hear the voice or block it out of their mind because it causes distress. On the other hand, they might argue with the voice to make it go away or even ruminate further about what the voice says because they believe the statement is true. In order to avoid the possibility of encountering this voice or similar feelings of rejection from others, individuals may decide that it is safer to stay indoors and isolate, and they may even stop leaving their home to even get the mail, resulting in significant life dysfunction. As part of an ever-expanding vicious cycle, chronic EA of these private events often simply produces more of them in the long term, not less.

In this way, EA is thought to be a critical component underlying various forms of psychopathology and is linked to depression, anxiety, distress, auditory hallucinations, paranoia, cognitive deficits, and poor insight in psychosis (Goldstone, Farhall, & Ong, 2011; Shawyer et al., 2007; Udachina, Varese, Myin-Germeys, & Bentall, 2014). Furthermore, research shows that suppression of auditory hallucinations, a "sealing-over" recovery style characterized by avoidance, and other "resistance coping efforts," are ineffective and associated with negative outcomes such as poor distress tolerance, lower treatment engagement, and increased negative self-evaluative beliefs (Escher, Delespaul, Romme, Buiks, & Van Os, 2003; Falloon & Talbot, 1981; Farhall & Gehrke, 1997; Tait, Birchwood, & Trower, 2003). Conversely, greater acceptance of voices is associated with improved outcomes such as increased quality of life and decreased depression (Shawyer et al., 2007).

Cognitive Fusion

Related to EA, cognitive fusion is the process by which people become entangled with their thoughts in ways that limit their flexibility in responding in adaptive ways. Thus, fusion with delusional thought content in patients with psychosis also is a target of ACTp. Emerging research suggests that fusion may be a key mechanism that produces psychotic experiences in prone individuals, especially in the context of cannabis use, developmental trauma, or schizotypy traits (Newman-Taylor et al., 2020). When individuals are fused with delusions or hallucinations, they act in inflexible and maladaptive ways that take them away from their values. The focus of ACTp is not on getting the person to directly evaluate the veracity of delusional thoughts or voices to determine whether they are "true" or "real." Instead, the goal is to help people recognize and respond to these thoughts as thoughts, thereby highlighting the fact that they are mental events that the person can choose to respond to or not, depending on the situation and their goals. Cognitive defusion in ACTp focuses less on the specific delusional ideation itself as the target, and more on disentangling the person from their thoughts in general, whether such thoughts are considered positive, negative, or neutral. This broader cognitive defusion approach can prevent the tendency for the therapist and patient to argue about the veracity of psychotic experiences, and at the same time help patients change their relationship to these experiences. Cognitive defusion thus indirectly reduces the overall believability of psychotic experiences and the tendency for psychotic experiences to influence the person's behavior in a values-inconsistent fashion.

Lack of Present Moment Awareness

Furthermore, lower levels of mindfulness, or the ability to be nonjudgmentally aware of mental events as they occur, are found in those with psychosis and are predictive of distress and other negative outcomes (Chien et al., 2020). Patients with psychosis are often unaware of their ongoing, present moment, internal experiences due to preoccupation with psychotic processes that result in detachment from reality and thus the environment around them. Present moment awareness is an important part of ACTp because it encourages patients to pay attention to their changing internal experiences instead of avoiding them. At the same time, mindfulness teaches people to let go of these unhelpful internal experiences, thereby decreasing the tendency to ruminate or become preoccupied with delusions and hallucinations. In this way, patients are able to contact a sense of self that is more stable and independent from their passing psychotic experiences, which then can be witnessed to ebb and flow just like other more mundane mental events.

Values-Actions Discrepancies

Finally, an important part of ACTp involves clarifying and building patients' personal values, or their global and desired life directions that create a sense of meaning and purpose. Values-actions discrepancies have been linked with functional impairment in those experiencing psychosis (Gaudiano, Primack, & Miller, 2016). For example, a person might value their family, but choose not to talk or visit them due to paranoia. Furthermore, while individuals with psychosis can exhibit significant and pervasive functional impairments across multiple domains, they still desire the same types of experiences and hold the same aspirations as those without psychosis (Fulford et al., 2018). In addition, patients with psychosis often experience discrimination and stigma from society, which can result in internalized self-stigma that inhibits valued-goal attainment (Brohan et al., 2010). ACTp situates acceptance, defusion, and mindfulness in the service of patients' freely chosen values as motivators of change and committed action. Negative symptoms, such as blunted affect, poverty of speech, anhedonia, lack of motivation, social disengagement, and inattention make behavior change more difficult and challenging to achieve for patients, and values can help support and sustain these efforts.

ACT versus CBT for Psychosis

ACTp differs in its theoretical framework and techniques from other psychological treatments for this population, such as in traditional cognitive-behavioral therapy for psychosis (CBTp). CBTp is one of the most widely studied psychosocial interventions for SZ and demonstrates small to medium, though clinically significant, effects on outcomes, including psychotic symptoms and functioning when added to medication and treatment as usual (Jauhar et al., 2014; Wykes, Steel, Everitt, & Tarrier, 2008). CBTp and ACTp share certain characteristics; notably, they seek to improve functioning by fostering a healthy working alliance, setting behavioral goals, and changing the relationship between the person and the world through manipulating how language and cognition influence behavior. However, in contrast to ACTp's focus on EA as described previously, CBTp uses behavioral strategies and reality testing to change automatic cognitions and biased appraisals about the self, others, and the world. In this way, CBTp focuses on altering psychotic experience *content*, whereas ACTp seeks to alter its *function*. Thus, ACTp does not seek to target symptom reduction directly by altering biased perceptions or dysfunctional cognitions, as is done in CBTp. Instead, ACTp focuses on meta-cognitive processes and seeks to manipulate contextual factors in order to create a more meaningful, rich, and present-focused life for the individual. ACTp also emphasizes compassion toward oneself and others, thereby affecting, albeit indirectly, the symptoms that cause impairment

(McLeod, 2009). Whereas CBTp intends to correct an individual's negative thinking patterns using behavioral exposures and reality testing, ACTp invites an individual to "make room" for, and nonjudgmentally observe, symptoms and mental experiences of all kinds, including those related to psychotic symptomatology such as hallucinations and delusions. Allowing an individual to notice these mental events as a product of their experience and to differentiate them from who they are as a person (i.e., their sense of "self") decreases the tendency to "hook" onto any distress resulting from these symptoms. In this way, ACTp helps people to change the way they relate to the symptom rather than changing the symptom itself. ACTp seeks to foster a richer, more meaningful life for the individual, who lives willingly with distress in the interest of pursuing worthwhile behaviors in line with their values.

Outcome Research

Currently, ACTp is listed as an empirically supported treatment with "modest research support" by the Society of Clinical Psychology (Division 12) of the American Psychological Association ("Acceptance and commitment therapy for psychosis," 2020). This designation is based on a growing literature supporting the feasibility, acceptability, and efficacy of ACTp, delivered across different formats, settings, and clinical populations. The research base can broadly be differentiated between ACTp delivered to inpatients (i.e., acutely ill, short-term treatment) vs outpatients (i.e., chronically ill, longer-term treatment). Notably, ACTp outpatient and inpatient trials differ with respect to the number of sessions, or "dosage" of treatment administered, and the severity of the samples treated. Outpatient randomized controlled trials (RCTs) of ACTp include multiple sessions delivered across many months (Gaudiano, Nowlan, Brown, Epstein-Lubow, & Miller, 2013), whereas the number of sessions delivered in inpatient settings is briefer based on the shorter length of stay (e.g., three sessions over 1 week) (Bach & Hayes, 2002; Gaudiano & Herbert, 2006).

Systematic Reviews and Meta-Analyses

Summarizing the findings of ACT for psychosis using meta-analysis and systematic reviews is challenging because of the heterogeneity existing among studies and samples, which hinders our ability to deduce accurate and generalizable effects. For this reason, the literature remains in a somewhat nascent phase, its findings perhaps more accurately portrayed through analysis of individual RCTs and less through the macro lens of a meta-analysis where differences across studies can become obscured. Nevertheless, systematic reviews and meta-analyses are informative insofar as they can give us an idea of the breadth and depth of the work in this area and provide relevant conclusions that can be deduced accurately across the trials conducted thus far.

In terms of systematic reviews, Wakefield, Roebuck, & Boyden, (2018) reviewed 13 open trials and RCTs and concluded that ACTp was generally effective in reducing rehospitalization rates, psychotic symptoms, psychological inflexibility, and functional impairment. Overall, ACTp was also more effective in studies using a briefer format conducted in more acutely ill samples (Wakefield et al., 2018). Another systematic review of 11 RCTs similarly concluded that ACTp was effective in improving hallucinations, depression, anxiety, help seeking, satisfaction, and psychological flexibility (Yıldız, 2020).

Of the preliminary meta-analyses conducted to date, ACTp shows promise with respect to improving psychotic symptom severity (with some variability depending on the sample and comparison condition) and rehospitalization rates in particular. For example, in a meta-analysis of four RCTs, participants in ACTp demonstrated significant improvements in negative symptoms (Standardized Mean Difference [SMD] = 0.65), but not positive symptoms, as well as significant reductions in rehospitalization rates (Relative Risk [RR] = .54; Tonarelli, Pasillas, Alvarado, Dwivedi, & Cancellare, 2016). In contrast, another meta-analysis of third-wave RCTs for psychosis reported that in the subanalysis of ACTp studies, results showed a reduction in positive symptoms (SMD = −0.57) and rehospitalizations (SMD = 0.41), but unlike the previous meta-analysis (Tonarelli et al., 2016) did not find an effect for negative symptoms (Cramer, Lauche, Haller, Langhorst, & Dobos, 2016). This is likely because the two meta-analyses examined a somewhat different set of studies. In addition, Wood, Williams, Billings, and Johnson (2020) examined 18 RCTs of both second- and third-wave therapies for inpatients, which included five studies of ACTp. They found that the third-wave interventions, including ACTp, had stronger effects on total symptom outcomes compared with traditional CBTp. However, direct comparisons of ACTp and CBTp within an individual study have yet to be conducted.

Individual RCTs

Not all relevant Randomized Controlled Trials (RCTs) have yet been included in previous meta-analyses of ACTp, and combining inpatient and outpatient samples may obscure the results on clinical outcomes. Therefore, given the mixed effects reported across trials of ACTp and other third-wave interventions for psychosis, it may be helpful to examine representative selected studies included in these reviews, particularly when separated based on their use of inpatient vs outpatient samples.

INPATIENT SAMPLES

The first RCT for ACTp (Bach & Hayes, 2002) was conducted within the last 20 years, preceded by one single-case study (García & Pérez, 2001). The initial RCT (Bach & Hayes, 2002) randomly assigned 80 inpatients with schizophrenia, schizoaffective disorder, and mood disorder with psychosis to either four, brief individual sessions of ACTp or treatment as usual alone (TAU) starting during hospitalization. TAU included group and individual psychoeducation, medication management, and post-discharge outpatient psychiatry and case management. Of the 35 patients remaining in each group by the 4-month follow-up, 40 percent of those assigned to TAU had been rehospitalized, compared to only 20 percent of those assigned to ACT. This difference emerged through survival analysis as being statistically significant (Bach & Hayes, 2002). Statistically significant differences in total number of days to hospitalization were observed favoring ACTp during follow-up as well. Despite patients self-reporting psychotic symptoms at a rate higher in ACTp compared with TAU, those assigned to ACTp demonstrated lower believability of symptoms as compared to TAU. Bach and Hayes (2002) interpreted this finding as suggesting that patients were more willing to report symptoms following ACTp; yet they learned not to engage with symptoms as though they were real, external stimuli that then decreased their negative impact on functioning.

The second RCT on ACTp emerged not long after (Gaudiano & Herbert, 2006) and expanded upon the findings of Bach and Hayes (2002) by examining differences in rehospitalization rates, psychiatric symptoms, impairment, and distress in 40 inpatients with schizophrenia. Participants were randomly assigned to either the experimental condition, ACTp plus enhanced TAU (ETAU), or the comparison condition, ETAU alone. Enhanced TAU entailed informal, brief, one-on-one check-ins with patients that were supportive in nature, as well as relaying symptom assessment information to the treatment team to inform patient care. Inpatient treatment for both conditions also included the typical therapy groups, occupational therapy, medication management sessions with a psychiatrist, and discharge planning and referral services. At hospital discharge, an average of three sessions of individual ACTp led to decreases in believability of hallucinations; changes in believability correlated with change in distress when frequency of hallucinations was controlled for (Gaudiano & Herbert, 2006). Impairment related to illness and clinically significant symptom change in overall psychiatric symptoms showed greater improvement by discharge in the ACTp condition as well. Rehospitalization rates were numerically lower for patients assigned to ACTp at the 4-month follow-up (Gaudiano & Herbert, 2006). After controlling for baseline severity of symptoms, days to rehospitalization emerged as being significantly longer for ACTp relative to ETAU alone, as reported in Bach, Gaudiano, Hayes, and Herbert (2013).

In a further inpatient study done in Sweden, Tyrberg, Carlbring, and Lundgren (2017) conducted an RCT involving 22 patients with acute psychosis, assigned randomly to TAU or an average of two sessions of ACTp plus TAU. Once again, rehospitalization rates were significantly lower for participants assigned to ACT after controlling for values-based living scores, age, and gender (Tyrberg et al., 2017).

Another RCT ($n = 30$) examined differences in general health indicators for inpatients diagnosed with methamphetamine use disorder with psychosis. Patients received either six sessions of ACTp plus weekly psychoeducation vs six sessions of psychoeducation alone. Participants assigned to ACTp demonstrated greater improvements in general health and aggressive behavior as compared to psychoeducation alone (Komala, Keliat, & Wardani, 2018).

Most recently, Jacobsen, Peters, Robinson, and Chadwick (2020) conducted an RCT comparing an average of three sessions of mindfulness-based crisis intervention (MBCI), an intervention composed mainly of ACTp elements, to a comparison condition (social activity therapy) with a sample of 50 inpatients with psychosis. Individuals assigned to MBCI demonstrated reductions in rehospitalization rates as compared to controls at a one-year follow-up, and no adverse events were related to trial participation (Jacobsen et al., 2020).

OUTPATIENT SAMPLES

Within the past decade, researchers also have begun investigating the efficacy of ACT for psychosis in outpatient settings. White et al. (2011) were the first to do so, reporting that 27 outpatients with depression following a psychotic episode showed significantly improved depression, increased mindfulness, reduced negative symptoms, and fewer crisis contacts at 3 months when randomized to 10 sessions of ACTp as compared to TAU. A follow-up study by Gumley et al. (2017) was then conducted using a parallel group, randomized, open blinded design ($n = 29$) of ACTp for depression following a psychotic episode. Participants assigned to ACTp showed a significant effect on depressive symptoms and psychological flexibility compared with those assigned to TAU at end of treatment at 5 months, although these group differences dissipated by the 10-month follow-up.

Shawyer et al. (2012) investigated the use of treatment of resistant command hallucinations (TORCH), which integrated elements of ACTp and CBTp, and compared TORCH to a "Befriending" condition in a sample of 43 outpatients with "problematic command hallucinations." A subsample also was randomized to a waitlist control. The Befriending comparison condition served as a manualized control meant to match for expectancy effects and time spent with a therapist, as used in other studies of CBT for psychosis (Bendall, Killackey, Jackson, & Gleeson, 2003). The TORCH intervention was delivered over 15 sessions for 5 months, incorporating both acceptance and reappraisal strategies to target voices. Both the TORCH and Befriending groups showed improvements in disruption and quality of life, but TORCH participants reported more robust improvements in quality of life and reported greater subjective improvement in command hallucinations (Shawyer et al., 2012). However, blinded assessments did not show differences between the two active treatment groups.

A follow-up RCT by Shawyer et al. (2017) compared eight sessions of ACTp to Befriending over 3 months for 96 outpatients with schizophrenia and schizoaffective disorder (Shawyer et al., 2017). Results showed that ACTp participants demonstrated significant improvements in positive symptoms by a 6-month follow-up. Process measures of acceptance, autonomous action, and defusion from illness did not significantly differ by group, but ACT participants reported voice-related distress significantly less than those assigned to the Befriending condition (Shawyer et al., 2017).

In another trial of group treatment, 10 sessions of ACTp produced significant improvements in anxiety, acceptance, and help-seeking behaviors for 50 outpatients with psychosis and childhood trauma as compared to TAU alone (Spidel, Daigneault, Kealy, & Lecomte, 2019). Most recently, van Aubel et al. (2020) conducted an RCT to explore the feasibility and efficacy of a "dedicated-device augmented, group-based, face-to-face ACT therapy (ACT-DL)" for non-help-seeking teens and young adults emerging with subthreshold depression and psychosis (van Aubel et al., 2020). This study used a control condition wherein participants watched documentaries in a group setting. Participants assigned to ACT-DL demonstrated significant improvements in negative affect and interviewer-rated depression severity relative to the control condition. However, groups did not significantly differ in self-reported depression, anxiety, overall symptomatology, and distress-related to psychosis (van Aubel et al., 2020). See Table 24.1 for a further summary of known RCTs of ACTp conducted to date.

Effectiveness and Implementation

Recent work also has been conducted to address the effectiveness and implementation of ACTp in routine clinical settings. An open trial (n = 26) of ACTp for inpatients on a routine hospital unit demonstrated high levels of patient and therapist satisfaction, along with significant improvements in psychiatric symptoms, distress, and mindfulness through a 4-month follow-up when delivered by non-ACT specialist hospital staff (e.g., social workers, psychiatric nurses, occupational therapists) (Gaudiano et al., 2020). In another inpatient study, Tyrberg et al. (2017) investigated the implementation of a 12-hour training program on ACTp for inpatient staff compared with staff at a separate unit acting as nonrandomized controls. Results showed that the training was acceptable and resulted in positive changes in psychological flexibility for the staff postintervention.

In terms of outpatient implementation, a pre-post designed trial (n = 65) showed that delivering 4 weeks of group ACTp to patients recruited from community psychosis teams in the UK was acceptable to patients and significantly improved functioning, mood, and experiential avoidance (Johns et al., 2016). Bloy, Morris, Johns, Cooke, and Oliver (2021) analyzed qualitative data from nine participants from the Johns et al. (2016) trial to identify themes in feedback from patients' experiences with ACTp. Participants reported increased awareness of internal experiences, changes in relating to thoughts, identification of goals, and pursuit of goals despite internal experiences (Bloy et al., 2021). An additional study by Butler et al. (2016) reported on the delivery of ACTp in 33 separate groups to 120 outpatients in a routine frontline psychosis service. Results showed that ACTp implemented in the community was feasible, acceptable, and potentially effective on clinical outcomes.

Finally, Jolley et al. (2020) conducted the first implementation RCT of group ACTp for psychosis delivered by frontline staff and co-facilitated by peer supports for both outpatients and their caregivers. Participants were randomized to ACTp with up to six sessions over 12 weeks provided immediately or after 12 weeks in a waitlist design. Results revealed that 71% of trained staff were able to deliver the intervention, patient refusal rates were low (9 percent),

Table 24.1 Summary of ACT for Psychosis RCTs Published in 2002–2020

Study	Sample	Comparison	Format	Results
Bach and Hayes (2002)	Inpatients with acute psychosis n = 80	Treatment as usual	Individual	ACT decreased rehospitalizations
Gaudiano and Herbert (2006)	Inpatients with acute psychosis n = 40	Enhanced treatment as usual	Individual	ACT decreased rehospitalizations, total symptoms, impairment, hallucination distress
White et al. (2011)	Outpatients with postpsychosis depression n = 27	Treatment as usual	Individual	ACT decreased negative symptoms and crisis calls; increased mindfulness
Shawyer et al. (2012)	Outpatients with command hallucinations n = 43	Active control	Individual	ACT decreased command hallucinations
Gaudiano et al. (2015)	Outpatients with psychotic depression n = 13	Enhanced treatment as usual	Individual	ACT decreased depression and experiential avoidance; increased functioning
Gumley et al. (2017)	Outpatients with postpsychosis depression n = 29	Treatment as usual	Individual	ACT decreased depression and experiential avoidance
Tyrberg et al. (2017)	Outpatients with acute psychosis n = 22	Treatment as usual	Individual	ACT decreased rehospitalizations
Shawyer et al. (2017)	Outpatients with residual psychosis n = 96	Active control	Group	ACT decreased positive symptoms and distress
Spidel, Lecomte, Kealy, and Daigneault (2018)	Outpatients with psychosis and trauma n = 50	Treatment as usual	Group	ACT decreased severity and anxiety; increased help-seeking and acceptance
Ghouchani et al. (2018)	Inpatients with aggression and drug use n = 30	Active control	Individual	ACT increased general health; decreased aggressiveness
Chowdhary and Jahan (2019)	Inpatient with psychosis n = 24	Treatment as usual	Individual	ACT increased medication adherence
van Aubel et al. (2020)	Outpatients with early psychosis and depression n = 55	Active control	Group + Mobile App	ACT decreased depression
Jacobsen et al. (2020)	Inpatients with acute psychosis n = 50	Active control	Individual	ACT decreased rehospitalizations

most who were invited to participate received at least 1 group session (60 percent), and outcomes generally favored ACTp with a range of small to large effects.

Potential Mediators and Moderators of Treatment Effects

Few studies to date have formally investigated moderators and mechanisms of ACTp. Some evidence exists supporting the mechanism of psychotic symptom "believability" (conceptualized in ACTp as a proxy for cognitive defusion), being a mediator of outcomes. Believability of hallucinations is the degree to which one believes that psychotic symptoms represent "real" or "true" external stimuli. Someone who is cognitively defused from hallucinations will be more likely to experience them as passing events that do not need to dictate behavior and choices. One study found that the significantly greater improvements in hallucinated-related distress in ACTp, versus the comparison condition, were statistically mediated by changes in believability of hallucinations (Gaudiano, Herbert, & Hayes, 2010). Believability was also indicated as a statistical mediator in a study combining data from two RCTs for ACTp for inpatients (Bach & Hayes, 2002; Gaudiano & Herbert, 2006), such that the effect of ACTp on rehospitalization rates was significantly mediated by the believability of psychotic symptoms (Bach et al., 2013).

Additional evidence for the potential mechanisms of ACTp comes from analyses of process changes that occur during treatment. For example, an open trial of outpatients with psychotic depression receiving ACTp demonstrated that improvements in depressive symptomatology were correlated with improvements in psychological flexibility, mindfulness, and valued living (Gaudiano et al., 2013). In addition, an RCT of ACTp by White et al. (2011) of outpatients with depression following a psychotic episode reported that improvements in mindfulness correlated with improvements in depression.

Furthermore, potential moderators of ACTp were investigated as part of a study by Spidel et al. (2019). In their RCT of outpatients with psychosis and childhood trauma comparing ACTp to TAU, Spidel et al. (2019) found that the effects of ACTp on symptom severity and treatment engagement were moderated by the number of sessions received and patients' attachment style. An avoidant attachment style and lower number of sessions received were both predictive of poorer treatment outcomes. However, trauma severity was hypothesized but was not found to be a moderator of outcomes in the study (Spidel et al., 2019).

Treatment Overview

ACTp protocols vary widely, but they are generally based on the same principles as ACT for other conditions, with some modifications that are considered clinically appropriate for patients with psychosis (Oliver, Joseph, Byrne, Johns, & Morris, 2013). Overall, the objectives of ACTp are to (1) foster acceptance of unavoidable distress associated with psychotic symptoms, (2) notice the experience of psychotic symptoms in a nonjudgmental way in the moment when they occur, and (3) build a values-driven life regardless of the presence of symptoms (Gaudiano et al., 2010). What follows is an example of what a typical ACTp treatment protocol might look like for an outpatient with psychosis.

First, as with other similar therapies for patients with psychosis, ACTp always emphasizes developing a strong working alliance, pacing the intervention according to the patient's willingness and capacity, and selecting intervention strategies and treatment targets based on a shared case conceptualization of problem areas to individualize and personalize the therapy process. In addition, the therapist needs to take into account the patient's symptom severity (e.g., withdrawal, disorganization), level of insight into illness, and any delusions that the person may hold that could interfere with the treatment process. If a patient is too acutely ill, then the therapist will need to proceed slowly and cautiously with treatment until their condition improves (e.g., provide initial support and encouragement). This may be the case in particular when treating hospitalized patients. As the psychotic episode improves, often with the passage of time and with the aid of medication, the person will be able to engage more actively in treatment sessions and ACTp elements can be added slowly. Regardless of severity level, it is always important for the therapist to meet the patient where they are at and to focus on practical goals or those aspects of treatment that both patient and therapist can agree are worthy to pursue at any given time.

The treatment typically starts with the therapist discussing the patient's history related to hallucinations, delusions, and negative symptoms, with an eye toward highlighting the role of EA-based coping attempts in causing increased distress and impairment over time. This will set the stage for proposing acceptance as an alternative approach. Patients with psychosis typically try blocking out psychotic symptoms (e.g., turning on loud music to drown out the voices) or struggling with them (e.g., arguing back to voices). This EA-focused discussion of coping is a modified version of what ACT would call developing "creative hopelessness," or an appreciation of what has not worked in the past to facilitate a willingness to try something different in therapy. For example, the therapist explores whether attempts to avoid or eliminate psychotic experiences have made them worse or better over time, or how perhaps increasing preoccupation with paranoid thoughts has led to increased impairment and dysfunction in life.

In addition, early ACTp sessions tend to be heavily rooted in values clarification work to help the individual identify what things are most important to them in a crucial effort to motivate and sustain the behavior change efforts that will follow. The therapist can explore with the patient how different life might look if hallucinations and delusions did not "get in the way" of valued pursuits and what the person would be doing differently, at least in a hypothetical sense initially. Once values are identified, values-consistent goals and action steps can be specified to guide future sessions. The focus here is on building small, short-term goals that evolve over time. For example, the patients may start by simply engaging in simple self-care behaviors such as dressing, eating, and hygiene, and work up to more complex behaviors such as attending a support group or volunteering their time.

Based on this initial discussion of how EA contributes to distress and impairment, as well as what values and goals are most important for the patient to pursue, the therapist creates an initial case conceptualization that is shared with the patient. This formulation is based on a functional analysis of the patient's strengths and weaknesses, which in turn is based on an exploration of how they relate to the whole individual, what the antecedents and consequences of the behaviors are, and how they fit into the broader context of the individual's life. Functional analysis of target behaviors can include both psychotic (delusions, hallucinations, negative symptoms) and nonpsychotic (e.g., depression, anxiety) symptoms, as well as other areas of life that are important to the patient's recovery (e.g., social functioning). Based on this functional case conceptualization of psychotic experiences, the therapist can start to select different processes to work on from the ACT hexaflex that might be particularly relevant to the specified treatment goals, including acceptance, defusion, self-as-context, present moment awareness, values, and committed action in the service of increasing psychological flexibility.

Although strategies and metaphors used in ACTp are typically the same as those used for other conditions, certain techniques may be particularly relevant when applied to psychotic symptoms (Gaudiano et al., 2010). For example, acceptance and cognitive defusion strategies can be helpful in addressing EA-focused coping with distressing voices. The "Tug of War with a Monster" metaphor can be used to explore how patients feel when they struggle with derogatory voices. In this example, the person's psychotic symptoms can be externalized as a "monster," and "letting go of the rope" is discussed as a way to accept but not change psychotic symptoms to foster the person's ability to pursue valued goals instead. A physical rope can be used as a reminder of this exercise in future sessions. The patient can be encouraged to identify when they are "holding" the rope (i.e., engaging in EA) in session, and then the therapist can invite them to put it down (literally and figuratively), and practice increasing their willingness in the moment with the therapist's support.

In addition, cognitive defusion strategies, as exemplified in the "Passengers on the Bus" exercise can be used to target delusional thinking patterns by helping the patient to attend less to the content of unhelpful thoughts (i.e., letting them say what they want to say, but not engaging them in a discussion or argument). Instead, the goal of this exercise is to focus on the values-driven behaviors that people have more direct control over in their lives (i.e., driving the bus and choosing their own route). In this metaphor, paranoid thoughts and derogatory voices may try to "boss" the bus driver around, and so the goal is for the driver to continue to move along the desired path without letting the undesirable mental "passengers" dictate the course. This "Passengers on the Bus" exercise can be acted out in a group setting, with other patients playing the various roles (O'Donoghue, Morris, Oliver, & Johns, 2018).

Furthermore, the therapist discusses the ways that psychotic symptoms can interfere with the patient's valued pursuits and how to deal with this in a more workable fashion. In the "Unwelcome Party Guest" metaphor, the patient first has to try to keep out a rude and undesirable guest from messing up their party. However, this effort results in the patient being unable to enjoy or participate in the party, as they have to always stand "guard" to block the entry of the unwelcome other. This scenario is likened to how the patient might try to wait for voices or paranoid beliefs to go away before they engage in certain desired activities. In this metaphor, the patient is then encouraged to allow the unwanted guest into the party while simultaneously hosting the party, with the guest also being present. In this way, the patient can explore ways of handling psychotic experiences that may be more workable in the moment and increase their ability to pursue valued activities despite symptoms. An animated version of this story is available online https://www.youtube.com/watch/VYht-guymF4? that can be shown to patients and discussed to aid in understanding and remembering this metaphor.

Over the course of treatment, the therapist continues to monitor the patient's progress toward values and goals and applies the ACT relevant processes to address EA issues that stand in the way of behavior change. In addition to working on psychotic symptoms, negative symptoms are also targeted in ACTp using similar strategies. For example, values work can address low motivation; values-based behavioral activation and exposure exercises can be applied to depression and anxiety; social skills training can be practiced to work on social functioning; and mindfulness meditation can be used to practice nonjudgmental awareness of experience with certain adaptations as described below (Gaudiano et al., 2013). Sometimes, negative symptoms can be targeted directly for change and improvement. For example, the therapist can help support the patient in socially engaging more with others in a values-consistent way. In other instances, patients may be encouraged to acknowledge and "carry forward" certain limitations that might be more difficult for them to directly change, such as cognitive challenges related to concentration and attention due to illness or medication effects. Instead, patients may be urged to pursue valued goals despite these deficits by finding more workable solutions or alternatives.

ACTp outpatient treatment (see Table 24.2) sessions typically last weekly for several months, similar to other cognitive-behavioral therapies, although the exact timeframe can vary based on the patient's goals and level of functioning. Latter sessions include discussions of longer-term goal setting based on evolving values clarification and relapse prevention by applying acceptance and mindfulness-based coping strategies to maintain and extend gains

Table 24.2 Sample Outpatient Treatment Outline of ACTp
• Provide informed consent for treatment and discuss treatment alternatives.
• Review patient's history, focusing on role of experiential avoidance in coping with psychotic symptoms and its associated unworkability.
• Clarify patient's values and specify values-consistent, short-term goals; then break them down into more manageable action steps.
• Develop a shared-case conceptualization of the patient's strengths and weaknesses based on a functional analysis of symptoms, functioning, and goals.
• Select ACT treatment processes as relevant to the patient's valued goal pursuits, including acceptance, defusion, mindfulness, self-as-context, values, and committed action as indicated.
• In addition to ACT processes, include other relevant behavioral strategies when applicable, including social skills training, behavioral activation, and exposure exercises to support valued goal attainment.
• Change exercises and metaphors so that they are appropriate for patients with cognitive limitations by making them briefer and less abstract and incorporating visual aids and multimedia to aid in learning and memory.
• Modify mindfulness exercises so that they are first delivered in an eye-opening fashion of shorter duration applied to everyday activities such as eating or walking.
• Address medication adherence through discussions of values-action consistency, workability, and the therapeutic alliance.
• Review session content frequently across sessions to ensure understanding and uptake of information.
• Monitor progress by collecting relevant measures of clinical outcomes and ACT-relevant processes of change throughout treatment.
• In later sessions, focus on using ACT processes to prevent relapse, specify longer-term valued goals, and offer "booster" sessions to continue to support recovery after the primary treatment phase is completed.

posttreatment. "Booster" sessions can be provided to aid the treatment transition process, increase the chances of success, and extend additional support when needed. Assessments are also collected before, during, and following treatment to track progress on clinical outcomes relevant to the patient (e.g., Psychotic Symptom Ratings Scales; Drake, Haddock, Tarrier, Bentall, & Lewis, 2007), as well as changes in ACT processes (e.g., Voices Acceptance and Action Scale; Shawyer et al., 2007).

Clinical Considerations

ACTp addresses the unique needs of those with psychosis in several ways. First, it is important to continually review and repeat content from session to session to facilitate learning. For example, perhaps a third of the sessions should be spent reviewing previous material, depending on the patient's level of functioning (Bach, Gaudiano, Pankey, Herbert, & Hayes, 2006). It is also helpful to deliver ACT exercises in shorter and less abstract ways. Metaphors can be simplified and supplemented with physical props or by acting out the concepts to illustrate ACT processes. It also is helpful to incorporate videos, worksheets, illustrations, and other visual aides to improve uptake.

In addition, mindfulness meditation exercises can be used safely and effectively with those patients with psychosis who are not acutely ill (Chadwick, Taylor, & Abba, 2005). However, certain patients may exhibit iatrogenic effects from intensive meditation practices because such exercises may inadvertently foster internal preoccupation and disengagement from reality in acutely ill individuals (Sharma, Mahapatra, & Gupta, 2019). Instead of practicing eyes-closed, internally focused meditation, patients can first learn to practice mindfulness in an eyes-open fashion as applied to everyday activities, such as eating, walking, or listening to music. When it is clinically appropriate to practice simple, eyes-closed meditation to the breath, the exercises should be kept briefer (5 minutes) and the therapist should check in and provide prompts during the practice.

Furthermore, most patients with psychosis will likely also be receiving pharmacotherapy while receiving ACTp. Therefore, the therapist should discuss contextual factors related to medication adherence and help the patient to address any problems in this area by conducting a functional analysis of nonadherence behaviors, focused on the potential role of EA. Common ACTp strategies can be used to address adherence, which include discussions of medication in terms of its workability, values-action consistency, and the therapeutic alliance with the provider (Moitra & Gaudiano, 2016).

Research and Clinical Directions

The limitations of the current ACTp research base include the use of small sample sizes leading to inadequate power to detect differences, differences in the comparison conditions and treatment protocols used across studies, and variability in sample severity and diagnoses. Complexity is further added by the variability in the number of treatment sessions delivered, length of follow-ups, and outcome measures utilized across both inpatient and outpatient trials. In general, the methodological quality of the ACTp clinical trials has been variable to date, with some having "gold standard" methodological features of RCTs, such as rater blinding and fidelity monitoring, while others lack these elements and are considered more feasibility or pilot studies. Larger and more methodologically rigorous studies are needed to confirm the effects reported from smaller trials.

Previous meta-analyses have sometimes produced conflicting conclusions based on the different studies they include (Cramer et al., 2016; Tonarelli et al., 2016). The practice of combining inpatient and outpatient studies in the same meta-analysis is questionable and may obscure potential treatment effects given differences in study design, methods, sample, and setting. So far, ACTp has not been directly compared to other evidence-based psychosocial interventions (e.g., traditional CBT or family therapy) in the same RCT. Thus, it is unclear if ACTp is more or less effective, or if it works through similar or different mechanisms of action compared with other psychotherapies. To date, little formal work has been done to investigate ACTp treatment mediators and moderators of outcomes. Some initial work suggests that the believability of psychotic symptoms may be a mediator of ACTp's treatment effects consistent with reductions in psychological inflexibility (Gaudiano et al., 2010). However, more research is needed, testing other ACT-consistent processes of change and using designs that can better establish temporal change in the presumed mediator prior to change in the observed clinical outcomes. More work also is needed on the real-world effectiveness and implementation of ACTp in typical clinical settings. Few therapists are trained in ACTp compared with traditional CBTp, and ACTp is not as yet typically offered in routine practice. Finally, given that patients with psychosis often receive a variety of treatments, including pharmacotherapy and other therapies, additional research should investigate how ACTp should be integrated with other common approaches so that it is complementary and not contradictory.

Despite these challenges, the available evidence from a growing number of RCTs shows that ACTp is a safe and efficacious treatment for patients with a range of schizophrenia-spectrum disorders. It is also one of the few treatments tested specifically for those with psychotic depression (Gaudiano et al., 2015; Gaudiano et al., 2013). Evidence-based treatment guidelines specify that, at present, the strongest support is for first-line use of traditional CBTp or family therapy for psychosis (NICE, 2014). Based on these guidelines, one can deduce that ACTp may be appropriate for use if patients have not responded to one of the other evidence-based therapies for psychosis first, when they are available. However, if CBTp or family therapy is not available, then ACTp may be considered based on factors such as therapist competence and patient preference, and following proper informed consent and review of alternative options. In addition, the research to date has only tested ACTp when it is added to ongoing pharmacotherapy for psychosis that typically includes antipsychotic medications.

Clinicians wishing to deliver ACTp should first be competent using the ACT model in general, and they also should have the requisite experience and training in working clinically with patients with severe mental illness. Clinical workshops on ACTp have been presented at conferences such as the Association for Contextual Behavior Science, and several books have been published describing the rationale and clinical application of ACTp to aid in training efforts (Gaudiano, 2015; Morris, Johns, & Oliver, 2013; O'Donoghue et al., 2018; Wright et al., 2014). However, it is recommended that clinicians with prior training in ACT who are comfortable working with patients with psychosis still receive additional peer consultation and supervision on early cases from therapists with established competence. This will ensure that the ACTp is being applied appropriately and safely.

One common misconception about ACTp is that the therapist's goal is to teach the patient to "accept" their psychotic experience for what they represent themselves to be (e.g., voices coming from an omnipotent external force). This is not the case, however, as the ACTp therapist does not attempt to reinforce psychotic symptom content or treat them literally. Instead, the therapist models an "agnostic" or nonjudgmental stance toward these experiences and encourages the patient to do likewise. The goal is not to ignore hallucinations or delusional thoughts when they are occurring. On the other hand, the goal also is not to engage or struggle with them in a preoccupied fashion. Instead of focusing on their literal veracity, the therapist helps patients to identify whether their responses to these psychotic experiences are workable or not for achieving their desired goals, and if not, to respond in ways that work better for this purpose as consistent with their values.

Furthermore, taking a nonjudgmental stance toward psychotic experiences when they occur in the moment does not mean that the therapist views psychotic symptom content as irrelevant or without meaning to the patient and their clinical context. For example, paranoia might be conceptualized as functioning for the patient to manage anxiety, and the specific delusional content is likely to be representative of the patient's individual learning history and past experiences. Instead of attempting to directly change paranoid thoughts, a functional analysis can be applied to hallucinations and delusions to better understand how they are being reinforced and maintained over time, and to identify healthier alternate behaviors to fulfill these needs for the patient that will lead to improved functioning and valued-goal attainment.

Conclusion

In summary, numerous clinical trials since 2002 have studied the effects of ACTp. These studies generally document the treatment's safety, feasibility, and acceptability to both patients and clinicians. Although symptom reduction is not the primary aim of ACTp, numerous research studies report significant improvements on multiple important clinical indicators, including positive symptoms, negative symptoms, depression, distress, impairment, quality of life, and help seeking (see Table 24.1 for a summary). As demonstrated in several studies of ACTp, the treatment's potential to reduce rehospitalizations constitutes a pragmatic, global indicator of functioning (Bach, Hayes, & Gallop, 2012), especially considering that symptomatic and functional recovery has been documented to occur at different times from one another (Tohen et al., 2000). However, the magnitude of ACTp's treatment effects has varied based on the types of measures collected, the characteristics of the sample, and the selection of comparison conditions used in prior research. Studies comparing ACTp to more active supportive therapies have often reported more equivocal results (Shawyer et al., 2017), which is similar to what is found in the CBTp literature when such comparisons are made (Lynch, Laws, & McKenna, 2010). Despite these limitations, it is important to note that ACTp has been used frequently in both inpatient and outpatient settings, including for those at various stages of illness and types of schizophrenia-spectrum disorders. In addition, ACTp has been provided in both group and individual session formats with positive effects. Therefore, ACTp provides a useful treatment alternative to offer those experiencing psychosis as part of the broader clinical armamentarium of care, potentially offering profound relief to those suffering from chronic mental illness.

References

Acceptance and commitment therapy for psychosis. (2020). Retrieved from https://div12.org/treatment/acceptance-and-commitment-therapy-for-psychosis

Bach, P. A., Gaudiano, B., Hayes, S. C., & Herbert, J. D. (2013). Reduced believability of positive symptoms mediates improved hospitalization outcomes of acceptance and commitment therapy for psychosis. *Psychosis, 5*, 166–174.

Bach, P. A., Gaudiano, B., Pankey, J., Herbert, J. D., & Hayes, S. C. (2006). Acceptance, mindfulness, values, and psychosis: Applying acceptance and commitment therapy (ACT) to the chronically mentally ill. In R. A. Baer (Ed.), *Mindfulness-based treatment approaches: Clinician's guide to evidence base and applications* (pp. 93–116). San Diego, CA: Elsevier Academic Press.

Bach, P. A., & Hayes, S. C. (2002). The use of acceptance and commitment therapy to prevent the rehospitalization of psychotic patients: A randomized controlled trial. *Journal of Consulting and Clinical Psychology, 70*(5), 1129–1139. doi:10.1037/0022-006X.70.5.1129

Bach, P., Hayes, S. C., & Gallop, R. (2012). Long-term effects of brief acceptance and commitment therapy for psychosis. *Behavior Modification, 36*(2), 165–181.

Barnes, T. R., Mutsatsa, S. H., Hutton, S. B., Watt, H. C., & Joyce, E. M. (2006). Comorbid substance use and age at onset of schizophrenia. *British Journal of Psychiatry, 188*(3), 237–242.

Beard, C., Hearon, B. A., Lee, J., Kopeski, L. M., Busch, A. B., & Björgvinsson, T. (2016). When partial hospitalization fails: Risk factors for inpatient hospitalization. *Journal of Nervous and Mental Disease, 204*(6), 431–436.

Bendall, S., Killackey, E., Jackson, H., & Gleeson, J. (2003). *Befriending manual.* Melbourne: ORYGEN Research Centre, University of Melbourne.

Bloy, S., Morris, E. M., Johns, L. C., Cooke, A., & Oliver, J. E. (2021). "My voices are just part of me, they don't own me": A qualitative investigation of acceptance and commitment therapy groups for people experiencing psychosis. *Psychosis, 13*(3), 1–14.

Braga, R. J., Petrides, G., & Figueira, I. (2004). Anxiety disorders in schizophrenia. *Comprehensive Psychiatry, 45*(6), 460–468.

Brohan, E., Elgie, R., Sartorius, N., Thornicroft, G., & Group, G.-E. S. (2010). Self-stigma, empowerment and perceived discrimination among people with schizophrenia in 14 European countries: The GAMIAN-Europe study. *Schizophrenia Research, 122*(1–3), 232–238.

Butler, L., Johns, L. C., Byrne, M., Joseph, C., O'Donoghue, E., Jolley, S., . . . Oliver, J. E. (2016). Running acceptance and commitment therapy groups for psychosis in community settings. *Journal of Contextual Behavioral Science, 5*(1), 33–38. doi:10.1016/j.jcbs.2015.12.001

Chadwick, P., Taylor, K. N., & Abba, N. (2005). Mindfulness groups for people with psychosis. *Behavioural and Cognitive Psychotherapy, 33*, 351–359.

Chien, W. T., Chow, K. M., Chong, Y. Y., Bressington, D., Choi, K. C., & Chan, C. W. H. (2020). The role of five facets of mindfulness in a mindfulness-based psychoeducation intervention for people with recent-onset

psychosis on mental and psychosocial health outcomes. *Frontiers in Psychiatry, 11*, 177. https://doi.org/10.3389/fpsyt.2020.00177
Chowdhary, M., & Jahan, M. (2019). Treatment adherence in patients with schizophrenia after acceptance and commitment therapy. *IAHRW International Journal of Social Sciences Review, 7*(5), 1067–1073.
Cloutier, M., Aigbogun, M. S., Guerin, A., Nitulescu, R., Ramanakumar, A. V., Kamat, S. A., . . . Henderson, C. (2016). The economic burden of schizophrenia in the United States in 2013. *Journal of Clinical Psychiatry, 77*(6), 764–771.
Cramer, H., Lauche, R., Haller, H., Langhorst, J., & Dobos, G. (2016). Mindfulness- and acceptance-based interventions for psychosis: A systematic review and meta-analysis. *Global Advances in Health and Medicine, 5*(1), 30–43.
De Hert, M., Correll, C. U., Bobes, J., Cetkovich-Bakmas, M., Cohen, D., Asai, I., . . . Ndetei, D. M. (2011). Physical illness in patients with severe mental disorders. I. Prevalence, impact of medications and disparities in health care. *World Psychiatry, 10*(1), 52.
Drake, R., Haddock, G., Tarrier, N., Bentall, R., & Lewis, S. (2007). The Psychotic Symptom Rating Scales (PSYRATS): Their usefulness and properties in first episode psychosis. *Schizophrenia Research, 89*(1–3), 119–122.
Eack, S. M., Bahorik, A. L., Newhill, C. E., Neighbors, H. W., & Davis, L. E. (2012). Interviewer-perceived honesty as a mediator of racial disparities in the diagnosis of schizophrenia. *Psychiatric Services, 63*(9), 875–880.
Escher, S., Delespaul, P., Romme, M., Buiks, A., & Van Os, J. I. M. (2003). Coping defence and depression in adolescents hearing voices. *Journal of Mental Health, 12*(1), 91–99. doi:10.1080/09638230021000058
Falloon, I. R., & Talbot, R. E. (1981). Persistent auditory hallucinations: coping mechanisms and implications for management. *Psychological Medicine, 11*(2), 329–339. doi:10.1017/s0033291700052144
Farhall, J., & Gehrke, M. (1997). Coping with hallucinations: Exploring stress and coping framework. *British Journal of Clinical Psychology, 36*(2), 259–261. doi:10.1111/j.2044-8260.1997.tb01411.x
First, M., Williams, J., Karg, R., & Spitzer, R. (2015). *Structured clinical interview for DSM-5*. Arlington, VA: American Psychiatric Association.
Fulford, D., Campellone, T., & Gard, D. E. (2018). Social motivation in schizophrenia: How research on basic reward processes informs and limits our understanding. *Clinical Psychology Review, 63*, 12–24.
García, J., & Pérez, M. (2001). ACT as a treatment for psychotic symptoms. The case of auditory hallucinations. *Análisis y modificación de conducta, 27*(113), 455–472.
Gaudiano, B. (Ed.). (2015). *Incorporating acceptance and mindfulness into the treatment of psychosis: Current trends and future directions*. New York: Oxford University Press.
Gaudiano, B., & Herbert, J. D. (2006). Acute treatment of inpatients with psychotic symptoms using acceptance and commitment therapy: Pilot results. *Behaviour Research and Therapy, 44*(3), 415–437. doi:10.1016/j.brat.2005.02.007
Gaudiano, B., Herbert, J. D., & Hayes, S. C. (2010). Is it the symptom or the relation to it? Investigating potential mediators of change in acceptance and commitment therapy for psychosis. *Behavior Therapy, 41*, 543–554.
Gaudiano, B. A., Busch, A. M., Wenze, S. J., Nowlan, K., Epstein-Lubow, G., & Miller, I. W. (2015). Acceptance-based behavior therapy for depression with psychosis. *Journal of Psychiatric Practice, 21*(5), 320–333. doi:10.1097/PRA.0000000000000092
Gaudiano, B. A., Ellenberg, S., Ostrove, B., Johnson, J., Mueser, K. T., Furman, M., & Miller, I. W. (2020). Feasibility and preliminary effects of implementing acceptance and commitment therapy for inpatients with psychotic-spectrum disorders in a clinical psychiatric intensive care setting. *Journal of Cognitive Psychotherapy, 34*(1), 80–96. doi:10.1891/0889-8391.34.1.80
Gaudiano, B. A., Nowlan, K., Brown, L. A., Epstein-Lubow, G., & Miller, I. W. (2013). An open trial of a new acceptance-based behavioral treatment for major depression with psychotic features. *Behavior Modification, 37*(3), 324–355.
Gaudiano, B. A., Primack, J., & Miller, I. W. (2016). Investigating the role of acceptance, mindfulness, and values in patients with psychosis in the context of depression. *Journal of Psychiatric Intensive Care, 12*, 79–87.
Ghouchani, S., Molavi, N., Massah, O., Sadeghi, M., Mousavi, S. H., Noroozi, M., . . . Farhoudian, A. (2018). Effectiveness of acceptance and commitment therapy (ACT) on aggression of patients with psychosis due to methamphetamine use: A pilot study. *Journal of Substance Use, 23*(4), 402–407. doi:10.1080/14659891.2018.1436602
Goldstone, E., Farhall, J., & Ong, B. (2011). Life hassles, experiential avoidance and distressing delusional experiences. *Behaviour Research and Therapy, 49*(4), 260–266. doi:10.1016/j.brat.2011.02.002
Green, M. F., Horan, W. P., & Lee, J. (2015). Social cognition in schizophrenia. *National Review of Neuroscience, 16*(10), 620–631. doi:10.1038/nrn4005
Gumley, A., White, R., Briggs, A., Ford, I., Barry, S., Stewart, C., . . . McLeod, H. (2017). A parallel group randomised open blinded evaluation of acceptance and commitment therapy for depression after psychosis: Pilot trial outcomes (ADAPT). *Schizophrenia Research, 183*, 143–150. doi:10.1016/j.schres.2016.11.026

Harris, C., & Barraclough, B. (1998). Excess mortality of mental disorder. *British Journal of Psychiatry, 173*(1), 11–53.

Harvey, P. D., Strassnig, M. T., & Silberstein, J. (2019). Prediction of disability in schizophrenia: Symptoms, cognition, and self-assessment. *Journal of Experimental Psychopathology, 10*(3), 2043808719865693.

Hayes, S. C., Levin, M. E., Plumb-Vilardaga, J., Villatte, J. L., & Pistorello, J. (2013). Acceptance and commitment therapy and contextual behavioral science: Examining the progress of a distinctive model of behavioral and cognitive therapy. *Behavior Therapy, 44*(2), 180–198. doi:10.1016/j.beth.2009.08.002

Heslin, K. C., & Weiss, A. J. (2015). Hospital readmissions involving psychiatric disorders, 2012: Statistical brief# 189. Rockville, MD: Agency for Healthcare Research and Quality.

Hudson, C. G. (2019). Five-year rehospitalization experience of a state-wide cohort of persons with schizophrenia. *Social Psychiatry and Psychiatric Epidemiology, 54*(7), 861–870.

Hughes, S., & Barnes-Holmes, D. (2016). Relational frame theory: The basic account. In R. D. Zettle (Ed.), *The Wiley handbook of contextual behavioral science* (pp. 129–178). Malden, MA: Wiley Blackwell.

Jablensky, A. (2010). The diagnostic concept of schizophrenia: Its history, evolution, and future prospects. *Dialogues in Clinical Neuroscience, 12*(3), 271–287. doi:10.31887/DCNS.2010.12.3/ajablensky

Jacobsen, P., Peters, E., Robinson, E. J., & Chadwick, P. (2020). Mindfulness-based crisis interventions (MBCI) for psychosis within acute inpatient psychiatric settings; A feasibility randomised controlled trial. *BMC Psychiatry, 20*, 1–12.

Jauhar, S., McKenna, P., Radua, J., Fung, E., Salvador, R., & Laws, K. (2014). Cognitive–behavioural therapy for the symptoms of schizophrenia: Systematic review and meta-analysis with examination of potential bias. *British Journal of Psychiatry, 204*(1), 20–29.

Johns, L. C., Oliver, J. E., Khondoker, M., Byrne, M., Jolley, S., Wykes, T., . . . Morris, E. M. J. (2016). The feasibility and acceptability of a brief acceptance and commitment therapy (ACT) group intervention for people with psychosis: The "ACT for life" study. *Journal of Behavior Therapy and Experimental Psychiatry, 50*, 257–263.

Jolley, S., Johns, L. C., O'Donoghue, E., Oliver, J., Khondoker, M., Byrne, M., . . . Morris, E. (2020). Group acceptance and commitment therapy for patients and caregivers in psychosis services: Feasibility of training and a preliminary randomized controlled evaluation. *British Journal of Clinical Psychology, 59*(4), 524–551. doi:https://doi.org/10.1111/bjc.12265

Kaskie, R. E., Graziano, B., & Ferrarelli, F. (2017). Schizophrenia and sleep disorders: links, risks, and management challenges. *Nature and Science of Sleep, 9*, 227–239. doi:10.2147/NSS.S121076

Kendler, K. S., & O'Donovan, M. C. (2014). A breakthrough in schizophrenia genetics. *JAMA Psychiatry, 71*(12), 1319–1320.

Komala, E. P. E., Keliat, B. A., & Wardani, I. Y. (2018). Acceptance and commitment therapy and family psycho education for clients with schizophrenia. *Enfermería Clínica, 28*, 88–93.

Lawrence, D. M., D'Arcy, C., Holman, J., Jablensky, A. V., & Hobbs, M. S. (2003). Death rate from ischaemic heart disease in Western Australian psychiatric patients 1980–1998. *British Journal of Psychiatry, 182*(1), 31–36.

Leucht, S., Arbter, D., Engel, R. R., Kissling, W., & Davis, J. (2009). How effective are second-generation antipsychotic drugs? A meta-analysis of placebo-controlled trials. *Molecular Psychiatry, 14*(4), 429–447.

Leucht, S., Burkard, T., Henderson, J., Maj, M., & Sartorius, N. (2007). Physical illness and schizophrenia: A review of the literature. *Acta Psychiatrica Scandinavica, 116*(5), 317–333.

Lilja, L., & Hellzén, O. (2008). Former patients' experience of psychiatric care: A qualitative investigation. *International Journal of Mental Health Nursing, 17*(4), 279–286.

Lorine, K., Goenjian, H., Kim, S., Steinberg, A. M., Schmidt, K., & Goenjian, A. K. (2015). Risk factors associated with psychiatric readmission. *Journal of Nervous and Mental Disease, 203*(6), 425–430.

Luo, Y., Zhang, L., He, P., Pang, L., Guo, C., & Zheng, X. (2019). Individual-level and area-level socioeconomic status (SES) and schizophrenia: Cross-sectional analyses using the evidence from 1.9 million Chinese adults. *BMJ Open, 9*(9), e026532.

Lynch, D., Laws, K., & McKenna, P. (2010). Cognitive behavioural therapy for major psychiatric disorder: does it really work? A meta-analytical review of well-controlled trials. *Psychological Medicine, 40*(1), 9–24.

Mander, H., & Kingdon, D. (2015). The evolution of cognitive–behavioral therapy for psychosis. *Psychology Research and Behavior Management, 8*, 63.

McLeod, H. J. (2009). ACT and CBT for psychosis: Comparisons and contrasts. In J. T. Blackledge, J. Ciarrochi, & F. P. Deane (Eds.), *Acceptance and commitment therapy: Contemporary theory, research and practice* (pp. 263–279). Sydney, Australia: Australian Academic Press.

Moitra, E., & Gaudiano, B. (2016). A psychological flexibility model of medication adherence in psychotic-spectrum disorders. *Journal of Contextual Behavioral Science, 5*(4), 252–257. doi:https://doi.org/10.1016/j.jcbs.2016.10.003

Moreno-Küstner, B., Martin, C., & Pastor, L. (2018). Prevalence of psychotic disorders and its association with methodological issues. A systematic review and meta-analyses. *PLOS One, 13*(4), e0195687.
Morris, E. M., Johns, L. C., & Oliver, J. E. (2013). *Acceptance and commitment therapy and mindfulness for psychosis.* Hoboken, NJ: Wiley Online Library.
Newman-Taylor, K., Richardson, T., Sood, M., Sopp, M., Perry, E., & Bolderston, H. (2020). Cognitive mechanisms in cannabis-related paranoia: Initial testing and model proposal. *Psychosis, 12*(4), 314–327.
NICE. (2014). *Schizophrenia in adults: Treatment and management.* London: National Institute for Health and Care Excellence.
O'Donoghue, E. K., Morris, E. M., Oliver, J., & Johns, L. C. (2018). *ACT for psychosis recovery: A practical manual for group-based interventions using acceptance and commitment therapy.* Oakland, CA: New Harbinger Publications.
Oliver, J. E., Joseph, C., Byrne, M., Johns, L. C., & Morris, E. M. J. (2013). Introduction to mindfulness and acceptance-based therapies for psychosis. In E. M. J. Morris, L C. Johns, and J. E. Oliver (Eds.), *Acceptance and commitment therapy and mindfulness for psychosis* (pp. 1–11). Hoboken, NJ: Wiley Blackwell.
Powers, A. R., III, Kelley, M. S., & Corlett, P. R. (2017). Varieties of voice-hearing: psychics and the psychosis continuum. *Schizophrenia Bulletin, 43*(1), 84–98.
Qin, P., & Nordentoft, M. (2005). Suicide risk in relation to psychiatric hospitalization: Evidence based on longitudinal registers. *Archives of General Psychiatry, 62*(4), 427–432.
Saha, S., Chant, D., & McGrath, J. (2007). A systematic review of mortality in schizophrenia: Is the differential mortality gap worsening over time? *Archives of General Psychiatry, 64*(10), 1123–1131. doi:10.1001/archpsyc.64.10.1123
Schulze, B., & Angermeyer, M. C. (2003). Subjective experiences of stigma. A focus group study of schizophrenic patients, their relatives and mental health professionals. *Social Science and Medicine, 56*(2), 299–312.
Sharma, P., Mahapatra, A., & Gupta, R. (2019). Meditation-induced psychosis: A narrative review and individual patient data analysis. *Irish Journal of Psychological Medicine*, 1–7. doi:10.1017/ipm.2019.47
Shawyer, F., Farhall, J., Mackinnon, A., Trauer, T., Sims, E., Ratcliff, K., . . . Copolov, D. (2012). A randomised controlled trial of acceptance-based cognitive behavioural therapy for command hallucinations in psychotic disorders. *Behaviour Research and Therapy, 50*(2), 110–121. doi:10.1016/j.brat.2011.11.007
Shawyer, F., Farhall, J., Thomas, N., Hayes, S. C., Gallop, R., Copolov, D., & Castle, D. J. (2017). Acceptance and commitment therapy for psychosis: Randomised controlled trial. *British Journal of Psychiatry, 210*(2), 140–148.
Shawyer, F., Ratcliff, K., Mackinnon, A., Farhall, J., Hayes, S. C., & Copolov, D. (2007). The voices acceptance and action scale (VAAS): Pilot data. *Journal of Clinical Psychology, 63*(6), 593–606. doi:10.1002/jclp.20366
Shumway, M., Saunders, T., Shern, D., Pines, E., Downs, A., Burbine, T., & Beller, J. (2003). Preferences for schizophrenia treatment outcomes among public policy makers, consumers, families, and providers. *Psychiatric Services, 54*(8), 1124–1128.
Spidel, A., Daigneault, I., Kealy, D., & Lecomte, T. (2019). Acceptance and commitment therapy for psychosis and trauma: Investigating links between trauma severity, attachment and outcome. *Behavioural and Cognitive Psychotherapy, 47*(2), 230–243.
Spidel, A., Lecomte, T., Kealy, D., & Daigneault, I. (2018). Acceptance and commitment therapy for psychosis and trauma: Improvement in psychiatric symptoms, emotion regulation, and treatment compliance following a brief group intervention. *Psychology and Psychotherapy: Theory, Research and Practice, 91*(2), 248–261. doi:10.1111/papt.12159
Stilo, S. A., & Murray, R. M. (2019). Non-genetic factors in schizophrenia. *Current Psychiatry Reports, 21*(10), 100.
Tait, L., Birchwood, M., & Trower, P. (2003). Predicting engagement with services for psychosis: insight, symptoms and recovery style. *British Journal of Psychiatry, 182*, 123–128. doi:10.1192/bjp.182.2.123
Tohen, M., Strakowski, S. M., Zarate Jr, C., Hennen, J., Stoll, A. L., Suppes, T., . . . Baldessarini, R. J. (2000). The McLean–Harvard first-episode project: 6-month symptomatic and functional outcome in affective and nonaffective psychosis. *Biological Psychiatry, 48*(6), 467–476.
Tonarelli, S. B., Pasillas, R., Alvarado, L., Dwivedi, A., & Cancellare, A. (2016). Acceptance and commitment therapy compared to treatment as usual in psychosis: A systematic review and meta-analysis. *Journal of Psychiatry, 19*, 366.
Torio, C. M., & Moore, B. J. (2006). National inpatient hospital costs: The most expensive conditions by payer, 2013: Statistical brief# 204. *Healthcare Cost and Utilization Project (HCUP) Statistical Briefs*, Rockville, MD, 2006–2016.
Tyrberg, M. J., Carlbring, P., & Lundgren, T. (2017). Usefulness of the ACT model for nurses in psychiatric inpatient care: A qualitative content analysis. *Journal of Contextual Behavioral Science, 6*, 208–214.
Udachina, A., Varese, F., Myin-Germeys, I., & Bentall, R. P. (2014). The role of experiential avoidance in paranoid delusions: An experience sampling study. *British Journal of Clinical Psychology, 53*(4), 422–432. doi:10.1111/bjc.12054
Valery, K.-M., & Prouteau, A. (2020). Schizophrenia stigma in mental health professionals and associated factors: A systematic review. *Psychiatry Research, 290*, 113068.

van Aubel, E., Bakker, J. M., Batink, T., Michielse, S., Goossens, L., Lange, I., . . . van Amelsvoort, T. (2020). Blended care in the treatment of subthreshold symptoms of depression and psychosis in emerging adults: A randomised controlled trial of acceptance and commitment therapy in daily-life (ACT-DL). *Behaviour Research and Therapy, 128*, 103592.

Van Os, J., Linscott, R. J., Myin-Germeys, I., Delespaul, P., & Krabbendam, L. (2009). A systematic review and meta-analysis of the psychosis continuum: Evidence for a psychosis proneness-persistence-impairment model of psychotic disorder. *Psychological Medicine, 39*(2), 179.

Wakefield, S., Roebuck, S., & Boyden, P. (2018). The evidence base of acceptance and commitment therapy (ACT) in psychosis: A systematic review. *Journal of Contextual Behavioral Science, 10*, 1–13.

White, R., Gumley, A., McTaggart, J., Rattrie, L., McConville, D., Cleare, S., & Mitchell, G. (2011). A feasibility study of acceptance and commitment Therapy for emotional dysfunction following psychosis. *Behaviour Research and Therapy, 49*(12), 901–907. doi:10.1016/j.brat.2011.09.003

Wood, L., Williams, C., Billings, J., & Johnson, S. (2020). A systematic review and meta-analysis of cognitive behavioural informed psychological interventions for psychiatric inpatients with psychosis. *Schizophrenia Research, 222*, 133–144. doi:https://doi.org/10.1016/j.schres.2020.03.041

Wright, N. P., Turkington, D., Kelly, O. P., Davies, D., Jacobs, A. M., & Hopton, J. (2014). *Treating psychosis: A clinician's guide to integrating acceptance and commitment therapy, compassion-focused therapy, and mindfulness approaches within the cognitive behavioral therapy tradition*. Oakland, CA: New Harbinger Publications.

Wykes, T., Steel, C., Everitt, B., & Tarrier, N. (2008). Cognitive behavior therapy for schizophrenia: effect sizes, clinical models, and methodological rigor. *Schizophrenia Bulletin, 34*(3), 523–537.

Yıldız, E. (2020). The effects of acceptance and commitment therapy in psychosis treatment: A systematic review of randomized controlled trials. *Perspectives in Psychiatric Care, 56*(3), 149–167.

SECTION 4

Implementation of ACT

CHAPTER

25 Effective Training and Delivery of ACT: The Dissemination and Implementation Issues

Robyn D. Walser *and* Emily Rachel Wharton

Abstract

The dissemination of acceptance and commitment therapy (ACT) as an evidence-based intervention is well underway. As a scientifically supported treatment approach, ACT may be considered a best practice in promoting well-being among those who suffer from psychological and emotional challenges. Optimizing mental health means not only understanding the mechanisms and processes by which individuals come to suffer and recover; it also means ensuring the successful dissemination and implementation of the practice. Sound dissemination processes for ACT include guiding researchers, policymakers, clinicians, and other stakeholders in the effective training and delivery of ACT as a best practice sustained over time. The process of widespread dissemination is subject to dilution of innovation—an adoption strategy wherein the "tools" of ACT are loosely adopted rather than the successful training of its principles and processes. Effective training concerns fidelity, adherence, and competency in ACT. There is a need for competency-based training that includes both workshops and ongoing consultation. This article proposes a model for disseminating and implementing ACT in clinics and large settings and reviews an example of ACT training in the Veterans Health Administration. Finally, it presents recommendations for future research and dissemination efforts of ACT training and supervision.

Key Words: ACT, dissemination, implementation, training, supervision

The dissemination and implementation of scientifically supported clinical interventions are paramount to best practice and to the promotion of well-being among those who suffer from psychological and emotional challenges. Optimizing public health means not only understanding the mechanisms and processes by which individuals come to suffer and recover, but also ensuring the effective dissemination and implementation (D&I) of the evidence-based practice (EBP) designed to reduce suffering and promote recovery. Acceptance and commitment therapy (ACT; Hayes et al., 2012) is considered an EBP for several health disorders (see Gloster et al., 2020) and is being disseminated internationally. Charting the future for the broad dissemination and implementation of ACT and focusing on competency-based training and sustainable practice will be crucial for its effective delivery.

ACT is a behavioral intervention that uses acceptance and awareness of internal experience practices, along with behavioral change commitments linked to values to alleviate human suffering. ACT, a third-wave behavioral intervention (Hayes, 2004), emerged from earlier behavioral and cognitive traditions, but with a new focus on the function of behavior over form, understanding behavior in context and creating flexible and effective repertoires of behavior to improve well-being (Hayes, 2004; Hayes & Hoffman, 2017). ACT's philosophical and theoretical underpinnings include functional contextualism (see Sandoz & Fogle, this volume), a philosophical approach that focuses on the behavior of individuals within their historical and situational contexts; and behavioral analysis of human cognition (see Harte & Barnes-Holmes, this volume).

Over the years, research on the intervention has ranged from basic accounts of human languaging (Dymond et al., 2010) to clinical application in different settings with differing populations, stretching across problems and issues such as mental and physical health populations (A-tjak et al., 2015; Graham et al., 2016), organizational behavior management (Bond et al., 2006), cultural issues and stigma (Luoma & Platt, 2015), and fit of intervention for diverse populations (Woidneck et al., 2012). A recent analysis of meta-analytic reviews (Gloster et al., 2020) showed that ACT was efficacious for all conditions examined, with positive effects for a broad range of target disorders and problems.

This broad and inclusive background of research on ACT sets the stage for the key elements in a successful D&I process. Indeed, effective dissemination includes understanding how EBPs fit with different clinical and other communities of practice and cultural backgrounds. Understanding how to create a beneficial implementation program while ensuring that it is effectively delivered and sustained within clinical and community settings requires extensive planning and commitment to implement on a large scale or bring the practice into a personal private practice setting.

The spread of ACT is well underway. International and online training and conferences have been held that include ACT workshops regularly occurring across the national and international conference itineraries. Nonetheless, without the issues of competency-based training and adherence to the model being addressed, ACT may experience a dilution (elements of an intervention being "loosely" adopted and applied) of innovation rather than a sustainable and effective diffusion (the spread of ideas among groups of people).

Implementation science (IS), an emerging field that involves the "scientific study of methods to promote the systematic uptake of clinical research findings and other evidence-based practices into routine practice" (Graham et al., 2006, p. 17), can inform sound dissemination and implementation processes for ACT, guiding researchers, policymakers, clinicians and other stakeholders in the effective training and delivery of ACT as a best practice sustained over time. Dissemination is the active spread of EBPs using planned strategies, while implementation is about integrating EBPs into a specific setting (Brownson et al., 2017), whether it be a hospital or private practice. The objects of D&I are interventions that have proven to be effective. This article will review broad issues related to disseminating and implementing ACT as an EBP, including challenges to effective dissemination and promising qualities of dissemination. We will also focus on issues specific to ACT such as ACT training and its implications for adherence to treatment, training to competency, and sustainability. An example of dissemination and an ACT roll out will be explored. We will then make a call to action concerning ways the ACT community can research and develop best practices in their dissemination and implementation efforts.

Dissemination and Implementation of ACT: Challenges and Opportunities

Over the past several decades, health care policy has increasingly stressed the importance of EBPs in health care delivery (McHugh & Barlow, 2010). As such, the emerging science of dissemination and implementation has played a central role in researching and implementing effective dissemination practices and understanding how to promote the adoption of an EBP in different settings, including private practice. Full discussion of IS remains beyond the scope of this article; interested readers can readily find descriptions of IS in many articles and books on the subject (see Backer et al., 1986; Brownson et al., 2017; Henggeler et al., 2002).

In recent years, IS has experienced an explosion of opportunity, with thousands of therapists trained in EBPs thanks to increased financial investment and institutional support in dissemination and implementation practices (McHugh & Barlow, 2010, Karlin & Cross, 2014). Patients who have received treatment from clinicians in these training programs have witnessed significant symptom improvement (e.g., Monson et al., 2018; Walser, et al., 2013). Despite the proliferation of research demonstrating the effectiveness of EBPs and the Herculean efforts to distribute effective treatment, studies have consistently found that these therapies are delivered infrequently in real-world clinical settings (e.g., Crits-Christoph, Wilson, & Hollon, 2005; Walser et al., 2013), calling into question the effectiveness of dissemination efforts.

EBP dissemination has likely lagged in part because integrating a new practice into a service setting or system (or, we would argue, private practice) past the duration of a training program faces many complex challenges (McHugh & Barlow, 2010; Rogers, 2003). For example, clinicians have reported several reasons for not offering EBPs, such as complex comorbidities, cognitive limitations, and low patient motivation (Cook et al., 2014), even though these perceived challenges do not correspond to research findings. Clinicians have also cited clinic-level barriers and beliefs that they need additional consultation to implement EBPs effectively (Cook et al., 2014; Osei-Bonsu et al., 2014); this is an argument we will ultimately support. The barriers reported by clinicians have significant implications and point to a key issue in therapy dissemination—ecological validity. Do EBPs translate to real-life situations, including therapist engagement in the EBP and the context of therapy.

The Case Against Broad Dissemination of Protocols for Syndromes

> *Where did the field get the idea that evidence of an intervention's efficacy from carefully controlled trials could be generalized as THE best practice for widely varied populations and settings?"*
>
> —L. W. Green (2001, p. 167)

The Institute of Medicine (2000) stated that the significant divide between medical research and actual medical practice is "not just a gap, but a chasm" (p. 1). The delay between science and practice for EBPs is even longer than the usual lengthy lag time of 15—20 years for medical interventions (Institute of Medicine, 2000; Karlin & Cross, 2014). One contributing factor to dissemination challenges is the aforementioned, either perceived or truly questionable, ecological validity and utility of many randomized controlled trials (RCTs) that help deem a psychotherapy "evidence-based." This is a much-debated topic in the field (Persons & Silberschatz, 1998). For many researchers and clinicians, evidence-based psychotherapy is synonymous with protocols for syndrome strategies, a likely outdated approach to understanding human suffering (see Hayes & Hoffman, 2020).

In part, due to methodological constraints and funding pressures, most RCTs assume that patients can be treated as if they have one discrete disorder; if they have more than one syndrome, they assume that such problems can be treated sequentially with different manuals (Westen et al., 2004; Wilson, 1998). These possibilities are potentially costly and inefficient strategies that can exclude therapists' clinical judgment and the client's needs and desires.

Indeed, evidence-based psychology practice is defined as "the integration of the best available research with clinical expertise in the context of patient characteristics, culture, and preferences" (APA Task Force on Evidence-Based Practice, 2006, p. 273).

This approach to evidence-based practice suggests at least one sound reason to pursue competency-based ACT training specific to its core competencies as currently defined (Luoma et al., 2007). The ACT competencies reflect the qualities described in the APA definition and include therapy that (1) tailors the interventions to fit the client's language and immediate life experience; (2) speaks to the client from an equal, vulnerable, genuine, and sharing point of view; and (3) sequences and applies specific ACT interventions in response to client needs, with therapists readying themselves to change course to fit those needs at any moment. Additionally, the behavioral underpinnings of ACT call for functional analysis of the client's behavior. By necessity, this relies on an idiographic approach fitted to each client, instituted across the treatment.

Another commonly held concern about psychotherapy research, consequently weakening clinician adoption of EBPs, is that they tend to focus on diagnosis and symptom reduction as the primary metric of treatment success (Kazdin, 2008). Many clinicians believe that psychotherapy "is not [as much] about reaching a destination (eliminating symptoms) as it is about the ride (the process of coping with life)" (Kazdin, 2008, p. 147). Even when symptoms are the focus of psychotherapy sessions, more than half of patients add new target problems or change their primary concerns throughout the course of treatment (Kazdin, 2008; Sorenson et al., 1985). RCTs rarely capture this process. They also tend to focus on reducing symptoms rather than larger issues of well-being. The less symptom-specific measures, such as quality of life, coping, and meaningful engagement, are often left out of RCTs (Kolovos et al., 2016). Understandably, many clinicians who are focused on client concerns and process versus outcome might be hesitant to integrate research findings into their clinical practice.

Another issue concerning ecological validity is the problem with RCTs focusing on analysis of averages. The "average person" in Western cultures has been accepted as a marker for outcomes in RCTs (Hayes & Hofmann, 2020) for an extended period. Yet, a problem arises; as Hayes and Hofmann (2020) state:

> *As we consider multiple variables, and their trajectories and interrelationships across time, our analysis at the level of the collective stops yielding information of known applicability to the individual.* (pp. 6–7)

A shift back to the idiographic understanding of working with clients in psychotherapy may be a useful future direction to help clinicians adopt EBPs into their practice writ large. This may be supported by turning the research focus to other forms of investigation such as dynamic assessment and modeling (see Fisher & Boswell, 2016; Hayes & Hofmann, 2020) or using different data analysis strategies such as the Group Iterative Multiple Model Estimation Method (see Gates & Molenaar, 2012). However, at the conceptual level, we would argue that understanding the idiographic nature of an individual's suffering is built into the ACT model. Appropriate intervention includes understanding the function of a behavior in context given a specific learning history, and not simply understanding a set of symptoms. Implementation of ACT is based on an ongoing functional analysis, with the selection and flexible use of the six core processes used in ACT fitting the conceptualization. However, arguing for this outcome makes specific issues such as fidelity to the model and training to competence the object of intense scrutiny. A critical look at training to fidelity and competence related to the dissemination of ACT is a worthwhile endeavor.

Treatment Adherence in ACT

Fidelity to an intervention refers to delivering the intervention as intended (Wiltsey Stirman et al., 2015). Competence in an intervention refers to the skill in understanding and delivering the therapy. Both adherence and competence are important aspects of effective D&I of an EBP, regardless of the clinician's work setting. Although fidelity to the model is a necessary component of delivering ACT, it is not sufficient. Fidelity and competence are intimately intertwined. A clinician may deliver certain exercises and metaphors in ACT well (occurring as intended according to protocol) but may do so in a manner that is not responsive to either client or context. Competence or skill in the model is still needed.

Madson and Campbell (2006) note that investigations of the delivery of EBPs have found that they are often delivered with low fidelity to the established psychotherapeutic model. Given this lack of fidelity to the treatment as published, many clients who are receiving an EBP may not be getting the effective version. Moreover, many clinicians receiving training in ACT as an EBP may not go on to receive supervision or consultation in the intervention, let alone fidelity checks to the model. Once a workshop training is completed, clinicians are often left to their own devices to implement the intervention as trained. Two issues arise concerning training and implementation. First, is the training being delivered expected to help therapists reach fidelity to and competence in the intervention, and second, is the therapist working to attain competency? More specifically to the present discussion, is this happening in ACT training and delivery? At this point, we would argue that the answer to this question is "no." We have found only three published studies that evaluate training to competency in ACT (Forman et al., 2012; Trompetter et al., 2014; and Walser et al., 2013). This is a critical issue in ACT D&I because effective delivery of ACT includes competent delivery of ACT.

Finally, ACT is unique because it is designed to allow tremendous innovation in technique, including the development of exercises and metaphors and other responsive, culturally sensitive, and context-driven procedures. Indeed, ACT's process orientation allows for a great deal of flexibility and the development of additional and tailored interventions. Nonetheless, each new development should link directly to ACT's underlying theory and philosophy of science, such that innovations remain inside the assumptions that make up the competency rubric.

THE TELEPHONE GAME EFFECT

The term *diffusion of innovation* (Rogers, 2003) describes how a product or idea spreads through a social community and is ultimately adopted through behavior change. The spread of ideas has long been relevant to psychology as interventions have been developed and circulated. Understanding how, why, and what gets disseminated has become even more important now that the EBP movement has become a central element of health care systems and health care policy (APA, 2006).

One problem related to the dissemination of innovation is the dilution of intervention. As diffusion of an innovation spreads, it can fall subject to "The Telephone Game Effect." Many readers may remember a childhood game in which each child lines up with others, and the first person in the line whispers a comment into the next person's ear. The whispered comment is passed along, person to person, each one whispering to the next the same comment whispered into their ear. By the time the comment reaches the end of the line, it is typically distorted, not nearly resembling the beginning whisper. Dissemination of psychotherapy theory and intervention can be subject to the same vagaries. The information and materials used to convey the intervention can become increasingly distorted as it moves further away from its source and foundational work.

The accuracy of theory and information related to an intervention can take various shapes and sizes outside of the academic setting (Ross, 2008). For instance, if clinicians believe that they understand an ACT process because they know the names and labels of the six core processes and have read descriptions of the same, they may mistakenly assume they know more than they actually do (Ross, 2008). For example, we have encountered situations where supervisors have claimed they can supervise ACT trainees because they have read materials about the intervention. Although they may have understood the read materials, we would argue that their effectiveness as a supervisor would depend greatly on what was read and other variables such as using the intervention in their own sessions and feedback on that use. Furthermore, a book on exercises and metaphors, for instance, versus the second edition of the original ACT book (see Hayes et al., 2012) published by the developers of ACT will constitute fairly different supervision experiences and transmission of understanding of theory and ideas related to ACT.

This scenario may be a matter of ethics. If a supervisor claims an ability to supervise in an intervention for which they have not been well trained, then they are risking an ethical dilemma as well as a lag in social responsibility. Nonetheless, these scenarios are fully possible, and students under such supervision may go on to believe that they have now been trained in ACT with the potential of amplifying the Telephone Game Effect.

Another example provides a sense of the potential dilution processes that may occur at the level of in-person training rather than reading written material. This particular example emerged in a conversation following training. A therapist attending an ACT workshop heard the Chinese Finger Trap Metaphor (Eifert & Forsyth, 2005, p. 146) and concluded that the way to *get out* of emotional pain is to approach emotional pain (i.e., push your fingers together into the trap instead of pulling). The trainer may have completed the exercise correctly (whispering it well following the telephone game metaphor), but what the trainee heard was not what was whispered. The trainee may then deliver ACT with the notion that moving toward internal experiences means getting away from negative experiences, delivering this message to both clients and perhaps their own trainees. In this case, the ACT intervention is about acceptance in the service of feeling good. If you move into your experience, you will no longer feel the so-called negative feelings. Given the reach and variety of information related to ACT, and given these types of possible misconstrues, at least some of what is called ACT is not truly ACT. A therapist may be engaging in behaviors that were subject to the distortions of the Telephone Game Effect.

Clearly, one of the key strategies for combating the Telephone Game Effect is the written word (Vaughan, 2017). To date, there are 67 protocols for different issues ranging from gambling disorders to agoraphobia to psychosis to pain management and diabetes management to obsessive-compulsive disorder and trichotillomania, to name a few. These are listed on the main ACT website, contextualscience.org. At least 182 books have been published, not counting those published in non-English languages (ACBS, 2020). These works help disseminate ACT, but it is unclear whether they contribute to the competent delivery of the intervention. Furthermore, adoption appears weakest when manuals alone are used for training, but it can remain weak if follow-up supervision is not provided (Sorenson et al., 1985)—a subject we turn to later in this article.

Additionally, the problem of fidelity takes on a slightly different form from those associated simply with the Telephone Game Effect when the concepts of interest are interrelated (e.g., fusion is interrelated with self-as-context/perspective-taking is interrelated with present moment) and highly nuanced (e.g., implementation of ongoing processes based on functional analysis of behavior as opposed to the application of techniques). Some forms of spreading ideas can inadvertently strip away the interrelated processes (e.g., presenting the six core processes in a book linearly) or nuance (e.g., reading materials may exclude other important data in an ACT session such as body language or felt experience, which is important information needed to formulate a case). When either or both get stripped away, the communication's intended message can be distorted or lost. Evaluating the breadth, depth, and form of written and other training materials related to ACT and the training context may be part of the training to competency rubric needing study. We would argue that feedback on implementing the processes in an interrelated and nuanced fashion is part of competency training and necessary for an effective implementation and sustainability process.

Strong communication efforts to govern the behavior of information providers (i.e., ACT trainers) and a solid set of guidelines and principles that specify training while allowing for innovation will help guard against the dilution of innovation or the Telephone Game Effect. Implementation of innovations is more consistent and positive when knowledge about them is clearly communicated (Edmondson, 2003).

Guarding against distortions of interrelated processes and highly nuanced interventions found in ACT may prove more difficult. Studies evaluating fidelity to the model and training to competency in the model include the six core processes, and other processes such as interpersonal, intrapersonal, and overarching processes (see Walser, 2019) are needed. Delivery of ACT in a way that does not violate the approach's spirit will be useful when considering the variability of training and supervision in the intervention. Importantly, ACT Recognized Trainers go through an extensive peer-review process (see ACBS Training Standards), assisting in promoting fidelity to and competence in the model. However, no long-standing evaluation of the trainer and their potential drift or training changes are monitored across time. Recognized trainers commit to a values-based process of engaging in training that includes self-awareness to ongoing learning processes and ongoing connection to the ACT community and research developments, but this is a self-assessment model with no monitoring by the community. Thus, it relies heavily on individual willingness and commitment to ethical behavior. Perhaps assessment and monitoring that support this values-based model may assist in preventing drift. Defining and monitoring the spirit of the training work while maintaining innovation will be a challenge for the ACT community.

FIDELITY MEASURES

Given the number of RCTs and open trials evaluating ACT, a fair number of ACT fidelity measures have been created to assess treatment adherence in these studies. We are aware of at least one Delphi study (i.e., gathering information through multiple rounds of questionnaires sent to experts) designed to create a measure of fidelity in ACT (O'Neill et al., 2019). The 25-item measure (ACT for Fidelity Measure or ACT-FM) resulting from this study was designed to be used across contexts and was found to have moderate to excellent interrater reliability. O'Neill and colleagues are one of the first to establish this type of sorely needed assessment. Further validation studies are needed for the measure to come to fruition. Working to rein in the proliferation of individualized ACT fidelity measures will help create a common language within the science of ACT. We are aware of at least five measures based on work directly familiar to us (Barnes et al., 2019; Borges et al., 2019; Gobin et al., 2017; Walser et al., 2013). Continuing O'Neill and colleagues' research is essential to robust dissemination processes.
Additionally, assessment concerning fidelity to a process rather than a protocol is also warranted. There is an important distinction between receiving a score indicating that a metaphor occurred or did not occur and receiving a score indicating that a process, such as self-as-context, occurred or did not occur (whether or not it contained a metaphor). The ACT Therapist Tape

Rating Scale (ACT-TRS; unpublished measure used in Walser et al., 2013) is likely one of the few measures assessing the delivery of six core processes. It is designed to assess skill or competency in implementing the core processes, not fidelity per se. Although, competency entails fidelity. The ACT-TRS also assesses the general ACT therapeutic stance, including the therapeutic relationship and modeling of ACT processes in session. ACT technology (e.g., strategy for behavior change/case conceptualization, ACT consistent homework, and implementation of metaphors and exercises) is also assessed. This instrument was developed via expert consensus, and validation research is underway, but much work is needed to understand its validity and psychometric properties.

Additional measures of skill have been created. As a multimethod assessment process in the Walser et al. (2013) dissemination project (described in detail later in this article), the Core Competency Rating Form (ACT-CRRF) was adapted from the Core Competencies Form found in Luoma et al. (2007) and originally developed by expert consensus and published in *A Practical Guide to Acceptance and Commitment Therapy* (Hayes & Strosahl, 2005). The ACT-CCRF and ACT-TRS were used to both assess and guide clinicians in becoming competent in the intervention. However, additional validation of the ACT-CCRF is needed. Other skill assessment tools exist, including self-rated competence (Trompetter et al., 2014), expert assessment of audio recordings (see Forman et al., 2012); Walser et al., 2013), and self-rated skills using visual analog (see Lappalainen et al., 2007). Finally, if knowledge is an indicator of competence, there are a few measures assessing knowledge of ACT and its model (e.g., Levin et al., 2015; Long, 2015). The psychometric properties of these tools need research and clarification as to their advantages and disadvantages depending on use.

Competent Delivery of ACT: Training Through Workshops and Supervision

Perhaps one of the more formidable challenges to disseminating and implementing ACT is training to competence in this complex treatment. McHugh and Barlow (2010) argue that competency training is difficult for at least two reasons: the complexity of therapeutic interventions and the challenges of commonly used models of training. We have previously written briefly about the complexity, noting ACT's interrelated and often highly nuanced qualities. We turn now more specifically to common training practices.

Training in a particular EBP often involves a shorter-term didactic that Stokes and Baer (1977) refer to as the "train and hope" model. Indeed, the most commonly used training strategy is a brief workshop (Herschell et al., 2004). While workshops may improve clinician attitudes toward and knowledge of therapy, they are often ineffective in changing clinician behavior in the therapy room (Beidas et al., 2012; Herschell et al., 2010).

Ongoing supervision or consultation in adopting a practice appears to be a critical element in changing clinician behavior (Beidas et al., 2012). Implementation literature has well-documented the need for consultation and ongoing support to shape clinician competence following training (Beidas & Kendall, 2010; Fixsen et al., 2005; Lyon et al., 2011). Indeed, training with ongoing supervised experience in delivering an intervention has been considered vital in any effort to implement a treatment with fidelity and competence (Schoenwald et al., 2013).

As a core component of behavior change in professional practice (Fixsen et al., 2005), supervision has been evaluated in several studies that are briefly reviewed here to demonstrate its importance. A workshop followed by weekly individual consultation with an expert was used as part of a dissemination program of prolonged exposure therapy for PTSD in the Veterans Health Administration (VHA). Results indicated that expert consultation enhanced clinicians' confidence in their ability to deliver the treatment beyond the effects found for the workshop alone (Karlin et al., 2010). This was also true for the ACT for depression implementation project in VHA (Walser et al., 2013). Even more important to this point, an RCT investigating three different post-workshop consultation processes (i.e., no consultation, consultation with audio review, and consultation without audio review) showed that patients whose therapists received ongoing consultation, compared with those who did not, experienced significantly greater improvement in symptoms of PTSD and functioning (Monson et al., 2018).

In a study conducted by Beidas et al. (2012), the number of supervision hours following training significantly predicted higher therapist adherence and skill at 3-month follow-up. The authors argued that ongoing supervision was indispensable, fully influencing therapist adherence and competence in the model trained. Ongoing consultation following the workshop improved therapist adherence by .4 points (on a scale of 0–6, with higher scores indicating better adherence) and skill by .3 points (on a scale of 1–7, with higher scores indicating greater competence). The authors found that approximately 7 hours of consultation occurring over a 3-month period increased adherence and skill by 23 and 20 percent, respectively. These findings suggest that even limited consultation following a training workshop can improve skills in a model (Beidas et al., 2012).

The number of clinicians seeking supervision following an ACT training is unknown. We wager that the percentages are relatively small, with only a handful of workshop attendees receiving ongoing supervision and support in implementing the model. We believe that therapists "hooked" by the model do return for more in-person and online workshop training, but they do not pursue supervision on the whole. Repeated attendance to workshops, though anecdotal, bodes well for continued learning that moves those attending ACT training closer to competence. Nevertheless, we still hold that supervision and consultation posttraining is perhaps the solitary path to skilled delivery of ACT.

Despite recognizing the need for ongoing supervision to train to competence, barriers to doing so remain. One barrier concerns the practical needs supervision. Supervision is time- and resource-intensive. Time dedicated to it is often not available or is created in "off hours." Many settings that therapists work in do not schedule consultation time as part of the regular workday. Furthermore, less supervision is provided in community clinics than in RCTs (Kolko et al., 2009), again showing the disparities between RCT outcomes and real-world clinical settings. In a large nationwide survey of practicing clinicians, Cook and colleagues (2009a) showed that concerns about time were the most frequently cited barrier to adopting new interventions. Time to engage in supervision and consultation remains a challenge.

A second barrier is training costs. Supervision following training may be organized in several ways, including weekly or monthly sessions, and can last many months (McHugh & Barlow, 2010). These types of arrangements become costly when considering the full range of supervision activities (e.g., lost clinical hours of clinician productivity, preparation for supervision, and cost of support materials) that may be part of the training to competence process. One study (Olmstead et al., 2011) found that 3 months of expert supervision and feedback following a Motivational Interviewing training session increased costs by 50 percent. Longer or more frequent supervision training sessions are likely to exceed the cost of a workshop alone. This may be a real disincentive. Discontinuing training prematurely by not including supervision may save money in the short run, but it will ultimately prove a "loss on investment" if those trained cannot skillfully implement the therapy as intended (Lyon et al., 2013).

A third barrier involves competing obligations. The reduction of competing responsibilities is undoubtedly an important facilitator of participation, as previous research has shown that productivity requirements can hinder EBP implementation (Schoenwald et al., 2008). Competing responsibilities are typically part of all settings, including private practice. To address this issue, providers of training and consultation programs may increase participation and engagement if there are opportunities to adapt the organizational (or private practice) context by negotiating changes in the productivity expectations maintained by participants' agencies (Aarons & Palinkas, 2007). However, given the high demands of varied service settings, this task could be difficult or even insurmountable. Therefore, it may be equally important to increase provider motivation to work within existing time constraints by creating compelling training opportunities. This goal could be accomplished by establishing policies that incentivize the implementation of an EBP at multiple levels (Goldman et al., 2001; Rapp et al., 2005) or by creating training perceived to have high utility, treatment effectiveness, and relevance in the target context. ACT may become one such intervention because of its transdiagnostic nature, functional outcomes focus, and broad appeal.

A fourth barrier concerns the limited availability of ongoing support by experts for the clinicians who have received training. Ongoing support typically involves supervision or consultation with an expert to encourage adoption, provide feedback, and increase proficiency. Locating and hiring experts can be challenging. For example, a study by Hipol and Deacon (2013) showed that few therapists (37.5 percent) reported having access to experts in cognitive-behavioral treatment for anxiety disorders in their community. When available, the services were both costly and time intensive.

THE QUESTION OF THE SKILLED SUPERVISOR

Given the research support for supervision following training as an effective path toward increased competence, what is being trained and the quality of supervision can play a role in diluting innovation.

Although supervised clinical practice is a widely recognized avenue of training (Greene & Dye, 2002), we should not assume that therapy skills will translate to the skills needed to become an effective supervisor who can train other therapists. Standards for supervisors have recently been developed that cover a broad range of issues. For instance, the American Psychological Association (APA) and the Association for State and Provincial Psychology Boards (ASPBB) have issued standards on topics such as ethics codes, defined and transparent processes for providing feedback, attention to cultural issues and power dynamics, and respect for supervisees' boundaries in self-disclosure in supervision (American Psychological Association, 2014; Association for State and Provincial Psychology Boards, 2020). These guidelines are important and provide foundational counsel about the supervisory relationship and its goals. Nonetheless, these guidelines call for supervisors to engage in self-assessment of competency in all aspects of supervision (Falender et al., 2014), including the above and the therapy model being supervised. Indeed, some research suggests that the effectiveness of general supervision is mixed and inconclusive (Watkins, 2011), increasing the need for clarification through research.

Didactic training with experiential exercises has been the main form of training in the ACT community. However, we are unaware of any research regarding the most effective approaches for training ACT therapists to competence in ACT supervision and consultation. More work is needed to understand the best training practices in workshop delivery, supervision, and consultation practices. Consultation and supervision as an implementation strategy have received little attention (Milne, 2010). Research in these areas specific to supervision in ACT will clarify and add to the published benefits of ongoing consultation in the implementation process (e.g., Miller et al., 2004), as well as guide supervisors and consultants in how to best assist providers in integrating ACT into their existing practices (e.g., Herschell et al., 2010). Investigations about best practices for training ACT trainers, supervisors, consultants, length of training and consultation needed for competence and sustainability, and optimal consultation formats (e.g., group versus individual) are needed.

One of the more notable features of the ACT community is its values-based qualities that focus on sharing the intervention freely. Its founder, Dr. Steven Hayes, has through the years insisted that the therapy be accessible. Through his approach and in conjunction with the Association of Contextual Behavioral Science (ACBS), the ACT community has focused on keeping training in ACT low cost while resisting the therapy certification process, which can support financial interests over dissemination interests related to promoting well-being. This noncertification and "open" approach can clearly assist with barriers related to cost. It does not, however, address the time and competing responsibilities issues. Nor does it necessarily mean that what is being disseminated is consistent with the model or that supervisors are training coherently and consistently. Despite these issues, ACT's "open-source" quality is attractive and possibly part of what keeps therapists returning for more. Expanding workshop training excitement to ongoing consultation may help prevent dilution and failure to implement therapy consistent with the ACT model.

Lastly, as with fidelity measures, measures of competency in ACT are also needed and remain a barrier to implementing the intervention as intended. Initial work is promising, as noted with the ACT-FM, ACT-CCRF, ACT-TRS, and other measures under development. Competent practice assessment is enhanced when competence assessment tools are available (Falender & Shafranske, 2004). This helps to operationalize the process, establishing quality measurement across studies and implementation work. These tools could also assist supervisors and consultants in guiding those learning ACT. The need to rely solely on clinical reports will decrease by instead using multiple methods to assess competence. Falender and Shafranske (2004) argue that these instruments are essential when the intervention involves complex concepts and behavioral interventions, as is the case with ACT. The lack of validated assessment tools concerning competence in ACT may result in numerous methods (Muse & McManus, 2013), potentially leading to problematic issues surrounding implementation.

A training to competency framework that includes supervision illustrates the potential positive results of these types of efforts. In its pioneering program, Improving Access to Psychological Therapies, the National Health Service of the United Kingdom enacted one of the most extensive and centralized efforts to disseminate and implement EBPs to date (Clark et al., 2009; McHugh & Barlow, 2010). An expert panel of clinical researchers identified basic and disorder-specific skills needed to demonstrate clinician competence across training areas (assessment, knowledge, diversity, etc.). Supervisors oversaw cases and assessed both written exams to measure didactic knowledge and effectiveness in delivering the interventions through standardized role plays. In line with efforts to promote sustainable adoption, staff received additional supervisory instruction to serve as future trainers. Patient outcomes reflected dissemination success; the EBP training program increased referrals and access to treatment and demonstrated clinical outcomes comparable to those found in research studies (50–60 percent recovery rates, with outcome measures effect sizes ranging from 0.98 to 1.26; Clark et al., 2009).

In sum, evaluating the competent delivery of therapy has only recently begun to emerge more broadly (Roth & Pilling, 2008); further research and development are needed. This is especially the case with ACT, given its relatively new status and its focus on processes rather than sets of techniques. Still, it is important to support clinicians in receiving supportive and supervisory services, given the general findings concerning improvement in the delivery of an intervention in dissemination programs.

Current Model: Experiential Training in Psychological Flexibility

For many new ACT practitioners, learning ACT may alter how they understand others' and their own relationships to sensations, emotions, thoughts, and memories. In the early phases of training, this process can prove challenging. ACT beginners may learn about techniques and exercises; however, the ACT model is not simply a collection of distinct tools but a "whole-cloth" intervention that weaves interpersonal, intrapersonal, and the six core processes together over the arc of the therapy (Walser, 2019). Training workshops often focus on practicing the intervention through role plays and experiencing the intervention from the "inside out" - training participants are often led through the intervention at a personal level. In addition to understanding ACT processes from this point of view, consultation, as it is currently understood, is critical in helping clinicians continually adapt their case conceptualizations while moving fluidly through the six core processes as treatment necessitates, rather than following a prescribed order or list of techniques. Recognizing their own relationship to internal experience is part of that learning process.

Luoma and Vilardaga (2013) provide an example. They explored how experiential phone consultation, as an adjunct to a standard ACT workshop, impacted psychological flexibility and burnout in therapists learning ACT. Participants were randomized to receive a two-day ACT workshop or the same workshop plus six phone coaching sessions that focused on experiential and emotion-focused elements designed to increase therapist psychological flexibility. Throughout the consultation calls, participants were encouraged to try out ACT techniques with clients and use ACT processes with themselves while interacting with clients. In this study, the ACT consultant focused on the trainee's emotional and cognitive experiences during sessions and used ACT processes to address their areas of struggle. Such interventions included brief meditative exercises, visualizations, or sharing a relevant metaphor or story, aligned with core processes therapists were learning in order to help conceptualize their clients and themselves in the therapeutic process.

The researchers found that over time psychological flexibility improved in the consultation group but not in the workshop-only group (d = 1.82 for between-group changes). The experiential nature of consultation used in this study and the subsequent psychological changes of therapists appear to depict a strong model of clinicians learning ACT from the "inside out," as therapists engage in a parallel process linked to treatment with their consultant. With this promising research at hand, further study of ACT training, including workshops and consultation, is needed to better train clinicians and supervisors in ACT.

Sustainability

Despite the problems encountered in defining sustainability in the implementation sciences (Moore et al., 2017), a broad definition that appears to fit the process emerged in the subject's literature. Moore and colleagues (2017) maintain that sustainability has five key parts: (1) after a defined period of time, (2) a program, clinical intervention, and/or implementation strategy continues to be delivered and/or (3) individual behavior change (i.e., clinician, patient) is maintained; (4) the program and individual behavior change may evolve or adapt while (5) continuing to produce benefits for individuals/systems (Moore et al., 2017). In other words, D&I endeavors can succeed only if the behavior change related to the training is sustained. Unfortunately, several studies show poor sustainability outcomes (Wiltsey Stirman et al., 2012).

For instance, Scheirer (2005) found that only one component of a dissemination program was sustained in 60 percent of the sites evaluated. Additionally, in a review of dissemination projects in health care, fewer than half of the projects continued the interventions at high-fidelity levels (Wiltsey Stirman et al., 2012). These findings may prove disappointing, given the investment of human and monetary efforts. Sustaining a behavior change (i.e., implementing a new model) is even less well understood and is likely more challenging in the private practice setting.

Scheirer (2005) iterated five important factors regarding the extent to which an intervention is sustainable: (1) the capacity for the intervention to be modified and adapted over time; (2) the presence of a "champion" or someone supporting ongoing implementation, learning, and problem solving; (3) the degree to which the intervention "fits" with an organization's procedures and mission; (4) the degree of benefit experienced by staff and clients and how well that benefit can be perceived; and (5) support from the key stakeholders in the organization.

Whether a clinician delivers services in a larger setting, group, or independent practice, time, effort, and finances dedicated to learning an EBP are significant. Training to competence in ACT should involve individual clinician change in behavior related to delivering the therapy as intended over time. With ACT this is likely to include major shifts in philosophical assumptions concerning human behavior and the role of language in human suffering, a challenging task given that many clinicians stick with their original graduate school training approach (Bitar et al., 2007; Cook et al., 2009b). Moreover, the degree to which competence training is maintained over time is not well known. Drifting away from the original training is problematic (McHugh et al., 2009). Self-assessment and ongoing consultation efforts may be part of true behavior change that is visible across time. We posit that training in principles and processes defined by benchmarks may assist as they tend to remain stable even if innovations in the model continue to develop. Evaluation of this premise is needed.

We encourage those interested in large D&I projects and those simply interested in learning ACT for implementation in their personal practice to consider how well ACT aligns with the organization's mission or personal understandings of human suffering and behavior change. In considering these aspects of uptake and sustainment, it will be useful to delve into evidence-supported processes of change and the competencies linked to effective implementation of the same (see Hayes & Hofmann, 2018). We argue that future ACT implementation projects consider the shift from protocols and simple procedures to process-based interventions linked to favorable outcomes (e.g., mediation analyses). This is not to say that techniques and procedures should be discarded. Rather, they should be used to support the process being delivered in treatment. Given that ACT is a process-based therapy, attitudes toward and experiences with this type of intervention will be integral to program success and sustainability (Gregory et al., 2007).

Promising Qualities for Disseminating ACT: Support for Effective Implementation

ACT, as a diffusion of innovation product, has been relatively successful. Its dissemination over the past 20 years, as evidenced by its international growth in research, training, and practice in regions such as Western Europe, Asia, Australia, Iran (Levin et al., 2019), and throughout the United States, is a testimony to this achievement. ACBS, the professional organization that houses ACT, has over 7,800 members internationally as well as a flagship journal titled *Journal of Contextual Behavioral Science*. To date, ACBS reports 912 randomized controlled trials of ACT (ACBS, 2022), and ACT has achieved recognition as an evidence-based psychotherapy by the American Psychological Association (see https://div12.org/treatments/). ACT's growth and appeal in terms of large-scale distribution may be due to several factors.

First, as a transdiagnostic, process-based intervention, ACT is suitable for a range of disorders and problems in living, targeting *psychological processes* relevant to human suffering (see A-tjak, et al., 2015, for process review). In addition to its benefit to clients (Gloster et al., 2020) and clinicians (e.g., Luoma & Vilardaga, 2013), this transdiagnostic approach allows ACT training to expand clinicians' skills in treating a wide range of therapy presentations, rather than simply focusing on treating a particular disorder. The ability to malleably conceptualize and treat multiple problems and comorbidities through the same framework may reduce clinicians' hesitation that a psychotherapy may only work for "pure" presentations, as seen in the research lab.

Second, clinicians may be more willing to incorporate ACT into their practice due to its focus on quality of life (Forman et al., 2007). In clinical practice, symptom-focused work may sometimes result in "moving targets," wherein a client experiences relief from one symptom or disorder, but other difficulties emerge (Sorenson et al., 1985; Westen et al., 2004). A client's frequency and intensity of symptoms may decrease, but they still feel unfulfilled and dissatisfied with their lives (Coryell et al., 1993). An approach that focuses on meaning and purpose in life may be especially beneficial, lining up with client and clinician desire to enhance well-being through vital living rather than simply focusing on losing a diagnosis. Openness to experience sets the stage for varying experiences of life that no longer need to be avoided.

Third, ACT's flexibility within its fidelity and competency criteria allows the intervention to be implemented in sync with the individual client presentation and context of delivery. The core processes are fluidly implemented depending on the presenting problem and case conceptualization, allowing a fairly large degree of freedom in approach while still maintaining consistency to the model and coherence in treatment application across time. The flexibility of the model permits variation, granting adaptation across what gets implemented and with whom. Highly fused clients may be met with defusion processes more so than those who are highly avoidant and need more acceptance process work, for instance. Clients in primary care can receive brief interventions, whereas clients in private practice can receive longer treatment depending on need. The core ACT processes do not need to be applied in a specific order but can be used based on the case conceptualization and the in-the-moment session material. This type of flexibility absolves hesitation, debunking the notion that therapists sometimes espouse the notion that adherence to EBPs is nonresponsive to client needs.

Most importantly, this flexibility within the model allows researchers and clinicians to assemble a workable set of change processes. Through these efforts, we can answer the question posed by Hayes and Hoffman (2018): "What core biopsychosocial processes should be targeted with this client given this goal in this situation, and how can they most efficiently and effectively be changed?" (p. 47). Adaptations of the model consider the client-specific needs given the current context (including alliance issues between therapist and client). Part of preserving the model means the therapist is sensitive to the client, basing variation in intervention on specific client needs, characteristics, and situations while remaining within an adaptable periphery (Kendall & Frank, 2018) of the ACT approach. Implementing ACT flexibly offers the opportunity to engage in an evidence-based practice more fully, bringing client, therapist expertise, and the intervention into play (see APA Presidential Task Force on Evidence-Based Practice, 2006). This process promotes ecological validity and implements the interventions in real-world settings to fit client needs and ultimately yield more successful dissemination efforts.

Fourth, this approach supports the integration of ACT processes into other evidence-based psychotherapies. Its focus on principles rather than on procedures allows clinicians to use other interventions while still being "adherent" if adaptations are made in an ACT-consistent way. For example, a clinician can engage a client with obsessive compulsive disorder in exposure therapy (Twohig et al., 2015) or can conduct prolonged exposure therapy with a PTSD client (Thompson et al., 2013) in an ACT-consistent way. ACT, in combination with other therapies, can be instrumental in strengthening motivation at the outset of treatment. Training can be elastic in giving clinicians more skills to enhance their existing clinical approaches, rather than replace or "convert" practitioners. This flexible training attitude increases the openness of mental health systems and providers to dissemination and implementation efforts.

A Model to Disseminate ACT in Clinics and Large Settings

Wiltsey Stirman and colleagues (2004a) describe an extensive plan to promote more effective dissemination of empirically supported psychotherapies. Principles of this integrated plan and specific considerations for ACT dissemination include two key foci: (1) planning, assessment, and collaboration, and (2) initial training, ongoing consultation, and support.

PLANNING, ASSESSMENT, AND COLLABORATION

Thoughtful planning is needed to address the challenges of integrating ACT into an existing framework of health care delivery. This phase of any dissemination project should include identifying a suitable system or organization, forming alliances with administrators and stakeholders, and securing needed funding.

Once a suitable system or organization has been identified or called for the implementation of ACT, forming alliances inside the organization will be critical. Administrator and stakeholder buy-in will be invaluable to success. Understanding the stakeholders' perspectives will help disseminate learning about potential divergent and even irreconcilable stakeholder viewpoints (Zimmerman et al., 2016). Using dynamic data models to promote stakeholder convergence in support of an implementation project may prove useful (see Zimmerman et al., 2016). Implementing strategies to assess organizational support and readiness, program, and implementer characteristics are part of forming alliances. For instance, aligning the implementation of ACT with the setting's mission and goals will promote sustainability (Tibbits et al., 2010). Those implementation projects that are clearly aligned with established organizational structures and processes are more likely to succeed (Scheirer, 2005).

Another factor in dissemination success is how the decisions to implement a new treatment are made (Wiltsey Stirman et al., 2004a). Top-down decisions, such as mandates or demands made by leadership, tend to result in faster but less effectively sustained dissemination (Backer et al., 1986; Rogers, 2003; Henggeler et al., 2002). "Mandate drift" (Wiltsey Stirman et al., 2004a) may occur because employees may think administrators are indifferent to their needs and preferences. If clinicians are not consulted in the dissemination decision-making process, they may be hesitant to incorporate new, unfamiliar methods and may resent being told how to conduct therapy, especially if they believe administrators lack clinical expertise (Wiltsey Stirman et al., 2004a). Decisions that include clinicians and administrators will likely make clinicians more amenable to new modalities, but the process will usually take more time (Rogers, 2003).

On the one hand, in top-down approaches, often called "push strategies," leaders push a service out to the field. For example, VHA enacts national policies that require veteran access to EBPs, triggering the competency-based training programs (Karlin & Cross, 2014). "Pull strategies," on the other hand, use a bottom-up approach of geanerating interest and demand for a service among users, stakeholders, or advocates, such as clients, family members, and clinicians. These strategies may include sharing patient success stories and positive patient outcomes, and therapist training outcomes (e.g., increased competency and self-efficacy, positive attitudes toward the training; Karlin & Cross, 2014).

ACT researchers and trainers should be aware of their role as "ambassadors" of the treatment (Wiltsey Stirman et al., 2004a). Schmidt and Taylor (2002) found that one of the greatest factors showing whether clinicians were willing to adopt a new EBP was the change agent's credibility and personal characteristics. Thus, the change agent should foster a strong alliance with the clinicians and administrators and work to accommodate the needs and preferences of potential adopters (Diamond, 1995).

As part of the planning, assessment, and collaboration process, clinicians' attitudes in the target organization should be assessed for their openness to learning and their enthusiasm for ACT training. The perceptions of a new treatment by clinicians and administrators have been found to strongly predict successful dissemination (Schmidt & Taylor, 2002; Backer et al., 1986). For instance, one study showed that views of an innovation account for 49–87 percent of the variance in the extent of its dissemination (Berwick, 2003). Dissemination efforts that do not have acceptance and support from clinicians implementing the treatment are likely to fail (Diamond, 1995; Torrey et al., 2001).

It is also imperative to understand how psychotherapy is currently practiced in an organization and to recognize how the current approach might influence clinician attitudes toward ACT. For example, if most clinicians in a setting practice psychodynamic therapy, are they aware of what the efforts to either apply ACT as is might include or how to integrate it into their current treatment of choice (Matoff, 2018)? If they are interested, working together with the clinicians to explore integration avenues will be paramount.

It might also be important to understand other attitudes toward ACT practices. For instance, it may be useful to assess clinicians' experience with or openness to mindful awareness practices, given their presence in ACT. Assessing these types of factors can prepare the dissemination team by helping them understand the current levels of experience in such practices and determining potential marketing or buy-in strategies. In the case of mindfulness practices, for instance, therapists may not be interested in or alerted to the psychological and physiological benefits of these practices to the client and the therapist themselves (Eberth & Sedlmeier, 2012). Indeed, therapist mindfulness has been positively correlated with therapeutic alliance, therapist self-efficacy, and treatment outcome (Padilla, 2010; Wexler, 2006), each of which is a potentially positive selling point in the initial phases of planning an ACT dissemination project.

Therapist psychological flexibility might also be an assessment focus. Psychological flexibility is positively associated with counseling self-efficacy through the mediating variable of having fewer experiences hindering self-focused attention (Wei et al., 2015). Wei and colleagues (2015) hypothesized that therapists with mindfulness skills and higher levels of psychological flexibility might more readily accept anxious or distracting thoughts, allowing them to remain more present with clients, and thus feeling more effective as a result. Psychological flexibility and mindfulness experience are not requirements for receiving training in ACT. However, an openness to developing such skills would likely facilitate increased adoption of ACT principles and interventions into clinical practice after training (Varra et al., 2008). Finally, training in ACT can both reduce burnout in clinicians (Hayes et al., 2004) and create openness to evidence-based training (Varra et al., 2008).

When collaborating with different health care settings, the proposed treatment must be appropriate for the patients served. ACT's transdiagnostic approach is beneficial for these considerations. However, ACT training may sometimes be implemented for specific disorders (Trompetter et al., 2014; Walser et al., 2013). When such specified training is being called upon, adapting the ACT training focus to fit the client population is needed. D&I in a specialty clinic would include additional conversations and agreements regarding the most common presentations. For example, an ACT training for a PTSD Residential Program would benefit from an explicit discussion of how to guide clients through trauma-informed mindfulness practices, how to respond to trauma reactions, and how to integrate ACT with specific trauma exposure methods. It is important to speak directly with clinicians about their needs and the common barriers they face in engaging and treating their specific client population.

While funding and resources are critical to the initial implementation of a new treatment, they are also vital in ensuring sustainability (Wiltsey Stirman et al., 2004a). If providers are to truly incorporate a new treatment into how they work with clients, "second-order change" (Watzlawick, Weakland, & Fisch, 1974) must be achieved—perhaps supporting a radical shift that challenges current assumptions and changes the way clinicians view treatment and its outcomes. The underlying structures of a health system must be adjusted to sustain psychotherapeutic changes, preventing the return to the old system of treatment (Wiltsey Stirman et al., 2004a). In the case of ACT dissemination, this type of second-order change might include a shift in clinicians' willingness to reconsider definitions of mental health, turning away from standard *Diagnostic and Statistical Manual* (DSM) diagnoses (see Hayes & Hofmann, 2020), instead prioritizing well-being in terms of life functioning and engagement in values. This change might also include reconceptualizing outcome data, focusing on quality and meaning in life rather than symptom reduction alone.

Creating second-order change is also likely to include ongoing supervision and consultation in ACT, extending well past the timeline of the initial training. It will be essential to consider the need to fund these ongoing measures when financially planning dissemination efforts. As Wiltsey Stirman and colleagues (2004a) state, "adequate resources must be available to support the adoption of a new intervention beyond the initial collaboration with the innovator" (p. 350).

INITIAL TRAINING, ONGOING CONSULTATION, AND SUPPORT

After identifying the target system, assessing needs, and collaborating with providers and administrators, planning and securing funding, training is the next dissemination step. Training will likely need to be intensive, although the intensity and duration of training will depend on therapists' familiarity with the therapy (Martin et al., 1998; Schmidt & Taylor, 2002; Wiltsey Stirman et al., 2004b). A common model involves providing a multi-day training workshop initially and sometimes throughout a dissemination project (Martin et al., 1998; Schmidt & Taylor, 2002). Training aspects of a dissemination program often include didactic presentations, videotapes of session examples, group discussion and exercises, and individual case evaluation (Wiltsey Stirman et al., 2004b). Foundational ACT training typically involves didactic presentations of the principles, core processes, and skills in ACT. Other teaching techniques might include experiential exercises, role plays in dyads, and master clinician role plays. As noted, the experiential nature of ACT has been an important and common part of ACT training. Learning the intervention from the "inside out" has helped connect clinicians to ACT material from an additional, personal perspective. The appeal is found in the experiential work that normalizes the therapists' own internal experience of their thoughts, emotions, and sensations. The effectiveness of this particular method for ACT trainees has yet to be fully researched.

Following workshop training, a plan for ongoing consultation should be at play. This is crucial for both promoting sustainability and strengthening the quality of care for receivers of the intervention. As explored previously, EBP training methods found that while reading, self-directed training, and workshops appear to increase knowledge of a given treatment (see Richards, et al., 2011 for ACT), they do not significantly change therapist behavior or competence (Herschell et al., 2010). Workshop participants will demonstrate an increase in knowledge and note some skill improvement. However, this does not translate into mastering the necessary skills to properly implement the intervention (Sholomskas et al., 2005). Maintenance of skills over time (Miller et al., 2004) and impact on patient outcome (Miller & Mount, 2001) are at risk if ongoing supervision is not provided. Expert consultation, supervision, and feedback are fundamental for refining clinical skills and increasing sustainable adoption of a new treatment (Herschell et al., 2010).

Competency-based training in ACT should be the target. Ratings on specific ACT competencies will ensure consistency with the model and will likely promote greater understanding of this process-based therapy. Feedback from expert clinicians can help new ACT practitioners adhere to the model, maintaining coherence across treatment and troubleshooting challenges as they arise. This will help refine the clinician's clinical skills on an ongoing basis, which is vital for developing competency in a new treatment.

Dissemination Case Example: ACT for Depression in VHA Training to Competency Program

The national dissemination and implementation initiative to promote ACT for Depression (ACT-D) in the VHA provides a helpful model for how to disseminate and train across a national health care system (Walser et al., 2013). The VHA has implemented multiple national programs to disseminate and implement evidence-based psychotherapies, all of which employ the competency-based training model (Karlin & Cross, 2014). The ACT-D initiative used the ACT Core Competency Rating Form (Luoma et al., 2007; Strosahl et al., 2004), a 30-item measure assessing ACT therapist competency and the ACT TRS, as well as other criteria, to this end.

The initiative was and remains a large-scale, multi-site, multi-cohort dissemination, and implementation project that started in the planning, assessment, and collaboration phase with a written dissemination proposal to obtain buy-in from VA leadership. This proposal was then used as a "push" strategy wherein top-down officials supported the intervention's roll-out upon the proposal's approval. Planning involved organizing written marketing material as well as presentations to leadership and other interested stakeholders. Planning also included multiple day-long meetings with leadership and ACT experts to review program evaluation, assessment tools, the process of training, material support (e.g., books, template progress notes, a website with materials, video examples of therapy) and possible barriers to and solutions regarding implementation. Program evaluation with the assessment of training, therapist self-efficacy and competency, and client outcomes were also developed. To promote implementation, first trainings were offered to therapists who were interested in and wanted training in the intervention. As the program grew, applications to attend were reviewed and approved based on a set of defined standards (e.g., engaged in clinical work 50 percent of the time, working in a setting offering clinical services).

Initial training, ongoing consultation, and support followed the initial planning, assessment, and collaboration phase. The dissemination project used three modes of training: (1) an experientially based 3-day workshop provided by an ACT trainer; (2) 6 months of 90-minute group weekly consultation calls guided by ACT-D "experts"; and (3) supportive reading materials, including a specially designed ACT protocol for veterans with depression (and/or comorbid anxiety). Therapists undergoing training needed to reach set training criteria before they were considered *certified as trained* (no official certification in ACT was promoted). These criteria included (1) attendance to the workshop in full, (2) attendance to at least 75 percent of the consultation calls, (3) a score of at least 90 out of 120 on one of three competency ratings taken at the end of month 1, 3, and 6, (4) a rating of at least 2.5 out of 4 (0–4 scale) on 5 of 10 therapy tapes rated across the protocol by the ACT-D consultant, and (6) implementation of the intervention with at least two clients during the 6-month consultation. Sustainability was supported and continues to be supported by ongoing volunteer monthly consultation and policies in VHA regarding the offering of EBPs to veterans seeking services.

Of the 334 therapists who successfully completed the training program at the time of the first publication (Walser et al., 2013), 96 percent of therapists achieved competency by the end compared to 21 percent during early training. The training was associated with significant increases in ACT-D therapist competency, therapist self-rated self-efficacy, positive attitudes toward ACT-D, and therapeutic alliance. Patients' depression symptoms decreased significantly, and the quality-of-life scores increased significantly. Post consultation surveys indicated that therapists trained in ACT-D used ACT with about half of their depressed patients.

Evaluation of the program demonstrated that the combination of intensive training in ACT-D and ongoing consultation yielded increased therapist competence, confidence, and sustained use of the intervention. The collected data suggest that those who completed the program improved in each of the six core processes implemented. Additional data analysis also revealed that improvement in acceptance as measured by the Acceptance and Action Questionnaire – II (AAQ-II; Hayes et al., 2004) predicted changes in depression (Walser et al., 2013). Reductions in suicidal ideation were also obtained, showing a positive change from 44.5 percent of veterans endorsing no suicidal ideation at baseline to 60 percent having no suicidal thoughts at the end of treatment. Finally, no differences were found between older and younger veterans or between men and women regarding treatment outcome, with all groups showing significant improvement (Walser et al., 2013). The ACT-D training continues, with over 1000 professionals trained and 5–10 trainings occurring per year.

Although this dissemination effort may be considered quite successful, there were several drawbacks. First, the roll-out of ACT was protocol-based and disorder-specific. Use of the 12-16 session protocol in training was helpful to clinicians, giving them guidance on what to implement in which session. However, many consultants and trainees found the protocol limiting by report, noting that it did not always match what was happening in the session. Flexible use of the protocol in these initial implementation efforts was and is expected to be limited due to the nature of initiating a training process – a protocol with specific guidance on what to do in the sessions was the starting point. However, it is unknown whether clinicians trained in the protocol are later able to move away from its structure, using ACT more fluidly.

Additionally, considering ACT's benefits as a transdiagnostic intervention, focusing on depression "shortchanges" ACT's utility to address a broad range of issues. Indeed, although rolling out this particular intervention in such a large hospital setting is a relatively remarkable achievement, rolling out multiple interventions for multiple diagnoses, as was done in the VA, seems cost-ineffective. Instead, it seems wiser to train clinicians in principle-based approaches, such as that found in ACT, in terms of cost and an overall improvement in clinician skill and delivery of services.

Finally, it is worth turning back to processes versus techniques and protocols. Training clinicians in processes that target the client's specific issues, given their learning history and contextual influences, may be a more fruitful endeavor, allowing the clinician to focus on moderators and mediators of change rather than first-order symptom reduction (see Hofmann & Hayes, 2019 and Hayes & Hofmann, 2020). Training to competency in process-based therapy may present its own unique set of challenges. However, it should be no more difficult than training to a protocol in terms of the initial dissemination efforts needed to create a successful program. Again, research to investigate these training issues is needed.

The Future of ACT Dissemination

In one of the first technology transfer training initiatives in ACT, Strosahl and colleagues (1998) tested the field effectiveness of the intervention. The study included a training workshop, followed by monthly group supervision with the full training lasting a year. This trial was a kind of "first" in terms of ACT's ecological implementation, laying the groundwork for possibilities in flexible dissemination of the same. In this trial, no restrictions were placed on the homogeneity of samples; clients with any diagnosis or problem were assessed and treated. The therapist, given the client's situation, determined the exact course, length of treatment, and any modifications given the client's situation. Clinicians were told to use their ACT training as they saw fit, and clients had a role in determining which therapy they received. Those patients of the therapists trained in ACT as compared to those in the control condition showed greater positive results. More of the ACT-trained therapists' patients completed therapy. The patients in this group were better able to cope with their initial problem and had fewer medication referrals. Although it clearly had its own limitations, this early trial heralded some of the very qualities we might wish to see in a D&I project today.

If we are to agree with the APA Presidential Task Force on Evidence-Based Practice, then working to disseminate ACT will include thoughtful and well-researched efforts that promote "the integration of the best available research with clinical expertise in the context of patient characteristics, culture, and preferences" (2006, p. 273). This trifecta of treatment, clinician expertise, and client characteristics is a call to action for those interested in the diffusion of innovation or dissemination of ACT and the competent delivery of ACT.

For those interested in formal ACT dissemination projects, we recommend using one of the dissemination and implementation models (see Tabak et al., 2012) to support these efforts. Choosing the model or integrating models (as in the example provided above) will depend on many factors, including finances and the targeted system. Regardless of the model, significant planning to include assessment and sustainability across the implementation project should be done in collaboration with the main stakeholders, including policymakers, leaders, clinicians, clients, and other essential personnel. One major challenge of technology transfer is an assessment that evaluates therapist competence. Including measures that evaluate the therapist's degree of skill and fidelity to the model and client outcomes should be part of the plan. Well-constructed training followed by ongoing consultation and support should be the hallmarks of any ACT dissemination effort. Indeed, whatever limited resources may be available for the project should be used to support supervision. In comparison to workshops alone, follow-up supervision that includes observation, feedback, and coaching strengthens adoption (Sorenson et al., 1985), assists in retaining skill proficiency (Miller et al., 2004), and, importantly, improves client outcomes (Monson et al., 2018). Sustainability that recognizes consistency to the model while permitting innovation and adaptation will be key to the success of any dissemination project.

Several of the dissemination and training challenges outlined in this article apply not only to implementing ACT in larger settings but also to broadly disseminating ACT. Hopefully, reviewing these issues will provide a multitude of research projects for ACT scientists and clinicians for years to come. If training to competency is a marker of success, then much work remains to be done. Assessing, outlining, and defining the best ACT training models that include ongoing supervision need development. Multiple models depending on the target audience (e.g., coaching, organizational/industrial, primary care, private practice) will need to be researched. The development of psychometrically sound tools assessing fidelity to and competence in ACT are beginning to emerge. Those evaluating competence in ACT processes and not just procedures will be useful given ACT's underlying principles and transdiagnostic approach. Strategies for addressing and studying adaptations, while remaining consistent with the theoretical model, will bolster dissemination. Building in course corrections may be a part of this process to prevent the Telephone Game Effect or dilution of the model. Variation and adaptation are essential. At the same time, too much flexibility can be problematic, moving the intervention away from fidelity to the principles.

As part of the competency evaluation effort, it is recommended that scientists and clinicians in the ACT community consider principles and standards for supervision, especially given its status in efforts to create competent clinicians. This may even include establishing supervision training programs that are specific to ACT. The content and quality of ACT supervision itself need investigation. The Portland Model (Thompson et al., 2015) and SHAPE (Morris & Bilich, 2017) are great launching points for this type of work. Research efforts that evaluate the supervisor's ability to train psychological flexibility (see Luoma & Vilardaga, 2013) in the therapist and its transfer to clients through assessment of clinical outcomes are first steps in addressing the lack of guidance and understanding in this area. Questions related to quality and amount of supervision, type of supervision (group versus individual), and their impact on training need answering. Other questions might include the following: How much supervision is needed to create a competent clinician who can sustain the model across time? Does observation matter or improve outcomes? Does focus on content or experiential work in supervision make a difference? What makes an ACT expert or an effective ACT supervisor? The study of ACT supervision in terms of its outcomes and what quality supervision looks like may improve dissemination efforts, guiding plans to create the most effective and cost-efficient supervision available.

Another essential area in need of development and study includes cultural adaptations to ACT that may involve "the systematic modification of an evidence-based treatment (EBT) to consider language, culture, and context in such a way that is compatible with the client's cultural patterns, meanings, and values" (Bernal, Bonilla, & Bellido, 1995, p. 362). Adaptations to ACT should be responsive to each client's unique cultural factors. However, any supplement, alteration, or deletion of core components needs to be tested so that it is clear that changes will not likely dilute the effectiveness of the intervention while still being capable of addressing idiographic needs.

The diffusion of ACT as an innovation is an exciting prospect. Disseminating an intervention that holds people as whole and acceptable, and promotes awareness, choice, and engagement in purposeful and values-based living is personally meaningful to both of us. We also care that the intervention is effective and implemented in ways that highlight client desires and integrate therapist expertise. This intervention will require a commitment to science and continuous practice improvement through lifelong learning. Our hope is to engage the reader in considering how to maximize dissemination to the full benefit of those who are suffering and seeking quality and competent care in the service of meaningful living.

References

Aarons, G. A., & Palinkas, L. A. (2007). Implementation of evidence-based practice in child welfare: Service provider perspectives. *Administration and Policy in Mental Health*, *34*(4), 411–419. https://doi.org/10.1007/s10488-007-0121-3

American Psychological Association. (2014). *APA guidelines for clinical supervision in health service psychology.* Washington DC. https://www.apa.org/about/policy/guidelines-supervision.pdf

APA Presidential Task Force on Evidence-Based Practice. (2006). Evidence-based practice in psychology. *American Psychologist, 61*(4), 271–285. https://doi.org/10.1037/0003-066X.61.4.271

Association for Contextual Behavioral Science. (2020). *ACT books: General purpose | Association for Contextual Behavioral Science.* ACBS. Retrieved November 25, 2020, fromhttps://contextualscience.org/actrft_books_general_purpose

Association for Contextual Behavioral Science. (2022). *ACT randomized controlled trials (1986 to present).* ACBS. Retrieved from https://contextualscience.org/act_randomized_controlled_trials_1986_to_present

Association for State and Provincial Psychology Boards. (2020). *The Association of State and Provincial Psychology Boards (ASPPB) supervision guidelines.* Tyrone, GA. https://cdn.ymaws.com/www.asppb.net/resource/resmgr/guidelines/asppb_supervision_guidelines.pdf

A-Tjak, J. G. L., Davis, M. L., Morina, N., Powers, M. B., Smits, J. A. J., & Emmelkamp, P. M. G. (2015). A meta-analysis of the efficacy of acceptance and commitment therapy for clinically relevant mental and physical health problems. *Psychotherapy and Psychosomatics, 84*(1), 30–36. https://doi.org/10.1159/000365764

Backer, T. E., Liberman, R. P., & Kuehnel, T. G. (1986). Dissemination and adoption of innovative psychosocial interventions. *Journal of Consulting and Clinical Psychology, 54* (1), 111–118. https://doi.org/10.1037/0022-006X.54.1.111

Barnes, S. M., Borges, L. M., Smith, G., Sorensen, D., & Walser, R. D. (2019, June). Empowering patients to thrive despite their desire for death: A workshop on ACT for suicide prevention workshop. Workshop presented at the Association for Contextual Behavioral Science World, Dublin, Ireland.

Beidas, R. S., Edmunds, J. M., Marcus, S. C., & Kendall, P. C. (2012). Training and consultation to promote implementation of an empirically supported treatment: A randomized trial. *Psychiatric Services* (Washington, DC), *63* (7), 660–665. https://doi.org/10.1176/appi.ps.201100401

Beidas, R. S., & Kendall, P. C. (2010). Training therapists in evidence-based practice: A critical review of studies from a systems-contextual perspective. *Clinical Psychology: A Publication of the Division of Clinical Psychology of the American Psychological Association, 17*(1), 1–30. https://doi.org/10.1111/j.1468-2850.2009.01187.x

Bernal, G., Bonilla, J., & Bellido, C. (1995). Ecological validity and cultural sensitivity for outcome research: Issues for the cultural adaptation and development of psychosocial treatments with Hispanics. *Journal of Abnormal Child Psychology, 23*(1), 67–82. https://doi.org/10.1007/BF01447045

Berwick, D. M. (2003). Disseminating innovations in health care. *JAMA, 289*(15), 1969–1975. https://doi.org/10.1001/jama.289.15.1969

Bitar, G. W., Bean, R. A., & Bermúdez, J. M. (2007). Influences and processes in theoretical orientation development: A grounded theory pilot study. *American Journal of Family Therapy, 35*(2), 109–121. https://doi.org/10.1080/01926180600553407

Bond, F. W., Hayes, S. C., & Barnes-Holmes, D. (2006). Psychological flexibility, ACT, and organizational behavior. *Journal of Organizational Behavior Management, 26*(1–2), 25–54. https://doi.org/10.1300/J075v26n01_02

Borges, L. M., Walser, R. D., Nieuwsma, J. A., Luoma, J., & Barnes, S. M. (2019, June). Perspectives on a process-based approach to moral injury: Targeting the pathways maintaining suffering. Panel presented at the Association for Contextual Behavioral Science World, Dublin, Ireland.

Brownson, R. C., Colditz, G. A., & Proctor, E. K. (2017). *Dissemination and implementation research in health: Translating science to practice.* Oxford University Press.

Clark, D. M., Layard, R., Smithies, R., Richards, D. A., Suckling, R., & Wright, B. (2009). Improving access to psychological therapy: Initial evaluation of two UK demonstration sites. *Behaviour Research and Therapy, 47*(11), 910–920. https://doi.org/10.1016/j.brat.2009.07.010

Cook, J. M., Biyanova, T., & Coyne, J. C. (2009a). Barriers to adoption of new treatments: An internet study of practicing community psychotherapists. *Administration and Policy in Mental Health and Mental Health Services Research, 36*(2), 83–90. https://doi.org/10.1007/s10488-008-0198-3

Cook, J. M., Dinnen, S., Simiola, V., Thompson, R., & Schnurr, P. P. (2014). VA residential provider perceptions of dissuading factors to the use of two evidence-based PTSD treatments. *Professional Psychology, Research and Practice, 45*(2), 136–142. https://doi.org/10.1037/a0036183

Cook, J. M., Schnurr, P. P., Biyanova, T., & Coyne, J. C. (2009b). Apples don't fall far from the tree: Influences on psychotherapists' adoption and sustained use of new therapies. *Psychiatric Services, 60*(5), 671–676. https://doi.org/10.1176/ps.2009.60.5.671

Coryell, W., Scheftner, W., Keller, M., Endicott, J., Maser, J., & Klerman, G. L. (1993). The enduring psychosocial consequences of mania and depression. *American Journal of Psychiatry, 150*(5), 720–727. https://doi.org/10.1176/ajp.150.5.720

Crits-Christoph, P., Wilson, G. T., & Hollon, S. D. (2005). Empirically supported psychotherapies: comment on Westen, Novotny, and Thompson-Brenner (2004). *Psychological Bulletin, 131*(3), 412–417. https://doi.org/10.1037/0033-2909.131.3.412

Diamond, M. (1995). Organizational change as human process, not technique. *NIDA Research Monograph, 155*, 119–131.

Dymond, S., May, R. J., Munnelly, A., & Hoon, A. E. (2010). Evaluating the evidence base for relational frame theory: A citation analysis. *The Behavior Analyst, 33*(1), 97–117.

Eberth, J., & Sedlmeier, P. (2012). The effects of mindfulness meditation: A meta-analysis. *Mindfulness, 3*(3), 174–189. https://doi.org/10.1007/s12671-012-0101-x

Edmondson, A. (2003). Speaking up in the operating room: How team leaders promote learning in interdisciplinary action teams. *Journal of Management Studies, 40*, 1419–1452. https://doi.org/10.1111/1467-6486.00386

Eifert, G. H., & Forsyth, J. P. (2005). *Acceptance and commitment therapy for anxiety disorders: A practitioner's treatment guide to using mindfulness, acceptance, and values-based behavior change.* New Harbinger Publications.

Falender, C. A., & Shafranske, E. P. (2004). *Clinical supervision: A competency-based approach* (pp. ix, 348). American Psychological Association. https://doi.org/10.1037/10806-000

Falender, C. A., Shafranske, E. P., & Ofek, A. (2014). Competent clinical supervision: Emerging effective practices. *Counselling Psychology Quarterly, 27*(4), 393–408. https://doi.org/10.1080/09515070.2014.934785

Fisher, A. J., & Boswell, J. F. (2016). Enhancing the personalization of psychotherapy with dynamic assessment and modeling. *Assessment, 23*(4), 496–506. https://doi.org/10.1177/1073191116638735

Fixsen, D. L., Naoom, S. F., Blase, K. A., Friedman, R. M. & Wallace, F. (2005). *Implementation research: A synthesis of the literature.* University of South Florida, Louis de la Parte Florida Mental Health Institute, The National Implementation Research Network.

Forman, E. M., Chapman, J. E., Herbert, J. D., Goetter, E. M., Yuen, E. K., & Moitra, E. (2012). Using session-by-session measurement to compare mechanisms of action for acceptance and commitment therapy and cognitive therapy. *Behavior Therapy, 43*(2), 341–354.

Forman, E. M., Herbert, J. D., Moitra, E., Yeomans, P. D., & Geller, P. A. (2007). A randomized controlled effectiveness trial of acceptance and commitment therapy and cognitive therapy for anxiety and depression. *Behavior Modification, 31*(6), 772–799. https://doi.org/10.1177/0145445507302202

Gates, K. M., & Molenaar, P. C. (2012). Group search algorithm recovers effective connectivity maps for individuals in homogeneous and heterogeneous samples. *NeuroImage, 63*(1), 310–319.

Gloster, A., Walder, N., Levin, M., Twohig, M., & Karekla, M. (2020). The empirical status of acceptance and commitment therapy: A review of meta-analyses. *Journal of Contextual Behavioral Science, 18*, 181–192. https://doi.org/10.1016/j.jcbs.2020.09.009

Gobin, R. L., Lang, A., Allard, C., Golshan J. S., Bomye, J., Schnurr, P., & Strauss, J. L. (2017, June 20). *Gender differences in response to acceptance and commitment therapy among U.S. military veterans.* ACBS Annual World Conference, Seville, Spain.

Goldman, H. H., Ganju, V., Drake, R. E., Gorman, P., Hogan, M., Hyde, P. S., & Morgan, O. (2001). policy implications for implementing evidence-based practices. *Psychiatric Services, 52*(12), 1591–1597. https://doi.org/10.1176/appi.ps.52.12.1591

Graham, C. D., Gouick, J., Krahé, C., & Gillanders, D. (2016). A systematic review of the use of acceptance and commitment therapy (ACT) in chronic disease and long-term conditions. *Clinical Psychology Review, 46*, 46–58. https://doi.org/10.1016/j.cpr.2016.04.009

Graham, I. D., Logan, J., Harrison, M. B., Straus, S. E., Tetroe, J., Caswell, W., & Robinson, N. (2006). Lost in knowledge translation: Time for a map? *Journal of Continuing Education in the Health Professions, 26*(1), 13–24. https://doi.org/10.1002/chp.47

Green, D., & Dye, A. L. (2002). How should we best train clinical psychology supervisors? A Delphi Survey. *Psychology Learning and Teaching, 2*(2), 108–115. https://doi.org/10.2304/plat.2002.2.2.108

Green, L. W. (2001). From research to "best practices" in other settings and populations. *American Journal of Health Behavior, 25*(3), 165–178. https://doi.org/10.5993/ajhb.25.3.2

Gregory, A., Henry, D. B., & Schoeny, M. E. (2007). School climate and implementation of a preventive intervention. *American Journal of Community Psychology, 40*(3–4), 250–260. https://doi.org/10.1007/s10464-007-9142-z

Hayes, S. C. (2004). Acceptance and commitment therapy, relational frame theory, and the third wave of behavioral and cognitive therapies. *Behavior Therapy, 35*(4), 639–665. https://doi.org/10.1016/S0005-7894(04)80013-3

Hayes, S. C., Bissett, R., Roget, N., Padilla, M., Kohlenberg, B. S., Fisher, G., Masuda, A., Pistorello, J., Rye, A. K., Berry, K., & Niccolls, R. (2004). The impact of acceptance and commitment training and multicultural training on the stigmatizing attitudes and professional burnout of substance abuse counselors. *Behavior Therapy, 35*(4), 821–835. https://doi.org/10.1016/S0005-7894(04)80022-4

Hayes, S. C., & Hofmann, S. (2020). *Beyond the DSM: Toward a process-based alternative for diagnosis and mental health treatment.* New Harbinger Publications.
Hayes, S. C., & Hofmann, S. G. (2018). *Process-based CBT: The science and core clinical competencies of cognitive behavioral therapy.* New Harbinger Publications.
Hayes, S. C., & Hofmann, S. G. (2017). The third wave of cognitive behavioral therapy and the rise of process-based care. *World Psychiatry, 16*(3), 245–246. https://doi.org/10.1002/wps.20442
Hayes, S. C., & Strosahl, K. D. (Eds.). (2005). *A practical guide to acceptance and commitment therapy.* Springer. https://doi.org/10.1007/978-0-387-23369-7
Hayes, S. C., Strosahl, K. D., & Wilson, K. G. (2012). *Acceptance and commitment therapy: The process and practice of mindful change.* Guilford press.
Hayes, S. C., Strosahl, K., Wilson, K. G., Bissett, R. T., Pistorello, J., Toarmino, D., Polusny, M. A., Dykstra, T. A., Batten, S. V., Bergan, J., Stewart, S. H., Zvolensky, M. J., Eifert, G. H., Bond, F. W., Forsyth, J. P., Karekla, M., & McCurry, S. M. (2004). Measuring experiential avoidance: A preliminary test of a working model. *The Psychological Record, 54*(4), 553–578. https://doi.org/10.1007/BF03395492
Henggeler, S. W., Lee, T., & Burns, J. A. (2002). What happens after the innovation is identified? *Clinical Psychology: Science and Practice, 9*(2), 191–194. https://doi.org/10.1093/clipsy/9.2.191
Herschell, A. D., Kolko, D. J., Baumann, B. L., & Davis, A. C. (2010). The role of therapist training in the implementation of psychosocial treatments: A review and critique with recommendations. *Clinical Psychology Review, 30*(4), 448–466. https://doi.org/10.1016/j.cpr.2010.02.005
Herschell, A. D., McNeil, C. B., & McNeil, D. W. (2004). Clinical child psychology's progress in disseminating empirically supported treatments. *Clinical Psychology: Science and Practice, 11*(3), 267–288. https://doi.org/10.1093/clipsy.bph082
Hipol, L. J., & Deacon, B. J. (2013). Dissemination of evidence-based practices for anxiety disorders in Wyoming: A survey of practicing psychotherapists. *Behavior Modification, 37*(2), 170–188. https://doi.org/10.1177/0145445512458794
Hofmann, S. G., & Hayes, S. C. (2019). The future of intervention science: Process-based therapy. *Clinical Psychological Science: A Journal of the Association for Psychological Science, 7*(1), 37–50. https://doi.org/10.1177/2167702618772296
Institute of Medicine (US) Committee on Quality of Health Care in America. (2000). In L. T. Kohn, J. M. Corrigan, & M. S. Donaldson (Eds.), *To err is human: Building a safer health system* (p. 1). National Academies Press. http://www.ncbi.nlm.nih.gov/books/NBK225182/
Karlin, B. E., & Cross, G. (2014). From the laboratory to the therapy room: National dissemination and implementation of evidence-based psychotherapies in the U.S. Department of Veterans Affairs Health Care System. *American Psychologist, 69*(1), 19–33. https://doi.org/10.1037/a0033888
Karlin, B. E., Ruzek, J. I., Chard, K. M., Eftekhari, A., Monson, C. M., Hembree, E. A., Resick, P. A., & Foa, E. B. (2010). Dissemination of evidence-based psychological treatments for posttraumatic stress disorder in the Veterans Health Administration. *Journal of Traumatic Stress, 23*(6), 663–673. https://doi.org/10.1002/jts.20588
Kazdin, A. E. (2008). Evidence-based treatment and practice: New opportunities to bridge clinical research and practice, enhance the knowledge base, and improve patient care. *The American Psychologist, 63*(3), 146–159. https://doi.org/10.1037/0003-066X.63.3.146
Kendall, P. C., & Frank, H. E. (2018). Implementing evidence-based treatment protocols: Flexibility within fidelity. *Clinical Psychology: Science and Practice, 25*(4), 40.
Kolko, D. J., Cohen, J. A., Mannarino, A. P., Baumann, B. L., & Knudsen, K. (2009). Community treatment of child sexual abuse: A survey of practitioners in the National Child Traumatic Stress Network. *Administration and Policy in Mental Health and Mental Health Services Research, 36*(1), 37–49. https://doi.org/10.1007/s10488-008-0180-0
Kolovos, S., Kleiboer, A., & Cuijpers, P. (2016). Effect of psychotherapy for depression on quality of life: Meta-analysis. *British Journal of Psychiatry, 209*(6), 460–468. https://doi.org/10.1192/bjp.bp.115.175059
Lappalainen, R., Lehtonen, T., Skarp, E., Taubert, E., Ojanen, M., & Hayes, S. C. (2007). The impact of CBT and ACT models using psychology trainee therapists: A preliminary controlled effectiveness trial. *Behavior Modification, 31*(4), 488–511. https://doi.org/10.1177/0145445506298436
Levin, M. E., Pistorello, J., Hayes, S. C., Seeley, J. R., & Levin, C. (2015). Feasibility of an acceptance and commitment therapy adjunctive web-based program for counseling centers. *Journal of Counseling Psychology, 62*(3), 529–536. https://doi.org/10.1037/cou0000083
Levin, M. E., Smith, B. M., & Smith, G. S. (2019). The potential benefits of flexibility for dissemination and implementation: acceptance and commitment therapy as an example. *Perspectives on Behavior Science, 42*(2), 223–232. https://doi.org/10.1007/s40614-019-00196-0

Long, D. M. (2015). *Development and evaluation of an acceptance and commitment therapy online competency assessment: A contextual behavioral building block approach.* University of Nevada, Reno ProQuest Dissertations Publishing, 3724133. https://scholarworks.unr.edu//handle/11714/2555

Luoma, J. B., Hayes, S. C., & Walser, R. D. (2007). *Learning ACT: An acceptance and commitment therapy skills-training manual for therapists* (Pap/DVD Edition). New Harbinger Publications.

Luoma, J. B., & Platt, M. G. (2015). Shame, self-criticism, self-stigma, and compassion in acceptance and commitment therapy. *Current Opinion in Psychology, 2,* 97–101. https://doi.org/10.1016/j.copsyc.2014.12.016

Luoma, J. B., & Vilardaga, J. P. (2013). Improving therapist psychological flexibility while training acceptance and commitment therapy: A pilot study. *Cognitive Behaviour Therapy, 42*(1), 1–8. https://doi.org/10.1080/16506073.2012.701662

Lyon, A. R., Ludwig, K., Romano, E., Leonard, S., Stoep, A. V., & McCauley, E. (2013). "If it's worth my time, I will make the time": School-based providers' decision-making about participating in an evidence-based psychotherapy consultation program. *Administration and Policy in Mental Health, 40*(6), 467–481. https://doi.org/10.1007/s10488-013-0494-4

Lyon, A. R., Stirman, S. W., Kerns, S. E. U., & Bruns, E. J. (2011). Developing the mental health workforce: Review and application of training approaches from multiple disciplines. *Administration and Policy in Mental Health, 38*(4), 238–253. https://doi.org/10.1007/s10488-010-0331-y

Madson, M., & Campbell, T. C. (2006). Measures of fidelity in motivational enhancement: A systematic review. *Journal of Substance Abuse Treatment, 31*(1), 67–73. https://doi.org/10.1016/J.JSAT.2006.03.010

Martin, G. W., Herie, M. A., Turner, B. J., & Cunningham, J. A. (1998). A social marketing model for disseminating research-based treatments to addictions treatment providers. *Addiction, 93*(11), 1703–1715. https://doi.org/10.1046/j.1360-0443.1998.931117038.x

Matoff, M. (2018). Circumstances to integrate acceptance and commitment therapy with short-term psychodynamic psychotherapies. *Cogent Psychology, 5*(1), 1453595. https://doi.org/10.1080/23311908.2018.1453595

McHugh, R. K., & Barlow, D. H. (2010). The dissemination and implementation of evidence-based psychological treatments: A review of current efforts. *American Psychologist, 65*(2), 73–84. https://doi.org/10.1037/a0018121

McHugh, R. K., Murray, H. W., & Barlow, D. H. (2009). Balancing fidelity and adaptation in the dissemination of empirically supported treatments: The promise of transdiagnostic interventions. *Behaviour Research and Therapy, 47*(11), 946–953. https://doi.org/10.1016/j.brat.2009.07.005

Miller, W., & Mount, K. (2001). A small study of training in motivational interviewing: Does one workshop change clinician and client behavior? *Behavioural and Cognitive Psychotherapy, 29,* 457–471. https://doi.org/10.1017/S1352465801004064

Miller, W. R., Yahne, C. E., Moyers, T. B., Martinez, J., & Pirritano, M. (2004). A randomized trial of methods to help clinicians learn motivational interviewing. *Journal of Consulting and Clinical Psychology, 72*(6), 1050–1062. https://doi.org/10.1037/0022-006X.72.6.1050

Milne, D. (2010). Can we enhance the training of clinical supervisors? A national pilot study of an evidence-based approach. *Clinical Psychology and Psychotherapy, 17*(4), 321–328. https://doi.org/10.1002/cpp.657

Monson, C. M., Shields, N., Suvak, M. K., Lane, J. E. M., Shnaider, P., Landy, M. S. H., Wagner, A. C., Sijercic, I., Masina, T., Wanklyn, S. G., & Stirman, S. W. (2018). A randomized controlled effectiveness trial of training strategies in cognitive processing therapy for posttraumatic stress disorder: Impact on patient outcomes. *Behaviour Research and Therapy, 110,* 31–40. https://doi.org/10.1016/j.brat.2018.08.007

Moore, J. E., Mascarenhas, A., Bain, J., & Straus, S. E. (2017). Developing a comprehensive definition of sustainability. *Implementation Science, 12*(1), 110. https://doi.org/10.1186/s13012-017-0637-1

Morris, E. M. J., & Bilich-Eric, L. (2017). A framework to support experiential learning and psychological flexibility in supervision: SHAPE. *Australian Psychologist, 52*(2), 104–113. https://doi.org/10.1111/ap.12267

Muse, K., & McManus, F. (2013). A systematic review of methods for assessing competence in cognitive-behavioural therapy. *Clinical Psychology Review, 33*(3), 484–499. https://doi.org/10.1016/j.cpr.2013.01.010

Olmstead, T., Carroll, K. M., Canning-Ball, M., & Martino, S. (2011). Cost and cost-effectiveness of three strategies for training clinicians in motivational interviewing. *Drug and Alcohol Dependence, 116*(1–3), 195–202. https://doi.org/10.1016/j.drugalcdep.2010.12.015

O'Neill, L., Latchford, G., McCracken, L. M., & Graham, C. D. (2019). The development of the acceptance and commitment therapy fidelity measure (ACT-FM): A Delphi study and field test. *Journal of Contextual Behavioral Science, 14,* 111–118.

Osei-Bonsu, P. E., Bokhour, B. G., Glickman, M. E., Rodrigues, S., Mueller, N. M., Dell, N. S., Zhao, S., Eisen, S. V., & Elwy, A. R. (2014). The role of coping in depression treatment utilization for VA primary care patients. *Patient Education and Counseling, 94*(3), 396–402. https://doi.org/10.1016/j.pec.2013.10.021

Padilla, A. (2010). *Mindfulness in therapeutic presence: How mindfulness of therapist impacts treatment outcome.* New School University, ProQuest Dissertations Publishing, 3413183. http://search.proquest.com/docview/746780879/abstract/1B23B68F37E24311PQ/8

Persons, J. B., & Silberschatz, G. (1998). Are results of randomized controlled trials useful to psychotherapists? *Journal of Consulting and Clinical Psychology, 66*(1), 126–135. https://doi.org/10.1037/0022-006X.66.1.126

Rapp, C. A., Bond, G. R., Becker, D. R., Carpinello, S. E., Nikkel, R. E., & Gintoli, G. (2005). The role of state mental health authorities in promoting improved client outcomes through evidence-based practice. *Community Mental Health Journal, 41*(3), 347–363. https://doi.org/10.1007/s10597-005-5008-8

Richards, R., Oliver, J. E., Morris, E., Aherne, K., Iervolino, A. C., & Wingrove, J. (2011). Acceptance and Commitment Therapy training for clinicians: an evaluation. *The Cognitive Behaviour Therapist, 4*(3), 114–121.

Rogers, E. M. (2003). *Diffusion of innovations, 5th Edition.* New York: Simon and Schuster.

Ross, S. N. (2008). Using developmental theory: When not to play telephone games. *Integral Review, 4*(1), 31–46.

Roth, A. D., & Pilling, S. (2008). Using an evidence-based methodology to identify the competences required to deliver effective cognitive and behavioural therapy for depression and anxiety disorders. *Behavioural and Cognitive Psychotherapy, 36*(2), 129–147. https://doi.org/10.1017/S1352465808004141

Scheirer, M. A. (2005). Is sustainability possible? A review and commentary on empirical studies of program sustainability. *American Journal of Evaluation, 26*(3), 320–347. https://doi.org/10.1177/1098214005278752

Schmidt, F., & Taylor, T. K. (2002). Putting empirically supported treatment into practice: Lessons learned in a children's mental health center. *Professional Psychology: Research and Practice, 33*(5), 483–489. https://doi.org/10.1037/0735-7028.33.5.483

Schoenwald, S. K., Chapman, J. E., Kelleher, K., Hoagwood, K. E., Landsverk, J., Stevens, J., Glisson, C., & Rolls-Reutz, J. (2008). A survey of the infrastructure for children's mental health services: Implications for the implementation of empirically supported treatments (ESTs). *Administration and Policy in Mental Health and Mental Health Services Research, 35*(1), 84–97.

Schoenwald, S., Mehta, T., Frazier, S., & Shernoff, E. (2013). Clinical supervision in effectiveness and implementation research. *Clinical Psychology Science and Practice, 20*, 44–59. https://doi.org/10.1111/cpsp.12022

Sholomskas, D. E., Syracuse-Siewert, G., Rounsaville, B. J., Ball, S. A., Nuro, K. F., & Carroll, K. M. (2005). We don't train in vain: a dissemination trial of three strategies of training clinicians in cognitive–behavioral therapy. *Journal of Consulting and Clinical Psychology, 73*(1), 106–115. https://doi.org/10.1037/0022-006X.73.1.106

Sorenson, R. L., Gorsuch, R. L., & Mintz, J. (1985). Moving targets: Patients' changing complaints during psychotherapy. *Journal of Consulting and Clinical Psychology, 53*(1), 49–54. https://doi.org/10.1037/0022-006X.53.1.49

Stokes, T. F., & Baer, D. M. (1977). An implicit technology of generalization. *Journal of Applied Behavior Analysis, 10*(2), 349–367. https://doi.org/10.1901/jaba.1977.10-349

Strosahl, K. D., Hayes, S. C., Bergan, J., & Romano, P. (1998). Assessing the field effectiveness of acceptance and commitment therapy: An example of the manipulated training research method. *Behavior Therapy, 29*(1), 35–63. https://doi.org/10.1016/S0005-7894(98)80017-8

Strosahl, K. D., Hayes, S. C., Wilson, K. G., & Gifford, E. V. (2004). An ACT primer. In S. C. Hayes & K. D. Strosahl (Eds.), *A practical guide to acceptance and commitment therapy* (pp. 31–58). New York, NY: Springer. https://doi.org/10.1007/978-0-387-23369-7_2

Tabak, R. G., Khoong, E. C., Chambers, D. A., & Brownson, R. C. (2012). Bridging research and practice: Models for dissemination and implementation research. *American Journal of Preventive Medicine, 43*(3), 337–350. https://doi.org/10.1016/j.amepre.2012.05.024

Thompson, B. L., Luoma, J. B., & LeJeune, J. T. (2013). Using acceptance and commitment therapy to guide exposure-based interventions for posttraumatic stress disorder. *Journal of Contemporary Psychotherapy: On the cutting edge of modern developments in psychotherapy, 43*(3), 133–140. https://doi.org/10.1007/s10879-013-9233-0

Thompson, B. L., Luoma, J. B., Terry, C. M., LeJeune, J. T., Guinther, P. M., & Robb, H. (2015). Creating a peer-led acceptance and commitment therapy consultation group: The Portland model. *Journal of Contextual Behavioral Science, 4*(3), 144–150. https://doi.org/10.1016/j.jcbs.2014.11.004

Tibbits, M. K., Bumbarger, B. K., Kyler, S. J., & Perkins, D. F. (2010). Sustaining evidence-based interventions under real-world conditions: Results from a large-scale diffusion project. *Prevention Science, 11*(3), 252–262.

Torrey, W. C., Drake, R. E., Dixon, L., Burns, B. J., Flynn, L., Rush, A. J., Clark, R. E., & Klatzker, D. (2001). Implementing evidence-based practices for persons with severe mental illnesses. *Psychiatric Services* (Washington, DC), *52*(1), 45–50. https://doi.org/10.1176/appi.ps.52.1.45

Trompetter, H. R., Schreurs, K. M. G., Heuts, P. H. T. G., & Vollenbroek-Hutten, M. M. (2014). The systematic implementation of acceptance and commitment therapy (ACT) in Dutch multidisciplinary chronic pain rehabilitation. *Patient Education and Counseling, 96*(2), 249–255. https://doi.org/10.1016/j.pec.2014.05.019

Twohig, M. P., Abramowitz, J. S., Bluett, E. J., Fabricant, L. E., Jacoby, R. J., Morrison, K. L., Reuman, L., & Smith, B. M. (2015). Exposure therapy for OCD from an acceptance and commitment therapy (ACT) framework. *Journal of Obsessive-Compulsive and Related Disorders, 6*, 167–173. https://doi.org/10.1016/j.jocrd.2014.12.007

Varra, A. A., Hayes, S. C., Roget, N., & Fisher, G. (2008). A randomized control trial examining the effect of acceptance and commitment training on clinician willingness to use evidence-based pharmacotherapy. *Journal of Consulting and Clinical Psychology, 76*(3), 449–458. https://doi.org/10.1037/0022-006X.76.3.449

Vaughan, K. (2017, May 4). *The fidelity model of spreading ideas*. Centre for Effective Altruism. https://www.centreforeffectivealtruism.org/blog/the-fidelity-model-of-spreading-ideas/

Walser, R. D. (2019). *The heart of ACT: Developing a flexible, process-based, and client-centered practice using acceptance and commitment therapy*. New Harbinger Publications.

Walser, R. D., Karlin, B. E., Trockel, M., Mazina, B., & Barr Taylor, C. (2013). Training in and implementation of acceptance and commitment therapy for depression in the Veterans Health Administration: Therapist and patient outcomes. *Behaviour Research and Therapy, 51*(9), 555–563. https://doi.org/10.1016/j.brat.2013.05.009

Watkins, E. (2011). Does psychotherapy supervision contribute to patient outcomes? considering thirty years of research. *The Clinical Supervisor, 30*(2), 235–256. https://doi.org/10.1080/07325223.2011.619417

Watzlawick, P., Weakland, J. H., & Fisch, R. (1974). *Change. Principles of problem formation and problem resolution*. Norton. http://www.sietmanagement.fr/wp-content/uploads/2016/04/Watzlawick-Change.pdf

Wei, M., Tsai, P.-C., Lannin, D. G., Du, Y., & Tucker, J. R. (2015). Mindfulness, psychological flexibility, and counseling self-efficacy: Hindering Self-Focused Attention as a Mediator. *The Counseling Psychologist, 43*(1), 39–63. https://doi.org/10.1177/0011000014560173

Westen, D., Novotny, C. M., & Thompson-Brenner, H. (2004). The empirical status of empirically supported psychotherapies: Assumptions, findings, and reporting in controlled clinical trials. *Psychological Bulletin, 130*(4), 631–663. https://doi.org/10.1037/0033-2909.130.4.631

Wexler, J. (2006). The relationship between therapist mindfulness and the therapeutic alliance. *Dissertation Abstracts International: Section B: The Sciences and Engineering, 67*(5-B), 2848.

Wilson, G. T. (1998). Manual-based treatment and clinical practice. *Clinical Psychology: Science and Practice, 5*(3), 363–375. https://doi.org/10.1111/j.1468-2850.1998.tb00156.x

Wiltsey Stirman, S., Crits-Christoph, P., & DeRubeis, R. J. (2004a). Achieving successful dissemination of empirically supported psychotherapies: A synthesis of dissemination theory. *Clinical Psychology: Science and Practice, 11*(4), 343–359. https://doi.org/10.1093/clipsy.bph091

Wiltsey Stirman, S., Finley, E. P., Shields, N., Cook, J., Haine-Schlagel, R., Burgess, J. F., Dimeff, L., Koerner, K., Suvak, M., Gutner, C. A., Gagnon, D., Masina, T., Beristianos, M., Mallard. K., Ramirez, V., & Monson, C. (2004b). Improving and sustaining delivery of CPT for PTSD in mental health systems: A cluster randomized trial. *Implementation Science, 12*(1), 32. https://doi.org/10.1186/s13012-017-0544-5

Wiltsey Stirman, S., Gutner, C., Crits-Christoph, P., Edmunds, J., Evans, A. C., & Beidas, R. S. (2015). Relationships between clinician-level attributes and fidelity-consistent and fidelity-inconsistent modifications to an evidence-based psychotherapy. *Implementation Science, 10*(1), 115. https://doi.org/10.1186/s13012-015-0308-z

Wiltsey Stirman, S., Kimberly, J., Cook, N., Calloway, A., Castro, F., & Charns, M. (2012). The sustainability of new programs and innovations: A review of the empirical literature and recommendations for future research. *Implementation Science, 7*(1), 17. https://doi.org/10.1186/1748-5908-7-17

Woidneck, M. R., Pratt, K. M., Gundy, J. M., Nelson, C. R., & Twohig, M. P. (2012). Exploring cultural competence in acceptance and commitment therapy outcomes. *Professional Psychology: Research and Practice, 43*(3), 227–233. https://doi.org/10.1037/a0026235

Zimmerman, L., Lounsbury, D. W., Rosen, C. S., Kimerling, R., Trafton, J. A., & Lindley, S. E. (2016). Participatory system dynamics modeling: Increasing stakeholder engagement and precision to improve implementation planning in systems. *Administration and Policy in Mental Health and Mental Health Services Research, 43*(6), 834–849. https://doi.org/10.1007/s10488-016-0754-1

CHAPTER

26 ACT in Schools: A Public Health Approach

Tyler L. Renshaw, Sean N. Weeks, Anthony J. Roberson, *and* Stephanie Vinal

Abstract

This article makes the conceptual and empirical case for using acceptance and commitment therapy (ACT) with youth in school settings. As background, a logical, evidence-based case is made for school-based mental health services more generally. The authors outline a public health approach to using ACT in schools via a multitiered system of supports (MTSS), which emphasizes scaled prevention at universal, targeted, and intensive levels. In addition, the existing literature on ACT in schools is reviewed, showing adequate evidence to support use at the targeted level. The limitations and challenges of using ACT in schools are discussed, and future directions for advancing research and practice are offered. Future work in this area might especially benefit from (1) enhancing the methodological rigor of research designs in school-based studies, (2) testing the viability of brief or focused ACT at the targeted level in schools, (3) investigating the treatment utility of ACT-related process measures in schools, and (4) expanding the scope of ACT in schools to promote the well-being of teachers and other educators.

Key Words: acceptance and commitment therapy, psychological flexibility, youth mental health, school mental health, public health, multitiered systems of supports, prevention, intervention

ACT in Schools: A Public Health Approach

Given that many types of schools serve different populations of people, we should first clarify what we mean by the term *schools*. For our present purposes, it refers to formal institutions that function to educate people by providing learning environments (e.g., buildings and classroom spaces) staffed by trained teachers who administer curricula to a defined population of students. Such schools can be compulsory or voluntary, may be sponsored by public or private entities, and can have broader (e.g., liberal arts) or narrower (e.g., technical skills) educational aims. Our primary concern here is with schools that serve youth or young people, who are pre-college or pre-university age. In the United States, this level of education is typically referred to as *primary* (serving children) or *secondary* (serving adolescents) schooling and is contrasted with *postsecondary* or *tertiary* schooling (serving adults). Schools for young people are typically held in person on a physical campus, with online or remote exceptions made for public health conditions, such as the COVID-19 pandemic, and they structure a large proportion of youths' waking hours (6–8 hours per day for at least 9 months per year) throughout their formative years of human development.

The use of ACT in schools to benefit youth has been warranted by both the broader literature suggesting that ACT is a promising treatment with youth *outside* of schools (e.g., Harris & Samuel, 2020) and the much larger and stronger literature indicating ACT's efficacy for improving the mental health concerns of adults in clinical and community settings (e.g., Gloster et al., 2020). For deeper background and more intellectual scaffolding on ACT with young people, see another article in this volume, which focuses more broadly on applications of ACT with youth (see Petersen et al.). Here we assume that ACT is a promising transdiagnostic intervention with youth outside of schools (again, see Petersen et al., this volume) and focus more narrowly on making the conceptual and empirical case for using ACT *in schools*.

The Case for School-Based Mental Health Services

Over the past two decades, youth mental health research has shown concerning trends regarding the increasing prevalence of psychopathology and risky behavior among young people (Collishaw, 2015; Twenge et al., 2019). Recent epidemiological studies indicate that approximately 16.5 percent of youth struggle with significant mental health problems (Whitney & Peterson, 2019). An earlier national sample of adolescents (Merikangas et al., 2010) showed an overall lifetime prevalence rate of 22.2 percent experiencing severe impairment or distress resulting from a mental health condition, and about a 50 percent prevalence rate when including lower levels of severity and distress. Although rates of specific problems have varied across gender, age, race/ethnicity, socioeconomic, and sexual orientation variables, longitudinal research indicates that mental health concerns in youth are elevated and rising. The surge in externalizing problems, such as conduct disorder, oppositional defiant disorder, and attention-deficit/hyperactivity disorder (ADHD), is especially salient in schools. However, internalizing problems, including anxiety and depression, are also growing at alarming rates and have been shown to be associated with substantial school and quality of life impairments (Bitsko et al., 2018; Mojtabai et al., 2016).

To date, some of the best available evidence estimates that 7.4 percent of youth had received a diagnosis for a disruptive behavior disorder, including oppositional defiant disorder and conduct disorder (Ghandour et al., 2019). Additionally, 9.4 percent of youth had a diagnosis of ADHD, 7.1 percent an anxiety related disorder, and 3.2 percent a mood disorder. Even more striking is the fact that externalizing and/or internalizing problems have been shown to co-occur or be comorbid in about three-quarters of cases (Ghandour et al., 2019). The risks associated with these mental health concerns is another, significant cause for concern. Over the past two decades, mental health problems among youth have been associated with higher rates of lawbreaking, violence, risky sexual behavior, drug and alcohol use, and incarceration (American Academy of Pediatrics, 2001; Skowyra & Cocozza, 2007). Additionally, youth mental health concerns have long been predictive of school performance problems, such as poor academic achievement, decreased classroom engagement, higher likelihood of dropout, and increased disciplinary action and expulsion (Dupéré et al., 2018; Murphy et al., 2015).

The most noteworthy and alarming outcome associated with youth mental health problems is suicide. The Centers for Disease Control and Prevention (CDC, 2016a) recently found that 49 states are seeing an average 25 percent increase in rates of suicide. Suicide accounts for more deaths among youth than all natural causes combined, making it the second leading cause of death (following accidents) for adolescents and young people (CDC, 2016b; Wyman et al., 2010). Another recent longitudinal study showed that suicide rates have steadily increased over the last decade for youth of all ages and that suicide has nearly tripled for young people ages 10–14 (Curtin & Heron, 2019). While the conditions contributing to these increased levels of suicidality and related mental health problems are far from understood, the current data is driving researchers, community organizations, and government task forces to attempt to answer this question. As part of this project, much work has been devoted to understanding the landscape of mental health service provision among youth.

Unfortunately, patterns of evidence strongly indicate that most youth who need mental health services do not consistently (or ever) receive treatment. Findings from the 2016 National Survey of Children's Health indicate that 49.4 percent of youth with a mental health disorder did not receive needed treatment from a mental health professional. Interestingly, however, there is also much variability in access rates, depending on geographic location—ranging from a low of 29.5 percent in Washington, DC, to a high of 72.2 percent in North Carolina (Whitney & Peterson, 2019). Similarly low service access rates were observed in a longitudinal study by Costello et al. (2014), who found that 55 percent of adolescents with significant mental health concerns did not receive treatment within the past 12 months. Findings from Costello et al. and others (e.g., Lipari et al., 2016) also highlight concerning disparities in youths' access to mental health services; these studies indicate that young people from diverse and minoritized communities are especially unlikely to get the mental health support they need.

The most frequently studied mental health service settings for youth include (1) inpatient settings, (2) outpatient clinics, (3) schools, (4) other general medical settings (e.g., pediatrics or family practice), (5) child welfare services, and (6) juvenile justice systems. Recent large-scale service access studies indicate that most youth who get mental health services do so within specialty mental health settings (~24%) and schools (~23%), with far fewer services received across all other settings (Costello et al., 2014; Lipari et al., 2016). A meta-analysis of service access studies spanning the last few decades yielded similar results, showing that schools were the most accessed mental health service setting for youth (22.1%), followed closely by outpatient mental health care (20.56%)—with substantially fewer services provided in primary care (9.93%), inpatient (9.05%), child welfare (7.9%), and juvenile justice (4.5%) settings (Duong et al., 2021). Given the generally low access rates among youth, as well as the fact that about 50 percent of youth obtaining services do so in schools, educational settings have developed a reputation as "gateway" or "de facto" mental health care systems for youth. This seems to be especially true for diverse and minoritized youth, whose families are more likely to be socioeconomically disadvantaged and therefore have greater need for public sector resources, such as schools, for mental health services (Villagrana, 2010).

Taken together, the literature can make a logical, evidence-based case for the import of school-based mental health services. Merrell et al. (2022) summarize the progression of these empirical points as follows: (1) many youth experience significant mental health problems; (2) most youth with mental health problems do not access treatment; (3) for youth who do get treatment, schools are a substantial source of services and often function as the de facto mental health care system; and (4) there are clear disparities related to service access for minoritized youth, which might be partially addressed via school-based service delivery. Given this line of reasoning, an increasing amount of empirical attention and public policy has turned toward establishing, maintaining, and evaluating the viability of school mental health services (Weist et al., 2014). An abundance of empirical literature demonstrates the effectiveness of school-based prevention and intervention efforts for improving the mental health of youth from diverse backgrounds, presenting with a variety of risks and problems, across both primary and secondary school settings (e.g., Sanchez et al., 2018; Mychailyszyn et al., 2012). Although investigating the relative effectiveness of services provided *in schools* compared to those provided *outside of schools* (e.g., outpatient clinics) has not been a priority to date, the literature that does exist suggests comparable outcomes across settings (Weist et al., 1999).

Like most mental health service sectors, the school-based mental health movement values and prioritizes evidence-based practice (EBP). Yet, as school mental health services have expanded and evolved over the years, so have the logistical growing pains associated with integrating EBP within educational settings. As noted by Shernoff et al. (2017), EBP protocols (1) "do not consistently address multiple referral concerns and have redundancies that are burdensome" for school-based practitioners (p. 221), (2) "lack cultural responsiveness and flexibility to adapt to the local context" (p. 225), and (3) show that "service delivery in schools is broad in scope" requiring applications across levels (e.g., schoolwide or classroom) that are often disconnected from how EBPs were developed (i.e., at the individual level of service delivery, p. 226). To successfully meet these challenges, Shernoff et al. and others (e.g., Marchette & Weisz, 2017) have advocated for a strong focus on transdiagnostic or common elements interventions that can be provided within a public health service delivery model and implemented across settings in real-world care.

A Public Health Framework for Using ACT in Schools

Taking a population-based, prevention-oriented approach to service delivery can reduce the prevalence and impact of youth mental health problems (Herman et al., 2020). The public health approach is often contrasted with the *medical model* or *clinical framework*, which emphasizes the diagnosis and treatment (as opposed to prevention) of individuals (as opposed to populations) who are presenting with already significant impairment or distress or disease (as opposed to varying levels of risk). However, it may be more helpful to view both frameworks as complementary rather than contrasting or mutually exclusive. The following parable about "the children in the river" nicely illustrates the importance of the public health and clinical approaches:

> To illustrate the point there is a fable concerning three people who were having a picnic beside the river. As they were enjoying their lunch in the sunshine, one looked up to see a child floating down the river. Immediately he leaped in and brought the child ashore. As he did so, his companions saw two more children helplessly bobbing in the water. Upon diving in to bring them out, they were dismayed to find still three more children in the river. Very quickly, they realized that the river was alive with struggling children in need of rescue. As they frantically worked to save as many as possible, one of the three suddenly left and began to run upstream along the bank. Seeing this, the others shouted after him in alarm, "Where are you going? Come back, we must help these children!" Continuing to run, he yelled, "You do the best you can there, I'm going up the river to try to stop them from falling in!"
>
> *(Drum & Figler, 1973, p. 13).*

In this parable, the situation at the outset is parallel to the clinical framework. Children potentially drowning in the river, and thus in dire need of help, are analogous to youth experiencing significant mental health concerns who could benefit from treatment. The bystanders who work to pull the imperiled children from the river are comparable to clinicians who treat youth in need. The analogy to the public health framework enters in, then, as soon one of the bystanders runs upstream. Recognizing that they do not have the capacity to help all the struggling children who are already in the river, this person endeavors to identify the source of the problem and prevent more children from endangering themselves. This person's goals are analogous to the preventive and population-based values of interventionists working within a public health framework. The important point of this scenario is that the goals of the work downstream in no way discounts or is incompatible with the intentions of the work upstream. Rather, both types of work are necessary and complementary functions that contribute to the children's well-being. And so it is with mental health professionals working within clinical and public health frameworks. Those practitioners metaphorically running upstream play no more or less critical a role than those working metaphorically downstream: both are collaborating to reduce the overall prevalence and impact of youth mental health concerns.

Multitiered Systems of Support in Schools

ACT can be applied within a common service delivery heuristic known as a *multitiered system of supports* (MTSS; Kilgus & von der Embse, 2019; Stoiber, 2014). This system is commonly operationalized through three tiers or levels of service delivery (see Figure 26.1). Within MTSS, *tier 1* or the *universal level* refers to low-intensity services that are provided to *all* students within a school population, regardless of risk status. The aim of this level of service delivery is to promote overall population wellness, which prevents the onset of new problems and buffers against existing problems. *Tier 2* or the *targeted level* refers to moderate-intensity services that are provided to *some* students, based on the presence of risk factors or early indicators of problems. The aim of tier 2 services is to support students at risk early and efficiently, preventing the possibility of worsening risk factors or developing more severe problems over time. Finally, *tier 3* or the *intensive level* refers to high-resource services that are provided to *few* students, who present with significant problems or extremely elevated levels of risk. The aim of this level of service delivery is to support students "in risk" immediately and effectively, preventing further development of chronic and costly problems throughout the lifespan.

The key features of the public health approach that shape MTSS in schools are not necessarily the percentage of students served within each tier, or the number of tiers included within the model, or the techniques or procedures employed at each tier. Rather, the critical aspects are (1) the scope of students receiving services and (2) the intensity of services provided to those students. In Figure 26.1, these two features are represented by interlocking triangles that form a comprehensive public health service delivery model, represented by the full rectangle. The relationship between these two triangles is scaled up or down, depending on need for supports within a target population. When taken together, these MTSS features function as a relative ratio that helps guide *the time or effort or resources that should be reasonably expended per pupil* (Merrell et al., 2022). Thus, at the universal level (tier 1), the cost-per-pupil for services should be relatively low, whereas this ratio thickens appreciably when moving to the targeted level (tier 2). The intensive level (tier 3), by contrast, will have the densest cost-per-pupil ratio and should therefore be engaged sparingly. Hearkening back to the parable of "the children in the river" can help further illustrate this ratio, as we can clearly intuit how it takes more time and effort per child to rescue them from the rushing river (analogous to tier 3 services) than it would to remove them from the water prior to wading too deeply (analogous to tier 2 services) or even preventing them from entering the river in the first place (analogous to tier 1 services).

When it comes to applying ACT within MTSS, we suggest that the two key characteristics (i.e., scope and intensity), three tiers (see Figure 26.1), and cost-per-pupil ratio are sufficient guiding principles. The multiple tiers of service delivery are not necessarily mutually exclusive, and school-based mental health professionals using ACT might provide services across all levels within MTSS—contingent, of course, upon their time, resources, and expertise. In addition to being transdiagnostic, then, a public health approach to ACT in schools should also be *trans-tiered*.

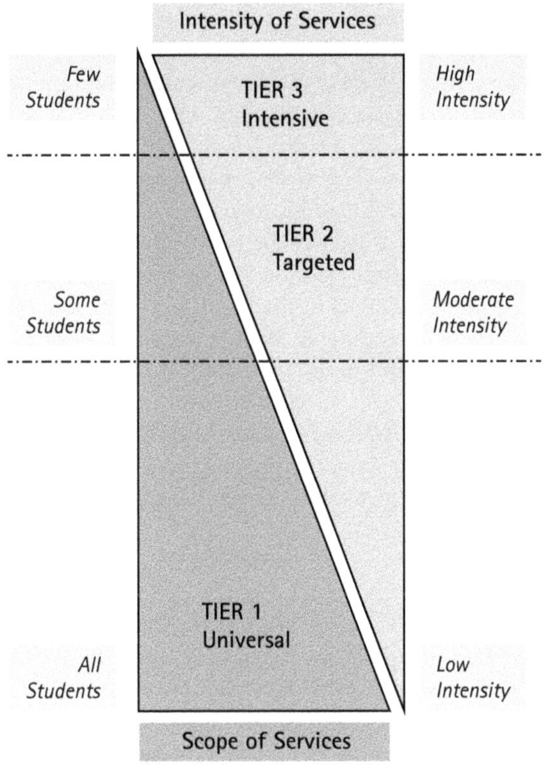

Figure 26.1. Visual representation of multitiered system of supports (MTSS) in schools.

Trans-tiered ACT in Schools

At tier 1 (or the universal level), ACT might be applied as a schoolwide or classroom-based prevention curriculum that aims to promote competencies that facilitate psychological flexibility within a general sample of students. This type of programming might be provided by a mental health professional, but it might also be feasibly implemented by a properly trained teacher or paraprofessional, as other effective interventions at this level have been (cf. Durlak et al., 2011; Klingbeil et al., 2017). The *Connect* curriculum, which is grounded in the DNA-V model of ACT (Hayes & Ciarrochi, 2015) and other well-being literature (Basarkod, 2019), is a recent example of potential applications at this tier. *Connec*t is a pay-for-use curriculum designed for implementation by teachers in classroom settings. It consists of over 250 lesson plans (with supplemental resources) for youth in primary schools (age range 4–11 years). In relation to the United Kingdom's education standards, *Connect* is considered a personal, social, and health education (PSHE) curriculum, which is analogous to a social-emotional learning (SEL) program in the United States. *Connect* is fitting for tier 1 because its implementation is unambiguously universal and its goals are clearly prevention-oriented, as the curriculum aims to lower the likelihood of mental health problems and promote the well-being and resilience of all children within a school. Inasmuch as one *Connect* session facilitated by an educator will reach 20 + youth, the cost-per-pupil ratio of this ACT-based intervention is relatively thin.

At tier 2 (or the targeted level), ACT can be used in schools as a pull-out, group-based intervention for select students identified with emerging or subclinical mental health problems. This level of service delivery is typically provided by well-trained and credentialed (or supervised) mental health professionals; yet, it is relatively short term and more structured than tier 3 applications. The *Get Out of Your Mind and Into Your Life for Teens* workbook (Ciarrochi et al., 2012) and the *Thriving Adolescent* curriculum and its associated DNA-V model (Hayes & Ciarrochi, 2015) are exemplars of what ACT might look like at this level within a public health approach. To illustrate a potential application at this level, imagine the hypothetical case of a secondary school classroom that has recently completed a PSHE or SEL program as a tier 1 intervention. Although most youth in the class are likely to respond positively to the curriculum, some may not and others, though benefiting somewhat, are likely to need more targeted support to address elevated risk or emerging mental health concerns. To keep things simple, let us say 4/20 (20%) of the pupils in this classroom fall into this "at-risk" zone. To further support these four students, then, a school-based mental health professional might transition them to a tier 2, ACT-based intervention, which involves pulling them out of class twice a week to participate in a 30-minute, short-term (e.g., 8 weeks) group intervention based on content in the *Thriving Adolescent* manual. This content includes various psychoeducational lessons, worksheets, exercises, and scripts that integrate ACT with positive psychology to help adolescents connect with their values, develop healthy relationships, and successfully transition into adulthood.

At tier 3 (or the intensive level), ACT in schools is relatively indistinguishable from ACT *outside* of schools (i.e., in clinical or other community settings). At this level, ACT is likely to be provided by mental health professionals in individual therapy contexts that are personalized, long-term, and targeted to significant mental health concerns. The primary difference, however, is that this ACT is provided on the school campus during regular school hours. Mental health professionals using ACT at this level may be full-time employees of the school (e.g., school psychologists, school counselors, or school social workers), or they may be contractors working for the school (e.g., child clinical psychologists, marriage and family therapists, or community mental health counselors) with the express purpose of providing intensive therapeutic services for the highest-risk students. The *ACT for Adolescents* manual (Turrell & Bell, 2016) and the *Mindfulness and Acceptance Workbook for Teen Anxiety* (Turrell et al., 2018) are good examples of potential ACT applications at this level. Extending the hypothetical case example provided at tier 2, imagine that one of the students involved in the pull-out, group-based ACT intervention fails to benefit from that targeted support—and even goes on to develop chronic, severe anxiety that contributes to school refusal and academic failure. To further support this one high-needs student "in risk," the school-based mental health professional might transition them to a tier 3 version of ACT. This treatment could consist of a pull-out, 50-minute, personalized, and longer-term (e.g., 16 weeks) regimen guided by the materials prepared by Turrell and colleagues (2018).

Additionally, considering that intensive-level interventions in schools are often multi-system, collaborative, and "wraparound" in nature, ACT at this top tier might benefit from coordinated supports for youths' caregivers, who are key stakeholders and often implementers for interventions that extend beyond school boundaries. *The Joy of Parenting* (Coyne & Murrell, 2009) and *Acceptance and Commitment Therapy: The Clinician's Guide for Supporting Parents* (Whittingham & Coyne, 2019) may be useful resources for supporting caregivers in these intensive, collaborative intervention situations. To further extend the hypothetical case example, an ACT-based approach to parent consultation might be a useful adjunct at tier 3 to increase the probability of a parent's successful adherence to a home–school behavioral intervention for reducing the youth's school refusal. Clearly, the cost-per-pupil ratio of the treatment at this most intensive level (tier 3) is much thicker than the ratio for the group-based intervention at the targeted level (tier 2), which, in turn, is denser than the rather thin ratio for classroom-based curriculum at the universal level (tier 1).

The examples of ACT applications within MTSS mentioned previously—as well as the several practical resources we highlighted—are intended to be illustrative, not exhaustive. Ultimately, ACT might take a variety of forms across the tiers in schools, being operationalized into countless curricula, workbooks, treatment manuals, and supporting materials. The most important consideration will always be how well any given form of ACT matches the aims and key characteristics of the MTSS level at which its applied (see Figure 26.1). Given that ACT is inherently a practical, flexible, principle-based approach to intervention (Hayes et al., 2012), its core processes and techniques might be adapted in myriad ways within schools to benefit local populations of students. Moreover, individual students might even benefit from ACT-based interventions across multiple levels of support within MTSS in schools.

Review of the Research Using ACT in Schools

Researchers have developed and tested ACT interventions across the three levels of MTSS: universal, targeted, and intensive. Results from these studies suggest promising—yet variable—outcomes across the tiers in schools and generally corroborate the findings supporting the promise of ACT with youth outside of schools (see Petersen et al., this volume). Yet, this line of research in schools is also more limited than that outside of schools, as it is characterized by fewer overall studies, less methodologically rigorous studies, and more questionable internal validity resulting from potential construct or content contamination. Our approach for this review is narrative in nature—highlighting the key features and findings of select studies that illustrate applications of ACT within a public health framework in schools. We begin by focusing on studies that seem to be conducted at tier 1 (or the universal level), followed by those that seem well suited for tier 2 (or the targeted level) and, finally, tier 3 (or the intensive level). We recognize at the outset that our tier-by-tier categorization of these studies is based on our personal interpretations of the match between a given study's research aims and scope with our understanding of the public health framework and MTSS in schools (see Figure 26.1). Reasonable people may therefore disagree with our classifications, and so we recommend focusing more on their heuristic value for fleshing out public health applications of ACT in schools.

Tier 1 or Universal ACT

The earliest evaluation we identified at this level was a schoolwide case study by Dixon (2013), who reported on a universal, ACT-based curriculum in an alternative elementary setting. In this project, the schoolwide implementation consisted of 30-minute ACT lessons delivered by school staff to each classroom at the beginning of each school day, with a supplementary ACT "book club" for teachers held once a week, which provided the opportunity to discuss ACT-related concepts. In addition, school staff facilitated some committed action components at the classroom level, including student goal setting and teacher contingency management to promote positive pupil behavior. While Dixon's (2013) report was mostly anecdotal, quantitative results indicated that students' attendance rates, psychological well-being, and grades improved school-wide. The curriculum piloted in this study eventually evolved into the *Accept–Identify–Move* (AIM) curriculum (Dixon & Paliliunas, 2018), which has since been tested with more rigorous empirical methods, albeit with more targeted samples and at more intensive levels of service delivery (for an example of the AIM curriculum at tier 3, see Wilson et al., 2022).

There is a compelling amount of literature indicating that (non-ACT) mindfulness-based interventions (e.g., Klingbeil et al., 2017) and traditional cognitive-behavioral strategies (e.g., Mychailyszyn et al., 2012) can be effective when implemented at the universal level in schools. Burckhardt et al. (2016) endeavored to expand this literature by evaluating the value-added of an ACT component to a universal prevention program. This culminated in a combination ACT and positive psychology curriculum known as *Strong Minds*. Burckhardt et al. (2016) conducted a pilot study with a sample of 267 secondary students in grades 10–11. *Strong Minds* consisted of 16 half-hour workshops held in the school auditorium over the course of 3 months, starting with sessions addressing the six core processes of psychological flexibility: present moment awareness, defusion, acceptance, self-as-context, values, and committed action (Hayes et al., 2012). Pre-/post-outcome data was collected on measures of depression, stress, anxiety, and subjective well-being. Students were randomly assigned to either the treatment group (i.e., *Strong Minds*) or an education-as-usual control group. So, although the implementation was not truly universal in nature (due to randomization), the study was open to all students regardless of risk status, and the implementation mirrored a universal approach across two secondary grades. Results are therefore reasonably generalizable to tier 1 supports in schools. Tenth graders participating in *Strong Minds* showed statistically significant and meaningful improvements in depression, anxiety, stress, and subjective well-being compared to the education-as-usual control. Interestingly, however, eleventh graders participating in the treatment did not show these same benefits relative to the control. Consideration of descriptive statistics indicated that high ratings of stress and anxiety at baseline were significantly reduced at posttest across grades and conditions, including the control. This finding suggests that a potential maturation effect among the eleventh graders may have limited detection of intervention effects.

As a follow-up to this *Strong Minds* study, Burckhardt et al. (2017) tested another universal ACT intervention—sans the positive psychology elements—with a separate sample of tenth-grade students. This second study used a similar research design, yet tested the ACT intervention against a "pastoral care" control condition, which was part of the standard educational curriculum within the parochial school of interest. But this time they found no statistically significant differences between groups for any pre-/post-measures across outcomes. In another and much larger universal ACT study, Van der Gucht et al. (2017) evaluated change on outcomes related to quality of life, psychological flexibility, and internalizing and externalizing problems across 34 classrooms, 14 schools, and 586 adolescents. Van der Gucht et al. (2017) used a similar research design as Burckhardt et al. (2016, 2017) and compared their intervention to an education-as-usual control. And like the second Burckhardt et al. (2017) study, they found no statistically significant differences in their pre-/post-measures across outcomes. However, unlike Burckhardt et al. (2017), their intervention protocol was teacher-led (as opposed to facilitated by a trained professional), classroom-based (as opposed to auditorium-based), and lasted only 4 weeks (as opposed to a few months). While Burckhardt et al. (2017) and Van der Gucht et al. (2017) found null results, we did identify at least one additional tier 1 study with more promising results. Specifically, Takahashi et al. (2020) found meaningful reductions in hyperactivity/inattention and avoidance behavior in their large-scale study investigating the malleability of psychological flexibility and emotional/behavioral problems in 299 adolescent students. The implementation in this study was composed of 6 biweekly, classwide ACT sessions (5 hours total dosage), which were loosely based on the content from Ciarrochi et al.'s (2012) *Get Out of Your Mind and Into Your Life for Teens* workbook and facilitated by clinical psychologists.

We classified the studies noted above at the universal or tier 1 level because they were all delivered in schools in either a classroom or other large-group environment (i.e., within a school auditorium) and involved general samples of students who participated in the intervention regardless of mental health risk or problem status. We estimate that, if implemented in real-world school settings, the cost-per-pupil ratio for each of these interventions would be reasonable and rather thin—appropriate for universal supports. That said, the amount of variability in the methodologies and outcomes of these studies is striking. Each evaluated a novel universal ACT-based intervention, with no available replication or generalizability studies (to our knowledge). The quality of research designs ranged from weak to strong, and results were mixed, ranging from null to meaningful. Overall, then, we conclude that the evidence is currently *weak* for supporting use of ACT at tier 1 in schools.

Tier 2 or Targeted ACT

One study at the tier 2 level was conducted by Barandeh et al. (2017), who compared the effects of two interventions in a high school setting for reducing procrastination among students who self-identified as having procrastination difficulties. Specifically, 60 high school girls participated in an eight-session treatment in which they were randomly assigned to an education-as-usual control group or one of two treatment conditions based on (1) ACT or (2) choice theory (a framework that emphasizes the importance of self-determination and assuming responsibility for choice-making; see Glasser, 1998). This intervention was targeted in nature in that these 60 students were selected for participation from a much larger sample of 260 students, based on baseline questionnaire scores indicating elevated levels of procrastination compared to the general sample. Additionally, unlike the universal interventions described in the previous subsection, which were broad in content scope, the content of this intervention was tailored to procrastination-related concerns. Pre-, post-, and follow-up data were collected on participants' self-reports of procrastination. Both interventions showed statistically significant improvements in self-ratings of procrastination compared to the education-as-usual control condition. No difference was discovered regarding the relative impact of the two treatment conditions, suggesting their beneficial effects on procrastination were comparable.

In another school-based tier 2 study, Pahnke et al. (2014) piloted the efficacy of group-based ACT for improving stress, hyperactivity, prosocial behaviors, anxiety, depression, and anger in students with high-functioning autism spectrum disorder (ASD). Although the outcomes of interest in this study were broad, we considered this intervention targeted because it focused specifically on youth with high-functioning ASD, who because of their disability status have a higher likelihood of risk for developing behavioral and mental health concerns. This pilot study used a quasi-experimental design, comparing participants in the ACT group to an education-as-usual control group. More specifically, 28 high-functioning adolescent students with ASD across six classrooms and two schools were assigned to either the treatment or control group based on their current class grouping. Participant data was collected at pre-, post-, and follow-up time points using multiple measures of teacher-report and self-report behavioral and emotional problems. The intervention was structured as a 6-week program that met twice weekly for 40 minutes per session. Overall, the ACT intervention showed statistically significant improvements on teacher- and self-reports of stress relative to the education-as-usual control. Teacher-reports of hyperactivity and prosocial behaviors also showed meaningful improvements in the treatment group compared to the control, although self-reports of similar outcomes were not different between the conditions. Self-reports of anxiety, depression, and anger were significantly improved in the ACT group relative to the control group.

Other studies at the tier 2 or targeted level have looked at the effects of ACT on measures of psychological flexibility and its subprocesses—including experiential avoidance, mindfulness, and valued living—though few have found significant improvements (Brookshier, 2016; Livheim et al., 2015; Livings, 2017; Mirzahosseini et al., 2016; Murrell et al., 2015; Pentchenva-Burns, 2015). While these process measures in targeted groups have yet to show much sensitivity to change, a good variety of mental health outcomes measures have demonstrated statistically significant and meaningful responses to ACT interventions. Indeed, emotion regulation, depression, anxiety, stress, healthy development, coping skills, school engagement, and positive psychological capital have all been found to significantly improve through ACT interventions targeting youth who have substantial risk factors (e.g., Fang & Ding, 2020) or who present with emerging mental health concerns (e.g., Livheim et al., 2015; Luciano et al., 2011; Saibini, 2013). Given the several studies identified at this level, we conclude that using ACT at tier 2 in schools has stronger and more consistent evidential support than applications at tier 1. Yet, as with tier 1, the literature at this level is still limited by an abundance of varying protocols and procedures, none of which have yet to be directly replicated or systematically generalized, as well as broad-ranging outcomes of interest, only few of which have been replicated. The key characteristic differentiating ACT studies at tier 1 and tier 2 in schools, then, is not so much the scope of outcomes as it is the scope of the population of interest: universal ACT has been provided to broad and general samples of students, whereas targeted ACT has narrowed in on sampling a variety of at-risk populations of students.

Tier 3 or Intensive ACT

Earlier we suggested that using ACT at the intensive level in schools could be relatively straightforward and comparable with using ACT in clinical or other community therapy contexts. We should note, however, that we only identified two studies at this level and that only one of them conforms with our recommendations. This study was conducted by Wilson et al. (2022) and consisted of an intensive-level application of the AIM curriculum (Dixon & Paliliunas, 2018). The study population consisted of three upper-primary students who were identified as displaying significant emotional, disruptive, and off-task behaviors in the classroom. The students were pulled from their classrooms for 30-minute ACT sessions once during the school day, which consisted of a mixture of psychoeducation, discussion and interaction, worksheets, metaphorical and experiential activities, and reflection on their experiences. Dixon and Paliliunas noted that although all sessions were based on content from the AIM curriculum, they were also tailored to participants' unique histories, presentations, and developmental level. Their study used a noncurrent multiple-baseline design across participants, with an embedded alternating treatments component that was intended to control for the potential confounding effect of simply pulling the students out of class to receive treatment. Following the course of 11 ACT sessions, intervention effects were analyzed for each participant, with results showing substantial improvements in disruptive and on-task behaviors in the classroom compared to both baseline and control conditions.

The only other study that seemed to meet the criteria for an intensive ACT intervention was an open-trial evaluation of a school-based substance use treatment program that incorporated ACT, motivational interviewing (MI), contingency management, family sessions, and medication management as a treatment package for 41 adolescents (Lintz et al., 2019). This treatment package was provided over 12 weeks for youth with identified substance use disorders who were being served in three school-based health clinics. Lintz et al. note that the ACT and MI components of the intervention were manual-standardized, yet individualized—and that this combination of approaches was chosen via collaboration among clinicians, researchers, and youth following the failure of a classical cognitive-behavioral therapy approach in these school-based health centers. Individual and family sessions of ACT + MI typically occurred weekly and lasted 45–60 minutes, whereas the frequency and duration of the contingency management and medication management components of the treatment package were not specified in the report. Ultimately, results following participation in the 12-week treatment package were promising, with students showing statistically significant improvements in substance use, school engagement, and emotional wellness. Interestingly, the average number of sessions completed by participants was only 7.4, yet the social validity ratings provided by participants for each session was extremely high (average of 38.2 out of 40 possible points). Furthermore, qualitative feedback received from the students, therapists (n = 3), and a school principal was likewise positive. Their comments indicated appreciation for the flexibility of the ACT + MI intervention model as well as the convenience of the school-based treatment approach.

Considered separately, these two studies (i.e., Lintz et al., 2019; Wilson et al., 2022) provide promising evidence supporting the use of ACT at tier 3 in schools. However, when compared directly with each other, sharp differences in study quality, scope, and intention become apparent. One study presents a single-case experimental design, whereas the other presents an open-trial, nonexperimental group design. One study implemented a relatively focused ACT treatment; the other implemented a multi-element treatment package with an ACT + MI component (among other potentially therapeutic components). One study targeted classroom-specific problem behaviors; the other targeted substance use plus subjective well-being outcomes. Indeed, when considered closely, these two studies seem incomparable across most methodological variables that matter. The thread that ties them together at the intensive level, then, is the fact that both studies endeavored to intervene with youth in schools that had been previously identified as having educationally or clinically significant mental health problems. Thus, the cost-per-pupil ratio for both treatments is relatively thick compared to the ratios for those intervention studies we cited at tier 2 and tier 1.

Given that we only identified two tier 3 studies—and considering their obvious methodological heterogeneity—the most realistic and low-inference conclusion we can offer for ACT at the intensive level is that the evidence is promising and yet extremely limited. To shore up evidence at this level, we recommend that future research be conducted to test purer applications of ACT in schools using more rigorous research designs, as has been done successfully with ACT outside of schools (see Petersen et al., this volume). If researchers continue testing ACT components within treatment packages at this level, as did Lintz et al. (2019), then we suggest that component analysis or dismantling studies will be necessary to quantify the value-added of ACT when applied in the context of other EBPs. Overall, considering the existing literature supporting applications of ACT across the tiers in schools, the strongest evidence is found at tier 2, with encouraging yet weaker evidence at tier 1 and promising yet extremely limited evidence at tier 3. Enough empirical support exists across the tiers to provide proof-of-concept for using ACT within a public health framework in schools. Yet, much work remains to be done to establish strong and consistent empirical support for this project at each respective prevention level.

Future Directions for ACT in Schools

Beyond the truism that "much more research is needed" on ACT across the tiers, we believe several other fruitful directions for advancing ACT in schools are possible. For example, at tier 3, the differential effectiveness of ACT for treating common presenting problems faced by school-based mental health professionals—such as externalizing problems (see Twohig et al.,

2008) and bereavement (see Renshaw et al., 2017)—is currently unknown. This is especially true when compared to other well-established EBPs for addressing similar concerns in schools. Thus, although we assume that ACT functions transdiagnostically at this tier, we do not yet have evidence either to support this claim or to demonstrate that ACT is superior (or inferior) to other EBPs with longer track records for improving youth mental health concerns (cf. Weisz et al., 2013). As another example at tier 3, the relative effectiveness of ACT *in schools* compared to ACT *outside schools* remains unspecified. Although we believe the public health approach warrants the use of ACT in schools regardless of whether it has comparable or diminished effects relative to ACT outside of schools, we suggest that explicitly testing and quantifying these relative effects is worthwhile. Indeed, it could uncover implementation moderators that might influence the usefulness of ACT with youth across settings. As yet another example, more rigorous research designs would be beneficial for evaluating ACT across the tiers, with a particular focus on probing the mechanisms of change that are purported to drive ACT's effects (see Kazdin & Nock, 2003, for an overview of methods toward this end). Although some studies of ACT in schools have shown changes in purported process variables (e.g., Sabaini, 2013, Takahashi et al., 2020), none have used rigorous enough designs to conclude that changes in these processes *precede* or *account for* or *have functional relationships with* changes in mental health outcomes. Thus, at bottom, the theory of psychological flexibility underlying ACT has yet to be systematically validated in schools.

All the future directions we just sketched focus on upgrading research designs and methodologies for evaluating ACT in schools. Many more possible improvements, beyond those we have mentioned, could be made on this theme. But we turn our attention now to key future directions that have more substantive implications for shifting and expanding the potential applications of ACT in schools. The three potential applications that are most compelling are: (1) exploring the viability of brief or focused ACT in schools, (2) improving the measurement of ACT-related processes with youth in schools, and (3) expanding the scope of ACT in schools to include intervention with teachers and other educators.

Trying Focused ACT in Schools

Over the past decade, Strosahl and colleagues (2012) have been developing a line of work known as *focused acceptance and commitment therapy* (FACT). This treatment approach aims to spark behavior change in a brief or few-session format, within often fast-paced and dynamic contexts, such as primary care. Beginning with short interviews to assess the function and impact of symptoms, FACT generates a quick case conceptualization that is grounded in psychological flexibility theory. The approach then moves speedily—usually within the same initial session—to introducing reframing strategies for promoting change-oriented motivation and then implementing awareness, openness, and/or engagement strategies that are intended to affect targeted behavior change. Some empirical data points have been generated to support the use of FACT with adults. For example, Glover et al. (2016) found that a 4-week group-based FACT implemented within a VA integrated care context produced statistically significant and meaningful improvements in patient quality of life, depressive symptoms, perceived stress, perceptions of mental health functioning, and physical health functioning. Furthermore, Kohtala et al. (2015) observed that a 4-week, individualized FACT implemented in a university lab-based setting resulted in statistically significant improvements in depressive symptoms, psychological inflexibility, general symptom severity, and subjective well-being. Most benefits were found to be maintained at the 6-month follow-up. To our knowledge, however, FACT has yet to be empirically evaluated with youth or in schools.

FACT might be particularly useful within school mental health service delivery models, and it is likely to fit especially well as a tier 2 or targeted-level intervention within MTSS (see Figure 26.1). At this level, interventions should be brief, easy to implement, adaptable to individual and group-based delivery formats, and capable of positively affecting multiple outcomes. FACT fits the bill for each of these characteristics. For example, a school-based mental health professional might provide FACT to groups of adolescent students who have screened positive for mental health risk at the universal level, indicating they warrant more focused intervention beyond what is currently available schoolwide. As another example, this same provider might use individualized FACT with students referred by teachers for mental health support as a first-line intervention—to see if their concerns might be remedied with a thinner cost-per-pupil ratio than would be required by engaging in individualized, intensive, longer-term ACT. Although FACT has yet to be tested with youth, we believe this model is viable. The promising and growing literature on brief—and even single-session—interventions implemented with youth across a variety of settings, including schools, demonstrates that this intervention approach can substantially improve multiple mental health outcomes (Schleider et al., 2020). Thus, we encourage researchers interested in this topic to systematically try FACT with youth in schools and to compare FACT with other (non-ACT) brief intervention options (e.g., growth-mindset interventions; Schleider & Weisz, 2018).

Measuring ACT-Related Processes in Schools

In addition to advancing intervention and treatment models, much work is needed to improve the measurement of ACT-related processes in schools. The public health approach and MTSS assume that evidence-based assessment will be employed to identify the scope and severity of problems, which can then be matched with the appropriate level of support (Kilgus & von der Embse, 2019). However, measurement within the MTSS framework typically focuses on risk factors and outcomes, largely ignoring treatment mechanisms and therapeutic process variables. Given that ACT is premised on a theory of multidimensional and interacting processes of behavior change (Hayes et al., 2012), measurement of these variables might facilitate more appropriate and precise decision making regarding how to match students with appropriate tiers and types of ACT-based support. As with any other measures of psychological variables, however, measures of ACT-related processes should have acceptable technical characteristics for the population and context in which the assessment data is used to support their construct validity (Strauss & Smith, 2009). Generalizations regarding the validity of measures developed with adults or within clinical contexts are therefore insufficient for guiding decision making with youth in schools. Although a variety of ACT-related process measures have been developed—such as the Multidimensional Experiential Avoidance Questionnaire (Gámez et al., 2011), Cognitive Fusion Questionnaire (Gillanders et al., 2014), Valuing Questionnaire (Smout et al., 2014), Committed Action Questionnaire (McCracken, 2013), and the Multidimensional Psychological Flexibility Inventory (MPFI; Rolffs et al., 2016)—the available construct validity evidence for these measures, which largely omits children and adolescents, does not yet justify their use in schools.

To date, the ACT-related measure that appears to have the most empirical support for use with youth and in schools is the Avoidance and Fusion Questionnaire for Youth (AFQ-Y; Greco et al., 2008). The AFQ-Y is a 17-item (full version) or 8-item (short version) self-report rating scale that contains item content relating to two core processes targeted by ACT—cognitive fusion and experiential avoidance—and was based heavily on the adult-oriented Acceptance and Action Questionnaire (Hayes et al., 2004). Youth respond to the AFQ-Y's items using a 5-point scale ranging from *Not at All True* to *Very True*. The measure is used by calculating a sum score, with higher scores interpreted as reflecting greater degrees of psychological inflexibility. Although several studies have generated validity evidence supporting use of the AFQ-Y with youth in clinical and nonclinical community samples (e.g., Greco et al., 2008; Muris et al., 2017), it seems that only a single validation study supports use of the AFQ-Y for school mental health purposes. Specifically, Renshaw (2017) found adequate reliability and validity evidence for interpretation and use of the AFQ-Y as a universal screener for clinical levels of depression and anxiety among secondary students. Although this one study is surely better than none, it does not provide evidence to justify broad, multitiered applications of the AFQ-Y within school mental health services. Evidence is still lacking for demonstrating that the AFQ-Y could be used for evaluating the effectiveness of universal ACT-based prevention programming (e.g., *Connect*) or for monitoring students' responsiveness to targeted, group-based ACT (e.g., *The Thriving Adolescent*) in schools. Some intervention studies in schools have indeed measured changes in process variables (e.g., Sabaini, 2013, Takahashi et al., 2020), yet these have not been conducted with an orientation toward measurement validation. Thus, systematic and thorough lines of school-based research are warranted not only with the AFQ-Y but also with other ACT-related measures that might have treatment utility for informing efforts across the tiers of prevention.

Using ACT with Teachers and Other Educators

ACT in schools might expand its capacity for promoting human well-being by broadening its scope to target teachers and other educators. Our earlier review of the literature on ACT in schools focused exclusively on studies with youth, yet we also mentioned that ACT might additionally be used to benefit caregivers (e.g., Whittingham & Coyne, 2019) when school-based mental health professionals are collaborating with them to support home–school interventions. This same logic that extends applications of ACT to parents also suggests the use of ACT with teachers and other educators, such as administrators and paraprofessionals working in schools, as school-based providers often consult and collaborate with them, too. Moreover, with the growing concern regarding teacher stress and burnout, educators themselves have become the focus of intervention (e.g., Iancu et al., 2018). ACT might not only help teachers better support students but also target and improve teacher well-being, both of which are worthy goals within the school mental health context.

A few studies have already tested ACT-based interventions with school staff, yielding promising results. Jeffcoat and Hayes (2012) conducted a randomized waitlist-controlled trial with 236 K-12 educators, wherein participants in the treatment group received a self-help ACT book. They found statistically significant improvements in the treatment group across teachers' anxiety, depression, and stress outcomes. In another study, Biglan et al. (2013) conducted a randomized waitlist-controlled trial in which preschool teachers working with children with special needs participated in an ACT-based workshop. Those in the treatment condition evidenced statistically significant increases in mindful awareness and valued living as well as reductions in experiential avoidance. Similarly, McConachie et al. (2014) conducted a waitlist-controlled study wherein support staff working with children diagnosed with an intellectual disability or behavioral disorder participated in an ACT-based workshop. Their findings showed statistically significant reductions in psychological distress at posttest and reductions of thought suppression at follow-up. Taken together, these studies provide proof-of-concept evidence for expanding the scope of ACT to promote the well-being of teachers and other educators. However, given that other cognitive-behavioral interventions (e.g., Iancu et al., 2018) and even (non-ACT) mindfulness-based interventions (e.g., Klingbeil & Renshaw, 2018) have been shown to be effective for reducing burnout and improving teacher well-being, future research would do well to focus on the value-added of ACT compared to other available EBPs for promoting teacher well-being.

Conclusions

As we conclude this work, we wish to reemphasize several key conclusions that are especially beneficial guidelines for researchers and practitioners using ACT in schools. Here are our "top 10 take-home messages," which we hope readers will find both memorable and useful:

1. Many youth experience significant mental health problems, and, unfortunately, most do not access appropriate treatment.
2. For youth who do access treatment, school-based services are a substantial (and often de facto) source of mental health intervention.
3. MTSS in schools is a useful heuristic for applying a public health framework to address the mental health concerns of a local school population (see Figure 26.1).
4. As the "children in the river" parable illustrates, the public health approach is best viewed as complementary—rather than contrasting or mutually exclusive—with the clinical framework of mental health services.
5. Given its practical, flexible, principle-based, and transdiagnostic features, ACT is well suited to functioning as a *trans-tiered* intervention within MTSS in schools.
6. So far, the available evidence for ACT in schools suggests adequate support for use at the targeted level (tier 2), encouraging yet weaker support for applications at the universal level (tier 1), and promising yet extremely limited evidence at the intensive level (tier 3).
7. Component analysis or dismantling studies are needed to determine the value-added of ACT when used within treatment packages and in combination with other EBPs in schools.
8. More rigorous research designs are warranted to validate the connection between ACT's purported mechanisms of change and the outcomes produced by ACT-based interventions in schools.
9. Fruitful directions for furthering applications of ACT with youth in schools include testing the viability of FACT at the targeted level (tier 2) and pursuing systematic measure development studies that focus on the treatment utility of ACT-related process measures for informing supports across the tiers.
10. ACT in schools might expand its capacity for promoting human well-being by broadening its scope to target teachers and other educators.

References

American Academy of Pediatrics. (2001). Committee on Psychosocial Aspects of Child and Family Health. The new morbidity revisited: A renewed commitment to the psychosocial aspects of pediatric care. *Pediatrics, 108*(5), 1227–1230. https://doi.org/10.1542/peds.108.5.1227

Barandeh, N., Shafiabadi, A., & Farzad, V. (2017). A comparison of the effectiveness of acceptance and commitment therapy (ACT) and choice theory on the procrastination among female third-grade high school students in Shahriar County. *Journal of Fundamentals of Mental Health, 19*(3), 319–326. https://doi.org/10.22038/JFMH.2017.10869

Basarkod, G. (2019). *The six ways to well-being (6W-WeB): A new measure of valued action that targets the frequency and motivation for six behavioural patterns that promote well-being.* [Thesis, Australian Catholic University]. https://doi.org/10.26199/5dcc7d5fab0e8

Biglan, A., Layton, G. L., Jones, L. B., Hankins, M., & Rusby, J. C. (2013). The value of workshops on psychological flexibility for early childhood special education staff. *Topics in Early Childhood Special Education, 32*(4), 196–210. https://doi.org/10.1177/0271121411425191

Bitsko, R. H., Holbrook, J. R., Ghandour, R. M., Blumberg, S. J., Visser, S. N., Perou, R., & Walkup, J. T. (2018). Epidemiology and impact of health care provider–diagnosed anxiety and depression among US children. *Journal of Developmental and Behavioral Pediatrics, 39*(5), 395–403. https://doi.org/10.1097/dbp.0000000000000571

Brookshier, A. R. (2016). *Ameliorating anxiety in the school setting using acceptance and commitment therapy and mindfulness.* PhD dissertation, Northern Arizona University.

Burckhardt, R., Manicavasagar, V., Batterham, P. J., & Hadzi-Pavlovic, D. (2016). A randomized controlled trial of strong minds: A school-based mental health program combining acceptance and commitment therapy and positive psychology. *Journal of School Psychology, 57,* 41–52. https://doi.org/10.1016/j.jsp.2016.05.008

Burckhardt, R., Manicavasagar, V., Batterham, P. J., Hadzi-Pavlovic, D., & Shand, F. (2017). Acceptance and commitment therapy universal prevention program for adolescents: A feasibility study. *Child and Adolescent Psychiatry and Mental Health, 11*(1), 27. https://doi.org/10.1186/s13034-017-0164-5

Centers for Disease Control and Prevention. (2016a). *Sexual identity, sex of sexual contacts, and health-risk behaviors among students in 9-12: Youth risk behavior surveillance.* U.S. Department of Health and Human Services.

Centers for Disease Control and Prevention. (2016b). *WISQARS leading causes of death reports.* Washington, DC: U.S. Department of Health and Human Services.

Ciarrochi, J., Hayes, L., & Bailey, A. (2012). *Get out of your mind and into your life for teens: A guide to living an extraordinary life.* New Harbinger Publications.

Collishaw, S. (2015). Annual research review: Secular trends in child and adolescent mental health. *Journal of Child Psychology and Psychiatry, 56*(3), 370–393. https://doi.org/10.1111/jcpp.12372

Costello, E. J., He, J. P., Sampson, N. A., Kessler, R. C., & Merikangas, K. R. (2014). Services for adolescents with psychiatric disorders: 12-month data from the National Comorbidity Survey–Adolescent. *Psychiatric Services, 65*(3), 359–366. https://doi.org/10.1176/appi.ps.201100518

Coyne, L., & Murrell, A. (2009). *The joy of parenting: An acceptance and commitment therapy guide to effective parenting in the early years.* New Harbinger Publications.

Curtin, S. C., & Heron, M. (2019). Death rates due to suicide and homicide among persons aged 10–24: United States, 2000–2017. *NCHS Data Brief,* no. 352. Hyattsville, MD: National Center for Health Statistics. https://www.cdc.gov/nchs/data/databriefs/db352-h.pdf

Dixon, M. R. (2013). Don't stop believing: Journeys school. *Behavior Analysis in Practice, 6*(1), 78–79. https://doi.org/10.1007/BF03391793

Dixon, M. R., & Paliliunas, D. (2018). *AIM: A behavior analytic curriculum for social-emotional development in children.* Shawnee Scientific Press.

Duong, M. T., Bruns, E. J., Lee, K., Cox, S., Coifman, J., Mayworm, A., & Lyon, A. R. (2021). Rates of mental health service utilization by children and adolescents in schools and other common service settings: A systematic review and meta-analysis. *Administration and Policy in Mental Health and Mental Health Services Research, 48,* 420–439. https://doi.org/10.1007/s10488-020-01080-9

Dupéré, V., Dion, E., Nault-Brière, F., Archambault, I., Leventhal, T., & Lesage, A. (2018). Revisiting the link between depression symptoms and high school dropout: Timing of exposure matters. *Journal of Adolescent Health, 62*(2), 205–211. https://doi.org/10.1016/j.jadohealth.2017.09.024

Durlak, J. A., Weissberg, R. P., Dymnicki, A. B., Taylor, R. D., & Schellinger, K. B. (2011). The impact of enhancing students' social and emotional learning: A meta-analysis of school-based universal interventions. *Child Development, 82*(1), 405–432. https://doi.org/10.1111/j.1467-8624.2010.01564.x

Drum, D. J., & Figler, H. E. (1973). *Outreach in counselling: Applying the growth and prevention model in schools and colleges.* Intext Educational Services.

Fang, S., & Ding, D. (2020). The efficacy of group-based acceptance and commitment therapy on psychological capital and school engagement: A pilot study among Chinese adolescents. *Journal of Contextual Behavioral Science, 16,* 134–143. https://doi.org/10.1016/j.jcbs.2020.04.005

Gámez, W., Chmielewski, M., Kotov, R., Ruggero, C., & Watson, D. (2011). Development of a measure of experiential avoidance: The Multidimensional Experiential Avoidance Questionnaire. *Psychological Assessment, 23,* 692–713. https://doi.org/10.1037/a0023242

Ghandour, R. M., Sherman, L. J., Vladutiu, C. J., Ali, M. M., Lynch, S. E., Bitsko, R. H., & Blumberg, S. J. (2019). Prevalence and treatment of depression, anxiety, and conduct problems in US children. *Journal of Pediatrics, 206,* 256–267. https://doi.org/10.1016/j.jpeds.2018.09.021

Gillanders, D. T., Bolderston, H., Bond, F. W., Dempster, M., Flaxman, P. E., Campbell, L., Kerr, S., Tansey, L., Noel, P., Ferenbach, C., Masley, S., Roach, L., Lloyd, J., May, L., Clarke, S., & Remington, R. (2014). The development and initial validation of the Cognitive Fusion Questionnaire. *Behavior Therapy, 45,* 83–101. https://doi.org/10.1016/j.beth.2013.09.001

Glasser, W. (1998). *Choice theory: Redefining your personal freedom.* HarperCollins.

Gloster, A. T., Walder, N., Levin, M., Twohig, M., & Karekla, M. (2020). The empirical status of acceptance and commitment therapy: A review of meta-analyses. *Journal of Contextual Behavioral Science, 18*, 181–192. https://doi.org/10.1016/j.jcbs.2020.09.009

Glover, N. G., Sylvers, P. D., Shearer, E. M., Kane, M.-C., Clasen, P. C., Epler, A. J., Plumb-Vilardaga, J. C., Bonow, J. T., & Jakupcak, M. (2016). The efficacy of focused acceptance and commitment therapy in VA primary care. *Psychological Services, 13*(2), 156–161. https://doi.org/10.1037/ser0000062

Greco, L. A., Lambert, W., & Baer, R. A. (2008). Psychological inflexibility in childhood and adolescence: Development and evaluation of the Avoidance and Fusion Questionnaire for Youth. *Psychological Assessment, 20*, 93–102. https://doi.org/10.1037/1040-3590.20.2.93

Harris, E., & Samuel, V. (2020). Acceptance and commitment therapy: A systematic literature review of prevention and intervention programs for mental health difficulties in children and young people. *Journal of Cognitive Psychotherapy, 34*(4), 280–305. https://doi.org/10.1891/JCPSY-D-20-00001

Hayes, L. L., & Ciarrochi, J. V. (2015). *The thriving adolescent: Using acceptance and commitment therapy and positive psychology to help teens manage emotions, achieve goals, and build connection.* New Harbinger Publications.

Hayes, S. C., Strosahl, K. D., & Wilson, K. G. (2012). *Acceptance and commitment therapy: The process and practice of mindful change* (2nd ed.). Guilford Press.

Hayes, S. C., Strosahl, K. D., Wilson, K. G., Bissett, R. T., Pistorello, J., Toarmino, D., Polusny, M. A., Dykstra, T. A., Batten, S. V., Bergan, J., Stewart, S. H., Zvolensky, M. J., Eifert, G. H., Bond, F. W., Forsyth, J. P., Karekla, M., & McCurry, S. M. (2004). Measuring experiential avoidance: A preliminary test of a working model. *The Psychological Record, 54*, 553–578. https://doi.org/10.1007/BF03395492

Herman, K. C., Reinke, W. M., & Thompson, A. M. (2020). Prevention science as a platform for solving major societal problems and improving population health. *Journal of Prevention and Health Promotion, 1*(1), 131–151. https://doi.org/10.1177/2632077020948786

Iancu, A. E., Rusu, A., Măroiu, C., Păcurar, R., & Maricuţoiu, L. P. (2018). The effectiveness of interventions aimed at reducing teacher burnout: A meta-analysis. *Educational Psychology Review, 30*(2), 373–396. https://doi.org/10.1007/s10648-017-9420-8

Jeffcoat, T., & Hayes, S. C. (2012). A randomized trial of ACT bibliotherapy on the mental health of K-12 teachers and staff. *Behaviour Research and Therapy, 50*(9), 571–579. https://doi.org/10.1016/j.brat.2012.05.008

Kazdin, A. E., & Nock, M. K. (2003). Delineating mechanisms of change in child and adolescent therapy: Methodological issues and research recommendations. *Journal of Child Psychology and Psychiatry, 44*(8), 1116–1129. https://doi.org/10.1111/1469-7610.00195

Kilgus, S. P., & von der Embse, N. P. (2019). General model of service delivery for school-based interventions. In K. C. Radley & E. H. Dart (Eds.), *Handbook of behavioral interventions in schools* (pp. 106–133). Oxford University Press.

Klingbeil, D. A., & Renshaw, T. L. (2018). Mindfulness-based interventions for teachers: A meta-analysis of the emerging evidence-base. *School Psychology Quarterly, 33*, 501–511. https://doi.org/10.1037/spq0000291

Klingbeil, D. A., Renshaw, T. L., Willenbrink, J. B., Copek, R. A., Chan, K. T., Haddock, A., Yassine, J., & Clifton, J. (2017). Mindfulness-based interventions with youth: A comprehensive meta-analysis of group-design studies. *Journal of School Psychology, 63*, 77–103. https://doi.org/10.1016/j.jsp.2017.03.006

Kohtala, A., Lappalainen, R., Savonen, L., Timo, E., & Tolvanen, A. (2015). A four-session acceptance and commitment therapy based intervention for depressive symptoms delivered by Masters degree level psychology students: A preliminary Study. *Behavioural and Cognitive Psychotherapy, 43*(3), 360–373. https://doi.org/10.1017/S1352465813000969

Lintz, M. J., Thurstone, C., Hull, M., & Ladegard, K. (2019). Development of a school-based substance treatment model. *Journal of Child and Adolescent Substance Abuse, 28*(2), 127–131. https://doi.org/10.1080/1067828X.2019.1623145

Lipari, R. N., Hedden, S., Blau, G., & Rubenstein, L. (2016). *Adolescent mental health service use and reasons for using services in specialty, educational, and general medical settings.* U.S. Substance Abuse and Mental Health Services Administration. https://www.samhsa.gov/data/sites/default/files/report_1973/ShortReport-1973.html

Livheim, F., Hayes, L., Ghaderi, A., Magnusdottir, T., Högfeldt, A., Rowse, J., Turner, S., Hayes, S. C., & Tengström, A. (2015). The effectiveness of acceptance and commitment therapy for adolescent mental health: Swedish and Australian pilot outcomes. *Journal of Child and Family Studies, 24*(4), 1016–1030. https://doi.org/10.1007/s10826-014-9912-9

Livings, J. E. (2017). *Taking ACTion on anger: A feasibility study investigating the effectiveness and acceptability of an ACT-based anger intervention for adolescent males in a school-context.* PhD dissertation, University of Surrey.

Luciano, C., Ruiz, F. J., Torres, R. M. V., Martín, V. S., Martínez, O. G., & López, J. C. L. (2011). A relational frame analysis of defusion interactions in acceptance and commitment therapy. A preliminary and quasi-experimental study with at-risk adolescents. *International Journal of Psychology and Psychological Therapy, 11*(2), 165–182. https://doi.org/10.1002/jeab.68

Marchette, L. K., & Weisz, J. R. (2017). Empirical evolution of youth psychotherapy toward transdiagnostic approaches. *Journal of Child Psychology and Psychiatry, 58*, 970–984. https://doi.org/10.1111/jcpp.12747

Merikangas, K. R., He, J. P., Burstein, M., Swanson, S. A., Avenevoli, S., Cui, L., Benjet, C., Georgiades, K., & Swendsen, J. (2010). Lifetime prevalence of mental disorders in US adolescents: results from the National Comorbidity Survey Replication–Adolescent Supplement (NCS-A). *Journal of the American Academy of Child and Adolescent Psychiatry, 49*(10), 980–989. https://doi.org/10.1016/j.jaac.2010.05.017

Merrell, K. W., Ervin, R., Gimpel Peacock, G., & Renshaw, T. L. (2022). *School psychology for the 21st century* (3rd ed.). Guilford Press.

McConachie, D. A. J., McKenzie, K., Morris, P. G., & Walley, R. M. (2014). Acceptance and mindfulness-based stress management for support staff caring for individuals with intellectual disabilities. *Research in Developmental Disabilities, 35*(6), 1216–1227. https://doi.org/10.1016/j.ridd.2014.03.005

McCracken, L. M. (2013). Committed action: An application of the psychological flexibility model to activity patterns in chronic pain. *Journal of Pain, 14*, 828–835. https://doi.org/10.1016/j.jpain.2013.02.009

Mirzahosseini, H., Pourabdol, S., & Sobhi Gharamaleki, N. (2016). Saravani Sh. [The effect of acceptance and commitment therapy in decreasing cognitive avoidance among students with specific learning disorder (SLD) (Persian)]. *Iranian Journal of Psychiatry and Clinical Psychology, 22*(3), 166–175. https://doi.org/10.18869/acadpub.ijpcp.22.3.166

Mojtabai, R., Olfson, M., & Han, B. (2016). National trends in the prevalence and treatment of depression in adolescents and young adults. *Pediatrics, 138*(6), e20161878. https://doi.org/10.1542/peds.2016-1878

Muris, P., Meesters, C., Herings, A., Jansen, M., Vossen, C., & Kersten, P. (2017). Inflexible youngsters: Psychological and psychopathological correlates of the Avoidance and Fusion Questionnaire for Youths in nonclinical Dutch adolescents. *Mindfulness, 8*(5), 1381–1392. https://doi.org/10.1007/s12671-017-0714-1

Murrell, A. R., Steinberg, D. S., Connally, M. L., Hulsey, T., & Hogan, E. (2015). Acting out to ACTing on: A preliminary investigation in youth with ADHD and co-morbid disorders. *Journal of Child and family Studies, 24*(7), 2174–2181. https://doi.org/10.1007/s10826-014-0020-7

Murphy, J. M., Guzmán, J., McCarthy, A. E., Squicciarini, A. M., George, M., Canenguez, K. M., Dunn, E. C., Baer, L., Simonsohn, A., Smoller, J. W., & Jellinek, M. S. (2015). Mental health predicts better academic outcomes: A longitudinal study of elementary school students in Chile. *Child Psychiatry and Human Development, 46*(2), 245–256. https://doi.org/10.1007/s10578-014-0464-4

Mychailyszyn, M. P., Brodman, D. M., Read, K. L., & Kendall, P. C. (2012). Cognitive-behavioral school-based interventions for anxious and depressed youth: A meta-analysis of outcomes. *Clinical Psychology: Science and Practice, 19*(2), 129–153. https://doi.org/10.1111/j.1468-2850.2012.01279.x

Pahnke, J., Lundgren, T., Hursti, T., & Hirvikoski, T. (2014). Outcomes of an acceptance and commitment therapy-based skills training group for students with high-functioning autism spectrum disorder: A quasi-experimental pilot study. *Autism, 18*(8), 953–964. https://doi.org/10.1177/1362361313501091

Pentcheva-Burns, M. (2015). *Effects of acceptance and commitment therapy for diverse symptomatology in immigrant youth.* PhD dissertation, Hofstra University.

Renshaw, T. L. (2017). Screening for psychological inflexibility: Initial validation of the Avoidance and Fusion Questionnaire for Youth as a school mental health screener. *Journal of Psychoeducational Assessment, 35*, 482–493. https://doi.org/10.1177/0734282916644096

Renshaw, T. L., Bolognino, S. J., Roberson, A. J., Upton, S. R., & Hammons, K. N. (2017). Using acceptance and commitment therapy to support bereaved students. In J. A. Brown & S. R. Jimerson (Eds.), *Supporting bereaved students at school* (pp. 223–235). Oxford University Press.

Rolffs, J. L., Rogge, R. D., & Wilson, K. G. (2016). Disentangling components of flexibility via the hexaflex model development and validation of the Multidimensional Psychological Flexibility Inventory (MPFI). *Assessment, 25*, 458–482. https://doi.org/10.1177/1073191116645905

Sabaini, K. D. (2013). *Evaluating the impact of acceptance and commitment therapy on children with emotional and behavioral disorders.* Master's thesis, Southern Illinois University.

Sanchez, A. L., Cornacchio, D., Poznanski, B., Golik, A. M., Chou, T., & Comer, J. S. (2018). The effectiveness of school-based mental health services for elementary-aged children: A meta-analysis. *Journal of the American Academy of Child and Adolescent Psychiatry, 57*(3), 153–165. https://doi.org/10.1016/j.jaac.2017.11.022

Schleider, J. L., Dobias, M. L., Sung, J. Y., & Mullarkey, M. C. (2020). Future directions in single-session youth mental health interventions. *Journal of Clinical Child and Adolescent Psychology, 49*(2), 264–278. https://doi.org/10.1080/15374416.2019.1683852

Schleider, J., & Weisz, J. (2018). A single-session growth mindset intervention for adolescent anxiety and depression: 9-month outcomes of a randomized trial. *Journal of Child Psychology and Psychiatry, 59*(2), 160–170. https://doi.org/10.1111/jcpp.12811

Shernoff, E. S., Bearman, S. K., & Kratochwill, T. R. (2017). Training the next generation of school psychologists to deliver evidence-based mental health practices: Current challenges and future directions. *School Psychology Review, 46*(2), 219–232. https://doi.org/10.17105/SPR-2015-0118.V46.2

Skowyra, K. R., & Cocozza, J. J. (2007). *Blueprint for change: A comprehensive model for the identification and treatment of youth with mental health needs in contact with the juvenile justice system.* Delmar, NY: Policy Research Associates.

Smout, M., Davies, M., Burns, N., & Christie, A. (2014). Development of the Valuing Questionnaire (VQ). *Journal of Contextual Behavioral Science, 3,* 164–172. http://dx.doi.org/10.1016/j.jcbs.2014.06.001

Stoiber, K. C. (2014). A comprehensive framework for multitiered systems of support in school psychology. In P. L. Harrison & A. Thomas (Eds.), *Best practices in school psychology: Data-based and collaborative decision making* (pp. 41–69). National Association of School Psychologists.

Strauss, M. E., & Smith, G. T. (2009). Construct validity: Advances in theory and methodology. *Annual Review of Clinical Psychology, 5,* 1–25. https://doi.org/10.1146/annurev.clinpsy.032408.153639

Strosahl, K., Gustavson, T., & Robinson, P. (2012). *Brief interventions for radical change: Principles and practice of focused acceptance commitment therapy.* New Harbinger Publications.

Takahashi, F., Ishizu, K., Matsubara, K., Ohtsuki, T., & Shimoda, Y. (2020). Acceptance and commitment therapy as a school-based group intervention for adolescents: An open-label trial. *Journal of Contextual Behavioral Science, 16,* 71–79. https://doi.org/10.1016/j.jcbs.2020.03.001

Turrell, S. L., & Bell, M. (2016). *ACT for adolescents: Treating teens and adolescents in individual and group therapy.* New Harbinger Publications.

Turrell, S. L., McCurry, C., & Bell, M. (2018). *The mindfulness and acceptance workbook for teen anxiety.* New Harbinger Publications.

Twenge, J. M., Cooper, A. B., Joiner, T. E., Duffy, M. E., & Binau, S. G. (2019). Age, period, and cohort trends in mood disorder indicators and suicide-related outcomes in a nationally representative dataset, 2005–2017. *Journal of Abnormal Psychology, 128*(3), 185–199. https://doi.org/10.1037/abn0000410.supp

Twohig, M. P., Hayes, S. C., & Berlin, K. S. (2008). Acceptance and commitment therapy for childhood externalizing disorders. In L. A. Greco & S. C. Hayes (Eds.), *Acceptance and mindfulness treatments for children and adolescents* (pp. 163–186). New Harbinger Publications.

Van der Gucht, K., Griffith, J. W., Hellemans, R., Bockstaele, M., Pascal-Claes, F., & Raes, F. (2017). Acceptance and commitment therapy (ACT) for adolescents: Outcomes of a large-sample, school-based, cluster-randomized controlled trial. *Mindfulness, 8*(2), 408–416. https://doi.org/10.1007/s12671-016-0612-y

Villagrana, M. (2010). Mental health services for children and youth in the child welfare system: A focus on caregivers as gatekeepers. *Children and Youth Services Review, 32*(5), 691–697. https://doi.org/10.1016/j.childyouth.2010.01.005

Weist, M. D., Evans, S. W., & Lever, N. A. (Eds.). (2014). *Handbook of school mental health: Advancing practice and research* (2nd ed.). Springer.

Weist, M. D., Myers, C. P., Hastings, E., Ghuman, H., & Han, Y. L. (1999). Psychosocial functioning of youth receiving mental health services in the schools versus community mental health centers. *Community Mental Health Journal, 35*(1), 69–81. https://doi.org/10.1097/CHI.0b013e318199970

Weisz, J. R., Kuppens, S., Eckshtain, D., Ugueto, A. M., Hawley, K. M., & Jensen-Doss, A. (2013). Performance of evidence-based youth psychotherapies compared with usual clinical care: A multilevel meta-analysis. *JAMA Psychiatry, 70*(7), 750–761. https://doi.org/10.1001/jamapsychiatry.2013.1176

Whitney, D. G., & Peterson, M. D. (2019). US national and state-level prevalence of mental health disorders and disparities of mental health care use in children. *JAMA Pediatrics, 173*(4), 389–391. https://doi.org/10.1001/jamapediatrics.2018.5399

Whittingham, K., & Coyne, L. (2019). *Acceptance and commitment therapy: The clinician's guide for supporting parents.* Academic Press.

Wilson, A.N., Dzugan, E. & Hutchinson, V.D. (2022). Using a nonconcurrent multiple-baseline across-participants design to examine the effects of individualized ACT at school. *Behavior Analysis Practice, 15,* 141–154. https://doi.org/10.1007/s40617-021-00558-8

Wyman, P. A., Brown, C. H., LoMurray, M., Schmeelk-Cone, K., Petrova, M., Yu, Q., Walsh, E., Tu, X., & Wang, W. (2010). An outcome evaluation of the sources of strength suicide prevention program delivered by adolescent peer leaders in high schools. *American Journal of Public Health, 100*(9), 1653–1661. https://doi.org/10.2105/AJPH.2009.190025

CHAPTER 27

ACT for Children and Adolescents

Julie M. Petersen, Louise Hayes, Duncan Gillard, *and* Joseph Ciarrochi

Abstract

Mental health concerns among children and adolescents are a common and growing international concern. Working with youth requires a developmental lens in order to capture the range of changes and contexts that younger populations experience. This article reviews the rationale, implementation, and research on acceptance and commitment therapy (ACT) for youth, with a specific focus on the DNA-V (Discoverer, Noticer, Advisor, and Values) model. Discussed here are challenges (e.g., working with parents) and future directions (e.g., diverse samples, longitudinal study designs) in researching and applying ACT. Overall, significant preliminary evidence supports the use of ACT with younger populations, particularly within certain conditions (e.g., chronic pain).

Key Words: children, adolescents, acceptance and commitment therapy, youth, DNA-V

Overview of Mental Health in Children and Adolescents

Mental health problems in youth are a serious global concern. In one larger meta-analysis of children and adolescents (n = 87,742 across 41 studies), the worldwide prevalence of mental disorders was 13.4% (Polanczyk, Salum, Sugaya, Caye, & Rohde, 2015). In children alone, international studies have established a high prevalence of mental health disorders; a European study (n = 7,682) found 12.8% of children report mental health concerns (Kovess-Masfety et al., 2016); a U.S. study (n = 46.6 million children) found 16.5% (7.7 million) reporting at least one mental health diagnosis (Whitney & Peterson, 2019); and a Canadian study found a 6-month prevalence of 18.2–21.8% for DSM-IV diagnoses in children (Georgiades et al., 2019). Adolescents are also considered at high risk, with up to two of every five adolescents meeting criteria for a mental disorder at the level labeled as severe impairment (Deighton et al., 2019).

Within these concerning numbers, certain disorders are more prevalent than others across age groups. Behavioral disorders are often considered more common in children, while anxiety disorders are most common in adolescents (Georgiades et al., 2019). Some international studies indicate that anxiety disorders are the most common in youth overall, with a worldwide prevalence of 6.5%, followed by depressive disorders (2.6%), attention-deficit/hyperactivity disorder (ADHD; 3.4%), oppositional defiant disorder (ODD; 3.6%), and conduct disorder (2.1%; Polanczyk et al., 2015). In the United States, anxiety disorders in youth are even more prevalent, with estimates as high as 31.9%, along with mood disorders at 14.3% (Erskine et al., 2017; Merikangas et al., 2010). The concern about youth mental health is only growing; for example, the 12-month prevalence of major depressive episodes in adolescents and young adults increased significantly from 8.8% in 2004 to 11.3% in 2014—an increase that is still significant even after controlling for sociodemographic variables and substance use (Mojtabai, Olfson, & Han, 2016). Finally, adolescence often marks the onset of lifelong problems, with 75% of mental illnesses emerging before the age of 25 years (McGorry & Mei, 2018).

Youth with anxiety and/or depressive disorders report significant life impairment across a wide range of domains such as school, social activities, and relationships (de Lijster et al., 2018). Mental health concerns are also associated with decreased overall well-being in adolescents and children (Arslan, 2018; Sharpe et al., 2016). Making matters worse, adolescents who need mental health support often fail to receive it (Sheppard, Deane, & Ciarrochi, 2018). These statistics speak to the need for developmentally appropriate and evidence-based psychological treatments for children and adolescents. Putting the largest investments in adult treatments is clearly the ambulance at the bottom of the cliff.

Development in Context

Working with children and adolescents requires the use of a developmental framework. The contextual behavioral science (CBS) approach (e.g., acceptance and commitment therapy) frames childhood and adolescence contextually, arguing that young people are adapting to whatever factors are presented during their development period, rather than only to symptoms (L. L. Hayes & Ciarrochi, 2015b). Therapists need to consider what is developmentally typical for a child's age (e.g., magical thinking is common in children ages 2–7; Arnold, 2017) and what might be outside norms but still adaptive within each child's context (e.g., yelling might be adaptive within one family's context but not another's). Typical development includes the ability to identify simple emotions in childhood ("I feel sad") and more complex emotional states in adolescence ("I feel sad and angry now but will feel better later"; Rowsell, Ciarrochi, Deane, & Heaven, 2016). However, an individual client's ability will depend on their own context (Sauter, Heyne, & Michiel Westenberg, 2009). For example, a young child may need more guidance in labeling, processing, and expressing their emotions than an adolescent—but not always (Arnold, 2017).

As youth develop, they become independent within ever widening external learning contexts (family, school, community) as well as their own internal learning context (behaviors, emotions, and verbal stimuli). For example, children are often taught that some feelings are "good" and desirable (e.g., happiness), while others are "bad" (e.g., anxiety) and should be avoided. A child may be told that crying is bad and thereby learns that crying should be avoided—and then may generalize this teaching to sadness overall. Thus, there is a gradual process of adapting *into* behaviors such as fear and avoidance, as well as inflexibly with thoughts, feelings, and meta-emotions (feelings about feelings).

Adolescence is particularly marked by strong emotions, risk-taking, sensation-seeking, and changes to family relationships (L. L. Hayes & Ciarrochi, 2015a). Notably, it is not just human adolescents that display these characteristics; animals show the same patterns (e.g., Spear, 2004). The similarities between human and nonhuman animals support the thesis that these characteristics have provided evolutionary advantage to adolescents. In modern contexts, risk-taking is frequently framed as inappropriate; however, across the history of humanity, it is necessary to build survival skills. Thus, a contextually informed approach allows problem behaviors to be seen as adaptive and an adolescent's context to be examined for contingent influences. For example, an adolescent lashing out at a teacher may actually be evidence of adaptive behavior if the adolescent's social context reinforced rebellion in order to "fit in" and gain social power among peers. As another example, to manage powerful emotions, an adolescent may turn to avoidance and rigid self-rules (e.g., staying in their room and self-harming) in order to adapt to a familial context where emotions are discouraged.

Metacognitive abilities improve throughout adolescence (Weil et al., 2013), but this improvement does not necessarily translate to greater flexibility as adults. There is evidence that youth are *more* flexible than adults in responding to new and novel situations (Gopnik et al., 2017), with some arguing that adolescence is a sweet spot primed for intervention before the full onset of the costs and concerns of adulthood are present (Riede, Johannsen, Högberg, Nowell, & Lombard, 2018). As humans approach adulthood, their verbal world gains strength, placing them at the mercy of internal self-created rules (e.g., "I am a loser," "I am not smart enough"). Thus, working with adolescents gives us opportunity for social and individual change. We need to be mindful of their developing internal world and build their flexibility in ways that foster vitality, helping them avoid being swept away by impulsivity or becoming rigid adults. Overall, childhood and adolescence are fruitful times for psychological intervention because there is a greater capacity for flexibly changing.

In addition to their internal worlds, young people's social context is critical for growth. Adolescents explore their own independence, push boundaries, and broaden their reliance to include friends and peers as well as parents (Moss, Land, & Tuttle, 2017). Their activities change too. Children's social relationships frequently revolve around play activities, whereas adolescent relationships focus on friendship qualities such as intimacy and loyalty (L. L. Hayes & Ciarrochi, 2015a). The struggle to feel close in relationships contributes to adolescent motivation to fit in, even if their actions are inconsistent with their personal values or goals. It is a complex task to navigate friendships, sexual/romantic relationships, school, and more, while also learning to stay true to themselves and their needs. Challenging transitions (e.g., the shift between dependence on family to independence, from high school to college) are distinct to youth and often inform self-esteem and self-perspectives, in the moment and into adulthood. With this idea in mind, social and identity exploration should be considered adaptations that will shift over time; this is why adolescence is synonymous with exploration. For example, an adolescent dying their hair blue may be "trying on" an identity while they navigate new friend circles.

Familial context is also central to youth social functioning. Across thousands of examples, families have been shown to teach and model rules about emotions, thoughts, or behaviors (e.g., Granic, Hollenstein, Dishion, & Patterson, 2003). For example, families may fail to teach the importance of emotional identification (e.g., a parent saying, "Don't tell me you're anxious") or may enforce unhelpful rules around self-worth or behavior (e.g., "You are only as good as your latest performance"). The rules children learn are often related to their caretaker's mental health too. For example, experiential avoidance in mothers is associated with distress and child behavior problems in preschoolers (Shea & Coyne, 2011). Authoritarian (cold and controlling) parenting style predicts the development of psychological inflexibility in adolescents (Williams, Ciarrochi, & Heaven, 2012). In contrast, nurturing familial contexts tend to report fewer negative outcomes (e.g., mental health concerns; Perry, Dollar, Calkins, Keane, & Shanahan, 2020). Adolescents may also struggle with finding meaning within their own familial context. For example, parents may set rules around an adolescent's behavior that is not reinforcing (e.g., encouraging good grades at the expense of mental health; valuing achievement as opposed to a love of exploration; L. L. Hayes & Ciarrochi, 2015b). In response, teenagers may rebel against their caretakers (e.g., neglect homework, break curfews) trying to get their needs met in their ever-changing social milieu.

Overarching Goals of Working with Children and Adolescents

Despite the concerning prevalence of youth mental health problems and the broader challenges of growing up, appropriate psychological health care is still difficult to find (Sheppard et al., 2018). In the United States and Canada, for example, 40–72% of families report not currently receiving necessary mental health care (Georgiades et al., 2019; Whitney & Peterson, 2019). Evidence-based care to improve child and adolescent mental health is crucially needed. The broad foundation of contextual behavioral science, and its applied technology of acceptance and commitment therapy, provides a way to step into this breach because it is a paradigm that can be developmental *and* contextual. It gives us a way to emphasize working with children and adolescents so that they develop functional behaviors and skills that will serve them their whole lives. We must look beyond psychopathology in youth and turn toward encouraging learning and growth—a holistic approach that goes beyond symptom reduction.

ACT is aimed at achieving psychological flexibility. Traditional adult ACT models define psychological flexibility as the ability to remain in the present moment and/or use attention flexibly in order to move toward what is functional and/or valued, despite difficult internal or external experiences (S. C. Hayes, Luoma, Bond, Masuda, & Lillis, 2006). Depending on the developmental level of youth, connecting psychological flexibility to values that are enduring is developmentally challenging and sometimes inappropriate. Younger populations cannot be expected to know what they want their life to be about, and they are exploring their identity in order to find out. Knowing what they value in an adult sense of the word takes years. However, they can value how they want to be today and work on what brings them vitality, as well as being consistent with a growing sense of self. For example, an adolescent may feel committed to physical health one week and yet go out binge drinking with friends another week. Considering their choices around these actions takes time. Nevertheless, to work with youth means to continually remember that they are still growing; they are still learning how to process internal experiences and orient to what they want their lives to be about. Thus, working with children and adolescents supports them as they move toward independence, psychological flexibility, and what a valued life might mean to *them*.

Conceptual Model of ACT for Children and Adolescents

A number of frameworks and tools can be used to put ACT processes into play, such as the hexaflex (S. C. Hayes, Strosahl, & Wilson, 2016), the "Matrix" (Polk & Schoendorff, 2014), and the choice point (Bailey, Ciarrochi, & Harris, 2014). However, further adaptations that account for the aforementioned developmental imperatives are necessary. One such adaptation is DNA-V (L. L. Hayes & Ciarrochi, 2015a). DNA-V demonstrates how the adaptation of adult work must avoid a top-down style (i.e., taking adult concepts and making them simpler), but instead account in a *growth-up* way for how young people grow and adapt in context.

The DNA-V Model for ACT with Youth

DNA-V is an applied model for youth nested within CBS and aims to address the evolutionary streams of human adaptation. It incorporates all multiple CBS streams of knowledge: evolutionary science (Wilson, Hayes, Biglan, & Embry, 2014), behavioral principles (Skinner, 1965), relational frame theory (S. C. Hayes, Barnes-Holmes, & Roche, 2001), acceptance and commitment therapy (S. C. Hayes et al., 2016), and positive psychology and self-determination theory (Ciarrochi, Atkins, Hayes, Sahdra, & Parker, 2016; Ciarrochi, Sahdra, Yap, & Dicke, 2020). It is a bottom-up model that considers how humans grow from birth into adulthood. DNA stands for three classes of behavior that are labeled Discoverer (D), Noticer (N), and Advisor (A). These classes of behavior are present in all humans and are optimally used in the service of vitality and valued action (V). This V is the target of the model, upskilling young people to use their behaviors to build well-being. A graphical representation of the model is presented in Figure 27.1.

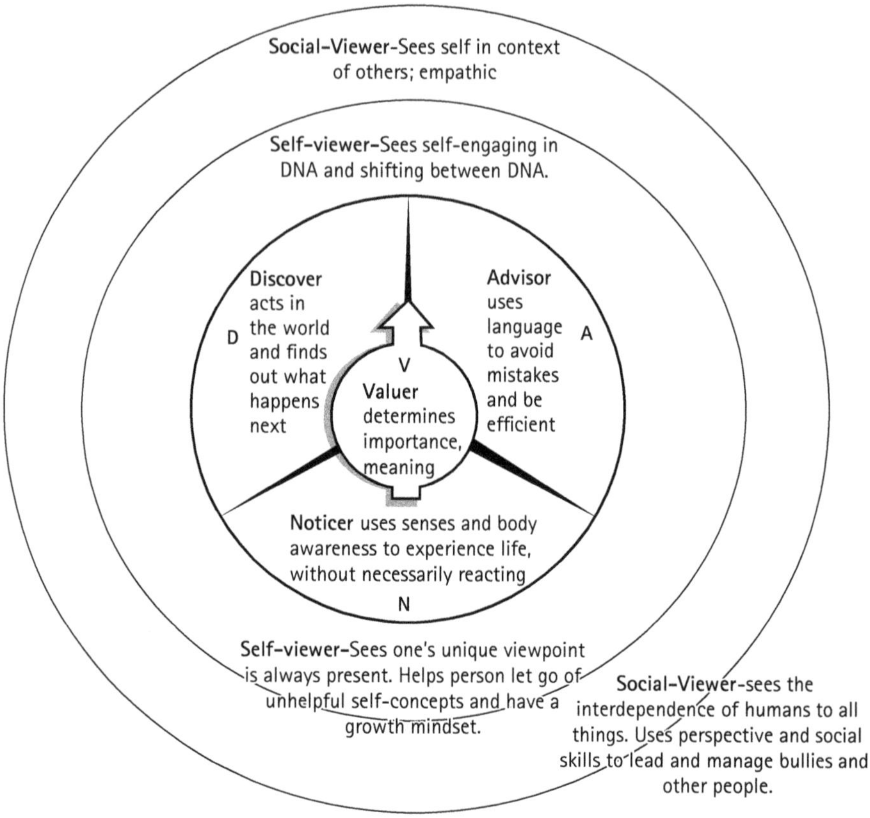

Figure 27.1: DNA-V

Values and vitality are the center of DNA-V. Everything we do in the DNA-V model is in the service of "The V," or what actions the young person considers meaningful, important, energizing, or fun. These actions also tend to create energy or vitality, benefiting them as a whole person. Examples might include connecting with others, being active, or challenging oneself. The values part of the disk is depicted with a dial, which indicates that we move the dial to one of the other elements (D, N, or A), depending on what builds their V within a given moment. It is surrounded by contexts of the self, social world (called self-view and social view to young people), and the external world (not depicted in the image). A brief description of each class of behavior follows (for more detail, see L. L. Hayes & Ciarrochi, 2015a).

ADVISOR

The advisor is a label that captures a person's inner voice or self-talk; technically, it represents using verbal behavior in order to navigate their life. and it includes such language behaviors as predicting, evaluating, judging, setting up rules for self and others, and problem-solving. All of these actions use past history and learning for the purpose of avoiding trial and error. A person's advisor is "trained" as they grow; for example, a parent might advise their child to always look both ways before crossing the street. Over time, the child will internalize this advice as a rule and say to themselves "look both ways." This human language capacity is a superb adaptation for survival, except when it is overused. Thus, the advisor is considered a helpful adaption when one's self-talk builds value, engages in constructive problem solving, or saves one from danger. It is less helpful when the advice is rigid rules, self-criticism (e.g., "My life is not worth living") or used for problem solving that does not help the child progress but instead becomes patterns of excessive worry or rumination (e.g., "What if something bad happens?"). If the self-advice is not helpful, we encourage young people to disengage from their advisor. We focus on four ways to build flexible self-advice: (1) understanding the advisor's role as that of looking out for danger, (2) testing the helpfulness of their self-talk (it is helpful if it builds their V), (3) defusing if they feel stuck by stepping into another part of DNA-V or using defusion tasks, and (4) creating and testing new rules.

NOTICER

The term *noticer* refers to the ability to have a somatic and sensory awareness of the world that is both inside and outside of us. We are all born as noticers, and, from the moment of birth, we take in the world with our senses. Over time, this ability changes so that our emotions and awareness can be *interpreted* rather than merely experienced as pleasant or unpleasant without judgment (Barrett, 2017). Noticer is informed by biological theories of adaptation and attachment learning (Bowlby, 1979). It focuses on building this skill so that the young person can learn to respond with awareness rather than be reactive to their inner self. Noticer involves not only attending to experience, but also allowing experiences to come and go, without destructive forms of clinging, avoiding, and impulsive actions. This process captures three ACT processes: acceptance, defusion, and contact-with-the-present moment.

DISCOVERER

The discoverer label denotes trial-and-error behavior with the goal of learning from experience. For children, it is the ability to manipulate the world; for toddlers, it is to stand up and fall down, to throw food off the high-chair, and delight in the ability to make things happen. Discoverer is children learning through play, which is a cross-species evolutionary adaptation that facilitates learning of the physical and social world (Gray, 2009). In adolescence, discovery shifts from play to risk-taking, sensation-seeking, and changes in relationships. Again, these changes are mimicked across the species, indicating evolutionary adaptations (Spear, 2004). Thus, a discover "acts" and then "tracks" the short-term consequences of action, and as the young person ages, they learn to track the long-term consequences of their action. The successful discoverer broadens and builds skills, resources, and social networks. Whereas the advisor helps us avoid trial and error, discoverer deliberately seeks out trial and error. The discoverer is most similar to ACT's notion of committed action and then brings in elements of self-determination theory (Ryan & Deci, 2017) and broad and build theory (Fredrickson, 2004).

One might think of D, N, and A as, respectively, doer, experiencer, and thinker. We can display all three of these classes of behavior within just one moment. DNA-V are foundational skills in the model. Outside these skills are factors that can influence DNA-V, including self-view, social view, and other aspects of context. (see Figure 27.1).

Self-view is most similar to the ACT notion of self-as-context and self-as-process (see McHugh & Stapleton, this volume), what we term simply as the "flexible self" (see Figure 27.2). Flexible self involves the ability to see one's discoverer, noticer, and advisor as changing and to recognize that each small action of thinking, feeling, or acting is only a small part of the whole self. In contrast, fixed view sees aspects of D, N, and A as being "true descriptions" of oneself, the same way that "ceramic" might be a description of a plate. Supporting young people to grow with a flexible view helps them to see that they can grow beyond their perceived limitations and to have a more compassionate view of themselves.

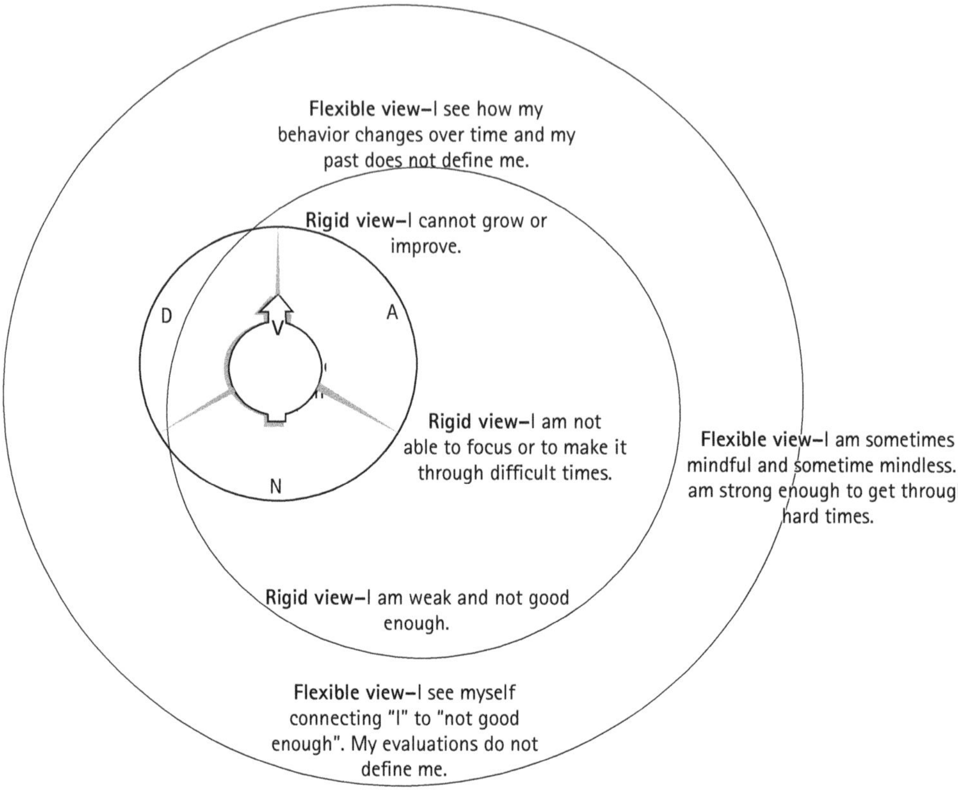

Figure 27.2. Self-view

Social view refers to the reciprocal changes that occur during development because humans grow within a social milieu. All of our being adapts within our social world, and we eventually change it, along with others around us. This adaptation begins with attachment and nurturing in infancy, resting on seminal attachment research by Bowlby (1979), neurodevelopmental work by Porges (e.g., Porges & Furman, 2011), and anthropological work such as Hrdy (2009). As young people grow, we look at how the social strategies they have learned in one context (e.g., adaptive avoidance within the family) can be overgeneralized to other contexts (e.g., maladaptive avoidance in school). Positive development involves young people taking on the broader perspectives of others, considering their views, having empathy, and building relationships. Social view rests on the ACT foundation of relational frame theory and evolutionary adaptation in context to consider perspective-taking skills and to build on them.

Assessment

Few measures of ACT and ACT-related processes exist for youth populations. The Avoidance and Fusion Questionnaire for Youth (AFQY) is the only validated measure of psychological inflexibility in youth (Greco, Lambert, & Baer, 2008). The AFQY, available in both short (8-item) and long (17-item) forms, focuses specifically on experiential avoidance and cognitive fusion in youth. Next, the Child and Adolescent Mindfulness Measure (CAMM) is a 20-item self-report of present moment awareness, with specific subscales of "observing" and "acting with awareness" (Ciarrochi, Kashdan, Leeson, Heaven, & Jordan, 2011). Elements of present moment awareness (e.g., emotional awareness, emotion identification abilities) can also be measured through the Levels of Emotional Awareness Scale for Children (LEAS-C; Bajgar, Ciarrochi, Lane, & Deane, 2005) and/or the Toronto Alexithymia Scale (TAS; Heaven, Ciarrochi, & Hurrell, 2010). Other ACT process measures designed for adults have been recently validated in youth populations: the Self-Compassion Scale (Donald et al., 2018), the Cognitive Fusion Questionnaire (Solé et al., 2015), the Valued Living Questionnaire (Swain, Hancock, Hainsworth, & Bowman, 2014), and other questionnaires of mindfulness processes (e.g., nonattachment; Sahdra, Ciarrochi, Parker, Marshall, & Heaven, 2015).

Lastly, there are two measures of psychological inflexibility in parents, the 6PAQ and the PAAQ. The Parental Acceptance Questionnaire (6-PAQ) is an 18-item questionnaire focusing on psychological inflexibility, with thoughts, feelings, and other behaviors around parenting specifically (Greene, Field, Fargo, & Twohig, 2015). The Parental Acceptance and Action Questionnaire (PAAQ) is a 15-item questionnaire assessing parental experiential avoidance via subscales of unwillingness and inaction (Cheron, Ehrenreich, & Pincus, 2009). The PAAQ focuses specifically on parents' psychological inflexibility in response to their own child's affect.

Evidence That ACT Processes Are Important to Youth Well-being

ACT is inherently a flexible, nonmanualized treatment approach that can be adapted to the developmental level of the child or adolescent. DNA-V is dynamic, encouraging young people to "move" between DNA "spaces" and different views of themselves and their social world, in the service of becoming stronger and their full potential. Importantly, the DNA-V model does not map one-to-one onto hexaflex processes but is built on the broad CBS foundation of ACT. Because childhood and adolescence are fruitful times of change, growing up with psychological flexibility might equip youth with important tools to handle changing contexts, roles, and relationships (Halliburton & Cooper, 2015). Furthermore, psychological inflexibility and experiential avoidance are known contributors to negative mental health and distress in younger populations too (e.g., worry, chronic medical concerns; Coyne, McHugh, & Martinez, 2011). In one study, experiential avoidance mediated 77% of the relationship between childhood psychological abuse and current mental health in 987 undergraduates (Reddy, Pickett, & Orcutt, 2006). In another study of youth with juvenile idiopathic arthritis ($n = 59$), child psychological flexibility contributed to improved psychosocial functioning and negative affect (Beeckman et al., 2019). Psychological flexibility and self-criticism also acted as mediators between verbal abuse and depression in a sample of LGBTQ youth (Armelie, Delahanty, & Boarts, 2010). Moreover, the increase in avoidance during the adolescent period is theorized to respond well to ACT techniques of encouraging acceptance, flexibility, and openness (i.e., psychological flexibility) in response to these challenges (Turrell & Bell, 2016).

While still nascent in terms of process-based evidence, there is support for the use of specific ACT processes to improve youth mental health, primarily focusing on adolescent populations. Concerning the processes of acceptance and contact with the present moment, one longitudinal study of 776 adolescents in grade 10 reported that "acting with awareness" and acceptance were both predictive of prosocial behaviors and well-being, even after one year (Ciarrochi et al., 2011). In another study of adolescents, those with chronic pain ($n = 122$), greater acceptance was associated with lowered distress and disability, but not less pain (McCracken, Gauntlett-Gilbert, & Eccleston, 2010). Acceptance in adolescents from the same study also accounted for variance in distress, disability, and family functioning, again suggesting the importance of developing acceptance in adolescents (McCracken et al., 2010). This finding is replicated in another study of pediatric chronic pain ($n = 59$) where child pain acceptance contributed to improved functioning and lower disability (Beeckman et al., 2019).

Lastly, in another study of adolescents (n = 657), low emotion identification abilities predicted lower quality and quantity of social support, along with low positive affect (Ciarrochi, Heaven, & Supavadeeprasit, 2008). These results suggest that skills related to present moment awareness and self-as-process (i.e., identifying and naming internal experiences as they occur—an element of present moment awareness, or *noticer* in DNA-V parlance) can help enhance adolescent behaviors within social contexts.

There is also clear evidence for ACT interventions focused on clarifying values and supporting the autonomy of youth (Ryan & Deci, 2017). For example, having disadvantaged youth write about their most important values improved their grades and response to stress (Cohen & Sherman, 2014; Sherman et al., 2013). With regard to the valued action component of ACT, research has demonstrated the value of encouraging youth to engage in exploratory behavior to broaden and build their skills and behavioral repertoires (Stifter, Augustine, & Dollar, 2020). Committed action in the presence of fear is encouraged in ACT via exposure, one of the most validated interventions in psychology (Abramowitz, Deacon, & Whiteside, 2019).

Concerning defusion (part of the advisor in DNA-V) or other processes that help youth unhook from unhelpful beliefs, there is now clear evidence that young people experience worse academic and well-being outcomes if they believe they cannot accomplish their goals, that they do not have social worth, and that problems are an overwhelming threat rather than a manageable challenge (Ciarrochi, Parker, Kashdan, Heaven, & Barkus, 2015; Marshall et al., 2015). ACT defusion interventions are designed to undermine the power of these beliefs, and there is clear evidence that we do not need to change the content of thinking, but instead can decouple the link between thoughts and unhelpful action (Levin, Luoma, & Haeger, 2015).

Finally, a major component of ACT interventions is teaching people to adopt broader perspectives on both themselves and others. There is evidence that taking a compassionate view of oneself promotes well-being and allows youth to bounce back from low self-esteem (Marshall et al., 2015). Perspective-taking of the self may also promote the belief that one can change and grow, which has been shown to promote resilience in youth (Yeager & Dweck, 2012). Finally, being able to see from another's perspective and have empathy helps youth to develop supportive social networks (Ciarrochi et al., 2017; Sahdra et al., 2015).

Evidence That ACT Promotes Youth Well-being

On the whole, ACT has been found to be useful for a range of mental and behavioral disorders in youth, as reported by a meta-analysis of 14 studies in children (Fang & Ding, 2020) and a meta-analysis of 21 studies in children and adolescents (Swain, Hancock, Dixon, & Bowman, 2015). We review the research in greater detail here and point towards area in need of further exploration.

Anxiety

Several studies have examined ACT for anxiety disorders in children and adolescents. The largest randomized controlled trial (RCT) is Hancock and colleagues' study (2018) comparing ACT, cognitive-behavioral therapy (CBT), and waitlist for anxiety in children and adolescents (n = 157). No differences between the ACT and CBT conditions were found, but both treatments were superior to waitlist, with the ACT condition reporting medium to large effect sizes (d = .5 – .7) for within-group increases in quality of life, psychological flexibility, and anxiety symptom severity following treatment (Hancock et al., 2018). For social anxiety specifically, one study compared ten 1-hour sessions of ACT to a waitlist for 40 middle school males with a learning disability (Rostami, Veisi, Jafarian Dehkordi, & Alkasir, 2014). Results indicated a 60% reduction in social anxiety symptoms after treatment as compared to the control (Rostami et al., 2014). Another RCT for social anxiety compared ten 90-minute sessions of ACT and a waitlist for social anxiety in female high schoolers (n = 30; Azadeh, Kazemi-Zahrani, & Besharat, 2016). At posttreatment, participants reported significantly decreased interpersonal problems (d = .71) and increased psychological flexibility (d=.61) as compared to the control group.

Several other smaller studies have examined ACT for anxiety in youth. In one pilot study of 10 adolescent females with anxiety, all participants received 6 hours total of weekly group ACT sessions at school; participants reported decreased anxiety (d = .74) and increased psychological flexibility (d = .38), with a trend toward a significant decrease in depression (Smith, Oxman, & Hayes, 2020). Second, in a multiple baseline, three community youth and four youth from a residential program completed a course of ACT for posttraumatic stress symptoms, resulting in a 69% symptom reduction at posttreatment and follow-up for community youth and 81% and 84% symptom reduction for residential youth (Woidneck, Morrison, & Twohig, 2014). Lastly, a sample (n = 43) of 8- to 12-year-old children with fear/anxiety about darkness were randomized to receive a 30-minute cognitive restructuring or cognitive defusion intervention (Simon, Driessen, Lambert, & Muris, 2020). Both conditions resulted in decreased fear of the dark, with a medium effect size favoring the cognitive restructuring condition (partial η = .08; Simon et al., 2020).

Obsessive-Compulsive and Related Disorders

Less research has looked at ACT for obsessive-compulsive and related disorders (OCRDs) in youth. One multiple baseline examined the effects of ACT for OCD in three adolescents; participants reported a 44% reduction in compulsions and a 12–61% total reduction in child Yale Brown Obsessive-Compulsive Scale (CY-BOCS) scores at follow-up (Armstrong, Morrison, & Twohig, 2013). In a larger RCT comparing group ACT + SSRIs, group CBT + SSRIs, and SSRIs-only in adolescents (n = 69), there was a 29.4% reduction in OCD symptoms at posttreatment (Hedge's g = 1.72) and a 21.8% reduction at follow-up (g = 1.04) in the ACT + SSRIs condition, but no differences between ACT and CBT conditions (Shabani et al., 2019).

Some research has also been done on trichotillomania, or problematic hair-pulling, on ACT alone or as a treatment adjunctive with habit reversal training (HRT) in adolescents. First, in a case series of acceptance-enhanced behavior therapy for two adolescents with trichotillomania, both adolescents reported clinically significant reductions in pulling, along with decreases in distress and functional impairment (Fine et al., 2012). In a study combining adolescent and adult participants, 14 adolescent participants reported 30.8% reduced hair-pulling, and 11.3% reported increases in psychological flexibility following 10 sessions of ACT (Lee et al., 2020). In a larger RCT, 29 adolescents with trichotillomania were randomized to ACT-enhanced behavior therapy (i.e., ACT with HRT) or waitlist control condition; adolescents receiving ACT-enhanced behavior therapy reported significantly decreased hair-pulling severity (g = 1.55; Twohig et al., 2021). Beyond trichotillomania, one pilot study (n = 13) compared HRT and ACT + HRT for tic disorder in adolescents. The study found that both treatments reported reductions in symptoms (to below the clinical cutoff) and functioning at posttreatment and 1-month follow-up (Franklin, Best, Wilson, Loew, & Compton, 2011).

Depression

To our knowledge, only three studies have examined ACT as a treatment for depression in adolescents. In an outpatient clinic RCT, 30 Australian adolescents were randomized to receive ACT or treatment as usual (TAU); after treatment, 58% of participants in the ACT condition reported clinically significant reductions (d = .38) in their depressive symptoms as compared to TAU (L. L. Hayes, Boyd, & Sewell, 2011). In a larger trial (n = 66), Australian adolescents received group ACT or a control condition utilizing individual support systems available through schools. Significant reductions in depression (d = .86) and psychological inflexibility (d = .73) were reported (Livheim et al., 2015). Lastly, in a smaller study (n = 11) of predominantly low-socioeconomic-status African American and multiracial adolescents, participants received a combination of ACT and motivational interviewing for depression (Petts, Duenas, & Gaynor, 2017). Adolescents reported significant reductions in depressive symptoms on two different measures (d = 1.50; g = 3.09), a 45% increase in behavioral activation (g = 2.83), and 27% increases in quality of life following treatment (g = 1.22; Petts et al., 2017).

Chronic Medical Conditions

A larger amount of research is available on the use of ACT for youth with chronic medical conditions (e.g., chronic illness, pain) in a combination of case, pilot, and RCT studies; ACT was recently approved by the World Health Organization as a treatment for pediatric chronic pain (World Health Organization, 2020). First, in a case study of a 14-year-old female with idiopathic generalized pain, the participant reported improved life functioning (100% reduction in impairment), lower pain (reductions from daily scores of 5 to 0 out of 10), and increased school attendance following a course of ACT (Wicksell, Dahl, Magnusson, & Olsson, 2005). In another case study, a 16-year-old African American male with sickle cell disease received eight sessions of ACT with his parents (Masuda, Cohen, Wicksell, Kemani, & Johnson, 2011). After treatment, he reported a 61% reduction in functional disability and a 71% increase in psychological flexibility at post and 3-month follow-up, along with general improvement in his life quality (e.g., his grades increased, he got a part-time job).

In a pilot study (n = 14) of adolescents with idiopathic chronic pain, ACT improved functioning, school attendance, pain intensity (46% reduction), and pain life interference (53% reduction) at posttreatment, with similar scores holding at 3- and 6-month follow-up (Wicksell, Melin, & Olsson, 2007). In another pilot study, adolescents (n = 21) with functional somatic syndromes (FSS) participated in a group ACT program (AHEAD); posttreatment scores indicated clinically significant improvements in physical health (an average increase of 9 points) and decreased psychological inflexibility into the healthy range (Kallesøe et al., 2020). Additionally, 68% of participants reported that the treatment made an overall positive difference in their lives (Kallesøe et al., 2020).

Three larger RCTs have demonstrated the effectiveness of ACT for chronic health problems in youth. One RCT compared ACT to multidisciplinary treatment for chronic pain, reporting that the ACT condition resulted in superior outcomes in pain intensity, health-related quality of life, and pain interference (ds = .22–.47) at posttreatment (Wicksell, Melin, Lekander, & Olsson, 2009). The ACT group also reported superior secondary outcomes, with decreases in pain discomfort, depression, and catastrophizing (ds = .18–.56). Another RCT compared outcomes of individual and group ACT for adolescents with chronic pain, finding no differences between the treatments; both reported medium to large effect sizes (r = .13–.59) in improved psychological flexibility, pain reactivity and interference, and depression (Kanstrup et al., 2016). Lastly, a larger trial (n = 98) examined the effects of 3-week residential ACT for chronic pain (Gauntlett-Gilbert, Connell, Clinch, & McCracken, 2013). Participants reported small to large improvements at 3-month follow-up across a range of areas: physical and social disability (d = .32 and.28), walking distances (d = .47), pain acceptance (d = 1.00), anxiety (d = .48), and school attendance (d = .45; Gauntlett-Gilbert et al., 2013).

Eating Disorders

Little research has examined the use of ACT for youth with disordered eating problems. In one case study, a 15-year-old female with anorexia nervosa (AN) received 14 sessions of ACT and reported reduced AN symptoms, weight gain into the healthy BMI range, and the return of her menstrual cycle at posttreatment (Heffner, Sperry, Eifert, & Detweiler, 2002). A small pilot trial of six adolescents with AN has also tested acceptance-based separated family treatment (ASFT); at posttreatment, five of six adolescents restored their weight to the appropriate BMI range, along with improved health and functioning (Merwin, Zucker, & Timko, 2013). Lastly, in a larger open trial (n = 47) of ASFT for adolescents with disordered eating, full remission was reported in 49% of participants and reduced disordered eating behaviors across participants (Timko, Zucker, Herbert, Rodriguez, & Merwin, 2015).

Other

Several studies have examined ACT for a range of other problems presenting in children and adolescents. One Spanish case study reported positive outcomes of biweekly ACT for a 17-year-old male with auditory hallucinations and a diagnosis of schizophrenia, resulting in a 40% decrease in hallucinations at posttreatment (Veiga-Martínez, Pérez-Álvarez, & García-Montes, 2008). In another case study, a 5-year-old with anger outbursts received four 20-minute RFT-based ACT sessions combined with a token economy over the course of 10 days (Ruiz & Perete, 2015). The child and mother reported reduced frequency and intensity of anger episodes, from once a day to once a month—even at 1-year follow-up (Ruiz & Perete, 2015). In another, smaller study, five adolescents with conduct and/or clinical impulsivity reported decreases in disruptive behavior (d = 2.85) and impulsivity (d = 1.14), along with increases in self-control (d = 1.29) and psychological flexibility (d = 1.40) after four 90-minute sessions of ACT (Gómez et al., 2014). In addition, preliminary results support the use of a brief, acceptance-based protocol for educating adolescents on safe sex and HIV prevention (Soriano, Salas, Martínez, Jiménez, & Blarrina, 2009). Lastly, a smaller RCT (n = 32) of Swedish adolescents with elevated stress levels were randomized to receive ACT or supportive care from the school system (Livheim et al., 2015). Adolescents in the ACT condition had a larger effect for reduction in stress (d = 1.20), a marginally significant decrease in anxiety (d = .8), and an increase in mindfulness (d = .75) as compared to the control condition.

Mediators and Moderators of Change

Only a few studies have examined mediators and moderators of change in ACT for youth. Because such research on ACT for youth is still nascent, much work remains. The first study investigated mediators of change in ACT and CBT for pediatric chronic pain and found that variables related to psychological flexibility (e.g., pain reactivity, beliefs about pain improvement) mediated the effects of treatment on follow-up outcomes (Wicksell, Olsson, & Hayes, 2011). These variables predicted improvements at follow-up when controlling for earlier improvements in treatment—but only in the ACT condition, suggesting that they are unique processes to ACT (Wicksell et al., 2011). Another study tested the six (i.e., hexaflex) processes of ACT as multiple mediators for treatment outcomes in the larger RCT comparing ACT, CBT, and waitlist (Swain, Hancock, Hainsworth, & Bowman, 2015). However, Swain and colleagues (2015) found that the ACT processes were only unique mediators for the ACT condition in the relationship between clinical severity ratings of anxiety and treatment condition. For other relationships, hexaflex processes were found as mediators in both conditions, suggesting that further research is needed to confirm that ACT is working via differing processes than other psychological treatments like CBT.

Applications beyond Traditional Clinic Settings

Around 75% of the published studies on the applications of psychological flexibility models (such as ACT Hexaflex and DNA-V) with young people report on interventions within clinical settings, most of which are one-to-one interventions (Swain, Hancock, Dixon, et al., 2015). However, psychological flexibility models have the potential for application far beyond the clinic settings and should be established where children grow—in schools and community. Indeed, applications beyond the clinic, within young peoples' own communities, may offer considerably greater opportunities for positive change than exclusively clinic-based applications. For example, fear of treatment has been highlighted as a common barrier to accessing psychological therapies within clinical settings (Rapp et al., 2007). It therefore seems sensible to suggest that these treatment fears may be absent—or at least less present—if an intervention were to take place within familiar physical and social environments.

Situational contexts within which community-based intervention programs can be delivered include the school/educational setting (Gillard, Flaxman, & Hooper, 2018; Szabo & Dixon, 2016), the home environment, often including direct work with immediate family members (Jones, Whittingham, Coyne, & Lightcap, 2016), and within young people's wider community settings. As the article by Renshaw et al. provides an extensive discussion of applications in schools, we restrict our discussions here to applications within other areas of youth community.

One relevant study (Livheim et al., 2020) reports on an ACT-based intervention with young people placed in residential care settings in Sweden (sometimes known as juvenile detention in other countries) due to substance misuse, psychosocial problems, and/or criminal convictions. In a quasi-experimental design, 160 young people across eight care home settings, ranging from 16 to 18 years of age, were allocated either a TAU group or a TAU + ACT intervention group. The intervention delivered to the TAU + ACT group was a slightly adapted version of the *ACT—Living Life Fully* Program, a manualized program consisting of six sessions of approximately two hours duration. Sessions were delivered by on-site staff who had received 8 days of ACT training from an experienced and peer-reviewed ACT trainer (the study's lead author) to a small group of between two and six young people per group. As the sessions were delivered by staff with no formal psychotherapeutic training, the sessions were primarily psychoeducational in nature and included activities such as group discussions, role playing hypothetical scenarios, use of exploration of metaphor, and perspective-taking exercises. Activities were designed to target core ACT processes (e.g., identifying and clarifying personal values, translating values into actions, exploring barriers to values-based action, and naming and normalizing painful psychological content).

Livheim's study reports significant and positive changes for the TAU + ACT group from pre- to postintervention, compared to the TAU group, across all depression scales, as well as within the Conduct Problems Scale, the Hyperactivity Scale, and the Prosocial Scale of the Strengths and Difficulties Questionnaire. Broadly, these encouraging findings were stable and maintained at 18-month follow-up. Administering the AFQ-Y (Greco et al., 2008) as an ACT process measure, the study concludes that *"the result from mediation analysis implies that a high proportion of the total effect of ACT on youth's anxiety level post-treatment is mediated by psychological flexibility"* (Livheim et al., 2020, p. 124).

A further emerging community-based application of the DNA-V model with young people can be found in a UK-based project supporting young care-leavers, individuals who are or have been living under government custody and/or independently from their families, between 16 and 25 years of age—the Reboot West Project. Young people who have spent much of their childhood in the care system are far more likely to experience poor life outcomes such as mental health issues, low educational achievement, poor physical health, higher prevalence of teenaged pregnancies, low socioeconomic status, and higher levels of involvement in criminal activity (Burch, Daru, & Taylor, 2018). As such, access to effective psychological support for this particular demographic, in order to improve their chances of more positive life-outcomes, is extremely important.

The Reboot West Project (Gillard, Hayes, McNally, & Willis, 2020) supports young people who were previously removed from their families and taken into care, usually because of issues related to abuse and/or neglect. As part of a larger charity organization called 1625 Independent People, Reboot West consists of a team of Education, Employment and Training (EET) Coaches, trained and supervised in the use of the DNA-V model. Each coach holds a caseload of young care-leavers, whom they support in moving in valued life directions, including supporting them into a career path linked to personal values. After 18 months with the project, 212 care-leavers were being supported, 101 of whom had started formal education programs. Of those 101 young people, at the time of writing, 73 had completed at least 50% of their educational programs and 56 had completed their studies and attained the relevant qualifications. Of the total 212, eight had started university degree programs and 73 were in sustained, paid employment. Further, almost all young people reported feeling safe in their daily lives and having at least one sustained, positive relationship (Gillard et al., 2020).

A critical aspect of this youth intervention program was the fact that it occurred flexibly, within the young people's own communities. Coaches were able to build sustained, trusting relationships with young people on their caseloads, in part by spending time with them wherever they felt safe, comfortable, and able to engage. For some, this was the local coffee shop, for others the local park, for others the gym. Targeting the psychological processes described within the DNA-V model in physical and social environments familiar to these young care-leavers undoubtedly helped tear down barriers to accessing psychological support such as treatment fear.

Challenges and Future Research Directions

Challenges

Working with youth brings multiple challenges and problems. First and foremost among these challenges is that therapists find working with adolescents challenging due to their developmental immaturity (Bolton Oetzel & Scherer, 2003). Furthermore, adolescents often require a more engaging and interactive therapy format (Halliburton & Cooper, 2015). Many are unwilling participants, and so they tend to drop out early (Oruche, Downs, Holloway, Draucker, & Aalsma, 2014). The typical 50-minute therapeutic session is not always suitable for many adolescents, with the "adult style" of speaking and listening in turns presenting a challenge for many. Thus, ACT with youth demands a flexible and creative therapist for the implementation of metaphors, experiential exercises, and ACT concepts into session. It may be especially helpful to use ACT in an experiential, process-based approach with youth (e.g., implementing present moment awareness in a walking meditation rather than a seated breathing exercise). As previously discussed, youth may also be experiencing many shifts in their own life as they try on new identities or enter new environments. This in itself can be a challenge in working with youth. Because youth may be exploring different ways of being, it is important to rely on nonjudgmental awareness and curiosity while working with them. The emphasis on functionality and a process-based approach (i.e., engaging with what is showing up in sessions) is key in this way as well.

Mental health services are stretched beyond capacity, leaving little time and money for research, and yet the field desperately needs more funded research with young people in order to test treatments. This testing must focus on treatments that can be delivered with the flexibility needed for the breadth of adolescent presentations and development. The addition of a research agenda adds complexity to a service. It is difficult to gather data from multiple participants, with adolescents, parents, and schools all needing informed consent and liaison activities. It is also a challenge for lab-based studies conducted by graduate students, which are often based on easily accessible participant groups such as those over 18 years. CBS functional-based approaches to treatment are able to meet this need, testing processes in the clinic and doing meditational and moderation studies in the lab.

Furthermore, working with youth demands that the practitioner work with the whole context, which inevitably involves school, parents, and family contexts. Some evidence suggests that working in schools is beneficial. For example, Keogh, Bond, and Flaxman (2006) demonstrated improvements in mental health and academic (exam grade) attainment through a brief intervention designed to support psychological preparation for exams in teenagers, as compared to a treatment-as-usual control group. While the intervention was not packaged as ACT, the program did include some ACT-consistent procedures. More generally, it demonstrates the feasibility of brief cognitive-behavioral interventions within school contexts (see Renshaw et al., this volume, for the current state of research for ACT in schools). There are also encouraging activities in the world of prevention science, evident in the recent development of ACT-based social and emotional learning programs such as the Connect Personal, Social, and Health Education (PSHE) curriculum and the Accept, Identify, and Move (AIM) curriculum. However, programs are in the evaluation stages and outcome data is yet to be published.

With regard to families, some evidence suggests that parental psychological inflexibility may be related to adolescent distress (e.g., Williams et al., 2012). Thus, it may be appropriate to actively involve parents and/or caretakers in treatment. However, the developmental level of the youth and the cultural context of the family must be considered in this decision. Integrating parents into treatment may involve explaining psychological flexibility models, actively working to enhance psychological flexibility in parents, or simply keeping the parent up to date on therapy homework. As one example of integrating parents, in a study using ACT for adolescents with trichotillomania, parents joined the last 10 minutes of the session to review material and were provided with handouts explaining different ACT concepts (Twohig et al., 2021). However, this structured approach may not be appropriate for all families or youth. It is important for the therapist to assess the appropriate level of familial involvement and support the youth accordingly.

Future Research Directions

In general, more research with youth and CBS frameworks is needed. Children and adolescent populations are underresearched, despite the need for additional evidence-based care. The adult CBS empirical literature dwarfs the available work on youth. Thus, it is important to add more research to better understand the effectiveness of ACT for youth struggling with mental health concerns. It may also benefit youth populations to invest further research in preventative programs based on CBS models. Treatment and preventative studies would also benefit from longitudinal tracking of long-term outcomes from treatment (e.g., psychological flexibility, future employment, or education).

Additionally, processes of change research in ACT for youth are needed. Process of change research in youth will allow a better understanding of how ACT works for youth and may possibly provide insight into what types of younger populations may best respond to ACT. With that in mind, greater research on measurement of the ACT process and CBS-related constructs is also needed. As of now, there are significantly fewer options for measuring psychological flexibility, values progression, cognitive defusion, and more in youth. While strong measurement research is still developing for adults and older groups, it is important to include youth in the conversation.

Lastly, more research with diverse participant populations is needed for CBS research in youth. For example, research on ACT for problems in youth is largely racially homogeneous beyond a few studies (e.g., Masuda et al., 2011; Petts et al., 2017). Because of the developmental approach and flexible contextual focus, ACT may benefit youth from marginalized groups (e.g., sexual and gender diverse youth). However, further research with these groups is needed. One way of targeting diverse groups may be for future CBS research in youth to focus on community-based psychological flexibility intervention programs. Implementation and dissemination research is just important as effectiveness trials.

Conclusion

More work is needed to understand how to best implement and disseminate ACT for youth. However, the present evidence demonstrates the strong promise and effectiveness of ACT models (e.g., DNA-V) for youth, particularly adolescents, in a variety of environments (e.g., communities, schools, and clinics). Given the demonstrated global need for addressing youth mental health concerns, ACT and CBS present a compelling evidence-based model for helping youth grow up into the person they most hope they can be.

References

Abramowitz, J. S., Deacon, B. J., & Whiteside, S. P. (2019). *Exposure therapy for anxiety: Principles and practice*: New York: Guilford Press.

Armelie, A. P., Delahanty, P. L., & Boarts, J. M. (2010). *The impact of verbal abuse on depression symptoms in lesbian, gay, and bisexual youth: The roles of self-criticism and psychological inflexibility*. Paper presented at the Association for Contextual and Behavioral Science, Reno, NV.

Armstrong, A. B., Morrison, K. L., & Twohig, M. P. (2013). A preliminary investigation of acceptance and commitment therapy for adolescent obsessive-compulsive disorder. *Journal of Cognitive Psychotherapy, 27*(2), 175–190.

Arnold, C. (2017). Developmental considerations for grieving youth. *Understanding Child and Adolescent Grief: Supporting Loss and Facilitating Growth*, 7–18.

Arslan, G. (2018). School-based social exclusion, affective wellbeing, and mental health problems in adolescents: A Study of mediator and moderator role of academic self-regulation. *Child Indicators Research, 11*(3), 963–980.

Azadeh, S. M., Kazemi-Zahrani, H., & Besharat, M. A. (2016). Effectiveness of acceptance and commitment therapy on interpersonal problems and psychological flexibility in female high school students with social anxiety disorder. *Global Journal of Health Science, 8*(3), 131.

Bailey, A., Ciarrochi, J., & Harris, R. (2014). *The weight escape: How to stop dieting and start living*. Boulder, CO: Shambhala Publications.

Bajgar, J., Ciarrochi, J., Lane, R., & Deane, F. P. (2005). Development of the levels of emotional awareness scale for children (LEAS-C). *British Journal of Developmental Psychology, 23*(4), 569–586.

Barrett, L. F. (2017). *How emotions are made: The secret life of the brain*. New York: Houghton Mifflin Harcourt.

Beeckman, M., Hughes, S., Van Ryckeghem, D., Van Hoecke, E., Dehoorne, J., Joos, R., & Goubert, L. (2019). Resilience factors in children with juvenile idiopathic arthritis and their parents: The role of child and parent psychological flexibility. *Pain Medicine, 20*(6), 1120–1131.

Bolton Oetzel, K., & Scherer, D. G. (2003). Therapeutic engagement with adolescents in psychotherapy. *Psychotherapy: Theory, Research, Practice, Training, 40*(3), 215.

Bowlby, J. (1979). *The making and breaking of affectional bonds*. London (Tavistock) 1979.

Burch, K., Daru, J., & Taylor, V. (2018). *Analysis of outcomes for children and young people 4 to 5 years after a final Care Order Cardiff: Welsh Government*. Retrieved from https://gov.wales/sites/default/files/statistics-and-research/2019-06/180515-placement-outcomes-children-young-people-4-5-years-after-final-care-order-summary-en.pdf

Cheron, D. M., Ehrenreich, J. T., & Pincus, D. B. (2009). Assessment of parental experiential avoidance in a clinical sample of children with anxiety disorders. *Child Psychiatry and Human Development, 40*(3), 383–403.

Ciarrochi, J. V., Atkins, P. W., Hayes, L. L., Sahdra, B. K., & Parker, P. (2016). Contextual positive psychology: Policy recommendations for implementing positive psychology into schools. *Frontiers in Psychology, 7*, 1561.

Ciarrochi, J. V., Heaven, P. C., & Supavadeeprasit, S. (2008). The link between emotion identification skills and socio-emotional functioning in early adolescence: A 1-year longitudinal study. *Journal of Adolescence, 31*(5), 565–582.
Ciarrochi, J. V., Kashdan, T. B., Leeson, P., Heaven, P., & Jordan, C. (2011). On being aware and accepting: a one-year longitudinal study into adolescent well-being. *Journal of Adolescence, 34*(4), 695–703.
Ciarrochi, J. V., Parker, P., Kashdan, T. B., Heaven, P. C., & Barkus, E. (2015). Hope and emotional well-being: A six-year study to distinguish antecedents, correlates, and consequences. *Journal of Positive Psychology, 10*(6), 520–532.
Ciarrochi, J. V., Parker, P. D., Sahdra, B. K., Kashdan, T. B., Kiuru, N., & Conigrave, J. (2017). When empathy matters: The role of sex and empathy in close friendships. *Journal of Personality, 85*(4), 494–504.
Ciarrochi, J. V., Sahdra, B. K., Yap, K., & Dicke, T. (2020). The role of nonattachment in the development of adolescent mental health: A three-year longitudinal study. *Mindfulness, 11*(9), 2131–2139.
Cohen, G. L., & Sherman, D. K. (2014). The psychology of change: Self-affirmation and social psychological intervention. *Annual Review of Psychology, 65*, 333–371.
Coyne, L. W., McHugh, L., & Martinez, E. R. (2011). Acceptance and commitment therapy (ACT): Advances and applications with children, adolescents, and families. *Child and Adolescent Psychiatric Clinics, 20*(2), 379–399.
de Lijster, J. M., Dieleman, G. C., Utens, E. M., Dierckx, B., Wierenga, M., Verhulst, F. C., & Legerstee, J. S. (2018). Social and academic functioning in adolescents with anxiety disorders: A systematic review. *Journal of Affective Disorders, 230*, 108–117.
Deighton, J., Lereya, S. T., Casey, P., Patalay, P., Humphrey, N., & Wolpert, M. (2019). Prevalence of mental health problems in schools: Poverty and other risk factors among 28,000 adolescents in England. *British Journal of Psychiatry*, 1–3.
Donald, J. N., Ciarrochi, J., Parker, P. D., Sahdra, B. K., Marshall, S. L., & Guo, J. (2018). A worthy self is a caring self: Examining the developmental relations between self-esteem and self-compassion in adolescents. *Journal of Personality, 86*(4), 619–630.
Erskine, H. E., Baxter, A. J., Patton, G., Moffitt, T. E., Patel, V., Whiteford, H. A., & Scott, J. G. (2017). The global coverage of prevalence data for mental disorders in children and adolescents. *Epidemiology and Psychiatric Science, 26*(4), 395–402.
Fang, S., & Ding, D. (2020). A meta-analysis of the efficacy of acceptance and commitment therapy for children. *Journal of Contextual Behavioral Science, 15*, 225–234.
Fine, K. M., Walther, M. R., Joseph, J. M., Robinson, J., Ricketts, E. J., Bowe, W. E., & Woods, D. W. (2012). Acceptance-enhanced behavior therapy for trichotillomania in adolescents. *Cognitive and Behavioral Practice, 19*(3), 463–471.
Franklin, M. E., Best, S. H., Wilson, M. A., Loew, B., & Compton, S. N. (2011). Habit reversal training and acceptance and commitment therapy for Tourette syndrome: A pilot project. *Journal of Developmental and Physical Disabilities, 23*(1), 49–60.
Fredrickson, B. L. (2004). The broaden–and–build theory of positive emotions. *Philosophical Transactions of the Royal Society of London. Series B: Biological Sciences, 359*(1449), 1367–1377.
Gauntlett-Gilbert, J., Connell, H., Clinch, J., & McCracken, L. M. (2013). Acceptance and values-based treatment of adolescents with chronic pain: Outcomes and their relationship to acceptance. *Journal of Pediatric Psychology, 38*(1), 72–81.
Georgiades, K., Duncan, L., Wang, L., Comeau, J., Boyle, M. H., & Ontario Child Health Study, T. (2019). Six-month prevalence of mental disorders and service contacts among children and youth in Ontario: Evidence from the 2014 Ontario Child Health Study. *Canadian Journal of Psychiatry, 64*(4), 246–255.
Gillard, D., Flaxman, P., & Hooper, N. (2018). Acceptance and commitment therapy: applications for educational psychologists within schools. *Educational Psychology in Practice, 34*(3), 272–281.
Gillard, D., Hayes, L. L., McNally, A., & Willis, K. (2020). Forging brighter futures with young care leavers. *The Psychologist, 34*, 44–48.
Gómez, M. J., Luciano, C., Páez-Blarrina, M., Ruiz, F. J., Valdivia-Salas, S., & Gil-Luciano, B. (2014). Brief ACT protocol in at-risk adolescents with conduct disorder and impulsivity. *International Journal of Psychology and Psychological Therapy, 14*(3), 307–332.
Gopnik, A., O'Grady, S., Lucas, C. G., Griffiths, T. L., Wente, A., Bridgers, S., . . . Dahl, R. E. (2017). Changes in cognitive flexibility and hypothesis search across human life history from childhood to adolescence to adulthood. *Proceedings of the National Academy of Sciences, 114*(30), 7892–7899.
Granic, I., Hollenstein, T., Dishion, T. J., & Patterson, G. R. (2003). Longitudinal analysis of flexibility and reorganization in early adolescence: A dynamic systems study of family interactions. *Developmental Psychology, 39*(3), 606.
Gray, P. (2009). Play as a foundation for hunter-gatherer social existence. *American Journal of Play, 1*(4), 476–522.

Greco, L. A., Lambert, W., & Baer, R. A. (2008). Psychological inflexibility in childhood and adolescence: Development and evaluation of the Avoidance and Fusion Questionnaire for Youth. *Psychological Assessment, 20*(2), 93.
Greene, R. L., Field, C. E., Fargo, J. D., & Twohig, M. P. (2015). Development and validation of the parental acceptance questionnaire (6-PAQ). *Journal of Contextual Behavioral Science, 4*(3), 170–175.
Halliburton, A. E., & Cooper, L. D. (2015). Applications and adaptations of acceptance and commitment therapy (ACT) for adolescents. *Journal of Contextual Behavioral Science, 4*(1), 1–11.
Hancock, K. M., Swain, J., Hainsworth, C. J., Dixon, A. L., Koo, S., & Munro, K. (2018). Acceptance and commitment therapy versus cognitive behavior therapy for children with anxiety: Outcomes of a randomized controlled trial. *Journal of Clinical Child and Adolescent Psychology, 47*(2), 296–311.
Hayes, L. L., Boyd, C. P., & Sewell, J. (2011). Acceptance and commitment therapy for the treatment of adolescent depression: A pilot study in a psychiatric outpatient setting. *Mindfulness, 2*(2), 86–94.
Hayes, L. L., & Ciarrochi, J. V. (2015a). *The thriving adolescent: Using acceptance and commitment therapy and positive psychology to help teens manage emotions, achieve goals, and build connection*: Oakland, CA: New Harbinger Publications.
Hayes, L. L., & Ciarrochi, J. V. (2015b). Using acceptance and commitment therapy to help young people develop and grow to their full potential. In B. Kirkcaldy (Ed.). *Promoting psychological well-being in children and families.* New York: Springer, pp. 102–122.
Hayes, S. C., Barnes-Holmes, D., & Roche, B. (2001). *Relational frame theory: A post-Skinnerian account of human language and cognition.* New York: Springer.
Hayes, S. C., Luoma, J. B., Bond, F. W., Masuda, A., & Lillis, J. (2006). Acceptance and commitment therapy: Model, processes and outcomes. *Behaviour Research and Therapy, 44*(1), 1–25.
Hayes, S. C., Strosahl, K. D., & Wilson, K. G. (2016). *Acceptance and commitment therapy: The process and practice of mindful change. New York*: Guilford Press.
Heaven, P. C., Ciarrochi, J., & Hurrell, K. (2010). The distinctiveness and utility of a brief measure of alexithymia for adolescents. *Personality and Individual Differences, 49*(3), 222–227.
Heffner, M., Sperry, J., Eifert, G. H., & Detweiler, M. (2002). Acceptance and commitment therapy in the treatment of an adolescent female with anorexia nervosa: A case example. *Cognitive and Behavioral Practice, 9*(3), 232–236.
Hrdy, S. (2009). Mothers and others. *The evolutionary origins of mutual understanding.* Cambridge, MA: The Belknap Press of Harvard University Press, 2009.
Jones, L. B., Whittingham, K., Coyne, L., & Lightcap, A. (2016). A contextual behavioral science approach to parenting intervention and research. In R. D. Zettle, S. C. Hayes, D. Barnes-Holmes, & A. Biglan (Eds.), *The Wiley handbook of contextual behavioral science* (p. 398). Chichester, UK: Wiley Blackwell.
Kallesøe, K. H., Schröder, A., Wicksell, R. K., Preuss, T., Jensen, J. S., & Rask, C. U. (2020). Feasibility of group-based acceptance and commitment therapy for adolescents (AHEAD) with multiple functional somatic syndromes: A pilot study. *BMC Psychiatry, 20*(1), 1–16.
Kanstrup, M., Wicksell, R. K., Kemani, M., Wiwe Lipsker, C., Lekander, M., & Holmström, L. (2016). A clinical pilot study of individual and group treatment for adolescents with chronic pain and their parents: Effects of acceptance and commitment therapy on functioning. *Children, 3*(4), 30.
Keogh, E., Bond, F. W., & Flaxman, P. E. (2006). Improving academic performance and mental health through a stress management intervention: Outcomes and mediators of change. *Behaviour Research and Therapy, 44*(3), 339–357.
Kovess-Masfety, V., Husky, M. M., Keyes, K., Hamilton, A., Pez, O., Bitfoi, A., . . . Mihova, Z. (2016). Comparing the prevalence of mental health problems in children 6-11 across Europe. *Social Psychiatry Psychiatric Epidemiology, 51*(8), 1093–1103.
Lee, E. B., Homan, K. J., Morrison, K. L., Ong, C. W., Levin, M. E., & Twohig, M. P. (2020). Acceptance and commitment therapy for trichotillomania: A randomized controlled trial of adults and adolescents. *Behavior Modification, 44*(1), 70–91.
Levin, M. E., Luoma, J. B., & Haeger, J. A. (2015). Decoupling as a mechanism of change in mindfulness and acceptance: A literature review. *Behavior Modification, 39*(6), 870–911.
Livheim, F., Hayes, L., Ghaderi, A., Magnusdottir, T., Högfeldt, A., Rowse, J., . . . Tengström, A. (2015). The effectiveness of acceptance and commitment therapy for adolescent mental health: Swedish and Australian pilot outcomes. *Journal of Child and Family Studies, 24*(4), 1016–1030.
Livheim, F., Tengström, A., Andersson, G., Dahl, J., Björck, C., & Rosendahl, I. (2020). A quasi-experimental, multicenter study of acceptance and commitment therapy for antisocial youth in residential care. *Journal of Contextual Behavioral Science, 16*, 119–127.
Marshall, S. L., Parker, P. D., Ciarrochi, J., Sahdra, B., Jackson, C. J., & Heaven, P. C. (2015). Self compassion protects against the negative effects of low self-esteem: A longitudinal study in a large adolescent sample. *Personality and Individual Differences, 74*, 116–121.

Masuda, A., Cohen, L. L., Wicksell, R. K., Kemani, M. K., & Johnson, A. (2011). A case study: Acceptance and commitment therapy for pediatric sickle cell disease. *Journal of Pediatric Psychology, 36*(4), 398–408.

McCracken, L. M., Gauntlett-Gilbert, J., & Eccleston, C. (2010). Acceptance of pain in adolescents with chronic pain: Validation of an adapted assessment instrument and preliminary correlation analyses. *European Journal of Pain, 14*(3), 316–320.

McGorry, P. D., & Mei, C. (2018). Early intervention in youth mental health: progress and future directions. *Evidence-based Mental Health, 21*(4), 182–184.

Merikangas, K. R., He, J. P., Burstein, M., Swanson, S. A., Avenevoli, S., Cui, L., . . . Swendsen, J. (2010). Lifetime prevalence of mental disorders in U.S. adolescents: Results from the National Comorbidity Survey Replication—Adolescent Supplement *(NCS-A). Journal of the American Academy of Child and Adolescent Psychiatry, 49*(10), 980–989.

Merwin, R. M., Zucker, N. L., & Timko, C. A. (2013). A pilot study of an acceptance-based separated family treatment for adolescent anorexia nervosa. *Cognitive Behavioral Practice, 20*(4), 485–500.

Mojtabai, R., Olfson, M., & Han, B. (2016). National trends in the prevalence and treatment of depression in adolescents and young adults. *Pediatrics, 138*(6):e20161878.

Moss, L., Land, C., & Tuttle, M. (2017). Counseling adolescents in school and clinical mental health settings. In J. Ziomek-Daigle (Ed.). *Counseling children and adolescents: Working in school and clinical mental health settings.* London, UK: Routledge, pp. 53–74.

Oruche, U. M., Downs, S., Holloway, E., Draucker, C., & Aalsma, M. (2014). Barriers and facilitators to treatment participation by adolescents in a community mental health clinic. *Journal of Psychiatric and Mental Health Nursing, 21*(3), 241–248.

Perry, N. B., Dollar, J. M., Calkins, S. D., Keane, S. P., & Shanahan, L. (2020). Maternal socialization of child emotion and adolescent adjustment: Indirect effects through emotion regulation. *Developmental Psychology, 56*(3), 541.

Petts, R. A., Duenas, J. A., & Gaynor, S. T. (2017). Acceptance and commitment therapy for adolescent depression: Application with a diverse and predominantly socioeconomically disadvantaged sample. *Journal of Contextual Behavioral Science, 6*(2), 134–144.

Polanczyk, G. V., Salum, G. A., Sugaya, L. S., Caye, A., & Rohde, L. A. (2015). Annual research review: A meta-analysis of the worldwide prevalence of mental disorders in children and adolescents. *Journal of Child Psychology and Psychiatry, 56*(3), 345–365.

Polk, K. L., & Schoendorff, B. (2014). *The ACT matrix: A new approach to building psychological flexibility across settings and populations.* Oakland, CA: New Harbinger Publications.

Porges, S. W., & Furman, S. A. (2011). The early development of the autonomic nervous system provides a neural platform for social behaviour: A polyvagal perspective. *Infant and Child Development, 20*(1), 106–118.

Rapp, R. C., Xu, J., Carr, C. A., Lane, D. T., Redko, C., Wang, J., & Carlson, R. G. (2007). Understanding treatment readiness in recently assessed, pre-treatment substance abusers. *Substance Abuse, 28*(1), 11–23.

Reddy, M. K., Pickett, S. M., & Orcutt, H. K. (2006). Experiential avoidance as a mediator in the relationship between childhood psychological abuse and current mental health symptoms in college students. *Journal of Emotional Abuse, 6*(1), 67–85.

Riede, F., Johannsen, N. N., Högberg, A., Nowell, A., & Lombard, M. (2018). The role of play objects and object play in human cognitive evolution and innovation. *Evolutionary Anthropology: Issues, News, and Reviews, 27*(1), 46–59.

Rostami, M., Veisi, N., Jafarian Dehkordi, F., & Alkasir, E. (2014). Social anxiety in students with learning disability: Benefits of acceptance and commitment therapy. *Practice in Clinical Psychology, 2*(4), 277–284.

Rowsell, H. C., Ciarrochi, J., Deane, F. P., & Heaven, P. C. (2016). Emotion identification skill and social support during adolescence: A three-year longitudinal study. *Journal of Research on Adolescence, 26*(1), 115–125.

Ruiz, F. J., & Perete, L. (2015). Application of a relational frame theory account of psychological flexibility in young children. *Psicothema, 27*(2), 114–119.

Ryan, R. M., & Deci, E. L. (2017). *Self-determination theory: Basic psychological needs in motivation, development, and wellness.* New York: Guilford Press.

Sahdra, B. K., Ciarrochi, J., Parker, P. D., Marshall, S., & Heaven, P. (2015). Empathy and nonattachment independently predict peer nominations of prosocial behavior of adolescents. *Frontiers in Psychology, 6,* 263.

Sauter, F. M., Heyne, D., & Michiel Westenberg, P. (2009). Cognitive behavior therapy for anxious adolescents: developmental influences on treatment design and delivery. *Clinical Child and Family Psychology Review, 12*(4), 310–335.

Shabani, M. J., Mohsenabadi, H., Omidi, A., Lee, E. B., Twohig, M. P., Ahmadvand, A., & Zanjani, Z. (2019). An Iranian study of group acceptance and commitment therapy versus group cognitive behavioral therapy for adolescents with obsessive-compulsive disorder on an optimal dose of selective serotonin reuptake inhibitors. *Journal of Obsessive-Compulsive and Related Disorders, 22,* 100440.

Sharpe, H., Patalay, P., Fink, E., Vostanis, P., Deighton, J., & Wolpert, M. (2016). Exploring the relationship between quality of life and mental health problems in children: Implications for measurement and practice. *European Child and Adolescent Psychiatry, 25*(6), 659–667.

Shea, S. E., & Coyne, L. W. (2011). Maternal dysphoric mood, stress, and parenting practices in mothers of Head Start preschoolers: The role of experiential avoidance. *Child and Family Behavior Therapy, 33*(3), 231–247.

Sheppard, R., Deane, F. P., & Ciarrochi, J. (2018). Unmet need for professional mental health care among adolescents with high psychological distress. *Australian and New Zealand Journal of Psychiatry, 52*(1), 59–67.

Sherman, D. K., Hartson, K. A., Binning, K. R., Purdie-Vaughns, V., Garcia, J., Taborsky-Barba, S., . . . Cohen, G. L. (2013). Deflecting the trajectory and changing the narrative: How self-affirmation affects academic performance and motivation under identity threat. *Journal of Personality and Social Psychology, 104*(4), 591.

Simon, E., Driessen, S., Lambert, A., & Muris, P. (2020). Challenging anxious cognitions or accepting them? Exploring the efficacy of the cognitive elements of cognitive behaviour therapy and acceptance and commitment therapy in the reduction of children's fear of the dark. *International Journal of Psychology, 55*(1), 90–97.

Skinner, B. F. (1965). *Science and human behavior.* New York: Simon and Schuster.

Smith, K. J., Oxman, L. N., & Hayes, L. (2020). ACT for adolescents: Impact of a pilot group intervention on psychological wellbeing. *Journal of Psychologists and Counsellors in Schools, 30*(2), 248–254.

Solé, E., Racine, M., Castarlenas, E., de la Vega, R., Tomé-Pires, C., Jensen, M., & Miró, J. (2015). The psychometric properties of the Cognitive Fusion Questionnaire in adolescents. *European Journal of Psychological Assessment, 32*(3), 181–186.

Soriano, M. C. L., Salas, S. V., Martínez, O. G., Jiménez, F. J. R., & Blarrina, M. B. P. (2009). Brief acceptance-based protocols applied to the work with adolescents. *International Journal of Psychology and Psychological Therapy, 9*(2), 237–257.

Spear, L. P. (2004). Adolescent brain development and animal models. *Annals of the New York Academy of Sciences, 1021*(1), 23–26.

Stifter, C., Augustine, M., & Dollar, J. (2020). The role of positive emotions in child development: A developmental treatment of the broaden and build theory. *Journal of Positive Psychology, 15*(1), 89–94.

Swain, J., Hancock, K., Hainsworth, C., & Bowman, J. (2014). Mechanism of change: Exploratory outcomes from a randomized controlled trial of acceptance and commitment therapy for anxious adolescents. *Journal of Contextual Behavioral Science, 4*(1), 56–67.

Swain, J., Hancock, K., Dixon, A., & Bowman, J. (2015). Acceptance and commitment therapy for children: A systematic review of intervention studies. *Journal of Contextual Behavioral Science, 4*(2), 73–85.

Swain, J., Hancock, K., Hainsworth, C., & Bowman, J. (2015). Mechanisms of change: Exploratory outcomes from a randomised controlled trial of acceptance and commitment therapy for anxious adolescents. *Journal of Contextual Behavioral Science, 4*(1), 56–67.

Szabo, T. G., & Dixon, M. R. (2016). Contextual behavioral science and education. In R. D. Zettle, S. C. Hayes, D. Barnes-Holmes, & A. Biglan (Eds.), *The Wiley handbook of contextual behavioral science.* Chichester, UK: Wiley Blackwell.

Timko, C. A., Zucker, N. L., Herbert, J. D., Rodriguez, D., & Merwin, R. M. (2015). An open trial of Acceptance-based Separated Family Treatment (ASFT) for adolescents with anorexia nervosa. *Behaviour Research and Therapy, 69,* 63–74.

Turrell, S. L., & Bell, M. (2016). *ACT for adolescents: Treating teens and adolescents in individual and group therapy*: Oakland, CA: New Harbinger Publications.

Twohig, M. P., Petersen, J. M., Fruge, J., Ong, C. W., Barney, J. L., Krafft, J., . . . Levin, M. E. (2021). A pilot randomized controlled trial of online-delivered act-enhanced behavior therapy for trichotillomania in adolescents. *Cognitive and Behavioral Practice, 28*(4), 653–668.

Veiga-Martínez, C., Pérez-Álvarez, M., & García-Montes, J. M. (2008). Acceptance and commitment therapy applied to treatment of auditory hallucinations. *Clinical Case Studies, 7*(2), 118–135.

Weil, L. G., Fleming, S. M., Dumontheil, I., Kilford, E. J., Weil, R. S., Rees, G., . . . Blakemore, S. J. (2013). The development of metacognitive ability in adolescence. *Conscious Cognition, 22*(1), 264–271.

Whitney, D. G., & Peterson, M. D. (2019). US national and state-level prevalence of mental health disorders and disparities of mental health care use in children. *JAMA Pediatrics, 173*(4), 389–391.

Wicksell, R. K., Dahl, J., Magnusson, B., & Olsson, G. L. (2005). Using acceptance and commitment therapy in the rehabilitation of an adolescent female with chronic pain: A case example. *Cognitive and Behavioral Practice, 12*(4), 415–423.

Wicksell, R. K., Melin, L., Lekander, M., & Olsson, G. L. (2009). Evaluating the effectiveness of exposure and acceptance strategies to improve functioning and quality of life in longstanding pediatric pain–a randomized controlled trial. *Pain, 141*(3), 248–257.

Wicksell, R. K., Melin, L., & Olsson, G. L. (2007). Exposure and acceptance in the rehabilitation of adolescents with idiopathic chronic pain–a pilot study. *European Journal of Pain, 11*(3), 267–274.

Wicksell, R. K., Olsson, G. L., & Hayes, S. C. (2011). Mediators of change in acceptance and commitment therapy for pediatric chronic pain. *Pain, 152*(12), 2792–2801.

Williams, K. E., Ciarrochi, J., & Heaven, P. C. (2012). Inflexible parents, inflexible kids: A 6-year longitudinal study of parenting style and the development of psychological flexibility in adolescents. *Journal of Youth and Adolescence, 41*(8), 1053–1066.

Wilson, D. S., Hayes, S. C., Biglan, A., & Embry, D. D. (2014). Evolving the future: Toward a science of intentional change. *The Behavioral and Brain Sciences, 37*(4), 395.

Woidneck, M. R., Morrison, K. L., & Twohig, M. P. (2014). Acceptance and commitment therapy for the treatment of posttraumatic stress among adolescents. *Behavior Modification, 38*(4), 451–476.

World Health Organization. (2020). Guidelines on the management of chronic pain in children.

Yeager, D. S., & Dweck, C. S. (2012). Mindsets that promote resilience: When students believe that personal characteristics can be developed. *Educational Psychologist, 47*(4), 302–314.

CHAPTER

28 Technology

Raimo Lappalainen, Katariina Keinonen, *and* Päivi Lappalainen

Abstract

With the increase in demand for mental health services globally, the need for technology-based interventions (e.g., mobile applications, self-help websites) has risen. Evidence suggests that guided online interventions can be as effective as in-person interventions, along with greater accessibility for populations that may otherwise struggle to receive evidence-based mental health care (e.g., lower income, rural populations). This article provides a detailed overview of and rationale for technology-based methods of psychological intervention, specifically acceptance and commitment therapy (ACT). The effectiveness of technology-based ACT interventions, with and without support, is reviewed. Suggestions for how to implement ACT over technology is discussed, along with challenges and future directions. Additionally, the wide evidence base, both outcome and process research, for technological implementations of ACT is reviewed across disorders and populations. Although the development of technology-based ACT interventions is still modest among some populations, the current evidence suggests that they are effective across various mental health concerns and are improving psychological flexibility and well-being.

Key Words: technology, acceptance and commitment therapy, self-help, mobile applications, online interventions

An Overview of Technology-based Interventions

There are vast mental health treatment gaps globally. Many individuals in need of treatment do not receive any services (e.g., Kessler et al., 2005). Because the dominant model of delivering psychosocial interventions involves a trained mental health professional in an in-person clinical setting, there are significant limitations to the scale and reach of many psychosocial interventions (Kazdin, 2019). Therefore, there is a need for multiple models of providing treatment (Kazdin, 2019). The advances that have been made in information technology, the internet, mobile phone apps, and other technology-based solutions have increased the reach and dissemination of psychological help (Andersson et al., 2019). Most of the internationally conducted internet interventions are based on cognitive-behavioral therapy (internet-based cognitive-behavioral therapy, ICBT), which is one of the most studied, effective forms of psychotherapy (Cuijpers et al., 2008). To date, more than 200 randomized controlled trials (RCTs) have been done on internet interventions for a range of psychological disorders and somatic conditions (Anderson, 2018).

Technology-based interventions, particularly Internet and mobile interventions, offer several benefits for both the individual and society. As compared to face-to-face therapy, online therapy is available regardless of time and place, so the client is free to decide when to work on therapy. Treatment thereby can be offered in sparsely populated, remote areas (Andersson et al., 2005). Online treatment can also help overcome reluctance to participate in treatments due to social or cultural barriers such as stigmatization and self-stigma (Andrade et al., 2014; Fiorillo et al., 2017). Using technology to disseminate treatments can also help overcome obstacles related to professional and financial resources (e.g., cost, working hours; Andrade et al., 2014). Technology-based interventions also allow for completing treatment at one's own pace, improved affordability of therapy, and privacy. Furthermore, some people may prefer nondirect communication or find it easier to report sensitive issues via computer rather than face-to-face (Andrews et al., 2010). Online interventions give clients significantly more opportunities to address issues related to psychological well-being more anonymously than in traditional face-to-face interventions. From a public health perspective, online interventions offer a significant benefit, allowing the therapist to treat large groups of clients without compromising the effectiveness of the treatment (Marks et al., 2003). Furthermore, strong evidence supports the cost effectiveness of online care, which, among other things, alleviates the financial burden of depression on society (McCrone et al., 2004; Warmerdam et al., 2010). Among the disadvantages of online interventions, nonadherence and high dropout rates are serious problems that merit much concern (Pots et al., 2016a).

The Effectiveness of Online Interventions

The effectiveness and efficiency of online therapies have been extensively studied in the treatment of various mental health problems (Carlbring et al., 2018; Green & Iverson, 2009; Kenwright et al., 2001). Increasing evidence shows that ICBT can be as effective as other treatment formats (Carlbring et al., 2018). The efficacy of supported web-based therapies is comparable to that of face-to-face therapies (e.g., Andersson, 2009; Andersson et al., 2007; Andrews et al., 2010; Kaltenthaler et al., 2004, 2008; Marks et al., 2007; Ruwaard et al., 2009; Vernmark et al., 2010). For example, Andrews et al. (2010) showed that the effect size of computer-based treatments at the end of treatment was large as compared to control groups ($d = 0.88$). In light of the current research literature, Internet-based therapies are an effective, acceptable, and cost-effective way to deliver empirically validated therapy to those who would otherwise go untreated.

In recent years, research on the effectiveness of online interventions has increasingly focused on identifying predictors of response. Studies have consistently reported that demographic factors such as age or educational level have low predictive power in explaining outcome (e.g., Fledderus et al., 2012; Pots et al., 2016a). One approach to understanding who benefits from online treatments is comparing treatment outcome among participants with varying symptom severity. For example, in an online treatment of panic disorder, lower severity of symptoms was associated with positive response (El Alaoui et al., 2013). In an online treatment program for depression, a higher level of symptoms of depression together with high positive psychological functioning predicted positive response, while high anxiety suggested lower changes in depression during treatment (Pots et al., 2016a). Another approach to understanding variance in response has been measuring the participants' expectations of the effectiveness of the online program. Research has shown that a positive expectation predicts better treatment outcome (Boettcher et al., 2013; El Alaoui et al., 2013; Hedman et al., 2012). In the treatment of depression, the expectations of the participants were found to strongly predict overall changes in symptoms (El Alaoui et al., 2013). Contrary to these findings, Zagorscak et al. (2020) reported that initial expectations had only a minor effect on treatment outcome.

Support in Online Interventions

A significant proportion of online treatments involve a therapist or a coach who guides and supports the client through the program, provides feedback on home assignments and answers to questions from the client (Andersson et al., 2019). Online treatments can differ considerably in regard to the amount of support or therapist contact provided. Glasgow and Rosen (1978) present a taxonomy to classify the nature and type of support provided for CBT self-help programs. It distinguishes between three types of support or guidance that could be provided in internet-based interventions: (1) self-administered in which no support is provided; (2) minimal contact in which a rationale with regular check-ins is incorporated in the intervention; and (3) guided self-help in which the clients receive an initial support session and support sessions throughout the treatment program (see Andersson, 2009). In guided or supported online/mobile interventions, the support can be provided via face-to-face sessions or online sessions using videoconferencing as well as via smartphones, email, text messages or other media (e.g., WhatsApp app).

Previous research suggests that treatments including support are more effective than treatments without any support (e.g., Andersson & Cuijpers, 2009; Farrand & Woodford, 2013). Meta-analyses and reviews comparing untreated control conditions with guided Internet-based and other computerized treatments indicate effect sizes between 0.42 and 0.78 in favor of guided treatments in which a therapist or a coach supports the client through the treatment program (Andersson & Cuijpers, 2009; Griffiths et al., 2010; Richards & Richardson, 2012). Self-administered or self-guided psychological treatments for depression without therapist support have shown smaller effect sizes ($d = 0.25–0.36$; Andersson & Cuijpers, 2009; Cuijpers et al., 2011; Richards & Richardson, 2012).

Some studies, however, have shown that the level of support (i.e., minimal support or extensive support) does not significantly affect treatment outcome (Fledderus et al., 2012). Indeed, minimal contact can be enough to produce outcomes that are comparable to those observed in face-to-face therapy (Cuijpers et al., 2010). Additionally, studies that compare the same online intervention delivered with varying levels of support suggest that support may not have a significant effect in all contexts (Berger et al., 2011).

Certain confounding factors may moderate or mediate the effect of therapist support (e.g., problem severity, type of problem, factors related to the content and delivery of the intervention or mode of delivering support). In summary, the research suggests that providing support is beneficial, although understanding the dose–effect relationship of therapist support in the context of online interventions requires further research (see Table 28.1. for estimated effectiveness of interventions with different types of support).

Internet-based traditional cognitive-behavioral therapy has existed for more than 20 years. However, acceptance and commitment therapy (ACT) research in this field is relatively young and has been available for less than 10 years. The solid research-based evidence and findings gained in ICBT studies has been valuable and highly useful in developing effective technology-based ACT interventions. In this article, we provide an overview of the technology-based ACT treatment approach and its evidence base.

How ACT Is Applied in Technology-Based Interventions

Many online ACT programs described in research have utilized existing face-to-face treatment protocols in designing web-based content. Specialists in a given field (e.g., chronic pain) can be used to revise and edit existing protocols to accommodate the online structure and the

Table 28.1. Type of support in technology-based interventions, and estimated effectiveness of these intervention models (e.g. Johansson & Andersson, 2012).

Type of support	Description	Estimated effectiveness
No support	No contact with a therapist; self-guided intervention	Small, d = 0.20
Guided: Minimal support	Brief contact via phone, text messages or written feedback, e.g. 10-15 minutes weekly	Small or moderate, d = 0.40–0.50 effect sizes often comparable with those reported for face-to-face treatments
Guided: Extensive support	Face-to-face contact via video conference technology or other real-time contact (e.g. phone) either through the intervention or before and after the intervention with lower intensity support during the program	Moderate or large, d = 0.50–0.90; effect sizes typically comparable with those reported for face-to-face treatments

desired length of the online treatment. Another common way to develop online or mobile ACT interventions is to take advantage of the existing self-help literature (i.e., using chapters of a book as content), ideally with revisions to increase interactivity. Overall, most forms of Internet treatments historically rely on text (Anderson, 2018). The user can read the text on screen instead of receiving the information from a therapist during a face-to-face meeting or reading the text from a book. However, an online format has an advantage over written material because it can utilize interactive questions, assessment procedures, exercises and tasks that would typically be included in a face-to-face session, as well as more engaging multimedia elements such as audio- or video-recorded exercises and content. However, the content of an effective online program should take the format into account and ensure that all material is sufficiently clear and easy to understand.

When it comes to the organization of an online treatment and choices regarding the format of content, the available programs typically consist of weekly modules or sections divided by specific topic or theme. It is important to use various ways of introducing the therapeutic content: readable self-care and psychoeducational text, self-assessment tasks, images, audio and video recordings or files, exercises asking the user to write down their thoughts concerning the text or questions presented in the program, cartoons, and games (e.g., Lappalainen and Lappalainen, 2020). For example, a program could include videos that provide information on ACT processes and concepts as well as video files that present experiential exercises and metaphors. Participants may also have access to a web diary, a discussion forum, or other interactive elements. Typically, web-based ACT programs consist of 6–15 modules of different length and follow a structure based on the processes of the ACT model: values, value-based actions, present moment, defusion, self-as-context, and acceptance, including self-compassion (e.g., Lappalainen and Lappalainen, 2020). Each module can present a set of psychological flexibility skills for the user to practice online and offline. In most cases, the user is instructed to follow one module per week or, alternatively, per two weeks. Home assignments to encourage practicing in real-life situations, such as writing tasks or behavioral tasks, are typically included in the intervention.

In addition to online interventions, ACT interventions can also be delivered or enhanced via mobile phones or apps. These apps make interventions more accessible by reaching people

24/7, thereby decreasing chances of dropout (Lee et al., 2018); they also have the potential to enhance therapy effects (Levin et al., 2017a). In addition, mobile apps and technologies make it easier to assess antecedents and consequences of target behaviors (e.g., specific triggers and short-term consequences), and interventions can be provided in their natural context, (e.g., prior to a feared situation; Vilardaga et al., 2014). Mobile apps may include psychoeducational text, pictures, or cartoons highlighting ACT processes, short experiential exercises in audio or text, self-monitoring, personalized feedback via text messages, diaries, games, social support, video clips, and quizzes (Lee et al., 2018).

What distinguishes online or mobile-provided interventions from face-to-face interventions is the lesser degree to which ACT can be tailored to the individual client. However, there are also many ways in which online treatment can be tailored when considering the different ways of providing support before, during, and after online treatment. For example, in guided online intervention models, preassessment procedures can include case formulation models that can help the therapist individualize the online intervention to the client. For example, the therapist can advise the user to pay attention to specific module/exercises or highlight the possible benefits of the intervention for the user. Thus, the clinician can highlight specific ACT processes based on the initial interview and behavioral assessment before online treatment begins. The therapist can also offer tailored feedback and support in this way during the treatment. A recent transdiagnostic meta-analysis found that across online ACT studies, therapist guidance was associated with greater effectiveness when compared to nonguided online ACT (Thompson et al., 2020).

Many online programs include written online feedback, which is typically asynchronous (i.e., the therapist and user are not writing at the same time but respond on their own schedule). Other ways to offer support include videoconferencing or phone calls, text messages, or other chat services. In some cases, automated reminders are used adjunctively to increase adherence to a preassigned schedule (e.g., Lappalainen et al., 2019a). Written support can also be partially predesigned or semistructured with individualized comments from the therapist. Regardless of the frequency and extensiveness of support (even if no support is included), it is important to discuss the schedule of communication and expected progress in the program with the user before online treatment begins. In fact, too much flexibility in progressing and completing assignments has been found to negatively affect treatment outcome (Paxling et al., 2013).

The optimal amount of support provided by a therapist has not yet been established (Griffiths et al., 2010). However, the therapist's main role is to encourage the user to work with the online program and to provide support during the course of the program. Because the purpose of using the technology-based interventions is often to decrease time spent by the therapist, 10–20 minutes a week can be sufficient. Whatever the type of support is, conveying to clients that a real person is available and will support them during the program is beneficial. Interestingly, the professional qualification of the therapist providing the web-based intervention seems to be of less importance (e.g., Andersson et al., 2019). Support can also be provided by a nonclinician and requires less therapeutic skills than those needed for face-to-face-delivered therapies.

While some research shows that support provided by a therapist during online intervention is important for treatment effectiveness (Anderson, 2018), other studies indicate that online programs can be effective even without the support of a therapist (e.g., Griffiths et al., 2010). An example of the latter is a self-help ACT-based online intervention without therapist support for subclinical and clinical insomnia (Lappalainen et al., 2019a). This intervention had a positive effect on sleep quality and duration as well as sleep-related dysfunctional cognitions and depressive symptoms, although the effect was small or moderate ($d = 0.21–0.53$).

Some Practical Guidelines for Therapist Support

When beginning an online treatment, it is important to communicate the aims and advantages of the web- or mobile-based treatment to the user or client, as well as present a general overview of the intervention. Such an introduction could include the following information: what is an online or mobile intervention; what are the benefits or advantages of this form of intervention; what is expected from the user; how long and how often the therapist recommends working with the program; what type of feedback or support is provided and when. Effective use of online interventions can also be facilitated by familiarizing the user with the intervention during the first session. Furthermore, a brief introduction to the content of the intervention and a demonstration on how to use the program can increase the ease of use. In practice, the service provider or therapist needs to have access to a computer or a tablet during the initial sessions and to familiarize themselves with the treatment program. If possible, an in-person meeting is recommended at the beginning and end of the program either face-to-face, via telephone call, or through videoconferencing. During the initial meeting, discussion of client motivation and potential barriers for intervention is also recommended. Further, clear schedules and deadlines for the completion of home assignments may help facilitate the impact of the intervention. Planning how the user is supported during use of the program is encouraged.

Evidence of Technology-based ACT Interventions

The number of technology-based interventions based on ACT is growing rapidly. Online ACT treatments have been investigated for a number of conditions. Meta-analyses show that web-based acceptance-, mindfulness- and value-based interventions are effective in enhancing well-being and mental health (Brown et al., 2016; Spijkerman et al., 2016). For example, in a meta-analysis of 10 RCTs of ACT-based online interventions (Brown et al., 2016), it was concluded that online ACT was effective in the management of depressive symptoms (between-group g = 0.24; within-group g = 0.73). Further, a meta-analysis by Thompson et al. (2020) concluded that, based on a transdiagnostic approach across 25 RCTs, online ACT produced small pooled effects (Hedge's g = 0.24 –0.38 across variables) that were maintained at follow-up (Hedge's g = 0.21–0.32). This meta-analysis also concluded that studies of clinical populations reported significantly larger effects on anxiety (Thompson et al., 2020). Thompson et al. (2020) also reported that online ACT produced small, but significant, effects on psychological flexibility at posttreatment and follow-up (Hedge's g = 0.32 and 0.36, respectively).

In the following sections, we describe technology-based ACT in the treatment of mood and anxiety disorders, stress (Table 28.2), and health behaviors and health-related problem (Tables 3). We also discuss interventions for young people and older people (Table 28.4). This review focuses mainly on online (i.e., web-based) interventions, as their evidence base and effectiveness are robust in treating mental health disorders. In addition, mobile apps, mobile games, videoconferencing and virtual reality (VR) are briefly covered. Tables 2–4 provide an overview of research literature with attention to various technologies investigated, modes of support offered during treatment, and treatment outcomes, including follow-up outcomes. These tables have been included to give a brief overview of the approaches of technology-based ACT among various populations. The current examples of studies are not totally representative and do not include all the studies in the field. There are approximately 70 studies investigating the impact of technology-based ACT interventions, and the number of studies is continuously increasing. This overview is intended to describe the rich variety and diversity of ACT-based interventions applying technology-based solutions. As we can see in the following sections, online and other technology-based ACT interventions can be delivered in several ways to a large variety of populations. In some studies, several technologies were combined.

Mood Disorders

Online ACT programs for depression are effective in reducing depressive symptomatology in comparison to both a waitlist control group and an active control (Buhrman et al., 2013; Carlbring et al., 2013; Fledderus et al., 2012; Jones et al., 2015; Lappalainen et al., 2014, 2015). For example, Pots et al. (2016b) found significant reductions in depressive symptoms as a result of a web-based ACT intervention compared with both a waitlist control group (between-group d = 0.56) and an active control group who received an expressive writing intervention (d = 0.36). Carlbring et al. (2013) reported similar results, in which ACT combined with behavioral activation produced larger changes in depression symptoms compared to a waitlist. Similar to how several studies demonstrate how guided online CBT is as effective as face-to-face CBT (Andersson & Cuijpers, 2009; Ruwaard et al., 2009; Titov, 2011), there is evidence that a supported ACT online intervention for depression can produce similar results compared to face-to-face ACT (Lappalainen et al., 2014). Interestingly, the guided online ACT intervention produced larger changes at 6-month follow-up compared to face-to-face ACT in depressive symptomatology, general health, and satisfaction with life (Lappalainen et al., 2014). This finding raises an interesting question: Could online treatment with brief therapist support be more effective than an intervention delivered face-to-face? There is also evidence that a therapist-supported online intervention for depressive disorders can be offered in a considerably shorter time compared to face-to-face intervention without diminishing the effectiveness and quality of the treatment. An ACT-based group + online rehabilitation intervention that included 6 days in a rehabilitation center produced equal results compared to a 15-day group intervention in the same center without the online intervention (Lappalainen et al., under review). These results suggest that, in the context of mood disorders, online interventions using very brief and low-intensity support can produce significant improvements in depressive symptomatology (see Table 28.2 for an overview).

Anxiety Disorders

A meta-analysis evaluating the impact of online ACT for anxiety found a small significant effect size (between-group g = 0.18; Brown et al., 2016). However, this meta-analysis only included seven RCTs, none of which included an intervention designed primarily to reduce anxiety, and all had evaluated anxiety as a secondary outcome (Brown et al., 2016). Dahlin et al. (2016a, 2016b) investigated the effects of a 9-week therapist-guided online program for generalized anxiety disorder (GAD) based on acceptance-based behavior therapy. The treatment was effective compared to a waitlist control condition, with moderate to large effect sizes on symptoms of GAD (d = 0.70–0.98) and depression (d = 0.51–0.56; Dahlin et al., 2016a, 2016b). This finding suggests that online ACT might be effective in reducing symptoms of GAD.

Studies have provided support for the effectiveness of online ACT for social anxiety disorder, with results that are comparable to those observed in face-to-face treatment (within group d = 1.18–1.47 with therapist support, d = 0.96 without support; Gershkovich et al., 2016; Gershkovich et al., 2017). Similarly, Ivanova et al. (2016) reported that online ACT is effective in reducing general anxiety (d = 0.39) and anxiety related to social situations (d = 0.70) among individuals with panic disorder and/or social anxiety disorder. Furthermore, online ACT combined with a mobile app was more effective than waitlist, regardless of whether or not participants received therapist support during the treatment. However, Ivanova et al. (2016) did not find significant reductions in panic disorder severity.

Support for the effectiveness of ACT for severe health anxiety was found in a pilot study by Hoffmann et al. (2018) reporting large effects in health anxiety symptoms (d = 1.06). Fiorillo et al. (2017) examined the effectiveness of an online ACT intervention in the treatment of PTSD symptoms among survivors of interpersonal trauma. Though preliminary, the results suggest the six-session intervention had a large effect on PTSD symptoms (d = 1.06) as well as on anxiety and depression (d = 0.89 and 0.79, respectively; Fiorillo et al., 2017). Technology-based ACT interventions for anxiety and stress are presented in Table 28.2.

Chronic Health Problems and Health Behavior

Online ACT programs for chronic health problems and health behaviors have been investigated in the context of various problems, such as pain, tinnitus, and smoking. In recent years, chronic pain in particular has attracted researchers' interest. Online ACT treatment has been found to have promising effects in the management of chronic pain (Buhrman et al., 2013) and in the treatment of fibromyalgia (Ljótsson et al., 2014). Another study investigating online ACT for fibromyalgia showed that, as an adjunct to treatment-as-usual, online ACT was effective in reducing the impact of fibromyalgia depression, pain and kinesiophobia, and fear of movement or injury (Simister et al., 2018). Another online ACT program was found to decrease chronic pain disability in several areas (e.g., work, household work, and social activities) among 28 percent of participants in comparison to 5 percent who received an expressive writing intervention (Trompetter et al., 2014). Hesser et al. (2012) compared guided online ACT with guided online CBT for tinnitus and found that both treatments were equally effective; they were significantly better than a monitored online discussion forum (d = 0.68–0.70). In line with these results, Lin et al. (2017) reported that a guided online ACT program was effective in reducing pain interference and increasing pain acceptance immediately after the intervention and at 6-month follow-up. The guided online ACT showed significantly less pain interference and higher pain acceptance than the waitlist group (d = 0. 58–0.76). Overall, online ACT has shown promise in the treatment of chronic pain conditions.

Puolakanaho et al. (2020) investigated the impact of an 8-week ACT intervention combining a group and web-based intervention for burnout symptoms and general well-being at work. The results showed that adding a brief ACT intervention to current occupational health care services (treatment-as-usual, TAU) decreased burnout, stress, and psychological symptoms, while general well-being and workability increased significantly compared to TAU alone. Stress and burnout symptoms were also significantly reduced in a RCT by Barrett and Stewart (2020), who compared an online ACT program to an online CBT program for stress management in health care workers. However, there were no significant differences between the groups receiving different programs (Barrett & Stewart, 2020). Online ACT has also been investigated in the context of eating disorders, specifically in a population with a diagnosis of bulimia or eating disorder not otherwise specified (Stranskov et al., 2017). This study suggested that online ACT was effective in reducing eating disorder symptoms and body dissatisfaction when compared to a waitlist control group; 36.6 percent of participants experienced clinically significant improvements compared to 7.1 percent in the control condition (Stranskov et al., 2017). Changes in health behavior were targeted in a pilot trial by Levin et al. (2017c) where an ACT matrix app was explored as an intervention to improve dietary choices, self-monitoring, physical activity, and psychological coping in relation to weight control. Though preliminary, the results indicate that a mobile ACT intervention

Table 28.2. Technology-based ACT interventions and other acceptance-based interventions targeting depressive symptoms, anxiety disorders, and stress.

Study	Population/treatment target (diagnosis or cutoff)	*N*	Study design (control if any)	Technology (support if any)	Primary outcome(s)	Pre-post outcome (d)	Follow-up outcome (F-U time[1]
Barrett & Stewart (2020)	Social and healthcare workers with stress	42 (22 + 20)	RCT: ACT or CBT	Internet-delivered	PSS	ACT = CBT (no sign. Time × Cond. interaction)	n/a
Carlbring et al. (2013)	Depression (MADRS-S ≥ 15 ≤ 30)	80 (40 + 40)	RCT: BA + ACT (WLC)	Internet-delivered, CD-ROM (written feedback)	BDI-II	0.98 BA + ACT > WLC	Effect was maintained (6 mo.)
Dahlin et al. (2016a)	GAD (diagnosis; PSWQ ≥ 45; MADRS-S ≤ 30)	103 (52 + 51)	RCT: ABBT (WLC)	Internet-delivered, audio CD and workbook (written support)	PSWQ	0.87 ABBT > WLC	Significant improvement (6 mo.)
Dahlin et al. (2016b)	GAD(diagnosis)	14	Single-arm: ABBT	Internet-delivered, audio CD and workbook (email, phone calls, 1 session)	PSWQ	2.14 (within)	Effect was maintained (2–3 mo.)
Fiorillo et al. (2017)	Interpersonal trauma (GHQ-12 ≥ 4)	25	Single-arm: ACT	Internet-delivered (calls and emails to prompt/ verify progress)	PCL-5 DASS-D DASS-A	1.06 0.79 0.89	n/a
Fledderus et al. (2012)	Depressive symptomatology (CES-D > 10 < 39; HADS-A > 3 < 15)	376 (125 + 125 + 126)	RCT: ACT extensive (ext.) support, ACT minimal (min.) support (WLC)	Internet-delivered (Email support)	CES-D	0.74 ext. 0.89 min. EXT = MIN Support > WLC	Effect was maintained (3 mo.)
Gershkovich et al. (2016)	SAD(diagnosis)	13	Single-arm: acceptance-based CBT	Internet-delivered (brief video-conferencing)	SPAI-SP LSAS-SR BFNE	1.47 0.92 1.17 (within)	1.39 0.86 1.08 (within) (3 mo.)

(*continued*)

Table 28.2. *Continued*

Study	Population/treatment target (diagnosis or cutoff)	*N*	Study design (control if any)	Technology (support if any)	Primary outcome(s)	Pre-post outcome (d)	Follow-up outcome (F-U time[1]
Gershkovich et al. (2017)	SAD (diagnosis)	42 (20+22)	RCT: acceptance-based CBT with support (s) or without support (ns)	Internet-delivered (brief video-conferencing, daily text messages)	SPAI-SP LSAS	1.18 (s) 0.96 (ns) 0.86 (s) 0.67 (ns) (within)	n/a
Hofer et al. (2018)	Stress and burnout (PSS ≥ 17)	119 (61 + 58)	RCT: ACT (WLC, WLC with study structure)	Online self-help book	PSS-10 MBI-GS Exhaustion Cynicism Personal efficacy	0.90 0.80 0.50 0.50 ACT > WLC	Continued improvement (3 mo.)
Hoffmann et al. (2018)	Severe health anxiety (WI-7 > 21.4)	15	Single-arm:ACT	Internet-delivered (written support)	WI-7	SRM = 1.63 (within)	SRM = 1.06 (within) (3 mo.)
Ivanova et al. (2016)	SAD, panic disorder (diagnosis; LSAS-SR ≥ 30 and/or PDSS-SR ≥ 8)	152 (50 + 51 + 51)	RCT:Guided ACT (G) or unguided ACT (UG) (WLC)	Internet-delivered with adjunct mobile app (in-app feedback)	GAD-7LSAS-SR PDSS-SR	0.39 0.70 NS G = UG ACT > WLC	n/a
Lappalainen et al. (2014)	Outpatients with depressive symptoms (positive screening for depression)	38 (19 + 19)	RCT: ACT online versus ACT face-to-face	Internet-delivered (two face-to-face sessions, written support)	BDI-II	g = 0.43 Face-to-face > online	g = -0.23 (18 mo.) Online > face to face
Lappalainen et al. (2015)	Depression (positive screening)	39 (19 + 20)	RCT: ACT (WLC)	Internet-delivered (written support)	BDI-II	g = 0.83 ACT > WLC	g = 1.33 (within) (12 mo.)

Lappalainen et al. (2013)	Men with stress-related psychological problems	24 (12 + 12)	RCT: CBT + ACT (WLC)	Various technologie s(group meetings)	BDI SCL-90 BBI-15	0.57 NS NS ACT > WLC	1.11 1.07 0.91 (within) (6 mo.)
Lappalainen et al., 2021	Parents of children with chronic conditions	110	RCT: online ACT self-help ACT	Internet-delivered with online support vs Self-help booklet + online exercises without support	SMBQ PHQ-9 CompACT FFMQ	NS 0.49 0.64 0.55	n/a
Levin et al. (2019)	Adults interested in self-help apps	69	RCT: Tailored app (TA) or random app (RA) (EMA only)	Mobile app-delivered (EMA check-in prompts via text message)	DASS	0.85 TA > RA 1.21 TA > RA	n/a
Ly et al. (2014a)	Stress (middle managers)	73 (36 + 37)	RCT: ACT (WLC)	Mobile app (text messages every other day)	GHQ-12 PSS-14	0.41 0.50 ACT > WLC	n/a
Pennefather et al. (2018)	Stress among parents of autistic children	23	Single-arm: ABA+ACT	Videoconferencing (weekly group meetings)	SDQ-P Emotional Conduct Hyperactivity Peer Prosocial DCI PSS	NS NS 0.74 NS 0.86 0.53 NS	n/a
Pots et al. (2016b)	Depressive symptoms	236 (82 + 67 + 87)	RCT: ACT (expressive writing, WLC)	Internet-delivered (email support)	CES-D	0.36 ACT > EW 0.56 ACT > WLC	Effects were maintained (12 mo.)

(continued)

Table 28.2. *Continued*

Study	Population/treatment target (diagnosis or cutoff)	N	Study design (control if any)	Technology (support if any)	Primary outcome(s)	Pre-post outcome (d)	Follow-up outcome (F-U time[1]
Proctor et al. (2018)	Multiple sclerosis patients with low mood	27 (14 + 13)	RCT: TAU+ACT (TAU)	Telephone-supported self-help book (8 weekly calls)	GAD-7 PHQ-9	n/a	0.84 NS (12 weeks) ACT > TAU
Sairanen et al. (2019)	Parents of children with type 1 diabetes or functional disabilities	74 (37 + 37)	RCT: ACT (WLC)	Internet-delivered (phone interview, online feedback, discussion forum)	SMBQ DASS	0.88 ACT 0.20 WLC 0.55 ACT 0.08 WLC	1.05 0.54 ACT > WLC
Yuen et al. (2013a)	SAD (diagnosis)	14	Single-arm: ABBT	Virtual environment in second life (12 weekly sessions)	SPAI-SP LSAS BFNE	1.42 1.07 1.21 (within)	1.50 1.21 1.29 (within) (3 mo.)
Yuen et al. (2013b)	SAD (diagnosis)	24	Single-arm: ABBT	Video-conferencing (12 weekly sessions)	SPAI-SP LSAS BFNE	1.91 1.40 1.23 (within)	2.10 1.30 1.41 (within) (3 mo.)
Yuen et al. (2019)	Public speaking anxiety (clinical/subclinical SAD, significant fear of public speaking)	11+15 (2 pilots)	Single-arm: ACT+exposure	Videoconferencing (additional video recording of the audience for one pilot)	PRCS-SF SSPS-P SSPS-N	1.06–1.72 1.00–1.20 0.86–1.33	1.63–1.69 1.06–1.12 0.94–1.33

Note: RCT = studies using a randomized controlled design (including, e.g., pilot, feasibility, etc.); single-arm = studies using a design without any control group; WLC = waiting-list control; for outcomes, effect size (between-group Cohen's *d* with direction of effect) reported unless indicated otherwise; *g* = Hedge's *g*; SRM = standardized response mean; NS = non-significant; F-U = follow-up, [1]if several follow-up points were reported, the longest follow-up period is reported; n/a = not applicable, was not reported.

Diagnosis, GAD = generalized anxiety disorder; SAD = social anxiety disorder.

Treatment, BA = behavior activation; ACT = acceptance and commitment therapy; ABBT = acceptance-based behavior therapy; CBT = cognitive behavioral therapy.

Screening and outcome measures, MADRS-S = MADRS-S = Montgomery Åsberg Depression Rating Scale; BDI-II = Beck Depression Inventory-II; PSWQ = Penn State Worry Questionnaire; GHQ-12 = General Health Questionnaire; PCL-5 = Posttraumatic Stress Disorder Checklist; DASS = Depression, Anxiety and Stress Scales; DASS-D = Depression subscale; DASS-A = Anxiety subscale; DASS-S = Stress subscale; CES-D = Center of Epidemiological Studies – Depression Scale; HADS-A = Hospital Anxiety and Depression Scale – anxiety subscale; SPAI-SP = Social Phobia and Anxiety Inventory; LSAS-SR = Liebowitz Social Anxiety Scale; BFNE = Brief Fear on Negative Evaluation Scale; PSS = Perceived Stress Scale; MBI-GS = Maslach Burnout Inventory – General Survey; WI-7 = Whiteley-7 Index; PDSS-SR = Panic Disorder Severity Scale-Self Rated; SCL-90 = 90-item symptom checklist; BBI-15 = Bergen Burnout Indicator; SDQ-P = Strengths and Difficulties Questionnaire – parent report; PSS = Parental Stress Scale; DCI = Daily Coping Inventory; SMBQ = Shirom-Melamed Burnout Questionnaire; PRCS-SF =

had medium to large effects on health behavior change efforts in relation to the waiting-list control group (Levin et al., 2017c).

Only a limited number of studies have examined the effectiveness of face-to-face delivered ACT interventions in treating insomnia (e.g., Baik, 2015; Zetterqvist et al., 2018). Similarly, few studies have investigated the effectiveness of online ACT for sleeping difficulties. In a RCT by Lappalainen et al. (2019a), an online ACT intervention without therapist support for subclinical and clinical insomnia had a significant effect on sleep quality and duration as well as sleep-related dysfunctional cognitions and depressive symptoms. The effect sizes between the treatment and control group were small to moderate (d = 0.21–0.53), suggesting that online ACT may be effective in relieving symptoms of insomnia (Lappalainen et al., 2019a). It has been suggested that ACT could be integrated in online CBT treatments for insomnia to enhance the intervention, specifically among those who do not benefit from online CBT for insomnia (Dalrymple, Fiorentino, Politi, & Posner, 2010).

ACT technology-based interventions appear to be a potential alternative for individuals interested in quitting smoking. Several RCTs investigating mobile-phone-delivered and online ACT interventions support the feasibility and efficacy of an online ACT approach (Bricker et al., 2010, 2013, 2014a, 2014b, 2018, 2020). A web-based ACT program for smoking cessation among smokers with depressive symptoms also showed promising results (Jones et al., 2015).

Online and mobile ACT interventions targeting health behaviors and health problems are depicted in Table 28.3.

Adolescents and Younger Adults

Several online ACT prevention and treatment programs have been developed for young adults, particularly for university students. For example, Levin et al. (2014) developed and tested a web-based program, with promising results in reducing depressive symptomatology (d = 0.40), though anxiety or stress did not decrease during the intervention. Further, an online ACT program for college students struggling with psychological problems reduced overall distress, general anxiety, social anxiety, depression, and academic concerns, along with improving positive mental health (d = 0.47–0.78; Levin et al., 2017a). In accordance with these findings, in a RCT by Räsänen et al. (2016), an online ACT intervention for university students improved well-being and reduced symptoms of stress and depression, and elevated satisfaction in life and self-confidence (d = 0.46–0.69). In addition, students' mindfulness skills significantly increased at postintervention (d = 0.49). These results were maintained at one-year follow-up (Räsänen et al., 2016). However, the web-based ACT intervention did not significantly impact anxiety and general psychological flexibility skills (as measured by the AAQ-II). Also, some studies using an active control condition, such as online psychoeducation, have reported equivalent effects between the intervention group and control group (e.g., Glick & Orsillo, 2015; Levin et al., 2016; Viskovich & Pakenham, 2018). Additionally, distressed university students reported an improvement in mental health symptoms after using an online ACT program that focused on open processes, engaged processes, or combined both when compared to a waitlist control (d = 0.71–0.86; Levin et al., 2020a). Online ACT programs have also been developed to improve academic skills among university students and young people. An online ACT program with a focus on values training improved the academic performance of undergraduate students (Chase et al., 2013). Interestingly, the online values training combined with goal-setting was more effective than goal-setting alone.

In addition, ACT has promise for use with children and adolescents (Halliburton & Cooper, 2015; Swain et al., 2015), but little research has examined online ACT for youth

Table 28.3. Technology-based ACT interventions and other acceptance-based interventions targeting health behavior and somatic health-related problems.

Study	Population/treatment target (diagnosis or cutoff)	N	Study design (control if any)	Technology (support if any)	Primary outcome(s)	Pre-post outcome (d)	Follow-up outcome (F-U time[1])
Boucher et al. (2016)	Intuitive eating (40–50-year-old women, IES < 65, BMI ≥ 26.5)	40	Single-arm: Intuitive eating + ACT	Internet-delivered (email reminders)	IES-2	Significant improvement	Effect was maintained (3 mo.)
Bricker et al. (2010)	Smoking cessation (daily smoker > 29 days)	14	Single-arm:ACT	Telephone-delivered (5 sessions)	Quit rate	29 %	29 % (12 mo.)
Bricker et al. (2013)	Smoking cessation(≥5 cigarettes per day ≥ 12 months)	222 (111 + 111)	RCT: ACT (website for smoking cessation)	Internet-delivered	Quit rate		23% ACT 10% control (3 mo.)
Bricker et al. (2014a)	Smoking cessation (≥10 cigarettes per day ≥ 12 months)	121 (59 + 62)	RCT: Nicotine-replacement + ACT (nicotine-replacement + CBT)	Telephone-delivered (5 sessions)	Quit rate	n/a	31% ACT 22% CBT (6 mo.)
Bricker et al. (2014b)	Smoking cessation (≥5 cigarettes per day ≥ 12 months)	196 (98 + 98)	RCT: ACT (app for smoking cessation)	Mobile app	Quit rate	n/a	13% ACT 8% control (2 mo.)
Bricker et al. (2018)	Smoking cessation (≥5 cigarettes per day ≥ 12 months)	2637 (1319 + 1318)	RCT: ACT (website for smoking cessation)	Internet-delivered (text message or email prompts, discussion forum in ACT condition)	Quit rate	n/a	24% ACT 26% control (12 mo.)
Bricker et al. (2020)	Smoking cessation	2415 (1214 + 1201)	RCT ACT (app for smoking cessation)	Mobile app	Quit rate	n/a	28% ACT 21% control (12 mo.)

Buhrman et al. (2013)	Chronic pain (functional impairment)	76 (38 + 38)	RCT: ACT (moderated online discussion forum)	Internet-delivered (written feedback, two phone calls)	CPAQ	0.41 ACT > WLC	Effect was maintained (6 mo.)
Hawkes et al. (2013)	Health in survivors of colorectal cancer (diagnosis within 12 mo., 1 ≥ poor health behavior)	410	RCT: ACT health counseling (TAU)	Telephone-delivered (bi-weekly calls for 5 mo. + after 4 weeks, handbook, postcards, pedometer, newsletter)	GLTEQ SF-36 FACITFS	No effect (6 mo.)	Significant effect only on moderate PA (12 mo.)
Hesser et al. (2012)	Tinnitus	99 (35 + 32 + 32)	RCT: ACT (CBT, monitored online discussion forum)	Internet-delivered (written support)	THI	0.70 (CBT) 0.68 (ACT) ACT = CBT	1.34 (within) (12 mo.) ACT = CBT
Jones et al. (2015)	Smokers with depressive symptoms (>5 cigarettes a day for 12 months, positive depression screening)	94 (47 + 47)	RCT: ACT (online intervention for smoking cessation)	Internet-delivered	Quitting rate Anxiety and depression detector	No significant effects	No significant effect s (3 mo.)
Lappalainen et al. (2019a)	Insomnia (ISI ≥ 8)	86 (43 + 40)	RCT: ACT (WLC)	Internet-delivered	BNSQ	0.42 ACT > WLC	0.69 (within) (6 mo.)
Levin et al. (2017a)	Health behaviors	23	Single-arm: ACT	Mobile app (in-person orientation, check-in calls)	WCSS	0.74	n/a
Lin et al. (2017)	Chronic pain	302 (100 + 101 + 101)	RCT: Guided ACT (G) or unguided ACT (UG) (WLC)	Internet-delivered (email support)	MPI	0.58 G > WLC G = UG UG = WLC	0.58 G > WLC (6 mo.)

(continued)

Table 28.3. *Continued*

Study	Population/treatment target (diagnosis or cutoff)	*N*	Study design (control if any)	Technology (support if any)	Primary outcome(s)	Pre-post outcome (d)	Follow-up outcome (F-U time[1])
Ljótsson et al. (2014)	Fibromyalgia (diagnosis for fibromyalgia)	41	Single-arm: Acceptance and values-based exposure	Internet-delivered (written support and online discussion forum)	FIQ	0.71 (within)	0.96 (within)
Moffitt and Mohr (2015)	Minimally active individuals	59 (27 + 32)	RCT: ACT + pedometer-based walking programme (WP) (only WP)	DVD-delivered	IPAQ	Cramer's $V = 0.45$ ACT > WP only	n/a
Molander et al. (2018)	Individuals with hearing problems (HHIE-S ≥ 8)	61 (31 + 30)	RCT: ACT (WLC)	Internet-delivered (online text messaging)	HHIE-S	0.93	n/a
Puolakanaho et al. (2020)	Individuals with burnout symptoms (BBI-15 scores > 75 percentile)	218 (109 + 109)	RCT: ACT (TAU)	Group-based ACT intervention combined with internet- delivered ACT	BBI-15 PSS WAQ	0.39 0.76 0.38	0.49 0.60 0.57 (12 mo.)
Rickardsson et al. (2020)	Chronic pain (continuous/recurring pain > 6 months)	39	Single-arm ACT	Internet-delivered (written support, phone support upon request)	PII	0.64 (within)	0.83 (within) (12 mo.)
Scott et al. (2018)	Complex pain (clinically significant pain, pain-related disability, and distress)	63(31 + 32)	Feasibility RCT: ACT + pain management (pain management)	Internet-delivered (written support, phone calls if needed)	Feasibility outcomes PGIC "much improved" or better	n/a	27% ACT. 15% TAU

Simister et al. (2018)	Fibromyalgi a (diagnosis for fibromyalgia)	67 (33 + 34)	RCT: ACT + TAU (TAU)	Internet-delivered (email reminders, written feedback)	FIQ-R	1.26	1.59 (3 mo.)
Strandskov et al. (2017)	Eating disorders (diagnosis of bulimia nervosa or EDNOS; BMI > 17.5)	92 (46 + 46)	RCT: ACT influenced CBT	Internet-delivered(online support, daily messaging possibility)	EDE-Q	0.54 ACT > WLC	n/a
Trompetter et al. (2014)	Chronic pain (momentary pain intensity score ≥ 4; pain ≥ 3 days a week for ≥ 6 months)	238 (82 + 79 + 77)	RCT: ACT (expressive writing, waiting-list control)	Internet-delivered	MPI interference	0.33 ACT > EW ACT = WLC * adh ACT > WLC 0.35	0.47 (6 mo.) ACT > EW ACT = WLC * adh ACT > WLC 0.40

Note: RCT = studies using a randomized controlled design (including, e.g., pilot, feasibility, etc.); single-arm = studies using a design without any control group; WLC = waiting-list control; for outcomes, effect size (between-group Cohen's *d* with direction of effect) reported unless indicated otherwise; NS = non-significant; F-U = follow-up, [1]if several follow-up points were reported, the longest follow-up period is reported; n/a = not applicable, was not reported.

For diagnosis, EDNOS = eating disorder not otherwise specified. *For treatment,* ACT = acceptance and commitment therapy; CBT = cognitive behavioral therapy; TAU = treatment-as-usual. *For screening and outcome measures,* IES = Intuitive Eating Scale; CPAQ = Chronic Pain Acceptance Questionnaire; GLTEQ = Godin Leisure-Time Exercise Questionnaire; SF-36 = Short Form-36; FACITFS = Functional Assessment of Chronic Illness Therapy Fatigue Scale; THI = Tinnitus Handicap Inventory; ISI = Insomnia Severity Index; BNSQ = Basic Nordic Sleep Questionnaire; WCSS = Weight Control Strategies Scale; MPI = Multidimensional Pain Inventory; FIQ = Fibromyalgia Impact Questionnaire; IPAQ = International Physical Activity Questionnaire; HHIE-S = Hearing Handicap Inventory for the Elderly, Screening version; BBI-15 = Bergen Burnout Inventory, PSS = Perceived Stress Scale, WAQ = Work Ability Questionnaire; PII = Pain Interference Index; PGIC = patient global impression of change; FIQ-R = Fibromyalgia Impact Questionnaire – Revised; EDE-Q = Eating Disorders Examination Questionnaire.

populations. One of these studies is *The Youth Compass,* an online program aimed at 15- to 16-year-old adolescents (Puolakanaho et al., 2019), which reduced stress and symptoms of depression while improving academic buoyancy (reflecting psychological flexibility related to school performance) and life satisfaction (Lappalainen et al., 2021c). Technology-based ACT interventions for adolescents and young adults are presented in Table 28.4.

Parents

Previous research shows that web-based interventions can support parental well-being (Hall & Bierman, 2015). However, online ACT interventions for parents have just started to be implemented (Whittingham et al., 2016, 2020), with very few studies available on the effectiveness of these interventions. A study by Sairanen et al. (2019) investigated a supported online ACT intervention among parents of children with chronic health conditions (e.g., type 1 diabetes, autism spectrum disorders, developmental disability, chromosomal abnormality, or genetic disorder). They found that, in comparison to waitlist, online ACT decreased burnout symptoms and depression (d = 0.54 and d = 1.05, respectively) and increased mindfulness skills (d = 0.98). Interestingly, the study design included only semistructured, written feedback without any face-to-face contact, which suggests that very low-intensity online interventions can be effective for supporting parental well-being (Sairanen et al., 2019). A study by Lappalainen et al. (2021b) confirmed the results of the Sairanen study. An online training program for the parents of children with autism combining components of applied behavior analysis and ACT was effective in reducing parental stress, increasing the children's prosocial behavior, and decreasing their hyperactive behavior (Pennefather et al., 2018).

Older Adults

There are an increasing number of elderly family caregivers, and these individuals often have difficulties obtaining health-promoting services. Studies indicate that many family caregivers experience high levels of distress, including depressive symptoms, stress, and reduced quality of life (Kuipers & Bebbington, 2005; Jansen et al., 2015). Lappalainen et al. (2021a) examined the effectiveness of a guided ACT-based online intervention (Lappalainen et al., 2019b) for enhancing the well-being of older family caregivers. The results suggest that an online ACT intervention is effective in decreasing depressive symptomatology, although the treatment effect was not fully sustained through the follow-up period of 10 months. These results are consistent with traditionally delivered psychosocial interventions to support caregivers that also suggest treatment gains may not be long-lasting (e.g., Bartels et al., 2019). Thus, there is a need to investigate how to best support caregivers over a long period of time in order to enhance long-term treatment results. Online ACT for older adults is still rare. However, an online ACT intervention for older adults with anxiety symptoms is currently being tested (Witlox et al., 2018). If proven effective, it will improve the accessibility of preventive interventions for older adults with anxiety problems. Technology-based interventions adapted to the older adult's needs and abilities are a feasible option that could be used to enhance quality of life for older adults.

Mobile ACT Applications

Information technology-based tools, typically mobile phones, enable various ways of self-monitoring and tracking one's own behavior, recording real-time momentary clinical assessments, and providing flexible access to therapeutic resources such as audio exercises or didactic instructions. There is evidence that mobile phones and apps are valid tools for self-monitoring, including mood, anxiety, life satisfaction, weight, calories, and exercise (e.g., Mattila et al.,

Table 28.4. Technology-based ACT interventions and other acceptance-based interventions for adolescents and young adults.

Study	Population/treatment target (diagnosis or cutoff)	N	Study design (control if any)	Technology (support if any)	Primary outcome(s)	Pre-post outcome (d)	Follow-up outcome (F-U time[1])
Chase et al. (2013)	Psychology majors	132 (51 + 48 + 33)	RCT: ACT-based values training (goal setting program, WLC)	Internet-delivered	GPA	0.63 ACT > WLC 0.41 ACT > goals	Non-significant deterioration
Eustis et al. (2018)	University students	156 (78 + 78)	RCT: ABBT (WLC)	Internet-delivered (email instructions and reminders, written feedback)	DASS-S DASS-A BFNE	0.44 NS NS	Effect was maintained
Firestone et al. (2019)	University students	137	Single-arm: Single-session values intervention	Internet-delivered	PVQ PWQ	0.27 NS (within)	n/a
Glick et al. (2015)	Undergraduate and graduate students	118	RCT: ABBT (time-management intervention)	Online video with PowerPoint slides	Behavioral measure	No significant difference	n/a
Krafft et al. (2019)	2 samples: University students[a] and help-seeking adults from community[b]	[a]63 (19 + 22 + 63) [b]35 (14 + 10 + 11)	RCT: Simple (SA) and complex (CA) version of ACT mobile app (WLC)	Mobile app (email check-in and reminders, optional summary with brief feedback)	DASS	[a]NS[b]SA = CA 0.29-0.39 App > WLC	Effect maintained (3 mo.)
Lappalainen et al. (2021)		249(83 + 82 + 84)	RCT:ACT with face-to-face and online support (FOS), with ACT online support (OS) and control group	Internet-delivered(face-to-face and online support or only online support)	DEPS SWLSAFQ-Y	whole sample NS; those who used at least 3 modules of 5 FOS = OS > control	n/a

(continued)

Table 28.4. *Continued*

Study	Population/treatment target (diagnosis or cutoff)	N	Study design (control if any)	Technology (support if any)	Primary outcome(s)	Pre-post outcome (d)	Follow-up outcome (F-U time[1])
Levin et al. (2016)	Undergraduate university students	234 (114 + 120)	RCT: Acceptance and commitment training (mental health education)	Internet-delivered (email and phone call reminders)	DASS	Equivalent effects	Equivalent effects (3 mo.)
Levin et al. (2014).	Undergraduate first-year university students	76 (37 + 39)	RCT: ACT (WLC)	Internet-delivered	DASS	0.40 (depression) ACT > WLC	Continued improvement (3 weeks)
Levin et al. (2017b)	Distressed university students	79 (40 + 39)	RCT: ACT (WLC)	Internet-delivered	CCAPS-34	0.66ACT > WLC	n/a
Levin et al. (2015)	Students receiving treatment at college counseling centers	82	Single-arm: ACT	Internet-delivered (adjunctive to sessions)	DASS-D DASS-A DASS-S	0.60 0.55 0.40 (within)	n/a
Levin et al. (2020a)	Distressed university students (1 ≥ cutoff for clinically sig. distress on CCAPS-34)	182 (46 + 46 + 45)	RCT: ACT Open only (O), ACT Engaged only (E), ACT combined (C) (WLC)	Internet-delivered (email prompts and reminders, phone support for 50%)	CCAPS-34	0.71–0.86 ACT > WLC O = E = C	0.92–1.03 ACT > WLC O = E = C (4 weeks)
Puolakanaho et al. (2019)	Ninth-grade adolescents (1/2 of sample: poor academic skills)	249 (83 + 82 + 84)	RCT: ACT with face-to-face and online support (FOS), with online support (OS), and control group	Internet-delivered (face-to-face and online support or only online support)	Stress School stress Academic Buoyancy	0.22 NS 0.27 FOS = OS > control	n/a

Sagon et al. (2018)	1st year university students	103 (52 + 51)	RCT: ABBT (WLC)	Internet-delivered	DASS-D	n/a	NS (2 mo.)
Räsänen et al. (2016)	University students	68 (33 + 35)	RCT: ACT (waiting-list control)	Internet-delivered	MHC-SF PSS-10	0.46 0.54 ACT > WLC	Effects were maintained (12 mo.)
Viskovich and Pakenham (2018)	University students	130 (40 + 43 + 47	RCT: ACT (varied instructions for completion)	Internet-delivered	DASS	NS (between) D: 0.36 A: 0.32 S: 0.48 (within)	n/a
Wollach et al. (2020)	University students	141	Single-arm: One-session cognitive defusion intervention	Internet-delivered	FSCS CFQ Emotional discomfort	n/a	NS *ES* = 0.40 *ES* = 0.56

Note: RCT = studies using a randomized controlled design (including, e.g., pilot, feasibility, etc.); single-arm = studies using a design without any control group; WLC = waiting-list control; for outcomes, effect size (between-group Cohen's *d* with direction of effect) reported unless indicated otherwise; *g* = Hedge's *g*; SRM = standardized response mean; NS = non-significant; F-U = follow-up; ES = effect size, [1]if several follow-up points were reported, the longest follow-up period is reported; n/a = not applicable, was not reported.

For treatment, ACT = acceptance and commitment therapy; ABBT = acceptance-based behavior therapy. *For screening and outcome measures*, GPA = grade point average; DASS = Depression, Anxiety and Stress Scales; DASS-D = depression subscale; DASS-A = anxiety subscale; DASS-S = stress subscale; BFNE = Brief Fear on Negative Evaluation Scale; PVQ = Personal Values Questionnaire; PWQ = Psychological Wellbeing Questionnaire; MHC-SF = Mental Health Continuum – Short Form; CCAPS-34 = Counseling Center Assessment of Psychological Symptoms; PSS = Perceived Stress Scale; FSCS = Functions of Self-Criticizing/Attacking Scale; CFQ = Cognitive Fusion Questionnaire.

2008). Mobile phones can automatically generate feedback to the user or send data to coaches, psychologists, counselor, or medical doctors. Lindhiem et al. (2015), in a meta-analysis of 26 articles, concluded that there is evidence for an added effect of mobile technology in the delivery of behavioral interventions. Thus, adding an ACT mobile app to in-person-delivered intervention can enhance skills training in ACT and thereby increase the impact of the intervention (Levin et al., 2017a). For example, mobile ACT can facilitate the utilization of skills of psychological flexibility in users' natural context and when it is most needed. However, more studies are needed in this area.

Several phone apps are already available that provide ACT-based content, including exercises and metaphors in written, audio, or video format. In fact, there are more than 30 ACT-relevant apps available at the moment. Many apps are a collection of exercises that can be used adjunctly to face-to-face sessions or online treatment. Some apps also have more sophisticated features, such as structured progress, tracking tools to evaluate changes over time, reminder notification systems, or check-in features to enable reflecting and planning use of the app. Most apps provide content that can also be used as homework assignments. Recently, the first ACT-based app and game for children has become available. The Magis—the Magical Adventure mobile game—is targeted for children aged 9–11 and is downloadable for free from the Google Play Store and Apple App Store. See Figure 28.1.

Pierce et al. (2016) examined practitioners′ perceptions of mental health apps in a survey among 356 professionals and students familiar with ACT. They found that practitioners were interested in using ACT-related apps, but that use of and familiarity with apps was low. The most helpful app functions related to supporting out-of-session skills practice and the maintenance of therapy gains. The greatest barriers to app use included little guidance about what apps to choose, app content inconsistent with ACT, and ethical concerns related to app use.

There are encouraging results showing that the ACT model is well suited for smartphones. Interestingly, mobile phones enable the gathering of information of specific exercises or skills in relation to observed changes during use of the mobile device. Data showing how often and how long the user has visited the app can be obtained. This type of information adds possibilities to investigate, for example, the dose-response, the magnitude of change in symptoms, or quality of life as a function of the use of the app (time of usage or number of exercises). Furthermore, data collected from smartphone devices could identify specific type of exercises causally linked to the outcomes. In the future, it is probable that some apps will automatically adjust to the individual needs of the user, giving continuous feedback over long periods of time. Additionally, log data or log files that record events in the app can also be collected from web interventions.

Bricker et al. (2014b) provide an example of an ACT-based mobile app for quitting smoking which delivers content while gathering information relevant to further developing the treatment. Study participants who reported opening the ACT-based app on average 37 times during an 8-week period showed a quit rate of 13 percent compared with 8 percent for the control app. Further, using data collected from an ACT-based mobile app, the investigators were able to identify several features that significantly predicted smoking abstinence (Heffner et al., 2013). Similarly, Ly et al. (2014b) successfully applied an ACT-based smartphone app in combination with web-based psychoeducation for stress management. Close to half of the participants adhered to the program for all of the 6 weeks of the intervention. Considering processes of change, it was also observed that active usage of a mobile ACT app was associated with improved psychological flexibility (Mattila et al., 2016) and that acceptance and cognitive defusion exercises were needed, in addition to self-as-context related exercises, in order to obtain gains in psychological flexibility (Mattila et al., 2016). Further, Ahtinen et al.

Figure 28.1. A screenshot from Magis, Magical Adventure, created by Anna Stanczyk (2020), courtesy of Mieli Mental Health Ostrobotnia.

(2013) observed that an ACT-based mobile app designed originally as a stress management app was reported as useful and acceptable by working-age participants. Interestingly, participants appreciated audio narrations and reported that they wanted to be guided through the program, but they did not want to narrow down the choices available for the user without any options to choose. This finding raises a question regarding the right balance between direct guidance and individual freedom to choose freely the content in an ACT mobile app as well as in other technology-based ACT interventions.

In addition to traditional tracking tools and journaling apps available, recent advancement has also been made available through various ecological momentary assessment (EMA) approaches. EMA includes assessment methods using mobile technology to gather data from users in their natural environment at various time points (e.g., McDevitt-Murphy, Luciano &

Zakarian, 2018). Typically, the mobile device prompts the user to complete assessment (e.g., to answer questions or complete rating scales) once or multiple times per day. This assessment procedure may occur at randomly determined times. An example of the usefulness of assessment methods using mobile technology is a study by Gloster et al. (2020). They examined whether a 15-minute microintervention would promote prosocial behaviors in couples. They observed an increase in prosocial behavior, using event sampling methodology and collecting participant experiences in real time with smartphones. Ecological momentary intervention (EMI) refers to the possibility of transporting the intervention to users' natural or home environment. EMI can include reminders, encouraging messages, instructions, and exercises or prompts, for example, for engaging in value-based actions. McDevitt-Murphy, Luciano, and Zakarian (2018) have pointed out that EMAs can be used as an additional assessment tool to develop a better understanding of functional relationships. They could, in turn, be used in planning or tailoring the intervention. EMI can expand the context in which therapeutic learning can occur from the therapy room to the user's real-world environment. Levin et al. (2019) evaluated whether using EMAs to tailor content delivered via an app would have benefits over delivering the same app where content was random or over only completing the EMA regularly (i.e., when prompted twice daily by text message). A sample of 69 adults used the self-help apps for 4 weeks, and equivalently high user satisfaction was reported in all apps. Participants in the tailored app providing ACT component skills based on the assessment evaluation showed better improvement on psychological distress and positive mental health compared to the random app and control conditions. Overall, this study suggests that tailoring ACT-skill coaching based on in-the-moment variables could be more effective compared to when no individual tailoring is used.

In summary, mobile technology offers various ways to enhance psychological interventions or even to deliver evidence-based interventions without professional support. The previously mentioned study by Bricker et al. (2020) with approximately 2500 participants highlights how apps can be easily distributed across large populations, even across the whole country. In addition, the cost of apps is typically relatively low, which can make supported mobile-based interventions a viable, effective and affordable option of receiving treatment.

Virtual Reality ACT Interventions

Highly interesting results have also been reported using virtual reality (VR) to produce therapeutic change. Though not a full ACT intervention, but still relevant in the context of ACT, a pilot study by Falconer et al. (2016) showed that using VR to enable participants to first give compassion to a virtual avatar of a child and then receive compassion from themselves as a child was effective in reducing depressive symptomatology (4-week follow-up $d = 1.11$) and self-criticism, as well as in increasing self-compassion. Additionally, the same design was previously reported to decrease self-criticism among healthy women who were high in self-criticism (Falconer et al., 2014). Though preliminary, these findings suggest that VR may offer new ways to target the effect of difficult thoughts as well as training new behaviors toward oneself in an experiential way. Future research should expand current understanding of how VR could be utilized in ACT treatments.

Acceptance and Feasibility of ACT Web- and Mobile Interventions

In general, studies examining clients' experiences of online interventions after treatment report that satisfaction with the form of therapy and its content has been high among clients (Andrews et al., 2010; Green & Iverson, 2009). In addition, the proportion of those who discontinue treatment is no higher in online therapy than in traditional face-to-face therapy (Green & Iverson, 2009), which suggests that online treatment is acceptable from a client perspective (Andrews et al., 2010). In a study by Waller and Gilbody (2009), 44 percent of subjects considered online treatment to be an even better option than face-to-face treatment.

When it comes to web-based ACT treatments, some studies report very low drop-out rates (e.g., 7%; Bricker et al., 2010; Hoffmann et al., 2018), whereas others have reported relatively large numbers of participants who decline participation after initial assessments (e.g., 33%; Rickardsson et al., 2020). Adherence to online treatments can also vary depending on several factors, such as the stage of development for the program (which can affect usability), the frequency and extensiveness of support or reminders that can help to increase compliance, and the amount of content included in the program. In some studies, users report preferring more time to complete modules and shorter overall length for the program (Rickardsson et al., 2020). Users have also reported that they do not appreciate rigid structures within online and mobile-based interventions and that they prefer the opportunity to personalize the intervention (Ahtinen et al., 2013; Köhle et al., 2017). Among the brief online interventions tested for feasibility, high completion rates have been reported; for example, in a two-session prevention program for university students, 93 percent completed both sessions (Levin et al., 2014). Further, Levin et al. (2017a) observed good engagement and satisfaction ratings when providing a cost-effective ACT self-help program to college students. A feasibility RCT by Scott et al. (2018) reported that among participants with complex chronic pain, 61 percent completed an online ACT program that was used adjunctively to specialty medical pain management. Scott et al. (2018) also reported that the online program was completed significantly more often by unemployed participants (80%) when compared to employed participants (44%) suggesting that it is important to consider the time required to complete the program when planning and implementing new online treatments.

Among the longer online ACT programs, evaluating adherence is often completed by using log data on times the program has been opened or activities have been completed (e.g., time spent using the program or total percentage content completed). Internet programs and mobile apps can be sensitive to flaws in the design of the content (e.g., confusing interface, excessive information or unclear instructions). Yet actual time spent with the program is associated with changes in psychological flexibility, suggesting a dose-response relationship (Mattila et al., 2016). Considering this important finding, the adherence data reported in current studies are encouraging in relation to time spent on the intervention (e.g., 2–3 hours a week; Ivanova et al., 2016), which can exceed time spent on face-to-face meetings.

Overall, acceptance of web-based ACT programs as well as mobile ACT apps has been good. It can be argued that, as the technological and pedagogic sophistication of these programs increases, user satisfaction and acceptance of technology-based ACT will likely also increase. Collecting feasibility data when the program is still being developed or refined may impact the results strongly. Larger-scale evaluations of the acceptability, credibility and usability of web-based and mobile ACT treatments are called for to draw strong conclusions and to compare satisfaction with equal treatment delivered face-to-face.

Processes of Change in Technology-based ACT Interventions

Studies focusing on possible mediators of online ACT programs are only recently starting to emerge (Pots et al., 2016a). Several reports suggest that improvements in psychological flexibility skills mediate the treatment effect on psychological distress with online ACT interventions (e.g., Trompetter et al., 2015). For example, in the treatment of tinnitus, Hesser et al. (2014) found that acceptance (measured as tinnitus suppression) mediated changes in tinnitus severity when participants received an ACT online program, but not when they received a CBT online program. However, when acceptance was measured as activity engagement, it mediated outcome in both treatment groups (Hesser et al., 2014). Bricker et al. (2010) reported that acceptance mediates the effect of a mobile-based ACT program on smoking cessation. In the treatment of depressive symptoms, psychological flexibility and mindfulness facets (i.e., nonreactivity compared to active control condition) were found to mediate the treatment effect of an online ACT treatment program (Pots et al., 2016a).

In a guided ACT intervention for university students including two face-to-face and five online sessions, changes in the nonreactivity subscale of mindfulness and sense of coherence subscale of meaningfulness mediated changes in well-being, depression, and stress (Räsänen et al., 2020). Interestingly, general psychological flexibility (AAQ-II) and cognitive defusion (Automatic Thoughts Questionnaire-Believability) did not mediate changes in outcomes. Another study by Levin et al. (2017a) found that acceptance mediated changes in psychological symptoms, especially symptoms of depression and anxiety, in an online ACT intervention for college students. Interestingly, in a dismantling trial, Levin et al. (2020a) found that when distressed college students (n = 181) were offered an online program that consisted of only Open components of ACT (cognitive defusion and acceptance), the intervention was less effective than an online program that consisted of Engaged components (values and committed action) or of all ACT components. Although all conditions led to significant improvement over the waitlist control, the finding suggests that addressing values and committed action is important to the effectiveness of online ACT (Levin et al., 2020a). In a further analysis, it was concluded that the combination of Open and Engaged ACT components improved mental health through a range of psychological flexibility processes, including acceptance, cognitive defusion, values, and committed action (Levin et al., 2020b).

Among participants reporting burnout symptoms, Puolakanaho et al. (2020) observed that psychological flexibility skills mediated the difference between supported online ACT and treatment-as-usual. In supplementary analyses, Kinnunen et al. (2020) investigated which of the five mindfulness facets (observing, describing, acting with awareness, nonjudging, and nonreacting) mediated the intervention effects on three burnout dimensions (exhaustion, cynicism, and reduced professional efficacy). It was concluded that nonjudging is possibly the most important mindfulness facet to improve in burnout interventions, given that it mediated the changes in all burnout dimensions during both the intervention and 10-month follow-up. Interestingly, there are indications that different mindfulness or psychological flexibility skills mediated changes in different dimensions of burnout. Sairanen et al. (2019) reported similar findings among parents of children with chronic conditions who were offered a supported ACT online intervention. Mindful nonreacting and describing mediated changes on burnout symptoms, while nonjudgment and describing mediated changes on stress. Regarding symptoms of depression, studies have found that nonreacting and nonjudging skills (Pots et al., 2016a; Räsänen et al., 2020) mediate the impact of online ACT interventions.

Overall, studies exploring mediators or, more generally, processes of change in online ACT are still relatively limited. There are indications that different mediators can be associated with distinct symptoms. Further, several mediators can predict changes in certain symptom measures. However, conclusions can vary dependent on the measures administrated in the study.

Advantages, Challenges, and Future Directions of Technology-Based ACT Interventions

Advantages

Providing treatment online has considerable advantages. The standardized content included in an online ACT program requires relatively light training to deliver with fidelity. Research supports the notion that ACT-based online treatments can be successfully crafted to the needs of a particular group and delivered in a systematically high-quality manner. Highly specialized ACT professionals can be consulted in creating the online intervention and even in designing semistructured feedback for the purposes of providing written support during the program. This process allows a large group of therapists and mental health professionals to harness the expertise of researchers and experts in ACT in the service of their clients. Indeed, even novice therapists can deliver online ACT interventions effectively when appropriate guidance is offered to ensure adherence. However, it is important to observe that online and mobile-based interventions are not intended to completely replace traditional face-to-face interventions. New technology provides alternative treatment delivery formats and can bring treatment to those who would otherwise be left without treatment. Easily accessible online and mobile apps could also be one option for preventing psychological problems. Disseminating effective interventions and making them available in various areas, countries, and cultures leads to more equality and consistency in receiving appropriate support or treatment. As we move toward an increasingly global society, the gap between research and implementation can widen due to local lack of resources or expertise. Online treatment delivery can help to overcome limitations with available professionals and experts in ACT. Online solutions allow a larger number of clients to utilize a professional's services as weekly time required to support individual clients decreases. If semistructured or automized feedback is used, weekly contact can take very little time, and any mental health professional can contact large amounts of individuals during a day. Online treatment can also help reduce the cost of treatment for the client, which helps to overcome treatment delay or lack of treatment due to financial constraints. In addition to the advantages from a financial point of view, online treatment delivery can also enable people living in remote areas to gain access to evidence-based ACT interventions. Further, underserved populations (e.g., individuals with visual or hearing impairments) can be provided with high-quality interventions if more resources are devoted to online services adapted to these populations. Thus, online-based services could increase equality among different populations.

An additional advantage of online interventions in comparison with face-to-face delivery is the possibility of individual dosage of treatment using automated prompts. Instead of the traditional schedule of a weekly hour of therapeutic work, a client can use a web-based program daily and receive reminders to complete recurring exercises or tasks. In fact, when applying web-based ACT interventions, the therapeutic content can be accessed at any time and at any frequency, and, consequently, more flexibility can be incorporated into the treatment program. As the technology advances, mobile devices, including wearable devices such as watches, can be used to deliver brief messages and prompts within the context of daily living. These mobile devices can also be used to monitor progress by collecting data on physical activity, sleep quality, heart rate variability, and more. Thus, technology-based interventions can increase the personalization of treatment and allow more freedom in the individual scheduling of the treatment. From the research point of view, online data collection can facilitate development of evidence-based interventions by providing continuous data during interventions.

Challenges

Although positive results and experiences have been reported for online ACT, their implementation poses some challenges. One of the major challenges of implementing online treatments on a systemic level is the need for an open attitude from the therapist. While the online ACT programs described in the research literature are designed to be intuitive and user-friendly, prejudice toward using technology may impact treatment adversely. The increased research, global interest, and use of technology to provide evidence-based interventions suggests that online and mobile interventions will become an integral part of health care delivery in the future. When online or technology-based treatment delivery is included in the training of therapist and counselors, biased views of technology may subside as new generations of professionals enter the field. However, in the short term, educating the currently working professionals on the advantages of online treatment delivery is important to overcome resistance when implementing technology-based interventions in order to respond to the rising need for psychological support.

Challenges may arise related to the ethical and confidentiality aspects of online and mobile applications. The quality of many programs has raised some concerns, as a wide range of commercial treatment sites may not be evidence-based (Ebert et al., 2018). Ethical guidelines are needed to protect users and provide guidance in selecting effective programs, as, at the moment, there are no regulations for assuring the quality of programs on a European level (Ebert et al., 2018). Important issues that remain to be resolved include development of standards for data protection, as at present there are no guidelines on quality criteria related to data protection and data safety (Ebert et al., 2018).

Future Directions

While the body of literature on the effectiveness of various online and mobile-based ACT programs continues to grow, few studies have discussed the development process in detail. As Vilardaga et al. (2020) state, more discussion is needed on both the theoretical basis of these technology-based interventions and the design process itself in order to increase consistency and accelerate the process of building an understanding of technology-based ACT processes. Future research should also aim to increase our understanding of individual differences in the effectiveness of online ACT treatment. The current studies of online ACT have given considerable attention to demographic factors that could be associated with better treatment outcome (e.g., level of education or age). Because the evidence for strong predicting variables is not consistent, research attention has turned to identifying processes of change that may mediate or moderate the result of an online program. Increased knowledge of mechanisms of change can guide program developers to emphasize evidence-based skills training in technology-delivered interventions. For example, online or mobile-delivered ACT interventions can increase the probability that the users practice essential skills for well-being more frequently compared with face-to-face treatment. Future research should also aim to increase understanding of factors related to adherence or nonadherence to online ACT programs to support participation and utilization of the technology. As the effectiveness of online ACT becomes more and more established, research efforts can be allocated to critical questions concerning implementation of the treatment model (e.g., who should be assigned to receive online ACT treatment instead of or in addition to face-to-face treatment).

The steady increase in the number of studies reporting promising findings with online ACT also raises the issue of implementation of technology-based interventions into the training of therapists or counselors. At the moment, no practical guidance on developing or designing an online ACT program is readily available to the professionals working in the field. Even though research protocols may include detailed information on the content of a program used in a trial, guidance may be needed on how to utilize the technology in clinical practice or the ways in which a clinical practitioner can apply the technology. In addition to understanding how online programs can be implemented with one's own clientele, training programs should also include information on how to provide support to users of online programs. In addition, therapists should also be trained in how to familiarize the user with technology-based interventions. The potential of technology-based interventions can be fully exploited not only if patients are keen to use them, but also only if therapists make use of them (Ebert et al., 2018).

Conclusions

Technology-based interventions have been extensively studied, and the number of ACT-based online applications has increased rapidly. Although the history of technology-based ACT interventions is relatively short and the number of high-quality RCTs is still modest, the current evidence suggests that they are effective in reducing symptoms related to various mental health problems and also have a positive impact on quality of life and psychological flexibility. In spite of the fact that only a limited number of controlled studies have investigated the impact of ACT-based online interventions, in comparison to online interventions based on the CBT model, the current evidence suggests that ACT-based interventions produce equivalent results. However, limited or no evidence exists regarding the application of ACT technology-based solutions for severe psychological problems such as eating disorders, obsessive-compulsive disorder (OCD), and psychosis.In addition, the currently available research literature has consistently reported that the effects of supported online ACT on various symptoms and measures of psychological flexibility are comparable to face-to-face delivered ACT. Indeed, there is no reason to assume that supported online treatment delivery is inferior to live-session delivery. The few studies that have directly compared different delivery methods (i.e., online vs. face-to-face) among the same population with therapists who received identical training support the noninferiority of internet-based ACT in relation to traditional ACT interventions. Research also suggests that online ACT with minimal support appears to be an adequate alternative if more extensive support is not available. The proportion of those who discontinue treatment does not appear to be higher in online ACT interventions than in traditional face-to-face treatment. However, the current results show that most ACT-based studies have provided support by a therapist or counselor during online intervention. The type of support provided can vary considerably. It is currently difficult to draw conclusions about the role of the quantity and quality of contact in relation to the observed impact of the interventions.

When investigating clients' experiences of online ACT interventions, satisfaction with the form of therapy and its content has been high among users. While the research evidence supporting online treatment delivery is increasing, technology that enables contact regardless of time and place is developing at a rapid pace. As both data on the effectiveness of online ACT programs and the sophistication and security of technological solutions are accumulating, it can be expected that health care services will increasingly turn to online alternatives. This larger, global development can help to respond to the need of psychological support more efficiently by utilizing evidence-based intervention protocols that are resource-conscious, easy to disseminate and easy to reach. Overall, studies suggest that ACT-based web and mobile apps are an efficient, acceptable, and cost-effective way to deliver empirically validated treatments to those who would otherwise go untreated.

In the future, various online and mobile interventions, as well as their integration in different ways with existing face-to-face treatments, will become more common. We will have different combinations of technology-assisted in-person interventions as well as stand-alone interventions providing, for example, automated support. Various technology-based assessment and measurement methods will also become more common. Instead of using pen and paper to fill in self-report questionnaires, behavioral diaries and other self-monitoring tasks, online solutions using mobile phones and other technological devices will be used. Information from these devices can be passed directly to the therapist and made available before the appointment. The client can also receive immediate, automatic feedback on the questionnaire or task. As devices become more and more affordable and available, the use of assessment and monitoring technologies will likely increase accordingly. The growing size and quality of the screens of hand-held devices will also make mobile apps increasingly easy to navigate. Online programs are also able to send reminders to assist the user in implementation of new skills. Clients can seek specialized treatment of certain problems, as geographical distances will not limit options in choosing a treatment provider.

The existing evidence and experiences imply that implementing the currently available technological approaches is improving the delivery of psychological interventions. In addition to online interventions, technology can offer possibilities of working with groups and facilitating peer support more broadly, providing supervision to therapists, or organizing networking and training opportunities to professionals. Technology brings us closer to each other. Technology can help to connect clients with rare somatic conditions or specific life history, or bring together professionals committed to advance contextual behavior therapy, regardless of the geographical location of each individual. By embracing the technological development, it may be possible to witness the advancement of contextual behavioral science around the world.

References

Ahtinen, A., Mattila, E., Välkkynen, P., Kaipainen, K., Vanhala, T., Ermes, M., Sairanen, E., Myllymäki, T., & Lappalainen, R. (2013). Mobile mental wellness training for stress management: feasibility and design implications based on a one-month field study. *JMIR mHealth and uHealth, 1*(2), e11.

Anderson, G. (2018). Internet interventions: Past, present and future. *Internet Interventions, 12*, 181–188.

Andersson, G. (2009). Using the internet to provide cognitive behaviour therapy. *Behaviour Research and Therapy, 47*(3), 175–180.

Andersson, G., & Cuijpers, P. (2009). Internet-based and other computerized psychological treatments for adult depression: A meta-analysis. *Cognitive Behaviour Therapy, 38*, 196–205.

Andersson, G., Bergström, J., Holländare, F., Carlbring, P., Kaldo, V., & Ekselius, L. (2005). Internet-based self-help for depression: Randomised controlled trial. *British Journal of Psychiatry, 187*(5), 456–461.

Andersson, G., Cuijpers, P., Carlbring, P., & Lindefors, N. (2007). Effects of internet-delivered cognitive behavior therapy for anxiety and mood disorders. *Helix Review Series, Psychiatry, 2*, 9–14.

Andersson, G., Titov, N., Dear, B. F., Rozental, A., & Carlbring, P. (2019). Internet-delivered psychological treatments: From innovation to implementation. *World Psychiatry, 18*(1), 20–28.

Andrade, L. H., Alonso, J., Mneimneh, Z., Wells, J. E., Al-Hamzawi, A., Borges, G., Bromet, E., Bruffaerts, R., de Girolamo, G., de Graaf, R., Florescu, S., Gureje, O., Hinkov, H. R., Hu, C., Huang, Y., Hwang, I., Jin, R., Karam, E. G., Kovess-Masfety, V., . . . Kessler, R. C. (2014). Barriers to mental health treatment: results from the WHO World Mental Health (WMH) Surveys. *Psychological Medicine, 44*(6), 1303–1317.

Andrews, G., Cuijpers, P., Craske, M. G., McEvoy, P., & Titov, N. (2010). Computer therapy for the anxiety and depressive disorders is effective, acceptable and practical health care: A meta-analysis. *PloS One, 5*(10), e13196.

Baik, K. D. (2015). Evaluating acceptance and commitment therapy for insomnia: A randomized controlled trial (2015). Doctoral thesis, the Graduate College of Bowling Green State University.

Barrett, K., & Stewart, I. (2020). A preliminary comparison of the efficacy of online acceptance and commitment therapy (ACT) and cognitive behavioural therapy (CBT) stress management interventions for social and health-care workers. *Health and Social Care in the Community, 20*(3), 113–126.

Bartels, S. L., Van Knippenberg, R. J., Dassen, F. C., Asaba, E., Patomella, A. H., Malinowsky, C., Verhey, F. R. J., & de Vugt, M. E. (2019). A narrative synthesis systematic review of digital self-monitoring interventions for middle-aged and older adults. *Internet Interventions, 18*, 100283.

Berger, T., Caspar, F., Richardson, R., Kneubühler, B., Sutter, D., & Andersson, G. (2011). Internet-based treatment of social phobia: A randomized controlled trial comparing unguided with two types of guided self-help. *Behaviour Research and Therapy, 49*(3), 158–169.

Boettcher, J., Renneberg, B., & Berger, T. (2013). Patient expectations in internet-based self-help for social anxiety. *Cognitive Behaviour Therapy, 42*, 203–214.
Boucher, S., Edwards, O., Gray, A., Nada-Raja, S., Lillis, J., Tylka, T. L., & Horwath, C. C. (2016). Teaching intuitive eating and acceptance and commitment therapy skills via a web-based intervention: a pilot single-arm intervention study. *JMIR Research Protocols, 5*(4), e180.
Bricker, J. B., Bush, T., Zbikowski, S. M., Mercer, L. D., & Heffner, J. L. (2014a). Randomized trial of telephone-delivered acceptance and commitment therapy versus cognitive behavioral therapy for smoking cessation: A pilot study. *Nicotine and Tobacco Research, 16*, 1446–1454.
Bricker, J. B., Mann, S. L., Marek, P. M., Liu, J., & Peterson, A.V. (2010). Telephone-delivered acceptance and commitment therapy for adult smoking cessation: A feasibility study. *Nicotine and Tobacco Research, 12*, 454–458.
Bricker, J. B., Mull, K. E., Kientz, J. A., Vilardaga, R., Mercer, L. D., Akioka, K. J., & Heffner, J. L. (2014b). Randomized, controlled pilot trial of a smartphone app for smoking cessation using acceptance and commitment therapy. *Drug and Alcohol Dependence, 143*, 87–94.
Bricker, J. B., Mull, K. E., McClure, J. B., Watson, N. L., & Heffner, J. L. (2018). Improving quit rates of web-delivered interventions for smoking cessation: Full scale randomized trial of WebQuit.org versus Smokefree.gov. *Addiction, 113*, 914–923.
Bricker, J. B., Watson, N. L., Mull, K. E., Sullivan, B. M., & Heffner, J. L. (2020). Efficacy of Smartphone Applications for Smoking Cessation: A randomized clinical trial. *JAMA Internal Medicine, 11*, 1472–1480.
Bricker, J., Wyszynski, C., Comstock, B., & Heffner, J. L. (2013). Pilot randomized controlled trial of web-based acceptance and commitment therapy for smoking cessation. *Nicotine and Tobacco Research, 15*, 1756–1764.
Brown, M., Glendenning, A., Hoon, A. E., & John, A. (2016). Effectiveness of web-delivered acceptance and commitment therapy in relation to mental health and well-being: A systematic review and meta-analysis. *Journal of Medical Internet Research,18*(8), e221.
Buhrman, M., Skoglund, A., Husell, J., Bergström, K., Gordh, T., Hursti, T., Bendelin, N., Furmark, T., & Andersson, G. (2013). Guided internet-delivered acceptance and commitment therapy for chronic pain patients: A randomized controlled trial. *Behaviour Research and Therapy, 51*(6), 307–315.
Carlbring, P., Andersson, G., Cuijpers, P., Riper, H., & Hedman-Lagerlöf, E. (2018). Internet-based vs. face-to-face cognitive behavior therapy for psychiatric and somatic disorders: An updated systematic review and meta-analysis. *Cognitive Behaviour Therapy, 47*(1), 1–18.
Carlbring, P., Hägglund, M., Luthström, A., Dahlin, M., Kadowaki, Å., Vernmark, K., & Andersson, G. (2013). Internet-based behavioral activation and acceptance-based treatment for depression: A randomized controlled trial. *Journal of Affective Disorders, 148*(2-3), 331–337.
Chase, J. A., Houmanfar, R., Hayes, S. C., Ward, T. A., Vilardaga, J. P., & Follette, V. (2013). Values are not just goals: Online ACT-based values training adds to goal setting in improving undergraduate college student performance. *Journal of Contextual Behavioral Science, 2*(3-4), 79–84.
Cuijpers, P., Donker, T., Johansson, R., Mohr, D. C., van Straten, A., & Andersson, G. (2011). Self-guided psychological treatment for depressive symptoms: A meta-analysis. *PloS One, 6*(6), e21274.
Cuijpers, P., Donker, T., van Straten A., Li, J, & Andersson, G. (2010). Is guided self-help as effective as face-to-face psychotherapy for depression and anxiety disorders? A systematic review and meta-analysis of comparative outcome studies. *Psychological Medicine, 40*, 1943–1957.
Cuijpers, P., van Straten, A., Andersson, G., & van Oppen, P. (2008). Psychotherapy for depression in adults: A meta-analysis of comparative outcome studies. *Journal of Consulting and Clinical Psychology, 76*(6), 909.
Dahlin, M., Andersson, G., Magnusson, K., Johansson, T., Sjögren, J., Håkansson, A., Pettersson, M., Kadowaki, Å., Cuijpers, P. & Carlbring, P. (2016a). Internet-delivered acceptance-based behaviour therapy for generalized anxiety disorder: A randomized controlled trial. *Behaviour Research and Therapy, 77*, 86–95.
Dahlin, M., Ryberg, M., Vernmark, K., Annas, N., Carlbring, P., & Andersson, G. (2016b). Internet-delivered acceptance-based behavior therapy for generalized anxiety disorder: A pilot study. *Internet Interventions, 6*, 16–21.
Dalrymple, K. L., Fiorentino, L., Politi, M. C., & Posner, D. (2010). Incorporating principles from acceptance and commitment therapy into cognitive-behavioral therapy for insomnia: A case example. *Journal of Contemporary Psychotherapy, 40*(4), 209–217.
Ebert, D. D., Van Daele, T., Nordgreen, T., Karekla, M., Compare, A., Zarbo, C., Brugnera, A., Øverland, S., Trebbi, G., Jensen, K. L., Kaehlke, F., & Baumeister, H. & Taylor, J. (2018). Internet- and mobile-based psychological interventions: Applications, efficacy, and potential for improving mental health: A report of the EFPA E-Health Taskforce. *European Psychologist, 23*(2), 167–187.
El Alaoui, S., Hedman, E., Ljótsson, B., Bergström, J., Andersson, E., Rück, C., & Lindefors, N. (2013). Predictors and moderators of internet- and group-based cognitive behaviour therapy for panic disorder. *PLoS One, 8*(11), e79024.

Eustis, E. H., Hayes-Skelton, S. A., Orsillo, S. M., & Roemer, L. (2018). Surviving and thriving during stress: A randomized clinical trial comparing a brief web-based therapist-assisted acceptance-based behavioral intervention versus waitlist control for college students. *Behavior Therapy, 49*(6), 889–903.
Falconer, C. J., Rovira, A., King, J. A., Gilbert, P., Antley, A., Fearon, P., Ralph, N., Slater, M., & Brewin, C. R. (2016). Embodying self-compassion within virtual reality and its effects on patients with depression. *BJPsych Open, 2*(1), 74–80.
Falconer, C. J., Slater, M., Rovira, A., King, J. A., Gilbert, P., Antley, A., & Brewin, C. R. (2014). Embodying compassion: A virtual reality paradigm for overcoming excessive self-criticism. *PloS One, 9*(11), e111933.
Farrand, P., & Woodford, J. (2013). Impact of support on the effectiveness of written cognitive behavioural self-help: A systematic review and meta-analysis of randomised controlled trials. *Clinical Psychology Review, 33*, 182–195.
Fiorillo, D., McLean, C., Pistorello, J., Hayes, S. C., & Follette, V. M. (2017). Evaluation of a web-based acceptance and commitment therapy program for women with trauma-related problems: A pilot study. *Journal of Contextual Behavioral Science, 6*(1), 104–113.
Firestone, J., Cardaciotto, L., Levin, M. E., Goldbacher, E., Vernig, P., & Gambrel, L. E. (2019). A web-based self-guided program to promote valued-living in college students: A pilot study. *Journal of Contextual Behavioral Science, 12*, 29–38.
Fledderus, M., Bohlmeijer, E. T., Pieterse, M. E., & Schreurs, K.M.G. (2012). Acceptance and commitment therapy as guided self-help for psychological distress and positive mental health: a randomized controlled trial. *Psychological Medicine, 42*, 485–495.
Gershkovich, M., Herbert, J. D., Forman, E. M., & Glassman, L. (2016). Guided internet-based self-help intervention for social anxiety disorder with videoconferenced therapist support. *Cognitive and Behavioral Practice, 23*(2), 239–255.
Gershkovich, M., Herbert, J. D., Forman, E. M., Schumacher, L. M., & Fischer, L. E. (2017). Internet-delivered acceptance-based cognitive-behavioral intervention for social anxiety disorder with and without therapist support: a randomized trial. *Behavior Modification, 41*(5), 583–608.
Glasgow, R. E., & Rosen, G. M. (1978). Behavioral bibliotherapy: A review of self-help behavior therapy manuals. *Psychological Bulletin, 85*(1), 1.
Glick, D. M., & Orsillo, S. M. (2015). An investigation of the efficacy of acceptance-based behavioral therapy for academic procrastination. *Journal of Experimental Psychology: General, 144*(2), 400.
Gloster, A. T., Rinner, M. T. B., & Meyer, A. H. (2020). Increasing prosocial behavior and decreasing selfishness in the lab and everyday life. *Scientific Reports, 10*, 21220.
Green, K. E., & Iverson, K. M. (2009). Computerized cognitive-behavioral therapy in a stepped care model of treatment. *Professional Psychology: Research and Practice, 40*(1), 96.
Griffiths, K. M., Farrer, L., & Christensen, H. (2010). The efficacy of internet interventions for depression and anxiety disorders: A review of randomised controlled trials. *Medical Journal of Australia, 192*, S4–S11.
Hall, C. M., & Bierman, K. L. (2015). Technology-assisted interventions for parents of young children: Emerging practices, current research, and future directions. *Early Childhood Research Quarterly, 33*, 21–32.
Halliburton, A. E., & Cooper, L. D. (2015). Applications and adaptations of acceptance and commitment therapy (ACT) for adolescents. *Journal of Contextual Behavioral Science, 4*(1), 1–11.
Hawkes, A. L., Chambers, S. K., Pakenham, K. I., Patrao, T. A., Baade, P. D., Lynch, B. M., Aitken, J. F., Meng, X., & Courneya, K. S. (2013). Effects of a telephone-delivered multiple health behavior change intervention (CanChange) on health and behavioral outcomes in survivors of colorectal cancer: A randomized controlled trial. *Journal of Clinical Oncology, 31*, 2313–2321.
Hedman, E., Ljótsson, B., & Lindefors, N. (2012). Cognitive behavior therapy via the Internet: A systematic review of applications, clinical efficacy and cost-effectiveness. *Expert Review of Pharmacoeconomics and Outcomes Research, 12*, 745–764.
Heffner, J. L., Wyszynski, C. M., Comstock, B., Mercer, L. D., & Bricker, J. (2013). Overcoming recruitment challenges of web-based interventions for tobacco use: The case of web-based acceptance and commitment therapy for smoking cessation. *Addictive Behaviors, 38*(10), 2473–2476.
Hesser, H., Gustafsson, T., Lundén, C., Henrikson, O., Fattahi, K., Johnsson, E., Westin, V. Z., Carlbring, P., Mäki-Torkko, E., Kaldo, V., & Andersson, G. (2012). A randomized controlled trial of internet-delivered cognitive behavior therapy and acceptance and commitment therapy in the treatment of tinnitus. *Journal of Consulting and Clinical Psychology, 80*(4), 649–661.
Hesser, H., Westin, V. Z., & Andersson, G. (2014). Acceptance as a mediator in internet-delivered acceptance and commitment therapy and cognitive behavior therapy for tinnitus. *Journal of Behavioral Medicine, 37*(4), 756–767.
Hofer, P. D., Waadt, M., Aschwanden, R., Milidou, M., Acker, J., Meyer, A. H., Lieb R., & Gloster, A. T. (2018). Self-help for stress and burnout without therapist contact: An online randomised controlled trial. *Work and Stress, 32*, 189–208.

Hoffmann, D., Rask, C. U., Hedman-Lagerlöf, E., Ljotsson, B., & Frostholm, L. (2018). Development and feasibility testing of internet-delivered acceptance and commitment therapy for severe health anxiety: Pilot study. *JMIR Mental Health, 5*(2), e28.

Ivanova, E., Lindner, P., Ly, K. H., Dahlin, M., Vernmark, K., Andersson, G., & Carlbring, P. (2016). Guided and unguided acceptance and commitment therapy for social anxiety disorder and/or panic disorder provided via the internet and a smartphone application: A randomized controlled trial. *Journal of Anxiety Disorders, 44*, 27–35.

Jansen, J. E., Harder, S., Haahr, U. H., Lyse, H. G., Pedersen, M. B., Trauelsen, A. M., & Simonsen, E. (2015). The role of metacognitions in expressed emotion and distress: A study on caregivers of persons with first-episode psychosis. *Clinical Psychology & Psychotherapy, 22*(6), 525–532.

Johansson, R., & Andersson, G. (2012). Internet-based psychological treatments for depression. *Expert Review of Neurotherapeutics, 12*(7), 861–870.

Jones, H. A., Heffner, J. L., Mercer, L., Wyszynski, C. M., Vilardaga, R., and Bricker, J. B. (2015) Web-based acceptance and commitment therapy smoking cessation treatment for smokers with depressive symptoms. *Journal of Dual Diagnosis, 11*(1), 56–62.

Kaltenthaler, E., Parry, G., & Beverley, C. (2004). Computerized cognitive behaviour therapy: A systematic review. *Behavioural and Cognitive Psychotherapy, 32*(1), 31–55.

Kaltenthaler, E., Parry, G., Beverley, C., & Ferriter, M. (2008). Computerised cognitive-behavioural therapy for depression: Systematic review. *British Journal of Psychiatry, 193*(3), 181–184.

Kazdin, A. E. (2019). Annual research review: Expanding mental health services through novel models of intervention delivery. *Journal of Child Psychology and Psychiatry, 60*(4), 455–472.

Kenwright, M., Liness, S., & Marks, I. (2001). Reducing demands on clinicians by offering computer-aided self-help for phobia/panic: Feasibility study. *British Journal of Psychiatry, 179*(5), 456–459.

Kessler, R. C., Demler, O., Frank, R. G., Olfson, M., Pincus, H. A., Walters, E. E., Wang, P., Wells, K. B., & Zaslavsky, A. M. (2005). Prevalence and treatment of mental disorders, 1990 to 2003. *New England Journal of Medicine, 352*(24), 2515–2523.

Kinnunen, S. M., Puolakanaho, A., Tolvanen, A., Mäkikangas, A., & Lappalainen, R. (2020). Improvements in mindfulness facets mediate the alleviation of burnout dimensions. *Mindfulness 11*(12), 2779–2792.

Köhle, N., Drossaert, C. H., Jaran, J., Schreurs, K. M., Verdonck-de Leeuw, I. M., & Bohlmeijer, E. T. (2017). User-experiences with a web-based self-help intervention for partners of cancer patients based on acceptance and commitment therapy and self-compassion: a qualitative study. *BMC Public Health, 17*(1), 225.

Krafft, J., Potts, S., Schoendorff, B., & Levin, M. E. (2019). A randomized controlled trial of multiple versions of an acceptance and commitment therapy matrix app for well-being. *Behavior Modification, 43*, 246–272.

Kuipers, E., & Bebbington, P. E. (2005). *Research on burden and coping strategies in families of people with mental disorders: Problems and perspectives.* In N. Sartorius (Ed.) & J. Leff, J. J. Lopez-Ibor, M. Maj, A. Okasha, *Families and mental disorders: From burden to empowerment* (pp. 217–234). John Wiley & Sons Ltd.

Lappalainen, P., Granlund, A., Siltanen, S., Ahonen, S., Vitikainen, M., Tolvanen, A., & Lappalainen, R. (2014). ACT internet-based vs face-to-face? A randomized controlled trial of two ways to deliver acceptance and commitment therapy for depressive symptoms: An 18-month follow-up. *Behaviour Research and Therapy, 61*, 43–54.

Lappalainen, P., Kaipainen, K., Lappalainen, R., Hoffrén, H., Myllymäki, T., Kinnunen, M. L., Mattila, E., Happonen, A. P., Rusko, H., & Korhonen, I. (2013). Feasibility of a personal health technology-based psychological intervention for men with stress and mood problems: Randomized controlled pilot trial. *JMIR Research Protocols, 2*(1), e1.

Lappalainen, P., Langrial, S., Oinas-Kukkonen, H., Muotka, J., & Lappalainen, R. (2019a). ACT for sleep—Internet-delivered self-help ACT for sub-clinical and clinical insomnia: A randomized controlled trial. *Journal of Contextual Behavioral Science, 12*, 119–127.

Lappalainen, P., Langrial, S., Oinas-Kukkonen, H., Tolvanen, A., & Lappalainen, R. (2015). Web-based acceptance and commitment therapy for depressive symptoms with minimal support - a randomized controlled trial. *Behavior Modification, 39*(6), 805–834.

Lappalainen, P., Lappi, M., Saari, E. -L., Kaipainen, K., Muotka, J., & Lappalainen, R. (under review). The mind journey—Acceptance and commitment therapy as a group- and online delivered rehabilitation for mood disorders: A randomized controlled pilot study.

Lappalainen, P., Pakkala, I., & Nikander, R. (2019b). CareACT—Internet-based intervention for enhancing the psychological well-being of elderly caregivers—a study protocol of a controlled trial. *BMC Geriatrics, 19*(1), 72.

Lappalainen, P., Pakkala, I., Lappalainen, R., & Nikander, R. (2021a). Supported web-based acceptance and commitment therapy for older family caregivers (CareACT) compared to usual care. *Clinical Gerontologist*, 1–17. Advance online publication.

Lappalainen, P., Pakkala, I., Strömmer, J., Sairanen, E., Kaipainen, K., & Lappalainen, R. (2021b). Supporting parents of children with chronic conditions: A randomized controlled trial of web-based and self-help ACT interventions. *Internet Interventions, 24*, 100382.

Lappalainen, R., & Lappalainen, P. (2020). Implementing ACT online. In M. E. Levin, M. P. Twohig, J. Krafft (Eds.), *Innovations in acceptance and commitment therapy: Clinical advancements and applications in ACT* (pp. 221–238). New Harbinger Publications.

Lappalainen, R., Lappalainen, P., Puolakanaho, A., Hirvonen, R., Eklund, K. Ahonen, T., Muotka, J., & Kiuru, N. (2021c). The youth compass—the effectiveness of an online acceptance and commitment therapy program to promote adolescent mental health: A randomized controlled trial. *Journal of Contextual Behavioral Science, 20*, 1–12.

Lee, M., Lee, H., Kim, Y., Kim, J., Cho, M., Jang, J., & Jang, H. (2018). Mobile app-based health promotion programs: A systematic review of the literature. *International Journal of Environmental Research and Public Health, 15*(12), 2838.

Levin, M. E., Haeger, J., & Cruz, R. A. (2019). Tailoring acceptance and commitment therapy skill coaching in the moment through smartphones: Results from a randomized controlled trial. *Mindfulness, 10*, 689–699.

Levin, M. E., Haeger, J., Pierce, B., & Cruz, R. A. (2017a). Evaluating an adjunctive mobile app to enhance psychological flexibility in acceptance and commitment therapy. *Behavior Modification, 41*(6), 846–867.

Levin, M. E., Haeger, J., Pierce, B., & Twohig, M. P. (2017b). Web-based acceptance and commitment therapy for mental health problems in college students: A randomized controlled trial. *Behavior Modification, 41*, 141–162.

Levin, M. E., Hayes, S. C., Pistorello, J., & Seeley, J. R. (2016). Web-based self-help for preventing mental health problems in universities: Comparing acceptance and commitment training to mental health education. *Journal of Clinical Psychology, 72*(3), 207–225.

Levin, M. E., Krafft, J., & Twohig, M. P. (2020b). Examining processes of change in an online acceptance and commitment therapy dismantling trial with distressed college students. *Journal of Contextual Behavioral Science, 17*, 10–16.

Levin, M. E., Krafft, J., Hicks, E. T., Pierce, B., & Twohig, M. P. (2020a). A randomized dismantling trial of the open and engaged components of acceptance and commitment therapy in an online intervention for distressed college students. *Behaviour Research and Therapy, 126*, 103557.

Levin, M. E., Pierce, B., & Schoendorff, B. (2017c). The acceptance and commitment therapy matrix mobile app: A pilot randomized trial on health behaviors. *Journal of Contextual Behavioral Science, 6*(3), 268–275.

Levin, M. E., Pistorello, J., Hayes, S. C., Seeley, J. R., & Levin, C. (2015). Feasibility of an acceptance and commitment therapy adjunctive web-based program for counseling centers. *Journal of Counseling Psychology, 62*(3), 529.

Levin, M. E., Pistorello, J., Seeley, J. R., & Hayes, S. C. (2014). Feasibility of a prototype web-based acceptance and commitment therapy prevention program for college students. *Journal of American College Health, 62*(1), 20–30.

Lin, J., Paganini, S., Sander, L., Lüking, M., Ebert, D. D., Buhrman, M., Andersson, G., & Baumeister, H. (2017). An internet-based intervention for chronic pain: A three-arm randomized controlled study of the effectiveness of guided and unguided acceptance and commitment therapy. *Deutsches Ärzteblatt International, 114*(41), 681.

Lindhiem, O., Bennett, C. B., Rosen, D., & Silk, J. (2015). Mobile technology boosts the effectiveness of psychotherapy and behavioral interventions: A meta-analysis. *Behavior Modification, 39*(6), 785–804.

Ljótsson, B., Atterlöf, E., Lagerlöf, M., Andersson, E., Jernelöv, S., Hedman, E., Kemani, M., & Wicksell, R. K. (2014). Internet-delivered acceptance and values-based exposure treatment for fibromyalgia: A pilot study. *Cognitive Behaviour Therapy, 43*(2), 93–104.

Ly, K. H., Trüschel, A., Jarl, L., Magnusson, S., Windahl, T., Johansson, R., Carlbring, P., & Andersson, G. (2014b). Behavioural activation versus mindfulness-based guided selfhelp treatment administered through a smartphone application: A randomised controlled trial. *BMJ Open, 4*, e003440.

Ly, K. H., Asplund, K., & Andersson, G. (2014a). Stress management for middle managers via an acceptance and commitment-based smartphone application: A randomized controlled trial. *Internet Interventions, 1*, 95–101.

Marks, I. M., Cavanagh, K., & Gega, L. (2007). *Hands-on help: Computer-aided psychotherapy*. Psychology Press.

Marks, I. M., Mataix-Cols, D., Kenwright, M., Cameron, R., Hirsch, S., & Gega, L. (2003). Pragmatic evaluation of computer-aided self-help for anxiety and depression. *British Journal of Psychiatry, 183*, 57–65.

Mattila, E., Lappalainen, R., Välkkynen, P., Sairanen, E., Lappalainen, P., Karhunen, L., Peuhkuri, K., Korpela, R., Kolehmainen, M., & Ermes, M. (2016). Usage and dose response of a mobile acceptance and commitment therapy app: secondary analysis of the intervention arm of a randomized controlled trial. *JMIR mHealth and uHealth, 4*(3), e90.

Mattila, E., Pärkkä, J., Hermersdorf, M., Kaasinen, J., Vainio, J., Samposalo, K., Merilahti, J., Kolari, J., Kulju, M., Lappalainen, R., & Korhonen, I. (2008). Mobile diary for wellness management—results on usage and usability in two user studies. *IEEE Transactions on Information Technology in Biomedicine, 12*(4), 501–512.

McCrone, P., Knapp, M., Proudfoot, J., Ryden, C., Cavanagh, K., Shapiro, D. A., Ilson, S., Gray, J. A., Goldberg, D., Mann, A., Marks, I., Everitt, B., & Marks, I. (2004). Cost-effectiveness of computerised cognitive-behavioural therapy for anxiety and depression in primary care: Randomised controlled trial. *British Journal of Psychiatry, 185*(1), 55–62.

McDevitt-Murphy, M. E., Luciano, M. T., & Zakarian, R. J. (2018). Use of ecological momentary assessment and intervention in treatment with adults. *Focus, 16*(4), 370–375.
Moffitt, R., & Mohr, P. (2015). The efficacy of a self-managed acceptance and commitment therapy intervention DVD for physical activity initiation. *British Journal of Health Psychology, 20*, 115–129.
Molander, P., Hesser, H., Weineland, S., Bergwall, K., Buck, S., Jäder Malmlöf, J., Lantz, H., Lunner, T., & Andersson, G. (2018). Internet-based acceptance and commitment therapy for psychological distress experienced by people with hearing problems: A pilot randomized controlled trial. *Cognitive Behaviour Therapy, 47*(2), 169–184.
Paxling, B., Lundgren, S., Norman, A., Almlov, J., Carlbring, P., Cuijpers, P., & Andersson, G. (2013). Therapist behaviours in internet-delivered cognitive behaviour therapy: analyses of e-mail correspondence in the treatment of generalized anxiety disorder. *Behavioural and Cognitive Psychotherapy, 41*, 280–289.
Pennefather, J., Hieneman, M., Raulston, T. J., & Caraway, N. (2018). Evaluation of an online training program to improve family routines, parental well-being, and the behavior of children with autism. *Research in Autism Spectrum Disorders, 54*, 21–26.
Pierce, B., Twohig, M. P., & Levin, M. E. (2016) Perspectives on the use of acceptance and commitment therapy related mobile apps: Results from a survey of students and professionals. *Journal of Contextual Behavioral Science, 5*(4), 215–224.
Pots, W. T., Fledderus, M., Meulenbeek, P. A., Peter, M., Schreurs, K. M., & Bohlmeijer, E. T. (2016b). Acceptance and commitment therapy as a web-based intervention for depressive symptoms: randomised controlled trial. *British Journal of Psychiatry, 208*(1), 69–77.
Pots, W. T., Trompetter, H. R., Schreurs, K. M., & Bohlmeijer, E. T. (2016a). How and for whom does web-based acceptance and commitment therapy work? Mediation and moderation analyses of web-based ACT for depressive symptoms. *BMC Psychiatry, 16*(1), 158.
Proctor, B. J., Moghaddam, N. G., Evangelou, N., & das Nair, R. (2018). Telephone-supported acceptance and commitment bibliotherapy for people with multiple sclerosis and psychological distress: A pilot randomised controlled trial. *Journal of Contextual Behavioral Science, 9*, 103–109.
Puolakanaho, A., Lappalainen, R., Lappalainen, P., Muotka, J. S., Hirvonen, R., Eklund, K. M., Ahonen, T. P. S., & Kiuru, N. (2019). Reducing stress and enhancing academic buoyancy among adolescents using a brief web-based program based on acceptance and commitment therapy: A randomized controlled trial. *Journal of Youth and Adolescence, 48*(2), 287–305.
Puolakanaho, A., Tolvanen, A., Kinnunen, S. M., & Lappalainen, R. (2020). A psychological flexibility-based intervention for burnout: A randomized controlled trial. *Journal of Contextual Behavioral Science, 15*, 52–67.
Räsänen, P., Lappalainen, P., Muotka, J., Tolvanen, A., & Lappalainen, R. (2016). An online guided ACT intervention for enhancing the psychological wellbeing of university students: A randomized controlled clinical trial. *Behaviour Research and Therapy, 78*, 30–42.
Räsänen, P., Muotka, J., & Lappalainen, R. (2020). Examining mediators of change in wellbeing, stress, and depression in a blended, Internet-based, ACT intervention for university students. *Internet Interventions, 22*, 100343.
Richards, D., & Richardson, T. (2012). Computer-based psychological treatments for depression: A systematic review and meta-analysis. *Clinical Psychology Review, 32*(4), 329–342.
Rickardsson, J., Zetterqvist, V., Gentili, C., Andersson, E., Holmström, L., Lekander, M., Persson, M., Persson, J., Ljótsson, B., & Wicksell, R. K. (2020). Internet-delivered acceptance and commitment therapy (iACT) for chronic pain—feasibility and preliminary effects in clinical and self-referred patients. *Mhealth*, 6, 27.
Ruwaard, J., Schrieken, B., Schrijver, M., Broeksteeg, J., Dekker, J., Vermeulen, H., & Lange, A. (2009). Standardized web-based cognitive behavioural therapy of mild to moderate depression: A randomized controlled trial with a long-term follow-up. *Cognitive Behaviour Therapy, 38*(4), 206–221.
Sagon, A. L., Danitz, S. B., Suvak, M. K., & Orsillo, S. M. (2018). The Mindful Way through the semester: Evaluating the feasibility of delivering an acceptance-based behavioral program online. *Journal of Contextual Behavioral Science, 9*, 36–44.
Sairanen, E., Lappalainen, R., Lappalainen, P., Kaipainen, K., Carlstedt, F., Anclair, M., & Hiltunen, A. (2019). Effectiveness of a web-based acceptance and commitment therapy intervention for wellbeing of parents whose children have chronic conditions: A randomized controlled trial. *Journal of Contextual Behavioral Science, 13*, 94–102.
Scott, W., Chilcot, J., Guildford, B., Daly-Eichenhardt, A., & McCracken, L. M. (2018). Feasibility randomized-controlled trial of online acceptance and commitment therapy for patients with complex chronic pain in the United Kingdom. *European Journal of Pain, 22*(8), 1473–1484.
Simister, H. D., Tkachuk, G. A., Shay, B. L., Vincent, N., Pear, J. J., & Skrabek, R. Q. (2018). Randomized controlled trial of online acceptance and commitment therapy for fibromyalgia. *Journal of Pain, 19*(7), 741–753.
Spijkerman, M. P. J., Pots, W. T. M., & Bohlmeijer, E. T. (2016). Effectiveness of online mindfulness-based interventions in improving mental health: A review and meta-analysis of randomised controlled trials. *Clinical Psychology Review, 45*, 102–114.

Strandskov, S. W., Ghaderi, A., Andersson, H., Parmskog, N., Hjort, E., Wärn, A. S., Jannert, M., & Andersson, G. (2017). Effects of tailored and ACT-influenced internet-based CBT for eating disorders and the relation between knowledge acquisition and outcome: A randomized controlled trial. *Behavior Therapy, 48*(5), 624–637.

Swain, J., Hancock, K., Dixon, A., & Bowman, J. (2015). Acceptance and commitment therapy for children: A systematic review of intervention studies. *Journal of Contextual Behavioral Science, 4*(2), 73–85.

Thompson, E. M., Destree, L., Albertella, L., & Fontenelle, L. F. (2020). Internet-based acceptance and commitment therapy: A transdiagnostic systematic review and meta-analysis for mental health outcomes. *Behavior Therapy, 52*(2), 492–507.

Titov, N. (2011). Internet-delivered psychotherapy for depression in adults. *Current Opinion in Psychiatry, 24*, 18–23.

Trompetter, H. R., Bohlmeijer, E. T., Fox, J. P., & Schreurs, K. M. (2015). Psychological flexibility and catastrophizing as associated change mechanisms during online acceptance and commitment therapy for chronic pain. *Behaviour Research and Therapy, 74*, 50–59.

Trompetter, H. R., Bohlmeijer, E. T., Veehof, M. M., & Schreurs, K. M. G. (2014). Internet-based guided self-help intervention for chronic pain based on acceptance and commitment therapy: A randomized controlled trial. *Journal of Behavioral Medicine, 38*, 66–80.

Vernmark, K., Lenndin, J., Bjärehed, J., Carlsson, M., Karlsson, J., Öberg, J., Carlbring, P., Eriksson, T., & Andersson, G. (2010). Internet administered guided self-help versus individualized e-mail therapy: A randomized trial of two versions of CBT for major depression. *Behaviour Research and Therapy, 48*(5), 368–376.

Vilardaga, R., Bricker, J. B., & McDonell, M. G. (2014). The promise of mobile technologies and single case designs for the study of individuals in their natural environment. *Journal of Contextual Behavioral Science, 3*(2), 148–153.

Vilardaga, R., Davies, P. S., Vowles, K. E., & Sullivan, M. D. (2020). Theoretical grounds of Pain Tracker Self Manager: An acceptance and commitment therapy digital intervention for patients with chronic pain. *Journal of Contextual Behavioral Science, 15*, 172–180.

Viskovich, S., & Pakenham, K. I. (2018). Pilot evaluation of a web-based acceptance and commitment therapy program to promote mental health skills in university students. *Journal of Clinical Psychology, 74*(12), 2047–2069.

Waller, R., & Gilbody, S. (2009). Barriers to the uptake of computerized cognitive behavioural therapy: A systematic review of the quantitative and qualitative evidence. *Psychological Medicine, 39*(5), 705.

Warmerdam, L., Smit, F., van Straten, A., Riper, H., & Cuijpers, P. (2010). Cost-utility and cost-effectiveness of internet-based treatment for adults with depressive symptoms: Randomized trial. *Journal of Medical Internet Research, 12*(5), e53.

Whittingham, K., Sheffield, J., & Boyd, R. N. (2016). Parenting acceptance and commitment therapy: A randomised controlled trial of an innovative online course for families of children with cerebral palsy. *BMJ Open, 6*(10), e012807.

Whittingham, K., Sheffield, J., Mak, C., Dickinson, C., & Boyd, R. N. (2020). Early parenting acceptance and commitment therapy "early PACT" for parents of infants with cerebral palsy: A study protocol of a randomised controlled trial. *BMJ Open, 10*, e037033.

Witlox, M., Kraaij, V., Garnefski, N., De Waal, M. W., Smit, F., Hoencamp, E., Gussekloo, J., Bohlmeijer, E. T., & Spinhoven, P. (2018). An internet-based acceptance and commitment therapy intervention for older adults with anxiety complaints: study protocol for a cluster randomized controlled trial. *Trials, 19*(1), 502.

Wollach, C. A. H., Cardaciotto, L., Levin, M., & Armstrong, S. L. (2020). Implementing a web-based cognitive defusion program to target negative self-referential thoughts in college students: A pilot study. *Journal of Contextual Behavioral Science, 16*, 183–191.

Yuen, E. K., Goetter, E. M., Stasio, M. J., Ash, P., Mansour, B., McNally, E., Sanchez, M., Hobar, E., Forte, S., Zulaica, K., & Watkins, J. (2019). A pilot of acceptance and commitment therapy for public speaking anxiety delivered with group videoconferencing and virtual reality exposure. *Journal of Contextual Behavioral Science, 12*, 47–54.

Yuen, E. K., Herbert, J. D., Forman, E. M., Goetter, E. M., Juarascio, A. S., Rabin, S., Goodwin, C. & Bouchard, S. (2013b). Acceptance based behavior therapy for social anxiety disorder through videoconferencing. *Journal of Anxiety Disorders, 27*, 389–397.

Yuen, E. K., Herbert, J. D., Forman, E. M., Goetter, E. M., Comer, R. & Bradley, J. C. (2013a). Treatment of social anxiety disorder using online virtual environments in Second Life. *Behavior Therapy, 44*, 51–61.

Zagorscak, P., Heinrich, M., Schulze, J., Böttcher, J., & Knaevelsrud, C. (2020). Factors contributing to symptom change in standardized and individualized Internet-based interventions for depression: A randomized-controlled trial. *Psychotherapy, 57*(2), 237–251.

Zetterqvist, V., Grudin, R., Rickardsson, J., Wicksell, R. K., & Holmström, L. (2018). Acceptance-based behavioural treatment for insomnia in chronic pain: A clinical pilot study. *Journal of Contextual Behavioral Science, 9*, 72–79.

CHAPTER
29 ACT in Groups

Joanna J. Arch, Lauren B. Finkelstein, *and* Lilian Dindo

Abstract

This article offers an up-to-date selective review of acceptance and commitment therapy (ACT) conducted in the group format. ACT in the group format differs from ACT in the individual format; its potential advantages and disadvantages are discussed in general and in terms of the six ACT hexaflex processes. Reviewed in this article are select large randomized clinical trials on ACT in groups, and highlighted are innovative group delivery modes and the diversity of problem areas to which this format has been applied. Major considerations for conducting ACT in groups are briefly discussed, including reasons to form an ACT group, who and what to include in an ACT group, how to start group sessions, and their length and frequency. The authors consider challenges, including the dearth of studies that directly compare group to individual delivery of ACT and whether group ACT operates similarly at the process level as individual ACT; address the needs of diverse individuals; and evaluate cost effectiveness. Building on the growing number of trials of group ACT interventions, the authors offer recommendations for future research, including strategies to evaluate how ACT groups work and for whom they work best.

Key Words: acceptance and commitment therapy (ACT), group, clinical trial, mental health, psychotherapy, behavioral therapy

Overview of ACT in Groups

Conducting ACT in groups is a widely used intervention strategy. We would not be surprised if half or nearly half of face-to-face ACT interventions were conducted in groups, and if this portion were even higher outside of the United States, Canada, Europe, Australia, and New Zealand. For example, significant ACT research has been conducted in Iran (e.g., Hasannezhad Reskati, Mirzaian, & Hosseini, 2018) and in South Korea (Choi & Kim, 2017), collectively covering dozens of ACT intervention studies, most or all of which were done in groups. Worldwide, the focus of ACT groups varies broadly, with groups conducted in myriad mental health, wellness, and behavioral medicine populations. Thus, an impressive breadth characterizes the literature on ACT in groups. In addition, group delivery formats have been creatively evolving. This article reviews a theoretical rationale and conceptual model for applying ACT in group formats, discusses research to date in this area, shares an overview of how ACT has been applied in groups, offers considerations for conducting ACT in groups, and delineates challenges and future directions of clinical research on ACT in groups.

Theoretical Rationale and Conceptual Model of ACT in Groups

In considering the popularity of delivering ACT in group format, it is important to underscore that ACT is a transdiagnostic model for understanding and intervening with problems of psychological suffering (Hayes, Strosahl, & Wilson, 1999, 2012). For example, experiential avoidance, defined as rigid and unhealthy "efforts to escape and avoid emotions, thoughts, memories, and other private experiences" and take steps to change their form, frequency, or the contexts that trigger them (Hayes, Wilson, Gifford, Follette, & Strosahl, 1996, p. 1152), is a core target of ACT interventions. It has been proposed as a functional dimension that serves a causal and maintenance role in diverse forms of psychopathology from substance abuse to anxiety disorders (e.g., Forsyth, Eifert, & Barrios, 2006). Similarly, psychological flexibility, an overarching aim of the ACT model, has been construed as a cornerstone of psychological health broadly (Kashdan & Rottenberg, 2010). ACT's core aims, principles, processes, and intervention strategies can be flexibly applied to many different problem areas and thus to different individuals in a group who are dealing with a range of problems—that is, to group interventions.

Conceptually, how does doing ACT in the group format differ from doing ACT in an individual format? What are its advantages and disadvantages? First, worldwide, most people who would benefit from mental health care do not receive it (Wang et al., 2007). Thus, an overarching advantage of delivering ACT in groups is that it reaches more people using fewer resources than individual therapy. As long as the outcomes of group ACT interventions approximate those of individual ACT interventions, group delivery represents a more efficient use of mental health resources.

In addition, ACT is meant to be an experiential intervention. On one hand, experiential exercises can be more individually tailored and extensively debriefed in individual therapy. On the other hand, we and others (Walser & Pistorello, 2004; Westrup & Wright, 2017) have found that many experiential exercises seem more powerful in a group setting. For example, similar to others (Juarascio, Shaw, Forman, Timko, Herbert, Butryn, & Lowe, 2013), we have found that acting out the Passengers on the Bus metaphor in a group setting allows participants the choice not only to experience driving the bus, but also to act out one of the passengers, or serve as an objective observer—each of which offers a valuable perspective that would not be readily available in individual therapy. Group settings also provide more routes to learning and perspective-taking than in individual therapy. Even quieter group members who avoid sharing can learn via modeling by observing others apply ACT processes to similar problems. Further, given the different ways each group member tends to conceptualize and apply ACT processes, groups provide modeling of more diverse understandings and applications of ACT principles, which may contribute to a deeper understanding of the concepts as well as facilitate psychological flexibility. For example, if a client does not grasp an ACT metaphor after the therapist shares it, they may grasp it after hearing other group members discuss the metaphor in their own words. Thus, other group members can serve as informal teachers and mentors simply by sharing their experience of ACT concepts. As Walser and Pistorello (2004) noted, sometimes group exercises and discussions lead to group members spontaneously offering their own metaphors or images that prove more helpful than the metaphor or image offered by the therapist.

On a conceptual level, it is worth further considering how conducting ACT in groups can facilitate or hinder each of the major ACT processes outlined in the ACT hexaflex (Hayes et al., 1999, 2012), as outlined in Table 29.1. These considerations are based on the underlying conceptual constructs and on our collective experience conducting ACT in groups. We also outline them with the intention of encouraging empirical evaluation of group versus individual ACT delivery.

Table 29.1. Examples of how ACT processes can be enhanced through group therapy	
Acceptance	Receiving validation and hearing shared experiences from peers with similar conditions can be a powerful path toward acceptance. "I am not alone in this; it's OK to feel this way."
Defusion	Recognizing that peers have thoughts that "hook" them, which have been around for a long time and cannot be simply removed, leads to greater perspective on one's own thoughts. This may enhance one's ability to "unhook" and reduce impact on behavioral choices. "Others have similar thoughts and have learned how to let the thoughts be there without letting them control their behaviors"
Values	Disclosing values and core yearnings facilitates a sense of common experience, shared humanity, mutual respect, and connection. "I can connect with the people in this room because we all care about our families, our health, and our community."
Committed action	Group members modeling committed action for one another and holding one another accountable to their commitments can facilitate change. "I can make a commitment to this group to go out of my comfort zone. If others can do it, so can I."
Self-as-context	Developing a flexible sense of perspective taking is facilitated when multiple different perspectives are on display in a group setting. "Hearing how others handle similar situations gives me new perspectives on how I can approach my challenges."
Mindfulness	Practicing being truly present and nonjudgmental with other group members facilitates greater presence in life outside of the group. "I appreciated how my peers listened to me without judgment and with presence. It made me feel closer to them. I will try that with the people in my life."

Acceptance.

Groups can strongly facilitate acceptance (see Boone & Canicci, 2013) by fostering a sense that "I am not alone with this. We all have these same difficult emotions and thoughts, and nobody else has been able to get rid of them either." If others in similar situations are saying "it's okay to have that," it becomes easier to accept the experience. Groups also validate a shared sense that "I can't control my thoughts and feelings and others can't either."

One of us (J.J.A.) facilitates groups for adults with anxiety and depression and incurable cancer. One group member had survived cancer far longer than expected, but her physical quality of life was poor. She tearfully admitted that she was haunted by the thought that she would have to physically suffer this way forever and that she would never get to die. She believed this was a very shameful thought to have, much less to share. But several other group members validated that they too felt that way, that they could fully relate to her mind-set. This validation from peers who also had incurable cancer radically shifted the participant's view on whether her thought was acceptable. She reported being able to have the thought and no longer needing to put so much energy into fighting it, while continuing to move toward her values. This shift would not likely have taken place as quickly or as fully in an individual therapy context with a healthy therapist. Particularly for stigmatized conditions and for those that severely compromise quality of life, receiving validation and hearing shared experiences from peers with similar conditions can be a powerful path toward acceptance. At the same time, depending on how safe the group feels and how extraverted the participants are, some may find it easier to experience difficult thoughts and emotions in private, in individual settings, than in group settings. Yet formal session feedback surveys have surprisingly revealed that quieter group members often find it powerful to witness others sharing their internal difficulties and report that this experience helps them to accept their own.

Cognitive Defusion.

Similar to acceptance, group settings can also facilitate cognitive defusion for challenging thoughts and beliefs. Compared to an individual in a 1:1 treatment setting, group members share a greater number and variety of difficult thoughts and beliefs. Witnessing others name their difficult thoughts out loud can promote defusion by offering group members a third-person perspective on their own thoughts and beliefs. It can also be easier to admit one's most shameful and embarrassing beliefs, at least to oneself, when numerous others who struggle with similar problems are naming theirs. Acknowledging and naming shameful and embarrassing thoughts and beliefs is a first step toward being able to defuse from them. For example, in another group, several participants shared that their religious faith served as their greatest source of psychological strength. In the face of current struggles, they felt devastated by the thought: "I've lost my faith." In acting out the Passengers on the Bus metaphor with "Lost Faith" as the Passenger, they were able to gain much-needed distance and perspective on the content of this thought and shift their relationship to it. The fact that more than one group member shared the "Lost Faith" Passenger appeared to facilitate defusion even for the members who were only observing the exercise.

Mindfulness.

On one hand, it is likely easier to "tune out" of the present moment in groups because the therapist's focus at any point may be on someone else. On the other hand, groups can generate an intensity of sharing around common experiences that may facilitate a sense of being present, not only for one's own therapy process (as in individual therapy), but for others as well—an experience unique to group therapy. In a well-run group, practicing being present and nonjudgmental with other group members and having them do the same for you provides a model of mindfulness in interpersonal contexts that has the potential to generalize to relationships outside of the group. For example, one member of a group we ran ("Tim") had a wife who complained that Tim was always distracted and not paying attention when she conversed with him. Tim admitted that his wife was correct—he was always thinking about what came next, not about the here-and-now. In group, Tim shared that for the first time, he experienced focusing on what others had to say in a truly present, unhurried, and open way—the fact that everyone in the group shared a stigmatized condition facilitated this change for him. By the middle of the 7-week group, his mindful listening skills began to generalize, and he reported that his wife noticed he was listening more carefully to her, as a result of which his marriage was benefiting.

Values.

At the level of values, experiencing ACT in a group context facilitates a sense of common experience, shared humanity, mutual respect, and connection. Groups can facilitate the sense that values are universal: that at the end of the day, we share our core yearnings, struggles, and motivations. This sense can be created in individual therapy, but rarely are the problems, struggles, and associated personal values as authentically shared between a therapist and client in individual therapy as they are among group members in group therapy for a shared problem or condition. A greater sense of intimacy emerges from shared values and shared vulnerability in a group setting, helping participants to more closely connect to their own values and to one another. For example, in another group for individuals with metastatic cancer, several participants admitted that treatment was failing to control their cancer and they no longer wanted to pursue aggressive treatment, yet they could not bring themselves to admit this to their oncologist or their family. These group members converged around a shared vulnerability of silencing their own wishes to please others, and a fear of appearing to have "given up" or "failed" in the face of their disease. They arrived at the shared value of "speaking the truth" about what they actually wanted for their health care and proceeding to support one another in moving toward this value.

Committed Action.

At the level of committed action, doing ACT in groups does not allow for the same level of individual tailoring of goals and actions, or exploring and overcoming individual barriers to enacting personal goals and actions. However, ACT groups have the major advantage that group members model committed action for one another and hold one another accountable to their commitments. Often, this creates positive synergy, at least in an active and engaged group. It is one thing to show up at individual therapy not having followed through on your commitments. It is quite another to show up to a group with peers who are struggling in the same ways as you, and not follow through. And if you do follow through on your committed actions, there are more people to positively reinforce you in a group setting. In contrast, a less active and committed group risks modeling a lack of committed action, thus functioning as a potential barrier.

Self-as-Context.

The process of self-as-context includes flexible perspective-taking and contacting a transcendent sense of self (Hayes et al., 1999, 2012); both facets may be facilitated by groups. First, at the level of human cognition, it may be easier to develop a flexible sense of perspective-taking when multiple perspectives are on display, as is the case in a group setting. This is particularly true when one feels safe and motivated to take others' perspectives seriously, a likely scenario given that groups convened around a shared problem may be particularly likely to foster mutual respect and a sense of common ground among group members. Second, the group's shared values and vulnerabilities facilitate a sense of a broader, collective self that transcends individual boundaries. Relative to individual therapy, the experience within ACT groups may more strongly engender a sense of common humanity, which in turn may facilitate a sense that "We are all connected . . . . This is a shared experience that transcends me alone." It is not a large leap to contacting a sense of the transcendent self.

The disadvantages of group delivery are largely not unique to ACT, but they are important to name. First, group ACT sessions usually take longer than individual ACT sessions to cover a similar breadth and depth of material. This is the case for at least two reasons. First, group members usually have a strong desire to share their experience with others who have experienced something similar—to trade personal narratives with other group members. Though ACT groups sometimes rein in sharing stories, we have found that allowing some degree of this form of sharing, particularly in the first week or two of a group, can be helpful for establishing a sense of common ground, intimacy, and trust among group members. However, even brief sharing takes time when multiplied by the number of group members. Second, facilitating ACT for a group of individuals, each of whom has their own learning style, and allowing each to share their experience of ACT, takes more time than it would in individual therapy. Thus, the efficiency of treating multiple individuals at once and the synergy of learning in a group must be weighed against the greater time required for each session.

Even with this extra time, group ACT does not permit as much time to focus on individual tailoring of the intervention content or applications to an individual's issues or learning style. Thus, individuals with unique learning needs that are challenging to address in groups (e.g., needing something explained many more times or in very different ways than most others)—common among individuals with significant neurological differences, relevant learning disabilities, or brain injury or functional deterioration—may benefit from individual intervention unless these features are shared among group members. Similarly, individuals in acute crisis, with very strong privacy needs or paranoia toward others, or with rare problems/issues not shared by other group members, may also require individual attention.

On one hand, these proposed disadvantages are largely speculative, as little research exists on whether they are relevant to ACT delivered in groups. On the other hand, it can be helpful to imagine their potential manifestations within a particular dimension of the hexaflex model of ACT. Let us imagine the impact on values work, for example.

For values work, one common conceptual pitfall we have observed is that it can be challenging for all group members to understand the distinction between values and goals. This distinction is simply more easily grasped by some than by others. Often, group leaders lack the time to give the individual attention needed to teach this distinction to those who struggle with it. This distinction sometimes matters functionally more for some group members or problems than for others, which can create challenges in group settings. For example, we once led an ACT group for physically ill individuals in which most members valued connecting with their family above all. These members showed varying degrees of success in understanding the distinction between values and goals, but each of them could imagine ways to meaningfully engage with family while ill. Thus, this conceptual distinction did not matter functionally for them. However, another member of the same group had little family, and she chiefly valued producing a specific and demanding art form that she could no longer physically do. She had focused her entire life on this art form but had great difficulty identifying or connecting with the values underneath it. In our group setting, the group leaders had limited time to engage her individually, and she shared neither the values nor a conceptual understanding of values (and their distinction from goals), with the rest of the group. Yet it was important for her to understand this distinction in order to move toward committed action. Thus, it was likely more challenging to engage her in values and related ACT processes in group therapy than it would have been in individual therapy.

Research on ACT in Groups

ACT group-based interventions have been evaluated in a robust and rapidly growing body of empirical research, including dozens of large-scale clinical trials and extensive pilot projects. Research on ACT groups covers diverse problem areas, including a broad spectrum of mental health problems from antisocial personality disorder (Livheim et al., 2020), eating disorders (Juarascio, Shaw, Forman, Timko, Herbert, Butryn, Bunnell, et al., 2013), obsessive-compulsive disorder (Shabani et al., 2019), psychosis (Spidel, Daigneault, Kealy, & Lecomte, 2019), behavioral medicine and communication problems from asthma management (Chong, Mak, Leung, Lam, & Loke, 2019), smoking cessation (McClure, Bricker, Mull, & Heffner, 2020), stuttering (Beilby, Byrnes, & Yaruss, 2012), work and school arenas, including workplace burnout and absence (Aasdahl et al., 2018) and academic procrastination (Wang et al., 2016), and other problem areas such as mental illness stigma (Kenny & Bizumic, 2016).

While a comprehensive review of this literature is beyond the scope of this article, we offer detailed overviews of one review and five clinical trials that illustrate the rigor and breadth of research on ACT in groups. In addition, we highlight others that use innovative group ACT delivery approaches.

We will begin our review of the literature with an overview of the one systematic review published in English on group ACT interventions (Coto-Lesmes, Fernandez-Rodriguez, & Gonzalez-Fernandez, 2020), followed by descriptions of exemplary clinical trials within mental health and behavioral medicine populations. Our aim is to sample the breadth of large and rigorous studies that evaluate group ACT interventions.

Select Large Randomized Clinical Trials and Reviews

The only known English-language review of ACT group interventions is that by Coto-Lesmes and colleagues (2020), who conducted a systematic review of group-based ACT for treating anxiety and depression. Their search yielded 10 randomized control trials (RCTs) comparing ACT to a no-intervention control group (six studies) or to cognitive-behavioral therapy (CBT)/cognitive therapy (CT) (four studies) as well as four single-arm group ACT clinical trials and one case study series. The trials were geographically diverse, including samples from Australia, the United States, Iran, Sweden, the Netherlands, and the United Kingdom. Sample sizes ranged from 13 to 193 participants, and interventions offered 4 to 12 group sessions of 1.5 to 2 hours each. Heterogeneity in evaluation methods complicated analysis; however, each of the 12 studies evaluating depression and the 11 studies evaluating anxiety found improvements in these outcomes. For the studies that carried out follow-up assessments, gains were maintained over time. Studies with active comparison conditions reported similar anxiety and depression outcomes for ACT versus CBT/CT, with the exception of one study (Zettle, Rains, & Hayes, 2011), which found that ACT outperformed CT for depression. Most studies evaluated change in psychological flexibility, with disparate results: eight found significant improvements, whereas three found no significant change. Again, CBT improved similarly in psychological flexibility as ACT, with the exception of one study where the ACT group showed a steeper rise on this dimension (Avdagic, Morrissey, & Boschen, 2014). Mediator analyses were limited, but three studies reported that psychological flexibility mediated improvements in anxiety and depression in the ACT condition. Qualitatively, participants reported high satisfaction with group-based ACT and had strong engagement ($< 25\%$ average attrition, $> 80\%$ sessions average attendance).

Given these findings, Coto-Lesmes et al. (2020) concluded that group-based ACT is useful in addressing anxiety and depression, but that further carefully controlled research is needed to identify the specific drivers of change and to show whether therapeutic mechanisms are specific to ACT. The authors noted that mechanism of change questions are especially pertinent given the challenges of targeting participant-level patterns of psychological inflexibility in a group format.

We next give an overview of five clinical trials selected to highlight three features of research on group ACT interventions: (1) large sample size, (2) breadth of topical focus, and (3) innovation in delivery methods.

The largest trial to date of group-delivered ACT evaluated classroom-based delivery toward the aim of preventing and improving youth mental health problems (Van der Gucht et al., 2017). The authors were motivated to investigate this intervention format because ACT targets common risk factors for mental health problems and thus may be especially conducive to prevention; schools are a prime setting for facilitating early intervention, improving service access, and destigmatizing mental health treatment. Students (average age 17) nested within

34 classes at 14 schools in Flanders, Belgium, were randomized by classroom to the ACT intervention (n = 288) or a no-intervention control (n = 298). The classroom-based intervention consisted of four weekly 2-hour sessions integrated into the school curriculum. The sessions included psychoeducation, experiential exercises, and workbook homework assignments aimed at helping students reduce experiential avoidance, experience the difference between "experiencing something" and "the person having the experience," and engage in committed actions. All sessions were teacher-led, following a 2-day teacher training, two 2-hour supervision sessions, and additional support as needed. Participating students completed psychological flexibility, quality of life, and behavioral/mental health symptom questionnaires pre- and postintervention, and a final follow-up one-year postintervention. Tests for all outcomes were nonsignificant, including for students with preexisting mental health symptoms. The authors speculated that the briefness of the intervention and the use of non-mental health professionals in delivering it were key reasons for its ineffectiveness.

In addition to mental health topics, the efficacy of group ACT has been evaluated across a variety of behavioral medicine concerns. In a randomized clinical trial conducted in Australia, 313 parents of children with newly diagnosed life-threatening illness or injury were randomized to either ACT (n = 152) or a waitlist control (n = 161) (Muscara et al., 2020). To be eligible, parents had to experience elevated levels of acute stress symptoms, which predict longer-term mental health disturbance including posttraumatic stress syndrome (PTSS). Parents in the ACT condition completed the Take a Breath program, which consisted of five 1.5-hour weekly therapy sessions followed by a final session 3 weeks later. This group-based intervention, designed to minimize PTSS in the population under investigation, was administered remotely in groups of three to eight parents and partners. Participants completed the intervention from their homes using Google Hangouts videoconferencing on study-provided iPads, and they were sent value cards, a session booklet, and a guided mindfulness audio file. Each session was delivered by two mental health clinicians trained by a senior ACT clinician. PTSS, depression, anxiety, stress, and psychological skills were measured at four time points before, during, and immediately after the intervention. The study had high attrition across both study arms, primarily due to time constraints or feelings that the intervention was not needed, with only 81 of 313 randomized participants completing postintervention measures. Among this smaller postintervention sample, parents in the ACT group experienced improved PTSS scores (Cohen's d = 1.10), emotional resources (d = 0.95), perceptions of uncertainty (d = 1.34), and negative appraisal (d = 0.98) compared to the waitlist control. These gains may be associated with the ACT group's relative improvement on a number of psychological skills, including experiential avoidance (d = 0.80), mindfulness (d = 1.51), values adherence (d = 1.14), and committed action (d = 0.86). Overall, these findings point to ACT videoconferencing as an effective and innovative method of administering group ACT intervention, albeit one with high attrition in this context. With about half of the sample living in rural or distant locations, the remote format overcame key barriers to access, and the interactive group video format provided the opportunity for peer support and normalization of experiences. However, additional research is needed to show whether the high attrition observed was specific to the targeted parent population, to home-based videoconferenced ACT groups, or to some other variable.

Like Muscara and colleagues, Järvelä-Reijonen et al. (2018) also explored virtual ACT delivery, this time comparing the effectiveness of the self-guided mobile app format plus a single in-person group session ("mobile ACT") to ongoing in-person group ACT. In this three-arm trial, Finnish adult participants who struggled with excess weight/obesity and psychological distress were randomly assigned to mobile ACT (n = 78), in-person group ACT (n =

70), or a no-intervention control (n = 71). The mobile and group ACT conditions were based on the same ACT program and therefore only differed in delivery method. The program incorporated ACT skills, with additions relevant to mindful eating, relaxation, and physical activity. The in-person group met a total of 6 times over an 8-week period, for ~1.5 hours each time. The groups of 6–12 participants were led by a psychologist who facilitated exercises and pair or group discussions, in addition to assigning homework guided by a workbook. The mobile group met once as a group in person to review key ACT principles and to pick up smartphones with a pre-installed app. The app, which was used individually and thus had no group element, contained dozens of videos and text or audio format exercises, which could be completed in any order and at any time. The control group simply completed measures of eating behavior and diet. Attrition was low and adherence across conditions was strong. Compared to the control group, eating for physical rather than emotional reasons significantly improved in both ACT conditions (d = 0.40 in-person, 0.33 mobile). In the in-person group condition, multiple additional outcomes improved, including uncontrolled eating (d = –0.34), food acceptance (d = 0.31), and integrated (d = 0.41) and identified (d = 0.15) regulation of eating behavior, whereas in the mobile app condition, only using food as a reward also decreased (d = –0.29). No impacts on dietary measures were observed. In summary, the ACT interventions improved participants' relationship with and regulation of eating, with stronger effects in the in-person group ACT intervention. However, the interventions did not impact diet. The authors point to the cost and access benefits of mobile delivery, while acknowledging that human support enhanced intervention effectiveness.

Using a similar three-armed trial design, Pederson et al. (2019) examined the effects of two different group ACT delivery intensities: a group workshop and weekly group sessions. Patients with functional somatic syndromes (characterized by bodily complaints with insufficient medical explanation) in Denmark were randomized to receive enhanced care (n = 60), a brief ACT intervention (n = 61), or an extended ACT intervention (n = 59). The brief ACT intervention included a one 1 to 1.5-hour manualized physician consultation aimed at enhancing understanding of diagnosis and treatment; a 1-day 6-hour workshop with 15 or fewer patients providing medical education and an introduction to ACT concepts through psychoeducation, experiential exercises, and group discussion; and an individual follow-up consultation with a therapist to personalize workshop content. The extended ACT intervention included the same manualized consultation, followed by nine weekly 3-hour sessions of in-person group ACT co-led by a psychiatrist and psychologist. Each session was based on core elements of the hexaflex model and incorporated experiential and mindfulness exercises, group discussions, and commitment processes. Finally, the enhanced care (EC) condition received the manualized consultation but no further treatment. On the primary outcome of self-rated global health at the 14-month time point, extended ACT outperformed EC (OR = 2.9), whereas brief ACT and EC performed similarly to one another. However, given that secondary outcomes did not show clinically relevant differences across conditions, the authors concluded that ACT had limited clinical impact compared to EC in this population. They speculated that the inflexibility of reliance on group-based processes may have limited therapeutic engagement and opportunity to address patients' individual challenges.

Whereas the aforementioned trials compared group ACT to no-intervention or minimally enhanced control groups, McClure et al. (2020) compared ACT to CBT, the existing group-based standard of care for smoking cessation. Smokers in Washington state in the United States were randomized to receive nicotine-replacement therapy (NRT) plus group ACT (n = 224) or CBT (n = 226). Both conditions included five weekly 1.5-hour sessions led by a trained master's-level counselor. The ACT sessions focused on metaphors and experiential exercises, followed by group discussion and feedback. In contrast to the CBT arm, the ACT group did not use a predefined quit date window to maintain flexibility and autonomy in committed actions. Self-reported 30-day point prevalence abstinence (PPA) at one year did not significantly differ between the two group types and was strongly associated with acceptance of cravings in both treatment arms. However, PPA was lower in the ACT arm at 1 week (OR = 0.44) and 6 months (OR = 0.56) posttreatment, although at the latter time point biochemically confirmed abstinence was not significantly different between the groups. Session attendance was the same for both conditions. NRT was used by 67.5 percent of the ACT group and 84.3 percent in the CBT group. Participants generally reported being at least somewhat satisfied with the intervention (92.4% ACT, 95.3% CBT) and found the intervention useful in quitting smoking (88.0% ACT, 94.3% CBT). Given these findings, the authors concluded that group-format ACT and CBT are comparable for smoking cessation, and they emphasized the value of having alternative treatment options: New treatments encourage smokers to make additional quit attempts, which in turn increase one's chances of successfully quitting. However, given that 74 percent of screened individuals declined study participation primarily due to lack of interest or inability to attend in-person sessions, these results may only generalize to those open to group-based treatment.

The literature we have described points to the broad transdiagnostic potential of group-format ACT, while also revealing this modality's mixed success across studies. The authors speculate that factors including intervention intensity, format, technology, problem focus, and staff expertise are critical in producing therapeutic engagement and change. Thus, the specifics of group design and facilitation may play key roles in promoting clinical improvement.

Innovative Group ACT Delivery Modes

The previous RCTs include examples of diverse group ACT delivery formats, varying in length, intensity, setting, and technology. In this section, we highlight additional delivery innovations that have been investigated in larger-scale or pilot studies. Group ACT is most commonly delivered through multiple weekly sessions in a health care setting, but several trials have implemented group ACT in more accessible or consolidated formats. For example, in a sample of adults with depression who have recurring migraines, Dindo et al. (2020) compared the efficacy of a 1-day 5- to 6-hour migraine education plus ACT workshop (n = 56) to a relaxation and social support-based workshop (n = 47). Each workshop included four to eight participants and was led by two psychologists. The ACT component focused on managing troubling thoughts, feelings, and pain sensations, resulting in significantly improved depression (OR = 2.70) and anxiety (OR = 4.25) symptoms, and headache-related disability (OR = 4.40) at 6-month follow-up compared to the support workshop. With effect sizes comparable to other psychotherapeutic depression treatments, this workshop format offers an attractive alternative to traditional psychotherapy: The single-day duration optimizes adherence, completion, and access, and the framing of this intervention as a "workshop" rather than "therapy" is less stigmatizing and has the potential to draw more people into treatment.

Hybrid remote and in-person group intervention ACT delivery can also help to reduce the scheduling, transportation, and financial costs of seeking treatment. This approach may be a particularly good match when full-day workshops are overly taxing or impractical due to the medical severity of the population. Arch et al. (2020) piloted this hybrid model in a study of 35 adults with metastatic cancer who were experiencing anxiety and depression, alternating in-person ACT group sessions held onsite in cancer care clinics with self-paced ACT online sessions and check-ins completed on their own. We predicted that in-person group support and connection would help to hold participants responsible for completing the online intervention components (which involved no therapist contact), thereby offsetting the weaker adherence rates and outcomes characteristic of online-only interventions (Baumeister, Reichler, Munzinger, & Lin, 2014). The online sessions and check-ins were designed to individualize and integrate ACT skills into the participants' daily lives. Among participants sufficiently well to begin the intervention (n = 26), the findings showed significant improvements in mental health, existential well-being, and advanced care planning outcomes—in addition to strong adherence and satisfaction with the intervention. Thus, pilot results support the feasibility, acceptability, and efficacy potential of this blended ACT treatment approach in a distressed population with metastatic disease.

Hosting group sessions onsite in the workplace offers an alternative means of lowering the transportation and time burdens associated with attending offsite therapy. O'Brien et al. (2019) implemented this approach through worksite nurse and nurse aide interventions. Participants were assigned to group ACT (n = 37) or a waitlist control (n = 34). For the ACT condition, two 2.5-hour group sessions were held at residential long-term care settings. The intervention was designed to encourage engagement between participants, which the authors hypothesized would promote coworker alliance-building useful for managing workplace stress and challenges. The intervention was effective, resulting in significantly fewer work absences due to workplace injury (d = 0.12) and improved mental health (d = 0.06), compared to the waitlist control group.

In the most well-integrated example of conducting ACT groups onsite in the location of care delivery, Vowles and McCracken (2008) investigated an immersive approach to chronic pain treatment by embedding ACT into a broader interdisciplinary treatment context where participants lived onsite for the duration of treatment. Participants were assigned to a 3-week (n = 145) or 4-week (n = 42) course of treatment, depending on illness severity and complexity. Integrative biopsychosocial treatment was delivered by a diverse group of health care professionals 5 days per week for 6.5 hours per day. Psychological content was delivered for 1.5 hours each day, with treatment targeting key ACT processes with the goal of improving flexibility and functioning rather than changing pain or emotional symptoms. These individuals with complex pain experienced significant improvements in pain, mental health, disability, health care use, work status, and physical performance, with almost uniformly medium to large effect sizes. Acceptance and values-based action were associated with improvements in functioning, pointing to the specific usefulness of ACT processes in this multimodal treatment model.

Thus far, we have discussed several models of group ACT delivery, implemented in diverse populations. However, a criticism common to all group-based therapies is that they fail to adequately personalize content or capitalize on the motivational and supportive elements characteristic of therapeutic relationships. Gifford et al. (2011) combined individual and group-based therapy in a smoking cessation RCT involving 303 people who smoked, randomized to receive bupropion alone or bupropion plus therapy. The therapy arm involved one group ACT session plus one individual functional analytic psychotherapy (FAP) session per week for 10 weeks. The two treatment modalities were intended to be mutually reinforcing: Skills learned in group could be individualized and reinforced during FAP, which was designed to maximize the impact of interpersonal treatment processes through intimate and reinforcing therapeutic relationships. The trial revealed promising results, with higher treatment satisfaction in the therapy + bupropion arm (d = 0.84) and significantly higher quit rates (d = 0.46) at posttreatment relative to bupropion alone, mediated by acceptance and the therapeutic alliance.

Academic Overview of Conducting ACT in Groups

Many excellent chapters and books (Boone & Canicci, 2013; Walser & Pistorello, 2004; Westrup & Wright, 2017) detail how to conduct ACT in groups from a clinical practice perspective. This section briefly summarizes major considerations involved in conducting ACT in groups, with more detailed clinical treatments available in these previous works.

Why Form an ACT Group?

Groups can be formed for reasons of resource conservation (e.g., Brown et al., 2011), therapeutic benefit, or both. As noted, the group format allows for conservation of institutional resources, as multiple people are being helped at once. Regarding therapeutic benefit, people struggling with psychological problems or chronic disease often become isolated; thus, the support of a group can be a powerful force in enacting therapeutic change. One group member's disclosure of shared struggles can leave participants with a sense that their struggles are not due to their personal weakness, that they are not alone, and that struggles are a natural consequence of being human. Participants with difficulties in interpersonal functioning can use a group therapy setting to improve social skills, learn from others, practice with others, and get feedback in a supportive and safe context.

Who and What to Include in an ACT Group.

ACT aims to enhance openness, awareness, and engagement in life values, transdiagnostic skills, and perspectives that offer the potential to enhance living for many different types of people. Thus, ACT group treatments could include people with different clinical problems, social challenges, behavioral issues, or physical health problems. At the same time, there is value in restricting groups to people with similar challenges or struggles. For example, individuals with chronic health conditions (e.g., HIV, inflammatory bowel disease, multiple sclerosis) often experience difficulties specific to their condition. The group's disclosure of their unique and shared struggles can be therapeutic. For example, in an ACT trial for people living with inflammatory bowel disease (Hou et al., 2017), one patient described his love of the outdoors (values), specifically being on a boat in the ocean (goal), and his inability to go on boats due to fear of needing a bathroom (barrier). Another patient, who also loved the outdoors and boating, humorously shared that he still took regular boat rides and simply leaned over the edge of the boat when needing a bathroom. These discussions between the patients, within the context of the ACT model (values, what gets in the way, how to overcome obstacles), were mutually validating and empowering because they concerned a shared problem unique to their medical condition (shared vulnerability) and a shared interest (shared goals and values). Shared vulnerabilities are easier to identify in a group that shares similar problems. Then, group members can share ways in which they continue living out values despite the unique challenges their condition poses.

When ACT groups are restricted to certain populations, it is worth considering whether to supplement ACT with other relevant information. In our experience, it can be useful to incorporate "education" into the ACT groups (Dindo, Weinrib, & Marchman, 2019). For example, patients with chronic disease often have surprisingly little understanding of their illness, the rationale of its treatment, and their own ability to influence its course. Combining ACT with illness education can be powerful. Among patients with interpersonal difficulties, it could be useful to include skills training and didactic information about interpersonal effectiveness linked to goals and values. Among patients with marital or relationship problems, it may be useful to incorporate exercises that enhance communication skills (e.g., empathic understandings, assertive versus aggressive communication), again linked to goals and values. It can be useful to include partners, caregivers, family, or other significant others in certain ACT sessions to share what is being learned and to increase the likelihood of its uptake at home.

It is also worth considering whether to have single-gender or mixed-gender groups (Ogrodniczuk, Piper, & Joyce, 2006). Single-gender group therapy allows for gender-relevant topics and enhanced feelings of safety. For example, in our work with veterans from the conflicts in Iraq and Afghanistan (Operations Iraqi Freedom, Enduring Freedom, and New Dawn), we learned that women and men both prefer to have single-sex groups in that context. Military sexual trauma is a significant problem among returning veterans, particularly women veterans. On the one hand, women reported feeling a greater sense of safety in woman-only groups, and men reported feeling more comfortable sharing among other men. On the other hand, sometimes perspectives from the other sex can be powerful motivators for change in mixed groups. For example, in a mixed ACT group for patients with inflammatory bowel disease, one man revealed significant shame about his body and his avoidance of intimacy as a result (and several other men could relate to this feeling). A woman in the group shared how important intimacy is to her and how painful it would be if her male partner avoided it due to shame. In this example, the (heterosexual) woman provided a different and valuable perspective for the (heterosexual) male patients in the group. Keeping the values of intimacy and connection front and center provided the motivation to engage in something meaningful even if it was uncomfortable.

Number of ACT Group Therapists.

Although one skilled ACT therapist can conduct the treatment, a two-member team of therapists or group facilitators is ideal for tracking client engagement and understanding. We have also found that interactions between two engaged and engaging therapists can provide powerful teaching moments in group sessions. For example, in situations when one therapist gets fused with content, the other therapist can humorously address this problem. This demonstrates that therapists are "human" and get fused. It also provides an opportunity for the therapist to model "defusing." One therapist may self-disclose when it is clinically useful, and the other therapist may model an empathic response. Overall, it is important for therapists to act as a team, welcoming mutual efforts to help each other be their best. Clients can observe collaborative, empathic, humorous, and even challenging but effective communication between therapists.

Participation.

It is important to encourage and facilitate everyone's participation. At the same time, therapists must honor the choice of anyone unwilling to do so. It is important not to argue with participants or to pressure them to do or commit to anything. It is also important to keep things on track in group interventions. People often want to share their story and personal problems with other group members. The facilitators can turn information shared by group members to effective uses by bringing the focus back to relevant ACT processes.

As noted, one especially powerful aspect of ACT group work is the opportunity to play with live metaphors. Many of the classic ACT metaphors, such as Tug of War with the Monster, Take Your Mind for a Walk, and Passengers on the Bus, readily lend themselves to group participation in an engaging and perspective-broadening manner.

Principle-Focused.

ACT is a principle-based rather than procedure-based intervention. Every group is unique in terms of the individuals, the specific content that is presented, and the problem focus. In order to be as effective as possible with each group of clients, therapists should be able to ascertain, moment to moment, which process(es) to focus on to move the group toward greater psychological flexibility. The procedures, techniques, exercises, and content are vehicles to accomplish that goal. Each therapist should have a repertoire of exercises to choose from for each process, tailored to work well in a group setting.

Starting a Group Session.

The usual conventions of therapy apply to the beginning of a group intervention. Initial topics to discuss include confidentiality (e.g., "you can discuss your own experience of the group but please do not share who else is here or what they share with anyone outside of the group"); the importance of respecting others in the group, which can include not giving unsolicited advice or asking others to "fix" their emotions (e.g., to stop crying, cheer up); and the importance of practicing skills in daily life. After discussing expectations and establishing ground rules, beginning an ACT group intervention with a brief eyes-closed centering exercise or a simple values-based exercise can be powerful. For an example of the latter, each group member could be asked to state their name and who or what is important to them. The therapist can write down each person's response on a board and ask if others have a similar value. This simple opening exercise will result in a list of valued domains, placing values at the center of the work. It will also allow the group members to recognize and appreciate that they share values such as family, friends, health, intimate relationships, and community, that bind them together as human beings. Once everyone has answered, the therapist can state: "This is what our work together is going to be about—the people and things in our lives that mean the most to us and how we can build our lives around what's important." Beginning a group intervention in this manner orients the conversation from the very start toward cultivating a life worth living. Values provide the motivation to do the hard work of therapy. Alternatively, beginning a group with shared challenges (written out for all to see) before shifting toward shared values can build a helpful foundation of trust and intimacy, plant the seeds of defusion and acceptance, and send the message that all dimensions of their experience are welcome in the group, including their difficulties.

Length and Frequency of Group Meetings.

ACT groups have been conducted in intensive 1-day workshops, 2-day workshops, weekly sessions, and hybrid formats (in which groups comprise one of several different treatment modalities). Each of these formats has advantages and disadvantages. For example, many barriers to care can be addressed by offering clients a 1-day (4–6-hour) workshop. Offering a "workshop" format rather than "therapy" is better suited for clients for whom mental health care is associated with stigma (e.g., veterans). A workshop is also better suited for primary or specialty care medical settings where clients often present with different expectations than those explicitly seeking mental health care. A 1-day workshop also ensures treatment adherence and completion. A meta-analysis of 669 studies on outpatient psychotherapy found that 20–40 percent of clients drop out of treatment prematurely (Swift & Greenberg, 2012). An effective intervention that can be completed in one day (6–7 hours) addresses this problem while providing clients with more contact time than is routinely available in outpatient settings. Finally, a 1-day workshop is more accessible and feasible than weekly treatments, particularly for clients who live in rural communities. A series of studies have shown that this approach can improve mental health symptoms and functioning (Dindo, Van Liew, & Arch, 2017). However, this approach may not suffice for all clients, including those not explicitly seeking mental health care. Some clients require more meetings over longer periods of time. For example, one study showed that clients undergoing surgery who attended an ACT workshop had lower levels of pain and opioid use compared to those in usual care. However, clients who had surgical complications did not show similar improvements and possibly needed more individualized support (Dindo et al., 2018). Clients with memory difficulties (e.g., traumatic brain injury, neurologic disease or deterioration) may not do as well with a 1-day approach because they often need information to be repeated over time. One option is to provide an individualized follow-up therapy session—either in person or via telephone/video (to reduce travel burden)—to clients who need more care. Thus, therapists could provide one or more individualized "booster" sessions following a workshop.

Others have used the "2 + 1" approach of psychotherapy whereby participants receive three 3-hour group sessions, two of them on consecutive weeks and a third 3 months later. This approach still limits the amount of time that people need to travel to the treatment, but it does gives people the opportunity to complete homework assignments, practice various strategies, and troubleshoot difficulties with the group and therapist in subsequent sessions. Bond and Bunce (2000), for example, have used this approach in the work setting and have found that ACT, presented this way, led to improvements in well-being and the tendency to innovate.

These intensive brief approaches can be used as a primary treatment modality, as a supplementary treatment to individual therapy, or as a trigger for initiating more extensive therapy. In fact, we have found that clients are more willing to seek regular mental health treatment after doing a workshop (Dindo, Roddy, et al., 2020).

Clients who present for mental health treatment may be more amenable to weekly group sessions over several months and may prefer the ability to connect with a group of people and to practice various strategies over time. However, meeting weekly requires more ongoing flexibility in schedules and an ability to present for care on a weekly basis.

Challenges and Future Directions

The biggest challenge in reflecting on the use of ACT in group formats is the dearth of empirical evidence for the specific advantages and disadvantages of group ACT delivery. Among the dozens of clinical trials using ACT group delivery, it is striking how few have aimed to directly compare ACT group delivery to individual delivery. Comparing group delivery of ACT to individual delivery of ACT is a first important step in establishing comparative effectiveness and in empirically investigating the potential advantages and disadvantages of group ACT delivery. Similar trials have compared group and individual forms of classic CBT for problems such as childhood anxiety disorders and adult social anxiety disorder (CBT; e.g., Bjornsson et al., 2011; Manassis et al., 2002; Mörtberg, Clark, Sundin, & Åberg Wistedt, 2007), internet-based CBT versus face-to-face group CBT for social anxiety disorder (Hedman et al., 2011), and others. One ACT trial in Finland compared six face-to-face ACT groups with a parallel mobile-based ACT app program (without provider contact), plus one group session to improve relationships to eating and diet (Jarvela-Reijonen et al., 2018). Both groups showed improvement in relationship to eating and diet relative to a control condition, with greater improvement in the face-to-face ACT group arm than the mobile app arm. However, although it is an important study, the two ACT conditions were not matched for dose or delivery modality (in person vs. online) and the processes between them were not compared.

One might ask if it is necessary to compare different ACT delivery formats if research has supported their efficacy in separate trials. After all, hundreds of separate ACT trials have established varying degrees of efficacy for individual and group versions of ACT. The answer depends on what type of evidence we desire. If we aim only to know whether a treatment is helpful for the target population, then the evidence to date may suffice. However, if we aim to know what form of ACT delivery is best for whom, and the comparative advantages of doing ACT in groups versus other forms, then comparing across treatment delivery modalities becomes necessary. Such comparisons facilitate identifying the participant characteristics that predict better outcomes in one form of ACT delivery versus another, reflecting treatment moderation. Identifying treatment moderators facilitates treatment matching (see DeRubeis et al., 2014). For example, in a sample of adults with heterogeneous anxiety disorders, we identified a composite index of treatment moderators that predicted differential dropout from individual ACT versus CBT (Niles, Wolitzky-Taylor, Arch, & Craske, 2017). Comparing the ACT group to individual (or other forms of) delivery would facilitate developing such knowledge for different forms of ACT delivery, as groups may work better for some individuals or clinical problems than for others.

In addition, studies that compare across delivery formats can address the critical question of whether ACT operates similarly at the process level in group delivery versus other formats. Because clinicians and clinical researchers have noted that experiential ACT exercises appear to be potentiated by group delivery (Walser & Pistorello, 2004; Westrup & Wright, 2017), this is an important empirical question in ACT. Different processes have been found to mediate individual versus group CBT in social anxiety disorder (Hedman et al., 2013), supporting the notion that different delivery formats of the same therapy can potentiate different change processes. Although an initial attempt focusing on the therapeutic alliance was unsuccessful (Rubel, Zilcha-Mano, Giesemann, Prinz, & Lutz, 2020), psychotherapy outcome research has begun applying machine learning approaches to predict personalized associations between therapeutic processes and outcomes. It may be that group ACT leads to different therapy process-outcome relationships than individual ACT—the study of which would be facilitated by directly comparing different forms of ACT delivery. Apart from this comparison, we encourage clinical researchers to apply intensive measurement and sophisticated statistical modeling to elucidate which processes change most in various ACT group interventions and to what extent these change processes depend on the dynamics of a particular group.

Another area that deserves mention is cost effectiveness. One advantage of group delivery of mental and behavioral health interventions more broadly is that they are more cost effective than individual delivery in terms of cost to the health care system (e.g., Brown et al., 2011). Directly comparing group delivery of ACT to other forms of delivery would create the opportunity to evaluate the cost effectiveness of group ACT relative to other forms of delivery.

One sudden change sparked by the COVID-19 pandemic is that most mental health care has shifted to online-only formats. This has been the case for group-based work as well, including the ACT group interventions conducted in the authors' research labs. Many mental health care systems, practitioners, and clients have needed to make this shift quickly and fully, and thus are growing accustomed and skilled at giving and receiving mental health care via telehealth. Given the upside of greater convenience in providing and accessing services, we imagine that online intervention will remain common after the pandemic passes. As yet, there is no significant published literature on conducting ACT groups online, and we encourage clinical researchers to address this timely gap.

Finally, another potential advantage of groups suggested by some clinical researchers is that groups may be a better-matched, more acceptable form of mental health treatment for some racial and ethnic minority youth and adult clients in North America, Europe, Australia, New Zealand (e.g., Tharp, 1991), and other nations. In support, as noted, reviews of ACT from Iran (Hasannezhad Reskati et al., 2018) and South Korea (Choi & Kim, 2017) showcased ACT trials, nearly all of which were conducted in groups, implying that groups were the delivery approach of choice in these contexts. Group-based intervention includes the possibility of expanding the definition of "group" to focus on the family, a class of professionals (e.g., health care workers), or the broader community, approaches that have been applied to train health care workers in group ACT workshops in Sierra Leone, for example (Stewart et al., 2016). That noted, the assumption that groups work better for many nonwhite North Americans or European Americans is based on grouping together extremely diverse cultures, groups, and individuals, and requires empirical investigation. For example, a recent large meta-analysis of various mental health interventions with Asian Americans, a highly diverse group, showed no difference in outcome between individual and group-based interventions (Huey & Tilley, 2018). However, tailoring of intervention content to Asian Americans and particularly to Asian American cultural subgroups (e.g., Cambodian refugees), but not to minorities in general, yielded superior outcomes. Although not ACT focused, these findings again point to the importance of evaluating assumptions about the presumed advantages (or disadvantages) of group interventions empirically. They also demonstrate the potential benefits of cultural tailoring.

In that a large number of clinical trials have already been conducted on group-delivered ACT, is the only way forward to conduct dozens of more large trials comparing group ACT to ACT delivered in other formats? In addition to large randomized clinical trials, other possibilities exist. Laboratory-based studies in the tradition of experimental psychopathology (Zvolensky, Lejuez, Stuart, & Curtin, 2001) have been widely used to evaluate ACT processes and components in brief experimental studies (Levin, Hildebrandt, Lillis, & Hayes, 2012). Such approaches could be applied to studying the immediate and short-term effects of experiential ACT exercises delivered in individual versus group format, for example. ACT researchers have also made excellent use of rigorous case-study series and small, intensive measurement trials of key ACT components (e.g., Villatte et al., 2016). These approaches too could be applied to studying the processes and outcomes associated with group ACT versus face-to-face individual and online forms of delivery. Finally, meta-analyses could compare group to individual therapy delivery as a moderator of process or outcome findings. Ruiz (2012) took this approach in his well-cited meta-analysis and found that group ($g+ = 0.50$) and individual ($g+ = 0.31$) ACT interventions for diverse problems, relative to classic CBT, did not show statistically significant differences in outcomes, though the pattern favored group approaches. Similar analyses should be conducted regularly in the ACT meta-analytic literature.

In summary, group ACT trials have produced a large evidence base but have rarely been compared to other forms of delivery. Numerous possibilities exist for advancing the field's understanding of the advantages and disadvantages of group ACT delivery for a variety of conditions, including identifying for whom group delivery works best, which distinct and shared processes emerge from group versus other forms of ACT delivery, as well as group delivery's relative cost effectiveness.

Conclusions

Conducting ACT in groups offers numerous potential advantages. These include leveraging the group to offer more avenues for peer learning and modeling of ACT processes, thus facilitating learning from diverse perspectives; conducting experiential exercises such as Passengers on the Bus from multiple vantage points within a single exercise, thus facilitating flexible perspective taking; treating multiple clients with fewer clinician resource, thus reducing intervention cost per participant; and taking a more collectivist approach to addressing psychological and behavioral medicine problems, which may provide a better-matched approach for some individuals, cultural groups, or problem foci. Many of these potential advantages are reflected in the impressively broad and numerous clinical trials conducted on group ACT interventions across dozens of distinct mental health and behavioral medicine populations. To advance the field's understanding of ACT in groups, we recommended more direct empirical investigation of the purported advantages and disadvantages of group delivery at the levels of process and outcome, and the relationships between them. Building on the burgeoning trials of group ACT interventions, we recommend ways to deepen the field's understanding of how ACT groups work and for whom they work best.

References

Aasdahl, L., Pape, K., Vasseljen, O., Johnsen, R., Gismervik, S., Halsteinli, V., . . . Fimland, M. S. (2018). Effect of inpatient multicomponent occupational rehabilitation versus less comprehensive outpatient rehabilitation on sickness absence in persons with musculoskeletal- or mental health disorders: A randomized clinical trial. *Journal of Occupational Rehabilitation, 28*(1), 170–179. doi: 10.1007/s10926-017-9708-z

Arch, J. J., Fishbein, J. N., Ferris, M., Mitchell, J. L., Levin, M. E., Andorsky, D. J., & Kutner, J. S. (2020). Acceptability, feasibility, and potential for efficacy of an acceptance-based intervention to address psychosocial and advance care planning needs among anxious and depressed adults with metastatic cancer. *Journal of Palliative Medicine, 23*(10), 1380–1385. doi: https://doi.org/10.1089/jpm.2019.0398

Avdagic, E., Morrissey, S. A., & Boschen, M. J. (2014). A randomised controlled trial of acceptance and commitment therapy and cognitive-behaviour therapy for generalised anxiety disorder. *Behaviour Change, 31*(2), 110–130.

Baumeister, H., Reichler, L., Munzinger, M., & Lin, J. (2014). The impact of guidance on Internet-based mental health interventions—A systematic review. *Internet Interventions, 1*(4), 205–215.

Beilby, J. M., Byrnes, M. L., & Yaruss, J. S. (2012). Acceptance and commitment therapy for adults who stutter: psychosocial adjustment and speech fluency. *Journal of Fluency Disorders, 37*(4), 289–299. doi: 10.1016/j.jfludis.2012.05.003

Bjornsson, A. S., Bidwell, L. C., Brosse, A. L., Carey, G., Hauser, M., Mackiewicz Seghete, K. L., . . . Craighead, W. E. (2011). Cognitive-behavioral group therapy versus group psychotherapy for social anxiety disorder among college students: A randomized controlled trial. *Depression and Anxiety, 28*(11), 1034–1042.

Bond, F. W., & Bunce, D. (2000). Mediators of change in emotion-focused and problem-focused worksite stress management interventions. *Journal of Occupational Health Psychology, 5*(1), 156–163.

Boone, M. S., & Canicci, J. (2013). Acceptance and commitment therapy (ACT) in groups. In J. Pistorello (Ed.), *Acceptance and mindfulness for counseling college students: Theory and practical applications for intervention, prevention, and outreach* (pp. 73–93). Oakland, CA: New Harbinger Publications.

Brown, J. S., Sellwood, K., Beecham, J. K., Slade, M., Andiappan, M., Landau, S., . . . Smith, R. (2011). Outcome, costs and patient engagement for group and individual CBT for depression: A naturalistic clinical study. *Behavioural and Cognitive Psychotherapy, 39*(3), 355.

Choi, D., & Kim, S. (2017). An integrative review of acceptance and commitment therapy (ACT) for mental health problem. *Korean Journal of Stress Research, 25*(2), 75–85.

Chong, Y. Y., Mak, Y. W., Leung, S. P., Lam, S. Y., & Loke, A. Y. (2019). Acceptance and commitment therapy for parental management of childhood asthma: An RCT. *Pediatrics, 143*(2), 1–16. doi: 10.1542/peds.2018-1723

Coto-Lesmes, R., Fernandez-Rodriguez, C., & Gonzalez-Fernandez, S. (2020). Acceptance and commitment therapy in group format for anxiety and depression. A systematic review. *Journal of Affective Disorders, 263*, 107–120. doi: 10.1016/j.jad.2019.11.154

DeRubeis, R. J., Cohen, Z. D., Forand, N. R., Fournier, J. C., Gelfand, L. A., & Lorenzo-Luaces, L. (2014). The Personalized Advantage Index: Translating research on prediction into individualized treatment recommendations. A demonstration. *PloS One, 9*(1), e83875.

Dindo, L., Roddy, M. K., Boykin, D., Woods, K., Rodrigues, M., Smith, T. L., . . . True, G. (2020). Combination outreach and wellness intervention for distressed rural veterans: results of a multimethod pilot study. *Journal of Behavioral Medicine, 44*(4), 440–453.

Dindo, L., Van Liew, J. R., & Arch, J. J. (2017). Acceptance and commitment therapy: A transdiagnostic behavioral intervention for mental health and medical conditions. *Neurotherapeutics, 14*(3), 546–553.

Dindo, L., Weinrib, A., & Marchman, J. (2019). One-day ACT workshops for patients with chronic health problems and associated emotional disorders. *Innovations in ACT.* Oakland, CA: New Harbinger Publications.

Dindo, L., Zimmerman, M. B., Hadlandsmyth, K., StMarie, B., Embree, J., Marchman, J., . . . Rakel, B. (2018). Acceptance and commitment therapy for prevention of chronic postsurgical pain and opioid use in at-risk veterans: A pilot randomized controlled study. *Journal of Pain, 19*(10), 1211–1221.

Dindo, L. N., Recober, A., Calarge, C. A., Zimmerman, B. M., Weinrib, A., Marchman, J. N., & Turvey, C. (2020). One-day acceptance and commitment therapy compared to support for depressed migraine patients: A randomized clinical trial. *Neurotherapeutics, 17*(2), 743–753. doi: 10.1007/s13311-019-00818-0

Forsyth, J. P., Eifert, G. H., & Barrios, V. (2006). Fear conditioning in an emotion regulation context: A fresh perspective on the origins of anxiety disorders. In M. G. Craske, D. Hermans & D. Vansteenwegen (Eds.), *From basic processes to clinical implications* (pp. 133–153). Washington, DC: American Psychological Association.

Gifford, E. V., Kohlenberg, B. S., Hayes, S. C., Pierson, H. M., Piasecki, M. P., Antonuccio, D. O., & Palm, K. M. (2011). Does acceptance and relationship focused behavior therapy contribute to bupropion outcomes? A randomized controlled trial of functional analytic psychotherapy and acceptance and commitment therapy for smoking cessation. *Behavior Therapy, 42*(4), 700–715. doi: https://doi.org/10.1016/j.beth.2011.03.002

Hasannezhad Reskati, M., Mirzaian, B., & Hosseini, S. H. (2018). A systematic review and meta-analysis of acceptance and commitment therapy on mental health and quality of life of women with breast cancer. *Journal of Mazandaran University of Medical Sciences, 28*(167), 192–207.

Hayes, S. C., Strosahl, K. D., & Wilson, K. G. (1999). *Acceptance and commitment therapy: An experiential approach to behavior change.* New York: Guilford Press.

Hayes, S. C., Strosahl, K. D., & Wilson, K. G. (2012). *Acceptance and commitment therapy: The process and practice of mindful change (2nd ed.).* New York: Guilford Press.

Hayes, S. C., Wilson, K. G., Gifford, E. V., Follette, V. M., & Strosahl, K. (1996). Experiential avoidance and behavioral disorders: A functional dimensional approach to diagnosis and treatment. *Journal of Consulting and Clinical Psychology, 64*(6), 1152–1168.

Hedman, E., Andersson, G., Ljótsson, B., Andersson, E., Rück, C., Mörtberg, E., & Lindefors, N. (2011). Internet-based cognitive behavior therapy vs. cognitive behavioral group therapy for social anxiety disorder: A randomized controlled non-inferiority trial. *PloS One, 6*(3), e18001.

Hedman, E., Mörtberg, E., Hesser, H., Clark, D. M., Lekander, M., Andersson, E., & Ljótsson, B. (2013). Mediators in psychological treatment of social anxiety disorder: Individual cognitive therapy compared to cognitive behavioral group therapy. *Behavior Research and Therapy, 51*(10), 696–705.

Hou, J. K., Vanga, R. R., Thakur, E., Gonzalez, I., Willis, D., & Dindo, L. (2017). One-day behavioral intervention for patients with inflammatory bowel disease and co-occurring psychological distress. *Clinical Gastroenterology and Hepatology, 15*(10), 1633–1634.

Huey, S. J., Jr., & Tilley, J. L. (2018). Effects of mental health interventions with Asian Americans: A review and meta-analysis. *Journal of Consulting and Clinical pPsychology, 86*(11), 915.

Jarvela-Reijonen, E., Karhunen, L., Sairanen, E., Muotka, J., Lindroos, S., Laitinen, J., . . . Kolehmainen, M. (2018). The effects of acceptance and commitment therapy on eating behavior and diet delivered through face-to-face contact and a mobile app: A randomized controlled trial. [Report]. *International Journal of Behavioral Nutrition and Physical Activity, 15,* Article 22.

Juarascio, A., Shaw, J., Forman, E., Timko, C. A., Herbert, J., Butryn, M., . . . Lowe, M. (2013). Acceptance and commitment therapy as a novel treatment for eating disorders: An initial test of efficacy and mediation. *Behavior Modification, 37*(4), 459–489. doi: 10.1177/0145445513478633

Juarascio, A., Shaw, J., Forman, E. M., Timko, C. A., Herbert, J. D., Butryn, M. L., & Lowe, M. (2013). Acceptance and commitment therapy for eating disorders: Clinical applications of a group treatment. *Journal of Contextual Behavioral Science, 2*(3-4), 85–94.

Kashdan, T. B., & Rottenberg, J. (2010). Psychological flexibility as a fundamental aspect of health. *Clinical Psychology Review, 30*(7), 865–887.

Kenny, A., & Bizumic, B. (2016). Learn and ACT: Changing prejudice towards people with mental illness using stigma reduction interventions. *Journal of Contextual Behavioral Science, 5*(3), 178–185. doi: 10.1016/j.jcbs.2016.06.004

Levin, M. E., Hildebrandt, M. J., Lillis, J., & Hayes, S. C. (2012). The impact of treatment components suggested by the psychological flexibility model: A meta-analysis of laboratory-based component studies. *Behavior Therapy, 43*(4), 741–756.

Livheim, F., Tengström, A., Andersson, G., Dahl, J., Björck, C., & Rosendahl, I. (2020). A quasi-experimental, multicenter study of acceptance and commitment therapy for antisocial youth in residential care. *Journal of Contextual Behavioral Science, 16,* 119–127. doi: 10.1016/j.jcbs.2020.03.008

Manassis, K., Mendlowitz, S. L., Scapillato, D., Avery, D., Fiksenbaum, L., Freire, M., . . . Owens, M. (2002). Group and individual cognitive-behavioral therapy for childhood anxiety disorders: A randomized trial. *Journal of the American Academy of Child & Adolescent Psychiatry, 41*(12), 1423–1430.
McClure, J. B., Bricker, J., Mull, K., & Heffner, J. L. (2020). Comparative effectiveness of group-delivered acceptance and commitment therapy versus cognitive behavioral therapy for smoking cessation: A randomized controlled trial. *Nicotine Tobacco Research, 22*(3), 354–362. doi: 10.1093/ntr/nty268
Mörtberg, E., Clark, D., Sundin, Ö., & Åberg Wistedt, A. (2007). Intensive group cognitive treatment and individual cognitive therapy vs. treatment as usual in social phobia: a randomized controlled trial. *Acta Psychiatrica Scandinavica, 115*(2), 142–154.
Muscara, F., McCarthy, M. C., Rayner, M., Nicholson, J. M., Dimovski, A., McMillan, L., . . . Anderson, V. A. (2020). Effect of a videoconference-based online group intervention for traumatic stress in parents of children with life-threatening illness: A randomized clinical trial. *JAMA Network Open, 3*(7), e208507. doi: 10.1001/jamanetworkopen.2020.8507
Niles, A. N., Wolitzky-Taylor, K. B., Arch, J. J., & Craske, M. G. (2017). Applying a novel statistical method to advance the personalized treatment of anxiety disorders: A composite moderator of comparative drop-out from CBT and ACT. *Behaviour Research and Therapy, 91*, 13–23.
O'Brien, W., Singh, S., Horan, K., Moeller, M., Wasson, R., & Jex, S. (2019). Group-based acceptance and commitment therapy for nurses and nurse aides working in long-term care residential settings. *Journal of Alternative and Complementary Medicine, 25*, 753–761. doi: 10.1089/acm.2019.0087
Ogrodniczuk, J. S., Piper, W. E., & Joyce, A. S. (2006). Differences in men's and women's responses to short-term group psychotherapy. *Psychotherapy Research, 14*(2), 231–243.
Pedersen, H. F., Agger, J. L., Frostholm, L., Jensen, J. S., Ørnbøl, E., Fink, P., & Schröder, A. (2019). Acceptance and commitment group therapy for patients with multiple functional somatic syndromes: A three-armed trial comparing ACT in a brief and extended version with enhanced care. *Psychological Medicine, 49*(6), 1005–1014. doi: 10.1017/S0033291718001666
Rubel, J. A., Zilcha-Mano, S., Giesemann, J., Prinz, J., & Lutz, W. (2020). Predicting personalized process-outcome associations in psychotherapy using machine learning approaches—A demonstration. *Psychotherapy Research, 30*(3), 300–309.
Ruiz, F. J. (2012). Acceptance and commitment therapy versus traditional cognitive behavioral therapy: A systematic review and meta-analysis of current empirical evidence. *International Journal of Psychology and Psychological Therapy, 12*(3), 333–358.
Shabani, M. J., Mohsenabadi, H., Omidi, A., Lee, E. B., Twohig, M. P., Ahmadvand, A., & Zanjani, Z. (2019). An Iranian study of group acceptance and commitment therapy versus group cognitive behavioral therapy for adolescents with obsessive-compulsive disorder on an optimal dose of selective serotonin reuptake inhibitors. *Journal of Obsessive-Compulsive and Related Disorders, 22*, 100440.
Spidel, A., Daigneault, I., Kealy, D., & Lecomte, T. (2019). Acceptance and commitment therapy for psychosis and trauma: Investigating links between trauma severity, attachment and outcome. *Behavioural and Cognitive Psychotherapy, 47*(2), 230–243. doi: 10.1017/S1352465818000413
Stewart, C., White, R. G., Ebert, B., Mays, I., Nardozzi, J., & Bockarie, H. (2016). A preliminary evaluation of acceptance and commitment therapy (ACT) training in Sierra Leone. *Journal of Contextual Behavioral Science, 5*(1), 16–22.
Swift, J. K., & Greenberg, R. P. (2012). Premature discontinuation in adult psychotherapy: A meta-analysis. *Journal of Consulting and Clinical Psychology, 80*(4), 547.
Tharp, R. G. (1991). Cultural diversity and treatment of children. *Journal of Consulting and Clinical Psychology, 59*(6), 799.
Van der Gucht, K., Griffith, J. W., Hellemans, R., Bockstaele, M., Pascal-Claes, F., & Raes, F. (2017). Acceptance and commitment therapy (ACT) for adolescents: Outcomes of a Large-sample, school-based, cluster-randomized controlled trial. *Mindfulness, 8*(2), 408–416. doi: 10.1007/s12671-016-0612-y
Villatte, J. L., Vilardaga, R., Villatte, M., Vilardaga, J. C. P., Atkins, D. C., & Hayes, S. C. (2016). Acceptance and commitment therapy modules: Differential impact on treatment processes and outcomes. *Behaviour Research and Therapy, 77*, 52–61.
Vowles, K. E., & McCracken, L. M. (2008). Acceptance and values-based action in chronic pain: a study of treatment effectiveness and process. *Journal of Consulting and Clinical Psychology, 76*(3), 397–407. doi: 10.1037/0022-006X.76.3.397
Walser, R. D., & Pistorello, J. (2004). ACT in group format *A practical guide to acceptance and commitment therapy* (pp. 347–372). New York: Springer.
Wang, P. S., Aguilar-Gaxiola, S., Alonso, J., Angermeyer, M. C., Borges, G., Bromet, E. J., . . . Gureje, O. (2007). Use of mental health services for anxiety, mood, and substance disorders in 17 countries in the WHO world mental health surveys. *The Lancet, 370*(9590), 841–850.

Wang, S., Zhou, Y., Yu, S., Ran, L.-W., Liu, X.-P., & Chen, Y.-F. (2016). Acceptance and commitment therapy and cognitive-behavioral therapy as treatments for academic procrastination. *Research on Social Work Practice, 27*(1), 48–58. doi: 10.1177/1049731515577890

Westrup, D., & Wright, M. J. (2017). *Learning ACT for group treatment: An acceptance and commitment therapy skills training manual for therapists.* Oakland, CA: New Harbinger Publications.

Zettle, R. D., Rains, J. C., & Hayes, S. C. (2011). Processes of change in acceptance and commitment therapy and cognitive therapy for depression: A mediation reanalysis of Zettle and Rains. *Behavior Modification, 35*(3), 265–283. doi: 10.1177/0145445511398344

Zvolensky, M. J., Lejuez, C., Stuart, G. L., & Curtin, J. J. (2001). Experimental psychopathology in psychological science. *Review of General Psychology, 5*(4), 371–381.

CHAPTER

30 Cultural Adaptations of Acceptance and Commitment Therapy

Akihiko Masuda, Lucas Morgan, Samuel D. Spencer, Joanne Qina'au, *and* Duckhyun Jo

Abstract

ACT is best understood functionally and contextually as the purposeful behavior of a clinician in a therapeutic context that is both principle-informed and experientially guided. From a functional and contextual account, every ACT case is subject to cultural adaptation because no two individuals have identical learning histories and situational contexts. If ACT is practiced functionally and contextually, no additional guidelines for cultural adaptation are needed. What is extremely difficult, however, is to practice and embody ACT *functionally and contextually*. The article offers some insights into how a clinician stays connected with the therapeutic context with a given client functionally and contextually.

Key Words: cultural adaptation, acceptance and commitment therapy, cultural humility, cultural competence, functional contextualism

Overview

Formally called comprehensive distancing, acceptance and commitment therapy (ACT) originated from a Western cultural worldview in the early 1980s (Hayes, 1987; Zettle & Hayes, 1986). Since then, ACT has been shaped into diverse forms (e.g., individual psychotherapy, group therapy, bibliotherapy, e-therapy) and adapted for use in various applied and clinical settings. These settings include independent practice, managed care, inpatient care, counseling and outreach, and, most recently, telehealth. For the past two decades, ACT has also been studied and practiced across the globe, including Africa, Asia, Central America, Oceania, and South America (Masuda, 2020). This global-level dissemination effort has been prompted in part by a large body of evidence pointing to ACT as a unified evidence-based procedure of behavior change (Twohig, Levin, & Ong, 2020).

The cultural adaptation of evidence-based procedures, such as those found in ACT, is not straightforward, however. In fact, scholars in diversity psychology have argued that a hasty adaptation of ACT may fall short of its intended clinical effects or may even cause harm to clients (Hall, Hong, Zane, & Meyer, 2011; Masuda, 2020). Some of the key questions raised in this context include (1) whether ACT is practiced effectively in *its original forms* with clients from diverse sociocultural backgrounds (e.g., racial/ethnic minority individuals); (2) whether key ACT concepts and methods are biased toward the social norms of a particular group of individuals, such as those of the Western, educated, industrialized, rich, and democratic (WEIRD; Henrich, Heine, & Norenzayan, 2010); (3) under what circumstances cultural adaptation of ACT is recommended; (4) when recommended, how the cultural adaptation of ACT should be implemented; and (5) what would be a guiding model for such adaptation efforts (Masuda, 2020).

It is also important to note that some cultural adaptation efforts that have been made in ACT seem to deviate from the philosophical assumptions of *functional contextualism*, the essential standpoint of ACT (Drossel, McCausland, Schneider, & Cattivelli, 2014; Pasillas & Masuda, 2014). As discussed elsewhere (Masuda, 2020, 2014b), carefully examining the aforementioned questions may help clarify the fundamental understanding of what ACT is (for) and how the "cultural adaptation of ACT" can be carried out effectively in a culturally humble and competent manner.

In this assessment of the cultural adaptations of ACT, we briefly present an overview of cultural competency, cultural humility, and cultural adaptation to orient readers to the present topic of interest. Subsequently, in comparison to a content-oriented approach to cultural adaptation, we present a functional contextual account of cultural adaptation and its application to ACT. Finally, we offer some examples of how the cultural adaptation of ACT can be done *functionally and contextually* (Drossel et al., 2014; Pasillas & Masuda, 2014), followed by an empirical review of ACT in the areas of diversity and cultural considerations.

Cultural Competence, Cultural Humility, and Cultural Adaptation

A given evidence-based procedure found to be effective in a specific sociocultural context cannot be assumed to be effective in other sociocultural contexts (Cheng & Sue, 2014). Despite its unified nature in theory and practice (Hayes, Pistorello, & Levin, 2012; Hayes, Strosahl, & Wilson, 2012), ACT is no exception. In behavioral health literature, *cultural competence, cultural humility,* and *cultural adaptation* are three major constructs that address the importance of implementing and disseminating evidence-based practice equally across individuals from various sociocultural backgrounds. As such, it may be worthwhile to touch on these concepts and on how ACT can be understood through these conceptual lenses.

The concept of *cultural competence* has been discussed at multiple levels, including individual, organizational, and systemic ones (S. Sue, 1998). At an individual and psychological level, it generally refers to a *clinician's skill sets,* or ongoing behavioral *processes,* that are aimed at effectively working with diverse groups of individuals (S. Sue, Zane, Hall, & Berger, 2009; Whaley & Davis, 2007). More specifically, Whaley and Davis (2007) operationalize cultural competence as "a set of problem-solving skills that include: (a) the ability to recognize and understand the dynamic interplay between the heritage and adaptation dimensions of culture in shaping human behavior; (b) the ability to use the knowledge acquired about an individual's heritage and adaptation challenges to maximize the effectiveness of assessment, diagnosis, and treatment; and (c) internalization (i.e., incorporation into one's clinical problem-solving repertoire) of this process of recognition, acquisition, and use of cultural dynamics so that it can be routinely applied to diverse groups" (p. 565). Similarly, Stanley Sue and colleagues conceptualize cultural competence as a multidimensional process of "*scientific mindedness* (i.e., forming and testing hypotheses), *dynamic sizing* (i.e., flexibility in generalization and individuation), and *culture-specific resources* (i.e., having knowledge and skills to work with other cultures) in response to different kinds of clients" (S. Sue et al., 2009, p. 529; italics added).

Cultural humility can be viewed as a clinician's fundamental attitude in the pursuit of cultural and clinical competence. Based on the principles of social justice, the perspective of cultural humility emphasizes the importance of a clinician's lifelong motivation to learn from others; critical self-examination of cultural awareness; interpersonal respect; development of mutual partnerships that address power imbalances; and an other-oriented stance open to new cultural information in theory and practice (e.g., Fisher, 2020; Hook, Davis, Owen, Worthington, & Utsey, 2013; Mosher et al., 2017). In the context of ACT, the concept of cultural humility offers insights into how clinicians and clinical researchers can work with a given individual client or group in an interpersonally genuine and humble way. This concept may be particularly relevant to ACT researchers and clinicians, as cultural considerations in ACT are examined predominantly from the perspective of WEIRD individuals. In fact, the fundamental framework of cultural consideration that many ACT researchers and clinicians follow in cultural adaptation work is predicated on the extent to which a given culturally adapted ACT deviates from the WEIRD-based, "original" and "pure," version of ACT. The concept of cultural humility invites us to make a fundamental shift in perspective from which cultural considerations of ACT are scrutinized (e.g., considering cultural adaptation of ACT from a perspective of racial and ethnic minority client or that of a foreign scholar, such as the first and last authors of this article).

Finally, *cultural adaptation* refers to "the systematic modification of existing evidence-based treatment (EBT) or intervention protocol to consider language, culture, and context in such a way as that it is compatible with the client's cultural patterns, meanings, and values" (Bernal, Jiménez-Chafey, & Domenech Rodríguez, 2009, p. 362). To date, the final product of cultural adaptation efforts in *content* and *form* are often emphasized, *more so than the guiding framework from which these adaptations are made.* This may be in part due to the assumption that a given treatment is best understood as a set of applied tools (e.g., specific procedures and therapeutic interactions) that are also defined in content and form. For example, culturally adapting an English-written ACT protocol for a Japanese client may include literally translating the protocol into the Japanese language, selecting and modifying therapeutic exercises in content for that client (e.g., using metaphors that will be intuitive to a particular Japanese client), and explicating treatment goals that are tailored to the sociocultural contingencies in that client's life context (Masuda, 2016, 2020; Masuda, Muto, Hayes, & Lillis, 2008). Once again, when the cultural adaptation of ACT is typically presented in extant literature, the topographical features of such efforts (*outcome*) are often highlighted, but not the very *context* that is taken into account for such topographical change (*process*) and the guiding framework of how to do so (Drossel et al., 2014).

Functional and Contextual Adaptation of ACT

From a functional and contextual perspective, not all accounts of cultural competence, cultural humility, and cultural adaptation are equally adequate (Masuda, 2014b). More specifically, from this perspective, these terms are best understood and practiced *functionally and contextually* through the framework of the "act-in-context." Similarly, from the clinician's perspective, a given ACT intervention is best viewed as the behavior of the whole clinician who serves as the therapeutic context for a given client's behavior change (Zettle & Hayes, 1986). For this very reason, the term *cultural adaptation* of ACT may be misleading, as it implies that ACT possesses an ontologically based *original form.*

Once again, if ACT is treated topographically (i.e., as a therapeutic tool to be fine-tuned in form), and not as the dynamic "act of a whole person in a given context," the focus on examining cultural adaptation will be fixed at the *content* level (Masuda, 2014a). This content-focused and ontological way of understanding ACT in the context of cultural adaptation efforts diverges from the very functional and contextual framework on which ACT is predicated. For this reason, one of the first peer-reviewed papers on ACT deliberately defined it as a set of contextually situated behavioral *processes of change* (Hayes & Wilson, 1994), not as a manualized protocol or set of topographically defined techniques.

Workability and Shortcomings of Content-focused Cultural Adaptation

From a functional and contextual perspective, *workability* is a key criterion of effective cultural adaptation of ACT. Workability requires us to ask, will this metaphor, activity, or therapeutic angle work for achieving a particular end? In ACT, or in any other functional and contextual therapy, the workability of a technique is determined not by its *form,* but by the contextually situated interaction between the behavior of the client and that of the therapist where the technique unfolds (Masuda, 2016, 2020). Take, for example, the Tug of War with a Monster metaphor (Hayes, Strosahl, et al., 2012, p. 276), whereby the clients are asked to see their distressing private event as a monster with whom they are engaging in a tug of war. This metaphor works only if the client is able to intuitively and experientially relate the narrative within the metaphor (e.g., pulling a rope against a powerful monster) to their own struggles with difficult private events, and then draw some wisdom from it (e.g., the awareness that they can respond to private events differently by letting go of the control agenda).

For some clients, the Tug of War with a Monster metaphor evokes such insight immediately; but for others, having such insight with this metaphor is extremely challenging. The latter may be the case if individuals do not have sufficient sociocultural learning history to make effective use of this metaphor. In other words, if a client has never played tug of war before, they will hardly know what the therapist is talking about—it may not be a *workable* metaphor for evoking the awareness that this metaphor intends to evoke. As discussed elsewhere (Drossel et al., 2014; Masuda, 2020), ACT's functional and contextual framework allows clinicians to attend to a given client's unique socioculturally shaped learning history and the workability of therapeutic work unfolding in a given moment in session, and to make adjustments to the therapeutic work accordingly. What follows is part of a metaphor that can be presented as an alternative to the Tug of War with a Monster metaphor when working with people in Hawaiʻi, especially Native Hawaiian-identified clients.

This alternative metaphor is tentatively called the Taro (Kalo) Plant in Nature metaphor, which was originally developed by the second author (L.M.) in the context of working with many Native Hawaiian-identified clients (see Figure 30.1). Functionally and contextually, this metaphor is presented with some of the clients in Hawaiʻi in order to help them become intuitively and experientially connected with (1) the transient nature of private events, including difficult emotions; (2) the futility of experiential avoidance; and (3) psychological openness (e.g., acceptance) as an alternative by highlighting the way a taro plant coexists and thrives with nebulous and dynamic conditions of nature.

Hawaiian culture has deeply intimate relationships with nature (i.e., dynamic natural forces) and offers notable cultural wisdom of how to coexist and thrive optimally in a dynamic tropical climate. For example, winds and rains of different types, textures, intensities, seasonality, and localities are honored and given different names and connotations (Akana, 2015). Many people in Hawaiʻi recognize that some rains are ominous, violent, and powerful, that some are soft and gentle, and that others are associated with the flourishing or blooming of particular plants. In this metaphor, emotions that clients experience are first reframed as forces in the body as if they are various natural forces in nature, such as rains and wind of the valley. Reframing emotions as if they are these naturally experienced forces allows clients to derive their emotions as *fundamentally natural,* allowing them to change the way they relate to their emotions, even difficult ones. The parallel with the Tug of War with a Monster metaphor in this case is the intuitive understanding that emotion, like weather, is something transient that

Figure 30.1. Taro (Kalo) Plant

comes and goes. In addition, it is obvious to most clients that no one is powerful enough to stop or change the weather, and that, for example, trying to stop the experience of a rainstorm will only cause undue struggle, in addition to getting one soaked. In this metaphor, the client and clinician connect emotions to rain and wind, all of which are temporary and will pass, all of which are potential sources of meaning and significance, and all of which will be felt differently the less one struggles to fight against them. In the words of this metaphor, sometimes hunkering down and waiting for a storm to pass over is the most advantageous course of action to take.

This part of the Taro (Kalo) Plant in Nature metaphor highlights the forceful, and yet transient, nature of difficult private events, including difficult emotions, as well as the futility of attempting to control them. This metaphor is particularly effective for many people in Hawaiʻi, especially Native Hawaiian-identified clients, who embrace the forceful, and yet transient, nature of the tropical climate they are in, as well as the cultural wisdom that highlights the futility of attempting to keep nature under control. By simply framing "private events" with "natural forces" (e.g., "emotions and thoughts that we have are like rains and winds in nature"), clients intuitively derive alternative, and more *natural* ways of relating to their private events. For this very reason, the Taro (Kalo) Plant in Nature metaphor or similar variants may also be particularly intuitive and experiential for clients from other cultures who have lived closely with this cultural wisdom. Later in this article, we will present the rest of this metaphor, which teaches clients the whole repertoire of psychological flexibility.

ACT as Contextually and Pragmatically Situated Acts of Clinicians

Because no two individuals have identical learning histories and situational contexts, cultural adaptation should occur in every clinical case, including the one that unfolds between client and therapist with a similar sociocultural background. In other words, every ACT case is subject to cultural adaptation, and for ACT, cultural adaptation is not a matter of whether or not it is necessary, but rather *to what extent* it occurs (Masuda, 2020). Theoretical and applied implications drawn from the perspective of functional contextualism highlight this very nature of cultural adaptation in ACT (Hayes, Barnes-Holmes, & Wilson, 2012; Hayes, Long, Levin, & Follette, 2013).

From the standpoint of the therapist, ACT can be viewed as a *contextually situated, purposeful act of a clinician* in a therapeutic context that is *principle-informed* and *experientially guided* (Masuda, 2020). ACT is said to be contextually situated, as the act of a clinician in a given therapeutic encounter represents the therapist's and client's contextually shaped learning histories unfolding in that very moment. ACT is said to be *purposeful* in that the clinician's actions are intentionally directed toward the promotion of the client's psychological flexibility. ACT is thus considered to be *principle-informed*, as the clinician's behavior is always guided by the psychological flexibility model (PFM) of well-being and behavior change. The following clinical implications are derived from the PFM (Hayes, Strosahl, et al., 2012; Masuda, 2016, 2020, 2014b).

1. From a larger functional and contextual perspective, many of a given client's presenting concerns (e.g., chronic worries, anxieties, trauma, negative self-appraisal, relationship conflicts, hopelessness, shame) are cognitively and socioculturally developed and maintained.
2. Within this sociocultural framework, client efforts to solve these concerns (e.g., experiential avoidance), which are often futile, are also cognitively and socioculturally regulated (e.g., rule-governed behavior).
3. An ACT case conceptualization is formulated in terms of the extent to which a client engages in meaningful and purposeful living. as well as the extent to which experiential avoidance dominates.
4. It is important to identify contextual factors that maintain the behavioral repertoires described in (3), especially the ones that can be systematically manipulated by the client, clinician, or both.
5. A client's sociocultural factors (e.g., cultural norms, cultural values, upbringing, learning history, verbal antecedents and consequences, and community) are functionally understood and are translated into the *contextually situated* target behavioral processes identified in (3).
6. The promotion of greater behavioral adaptation and flexibility does not necessarily require the elimination of presenting concerns in their form or frequency.
7. Practicing meaningful and purposeful living with psychological openness represents greater behavioral adaptation and flexibility.
8. In practice, the client and clinician identify and examine ways to move the abovementioned behavioral processes in (7), while taking into account information gathered in (4).

These clinical implications may appear to be too general for many ACT researchers and clinicians, and not specific enough to the cultural adaptation of ACT. However, these are the very implications that we feel are necessary and useful to follow for the effective cultural adaptation of ACT (Masuda, 2020). These implications become especially salient when we consider that every ACT case is subject to cultural adaptation to some degree. In fact, we believe that no additional psychological principles or guidelines are required for the effective cultural adaption of ACT (Pasillas & Masuda, 2014). What many often overlook is how difficult it is to follow these clinical implications, especially for those from WEIRD sociocultural backgrounds. In other words, for effective clinical work to take place, it is imperative to understand and follow these clinical implications *functionally and contextually for each clinical case.*

Finally, *when understood functionally and contextually*, the PFM is theorized to be universally applicable. However, as discussed previously, the practice of PFM-informed ACT is extremely idiographic (Hayes et al., 2019; Hayes, Strosahl, et al., 2012). That is, the behavior of an ACT clinician is shaped and adjusted functionally and contextually through the *ongoing* interaction with a given client. This is the ongoing and *experientially guided* aspect of ACT that was mentioned earlier.

Cultural Adaptation of ACT

Given its functional and contextual foci, ideally the cultural adaptations of ACT should align with the conceptual and applied foundations of clinical behavior analysis (Dougher & Hayes, 2000; Vilardaga, Hayes, Levin, & Muto, 2009). More specifically, unlike a content-focused intervention approach, intervention work in ACT does not begin in earnest until the client's presenting concerns, general functioning, and treatment goals are understood functionally and contextually using the PFM conceptual framework (Masuda, 2020).

Psychological Flexibility as a Socioculturally Situated Overarching Behavioral Repertoire

The promotion of psychological flexibility (e.g., engaging in meaningful and purposeful living with psychological openness) in clients is the overarching treatment goal of ACT (Hayes, Strosahl, et al., 2012). It is important to emphasize that the way in which the behavioral repertoire of psychological flexibility is manifested topographically can vary significantly across clients (Masuda, 2020). This variability is theorized to occur because of different sociocultural contingencies, both historical and situational, that operate for different individuals within their unique sociocultural environments.

For example, social contingencies that are aligned with an *individualistic* world view are likely to shape psychological flexibility in particular forms (Markus & Kitayama, 1991; Weisz, Rothbaum, & Blackburn, 1984). More specifically, any behaviors under the contingencies that reflect values of individuality, justice, and autonomy, such as self-assertiveness, may be promoted as part of psychological flexibility. For clients who draw their values from a *collective and interdependent* culture, sociocultural contingencies that promote and maintain interpersonal harmony and conformity to the collective whole are likely to shape their psychological flexibility into collectivistic forms (Markus & Kitayama, 2010). In a collective culture, behavioral pursuits of self-efficacy and self-worth may not be a culturally situated form of psychological flexibility unless they reflect the self as part of a communal whole (Kaholokula, 2017; Odom, Jackson, Derauf, Inada, & Aoki, 2019). Once again, as discussed extensively elsewhere (Drossel et al., 2014; Masuda, 2020), it is crucial for ACT clinicians to be mindful of the situational and context-dependent nature of psychological flexibility *for each client.*

Awareness of One's Own Assumptions

Clinicians are also historical beings who are influenced by their previous and current learning history (Masuda, 2020). This means that a therapist's standards and views of adaptive and maladaptive behavior are also functionally and contextually shaped within a given sociocultural context (e.g., verbal community). As such, it is imperative that the clinician not make assumptions regarding which client's behaviors are adaptive or not adaptive without carefully assessing their functions in the context in which they occur. Here we will focus on potential biases in the domain of actual practice, using values and commitment work as an example.

As discussed elsewhere (Markus & Kitayama, 1991, 2010; Masuda, 2020), striving for personal achievement in the domains of occupation and education is often viewed as a value-consistent action in Western cultural contexts. This focus is also the case for many clients in non-Western cultural contexts (e.g., those in collectivistic cultures). However, while the pursuit of personal growth tends to be individualistic in mainstream Western cultures, such pursuits are more collectivistic and interpersonal in collectivistic cultures (e.g., the collectivist view may be, "I will pursue education *as a member of my family for the prosperity of my family*"). For therapists with a Western world view, this collectivistic quality may come across as being passive or an indication of arrested development. However, within these collectivistic cultural views, such relational and collective qualities are the very essence of adaptive and intrinsically rewarding personal values.

Assertiveness is another example that has been discussed in the domains of values and committed action. Speaking up for one's own thoughts, beliefs, and "wants" is often valued in many Western cultural contexts, including those in the United States (Duckworth, 2008; Markus & Kitayama, 2010; Weisz et al., 1984). For example, ACT therapists often encourage clients to be assertive to their partners in their intimate relationships. As the proverb "the squeaky wheel gets the grease" goes, the act of assertiveness is often followed by favorable outcomes, and this is in part because Western sociocultural contexts tend to encourage such interpersonal communication styles (Masuda, 2020). However, in other cultural contexts, such as those of many racial and ethnic minority individuals in the United States, directly expressing assertiveness can be viewed as a sign of hostility, self-centeredness, and disruption of interpersonal harmony (D. W. Sue, Sue, Neville, & Smith, 2019). It is important to clarify that we do not contend that directly communicated assertiveness should be discouraged for all non-Western clients from non-Western cultures. Instead, what we attempt to clarify here is that the *form* of assertiveness that is adaptive in Western cultural contexts (e.g., "I want . . . ", or even, "I need . . . ") may not be so in other sociocultural contexts. As the Japanese proverb "a nail that stands will be hammered down" goes, directly communicated assertiveness may actually result in unintended negative outcomes, especially when it emerges from a sense of self as a unique being that is separated from others. Once again, it is important for the therapist to become cognizant of the *function* of the target behavior, which depends on the context in which it occurs. To do so, it is important for the therapist to become aware of their own socioculturally situated assumptions and biases.

Therapeutic Relationship and Stance of the Therapist

In ACT, a therapeutic relationship is the *contextually situated*, ongoing, and dynamic interplay between the client and the therapist as *historical and situational beings* (Hayes, Strosahl, et al., 2012, see pp. 141–149). For clients, the therapeutic relationship is a context where they can learn a new set of behaviors or insights through interacting with a clinician as a crucial contextual factor (Robins, Schmidt, & Linehan, 2004). For clinicians, the therapeutic relationship is also an interpersonal context that requires them to be flexible in response to ongoing changes in each therapeutic moment with the client (Kohlenberg & Tsai, 1991).

As reflected in the work of many celebrated ACT clinicians and trainers (e.g., Wilson & Dufrene, 2008), extant ACT manuals (e.g., Hayes, Strosahl, et al., 2012, pp. 141–142) often encourage a therapeutic relationship to be horizontal with a powerful interpersonal connection between client and therapist. However, from a functional and contextual perspective, one cannot assume that this particular *form* of interpersonal style will be universally effective for all clients (Masuda, 2020). In fact, a therapeutic interaction that is vertical, prescriptive, and directive may be more effective for some clients from certain sociocultural backgrounds. For example, when A.M. worked with Black and Latinx clients in Atlanta, Georgia, he tended to present himself politely as an expert, at least initially, and he interacted with them in a humble, and yet directive, manner more so than when he was working with White American clients in the same city. Once again, A.M. chose this style of therapeutic interaction based on its *workability* (i.e., function), not simply because a given client identified as Black and Latinx (i.e., content). Similarly, many Latinx and Black clients, regardless of their ages, also preferred to call him "Dr. Masuda" or "Dr. Aki," rather than calling him "Aki," which was more common among White American clients. A.M. then called them, "Mr. . . . " or "Mrs. . . . " in return to express his respect and humility to them, especially when they were older than he was. In sum, A.M.'s therapeutic relationship is not always horizontal in form, as is often suggested by ACT manuals. However, this vertical and more polite *form* of therapeutic relationship is still ACT-consistent if it *functions* to promote greater psychological flexibility (Drossel et al., 2014; Pasillas & Masuda, 2014). The key takeaway here is that effective styles of therapeutic relationships can vary widely in form or content across different client-therapist dyads. As such, it is crucial for the therapist to cultivate this careful discernment of function, such that they may finetune the form of therapeutic relationship with a given client in each moment based on its workability, in service of promoting the psychological flexibility of that client.

Another important topic to discuss here is therapist self-disclosure. A therapist's self-disclosure in session is a central topic in ACT therapist training (Hayes, Strosahl, et al., 2012). It is also discussed extensively in cultural adaptations of ACT (Masuda, 2020; Pasillas & Masuda, 2014). For example, ACT therapists are often encouraged to share their personal struggles with their clients in session to highlight the ubiquitous nature of human suffering (e.g., a clinician saying "we are in the same stew, and the truth is I've also been struggling with chronic depression for years"). One major purpose of therapist self-disclosure in session is to help clients to relate to and experience their own internalized struggles openly as they are without attempting to change them.

Note, however, that the therapist's self-disclosure of their own psychological struggles may not always be therapeutic for all clients, especially during the initial phase of the therapeutic relationship. This is because, for some clients, mental health issues are cultural taboos, and self-disclosure of one's own mental health issues is not part of their sociocultural norms and contingencies in interpersonal contexts (Komiya, Good, & Sherrod, 2000; D. W. Sue et al., 2019). Once again, when A.M. worked with racial and ethnic minority (REM) clients in Atlanta, Georgia, he learned to avoid sharing his personal psychological struggles with them until they perceived him as a behavioral health expert whom they could trust. A.M. also found that his strategic self-disclosure of his own psychological issues with REM clients was effective when it was presented with them genuinely, but more descriptively and calmly as a matter of fact, rather than emotionally or intimately, as it is often done in experiential ACT workshops for professionals. Once again, given the potential pitfalls of a therapist's self-disclosure, clinicians must be mindful of the timing and content of self-disclosure. Similar to that of the therapeutic relationship, the general consensus here is to self-disclose only if it is considered to be therapeutic for the client.

Case Example: ACT Case Conceptualization and Cultural Considerations

ACT is not suitable for every client. For this very reason, it is imperative that an ACT clinician first examine (1) whether the PFM can adequately conceptualize a given client and their presenting concerns and (2) if so, whether a tentative treatment goal(s) derived from the PFM-informed case conceptualization is *socioculturally* sound for that client. Once again, while ACT offers a generic case formulation framework (e.g., Bach & Moran, 2008), understanding a given client must be extremely idiographic (Hayes, Strosahl, et al., 2012; Masuda, 2020). Next, we discuss how a culturally and idiographically informed ACT case can be formulated by using one of our previously published ACT case studies as an example (e.g., Masuda et al., 2008).

"Yoko" was a 23-year-old Japanese international student who endorsed fatigue, body dissatisfaction, and restrictive eating as her presenting concerns (Masuda et al., 2008). This was an outpatient individual ACT case completed by the first author of this chapter (A.M.) when he worked as a predoctoral psychotherapist in a university counseling center. A.M. was assigned as Yoko's therapist after she completed the intake assessment with another predoctoral therapist, who was a White woman. He was assigned to this case primarily because he was the only Japanese-speaking therapist in the counseling center at the time, and also because he was familiar with Japanese culture as well as challenges that Japanese international college students often experience in the United States. Yoko was a senior student, and she attended a total of 26 individual sessions from July 200x to May 200x + 1.

Besides the presenting concerns mentioned previously, one other notable concern that A.M. noticed in Yoko was her strong entanglement with internalized shame, which can be understood in part through an Asian cultural practice of *saving face* (or saving honor). As discussed elsewhere (e.g., S. Sue, Cheng, Saad, & Chu, 2012), *saving face* is an Asian and Asian American cultural practice that signifies a desire or behavioral effort to avoid humiliation or embarrassment, maintain dignity, and preserve the reputation of oneself and one's family. For many Asians and Asian Americans, this cultural practice is pervasive across various life domains, including work, education, family, and interpersonal relationships. Furthermore, relevant to the topic of the present article, many Asians and Asian Americans view personally having mental health issues as a major threat to their *face*.

This seemed to be the case for Yoko as well. Later during ACT sessions, Yoko disclosed to A.M. that a significant portion of her suffering came from internalized shame related to the implication of having mental health issues and that, because of the shame, she had kept her "mental health issues" to herself for years. As a result, for Yoko, the ACT therapy was her first behavioral health service experience. The following section presents the PFM-informed case formulation where Yoko's presenting concerns were understood in part through the cultural framework of *saving face*.

Yoko's entanglement with internalized shame was theorized to have been maintained for years in part under the sociocultural contingencies of saving face. These contingencies of saving face and resultant internalized shame were also theorized to serve as the context for perpetuating her presenting concerns of body dissatisfaction and restrictive eating, which began 2 years prior. More specifically, under the influence of these sociocultural practices, Yoko seemed to have begun to evaluate her body shape and weight to be unacceptable and her experience of body dissatisfaction to be shameful. To downregulate her body dissatisfaction and internalized shame, she began engaging in restrictive eating and other compensatory behaviors (e.g., running and walking), and she did so *secretively* to save her *face*. However, as her body dissatisfaction continued to grow over time despite her continuing efforts to keep it under control, so did her restrictive eating and other compensatory behaviors (see Hayes, Wilson, Gifford, Follette, & Strosahl, 1996 for the paradoxical effects of experiential avoidance). Furthermore, to conceal restrictive eating and other compensatory behaviors, she began to isolate herself from others more and more. At the beginning phase of ACT therapy, Yoko appeared to be preoccupied with her body dissatisfaction and internalized shame, although she initially denied them as her primary concerns (see below). She also did not seem to allocate much of her time and effort to activities that were purposeful and meaningful to her. The often secretive nature of disordered eating concerns was theorized to be particularly salient for Yoko, as her behavior was influenced by the contingencies of *saving face* and other Asian and Asian American cultural practices that she used to maintain face.

Cultural Considerations and Treatment Plan and Delivery

As discussed previously, sociocultural contingencies operating in a client's life context must be taken into consideration in an ACT treatment plan and delivery. To highlight this importance, we continue to present the ACT case with Yoko (Masuda et al., 2008).

At the time of ACT with A.M., Yoko mainly socialized with other Japanese international students. She also told A.M. that she planned to go back to Japan after graduation. For this reason, Yoko was expected to continue to remain under contingencies of *saving face* (i.e., "世間体、面子、見栄" in Japanese) and other Japanese cultural practices, and therefore the present ACT work with Yoko was done while taking these cultural considerations into account. For example, when working on normalization and validation of her psychological suffering (悩み; "having mental health issues"), Yoko and A.M. conceptualized her sociocultural environment as invalidating and dismissive of her experience of psychological distress. More specifically, A.M. encouraged Yoko to openly acknowledge and experience psychological suffering as common human experiences *within the skin*, while adhering to the cultural practice of saving face *outside the skin*. This context-specific encouragement of psychological acceptance may be in sharp contrast with how ACT is typically conducted with clients from WEIRD backgrounds in the United States, where psychological acceptance is encouraged indiscriminately across all contexts, both inside and outside the skin. What follows is the vignette between Yoko and A.M., which highlights the context-specific encouragement of psychological acceptance:

Therapist (A.M.): (*gently and kindly*) Maybe everyone has a story kept from others . . . like the story that you had shared with me that was kept to yourself for years . . . . What if I say we're all struggled within, and yet we just don't show that to others? What if I say I also have a shameful secret about myself that had been kept to me for years?

Yoko: (nodding quietly and listening to A.M. thoughtfully)

Therapist: What if I say because we don't see it in others when we are with them or when we see them, each of us comes to believe, "It must be just me who has this shameful secret . . . and to fit in or to be accepted, I must keep it to myself, and it can't spill out from me."

Yoko: (nodding quietly and looking the therapist in the eyes)

Therapist: . . . and then we all get tired, and what's worse is that we feel disconnected from others and we even feel disconnected from ourselves . . . . like I don't know myself. It's ironic isn't it?

Yoko: (nodding and looking at the therapist thoughtfully)

Therapist: . . . What if I say, although we are expected not to show these to others, whatever these are . . . and although we're not expected to express our feelings on these secrets . . . it is *okay* for us to have them and have them with us inside. What if I say it's okay to give us permission to have them with us, *within*?

Therapist's Awareness of Own Stimulus Function for a Given Client

It is imperative for clinicians to become cognizant of their own *stimulus function* for a given client. A clinician may ask themselves, "how might I be serving as a stimulus (i.e., antecedent) of client behaviors?" This question is critical, as clinicians evoke certain forms of behavior from their clients more regularly than other forms of behavior in their therapeutic relationships (e.g., Zane & Ku, 2014). Consider the therapeutic work between Yoko and A.M. as an example. As noted above, Yoko completed an intake assessment with another predoctoral therapist prior to seeing A.M. As noted earlier, the intake clinician was a White American woman, and she informed A.M. that Yoko's primary concerns were likely to be her body dissatisfaction and restrictive eating, as they discussed these concerns extensively during the intake assessment. For this reason, during his first session with Yoko, A.M. asked her to confirm that these were the concerns that she wanted to work on in psychotherapy. However, Yoko denied that these were her presenting concerns and told A.M. that instead she wanted to work on improving her English communication skills, which was much less stigmatizing. As discussed briefly above, A.M. viewed this as Yoko's "possible guardedness" driven in part by internalized shame that was evoked by her cultural adherence to *saving face*.

In hindsight, this case formulation was not inaccurate, but it was incomplete. What should also have been taken into consideration was A.M.'s stimulus function for Yoko. More specifically, one might, speculate that A.M. being a *Japanese male*, might have evoked certain cultural and power dynamics, perhaps making her extremely hesitant to discuss her body dissatisfaction and restrictive eating concerns in therapy with him, which she openly disclosed to her intake therapist. We can also speculate that for Yoko, A.M. might have served as part of the sociocultural contingencies of saving face and other Japanese cultural practices during the earlier phase of therapy (Zane & Ku, 2014). As discussed elsewhere (Masuda et al., 2008), Yoko and A.M. spent the next two sessions primarily on improving her communication skills. Then after a gentle prompt from A.M at the end of that second session, she finally disclosed to A.M., with hesitation, her struggles with internalized shame and body dissatisfaction. If A.M. was cognizant of the cultural dynamic that he unknowingly brought to the therapeutic dynamics between Yoko and him back then, he could have moved forward in these sessions differently. Since this experience, A.M. has intentionally discussed with clients potential cultural issues both at the outset and throughout the course of therapy, which may show up during therapeutic work (e.g., see Masuda, Ng, Moore, Felix, & Drake, 2016).

Modification of Therapeutic Techniques

As described previously, from a functional contextualist perspective, modifications of treatment in form (e.g., cultural adaptation) are always expected (Masuda, 2016, 2020). In ACT, these content modifications can take place within therapeutic procedures/techniques used (e.g., experiential exercises, metaphors, and activities), their length, session format, or across other relevant domains, such as client-therapist match in gender and inclusion of "key brokers" (see Pasillas & Masuda, 2014).

Once again, consider ACT values and committed action work with Yoko as an example (Masuda et al., 2008). Unlike a content-focused adaptation, a *functional and contextual* adaptation of ACT started with identifying behavioral processes that might increase or undermine greater psychological flexibility for Yoko. Here, primary behavioral processes identified as supportive of psychological flexibility were (1) the construction of freely chosen meaningfulness and purposefulness as a guiding direction in her life (i.e., values); (2) identification of actions that reflected these values; and (3) continuous engagement in these values-directed actions.

The next step in this cultural adaptation of ACT was to identify potential strategies to move these behavioral processes forward. ACT manuals often suggest the use of the Skiing metaphor (Hayes, Strosahl, & Wilson, 1999, pp. 220–221), the Path Up the Mountain metaphor (Hayes et al., 1999, pp. 221–222), or the Passengers on the Bus metaphor (Hayes et al., 1999, pp. 157–158) to promote these behavioral processes. If the use of these recommended metaphors were judged to be effective for Yoko, there would be no reason not to use them and see if they in fact yielded the intended functional effects (e.g., Yoko became more willing to pursue values-directed action). If not, it would be important to identify other potential strategies that could be valuable to her. For Yoko, the latter was the case.

More specifically, A.M. incorporated proverbs and common personal mottos that were familiar to many Japanese people, including Yoko, and that adequately captured the behavioral processes of values-directed action and purposeful and meaningful living. These included "思い立ったが吉日 (Never put off until tomorrow what you can do today)," "七転び八起き (Fall seven times, stand up eight)," "継続は力なり (Perseverance is power)," and similar others. Yoko appeared to relate well to these proverbs at both a personal and an experiential level. If the use of these proverbs did not yield the intended effects, A.M. reviewed why that was the case and explored potential alternatives (i.e., functional analysis). In sum, the modification of ACT must be done functionally and individually with a given client in the service of promoting greater behavioral adaptation and psychological flexibility.

Another example of modification in therapeutic technique is use of the Taro (Kalo) Plant in Nature metaphor. As noted previously, traditional Native Hawaiian culture and world views have a rich, complex relationship with elements and forces of nature, such as winds, water, rains, and waves, and with spiritual significance associated with different types of animals and plants (Abbot, 1992; Akana, 2015). As such, metaphors involving such forces or aspects of nature may be particularly salient to Native Hawaiian clients who identify more strongly with traditional Hawaiian culture and world views. We presented the earlier part of the Taro (Kalo) Plant in Nature metaphor in a previous section; following is the rest of this metaphor that is used to enhance psychological flexibility, with particular salience to many Native Hawaiian-identified clients.

This metaphor aims to promote client psychological flexibility by using the image of a kalo (taro) plant in a blowing wind as a parallel with the client's relationship to their emotional and physiological challenges. Kalo (also known as taro and *Colocasia esculaenta*) is one of the most important plants in Hawaiian culture. It is not only the source of poi, a staple food in the Hawaiian Islands prior to the devastating impacts of colonization and colonialism, but also is symbolized as the older sibling of the first Hawaiian in the traditional story of creation (Handy & Handy, 1972). Because it remains an important plant, food, and symbol of Hawaiian culture and identity in Hawaiʻi today, many Native Hawaiian clients are readily familiar with the image of kalo plants growing in kalo patches or loʻi. As such, it was deemed a potentially apt symbol to include in a metaphor about one's relationship to their thoughts and feelings and therefore useful in therapy to increase psychological flexibility and value-based actions.

As shown in Figure 30.1, kalo are plants with large heart-shaped leaves at the ends of tall slender stalks. These stalks, called hā in the Hawaiian language, connect to the edible corm and roots in the soil. If one has seen kalo growing in loʻi, they will notice that when the wind blows, the leaves of the kalo twist and turn, a motion that can be called "lau kapalili" or quivering, throbbing, or palpitating leaf (Pukui & Elbert, 1986). The rest of Taro Plant in Nature metaphor goes as follows:

Therapist (L.M.): What if I say that we are like kalo plants? When a wind blows, the leaf may quiver and shake, but the roots are still connected firmly in the ground . . . . As we have discussed together before, the winds can symbolize strong and uncontrollable feelings we experience. The wind's/emotions then cause our body and mind to flutter and quiver, which can manifest as distressing thoughts and memories, rumination, heart palpitations, body tension, restlessness, and other psychosomatic experiences.

Client: (nodding quietly and listening to L.M. thoroughly)

Therapist: We recognize that we cannot control the wind and that doing so would only cause us to struggle harder and in vain. Like the kalo, we can remember that although our mind and body are quivering or trembling in different ways, we are always connected to our breath (hā), just as the leaf is connected to the hā (stem). When we remember and reconnect with the breath, while allowing the wind to continue blowing as it is and allowing the leaf to quake as it is, we follow the long slender stalk down to the solidity of the roots down in the earth, and in doing so we bring our awareness down with our breath into our body, our center, where we remember we are rooted, no matter how strong the wind is blowing.

In Hawaiian language, the belly, guts, or intestines are called "na'au," which can refer to one's "heart/mind/feelings/intuition" and is also connected to the concept of "na'auao," meaning wisdom and knowledge, literally "daylight (enlightened) mind".

Therapist (L.M.): What if I say the wisdom from your culture and your ancestors that is particularly relevant here is that we live and breathe like a kalo plant? If we reconnect with our hā (breath), which is connected with the "na'au," and if we remember to reconnect with the awareness of "na'auao," a deeper wisdom that is underneath the vicissitudes of thoughts and feelings perhaps, we may stop trying to fight the winds and the kapalili inside (representing anxiety, worrying mind, etc.) . . . .

Client: (nodding quietly and listening to L.M. thoroughly)

Therapist: Also see if you can notice that as a kalo, we are rooted into our land, or perhaps we can say, we are connected to our land as if there are no separations between us and the land. From this perspective, perhaps, you are more than who you feel you are . . . perhaps you are truly part of nature, part of the past and future, and of the wisdom of interconnectedness handed down from your ancestors . . . From this standpoint, how would you like to live your life?

Once again, this part of the Taro Plant in Nature metaphor is intended to help a client develop a more defused and flexible relationship to distressing thoughts and feelings for the purpose of pursuing values-directed living. At the same time, this part of the metaphor also serves as an easy-to-remember mindfulness of breath practice, which is often included in the second author's (L.M.) therapeutic work. L.M. often presents this metaphor to his clients in Hawai'i because it could intuitively teach them the perspective of psychological flexibility. For many of his clients, it has been helpful to generalize their repertoires of psychological flexibility from their intuitive relationship with nature to the context of their often-unwanted private events and internal experiences.

Research Support

The synthesis of knowledge and evidence regarding the *cultural adaptation* of ACT is still in its infancy (Masuda, 2020). To date, the importance of effective cultural adaptation of ACT has been discussed conceptually in the context of multicultural competencies and mindfulness- and acceptance-based cognitive behavioral therapies (Masuda, 2014b), treatment development (Hayes et al., 2013), and the inclusion of underrepresented groups in ACT research (Woidneck, Pratt, Gundy, Nelson, & Twohig, 2012). Similarly, ACT scholars have begun to examine the *cross-cultural utility and validity* of ACT and the psychological flexibility model to various cultural and anthropological contexts (e.g., Fung, 2015; Pasillas & Masuda,

2014; Perry, Gardener, Oliver, Taş, & Özenç, 2019; Sabucedo, 2017; Stewart et al., 2016; White, Gregg, Batten, Hayes, & Kasujja, 2017).

For example, Masuda (2014a) has argued that ACT can be a highly pragmatic, experiential, and collaborative therapeutic approach across diverse clients through connecting them to their *contextually situated values* and using this information to guide the therapeutic process and promote flexible and purposeful living. Similarly, Perry et al. (2019), in their examination of the cultural flexibility of the ACT model, assert that the emphasis on values and context, two central tenets of the ACT model, offers potential for its cultural adaptability for underserved populations, such as Turkish-speaking communalities in East London, while taking into account their collectivistic structure, religious beliefs, and many experiences of distress due to collective experiences of loss, displacement, and existence as a refugee. Thus, it is crucial to reiterate that ACT is culturally adaptative only when it is idiographically tailored for a given client(s) in a functional and contextual manner (White et al., 2017).

Despite the dearth of empirical research on key questions regarding the cultural adaptation of ACT, some understanding can be gained through examining the methods and processes of cultural adaptation that have been described briefly in previously published ACT outcome studies in socioculturally diverse contexts. For example, in designing an ACT therapist training program in Sierra Leone, Stewart et al. (2016) met with key local stakeholders about how to best tailor core ACT processes to local customs for therapist training as well as the resources available in the training setting (e.g., intervention delivery without the use of electricity). Additionally, Hassinen and Lappalainen (2018) adapted ACT for deaf Finnish individuals through the creation of videos of ACT metaphors and exercises translated into Finnish sign language. A professional Finnish translator and extant Finnish ACT protocols were also used to further enhance the development of this video-augmented ACT intervention through Finnish sign language. Unfortunately, space limitations in journal articles often preclude detailed descriptions of *how* the cultural adaption of ACTs were implemented in many research studies examining ACT in diverse cultural contexts. As such, more research will be needed to bridge the gap between conceptual and empirical work in the cultural adaptation of ACT to attain a better understanding of key functional processes necessitated in this context.

Finally, it has been historically challenging to include individuals from underrepresented populations across the globe in ACT studies, despite the fact that the cultural adaption of ACT is most relevant to these groups. At the time of writing, there remains a disproportionately small number of studies examining ACT outcomes and processes with a range of hard-to-access minority groups, though the trend is certainly on the rise. Similarly, there are disproportionately smaller numbers of ACT researchers and clinicians from these underrepresented groups, resulting in slower progress in cultural adaptation of ACT. These underrepresented groups include ethnic minorities; sexual minorities (e.g., lesbian, gay, bisexual, pansexual, and queer folx); gender minorities (e.g., transgender and gender nonconforming or gender fluid folx); the differently abled; and elderly populations. These groups of individuals may benefit most from further empirical exploration into their psychological health and well-being. While this inequity in representation is generally paralleled in social science research writ large (e.g., Henrich et al., 2010), leaders in ACT research call for greater conscientiousness from the community in filling these gaps in knowledge and, ultimately, service delivery (Hayes et al., 2013; Masuda, 2014b; Skinta & Curtin, 2016).

Conclusions and Final Notes

ACT is best understood as the purposeful behavior of a clinician in a therapeutic context that is both principle-informed and experientially guided. Every ACT case is subject to cultural adaptation because no two individuals have identical learning histories and situational contexts, including the one that unfolds between client and therapist of a similar sociocultural background. With respect to the very topic of this article, it is extremely difficult to practice and embody ACT *functionally and contextually*. If followed functionally and contextually, an ACT framework allows a clinician to adapt and finetune their clinical work with a given client while staying connected to the promotion of psychological flexibility as the ultimate treatment goal. If the PFM is followed functionally and contextually, therefore idiographically to a given client, no additional guidelines for cultural adaptation are needed. The very fact that the present article is placed as a standalone entry toward the end of this volume suggests the importance of explicating functional contextualism as the standpoint of learning and practicing ACT further, so that we do not fall prey to the same pitfalls of symptom-oriented, content-based treatment development approaches (Hayes & Hofmann, 2020) in our cultural adaptation efforts (e.g., ACT for Japanese, ACT for multiracial clients, ACT for Muslim, ACT for the democrat). At last, given its importance, we hope that the same level of careful investigation will continue to be implemented for the cultural adaptation of ACT, as our field has done for a wide variety of behavioral health issues (e.g., depression, anxiety, chronic pain) in service of our clients' well-being. As ACT has shifted from a symptom-focused paradigm to a unified and process-based one in recent years (Hayes & Hofmann, 2018), we hope that our cultural adaptation efforts also shift from content-focused cultural adaptation of ACT to a more process-based, principle-informed cultural adaptation of this therapy.

References

Abbot, I. A. (1992). *Lā'au Hawai'i; traditional Hawaiian uses of plants*. Honolulu, HI: Bishop Museum Press.

Akana, C. L. (2015). *Hānau Ka Ua; Hawaiian Rain Names*. Honolulu, HI: Kamehameha Publishing.

Bach, P. A., & Moran, D. J. (2008). *ACT in practice: Case conceptualization in acceptance and commitment therapy*. Oakland, CA: New Harbinger Publications.

Bernal, G., Jiménez-Chafey, M. I., & Domenech Rodríguez, M. M. (2009). Cultural adaptation of treatments: A resource for considering culture in evidence-based practice. *Professional Psychology: Research and Practice, 40*(4), 361–368. doi:10.1037/a0016401

Cheng, J. K. Y., & Sue, S. (2014). Addressing cultural and ethnic minority issues in the acceptance and mindfulness movement. In A. Masuda & A. Masuda (Eds.), *Mindfulness and acceptance in multicultural competency: A contextual approach to sociocultural diversity in theory and practice* (pp. 21–37). Oakland, CA: Context Press/New Harbinger Publications.

Dougher, M. J., & Hayes, S. C. (2000). Clinical behavior analysis. In M. J. Dougher (Ed.), *Clinical behavior analysis* (pp. 11–25). Reno, NV: Context Press.

Drossel, C., McCausland, C., Schneider, N., & Cattivelli, R. (2014). Functional adaptation of acceptance- and mindfulness-based therapies: An ethical imperative. In A. Masuda (Ed.), *Mindfulness and acceptance in multicultural competency: A contextual approach to sociocultural diversity in theory and practice* (pp. 129–146). Oakland, CA: Context Press.

Duckworth, M. P. (2008). Assertiveness skills and the management of related factors. In W. T. O'Donohue & J. E. Fisher (Eds.), *Cognitive behavior therapy: Applying empirically supported techniques in your practice* (2nd ed.) (pp. 26–34). Hoboken, NJ: John Wiley.

Fisher, E. S. (2020). Cultural humility as a form of social justice: Promising practices for global school psychology training. *School Psychology International, 41*(1), 53–66.

Fung, K. (2015). Acceptance and commitment therapy: Western adoption of Buddhist tenets? *Transcultural Psychiatry, 52*(4), 561–576.

Hall, G. C. N., Hong, J. J., Zane, N. W. S., & Meyer, O. L. (2011). Culturally competent treatments for Asian Americans: The relevance of mindfulness and acceptance-based psychotherapies. *Clinical Psychology: Science and Practice, 18*(3), 215–231. doi:10.1111/j.1468-2850.2011.01253.x

Handy, E. S. C., & Handy, E. G. (1972). *Native planters in old Hawaii: their life, lore, and environment*. Honolulu, HI: Bishop Muscum Press.

Hassinen, L., & Lappalainen, R. (2018). Acceptance and commitment therapy using Finnish sign language: Training counselors in signed ACT for the deaf—A pilot study. *Journal of Contextual Behavioral Science, 8*, 74–81.

Hayes, S. C. (1987). A contextual approach to therapeutic change. In N. S. Jacobson (Ed.), *Psychotherapists in clinical practice: Cognitive and behavioral perspectives* (pp. 327–387). New York: Guilford Press.

Hayes, S. C., Barnes-Holmes, D., & Wilson, K. G. (2012). Contextual behavioral science: Creating a science more adequate to the challenge of the human condition. *Journal of Contextual Behavioral Science, 1*(1–2), 1–16. doi:http://dx.doi.org/10.1016/j.jcbs.2012.09.004

Hayes, S. C., & Hofmann, S. G. (2020). *Beyond the DSM: Toward a process-based alternative for diagnosis and mental health treatment.* Oakland, CA: New Harbinger Publications.

Hayes, S. C., & Hofmann, S. G. (Eds.). (2018). *Process-based CBT: The science and core clinical competencies of cognitive behavioral therapy.* Oakland, CA: New Harbinger Publications.

Hayes, S. C., Hofmann, S. G., Stanton, C. E., Carpenter, J. K., Sanford, B. T., Curtiss, J. E., & Ciarrochi, J. (2019). The role of the individual in the coming era of process-based therapy. *Behavior Research and Therapy, 117,* 40–53.

Hayes, S. C., Long, D. M., Levin, M. E., & Follette, W. C. (2013). Treatment development: Can we find a better way? *Clinical Psychology Review, 33*(7), 870–882. doi:10.1016/j.cpr.2012.09.009

Hayes, S. C., Pistorello, J., & Levin, M. E. (2012). Acceptance and commitment therapy as a unified model of behavior change. *The Counseling Psychologist, 40*(7), 976–1002.

Hayes, S. C., Strosahl, K. D., & Wilson, K. G. (1999). *Acceptance and commitment therapy: An experiential approach to behavior change.* New York: Guilford Press.

Hayes, S. C., Strosahl, K. D., & Wilson, K. G. (2012). *Acceptance and commitment therapy: The process and practice of mindful change* (2nd ed.). New York: Guilford Press.

Hayes, S. C., & Wilson, K. G. (1994). Acceptance and commitment therapy: Altering the verbal support for experiential avoidance. *The Behavior Analyst, 17*(2), 289–303.

Hayes, S. C., Wilson, K. G., Gifford, E. V., Follette, V. M., & Strosahl, K. (1996). Experiential avoidance and behavioral disorders: A functional dimensional approach to diagnosis and treatment. *Journal of Consulting and Clinical Psychology, 64*(6), 1152–1168.

Henrich, J., Heine, S. J., & Norenzayan, A. (2010). The weirdest people in the world? *Behavioral and Brain Sciences, 33*(2–3), 61–83.

Hook, J. N., Davis, D. E., Owen, J., Worthington, E. L., Jr., & Utsey, S. O. (2013). Cultural humility: Measuring openness to culturally diverse clients. *Journal of Counseling Psychology, 60*(3), 353–366.

Kaholokula, J. K. (2017). Mauli Ola: Pathways to optimal Kanaka 'Ōiwi Health. In W. K. M. Lee & M. A. Look (Eds.), *Ho'i Hou Ka Mauli Ola* (pp. 2–22). Honolulu, HI: University of Hawai'i Press.

Kohlenberg, R. J., & Tsai, M. (1991). Functional analytic psychotherapy: Creating intense and curative therapeutic relationships. Plenum Press. https://doi-org.eres.library.manoa.hawaii.edu/10.1007/978-0-387-70855-3

Komiya, N., Good, G. E., & Sherrod, N. B. (2000). Emotional openness as a predictor of college students' attitudes toward seeking psychological help. *Journal of Counseling Psychology, 47*(1), 138–143. doi:10.1037/0022-0167.47.1.138

Markus, H. R., & Kitayama, S. (1991). Culture and the self: Implications for cognition, emotion, and motivation. *Psychological Review, 98*(2), 224–253.

Markus, H. R., & Kitayama, S. (2010). Cultures and selves: A cycle of mutual constitution. *Perspectives on Psychological Science, 5*(4), 420–430. doi:10.1177/1745691610375557

Masuda, A. (2014a). Psychotherapy in cultural context. In A. Masuda (Ed.), *Mindfulness and acceptance in multicultural competency: A contextual approach to sociocultural diversity in theory and practice* (pp. 39–55). Oakland, CA: New Harbinger Publications.

Masuda, A. (2016). Principle-based cultural adaptation of cognitive behavior therapies: A functional and contextual perspective as an example. *Japanese Journal of Behavior Therapy, 42*(1), 11–19.

Masuda, A. (2020). Adapting acceptance and commitment therapy to diverse cultures. In M. E. Levin, M. P. Twohig, & J. Kraft (Eds.), *Innovations in acceptance and commitment therapy: Clinical advancements and applications in ACT* (pp. 239–251). Oakland, CA: Context Press.

Masuda, A. (Ed.) (2014b). *Mindfulness and acceptance in multicultural competency: A contextual approach to sociocultural diversity in theory and practice.* Oakland, CA: Context Press/New Harbinger Publications.

Masuda, A., Muto, T., Hayes, S. C., & Lillis, J. (2008). Acceptance and commitment therapy: application to a Japanese client. *Japanese Journal of Behavior Therapy, 34,* 137–148.

Masuda, A., Ng, S. Y., Moore, M., Felix, I., & Drake, C. E. (2016). Acceptance and commitment therapy as a treatment for a Latina young adult woman with purging: A case report. *Practice Innovations, 1*(1), 20–35.

Mosher, D. K., Hook, J. N., Captari, L. E., Davis, D. E., DeBlaere, C., & Owen, J. (2017). Cultural humility: A therapeutic framework for engaging diverse clients. *Practice Innovations, 2*(4), 221–233.

Odom, S. K., Jackson, P., Derauf, D., Inada, M. K., & Aoki, A. H. (2019). Pilinahā: An indigenous framework for health. *Current Developments in Nutrition, 3,* 32–38.

Pasillas, R. M., & Masuda, A. (2014). Cultural competency and acceptance and commitment therapy. In A. Masuda (Ed.), *Mindfulness and acceptance in multicultural competency: A contextual approach to sociocultural diversity in theory and practice* (pp. 109–125). Oakland, CA: Context Press/New Harbinger Publications.

Perry, A., Gardener, C., Oliver, J. E., Taş, Ç., & Özenç, C. (2019). Exploring the cultural flexibility of the ACT model as an effective therapeutic group intervention for Turkish speaking communities in East London. *The Cognitive Behaviour Therapist, 12*(e2), 1–25.

Pukui, M. K., & Elbert, S. H. (1986). *Hawaiian dictionary*. Honolulu, HI: University of Hawai'i Press.

Robins, C. J., Schmidt, H., III, & Linehan, M. M. (2004). Dialectical behavior therapy: Synthesizing radical acceptance with skillful means. In S. C. Hayes, V. M. Follette, & M. M. Linehan (Eds.), *Mindfulness and acceptance: Expanding the cognitive-behavioral tradition*. (pp. 30–44). New York: Guilford Press.

Sabucedo, P. (2017). The psychological flexibility model from a cultural perspective: An interpretative analysis of two Native American healing rituals. *International Journal of Culture and Mental Health, 10*(4), 367–375.

Skinta, M. D., & Curtin, A. (2016). *Mindfulness and acceptance for gender and sexual minorities: A clinician's guide to fostering compassion, connection and equality using contextual strategies*. Oakland, CA: Context Press/New Harbinger Publications.

Stewart, C., G. White, R., Ebert, B., Mays, I., Nardozzi, J., & Bockarie, H. (2016). A preliminary evaluation of Acceptance and commitment therapy (ACT) training in Sierra Leone. *Journal of Contextual Behavioral Science, 5*(1), 16–22. doi:https://doi.org/10.1016/j.jcbs.2016.01.001

Sue, D. W., Sue, D., Neville, H. A., & Smith, L. (2019). *Counseling the culturally diverse: Theory and practice* (8th ed.). Hoboken, NJ: John Wiley.

Sue, S. (1998). In search of cultural competence in psychotherapy and counseling. *American Psychologist, 53*(4), 440–448. doi:10.1037/0003-066x.53.4.440

Sue, S., Cheng, J. K. Y., Saad, C. S., & Chu, J. P. (2012). Asian American mental health: A call to action. *American Psychologist, 67*(7), 532–544. doi:10.1037/a0028900

Sue, S., Zane, N., Hall, G. C. N., & Berger, L. K. (2009). The case for cultural competency in psychotherapeutic interventions. *Annual Review of Psychology, 60*, 525–548. doi:10.1146/annurev.psych.60.110707.163651

Twohig, M. P., Levin, M. E., & Ong, C. W. (2020). *ACT in steps: A transdiagnostic manual for learning acceptance and commitment therapy*. New York: Oxford University Press.

Vilardaga, R., Hayes, S. C., Levin, M. E., & Muto, T. (2009). Creating a strategy for progress: A contextual behavioral science approach. *The Behavior Analyst, 32*(1), 105–133.

Weisz, J. R., Rothbaum, F. M., & Blackburn, T. C. (1984). Standing out and standing in: The psychology of control in America and Japan. *American Psychologist, 39*(9), 955–969.

Whaley, A. L., & Davis, K. E. (2007). Cultural competence and evidence-based practice in mental health services: A complementary perspective. *American Psychologist, 62*(6), 563–574. doi:10.1037/0003-066x.62.6.563

White, R. G., Gregg, J., Batten, S., Hayes, L. L., & Kasujja, R. (2017). Contextual behavioral science and global mental health: synergies and opportunities. *Journal of Contextual Behavioral Science, 6*(3), 245–251. doi:https://doi.org/10.1016/j.jcbs.2017.07.001

Wilson, K. G., & Dufrene, T. (2008). *Mindfulness for two: An acceptance and commitment therapy approach to mindfulness in psychotherapy*. Oakland, CA: New Harbinger Prblications.

Woidneck, M. R., Pratt, K. M., Gundy, J. M., Nelson, C. R., & Twohig, M. P. (2012). Exploring cultural competence in acceptance and commitment therapy outcomes. *Professional Psychology: Research and Practice, 43*(3), 227–233.

Zane, N., & Ku, H. (2014). Effects of ethnic match, gender match, acculturation, cultural identity, and face concern on self-disclosure in counseling for Asian Americans. *Asian American Journal of Psychology, 5*(1), 66–74.

Zettle, R. D., & Hayes, S. C. (1986). Dysfunctional control by client verbal behavior: The context of reason-giving. *The Analysis of Verbal Behavior, 4*(1), 30–38.

CHAPTER

31 Acceptance and Commitment Therapy Inside Behavior Analysis

Jonathan Tarbox, Amanda N. Chastain, *and* Thomas G. Szabo

Abstract

Acceptance and commitment therapy (ACT) is a widely adopted and well-supported contemporary approach to psychotherapy. However, the basic research and learning principles that ACT is based on originated in the science of behavior analysis; therefore, ACT remains linked to behavior analysis at the conceptual level. In recent years, a flurry of interest in ACT among applied behavior analytic practitioners has developed, and research on the application of ACT inside of behavior analysis has been flourishing as well. This chapter discusses the conceptual foundations for ACT inside behavior analysis, including a brief conceptual analysis of the six core ACT processes in terms of behavior analytic principles of learning and motivation. The chapter reviews research on ACT inside of behavior analysis, especially as it has been applied to individuals with autism, their caregivers and staff. Also discussed are the extent to which the research reviewed adheres to the defining characteristics of applied behavior analysis, as well as directions for the future research that could both enhance the precision of the ACT literature, as well as expand the scope of applied behavior analysis.

Key Words: acceptance and commitment therapy, acceptance and commitment training, behavior analysis, applied behavior analysis, autism, parent training, staff training

Introduction

Acceptance and commitment therapy (ACT) is among the most well-known contemporary treatment approaches in mainstream psychology but its roots are to be found in the science of behavior analysis. ACT was developed by combining careful basic behavior analytic laboratory research on human language and cognition with contemporary values and mindfulness-based approaches to behavior change (Sandoz, Boullion, & Rachal, 2020). As we will describe in the conceptual analysis section, ACT has always been conceptualized as behavior analysis, even while, as a treatment model, it has been disseminated and popularized outside of behavior analysis. In some very real sense, behavior analysis has always been the proper home of ACT.

Despite the natural fit of ACT with behavior analysis, the vast majority of research on ACT has been done in psychotherapeutic contexts, outside of behavior analysis. In this chapter, we will refer to ACT that is practiced inside psychotherapeutic contexts as acceptance and commitment *therapy*, as contrasted with ACT practiced outside of psychotherapy, which we will refer to as acceptance and commitment *training*. We will discuss how the relationship between ACT and behavior analysis is mutually beneficial. Behavior analysis helps keep ACT rooted in the basic science of learning and motivation from which it came, and ACT may help the science of behavior analysis achieve a more comprehensive scope, as has been aspirational for the science beginning with the early works of B. F. Skinner (1938). In turn, as an understanding of a broader scope of socially significant human behavior is achieved through the contributions of ACT, such expansion promises to further expand the scope of practice for practitioners of applied behavior analysis (ABA) into ever-broader ranges of human behavior.

Conceptual Foundations for ACT in Behavior Analysis

At the most fundamental level, ACT has always been an application of behavior analytic principles of learning and motivation, extended into basic behavioral accounts of human language and cognition (Hayes & Wilson, 1994). Although ACT has largely flourished in parallel to the science and practice of behavior analysis most or all major ACT books make explicit reference to the behavior analytic basic principles from which it came. In what follows, we expand commonly available behavioral accounts of ACT by attempting an extended behavioral conceptual account of the behavioral repertoires that ACT targets.

Behavior Analytic Account of ACT as Explained through the Choice Point

Books on ACT commonly emphasize that, at the broadest level, ACT aims to help people make difficult choices, specifically choices of committed action toward values, over experiential avoidance. This has been referred to as the "pivot" (Hayes, 2020) or the "choice point" (Ciarrochi, Bailey, & Harris, 2014). We have argued that this choice point can be conceptualized as a concurrent operants paradigm, much like those studied in the self-control and delay discounting behavior analytic basic literatures (Tarbox, Szabo, & Aclan, 2020). The circle at the bottom of Figure 31.1 depicts choice points that are commonly available throughout daily life when things are difficult, that is, when aversive overt or covert stimuli are present (e.g., the aversive stimuli produced by engaging in hard exercise, hearing oneself have negative thoughts about oneself at work, hearing one's child crying). Myriad times per day, choice points that involve concurrently available choices on two different "levers" are presented to all of us. One option, depicted by the left arrow, leads to short-term escape/avoidance of that

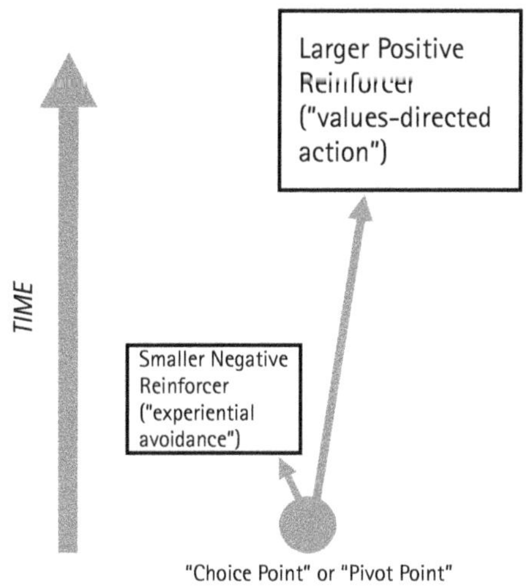

Figure 31.1. A diagram of the "choice point" or "pivot point," which involves choices between smaller, sooner negative reinforcement (aka "experiential avoidance"), versus larger, later positive reinforcement (aka "valued action").

aversive stimulus, while the other option, depicted by the right arrow, fails to terminate that aversive stimulus but leads to a relatively larger positive reinforcer in the longer term. For example, when performing at work, one often has a choice between avoiding doing something important, which avoids the anxiety or boredom produced by that behavior (depicted by the left arrow), versus doing that important task, which may still be anxiety-producing or boring but leads to some important delayed outcome, for example, getting a promotion. We posit that many of life's most important circumstances involve choices between immediate escape/avoidance versus long-term positive reinforcement. These choices are also often referred to as "away moves" versus "toward moves." These away moves constitute experiential avoidance, whereas the toward moves constitute action toward one's values.

Although we fundamentally appreciate the choice point framework introduced by Ciarrochi et al. (2014), we suggest an evidence-based modification derived from the experimental analysis of behavior literature and depicted in Figure 31.2. Note that in the procedure and conceptualization offered previously and in Figure 31.1, there is *one* choice point—that moment at which a nonpreferred event with a large payoff is often avoided in favor of a preferred event with a smaller yield. But in an early study on the matching law and delay discounting, Rachlin and Green (1972) showed that pigeons could be taught to choose a large reinforcer with a long delay over a smaller reinforcer with a short delay at a given point at time Y by progressively lengthening a temporal interval between Y and an earlier Choice Point X at which time the larger reinforcer with a longer delay is preferred. In other words, Rachlin and Green showed that preference shifts between *two* distinct choice points and that a commitment made at the earlier choice point can change a suboptimal preference for the better.

Consider the dilemma facing students of behavior analysis who are preparing for the exam they must take on Saturday, again shown in Figure 31.2. A week before the exam (Choice Point X), the student would prefer studying on Friday night and getting a good night's sleep before the exam. But when a friend calls Friday afternoon alerting the student to an impromptu party that night (Choice Point Y), the student is likely to go out, accepting the smaller, immediate reinforcer of avoiding studying to the larger, delayed reinforcer available for hard work in preparation for the exam. Were the student to make a commitment to a friend a week in advance of the exam (Choice Point X) to study together at their house Friday night (Choice Point Y), the probability of their studying and forgoing the party increases.

Of course, not all choices that humans face are as easy as making a commitment to a friend for studying together on Friday night. But those that applied behavior analysts help parents, staff, and consumers with are often ripe for equivalent public commitment strategies. And when they are not, other conditioned reinforcement contingencies can be programmed. For example, a behavior analyst could ask a parent to text after their child has left for school and an hour before the child comes home and settles in to do ABA with their parent. In these texts, the parent can tell the behavior analyst what they have done (e.g., laundry, food prep) to make sure they are allotting enough time for ABA. Then the parent can text the behavior analyst after completing the ABA session with their child and access social reinforcers for their effort. In cases where the parent cannot text the behavior analyst, they may be taught to supply appetitive or reinforcing self-statements for themselves. Renewed commitment responses in the form of intermittent social engagement and self-statements serve as conditioned reinforcers and discriminative stimuli. These repeated events in between Choice Points X and Y strengthen the probability of forgoing smaller reinforcers available at Y in favor of larger, later ones. With a long enough history of employing these strategies, the parent may cease "seeing" the smaller immediate alternative because they make these advance commitments and access smaller reinforcements along the way, as portrayed in Figure 31.2. In this regard, the modified

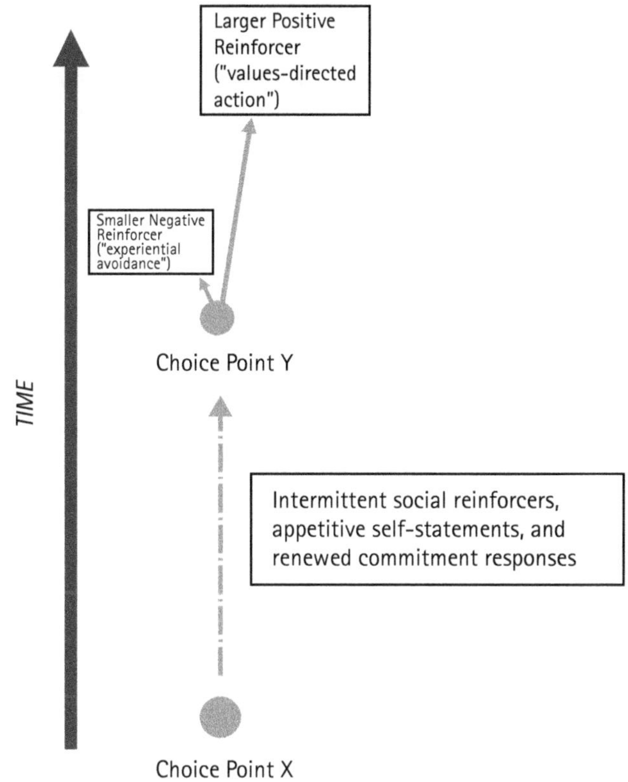

Figure 31.2. The "modified choice point." A commitment is made at Choice Point X, followed by intermittent renewed commitments and conditioned reinforcers assuring that at the often-observed preference reversal at Choice Point Y does not occur. The choice at Point Y is weakened, reducing the lure of smaller, sooner negative reinforcement (aka "experiential avoidance") and increasing the likelihood of responses that access larger, later positive reinforcers (aka "valued action").

choice point procedure and conceptualization offer behavior analysts using ACT many opportunities to promote effective action.

From a behavior analytic perspective, we conceptualize that the primary goal of ACT training is to help trainees press the left lever less and the right lever more. Of course, negative reinforcement is a natural behavioral learning process that cannot be eliminated from life. But we believe that many of life's most important problems can be usefully analyzed as a person avoiding too much and behaving for long-term positive reinforcers too infrequently. For example, avoid recycling now or have a livable environment later, avoid the effort of exercise now or have a healthy body later, avoid intimate conversations now or have a loving relationship later, avoid studying now or pass the exam later, and so on. The goal of ACT, from this perspective, is to help people reallocate their behavior such that they spend more behavior on valued action and less behavior on avoidance, at least when it is workable for moving them in life directions that they genuinely value.

By definition, if a person is consistently choosing one response option over another, then the environmental contingencies controlling those choices are effective in maintaining that pattern of behavior. Put simply, if someone is consistently engaging in experiential avoidance, it is not "wrong," it is the natural and expected outcome of their learning history and current circumstances. How, then, might we expect to help people shift allocation of their responding from "pressing the experiential avoidance" lever to "pressing the valued action lever"? The six points of the hexaflex comprise six behavioral repertoires that, when strengthened, give a person behavioral tools that help them allocate more of their responding to valued action and less to experiential avoidance. In what follows, we provide a brief behavioral conceptual analysis of each point of the ACT hexaflex. We refer readers to Tarbox et al. (2020) and Dixon, Hayes, Stanley, Law, and al-Nasser (2020) for further behavioral treatments of the hexaflex.

The ACT Hexaflex in Behavior Analytic Perspective

VALUES

As mentioned in previous chapters (see LeJeune & Luoma, this volume), values lie at the center of ACT. They provide motivation for an individual to pivot toward contact with aversive stimuli for the purpose of achieving a life filled with greater meaning and purpose. Values are somewhat abstract and are thus not achievable "things." Rather, they make up a set of verbally constructed reinforcers that one comes into contact with when behaving in line with that value. More specifically, a value serves as an *augmental*, or a type of rule-governed behavior that influences the reinforcing effectiveness of a given stimulus, establishing a stimulus as a reinforcer (*formative augmental*) or increasing the momentary reinforcing effectiveness of an already established reinforcer (*motivative augmental*). Values transform the function of a given stimulus into an appetitive one, such that reinforcing consequences can be more immediately contacted in the present environment. For example, let us consider a situation where an individual has identified "health" as a value. When it comes time to work out, this individual may be exposed to aversive stimuli (e.g., feeling too tired, muscle aches from the day before, the thought of not having enough time). If, however, this individual has identified health as a value, the stimuli involved in steps that are in line with that value (getting gym bag, workout clothes, driving to the gym, etc.) can be transformed into appetitive stimuli, thereby increasing the likelihood that the behaviors that lead to them will occur.

ACCEPTANCE

One of the most fundamental principles in behavior analysis is that organisms engage in escape or avoidance responses in the presence of aversive stimuli or warning of their forthcoming. When humans acquire a complex language repertoire (specifically arbitrarily applicable derived relational responding), private verbal stimuli can readily become members of a larger class of aversives. When we experience private events (covert stimuli including thoughts, visual images, physical sensations, or emotions; Skinner, 1974) with aversive properties, the natural response is to try and escape. Part of the challenge of being human is that when an attempt to escape private stimuli is made (e.g., think of something else), new stimuli become verbally related to those already present within that class of aversives. When aversive Stimulus A is related to both Stimulus B and Stimulus C, then B and C also become related to one another and acquire the aversive properties of Stimulus A (Hayes et al., 2001). In other words, that new relation becomes "tangled in a web" of existing relations, creating a more restrictive and aversive environment. Because private events themselves cannot be escaped, people tend to escape or avoid the environmental events by which they are evoked. For example, giving a talk in a room full of people may evoke thoughts of "They're going to think I'm so stupid," or "I can't do this" and may elicit fear responses such as sweating, shaking, or increased heart rate. Thus, giving a talk in a room full of people might be avoided; indeed, even thinking about or talking about giving a talk may be avoided. Acceptance as a behavioral skill repertoire involves strengthening approach responses toward those aversive stimuli that would normally evoke escape, when doing so is in line with one's values. It is pivoting toward those reinforcers we described in our discussion of values, even if it means initially or concurrently tolerating aversive stimuli in the immediate environment.

DEFUSION

Verbally sophisticated humans build up an incredibly complex repertoire of rules about behavior–environment relations. Pliance, one of the initial forms of rule-governed behavior, involves following a rule simply because rule following is, in and of itself, reinforcing due to a long history of social reinforcement for rule-following behavior (Hayes, Barnes-Holmes, & Roche, 2001). While pliance seems to be important to the overall development of an effective rule-following repertoire, it is also necessary for healthy human development to establish a relationship between rules and the actual environmental contingencies at play (i.e., tracking). Pliance can result in contingency insensitivity, restricted access to reinforcement, and potentially even unnecessary exposure to aversive stimuli. One aim of defusion is to build flexibility around rule-following by teaching an individual to recognize that rule for what it really is—a verbal stimulus in their environment. Learning to discriminate between private verbal stimuli and actual environmental contingencies may decrease the likelihood that these verbal stimuli will influence one's behavior.

A second function of defusion is the deliteralization of language. When stimuli are related through a frame of coordination, they become equivalent to one another, thereby serving the same functions in a given context. For example, if the word "Dog" is equivalent to an actual dog, then the word "dog" comes to evoke the same responses that may be brought to bear in the presence of an actual dog. If the presence of an actual dog elicits a fear response, then the presence of the word "Dog" will also elicit that fear response. When this occurs in a context where it may be maladaptive, defusion exercises (e.g., saying "Dog" in a silly voice) transform the function of that stimulus (i.e., the word "Dog") such that it acquires new functions (e.g., it is now also related to "funny") and minimizes the strength of those fear responses in that context. Overall, defusion training strengthens more flexible repertoires of responding to one's private verbal stimuli, thereby decreasing overly rigid avoidant behavior and making room for more flexible responding to aversive private events, including valued action.

SELF-AS-CONTEXT

In behavior-analytic terms, the conceptualized self can be described broadly as rules about self. As with the rules described in the section on defusion, rules about self can be directly trained or derived. Self-as-context involves strengthening two repertoires. The first targets recognizing the verbal stimuli that make up the rule as mere stimuli in the environment. The second repertoire allows for fluid shifting between different conceptualizations of self across varying contexts (i.e., self-as-context as opposed to self-as-content). The former seems to be a product of a repertoire similar to that described in the section on defusion. A difference between defusion and self-as-context is the nature of the rules being recognized. While defusion focuses on rules that are about the world outside of the self, self-as-context involves rules regarding the conceptualized self (e.g., "I waste time by asking questions" vs. "I am smart, and asking that question will make me look stupid"). Fluidly shifting between roles depending on the context occurs as a product of relational responding, primarily via deictic framing where "I" then participates in a number of other relational frames. In the previous example, "I" participates in a frame of coordination with "SMART" and "question asking" participates in a frame of opposition with SMART. This may influence behavior such that the person does not ask a question to ultimately gain information that is necessary to effectively complete a task. In instances where these relations negatively impact socially significant behavior, strengthening the relations between "I" and members of other relational networks (e.g., "I" in a frame of coordination with "learner") and strengthening a repertoire of fluidly shifting between them depending on current context may promote more adaptive behavior (e.g., asking that question).

In summary, self-as-context involves building a repertoire in which one recognizes the conceptualized self (i.e., rules about self) as part of the environment, and not as a separate "thing" that *is* a certain way (e.g., "good," "bad," "lazy"). Stated differently, self-as-context involves teaching a repertoire of noticing one's verbal descriptions of self and behaving more flexibly in relation to those descriptions in a way that is more adaptive for a given context and that can shift flexibly as the context changes.

PRESENT MOMENT

Yet another layer of the double-edged language sword we humans carry is our ability to verbally construct and, to some extent, actually experience moments that were either lived in the past or have not yet been experienced and may never actually be. We are able to time-travel due to a history of relating stimuli via deictic framing, where "I" can participate in several larger networks, which then, through transformation of stimulus function, can be experienced as though the actual event were taking place in that moment. For example, because they are members of the same stimulus class, hearing the word "Run" may lead to one visualizing running, which may be verbally related to going for a run that morning, which is related to almost getting hit by that guy in the red car, which elicits responses similar to those present when you almost got hit by that car.

This verbal time traveling becomes maladaptive when an individual is overly focused on the stimuli involved in experiencing the past or future and is thus not attending to stimuli in their immediate environment that are relevant to meaningful behavior in that moment. For example, if a person is driving while attending to private verbal stimuli related to how badly they messed up at work that day, they may not see the car in front of them stop and might crash into it. Another example is a nervous student who is so focused on thoughts about not understanding what their teacher is saying that they completely miss what is being communicated. Attending to stimuli in the immediate environment can increase contact with reinforcement for behavior happening in that moment. Strengthening this present moment attending response allows for one to more flexibly shift their attention to relevant stimuli in their environment when necessary to engage in valued action.

COMMITTED ACTION

Committed action is perhaps most easily understood through a behavior-analytic lens. Committed action refers to the socially significant behavior that occurs for the purpose of accessing the delayed verbally constructed reinforcer in line with one's values, even though aversive stimuli are present prior to and/or co-occur with that target behavior. Committed action is made up of specific, observable, and measurable behavior that is accomplished via common behavior-analytic techniques (e.g., behavior contracts, goal-setting, self-management strategies, reinforcement). For example, if a person identifies health as a value, a committed action may be to go to the gym on Tuesday at 6 p.m. for 60 minutes. Unlike values, committed actions are achievable and attainable. The ultimate aim of ACT is to follow these committed actions in service of one's values, and the remaining pieces of the hexaflex help with this process.

ACT WITHOUT THE HEXAFLEX

If ACT is understood purely in behavior-analytic principles, as described previously, then it should be possible to use behavioral principles and procedures to strengthen the repertoires described previously, without the need for the "middle level" (easy-to-use constructs based on basic principles) terms comprising the hexaflex (acceptance, values, etc.). One potential rationale for taking this approach is to avoid the potential limitations of using middle-level terms. Perhaps most concerning is the possibility that practitioners will implement the procedures named in the hexaflex as mere technology, without the hexaflex being systematically understood in terms of basic behavioral principles. In the worst case scenario, implementation of ACT may be completely divorced from an understanding of how it works in terms of behavior-analytic principles, for example, by using the terms contained in the hexaflex as hypothetical causal constructs. Another potential challenge one might imagine is using ACT procedures, in name and in topography, but in such a way as to change behavior because of the *wrong* processes entirely. For example, if one discusses "values" with a client in a way that comes off as authoritarian and judgmental, then the client's behavior may indeed change in the desired direction. But this result is more because of avoidance of aversive interactions with the behavior analyst than because of the transformation and augmenting of positive reinforcement functions that values procedures are intended to bring about.

Any time that a new body of work is disseminated, a profession runs the risk of adopting it in a piecemeal fashion, inconsistently, or just generally at a low level of quality. This would presumably be the case for the adoption of ACT within ABA, just like any other new area of research and practice within ABA. ABA's adoption of ACT may be at especially high risk for being done as mere technology, without sufficient training in the behavioral principles underlying it for a number of reasons. First, the behavioral repertoires that are addressed in ACT are different from those that are typically addressed and understood functionally in mainstream ABA. For example, it is far easier to understand tantrums or manding (aka requesting) in terms of behavioral principles than it is to understand the behavior of a parent saying they "feel like a bad mother." Reducing such a statement to traditional behavioral functions such as tangible, attention, and escape, which result in immediate access to overt operant reinforcement, without regard to relational frames, rule governance, and so on, would be naively simplistic. It may not be surprising, then, that many articles published on ACT inside ABA have not attempted to discuss the hexaflex from the standpoint of behavioral principles. And it is possible, still, that ACT procedures are powerful enough that they may often actually work, even without a meaningful functional understanding of how or why. However, even if this is the case, in order to remain conceptually systematic, it is critical that behavior analysts not ignore addressing ACT in a behavior-analytic way.

One option for addressing the potential challenge of ABA researchers and practitioners adopting the ACT hexaflex only as technology would be to simply omit the hexaflex in adopting ACT into the ABA pantheon. One might think of ACT as a very complex treatment package with many components. It is common in the field of ABA to identify and implement individual treatment components, often one at a time, and usually referring only to their technical names. Doing so with ACT procedures might proceed along the lines of identifying the particular behaviors one wants to strengthen and identify the behavioral procedures for doing so. For example, rather than "working on values" with a client, one might notice a lack of motivation in one's client and then work on identifying "verbally mediated motivating operations or augmentals." Or, instead of "training a client on defusion strategies," one might notice particularly rigid rule-governed behavior in one's client and work on training more flexible rule-governed behavior. It is possible that the verbal repertoires of ABA researchers and practitioners will evolve in this direction. However, given that virtually all ACT literature has been communicated using the hexaflex, virtually all ACT trainers have been trained using the hexaflex, and virtually all published treatment studies supporting ACT have been conducted by experimenters who were trained using the hexaflex, We believe that adopting the hexaflex by translating it purely in terms of behavior analytic principles, as we have done here, is likely to be the most efficient tactic for disseminating ACT within the ABA community at this time. Applied behavior analysts may still utilize the techniques taught in ACT much like we learned useful techniques for discrete trial teaching and mand training, but hopefully we are all aware of the basic principles that underlie such techniques and can adjust our procedures as appropriate.

Review of Research on ACT Inside Behavior Analysis

There are likely many different ways to conceptualize research on ACT inside behavior analysis, stemming from the various ways in which one might answer the question, what qualifies a study as ACT inside behavior analysis? Is it the presence of a behavior analytic conceptual analysis, the participant population, the behavior analytic training/credentials of the researchers implementing the intervention, the use of single-case designs, the inclusion of direct measures of behavior, publication in a behavioral journal, or some combination of any or all of these? There is no widely agreed upon definition of what "counts" as ACT inside behavior analysis, nor would such a rigid definition be useful. In the following section, we review research from each of these perspectives. We also refer readers to a recent systematic review paper by Suarez, Moon, and Najdowski (2022) on research on ACT in the context of supporting individuals with autism and other developmental challenges.

Acceptance and Commitment Training for Staff

Although the majority of the literature on ACT in the workplace discusses how ACT is correlated with indirect measures such as decreased burnout, increased job satisfaction, increased psychological flexibility, and so on, a handful of studies have evaluated how it might influence direct measures of behavior change in the workplace (e.g., Bond & Flaxman, 2006; Brooker et al., 2014; Dahl, Wilson, & Nilsson, 2004). For example, Bond and Flaxman (2006) demonstrated a correlation between psychological flexibility scores and a person's ability to learn a new work skill (i.e., utilization of a computer software program). While correlational, these results demonstrate a potential relationship between psychological flexibility and overt behavior. In another study, Dahl and colleagues (2004) compared participants who received four 1-hour weekly ACT interventions to those who received regular medical treatment in a randomized trial, and showed that members of the ACT group used fewer sick days and fewer medical resources relative to the control group.

A growing body of literature is using multiple baseline designs to demonstrate a functional relationship between the ACT intervention and the behavior of staff working with individuals who have developmental disabilities. Castro and colleagues (2016) evaluated the effects of values and committed action interventions on frequency of client engagement for a three-day program for staff working with adults with severe developmental disabilities. During their initial baseline observations, which consisted of 15-minute sessions occurring at a rate of two to three times per week in the normal classroom environment, participants were observed to engage with their clients at low rates, with stable data ranging from zero to three instances per observation period just prior to intervention. Following protocol for a multiple baseline design across participants, each staff member was systematically exposed to a workshop series consisting of three brief (20–40 minute) intervention sessions. During each workshop session, participants walked through a values exercise (the Bullseye Activity, a version of the Cycling Race Metaphor, and a paper t-shirts exercise) for the purpose of clarifying their work values and established committed actions. Updates on committed actions were shared at the beginning of each subsequent session. Following this series of values interventions, increases in staff engagement were observed for all three participants. In a second intervention, each participant revisited the same values and committed action workshop series, but with an emphasis on client-centered values rather than overall work values. Data showed further increases in staff interactions with clients for two of the three participants, and social validity reports were positive overall. While the values and committed action treatment clearly had a substantial effect on staff engagement with clients, it is unknown whether these increases would be maintained over time.

In a subsequent study, Chancey and colleagues (2019) used a multiple baseline design across participants to measure changes in the frequency of staff engagement following a brief present moment intervention. Participants consisted of three staff members who worked with adults with developmental disabilities, supporting them with their daily living skills. The intervention consisted of five workshops, each lasting 15 minutes per day and occurring at a rate of two to three times per week. The first three workshops in the series consisted of didactic training on the definition and purpose of mindfulness, a discussion of mindfulness, and a review of the definition of mindfulness, respectively. Following the discussion in each session, participants were walked through a present moment exercise (Notice Five Things, Mindfulness of the Body, and a mindful eating exercise, respectively). In the fourth workshop of the series, participants were guided through another present moment exercise (Mindfulness of Your Hand). In the final workshop, a brief discussion about the definition of mindfulness was conducted, followed by a final mindfulness exercise that consisted of imagining mindfully completing a chore.

Increases in client interactions were observed for all three participants following intervention, with these increases continuing through the remainder of treatment, as well as during maintenance observations, and with overall positive responses on the staff's social validity measurement. It should be noted that the experimenters' definition of "staff interactions" did not separate negative from positive interactions, and authors suggested that future research specifically evaluate increases in positive interactions (though it seems hard to imagine why present moment training would increase negative staff interactions). Moreover, while maintenance data were collected, observations were conducted close in time to the intervention, approximately 2 days following the intervention phase. Another interesting detail is that scores on AAQ-II increased for two participants from baseline to posttest, indicating increased levels of experiential avoidance following the mindfulness intervention. However, it is possible that decreases in psychological flexibility as measured by the AAQ-II occur subsequent to a history of reinforcement with direct contingencies being established. In other words, behavioral flexibility and willingness to experience the aversive stimuli may precede changes in psychological flexibility. It is also worth noting that the ultimate goal of ACT is to increase values-directed overt behavior and that merely endorsing questions on a self-report measure of psychological flexibility, in itself, may not be a socially meaningful outcome.

Recent research has also evaluated ACT in combination with typical behavior-analytic staff training techniques. In an A-B-BC multiple baseline design across participants, Pingo and colleagues (2020a) measured behavior change for five direct service provider staff following feedback and combined feedback and ACT intervention conditions. Direct measures included percent of time which staff engaged in active treatment during the observation intervals, percent of time that this active treatment was taking place at the beginning of the observation period, and fidelity of behavior-analytic teaching skills observed to occur (e.g., immediate delivery of reinforcement, utilization of differential reinforcement). Staff observations were conducted for 15 minutes in the natural care environment with individuals with disabilities. Following baseline, participants contacted the feedback training condition during which the specific behavior change goals (outlined previously) were provided to them in written form. Verbal and written feedback was given to participants following each observation in this condition, with observations occurring at a rate of about three times per week. Participants received written feedback on their performance weekly.

In the combined feedback and ACT condition, a single-day 8-hour didactic and experiential ACT training was delivered either on a computer or in person. The training was completed in a single day and consisted of a general overview of ACT and each area of the hexaflex. More specifically, the first segment of training consisted of a description of ACT along with present moment, defusion, and acceptance, and participants practiced activities consistent with each (i.e., Mindfulness of Your Hand, Leaves on a Stream, and Mindfulness of Emotions). In the subsequent session, values and committed action were described and participants were guided through a values activity during which they identified their own work values, assessed their values in relation to those of the organization, and were asked to create short- and long-term committed actions in line with those values.

While the feedback-only condition produced an increase in all three overt measures being targeted, further change was observed for all three participants when the verbal and written feedback condition was combined with the ACT intervention. When interpreting these results, however, one must also consider the limitations of the study. Data from three of the five participants followed slight increasing trends in the feedback-only condition, making it unclear whether further progress observed within the combined feedback and ACT condition was a product of the combined training or a continuation of the feedback-only intervention. Additionally, two participants demonstrated such an improvement following the feedback-only condition that further change was not obviously detectable moving into the combined condition due to a ceiling effect.

In a between-subjects pretest–posttest design, Pingo and colleagues (2020b) evaluated the same measures outlined in their previous study in addition to the percentage of clients who had learning or leisure materials nearby, and who were engaged in purposeful activities at the beginning of each observation. Indirect measures of job satisfaction, workplace stress, and psychological flexibility were also administered at the beginning and end of their participation in the study. Forty-one full-time direct support staff working with individuals with developmental disabilities of all ages were separated into one of two experimental groups or a control group. Those in the experimental groups participated in a Performance Enhancement Intervention (PEI) Training Group following baseline. This training consisted of direct contingency management via verbal and written feedback and a lottery reinforcement system, with tickets awarded contingent on specific behavioral criteria being met by the individual and/or the group. Barriers to desired performance were evaluated using the Performance Diagnostic Checklist (PDC). Participants in the PEI plus the ACT experimental group were additionally asked to participate in two 4-hour ACT training sessions, occurring 1 to 2 weeks apart. Training procedures were similar to the methods outlined in Pingo and colleagues (2020a). For those in the control group, measurements were collected during pretest and posttest, though no intervention was included. As with Pingo et al. (2020a), results indicated that while statistically significant improvements across all observable measures followed Performance Enhancement Training, the combined PEI and ACT condition yielded significantly better results across observational measures. No significant changes in self report measures were observed.

To add to the growing body of literature on enhancing effective behavior-analytic staff training methods with ACT, Little and colleagues (2020) investigated how ACT might strengthen the outcomes of Behavior Skills Training (BST) with three staff members at a clinic for children with autism. Participants in this study were senior therapists who were responsible for training direct implementation staff. A multiple baseline design across participants was used with an A-B-BC intervention to measure the effect of BST alone, with a subsequent combined BST and ACT condition, on the percent of opportunities in which staff used BST when delivering feedback to the direct instructors. Each 20-minute observation was conducted while the participant performed their normal job responsibilities. Following baseline, each participant met with the experimenter and completed BST on how to implement BST with the direct care staff. All three staff members used more BST immediately following training, with data for all three participants stabilizing around 50 percent occurrence of the target behavior (i.e., BST use). Subsequently, each participant was provided a single one-hour ACT training session, which exposed them to present moment (5-senses and Drop the Anchor), work values identification, and committed action via the Willingness and Action Plan, which involves having participants write down their most important work value, identify a committed action in line with that value, identify difficult private events that may come up that they are willing to make room for (i.e., accept), and then note specific details about when they were going to take this action. All three participants independently identified increasing BST training with staff as their committed action. The experimenter then sent a text prompt to review the committed action worksheet post-ACT intervention and again immediately preceding follow-up. About 24 hours post-ACT training, data revealed increases in the use of BST training for all three participants, with scores remaining high throughout the maintenance and generalization phases. It is unknown whether all components of the ACT intervention were necessary to yield increases in BST use, or whether the text message prompts served as an additional variable, which, in itself, increased the use of BST further. Additionally, no treatment fidelity data were collected on implementation of the ACT intervention.

Acceptance and Commitment Training for Parents

Research has been slow to expand on ACT for parents of children with autism and other challenges, but it is currently increasing. Certainly, the area is ripe for applied behavior-analytic ACT investigations. We review 10 studies involving ACT for parents of children with neurodevelopmental disorders. Of these, only two evaluated changes in socially significant responding measured across behavioral dimensions, such as frequency, duration, or latency.

The earliest study on ACT for parents of children with autism was conducted by Blackledge and Hayes (2006). The authors used a repeated measures approach to evaluate the effects of a 2-day ACT workshop on depression, general health, and ACT processes in 20 participants. ACT reduced general distress and depression at posttreatment, and these results were maintained at 3-month follow-up. Generalized health outcomes showed improvement after 3 months but not at posttreatment assessment. Importantly, Blackledge and Hayes reported reductions in both fusion and experiential avoidance. Although these authors did not employ a straightforward analytic strategy such as that advocated by Baron and Kenny (1986), they used repeated outcome assessments after the intervention to evaluate mediators and found evidence that defusion and acceptance treatment efforts were responsible for the results obtained. Because this was a small sample trial with no control group, the authors conducted some within-subject analysis of outcome variables. Overall effects were not large, but depression scores were greatly reduced compared to other measures in the five participants that started with clinically significant depression scores (Beck Depression Inventory II, 18 or above at baseline). These outcomes were maintained at follow-up.

Also in 2006, Singh et al. published outcomes of a mixed-methods study involving three parent–child dyads trained in mindfulness. The authors used a within-subject, multiple baseline across participants design to evaluate reductions in child noncompliance and aggression. Additionally, Singh et al. reported pre-, mid-, and posttraining practice self-reports of parenting and interaction satisfaction as well as use of mindfulness exercises. Though promising, the child behavioral data showed a large percentage of overlapping data points; thus, these results lacked strong experimental control. It is noteworthy that the investigators in this study did not ask parents to use direct contingencies of reinforcement. It might have been interesting to determine whether the combination of mindfulness and direct contingency management could have produced more rapid or robust child outcomes than either of these strategies by themselves. Nevertheless, mindfulness use, parenting satisfaction, and interaction satisfaction ratings steadily improved across all three parents. Although mindfulness is not equivalent to ACT, the procedures used in this study overlap greatly with procedures commonly used in present moment training in the ACT literature.

After a decade-long gap, Joekar, Farid, Birashk, Gharraee, and Mohammadian (2016) evaluated two forms of counseling to 24 mothers of children with autism. Twelve received an eight-session group ACT workshop; the other 12 received eight sessions of individual counseling, the usual treatment offered in their study's clinical setting. None of the participants were diagnosed with mental or physical health issues, and although they signed up for the study, none of the participants sought formal mental health care before or afterward. Joeckar et al. found that depression and experiential avoidance decreased more among mothers in the ACT group but found no differences between groups with respect to changes in anxiety or quality of life. Unlike Singh et al., the investigators in this study did not evaluate changes in either parent or child behavior. Notably, however, this study was conducted in Iran and added to a rapidly growing base of Middle Eastern reports on the effectiveness of ACT in various populations (e.g., Abasi, Fati, Molodi, & Zarabi, 2013; Asghari, Saed, Dibajnia, & Zangeneh, 2008).

In 2018, several teams investigated ACT with parents of children with autism. Corti et al. (2018) compared an ACT-oriented parent training plus early intensive behavioral intervention (EIBI) to an EIBI-alone control group and, as had Blackledge and Hayes (2006), measured fusion, experiential avoidance, and stress. Corti et al. reported no effect for fusion, a "trend toward" statistical significance for stress, and a paradoxical reduction in mindfulness awareness, which they attributed either to the questionnaires being too complicated or the parents receiving mindfulness training becoming aware of their inner states for the first time. Although it is not unusual that individuals that have been explicitly taught to ignore their physiologies and emotions become aware for the first time during mindfulness training of these inner states (e.g., injured athletes; Mahoney & Hanrahan, 2011), the Corti et al. participant sample was large and diverse enough ($n = 20$) to likely rule out such interpretations. That said, the fact that parents in the ACT + EIBI group worsened in mindfulness awareness and did not improve defusion skills after 12 sessions requires some interpretation. The authors did offer other possible explanations and suggested that future research was needed to parse the discrepancies in their findings with those of other studies.

In two connected studies, Fung et al. (2018) and Lunsky et al. (2018) evaluated ACT delivered to mothers of children with acute stress disorder (ASD) by other mothers of children with ASD. These studies involved a cohort of 33 parents that were exposed to an evening session followed by a full-day session and a booster session after 1 month. Lunsky et al. published data suggesting that ACT presented by other parents was feasible, easy to recruit for, well attended, and satisfactory to participants. The authors also evaluated stress, depression, health, and isolation. Of the four outcome variables assessed, only isolation did not reach statistical significance at posttest and follow-up. Fung et al. evaluated changes from pretest, posttest, and follow-up in depression and stress as well as ACT process measures, specifically, psychological flexibility, fusion, and values. Parents were also asked to report whether they changed behavior with respect to parenting, relationships, and self-care. All three process measures showed positive changes at posttest and follow-up. Reductions in depression and stress correlated at posttest, with self-reported changes in valued activity frequencies and at follow-up with decreased cognitive fusion. Taken together, these reports suggest that a train-the-trainer model in which brief ACT workshops are delivered to parents by other parents of children with autism is potentially useful and cost effective.

Also in 2018, Gould et al. reported results from a nonconcurrent multiple baseline design across participants with three parents of children with ASD exposed to six 90-minute training sessions. The authors delivered exercises targeting all six ACT processes and measured self-reported changes in psychological flexibility, self-compassion, and the positive and negative impacts of having a child with a disability. Importantly, the authors also asked parents to collect data on the frequency of their own values-directed overt behaviors that they targeted for change prior to baseline. Results were favorable across all process measures, and values-directed behaviors seemed to increase even more dramatically at 7- and 8-month follow-up for two participants than at postevaluations. The behavioral data should be viewed with caution, however, because the records were collected by the participants themselves. Formal interobserver agreement data were not collected. Rather, participants submitted corroborating evidence that the behaviors occurred, in the form of photographs (e.g., "selfies") of the participants engaging in the behaviors or credit card receipts documenting purchases associated with the behaviors. This method was used because the dependent variables consisted of socially meaningful behaviors that occurred in the absence of clinicians; therefore, no professionals could be present to collect formal interobserver agreement data. Moreover, many of the behaviors occurred in community locations (e.g., restaurants, parks), where videotaping would be unwieldy or inappropriate. Although the primary dependent variable consisted of self-monitored frequency data, the corroborating evidence was unconventional by ABA standards because it did not measure the dimensional properties of actual responding. Nevertheless, the primary dependent variable consisted of frequency data. As far as we are aware, this was the first published study on ACT-based parent training for parents of children with autism that included direct measures of overt parent behavior.

Hahs et al. (2019) compared ACT delivered in two 2-hour sessions to a concurrent no treatment control condition and evaluated statistical and effect-size outcomes on self-report measures of psychological flexibility, mindfulness, cognitive fusion, values, depression, and shame. Significant effects found in six of the eight measures suggest that this format of ACT could be efficacious for increasing elements of psychological flexibility and decreasing depression and shame. The experimental strategy, a pre-/post randomized controlled trial, is not a commonly used design in ABA, but it yielded favorable preliminary findings. Although the small sample size (n = 18) limits the generality of these findings, the statistical significance of the outcomes and moderate effect sizes on six of the eight measures is promising.

From the same research group, Yi and Dixon (2020) published randomized controlled trial (RCT) data and a manual for providing telehealth ABA parent training including ACT to enhance parent adherence in the context of the COVID-19 pandemic that began in 2020. After an initial onboarding meeting that included a 30-minute ACT session, the model involved five self-paced skill development lessons delivered on an online learner management platform and five individual consultations with follow-up coaching that was available contingent upon completion of online lessons. The 30-minute ACT session embedded in the onboarding meeting included present moment awareness, acceptance, and valuing exercises, followed by a description of 10 tips for increasing motivation for practicing new skills and pursuing valued goals. The five self-paced lessons included instruction in the principles of behavior, behavior management, and teaching skills to children. Parents who received the supplemental ACT material made significantly more progress than controls and were less likely to drop out. Despite the very small sample and delivery during the chaotic early stages of the pandemic, the results of this study are promising, and the manual, blending ABA and ACT instruction, could potentially be valuable to providers during and after the global health crisis.

The final study on parent training reviewed here was conducted in outpatient and inpatient clinics located in India. Poddar, Sinha, and Urbi (2015) used a repeated measures design to evaluate ACT delivered in 10 sessions over 2 months for treating anxiety, depression, psychological inflexibility, and diminished quality of life after parents received the diagnosis of autism for their children. Pre- to post results were significant on all measures. As was the case for Joekar et al. (2016), this study took place in a nation with limited support for psychosocial interventions for parental distress. Thus, it is a noteworthy contribution to an area of research with substantial need in lower- and middle-income nations.

Taken together, literature on the use of ACT to help parents of children with neurodevelopmental disorders is in its infancy. The increased levels of distress and alienation that parents of children with these disorders experience is well documented, but evidence-based treatments for parents in comparison to their children with disabilities have been slow to develop. In this section, we presented the emerging ACT literature in this area chronologically to provide evidence that there is a growing global interest among ACT researchers in developing interventions for this population and that the existing evidence shows promise. Additional research is needed to address issues with respect to mediation and moderation of treatment outcomes, durability of outcomes, level of clinician training and competency, and in some nations, the issue of whether paraprofessionals can be taught to implement ACT with parents who are in need of assistance. Also, researchers ought to collect data on dimensional aspects of behavior (i.e., frequency, latency, and duration). Self-report measures provide a useful index, but unless valued behavior is observed and measured, the extent of change cannot be evaluated or verified. RCTs are vital to research programs aiming to expand the use of contextual behavior treatments outside the small bubble of applied behavior analysis autism clinics. However, the results reported in this section suggest that more fine-grained analyses of treatment components are needed to fully answer the question Gordon Paul asked over 50 years ago: "What treatment, by whom, is most effective for this individual, with what specific problem, under which set of circumstances, and how does it come about?" (Paul, 1969, p. 44). This question, often dubbed the *ultimate* clinical question, begs an answer. Behavior analysts are in a good position to use within-subject designs for measuring dimensional changes in behavior to help answer this question with respect to parents of children with developmental disorders.

Acceptance and Commitment Training for Individuals with Autism

The body of evidence supporting the application of ACT to individuals with autism and related disorders has been expanding in recent years. Although the research is still emerging, ACT could be particularly useful for individuals with ASD because the diagnosis is characterized by behavioral rigidity (American Psychiatric Association, 2013) and there is some evidence that individuals with autism may experience higher levels of fusion than neurotypical peers (Maisel, Stephenson, Cox, & South, 2019). An early study involved a quasi-experimental comparison of small-group ACT training for adolescents with ASD to a waitlist control, in the context of a special education setting (Pahnke, Lundgren, Hursti, & Hirvikoski, 2014). ACT training consisted of twice-weekly 40-minute small-group training, for 6 weeks, for a total of approximately 8 hours of small-group training with an ACT trainer. In addition, special education teachers facilitated 6- to 12-minute daily mindfulness exercises in the classrooms, and students were asked to complete brief homework assignments that touched on mindfulness and self-monitoring of values-directed behaviors. Dependent variables consisted of teacher and student reports on questionnaires, and results indicated that the ACT group experienced decreases in stress, hyperactivity, and emotional distress, as well as increases in reports of prosocial behavior, and that the improvements were maintained or increased at 2-month follow-up.

In what was among the first studies applying ACT to individuals with autism in an ABA context, Eilers and Hayes (2015) conducted two experiments that evaluated defusion and exposure for decreasing direct measures of overt challenging behaviors displayed by six children with ASD. All children in the study displayed challenging behaviors (e.g., crying, aggression, running away) when experiencing situations that were disruptive to their preferred routines. Disruptions in routines were unique for each child but included scenarios such as a toy train track being disconnected, another person attempting to take turns during block play, and presentation of novel foods. In the first multiple baseline experiment across three children, experimenters implemented a combined defusion and exposure treatment package, in which experimenters asked the participants to use a "silly voice" to repeat their thoughts about the problematic situation for 30 seconds. After 30 seconds, the participants were told to continue to repeat the thoughts to themselves, while experiencing 5 minutes of a scenario that broke their preferred routine. All three participants demonstrated substantial decreases in challenging behavior after defusion and exposure training.

In Eilers and Hayes's (2015) second experiment, the researchers attempted to evaluate the separate effects of the defusion and exposure components by comparing their separate effects in an alternating treatments design with four children with autism, one of whom had participated in the first experiment. The defusion plus exposure condition was the same as the one that was evaluated in experiment 1, and it was compared to an exposure-only control condition. In the exposure-only control condition, participants were instructed to repeat statements (e.g., "The sky is blue") that were not related to their challenging behavior surrounding rigid routines. Both conditions involved the participant then experiencing their routine being broken; therefore, both involved exposure, but only one included defusion. Both procedures resulted in decreases in challenging behaviors and increases in socially meaningful replacement behaviors, but the defusion procedure produced larger and/or more rapid effects for three of four participants.

Brazeau and colleagues (2017) used a multiple baseline across participants design to evaluate the effectiveness of present moment and defusion components of ACT in supporting three young adults in developing job interviewing skills. The dependent variable consisted of the percentage of correct responses on a job interview skill checklist, which included nonvocal behaviors (e.g., posture, eye contact, fidgeting) and vocal behaviors (e.g., answering job interview questions on-topic and related to the particular job being interviewed for), administered in the context of simulated job interviews. ACT training consisted of mindful walking, mindful breathing, and mindful body scan procedures. Defusion procedures (e.g., Name That Tune) were added for one participant who reported that she did not prefer the mindfulness training procedures. Training sessions were conducted for approximately 15 minutes before each simulated job interview. Two of the three participants demonstrated substantially improved performance during the ACT training condition, and behavioral skills training was added to further enhance the effects for one, as well as produce initial effects for the third. Across the two participants for whom ACT training alone was effective, the total duration before a substantial effect was observed ranged from 15 to 75 minutes, representing rapid treatment effects.

Szabo (2019) used a multiple baseline to evaluate a 4-hour one-on-one ACT training for addressing inflexibility in children with ASD. Three 8- to 10-year-old boys with ASD participated. All participants had a history of engaging in inflexible behavior, consisting of vocal protesting, aggression, and refusal to participate when routines were changed, especially when the rules for games were altered. Standard experimental functional analyses yielded inconclusive results for the inflexible behavior. ACT training consisted of games that physicalized ACT processes, such as reading a book that makes adults say silly things (defusion), holding ice cubes (acceptance), walking in unison with the experimenter (present moment), wearing nametags with "I . . . " statements (self-as-context), and playing blob tag and doing trust falls (values). After each exercise, the researcher debriefed the child by coaching the child through discussion of the questions "What happened?", "So what?", and "Now what?", in order to practice present moment, contact values, and make commitments. After ACT training, inflexible behaviors were reduced substantially across all participants, and participants began to request that rules be changed during subsequent games. This suggested that the function of flexibility per se may have been transformed to be less aversive, or perhaps even positively reinforcing.

Not all published research on ACT for individuals with ASD have shown it to be effective. For example, Maisel, Stephenson, Cox, and South (2019) compared the effects of defusion to distraction in adults with autism in a brief lab study. Thought identification, thought rating, and defusion strategies were implemented, and effects were compared to distraction strategies on measures of thought believability and thought discomfort, across individuals with autism and neurotypical individuals. Results showed no difference in effects when comparing defusion to distraction, but both groups demonstrated substantial improvements compared to pretest. A no-treatment control group was not included. The authors interpreted the findings as evidence for equal effectiveness of defusion and distraction, but in the absence of a no-treatment control, it also seems possible that neither treatment was effective. Instead, it is possible that other factors (e.g., repeated exposure to testing) were responsible for the changes seen in the dependent variables.

Similarly, Garcia-Zambrano and colleagues (2019) used a randomized between-groups design to evaluate a brief defusion and self-as-context intervention for increasing self-as-context statements and decreasing self-as-content statements in individuals with ASD, ages 13–21. The dependent variable consisted of the rate of directly measured verbal statements during interviews that were 8–11 minutes in duration. The intervention consisted of a single implementation of the chessboard procedure, with an actual chessboard present. Participants in the control condition engaged in a general conversation about themselves and their therapy, not directed toward defusion or self-as-context. Self-as-context statements increased and self-as-content statements decreased for the treatment group after treatment, but the differences in outcome between groups were not statistically significant. The intervention could likely have been too brief (i.e., a single brief conversation), or the sample sizes could have been too small (i.e., only 10 participants per group) to detect an effect, especially considering that there was large intragroup variability.

ACT Research Expanding the Scope of Behavior Analytic Intervention

One of the greatest potential contributions of ACT to behavior analysis is the potential to expand the reach of behavior analysis into a broader and more comprehensive scope of complex human behavior. Behavior analysts have published a small number of studies on the application of ACT to populations and/or behaviors that they less commonly address. A small number of studies on ACT have also been published by researchers who are perhaps best thought of as clinical psychologists but are also behavior analysts, applying ACT to populations that occupy the "gray area" between the two disciplines. We describe several studies of both kinds. We intentionally leave out studies on ACT that use single-case designs applied to more traditionally clinical populations (e.g., obsessive-compulsive disorder), as well as studies that use single-case designs but use indirect measures rather than direct measures of behavior, as these studies are addressed by other chapters in this volume.

Sports and Fitness

A recent study by Wang, Tarbox, Chastain, and Cameron (2020) evaluated the effects of an ACT coaching program for increasing physical activity in bilingual international university students. The study used a multiple baseline design across participants to evaluate the effects of a one-on-one coaching program, consisting of weekly brief (approximately 20 minutes) sessions, for 5 weeks. All four participants went from being completely sedentary in baseline to meeting or exceeding all of their exercise goals during intervention and throughout follow-up.

In another application of ACT and ABA to sports and fitness, Szabo, Willis, and Palinski (2019) evaluated the effects of adding ACT to traditional contingency management ABA procedures to improve the performance of athletes in competitive rock climbing. They used a multiple baseline to measure the effects on three dependent variables: (1) arriving late for team practice, (2) heart rate, and (3) length of falls (an indirect measure of assertive performance). Participants consisted of young adults with ASD who were living and working in typical community settings and had highly developed verbal repertoires. The traditional ABA procedures consisted of instructions, shaping, stimulus control, goal-setting, and feedback. The ACT intervention consisted of three approximately 2-hour training sessions, referred to as the Watch Me Try approach. The first session focused on present moment attention, the second on acceptance and self-as-context, and the third on values and committed action. One participant's performance improved substantially with traditional ABA procedures, while the other two participants required the ACT intervention for their behavior to change substantially. The study is relatively unique in that it evaluated the separate additive effects of ACT, above and beyond traditional ABA approaches, as opposed to the majority of research on ACT inside ABA, which has evaluated ACT either alone or as part of a multicomponent intervention with ABA procedures.

Trichotillomania

Several studies have evaluated a combination of ACT with habit reversal training for the treatment of trichotillomania (i.e., hairpulling disorder) in the context of single-case designs, using self-monitored direct measures of the overt behavior of hairpulling. Twohig and Woods (2004) evaluated the effects of ACT and habit reversal for decreasing hairpulling behavior in six neurotypical adults, ages 20–50, who were diagnosed with trichotillomania. Treatment was conducted in seven weekly sessions. The first four sessions consisted of 60 minutes of ACT training each, while sessions 5–7 consisted of habit reversal training in the context of ACT, session 5 lasting 60 minutes and sessions 6 and 7 lasting 30 minutes each. Treatment was conducted according to a manual, and treatment integrity data were assessed during 25 percent of the sessions, yielding an overall treatment integrity score of 100 percent. ACT alone produced substantial reductions in hairpulling for four of six participants. The addition of habit reversal produced robust effects for one additional participant, while the sixth participant did not experience a substantial reduction in the behavior. Of the five participants who demonstrated robust treatment effects, three maintained their reductions at 3-month follow-up, one did not, and one was not available for follow-up data.

Similar methods and results were reported by Crosby, Dehlin, Mitchell, and Twohig (2012). They evaluated the effects of adding habit reversal to ACT training for reducing hair-pulling behavior in five neurotypical participants, ages 18–32 years, in a multiple baseline design. ACT alone produced substantial reductions in the behavior for three of five participants, with the remaining two participants requiring the addition of habit reversal training to reduce the behavior. At 3-month follow-up, two maintained substantial treatment gains, two maintained some gains, and one demonstrated behavior at pretreatment levels.

Skin Picking

Twohig, Hayes, and Masuda (2006) conducted a preliminary evaluation of ACT for the treatment of chronic skin picking in a multiple baseline across five neurotypical white women, ages 19–28. Participants were trained to collect frequency data on their own behavior of picking skin, operationally defined as "using one's fingers or an instrument to attempt or actually remove a piece of skin." ACT was conducted according to a manual and consisted of eight weekly sessions that covered commonly used ACT procedures, tailored to skin picking, and the treatment intentionally excluded any habit reversal treatment components. Treatment integrity data were collected, and the mean integrity score was 4.4 out of 5, indicating high procedural fidelity. Skin picking reduced to near-zero levels for four of the five participants, with the fifth participant achieving a substantial reduction. At 3 months posttreatment, substantial reductions in skin picking maintained for only one participant, with partial reductions maintaining for two of the other four participants.

Discussion of Research

ACT from the Lens of the Seven Dimensions of Applied Behavior Analysis

Elsewhere (Tarbox, 2018; Tarbox et al., 2020) we have written about how to assess ACT from the standpoint of the seven dimensions of ABA proposed by Baer, Wolf, and Risley (1968). We will not repeat our previously published discussions here, but a brief discussion of the research reviewed previously from the standpoint of the seven dimensions is in order.

APPLIED

The majority of the research studies reviewed included behaviors of clear social importance, for example, implementation of evidence-based staff training procedures, engaging in parental self-care, decreases in child destructive behaviors, and decreases in hairpulling or skin picking. To date, research on ACT inside behavior analysis appears to be strong in the dimension of *applied.*

BEHAVIORAL

Some behavior analysts have been concerned about the common use of indirect self-report measures in ACT research published in the context of clinical psychology, as opposed to including direct measures of overt behavior. There is a place for indirect self-report measures, particularly in randomized trials and in research where the experimenters do not have direct access to measure overt behaviors and the participants cannot reasonably be trained to directly measure their own overt behavior. However, most of the research reviewed previously also demonstrates that direct measures of behavior can be included when evaluating ACT interventions, and that ACT consistently produces substantial changes in overt behaviors. In the case of behavior displayed by typically developing adults during their normal everyday lives, where behavioral professionals cannot possibly follow them around to collect data, participants were trained to self-monitor and directly measure their own overt behaviors (Gould, Tarbox, & Coyne, 2018; Twohig & Woods, 2004; Crosby et al., 2012). A notable exception to direct measurement of overt behavior is the parent training research described previously, in which only two of ten studies included direct measures of behavior. Future research on ACT approaches to parent training within ABA should include direct measures of overt parent behavior, whenever possible.

ANALYTIC

The characteristic of research being analytic, meaning that it uses valid experimental designs to evaluate a functional relationship between dependent and independent variables, is a common feature of most intervention research published in current peer-reviewed journals. So it is perhaps not surprising that the vast majority of research reviewed previously used single-case experimental designs, primarily multiple baselines, to demonstrate control of behavior by implementing ACT-based interventions. However, several of the studies described previously used within-group pre-post designs, which lack experimental control. These designs can certainly be appropriate for initial proof-of-concept, but future research on ACT inside ABA must endeavor to use valid experimental designs, both single-case and randomized trials.

CONCEPTUALLY SYSTEMATIC

A substantial area for potential for further development of the research described previously is the extent to which it is conceptually systematic with behavioral principles. Being conceptually systematic is important when research is communicated in peer-reviewed journals and in how behavioral principles are used to design, execute, and fine-tune interventions. In the research reviewed in this chapter, ACT is most commonly described in middle-level terms, which are useful for communicating to a broad audience. But within any science, conceptual coherence is important to ensure that continued developments in research contribute to extending the science in a cumulative manner and prevent conceptual eclecticism. Use of middle-level terms in place of conceptually systematic accounts will likely contribute to conceptual confusion and incoherence. However, if middle-level terms are used as nothing more than names for more complex sets of phenomena that are communicated and understood in conceptually systematic technical terms, then they should pose no risk. We hope that adoption of the hexaflex within the field of ABA will proceed along these lines and that future research on ACT inside ABA will endeavor to include more thorough analyses of their procedures from the standpoint of basic behavioral principles.

TECHNOLOGICAL

The need to define and communicate behavior-analytic procedures in a manner that is sufficiently technological so as to be replicated by others is another area in which ACT research inside behavior analysis could be developed. Although many manualized protocols for ACT exist and many scripts for implementing ACT are freely available online, most research described previously did not state that the intervention was implemented according to a manual, did not clearly operationally define the procedures, and did not report procedural fidelity data (with Gould, Tarbox, & Coyne, 2018; Twohig & Woods, 2004; Crosby, Dehlin, Mitchell, & Twohig, 2012 as notable exceptions). To some extent, this may be expected, given that, by definition, ACT is a flexible, contextually sensitive training approach. In some sense, proper implementation of ACT requires some level of flexibility. Still, future behavior analytic research on ACT should endeavor to clearly define trainer competencies and operationally define procedural fidelity to a more precise degree, in order to aid in replication and dissemination.

GENERALITY

The vast majority of the studies reviewed previously did not assess generalization of the effects of the ACT interventions that were evaluated. This may be considered strange, given that the very purpose of ACT is to address verbal processes that are highly portable across time and contexts. As a very new area of research, perhaps it is not surprising that research on ACT inside behavior analysis has not yet matured to the point of addressing generalization, as is common in many newer areas of research. Still, future research on ACT in ABA should explicitly program for generalization, for example, by training ACT skills across multiple exemplars of settings or behaviors, and explicitly measure the generalization of those skills and resulting behavior changes, across untrained settings, contexts, and behaviors.

EFFECTIVE

In the majority of the research described previously, participant behaviors changed substantially as a function of receiving ACT training, suggesting that ACT can be highly effective. Of course, no intervention is perfect, and some studies produced more mild effects as well. Now that a significant selection of studies have demonstrated initial efficacy of ACT inside ABA, future research should attempt to *compare* the effectiveness of ACT-based approaches to more traditional ABA approaches and/or evaluate the *additive* effects of implementing ACT on top of a baseline of traditional ABA procedures (e.g., Little et al., 2020).

Summary of ACT Research Methods in Behavior Analytic Research

COMPONENTS OF ACT COMMONLY INCLUDED

The research described previously varies, from implementing the full ACT treatment package to implementing only one or two components. For example, Chancey and colleagues (2019) demonstrated that present moment training alone changed staff behavior, while Little and colleagues (2020) implemented present moment training combined with values and committed action to change staff behavior. Similarly, Brazeau and colleagues (2017) implemented defusion and present moment with individuals with autism, whereas Szabo (2019) implemented a comprehensive ACT protocol with individuals with autism, and both studies produced substantial changes in behavior. At the current state of the literature on ACT inside ABA, it is not clear to what extent and under what conditions the full ACT protocol versus piecemeal implementation is necessary or sufficient to produce socially meaningful behavior change. Future research should attempt to systematically evaluate procedures for helping clinicians and researchers decide which, if any, ACT components to use with which client, for which behaviors, and in which settings. Developing something akin to a pretreatment ACT functional analysis procedure may increase the precision of the ACT treatment literature inside ABA, as well as potentially make ACT treatment more targeted and therefore perhaps more effective.

DURATION AND DOSE

The number of sessions of ACT that were implemented in the research described in this chapter range from 1 (Little et al., 2020) to about 12 (Corti et al., 2018). The duration of each individual training session ranged from very brief (e.g., 15 minutes; Chancey et al., 2019) to longer "workshop" formats (e.g., 8 hours; Pingo et al., 2020a). The total duration of session time ranged from approximately one hour (Little et al., 2020) to about 9 hours (Gould et al., 2018). The total duration, in calendar days, is often not reported but can be deduced to be 1 day (Little et al., 2020) to 12 weeks (Corti et al., 2018). With a few exceptions, the total dose and duration of ACT that have been researched inside of ABA has been quite brief, suggesting that ACT interventions inside of behavior analysis can be efficient. However, in one of the few published studies on ACT in ABA showing a lack of effectiveness, the intervention was very brief; only about 15 minutes in duration (Garcia-Zambrano et al., 2019). Thus, it seems possible that extremely brief interventions are less likely to be effective. However, much further research is needed to determine the approximate dose and duration of ACT that may be required to produce relatively easy behavior changes (e.g., giving feedback at work), versus relatively difficult ones (e.g., moving from a sedentary to physically active lifestyle).

RESEARCH SETTINGS

Much of the research described previously was carried out in traditional behavior-analytic settings, for example, clinics that serve individuals with autism. This makes good sense from the standpoint of establishing ACT within the behavior analytic community. However, it would be encouraging to see ACT research used as a context for creating greater collaboration between researchers and practitioners from ABA and other allied disciplines. For example, if behavior analysts collaborated with other disciplines on ACT research in settings that traditionally do not include behavior analysts, it could lead to further inroads into expanding the scope of behavior analytic practice, as well as fostering greater interdisciplinary collaboration. Community mental health settings, primary care clinics, hospitals, substance abuse treatment centers, and public schools all seem to be settings ripe for fruitful collaboration.

EXPERIMENTAL DESIGNS

Single-case designs are a defining feature of behavior analytic research (Kazdin, 2011). It is perhaps no surprise, then, that a large proportion of research on ACT inside behavior analysis has used single-case designs. A small but growing amount of research has used group designs to investigate ACT with populations that are typically served by behavior analytic practitioners. The choice between single-case versus group designs when researching behavior analytic applications of ACT is an interesting one and may be largely driven by the intended primary audience for the study. If the primary purpose of the publication is to evaluate and disseminate ACT within the behavior analytic community, then a small, well-controlled multiple baseline design is likely going to be more effective than a much larger, much more resource-intensive randomized trial. However, if the intent of the publication is to demonstrate to the larger scientific and policymaking community that behavior analysts can effectively implement ACT to bring about meaningful outcomes, then large-scale RCTs are almost certain to be more effective.

Challenges and Future Directions

Behavior-Analytic Research on Components of ACT

ACT is a complex multicomponent intervention. Ample research has supported the effectiveness of the package as a whole, but, from both a scientific and practical perspective, it is important to consider carefully which components are necessary and sufficient to optimize meaningful behavior change. This question can be considered from the standpoint of pure procedures or technology, but, more importantly in the behavior analytic perspective, it can be asked from a functional standpoint. In the case of the latter, group designs that compare outcomes between groups of participants who receive one particular combination of treatment components to another group who receive a different combination of treatment components cannot expect to meaningfully address the issue. The contribution of individual behavioral principles will be masked behind middle-level terms, the individual effect of which will be masked behind the mean effect across the group. Behavior analytic single-case designs are uniquely suited to evaluate the unique contributions of individual variables on the behavior of the individual participant because that is the analytic level at which the designs work. Much more single-case behavioral research is needed on the necessary and sufficient components that make ACT effective in producing socially meaningful behavior change.

Basic Operant and Bridge Research for Innovating and Fine-tuning ACT

Although more members of the behavior analytic community are embracing ACT, our understanding of how to best use ACT with the populations that behavior analysts often serve is far from complete. The steadily growing body of literature on ACT within behavior analysis brings to bear many questions regarding exactly *which pieces of ACT are effective in changing behavior, why, and under what conditions.* Initiating empirical investigations to answer these questions will fine-tune ACT in practice and may answer some "big questions" behavior scientists have about how our verbal behavior and private events influence our actions. This begins and ends with the applied scientist-practitioners who are using current research and systematically applying these methods to their cases. As they do, questions will arise such as: *How do I assess my client's behavior to know where to start with ACT? Which parts of ACT are necessary to change a given behavior? What are the necessary prerequisites for ACT to be effective? Which variables can I manipulate to individualize this treatment so that my client is engaged and benefiting from it? Is ACT a socially valid treatment for the clients that we serve?* and so forth.

While scientist-practitioners can and should evaluate answers to these questions in the real-life clinical environment, more controlled analyses are also needed. In order to answer questions related to which parts of ACT are effective and under what conditions, bridge researchers should set up controlled lab studies using models of applied problems developed in tandem with basic researchers (e.g., models of experiential avoidance, impulsivity, contingency insensitivity). It is also necessary for basic researchers to bring some of these clinical questions back to the Skinner Box, so to speak, where investigations can be conducted at a molecular level to provide a better understanding of the conditions under which we can strengthen or weaken the immediate influence of these indirect acting contingencies on overt behavior (e.g., rule-governed behavior, sensitivity of derived relations to different environmental variables, transformation of stimulus function). When these forces combine, we will likely be able to generate extremely effective means of intervention for behavior under the control of these indirect acting contingencies across a variety of populations and applied problems. Figure 31.3 depicts a few of the many potential overlapping and cross-fertilizing avenues for future bridge, basic, and applied research to enhance the precision and scope of research on ACT inside of ABA.

Scope of Practice

Although ABA has always been conceptualized as a comprehensive applied science of human behavior, the field has flourished in addressing developmental disorders, while relatively little expansion has been achieved into other areas of socially meaningful behavior. As Skinner (1953) and legions of behavior analysts have noted, there are few problems of humanity that do *not* involve human behavior, and yet the forward progress of ABA into mainstream society has occurred particularly slowly. One possible reason is that more traditional approaches to language in behavior analysis, particularly Skinner's analysis of verbal behavior, struggled to give birth to basic and applied research that productively addressed complex human language and cognition (Hayes, Barnes-Holmes, & Roche, 2001). One of the greatest promises of ACT, and of RFT upon which it is based, is to provide tools for expanding the scope of practice of

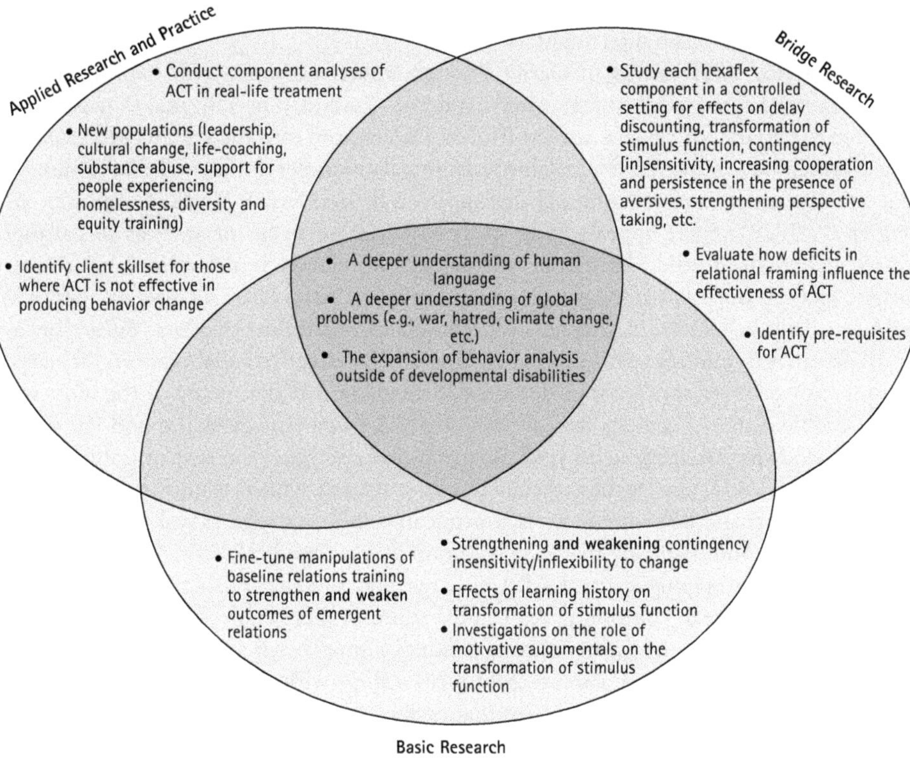

Figure 31.3. Venn diagram depicting potential areas for future applied, basic, and bridge research on ACT inside behavior analysis.

ABA. The rationale for this is that the transition from working with individuals with developmental disabilities to working with typically developing individuals largely consists of transitioning from clients for whom the ABA practitioner has direct and frequent access to the direct consequence of the person's behavior, to working with clients with whom the ABA clinician has very infrequent, even totally absent, direct access to the consequences of some of the most important client behaviors.

Many of humanity's greatest causes of preventable death can be attributed to human behavior, for which clinicians do not have direct access. For example, eating healthier and less calorically dense foods can help prevent heart disease and diabetes (e.g., Pallazola et al., 2019). Even if a behavior analyst trains a client for an hour per week, the amount of food choosing, cooking, and eating behavior that can be evoked and directly reinforced in that setting is incredibly small, compared to the proportion of the same behavior that occurs outside of session. In addition to nutrition, regular exercise is known to guard against heart disease and diabetes (Warburton, Nicol, & Bredin, 2006), as well as having beneficial effects on mental health (Stojanovska, Polenakovic, Bosevski, & Apostolopoulos, 2017). But the same challenge is present as for eating: the clinician does not have direct access to a substantial proportion of exercise behavior in their clients, nor to the particularly challenging environments in which exercise must often occur (e.g., early in the morning or late at night). In the case of diabetes, life and limb can be affected in powerful ways by behavioral choices (blood sugar testing, sugar, and insulin administration) made by patients on a daily basis, the vast majority of which the clinician has little or no direct contact with.

The fact that ACT works primarily through indirect contact with contingencies, via derived relational responding and transformation of stimulus function, makes it particularly well suited to helping the science and practice of ABA expand into these underaddressed areas, many of which have much broader mainstream impact than developmental disabilities. Some of the initial research is encouraging, for example, in fitness (Szabo, Willis, & Palinski, 2019; Wang et al., 2020). There appears to be great potential for behavior analysts to collaborate with researchers from other disciplines who struggle to change health-related behaviors, for example, medical doctors working with patients with diabetes, heart disease, or obesity, who would especially benefit from changes in exercise and nutrition behaviors. Future behavior analytic research should identify and evaluate models for effective collaboration, for example, in hospitals or primary care settings. It seems particularly odd that many of the most vexing medical problems that hospitals face are majorly tied to patient behavior, and yet very few hospitals have behavior analysts on staff. Research that combines the best of traditional ABA procedures with ACT approaches, executed and evaluated within traditional medical contexts, may help expand behavior analysts' practice into these settings, as well as bridge the gap between behavior and medicine that is so common in most medical settings.

In addition to helping expand ABA research and practice further into health-related behaviors, future research combining ACT and traditional ABA methods likely has the potential to expand ABA's reach into other areas of complex human behavioral challenges that do not yet warrant a formal diagnosis. Parent–child relationships with typically developing children seem to be one such area. Many problems that appear acute in later years likely could be prevented by early intervention (Biglan, Hayes, & Pistorello, 2008). For example, effective parent training provided much earlier in the child's life will likely prevent the need for more intensive intervention for behavioral disorders, such as conduct disorders. Traditional behavioral parent training likely has the potential to be effective in this manner, but if complementing ABA parent training with an ACT approach may make it more effective and potentially longer-lasting, then perhaps implementing it early in life would be an effective and efficient approach to preventing more acute problems later. In addition, behavior analysts typically are not called in to help a family until the problem has become severe. Future research should attempt to develop low-intensity models for providing ACT-informed ABA parent training to parents who may be at risk for their children developing challenges later in life. Examples are families who are severely underresourced, and families with one or more parents struggling with substance abuse. If implemented early and evaluated on a large scale, it may be possible to identify, at a group level, whether negative outcomes such as involvement in the penal system, dropping out of school, teen pregnancy, or substance abuse challenges can be prevented (Kellam et al., 2014). This potential future for the field of ABA could envision behavior analysts preventing problems, rather than being called in to "put out fires" after they have already become severe.

Scope of Competence

Recent research (Enoch & Nicholson, 2020) has revealed that the practitioner community is accepting ACT as part of ABA; however, concerns remain about scope of practice and standards of competence. As discussed in the section on the *technological* dimension of ACT inside ABA, research has a long way to go in operationally defining competence in implementing ACT, inside or outside of behavior analysis. Much more future research is needed in this regard. Until such research has been published, behavior analysts will need to adopt ACT procedures in the same way in which they adopt any other new behavior-analytic procedures:

gradually, cautiously, and only with expert training and mentorship. There is not yet any data-based reason to believe that competence in ACT is any less attainable than competence in any other behavior analytic treatment approach.

Conclusion

The relationship between ACT and behavior analysis has been and continues to be mutually beneficial. The current explosion of popularity that ACT is experiencing within the mainstream behavior analytic community is exciting and will no doubt usher in challenges and opportunities. In this chapter, we have attempted to establish that ACT can not only reasonably be practiced within behavior analysis but also that behavior analysis is the proper home for ACT. Much more research is still needed on implementing ACT within mainstream ABA settings and populations, on methods for training behavior analysts to competence in ACT, and ultimately, on using ACT to expand the scope of ABA to include a fuller range of human behaviors, more closely approaching B. F. Skinner's dream of a comprehensive science of human behavior.

References

Abasi, E., Fati, L., Molodi, R., & Zarabi, H. (2013). Psychometric properties of Persian version of acceptance and action questionnaire-ii. *Journal of Psychological Models and Methods, 3*(10), 65–80.

American Psychiatric Association. (2013). *Diagnostic and statistical manual of mental disorders* (5th ed.). Washington, DC: American Psychiatric Association. https://doi.org/10.1176/appi.books.9780890425596

Asghari, M. M., Saed, F., Dibajnia, P., & Zangeneh, J. (2008). A preliminary validation of the depression, anxiety and stress scales (DASS) in non-clinical sample. *Journal of Clinical Psychology and Personality, 15*, 23–38.

Baer, D. M., Wolf, M. M., & Risley, T. R. (1968). Some current dimensions of applied behavior analysis. *Journal of Applied Behavior Analysis, 1*(1), 91.

Baron, R. M., & Kenny, A. A. (1986). The moderator-mediator variable distinction in social psychological research: Conceptual, strategic, and statistical considerations. *Journal of Personality and Social Psychology, 51*, 1173–1182. https://doi.org/10.1037/0022-3514.51.6.1173

Biglan, A., Hayes, S. C., & Pistorello, J. (2008). Acceptance and commitment: Implications for prevention science. *Prevention Science, 9*(3), 139–152.

Blackledge, J. T., & Hayes, S. C. (2006). Using acceptance and commitment training in the support of parents of children diagnosed with autism. *Child and Family Behavior Therapy, 28*, 1–18. https://doi.org/10.1300/J019v28n01_01

Bond, F. W., & Flaxman, E. P. (2006). The ability of psychological flexibility and job control to predict learning, job performance, and mental health, *Journal of Organizational Behavior Management, 26*(1–2), 113–130. https://doi.org/10.1300/J075v26n01_05

Brazeau, K., Rehfeldt, R. A., Mazo, A., Smalley, S., Krus, S., & Henson, L. (2017). On the efficacy of mindfulness, defusion, and behavioral skills training on job interviewing skills in dually-diagnosed adults with developmental disorders. *Journal of Contextual Behavioral Science, 6*(2), 145–151.

Brooker, J. E., Webber, L., Julian, J., Shawyer, F., Graham, A. L., Chan, J., & Meadows, G. N. (2014). Mindfulness-based training shows promise in assisting staff to reduce their use of restrictive interventions in residential services. *Mindfulness, 5*, 598–603. https://doi.org/10.1007/s12671-014-0306-2

Castro, M., Rehfeldt, R. A., & Root, W. B. (2016). On the role of values clarification and committed actions in enhancing the engagement of direct care workers with clients with severe developmental disorders. *Journal of Contextual Behavioral Science, 5*(4), 201–207. https://doi.org/10.1016/j.jcbs.2016.09.003

Chancey, C., Weihl, C., Root, W. B., Rehfeldt, R., McCauley, D., Takeguchi, K., & Pritchard, J. (2019). The impact of mindfulness skills on interactions between direct care staff and adults with developmental disabilities. *Journal of Contextual Behavioral Science, 12*, 160–169. https://doi.org/10.1016/j.jcbs.2018.07.004

Ciarrochi, J., Bailey, A., & Harris, R. (2014). *The weight escape*. Melbourne, Australia: Penguin Group.

Corti, C., Pergolizzi, F., Vanzin, L., Cargasacchi, G., Villa, L., Pozzi, M., & Molteni, M. (2018). Acceptance and commitment therapy-oriented parent-training for parents of children with autism. *Journal of Child and Family Studies, 27*, 1–14. https://doi.org/10.1007/s10826-018-1123-3

Crosby, J. M., Dehlin, J. P., Mitchell, P. R., & Twohig, M. P. (2012). Acceptance and commitment therapy and habit reversal training for the treatment of trichotillomania. *Cognitive and Behavioral Practice, 19*, 595–605.

Dahl, J., Wilson, K. G., & Nilsson, A. (2004). Acceptance and commitment therapy and the treatment of persons at risk for long-term disability resulting from stress and pain symptoms: A preliminary randomized trial. *Behavior Therapy, 35*, 785–802.

Dixon, M. R., Hayes, S. C., Stanley, C., Law, S., & al-Nasser, T. (2020). Is acceptance and commitment training or therapy (ACT) a method that applied behavior analysts can and should use? *The Psychological Record, 70*(4), 559–579.

Eilers, H. J., & Hayes, S. C. (2015). Exposure and response prevention therapy with cognitive defusion exercises to reduce repetitive and restrictive behaviors displayed by children with autism spectrum disorder. *Research in Autism Spectrum Disorders, 19*, 18–31.

Enoch, M. R., & Nicholson, S. L. (2020). Acceptance and commitment therapy and relational frame theory in the field of applied behavior analysis: The acceptability and perspective of the practicing BCBA. *Behavior Analysis in Practice, 13*(3), 609–617.

Fung, K., Lake, J., Steel, L., Bryce, K., & Lunsky, Y. (2018). ACT processes in group intervention for mothers of children with autism spectrum disorder. *Journal of Autism and Developmental Disorders, 48*(8), 2740–2747. https://doi.org/10.1007/s10803-018-3525-x

García-Zambrano, S., Rehfeldt, R. A., Hertel, I. P., & Boehmert, R. (2019). Effects of deictic framing and defusion on the development of self-as-context in individuals with disabilities. *Journal of Contextual Behavioral Science, 12*, 55–58.

Gould, E. R., Tarbox, J., & Coyne, L. (2018). Evaluating the effects of acceptance and commitment training on the overt behavior of parents of children with autism. *Journal of Contextual Behavioral Science, 7*, 81–88. https://doi.org/10.1016/j.jcbs.2017.06.003

Hahs, A. D., Dixon, M. R., & Paliliunas, D. (2019). Randomized controlled trial of a brief acceptance and commitment training for parents of individuals diagnosed with autism spectrum disorders. *Journal of Contextual Behavioral Science, 12*, 154–159. https://doi.org/10.1016/j.jcbs.2018.03.002

Hayes, S. C. (2020). *A liberated mind: How to pivot toward what matters*. New York: Avery.

Hayes, S. C., Barnes-Holmes, S. C. H. D., & Roche, B. (2001). *Relational frame theory: A post-Skinnerian account of human language and cognition*. New York: Springer Science & Business Media.

Hayes, S. C., & Wilson, K. G. (1994). Acceptance and commitment therapy: Altering the verbal support for experiential avoidance. *The Behavior Analyst, 17*(2), 289–303. https://doi.org/10.1007/BF03392677

Joekar, S., Farid, A.A., Birashk, B., Gharraee, B., & Mohammadian, M. (2016). Effectiveness of acceptance and commitment therapy in the support of parents of children with high-functioning autism. *International Journal of Humanities and Social Sciences, 2*, 2763–2772.

Kazdin, A. E. (2011). *Single-case research designs: Methods for clinical and applied settings* (2nd ed.). New York: Oxford University Press.

Kellam, S. G., Wang, W., Mackenzie, A. C., Brown, C. H., Ompad, D. C., Or, F., . . . Windham, A. (2014). The impact of the Good Behavior Game, a universal classroom-based preventive intervention in first and second grades, on high-risk sexual behaviors and drug abuse and dependence disorders into young adulthood. *Prevention Science: 15 Suppl. 1*(0 1), S6–S18. https://doi.org/10.1007/s11121-012-0296-z

Little, A., Tarbox, J., Alzaabi, K. (2020). Using acceptance and commitment training to enhance the effectiveness of behavioral skills training, *Journal of Contextual Behavioral Science, 16*, 9–16. https://doi.org/10.1016/j.jcbs.2020.02.002

Lunsky, Y., Fung, K., Lake, J., Steel, L., & Bryce, K. (2018). Evaluation of acceptance and commitment therapy (ACT) for mothers of children and youth with autism spectrum disorder. *Mindfulness, 9*(4), 1110–1116. https://doi.org/10.1007/s12671-017-0846-3

Mahoney, J., & Hanrahan, S. J. (2011). A brief educational intervention using acceptance and commitment therapy: Four injured athletes' experiences, *Journal of Clinical Sport Psychology, 5*(3), 252–273. https://doi.org/10.1123/jcsp.5.3.252

Maisel, M. E., Stephenson, K. G., Cox, J. C., & South, M. (2019). Cognitive defusion for reducing distressing thoughts in adults with autism. *Research in Autism Spectrum Disorders, 59*, 34–45.

Mikkelsen, K., Stojanovska, L., Polenakovic, M., Bosevski, M., & Apostolopoulos, V. (2017). Exercise and mental health. *Maturitas, 106*, 48–56.

Pahnke, J., Lundgren, T., Hursti, T., & Hirvikoski, T. (2014). Outcomes of an acceptance and commitment therapy-based skills training group for students with high-functioning autism spectrum disorder: A quasi-experimental pilot study. *Autism, 18*(8), 953–964. https://doi.org/10.1177/1362361313501091

Pallazola, V. A., Davis, D. M., Whelton, S. P., Cardoso, R., Latina, J. M., Michos, E. D., Sarkar, S., . . . & Welty, F. K. (2019). A clinician's guide to healthy eating for cardiovascular disease prevention. *Mayo Clinic Proceedings. Innovations, Quality and Outcomes, 3*(3), 251–267. https://doi.org/10.1016/j.mayocpiqo.2019.05.001

Paul, G. L. (1969). Behavior modification research: Design and tactics. In C. M. Franks (Ed.), *Behavior therapy: Appraisal and status* (pp. 29–62). New York: McGraw-Hill.
Pingo, J. C., Dixon, M. R., & Paliliunas, D. (2020a). Intervention enhancing effects of acceptance and commitment training on performance feedback for direct support professional work performance, stress, and job satisfaction. *Behavior Analysis in Practice, 13*(1), 1–10. https://doi.org/10.1007/s40617-019-00333-w
Pingo, J. C., Dixon, M. R., & Piliiunas, D. (2020b). An examination of the intervention-enhancing effect of acceptance and commitment therapy-based training on direct service professionals' performance in the workplace. *Behavior Analysis in Practice, 15*, 192–202. https://doi.org/10.1007/s40617-018-00275-9
Poddar, S., Sinha, V. K., Urbi, M. (2015). Acceptance and commitment therapy on parents of children and adolescents with autism spectrum disorders. *International Journal of Education and Psychological Research, 1*, 221–225.
Rachlin, H., & Green, L. (1972). Commitment, choice and self-control 1. *Journal of the Experimental Analysis of Behavior, 17*(1), 15–22.
Sandoz, E. K., Boullion, G. Q., & Rachal, D. O. (2020). Second and third wave behavior therapy. In R. A. Rehfeldt, J. Tarbox, M. Fryling, and L. Hayes (Eds.), *Applied behavior analysis of language and cognition: core concepts and principles for practitioners*, pp. 250–263. Oakland, CA: New Harbinger Publications.
Singh, N. N., Lancioni, G. E., Winton, A. S. W., Fisher, B. C., Wahler, R. G., Mcaleavey, K., . . . Sabaawi, M. (2006). Mindful parenting decreases aggression, noncompliance, and self-injury in children with autism. *Journal of Emotional and Behavioral Disorders, 14*(3), 169–177. https://doi.org/10.1177/10634266060140030401
Skinner, B. F. (1938). *The behavior of organisms: An experimental analysis*. New York: Appleton-Century.
Skinner, B. F. (1953). *Science and human behavior*. New York: Macmillan.
Skinner, B. F. (1974). *About behaviorism*. New York: Knopf.
Suarez, V. D., Moon, E. I., & Nadjowski, A. (2022). A systematic review of acceptance and commitment training in the behavioral intervention of individuals with autism and developmental disorders. *Behavior Analysis in Practice, 15*, 126–140.
Szabo, T. G. (2019). Acceptance and commitment training for reducing inflexible behaviors in children with autism. *Journal of Contextual Behavioral Science, 12*, 178–188.
Szabo, T. G., Willis, P. B., & Palinski, C. J. (2019). Watch me try: ACT for improving athletic performance of young adults with ASD. *Advances in Neurodevelopmental Disorders, 3(4)*, 434–449.
Tarbox, J. (2018). ACT through the lens of Baer, Wolf, and Risley: A guest blog. Behavior science dissemination. https://science.abainternational.org/2018/04/09/act-through-the-lens-of-baer-wolf-risley-a-guest-blog-by-jonathan-tarbox/
Tarbox, J., Szabo, T. G., & Aclan, M. (2020). Acceptance and commitment training within the scope of practice of applied behavior analysis. *Behavior Analysis in Practice, 15*(1), 11–32. https://doi.org/10.1007/s40617-020-00466-3
Twohig, M. P., Hayes, S. C., & Masuda, A. (2006). A preliminary investigation of acceptance and commitment therapy as a treatment for chronic skin picking. *Behavior Research and Therapy, 44*, 1513–1522.
Twohig, M. P., & Woods, D. W. (2004). A preliminary investigation of acceptance and commitment therapy and habit reversal as a treatment for trichotillomania. *Behavior Therapy, 35*, 803–820.
Wang, Y., Tarbox, J., Chastain, A. N., & Cameron, M. J. (2020). The effects of bilingual acceptance and commitment training (ACT) on exercise in bilingual international university students. *Journal of Contextual Behavioral Science, 18*, 1–8.
Warburton, D. E., Nicol, C. W., & Bredin, S. S. (2006). Health benefits of physical activity: The evidence. *Cmaj, 174*(6), 801–809.
Yi, Z., & Dixon, M. R. (2020). Developing and enhancing adherence to a telehealth ABA parent training curriculum for caregivers of children with autism. *Behavior Analysis in Practice, 14*, 58–74. https://doi.org/10.1007/s40617-020-00464-5

Conclusion

CHAPTER
32 Future Directions of Contextual Behavioral Science

Rikard K. Wicksell, Niklas Törneke, Lance M. McCracken, Jonathan B. Bricker, Amy R. Murrell, Akihiko Masuda, *and* Anthony Biglan

Abstract

This article reflects on future directions within the field of contextual behavioral science (CBS), focusing on (1) *refinement of the theory* of CBS and implications for clinical practice; (2) *methodological aspects*, particularly the utility of individual-level analyses for understanding change processes and customized interventions; (3) how *digital resources* can be utilized to improve research and clinical interventions, including accessibility to empirically supported treatments; (4) how a *systems-oriented approach* can improve the ability to address complex problems in, for example, young individuals and their families; (5) why and how dissemination across *cultural contexts* is an important area of development; and (6) how CBS can be used at a societal level to promote *public health*, including policymaking and key research studies. It is hoped that directing attention to key challenges and opportunities will inspire other researchers, Finally, suggestions are offered on how to develop the field to gain further knowledge, improve methods, increase evidence, and, ultimately, promote health and well-being.

Key Words: relational frame theory, methodology, individual-level data analyses, digital tools, technical innovations, systems-approach, cultural adaptation, public health

Refinement of Theory and the Bridge to Clinical Practice

Even though acceptance and commitment therapy (ACT) has been influenced by a variety of factors (see Zettle & Wilson, this volume), its main scientific context was behavior analysis—more specifically, the efforts to analyze the overlapping areas traditionally labeled rule-governed and verbal behavior, respectively (e.g., Hayes & Hayes, 1992). This specific research program was presented in a comprehensive manner in 2001 in the book on relational frame theory (RFT) edited by Hayes, Barnes-Holmes, and Roche. The specific relationship between this research program and the clinical model of ACT can be described as that of two siblings growing up together. As ACT is the result of many factors, it would be an exaggeration to say that the model is built on RFT, but it is beyond doubt that this specific way of analyzing human language has been extremely influential in the development of the clinical model. This can be illustrated by focusing on perhaps the most central concept in ACT, the cognitive fusion/defusion dichotomy. Fusion refers to the tendency of language-capable humans to coordinate their actions with certain verbal functions, regardless of the problematic long-run effects. Defusion refers to the process of disentangling from this verbal power. As defined in the first book-length presentation of ACT (Hayes, Strosahl, & Wilson, 1999, p. 74): "To deliteralize[1] means to disrupt ordinary meaning functions of language such that the ongoing process of framing events relationally is evident in the moment and competes with the stimulus products of relational activity". The terminology used confirms ACT's close relationship to RFT. Processes described using RFT is at the root of ACT. The fact that this was so from the very start is confirmed by the fact that the same process is described in the earliest publication (Hayes, 1984) presenting the ideas that eventually became ACT.

Where Do We Go from Here? Dig Where You Stand!

The previous argument brings us to the first recommendation regarding refinements of theory and the bridge to clinical practice: Move forward with theoretical integrity, that is, base further clinical development on the key principles that are established! Even though the central processes of ACT were identified early, our understanding of them has increased over the years, as a result of the continued basic research program of RFT. As our understanding of different types of relational behavior (different types of "frames") have increased, it has become clear that the process of defusion can be described with better precision by using RFT concepts of deictic (perspective-taking) and hierarchical frames. Still, there is a continued need for more research focusing on these processes. Regarding deictic framing, most research concerns the repertoire of taking the perspective of another person (e.g., Hooper, Erdogan, Keen, Lawton, & McHugh, 2015). From a clinical point of view, there is a need for more research on the behavior repertoire that relates to taking perspective on your own responding, including work on defusion or deliteralization—in other words, the phenomena which early in RFT literature was called I-Here-Now versus I-There-Then (Barnes-Holmes, Hayes, & Dymond, 2001).

As for hierarchical framing, the behavior as such has been described in a laboratory context (e.g., Callejón, 2020; Gil, Luciano, Ruiz, & Valdivia- Salas, 2012) It has also been demonstrated that this repertoire, in conjunction with deictic framing, is part of the central clinical process of being able to interact with your own responding in a flexible way, what is called defusion in ACT (e.g., Foody, Barnes-Holmes, Barnes-Holmes, & Luciano, 2013; Luciano et al., 2011). Still, this work is in its infancy and there is a great need to expand on and deepen the work already done. The word "deepen" is used here in the sense that we need to know more about how to predict and influence this process, and the word "expand" is used in the sense that we need to test different related interventions to get closer to everyday clinical work.

Another important area of research that represents a starting point for ACT is the phenomenon of rule-governed behavior, which is very much connected to fusion/defusion as the tendency to follow self-rules is at the core of the problematic effects of fusion (Törneke, Luciano, Barnes-Holmes, & Bond, 2016). So, the advice to dig deeper for one is also advice to dig for the other.

Scientists and clinicians from theoretical backgrounds other than behavior analysis are pointing out the relevance of similar psychological or behavioral processes, although they are using different terminology (Bernstein et al., 2015). This brings us to a second recommendation regarding the refinements of theory and bridge to clinical practice.

Talk to Those Digging Nearby!

The contextual behavior wing of behavior analysis has already managed to launch fruitful dialogues with neighboring researchers. An example is the communication and collaboration with researchers rooted in cognitive (e.g., De Houwer, Barnes-Holmes, & Moors, 2013) and evolutionary science (e.g., Wilson, Hayes, Biglan, & Embry, 2014). At the same time, one other neighbor has been digging close by for a long time, where the dialogue is yet almost nonexistent: the science of linguistics. This is strange in many ways, as the main tool of any psychotherapy model is talking, that is, using language. A collaboration with linguists is particularly relevant to those with a great interest in RFT because RFT is a research program focusing on human language and linguistics is the science of that very subject.

It is well known that the problematic relationship between behavioral analysis and linguistics has been formed by the way the prominent linguist Noam Chomsky responded to B. F. Skinner's attempt to analyze human language around 70 years ago (Chomsky, 1959; Skinner, 1957). However, refinement of theory and improvement of clinical models require scientific collaborations between researchers from different fields and traditions. Thus, the time has come to move beyond that conflict.

Modern linguistics share many assumptions with contextual behavioral science. Perhaps the most obvious one is the description of language as an activity of the whole person, acting in an ecological setting (context). Language is "languaging" (Thibault, 2011). Of special interest to those familiar with RFT is that this trend is very influential in modern linguistic work on the phenomenon of metaphors (Müller, 2008), an area in which RFT research has contributed and shed substantial light (Stewart & Barnes-Holmes, 2001). And this goes beyond basic science. Within the linguistic community there is a growing interest in using metaphors in clinical work, in psychotherapy (Tay, 2013) and in other areas of health care (Demjén & Semino, 2017). Taken together, converging research conducted in different fields makes it clear that it is time to open up for a dialogue that will likely be vital but that has been unheard of for decades.

Methodological Aspects of Future Clinical Research

In many areas where broadly cognitive-behavioral treatments are applied, there is no longer a need for more randomized clinical trials (RCTs) focused on efficacy and clinical outcomes from treatments based on protocols designed for particular syndromes (Hayes & Hofmann, 2018). We have reached a saturation point, and even comparisons of conventional with newer variants of CBT do not appear to offer progress. Little or no new knowledge has been gained in these studies. Instead, to improve treatments, we now need different trial designs to provide answers to critically important questions. Where we continue with randomized group comparison designs, these need to be set up to enable examinations of change processes and/or analyze treatment components linked to processes of change. In both cases, the ability to determine individual variability in response is imperative. Reporting statistical differences in group means, or even reporting summary effect sizes, is not enough. What is called for is individualized (Hayes et al. 2019) or "personalized and precision treatments" (Fisher et al., 2019).

The Need for Idiographic Research

Idiographic research is needed on specific individuals or contexts to extend knowledge in areas where nomothetic research at a group level has dominated. It is now clear that findings based in aggregated group data do not typically generalize to the individual (e.g., Fisher, Medaglia, & Jeronimus, 2018). Even where measures of central tendency derived from group versus individual data may be similar, the variability in the individual data is so large that it will not be appropriate to regard the group data as providing an accurate estimate of any of the individuals in the population (Fisher et al., 2018).

Thus, there is a need to shift study methods from those that have historically included large sample sizes to methods that instead include a large number of *observations within each individual over time*. The latter are commonly called intensive longitudinal designs, which include single-case experimental designs as an example. These designs are perfectly suited to conduct analyses of treatments that are process-focused and idiographic (Bentley, Kleiman, Elliott, Huffman, & Knock, 2019), particularly with regard to developments in ecological momentary assessment and so-called real-time monitoring using mobile technologies (Bentley et al., 2019; Vilardaga, Bricker, & McDonell, 2014), as well as statistical approaches such as cross-lagged correlation analyses (e.g., Caneiro, Smith, Linton, Moseley, & O'Sullican, 2019) and simulation modeling analysis (Borckardt et al., 2008).

To capture the dynamics of change processes over time, frequent session-by-session, day-to-day, and preferably, where possible, moment-to-moment assessment will be needed (e.g., Hayes et al., 2019). Without such detailed information, therapists will not be equipped to assess, track, and customize treatment by linking critical change processes to specific interventions.

Intensive Longitudinal Studies Require New Instruments for Assessment

To support intensive longitudinal studies of process and outcome, appropriate measures are needed. Such measures should be *brief* enough for repeated use, *sensitive* to change for the respective intervention, and *direct* in the sense of capturing behavior patterns of interest in the situation and at the time where they occur. This will require approaches to instrument design that are unlike conventional psychometric instrument design (e.g. based on classical test theory), including daily diary methods (e.g., Berghoff, Ritzert, & Forsyth, 2018), statistical methods for managing complex individual data, such as the dynamic p-technique (Kurz, Johnson, Kellum, & Wilson, 2019), and network analysis (Christodoulou, Michaelides, & Karekla, in press). While traditional psychometric questionnaires will continue to have a place in group research designs, they are not suited for intensive idiographic assessment for reasons including their length, the time required to complete them, their complexity (inadvertently combining functionally distinct behavior patterns), and the indirect quality of the data (e.g., imprecision in behavior of interest, time, and context of interest). Also, the framing of the questions over extensive periods of time (e.g., the past 2 weeks) results in a failure to capture important variability, as well as the sources of that variability. Furthermore, such retrospective ratings often succumb to reporting biases. Hence, instruments developed using traditional psychometric approaches are generally unsuitable for the idiographic approaches described here.

Distinctions between types of therapy appear too coarse to best promote progress in therapy development and certainly too coarse to fit the future of individual process-based therapy. What is envisioned is a future where types of CBT or psychotherapy in general drop away and are replaced by lists of known effective behavior change processes linked to specific methods known to drive them (Hayes et al., 2019). However, such aspirations call for a paradigm shift in which idiographic research designs are emphasized (on top of nomothetic approaches that adhere to the same spirit) to enhance the focus on individual needs, specific change processes, and customized interventions.

Utilizing Digital Resources in Future Research and Clinical Practice

Early initiatives designed to transform ACT into a digital intervention in 2010 were met by skepticism from CBS clinical and research colleagues, as well as grant reviewers, who argued that this change would be too challenging because ACT had usually been delivered by highly trained clinicians in lengthy face-to-face experiential exercises. The past 10 years of research have shown the opposite pattern: there are numerous examples of ACT, and contextual behavioral science in general, being successfully adapted into and tested in a digital intervention for a variety of clinically relevant problems, including smoking cessation, obesity, pain management, and depression (Anthony et al., 2020; Bricker, Watson, Mull, Sullivan, & Heffner, 2020; Järvelä-Reijonen et al., 2020). This decade of learning has highlighted the notion that, to be effective, these digital adaptations required contextual behavioral researchers to rethink their scientific questions, form transdisciplinary collaborations, employ a broad range of study designs, and address the challenges of recruiting and retaining study participants. This future directions section highlights each of these elements and their critical role in the next decade of digital contextual behavioral research.

Rethinking Research Questions

Digital technologies are fundamentally changing the clinical and basic research questions that contextual behavioral scientists are asking. Clinically, digital technologies are leading to a focus on questions of whether contextual behavioral interventions can be tested and later disseminated on a population level. Compared to traditional interventions that deliver interventions face-to-face, digital interventions can be delivered on a broader scale at a fraction of the cost, which in turn elevates the population-level impact of the behavioral interventions. For example, smartphone applications for English-language cigarette smoking cessation have already been downloaded 33 million times (Bricker et al., 2020). Clinical intervention research questions include the following query: to what extent does acceptance of internal experiences (e.g., thoughts and emotions) mediate the relationship between objective behaviors and clinical outcomes? With the advent of widely available low-cost and easily worn sensors that can passively track a variety of behaviors, including heart rate, pulse, location, and physical activity, it is now possible to ask new basic research questions, including what are the bidirectional relationships between objective behaviors and avoidance of internal processes? Contextually collected digital data on antecedents, behaviors, and consequences are allowing for more valid, reliable, and fine-grained functional analysis of target behaviors (Levin, Krafft, Pierce, & Potts, 2018;). Ecological momentary assessments, which provide random prompting of short real-time self-report measures of internal experiences (e.g., thoughts and emotions), address the recall bias of traditional self-report surveys (Shiffman, 2007). Also, frequent assessment (e.g., up to multiple times per day) provides a more valid analysis of mediators and basic processes linking behaviors and objective behavioral measures. Patients and study participants who never before considered using a behavioral intervention to address a given problem (e.g., depression) are now engaging in treatments because the digital delivery is more accessible than in-person delivery. However, an important question that contextual behavioral researchers need to address is how to design digital interventions to optimize accessibility to a broad range of populations, such as those with cognitive and visual impairments, as well as those experiencing structural barriers that limit their access to technologies (e.g., poverty, living in a rural area, lack of WIFI access).

Transdisciplinary Science

Scientists in the allied fields of public health, medicine, computer science, engineering, and statistics are needed for collaborating with contextual behavioral scientists on digital technology research. Public health researchers have a valuable role in understanding systemic barriers to accessing digital interventions (e.g., geographic areas of low WIFI access), principles of epidemiology (e.g., to determine population-level impact), and community-based participatory research (e.g., including potential end-users, clinicians, and digital technology companies in the development team) in the development, testing, dissemination, and implementation of CBS digital research (Rutter et al., 2017). Medical researchers (i.e., physician scientists) can provide valuable expertise on how to conduct CBS digital research for specific medical populations and settings, with a special understanding of how these medical conditions would influence these questions (e.g., adapting user interfaces for cancer patients experiencing the side effects of chemotherapy). Computer scientists bring in a broad range of expertise, including passive sensing (e.g., accelerometers, global positioning systems), machine learning, and natural language processing (Milne-Ives et al., 2020; Thomas Craig et al., 2020), all of which are important areas for the conceptualization of a wide variety of CBS digital research. Perhaps engineering's most important contribution to CBS digital research has been in the subfield of human-centered design, which focuses on using multiple research methods (e.g., interviews, focus groups, diary studies) to conceptualize and iterate designs of technologies that are engaging to the end user (Matheson, Pacione, Shultz, & Klügl, 2015).

Finally, statistics has been an important academic field, providing expertise in study methods such as adaptive research designs (see the next heading). Part of this transdisciplinary collaboration has included forming partnerships with vendors in the field of technology and digital health. These businesses have included in-house designers, programmers, and managers who usually serve the private sector, so developing a shared vision and set of expectations is critical (Roth, Vilardaga, Wolfe, Bricker, & McDonell, 2014). The emergence of this type of transdisciplinary research within CBS is mirrored within digital technology behavior research. There is a newer academic field of technology intervention research that bridges the disciplines mentioned previously (e.g., engineering, computing, medicine, and behavioral science) with journals devoted solely to this area. The *Journal of Medical Internet Research (JMIR)* is a good example (impact factor= 5) (JMIR, 2020) of this new field, with multiple subjournals focused on the intervention protocols (*JMIR Res Prot*), formative research (*JMIR Form Res*), small-scale trials (*JMIR mhealh and uhealth*), and gaming (*JMIR Serious Games*). For these transdisciplinary collaborations to be effective, CBS researchers must "get out of their comfort zone" by reaching out to their colleagues across their institutions and around the globe and work to find common language and vocabulary to communicate CBS concepts and assumptions, and vice versa.

Broader Research Designs

New CBS digital research questions formed in transdisciplinary collaborations are now supporting study designs that go beyond the two-arm randomized controlled trial design. Starting in the design phase, user-centered study designs include qualitative theme analyses from interviews, focus groups, open-ended surveys, and diary studies (Davies & Mueller, 2020). Single-case and N-of-1 designs (see the section on method development) have been valuable in the development phase for establishing the causality of CBS intervention effects on a small scale (Thorsell Cederberg, Dahl, von Essen, & Ljungman, 2017; Vilardaga et al., 2014). For determining which components of a CBS intervention and their combination are effective, the multiphase optimization strategy (MOST) is a valuable engineering-based design framework for optimizing CBS intervention content (Collins et al., 2011). Study designs such as factorial experiments, micro-randomized trials, and sequential multiple assignment randomized trials (SMART) are being used to optimize interventions (Klasnja et al., 2015). As an example of how these novel methods are applied in CBS research, a micro-randomized trial to test the causal effects of specific ACT messages on coping with urges to smoke will be conducted soon, with the goal of determining what message has impact on proximal outcomes such as cravings (Thrul, 2020). Also, a SMART design will be used to test the effects of push notifications for those not engaging in a web-based ACT intervention (Watson, 2020). Finally, just-in-time adaptive intervention (JITAI) designs are a special type of adaptive intervention that uses a sequence of decision rules to specify an intervention depending on treatment needs (Nahum-Shani et al., 2018). In JITAIs, continuously collected digital data (e.g., EMA-based mood data) can be used to randomly assign participants to receive (or not) specific digitally delivered intervention content. Taken together, this broader set of qualitative and experimental research designs, which optimize an intervention that adapts to the changing contexts of the individual, are providing methods that are "catching up" to the way that contextual behaviorists have always thought about behavior: a specific intervention in a specific moment for a specific person. A main challenge ahead is to show the broader research community how these research designs work and why they are valuable in the overall spectrum of contextual behavioral research methods.

Participant Recruitment and Retention

Two serious and recurrent sources of bias in all behavioral research are participant recruitment and retention. Regarding recruitment, behavioral clinical trials often failed to recruit an adequate and generalizable sample of study participants (Walters et al., 2017). The lack of adequate sample size severely restricts statistical power, thereby making confidence intervals wide and results uninterpretable. Lack of broad reach in recruitment will often mean that people of color and other marginalized populations will not be included in the study, which implies that trial results will not apply to them (Chen, Lara, Dang, Paterniti, & Kelly, 2014). Fortunately, digital technologies are providing a platform for more efficient recruitment of harder-to-reach and traditionally underrepresented study populations. All major forms of digital social media (e.g., Facebook), as well as digital forms of traditional media (major newspapers), are now a vehicle for recruiting study participants. Often, these recruitment platforms include targeted advertisements designed to reach special populations such as youth, racial or ethnic minorities, sexual minorities, and rural populations. Compared to nondigital recruiting methods, such as flyers, bus ads, and radio ads, digital recruitment methods can yield a large and geographically broad study population in less time, lower cost, and with greater representation. For example, a recent study tested 16 research-designed Facebook ads to recruit for a digital ACT smoking cessation intervention trial. Within 32 days, the top three performing ads were identified, which altogether randomized 1299 participants from all 50 U.S. states at a cost of $40.51 USD per randomized participant (Watson, Mull, Heffner, McClure, & Bricker, 2018).

An ongoing problem in behavioral intervention research is participant attrition. Missing follow-up data can bias a result in favor of those who responded to treatment, as those participants are more likely to complete outcome assessments (Little et al., 2012). Often, missing participants are racial/ethnic minorities and those with lower education and income (Flores et al., 2017). Digital technologies have been helpful in preventing attrition because of their ability to track study participants and offer a convenient method for them to provide objective and self-reported data. For example, by providing such methods as time-limited reinforcers for outcome survey completion (e.g., a $10 bonus for completing an online survey within 24 hours), 12-month follow-up rates of nearly 90% can be obtained (Bricker et al., 2020). Because surveys were initially offered online, such a 24-hour reinforcer was practical, and would not have been possible with traditional mailed survey methods. Future contextual behavioral research can collaborate with public opinion and communications researchers in applying contextual behavioral principles in the design of study recruitment social media message framing (e.g., appealing to values) and online retention methods (e.g., reinforcement schedules for incentives). Such research would have broad implications across all fields of clinical research.

As this section has shown, contextual behavioral scientists conducting digital research adaptations have spent the past decade rethinking their scientific questions, forming transdisciplinary collaborations, employing a broad range of study designs, and addressing the challenges of recruiting and retaining study participants. For the next decade to grow in impact, contextual behavioral researchers will need to stay informed of developments in a broad array of *nonbehavioral* disciplines (e.g., engineering) by reading their literature, attending digital technology conferences, remaining aware of changes in available technology, and forming transdisciplinary collaborations. Contextual behavioral research in technology is an emerging area, so scientists have many opportunities to develop research programs in this domain.

The Importance of Systemic Influences in Treatment

Most of the gold standard therapies for physical and psychological health concerns in adulthood focus on the individual (American Psychological Association, Division 12).[2] According to the Society of Child Clinical and Adolescent Psychology, however, many of the most effective treatments for youth include the family and other systemic factors.[3] For example, the existing literature on evidenced-based treatments for anxiety in young children and teens indicates that family-based cognitive-behavioral treatment (CBT) and CBT for parents, along with their affected children, have the most support. Similar treatment is recommended for disruptive behavior problems, obsessive-compulsive, and bipolar disorders. The strongest evidence supports inclusion of teachers in addressing problematic issues associated with autism spectrum disorder and specific learning disorders (APA Division 53 website, 2021).

Although youth obviously have different needs than adults, historically child interventions have been "scaled-down" versions of adult treatment models that ignore developmental aspects and relationships that affect developmental pathways. In the last 25 years or so, evidence has accumulated indicating that inclusion of parents, siblings, peers, and teachers can bolster treatment effects (Kazdin, 1995). Systems-oriented approaches such as multisystemic therapy (MST; Henggeler, Schoenwald, Borduin, Rowland, & Cunningham, 1998) or the EcoFIT model (Dishion & Stormshak, 2007) account for not only the inclusion of these multiple variables (e.g., maternal influence, peer modeling) but also bidirectional relationships among them (e.g., parents' relationships with teachers affecting child behavior).

Systems-oriented approaches are grounded in the principles of ecological treatment (Brofenbrenner, 1979) in which child, family, peer, teacher, community, and cultural factors are all considered. MST (Henggeler, Schoenwald, Borduin, Rowland, & Cunningham, 1998) has been utilized primarily for externalizing disorders but has also been applied to internalizing problems and physical health concerns. In terms of addressing externalizing problems, MST has become a gold standard; it is used in more than 500 sites internationally, and over 100 peer-reviewed articles have been published on its efficacy. MST works well for criminal offending, substance use, sexual offending, and other conduct problems (Henggeler & Schaeffer, 2019). In a review of the literature, MST for health problems was found to lead to greater benefits than treatment as usual for obesity and diabetes, but the need for further study was noted (Pane, White, Nadorff, Grills-Taquechel, & Stanley, 2013). The same review of MST showed mixed results for internalizing symptoms, primarily finding that MST did work better than treatment as usual for serious emotional difficulties at immediate treatment conclusion and short-term follow-up, but the difference in MST and effects of the treatment as usual were not significant by one-year follow-up (Pane et al., 2013).

The EcoFIT model has several core similarities to the MST; it is an ecological model, empirically based and assessment driven. In this model, caregivers are utilized to propel changes in child behavior. Mindful and engaged caregivers change their interactions with their children as needed and advocate for their children appropriately in school and in broader family settings. It is equally effective across several diverse cultural groups (Stormshak et al., 2011). The model can be modified such that it is implemented in school settings, which fits a public health prevention model (O'Connell, Boat, & Warner, 2009), and it can be scaled up or down to include a variety of prevention and intervention services. The Eco-FIT model was designed to link individual family and community resources such as scouts' programs, sports leagues, library programs, and school tutors. Recent research shows that if the model is implemented as "school readiness," parents and school staff are more receptive to it than if it were to be labeled as treatment for "at-risk" youth (O'Connell et al., 2009).

Other systemic approaches to child treatment are available—for example, the Maudsley approach to eating disorders (Rhodes, 2003) and trauma systems therapy for trauma and stressor-related disorders (Brown, Laitner, & Saxe, 2017). In every case, these systems-oriented approaches include family and school factors at varying levels, thereby bolstering treatment effectiveness. Given that these ecological models are intentionally built to be melded with community resources, they can reach a larger number of youth and can be implemented at a wide prevention level. Systems-oriented approaches can provide support for families—and even communities—as opposed to individual youth. Finally, given the multitude of factors addressed, and the ways in which the model addresses relationships among factors, systems approaches are far more likely to address comorbidity and complex problem sequelae.

How ACT Is a Systems-Oriented Approach, the Work Thus Far, and Where It Needs to Go

Given that the root metaphor of contextualism, the philosophy of science that underlies ACT, is "the act in context" (Pepper, 1942), it is logical that the principles of ecological treatment would apply. These systems-oriented principles dictate inclusion of multidirectional influence at varied levels of a youth's environment. With regard to the ecological model, the most proximal level of influence includes a child's individual factors such as genetic predisposition and phenotypic expression of physical traits, as well as their typical ways of interacting with the world. Within an ACT framework, individual-level factors also include private events such as thoughts, feelings, and bodily sensations (Hayes, Strosahl, & Wilson, 1999). While the ACT work with youth is not yet as advanced as it is with adults, as of December 2020, there were 14 randomized controlled trials targeting youth's processes (e.g., mindfulness, valuing, acceptance) or outcomes (e.g., anxiety, depression, chronic pain) at the individual level. There are multiple case studies and noncontrolled group studies as well.[4]

Individual factors are thought to be dynamic, especially at certain times during development (e.g., middle childhood; Collins, Madsen, & Susman-Stillman, 2002). Further, these ever-changing and interacting factors influence and are influenced by other contextual variables. Such variables may include the quality of parent–child relationship, sibling relationship factors, economic resources of the school the youth attends, the ethnic culture in which the youth primarily develops, the parents' relationship with one another, the mother's work stress, and so on.

As of today, a fair number of studies have been completed that directly target parents' responses to their children's varied difficulties. Several studies (e.g., Gould, Tarbox, & Coyne, 2018) address the difficulties of parenting a child who has autism spectrum disorder. There are also several empirical articles, many of them RCTs, about parenting a child with chronic illness (e.g., Whittingham, Sanders, McKinlay, & Boyd, 2015). In addition, a handful of studies address the parent–child interaction while targeting issues such as parental posttraumatic stress disorder (PTSD; Lane, 2018), COVID (Szabo, Richling, Embry, Biglan, & Wilson, 2020), and youth chronic pain (Kemani, Kanstrup, Jordan, Caes, & Gauntlett-Gilbert, 2018).

As a reminder, all these larger factors are also theorized to be dynamic and to influence each other in multidirectional ways (Brofenbrenner, 1979). Although we have made a great start, we have a long way to go; for example, little investigation has been done on sibling influence or political climate. It is impossible to identify all the ways in which youth, or the system in which they function, is influenced in ever-changing fashion. Fortunately, ACT is grounded in a specific type of contextualism—that of functional contextualism. This specific philosophy of science, like all contextualism, is about pragmatism (Pepper, 1942). The explicit goal of functional contextualism is to predict and influence human behavior with precision, scope, and depth. Therefore, the level of variable selection and manipulation that is chosen is designed to help move youth forward in their lives. Going back to the evidenced-based literature, we find, however, that broad influence appears to lead to big impact.

That is why we are embracing ACT as a systemic approach to youth treatment. A few studies of ACT with families have been done that are broader than parent–child dyads. Masuda and colleagues provided eight family sessions (minus a sibling) to help a family cope with the stresses of a member having sickle-cell disease (Masuda, Cohen, Wicksell, Kemani, & Johnson, 2011). While they met separately, Timko et al. (2015) provided ACT to all family members of a youth presenting with anorexia nervosa (Timko, Zucker, Rodriguez, & Merwin, 2015). A recent dissertation on ACT (Bisetty, 2018) examined the influence of cultural factors on family treatment, truly exemplifying the systemic nature of the model.

Another area in which systemic emphasis has been high is within the recent incorporation of ACT into school systems by using the Connect PSHE Curriculum, for example (Gillard, Flaxman, & Hooper, 2018). Previous attempts have been made to integrate mindfulness and acceptance-based treatments into schools. One of these attempts has come from ACT developers (Ciarrochi, Atkins, Hayes, Sandra, & Parker, 2016). In the article in which they suggest using positive psychology, they state that the context must be relied upon heavily, and they make six specific recommendations. And as Ciarrochi et al. themselves hint at in six steps (i.e., they write that the first five steps should also be applied to social groups as well as individuals), the recommendations should be applied not only to an individual youth but to each of the ecological system levels within which they function. While this may seem to be an overwhelming task to a functional contextual psychologist, the direction is simple: do whatever works!

Promoting Contextual Behavioral Science across Cultural Contexts

ACT, the poster child of CBS, originated from a Western cultural world view in the early 1980s (Hayes, 1987). Since then, ACT has been shaped into diverse forms (e.g., individual psychotherapy, group therapy, bibliotherapy, e-therapy) and adapted for use in various applied and clinical settings for promoting health and well-being. For the past two decades, ACT and CBS also have been disseminated across the globe, including Africa, Asia, Central America, Oceania, and South America (Masuda, 2020). This global-level dissemination effort is prompted in part by a large body of evidence pointing to ACT and CBS as a unified framework for promoting well-being and adaptive behavior change (Twohig, Levin, & Ong, 2020).

Which Regions in the World Represent the CBS?

To date, despite their global-level recognition, ACT and CBS have not been disseminated uniformly across all regions of the world. One index for explicating differential dissemination efforts across the globe is to count the number of ACT RCTs completed in a given geographic region during a given period of time. To do so, we have looked into ACT RCTs published in a peer-reviewed journal since 2018. To be included in this analysis, the entire manuscript had to be available in English. To make this analysis as parsimonious as possible, we simply reviewed the country where participants of these study were recruited (e.g., the United States, Iran, and Sweden) and then categorized the respective country into one of seven regional groups: Africa, the European Union plus the United Kingdom; North America; Central and South America; East, South, and Central Asia; West Asia (Middle East); and Oceania.

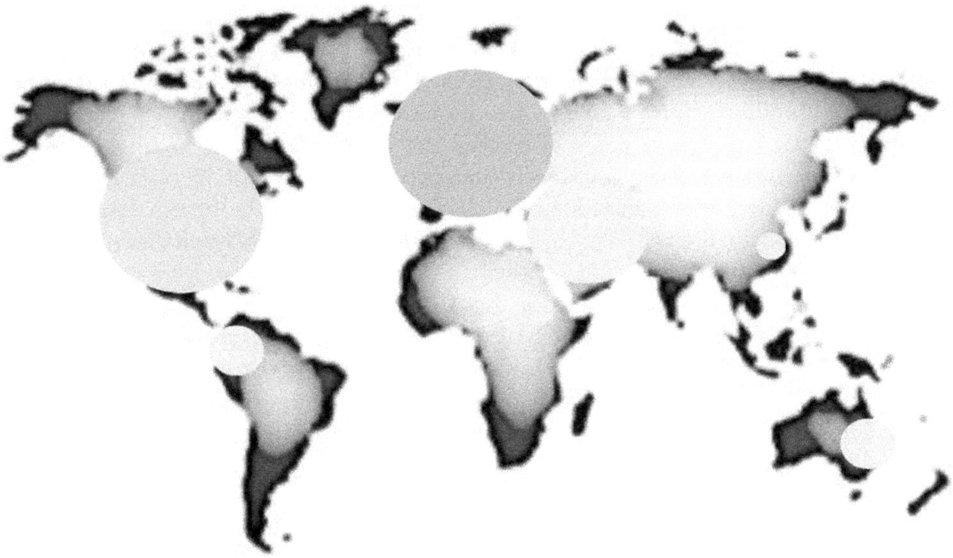

Figure 32.1. The number of ACT randomized control trials (RCT) published since 2018 across different geographic regions in the world (n = 145).

Of 195 RCTs presented in the Association for Contextual Behavioral Science (ACBS) website (2021),[5] the full texts of 145 RCT studies were available in English. Figure 32.1 is a visual presentation of the regions in the world map where the participants of ACT RCTs since 2018 were recruited. Seven circles on the map represent the seven regional groups, and the size of a circle visually reflects the number of published RCTs in that region (bigger circle for more published RCTs). As seen in Figure 32.1, 67 percent% of ACT RCTs published since 2018 were conducted in either EU plus UK (n = 56 studies) or North America (n = 41 studies). Somewhat surprisingly, West Asia (almost exclusively from Iran) produced 32 ACT RCTs, which has yielded approximately 22 percent of the total ACT RCTs published since 2018. As expected, a smaller number of ACT RCTs are conducted in Central and South America (n = 5), Oceania (n = 5), East, South, and Central Asia (n = 4), and Africa (n = 2). Again, this analysis has several limitations (e.g., relying almost exclusively on peer-reviewed English-language journals published in Western cultures; regional disparities in resources available to conduct an RCT). That being said, the present analysis sheds light on the current geographic trend within ACT research by providing an estimate of the extent to which different regions in the world are represented in CBS research.

What Can Be Done to Promote CBS Research in Underrepresented Regions?

Importantly, CBS is one among several approaches that contribute to health and well-being in the world. Thus, as discussed elsewhere (Masuda, 2020), because other relevant approaches are available, the utility of ACT may be limited in some geographical areas and potentially may sometimes even be inappropriate. This may also be the case for CBS, and so we want to highlight the importance of being aware of assumptions regarding the generalizability of CBS to different cultural and/or geographical contexts that are not yet empirically validated.

Across the globe many culturally situated and sustainable practices have nurtured humans for thousands of years (e.g., Masuda & O'Donohue, 2017). From a larger CBS perspective, some of the underrepresented regions (Figure 32.1) may contain cultures with social contingencies and infrastructures established to promote health and well-being (see Hayes & Toarmino, 1995, for a CBS account of cultural and individual levels of contingencies). For example, although Japan remains relatively underrepresented within CBS, various indices of health and well-being (e.g., average life expectancy, access to public health care system, rate of obesity and metabolic disease) may suggest that Japan has reasonably well-established infrastructures for promoting health and well-being as well as cultural contingencies to do so. In cultural contexts such as Japan, it may be that CBS is most useful when augmenting extant infrastructures and cultural practices of health and well-being, rather than replacing or modifying them. Conversely, however, in some contexts CBS can have a large impact on health and well-being by altering the common approach (White, Gregg, Batten, Hayes, & Kasujja, 2017). For example, fruitful efforts of CBS as a *commit and act* approach were recently seen during the ebola crisis in Sierra Leone (Stewart et al., 2016).

Therefore, when analyzing the geographical distribution of CBS research, as illustrated in Figure 32.1, particularly the parts of the world where CBS is underrepresented, it is important to critically assess and evaluate factors that may explain this underrepresentation, and whether CBS can bring any additive benefits to these cultural and regional contexts without exploiting them unduly.

Does the CBS Model Need to Be Culturally Adapted?

Given its functional and contextual nature, when applied to diverse sociocultural contexts, the CBS model of behavior change does not need to be modified significantly at the basic-principle or philosophical level (Masuda, 2014b). Importantly, however, the specific methods (ACT) should always be applied in a contextually sensitive way, that is, adapted to a given individual(s) in particular sociocultural contexts (Masuda, 2020).

One area where CBS can be particularly relevant to these underrepresented regions is *public health* (see also the material regarding the application of CBS at a societal level). One common feature of many underrepresented regions in CBS is the lack of mental health literacy or mental health service literacy. This lack may, in part, be due to an absence of a clear mind–body dichotomy in their native cultures or to a difference in the language used to describe these phenomena. It is important to note that this may not necessarily imply that the significance of mental health/behavioral health issues is overlooked, but rather it may reflect a different view on mental health/behavioral health issues (e.g., holistically as part of "health," "lifestyle," and "socialization").

Additionally, cultures of underrepresented regions seem to be more communal and collectivistic than individualistic (Markus & Kitayama, 2010). As such, the framework of *public health* can be particularly suitable to people of these cultures. As discussed previously, the *commit and act* initiative is a salient example of how a CBS approach was successfully adapted for offsetting a series of public health crises in Sierra Leone. Furthermore, the importance of adapting CBS and other approaches concerning human behavior to optimize the effectiveness across different cultural contexts has been illustrated during the ongoing global challenge of the COVID-19 pandemic.

What Kinds of Research Needs to Be Done?

The synthesis of knowledge and evidence regarding the *cultural considerations* of ACT and CBS is still in its infancy (Masuda, 2020). To date, the importance of effective cultural adaptation of ACT has been investigated conceptually more so than empirically in the context of third-wave cognitive-behavioral therapies (Masuda, 2014a,b), treatment development (Hayes, Long, Levin, & Follette, 2013), and the inclusion of underrepresented groups in ACT research (Woidneck, Pratt, Gundy, Nelson, & Twohig, 2012). Similarly, ACT scholars have begun to examine the *cross-cultural utility and validity* of ACT and the psychological flexibility model (PFM) in various cultural contexts (e.g., see Masuda et al., this volume). Given its importance, we hope that the same level of careful investigation is done for the cultural adaption of ACT and CBS, as we have done for a wide variety of specific behavioral health issues (e.g., depression, anxiety, chronic pain).

Cultural considerations of ACT and CBS can be examined through *two pathways* of empirical verification. One pathway is through generalizability studies across all theoretical and applied aspects of ACT and CBS, using the empirical evidence from European and North American regions as a reference point. Although it would be reasonable to assume that ACT and CBS strategies are broadly applicable to a wide range of sociocultural contexts, universality assumptions are often not supported by data because of the sample- and context-dependent nature of psychological model and applied methods (e.g., Hall, Yip, & Zárate, 2016). Similarly, the field of diversity psychology has emphasized the importance of directly testing a given conceptual model or applied method of interest with the target sample of interest (Cheng & Sue, 2014). These include ACT and other CBS-informed treatment interventions in a given format of delivery (e.g., individual therapy, digital interventions) as well as various assessment methods.

Given the scarcity of research evaluating the generalizability of theoretical constructs and applied methods across cultural contexts, this pathway requires careful considerations of the psychometric properties of instruments developed and evaluated in one context and subsequently applied to a new and culturally distinct population. For example, studying psychological inflexibility among chronic pain patients in Japan using instruments developed in, for example, Europe or the United States requires not only a proper translation but also psychometric examinations to ascertain the adequacy of the Japanese version of the instrument (Nagasawa et al., 2021).

Another pathway to accumulate evidence of functional and contextual accounts of cultural adaption is to encourage researchers and clinicians to conduct a series of studies utilizing individual-level data. For example, studies using single-case experimental design (see the section on research methods) or simple clinical case studies can offer a detailed description of how, and in what context, a given intervention is provided with a client and how key variables of interest are identified and measured.

Finally, it has been historically challenging to include individuals from underrepresented populations across the globe in ACT research. Relatedly, there are disproportionately smaller numbers of ACT researchers and clinicians from these underrepresented groups, resulting in slower progress in cultural considerations of ACT. While this inequity in representation is generally paralleled in behavioral science research writ large (e.g., Henrich, Heine, & Norenzayan, 2010), leaders in ACT research call for greater conscientiousness from the community in filling these gaps in knowledge and, ultimately, service delivery (Hayes et al., 2013).

CBS at a Societal Level to Promote Public Health and Well-being

The ultimate benefit of our work could be stated as a significant increase in the prevalence of people living in nurturing environments. Such environments minimize physical and social conditions that threaten or harm people, richly reinforce all kinds of prosocial behavior, limit opportunities and influences for harmful behavior, and promote psychological flexibility (Biglan, Johansson, Van Ryzin, & Embry, 2020).

CBS, broadly conceived, has made enormous progress in identifying treatment and prevention interventions that can increase the prevalence of nurturing environments. By "broadly conceived," we mean all research that has studied how contexts affect well-being, not just research explicitly identified as contextual behavioral science. This point is important for future efforts to expand the benefit of what we have learned about human well-being. In addition to developing a rich array of clinical interventions that affect all of the most common and costly psychological and behavioral problems, today we have access to a wide variety of interventions to prevent these problems (Biglan, 2015). At the same time, economists and public health specialists have pinpointed more macro conditions that affect well-being and policies that can ameliorate those conditions. These conditions include poverty (Child Trends Databank, 2019), economic inequality (Wilkinson & Pickett, 2009), discrimination (Bailey et al., 2017), as well as the marketing of harmful substances such as tobacco (Biglan, 2020b), unhealthful food (Biglan, 2020a), guns (Biglan, 2020c), and alcohol (Pechmann, Biglan, Grube, & Cody, 2012). This body of evidence lays the foundation for expanding our work to affect well-being in entire populations. Based on a recent analyses of how we can scale up our impact (Biglan et al., 2020), following is a brief summary of what is yet needed.

Build a Coalition of All the Organizations Working to Improve Human Well-being

Elsewhere, the synthesis just summarized is labeled the Nurture Consilience (Biglan et al., 2020). A consilience involves "the linking of facts and fact-based theory across disciplines to create a common groundwork of explanation" (Wilson, 2012). Although there may be a better term for it, it is vital that all of the disparate groups working on one or another aspect of well-being recognize how their work fits with the work of others in defining not only the conditions humans need to thrive, but the values, norms, programs, policies, and practices that will foster those conditions. It is on this basis that not only behavioral science organizations, but all of the organizations that are working to advance well-being, need to find ways to speak with one voice about what is needed.

One of the most important reasons for speaking with one voice is that much of the current malaise that exists in societies across the world is due to the well-organized, but not well-understood, advocacy for free market economics. Its impact on well-being in the United States is well documented (Mayer, 2016). The core belief of free market ideology is that individuals' pursuit of their own economic well-being will necessarily benefit society. This view is not only not supported by the evidence (Biglan, 2020), but it is directly contrary to the evidence that humans are most likely to thrive when they work together for common goals.

Much of the current efforts to promote well-being are not connected with other efforts. For example, work on preventing harmful marketing through regulation has some groups opposing the marketing of tobacco, others opposing the marketing of unhealthful food, and still others opposing the marketing of guns. This advocacy occurs in the context of the widespread default assumption that government regulation is harmful. What is needed is advocacy for regulating *any* corporate practice that can be shown to harm a significant segment of the population. Imagine how much more powerful forces for nurturance would be if we had a network of organizations, all of which were supporting every effort to promote nurturing environments. Such a coalition would be more effective in assisting individual organizations in pursuing the improvements in well-being that they are working toward.

Build a Public Health Monitoring System That Tracks All Aspects of Human Well-Being Down to the Community Level

In any effort to influence a behavior, ongoing measurement is required. This is true for efforts that may affect the incidence and prevalence of behaviors in populations and the prevalence of nurturing environments. Technology and measures are available to track virtually any aspect of well-being. In the United States, at the national and to a lesser extent at the state level, as well as in other countries, systems are in place for tracking important aspects of public health, such as the prevalence of tobacco use, the incidence of suicide, and many other aspects of human well-being. The COVID-19 pandemic has shown us the importance of monitoring well-being in populations. However, if we are going to increase the prevalence of nurturance, every community will need at least annual data on the well-being of its residents. Such data will enable communities to motivate its members to adopt more effective policies and programs. Also, it will enable experimental comparisons of different strategies for improving well-being. Finally, it will direct attention to conditions, such as poverty and discrimination, which contribute to multiple, interconnected problems. This is important because we tend to focus on individual problems, and we ignore the larger context influencing multiple problems. For example, many schools and communities have programs to prevent substance use, other programs to prevent delinquency, and still others to prevent depression and suicide. These programs tend to focus on ameliorating proximal influences on the problem. For example, a depression prevention program may teach skills for dealing with depressive thoughts and feelings. This program can be helpful, but depression along with substance use and delinquency are made more likely by poverty. Monitoring the co-occurrence of these problems could increase the attention to modifying contextual conditions such as poverty and discrimination that contribute to the entire range of problems.

Get Much Better at Scaling Up Our Impact

Embracing the goal of affecting population well-being can become the consequence that selects our practices. That is, to the extent that our communities and our public health and health care system are seeking to affect population well-being, they will retain practices that are affecting population well-being and abandon or modify those that are not affecting population well-being. This is simply the application of evolutionary principles to the problem of public health. Another evolutionary principle that is relevant here is variation and selection. We should promote a wide variety of efforts to increase the reach of policies and programs that enhance well-being, assess their impact on population well-being, and retain those that are working. Of particular value will be technological developments (see the section on how technology can help us reach many more people).

Other things needed are strategies for getting entire health care systems to invest more in treatment and preventive interventions to affect substance use, depression, anxiety, antisocial behavior, and academic failure - all of which contribute to premature death. A wide variety of tested and effective treatment and prevention programs have been established (Komro, Flay, Biglan, & Promise Neighborhoods Research Consortium, 2011), but, perhaps because these are psychological and behavioral rather than medical interventions, health care systems are not implementing them to the extent that they should, given their efficacy. To the extent that the effectiveness of a health care system is measured in terms of its impact on population health, it will be more likely to adopt such practices.

Get Much Better at Affecting Public Policy

A large proportion of the behavioral science community is working on strategies for influencing the behavior of individuals, families, and small groups. This work has been foundational for much of the progress we have made. However, more efforts are needed at the population level. Public policy provides a way to affect the populations of individuals without the need for an individual change agent. Two types of policy are important for public health.

The first is policy that directly affects the behavior of individuals (Markowitz, Komro, Livingston, Lenhart, & Wagenaar, 2017a, 2017b). For example, increasing taxation on tobacco, alcohol, and unhealthful food can reduce the use of these substances and thereby prevent use and addiction (Biglan 2020). Similarly, a variety of policies have been shown to affect family economic well-being (National Academies of Sciences, Engineering, & Medicine, 2019).

The second type of policy consists of regulations that increase research and practices that affect entire populations. We need increased investment in treatment and prevention programs. We need policies that build the monitoring systems so that communities and the health care community are routinely reminded that their ultimate impact needs to be on population health. We need policies that require the use of evidence-based programs and policies. We need legislation that funds the research required to scale up our interventions.

What Members of the Contextual Behavioral Science Community Can Do

As a reader of this article, you are probably connected to the CBS community. Also, you are likely working on problems at the level of the individual (or group). Hopefully, after reading this section, you will understand the utility in addressing public health concerns at a societal level. If so, you can make a difference by joining us in efforts to (1) increase interdisciplinary work aimed at scaling up individual-focused interventions to reach a larger proportion of the population, (2) support ACBS and other behavioral science organizations advocating for public policies that advance population well-being, and (3) encourage the next generation of behavioral scientists to work in communities and policymaking contexts to affect population health.

Concluding Remarks

In the past two decades, developments within the field of contextual behavioral science have been remarkable. During this same period of time, the world has undergone several major changes. Some processes were rather quick, such as digitalization, but others, such as global warming, are more gradual. But all have clear implications for the years to come. Foreseeing the future has always been important, providing clear advantages to those who excel in this complex task. The term *megatrend* is sometimes used to describe developments with great impact, commonly referring to events with the potential to represent a global threat but also contextual changes that may facilitate growth and equity. Right now, as the world is currently facing one of the most severe challenges of our time, trends, trajectories, and predictions of the future are discussed everywhere. And these discussions inform decisions in areas ranging from local businesses and child sport activities to regional health care strategies and international travel policies. The COVID-19 pandemic has in a brutal way pointed at the importance of understanding behaviors in context (although this disease is caused by a virus, arguably the key ingredient of a pandemic is human behavior), and the necessity of collaborating across any form of border.

In this last article of this volume, experts in contextual behavioral science share their thoughts on future directions, pointing out challenges as well as opportunities. Our hope is to inspire and direct attention toward some of the key areas of further development: Continuous efforts to refine the theoretical framework is an exciting, yet challenging, endeavor, ideally undertaken in close collaboration with fellow researchers in related disciplines. New, and not so new, methods to understand a person in context, as well as the individual change processes, can generate a more precise description of how we can tailor interventions to meet specific needs. Because much of our digital literacy is rapidly increasing, we are only in the beginning of an era when access to new technical resources will provide unprecedented opportunities to enhance behavioral health for individuals and societies, if used wisely. The recent years showed with clarity the importance of the social context for resilience in individuals as well as groups and societies, emphasizing the utility of a systems-oriented approach to complex clinical challenges. Scientific literature on CBS illustrates a strikingly uneven geographical distribution of research, and many questions regarding the applicability across different cultural contexts remain. The flexibility of the CBS approach makes it ideal to address public health, and although some problems require individual interventions, well-orchestrated efforts at a societal level are both needed and feasible.

In conclusion, reflecting on past achievements and current activities gives us a sense of optimism regarding the future. We are grateful to friends and colleagues around the world for all the hard work, and we hope for more and new collaborations adding to the growth and development of the field. A better world requires better research, treatments, educational programs, and public health policies. If we can be useful, please reach out—for collaboration, advice, or simply a chat. Making a difference takes a village.

Notes

1. An early term used for the same process as defusion.
2. Retrieved from https://div12.org/diagnoses/ in 2020.
3. Retrieved from https://effectivechildtherapy.org/concerns-symptoms-disorders in 2020.
4. Results retrieved from https://contextualscience.org/state_of_the_act_evidence on December 13, 2020.
5. https://contextualscience.org/ACT_Randomized_Controlled_Trials, November 12, 2020.

References

ACBS website. (2021). https://contextualscience.org

Anthony, C. A., Rojas, E. O., Keffala, V., Glass, N. A., Shah, A. S., Miller, B. J., . . . & Marsh, J. L. (2020). Acceptance and commitment therapy delivered via a mobile phone messaging robot to decrease postoperative opioid use in patients with orthopedic trauma: Randomized controlled trial. *Journal of Medical Internet Research, 22*(7), e17750.

APA Division 12 website. (2021). https://div12.org/

APA Division 53 website. (2021). https://sccap53.org/

Bailey, Z. D., Krieger, N., Agénor, M., Graves, J., Linos, N., & Bassett, M. T. (2017). Structural racism and health inequities in the USA: evidence and interventions. *The Lancet, 389*(10077), 1453–1463. doi:https://doi.org/10.1016/S0140-6736(17)30569-X

Barnes-Holmes, D., Hayes, S. C., & Dymond, S. (2001). Self and self-directed rules. In S. C. Hayes, D. Barnes-Holmes, & B. Roche. (Eds.). *Relational frame theory: A post-skinnerian account of human language and cognition* (pp. 103–118). New York: Kluwer Academic/Plenum Publishers.

Bentley, K. H., Kleiman, E. M., Elliott, Huffman, J. C., & Knock, M. K. (2019). Real-time monitoring technology in single-case experimental design research: Opportunities and challenges. *Behavior Research and Therapy, 117,* 87–96.

Berghoff, C. R., Ritzert, T. R., & Forsyth, J. P. (2018). Value-guided action: Within-day and lagged relations of experiential avoidance, mindful awareness, and cognitive fusion in a non-clinical sample. *Journal of Contextual Behavioral Science, 10,* 19–23.

Bernstein, A., Hadash, Y., Lichtash, Y., Tanay, G., Shepherd, K., & Fresco, D. M (2015) Decentering and related construct: A critical review and metacognitive processing model. *Perpectives on Psychological Science, 10,* 599–617

Biglan, A. (2015). *The nurture effect: How the science of human behavior can improve our lives and our world.* Oakland, CA: New Harbinger Publications.

Biglan, A. (2020). *Rebooting capitalism: How behavioral science can forge a society that works for everyone.* Eugene, OR: Values to Action.

Biglan, A. (2020a). How and why the food industry makes Americans sick. Social Pathologies Series. Retrieved from https://evolution-institute.org/how-and-why-the-food-industry-makes-americans-sick.

Biglan, A. (2020b). How cigarette marketing killed 20 million people. Social Pathologies Series. Retrieved from https://evolution-institute.org/how-cigarette-marketing-killed-20-million-people.
Biglan, A. (2020c). The right to sell arms. Retrieved from https://evolution-institute.org/the-right-to-sell-arms.
Biglan, A., Johansson, M., Van Ryzin, M., & Embry, D. (2020). Scaling up and scaling out: Consilience and the evolution of more nurturing societies. *Clinical Psychology Review, 81.*
Bisetty, M. (2018). *Multiculturally Conscious Acceptance and Commitment Therapy: A Proposed Treatment Intervention for Latino and Mexican-American Families Affected by Childhood Cancer* [Doctoral dissertation, Antioch University]. OhioLINK Electronic Theses and Dissertations Center. http://rave.ohiolink.edu/etdc/view?acc_num=antioch1527527955816642
Borckardt, J. J., Nash, M. R., Murphy, M. D., Moore, M., Shaw, D., & O'Neil, P. (2008). Clinical practice as natural laboratory for psychotherapy research. *American Psychologist, 63,* 77–93.
Bricker, J. B., Watson, N. L., Mull, K. E., Sullivan, B. M., & Heffner, J. L. (2020). Efficacy of smartphone applications for smoking cessation: A randomized clinical trial. *Journal of the American Medical Association: Internal Medicine,* 4(1). doi:10.2196/16652
Brofenbrenner, U. (1979). *The ecology of human development: Experiments by nature and design.* Cambridge, MA: Harvard University Press.
Brown, A., Laitner, C., & Saxe, G. (2017). Trauma systems therapy for children and adolescents. In M. A. Landolt, M. Cloitre, U. Schnyder, M. A. Landolt, M. Cloitre, & U. Schnyder (Eds.), *Evidence-based treatments for trauma related disorders in children and adolescents* (pp. 363–384). New York: Springer International Publishing. https://doi-org.ezproxy.memphis.edu/10.1007/978-3-319-46138-0_17
Callejón, Z. (2020) Training the hierarchical responding. Unpublished doctoral thesis Facultad de Psicología Universidad de Almeria.
Caneiro, J. P., Smith, A., Linton, S. J., Moseley, G. L., & O'Sullican, P. (2019). How does change unfold? An evaluation of the process of change in four people with chronic low back pain and high pain-related fear management with cognitive functional therapy: A replicated single-case experimental design. *Behavior Research and Therapy, 117,* 28–39.
Chen, M. S., Lara, P. N., Dang, J. H., Paterniti, D. A., & Kelly, K. (2014). Twenty years post NIH revitalization act: Enhancing minority participation in clinical trials (EMPaCT): laying the groundwork for improving minority clinical trial accrual. *Cancer, 120,* 1091–1096. doi:10.1002/cncr.28575
Cheng, J. K. Y., & Sue, S. (2014). Addressing cultural and ethnic minority issues in the acceptance and mindfulness movement. In A. Masuda (Eds.), *Mindfulness and acceptance in multicultural competency: A contextual approach to sociocultural diversity in theory and practice* (pp. 21–37). Oakland, CA: Context Press/New Harbinger Publications.
Child Trends Databank. (2019). Children in poverty. Retrieved from https://www.childtrends.org/?indicators=children-in-poverty
Chomsky, N. (1959). Reviews. Verbal behavior by B. F. Skinner. *Language, 35,* 26–58.
Christodoulou, A., Michaelides, M., & Karekla, M. (in press). Network analysis: A new psychometric approach to examine the underlying ACT model components. *Journal of Contextual Behavioral Science, 12,* 285–289.
Ciarrochi, J., Atkins, P. W. B., Hayes, L. L., Sahdra, B. K., & Parker, P. (2016). Contextual positive psychology: Policy recommendations for implementing positive psychology into schools. *Frontiers in Psychology, 7.*
Collins, L. M., Baker, T. B., Mermelstein, R. J., Piper, M. E., Jorenby, D. E., Smith, S. S., . . . & Fiore, M. C. (2011). The multiphase optimization strategy for engineering effective tobacco use interventions. *Annals of Behavioral Medicine, 41*(2), 208–226. doi:10.1007/s12160-010-9253-x
Collins, W. A., Madsen, S. D., & Susman-Stillman, A. (2002). Parenting during middle childhood from: *Handbook of parenting, children and parenting.* London: Routledge. Accessed on: 13 Dec 2020. https://www.routledgehandbooks.com/doi/10.4324/9781410612137.ch3
Davies, A., & Mueller, J. (2020). *Developing medical apps and MHealth interventions: A guide for researchers, physicians and informaticians*: Cham, Switzerland: Springer International Publishing AG.
De Houwer, J., Barnes-Holmes, D., & Moors, A. (2013) What is learning? On the nature and merits of a functional definition of learning. *Psychonomic Bulletin and Review, 20,* 631–642.
Demjén, Z, & Semino, E. (2017) Using metaphor in health care. Physical health. In Z. Demjén & E. Semino (Eds.), *The Routledge handbook of metaphor and language* (pp. 385–399). New York: Taylor and Francis.
Dishion, T. J., & Stromshak, E. A. (2007). Intervening in children's lives: An ecological, family-centered approach to mental health care. Washington, DC: APA Press.
Fisher, A. J., Bosley, H. G., Fernandez, K. C., Reeves, J. W., Soyster, P. D., Diamond, A. E., & Barken, J. (2019). Open trial of a personalized modular treatment for mood and anxiety. *Behavior Research and Therapy, 116,* 69–79.
Fisher, A. J., Medaglia, J. D., & Jeronimus, B. F. (2018). Lack of group-to-individual generalizability is a threat to human subjects research. *PNAS, 115,* E6106–E6115.

Flores, G., Portillo, A., Lin, H., Walker, C., Fierro, M., Henry, M., & Massey, K. (2017). A successful approach to minimizing attrition in racial/ethnic minority, low-income populations. *Contemporary Clinical Trials Communications, 5*, 168–174. doi:10.1016/j.conctc.2017.01.009

Foody, M., Barnes-Holmes, Y., Barnes-Holmes, D., & Luciano, C. (2013). An empirical investigation of hierarchical versus distinction relations in a self-based ACT exercise. *International Journal of Psychology and Psychological Therapy, 13*(3), 373–388.

Gil, E., Luciano, C., Ruiz, F. J., & Valdivia-Salas, V. (2012). A preliminary demonstration of transformation of functions through hierarchical relations. *International Journal of, Psychology and Psychological Therapy, 12*(1), 1–19.

Gillard, D., Flaxman, P., & Hooper, N. (2018). Acceptance and commitment therapy: applications for educational psychologists within schools. *Educational Psychology in Practice*, 34(3), 272–281. https://doi-org.ezproxy.memphis.edu/10.1080/02667363.2018.1446911

Gould, E. R., Tarbox, J., & Coyne, L. (2018) Evaluating the effects of acceptance and commitment training on the overt behavior of parents of children with autism. *Journal of Contextual Behavioral Science, 7*, 81–88.

Hall, G. C. N., Yip, T., & Zárate, M. A. (2016). On becoming multicultural in a monocultural research world: A conceptual approach to studying ethnocultural diversity. *American Psychologist, 71*(1), 40–51. doi:10.1037/a0039734

Hayes, S. C. (1984) Making sense of spirituality. *Behaviorism, 12*(2), 99–110.

Hayes, S. C. (1987). A contextual approach to therapeutic change. In N. S. Jacobson (Ed.), *Psychotherapists in clinical practice: Cognitive and behavioral perspectives* (pp. 327–387). New York: Guilford Press.

Hayes S. C., Barnes-Holmes, D. & Roche, B. (Eds.). (2001). *Relational frame theory: A post-Skinnerian account of human language and cognition.* New York: Kluwer Academic/Plenum Publishers.

Hayes, S. C., & Hayes, L. J. (1992). Verbal relations and the evolution of behavior analysis. *American Psychologist, 47*, 1383–1395.

Hayes, S. C., & Hofmann, S. G. (2018). The third wave of cognitive behavioral therapy and the rise of process-based care. *World Psychiatry, 16*, 245–246.

Hayes, S. C., Hofmann, S. G., Stanton, C. E., Carpenter, J. K., Sanford, B. T., Curtiss, J. E., & Ciarrochi, J. (2019). The role of the individual in the coming era of process-based therapy. *Behavior Research and Therapy, 117*, 40–53.

Hayes, S. C., Long, D. M., Levin, M. E., & Follette, W. C. (2013). Treatment development: Can we find a better way? *Clinical Psychology Review, 33*(7), 870–882. doi:10.1016/j.cpr.2012.09.009

Hayes, S. C., Strosahl, K., & Wilson, K. G. (1999). *Acceptance and commitment therapy: An experiential approach to behavior change.* New York: Guilford Press.

Hayes, S. C., & Toarmino, D. (1995). If behavioral principles are generally applicable, why is it necessary to understand cultural diversity? *The Behavior Therapist, 18*, 21–23.

Henggeler, S. W., & Schaeffer, C. M. (2019). Multisystemic therapy®: Clinical procedures, outcomes, and implementation research. In B. H. Fiese, M. Celano, K. Deater-Deckard, E. N. Jouriles, & M. A. Whisman (Eds.), *APA handbooks in psychology®. APA handbook of contemporary family psychology: Family therapy and training* (pp. 205–220). Washington, DC: American Psychological Association. https://doi.org/10.1037/0000101-013

Henggeler, S. W., Schoenwald, S. K., Borduin, C. M., Rowland, M. D., & Cunningham, P. B. (1998). *Multisystemic treatment of antisocial behavior in children and adolescents.* New York: Guilford Press.

Henrich, J., Heine, S. J., & Norenzayan, A. (2010). The weirdest people in the world? *Behavioral and Brain Sciences, 33*(2–3), 61–83.

Hooper, N., Erdogan, A., Keen, G., Lawton, K. & McHugh, L. (2015). Perspective taking reduces the fundamental attribution error. *Journal of Contextual Behavioral Science, 4*, 69–72.

Järvelä-Reijonen, E., Puttonen, S., Karhunen, L., Sairanen, E., Laitinen, J., Kolehmainen, M., . . . & Kolehmainen, M. (2020). The effects of acceptance and commitment therapy (ACT) intervention on inflammation and stress biomarkers: A randomized controlled trial. *International Journal of Behavioral Medicine, 27*, 539–555.

JMIR. (2020). *Journal of Medical Internet Research.* Retrieved from https://www.jmir.org

Kazdin, A. E. (1995). Bridging child, adolescent, and adult psychotherapy: Directions for research. *Psychotherapy Research, 5*, 258–277.

Kemani, M. K., Kanstrup, M., Jordan, A., Caes, L., & Gauntlett-Gilbert, J. (2018). Evaluation of an intensive interdisciplinary pain treatment based on acceptance and commitment therapy for adolescents with chronic pain and their parents: A nonrandomized clinical trial. *Journal of Pediatric Psychology*, 43(9), 981–994. https://doi-org.ezproxy.memphis.edu/10.1093/jpepsy/jsy031

Klasnja, P., Hekler, E. B., Shiffman, S., Boruvka, A., Almirall, D., Tewari, A., & Murphy, S. A. (2015). Micro-randomized trials: An experimental design for developing just-in-time adaptive interventions. *Health Psychology, 34*, 1220–1228. doi:10.1037/hea0000305

Komro, K. A., Flay, B. R., Biglan, A., & Promise Neighborhoods Research Consortium (2011). Creating nurturing environments: a science-based framework for promoting child health and development within high-poverty

neighborhoods. *Clinical child and family psychology review, 14*(2), 111–134. https://doi.org/10.1007/s10567-011-0095-2
Kurz, A. S., Johnson, Y. L., Kellum, K. K., & Wilson, K. G. (2019). How can process-based researchers bridge the gap between individuals and groups? Discover the dynamic p-technique. *Journal of Contextual Behavioral Science, 13*, 60–65.
Lane, M. M. (2018). Acceptance and commitment therapy (ACT) adapted for use with adolescents of veterans with PTSD [ProQuest Information & Learning]. In *Dissertation Abstracts International*: Section B: The Sciences and Engineering, *78*(10),–B(E).
Levin, M. E., Krafft, J., Pierce, B., & Potts, S. (2018). When is experiential avoidance harmful in the moment? Examining global experiential avoidance as a moderator. *Journal of Behavior Therapy and Experimental Psychiatry, 61*, 158–163. doi:10.1016/j.jbtep.2018.07.005
Little, R. J., D'Agostino, R., Cohen, M. L., Dickersin, K., Emerson, S. S., Farrar, J. T., . . . & Stern, H. (2012). The prevention and treatment of missing data in clinical trials. *New England Journal of Medicine*, 367(14), 1355–1360.
Luciano, C., Ruiz, F. J., Vizcaíno-Torres, R. M., Sánchez-Martín, V., Gutiérrez-Martínez, O., & López-López, J. C. (2011). A relational frame analysis of defusion interactions in acceptance and commitment therapy: A preliminary and quasi-experimental study with at- risk adolescents. *International Journal of Psychology and Psychological Therapy, 11*, 165–182.
Markowitz, S., Komro, K. A., Livingston, M. D., Lenhart, O., & Wagenaar, A. C. (2017a). Effects of state-level earned income tax credit laws in the U.S. on maternal health behaviors and infant health outcomes. *Social Science and Medicine, 194*, 67–75. doi:10.1016/j.socscimed.2017.10.016
Markowitz, S., Komro, K. A., Livingston, M. D., Lenhart, O., & Wagenaar, A. C. (2017b). Effects of state-level earned income tax credit laws in the U.S. on maternal health behaviors and infant health outcomes. National Institute on Minority Health and Health Disparities, NIH. National Bureau of Economic Research. Retrieved from http://www.nber.org/papers/w23714
Markus, H. R., & Kitayama, S. (2010). Cultures and selves: A cycle of mutual constitution. *Perspectives on Psychological Science*, 5(4), 420–430. doi:10.1177/1745691610375557
Masuda, A. (2014a). Psychotherapy in cultural context. In A. Masuda (Ed.), *Mindfulness and acceptance in multicultural competency: A contextual approach to sociocultural diversity in theory and practice* (pp. 39–55). Oakland, CA: New Harbinger Publications.
Masuda, A. (Ed.). (2014b). *Mindfulness and acceptance in multicultural competency: A contextual approach to sociocultural diversity in theory and practice*. Oakland, CA: Context Press/New Harbinger Publications.
Masuda, A. (2020). Adapting acceptance and commitment therapy to diverse cultures. In M. E. Levin, M. P. Twohig, & J. Kraft (Eds.), *Innovations in acceptance and commitment therapy: Clinical Advancements and Applications in ACT* (pp. 239–251). Oakland, CA: Context Press.
Masuda, A., Cohen, L, Wicksell, R. K, Kemani, M, & Johnson, A. (2011). A case study: acceptance and commitment therapy for pediatric sickle cell disease. *Journal of Pediatric Psychology, 36*, 398–408.
Masuda, A., & O'Donohue, W. T. (2017). *Handbook of zen, mindfulness, and behavioral health*. New York: Springer.
Matheson, G. O., Pacione, C., Shultz, R. K., & Klügl, M. (2015). Leveraging human-centered design in chronic disease prevention. *American Journal of Preventive Medicine, 48*(4), 472–479.
Mayer, J. (2016). *Dark money: The hidden history of the billionaires behind the rise of the radical right*. New York: Penguin Random House.
Milne-Ives, M., de Cock C, Lim, E., Shehadeh, M. H., de Pennington, N., Mole, G., . . . & Meinert, E. (2020). The effectiveness of artificial intelligence conversational agents in health care: Systematic review. *Journal of Medicine and Internet Research*, e20346.
Müller, C. (2008). *Metaphors dead and alive, sleeping and walking: A dynamic view*. Chicago: University of Chicago Press.
Nagasawa, Y., Shibata, A., Fukamachi, H., Ishii, K., Wicksell, R. K., & Oka, K. (2021). The Psychological Inflexibility in Pain Scale (PIPS): Validity and Reliability of the Japanese Version for Chronic Low Back Pain and Knee Pain. *Journal of pain research, 14*, 325–332. https://doi-org.proxy.kib.ki.se/10.2147/JPR.S287549
Nahum-Shani, I., Smith, S. N., Spring, B. J., Collins, L. M., Witkiewitz, K., Tewari, A., & Murphy, S. A. (2018). Just-in-time adaptive interventions (JITAIs) in mobile health: key components and design principles for ongoing health behavior support. *Annaks of Behavioral Medicine, 52*(6), 446–462. doi:10.1007/s12160-016-9830-8
National Academies of Sciences, Engineering, and Medicine. (2019). *A roadmap to reducing child poverty*. Washington, DC: National Academies Press.
O'Connell, M. E., Boat, T., & Warner, K. E. (2009). Preventing mental, emotional, and behavioral disorders among young people: Progress and possibilities. Washington, DC: National Academies Press. Committee on

the Prevention of Mental Disorders and Substance Abuse Among Children, Youth and Young Adults: Research Advances and Promising Interventions; Institute of Medicine; National Research Council.

Pane, H. T., White, R. S., Nadorff, M. R., Grills-Taquechel, A., & Stanley, M. A. (2013). Multisystemic therapy for child non-externalizing psychological and health problems: A preliminary review. *Clinical Child and Family Psychology Review, 16*(1), 81–99. https://doi-org.ezproxy.memphis.edu/10.1007/s10567-012-0127-6

Pechmann, C., Biglan, A., Grube, J. W., & Cody, C. (2012). Transformative consumer research for addressing tobacco and alcohol consumption. In D. G. Mick, S. Pettigrew, C. Pechmann, & J. L. Ozanne (Eds.), *Transformative consumer research for personal and collective well-being* (pp. 353–389). Routledge/Taylor & Francis Group.

Pepper, S. C. (1942). *World hypotheses: A study in evidence.* Berkeley: University of California Press.

Rhodes, P. (2003). The Maudsley Model of Family Therapy for Children and Adolescents with anorexia nervosa: Theory, clinical practice, and empirical support. *ANZJFT Australian and New Zealand Journal of Family Therapy, 24*(4), 191–198. https://doi-org.ezproxy.memphis.edu/10.1002/j.1467-8438.2003.tb00559.x

Roth, W. R., Vilardaga, R., Wolfe, N., Bricker, J. B., & McDonell, M. (2014). Practical considerations in the design and development of smartphone apps for behavior change. *Journal of Contextual Behavioral Science, 3*(4), 269–272. doi:10.1016/j.jcbs.2014.08.006

Rutter, H., Savona, N., Glonti, K., Bibby, J., Cummins, S., & Finegood, D. T. (2017). The need for a complex systems model of evidence for public health. *The Lancet, 390*(10112), 2602–2604.

Shiffman, S. (2007). Designing protocols for ecological momentary assessment. In A. A. Stone, S. Shiffman, A. Atienza, & L. Nebeling (Eds.). *The science of real-time data capture: self-reports in health research* (pp. 27–53). New York: Oxford University Press.

Skinner, B. F. (1957). *Verbal behavior.* New York: Appleton-Century-Crofts.

Stewart, C., G. White, R., Ebert, B., Mays, I., Nardozzi, J., & Bockarie, H. (2016). A preliminary evaluation of acceptance and commitment therapy (ACT) training in Sierra Leone. *Journal of Contextual Behavioral Science, 5*(1), 16–22. doi:https://doi.org/10.1016/j.jcbs.2016.01.001

Stewart, I., & Barnes-Holmes, D. (2001). Understanding metaphor: A relational frame perspective. *The Behavior Analyst, 24*, 191–199.

Stormshak, E. A., Connell, A. M., Véronneau, M.-H., Myers, M. W., Dishion, T. J., Kavanagh, K., & Caruthers, A. S. (2011). An ecological approach to promoting early adolescent mental health and social adaptation: Family-centered intervention in public middle schools. *Child Development, 82*, 209–225.

Szabo, T. G., Richling, S., Embry, D. D., Biglan, A., & Wilson, K. G. (2020). From Helpless to Hero: Promoting Values-Based Behavior and Positive Family Interaction in the Midst of COVID-19. *Behavior Analysis in Practice, 13*(3), 568–576. https://doi.org/10.1007/s40617-020-00431-0

Tay, D. (2013). *Metaphor in psychotherapy: A descriptive and prescriptive analysis.* Amsterdam: John Benjamins Publishing Company Teasdale.

Thibodeau, P. H., & Boroditsky, L. (2011). Metaphors we think with: The role of metaphor in reasoning. *PLoS ONE 6*(2): e16782. doi:10.1371/journal.pone.0016782.

Thomas Craig, K. J., Morgan, L. C., Chen, C. H., Michie, S., Fusco, N., Snowdon, J. L., . . . & Sill, S. (2020). Systematic review of context-aware digital behavior change interventions to improve health. *Translational Behavioral Medicine, 11*(5), 1037–1048. doi:10.1093/tbm/ibaa099

Thorsell Cederberg, J., Dahl, J., von Essen, L., & Ljungman, G. (2017). An acceptance-based intervention for children and adolescents with cancer experiencing acute pain: A single-subject study. *Journal of Pain Research, 10*, 2195–2203. doi:10.2147/JPR.S139087

Thrul, J. (2020). Testing the impact of smartphone-based messaging to support young adult smoking cessation. Retrieved from https://projectreporter.nih.gov/project_info_description.cfm?aid=10049469&icde=52498074&ddparam=&ddvalue=&ddsub=&cr=1&csb=default&cs=ASC&pball=

Timko, C. A., Zucker, N. L., Herbert, J. D., Rodriguez, D., & Merwin, R. M. (2015). An open trial of acceptance-based separated family treatment (ASFT) for adolescents with anorexia nervosa. *Behavior Research and Therapy, 69*, 63–74.

Törneke, N., Luciano, C., Barnes-Holmes, Y., & Bond, F. (2016). RFT for clinical practice: Three core strategies in understanding and treating human suffering. In R. D. Zettle, S. C. Hayes, D. Barnes-Holmes, & T. Biglan (ed.), *Wiley handbook of contextual behavioral science* (p. 254–272). Chichester: John Wiley & Sons.

Twohig, M. P., Levin, M. E., & Ong, C. W. (2020). *ACT in steps: A transdiagnostic manual for learning acceptance and commitment* therapy. New York: Oxford University Press.

Vilardaga, R., Bricker, J., & McDonell, M. (2014). The promise of mobile technologies and single case designs for the study of individuals in their natural environment. *Journal of Contextual Behavioral Science, 3*(2), 148–153. doi:10.1016/j.jcbs.2014.03.003

Walters, S. J., Bonacho Dos Anjos Henriques-Cadby, I., Bortolami, O., Flight, L., Hind, D., Jacques, R. M., . . . Julious, S. A. (2017). Recruitment and retention of participants in randomised controlled trials: A review of trials funded and published by the United Kingdom Health Technology Assessment Programme. *BMJ Open, 7,* e015276. doi:10.1136/bmjopen-2016-015276

Watson, N. L. (2020). A smart pilot of adaptive treatment strategies to improve engagement with a web-based smoking intervention for socially anxious smokers. Retrieved from https://projectreporter.nih.gov/project_info_details.cfm?aid=9891751&icde=52498078

Watson, N. L., Mull, K. E., Heffner, J. L., McClure, J. B., & Bricker, J. B. (2018). Participant Recruitment and Retention in Remote eHealth Intervention Trials: Methods and Lessons Learned from a Large Randomized Controlled Trial of Two Web-Based Smoking Interventions. *Journal of Medical Internet Research, 20*(8), e10351. https://doi-org.proxy.kib.ki.se/10.2196/10351

White, R. G., Gregg, J., Batten, S., Hayes, L. L., & Kasujja, R. (2017). Contextual behavioral science and global mental health: Synergies and opportunities. *Journal of Contextual Behavioral Science, 6*(3), 245–251. doi:https://doi.org/10.1016/j.jcbs.2017.07.001

Whittingham, K., Sanders, M., McKinlay, L., & Boyd, R. N. (2015). Interventions to reduce behavioral problems in children with cerebral palsy: An RCT. *Pediatrics, 133,* 1–9. doi: 10.1542/peds.2013-3620

Wilkinson, R., & Pickett, K. (2009). *The spirit level: Why greater equality makes societies stronger.* London: Bloomsbury Press.

Wilson, D. S. (2012). Consilience: Making contextual behavioral science part of the United Ivory Archipelago. *Journal of Contextual Behavioral Science, 1*(1–2), 39–42. Retrieved from http://www.sciencedirect.com/science/article/pii/S2212144712000099

Wilson, D., Hayes, S., Biglan, A., & Embry, D. (2014). Evolving the future: Toward a science of intentional change. *Behavioral and Brain Sciences, 37*(4), 395–416.

Woidneck, M. R., Pratt, K. M., Gundy, J. M., Nelson, C. R., & Twohig, M. P. (2012). Exploring cultural competence in acceptance and commitment therapy outcomes. *Professional Psychology: Research and Practice, 43*(3), 227–233.

CHAPTER

33 Creating Progress in Contextual Behavioral Science: Overcoming the Hurdles of the Past—Facing the Challenges of the Future

Neal Falletta-Cowden, Steven C. Hayes, *and* Michelle Forman

Abstract

Acceptance and commitment therapy (ACT) should be understood as a piece of the larger puzzle being constructed by contextual behavioral science (CBS). The goal of this scientific endeavor is not only to reduce suffering but also to understand complex human behavior to the degree necessary for bringing about large-scale changes in the world and facing the existential crises that threaten us. To accomplish these goals, the CBS community must be directed toward conducting research that is process-based, multilevel, multidimensional, prosocial, and pragmatic. In 2021, the ACBS Task Force developed a list of 33 recommendations for the CBS community that will help orient the path forward for this corner of science. This article addresses the hopes and dreams for behavioral science, the missteps taken along the way, and how the Task Force recommendations have numerous implications for the field of CBS as it evolves.

Key Words: acceptance and commitment therapy, contextual behavioral science, Association for Contextual Behavioral Science Task Force, psychological flexibility, Walden Two

Walden Two and the Vision of Contextual Behavioral Science

The ultimate goal of work on acceptance and commitment therapy or training (ACT; Hayes, Strosahl, & Wilson, 2011) needs to be seen in the context of its underlying principles and assumptions, as this volume has done. ACT is part of contextual behavioral science (CBS; Zettle, Hayes, Barnes-Holmes, & Biglan, 2016) as even a naïve reader will now fully appreciate. CBS, in turn, needs to be seen as part of a longer historical tradition with unusually expansive goals to understand both where it comes from and where it is going. ACT can then be seen in context, as part of the scientific journey taken by many thousands of people.

That is the topic of this article.

The goals that behavioral scientists set for their field can be lofty. While this is by no means an aspiration exclusive to behavioral science, the relevance of human action to everything we are about or hope for means it is an especially powerful idea in this area of science and practice. Having expansive visions for careful scientific work has been a vein of thought in behavioral psychology for its entire history. This is clearly so, or perhaps especially so, within the functional contextual wing of behavior analysis.

Even as a young academic, B. F. Skinner saw the field he helped develop out of his animal learning lab to be an essential step toward a science-led global salvation. Skinner brought this grand vision to life in his novel *Walden Two* (1948), which told the story of a skeptical professor visiting a behavioral scientist by the name of Frazier who had helped found a utopia built from the ground up using behavioral principles. This reimagined community was a place filled with art, education, and purpose for each individual. Skinner used *Walden Two* to paint a picture of what a society governed by behavioral principles could look like, complete with minute details such as teacups carried in a sling rather than a saucer (to prevent spillage) and radical visions such as workdays whose length was determined by results rather than set hours.

Skinner did not mean this vision as a declaration of accomplishment—it was an aspirational vision to be taken seriously. As if to underline its serious purpose, some features of his specific vision have survived to the present day, and not just in the form of communes that continue to exist based on its principles (Ardila, 2008). For example, centering the workday around results has been encouraged by industrial consultants such as William Abernathy (2009). And while it is true that for Skinner himself the optimism that guided his pen during much of his career faded during the latter years of his life as he argued that behavioral principles themselves explained why we are *not* acting to save the world (1987), the grand vision that characterized behavioral psychology never fully left him. In the modern era, that appears to be true in the hands of behavioral psychologists who believe that a deeper understanding of human language and cognition might give us a better toehold on the climb to a better human future (e.g., Dixon, Belisle, Rehfeldt, & Rung, 2018; Hayes, 2019a).

It is obvious that the need for a powerful and useful behavioral science is as great or greater than ever. Humans as a species simultaneously act in ways that harm the world they live in while also being *aware* of the fact that they are acting in these destructive ways. In his effort to explain how dilemmas such as this can exist, Skinner wrote that we are "being asked to do something about the future. But the future does not exist. It cannot act upon us; we cannot act upon it" (Skinner, 1987. p. 2).

Direct contingency principles operate by the principle of *selection*, which is very effective in preparing organisms for future environments that are similar to the current environment but less effective in preparing organisms for periods of rapid change. Operant conditioning allows organisms to learn new practices during their lifetime, but that process needs to be directed to adjust to important changes that are known to be coming. In Skinner's conception of cultural practices, behavior is passed on to others through language without the need for direct experience, which allows humans to position themselves well in a shifting world through cultural evolution. Skinner asked, "Can we not *design* a way of life that will have a better chance of a future?" (Skinner, 1987, p. 8). But why would cultures do so? Here the analysis became less pointed and less clear, and the role of psychology per se faded into a sociological level of analysis.

In the three and one-half decades since Skinner spoke his final words on the matter, we are facing global crises in the form of climate change, economic disparities, immigration policies, racism, global pandemics, and the threat of nuclear war. Humans are growing more and more *aware* of the fact that the current trajectory of the world will lead to certain disaster, and yet drastic collective action to reverse this path remains elusive. Skinner had correctly identified the issue facing humanity when he wrote about of a lack of *purpose,* but the behavioral science and evolutionary principles available to him were too limited to picture how the problem could be solved at the psychological level as well as at the level of cultural practices.

We as behavioral scientists should ask ourselves whether the progress in our field over the last 30 years has brought us any closer to acting with purpose in areas such as this. In the same vein as others (e.g., Dixon et al., 2018), this article argues that the rise of CBS and its applied technologies such as acceptance and commitment training (ACT) or prosocial (Atkins, Wilson, & Hayes, 2019) does indeed give behavioral science a foothold from which we can take steps toward fulfilling the responsive vision that Skinner felt was just out of reach.

CBS arose to solve a small set of problems that are reflected in what led to Skinner's skepticism at the end of his life. ACT is possible only because of the solutions that were reached. They have all been touched on in this volume, so after a brief review of them we will then turn to the future development of CBS research, including ACT, using as our touchstone a set of steps and strategies that have been formally developed by a multiyear consensus building process within ACBS and adopted by the Association as its plan for creating empirical progress (Hayes et al., 2021b). In each of the main areas, we will describe how ACT can fit into these strategies.

Missteps Taken in Behavioral Science

A first step in understanding how behavioral science has evolved to the point where it may be able to take on the challenges of the modern world is to examine the missteps that have been taken along the way to where we are now. These missteps included an overreliance on an inadequate account of human language and cognition, a failure to build allies within other scientific fields, an oversimplified understanding of the relationship between the environment and behavior, and a lack of attention to underlying theory.

Inadequate Theories of Language

Skinner's *Verbal Behavior* (1957) laid out a series of concepts, principles, and forms of operant behavior that he developed in an attempt to piece together human language and cognition using operant conditioning as the binding agent. His conception of human language is immensely well known; at the time of this writing, it had been cited at least 13,000 times. It has led to multiple curriculums used by practitioners in the field of applied behavior analysis and has proven quite effective in the early stages of intervention for children diagnosed with developmental disabilities who lack language (Esch, LaLonde, & Esch, 2010; Frost & Bondy, 2006).

Skinner understood very well that verbal language would be among the most difficult frontiers in the study of human behavior, and it is unlikely that he believed the theory he elaborated in 1957 to be the final word on this complex topic. Unfortunately, more than 50 years later Skinner's theory has still not led to a robust empirical research program that rises to the challenge of human cognition across a wider range of verbal abilities; for a scientific field with an insistence on empirical validity, this does not bode well. Between 1984 and 2004, 80 percent of the articles citing *Verbal Behavior* were nonempirical and just 1.4 percent were basic experimental articles (Dymond, O'Hora, Whelan, & O'Donovan, 2006). The vast majority of empirical studies on Skinner's book targeted children with significant developmental disabilities (Dixon, Small, & Rosales, 2007). The "verbal operants" that Skinner describes in his book are able to explain fairly rudimentary behaviors such as identifying objects in the environment and requesting items from others. However, more complex forms of verbal behavior such as the conversations that occur in a heated academic discussion felt out of reach.

One of the likely causes for the lack of research programs studying verbal behavior from the Skinnerian perspective is that distinguishing between verbal operants can sometimes depend on analyzing response *form* rather than *function*. This issue stems from a conceptual problem, namely, that Skinner's definition of verbal behavior is behavior reinforced by the actions of a listener. For example, a request (or "mand") from a speaker for a listener to open a door is reinforced upon the listener's behavior of opening a door. Thus, Skinner's "definition turns not on the history of the organism of interest, but on the history of another organism" (Hayes, Barnes-Holmes, & Roche, 2001, p. 12). This conceptual problem is coupled with the problem of Skinner's definition being too broad to ensure that complex verbal behavior is unique to humans. Skinner himself stated that the relationship between an experimenter and the rat they are training may constitute "a small but genuine verbal community" (1957, footnote 11, p. 108). What remained needed within behavioral science was a theory of language and cognition that is still rooted in operant psychology, but with principles adequate for capturing the complexity and richness of human verbal behavior.

Failure to Build an Alliance with Evolutionary Science

Contextual behavioral science has its philosophical roots in functional contextualism, which is a refinement of radical behaviorism (Hayes, Sanford, & Chin, 2017). Both are radically pragmatic approaches that have sought to weave evolutionary theory into their assumptions to empower an understanding of human behavior (Biglan & Hayes, 1996). It is odd, then, that behavioral scientists have until recently been relatively unsuccessful in garnering the attention and interest of evolutionary scientists. As a result, this wing of behavioral science has not been able to create a proper role for itself in the life sciences more generally.

The cause for this disconnect seems to lie in an assumption made by leading evolutionary theorists, namely, that behaviorists believe that the behavior of an organism can be understood independently from its genes and biological makeup (Pinker, 2003). That has never been the case. It was fed in part by the search for learning principles that apply across tips of evolutionary branches in behavioral psychology, as contrasted with a focus on differences between branches of the evolutionary tree in most evolutionary approaches. While these two viewpoints could have been complementary, effective community building was limited from both sides. Evolutionary theory was dominated by gene-centric accounts, and behaviorists failed to make a convincing effort to form an in-depth understanding of the biological underpinnings of behavioral science. Skinner himself discussed how a research program tying learning principles and genetic modification could work, but the project was never mounted (Hayes et al, 2017). The lack of effective effort limited any alliance between these fields.

Lack of Concepts Needed to Address Behavior–Behavior Relations

The goal of science from a behavior-analytic perspective has been described as prediction and control, or influence. Behaviorists are driven by these goals (Hayes & Brownstein, 1986), which causes them to focus on the external environment in both their empirical and applied work because the determinants of an "act in context" within the analyst's control reside there.

The problem arises when private events need to enter into the account. Private events are actions or environmental shifts that are not directly observable except by the individual. It is important not to appeal to behavioral "causes" because this puts analysis linked to prediction and influence beyond the analyst's reach, leading easily to the problem of dualism—the belief that there is an immaterial plane in which a person's "soul" or mind finds refuge and that determines human action. Behaviorism's early proponents, such as John B. Watson (1925), claimed at times that private behaviors such as thoughts are not real in their own right because they cannot be measured by a separate observer. Skinner overturned that view on the grounds that any observation of an action, public or private, required a history needed to bring observations under control of events. That approach opened the doorway to issues having to do with how "behavior–behavior" relations (Hayes & Brownstein, 1986) might be addressed conceptually and empirically. But until that area is fully explored, behavioral psychology cannot take full advantage of Skinner's functional approach to the issue of privacy.

For example, when a person has the thought "I'd like an ice cream" and then gets in their car to go to the store, we may be tempted to say that the behavior of getting in the car was caused by the thought of ice cream. This is an incomplete account, however, as the contextual source of both the thought and the relation of the thought to getting into the car must still be specified.

The lack of clarity in this area allowed private events to be fully conflated with "mentalism." That in turn meant that any expansion beyond direct contingency analysis needlessly threatened the conceptual superstructure of a behavioral approach. Skinner's approach to verbal events did not demand that these issues be addressed, and they were not by the behavior-analytic mainstream. In practice, this meant that sequences of psychologically relevant actions—processes of change that involved the private experiences of people—were given short shrift. Ironically, this actually encouraged a mentalistic account in two ways. Having no alternative, applied behavioral workers often reverted to lay language when trying to address private events with their clients, and basic researchers appealed to processes to explain symbolic events (e.g., "mediated generalization"—see Eilifsen & Arntzen, 2021) that sounded "behavioral" but were the very historical roots of traditional cognitive accounts.

Lack of Theory

A final problem faced by traditional behavior analysis is the lack of clarity about theory. It is not enough to be clear about principles, processes, and procedures. It is also critical to have models and theories that help summarize these features in coherent and useful intellectual and practical systems.

Ironically, the source of these problems was Skinner's (1950) useful rejection of hypothetico-deductive theory and of theories conceived of as models of what cannot be manipulated (e.g., for a powerful and negative example of what was rejected, see Spence, 1944, p. 71). Skinner's arguments were so powerful, and the title of his initial work in this area was so broad ("Are theories of learning necessary") that for the rest of his career Skinner tried to undo the overgeneralization of that argument, even putting the word "theory" into the titles of his own books. Unfortunately, he was less clear about the kind of theory he was *for*, and to this day use of the term *theory* can cause hand wringing in behavioral circles.

Correcting Missteps and Moving Ahead

Contextual behavioral science is a modern face of functional contextual thinking. One could say that CBS is a modern form of behavior analysis and be done with it, but it's no longer fully communicative to say it that way because behavior analysis itself has evolved to be a profession in its own right. In that form, it has generally narrowed its purview to developmental disabilities and a few other key areas. In addition, many behavior analysts are actively opposed to CBS thinking in a range of areas. Thus, the situation is likely to remain as it is, with CBS researchers and practitioners increasingly viewing its development as a related but distinct approach to behavior analysis, with historical linkages and its own journey ahead.

We have reviewed this history in order to begin to put meat on the bones of CBS itself. Once these four missteps are corrected, the broad agenda we began with in this article can be given proper attention and due weight. That needs to be done in new ways, and yet at times in ways that reaffirm some of the features of the functional contextual behavioral tradition from William James forward. For example, the functional contextual behavioral tradition has long sought analyses that are "idiographic" in origin. The reason for this is largely philosophical: a focus on actions in their historical and situational context cannot be readily applied to collectives with different histories and in different circumstances. Despite that, throughout its history psychology has overemphasized the study of collectives, and its methods, analytic strategies, and concepts are largely tied to that level of analysis. As CBS explores more fully how the functional contextual tradition can make a difference with these previous missteps solved, it can turn its full energy to the changes needed to make full use of idiographic data and concepts, and yet to embed them in large *N* studies with a nomothetic purpose. That approach in turn informs how ACT and other CBS methods might be used to address critical problems the world is now facing.

Several of the articles in the present volume have discussed how human verbal complexity can be addressed with relational frame theory (RFT; Hayes et al., 2001). RFT is an analytic-abstractive behavioral theory—it is not hypothetico-deductive. It consists entirely of (1) systematic and generally applicable analyses of important classes of behavioral observations (2) stated in terms of coherently related sets of behavioral principles, that (3) allow behavioral phenomena within that class to be predicted-and-influenced as a unified goal with greater precision, scope, and depth. No new behavioral principles are needed to understand RFT, although new principles do arise as an empirical *result* of relational operants because the transformation of stimulus functions is itself a new phenomenon.

The environmentalism of RFT allows researchers and practitioners to address private events and the behavior–behavior relations established by relational operants without succumbing to mentalism. Consider the situation faced by a parent having the thought "I am a bad parent" while observing their child having a tantrum. In the normal social-verbal context, with its reason-giving, excessive push for coherence, and support of emotional avoidance, relational events of this kind can produce strong transformations of stimulus functions that evoke avoidance or impaired parenting practices. It is all too easy to respond by giving the child a candy to end the tantrum and reduce the aversiveness of the context (Coyne & Wilson, 2004), thus increasing a behavior–behavior relation between a self-judgmental thought and overt action due to the immediate consequences, even if they are likely to be negative later. The use of "defusion" methods alters these contexts and thus weakens the transformation of stimulus functions and the linkage between thoughts and actions (Leech, Barnes-Holmes, & McEnteggart, 2017).

The key processes of change in ACT's psychological flexibility model are contextually bound and are all analyzable as functionally important parts of overall causal sequences without being viewed as causes in and of themselves. The result is that despite its development and validation in CBS, ACT now meets the requirements of traditional behavior-analytic methods as originally outlined by Baer, Wolf, and Risley (1968) in being applied, behavioral, analytic, effective, technological, conceptually systematic, and generative (Dixon, Hayes, Stanley, Law, & al-Nasser, 2020).

Earlier articles in this book have repeatedly demonstrated the effectiveness of ACT across an expansive range of topics. In the context of the extraordinary human challenges we face, it's worth noting how much the evidentiary basis of CBS has evolved in recent times. Unlike previous behavior-analytic accounts of language and cognition, RFT has spurred a very large and increasing number of studies over the last 35 years, during which its empirical research program has developed (Hayes et al., 2021a). A recent literature review analyzing 521 studies of RFT between 2009 and 2016 found that over 55 percent were empirical and dealt with a vast range of topics (O'Connor, Farrell, Munnelly, & McHugh, 2017). On an annualized basis, the rate of RFT-based experimental studies increased from 2.5 per year in the 1991 and

2008 period (Dymond, May, Munnelly, & Hoon, 2010) to 41.1 per year between 2009 and 2006, an increase of 1,665 percent.

The same kind of exponential grown has been seen in ACT. Well over 500 randomized controlled trials have been published since 1986 (as of late May 2021; see bit.ly/ACTRCTs), but only a little more than a quarter of those studies occurred in the first 30 years following the first RCT. Nearly three quarters have been published in the 6 years since.

The reason this growth is so important is that it creates a context for adoption and testing of CBS methods in the context of major crises being faced by the world. An example is the promulgation of ACT by the World Health Organization (WHO) to help with COVID-related distress (World Health Organization, 2020a), based on its proven usefulness with refugees in Africa (Tol et al., 2020).

The Evolutionary Umbrella over CBS

One place that "moving ahead" can be easily seen as a fulfillment of the original vision of behavior analysis is in the area of evolutionary science. Skinner viewed behavioral science and evolutionary science as conceptually nested, and he stated that the "story" of human behavior would only be fully told through "the joint action of the science of genetics, behavior, and culture" (Skinner, 1988, p. 83). Exactly how to do this is a work in progress, but it has been made much easier by the rise of an extended evolutionary model (Wilson & Hayes, 2018).

Nesting any applied science in evolutionary science requires at least six core concepts: "**variation** and **retention** of what is **selected** in **context** at the right **dimension** and **level**" (Hayes, Stanton, Sanford, Law, & Ta, 2020, p. 56). In CBS, efforts have been made to apply these concepts to the evolution of relational framing via multilevel evolution linked to human cooperation (Hayes & Sanford, 2014). In ACT, efforts have been made to view processes of change within an Extended Evolutionary Meta-Model (EEMM) that applies variation and selective retention in context to six psychological dimensions (affect, cognition, attention, self, motivation, and overt behavior) and two additional levels of analysis: the sociocultural and the biophysiological (Hayes et al, 2019, p. 9).

The EEMM can be readily understood as a more generally applicable form of the psychological flexibility model. Classic ACT inflexibility processes restrict healthy variation, reduce needed context sensitivity, alter useful forms of selection, and undermine retention of actions that lead to larger later gains.

For example, experiential avoidance refers to the repertoire-narrowing impact of private events that lead to various forms of needless escape and avoidance at the cost of functionally useful alternatives. Driven by context-insensitive short-term gains, this process undermines the ability to construct broad and flexible repertoires that lead to long-term reinforcers. Conversely, acceptance skills can be thought of as emotional flexibility skills, as private events can be experienced without attachment or avoidance. This allows these results of past history to occur and to inform the person about key features and motives of present context, thus increasing useful context sensitivity and reducing the needless and excessive impact of short-term reactions that do not necessarily foster long-term gains.

This same style of analysis can be applied to all of the inflexibility and flexibility processes (see Hayes, 2019a for such an attempt). For the account to be well rounded, however, other levels of analysis, such as the biophysiological and the sociocultural, also need to be considered.

The ties between applied psychology and genetics or epigenetics are a cutting-edge area of science. Environment and behavior alter how genetic factors influence behavior via epigenetic activation (Crespi, 2020). Training in evolutionary science is necessary to understand how evolution resulted in the learning principles and capacities that psychologists use to influence behavior (Abed, Ayton, St. John-Smith, Swanepoel, & Tracy, 2019). CBS is well positioned to lead this charge, as much of the theoretical groundwork has already been laid to allow CBS to discuss how an evolutionary selectivist approach has implications for the study of human behavior, including but not limited to language and cognition (Hayes & Long, 2013).

CBS and evolutionary science can also be combined to help address the sociocultural level of analysis. An example is Prosocial, an applied method of influencing the functioning of small groups based on the combination of psychological flexibility and Elinor Ostrom's core design principles (CDPs; Atkins et al., 2019). Like psychological flexibility itself, Ostrom's CDPs can be readily viewed through the lens of evolutionary theory (Wilson, Ostrom, & Cox, 2013), which is part of why they can so easily be combined. Evolutionary theory provides the consilience needed to take that important step.

Ostrom's work identified a series of principles that appeared to surface across organized groups she studied who were managing common pool resources. Her work paved the road for further research on how some human groups have avoided the so-called Tragedy of the Commons (Ostrom, 1990). Out of her analyses, eight core design principles were derived, which were present in the groups she studied that successfully manage common pool resources. These principles were a shared group identity, inclusive decision making, equitable distribution of benefits and costs, monitoring of member behavior, sanctions upon those who behaved poorly, quick and fair conflict resolution, the ability to self-govern, and a nesting of the group within a larger community of groups. As the goal of CBS is not only to predict human behavior (and by extension the behavior of humans in groups) but also to influence it, Prosocial as a joint effort between EvoSci and CBS has produced a method of influencing small groups that uses the psychological flexibility model to understand how individuals within a group may respond to a sociocultural context. Prosocial thus serves as an example of how CBS can cooperate with other scientific fields and stay true to its idiographic roots, while developing concepts that are applicable at the group level.

To summarize this article so far, CBS is part of a pragmatic functional contextual tradition. The CBS journey has been based on an analysis of the missteps that occurred in the history of behavior analysis and a careful attempt to remediate them so as to carry the field forward toward in meeting its original mission, namely, creating a behavioral science that is more adequate to the human condition.

Relational frame theory has bridged the gap in understanding complex human language as the result of a learned pattern of derived relational responding. In addition, ACT has produced a large amount of empirically supported research for beneficial behavior change through increased psychological flexibility, but much more remains to be done. By building on the foundation laid for CBS as a form of evolutionary science, CBS seems ready to proceed in advancing the mission of functional contextual behavioral thinking.

Here we turn to the future, but instead of merely stating and defending our preferences, we are in the extraordinary position of being able to describe the results and explore the implications of a multiyear process of consideration by some of the leading researchers and practitioners in all of CBS.

Introduction to the Task Force on the Strategies and Tactics of CBS Research

In the fall of 2018, the Association for Contextual Behavioral Science (ACBS) created the Task Force on the Strategies and Tactics of Contextual Behavioral Science Research (hereinafter Task Force) to construct a progressive research strategy for contextual behavioral research. Task Force members were appointed by then ACBS president Louise Hayes, in consultation with an author of the present article (SCH), who was appointed chair of the Task Force. Over the next two and a half years, the Task Force put together a series of recommendations that they thought, going forward, would ensure that the field had a clear strategy and set of tactics, with the end goal of overcoming the challenges behavioral science has encountered in the past. The Task Force settled upon five different features of CBS research which should be emphasized: namely, it should be multilevel, process-based, multidimensional, prosocial, and pragmatic. A total of 33 recommendations, several in each of these five areas, were promulgated to the community in late April 2021 in the form of the *Report of the ACBS Task Force on the Strategies and Tactics of Contextual Behavioral Science Research* (Hayes, 2021).

The recommendations regarding what should become central to CBS research is meant to be a key step in developing a comprehensive and cohesive science. Contextual behavioral science can be defined as follows:

> Contextual Behavioral Science (CBS) is a principle-focused, communitarian strategy of reticulated scientific and practical development. Grounded in contextualistic philosophical assumptions, and nested within multidimensional, multi-level evolution science as a contextual view of life, it seeks the development of basic and applied scientific concepts and methods that are useful in predicting-and-influencing the contextually embedded actions of whole organisms, individually and in groups, with precision, scope, and depth; and extends that approach into knowledge development itself so as to create a behavioral science more adequate to the challenges of the human condition.
> *(Hayes, Barnes-Holmes, & Wilson, 2012, p. 2)*

Let us begin breaking down this hefty definition by pointing out that CBS maintains a strategy of reticulated scientific as well as practical development. This means that as researchers within universities or other research institutions produce research that leads to the identification of potential principles of behavior or learning, practitioners in the field then apply this knowledge to determine fidelity in less contrived environments. The feedback that these practitioners provide to researchers then leads to the next round of studies, and the process repeats itself. This is one of the most important features of CBS because it ensures that the methods used by those providing needed services to the public in the domain of behavioral health are empirically validated and based on universal principles of behavior.

Another important element of the definition of CBS is the philosophical grounding in contextualistic assumptions. This issue will be discussed in more detail later in this article; for now we may simply define the philosophical underpinning of CBS as *functional contextualism,* which is a pragmatic perspective that takes the Act in Context to be the only "capital T" Truth to be analyzed and understood. Continuing through the definition of CBS, we come to the purpose of CBS, which is to aid in the prediction-and-influence of the behavior of organisms, while taking into account the entire context in which that behavior occurred. In other words, we must understand the contexts in which organisms behave in certain ways so that we can predict this behavior into the future and ideally influence it to be more adaptive for the individual and their communities at large. Precision, scope, and depth are also terms used within CBS that require some definition. *Precision* means that out of a range of principles and findings within the field of CBS, a select few of these principles must apply to a given case. *Scope* means that one must be able to take one such principle and apply it across a series of cases to ensure that our principles are sufficiently applicable to various individuals. And finally, *depth* means that the concepts delineated in CBS do not contradict the scientific findings of other respectable fields of science. We must be able to take our principles and ensure that they fit what we know about other domains of science such as evolutionary theory.

The Task Force report was created to keep CBS true to its purpose and to help guide future research toward studies that will ensure that CBS can have the highest impact possible. CBS intends to break free of the "norms" that have developed within behavioral science such as the focus on syndromal categories rather than functional relationships between an individual and their environment. These elements of the "status quo" within behavioral science can threaten the ability of researchers in CBS to ensure that their work aligns with the previous definition of the field. The Task Force's recommendations, as discussed in the following section, have many implications for these research lines.

Incorporating the Task Force Recommendations

ACT, RFT, and CBS are helping to change the role of behavioral science in the world. For CBS to reach its full potential, we need to understand ACT and RFT more as squares in the quilt of science than as a final answer to anything. Implementing the recommendations of the Task Force would mark a major step toward fulfilling that role. Each of the Task Force recommendations will be discussed here in the context of the issues and concepts discussed so far and the range of topics considered in this volume. In working to incorporate these recommendations, we not only change the role of behavioral science, but also work together to build a better future.

The Task Force agreed that CBS had at least five critical features. Concrete recommendations were then offered in each of these five areas.

Characteristic One: Contextual Behavioral Science Is a Multilevel Approach

The Task Force argued that CBS is a multilevel approach. That is, knowledge in the life sciences needs to be seen at multiple levels of organization, without reductionism or expansionism. Biophysiological, psychological, and sociocultural factors all impact human behavior, and to be used effectively, knowledge at any one level often needs to be appreciated in the context of other levels of organization. Thus, our analysis must also be multilevel. These recommendations are as follows:

- Recommendation 1: CBS research should examine relevant variables across levels of analysis, facilitated by more cross-disciplinary research, and with the explicit aim of coherence across levels of analysis within a broad evolutionary science framework.
- Recommendation 2: CBS research needs more basic experimental research into sources of behavioral influence across levels of analysis.
- Recommendation 3: CBS research needs middle-level terms to be examined for their utility in different contexts and for them to be increasingly specified and tested in basic analytic terms that allow for identification of multilevel influences on behavior.
- Recommendation 4: CBS research needs to carefully measure multilevel factors that for ethical or practical reasons cannot be manipulated.
- Recommendation 5: CBS research needs to emphasize more longitudinal measurement that situates a psychological event in a behavioral stream and the context in which that stream occurs.
- Recommendation 6: CBS research needs to focus on analyses with depth that encourage the identification of principles and processes that can scale hierarchically across complex multilevel systems.

It will not be lost on the reader that the very first recommendation of the Task Force is a call for more cross-disciplinary research. Behavioral science is not an island of its own, so to speak. The field is instead nested within a much broader context that includes physiological, neurological, genetic, and epigenetic underpinnings—all of which can be said to be nested within the complex individuals we research and seek to understand. Going back to the EEMM and the six levels of analysis discussed previously, we can think of this problem as one of variation and selection. Enhanced understanding through following this recommendation will assist the field in avoiding issues such as reductionism while moving forward in a progressive and cooperative way with other fields of scientific research. Behavioral science research also tends to lean heavily on randomized controlled trials and case studies as its chosen avenue of application. As the Task Force has noted, increases in longitudinal research are recommended. It is important that we generate an understanding of each level of our chosen analysis in order to allow us to move from basic theory to applied methodologies, while also respecting each level (including physiological and biological processes). CBS research needs to work to consider when midlevel terms require technically precise analyses for given research and practice purposes—and when they do not.

As these recommendations apply to ACT specifically, they point to many important areas of research and practice that are underdeveloped. How does ACT impact epigenetic and neurobiological substrates? How can psychological flexibility processes extend to couples, small groups, or cultural processes? How do psychological flexibility processes interact with context and behavior over time? Are there cultural processes that interact with the psychological flexibility model? Answering questions such as these would vitalize CBS research in general and ACT research in particular.

Characteristic Two: Contextual Behavioral Science Is a Process-Based Approach

The Task Force viewed CBS as a process-based approach to science and practice, meaning that rather than seek syndromal or other normative and categorical explanations for behavior, the focus of CBS is to discover "processes of behavioral change that allow psychological events to be predicted and influenced" and to do so in a way that helps analysts reach "desired analytic, prosocial, and practical goals" (Hayes et al., 2021b, p. 16). One such set of processes are *basic behavioral* processes, such as reinforcement, stimulus generalization, or derived relational responding. Another set of processes are *evolutionary processes,* such as epigenetics in the form of various gene expressions or phenotypical development. *Therapeutic processes* involve largely middle-level terms such as acceptance, defusion, or values, which are helpful for the identification of functional relationships in therapeutic practice but still require basic and evolutionary accounts to be fully understood. The recommendations of the Task Force in this area urge the CBS community to further explore processes of change at various levels of analysis, ranging from basic behavioral research to therapeutic kernels that can be used to influence processes at each level of analysis, from the biophysiological to the cultural. These recommendations are as follows:

- Recommendation 7: CBS research needs basic and applied behavioral research to identify processes of change.
- Recommendation 8: CBS research needs to identify and conceptualize intervention "kernels" using a range of basic, applied, experimental analog, and inductive research methods.
- Recommendation 9: CBS research needs more behavioral and biophysiological measures of processes of change.

- Recommendation 10: CBS researchers need to conduct RCTs in a way that fosters idiographic analyses of process of change.
- Recommendation 11: CBS research acknowledges the need for adaptive clinical research methods to rigorously test treatment components.
- Recommendation 12: CBS research needs more idiographic and longitudinal, dynamic network-based research, especially in conjunction with high temporal density behavioral and biophysiological measures.
- Recommendation 13: CBS research needs more focus on the empirical evaluation of interventions and intervention components, or kernels based on the degree to which they move processes of change.
- Recommendation 14: CBS research needs to develop alternatives to traditional psychometrics as quality standards for measures that are idiographically useful; sensitive to context; appropriate for repeated, frequent measurement; and that emphasize observable behavioral and biophysiological changes in addition to self-report.
- Recommendation 15: CBS research needs to integrate research findings into underlying models of applied work.
- Recommendation 16: CBS research needs to study processes of change in different contexts to facilitate generalization or adaptation of principles and interventions and to examine their ability to scale across levels of analysis.

The implications for CBS if these recommendations are followed are that, in terms of prediction and influence of behavioral change, CBS can remain at the cutting edge as biological, evolutionary, and psychological science progresses. One of the major setbacks within psychology was the development of the *DSM* (*Diagnostic and Statistical Manual of Mental Disorders*) model, which biomedicalized human functioning in ways that override the role of the history and circumstances of the individual's behavior. This syndromal focus led to the stigmatization of common human experiences such as grief over the loss of a loved one, and furthermore stigmatized marginalized populations such as those whose sexual orientations fell outside of "normal" cultural assumptions (Drescher, 2015). A closer look at the history of diagnoses and syndromes reveals that efforts to define what is psychologically "abnormal" in any given era hinges upon the cultural context and societal structures of the time. For example, in a time when slavery was the "norm," diagnoses such as *drapetomania* were formed to identify slaves who supposedly had a biological predisposition that caused them to continually attempt to run away from slaveowners (Schwartz, 1998). As Schwartz (1998) puts it, researchers of the time "considered slavery as a given and therefore looked to problems in the slaves as to why they would run away" (p. 357). Although this example may seem extreme, diagnoses within the DSM have repeatedly been cast out of the manual due to cultural shifts and public outcry, such as the Stonewall riots of the 1969, which signaled a cultural shift that eventually resulted in homosexuality being dropped from the *DSM* in 1973 (Drescher, 2015).

The focus on diagnoses of syndromes has resulted in a continual game of cat and mouse in which boards of psychologists determine what clusters of behaviors appear to fall outside of the normative range and researchers attempt to discover therapies that target each specific diagnosis. The underlying assumption of this game is that there *is* a "normal" set of human behaviors and dispositions, and psychology is in some sense the science of understanding and treating the abnormal, or as the American Psychiatric Association defines it, "to understand and treat mental, emotional, physical, and social dysfunction" (VandenBos, 2007). While the APA's definition also includes the notion that the science of psychology seeks to understand and enhance behavior across settings such as school, sports, or the workplace, these efforts in the field of psychology tend to be overshadowed by the dominating cultural influence of the *DSM*.

Although ACT has been shown to be effective in reducing stigma toward those with psychological disorders, much remains to be done in this area (Masuda et al., 2007). In the United States, the influence of syndromal thinking is felt particularly strongly because of the direct-to-consumer (DTC) marketing strategies that pharmaceutical companies use to promote self-diagnosis. In the first 6 months of 2009, DTC marketing expenditures reached $2.9 billion (Ebeling, 2011), and given the onslaught of pharmaceutical ads encouraging individuals to examine their own experiences in light of specific DSM criteria, it is no wonder that between 2015 and 2018, 13.2 percent of U.S. adults had used antidepressants in the last 30 days (Brody & Gu, 2020). What we need in the field of psychology is not an updated version of the *DSM*, but a shift in how behavioral science approaches the goal of behavioral change and how to produce adaptive behavioral outcomes in the individuals we serve.

A process-based approach avoids the pitfalls of a syndromal focus by developing and refining a set of empirically validated processes at the behavioral, evolutionary, and therapeutic levels. While the processes identified across these levels of analysis will of course be products of the time during which they were developed, the focus will not be on attaching a diagnosis to individuals whose behavior falls outside of the normative range but rather on identifying how processes at any given level may have led to maladaptive behavioral outcomes that can be positively influenced through kernels of intervention. The Task Force's recommendations encourage rigorous idiographic research into processes of change at the behavioral and biophysiological levels, with the goal of developing kernels of intervention that influence processes of change. If these recommendations are implemented, CBS research will lead to alternatives to traditional psychometrics that are contextually sensitive and reliable across time, such that the effect of changes at the process level can be measured in terms of observable behavioral and biophysiological outcomes. The focus on processes of change across every level (suborganismic; whole organism; small group) also allows for a program of study to evolve over time as CBS and EvoSci develop more refined tools of analysis.

The plan of study and research in ACT envisioned in this part of the document is bold. Consider the list of central organizing ideas in a traditional research study that are put on the chopping block: syndromes, protocols, excessive use of self-report, traditional randomized controlled trials, psychometrics, and pre-/post-follow-up measurement. In its place are new forms of high-density, longitudinal measurement focused on the individual, linked to models of change processes linked in turn to intervention kernels. ACT research has all of these features to some small degree, but this is the agenda we are just beginning.

Characteristic Three: Contextual Behavioral Science Is a Multidimensional Approach

Behavioral science was defined as an essence of evolutionary science through Skinner's account that behavioral principles would be better served, in part, as the science of selection by consequences (Skinner, 1981). While this was a heavy lift at the time, current evolutionary science can be incorporated and understood within the lens of behavioral science through the use of current multilevel and multidimensional concepts. We know that selection occurs at more than just one level of organization. It is multilevel, as discussed previously.

It is also multidimensional in that variation and selection operate on different streams of events within a given level of organization in different ways. At the biophysiological level, selection may operate differently on genes and epigenes; at the psychological level, variation and selection in symbolic behavior may need to be analyzed differently than overt behavior, or emotional responses differently than sense of self. For example, relational framing may have evolved in part through the impact of perspective-taking on human cooperation (Hayes & Sanford, 2015). That statement is multilevel (involving both the psychological and sociocultural level) and also multidimensional (perspective-taking and relational framing are different contingency streams, but they are both at the psychological level).

The Task Force recommendations for a multidimensional behavioral science include the following:

- Recommendation 17: CBS research needs to track change in a multidimensional way, using functional-analytic concepts with precision and good fit to the underlying analytic purposes of a particular research study.
- Recommendation 18: CBS research needs to assess the extent to which each identified dimension can be functionally measured, using multiple methods, and in a way that fosters successful functional analysis.
- Recommendation 19: CBS research needs to address how different dimensions can be measured in ways that are valid at the individual level.
- Recommendation 20: CBS research needs to assess the extent to which intervention outcomes are due to various change dimensions at the idiographic level.
- Recommendation 21: CBS research needs to assess the extent to which different dimensions link to and influence each other.
- Recommendation 22: CBS research needs a more transdisciplinary approach.

An easy way to consider the relevance of a multidimensional approach to ACT is to recognize that psychological flexibility is traditionally divided into six different areas defined by particular dimensions of psychological experience: affect, cognition, attention, sense of self, motivation, and overt behavior. Thus, each of the recommendations applies to the ways that psychological flexibility is understood and researched. Recommendations 17–19 suggest that the particular dimensions of psychological flexibility (affect, cognition, motivation, and so on) be considered and measured in multiple ways idiographically. Recommendations 20–22 suggest that these various dimensions be examined in an interactive way and then linked to outcomes, while recognizing that this will take a more transdisciplinary approach given the current barriers to cooperation among cognitive scientists, emotion scientists, and so on.

Characteristic Four: Contextual Behavioral Science Is Prosocial in Its Purpose

A pragmatic approach to science derives its truth criteria from functionality. Characteristic four suggests that CBS researchers should hold themselves accountable to the overall prosocial purpose of their own research. This is part of what is meant by the CBS goal of "creating a behavioral science more worthy of the challenge of the human condition"—the creation of a science that is accountable for its impact on psychological, social, and physical well-being. It also recognizes that the principles and concepts derived within RFT and ACT can be extended into the sociocultural level.

In line with the opening focus of the present article, the recommendations that flow from this characteristic suggest that psychological researchers keep their eyes on the overall social good that research can do for critical problems identified within the culture, such as systemic racism, violence, climate change, authoritarianism, lack of caring toward immigrants, and so on. An example is the relationship of deictic framing (a particular relational operant) within RFT research to perspective-taking and empathy toward other individuals (Davis, Krafft, Hicks, & Levin, 2021; Vilardaga, 2009). Basic RFT research has also shown how the transformation of stimulus function as a basic behavioral process can lead to the stigmatization of obesity and social categorization more broadly (Weinstein, Wilson, Drake, & Kellum, 2008). Larger cultural questions, such as how prejudice may form following acts of terrorism, have also been topics of study within the CBS and RFT community (Dixon, Dymond, Rehfeldt, Roche, & Zlomke, 2003).

Contextual behavioral science cannot turn a blind eye to the issues facing the world at large because addressing these issues is a goal of the analysis. These issues will not solve themselves, and indeed issues such as climate change appear to be continually worsening. A self-consciously pragmatic field cannot follow the pathway that other scientific efforts have taken in the past and remain in the ivory tower while the needs of the world are ignored. Contextual behavioral science takes the prediction and influence of behavior to be its goal, and each of the global issues named above maintains its momentum through perpetuation at the individual level, whether this be in the form of individuals continuing to purchase plastic water bottles they have no intention of recycling or changing the news channel when facing yet another instance of police brutality.

The following recommendations are provided to direct behavioral science in a more prosocial direction, so that the CBS community may account for, understand, and intervene in these large-scale cultural and systemic issues.

- Recommendation 23: CBS research needs to be explicit about its prosocial purpose and to seek scientific knowledge that fosters social justice.
- Recommendation 24: CBS research needs to address diversity issues (gender; language; race, ethnicity; sexual orientation and identity, etc.) in treatment and process of change research.
- Recommendation 25: CBS research needs to focus on conditions that promote human cooperation.
- Recommendation 26: CBS needs more research on variables that influence social networks for prosocial purposes.
- Recommendation 27: CBS research needs to be considered within an extended evolutionary science framework for the purpose of fostering greater scientific consilience. At the same time, CBS researchers need to encourage an expansion of evolutionary and cultural science research beyond observation and description to include studies of influence and change.

Recommendations 23 and 24 encourage the CBS community to become explicit in their goal of facing these issues through an empirical lens and building an understanding of not only the behavioral processes which underlie social problems, but also which processes of change are the most important to target through intervention. This may require scaling up the unit of analysis from the individual's behavior in a given present and historical context to the analysis of small groups operating in societal and cultural contexts.

One such effort discussed earlier is *Prosocial*, which represents an opportunity for CBS to work together with EvoSci to develop an understanding of key processes of change that appear important at the group level (Atkins et al., 2019). In the example of *Prosocial*, these are the Core Design Principles. However, other social processes may be operating at the group level which require analysis and explanation grounded in a coherent account of language and cognition, namely, RFT.

CBS is in a position to successfully develop interventions at the group level that are sensitive to the effects such interventions may have on individuals within the group. The empirical foundation that is built by studying individuals must be understood in light of how processes controlling individual behavior are affected by group-level intervention. Only through the interplay between these two levels of analysis will human cooperation be better understood. The recommendations explicitly ask for further research on variables influencing social networks that are to be analyzed for prosocial purposes. The implications for behavioral science more generally, should these recommendations be followed, are expansive in that CBS will have something empirically valid and valuable to say at levels of analysis that have previously belonged to the field of sociology or anthropology. The dreams of behavioral science have always been loftier than the behavior of the individual, and CBS research bolstered by an extended evolutionary approach to studying prosocial behavior can make these dreams a reality.

ACT work in CBS is noteworthy for the degree to which it has touched upon all of these issues, so it should be noted that ACT research is not starting from a standstill. As was mentioned earlier, ACT has been successfully tested by the WHO to alleviate the distress of displaced refugees in Africa. Two more trials recently completed with a range of displaced persons show that ACT also prevents the development of mental disorders in communities impacted by adversity such as wars, terrorism, or natural disasters (Purgato et al., 2019; White et al., 2021). No other method of what the WHO calls "scalable psychological interventions" can yet make that claim, and full-scale promulgation of ACT by the WHO should soon follow.

A similar story can be told in ACT for domestic violence in which significant reductions of violence by perpetrators (Zarling, Lawrence, & Marchman, 2015) have now led to statewide implementation of ACT for perpetrators in Iowa (Zarling, Bannon, & Berta, 2019). Results of ACT interventions for reducing prejudice (Kenny & Bizumic, 2016) or for ameliorating self-stigma (Lillis & Hayes, 2007; Potts, Krafft, & Levin, 2020) are also positive. Thus, while basic research within a CBS on systemic social problems such as racism, violence, or climate change is limited (Davis et al., 2021), and much more needs to be done in this area (Matsuda, Garcia, Catagnus, & Brandt, 2020), ACT is making notable progress. That progress seems destined to continue if the recommendations of the Task Force in this area are followed.

Characteristic Five: Contextual Behavioral Science Is a Pragmatic Approach

The final recommendation category is that of pragmatism. CBS research is not about truth with a capital "T"; rather, it is about making a difference. Research on abstract principles disconnected from making a practical difference will never move the field in a "Walden Two" direction. What is required here is an approach that looks at the four areas discussed thus far, keeping practicality in mind. The CBS Task Force understood that to do so, we should develop tools and methods that are "useful, available, easy to use, and inexpensive" (Hayes et al, 2021, p. 42). The following recommendations are meant to ensure that behavioral science is pragmatic in its approach:

- Recommendation 28: CBS research needs to develop practical research and intervention tools, focused on functionally important processes of change, meaningful intervention goals, and user-friendly methodological and statistical approaches that meet its underlying assumptions.
- Recommendation 29: CBS research needs more cross-cultural focus and greater attention to biases or assumptions that may influence the research that is conducted and the explication of its implications.
- Recommendation 30: CBS research needs to maximize the external validity of research by including key stakeholders in the research enterprise.

- Recommendation 31: CBS research needs to focus on how best to train CBS researchers and practitioners.
- Recommendation 32: CBS research needs to help ensure the promulgation and use of research that meets human needs.

Criticisms of ACT and RFT sometimes point to the lack of clarity with regard to concepts within the basic theory. Assumed processes of change with the psychological flexibility model such as "acceptance" and "values" are often defined functionally, though their definitions often stop short of being fully explained through basic behavioral processes. This problem is as much about the basic account as it is about the applied account (Gross & Fox, 2009). One reason why the issue of midlevel constructs has not stopped their use is a pragmatic one: namely, empirical evidence for successful mediation of outcomes through demonstrable changes in these midlevel constructs solidifies the value of these constructs despite lacking a full technical understanding (Rector, 2013). In other words, ACT research has been able to make progress on the goal of identifying functionally relevant change processes that lead to meaningful interventions despite using midlevel constructs. Furthermore, the use of midlevel terms has aided in the development of empirically validated interventions that can be easily passed on to practitioners learning to implement ACT techniques and target processes of change. The further study of these processes of change and what basic behavioral processes may be related to midlevel constructs is still a required next step in the research arc of CBS, but research and applied practice in the field of CBS should not cease while these definitions are being formed.

That is in the spirit of Recommendation 28. Yes, more research is needed, but it also requires user-friendly methodological and statistical approaches, as well as practical research and intervention tools.

Recommendation 29 zeroes in on an important issue that has come to light more fully in current societal mediums and that has become the issue of cross-cultural focus and bias. Implications of race and bias have seen increased scrutiny in some areas, such as in the medical fields. For example, one article reported on how members of minority groups tended to report poorer health than did members of racial or ethnic majority groups; the thoughts and feelings related to minority versus majority groups could play a role in those health care disparities (Penner et al., 2013). It is up to the CBS community to identify these areas where our science can provide not only an explanation of how these disparities form, but also how behavioral science can be used to influence change to alleviate these disparities.

It would be detrimental to the future of behavioral science to concern itself only with issues of less complex overt behavior or to resist answering the call to action in other areas of need. As such, CBS must maintain close contact with stakeholders to ensure that behavioral science is able to provide answers to the questions that those we serve may be asking. This seems simple, but Recommendations 30 and 31 represent a shift in thinking in which the CBS community holds itself accountable not only to the community that practitioners within the field serve, but also to the students who will be future practitioners and who must be given an opportunity to critically examine the state of behavioral science and influence change as necessary. This means doctoral programs that produce highly trained scientist practitioners and efforts to serve the community and that not only provide grant funding for students but also address the specific needs of the societal moment and context. Finally, Recommendation 32 asks that CBS researchers be as committed to the promulgation of knowledge as to its development.

Conclusion

ACT is not very important when viewed merely as a set of intervention techniques. It is better thought of functionally, as a dynamic and evolving set of intervention kernels that are consciously linked to an underlying functional contextual model. Stated another way, an "ACT method" is any method that is consciously designed and ultimately empirically shown to modify psychological flexibility processes. The psychological flexibility model in turn is based on an analytic abstractive theory of language and cognition, RFT, as influenced by behavioral principles and evolutionary science principles more generally. This model, in turn, is based on functional contextual philosophical assumptions and on empirical findings throughout the history of functional contextual behavioral science.

Understood that way, ACT is part of the unified fabric of an entire approach to behavioral science. It is evolving and changing as the data come in. ACT is not controlled by any person or any set of persons. The development of ACT is driven not only by the data but also by the philosophical assumptions, values, and goals of the community itself. In the beginning of this article, we described how CBS was formed in part based on an attempt to help the behavioral tradition address a small set of key obstacles. These obstacles appear to have been largely overcome. The challenge now is how to address the future.

When the five characteristics of CBS research are considered and linked to ACT, it is clear that ACT itself needs to be thought of as consciously multilevel, process-oriented, multidimensional, prosocial, and pragmatic. Clarity about its characteristic features is all the more important in this new era of success in which ACT is listed as a treatment for chronic pain in adolescents by the WHO (2020b) or is recommended for tinnitus and chronic pain by the United Kingdom's National Institute for Health and Care Excellence (NICE) guidelines (Carville, Constanti, Kosky, Stannard, & Wilkinson, 2021). ACT, RFT, and CBS are no longer on the outside looking in. It is essential for the field that the CBS community not rest on its laurels and instead take the bold steps needed to continue to ensure that it remains empirically validated, practically focused, grounded in evolutionary theory, and able to be applied to challenges of the human condition at both the individual and global level.

The Task Force's final recommendation anticipated the possibility of entropy. This recommendation is not part of the five characteristic areas, but rather is in a category of its own. It states that:

> the CBS community should foster the recommendations of the ACBS Task Force on the Strategies and Tactics of Contextual Behavioral Science Research in their laboratories, classrooms, scientific reports, and applied agencies. ACBS should foster these recommendations in association policy, association conferences and committees, and in association publications such as the Journal of Contextual Behavioral Science. In due time, the CBS community should revisit, review, and refresh these recommendations as part of an ongoing process of attempting to create a behavioral science more worthy of the challenge of the human condition.
>
> *(pp. 47–48)*

Contextual behavioral science is ready to assume the role of a leading force within behavioral science at large. The recommendations proposed by the Task Force demonstrate that CBS is not a field characterized by any particular concept or process, but rather is a corner of behavioral science characterized by the functional outcomes it seeks to bring about. As such, it is a science unafraid of change and is especially unafraid of being critical of the theories and therapeutic interventions developed under its auspices. One of the greatest assets of ACT and the psychological flexibility model is its "focus on variation and selective retention in context at the right dimension and level," which can ensure that the model will adapt and evolve as CBS progresses in the direction laid out in these recommendations (Hayes, 2019b, p. 227). CBS as a behavioral system is primed for evolution as the empirical groundwork that has already been done in ACT, and RFT continues to narrow in on processes of change that allow us to better predict and influence behavioral and biophysiological outcomes across multiple levels and dimensions, and in turn create a world in which humans can thrive instead of merely survive.

References

Abed, R., Ayton, A., St John-Smith, P., Swanepoel, A., & Tracy, D. K. (2019). Evolutionary biology: An essential basic science for the training of the next generation of psychiatrists. *British Journal of Psychiatry, 215*(6), 699–701.

Abernathy, W. B. (2009). Walden Two revisited: Optimizing behavioral systems. *Journal of Organizational Behavior Management, 29*(2), 175–192.

Ardila, R. (2008). Walden Two, 60 years later (1948–2008). *Revista Latinoamericana de Psicología, 40* (3), 595–597.

Atkins, P. W., Wilson, D. S., & Hayes, S. C. (2019). *Prosocial: Using evolutionary science to build productive, equitable, and collaborative groups.* Oakland, CA: Context Press/New Harbinger Publications.

Baer, D. M., Wolf, M. M., & Risley, T. R. (1968). Some current dimensions of applied behavior analysis. *Journal of Applied Behavior Analysis, 1*(1), 91.

Biglan, A., & Hayes, S. C. (1996). Should the behavioral sciences become more pragmatic? The case for functional contextualism in research on human behavior. *Applied and Preventive Psychology, 5*(1), 47–57.

Brody, D. J., & Gu, Q. (2020, September 4). Products—Data Briefs—Number 377—September 2020. Centers for Disease Control and Prevention. https://www.cdc.gov/nchs/products/databriefs/db377.htm#:~:text=During%202015%E2%80%932018%2C%2013.2%25%20of%20adults%20used%20antidepressants%20in,those%20aged%2060%20and%20over.

Carville, S., Constanti, M., Kosky, N., Stannard, C., & Wilkinson, C. (2021). Chronic pain (primary and secondary) in over 16s: Summary of NICE guidance. *BMJ* 2021;373:n895

Coyne, L. W., & Wilson, K. G. (2004). The role of cognitive fusion in impaired parenting: An RFT analysis. *International Journal of Psychology and Psychological Therapy, 4*(3), 469–486.

Crespi, B. J. (2020). Evolutionary and genetic insights for clinical psychology. *Clinical Psychology Review, 78,* 101857. doi: 10.1016/j.cpr.2020.101857

Davis, C. H., Krafft, J., Hicks, E. T., & Levin, M. E. (2021). The role of psychological inflexibility and perspective taking in anti-racism and anti-sexism. *Personality and Individual Differences, 175,* 110724. doi: 10.1016/j.paid.2021.110724

Dixon, M. R., Belisle, J., Rehfeldt, R. A., & Root, W. B. (2018). Why we are still not acting to save the world: The upward challenge of a post-Skinnerian behavior science. *Perspectives on Behavioral Science, 41,* 241–267. doi: 10.1007/s40614-018-0162-9

Dixon, M. R., Dymond, S., Rehfeldt, R. A., Roche, B., & Zlomke, K. R. (2003). Terrorism and relational frame theory. *Behavior and Social Issues, 12*(2), 129–147.

Dixon, M. R., Hayes, S. C., Stanley, C., Law, S., & al-Nasser, T. (2020). Is acceptance and commitment training or therapy (ACT) a method that applied behavior analysts can and should use? *The Psychological Record, 70*(4), 559–579.

Dixon, M. R., Small, S. L. & Rosales, R. (2007). Extended analysis of empirical citations with Skinner's *Verbal Behavior*: 1984–2004. *The Behavior Analyst, 30,* 197–209. doi: 10.1007/BF03392155

Drescher, J. (2015). Out of DSM: Depathologizing homosexuality. *Behavioral Sciences, 5*(4), 565–575. https://doi.org/10.3390/bs5040565

Dymond, S., May, R. J., Munnelly, A., & Hoon, A. E. (2010). Evaluating the evidence base for relational frame theory: A citation analysis. *The Behavior Analyst, 33*(1), 97–117.

Dymond, S., O'Hora, D., Whelan, R., & O'Donovan, A. (2006). Citation analysis of Skinner's verbal behavior: 1984–2004. *The Behavior Analyst, 29*(1), 75–88.

Ebeling, M. (2011). "Get with the program!": Pharmaceutical marketing, symptom checklists and self-diagnosis. *Social Science and Medicine, 73*(6), 825–832. https://doi.org/10.1016/j.socscimed.2011.05.054

Eilifsen, C., & Arntzen, E. (2021). Mediated generalization and stimulus equivalence. *Perspectives on Behavior Science, 44*(1), 1–27.

Esch, B. E., LaLonde, K. B., & Esch, J. W. (2010). Speech and language assessment: A verbal behavior analysis. *Journal of Speech and Language Pathology–Applied Behavior Analysis, 5*(2), 166.

Frost, L., & Bondy, A. (2006). A common language: Using BF Skinner's verbal behavior for assessment and treatment of communication disabilities in SLP-ABA. *Journal of Speech and Language Pathology–Applied Behavior Analysis, 1*(2), 103.

Gross, A. C., & Fox, E. J. (2009). Relational frame theory: An overview of the controversy. *The Analysis of Verbal Behavior, 25*(1), 87–98.

Hayes, S. C. (2019a). *A liberated mind: How to pivot toward what matters.* New York: Penguin/Avery.

Hayes, S. C. (2019b). Acceptance and commitment therapy: Towards a unified model of behavior change. *World Psychiatry, 18*(2), 226.

Hayes, S. (2021, March). ACT randomized controlled trials since 1986. contextualscience.org. https://contextualscience.org/act_randomized_controlled_trials_since_1986.

Hayes, S., Barnes-Holmes, D., & Roche, B. (2001). *Relational frame theory: A post-Skinnerian account of human language and cognition.* New York: Kluwer Academic/Plenum Publishers.

Hayes, S. C., Barnes-Holmes, D., & Wilson, K. G. (2012). Contextual behavioral science: Creating a science more adequate to the challenge of the human condition. *Journal of Contextual Behavioral Science, 1*(1-2), 1–16.

Hayes, S. C., & Brownstein, A. J. (1986). Mentalism, behavior–behavior relations, and a behavior-analytic view of the purposes of science. *The Behavior Analyst, 9*(2), 175–190.

Hayes, S. C., Hofmann, S. G., Stanton, C. E., Carpenter, J. K., Sanford, B. T., Curtiss, J. E., & Ciarrochi, J. (2019). The role of the individual in the coming era of process-based therapy. *Behavior Research and Therapy, 117,* 40–53.

Hayes, S. C., Law, S., Assemi, K., Falletta-Cowden, N., Shamblin, M., Burleigh, K., . . . Smith, P. (2021a). Relating is an operant: A fly over of 35 years of RFT research. *Perspectivas em Análise do Comportamento, 12.* doi: 10.18761/PAC.2021.v12.RFT.02

Hayes, S. C., & Long, D. M. (2013). Contextual behavioral science, evolution, and scientific epistemology. In S. Dymond & B. Roche (Eds.), *Advances in relational frame theory: Research and application* (pp. 5–26). Oakland, CA: New Harbinger Publications.

Hayes, S. C., Merwin, R. M., McHugh, L., Sandoz, E., Jacqueline, A., Ruiz, F. J., . . . McCracken, L. M. (2021b). Report of the ACBS Task Force on the Strategies and Tactics of Contextual Behavioral Science Research. *Journal of Contextual Behavioral Science, 20,* 172–183. doi: 10.1016/j.jcbs.2021.03.007

Hayes, S. C., & Sanford, B. T. (2014). Cooperation came first: Evolution and human cognition. *Journal of the Experimental Analysis of Behavior, 101*(1), 112–129.

Hayes, S. C., & Sanford, B. T. (2015). Modern psychotherapy as a multidimensional multilevel evolutionary process. *Current Opinion in Psychology, 2,* 16–20.

Hayes, S. C., Sanford, B. T., & Chin, F. T. (2017). Carrying the baton: Evolution science and a contextual behavioral analysis of language and cognition. *Journal of Contextual Behavioral Science, 6*(3), 314–328.

Hayes, S. C., Stanton, C., Sanford, B., Law, S., & Ta, J. (2020). Becoming more versatile (VRSCDL) using evolutionary science to suggest innovations in ACT. In M. E. Levin, M. P. Twohig, & J. Krafft (Eds.). *Innovations in acceptance and commitment therapy: Clinical advancements and applications in ACT* (pp. 53–65). Oakland, CA: Context Press.

Hayes, S. C., Strosahl, K. D., & Wilson, K. G. (2011). *Acceptance and commitment therapy: The process and practice of mindful change.* New York: Guilford Press.

Kenny, A., & Bizumic, B. (2016). Learn and ACT: Changing prejudice towards people with mental illness using stigma reduction interventions. *Journal of Contextual Behavioral Science, 5*(3), 178–185. doi: 10.1016/j.jcbs.2016.06.004.

Leech, A., Barnes-Holmes, D., & McEnteggart, C. (2017). Spider fear and avoidance: A preliminary study of the impact of two verbal rehearsal tasks on a behavior–behavior relation and its implications for an experimental analysis of defusion. *The Psychological Record, 67*(3), 387–398.

Lillis, J., & Hayes, S. C. (2007). Applying acceptance, mindfulness, and values to the reduction of prejudice: A pilot study. *Behavior Modification, 31*(4), 389–411.

Masuda, A., Hayes, S. C., Fletcher, L. B., Seignourel, P. J., Bunting, K., Herbst, S. A., . . . Lillis, J. (2007). Impact of acceptance and commitment therapy versus education on stigma toward people with psychological disorders. *Behavior Research and Therapy, 45*(11), 2764–2772.

Matsuda, K., Garcia, Y., Catagnus, R., & Brandt, J. A. (2020). Can behavior analysis help us understand and reduce racism? A review of the current literature. *Behavior Analysis in Practice, 13*(2), 336–347.

O'Connor, M., Farrell, L., Munnelly, A., & McHugh, L. (2017). Citation analysis of relational frame theory: 2009–2016. *Journal of Contextual Behavioral Science, 6*(2), 152–158.

Ostrom, E. (1990). *Governing the commons: The evolution of institutions for collective action.* Cambridge: Cambridge University Press.

Penner, L. A., Hagiwara, N., Eggly, S., Gaertner, S. L., Albrecht, T. L., & Dovidio, J. F. (2013). Racial healthcare disparities: A social psychological analysis. *European Review of Social Psychology, 24*(1), 70–122.

Pinker, S. (2003). *The blank slate: The modern denial of human nature.* New York: Penguin.

Potts, S., Krafft, J., & Levin, M. E. (2020; in press). A pilot randomized controlled trial of acceptance and commitment therapy guided self-help for overweight and obese adults high in weight self-stigma. *Behavior Modification, 46*(1), 178–201 doi:10.1177/0145445520975112

Purgato, M., Carswell, K., Acarturk, C., Au, T., Akbai, S., Anttila, M., . . . Van Ommeren, M. (2019). Effectiveness and cost-effectiveness of Self-Help Plus (SH+) for preventing mental disorders in refugees and asylum seekers in Europe and Turkey: Study protocols for two randomised controlled trials. *BMJ Open, 9*(5), e030259.

Rector, N. A. (2013). Acceptance and commitment therapy: Empirical considerations. *Behavior Therapy, 44*(2), 213–217. https://doi.org/10.1016/j.beth.2010.07.007

Schwartz, S. (1998). The role of values in the nature/nurture debate about psychiatric disorders. *Social Psychiatry and Psychiatric Epidemiology, 33*(8), 356–362. https://doi.org/10.1007/s001270050066

Skinner, B. F. (1948). *Walden two.* New York: Hackett Publishing.

Skinner, B. F. (1950). Are theories of learning necessary? *Psychological Review, 57*(4), 193.

Skinner, B. F. (1957). *Verbal behavior.* New York: Appleton-Century-Crofts.

Skinner, B. F. (1987). Why we are not acting to save the world. In *Upon further reflection* (pp. 1–14). New York: Prentice-Hall.

Skinner, B. F. (1988). *The selection of behavior: The operant behaviorism of BF Skinner: Comments and consequences.* Cambridge: Cambridge University Press Archive.

Skinner, B.F. (1981). Selection by consequence. *Science, 213*, 501–504.

Spence, K. W. (1944). The nature of theory construction in contemporary psychology. *Psychological Review, 51*(1), 47.

Tol, W. A., Leku, M. R., Lakin, D. P., Carswell, K., Augustinavicius, J., & Adaku, A. (2020). Guided self-help to reduce psychological distress in South Sudanese female refugees in Uganda: A cluster randomised trial. *Lancet Global Health, 8*(2), E254–E263. doi: 10.1016/S2214-109X(19)30504-2

VandenBos, G. R. (2007). *APA dictionary of psychology.* Washington, DC: American Psychological Association.

Vilardaga, R. (2009). A relational frame theory account of empathy. *International Journal of Behavioral Consultation and Therapy, 5*(2), 178.

Watson, J. B. (1925). *Behaviorism.* New York: Norton.

Weinstein, J. H., Wilson, K. G., Drake, C. E., & Kellum, K. K. (2008). A relational frame theory contribution to social categorization. *Behavior and Social Issues, 17*(1), 40–65.

White, R. G., Barbui, C., Purgato, M., Acarturk, C., Van Ommeren, M., & Carswell, K. (June 2021). *Evaluating the effectiveness of the WHO Self-Help Plus (SH+) intervention for preventing mental disorders among refugees in the EU and Turkey.* Paper presented at the virtual World Conference of the Association for Contextual Behavioral Science.

Wilson, D. S. & Hayes, S. C. (Eds.). (2018). *Evolution and contextual behavioral science: An integrated framework for understanding, predicting, and influencing human behavior.* Oakland, CA: Context Press/New Harbinger Publications.

Wilson, D. S., Ostrom, E., & Cox, M. E. (2013). Generalizing the core design principles for the efficacy of groups. *Journal of Economic Behavior and Organization, 90*, S21–S32.

World Health Organization. (2020a). *Doing what matters in times of stress: An illustrated guide.* Geneva: World Health Organization.

World Health Organization. (2020b). *Guidelines on the management of chronic pain in children.* Geneva: World Health Organization.

Zarling, A., Bannon, S., & Berta, M. (2019). Evaluation of acceptance and commitment therapy for domestic violence offenders. *Psychology of Violence, 9*(3), 257.

Zarling, A., Lawrence, E., & Marchman, J. (2015). A randomized controlled trial of acceptance and commitment therapy for aggressive behavior. *Journal of Consulting and Clinical Psychology, 83*(1), 199.

Zettle, R. D. (Ed.)., Hayes, S. C., Barnes-Holmes, D., & Biglan, A. (2016). *The Wiley handbook of contextual behavioral science.* Chichester, UK: Wiley Blackwell.

INDEX

Tables and figures are indicated by *t* and *f* following the page number

D

Q

R

W

Y

Z

www.ingramcontent.com/pod-product-compliance
Ingram Content Group UK Ltd.
Pitfield, Milton Keynes, MK11 3LW, UK
UKHW051348240926
475595UK00048B/162

9 780197 550076